# Brief Contents

# WileyPLUS

## WileyPLUS is a research-based online environment for effective teaching and learning.

*WileyPLUS* builds students' confidence because it takes the guesswork out of studying by providing students with a clear roadmap:

- what to do
- how to do it
- if they did it right

It offers interactive resources along with a complete digital textbook that help students learn more. With *WileyPLUS*, students take more initiative so you'll have greater impact on their achievement in the classroom and beyond.

For more information, visit www.wileyplus.com

# WileyPLUS

## ALL THE HELP, RESOURCES, AND PERSONAL SUPPORT YOU AND YOUR STUDENTS NEED!
### www.wileyplus.com/resources

## 1st DAY OF CLASS ...AND BEYOND!

2-Minute Tutorials and all of the resources you and your students need to get started

## WileyPLUS
### Student Partner Program

Student support from an experienced student user

## Wiley Faculty Network

Collaborate with your colleagues, find a mentor, attend virtual and live events, and view resources
www.WhereFacultyConnect.com

## WileyPLUS
### Quick Start

Pre-loaded, ready-to-use assignments and presentations created by subject matter experts

Technical Support 24/7
FAQs, online chat, and phone support
www.wileyplus.com/support

(Courtney Keating/iStockphoto)

Your *WileyPLUS* Account Manager, providing personal training and support

# MANAGEMENT

## TWELFTH EDITION

JOHN R. SCHERMERHORN, JR.

WILEY

VICE PRESIDENT & EXECUTIVE PUBLISHER   George Hoffman
EXECUTIVE EDITOR   Lisé Johnson
SENIOR PRODUCT DESIGNER   Allison Morris
EDITORIAL OPERATIONS MANAGER   Yana Mermel
CONTENT EDITOR   Jennifer Manias
ASSOCIATE DIRECTOR OF MARKETING   Amy Scholz
MARKETING MANAGER   Kelly Simmons
SENIOR CONTENT MANAGER   Dorothy Sinclair
SENIOR PRODUCTION EDITOR   Erin Bascom
DESIGN DIRECTOR   Harry Nolan
PHOTO DEPARTMENT MANAGER   Hilary Newman
EDITORIAL ASSISTANT   Melissa Solarz
SENIOR MARKETING ASSISTANT   Ashley Tomeck
SENIOR MEDIA SPECIALIST   Elena Santa Maria
PRODUCTION MANAGEMENT SERVICES   Ingrao Associates
COVER DESIGNER   Wendy Lai
PHOTO RESEARCHER   Susan McLaughlin
INTERIOR DESIGN   Tom Nery
COVER PHOTO   ©Simon Ingate/iStockphoto

REPEATED DESIGN ELEMENT PHOTO CREDITS   (opener blue background) Viktoriya Sukhanova/iStockphoto; (opener GPS navigation screen) pagadesign/iStockphoto; (opener keyboard) tioloco/iStockphoto; (Facts for Analysis) George Diebold/Purestock/SuperStock; (Learning Check Summary, Self-Test, Recommended Reading and Management in Popular Culture) vanias/iStockphoto; (Team Exercise) RelaxFoto.de/iStockphoto; (Career Situations) sweetym/iStockphoto; (Case Study) 123render/iStockphoto

This book was set in 11/14 Kepler by Aptara, Inc. and printed and bound by Courier/Kendallville. The cover was printed by Courier/Kendallville.

This book is printed on acid free paper. ∞

Founded in 1807, John Wiley & Sons, Inc. has been a valued source of knowledge and understanding for more than 200 years, helping people around the world meet their needs and fulfill their aspirations. Our company is built on a foundation of principles that include responsibility to the communities we serve and where we live and work. In 2008, we launched a Corporate Citizenship Initiative, a global effort to address the environmental, social, economic, and ethical challenges we face in our business. Among the issues we are addressing are carbon impact, paper specifications and procurement, ethical conduct within our business and among our vendors, and community and charitable support. For more information, please visit ourwebsite: www.wiley.com/go/citizenship.

*Library of Congress Cataloging in Publication Data:*
Schermerhorn, John R.
Management / John R. Schermerhorn. — 12th ed.

   p. cm.
   ISBN 978-1-118-11392-9 (cloth)
   1.  Management.   I. Title.
HD31.S3325 2013
658—dc23

978-1-118-11392-9 (Main Book ISBN)
978-1-118-39742-8 (Binder-Ready Version ISBN)

Printed in the United States of America

10 9 8 7 6 5 4 3 2 1

# TO MY SONS, JOHN CHRISTIAN AND CHARLES PORTER

*While you played*
*I wrote.*
*But always,*
*I was listening*
*and loving*
*you.*

1984

*It's later now.*
*Don't worry.*
*Time*
*means love shared,*
*by you*
*and me.*

1986

*Think*
*of all the fun*
*we have.*
*Here, there, everywhere,*
*doing things*
*together.*

1989

*Home,*
*now and forever,*
*will always be*
*wherever*
*I can be*
*with you.*

1992

*Time*
*has its ways,*
*doesn't it?*
*Not enough,*
*not enough,*
*I often say.*

1996

*Hurry home*
*when you can.*
*Come laughing, sons.*
*Tell us*
*your*
*wonderful stories.*

1999

*Songs riding winds.*
*Mimi,*
*Uncle George,*
*Uncle Nelson.*
*Whispers and choirs.*
*Silence speaks.*

2002

*On the mountain,*
*by Irish lakes,*
*find beauty and*
*peace.*
*Fairies dance*
*there.*

2004

*Mom loves*
*us, cats*
*and rainy days.*
*Nana and Poppy*
*loved us*
*too.*

2007

*Bookstores, museums,*
*stories, paintings.*
*And dreams.*
*We travel,*
*we laugh,*
*joined in life.*

2009

*While you work,*
*I'm starting to play*
*again.*
*Still listening,*
*and loving*
*you.*

2011

*When I*
*was young*
*I never knew*
*you would make*
*dreams*
*come true.*

2013

# About the Author

Ohio University named Dr. Schermerhorn a University Professor, the university's highest campus-wide honor for exellence in undergraduate teaching.

**Dr. John R. Schermerhorn, Jr.** is the Charles G. O'Bleness Professor of Management Emeritus in the College of Business at Ohio University, where he teaches graduate and undergraduate courses in management. Dr. Schermerhorn earned a Ph.D. in organizational behavior from Northwestern University, an MBA (with distinction) in management and international business from New York University, and a BS in business administration from the State University of New York at Buffalo. He previously taught at Tulane University, the University of Vermont, and Southern Illinois University at Carbondale, where he also served as head of the Department of Management and associate dean of the College of Business Administration.

International experience adds a unique global dimension to Dr. Schermerhorn's teaching and writing. He holds an honorary doctorate from the University of Pécs in Hungary. He was a visiting professor of management at the Chinese University of Hong Kong, on-site coordinator of the Ohio University MBA and Executive MBA programs in Malaysia, and Kohei Miura visiting professor at Chubu University in Japan. He has served as adjunct professor at the National University of Ireland at Galway and advisor to the Lao-American College in Vientiane, Laos. He presently teaches an MBA course at Università Politecnica Delle Marche in Ancona, Italy, and PhD seminars in the Knowledge and Innovation Management doctoral program at Bangkok University, Thailand. At Ohio University he has twice been Director of the Center for Southeast Asian Studies.

A member of the Academy of Management, Dr. Schermerhorn was chairperson of the Management Education and Development Division. Management educators and students alike know him as author of *Exploring Management* 3e (Wiley, 2012), *Management* 12e (Wiley, 2013), and senior co-author of *Organizational Behavior* 12e (Wiley, 2011). Dr. Schermerhorn has also published numerous articles, including ones in the *Academy of Management Journal, Academy of Management Review, Academy of Management Executive, Organizational Dynamics, Asia-Pacific Journal of Management,* the *Journal of Management Development,* and the *Journal of Management Education.*

Dr. Schermerhorn is a popular guest speaker at colleges and universities. He is available for student lectures and classroom visits, as well as for faculty workshops on scholarly manuscript development, textbook writing, high engagement teaching, and instructional and curriculum innovations.

# Preface

From the beautiful cover of this book to the realities of organizations today, great accomplishments are much like inspired works of art. Whether one is talking about arranging objects or bringing together people and other resources in organizational systems, it is a balancing act. But the results are spectacular when goals and talent combine to create a lasting and positive impact.

Just as artists find inspiration in all the senses that bring our world to life, managers find inspiration in daily experiences, from the insights of management scholars, through relationships with other people, and among the goals that guide organizations in an ever more demanding society. And like artists, managers must master many challenges as they strive to create the future from the resources of the present.

While a beautiful formation of feathers, wood, and stones in the cover art shows balance and harmony in a visual masterpiece, a well-managed workplace can build, mix, and integrate all the beauties of human talent to achieve great things. This capacity for positive impact is the goal bound into the pages of *Management 12e*. It is an opportunity to gain knowledge, find inspiration, and learn practices that can help build the organizations we need to forge a better world.

> A well-managed workplace can build, mix, and integrate all the beauties of human talent to achieve great things.

## *Management 12e* Philosophy

Today's students are tomorrow's leaders and managers. They are our hope for the future. When well prepared, they can be major contributors during this time of social transformation. But the workplace is rapidly changing, and so too must our teaching and learning environments change from the comforts and successes of days gone by. New values and management approaches are appearing; organizations are changing forms and practices; jobs are being redefined and relocated; the age of information is a major force in our lives; and the intricacies of globalization are presenting major organizational and economic challenges.

*Management 12e* is designed for this new world of work. It is crafted to help students not just explore the essentials of the management discipline, but also to discover their true potential and accept personal responsibilities for developing useful career skills. The content, pedagogy, and features of this edition were carefully blended to support management educators who want their courses to:

> *Management 12e* is designed to help students discover their true potential and accept personal responsibilities for developing career skills.

- enhance our students' career readiness;
- make our students more attractive as intern and job candidates;

- improve our students' confidence in critical thinking;
- raise our students' awareness of timely social and organizational issues;
- inspire our students to embrace life-long learning for career success.

## *Management 12e* Pedagogy

Our goal as educators should be to make good content choices that set the best possible foundations for lifelong learning.

The pedagogical foundations of *Management 12e* are based on four constructive balances that are essential to higher education for business and management.

- *The balance of research insights with formative education.* As educators we must be willing to make choices when bringing the theories and concepts of our discipline to the attention of the introductory student. We cannot do everything in one course. The goal should be to make good content choices that set the best possible foundations for lifelong learning.

- *The balance of management theory with management practice.* As educators we must understand the compelling needs of students to learn and appreciate the applications of the material they are reading and thinking about. We must continually bring to their attention good, interesting, and recognizable examples.

- *The balance of present understandings with future possibilities.* As educators we must continually search for the directions in which the real world of management is heading. We must select and present materials that can both point students in the right directions and help them develop the confidence and self-respect needed to best pursue them.

We are role models . . . we must be willing to take stands on issues such as managerial ethics and social responsibility.

- *The balance of what "can" be done with what is, purely and simply, the "right" thing to do.* As educators we are role models; we set the examples. We must be willing to take stands on issues such as managerial ethics and social responsibility. We must be careful not to let the concept of "contingency" betray the need for positive "action" and "accountability" in managerial practice.

Today, more than ever before, our students have pressing needs for direction as well as suggestion. They have needs for application as well as information. They have needs for integration as well as presentation. And they have needs for confidence built upon solid understanding. Our instructional approaches and materials must deliver on all of these dimensions and more. My goal is to put into your hands and into those of your students a learning resource that can help meet these needs. *Management 12e* and its supporting online resources are my contributions to the future careers of your students and mine.

## *Management 12e* Highlights

*Management 12e* is written for students seeking career success in today's challenging and ever-changing work environment. It introduces the essentials of management as they apply to organizations and careers in a complex global society. The subject matter is carefully chosen to meet AACSB accreditation guidelines, while still allowing extensive flexibility to fit various course designs and class sizes.

## Content and Organization

The chapter content is timely and the organization is flexible in meeting a wide variety of course objectives and instructor preferences. All chapters have been updated and enriched with new features and examples from the latest current events.

Chapter content is timely and the organization is flexible in meeting a wide variety of course objectives and instructor preferences.

- **Part 1: Management**—Three chapters introducing management in terms of present-day dynamics and historical foundations—Introducing Management, Management Learning Past to Present, and Ethics and Social Responsibility.

- **Part 2: Environment**—Three chapters setting the environmental context within which today's managers function—Environment, Innovation, and Sustainability, Global Management and Cultural Diversity, and Entrepreneurship and New Ventures.

- **Part 3: Planning and Controlling**—Four-chapter sequence covering Information and Decision Making, Planning Processes and Techniques, Control Processes and Systems, and Strategy and Strategic Management.

- **Part 4: Organizing**—Three chapters on the essential building blocks of organizations—Organization Structures and Design, Organizational Culture and Change, and Human Resource Management.

- **Part 5: Leading**—Five chapters exploring key leadership skills and competencies—Leading and Leadership Development, Individual Behavior, Motivation Theory and Practice, Teams and Teamwork, and Communication and Collaboration.

## Learning Model

*Management 12e* is written with a learning model that helps students read, study, reflect, and use critical thinking. Attention is focused on building management skills and competencies through active learning, and discovering how management issues and themes apply to current events that affect everyday living.

*Management 12e* is written with a learning model that helps students study, reflect, and use critical thinking as they read.

Each chapter begins with a *Learning Dashboard* linked to the major headings in the chapter. A *Learning Check* follows each text section with a *Takeaway Question* and bullet list of mastery learning assessments to complete before reading on.

Major *Figures* within chapters provide visual support for student comprehension as concepts, theories, and terms are introduced. Where appropriate, *Small Boxed Figures and Summaries* are embedded with the discussion to help summarize and clarify major points. The *Management Learning Review* section at the end of chapter contains a *Study Question Summary* and a *Chapter Self-Test* to tie things together at the end of the chapter.

## Self-Reflection and Active Learning

A two-page opening spread focuses student attention on wisdom and insight relevant to chapter content. The left-page *Wisdom: Learning from Others* feature highlights a person or organization doing something worth thinking about from a benchmarking standpoint. It ends with a "More to Look for Inside" list of chapter highlights. The right-page *Insight: Learning About Yourself* feature introduces a skill or personal characteristic of career relevance. It ends by asking the reader to "Get to Know Yourself Better" through special active learning options in the end-of-chapter *Management Skills and Competencies* section. This includes *Further Reflection* on the chapter opening skill or personal characteristic, a *Self-Assessment* to deepen self-awareness, a *Team Exercise* to experience chapter content in a team setting, *Career Situations* to apply chapter learning to common early-career situations, and a recommended *Case Study* for analysis and further research.

## Critical Thinking

Special chapter features engage students in critical thinking about timely examples, current events, and applications of chapter material. *Ethics on the Line* challenges students to respond to an ethics problem or dilemma. *Follow the Story* presents exemplars and raises awareness about success in career and work situations. *Facts for Analysis* presents interesting facts for reflection and discussion. *Research Brief* summarizes recent research on a chapter topic and asks students to consider further research of their own.

   *Management Cases for Critical Thinking* is a rich and useful learning resource. It contains timely *Case Studies* for each chapter that ask students to answer three types of questions—discussion, problem solving, and further research. The cases are useful for in-class activities, as well as both individual and team writing and presentation assignments.

# *Management 12e* Teaching and Learning Resources

**Instructor's Resource Manual.** The Instructor's Resource Manual offers helpful teaching ideas. It has advice on course development, sample assignments, and recommended activities. It also offers chapter-by-chapter text highlights, learning objectives, lecture outlines, class exercises, lecture notes, answers to end-of-chapter material, and tips on using cases.

**Test Bank.** This comprehensive Test Bank (available on the instructor portion of the *Management 12e* Web site) has more than 175 questions per chapter. The true/false, multiple-choice, and short-essay questions vary in degree of difficulty. All questions are tagged with learning objectives, Bloom's Taxonomy categories, and AACSB Standards. The Computerized Test Bank allows instructors to modify and add questions to the master bank, and to customize their exams.

**Practice Quizzes.** An online study guide with quizzes of varying levels of difficulty helps students evaluate their progress through a chapter. It is available on the student portion of the Schermerhorn, *Management 12e* Web site.

**Pre- and Post-Lecture Quizzes.** Included in WileyPLUS, the Pre- and Post-Lecture Quizzes focus on the key terms and concepts. They can be used as stand-alone quizzes, or in combination to evaluate students' progress before and after lectures.

**PowerPoint Presentation Slides.** This robust set of slides can be accessed on the instructor portion of the *Management 12e* Web site. Lecture notes accompany each slide.

**Lecture Launcher Videos.** Short video clips developed from CBS News source materials provide an excellent starting point for lectures or for general class discussion. Teaching Notes are available and include video summaries and quiz and discussion questions.

**Movies and Music.** The *Art Imitates Life* supplement, prepared by Robert L. Holbrook of Ohio University, offers tips for those interested in integrating popular culture and the humanities into their courses. It provides innovative teaching ideas and scripts for using movies and music to enrich day-to-day classroom activities. It is widely praised for increasing student involvement and enthusiasm for learning.

*The* Art Imitates Life *supplement offers tips for those interested in integrating popular culture and the humanities into their courses.*

**Personal Response System.** The Personal Response System (PRS) questions for each chapter are designed to spark classroom discussion and debate. For more information on PRS, please contact your local Wiley sales representative.

**MP3 Downloads.** A complete playlist of MP3 downloads provides easy-to-access and ever-ready audio files that overview key chapter topics, terms, and potential test materials.

**Student Portfolio Builder.** This special guide to building a student portfolio is complete with professional résumé and competency documentation templates. It is on the student Companion Web site.

**Wiley Business Study Center.** With the new Wiley Business Study Center app, all of your review materials are in a single location. It's a one-stop resource for students to download and review classroom material on their mobile devices. Using Flash Cards to drill key terms and definitions, and Self Tests to quiz on applied knowledge of the content, we're constantly working to add new material for study and review.

**Companion Website.** The *Management 12e* Web site at http://www.wiley.com/college/schermerhorn contains a myriad of tools and links to aid both teaching and learning, including resources described above.

## WileyPlus

*WileyPLUS* is an innovative, research-based online environment for effective teaching and learning.

*WileyPLUS offers 24/7 online student engagement for enhanced learning while streamlining course management for instructors.*

*WileyPLUS* builds students' confidence because it takes the guesswork out of studying by providing students with a clear roadmap: **what to do, how to do it, if they did it right**. This interactive approach focuses on:

CONFIDENCE Research shows that students experience a great deal of anxiety over studying. That's why we provide a structured learning environment that helps students focus on **what to do**, along with the support of immediate resources.

MOTIVATION To increase and sustain motivation throughout the semester, *WileyPLUS* helps students learn **how to do** it at a pace that's right for them. Our integrated resources—available 24/7—function like a personal tutor, directly addressing each student's demonstrated needs with specific problem-solving techniques.

SUCCESS *WileyPLUS* helps to assure that each study session has a positive outcome by putting students in control. Through instant feedback and study objective reports, students know **if they did it right**, and where to focus next, so they achieve the strongest results.

With *WileyPLUS*, our efficacy research shows that students improve their outcomes by as much as one letter grade. *WileyPLUS* helps students take more initiative, so you'll have greater impact on their achievement in the classroom and beyond.

## What do students receive with *WileyPLUS*?

- The complete digital textbook, saving students up to 60% off the cost of a printed text.
- Question assistance, including links to relevant sections in the online digital textbook.
- Immediate feedback and proof of progress, 24/7.
- Integrated, multi-media resources—including virtual cases, visual exhibits, crossword puzzles, and much more—that provide multiple study paths and encourage more active learning.

## What do instructors receive with *WileyPLUS*?

- Reliable resources that reinforce course goals inside and outside of the classroom.
- The ability to easily identify those students who are failing behind.
- Media-rich course materials and assessment content including—Instructor's Manual, Test Bank, PowerPoint® Slides, Learning Objectives, Management Weekly Updates, Video Clips, Computerized Test Bank, Pre- and Post- Lecture Quizzes, and much more.

**www.wileyplus.com. Learn More.**

# Acknowledgments

*Management 12e* was initiated and completed with the support of my talented and dedicated development editor Susan McLaughlin, Executive Editor Lise Johnson who never failed to support the project and the entire team through all of its ups and downs, and ever-helpful Content Editor Jennifer Manias. We have all benefitted from the further support of an expert Wiley team that includes George Hoffman (publisher), Yana Mermel (Editorial Operations Manager), Harry Nolan (designer), Hilary Newman, Susan McLaughlin and Jeri Stratford (photo research), Suzanne Ingrao (Ingrao Associates), Erin Bascom (production), Kelly Simmons and Amy Scholz (marketing), as well as the help of Teri Stratford (photos). As always, I have been fortunate during this revision to have worked with the support and encouragement of my wife Ann. She perseveres even when "the book" overwhelms many of life's opportunities. I am also grateful to be working in a college and university that values teaching most highly, and to have the special advantages of scholarly challenge and inspiration from my colleagues Lenie Holbrook and Will Lamb.

I thank William Turnley of Kansas State University for his contributions to updating Chapters 13 and 16. I also thank the following colleagues whose help with this book at various stages of its life added to my understanding.

Carl Adams, *University of Minnesota*; Todd Allessandri, *Northeastern University*; Allen Amason, *University of Georgia*; Lydia Anderson, *Fresno City College*; Hal Babson, *Columbus State Community College*; Marvin Bates, *Benedictine University*; Joy Benson, *University of Wisconsin-Green Bay*; Santanu Borah, *University of Northern Alabama*; Peggy Brewer, *Eastern Kentucky University*; Jon Bryan, *Bridgewater State University*; Jim Buckenmyer, *Southeast Missouri State University*; Michael Buckley, *University of Oklahoma-Norman*; Barry Bunn, *Valencia Community College*; Jim Cashman, *University of Alabama*; Bruce Charnov, *Hofstra University*; Larry Chasteen, *Stephen F. Austin State University*; William Clark, *Leeward Community College*; Frederick Collett, *Mercy College*; Jeanie Diemer, *Ivy Tech State College*; Richard Eisenbeis, *Colorado State University-Pueblo*; Jud Faurer, *Metropolitan State University*; Linda Ferraro, *Central Connecticut State University*; Phyllis Flott, *Tennessee State University*; Dwight Frink, *Mississippi State University*; Shelly Gardner, *Augustana College*; Tommy Georgiades, *DeVry University*; Marvin Gordon, *University of Illinois-Chicago*; Fran Green, *Pennsylvania State University-Brandywine*; Dan Hallock, *University of North Alabama*; Joe Hanson, *Des Moines Area Community College*; Carol Harvey, *Assumption College*; Samuel Hazen, *Tarleton State University*; Lenie Holbrook, *Ohio University*; Gary Insch, *West Virginia University*; Camille Johnson, *San Jose State University*; Kathleen Jones, *University of North Dakota*; Marvin Karlins, *University of South Florida*; John Lipinski, *University of Pittsburgh*; Beverly Little, *Western Carolina University*; Kristie Loescher, *University of Texas*; James LoPresti, *University of Colorado-Boulder*; Susan Manring, *Elon University*; Kurt Martsolf, *California State University-Hayward*; Brian Maruffi, *Fordham University*; Brenda McAleer and Grace McLaughlin, *University of California-Irvine*; Val D. Miskin, *Washington State University*; Donald Mosley, *University of South Alabama*; Behnam Nakhai, *Millersville University of Pennsylvania*; Robert Nale, *Coastal Carolina University*; Augustine Obiaku, *Allegheny County Community College*; Michael Okrent, *Southern Connecticut State University*; John Overby, *The University of Tennessee-Martin*; Javier Pagan, *University of Puerto Rio—Piedras*; Diana Page, *University of West Florida*; Fernando Pargas, *James Madison University*; Richard Pena, *University of Texas-San Antonio*; Wendy Pike, *Benedictine University*; Newman Pollack, *Florida Atlantic University*; Anthony Racka, *Oakland Community College*; Jenny Rink, *Community College of Philadelphia*; Joseph Santora, *Essex County College*; Rajib Sanyal, *The College of New Jersey*; Amit Shah, *Frostburg State University*; Roy Shin, *Indiana University*; Brien N. Smith, *Ball State University*; Shane Spiller, *Western Kentucky University*; Shanthi Srinivas, *California State Polytechnic University-Pomona*; Howard Stanger, *Canisius College*; Jerry Stevens, *Texas Tech University*; William Stevens, *Missouri Southern State College*; Chuck Stubbart, *Southern Illinois University*; Harry Stucke, *Long Island University*; Thomas Thompson, *University of Maryland*; Judy Thompson, *Briar Cliff University*; Michael Troyer, *University of Wisconsin-Green Bay*; Susan L. Verhulst, *Des Moines Area Community College*; Jeffrey Ward, *Edmonds Community College*; Marta White, *Georgia State University*; James Whitney, *Champlain College*; Garland Wiggs, *Radford University*; Eric Wiklendt, *University of Northern Iowa*; Jiaqin Yang, *Georgia College and State University*; Greg Yon, *Florida State University*; Yichuan Zhao, *Dalian Maritime University*.

# Brief Contents

# Contents

Part Five Leading

14 Leading and Leadership Development   350

15 Individual Behavior   376

# Management Cases for Critical Thinking   C-1

# Features

## Wisdom: Learning From Others

Chapter 1 Smart People Create Their Own Futures
Chapter 2 There Are Many Pathways to Goal Achievement
Chapter 3 Everyone Gains When Our Planet Is a Priority
Chapter 4 A Keen Eye Will Spot Lots of Opportunities
Chapter 5 Globalization Makes Businesses World Travelers
Chapter 6 Entrepreneurs Are Changing Our World
Chapter 7 Decisions Turn Potential into Achievement
Chapter 8 Think Now and Embrace the Future
Chapter 9 Control Leaves No Room for Complacency
Chapter 10 Passion and Values Make for Strategic Success
Chapter 11 It's All About How You Put the Pieces Together
Chapter 12 Healthy Living Sets a Positive Tone
Chapter 13 Great Employers Respect Diversity and Value People
Chapter 14 Leaders Provide the Roadmaps
Chapter 15 There Are Personalities Behind Those Faces
Chapter 16 Great Employers Bring Out the Best in US
Chapter 17 The Beauty is in the Teamwork
Chapter 18 Impact is Just a Tweet Away

## Insight: Learning About Yourself

Chapter 1 Self-Awareness
Chapter 2 Learning Style
Chapter 3 Individual Character
Chapter 4 Risk Taking
Chapter 5 Cultural Awareness
Chapter 6 Self-Management
Chapter 7 Self-Confidence
Chapter 8 Time Management
Chapter 9 Resiliency
Chapter 10 Critical Thinking
Chapter 11 Empowerment
Chapter 12 Tolerance for Ambiguity
Chapter 13 Conscientiousness
Chapter 14 Integrity
Chapter 15 Ambition
Chapter 16 Engagement
Chapter 17 Team Contributions
Chapter 18 Communication and Networking

## Ethics On the Line

Chapter 1 Access to Coke's Secret Formula Is a Tantalizer
Chapter 2 CEO Golden Parachutes Fly in Face of Public Outrage
Chapter 3 Your Social Media History Might Be a Job Hurdle
Chapter 4 Offshore E-Waste Graveyards Bury a Problem
Chapter 5 Who Wins when Nationalism Meets Protectionism
Chapter 6 Entrepreneurship Meets Caring Capitalism Meets Big Business
Chapter 7 Climber Left to Die on Mt. Everest
Chapter 8 What Really Works When Fighting World Poverty?
Chapter 9 Firms Find Global Traveling Rough on Privacy and Censorship
Chapter 10 Life and Death at an Outsourcing Factory
Chapter 11 Help! I've been Flattened into Exhaustion
Chapter 12 Hidden Agendas in Organizational Change

Chapter 13 Are Employers Checking Your Facebook Page?
Chapter 14 Would You Put Your Boss Above Your Organization?
Chapter 15 Is Personality Testing in Your Future?
Chapter 16 Information Goldmine Creates Equity Dilemma
Chapter 17 Social Loafing Is Getting in the Way
Chapter 18 Blogging Is Easy, But Bloggers Should Beware

## Follow the Story

Chapter 1 Indra Nooyi Pushes Pepsi Toward Responsibility and Sustainability
Chapter 2 Former Microsoft Executive Finds Fulfillment Fighting Illiteracy
Chapter 3 Business School Students Challenged to Serve the Greater Good
Chapter 4 Disruptive Innovation the Steve Jobs Way (1955–2011)
Chapter 5 Wal-Mart Holds a Chinese Tiger by the Tail
Chapter 6 Entrepreneurs Find Rural Setting Fuels Solar Power
Chapter 7 No. 2 at Facebook a Good Fit for Sheryl Sandberg
Chapter 8 Don Thompson Sets Goals for Winning Role at McDonald's
Chapter 9 Roger Ferguson Provides Strategic Leadership for Retirement Security
Chapter 10 Ursula Burns Sets Strategic Directions for Xerox
Chapter 11 Dancing Deer Baking Sweetens Growth with Values
Chapter 12 Alan Mulally Makes His Mark on Ford's Culture
Chapter 13 Tony Hsieh Taps HRM to Keep Zappos One Step Ahead
Chapter 14 Educator's Leadership Turns Vision into Inspiration
Chapter 15 Little Things Are Big Things at Life Is Good
Chapter 16 The King of Coffee Brews for Engagement
Chapter 17 Teams and Teamwork Help Put the Lift into Boeing's New Planes
Chapter 18 The Limited's Linda Heasley Gives Others Reasons to Work with Her

## Research Brief

Chapter 1 Worldwide Study Identifies Success Factors in Global Leadership
Chapter 2 Setting Personal Goals Improves Academic Performance
Chapter 3 Prioritizing Stakeholders for Organizational Action
Chapter 4 Generations Show Differences on Important Values
Chapter 5 Personality Traits, Behavioral Competencies, and Expatriate Effectiveness
Chapter 6 Do Founders of New Ventures Take Less Compensation than Other Senior Managers in Their Firms?
Chapter 7 Escalation Increases Risk of Unethical Decisions
Chapter 8 You've Got to Move Beyond Planning by the Calendar
Chapter 9 Restating Corporate Financial Performance Foreshadows Significant Executive Turnover
Chapter 10 Female Directors on Corporate Boards Linked with Positive Management Practices
Chapter 11 Making Schools Work Better with Organizational Design
Chapter 12 Top Management Must Get—and Stay—Committed for Shared Power to Work in Tandem with Top-Down Change
Chapter 13 Racial Bias May Exist in Supervisor Ratings of Workers

# MANAGEMENT

## TWELFTH EDITION

Bryce Vickmak 2009/Redux Pictures

# Wisdom
## Learning
## From Others

## > SMART PEOPLE CREATE THEIR OWN FUTURES

It's been a tough economy for job seekers. But isn't it time to take the future in your own hands?

There's a major shift toward online recruiting. The head of consulting firm Accenture's global recruiting says "this is the future of recruiting for our company." Sites like Monster.com and Careerbuilder.com are a good start for new graduates. On Facebook, apps like BranchOut and Jobvite help recruiters and job seekers find one another. LinkedIn.com is a destination for those with job experience. It claims over 150 million professionals use its site for networking and career visibility.[1]

Starting your own business can also be a great career choice. Not everyone wants to work for someone else. Monster.com began when founder Jeff Taylor, shown here, jotted an idea on a sketch pad, made an early-morning trip to a coffee shop, and turned his notes into a business concept.[2]

Whatever your career direction—entrepreneurship, corporate employer, nonprofit manager—there's one thing for sure: The future is yours, but you have to take charge and go for it. You have to keep developing and even reinventing yourself with every passing day. If smart people really do create their own futures, what path are you on? Don't ever forget, what happens next is up to you!

## MORE TO LOOK FOR INSIDE>

### FOLLOW THE STORY
Indra Nooyi Pushes Pepsi Toward Responsibility and Sustainability

### ETHICS ON THE LINE
Access to Coke's Secret Formula Is a Tantalizer

### FACTS FOR ANALYSIS
Employment Contradictions in Workforce Diversity

### RESEARCH BRIEF
Worldwide Study Identifies Success Factors in Global Leadership

# Introducing Management

## > SELF-AWARENESS

Although it's an important career skill, **self-awareness** can be easy to talk about but hard to master.[3] Self-Awareness helps us build on strengths and overcome weaknesses, and it helps us avoid seeing ourselves more favorably than is justified.

How often do you take a critical look at your attitudes, behaviors, skills, personal characteristics, and accomplishments? When was the last time you thought about them from a career perspective— as you see them and as others do?

The *Johari Window* is one pathway to self-awareness. It's a way of comparing what we know about ourselves with what others know about us.[4] The "open" areas known to ourselves and others are often small. The "blind spot," "the unknown," and the "hidden" areas can be quite large. They challenge our capacities for self-discovery.

Self-awareness is a pathway to adaptability, something we need to keep learning and growing in changing times. But remember the insights of the Johari Window. True self-awareness means not just knowing your idealized self—the person you want or hope to be. It also means knowing who you really are in the eyes of others and as defined by your actions.

## Insight
### Learning About Yourself

| | Unknown to you | Known to you |
|---|---|---|
| **Known to others** | Blind Spot | Open Area |
| **Unknown to others** | The Unknown | Hidden Self |

## BUILD SKILLS AND COMPETENCIES AT END OF CHAPTER

- Engage in *Further Reflection on Self-Awareness*
- Take the *Self-Assessment on Career Readiness*
- Complete the *Team Exercise—My Best Manager*
- Solve the *Career Situations for New Managers*
- Analyze the *Case Study—Trader Joe's: Keeping a Cool Edge*

**<GET TO KNOW YOURSELF BETTER**

| TAKEAWAY 1 | TAKEAWAY 2 | TAKEAWAY 3 | TAKEAWAY 4 | TAKEAWAY 5 |
|---|---|---|---|---|
| **Working Today** <br> • Talent <br> • Technology <br> • Globalization <br> • Ethics <br> • Diversity <br> • Careers | **Organizations** <br> • What is an organization? <br> • Organizations as systems <br> • Organizational performance <br> • Changing nature of organizations | **Managers** <br> • What is a manager? <br> • Levels of managers <br> • Types of managers <br> • Managerial performance <br> • Changing nature of managerial work | **The Management Process** <br> • Functions of management <br> • Managerial roles and activities <br> • Managerial agendas and networks | **Learning How to Manage** <br> • Essential managerial skills <br> • Developing managerial potential |
| LEARNING CHECK 1 | LEARNING CHECK 2 | LEARNING CHECK 3 | LEARNING CHECK 4 | LEARNING CHECK 5 |

Welcome to *Management 12/e* and its themes of personal development and career readiness. We live and work in a very complex world. Job scarcities, ethical miscues by business and government leaders, financial turmoil and uncertainties, great environmental challenges, and complex global economics and politics are regularly in the news. Today's organizations are fast changing, as is the nature of work itself. In most jobs, talent and technology reign supreme. Learning, quality, and speed are in; habit, complacency, and even security are out. Employers expect and demand high performance. The best of them provide creative and inspiring leadership and supportive work environments built around themes of respect, participation, empowerment, involvement, teamwork, and self-management.[5] All of this, and more, is what *Management 12/e* and your management course are about.

## Working Today

In her book *The Shift: The Future of Work Is Already Here*, scholar Lynda Gratton describes the difficult times in which we live and work. "Technology shrinks the world but consumes all of our time," she says, while "globalization means we can work anywhere, but must compete with people from everywhere."[6] What does this mean when planning for career entry and advancement? At a minimum there are few guarantees of long-term employment. Jobs are increasingly earned and re-earned every day through one's performance accomplishments. Careers are being redefined along the lines of "flexibility," "free agency," "skill portfolios," and "entrepreneurship." Career success requires lots of initiative and self awareness, as well as continuous learning. The question is: Are you ready?

## Talent

In a study of high-performing companies, management scholars Charles O'Reilly and Jeffrey Pfeffer report that they achieve success by being better than competitors at getting extraordinary results from the people working for them. "These companies have won the war for talent," they say, "not just by being great places to work—although they are that—but by figuring out how to get the best out of all of their people, every day."[7]

People and their talents—what they know, what they learn, and what they do with it—are the ultimate foundations of organizational performance. They represent what managers call **intellectual capital**, the collective brainpower or shared knowledge of a workforce that can be used to create value.[8] Intellectual capital is a strategic asset for organizations. It is the pathway to performance through human creativity, insight, and decision making. Intellectual capital is a personal asset for individuals. It is the package of intellect, skills, and capabilities that differentiates us from others and that makes us valuable to potential employers.

**Intellectual capital** is the collective brainpower or shared knowledge of a workforce.

When we talk in the chapter openers about Wisdom—Learning From Others and Insight—Learning About Yourself, the focus is really on developing your intellectual capital. Think about this **intellectual capital equation**: Intellectual Capital = Competency × Commitment.[9] **Competency** represents your talents or job-relevant capabilities, while **commitment** represents your willingness to work hard in applying them to important tasks. Both are essential. One without the other is not enough to meet anyone's career needs or any organization's performance requirements.

The **intellectual capital equation** states: Intellectual Capital = Competency × Commitment.

Today's workplaces are dominated by **knowledge workers**—persons whose minds, not just their physical capabilities, are critical assets.[10] Futurist Daniel Pink says that we are entering the *conceptual age*, which belongs to people with "whole mind" competencies that are both "high concept"—creative and good with ideas—and "high touch"—joyful and good with relationships.[11] Management scholar and consultant Gary Hamel says we have a *creative economy* "where even knowledge itself is becoming a commodity" and "the most important differentiator will be how fast you can create something new."[12] Such challenges will be best mastered by those who develop multiple skill sets that always keep personal competencies well aligned with emerging job trends.

A **knowledge worker** is someone whose mind is a critical asset to employers.

David Paul Morris/Bloomberg/Getty Images, Inc.

### Salesforce.com Puts Software in the Cloud

Cloud computing, or software and storage on demand through the Internet, is the power behind Salesforce.com. Created by Marc Neioff and a colleague in a San Francisco apartment, the firm provides software that companies use to track potential customers, keep track of existing ones, and track sales performance. The beauty is that all is done "in the cloud" with no required software resident on company computers. This means users save on costs and complications. Also, the products keep getting better as Salesforce.com constantly seeks feedback from its users and tweaks products to best fit their needs.

## Technology

Technology continuously tests our talents. We are bombarded with offers for the latest in smartphones, urged to join the shift from PCs to tablets, and struggle to keep up with our social media involvements. You might even be reading this book on an Amazon Fire or iPad. What will it be tomorrow?

It is essential to build and maintain what we might call a high **Tech IQ**—a person's ability to use technology at work and everyday living, and a commitment to stay informed on the latest technological developments. Tech IQ is required in basic operations of organizations, whether one is checking inventory, making a sales transaction, ordering supplies, or analyzing customer preferences. It is required in new ways of working as more and more people spend at least part of their work time "telecommuting" or "working from home" or in "mobile offices" that free them from the constraints of the normal "8–5" schedules. It is also required in the rapidly growing numbers of "virtual teams" whose members hold meetings, access common databases, share information and files, make plans, and solve problems together—all without ever meeting face to face.

Even the process of job seeking and employment screening is increasingly technology driven. The chapter opener introduced Monster.com and LinkedIn.com as online career sites used by job hunters and employers. To take advantage you have to be online and also use the right protocols—Tech IQ again. Poor communication like "Hey dude, you got any jobs in Texas?" doesn't work in the world of electronic job searches. Filling your online profile with the right key words does work. Employers use special software to scan online profiles for indicators of real job skills and experiences that fit their needs. And don't forget, many if not most recruiters are now checking social media sites for negative indicators about their job applicants.

**Tech IQ** is ability to use technology and to stay informed on the latest technological developments.

## Globalization

National boundaries hardly count anymore in the world of business.[13] Over 5 million Americans work in the United States for foreign employers.[14] We buy foreign cars like Toyota, Nissan, and Mercedes-Benz that are assembled in America. We buy appliances from the Chinese firm Haier and Eight O'Clock Coffee from India's Tata Group. Top managers at Starbucks, IBM, Sony, Ford, and other global corporations have little need for the words "overseas" or "international" in everyday business vocabulary. They operate as global businesses that serve customers wherever in the world they are located. And, they source materials and hire talent wherever in the world they are available at the lowest costs.

These are among the many faces of **globalization**, the worldwide interdependence of resource flows, product markets, and business competition that characterizes our economy.[15] In our global world, government leaders now worry about the competitiveness of nations, just as corporate leaders worry about business competitiveness.[16] Countries and people are not just interconnected through the news, in travel, and lifestyles; they are interconnected in labor markets and employment patterns, and in financial and business dealings. At a time when many Americans find that their customer service call is answered in Ghana, their CAT scan read by a radiologist in India, and their tax return prepared by an accountant in the Philippines, the fact that globalization offers both opportunities and challenges is quite clear indeed.

**Globalization** is the worldwide interdependence of resource flows, product markets, and business competition.

## Teach for America Offers Chance to Do Good While Gaining Experience

Founded by Wendy Kopp and based on her undergraduate thesis at Princeton University, Teach for America's nonprofit organization's mission "is to build the movement to eliminate educational inequity by enlisting our nation's most promising future leaders in the effort." Teach for America recruits college graduates to serve for two years in urban and rural public schools. Over 4,000 new teachers join the corps each year, and Kopp says: "We believe that education is the great enabler [and that] it's the foundation for life opportunity."

Press-Telegram, Stephen Carr/AP/Wide World Photos

One controversial side effect to globalization is **job migration**, the shifting of jobs from one country to another. The U.S. economy has been a net loser to job migration while countries like China, India, and the Philippines are net gainers. Politicians and policymakers regularly debate the high costs of job migration as local workers lose jobs and their communities lose economic vitality. One side looks for new government policies to stop job migration and protect the jobs of U.S. workers. The other side calls for patience, believing that the national economy will strengthen and grow jobs in the long run as the global economy readjusts.

**Job migration** occurs when firms shift jobs from one country to another.

As costs of manufacturing in countries like China rise, some firms like Caterpillar, Ford, and General Electric have started shifting some manufacturing and jobs back to the United States.[17] Worries about intellectual property theft in foreign operations also make domestic manufacturing more appealing to some. When Intel announced an expansion of its semiconductor plant in Arizona, an industry analyst said: "The huge advantage of keeping manufacturing in the U.S. is you don't have to worry about your intellectual property walking out the door every evening."[18]

## Ethics

When Bernard Madoff was sentenced to 150 years in jail for a fraudulent Ponzi scheme that cost investors billions of dollars, the message was crystal clear: Commit white-collar crime and you will be punished.[19] Madoff's crime did terrible harm to individuals who lost lifelong and retirement savings, foundations that lost millions in charitable gifts, and employees who lost jobs. Society at large paid a price, too, as faith in the nation's business system was damaged by the scandal. If this was a unique or limited case of bad behavior by a business executive it would be one thing, but the problem is bigger. It seems like a new scandal hits the news almost every week.

The issue raised here goes beyond criminal behavior to embrace the broader notion of **ethics**—a code of moral principles that sets standards for what is "good" and "right" as opposed to "bad" and "wrong" in the conduct of a person or group.[20] At the end of the day we depend on individual people, working at all levels of organizations, to act ethically in all aspects of their jobs and in all their working relationships. In his book, *The Transparent Leader*, the former CEO of Dial Corporation, Herb Baum, argues that integrity is a key to leadership success and that the responsibility for

**Ethics** set moral standards of what is "good" and "right" in one's behavior.

setting the ethical tone of an organization begins at the top. Believing that most CEOs are overpaid, he once gave his annual bonus to the firm's lowest-paid workers.[21]

Ethics, social responsibility, and sustainability are recurring topics in this book. And you'll find many examples of people and organizations that are exemplars of ethical behavior and integrity. Each chapter also has an Ethics on the Line feature that helps you to think through and consider ethical challenges from everyday life and work situations.

---

**ETHICS ON THE LINE**

> IT MAY BE A WAY TO GAIN VISIBILITY WITH THE BIG BOSS.
BUT IS IT THE RIGHT THING TO DO?

## Access to Coke's Secret Formula Is a Tantalizer

Thomas Tolstrup/Newscom

**Scene:** *Corporate headquarters of PepsiCo.*
A young executive is gesturing excitedly, and three more obviously senior ones listen attentively. The CEO sits at her desk, swiveling occasionally in the chair while listening carefully to the conversation.

YOUNG EXECUTIVE, *acting a bit proud to be there*
It started with a telephone call. I agreed to meet with a former employee of Coca-Cola at his request. We met and, lo and behold, he offered me the "secret formula."

ONE OF THE SENIOR EXECUTIVES, *cautiously*
Let me be sure I understand. You received a call from someone who said he used to work at Coke, and that person was requesting a face-to-face meeting. Correct?

YOUNG EXECUTIVE, *quickly and proudly*
Right!

THE SENIOR EXECUTIVE, *with a bit of challenge*
Why? Why would you meet with someone who said he just left Coke?

YOUNG EXECUTIVE, *tentative now*
Well . . . I . . . uh . . . It seemed like a great chance to get some competitive information and maybe even hire someone who really knows their strategies.

SECOND SENIOR EXECUTIVE
So, what happened next?

YOUNG EXECUTIVE, *excited again*
Well, after just a minute or two conversing, he said that he had the formula!

SECOND SENIOR EXECUTIVE
And . . .?

YOUNG EXECUTIVE, *uncertain all of a sudden and now speaking softly*
He said it was "for sale."

THIRD SENIOR EXECUTIVE, *with a bit of edge in her voice*
So, what did you say?

YOUNG EXECUTIVE, *looking down and shuffling slightly backward*
I said that I'd take it "up the ladder." I'm supposed to call him back . . .

CEO, *breaking into the conversation*
And we're glad you did "bring it up the ladder," as you say. But now that you have, what do you propose we do about this opportunity to buy Coke's most important secret?
*As CEO speaks, other senior executives move over to stand behind her. Everyone looks in the direction of the young executive.*

 **YOU DECIDE**

This young executive's career prospects might depend on his answer. What do you think he will recommend? Perhaps more importantly, what would you do? What are the key ethical tradeoffs that need to be considered here?

# Diversity

The term **workforce diversity** describes the composition of a workforce in terms of such differences as gender, age, race, ethnicity, religion, sexual orientation, and able-bodiedness.[22] Diversity trends of changing demographics in society are well recognized. Minorities now constitute more than one-third of the U.S. population; by 2050, African Americans, American Indians, Asians, and Hispanics will be the new majority. Also by 2050, the U.S. Census Bureau expects that more than 20% of the population will be aged 65+ years. And, women may already outnumber men in the U.S. workforce.[23]

Even though society is diverse, the way we deal with diversity in the workplace remains an issue. Women now lead global companies like IBM, PepsiCo, Xerox, and Kraft, but they hold only 2% of all top jobs in American firms.[24] Why do so few women make it to the top? And what about people of color? Researchers have found that résumés with white-sounding first names, such as Brett, received 50% more responses from potential employers than those with black-sounding first names, such as Kareem.[25] The résumé credentials were equal. Researchers have also found that experimental subjects view white leaders as more successful than minority leaders, most often expect business leaders to "be White," and believe that white leaders succeed because of competence and non-white leaders succeed despite incompetency.[26] Where does such diversity bias come from?

The stage for diversity bias is set by **prejudice**—the holding of negative, irrational opinions and attitudes regarding members of diverse populations. An example is lingering prejudice against working mothers. The nonprofit Families and Work Institute reports that in 1977 49% of men and 71% of women believed that mothers can be good employees; by 2008 the figures had risen to 67% and 80%.[27] Don't you wonder why the figures aren't 100% in support of working mothers?

Prejudice becomes active **discrimination** when minority members are unfairly treated and denied the full benefits of organizational membership. An example is when a manager fabricates reasons not to interview a minority job candidate, or refuses to promote a working mother for fear that parenting responsibilities may make it hard for her to do a good job. Such thinking shows a subtle form of discrimination called the **glass ceiling effect**, an invisible barrier or "ceiling" that prevents women and minorities from rising above a certain level of organizational responsibility. Scholar Judith Rosener warns that the loss caused by any form of discriminatory practices is "undervalued and underutilized human capital."[28]

The position of Chief Diversity Officer, or CDO, is gaining stature in organizations. Its presence recognizes that diversity is not only a moral issue but an opportunity for real performance gains. The job of CDO to make sure the work environment supports women and minorities, allows them to flourish, and fully utilizes their talents.[29]

**Workforce diversity** describes differences among workers in gender, race, age, ethnicity, religion, sexual orientation, and able-bodiedness.

**Prejudice** is the display of negative, irrational attitudes toward members of diverse populations.

**Discrimination** actively denies minority members the full benefits of organizational membership.

The **glass ceiling effect** is an invisible barrier limiting career advancement of women and minorities.

# Careers

When the economy is down and employment markets are tight, the task of finding a career entry point can be daunting. It always pays to remember the importance of online résumés and job searches, and the power of social networking with established professionals. It's also helpful to pursue internships as pathways to first-job placements. But don't forget the importance of the skills you can offer a potential employer and how well you communicate. Picture yourself in a job interview. The recruiter asks this question: "What can you do for us?" How do you reply?

# Employment Contradictions in Workforce Diversity

The nonprofit research group Catalyst points out that "Now more than ever, as companies examine how to best weather an economy in crisis, we need talented business leaders, and many of these leaders, yet untapped, are women." Susan Sandberg, Facebook's Chief Operating Officer, says the small number of women found in top jobs in U.S. companies represents a "stalled revolution." Research studies and news reports continue to show contradictions in workforce diversity.

- Women earn some 60% of college degrees but hold just over 50% of managerial jobs.
- Women hold 3.6% of CEO jobs and 15% of senior manager jobs in *Fortune* 500 firms.
- Women hold 16% of board seats at *Fortune* 500 firms; women of color hold 3% of board seats.

- The median compensation of female CEOs in North American firms is 85% that of males; in the largest firms it is 61%.
- For each $1 earned by male managers, female managers earn 79 cents and female managers in finance earn just 59 cents.

 **YOUR THOUGHTS?**

How can these data be explained? How can contradictions like these be justified? How can they be corrected? What are the implications of these data for you and your career aspirations?

---

A **shamrock organization** operates with a core group of full-time long-term workers supported by others who work on contracts and part-time.

In a **free-agent economy** people change jobs more often, and many work on independent contracts with a shifting mix of employers.

**Self-management** is the ability to understand oneself, exercise initiative, accept responsibility, and learn from experience.

Today's career challenge isn't just about finding your first job; it's also about successful career planning in changing times. British scholar and consultant Charles Handy uses the analogy of the **shamrock organization** to highlight the challenges.[30] The first leaf in the shamrock is a core group of permanent, full-time employees who follow standard career paths. And, the number of people in this first leaf is shrinking.[31] They are being replaced by growth in a second leaf of "freelancers" and "independent contractors". They provide organizations with specialized skills and talents on a contract basis, and then change employers when projects are completed.[32] Full-time employees are also being replaced by a growing third leaf of temporary part-timers. They often work without benefits and are the first to lose their jobs when an employer runs into economic difficulties.

You will have to succeed in a **free-agent economy**, one where people change jobs more often and work on flexible contracts with a shifting mix of employers over time. Skills like those in Management Smarts must be kept up-to-date, portable, and always of value.[33] These skills can't be gained once and then forgotten. They must be carefully maintained and upgraded all the time. All this places a premium on your capacity for **self-management**—being able to realistically assess yourself, make constructive changes, and manage your personal development.

## ManagementSmarts

### Early Career Survival Skills

*Mastery:* You need to be good at something; you need to be able to contribute real value to your employer.

*Networking:* You need to know people; networking with others within and outside the organization is essential to get things done.

*Entrepreneurship:* You must act as if you are running your own business, spotting ideas and opportunities and running with them.

*Technology:* You have to embrace technology; you have to stay up to date and fully utilize what becomes newly available.

*Marketing:* You need to communicate your successes and progress, both yours personally and those of your work team.

*Passion for renewal:* You need to be continuously learning and changing, always updating yourself to best match future demands.

**TAKEAWAY QUESTION 1 What are the challenges of working in the new economy?**

**Be sure you can** • describe how intellectual capital, ethics, diversity, globalization, technology, and the changing nature of careers influence working in the new economy • define *intellectual capital, workforce diversity,* and *globalization* • explain how prejudice, discrimination, and the glass ceiling can hurt people at work

# Organizations

As pointed out earlier, what happens from this point forward in your career is largely up to you. So, let's start with organizations. In order to make good employment choices and perform well in a career, you need to understand the nature of organizations and how they work as complex systems.

## What Is an Organization?

An **organization** is a collection of people working together to achieve a common purpose. It is a unique social phenomenon that enables its members to perform tasks far beyond the reach of individual accomplishment. This description applies to organizations of all sizes and types that make up the life of any community, from large corporations to small businesses, and nonprofit organizations such as schools, government agencies, and community hospitals.

> An **organization** is a collection of people working together to achieve a common purpose.

The broad purpose of any organization is to provide goods or services of value to customers and clients. A clear sense of purpose tied to "quality products and services," "customer satisfaction," and "social responsibility" can be an important source of organizational strength and performance advantage. IBM's former CEO, Samuel Palmisano, once said: "One simple way to assess the impact of any organization is to answer the question: How is the world different because it existed?" He answered this question by launching the firm's Smarter Planet initiative to address everything "from clean water, to safe food, to sustainable and vibrant cities, to green energy, to better schools, to smarter work, and an empowered workforce."[34] Whole Foods founder John Mackey says: "I think that business has a noble purpose. It means that businesses serve society. They produce goods and services that make people's lives better." On the Whole Foods website this is stated as a commitment to "Whole Foods—Whole People—Whole Planet."[35]

## Organizations as Systems

All organizations are **open systems** that interact with their environments. They do so in a continual process of obtaining resource inputs—people, information, resources, and capital—and transforming them into outputs in the form of finished goods and services for customers.[36]

> An **open system** transforms resource inputs from the environment into product outputs.

As shown in Figure 1.1, feedback from the environment indicates how well an organization is doing. When Starbucks started a customer blog, for example, requests for speedier service popped up. The company quickly made changes that

FIGURE 1.1 **Organizations as open systems interacting with their environments.**

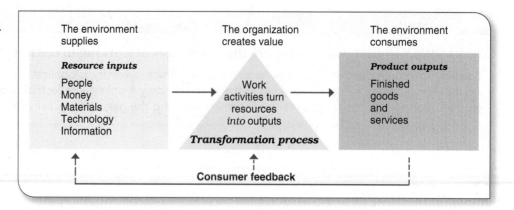

eliminated required signatures on credit card charges less than $25. Salesforce.com is another company that thrives on feedback. It set up a website called Idea Exchange to get customer suggestions, even asking them at one point to vote on a possible name change—the response was "No!"[37] Gathering and listening to customer feedback is important; without loyal customers, a business can't survive. When you hear or read about bankruptcies, they are stark testimonies to this fact of the marketplace.

## Organizational Performance

Organizations create value when they use resources well to produce good products and take care of their customers. When operations add value to the original cost of resource inputs, then (1) a business organization can earn a profit—that is, sell a product for more than the costs of making it—or (2) a nonprofit organization can add wealth to society—that is, provide a public service like fire protection that is worth more than its cost.

One of the most common ways to assess performance by and within organizations is **productivity**. It measures the quantity and quality of outputs relative to the cost of inputs. And as Figure 1.2 shows, productivity involves both performance effectiveness and performance efficiency.

**Performance effectiveness** is an output measure of task or goal accomplishment. If you are working as a software engineer for a computer game developer, performance effectiveness may mean that you meet a daily production target in terms of the quantity and quality of lines of code written. This productivity helps the company meet customer demands for timely delivery of high-quality gaming products.

**Productivity** is the quantity and quality of work performance, with resource utilization considered.

**Performance effectiveness** is an output measure of task or goal accomplishment.

FIGURE 1.2 **Productivity and the dimensions of organizational performance.**

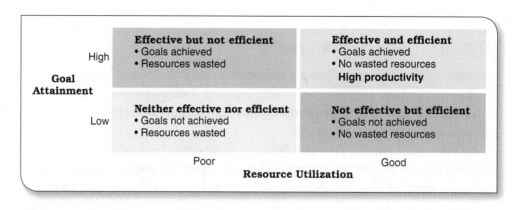

**Performance efficiency** is an input measure of the resource costs associated with goal accomplishment. Returning to the gaming example, the most efficient software production is accomplished at a minimum cost in materials and labor. If you are producing fewer lines of code in a day than you are capable of, this amounts to inefficiency; if you make a lot of mistakes that require extensive rewrites, this is also inefficient work. All such inefficiencies drive up costs and reduce productivity.

**Performance efficiency** is an input measure of resource cost associated with goal accomplishment.

## Changing Nature of Organizations

Change is a continuing theme in our society, and organizations are no exception. The following list shows some of the organizational trends and transitions relevant to the study of management.[38]

- *Focus on valuing human capital:* The premium is on high-involvement work settings that rally the knowledge, experience, and commitment of all members.
- *Demise of "command-and-control":* Traditional top-down "do as I say" bosses are giving way to participatory bosses who treat people with respect.
- *Emphasis on teamwork:* Organizations are more horizontal in focus, and driven by teamwork that pools talents for creative problem solving.
- *Preeminence of technology:* New developments in computer and information technology continually change the way organizations operate and how people work.
- *Importance of networking:* Organizations and their members are networked for intense, real-time communication and coordination.
- *New workforce expectations:* A new generation of workers is less tolerant of hierarchy, more informal, attentive to performance merit, and concerned for work–life balance.
- *Priorities on sustainability:* Social values show more attention to preservation of natural resources for future generations and understanding how work affects human well-being.

---

**LEARNING CHECK 2**

**TAKEAWAY QUESTION 2 What are organizations like in the new workplace?**

**Be sure you can** • describe how organizations operate as open systems • explain productivity as a measure of organizational performance • distinguish between performance effectiveness and performance efficiency • list several ways in which organizations are changing today

---

# Managers

In an article entitled "Putting People First for Organizational Success," Jeffrey Pfeffer and John F. Veiga argue forcefully that organizations perform better when they treat their members better.[39] Managers in these high-performing organizations don't treat people as costs to be controlled; they treat them as valuable strategic assets to be carefully nurtured and developed. So, who are today's managers and just what do they do?

## What Is a Manager?

A **manager** is a person who supports, activates, and is responsible for the work of others.

You find them in all organizations and with a wide variety of job titles—team leader, department head, supervisor, project manager, president, administrator, and more. We call them **managers**, people in organizations who directly support, supervise, and help activate the work efforts and performance accomplishments of others. Whether they are called direct reports, team members, work associates, or subordinates, these "other people" are the essential human resources whose contributions represent the real work of the organization. And as pointed out by management scholar Henry Mintzberg, being a manager remains an important and socially responsible job. "No job is more vital to our society than that of the manager," he says. "It is the manager who determines whether our social institutions serve us well or whether they squander our talents and resources."[40]

## Levels of Managers

Members of a **board of directors** or board of trustees are supposed to make sure an organization is run right.

At the highest levels of business organizations, as shown in Figure 1.3, we find a **board of directors** whose members are elected by stockholders to represent their ownership interests. In nonprofit organizations such as a hospital or university, this level is often called a *board of trustees*, and it may be elected by local citizens, appointed by government bodies, or invited by existing members. The basic responsibilities of board members are the same in both business and the public sector—to make sure that the organization is always being run right.[41]

Common job titles just below the board level are chief executive officer (CEO), chief operating officer (COO), chief financial officer (CFO), chief information officer (CIO), chief diversity officer (CDO), president, and vice president. These **top managers** constitute an executive team that reports to the board and is responsible for the performance of an organization as a whole or for one of its larger parts.

**Top managers** guide the performance of the organization as a whole or of one of its major parts.

Top managers are supposed to set strategy and lead the organization consistent with its purpose and mission. They should pay special attention to the external environment and be alert to potential long-run problems and opportunities. The best top managers are strategic thinkers able to make good decisions under highly competitive and even uncertain conditions. A CEO at Procter & Gamble

FIGURE 1.3 **Management levels in typical business and nonprofit organizations.**

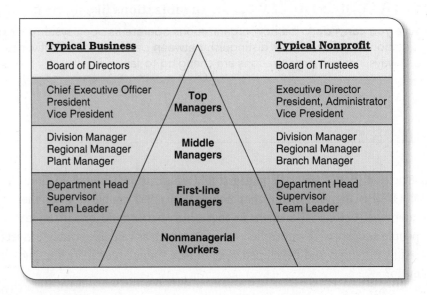

| Typical Business | | Typical Nonprofit |
|---|---|---|
| Board of Directors | | Board of Trustees |
| Chief Executive Officer<br>President<br>Vice President | **Top Managers** | Executive Director<br>President, Administrator<br>Vice President |
| Division Manager<br>Regional Manager<br>Plant Manager | **Middle Managers** | Division Manager<br>Regional Manager<br>Branch Manager |
| Department Head<br>Supervisor<br>Team Leader | **First-line Managers** | Department Head<br>Supervisor<br>Team Leader |
| | **Nonmanagerial Workers** | |

once said the job of top managers is to "link the external world with the internal organization . . . make sure the voice of the consumer is heard . . . shape values and standards."[42]

Reporting to top managers are the **middle managers**, who are in charge of relatively large departments or divisions consisting of several smaller work units. Examples are clinic directors in hospitals; deans in universities; and division managers, plant managers, and regional sales managers in businesses. Middle managers work with top managers, coordinate with peers, and support lower levels to develop and pursue action plans that implement organizational strategies to accomplish key objectives.

> **Middle managers** oversee the work of large departments or divisions.

A first job in management typically involves serving as a **team leader** or supervisor—someone in charge of a small work group composed of nonmanagerial workers.[43] Typical job titles for these *first-line* managers include department head, team leader, and supervisor. The leader of an auditing team, for example, is considered a first-line manager as is the head of an academic department in a university. Even though most people enter the workforce as technical specialists such as engineer, market researcher, or systems analyst, they most often advance sooner or later to positions of initial managerial responsibility.

> **Team leaders** report to middle managers and supervise nonmanagerial workers.

## Types of Managers

There are many types of managers in organizations. **Line managers** are responsible for work that makes a direct contribution to the organization's outputs. For example, the president, retail manager, and department supervisors of a local department store all have line responsibilities. Their jobs in one way or another are directly related to the sales operations of the store. **Staff managers**, by contrast, use special technical expertise to advise and support the efforts of line workers. In a department store chain like Nordstrom's or Macy's, the corporate director of human resources and chief financial officer would have staff responsibilities.

> **Line managers** directly contribute to producing the organization's goods or services.
>
> **Staff managers** use special technical expertise to advise and support line workers.
>
> **Functional managers** are responsible for one area, such as finance, marketing, production, personnel, accounting, or sales.
>
> **General managers** are responsible for complex, multifunctional units.
>
> An **administrator** is a manager in a public or nonprofit organization.
>
> **Accountability** is the requirement to show performance results to a supervisor.

**Functional managers** have responsibility for a single area of activity such as finance, marketing, production, human resources, accounting, or sales. **General managers** are responsible for activities covering many functional areas. An example is a plant manager who oversees everything from purchasing to manufacturing to human resources to finance and accounting functions. In public or nonprofit organizations, managers may be called **administrators**. Examples include hospital administrators, public administrators, and city administrators.

## Managerial Performance

All managers help people, working individually and in teams, to perform. They do this while being personally accountable for results achieved. **Accountability** is the requirement of one person to answer to a higher authority for performance results in his or her area of work responsibility.

In the traditional organizational pyramid, accountability flows upward. The team leader is accountable to a middle

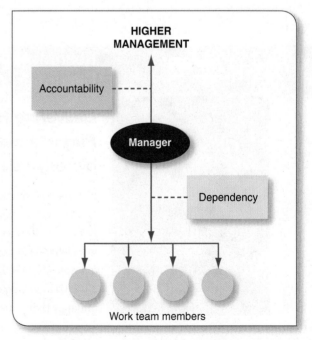

manager, the middle manager is accountable to a top manager, and even the top manager is accountable to a board of directors or board of trustees. This accountability was evident when Hewlett Packard's board fired CEO Leo Apotheker after only 11 months on the job. The board chairman, Ray Lane, said Apotheker had missed quarterly performance targets and failed to communicate well on important issues.[44] This termination decision showed **corporate governance** in action. HP's board was holding the CEO accountable for the firm's poor performance.

But what, you might ask, constitutes excellence in managerial performance? When is a manager "effective"? A good answer is that **effective managers** successfully help others achieve both high performance *and* satisfaction in their work. This dual concern for performance and satisfaction introduces **quality of work life** (QWL) as an indicator of the overall quality of human experiences at work. A "high-QWL" workplace offers such things as respect, fair pay, safe conditions, opportunities to learn and use new skills, room to grow and progress in a career, and protection of individual rights and wellness.

Scholar Jeffrey Pfeffer considers QWL a high priority sustainability issue. Why, Pfeffer asks, don't we add to our concerns for natural environment sustainability further concerns for human sustainability and "organizational effects on employee health and mortality"?[45] What do you think? Should managers be held accountable not just for performance accomplishments of their teams and work units, but also for the human sustainability of those who work with and for them? In other words, shouldn't productivity and quality of working life go hand in hand?

**Corporate governance** occurs when a board of directors holds top management accountable for organizational performance.

An **effective manager** helps others achieve high performance and satisfaction at work.

**Quality of work life** is the overall quality of human experiences in the workplace.

## Changing Nature of Managerial Work

Cindy Zollinger, president and CEO of Cornerstone Research, directly supervises over 20 people. But she says: "I don't really manage them in a typical way; they largely run themselves. I help them in dealing with obstacles they face, or in making the most of opportunities they find."[46] These comments suggest we are in a time when the best managers are known more for "helping" and "supporting" than for

## Recommended Reading

Brad Swonetz/Redux Pictures

### *Delivering Happiness: A Path to Profits, Passion and Purpose* (Business Plus, 2010)
### by Tony Hsieh

If you've ever ordered shoes or other items from Zappos.com, you should have had a great customer experience. That's part of CEO Tony Hsieh's successful business model. But if you talk with any of Zappos' employees—Zapponians—you'll also find they thrive in Hsieh's "work hard, play hard" culture—one that includes a "culture fit" job interview followed by such things as free food, fully paid health and dental insurance, and even a $2,000 bonus for quitting. Yes, it's true! Hsieh says he'd rather pay you to leave if you are unhappy than suffer the cost of having an unhappy employee on board.

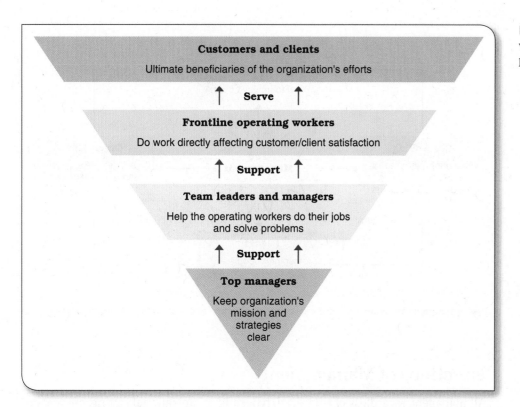

FIGURE 1.4 **The organization viewed as an upside-down pyramid.**

"directing" and "order giving." The words *coordinator*, *coach*, and *team leader* are heard as often as *supervisor* or *boss*.

The concept of the **upside-down pyramid** shown in Figure 1.4 fits well with the changing mindset of managerial work today. Notice that the operating and front-line workers are at the top of the upside-down pyramid, just below the customers and clients they serve. They are supported in their work efforts by managers below them. These managers aren't just order-givers; they are there to mobilize and deliver the support others need to do their jobs best and serve customer needs. Sitting at the bottom are top managers and executives; their jobs are to support everyone and everything above them. The upside-down pyramid view leaves no doubt that the whole organization is devoted to serving customers and that the job of managers is to support the workers who make this possible.

The **upside-down pyramid** view of organizations shows customers at the top being served by workers who are supported by managers.

## The Management Process

The ultimate "bottom line" in every manager's job is to help an organization achieve high performance by best utilizing its human and material resources. This is accomplished through the four functions of management in what is called the **management process**—planning, organizing, leading, and controlling.

The **management process** is planning, organizing, leading, and controlling the use of resources to accomplish performance goals.

FIGURE 1.5 **Four functions of management—planning, organizing, leading, and controlling.**

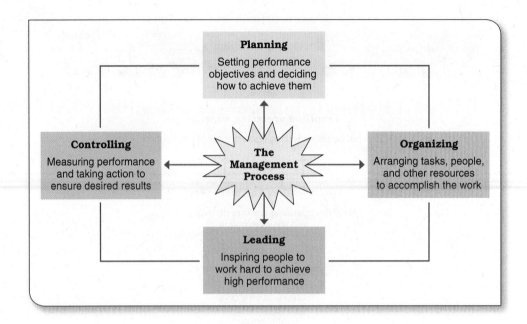

## Functions of Management

All managers, regardless of title, level, type, and organizational setting, are responsible for the four management functions shown in Figure 1.5. These functions are continually engaged as a manager moves from task to task and opportunity to opportunity in his or her work.

### Planning

**Planning** is the process of setting objectives and determining what should be done to accomplish them.

In management, **planning** is the process of setting performance objectives and determining what actions should be taken to accomplish them. Through planning, a manager identifies desired results and ways to achieve them.

Take, for example, an Ernst & Young initiative that was developed to better meet the needs of the firm's female professionals. This initiative grew out of top management's concern about the firm's retention rates for women.[47] Then-chairman Philip A. Laskawy launched a Diversity Task Force with the planning objective to reduce turnover rates for women. When the task force began its work, this turnover was running some 22% per year, and it cost the firm about 150% of a departing employee's annual salary to hire and train each replacement. Laskawy considered this performance unacceptable and put plans in place to improve it.

### Organizing

**Organizing** is the process of assigning tasks, allocating resources, and coordinating work activities.

Once plans are set, they must be implemented. This begins with **organizing**, the process of assigning tasks, allocating resources, and coordinating the activities of individuals and groups to accomplish plans. Organizing is how managers turn plans into actions by defining jobs, assigning personnel, and supporting them with technology and other resources.

At Ernst & Young, Laskawy organized by convening and personally chairing a Diversity Task Force to meet his planning objective. He also established a new Office of Retention and hired Deborah K. Holmes, now serving as global director of corporate responsibility, to head it. As retention problems were identified in

# Indra Nooyi Pushes Pepsi Toward Responsibility and Sustainability

Natalia Kolesnikova/AFP/Getty Images/Newscom

Indra Nooyi, PepsiCo's Chairman and CEO, says the best advice she ever got came from her father: "Always assume positive intent." If you do, she says, "you will be amazed at how your whole approach to a person or problem becomes very different. . . . You are trying to understand and listen because at your basic core you are saying, 'Maybe they are saying something to me that I am not hearing.'"

This advice has helped carry Nooyi from childhood in India to the top ranks of global business. *BusinessWeek* has described her as a leader with "prescient business sense." Former PepsiCo CEO Roger Enrico says, "Indra can drive as deep and hard as anyone I've ever met, but she can do it with a sense of heart and fun."

Nooyi believes that a firm's "real profit" should be measured as Revenue less Cost of Goods Sold less Costs to Society. "It's critically important that we take that responsibility very, very seriously," she says. "We have to make sure that what corporations do doesn't add costs to society."

Lots of people would argue that a firm that sells soft drinks and snack food has a lot of social costs to bear. For her part, Nooyi has invested more than $50 billion in a "Good for You" initiative to bring to market healthier snacks and beverage selections, ones with less sugar and salt and more healthful oils. She has also pushed the firm to cut back its energy use and improve environmental sustainability.

Nooyi's initiatives with healthier products have taken a toll on profits. Pepsi-Cola has lost U.S. market share to Coca-Cola, and Coke's stock price has vastly outperformed Pepsi's. Critics claim Nooyi "took her eye off the ball" in the push toward healthier products. She has responded with a major company-wide strategic review and increased ad spending. But she's also sticking with her commitment to healthier products. So far, at least, Nooyi's moves have the support of PepsiCo's board.

 **YOUR TAKE?**

Indra Nooyi makes lots of decisions every day that have consequences for her firm, customers, and society at large. But she seems to lead with personal confidence and a strong sense of ethical direction. Is she a leadership role model worth thinking more about? Can she really make "costs to society" part of her firm's bottom line? Does Nooyi have what it takes to maintain investor and board support while she remakes PepsiCo into a "healthier" success story?

---

various parts of the firm, Holmes also organized special task forces to tackle them and recommend location-specific solutions.

## Leading

**Leading** is the process of arousing people's enthusiasm and inspiring their efforts to work hard to fulfill plans and accomplish objectives. Managers lead by building commitments to a common vision, encouraging activities that support goals, and influencing others to do their best work on the organization's behalf.

Deborah K. Holmes actively pursued her leadership responsibilities at Ernst & Young. She noticed that, in addition to stress caused by intense work at the firm, women often faced more stress because their spouses also worked. She became a champion for improved work–life balance and pursued it vigorously. She

**Leading** is the process of arousing enthusiasm and inspiring efforts to achieve goals.

# Worldwide Study Identifies Success Factors in Global Leadership

Robert J. House and colleagues developed a network of 170 researchers to study leadership around the world. Over a 10-year period they investigated cultural frameworks, cultural differences, and their leadership implications as part of Project GLOBE. The results are summarized in the book *Culture, Leadership and Organizations: The GLOBE Study of 62 Societies*.

Data from over 17,000 managers working in 62 national cultures were collected and analyzed. The researchers found that the world's cultures do have some differences in what constitutes leadership effectiveness. But they also share some universal facilitators to leadership success—such as leaders being honest and trustworthy, and impediments—such as leaders being self-protective and dictatorial.

In terms of leadership development, the GLOBE researchers concluded that global mindsets, tolerance for ambiguity, cultural adaptability, and flexibility are essential as leaders seek to influence persons whose cultural backgrounds are different from their own. Personal aspects that seemed most culturally sensitive in terms of leadership effectiveness were being individualistic, being status conscious, and being open to risk.

 **YOU BE THE RESEARCHER**

Take a survey of workers at your university, your place of employment, or a local organization. Ask them to describe their best and worst leaders. Use the results to answer the

question: How closely do local views of leadership match with findings of the GLOBE study? Don't you agree that we still have a lot more to learn about how leadership success is viewed in the many cultures of the world? The links between culture and leadership seem particularly important, not only in a business context, but also as governments try to work together both bilaterally and multilaterally in forums such as the United Nations.

---

**Universal facilitators of leadership effectiveness**
- Trustworthy, honest, just
- Foresight, ability to plan ahead
- Positive, dynamic, encouraging, motivating
- Communicative, informed, integrating

**Universal impediments to leadership effectiveness**
- Loner, asocial, self-protective
- Noncooperative, irritable
- Dictatorial and autocratic

---

*Reference:* Robert J. House, P. J. Hanges, Mansour Javidan, P. Dorfman, and V. Gupta (eds.), *Culture, Leadership and Organizations: The GLOBE Study of 62 Societies* (Thousand Oaks, CA: Sage Publications, 2004); Mansour Javidan, Peter W. Dorfman, Mary Sully de Luque, and Robert J. House, *Academy of Management Perspective*, vol. 20 (2006), pp. 67–90.

---

started "call-free holidays" where professionals did not check voice mail or e-mail on weekends and holidays. She started a "travel sanity" program that limited staffers' travel to four days a week so that they could get home for weekends. And, she started a Woman's Access Program to provide mentoring and career development.

## Controlling

**Controlling** is the process of measuring performance and taking action to ensure desired results.

The management function of **controlling** is the process of measuring work performance, comparing results to objectives, and taking corrective action as needed. Managers exercise control by staying in active contact with people as they work, gathering and interpreting performance measurements, and using this information to make constructive changes. Control is indispensable in the management process. Things don't always go as anticipated, and plans must often be modified and redefined to best fit new circumstances.

At Ernst & Young, Laskawy and Holmes documented what the firm's retention rates for women were when they started the new programs. This gave them a clear baseline against which they were able to track progress. They regularly measured retention rates for women and compared them to the baseline. By comparing results with plans and objectives, they were able to identify successes and also pinpoint where they needed to further improve their work–life balance programs. Over time, turnover rates for women were reduced at all levels in the firm.

## Managerial Roles and Activities

The management process and its responsibilities for planning, organizing, leading, and controlling are more complicated than they appear at first glance. They must be successfully accomplished during a work day that can be very challenging. In his classic book, *The Nature of Managerial Work*, for example, Henry Mintzberg describes the daily work of corporate chief executives as follows: "There was no break in the pace of activity during office hours. The mail . . . telephone calls . . . and meetings . . . accounted for almost every minute from the moment these executives entered their offices in the morning until they departed in the evenings."[48] Today we would complicate things even further by adding ever-present e-mail, instant messages, and social media attention to Mintzberg's list of executive preoccupations.

### Managerial Roles

In trying to better understand and describe the nature of managerial work, Mintzberg identified a set of 10 roles commonly filled by managers.[49] The roles fall into three categories—informational, interpersonal, and decisional roles.

A manager's informational roles involve the giving, receiving, and analyzing of information. A manager fulfilling these roles will be a *monitor*, scanning for information; a *disseminator*, sharing information; and a *spokesperson*, acting as official communicator. The interpersonal roles involve interactions with people inside and outside the work unit. A manager fulfilling these roles will be a *figurehead*, modeling and setting forth key principles and policies; a *leader*, providing direction and instilling enthusiasm; and a *liaison*, coordinating with others. The decisional roles involve using information to make decisions to solve problems or address opportunities. A manager fulfilling these roles will be a *disturbance handler*, dealing with problems and conflicts; a *resource allocator*, handling budgets and distributing resources; a *negotiator*, making deals and forging agreements; and an *entrepreneur*, developing new initiatives.

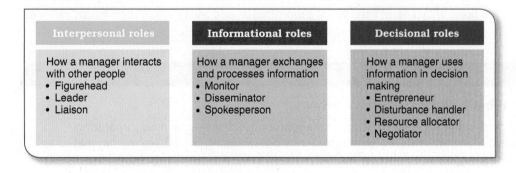

| Interpersonal roles | Informational roles | Decisional roles |
|---|---|---|
| How a manager interacts with other people<br>• Figurehead<br>• Leader<br>• Liaison | How a manager exchanges and processes information<br>• Monitor<br>• Disseminator<br>• Spokesperson | How a manager uses information in decision making<br>• Entrepreneur<br>• Disturbance handler<br>• Resource allocator<br>• Negotiator |

## Managerial Activities

Managers must not only master key roles, they must implement them in intense and complex work settings. Their work is busy, demanding, and stressful at all levels of responsibility. The managers Mintzberg studied had little free time to themselves; in fact, unexpected problems and continuing requests for meetings consumed almost all available time. The nearby box shows their workdays were hectic; the pressure for continuously improving performance was all-encompassing.[50] Mintzberg summarized his observations this way: "The manager can never be free to forget the job, and never has the pleasure of knowing, even temporarily, that there is nothing else to do. . . . Managers always carry the nagging suspicion that they might be able to contribute just a little bit more. Hence they assume an unrelenting pace in their work."[51]

---

**A manager's workday**

- long hours.
- intense pace.
- fragmented and varied tasks.
- many communication media.
- filled with interpersonal relationships.

---

## Managerial Agendas and Networks

On his way to a meeting, a general manager bumped into a staff member who did not report to him. Using this opportunity, in a two-minute conversation he (a) asked two questions and received the information he needed; (b) reinforced their good relationship by sincerely complimenting the staff member on something he had recently done; and (c) got the staff member to agree to do something that the general manager needed done.

This brief incident provides a glimpse of an effective general manager in action.[52] It also portrays two activities that consultant and scholar John Kotter considers critical to a manager's success—agenda setting and networking.

**Agenda setting** develops action priorities for accomplishing goals and plans.

Through **agenda setting**, good managers develop action priorities that include goals and plans spanning long and short time frames. These agendas are usually incomplete and loosely connected in the beginning, but they become more specific as the manager utilizes information continually gleaned from many different sources. The agendas are always present in the manager's mind and are played out or pushed ahead whenever an opportunity arises, as in the preceding example.

**Networking** is the process of creating positive relationships with people who can help advance agendas.

**Social capital** is a capacity to get things done with the support and help of others.

Good managers implement their agendas by **networking**, the process of building and maintaining positive relationships with people whose help may be needed to implement one's agendas. Such networking creates **social capital**—a capacity to attract support and help from others in order to get things done. In Kotter's example, the general manager received help from a staff member who did not report directly to him. His networks and social capital would also include relationships with peers, a boss, higher-level executives, subordinates, and members of their work teams, as well as with external customers, suppliers, and community representatives.

---

**LEARNING CHECK 4**

**TAKEAWAY QUESTION 4 What is the management process?**

**Be sure you can** • define and give examples of each of the management functions—*planning, organizing, leading,* and *controlling* • explain Mintzberg's view of what managers do, including the 10 key managerial roles • explain Kotter's points on how managers use agendas and networks to fulfill their work responsibilities

# Learning How to Manage

Career success in today's turbulent times depends on your commitment to **learning**—changing behavior through experience. The learning focus in management is on developing skills and competencies to deal with the complexities of human behavior and problem solving in organizations. This is why the Wisdom—Learning From Others and Insight—Learning About Yourself features begin each chapter in this book. When you read them, be sure to think about your career readiness. And, don't forget that it's not just formal learning in the classroom that counts. Long-term career success depends on **lifelong learning**—the process of continuous learning from all of our daily experiences and opportunities.

**Learning** is a change in behavior that results from experience.

**Lifelong learning** is continuous learning from daily experiences.

## Essential Managerial Skills

A **skill** is the ability to translate knowledge into action that results in desired performance.[53] Harvard scholar Robert L. Katz described the essential, or baseline, skills of managers in three categories: technical, human, and conceptual.[54] He suggests that all three sets of skills are necessary for management success, and that their relative importance varies by level of managerial responsibility as shown in Figure 1.6.

A **skill** is the ability to translate knowledge into action that results in desired performance.

### Technical Skills

A **technical skill** is the ability to use a special proficiency or expertise to perform particular tasks. Accountants, engineers, market researchers, financial planners, and systems analysts, for example, possess technical skills within their areas of expertise. Knowing how to write a business plan, use statistics to analyze data from a market survey, and prepare visual aids and deliver a persuasive oral presentation are also technical skills. Although initially acquired through formal education, they should be nurtured and further developed by training and job experience.

A **technical skill** is the ability to use expertise to perform a task with proficiency.

Figure 1.6 shows that technical skills are very important at job entry and early career levels. As you look at this figure, take a quick inventory of your technical skills. They are things you could tell a prospective employer when asked: "What exactly can you do for us?"

### Human and Interpersonal Skills

Recruiters today put a lot of weight on a job candidate's "soft" skills—things like ability to communicate, collaborate, and network, and to engage others with a spirit

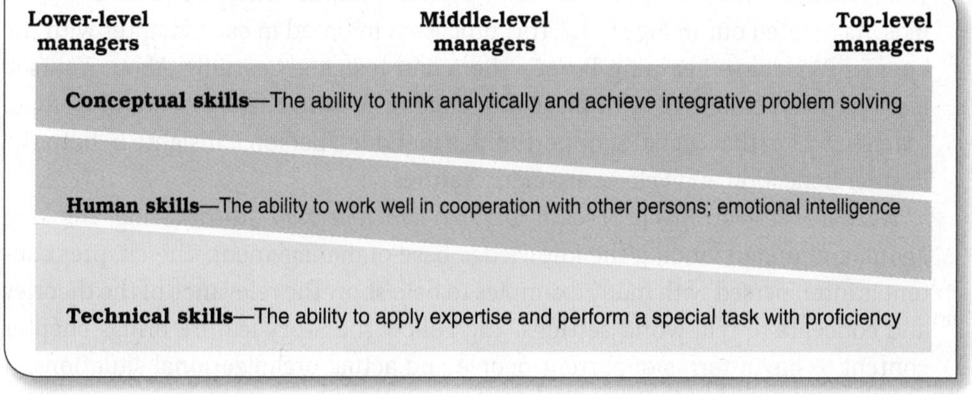

FIGURE 1.6 **Katz's essential managerial skills—technical, human, and conceptual.**

A **human skill** or interpersonal skill is the ability to work well in cooperation with other people.

of trust, enthusiasm, and positive impact.[55] These are all part of what Katz called the ability to work well in cooperation with other persons, or **human skill**. As pointed out in Figure 1.6, the interpersonal nature of managerial work makes human skills consistently important across all levels of managerial responsibility.

A manager with good human skills will have a high degree of self-awareness, as discussed in the chapter opener. It's a foundation for something called **emotional intelligence**, defined by scholar and consultant Daniel Goleman as the "ability to manage ourselves and our relationships effectively."[56]

**Emotional intelligence** is the ability to manage ourselves and our relationships effectively.

Your strength or weakness in emotional intelligence is reflected in how well you recognize, understand, and manage feelings while interacting and dealing with others. Someone high in emotional intelligence will know when her or his emotions are about to become disruptive, and act to control them. This same person will sense when another person's emotions are negatively influencing a relationship, and act to understand and better deal with them.[57] Check your interpersonal skills and emotional intelligence by asking and answering this question: "Just how well do I relate with and work with others?"

## Conceptual and Analytical Skills

A **conceptual skill** is the ability to think analytically to diagnose and solve complex problems.

The ability to think critically and analytically is a **conceptual skill**. It involves the capacity to break problems into smaller parts, see the relations between the parts, and recognize the implications of any one problem for others. We often call this "critical thinking."[58]

Figure 1.6 shows that conceptual skills gain in importance as one moves from lower to higher levels of management. This is because the problems faced at higher levels of responsibility are often ambiguous and unstructured, full of complications and interconnections, and pose longer-term consequences. The recommended chapter case for critical thinking is there to help further develop your conceptual skills in management. For now, the question to ask is: "Am I developing the strong critical thinking and problem-solving capabilities I will need for long-term career success?"

# Developing Managerial Potential

*Management 12/e* is written and organized to help you learn managerial skills and competencies. It will also deepen your understanding of the key concepts, theories, and research upon which they are based.

Real management learning starts with the all-important commitment to *experience and self-assessment*—engaging experience and coming to terms with where you presently stand in respect to skills, personal characteristics, and understandings. As pointed out in Figure 1.7, this process is initiated in each chapter with the opening Wisdom—Learning From Others and Insight—Learning About Yourself features. It is reinforced with an end-of-chapter Management Skills and Competencies section that includes opportunities for added personal insights in both the Further Reflection and Self-Assessment features.

Next in the learning process is *inquiry and reflection*—discovering, thinking about, and understanding the knowledge base of management. The chapter content is interspersed with many examples to help show the relevance of the theories and concepts to real-world settings. The Follow the Story feature brings chapter content to life in terms of current people and actual organizational situations. A

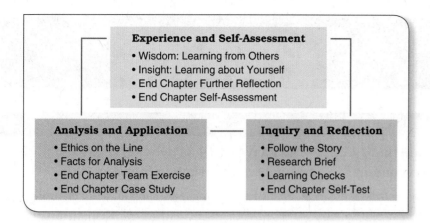

Research Brief illustrates the types of questions researchers are trying to answer in their scientific inquiries. Learning Checks at the end of each major section are chances to pause and reflect back on your understanding before reading further. The end-of-chapter Management Learning Review includes a Learning Check Summary and a Self-Test with multiple-choice, short-answer, and essay questions to double check comprehension and exam readiness.

The learning process completes with *analysis and application. Management 12/e* facilitates this by asking thought questions during text presentation and in chapter features. Facts for Analysis summarizes interesting data on worklife and organizations, and ask questions on interpretations and implications. Ethics on the Line feature presents real ethics dilemmas and then asks you to engage in critical thinking about how to best deal with them. Management Smarts provides bullet-list pointers on how to put the theories and concepts into practice. And, the end-of-chapter Career Situations, Team Exercise, and recommended Case Study offer further opportunities to wrestle with theory-into-practice applications that will test your skills and competencies management.

---

**LEARNING CHECK 5**

**TAKEAWAY QUESTION 5 How do you learn essential managerial skills and competencies?**

**Be sure you can** • define three essential managerial skills—*technical, human,* and *conceptual skills* • explain Katz's view of how these skills vary in importance across management levels • define *emotional intelligence* as an important human skill • list and give examples of personal competencies important for managerial success

# MANAGEMENT LEARNING REVIEW

## LEARNING CHECK SUMMARY

### TAKEAWAY QUESTION 1 What are the challenges of working in the new economy?

- Work in the new economy is increasingly knowledge based, and intellectual capital is the foundation of organizational performance.
- Organizations must value the talents of a workforce whose members are increasingly diverse with respect to gender, age, race and ethnicity, able-bodiedness, and lifestyles.
- The forces of globalization are bringing increased interdependencies among nations and economies, as customer markets and resource flows create intense business competition.
- Ever-present developments in information technology are reshaping organizations, changing the nature of work, and increasing the value of knowledge workers.
- Society has high expectations for organizations and their members to perform with commitment to high ethical standards and in socially responsible ways.
- Careers in the new economy require great personal initiative to build and maintain skill "portfolios" that are always up-to-date and valuable in a free agent economy.

**For Discussion** How is globalization creating career risks and opportunities for today's college graduates?

### TAKEAWAY QUESTION 2 What are organizations like in the new workplace?

- Organizations are collections of people working together to achieve a common purpose.
- As open systems, organizations interact with their environments in the process of transforming resource inputs into product and service outputs.
- Productivity is a measure of the quantity and quality of work performance, with resource costs taken into account.
- High-performing organizations achieve both performance effectiveness in terms of goal accomplishment, and performance efficiency in terms of resource utilization.

**For Discussion** Is it ever acceptable to sacrifice performance efficiency for performance effectiveness?

### TAKEAWAY QUESTION 3 Who are the managers and what do they do?

- Managers directly support and facilitate the work efforts of other people in organizations.
- Top managers scan the environment, create strategies, and emphasize long-term goals; middle managers coordinate activities in large departments or divisions; team leaders and supervisors support performance of front-line workers at the team or work-unit level.
- Functional managers work in specific areas such as finance or marketing; general managers are responsible for larger multifunctional units; administrators are managers in public or nonprofit organizations.
- The upside-down pyramid view of organizations shows operating workers at the top, serving customer needs while being supported from below by various levels of management.
- The changing nature of managerial work emphasizes being good at "coaching" and "supporting" others, rather than simply "directing" and "order-giving."

**For Discussion** In what ways could we expect the work of a top manager to differ from that of a team leader?

### TAKEAWAY QUESTION 4 What is the management process?

- The management process consists of the four functions of planning, organizing, leading, and controlling.
- Planning sets the direction; organizing assembles the human and material resources; leading provides the enthusiasm and direction; controlling ensures results.
- Managers implement the four functions in daily work that is often intense and stressful, involving long hours and continuous performance pressures.
- Managerial success requires the ability to perform well in interpersonal, informational, and decision-making roles.
- Managerial success also requires the ability to build interpersonal networks and use them to accomplish well-selected task agendas.

**For Discussion** How might the upside-down pyramid view of organizations affect a manager's approach to planning, organizing, leading, and controlling?

**TAKEAWAY QUESTION 5 How do you learn essential managerial skills and competencies?**

- Careers in the new economy demand continual attention to lifelong learning from all aspects of daily experience and job opportunities.
- Skills considered essential for managers are broadly described as technical—ability to use expertise; human—ability to work well with other people; and conceptual—ability to analyze and solve complex problems.

- Human skills are equally important for all management levels, whereas conceptual skills gain importance at higher levels and technical skills gain importance at lower levels.

**For Discussion** Among the various managerial skills and competencies, which do you consider the most difficult to develop, and why?

## SELF-TEST 1

### Multiple-Choice Questions

1. The process of management involves the functions of planning, _____, leading, and controlling.
   (a) accounting
   (b) creating
   (c) innovating
   (d) organizing

2. An effective manager achieves both high-performance results and high levels of _____ among people doing the required work.
   (a) turnover
   (b) effectiveness
   (c) satisfaction
   (d) stress

3. Performance efficiency is a measure of the _____ associated with task accomplishment.
   (a) resource costs
   (b) goal specificity
   (c) product quality
   (d) product quantity

4. The requirement that a manager answer to a higher-level boss for performance results achieved by a work team is called _____.
   (a) dependency
   (b) accountability
   (c) authority
   (d) empowerment

5. Productivity is a measure of the quantity and _____ of work produced, relative to the cost of inputs.
   (a) quality
   (b) cost
   (c) timeliness
   (d) value

6. _____ managers pay special attention to the external environment, looking for problems and opportunities and finding ways to deal with them.

(a) Top
(b) Middle
(c) Lower
(d) First-line

7. The accounting manager for a local newspaper would be considered a _____ manager, whereas the editorial director would be considered a _____ manager.
   (a) general, functional
   (b) middle, top
   (c) staff, line
   (d) senior, junior

8. When a team leader clarifies desired work targets and deadlines for a work team, he or she is fulfilling the management function of _____.
   (a) planning
   (b) delegating
   (c) controlling
   (d) supervising

9. The process of building and maintaining good working relationships with others who may help implement a manager's work agendas is called _____.
   (a) governance
   (b) networking
   (c) authority
   (d) entrepreneurship

10. In Katz's framework, top managers tend to rely more on their _____ skills than do first-line managers.
    (a) human
    (b) conceptual
    (c) decision-making
    (d) technical

11. The research of Mintzberg and others concludes that managers _____.
    (a) work at a leisurely pace
    (b) have blocks of private time for planning

(c) are never free from the pressures of performance responsibility

(d) have the advantages of flexible work hours

12. When someone with a negative attitude toward minorities makes a decision to deny advancement opportunities to a Hispanic worker, this is an example of _____.
(a) discrimination
(b) emotional intelligence
(c) performance efficiency
(d) prejudice

13. Among the trends in the new workplace, one can expect to find _____.
(a) more order-giving
(b) more valuing people as human assets
(c) less teamwork
(d) reduced concern for work–life balance

14. The manager's role in the "upside-down pyramid" view of organizations is best described as providing _____ so that operating workers can directly serve _____.
(a) direction, top management
(b) leadership, organizational goals
(c) support, customers
(d) agendas, networking

15. The management function of _____ is being performed when a retail manager measures daily sales in the women's apparel department and compares them with daily sales targets.
(a) planning
(b) agenda setting
(c) controlling
(d) delegating

## Short-Response Questions

16. Discuss the importance of ethics in the relationship between managers and the people they supervise.

17. Explain how "accountability" operates in the relationship between (a) a team leader and her team members, and (b) the same team leader and her boss.

18. Explain how the "glass ceiling effect" may disadvantage newly hired African American college graduates in a large corporation.

19. What is globalization, and what are its implications for working in the new economy?

## Essay Question

20. You have just been hired as the new head of an audit team for a national accounting firm. With four years of experience, you feel technically well prepared for the assignment. However, this is your first formal appointment as a "manager." Things are complicated at the moment. The team has 12 members of diverse demographic and cultural backgrounds, as well as work experience. There is an intense workload and lots of performance pressure. How will this situation challenge you to develop and use essential managerial skills and related competencies to successfully manage the team to high levels of auditing performance?

## MANAGEMENT SKILLS AND COMPETENCIES

# Further Reflection: Self-Awareness

The chapter opener used the Johari Window to introduce you to possible blind spots, hidden areas and unknowns in your **self-awareness**. Now that you have had the chance to think about current trends in the workplace, how organizations are changing today, and the nature of managerial work, the importance of self-awareness to your career should be very evident. It's only through a willingness to discover the "real" self that we can build on strengths, overcome weaknesses, and avoid viewing ourselves more favorably than is justified.[59] True self-awareness is achieved only when we are able to objectively see ourselves through the eyes of others. This is an important career skill, but it isn't easy to master. Why not use the many self-assessments in this book to build your self-awareness skills?

 **DO IT NOW . . .**
**LOOK IN THE MIRROR**

- **Map your Johari Window**
- **Make notes on your "Open Area" and "Hidden Self," speculate about your "Unknown"**
- **Ask friends, family, coworkers for insights to your "Blind Spot."**
- **Write a summary of what your Johari Window map says about your possible career strengths and weaknesses.**

# Self-Assessment: Career Readiness

## Instructions

Use the following scale to rate yourself on personal characteristics.[60]

S   Strong, I am very confident with this one.
G   Good, but I still have room to grow.
W   Weak, I really need work on this one.
U   Unsure, I just don't know.

1. *Inner work standards:* The ability to personally set and work to high performance standards.

2. *Initiative:* The ability to actively tackle problems and take advantage of opportunities.

3. *Cognitive intelligence:* The ability to think systematically and identify cause–effect patterns in data and events.

4. *Tolerance for uncertainty:* The ability to get work done even under ambiguous and uncertain conditions.

5. *Social objectivity:* The ability to act free of racial, ethnic, gender, and other prejudices or biases.

6. *Social intelligence:* The ability to understand another person's needs and feelings.

7. *Emotional intelligence:* The ability to exercise self-awareness and self-management of emotions.

8. *Stamina:* The ability to sustain long work hours.

9. *Resistance to stress:* The ability to get work done even under stressful conditions.

10. *Adaptability:* The ability to be flexible and adapt to changes.

11. *Self-confidence:* The ability to be consistently decisive and willing to take action.

12. *Self-objectivity:* The ability to evaluate personal strengths and weaknesses and motives and skills relative to a job.

13. *Impression management:* The ability to create and sustain a positive impression in the eyes of others.

14. *Introspection:* The ability to learn from experience, awareness, and self-study.

## Self-Assessment Scoring

Give yourself 1 point for each S, and 1/2 point for each G. Do not give yourself points for W and U responses. Total your points and enter the result here [_____].

## Interpretation

This assessment is a good starting point for considering where and how you can further develop useful managerial skills and competencies. It offers a self-described profile of your personal management foundations—things that establish strong career readiness.

The higher you score the better. Are you a perfect 10, or something less? There shouldn't be too many 10s around.

Ask someone you know to also assess you on this instrument. You may be surprised at the differences between your score and the one they come up with.

## Team Exercise: My Best Manager

## Preparation

Working alone, make a list of the *behavioral attributes* that describe the "best" manager you have ever had. This could be someone you worked for in a full-time or part-time job, summer job, volunteer job, student organization, or elsewhere. If you have trouble identifying an actual manager, make a list of behavioral attributes of the manager you would most like to work for in your next job.

1. Make of list of the behavioral attributes that describe the "worst" manager you have ever had.

2. Write a short synopsis of things that this bad manager actually did or said that would qualify for "Believe it or not, it's really true!" status.

3. If you also made a list of attributes for your "best" manager, write a quick summary of the most important differences that quickly sort out your best from your worst.

## Instructions

Form into groups as assigned by your instructor, or work with a nearby classmate. Share your list of attributes and listen to the lists of others. Be sure to ask questions and make comments on items of special interest.

Work together in the group to create a master list that combines the unique attributes of the "best" and/or "worst" managers experienced by members. Have a spokesperson share that list with the rest of the class for further discussion. Be sure to also share "Believe it or not!" stories provided by group members.

## Career Situations for New Managers: What Would You Do?

1. **The Foreign Employer** One of the plus sides of globalization is that a growing number of locals are now working for foreign employers in their local communities. How about you: Does it make any difference if you receive a job offer from a foreign employer such as Honda or a domestic one such as Ford? Assume you just had such an offer. Prepare a Job Hunter's Balance Sheet. On the left list the "pluses" and on the right the "minuses" of working at home for a foreign employer.

2. **Interview for Dream Job** It's time to take your first interview for a "dream" job. The interviewer is sitting across the table from you. She smiles, looks you in the eye, and says: "You have a very nice academic record and we're impressed with your extracurricular activi-

ties. Now tell me, just what can you do for us that will add value to the organization right from day one?" You're on the spot. How will you answer? And, what can you add to the conversation that clearly shows you have strong human and conceptual skills, not just technical ones?

3. **New Manager Supervising Old Friends** When people are promoted into management they sometimes end up supervising friends and colleagues they previously worked with. This could happen to you. When it does, how can you best deal with this situation right from the start? What will you do to earn the respect of everyone under your supervision and set the foundations for what will become a well-regarded and high-performing work team?

## Case Study

# Trader Joe's

Go to *Management Cases for Critical Thinking* at the end of the book to find the Chapter 1 case—"Trader Joe's: Keeping a Cool Edge."

It's never just an average day at Trader Joe's. Found in almost thirty states, the gourmet, specialty, and natural-foods store offers staples such as milk and eggs along with more curious, one-of-a-kind foods. Foodies, hipsters, and recessionistas alike are attracted to the chain's charming blend of low prices, tasty treats, and laid-back but enthusiastic customer service.

Shopping at Trader Joe's is less a chore than it is immersion into another culture. In keeping with its

whimsical faux-nautical theme, crew members and managers wear loud tropical-print shirts. Chalkboards around every corner unabashedly announce slogans such as, "You don't have to join a club, carry a card, or clip coupons to get a good deal." Take a walk down the aisle of Trader Joe's and learn how sharp attention to the fundamentals of retail management made this chain more than the average Joe.

Peter DaSilva/The New York Times/Redux Pictures

# Wisdom
## Learning From Others

## > THERE ARE MANY PATHWAYS TO GOAL ACHIEVEMENT

Facebook and Zappos were both entrepreneurial startups that made it big while following very different approaches to employee hiring and retention.[1] Is one right and the other wrong?

Facebook's founder and CEO, Mark Zuckerberg, likes to hire "hackers" with an entrepreneurial side. He's interested in people who like to create new things quickly rather than those who want long-term employment. He compares Facebook to great collegiate sports schools where athletes go to play and excel, while also preparing for later careers in professional sports. The great "hackers," according to Zuckerberg, don't "want to stay at one place forever."

Zappos CEO Tony Hsieh says, "We have a different approach from what Mark was talking about. We actually want our employees to stay with the company for a long time, for 10 years, maybe for their entire life." Internal career paths are clear at Zappos, promotions are frequent, and time off for personal affairs is not a problem. Zappos invests heavily in staff training and mentoring. The key, according to Hsieh, is "constant growth" along with a strong dose of satisfaction.

The lesson here is there are many pathways to goal achievement. But which firm would you most like to join—Facebook or Zappos? What does this choice say about your career needs and aspirations?

## MORE TO LOOK FOR INSIDE>

### FOLLOW THE STORY
Former Microsoft Executive Finds Fulfillment Fighting Illiteracy

### ETHICS ON THE LINE
CEO Golden Parachutes Fly in Face of Public Outrage

### FACTS FOR ANALYSIS
Generations Differ When Rating Their Bosses

### RESEARCH BRIEF
Setting Personal Goals Improves Academic Performance

# Management Learning Past to Present

## > LEARNING STYLE

This is a good time to examine your **learning style**. Think of it as how you like to learn through receiving, processing, and recalling new information.

Each of us tends to learn in slightly different ways. Look how some students do well in lecture classes, while others do not. But these others might excel in case study or project classes that emphasize discussion and problem solving rather than digesting information.

There's no right or wrong when it comes to learning styles. But we should recognize and understand them. Some people learn by watching. They observe others and model what they see. Others learn by doing. They act and experiment, learning as they go. Some people are feelers for whom emotions and val-ues count a lot. Others are thinkers who emphasize reason and analysis.[2]

Look at the diagram of learning styles and think about your preferences. Shade in each circle to show the degree to which that description fits you. This portrait of your personal learning style is good food for thought.

Everyone a manager deals with is unique, most problem situations are complex, and things are always changing. Success comes only to managers who thrive on learning.

It's a personal challenge to learn something new every day, and it's a managerial challenge to consistently help others learn things as well.

## Insight
### Learning About Yourself

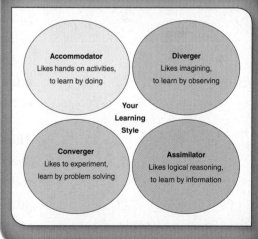

## BUILD SKILLS AND COMPETENCIES AT END OF CHAPTER

- Engage in *Further Reflection on Individual Character*
- Take the *Self-Assessment on Managerial Assumptions*
- Complete the *Team Exercise—Evidence-based Management Quiz*
- Solve the *Career Situations for Today*
- Analyze the *Case Study—Zara International: Fashion at the Speed of Light*

## <GET TO KNOW YOURSELF BETTER

| TAKEAWAY 1 | TAKEAWAY 2 | TAKEAWAY 3 |
|---|---|---|
| **Classical Management Approaches**<br>• Scientific management<br>• Administrative principles<br>• Bureaucratic organization | **Behavioral Management Approaches**<br>• Follett's organizations as communities<br>• The Hawthorne studies<br>• Maslow's theory of human needs<br>• McGregor's Theory X and Theory Y<br>• Argyris's theory of adult personality | **Modern Management Foundations**<br>• Quantitative analysis and tools<br>• Organizations as systems<br>• Contingency thinking<br>• Quality management<br>• Knowledge management and organizational learning<br>• Evidence-based management |
| LEARNING CHECK 1 | LEARNING CHECK 2 | LEARNING CHECK 3 |

In *The Evolution of Management Thought*, Daniel Wren traces management as far back as 5000 B.C., when ancient Sumerians used written records to assist in governmental and business activities.[3] Management was important to the construction of the Egyptian pyramids, the rise of the Roman Empire, and the commercial success of 14th-century Venice. By the time of the Industrial Revolution in the 1700s, great social changes had helped prompt a major leap forward in the manufacture of basic staples and consumer goods. Industrial development was accelerated by Adam Smith's ideas of efficient production through specialized tasks and the division of labor. At the turn of the 20th century, Henry Ford and others were making mass production a mainstay of the emerging economy. Since then, the science and practices of management have been on a rapid and continuing path of development.[4]

There are many useful lessons in the history of management thought. Rather than naively believing that we are always reinventing management practice today, it is wise to remember the historical roots of many modern ideas and admit that we are still trying to perfect them.

## Classical Management Approaches

Our study of management begins with the classical approaches: (1) scientific management, (2) administrative principles, and (3) bureaucratic organization.[5] Figure 2.1 associates each with a prominent person in the history of management thought—Taylor, Weber, and Fayol. The figure also shows that the classical approaches share a common assumption: People at work rationally consider opportunities made available to them and do whatever is necessary to achieve the greatest personal and monetary gain.[6]

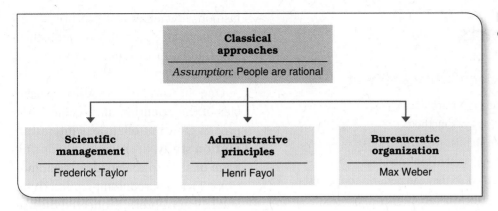

FIGURE 2.1   **Major branches in the classical approach to management.**

## Scientific Management

In 1911, Frederick W. Taylor published *The Principles of Scientific Management*, in which he made the following statement: "The principal object of management should be to secure maximum prosperity for the employer, coupled with the maximum prosperity for the employee."[7] Taylor, often called the "father of scientific management," noticed that many workers did their jobs their own ways and without a clear and consistent approach. He believed this caused inefficiency and low performance. He also believed that this problem could be corrected if workers were taught and then helped by supervisors to always do their jobs in the right ways.

Taylor's goal was to improve the productivity of people at work. He used the concept of "time study" to analyze the motions and tasks required in any job and to develop the most efficient ways to perform them. He then linked these job requirements to both training for the worker and support from supervisors in the form of proper direction, work assistance, and monetary incentives. Taylor's approach is known as **scientific management** and includes four guiding principles.

> **Scientific management** emphasizes careful selection and training of workers and supervisory support.

1.  Develop for every job a "science" that includes rules of motion, standardized work implements, and proper working conditions.
2.  Carefully select workers with the right abilities for the job.
3.  Carefully train workers to do the job and give them the proper incentives to cooperate with the job "science."
4.  Support workers by carefully planning their work and by smoothing the way as they go about their jobs.

Although Taylor called his approach "scientific" management, contemporary scholars have questioned his truthfulness in reporting and the scientific rigor of his studies.[8] But Taylor's ideas still influence management thinking.[9] A ready example can be seen at United Parcel Service where many workers are guided by carefully calibrated productivity standards. Sorters at regional centers are timed according to strict task requirements and are expected to load vans at a set number of packages per hour. GPS technology plots the shortest delivery routes; stops register in on-board computers that are studied to identify wasted time. Industrial engineers devise precise routines for drivers—things like avoid left turns in traffic and walk at a "brisk" pace. In classic scientific management

## ManagementSmarts

### Practical Insights from Scientific Management

- Make results-based compensation a performance incentive.
- Carefully design jobs with efficient work methods.
- Carefully select workers with the abilities to do these jobs.
- Train workers to perform jobs to the best of their abilities.
- Train supervisors to support workers so they can perform to the best of their abilities.

**Motion study** is the science of reducing a task to its basic physical motions.

fashion, efficiency is a top priority at UPS; savings of seconds on individual stops adds up to significant increases in productivity.[10]

One of the most enduring legacies of the scientific management approach grew out of Taylor's interest in **motion study**, the science of reducing a job or task to its basic physical motions. Two of his contemporaries, Frank and Lillian Gilbreth, pioneered the use of motion studies as a management tool.[11] In one famous case they reduced the number of motions used by bricklayers and tripled their productivity.

Insights from scientific management (see Management Smarts) led to advances in the areas of job design, work standards, and incentive wage plans—all techniques still used in the modern workplace. At Worthington Industries, an Ohio-based steel producer, for example, time clocks were installed at workstations in a drive to improve productivity. Work teams track how long it takes to perform tasks using time clocks that display both a goal for the task—say 30 minutes—and actual time elapsed—say 35 minutes. The goal is continuous improvement in task efficiency.[12]

## Administrative Principles

In 1916, after a career in French industry, Henri Fayol published *Administration Industrielle et Générale*.[13] The book outlines his views on the proper management of organizations and of the people within them. It identifies the following five "rules" or "duties" of management, which are foundations for the four functions of management—planning, organizing, leading, and controlling—that we talk about today:

1. *Foresight*—to complete a plan of action for the future.
2. *Organization*—to provide and mobilize resources to implement the plan.
3. *Command*—to lead, select, and evaluate workers to get the best work toward the plan.
4. *Coordination*—to fit diverse efforts together and to ensure information is shared and problems solved.
5. *Control*—to make sure things happen according to plan and to take necessary corrective action.

Importantly, Fayol believed that management could be taught. He wanted to improve the quality of management and set forth a number of "principles" to guide managers in action. A number of them are still part of the management vocabulary. They include the *scalar chain principle*—there should be a clear and unbroken line of communication from the top to the bottom in the organization; the *unity of command principle*—each person should receive orders from only one boss; and the *unity of direction principle*—one person should be in charge of all activities that have the same performance objective.

Wu Jingdan/Xinhua/Photoshot/Newscom

## Taco Bell Wraps Things Up with Scientific Management

Fast food may not be your choice, but there are days when a drive-up stop at Taco Bell might be in your future. When it is, think scientific management at work. Think also 164—164 seconds that is. It's the average time per customer from point of order to taco in hand. The company measures performance on time and accuracy criteria. Both are linked to standardized systems for order taking, money handling, food preparation, and order delivery. It's all carefully scripted in assembly-line style, where each worker learns the script for his or her station and then does it over and over again. The whole process is backed by lots of training, and reinforcement is given for doing things right.

## Bureaucratic Organization

Max Weber was a late-19th-century German intellectual whose insights had a major impact on the field of management and the sociology of organizations. His ideas developed after noticing organizations of his day often performed poorly. Among other things, Weber saw people holding positions of authority not because of their capabilities, but because of their "privileged" social status in German society.

At the heart of Weber's thinking was an ideal, intentionally rational, and very efficient form of organization called a **bureaucracy**.[14] It was founded on principles of logic, order, and legitimate authority. The defining characteristics of Weber's bureaucratic organization are:

A **bureaucracy** is a rational and efficient form of organization founded on logic, order, and legitimate authority.

- *Clear division of labor:* Jobs are well defined, and workers become highly skilled at performing them.
- *Clear hierarchy of authority:* Authority and responsibility are well defined for each position, and each position reports to a higher-level one.
- *Formal rules and procedures:* Written guidelines direct behavior and decisions in jobs, and written files are kept for historical record.
- *Impersonality:* Rules and procedures are impartially and uniformly applied, with no one receiving preferential treatment.
- *Careers based on merit:* Workers are selected and promoted on ability, competency, and performance, and managers are career employees of the organization.

Weber believed that bureaucracies would have the advantages of efficiency in utilizing resources, and of fairness or equity in the treatment of employees and clients. These are his words.[15]

The purely bureaucratic type of administrative organization . . . is, from a purely technical point of view, capable of attaining the highest degree of efficiency. . . . It is superior to any other form in precision, in stability, in the stringency of its discipline, and in its reliability. It thus makes possible a particularly high degree of calculability of results for the heads of the organization and for those acting in relation to it.

The Classic Bureaucracy

Fair
Impersonal
Career managers
Clear division of labor
Promotion based on merit
Formal hierarchy of authority
Written rules and standard procedures

Today we recognize that bureaucracy works well sometimes, but not all the time. In fact, we often hear the terms *bureaucracy* and *bureaucrat* used with negative connotations. The possible disadvantages of bureaucracy include excessive paperwork or "red tape," slowness in handling problems, rigidity in the face of shifting customer or client needs, resistance to change, and employee apathy.[16] These disadvantages cause problems for organizations that must be flexible and quick in adapting to changing circumstances—a common situation today. A major management challenge is to know when bureaucratic features work well and what the best alternatives are when they don't. Later in the chapter we'll call this "contingency thinking."

---

**LEARNING CHECK 1**

**TAKEAWAY QUESTION 1 What can be learned from classical management thinking?**

**Be sure you can** • state the underlying assumption of the classical management approaches • list the principles of Taylor's scientific management • identify three of Fayol's principles for guiding managerial action • list the key characteristics of bureaucracy and explain why Weber considered it an ideal form of organization • identify possible disadvantages of bureaucracy in today's environment

---

# Behavioral Management Approaches

During the 1920s, an emphasis on the human side of the workplace began to influence management thinking. Major branches in these behavioral or human resource approaches to management are shown in Figure 2.2. They include Follett's notion of organizations as communities, the Hawthorne studies, Maslow's theory of human needs, and related ideas of Douglas McGregor and Chris Argyris.

The behavioral approaches assume that people are social and self-actualizing, enjoying social relationships, responding to group pressures, and searching for personal fulfillment. These historical foundations set the stage for what is now known as the field of **organizational behavior**, the study of individuals and groups in organizations.

**Organizational behavior** is the study of individuals and groups in organizations.

FIGURE 2.2  **Foundations in the behavioral or human resource approaches to management.**

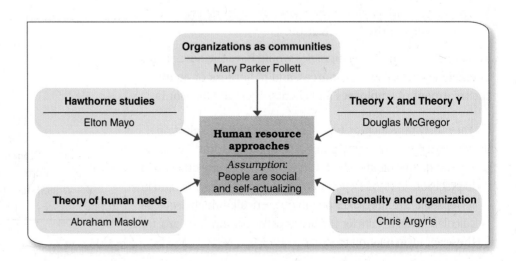

## Follett's Organizations as Communities

The work of Mary Parker Follett was part of an important transition from classical thinking into behavioral management. As summarized in *Mary Parker Follett—Prophet of Management: A Celebration of Writings from the 1920s*, it is a good reminder of the wisdom of history. Although Follett wrote in a different day and age, her ideas are rich with foresight. She taught respect for the experience and knowledge of workers, warned against the dangers of too much hierarchy, and called for visionary leadership. Follett was eulogized upon her death in 1933 as "one of the most important women America has yet produced in the fields of civics and sociology."[17]

In her writings, Follett describes organizations as "communities" in which managers and workers should labor in harmony without one party dominating the other, and with the freedom to talk over and truly reconcile conflicts and differences. For her, groups were mechanisms through which diverse individuals could combine their talents for a greater good. And she believed it was the manager's job to help people in organizations cooperate with one another and achieve an integration of interests.

Follett's emphasis on groups and her commitment to human cooperation are still highly relevant themes today.[18] She believed that making every employee an owner in a business would create feelings of collective responsibility. Today, we address the same issues under such labels as *employee ownership*, *profit sharing*, and *gain-sharing plans*. She believed that business problems involve a wide variety of factors that must be considered in relationship to one another. Today, we talk about "systems" and "contingency thinking." She also believed that businesses were service organizations and that private profits should always be considered vis-à-vis the public good. Today, we pursue the same issues under the labels *managerial ethics* and *corporate social responsibility*.

**FACTS FOR ANALYSIS** > MILLENNIALS TEND TO GIVE THEIR BOSSES HIGHER RATINGS THAN DO GEN XERS AND BABY BOOMERS

## Generations Differ When Rating Their Bosses

Would it surprise you that Millennials have somewhat different views of their bosses than their older coworkers, Generation Xers and Baby Boomers? Check these data from a Kenexa survey that asked 11,000 respondents to rate the performance of their managers.

- Overall performance positive—Boomers 55%, Gen Xers 59%, Millennials 68%.

- People management positive—Boomers 50%, Gen Xers 53%, Millennials 62%.

- Work management positive—Boomers 52%, Gen Xers 55%, Millennials 63%.

- Keeping commitments positive—Boomers 59%, Gen Xers 60%, Millennials 65%.

- Outstanding leader—Boomers 39%, Gen Xers 43%, Millennials 51%.

 **YOUR THOUGHTS?**

A Kenexa researcher says Millennials may be "more willing to take direction and accept authority" while "as we grow older, our ideas become more concrete and less flexible." Does this seem like an accurate conclusion from these data? How can these generational differences in evaluating mangers be explained? Have you observed generational differences in your work settings? And, what do the Kenexa data suggest for someone managing a team composed of members from different generations?

# The Hawthorne Studies

The shift toward behavioral thinking in management was given an important boost in 1924 when the Western Electric Company commissioned a research program to study individual productivity at the Hawthorne Works of the firm's Chicago plant.[19] The initial Hawthorne studies applied a scientific management perspective to understand how economic incentives and physical conditions of the workplace affected the output of workers. But after failing to find a link between improved lighting and productivity, the researchers concluded that unforeseen "psychological factors" somehow interfered with their experiments.

## Social Setting and Human Relations

In a study of worker fatigue and output, a team led by Harvard's Elton Mayo was careful to design a scientific test that would be free of the psychological effects thought to have confounded the earlier studies. Six workers who assembled small electrical relays were isolated for intensive study in a special test room. They were given various rest pauses, as well as workdays and workweeks of various lengths, and production was regularly measured. Once again, researchers failed to find any direct relationship between changes in physical working conditions and output. Productivity increased regardless of the changes made.

Mayo and his colleagues concluded that the new "social setting" created for workers in the test room made them want to do a good job. They shared pleasant social interactions with one another and received special attention that made them feel important. They were given a lot of information and were frequently asked for their opinions. None of this was the case in their regular jobs back in the plant. In other words, good "human relations" in the test room seemed to result in higher productivity.

## Employee Attitudes and Group Processes

The Hawthorne research team's interest in the human factor broadened to include employee attitudes, interpersonal relations, and group dynamics. One study interviewed over 21,000 employees to learn what they liked and disliked about their work environment. "Complex" and "baffling" results led the researchers to conclude that things like work conditions or wages could be sources of satisfaction for some workers and of dissatisfaction for others.

The final study was conducted in the bank wiring room and centered on the role of the work group. A "surprising" finding was that people would restrict their output to avoid the displeasure of the group, even if it meant sacrificing pay that could otherwise be earned by increasing output. The researchers concluded that groups can have strong negative, as well as positive, influences on individual productivity.

## Lessons of the Hawthorne Studies

Scholars now criticize the Hawthorne studies for poor research design, weak empirical support for the conclusions drawn, and the tendency of researchers to overgeneralize their findings.[20] Yet their significance as turning points in the evolution of management thought remains intact. The studies pointed the attention of managers and researchers toward social and human factors as keys to productivity.

## CEO Golden Parachutes Fly in Face of Public Outrage

© Masterfile

In many ways it's like winning the lottery. Many CEOs in corporate America get paid very well whether their companies do well or not. Even getting fired can mean a heck of a payday. Consider these examples of what some might call outrageous CEO golden parachutes.

Leo Apotheker—fired as CEO of Hewlett-Packard after only 11 months on the job. Severance package = $13.2 million.

Robert Kelly—ousted as CEO of Bank New York Mellon. Severance package = $17.2 million.

Carol Bartz—fired as CEO of Yahoo. Severance package = about $10 million.

John Chidsey—resigned as CEO of Burger King after the firm struggled to keep up with McDonalds. Severance package = almost $20 million.

CEO compensation packages are largely negotiated at initial hiring, a time when the person seems to be the "best fit" for the task at hand. Hiring firms usually try to match what others are offering their CEOs and top executives. Many people are shocked by high CEO salaries and bonuses, and the rich golden parachutes they get upon departure.

### ETHICS QUESTIONS

At times when firms may be laying off employees and performing poorly, is it morally right for a board to give a departing CEO a multimillion-dollar parachute? Should a CEO accept millions in compensation when front-line employees are given minimal or even zero raises? What about pay disparity itself? Do you think CEO pay should be capped at some multiple of the average worker's pay? Should CEOs take pay cuts during difficult financial times? But how about you? If hired as CEO, wouldn't you go for the big compensation contract and severance package?

They brought visibility to the notions that people's feelings, attitudes, and relationships with coworkers affected their work, and that groups were important influences on individuals. They also identified the **Hawthorne effect**—the tendency of people who are singled out for special attention to perform as anticipated because of expectations created by the situation.

> The **Hawthorne effect** is the tendency of persons singled out for special attention to perform as expected.

## Maslow's Theory of Human Needs

The work of psychologist Abraham Maslow in the area of human "needs" has also had a major impact on the behavioral approach to management.[21] He described a **need** as a physiological or psychological deficiency a person feels the compulsion to satisfy, suggesting that needs create tensions that can influence a person's work attitudes and behaviors. He also placed needs in the five levels shown in Figure 2.3. From lowest to highest in order, they are physiological, safety, social, esteem, and self-actualization needs.

> A **need** is a physiological or psychological deficiency that a person wants to satisfy.

Maslow's theory is based on two underlying principles. The first is the **deficit principle**—a satisfied need is not a motivator of behavior. People act to satisfy "deprived" needs, those for which a satisfaction "deficit" exists. The second is the

> According to the **deficit principle** a satisfied need does not motivate behavior.

FIGURE 2.3 **Maslow's hierarchy of human needs.**

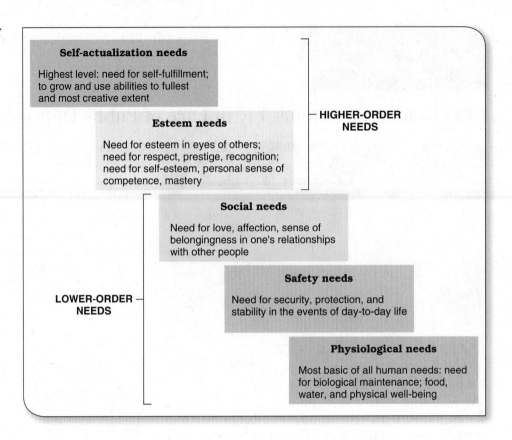

According to the **progression principle** a need is activated only when the next-lower-level need is satisfied.

**progression principle**—the five needs exist in a hierarchy of "prepotency." A need at any level is activated only when the next-lower-level need is satisfied. Maslow suggests people try to satisfy the five needs in sequence. They progress step by step from the lowest level in the hierarchy up to the highest. Along the way, a deprived need dominates individual attention and determines behavior until it is satisfied. Then, the next-higher-level need is activated. At the level of self-actualization, the deficit and progression principles cease to operate. The more this need is satisfied, the stronger it grows.

Consistent with human relations thinking, Maslow's theory implies that managers who understand and help people satisfy their important needs at work will achieve productivity. Although scholars now recognize things are more complicated than this, Maslow's ideas are still relevant. Consider the case of volunteer workers at the local Red Cross or other community organizations. How can you motivate people who aren't paid? Maslow's ideas point managers toward finding ways to link volunteer work with opportunities to satisfy higher-order needs like esteem and self-actualization.

## McGregor's Theory X and Theory Y

Douglas McGregor was heavily influenced by both the Hawthorne studies and Maslow. His classic book, *The Human Side of Enterprise*, advances the thesis that managers should give more attention to the social and self-actualizing needs of people at work.[22] McGregor called upon managers to shift their view of human nature away from a set of assumptions he called Theory X and toward ones he called Theory Y. You can check your managerial assumptions by completing the self-assessment at the end of the chapter.

According to McGregor, managers holding **Theory X** assumptions approach their jobs believing that those who work for them generally dislike work, lack ambition, are irresponsible, are resistant to change, and prefer to be led rather than to lead. McGregor considers such thinking inappropriate. He argues instead for **Theory Y** assumptions in which the manager believes people are willing to work, capable of self-control, willing to accept responsibility, imaginative and creative, and capable of self-direction.

**Theory X** assumes people dislike work, lack ambition, act irresponsibly, and prefer to be led.

**Theory Y** assumes people are willing to work, like responsibility, and are self-directed and creative.

---

**FOLLOW THE STORY**

> HIS LIFE CHANGED AND ITS "SECOND CHAPTER" STARTED AFTER A TREKKING HOLIDAY IN NEPAL

## Former Microsoft Executive Finds Fulfillment Fighting Illiteracy

AFP Photo/Room To Read/NewsCom

There are many ways to help build a better society. John Wood's choice is social entrepreneurship that promotes literacy for children of the developing world. During a successful career as Microsoft executive, his life changed after he went on a trekking vacation to the Himalayas of Nepal. While there, Wood was shocked at the lack of schools and poor access to children's reading materials. He pledged to collect books for a Nepalese school that he visited and, indeed, returned a year later with 3,000 in hand. But the impact on his future didn't end there. He was inspired to rally his years of executive experience to accomplish more through nonprofit work.

Woods quit his Microsoft job to found Room to Read. It builds libraries and schools in poor nations like Nepal, Cambodia, Vietnam, and Laos, and publishes local language books to help fill them. Now in what he calls the "second chapter" in his life, Wood's passion is to provide the lifelong benefits of education to poor children. His organization's website describes the vision this way: "We envision a world in which all children can pursue a quality education that enables them to reach their full potential and contribute to their community and the world."

Picture this scene in Laos, one of the world's poorest nations. Children sit happily in a small library full of books reading a story with their teacher. It's a Room to Read project. So far the organization has put in place over 700 libraries and built 140 schools in this small land-locked Southeast Asian country. Laos has just over 8,000 primary schools nation-wide and the majority offer only incomplete educational experiences.

The Room to Read model is so efficient that it can build schools for as little as $6,000 and is now setting up five or six new libraries each day. Over 10,000 libraries are already in place in Asia and Sub-Saharan Africa. *Time* magazine called Wood and his team "Asian Heroes," and *Fast Company* magazine gave Room to Read its Social Capitalist Award.

Noting that one-seventh of the global population can't read or write, Wood says: "I don't see how we are going to solve the world's problems without literacy."

 **WHAT'S YOUR TAKE?**

Room to Read builds one school or library at a time, but the results add up quickly—some 10 million children have benefited to date. Is the success of Room to Read due in part to Wood's prior business and management experience? How can such experience help nonprofit organizations? Can you identify a social problem in your community that might be addressed using John Wood and his work with Room to Read as a role model?

A **self-fulfilling prophecy** occurs when a person acts in ways that confirm another's expectations.

An important aspect of McGregor's ideas is his belief that managers who hold either set of assumptions can create **self-fulfilling prophecies**—that is, through their behavior they create situations where others act in ways that confirm the original expectations.[23] Managers with Theory X assumptions tend to act in a very directive "command-and-control" fashion that gives people little personal say over their work. These supervisory behaviors create passive, dependent, and reluctant subordinates, who tend to do only what they are told to or required to do. This reinforces the original Theory X viewpoint.

In contrast to Theory X, managers with Theory Y assumptions tend to behave in engaging ways that allow subordinates more job involvement, freedom, and responsibility. This creates opportunities for them to satisfy esteem and self-actualization needs. They respond by performing with initiative and high performance, and the self-fulfilling prophecy becomes a positive one.[24] Theory Y thinking is reflected in a lot of the ideas and developments discussed in this book, such as valuing diversity, employee involvement, job enrichment, empowerment, and self-managing teams.

## Argyris's Theory of Adult Personality

The ideas of Maslow and McGregor inspired the well-regarded scholar and consultant Chris Argyris. In his book *Personality and Organization*, Argyris contrasts the management practices found in traditional and hierarchical organizations with the needs and capabilities of mature adults.[25] He believes common problems of employee absenteeism, turnover, apathy, alienation, and low morale may be signs of a mismatch. And, he argues that managers who treat people positively and as responsible adults will achieve the highest productivity.

Consider these examples. In scientific management, the principle of specialization assumes that people will work more efficiently as tasks become simpler and better defined. Argyris believes that this limits opportunities for self-actualization. In Weber's bureaucracy, people work in a clear hierarchy of authority, with higher levels directing and controlling lower levels. Argyris worries that this creates dependent, passive workers who feel they have little control over their work environments. In Fayol's administrative principles, the concept of unity of direction assumes that efficiency will increase when a person's work is planned and directed by a supervisor. Argyris suggests that this may create conditions for psychological failure; conversely, psychological success occurs when people define their own goals.

**LEARNING CHECK 2**

**TAKEAWAY QUESTION 2 What insights come from the behavioral management approaches?**

**Be sure you can** • explain Follett's concept of organizations as communities • define the *Hawthorne effect* • explain how the Hawthorne findings influenced the development of management thought • explain how Maslow's hierarchy of needs operates in the workplace • distinguish between Theory X and Theory Y assumptions, and explain why McGregor favored Theory Y • explain Argyris's criticism that traditional organizational practices are inconsistent with mature adult personalities

# Modern Management Foundations

The concepts, models, and ideas discussed so far helped set the stage for continuing developments in management thought. They ushered in modern management approaches that include the use of quantitative analysis and tools, a systems view of organizations, contingency thinking, commitment to quality management, the role of knowledge management learning organizations, and the importance of evidence-based management.

## Quantitative Analysis and Tools

In our world of vast computing power and the easy collection and storage of data, there is renewed emphasis on how to use quantitative analysis to mine available data and make management decisions. This is an area known as **analytics**, the systematic analysis of large databases to solve problems and make informed decisions.[26] Delivery drivers at Schwan Food Company, for example, used to rely on six-week old lists of customers' prior orders to decide who to visit and what to offer them. Sales were flat and inventories high. Things improved greatly after a new analytics program was put into place. Computers now churn vast historical data to identify likely customer preferences and send daily sales recommendations direct to each driver's hand-held device. And at Google, retention of talented engineers is a big issue. An analytics program pools information from performance reviews, surveys, and pay and promotion histories, and uses a math formula to identify employees who might be open to offers from other firms. Human resource management plans are then made to try and retain them.[27]

**Analytics** is the systematic analysis of large databases to solve problems and make informed decisions.

A typical quantitative approach to managerial problem solving proceeds as follows. A problem is encountered, it is systematically analyzed, appropriate mathematical models and computations are applied, and an optimum solution is identified. Consider these further examples of real management problems and how they can be addressed with analytics and quantitative tools.

*Problem:* An oil exploration company is worried about future petroleum reserves in various parts of the world. *Quantitative approach—Mathematical forecasting* makes future projections for reserve sizes and depletion rates that are useful in the planning process.

*Problem:* A "big box" retailer is trying to deal with pressures on profit margins by minimizing costs of inventories, but must also avoid going "out of stock" for customers. *Quantitative approach—Inventory analysis*, discussed in Chapter 19 on operations and services management, helps control inventories by mathematically determining how much to automatically order and when.

*Problem:* A grocery store is getting complaints from customers that waiting times are too long for checkouts during certain times of the day. *Quantitative approach—Queuing theory* allocates service personnel and workstations based on alternative workload demands and in a way that minimizes both customer waiting times and costs of service workers.

*Problem:* A manufacturer wants to maximize profits for producing three different products on three different machines, each of which can be used for different periods of times and runs at different costs. *Quantitative approach—Linear programming* calculates how best to allocate production among different machines.

*Problem:* A real estate developer wants to control costs and finish building a new apartment complex on time. *Quantitative approach—Network models* break large tasks into smaller components and diagram them in step-by-step sequences. This allows project managers to better analyze, plan, and control timetables for completion of many different activities.

## Organizations as Systems

Organizations have long been described as cooperative systems that achieve great things by combining resources and the contributions of many individuals to achieve a common purpose. But the reality is that cooperation among the many people and parts is often imperfect and can be improved upon. This is why it's important to understand the full complexity of an organization as a **system** of interrelated parts or **subsystems** that work together to achieve a common purpose.[28]

It is helpful to view organizations as **open systems** that interact with their environments in the continual process of transforming inputs—people, technology, information, money, and supplies—into outputs—goods and services for their customers and clients. Figure 2.4 shows how the inside of an organization looks as an interlocking network of subsystems whose activities individually and collectively support the work of the larger system and make things happen. In the figure, the operations and service management subsystems anchor the transformation process

A **system** is a collection of interrelated parts working together for a purpose.

A **subsystem** is a smaller component of a larger system.

An **open system** interacts with its environment and transforms resource inputs into outputs.

FIGURE 2.4 **Organizations as complex networks of interacting subsystems.**

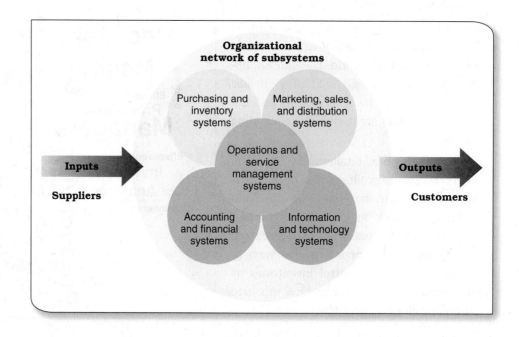

Organizational network of subsystems

Purchasing and inventory systems

Marketing, sales, and distribution systems

Operations and service management systems

Accounting and financial systems

Information and technology systems

Inputs

Suppliers

Outputs

Customers

while linking with other subsystems such as purchasing, accounting, sales, and information. High performance by the organization occurs only when each subsystem both performs its tasks well and works well in cooperation with others.

## Contingency Thinking

Modern management tries to identify practices that are best fits with the demands of unique situations. This requires **contingency thinking** that matches managerial responses with problems and opportunities specific to different people and settings. There is no "one best way" to manage in all circumstances. Rather, the contingency perspective tries to help managers understand situational differences and respond to them in ways that fit their unique characteristics.[29]

**Contingency thinking** tries to match management practices with situational demands.

Contingency thinking is an important theme in this book, and its implications extend to all of the management functions—from planning and controlling for diverse environmental conditions, to organizing for different strategies, to leading in different performance situations. To clarify this notion, consider once again the concept of bureaucracy. Weber offered it as an ideal form of organization. But from a contingency perspective, the bureaucratic form is only one possible way of organizing things. What turns out to be the "best" structure in any given situation will depend on many factors, including environmental uncertainty, an organization's primary technology, and the strategy being pursued. As the nearby figure suggests, a tight bureaucracy works best when the environment is relatively stable and operations are predictable and uncomplicated. In complex and changing situations more flexible structures are needed.[30]

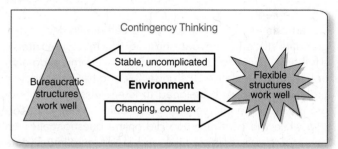

## Quality Management

The work of W. Edwards Deming is a cornerstone of the quality movement in management.[31] His story begins in 1951 when he was invited to Japan to explain quality control techniques that had been developed in the United States. "When Deming spoke," we might say, "the Japanese listened." The principles he taught the Japanese were straightforward and they worked: Tally defects, analyze and trace them to the source, make corrections, and keep a record of what happens afterward. Deming's approach to quality emphasizes use of statistical methods, commitment to training in the fundamentals of quality assurance, and constant innovation.[32]

These ideas contributed to the emergence of **total quality management**, or TQM. It makes quality principles part of the organization's strategic objectives, applying them to all aspects of operations and striving to meet customers' needs by doing things right the first time. Most TQM approaches begin with an insistence that the total quality commitment applies to everyone and every subsystem in an organization—from resource acquisition and supply chain management, through production and into the distribution of finished goods and services, and ultimately to the customer–management relationship. This search for and commitment to quality shows up as an emphasis on **continuous improvement**—always looking for new ways to improve on current performance. The point is that one must never be satisfied; something always can and should be improved upon.

**Total quality management** is an organization-wide commitment to continuous improvement, product quality, and customer needs.

**Continuous improvement** involves always searching for new ways to improve work quality and performance.

RESEARCH BRIEF

# Setting Personal Goals Improves Academic Performance

University graduates out-earn and suffer less unemployment than non-completers. But, as many as 25% of U.S. students that begin college fail to graduate. Even among those who do graduate, only about 35% do so in four years of study, while only 57% graduate after six years. What can schools do to fight this problem?

Dominique Morisano, Jacob Hirsh, Jordan Peterson, Robert Phil, and Bruce Shore set out to determine if a goal-setting intervention could help by improving students' academic performance. They used longitudinal research to study the impact of a structured online personal goal-setting program on student grades, enrolled credits, and motivation. The basic hypothesis was that students engaged in personal goal setting would show academic improvement.

Participants in the study were 85 self-nominated undergraduate students from one university that met three criteria: a full-time course load, having been on academic probation or having a cumulative GPA under 3.0, and having academic problems. They were assigned to intervention and control groups, with the intervention group doing online goal-setting while the control group did online questionnaires on personal characteristics. GPA and credit enrollment data were gathered both before and after the online activities, and a motivational questionnaire was completed at the end of the study.

Results, as shown in the figure, showed that students in the goal-setting intervention had higher GPAs after the intervention. The researchers concluded that: "This low-cost intervention could potentially be used by academic institutions to help 1st-year students establish goals and increase

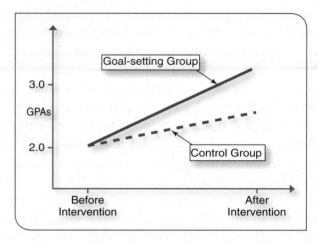

their academic prospects; it could also be used as a treatment for students on academic probation."

### YOU BE THE RESEARCHER

Is the conclusion of this study sufficiently evidence-based for department heads and deans to seriously consider starting personal goal-setting interventions to improve their students' academic performance? What weaknesses can you spot in the study design? If you were to replicate this study at your college or university, what would you change to get even better ideas to improve students' grades, retention, and graduation rates?

*Reference:* Dominique Morisano, Jacob B. Hirsh, Jordan B. Peterson, Robert O. Phil, and Bruce M. Shore, "Setting, Elaborating, and Reflecting on Personal Goals Improves Academic Performance," *Journal of Applied Psychology*, vol. 95, no. 2 (2010), pp. 255–264.

**ISO certification** indicates conformance with a rigorous set of international quality standards.

A global indicator of just how important quality management has become is **ISO certification** by the International Standards Organization in Geneva, Switzerland. Businesses and nonprofits that want to be viewed as "world-class" are increasingly expected to have ISO certification at various levels. To do so, they must refine and upgrade quality in all operations, and then undergo a rigorous assessment by outside auditors to determine whether they meet ISO requirements.

## Knowledge Management and Organizational Learning

The late and noted management scholar Peter Drucker once issued this warning: "Knowledge constantly makes itself obsolete."[33] His message suggests that neither people nor organizations can afford to rest on past laurels. Future success will be earned only by those who continually build and use knowledge to the fullest extent possible.

The term **knowledge management** describes the processes through which organizations use information technology to develop, organize, and share knowledge to achieve performance success.[34] You can spot the significance of knowledge management with the popularity of an executive job title—chief knowledge officer. The CKO is responsible for energizing learning processes and making sure that an organization's intellectual assets are well managed and continually enhanced. These assets include patents, intellectual property rights, trade secrets, and special processes and methods, as well as the accumulated knowledge and understanding of the entire workforce.

**Knowledge management** is the process of using intellectual capital for competitive advantage.

An emphasis on knowledge management is characteristic of what consultant Peter Senge calls a **learning organization**, popularized in his book *The Fifth Discipline*.[35] A learning organization, he says, is one that "by virtue of people, values, and systems is able to continuously change and improve its performance based upon the lessons of experience." He describes learning organizations as encouraging and helping all members to learn continuously, while emphasizing information sharing, teamwork, empowerment, and participation.

A **learning organization** continuously changes and improves, using the lessons of experience.

## Evidence-Based Management

One concern of today's management scholars is that we may be too quick in accepting as factual the results of studies that are based on poor science or questionable evidence. If studies are flawed, extra care needs to be exercised when trying to interpret and apply their insights.[36]

Managers are always searching for solid answers to questions on how to deal with day-to-day dilemmas and situations.[37] What is the best way to do performance appraisals? How do you select members for high-performance teams? How should a merit pay system be designed and implemented? When does directive leadership work best? How do you structure organizations for innovation? As such questions are posed, it only makes sense to be cautious and a bit skeptical when it comes to separating fads from facts and conjecture from informed insight.

Scholars Jeffrey Pfeffer and Robert Sutton make the case for **evidence-based management**, making management decisions based on "hard facts"—that is, about what really works—rather than on "dangerous half-truths"—things that

**Evidence-based management** involves making decisions based on hard facts about what really works.

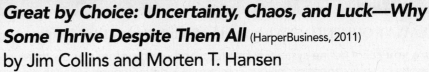

## Recommended Reading

### *Great by Choice: Uncertainty, Chaos, and Luck—Why Some Thrive Despite Them All* (HarperBusiness, 2011)
### by Jim Collins and Morten T. Hansen

BCarrie Devorah/WENN/NewsCom

When Jim Collins wrote a book entitled *Good to Great* and described characteristics of high-performing companies, it became a best-seller. So did his follow-up book, *How the Mighty Fall.* It discussed why some of his previous picks for greatness had major problems due to management egos that fueled excessive risks in the quest for fast growth. His latest book, *Great by Choice*, focuses on foundations for success in a world of uncertainty and rapid change. Interestingly, the researchers says it's not making fast decisions that counts for success, but rather making them in empirical and disciplined ways.

sound good but lack empirical substantiation.[38] Pfeffer and Sutton want managers to be well informed and discerning as they make decisions. Evidence-based management, they say, is about managers "making decisions through the conscientious, explicit, and judicious use of four sources of information: practitioner expertise and judgment, evidence from the local context, a critical evaluation of the best available research evidence, and the perspectives of those people who might be affected by the decision."[39]

Management scholars support and inform evidence-based management by pursuing solid and meaningful research using scientific methods, and by rigorously examining and reporting case studies and insights from managers' experiences.[40] The Research Brief feature found in each chapter of *Management 12/e* introduces the types of studies that are being done. Some carve out new and innovative territories while others refine and extend knowledge that has come down in building-block fashion over time.

Management research involves data collection and analysis in one form or another. But just because a reported study uses data doesn't make it solid and scientific. The following criteria are a helpful first-test in determining whether or not good scientific methods have been used by the researchers.

1. A research question or problem is clearly identified.
2. One of more hypotheses is stated to describe possible explanations.
3. The research design provides for a good test of the hypotheses.
4. Data are rigorously gathered, analyzed, and interpreted.
5. Hypotheses are accepted or rejected and conclusions made based on the evidence.

When research satisfies the scientific methods test, managers can have more confidence in accepting and applying the results in actual practice. Gathering data from a sample of some 1,000 firms, for example, Pfeffer and a colleague studied the link between human resource management and organizational performance.[41] They found that firms using a mix of positive human resource management practices had more sales per employee and higher profits per employee than those that didn't. These positive practices included employment security, selective hiring, self-managed teams, high wages based on performance merit, training and skill development, minimal status differences, and shared information.[42]

---

**LEARNING CHECK 3**

**TAKEAWAY QUESTION 3 What are the foundations of modern management thinking?**

**Be sure you can** • define *system*, *subsystem*, and *open system* • apply these concepts to describe the operations of an organization in your community • define *contingency thinking, knowledge management,* and *learning organization* • list characteristics of learning organizations • describe evidence-based management and its link with scientific methods

# MANAGEMENT LEARNING REVIEW

## LEARNING CHECK SUMMARY

### TAKEAWAY QUESTION 1 What can be learned from classical management thinking?

- Frederick Taylor's four principles of scientific management focused on the need to carefully select, train, and support workers for individual task performance.
- Henri Fayol suggested that managers should learn what are now known as the management functions of planning, organizing, leading, and controlling.
- Max Weber described bureaucracy with its clear hierarchy, formal rules, and well-defined jobs as an ideal form of organization.

**For Discussion Should Weber's notion of the ideal bureaucracy be scrapped altogether, or is it still relevant today?**

### TAKEAWAY QUESTION 2 What insights come from the behavioral management approaches?

- The behavioral approaches shifted management attention toward the human factor as a key element in organizational performance.
- Mary Parker Follett describes organizations as communities within which people combine talents to work for a greater good.
- The Hawthorne studies suggested that work behavior is influenced by social and psychological forces and that work performance may be improved by better "human relations."
- Abraham Maslow's hierarchy of human needs introduced the concept of self-actualization and the potential for people to experience self-fulfillment in their work.
- Douglas McGregor urged managers to shift away from Theory X and toward Theory Y thinking, which views people as independent, responsible, and capable of self-direction in their work.
- Chris Argyris pointed out that people in the workplace

are adults and may react negatively when constrained by strict management practices and rigid organizational structures.

**For Discussion How can a manager still benefit by using insights from Maslow's hierarchy of needs theory?**

### TAKEAWAY QUESTION 3 What are the foundations of modern management thinking?

- Analytics that use advanced quantitative analysis techniques in decision sciences and operations management can help managers solve complex problems.
- Organizations are open systems that interact with their external environments, while consisting of many internal subsystems that must work together in a coordinated way to support the organization's overall success.
- Contingency thinking avoids "one best way" arguments, instead recognizing the need to understand situational differences and respond appropriately to them.
- Quality management focuses on making a total commitment to product and service quality throughout an organization, maintaining continuous improvement and meeting worldwide quality standards such as ISO certification.
- Knowledge management is a process for developing, organizing, sharing, and using knowledge to facilitate organizational performance and create an environment for ongoing organizational learning.
- Evidence-based management uses findings from rigorous scientific research to identify management practices for high performance.

**For Discussion Can system and subsystem dynamics help describe and explain performance problems for an organization in your community?**

## SELF-TEST 2

### Multiple-Choice Questions

1. The assumption that people are complex with widely varying needs is most associated with the _____ management approaches.
   (a) classical
   (b) neoclassical
   (c) behavioral
   (d) modern

2. The father of scientific management is _____.
   (a) Weber
   (b) Taylor
   (c) Mintzberg
   (d) Katz

3. When the registrar of a university deals with students by an identification number rather than a name,

which characteristic of bureaucracy is being displayed and what is its intended benefit?
(a) division of labor, competency
(b) merit-based careers, productivity
(c) rules and procedures, efficiency
(d) impersonality, fairness

4. If an organization was performing poorly and Henri Fayol was called in as a consultant, what would he most likely suggest to improve things?
(a) Teach managers to better plan and control.
(b) Teach workers more efficient job methods.
(c) Promote to management only the most competent workers.
(d) Find ways to increase corporate social responsibility.

5. One example of how scientific management principles are applied in organizations today would be:
(a) conducting studies to increase efficiencies in job performance.
(b) finding alternatives to a bureaucratic structure.
(c) training managers to better understand worker attitudes.
(d) focusing managers on teamwork rather than individual jobs.

6. The Hawthorne studies raised awareness of how _____ can be important influences on productivity.
(a) structures
(b) human factors
(c) physical work conditions
(d) pay and rewards

7. Advice to study a job, carefully train workers to do that job, and link financial incentives to job performance would most likely come from _____.
(a) scientific management
(b) contingency management
(c) Henri Fayol
(d) Abraham Maslow

8. The highest level in Maslow's hierarchy includes _____ needs.
(a) safety
(b) esteem
(c) self-actualization
(d) physiological

9. A possible misfit between the mature adult personality and rigid practices of a bureaucratic organization was a major concern of _____.
(a) Argyris
(b) Follett
(c) Weber
(d) Fuller

10. When people perform in a situation as they are expected to, this is sometimes called the _____ Effect.
(a) Hawthorne
(b) systems
(c) contingency
(d) open-systems

11. Resource acquisition and customer satisfaction are important when an organization is viewed as a(n) _____.
(a) bureaucracy
(b) closed system
(c) open system
(d) pyramid

12. The loan-processing department would be considered a _____ of your local bank or credit union.
(a) subsystem
(b) closed system
(c) resource input
(d) cost center

13. When a manager notices that Sheryl has strong social needs and assigns her a job in customer relations and gives Kwabena lots of praise because of his strong ego needs, the manager is displaying _____.
(a) systems thinking
(b) Theory X
(c) motion study
(d) contingency thinking

14. Which is the correct match?
(a) Senge–motion study
(b) McGregor–analytics
(c) Deming–quality management
(d) Maslow–Theory X and Y

15. When managers try to avoid hearsay and make decisions based on solid facts and information, this is known as _____.
(a) continuous improvement
(b) evidence-based management
(c) TQM
(d) Theory X management

## Short-Response Questions

16. Explain how McGregor's Theory Y assumptions can create self-fulfilling prophecies consistent with the current emphasis on participation and involvement in the workplace.

17. How do the deficit and progression principles operate in Maslow's hierarchy-of-needs theory?

18. Define contingency thinking and give an example of how it might apply to management.

19. Explain why the external environment is so important in the open-systems view of organizations.

## Essay Question

20. Enrique Temoltzin has just been appointed the new manager of your local college bookstore. Enrique would like to make sure the store operates according to Weber's bureaucracy. Describe the characteristics of bureaucracy and answer this question: Is the bureaucracy a good management approach for Enrique to follow? Discuss the possible limitations of bureaucracy and the implications for managing people as key assets of the store.

# Further Reflection: Learning Style

People tend to learn in different ways. You should think about your **learning style**—how you learn by receiving, processing, and sharing information. And, you should understand the learning styles of others. One of our most significant challenges is to always embrace experiences at school, at work, and in everyday living and try our best to learn from them. And when it comes to experience as a foundation for learning, let's not forget the wisdom of the past. This chapter has offered a reminder about the importance of management history and how past achievements provide insights that can help us deal with the present.

 **DO IT NOW . . .**
**LOOK IN THE MIRROR**

- Ask: "What are the implications of my learning style for how I perform academically and how well I perform at work?"
- Ask also: "How does my learning style influence my relationships with others in study groups and work teams?"
- Write a memo describing your learning style and how it might positively and negatively affect your relationships with people at work.

# Self-Assessment: Managerial Assumptions

## Instructions

Read the following statements. Use the space in the margins to write "Yes" if you agree with the statement, or "No" if you disagree with it. Force yourself to take a Yes or No position.

1. Is good pay and a secure job enough to satisfy most workers?
2. Should a manager help and coach subordinates in their work?
3. Do most people like real responsibility in their jobs?
4. Are most people afraid to learn new things in their jobs?
5. Should managers let subordinates control the quality of their work?
6. Do most people dislike work?
7. Are most people creative?
8. Should a manager closely supervise and direct the work of subordinates?
9. Do most people tend to resist change?
10. Do most people work only as hard as they have to?
11. Should workers be allowed to set their own job goals?
12. Are most people happiest off the job?
13. Do most workers really care about the organization they work for?
14. Should a manager help subordinates advance and grow in their jobs?

## Scoring

Count the number of yes responses to items 1, 4, 6, 8, 9, 10, 12.
Write that number here as [X = _____].

Count the number of yes responses to items 2, 3, 5, 7, 11, 13, 14.
Write that score here as [Y = _____].

## Interpretation

This assessment provides insight into your orientation toward Douglas McGregor's Theory X (your "X" score) and Theory Y (your "Y" score) assumptions as discussed earlier in the chapter. You should review the discussion of McGregor's thinking in this chapter and consider further the ways in which you are likely to behave toward other people at work. Think, in particular, about the types of "self-fulfilling prophecies" your managerial assumptions are likely to create.

## Team Exercise:
## Evidence-based Management Quiz

### Instructions

1. For each of the following questions answer "T" (true) if you believe the statement is backed by solid research evidence, or "F" (false) if you do not believe it is an evidence-based statement.[42]

   T F 1. Intelligence is a better predictor of job performance than having a conscientious personality.

   T F 2. Screening job candidates for values results in higher job performance than screening for intelligence.

   T F 3. A highly intelligent person will have a hard time performing well in a low-skill job.

   T F 4. "Integrity tests" are good predictors of whether employees will steal, be absent, or take advantage of their employers in other ways.

   T F 5. Goal setting is more likely to result in improved performance than is participation in decision making.

   T F 6. Errors in performance appraisals can be reduced through proper training.

   T F 7. People behave in ways that show pay is more important to them than what they indicate on surveys.

   T F 8. People hired through employee referrals have better retention rates than those hired from other recruiting sources.

   T F 9. Workers who get training and development opportunities at work tend to have lower desires to change employers.

   T F 10. Being "realistic" in job interviews and telling prospective employees about both negative and positive job aspects improves employee retention.

2. Share your answers with others in your assigned group. Discuss the reasons members chose the answers they did; arrive at a final answer to each question for the group as a whole.

3. Compare your results with these answers "from the evidence."

4. Engage in a class discussion of how common-sense answers can sometimes differ from answers provided by evidence. Ask: What are the implications of this discussion for management practice?

## Career Situations for Today:
## What Would You Do?

1. **Paying a Summer Worker**   It's summer job time and you've found something that just might work— handling technical support inquiries at a local Internet provider. The regular full-time employees are paid by the hour. Summer hires like you fill in when they go on vacation. However, you will be paid by the call for each customer that you handle. How will this pay plan affect your work behavior as a customer service representative? Is this summer pay plan a good choice by the management of the Internet provider?

2. **No Pay Raises for Good Performance**   As a manager in a small local firm you've been told that because of the poor economy workers can't be given any pay raises this year. You have some really hard-working and high-performing people on your team that you were counting on giving solid raises to. Now what can you do? How can you use insights from Maslow's hierarchy of needs to solve this dilemma of finding suitable rewards for high performance?

3. **I've Got this Great Idea**   You've just come up with a great idea for improving productivity and morale in a shop that silk-screens t-shirts. You want to allow workers to work four 10-hour days if they want instead of the normal five day/40-hour week. With the added time off, you reason, they'll be happier and more productive while working. But your boss isn't so sure. "Show me some evidence," she says. Can you design a research study that can be done in the shop to show whether your proposal is a good one?

# Case Study

# Zara International

Go to *Management Cases for Critical Thinking* to find the recommended case for Chapter 2—"Zara International: Fashion at the Speed of Light."

Shoppers in 77 countries are fans of Zara's knack for bringing the latest styles from sketchbook to clothing rack at lightning speed. New items can be in stores within two weeks of original design. This rapid response to fashion trends gives Zara a top ranking among global clothing vendors. You can't wait for sales when shopping at Zara; merchandise moves too fast. The stores carry as many as 10,000 new designs each year. And, it all comes at prices tailored to the young—reasonable by market standards.

Zara is owned by Spanish parent Inditex, and its fast-fashion model is the brainchild of founder Armancio Ortega. By way of tribute, Louis Vuitton fashion director Daniel Piette described Zara as "possibly the most innovative and devastating retailer in the world." Zara is experimenting with a move online. And if the popularity of its midtown Manhattan flagship American store is any indicator, other fashion retailers best beware. Before you know it there'll be a Zara at the local shopping mall.

JODI HILTON/The New York Times/Redux Pictures

# Wisdom
## Learning
## From Others

### > EVERYONE GAINS WHEN OUR PLANET IS A PRIORITY

"Business is the most powerful force in the world," says Gary Hirshberg, "I believe that virtually every problem in the world exists because business hasn't made finding a solution a priority." Co-founder, former CEO, and current chairman of Stonyfield Farm, the world's largest producer of organic yogurt, he's the author of *Stirring It Up: How to Make Money and Save the World* and was named one of "America's Most Promising Social Entrepreneurs" by *BusinessWeek* magazine.

The mission of Stonyfield Farm is straightforward: "Offer a pure and healthy product that tastes good and earn a profit without harming the environment." This translates into a triple bottom line of being economi-cally, socially, and environmentally responsible.

Hirshberg says that Stonyfield Farm "factors the planet into all our deci-sions. . . . It's a simple strategy but a powerful one." "Going green is not just the right thing to do, but a great way to build a successful business."

That thinking has helped grow Stonyfield Farm into the number one maker of organic yogurt in the world. The company uses dairy-farm suppliers who pledge not to use bovine growth hormone (BGH) and operates on the principle that "healthy food can only come from a healthy planet." Hirshberg's current focus is on getting better labeling for genetically engineered foods and new national food and agriculture policies.[1]

MORE TO LOOK FOR INSIDE>

# Ethics and Social Responsibility

**3**

## > INDIVIDUAL CHARACTER

There is no doubt that **individual character** is evident in all we do. Persons of high character act confidently due to the self-respect it provides, even in difficult situations. Those who lack it are more insecure. They act inconsistently and suffer in self-esteem and in the esteem of others.

Our character links directly with our personal integrity. It provides an ethical anchor for how we behave at work and in life overall. Think of it as demonstrated honesty, civility, caring, and sense of fair play.

Ethics and social responsibility issues facing organizations today can put individual character to a very stiff test. We need to know ourselves well enough to make principled decisions that we can be proud of and that others will respect. After all, it's the character of the people making key decisions that determines whether our organizations act in socially responsible or irresponsible ways.[2]

One trait that can undermine individual character is hypercompetitiveness. You see it in individuals who think that winning—or getting ahead—is the only thing that matters. They hate to lose. They judge themselves more on outcomes achieved than methods used to get there. And, they may be quick to put aside virtues in competitive situations like the business world.[3]

## Insight
### Learning About Yourself

## BUILD SKILLS AND COMPETENCIES AT END OF CHAPTER

- Engage in *Further Reflection on Individual Character*
- Do the *Self-Assessment on Terminal Values*
- Complete the *Team Exercise—Confronting Ethical Dilemmas*
- Solve the *Career Situations for Ethical Behavior*
- Analyze the *Case Study—Patagonia: Leading a Green Revolution*

## <GET TO KNOW YOURSELF BETTER

| TAKEAWAY 1 | TAKEAWAY 2 | TAKEAWAY 3 | TAKEAWAY 4 |
|---|---|---|---|
| **What Is Ethical Behavior?** | **Ethics in the Workplace** | **Maintaining High Ethical Standards** | **Social Responsibility** |
| • Laws and values as determinants of ethical behavior<br><br>• Alternative views of ethics<br><br>• Cultural issues in ethical behavior | • Ethical dilemmas<br><br>• Influences on ethical decision making<br><br>• Rationalizations for unethical behavior | • Moral management<br><br>• Ethics training<br><br>• Codes of ethical conduct<br><br>• Whistleblower protection | • Stewardship<br><br>• Stakeholder management<br><br>• Perspectives on corporate social responsibility<br><br>• Evaluating corporate social performance<br><br>• Corporate governance |
| LEARNING CHECK 1 | LEARNING CHECK 2 | LEARNING CHECK 3 | LEARNING CHECK 4 |

The opening example of Gary Hirshberg and Stonyfield Farm should get you thinking about ethics, social responsibility, and principled leadership. Look around; there are many cases of people and organizations operating in admirable ways. Some are quite well known—Ben and Jerry's, Burt's Bees, Tom's of Maine, and Whole Foods Markets, for example. Surely there are others right in your local community. But as you think of the organizations, don't forget the people that run them—the ones whose behavior ultimately influences their organizations' performance. Consider also this reminder from Desmond Tutu, archbishop of Capetown, South Africa, and winner of the Nobel Peace Prize.

You are powerful people. You can make this world a better place where business decisions and methods take account of right and wrong as well as profitability. . . . You must take a stand on important issues: the environment and ecology, affirmative action, sexual harassment, racism and sexism, the arms race, poverty, the obligations of the affluent West to its less-well-off sisters and brothers elsewhere.[4]

## What Is Ethical Behavior?

**Ethics** establish standards of good or bad, or right or wrong, in one's conduct.

For our purposes, **ethics** is defined as the moral code of principles that sets standards of good or bad, or right or wrong, in one's conduct.[5] A person's moral code is influenced by a variety of sources including family, friends, local culture, religion, educational institutions, and individual experiences.[6] Ethics guide and help people make moral choices among alternative courses of action. And in practice, **ethical behavior** is that which is accepted as "good" and "right" as opposed to "bad" or "wrong" in the context of the governing moral code.

**Ethical behavior** is "right" or "good" in the context of a governing moral code.

58

## Laws and Values as Determinants of Ethical Behavior

Individuals often assume that anything that is legal should be considered ethical. Slavery was once legal in the United States, and laws once permitted only men to vote.[7] But that doesn't mean the practices were ethical. Sometimes legislation lags behind changes in moral positions within a society. The delay makes it possible for something to be legal during a time when most people think it should be illegal.[8]

By the same token, just because an action is not strictly illegal doesn't make it ethical.[9] Living up to the "letter of the law" is not sufficient to guarantee that one's actions will or should be considered ethical. Is it truly ethical, for example, for an employee to take longer than necessary to do a job? To call in sick so that you can take a day off work for leisure? To fail to report rule violations by a coworker? Although none of these acts is strictly illegal, many would consider them to be unethical.

Most ethical problems in the workplace arise when people are asked to do, or find they are about to do, something that violates their personal beliefs. For some, if the act is legal, they proceed without worrying about it. For others, the ethical test goes beyond legality and into personal **values**—the underlying beliefs and attitudes that help determine individual behavior.

The psychologist Milton Rokeach makes a distinction between "terminal" and "instrumental" values.[10] **Terminal values** (see the end-of-chapter self-assessment) are preferences about desired ends, such as the goals one strives to achieve in life. Examples of terminal values considered important by managers include self-respect, family security, freedom, and happiness. **Instrumental values** are preferences regarding the means for accomplishing these ends. Among the instrumental values held important by managers are honesty, ambition, imagination, and self-discipline.

The value pattern for any one person is very enduring. But, values vary from one person to the next. And to the extent that they do, we can expect different interpretations of what behavior is ethical or unethical in a given situation. When commenting on cheating tendencies, an ethics professor at Insead in France once told business school students: "The academic values of integrity and honesty in your work can seem to be less relevant than the instrumental goal of getting a good job."[11] And when about 10% of an MBA class at a major university was caught cheating on a take-home final exam, some said that we should expect such behavior from students who are taught to collaborate and work in teams and utilize the latest communication technologies. For others, the instrumental values driving such behavior are totally unacceptable—it was an individual exam, the students cheated, and they should be penalized.[12]

> **Values** are broad beliefs about what is appropriate behavior.

> **Terminal values** are preferences about desired end states.

> **Instrumental values** are preferences regarding the means to desired ends.

FIGURE 3.1 **Four views of ethical behavior.**

## Alternative Views of Ethics

Figure 3.1 shows four views of ethical behavior—the utilitarian, individualism, moral rights, and justice views.[13] Depending on which perspective one adopts in a given situation, the resulting behaviors may be considered ethical or unethical.

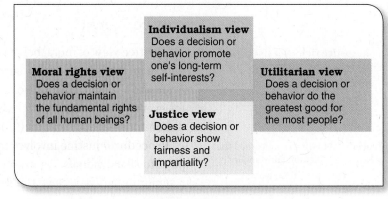

**Moral rights view**
Does a decision or behavior maintain the fundamental rights of all human beings?

**Individualism view**
Does a decision or behavior promote one's long-term self-interests?

**Justice view**
Does a decision or behavior show fairness and impartiality?

**Utilitarian view**
Does a decision or behavior do the greatest good for the most people?

## Utilitarian View

The **utilitarian view** considers ethical behavior to be that which delivers the greatest good to the greatest number of people. Based on the work of 19th-century philosopher John Stuart Mill, this results-oriented point of view assesses the moral implications of actions in terms of their consequences. Business decision makers, for example, are inclined to use profits, efficiency, and other performance criteria to judge what is best for the most people. In a recession or when a firm is suffering through hard times, an executive may decide to cut 30% of the workforce in order to keep the company profitable and save the jobs of remaining workers. She could justify this decision based on a utilitarian sense of business ethics.

## Individualism View

The **individualism view** of ethical behavior is based on the belief that one's primary commitment is to the long-term advancement of self-interests. The basic idea of this approach is that society will be best off if everyone acts in a way that maximizes his or her own utility or happiness. According to this viewpoint, people are supposedly self-regulating as they seek long-term individual advantage. For example, lying and cheating for short-term gain should not be tolerated because if everyone behaves this way then no one's long-term interests will be served. The individualism view is supposed to promote honesty and integrity. But in business practice it may result in greed, a pecuniary ethic described by one executive as the tendency to "push the law to its outer limits" and "run roughshod over other individuals to achieve one's objectives."[14]

> ### SELECTIONS FROM UNIVERSAL DECLARATION OF HUMAN RIGHTS
>
> • All human beings are born free and equal in dignity and rights.
>
> • Everyone has the right to life, liberty, and security of person.
>
> • No one shall be held in slavery or servitude.
>
> • No one shall be subjected to torture or to cruel, inhuman, or degrading treatment or punishment.
>
> • All are equal before the law and are entitled without any discrimination to equal protection of the law.

## Moral Rights View

Ethical behavior under a **moral rights view** is that which respects and protects the fundamental rights of people. From the teachings of John Locke and Thomas Jefferson, for example, the rights of all people to life, liberty, and fair treatment under the law are considered inviolate. In organizations, the moral rights concept extends to ensuring that employees are protected in rights to privacy, due process, free speech, free consent, health and safety, and freedom of conscience. The issue of human rights, a major ethical concern in the international business environment, is central to this perspective. The United Nations, as indicated in the accompanying box, stands by the Universal Declaration of Human Rights passed by the General Assembly in 1948.[15]

## Justice View

The **justice view** of moral behavior is based on the belief that ethical decisions treat people impartially and fairly, according to legal rules and standards. This approach evaluates the ethical aspects of any decision on the basis of whether it is "equitable" for everyone affected.[16] Justice issues in organizations are often addressed on four dimensions—procedural, distributive, interactional, and commutative.[17]

**Procedural justice** involves the degree to which policies and rules are fairly applied to all individuals. For example, does a sexual harassment charge levied against a senior executive receive the same full hearing as one made against a first-level supervisor? **Distributive justice** involves the degree to which outcomes are allocated fairly among people and without respect to individual characteristics based on ethnicity, race, gender, age, or other particularistic criteria. For example, are women and minorities treated fairly when pay raises and promotions are made? Do universities allocate a proportionate share of athletic scholarships to males and females?

**Interactional justice** involves the degree to which people treat one another with dignity and respect. For example, does a bank loan officer take the time to fully explain to an applicant why he or she was turned down for a loan?[18] **Commutative justice** focuses on the fairness of exchanges or transactions. Things are fair if all parties enter freely, have access to relevant information, and obtain some benefit.[19] Does a bank loan officer make it clear, for example, that a applicant may have difficulty repaying the loan if interest rates increase and the applicant's income does not?

**Distributive justice** focuses on the degree to which outcomes are distributed fairly.

**Interactional justice** is the degree to which others are treated with dignity and respect.

**Commutative justice** is the degree to which an exchange or a transaction is fair to all parties.

## Contrasts and Drawbacks

Examining issues through all four of the prior viewpoints helps to provide a more complete picture of the ethicality of a decision than merely relying on a single point of view. However, each viewpoint has some drawbacks that should be recognized.

The utilitarian view relies on the assessment of future outcomes that are often difficult to predict and that are tough to measure accurately. What is the economic value of a human life when deciding how rigid safety regulations need to be, especially when it is unclear exactly how many individuals might be affected? The individualism view presumes that individuals are self-regulating; however, not everyone has the same capacity or desire to control their behaviors. Even if only a few individuals take advantage of the freedom allowed under this perspective, such instances can disrupt the degree of trust that exists within a business community and make it difficult to predict how others will act.

The moral rights view provides for individual rights, but does not ensure that the outcomes associated with protecting those rights are beneficial to the majority of society. What happens when someone's right to privacy makes the workplace less safe for everyone? The justice view places an emphasis on fairness and equity, but this viewpoint raises the question of which type of justice is paramount. Is it more important to ensure that everyone is treated exactly the same way (procedural justice) or to ensure that those from different backgrounds are adequately represented in terms of the final outcome (distributive justice)?

## Cultural Issues in Ethical Behavior

Picture the situation: A 12-year-old boy is working in a garment factory in Bangladesh. He is the sole income earner for his family. He often works 12-hour days and was once burned quite badly by a hot iron. One day he is fired. His employer had been given an ultimatum by a major American customer: "No child workers if you want to keep our contracts." The boy says: "I don't understand. I could do my job very well. I need the money."

Should the boy be allowed to work? This difficult and perplexing situation is one example of the many ethics challenges faced in international business. Former Levi Strauss CEO Robert Haas once said that an ethical problem "becomes even more difficult when you overlay the complexities of different cultures and values systems that exist throughout the world."[20]

## Child Labor Controversies Are an International Business Reality

The International Labour Organization reports there are some 215 million child laborers worldwide; 115 million of them work in hazardous conditions. It was once commonplace for children to work in factories in the United States. Some would say it was a contributor to the country's economic development. Now there are strict laws that govern the employment of children. In some other countries child labor remains common. It's part of their economies and many families depend for their daily sustenance on the income that children provide. The photo shows a young African child carrying goods which are to be sold in the market. What is your position on child labor around the world?

Thomas Cockrem/Alamy

**Cultural relativism** suggests there is no one right way to behave; ethical behavior is determined by its cultural context.

**Moral absolutism** suggests ethical standards apply universally across all cultures.

**Ethical imperialism** is an attempt to impose one's ethical standards on other cultures.

Those who believe that behavior in foreign settings should be guided by the classic rule of "when in Rome, do as the Romans do" reflect an ethical position known as **cultural relativism**.[21] This is the belief that there is no one right way to behave and that ethical behavior is always determined by its cultural context. An American international business executive guided by rules of cultural relativism, for example, would argue that the use of child labor is acceptable in another country as long as it is consistent with local laws and customs.

Figure 3.2 contrasts cultural relativism with **moral absolutism**. This is the belief that if a behavior or practice is not okay in one's home environment, it is not an acceptable practice anywhere else. In other words, ethical standards are universal and should apply absolutely across cultures and national boundaries. In the former example, the American executive would not do business in a setting where child labor was used since it is unacceptable at home. Critics of such an absolutist approach claim that it is a form of **ethical imperialism**, an attempt to impose one's ethical standards on others.

Business ethicist Thomas Donaldson finds fault with both cultural relativism and ethical imperialism. He argues instead that certain fundamental rights and ethical standards can be preserved at the same time that values and traditions of a given culture are respected.[22] The core values or "hyper-norms" that should transcend cultural boundaries focus on human dignity, basic rights, and good citizenship. Donaldson believes international business behaviors can be tailored to local and regional cultural contexts while still upholding these core values. In the case of child

| Cultural relativism | Moral absolutism |
| --- | --- |
| No culture's ethics are superior. The values and practices of the local setting determine what is right or wrong. | Certain absolute truths apply everywhere. Universal values transcend cultures in determining what is right or wrong. |
| *When in Rome, do as the Romans do.* | *Don't do anything you wouldn't do at home.* |

FIGURE 3.2 **Cultural relativism and universalism in international business ethics.**
*Source:* Developed from Thomas Donaldson, "Values in Tension: Ethics Away from Home," *Harvard Business Review*, vol. 74 (September–October 1996), pp. 48–62.

labor, the American executive might take steps so that any children working in a factory under contract to his or her business would be provided daily scheduled schooling as well as employment.[23]

---

**LEARNING CHECK 1**

**TAKEAWAY QUESTION 1 What is ethical behavior?**

**Be sure you can** • define *ethics* • explain why obeying the law is not always the same as behaving ethically • explain the difference between terminal and instrumental values • identify the four alternative views of ethics • contrast cultural relativism with moral relativism?

---

# Ethics in the Workplace

A college student gets a job offer and accepts it, only to get a better offer two weeks later. Is it right for her to reject the first job to accept the second? A student knows that his roommate submitted a term paper purchased on the Internet. Is it right for him not to tell the instructor? One student confides to another that a faculty member promised her a high final grade in return for sexual favors. Is it right for him to inform the instructor's department head?

The real test of ethics occurs when individuals encounter a situation that challenges their personal values and standards. Often ambiguous and unexpected, these ethical challenges are inevitable. Everyone has to be prepared to deal with them, even students.

## Ethical Dilemmas

An **ethical dilemma** is a situation that requires a choice regarding a possible course of action that, although offering the potential for personal or organizational benefit, or both, may be considered unethical. It is often a situation in which action must be taken but for which there is no clear consensus on what is "right" and "wrong." An engineering manager speaking from experience sums it up this way: "I define an unethical situation as one in which I have to do something I don't feel good about."[24] Here are some common examples of situations that present managers with ethical dilemmas.[25]

An **ethical dilemma** is a situation that offers potential benefit or gain and that may also be considered unethical.

- *Discrimination*—Your boss suggests that it would be a mistake to hire a qualified job candidate because she wears a headscarf for religious purposes. The boss believes your traditional customers might be uncomfortable with her appearance.
- *Sexual harassment*—A female subordinate asks you to discipline a coworker that she claims is making her feel uncomfortable with inappropriate sexual remarks. The coworker, your friend, says that he was just kidding around and asks you not to take any action that would harm his career.
- *Conflicts of interest*—You are working in another country and are offered an expensive gift in return for making a decision favorable to the gift giver. You know that such exchanges are common practice in this culture and that several of your colleagues have accepted similar gifts in the past.
- *Product safety*—Your company is struggling financially and can make one of its major products more cheaply by purchasing lower-quality materials, although doing so would slightly increase the risk of consumer injury.

## ManagementSmarts

### Quick Check for Dealing with Ethical Dilemmas

**Step 1.** Recognize the ethical dilemma.

**Step 2.** Get the facts and identify your options.

**Step 3.** Test each option: Is it legal? Is it right? Whom does it affect? Who benefits? Who gets hurt?

**Step 4.** Decide which option to follow.

**Step 5.** Double-check with the *spotlight questions:*

*"How will I feel if my family finds out about my decision?"*

*"How will I feel about this if my decision is reported in the local newspaper or posted on the Internet?"*

*"What would the person I admire most for their character and ethical judgement say about my decision?"*

**Step 6.** Take action.

• Use of *organizational resources*—You bring an office laptop computer home so that you can work after hours. Your wife likes this computer better than hers, and asks if she can use it for her online business during the weekends.

It is almost too easy to confront ethical dilemmas from the safety of a textbook or a classroom discussion. In real life it's a lot harder to consistently choose ethical courses of action. We end up facing ethical dilemmas at unexpected and inconvenient times, in situations where events and facts are ambiguous, and when pressures to perform seem unforgiving and intense. Is it any surprise, then, that 56% of U.S. workers in one survey reported feeling pressured to act unethically in their jobs? Or that 48% said they had committed questionable acts within the past year?[26]

Management Smarts presents a six-step checklist for dealing with an ethical dilemma.[27] It is a way to double-check the ethics of decisions before taking action. Step 5 highlights a key test: the risk of public disclosure. Asking and answering the recommended *spotlight questions* is a powerful way to test whether a decision is consistent with your personal ethical standards. Think about this the next time you're making an uncomfortable decision: "How will I feel if my family finds out, or if this gets reported in the local newspaper or posted on the Internet?" "What would the person I admire most for their character and ethical judgement say about my decision?"

## Influences on Ethical Decision Making

Standing up for what you believe in isn't always easy, especially in a social context full of contradictory or just plain bad advice. Consider these words from a commencement address delivered some years ago at a well-known school of business administration. "Greed is all right," the speaker said. "Greed is healthy. You can be greedy and still feel good about yourself." The students, it is reported, greeted these remarks with laughter and applause. The speaker was Ivan Boesky, once considered the "king of the arbitragers."[28] It wasn't long after his commencement speech, however, that Boesky was arrested, tried, convicted, and sentenced to prison for trading on inside information.

An **ethical framework** is a personal rule or strategy for making ethical decisions.

### Personal Influences on Ethics

Values, family, religion, and personal needs all help determine a person's ethics. Managers who lack a strong and clear set of personal ethics will find that their decisions vary from situation to situation. Those with solid **ethical frameworks**, ones that provide personal rules or strategies for ethical decision making, will act more consistently and confidently. These frameworks are moral anchors based in individual character and personal values that give priority to such virtues as honesty, fairness, integrity, and self-respect. They help us make ethical decisions even in difficult circumstances.

## Stages of Moral Development

Lawrence Kohlberg describes the three levels of moral development shown in Figure 3.3—preconventional, conventional, and postconventional.[29] There are two stages in each level, and Kohlberg believes that we move step by step through them as we grow in maturity and education. Most people are at a preconventional or conventional level of moral development; very few consistently act at the postconventional level. And, people at the different levels of moral development may approach the same ethical dilemma very differently.

In Kohlberg's *preconventional level* of moral development the individual is self-centered. Moral thinking is largely limited to issues of punishment, obedience, and personal interest. Decisions made in the preconventional stages of moral development are likely to be directed toward achieving personal gain or avoiding punishment and are based on obedience to rules.

In the *conventional level* of moral development, the individual is more social-centered. Decisions made in these stages are likely to be based on following social norms, meeting the expectations of group memberships, and living up to agreed-upon role obligations.

At the *postconventional level* of moral development, the individual is strongly principle-centered. This is where a strong ethics framework is evident. The individual is willing to break with norms and conventions, even laws, to make decisions consistent with universal principles. Kohlberg believes that only a small percentage of people progress to the postconventional stages. An example might be the student who doesn't cheat on a take-home examination because he or she believes it is wrong, even while knowing that other students will cheat, there is almost no chance of getting caught, and the consequence of not cheating might be getting a lower grade on the test.

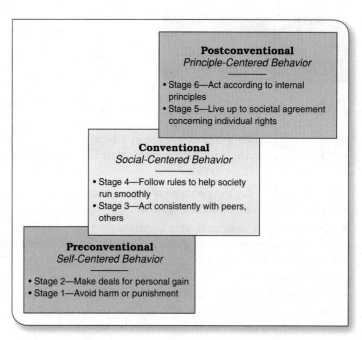

**FIGURE 3.3** **Kohlberg's levels of individual moral development.**

## Situational Context and Ethics Intensity

Ethical dilemmas sometimes catch us off guard and we struggle to respond. Other times, we might even fail to see that an issue or a situation has an ethics component. This may happen, for example, when students find cheating so commonplace on campus that it becomes an accepted standard of behavior. Scholars discuss this as an issue of **ethics intensity** or **issue intensity**, the extent to which a situation is perceived to pose important ethics challenges.[30]

The greater the ethical intensity of the situation, the more aware the decision maker generally is about ethics issues and the more likely that his or her behavior will be ethical. The conditions that raise the ethics intensity of a situation include the magnitude, probability, and immediacy of any potential harm, the proximity and concentration of the effects, and social consensus. A decision situation will elicit greater ethical attention when the potential harm is perceived as great, likely, and imminent, when the potential victims are visible and close by, and when there is more social agreement on what is good or bad about what is taking place. How, for example, does the issue of pirated music or movie downloads stack up on each of these ethics intensity factors? Can we say that low ethics intensity contributes to the likelihood of pirating?

**Ethics intensity** or **issue intensity** indicates the degree to which an issue or a situation is recognized to pose important ethical challenges

# Behavior of Managers Key to Ethical Workplace

Managers make a big difference in ethical behavior at work, according to a survey conducted for Deloitte & Touche USA.

- 42% of workers say the behavior of their managers is a major influence on an ethical workplace.

- Most common unethical acts by managers and supervisors include verbal, sexual, and racial harassment, misuse of company property, and giving preferential treatment.

- 91% of workers are more likely to behave ethically when they have work–life balance; 30% say they suffer from poor work–life balance.

- Top reasons for unethical behavior are lack of personal integrity (80%) and lack of job satisfaction (60%).

- Most workers consider it unacceptable to steal from an employer, cheat on expense reports, take credit for another's accomplishments, and lie on time sheets.

- Most workers consider it acceptable to ask a work colleague for a personal favor, take sick days when not ill, or use company technology for personal affairs.

### ■ YOUR THOUGHTS?

Are there any surprises in these data? Is this emphasis on manager and direct supervisor behavior justified as the key to an ethical workplace? What is your reaction to what the workers in this survey reported as acceptable and unacceptable work behaviors? Based on your experiences, what would you add to the list of unacceptable behaviors?

## Organizational Culture

The culture and values of an organization are important influences on ethics in the workplace. Some organizations try to set the ethics culture by issuing formal policy statements and guidelines. But these ethics codes often have limited impact on their own. How a supervisor acts, what he or she requests, and what is rewarded or punished, by contrast, has a strong impact. The expectations of peers and group norms are also influential. In some cases, a person won't be fully accepted on a team if he or she doesn't join in actions outsiders might consider unethical—for example, slacking off or abusing privileges. In other cases, the ethics culture sets high standards and may even push people to behave more ethically than they otherwise would.

## External Environment, Government Regulation, and Industry Norms

Government laws and regulations are important influences on ethical behavior. Laws interpret social values to define appropriate behaviors for organizations and their members; regulations help governments monitor these behaviors and keep them within acceptable standards. After a spate of corporate scandals, for example, the U.S. Congress passed the Sarbanes-Oxley Act of 2002 to make it easier for corporate executives to be tried and sentenced to jail for financial misconduct.

The climate of competition in an industry also sets standards for what may be considered ethical or unethical behavior. Former American Airlines president Robert Crandall once telephoned Howard Putnam, then president of the now-defunct Braniff Airlines. Both companies were suffering from money-losing competition on routes from their home base of Dallas. A portion of their conversation follows.[31]

PUTNAM:    Do you have a suggestion for me?

CRANDALL:  Yes . . . Raise your fares 20 percent. I'll raise mine the next morning.

PUTNAM:     Robert, we—
CRANDALL:   You'll make more money and I will, too.
PUTNAM:     We can't talk about pricing.
CRANDALL:   Oh, Howard. We can talk about anything we want to talk about.

In fact, the U.S. Justice Department strongly disagreed with Crandall. It alleged that his suggestion of a 20% fare increase amounted to an illegal attempt to monopolize airline routes.

## Rationalizations for Unethical Behavior

*Situation:* A college professor sends students an e-mail containing the school's honor code and a link to answers for the prior year's final exam. It was an experiment; 41% of students clicked on the link. *Situation:* An internal audit by Avon discloses that executives in its China operation may have used money payments to obtain local direct sales licenses for the firm. Avon faces investigation and possible prosecution under the U.S. Foreign Corrupt Practices Act.[32] How do people explain doing things like this? The fact is that they very often rationalize with after-the-fact justifications like these.[33]

- Convincing yourself that a behavior is not really illegal.
- Convincing yourself that a behavior is in everyone's best interests.
- Convincing yourself that nobody will ever find out what you've done.
- Convincing yourself that the organization will "protect" you.

After doing something that might be considered unethical, a rationalizer says: "*It's not really illegal.*" This expresses a mistaken belief that one's behavior is acceptable, especially in ambiguous situations. When dealing with shady or borderline situations in which you are having a hard time precisely determining right from wrong, the advice is quite simple: When in doubt about a decision to be made or an action to be taken, don't do it.

Another common statement by a rationalizer is "*It's in everyone's best interests.*" This response involves the mistaken belief that because someone can be found to benefit from the behavior, the behavior is also in the individual's or the organization's best interests. Overcoming this rationalization depends in part on the ability to look beyond short-run results to address longer-term implications, and to look beyond results in general to the ways in which they are obtained. In response to the question "How far can I push matters to obtain this performance goal?" the best answer may be, "Don't try to find out."

Sometimes rationalizers tell themselves that "*no one will ever know about it.*" They mistakenly believe that a questionable behavior is really "safe" and will never be found out

Timothy A. Clary/AFP Getty Images, Inc.

## Bernie Madoff's Ponzi Scheme

Bernard (Bernie) Madoff, a stock broker and financial advisor, founded the Wall Street firm Madoff Investment Securities LLC in 1960. He was its chairman until his arrest for securities fraud. Madoff is the admitted operator of what has been described as the largest Ponzi scheme in history. He defrauded thousands of investors out of billions of dollars. Madoff pleaded guilty to 11 federal offenses including securities fraud, wire fraud, and money laundering. He was sentenced to 150 years in prison and is now prisoner number 61727-054 at Butner Federal Correctional Institute.

> WANT A CAR LOAN? GET A CREDIT CHECK. WANT A JOB?
  GET A SOCIAL MEDIA CHECK

## Your Social Media History Might Be a Job Hurdle

Anatolii Babii/Alamy Limited

It's true: A check of someone's social media sites and histories is now pretty much a standard practice for employment recruiters. There's even a company—Social Intelligence—that does this Internet screening for employers. But is this all invasion of your privacy? The CEO of Social Intelligence says: "We are not detectives. All we assemble is what is publicly available on the Internet today."

What social media signals warn that a job candidate should be taken off the interview list? Think off-color or racist language; think sexually explicit or "racy" photos; think lots of things, from party photos or videos to comments posted by friends or acquaintances.

Already employed? Watch what you say online about an employer. Employment law on social media use is still developing. Your online rants may have legal consequences. One employee was fired after posting negative comments about a boss. After coworkers "liked it" and added more of their own, the employee was fired. An appeal to the National Labor Relations Board supported the employee because the employer's policy was "vague." Many organizations are adding and updating social media policies.

### ETHICS QUESTIONS

What rights do employers have when it comes to their employees' use of social media—both on and off the job? Just how far should a recruiter or employer be able to go in using social media postings in job-related decisions? Where does individual privacy begin and end in employment? Is it ethical for a recruiter to conduct Internet searches without first informing the job candidate that this will done? If a conversation among coworkers includes comments that "trash" the boss and no one is penalized, is it ethical that those same comments posted to an Internet site may result in someone being disciplined or even fired?

---

or made public. Unless it is discovered, the argument implies, no crime was really committed. Lack of accountability, unrealistic pressures to perform, and a boss who prefers "not to know" can all reinforce such thinking. In this case, the best deterrent is to make sure that everyone knows that wrongdoing will be punished whenever it is discovered.

Finally, rationalizers may proceed with a questionable action because of a mistaken belief that *the organization will stand behind me.* This is misperceived loyalty. The individual believes that the organization's best interests stand above all others. In return, the individual believes that top managers will condone the behavior and protect the individual from harm. But loyalty to the organization is not an acceptable excuse for misconduct; it should not stand above the law and social morality.

---

### LEARNING CHECK 2

**TAKEAWAY QUESTION 2 How do ethical dilemmas complicate the workplace?**

**Be sure you can** • define *ethical dilemma* and give workplace examples • identify Kohlberg's stages of moral development • explain how ethics intensity influences ethical decision making • explain how ethics decisions are influenced by an organization's culture and the external environment • list four common rationalizations for unethical behavior

# Maintaining High Ethical Standards

*Item:* Bernard Madoff masterminded the largest fraud in history by swindling billions of dollars from thousands of investors. *Item:* Company admits overcharging consumers and insurers more than $13 million for repairs to damaged rental cars. *Item:* Former Tyco CEO Dennis Kozlowski convicted on 22 counts of grand larceny, fraud, conspiracy, and falsifying business records. *Item:* U.S. lawmakers charge that BP was negligent in inspecting oil pipelines, and that workers complained of excessive cost-cutting and pressures to falsify maintenance records.

News from the corporate world isn't always positive when it comes to ethics. But as quick as we are to recognize the bad, we shouldn't forget that there is a lot of good news, too. There are many organizations, like Stonyfield Farm as featured in the chapter opener, whose leaders and members set high ethics standards for themselves and others. In the final analysis, there is no replacement for effective management practices that staff organizations with honest people. And, there is no replacement for having ethical leaders that set positive examples and always act as ethical role models.

## Moral Management

Management scholar Archie Carroll makes a distinction between immoral, amoral, and moral managers.[34] The **immoral manager** chooses to behave unethically. He or she does something purely for personal gain and knowingly disregards the ethics of the action or situation. The **amoral manager** also disregards the ethics of an act or a decision, but does so unintentionally or unknowingly. This manager simply fails to consider the ethical consequences of his or her actions, and typically uses the law as a guideline for behavior. The **moral manager** considers ethical behavior as a personal goal. He or she makes decisions and acts in full consideration of ethical issues. In Kohlberg's terms, this manager is likely to be operating at the postconventional or principled level of moral development.[35]

Although it may seem surprising, Carroll suggests that most managers act amorally. Though well intentioned, they remain mostly uninformed or undisciplined in considering the ethical aspects of our behavior. The moral manager, by contrast, is an ethics leader who always serves as a positive role model.

> An **immoral manager** chooses to behave unethically.
>
> An **amoral manager** fails to consider the ethics of her or his behavior.
>
> A **moral manager** makes ethical behavior a personal goal.

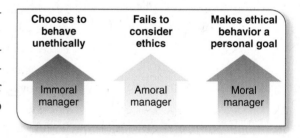

## Ethics Training

**Ethics training** is one way to try to instill ethical behavior in an organization. It takes the form of structured programs to help participants understand the ethical aspects of decision making and better integrate high ethical standards into their daily behaviors. The decision checklist shown in the prior Management Smarts is an example of what might be discussed in an ethics training session. Other topics might include ways to deal with such issues as bullying, harassment, conflicts of interest, gifts, and bribery. Colleges and universities are also strengthening their coverage of ethics in academic curricula.

> **Ethics training** seeks to help people understand the ethical aspects of decision making and to incorporate high ethical standards into their daily behavior.

Regardless of where or how ethics training is conducted, it is important to keep things in perspective. Training is an ethics development resource; it isn't a guarantee of ethical behavior. A banking executive once summed things up this way: "We aren't teaching people right from wrong—we assume they know that. We aren't giving people moral courage to do what is right—they should be able to do that anyhow. We focus on dilemmas."[36]

## Management in Popular Culture

### Ambition is on the Line in *The Social Network*

Jesse Eisenberg's portrayal of Facebook CEO Mark Zuckerberg in *The Social Network* won rave reviews from moviegoers and critics alike. But Zuckerberg's behavior during the start-up days of Facebook may be less praiseworthy, at least based on the movie version of key events. There are times in the movie when ambition may have gotten the better of him. Watch the movie pick out scenes about his dealings with former classmates at Harvard, Cameron and Tyler Winklevoss, and also with early collaborator and Facebook co-founder Eduardo Saverin. In reviewing the movie, *Entertainment Weekly* asked: "Why did Zuckerberg betray these people? Or, in fact, did he really?" Check out the film; come to your own conclusions.

Columbia Pictures/Photofest

## Codes of Ethical Conduct

A **code of ethics** is a formal statement of values and ethical standards.

It is now common for organizations to have **codes of ethics**; in fact you may be asked to sign one as a condition of employment. They are formal statements of an organization's values and ethical principles that set expectations for behavior. Ethics codes typically address organizational citizenship, illegal or improper acts, and relationships with coworkers and customers. Specific guidelines are often set for bribes and kickbacks, political contributions, honesty of books or records, and confidentiality of corporate information.

Ethics codes are common in the complicated world of international business. For example, global manufacturing at Gap, Inc., is governed by a Code of Vendor Conduct.[37] The document addresses:

*Discrimination*—"Factories shall employ workers on the basis of their ability to do the job, not on the basis of their personal characteristics or beliefs."

*Forced labor*—"Factories shall not use any prison, indentured or forced labor."

*Working conditions*—"Factories must treat all workers with respect and dignity and provide them with a safe and healthy environment."

*Freedom of association*—"Factories must not interfere with workers who wish to lawfully and peacefully associate, organize or bargain collectively."

But even as global firms like the Gap have ethics codes in place, it is hard for them to police practices when they have many, even hundreds, of suppliers from different parts of the world. In international business, as elsewhere, ethics codes are good at describing ethical expectations but they do not always guarantee ethical conduct.

## Whistleblower Protection

- Agnes Connolly pressed her employer to report two toxic chemical accidents.
- Dave Jones reported his company used unqualified suppliers in the construction of a nuclear power plant.
- Margaret Newsham revealed that her firm allowed workers to do personal business while on government contracts.
- Herman Cohen charged that the ASPCA in New York was mistreating animals.
- Barry Adams complained that his hospital followed unsafe practices.[38]

These five people come from different work settings and are linked to different issues. But, they share two important things in common. First, each was a **whistleblower** who exposed misdeeds in their organizations in order to preserve ethical standards and protect against further wasteful, harmful, or illegal acts.[39] Second, each was fired from their job.

At the same time that we can admire whistleblowers for their ethical stances, there is no doubt that they face risks of impaired career progress and other forms of organizational retaliation, up to and including termination. Although laws such as the Whistleblower Protection Act of 1989 offer some defense against "retaliatory discharge," legal protections for whistleblowers are continually being tested in court and many consider them inadequate.[40] Laws vary from state to state, and federal laws mainly protect government workers.

Research by the Ethics Resource Center has found that some 44% of workers in the United States fail to blow the whistle to report wrongdoings they observe at work. The top reasons are "(1) the belief that no corrective action would be taken and (2) the fear that reports would not be kept confidential."[41] Within an organization, furthermore, typical barriers to whistleblowing include a strict chain of command that makes it hard to bypass the boss; strong work group identities that encourage loyalty and self-censorship; and ambiguous priorities that make it hard to distinguish right from wrong.[42]

A **whistleblower** exposes the misdeeds of others in organizations.

---

**LEARNING CHECK 3**

**TAKEAWAY QUESTION 3 How can high ethical standards be maintained?**

**Be sure you can** • compare and contrast ethics training and codes of ethical conduct as methods for encouraging ethical behavior in organizations • differentiate between amoral, immoral, and moral management • define *whistleblower* • identify common barriers to whistle blowing and the factors to consider when determining whether whistle blowing is appropriate

---

# Social Responsibility

**Sustainability** is an important word in management these days. Procter & Gamble defines it as acting in ways that help ensure "a better quality of life for everyone now and for generations to come."[43] Think sustainability opportunities when you hear terms like alternative energy, recycling, and waste avoidance. Think sustainability problems when you ponder the aftermath of the enormous Gulf of Mexico oil spill or read about hazardous chemicals in our medicines and food sources.

We'll talk more about sustainability issues in the next chapter. For now, they all come into play with an important management concept known as **corporate social responsibility**. Often called *CSR* for short, it describes the obligation of an organization to act in ways that serve both its own interests and the interests of society at large. Consider these brief examples.[44]

**Sustainability** in management means acting in ways that support a high quality of life for present and future generations.

**Corporate social responsibility** is the obligation of an organization to serve the interests of society in addition to its own interests.

• Trish Karter co-founded the Dancing Deer Bakery in Boston with a winning recipe for social responsibility. She hires people who lack skills, trains them, and provides them with a financial stake in the company. She also donates 35% of company proceeds to fund action programs to end family homelessness.

- Ori Sivan started a Chicago company called Greenmaker Building Supply. It supplies builders with a variety of green products—things like kitchen tiles from coal combustion residue, countertops from recycled paper, and insulation made from old blue jeans.
- Deborah Sardone owns a housekeeping service in Texas. Noticing that clients with cancer really struggled with chores, she started Cleaning for a Reason. The nonprofit organization networks with cleaning firms around the country to provide free home cleaning to cancer patients.

## Stewardship and the Triple Bottom Line

**Stewardship** in management means taking personal responsibility to always respect and protect the interests of society at large.

Corporate social responsibility comes to life in day-to-day management through **stewardship**, the notion that managers at all levels should act in ways that respect and protect the interests of society. A good steward, for example, supports and displays sustainable practices; a poor steward could care less.

It has always been common for managers to make decisions while paying attention to what accountants call the "bottom line"—that is, considering how the decision will

FOLLOW
THE STORY

> "BUSINESS EDUCATION MUST REFRAME THE 'WINNER TAKES ALL' MENTALITY"

## Business School Students Challenged to Serve the Greater Good

Philip Laubner, Catholic Relief Services

She didn't fit the stereotype—visiting Afghanistan, Pakistan, Ethiopia, Zambia, and more. But when Carolyn Y. Woo was dean of the Mendoza College of Business at the University of Notre Dame, she was a dean with a purpose—business schools and their graduates must better serve the social good. She says "a true business education must ultimately engage and enlighten students," causing them to "feel a sense of urgency that the collective good of society depends on them."

Dr. Woo grew up in Hong Kong, works on corporate and non-profit boards, and has had a long career in academe.

She believes that "business and business education are powerful forces able to transform lives, for better or worse," and points to the U.N. Global compact as an exemplar of values that should guide business behavior. The compact focuses attention on human rights (protect rights and avoid abuses), labor (uphold free association and eliminate slave labor, child labor, and discrimination), environment (act responsibly and use environmentally friendly technologies), and corruption (work against it in all forms).

Now President and CEO of Catholic Relief Services, Dr. Woo is leading its mission to "assist the poor and vulnerable overseas." But her many contributions as a business school dean serve as a good reminder that times have changed and business students must change with them. In her words: "Business is a necessary good, not a tolerated evil" . . . "corporate social responsibility is no longer exogenous to business" . . . "business education must reframe the 'winner takes all' mentality."

### WHAT'S YOUR TAKE?

Dr. Woo says that business can be a force for the better or worse in society. Can you describe recent examples or situations from your experiences that would fit in the "best" and "worst" categories? What does she mean by saying business students should abandon the "winner takes all" mentality? Is it possible for an undergraduate business education to really make a difference in a person's ethics and the way they will approach business decisions later in life?

affect the profitability of the firm. But now, we are talking more and more about stewardship in management as a commitment to the **triple bottom line** of economic, social, and environmental performance.[45] Some call this triple bottom line the concern for the **3 P's of organizational performance**—profit, people, and planet.[46]

You might think of stewardship, the triple bottom line, and the 3 P's more generally as acting with social responsibility. And by the way, that's most likely how you'd like your future employers to behave. "Students nowadays want to work for companies that help enhance the quality of life in their surrounding community," says one recruiter.[47] Surveys report that 70% of students believe "a company's reputation and ethics" is "very important" when deciding whether or not to accept a job offer; and that 79% of 13–25-year-olds "want to work for a company that cares about how it affects or contributes to society."[48]

FIGURE 3.4   **The many stakeholders of organizations.**

The **triple bottom line** evaluates organizational performance on economic, social, and environmental criteria.

The **3 P's of organizational performance** are profit, people, and planet.

**Stakeholders** are the persons, groups, and other organizations that are directly affected by the behavior of the organization and that hold a stake in its performance.

## Stakeholders and Stakeholder Management

All organizations have **stakeholders**. They are persons, groups, and other organizations directly affected by the behavior of the organization and that hold a stake in its performance.[49] Figure 3.4 shows that stakeholder networks include owners or shareholders, employees, customers, suppliers, business partners, government representatives and regulators, community members, and future generations.

Given the sheer complexity of stakeholders facing an organization, it's to be expected that they may have somewhat different interests. This often makes a manager's responsibility for stakeholder management quite complicated. For example, customers may demand low-priced products, while environmental activists may pressure the company to utilize manufacturing processes that make products more expensive. Or, shareholders may push the company to cut costs and improve the organization's financial performance, while employees may demand higher levels of healthcare benefits or protection against layoffs.

One way for managers to deal with conflicting stakeholder demands is to evaluate them using three criteria—the power of the stakeholder, the legitimacy of the demand, and the urgency of the issue.[50] **Stakeholder power** refers to the capacity of the stakeholder to positively or negatively affect the operations of the organization. **Demand legitimacy**, which reflects the extent to which the stakeholder's demand is perceived as valid and the extent to which the demand comes from a party with a legitimate stake in the organization. **Issue urgency** deals with the extent to which the issues require immediate attention or action.

**Stakeholder power** refers to the capacity of the stakeholder to positively or negatively affect the operations of the organization.

**Demand legitimacy** indicates the validity and legitimacy of a stakeholder's interest in the organization.

**Issue urgency** indicates the extent to which a stakeholder's concerns need immediate attention.

## Perspectives on Corporate Social Responsibility

It may seem that corporate social responsibility is one of those concepts that most everyone agrees upon. But stakeholders can hold differing views on the ethicality of an organization's actions.[51] Even the pros and cons of CSR as a business priority are subjects of debate.[52]

## Classical View

The **classical view of CSR** is that business should focus on profits.

The **classical view of CSR** holds that management's only responsibility in running a business is to maximize profits. In other words, "the business of business is business" and the principal obligation of management should be to owners and shareholders. This narrow stakeholder perspective is linked to the respected economist and Nobel Laureate, Milton Friedman. He once said: "Few trends could so thoroughly undermine the very foundations of our free society as the acceptance by corporate officials of social responsibility other than to make as much money for their stockholders as possible."[53]

Although not against corporate social responsibility in its own right, proponents of the classical view believe that society's interests are best served in the long run by executives who focus on maximizing their firm's profits. They believe that society gains when businesses pursue their own interests in competitive settings that make things like healthier foods and energy-efficient products attractive to produce because they

## RESEARCH BRIEF

# Prioritizing Stakeholders for Organizational Action

Writing in the *Journal of Business Ethics*, Milena M. Parent and David L. Deephouse discuss how organizations can identify which stakeholder demands should get the most attention. Organizations typically cannot carry out all of the requests of stakeholders. Some are too expensive and time consuming, while others would interfere with an organization's ability to effectively conduct its business. Thus, it becomes important for organizations to discern which stakeholders should be listened to and how such requests should be prioritized.

Parent and Deephouse wanted to see if managers actually determine the importance of stakeholder demands based on the characteristics of power, legitimacy, and urgency. They studied organizations handling two major athletic contests, the Jeux de la Francophonie (Francophone Games) and the Pan American Games. Both organizations had to deal with a large number of stakeholders and a wide variety of demands in order to be successful.

The researchers found that having more than one of the characteristics of power, urgency, and legitimacy increased the importance of the stakeholder to managers. They also found that power was the single most important characteristic, followed by urgency and then legitimacy. Stakeholders with a lot of power relative to the organization are likely to be listened to; stakeholders with urgent requests were also given a reasonable amount of attention. In contrast, even legitimate demands were likely to be ignored when they lacked urgency and were made by relatively nonpowerful stakeholders. Because managers at different levels often evaluated stakeholder demands in a variety of ways, Parent and Deephouse recommend that more than one manager rate the stakeholders in order to increase the reliability with which such judgments are made.

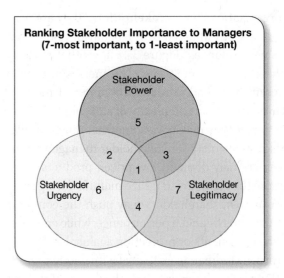

Ranking Stakeholder Importance to Managers (7-most important, to 1-least important)

### YOU BE THE RESEARCHER

Think of the important stakeholders associated with the organization at which you work or volunteer. Talk to others and develop a map of these stakeholders and their interests. Which ones seem most powerful? Whose demands seem legitimate or urgent? Ask: How are these demands reflected—or not—in the goals and actions of this organization?

*Reference:* Milena M. Parent and David L. Deephouse, "A Case Study of Stakeholder Identification and Prioritization by Managers," *Journal of Business Ethics* (September 2007), pp. 1–23.

are profitable.[54] They fear that pursuit of corporate social responsibility as a separate business goal will reduce profits, raise costs, reduce competitiveness with foreign firms, and give business too much social power with too little accountability to the public.

## Socioeconomic View

The **socioeconomic view of CSR** holds that managers must be concerned with the organization's effect on the broader social welfare and not just with corporate profits. This broad stakeholder perspective puts the focus on the triple bottom line of not just financial performance but also social and environmental performance. In its support, another distinguished economist and Nobel Laureate, Paul Samuelson, has said: "A large corporation these days not only may engage in social responsibility, it had damn well better try to do so."[55]

Arguments in favor of corporate social responsibility are that its pursuit by a business will enhance long-run profits, improve public image, make the organization a more attractive place to work, and help avoid government regulation. Furthermore, because society provides the infrastructure that allows businesses to operate, they should act consistent with society's best interests.

> The **socioeconomic view of CSR** is that business should focus on broader social welfare as well as profits.

## Shared Value View

One of the problems with the prior debate is that it seems to pit the interests of shareholders and owners against other stakeholders in win-lose fashion. Another problem is that even when CSR is made a priority it becomes more of an add-on initiative than a strategically integrated one. Although a company may fund useful things like local philanthropy and environment projects, such CSR practices end up serving mainly reputational and branding goals for the firm rather than being part of the core business model. The notion of **shared value** has been advocated by Michael Porter and Mark Kramer as an alternative way of thinking.[56] They say: "The purpose of a corporation must be redefined as creating shared value, not just profit per se."[57]

The shared value concept is that economic progress for the firm and social progress for the broader community are fundamentally interconnected. Rather than pursue a narrow stakeholder perspective focused on short-term profits or displaying corporate citizenship in broad-brush public ways. Business decisions should be made so that economic value is created by pursuing social value.

The point of the shared value approach is to seek business advantage by following practices and aligning strategies with social issues like aging, illiteracy, nutrition, resource conservation, and poverty. It suggests a **virtuous circle** in which

> **Shared value** approaches business decisions with the understanding that economic and social progress are interconnected.

> The **virtuous circle** occurs when socially responsible behavior improves financial performance, which leads to more responsible behavior in the future.

---

## IBM Finds That Shared Value Links Better Cities with Business Profits

Courtesy International Business Machines Corporation, ©International Business Machines Corporation

You don't have to give up profit to do social good according to the notion of shared value as described by Michael Porter and Mark Kramer. They believe businesses gain by focusing attention on important social problems. IBM found a new market when it realized cities could benefit from more integrated computer systems and analytics. It started a "Smarter Cities" business to help cities use its technologies to solve problems with traffic flows, public health, schools, housing, and crime. IBM systems in Rio de Janeiro help city planners gather and analyze data from multiple sources.

corporate social responsibility leads to improved financial performance for the firm which, in turn, leads to more socially responsible actions in the future.[58]

We can consider shared value, as creating wins for both companies and society, as these examples suggest. Len Sauers, Procter & Gamble's vice president of global sustainability, says that reducing waste is a top priority and that doing so "almost always results in cost savings." Nestlé pushes local sourcing and supports rural businesses near its factories, while reducing distribution costs and ensuring supplies of high-quality products. Carpet manufacturer Desso's green supply chain and cradle-to-grave manufacturing allows products to be disassembled at the end of their lives as biodegradable waste or new products. CEO Stef Kranendijk says the approach has been a stimulus to innovation.[59]

## Evaluating Corporate Social Performance

If we are to get serious about social responsibility and shared value, we need to get rigorous about measuring social performance and holding business leaders accountable for the results. It is increasingly common to take **social responsibility audits** at regular intervals. They measure and report an organization's social performance. And, research finds that mandatory social reporting of this nature improves socially responsible behavior.[60] In other words, what gets measured tends to happen.

When social responsibility audits are done, the performance of firms ranges from *compliance*—acting to avoid adverse consequences—to *conviction*—acting to create positive impact.[61] Compliance behaviors focus on being profitable and obeying the law, while conviction behaviors focus on doing what is right and contributing to the broader community. Figure 3.5 displays these as alternative social responsibility strategies, ones you may recognize in news reports and current events.[62]

On the compliance side, an **obstructionist strategy** ("Fight social demands") focuses mainly on economic priorities. Social demands lying outside the organization's perceived self-interests are resisted. Cigarette manufacturers, for example, tried to minimize the negative health effects of smoking for decades until indisputable evidence became available. A **defensive strategy** ("Meet legal and market requirements") focuses on protecting the organization by meeting minimum legal requirements and responding to competitive market forces, perhaps even activist pressures. Mortgage lenders are required to provide certain information to customers concerning loans they may be receiving. But whereas some take time to carefully review everything with customers, others may rush in hopes the customer won't question the details.

On the conviction side, an **accommodative strategy** ("Meet ethical requirements") focuses on satisfying society's ethical expectations. An oil firm, for example, may engage in appropriate cleanup activities after a spill occurs and provide compensation to communities that may have been harmed. But it may be slow to invest in new technology to prevent spills in the first place. The oil firm, following a more **proactive strategy** ("Take leadership in social initiatives"), does make such investments and even invests in the search for alternative energy

A **social responsibility audit** measures an organization's performance in various areas of social responsibility.

An **obstructionist strategy** tries to avoid and resist pressures for social responsibility.

A **defensive strategy** does the minimum legally required to display social responsibility.

An **accommodative strategy** accepts social responsibility and tries to satisfy society's basic ethical expectations.

A **proactive strategy** actively pursues social responsibility by taking discretionary actions to make things better in the future.

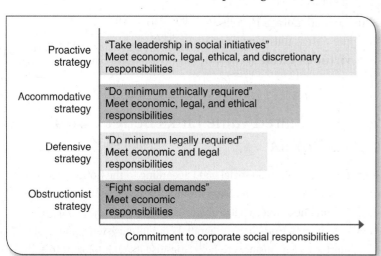

| | |
|---|---|
| Proactive strategy | "Take leadership in social initiatives" Meet economic, legal, ethical, and discretionary responsibilities |
| Accommodative strategy | "Do minimum ethically required" Meet economic, legal, and ethical responsibilities |
| Defensive strategy | "Do minimum legally required" Meet economic and legal responsibilities |
| Obstructionist strategy | "Fight social demands" Meet economic responsibilities |

Commitment to corporate social responsibilities

**FIGURE 3.5**  **Four strategies of corporate social responsibility—from obstructionist to proactive behavior.**

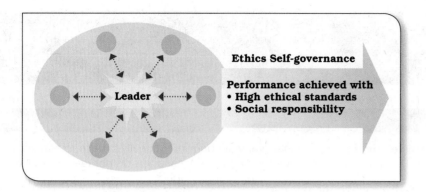

FIGURE 3.6 **Ethics self-governance in leadership and the managerial role.**

sources. It takes discretionary actions in the hopes of making things better in the future. Desso, the carpet firm mentioned earlier, shows a proactive strategy in its industry by pursuing a green supply chain and cradle-to-grave manufacturing.

## Corporate Governance

Issues relating to **corporate governance** are often raised when you read and hear about business ethics failures and poor corporate social responsibility. The term refers to the active oversight of management decisions and company actions by boards of directors.[63] Businesses are required by law to have boards of directors that are elected by stockholders to represent their interests. The governance exercised by these boards most typically involves hiring, firing, and compensating the CEO and top management; assessing strategy; and verifying financial records. The expectation is that board members will hold management accountable for ethical and socially responsible leadership.

When corporate failures and controversies occur, weak governance often gets blamed. And when it does, you will sometimes see government stepping in to try to correct things for the future. Hearings are held, laws are proposed and passed, and government agencies are directed or created to better control business behavior. The Sarbanes-Oxley Act, for example, was passed by Congress in response to public outcries over major ethics and business scandals. Its goal is to ensure that top managers properly oversee and are held accountable for the financial conduct of their organizations.

Even as one talks about corporate governance and top management accountability, it is important to remember that all managers must accept personal responsibility for doing the "right" things. Figure 3.6 highlights **ethics self-governance** in day-to-day work behavior. It is not enough to fulfill one's performance accountabilities; it must be fulfilled in an ethical and socially responsible manner. The full weight of this responsibility holds in every organizational setting, from small to large and from private to nonprofit, and at every managerial level from top to bottom. There is no escaping the ultimate reality—every manager is a steward of stakeholder interests, and being a manager at any level is a very socially responsible job!

**Corporate governance** is the oversight of top management by a board of directors.

**Ethics self-governance** is making sure day-to-day performance is achieved ethically and in socially responsible ways.

**LEARNING CHECK 4**

**TAKEAWAY QUESTION 4  What are social responsibility and corporate governance?**

**Be sure you can** • discuss stakeholder management and identify key organizational stakeholders • define *corporate social responsibility* • summarize arguments for and against corporate social responsibility • identify four criteria for measuring corporate social performance • explain four possible social responsibility strategies • define *corporate governance* and discuss its importance

# MANAGEMENT LEARNING REVIEW

## LEARNING CHECK SUMMARY

### TAKEAWAY QUESTION 1 What is ethical behavior?

- Ethical behavior is that which is accepted as "good" or "right" as opposed to "bad" or "wrong."
- Because an action is not illegal does not necessarily make it ethical in a given situation.
- Because values vary, the question "What is ethical behavior?" may be answered differently by different people.
- The utilitarian, individualism, moral-rights, and justice views offer alternative ways of thinking about ethical behavior.
- Cultural relativism argues that no culture is ethically superior to any other; universalism argues that certain ethical standards apply everywhere.

**For Discussion** Is there ever a justification for cultural relativism in international business ethics?

### TAKEAWAY QUESTION 2 How do ethical dilemmas complicate the workplace?

- An ethical dilemma occurs when someone must decide whether to pursue a course of action that, although offering the potential for personal or organizational benefit or both, may be unethical.
- Managers report that their ethical dilemmas often involve conflicts with superiors, customers, and subordinates over such matters as dishonesty in advertising and communications, as well as pressure from bosses to do unethical things.
- Common rationalizations for unethical behavior include believing the behavior is not illegal, is in everyone's best interests, will never be noticed, or will be supported by the organization.

**For Discussion** Are ethical dilemmas always problems, or can they also be opportunities?

### TAKEAWAY QUESTION 3 How can high ethical standards be maintained?

- Ethics training can help people better deal with ethical dilemmas in the workplace.
- Written codes of ethical conduct formally state what an organization expects of its employees regarding ethical behavior at work.

- Immoral managers intentionally choose to behave unethically; amoral managers do not really pay attention to or think through the ethics of their actions or decisions; moral managers consider ethical behavior a personal goal.
- Whistleblowers expose the unethical acts of others in organizations, even while facing career risks for doing so.

**For Discussion** Is it right for organizations to require employees to sign codes of conduct and undergo ethics training?

### TAKEAWAY QUESTION 4 What are social responsibility and corporate governance?

- Social responsibility is an obligation of the organization to act in ways that serve both its own interests and the interests of its many stakeholders.
- The triple bottom line for assessing organizational performance evaluates how well organizations are doing on economic, social, and environmental performance criteria.
- The argument against corporate social responsibility says that businesses should focus on making profits; the argument for corporate social responsibility says that businesses should use their resources to serve broader social concerns.
- The shared value concept links business and social goals with the idea that businesses can find economic value by pursuing opportunities and practices that advance the well-being of society.
- An organization's social performance can be evaluated on how well it meets economic, legal, ethical, and discretionary responsibilities.
- Corporate strategies in response to demands for socially responsible behavior include obstruction, defense, accommodation, and proaction.
- Corporate governance is the responsibility of a board of directors to oversee the performance of the organization's top management.

**For Discussion** What questions would you include on a social audit for an organization in your community?

## SELF-TEST 3

## Multiple-Choice Questions

1. Values are personal beliefs that help determine whether a behavior will be considered ethical or unethical. An example of a terminal value is _____.
   (a) ambition
   (b) self-respect
   (c) courage
   (d) imagination

2. Under the _____ view of ethical behavior, a business owner would be considered ethical if she reduced a plant's workforce by 10% in order to cut costs to keep the business from failing and thus save jobs for the other 90%.
   (a) utilitarian
   (b) individualism
   (c) justice
   (d) moral rights

3. A manager's failure to enforce a late-to-work policy the same way for employees on the day shifts and night shifts is an ethical violation of _____ justice.
   (a) ethical
   (b) moral
   (c) distributive
   (d) procedural

4. The Sarbanes-Oxley Act of 2002 makes it easier for corporate executives to _____.
   (a) protect themselves from shareholder lawsuits
   (b) sue employees who commit illegal acts
   (c) be tried and sentenced to jail for financial misconduct
   (d) shift blame for wrongdoing to boards of directors

5. Two "spotlight" questions for conducting the ethics double-check of a decision are (a) "How would I feel if my family found out about this?" and (b) "How would I feel if _____?"
   (a) my boss found out about this
   (b) my subordinates found out about this
   (c) this was published in the local newspaper
   (d) this went into my personnel file

6. Research on ethical dilemmas indicates that _____ is/are often the cause of unethical behavior by people at work.
   (a) declining morals in society
   (b) lack of religious beliefs
   (c) the absence of whistleblowers
   (d) pressures from bosses and superiors

7. Customers, investors, employees, and regulators are examples of _____ that are important in the analysis of corporate social responsibility.
   (a) special-interest groups
   (b) stakeholders
   (c) ethics advocates
   (d) whistleblowers

8. A(n) _____ is someone who exposes the ethical misdeeds of others.
   (a) whistleblower
   (b) ethics advocate
   (c) ombudsman
   (d) stakeholder

9. A proponent of the classical view of corporate social responsibility would most likely agree with which of these statements?
   (a) Social responsibility improves the public image of business.
   (b) The primary responsibility of business is to maximize business profits.
   (c) By acting responsibly, businesses avoid government regulation.
   (d) Businesses can and should do "good" while doing business.

10. An amoral manager _____.
    (a) always acts in consideration of ethical issues
    (b) chooses to behave unethically
    (c) makes ethics a personal goal
    (d) acts without considering whether or not the behavior is ethical

11. An organization that takes the lead in addressing emerging social issues is being _____, showing the most progressive corporate social responsibility strategy.
    (a) accommodative
    (b) defensive
    (c) proactive
    (d) obstructionist

12. The criterion of _____ identifies the highest level of conviction by an organization to operate in a socially responsible manner.
    (a) economic justice
    (b) legal requirements
    (c) ethical commitment
    (d) discretionary responsibility

**13.** Which viewpoint emphasizes that business can find ways to profit by doing things that advance the well being of society?
(a) classical
(b) shared value
(c) defensive
(d) obstructionist

**14.** A manager shows self-governance when he or she always tries to achieve performance objectives in ways that are _____.
(a) performance effective
(b) cost efficient
(c) quality oriented
(d) ethical and socially responsible

**15.** The triple bottom line of organizational performance focuses on the "3 Ps" of profit, people, and _____.
(a) principle
(b) procedure
(c) planet
(d) progress

## Short-Response Questions

**16.** Explain the difference between the individualism and justice views of ethical behavior.

**17.** List four common rationalizations for unethical managerial behavior.

**18.** What are the major arguments for and against corporate social responsibility?

**19.** What is the primary difference between immoral and amoral management?

## Essay Question

**20.** A small outdoor clothing company has just received an attractive offer from a business in Bangladesh to manufacture its work gloves. The offer would allow for substantial cost savings over the current supplier. The company manager, however, has read reports that some Bangladeshi businesses break their own laws and operate with child labor. How would differences in the following corporate responsibility strategies affect the manager's decision regarding whether to accept the offer: obstruction, defense, accommodation, and proaction?

# MANAGEMENT SKILLS AND COMPETENCIES

## Further Reflection: Individual Character

Character is something that people tend to think more about during presidential election years or when famous people, such as professional athletes or politicians, do bad things. As suggested in the chapter opener, however, **individual character** and its underlying foundation of personal integrity shouldn't be just occasional concerns. They deserve constant attention. Ethical dilemmas can arise unexpectedly. To deal with them we have to know ourselves well enough to make principled decisions that we can be proud of and that others will respect. After all, it's the character of people making key decisions that determines whether our organizations act in socially responsible or irresponsible ways.

 DO IT NOW . . .
LOOK IN THE MIRROR

- **Check yourself for signs of hypercompetitiveness in school and in work situations.**
- **Ask: What are the implications for the ethics of my behavior?**
- **Make notes on two situations that presented you with some ethical test.**
- **Using the vantage points of a parent, loved one, or good friend, write a critique of how you handled each incident and what this shows about your individual character.**

## Self-Assessment: Terminal Values

### Instructions

1. Read the following list of things people value. Think about each value in terms of its importance as a guiding principle in your life.

| | |
|---|---|
| A comfortable life | Inner harmony |
| An exciting life | Mature love |
| A sense of accomplishment | National security |
| A world at peace | Pleasure |
| A world of beauty | Salvation |
| Equality | Self-respect |
| Family security | Social recognition |
| Freedom | True friendship |
| Happiness | Wisdom |

2. Circle six of these 18 values to indicate that they are most important to you. If you can, rank-order these most important values by writing a number above them—with "1" = the most important value in my life, and so on through "6."

3. Underline the six of these 18 values that are least important to you.

### Interpretation

Terminal values reflect a person's preferences concerning the ends to be achieved. They are the goals individuals would like to achieve in their lifetimes. As you look at the items you have selected as most and least important, what major differences exist among the items in the two sets? Think about this and then answer the following questions.

(A) What does your selection of most and least important values say about you as a person?

(B) What does your selection of most and least important values suggest about the type of work and career that might be best for you?

(C) Which values among your most and least important selections might cause problems for you in the future—at work and/or in your personal life? What problems might they cause and why? How might you prepare now to best deal with these problems in the future?

(D) How might your choices of most and least important values turn out to be major strengths or assets for you—at work and/or in your personal life, and why?

## Team Exercise: Confronting Ethical Dilemmas

### Preparation

Read and indicate your response to each of the following situations.

**A.** Ron Jones, vice president of a large construction firm, receives in the mail a large envelope marked "personal." It contains a competitor's cost data for a project that both firms will be bidding on shortly.

The data are accompanied by a note from one of Ron's subordinates. It says: "This is the real thing!"

Ron knows that the data could be a major advantage to his firm in preparing a bid that can win the contract. What should he do?

**B.** Kay Smith is one of your top-performing subordinates. She has shared with you her desire to apply for promotion to a new position just announced in a different division of the company. This will be tough on you since recent budget cuts mean you will be unable to replace anyone who leaves, at least for quite some time.

Kay knows all of this and, in all fairness, has asked your permission before she submits an application. It is rumored that the son of a good friend of your boss is going to apply for the job. Although his credentials are less impressive than Kay's, the likelihood is that he will get the job if she doesn't apply. What will you do?

**C.** Marty was pleased to represent her firm as head of the local community development committee. In fact, her supervisor's boss once held this position and told her in a hallway conversation, "Do your best and give them every support possible."

Going along with this advice, Marty agreed to pick up the bill (several hundred dollars) for a dinner meeting with local civic and business leaders. Shortly thereafter, her supervisor informed everyone that the entertainment budget was being eliminated in a cost-saving effort.

Not wanting to renege on supporting the community development committee, Marty charged the dinner bill to an advertising budget. An internal auditor discovered the charge and reported it to you, the firm's human resource manager.

Marty is scheduled to meet with you in a few minutes. What will you do?

### Instructions

1. Working alone, make the requested decisions in each of these incidents. Think carefully about your justification for the decision.

2. Meet in a group assigned by your instructor. Share your decisions and justifications in each case with other group members. Listen to theirs.

3. Try to reach a group consensus on what to do in each situation and why.

4. Be prepared to share the group decisions, and any dissenting views, in general class discussion.

## Career Situations for Ethical Behavior: What Would You Do?

1. **Window to the Future**   You have just seen one of your classmates snap a cell phone photo of an essay question on the exam everyone is taking. The instructor missed it and you're not sure if anyone else saw it. You know that the instructor is giving an exam to another section of the course next class period. Do you let this pass and pretend it isn't all that important? Or, do you take some action?

2. **Intern's Assignment**   One of your first tasks as a summer intern is to design an ethics training program for the firm's new hires. Your boss says that the program should familiarize participants with the cor-porate code of ethics. But it should also go beyond this to help set good foundations for handling ethical dilemmas in a confident and moral way. What would your training program look like?

3. **Gen Ys at the Table**   Your employer brings younger hires (Gen Ys) together with senior executives on a monthly basis. Each session tackles a topic. This month it's "CSR as a business priority." You've heard that some of the seniors are skeptical, believing that business is business and the priority should be on profits alone. What arguments might you be prepared to make in support of CSR and the concept called "shared value"?

## Case Study

# Patagonia

Go to *Management Cases for Critical Thinking* to find the recommended case for Chapter 3—"Patagonia: Leading a Green Revolution."

Patagonia has stayed both green and profitable at a time when the economy is down, consumers are tight for cash, and doing the profitable thing is not necessarily doing the right thing. How has Patagonia achieved its success without compromising the ideals of founder Yves Chouinard and the company's stated values?

There's no doubt that Patagonia succeeds by staying true to Chouinard's vision. "It's good business to make a great product, and do it with the least amount of damage to the planet," he says. His standards have set the pace in the industry for outdoor clothing and gear. "They've become the Rolls-Royce of their product category," says Marshal Cohen, chief industry analyst with market research firm NPD Group. "When people were stepping back, and the industry became copycat, Chouinard didn't sell out, lower prices, and dilute the brand. Sometimes, the less you do, the more provocative and true of a leader you are."

Jim Wilson/Redux Pictures

# Wisdom
## Learning From Others

### > A KEEN EYE SPOTS LOTS OF OPPORTUNITIES

Cloud computing now handles lots of our personal music, videos, and files. But who would have predicted ten years ago that it would change the way software firms sell to customers? Marc Benioff did. He started Salesforce.com to sell customer relationship management software not as a product but as a service fed from the cloud.

The whole notion is to free users from costly software ownership. Instead, they basically "rent" services delivered from remote servers. Benioff's genius in anticipating this market scored a bull's-eye.

Forward looking and confident in taking risk, Benioff recognized how a changing technological environment created opportunity. Benioff's breakthrough idea started with his admiration for the online businesses pioneered by Amazon and eBay. He realized enterprise software could be sold the same way. The result was a new business model. Customers buy only what they want and drop the service if they become dissatisfied.

Salesforce.com even has a website called IdeaExchange where customers provide suggestions and comments to spur continued improvements. And when the firm ran into difficulty handling computer crashes at one point, Benioff communicated with full disclosure and transparency so that customers always knew what was happening.

In respect to corporate philanthropy Benioff still follows what he calls the 1-1-1 rule. Donate to charity 1% of equity, 1% of profit, 1% of employee time.[1]

## MORE TO LOOK FOR INSIDE>

### FOLLOW THE STORY
Disruptive Innovation the Steve Jobs Way (1955–2011)

### ETHICS ON THE LINE
Offshore E-Waste Graveyards Bury a Problem

### FACTS FOR ANALYSIS
Workers May Be Unhappy, But They Aren't Changing Jobs

### RESEARCH BRIEF
Generations Show Differences on Important Values

# Environment, Innovation, and Sustainability

**4**

## > RISK TAKING

Why is there such interest today in adventure sports like ice climbing, river running, cliff parachuting, and more? Some say it's a quest for the adrenaline rush: others claim the "thrill" is addictive. For sure the issue is **risk taking** and the degree to which we are uncomfortable or comfortable taking action in situations that are high in uncertainty.

Risk taking is a way to step forward and try new things. But there's need for caution as well. The risks we take in our personal lives and in our careers aren't always for the best.

Research finds executives in higher-performing organizations take risks while motivated by confidence. This helps them adapt and deal positively with problems as they arise.

Executives in lower-performing organizations may take risks while motivated by desperation to escape existing difficulties. Because they lack confidence, they are likely to jump from one problem to the next without making any real sustainable gains.

Look at the box. On which side of the "risk line" do you most often fall—the positive side motivated by confidence, or the negative side motivated by desperation?

By the way, research links high risk taking with boredom and dissatisfaction. Can this explain why some people engage in risky sports or personal behaviors?[2]

## Insight
## Learning About Yourself

### WALKING THE FINE LINE OF RISK TAKING

**Positive Side of Risk-Taking Behavior**
Risk taking from base of performance success; motivated by confidence in moving to even better situation; able to deal with problems as they arise; lots of staying power

Risk Line -------------------------- Risk Line

**Negative Side of Risk-Taking Behavior**
Risk taking from position of performance difficulty; motivated by desperation to get out of bad situation; hard time dealing with problems without losing focus; little staying power

## BUILD SKILLS AND COMPETENCIES AT END OF CHAPTER

- Engage in *Further Reflection on Risk Taking*
- Take the *Self-Assessment on Tolerance for Ambiguity*
- Complete the *Team Exercise—Organizational Commitment to Sustainability Scorecard*
- Solve the *Career Situations for a Complex Environment*
- Analyze the *Case Study—Timberland: Walking with Sustainability*

## <GET TO KNOW YOURSELF BETTER

| TAKEAWAY 1 | TAKEAWAY 2 | TAKEAWAY 3 | TAKEAWAY 4 |
|---|---|---|---|
| **The General or Macro Environment** | **The Specific or Task Environment** | **Environment and Innovation** | **Environment and Sustainability** |
| • Economic conditions<br>• Legal-political conditions<br>• Sociocultural conditions<br>• Technological conditions<br>• Natural environment conditions | • Stakeholders and value creation<br>• Competitive advantage<br>• Uncertainty, complexity, and change | • Types of innovations<br>• The innovation process<br>• Disruptive innovation and technology | • Sustainable development<br>• Sustainable business<br>• Sustainability goals, measurement, and reporting<br>• Human sustainability |
| LEARNING CHECK 1 | LEARNING CHECK 2 | LEARNING CHECK 3 | LEARNING CHECK 4 |

*"I'm deeply sorry for any accident that Toyota drivers have experienced.... I myself, as well as Toyota, am not perfect. We never run away from our problems or pretend we don't notice them."* Toyota President Akio Toyoda, testifying before U.S. Congress

*"Every single Toyota owner deserves a full accounting of what happened and what went wrong.... The U.S. government has to do a much better job of keeping the American people safe."* Senator Jay Rockefeller, Chairman, U.S. Senate Commerce Committee

When Toyota recalled millions of vehicles for accelerator problems and quality defects, it wasn't just customers and the marketplace that reacted; U.S. lawmakers did too.[3] Toyota's president Akio Toyoda felt the full brunt of American anger when called to testify before the Senate Commerce Committee. Although he apologized and pledged a complete response by the firm, he was criticized that Toyota had acted with "greed and insensitivity."

This interaction between Toyota, its customers, and U.S. lawmakers is an example of the complex relationship that organizations maintain with their external environments. We saw a more positive one in the opening vignette of Marc Benioff's accomplishment creating Salesforce.com. He showed what can be achieved by facing risk and uncertainty with discipline and insight. The fact is some managers look at conditions in our world and see hopeless problems while others look and see endless opportunities. Some read environmental trends and spot innovation potential. Some don't even bother to look.

## The General or Macroenvironment

The **general environment** consists of economic, legal-political, sociocultural, technological, and natural environment conditions.

The **general environment** of organizations consists of all external conditions that set the context for managerial decision making. You might think of it as a broad envelope of dynamic forces that surround and influence an organization. We most

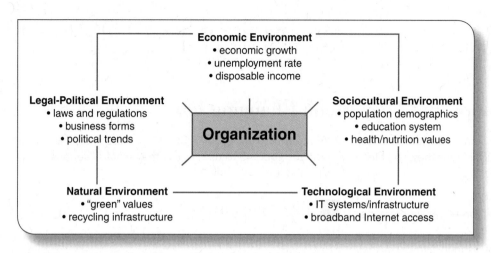

FIGURE 4.1   **Sample elements in the general environments of organizations.**

often classify these forces as economic, legal-political, sociocultural, technological, and natural environment conditions, as shown in Figure 4.1.

## Economic Conditions

> Unemployment stubbornly high; income disparity between rich and poor Americans increasing; middle-class income decreasing, and consumer confidence falling for low income families.

When the environment presents evidence like this, what does it mean for organizations and their managers?[4] Such data represent *economic conditions in the general environment*. Things like the overall health of the economy in terms of financial markets, inflation, income levels, and job outlook are always important. All such economic conditions affect the prospects for individual companies, the spending patterns and lifestyles of consumers, and even a nation's priorities. They must be assessed, forecasted, and considered when executives make decisions about the strategies and operations of their organizations.

For years, Procter & Gamble has sold products to America's rising middle class. But now, with facts like the above in evidence, its executives are reevaluating their strategies. As the middle class struggles, P & G's profits will suffer unless conditions change—which may take awhile, or changes are quickly made in the firm's business approach. One of the ways P & G is responding is to refocus attention on two market tiers: one high where price isn't an issue, and the other low where price makes a big difference. In dish soaps, for example, it sells Dawn Hand Renewal at the high end and Gain at the low end. But for a firm that for years prospered with a one-market approach, it's challenging. A company spokesperson calls the situation "humbling."[5]

Global economic trends are highly important as well. For years companies have pursued **offshoring**, which involves the outsourcing of work and jobs to lower cost foreign locations. But new economic signals are showing signs of a shift toward **reshoring**, which moves jobs back home. Rising labor costs in foreign countries, higher shipping costs, complicated logistics, complaints about poor customer service, public criticisms about destroying local jobs, and economic incentives offered by communities are causing global firms to rethink their offshoring strategies and start to relocate more jobs back home.[6]

**Offshoring** is the outsourcing of jobs to foreign locations.

**Reshoring** is the return of jobs from foreign locations as companies establish new domestic operations.

FACTS
FOR ANALYSIS

> YOUNGER WORKERS PAYING THE PRICE AS LACK OF
JOB ALTERNATIVES KEEPS THEM WHERE THEY ARE

## Workers May Be Unhappy, But They Aren't Changing Jobs

With everyone so concerned about getting jobs, it's easy to overlook those who are stuck in jobs they don't like.

- American teens and young adults under 25 face the most difficult job market in recent history.
- Compared with past years, 1 million fewer workers per month are quitting jobs.
- Some 28 million Americans are working in jobs they would prefer to leave.
- About 1 of every 3 workers say they would change jobs if they could.
- Voluntary labor turnover in the U.S. workforce is at the lowest since data were first collected in 2000.

- Younger workers aged 16 to 34 are more likely than older workers aged 45 to 65+ to say they would "seriously considering leaving" their jobs.

 **YOUR THOUGHTS?**

Many people have traditionally relied on changing jobs to improve their wages and career advancement. But what happens when a bad economy thwarts this process? What are the potential costs to a worker, the organization, and society at large when someone stays on a job he or she would really like to leave behind? What's an ambitious younger worker to do when job alternatives just aren't there?

## Legal-Political Conditions

> Yahoo sues Facebook for infringement on privacy controls and advertising patents; Oracle sues Google over alleged infringements on its Android patents; Apple sues Samsung and Samsung sues Apple—all over supposed patent infringements.

Patents and intellectual property are hot topics these days.[7] They are just one area among many that highlight the importance for managers to stay abreast of developments in the complex *legal-political conditions in the general environment.* These conditions reflect existing and proposed laws and regulations, government policies, and the philosophy and objectives of political parties. U.S. lawmakers, for example, have been debating many issues such as regulation of banks and the financial services industry, foreign trade agreements, and protection of U.S. jobs and industries. Corporate executives follow such debates to monitor trends that can affect the regulation, oversight, and competitive directions of their businesses.

As if the domestic legal and political environment wasn't complicated enough, the legal-political conditions in the global business environment vary significantly from one country to the next. Just as foreign firms like Toyota have to learn to deal with U.S. laws and political conditions, so, too, must U.S. firms adjust to those of foreign countries. The European Union once fined Microsoft $1.35 billion for antitrust violations involving the practice of bundling media and Windows software and making the source code for interoperability unavailable to competitors.[8] Apple was sued in both Chinese and U.S. courts by Proview Electronics Co. The firm claimed Apple was illegally selling in China products with a name Proview, a Chinese company, had previously trademarked—"iPad".[9]

Not all countries stand up for international copyright and intellectual property protection. Music, movie, product, and software piracy plagues companies from SONY pictures to Louis Vuitton to Microsoft. Lots of the piracy originates outside of the United States and in countries where legal protections are minimal or largely unenforced.

## Nobel Prize Recognizes Women for Leadership Roles in Peace-Building

Some call it *Management 3.0*. Others describe it as a time when we expect organizations and the people who run them to make the world a better place, now and for the future. And it's a world complicated by many social, legal, and political issues. When the Nobel Peace Prize committee announced its 2011 winners, Tawakkul Karman (Yemeni Rights Campaigner), Ellen Johnson Sirleaf (President of Liberia), and Leymah Gbowee (Liberian Activist) shared the award. The committee praised them for "nonviolent struggle for the safety of women and for women's rights to full participation in peace-building work."

Fosaas Roger/Stella Pictures/ABACA/Newscom

National policies also vary on **Internet censorship**—the deliberate blockage and denial of public access to information posted on the Internet, and global firms face many dilemmas in dealing with them. Google, Yahoo, and Twitter, for example, face ongoing problems in China where laws restrict access to Internet sites with content deemed off limits by the government. After Google complied in one instance by censoring its Google.cn site, it was then criticized for reneging on its avowed commitments to information freedom. A Google spokesperson said it's "a delicate balancing act between being a platform for free expression and also obeying local laws around the world."[10]

> **Internet censorship** is the deliberate blockage and denial of public access to information posted on the Internet.

## Sociocultural Conditions

Unemployment among Blacks hits 16.5% and for Whites 8%; White households out earn Black households by 20 times and Hispanic households by 18 times.[11]

Data like these aren't only economic in significance; they reflect more broadly on diversity issues relating to educational opportunity, access to technology, housing options, job options, and more. Such things are part of the *sociocultural conditions in the general environment*. Think of them as norms, customs, and demographics of a society or region, as well as social values on such matters as ethics, human rights, gender roles, and lifestyles. Sociocultural conditions can have major consequences for organizations and how they are managed.

In respect to age demographics, for example, managers should stay abreast of differences among **generational cohorts**—people born within a few years of one another and who experience somewhat similar life events during their formative years.[12] Baby Boomers are "digital immigrants" that have had to learn about technology as it became available. The Millennials or Gen Ys, along with their younger counterparts the iGeneration, are "digital natives" who grew up in technology-enriched homes, schools, and friendship environments. This affects everything from how they shop to how they learn to how they like to work. Characteristics often described for digital natives are ease of multitasking, desire for immediate gratification, continuous contact with others, and less concern with knowing things than with knowing where to find out about things.[13]

In respect to social values, shifting currents and trends affect how organizations deal with reputation management, product development, advertising messages, and internal policies and practices. There was a time, for example, when the pay of

> **Generational cohorts** consist of people born within a few years of one another and who experience somewhat similar life events during their formative years.

## Generations Show Differences on Important Values

In an economy with an aging workforce, scholars Jean Twenge, Stacy Campbell, Brian Hoffman, and Charles Lance decided to investigate value differences across generational cohorts—groups of individuals born about the same time and experiencing similar life events during their development years. The authors wanted to understand how values may differ among generations in the same workplace and what the implications might be for managing these differences.

Twenge et al. focused their attention on comparing Baby Boomers (born 1946–1964, grew up during the Vietnam War and civil rights movement) with Generation X (born 1965–1981, saw fall of the Soviet Union and advent of the AIDS epidemic) and with Generation Y or the Millennials (born 1982–1999, grew up digital and saw major corporate ethics scandals). Their data was from a program called Monitoring the Future, which has surveyed high school seniors each year since 1976.

The main findings were in values toward leisure, with GenX increasing over Boomers and Millennials further increasing over GenX. The researchers interpret this as a growing desire for work–life balance. Extrinsic values for money and status, however, increased for GenX and then decreased for Millennials. The researchers say GenX and Millennials may be attracted to work settings that offer work–life balance and support leisure pursuits, things often associated with alternative and more flexible work scheduling.

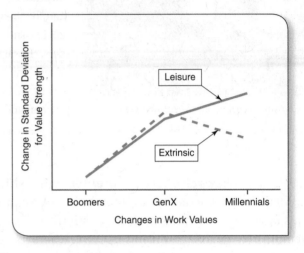

### YOU BE THE RESEARCHER

Do these findings confirm your observations and experiences? Assume you are a summer intern in a large organization and your boss says: "I'd like you to conduct a study to learn what our different generations of employees want from work and what problems they have working with one another." Just how would you design this study so that your findings would have real credibility and value?

*Reference:* Jean M. Twenge, Stacy M. Campbell, Brian J. Hoffman, and Charles E. Lance, "Generational Difference in Work Values: Leisure and Extrinsic Values Increasing, Social and Intrinsic Values Decreasing," *Journal of Management Online First* (March 1, 2010), www.jom.sagepub.com.

American CEOs wasn't a hot-button topic. Not even Apple CEO Tim Cook's $189,000 per hour.[14] No more. With high unemployment and big wide gaps between the average workers and executives, public values show more intolerance on executive pay. We have reached the point where Congressional discussions have been held, and a growing number of firms are facing shareholder resolutions asking for more input on executive compensation.

## Technological Conditions

Facebook—845 million users and growing; Twitter—175 million Tweets per day; YouTube—one hour of video uploaded each second and 4 billion videos viewed each day; web access by mobile devices doubling each year.

With data like these available it shouldn't be any surprise that businesses are quickly ramping up their spending on social media usage for product promotions, reputation management, and more.[15] No one doubts that continuing developments in the *technological conditions in the general environment* affect everything from the way we work to how we live and how we raise our children. The role of technology in organizations is advancing as rapidly as our personal use of YouTube, Facebook, and other features and "apps" on our smart phones. The ongoing wave of social media applications in the workplace ranges from new product development and advertising to employee networking and data sharing to virtual meetings and always-available chats. Between new applications and fast-developing mobile and smart device technologies, some say that e-mail will soon be used mainly by "old" people or for talking with your parents.

Employers are finding this new era of ever-present and ever-changing technology is full of potential problems, as well as opportunities. It's a fact that many employees spend lots of time doing personal things online. Some employers call this loss of productive time "social *not*working." After finding out that 70% of workers spent over an hour a day watching Web-based videos, one employer said: "I almost fell out of my chair when I saw how many people were doing it."[16] This problem isn't limited to the work environment; it's a classroom issue as well. In one survey, 65% of business students said they sent at least one text message during each class, but only 49% felt guilty about it.[17]

On the employee side of things, technology is often a factor in work–life issues. Do you realize how easily it carries work responsibilities into our non-work lives? How often do you hear people complaining that they're "never free" from the job" and that their work follows them home, on vacation, and just about everywhere else on their latest tablet or smart phone device? And what about all the warnings on social media usage? A CareerBuilder.com survey reports that about one-third of executives visiting social-network sites of job candidates said they found information that caused them to not hire the person.[18]

## Natural Environment Conditions

On March 11, 2011, a magnitude 9.0 earthquake and large tsunami hit Japan, killed 20,000 people, and damaged the Fukushima Daiichi nuclear power station; 80,000 residents were evacuated; nuclear radiation may prohibit return to some communities for decades.

We often think most about them in times of disaster—a nuclear plant that fails, a major oil spill, or an enormous hurricane.[19] But *natural environment conditions* are ever-present and increasingly a source of global concerns. Calls for being "carbon neutral," "green," and "sustainable" are common on our campuses, in our communities, and in our everyday lives. It's all about the natural resources that the environment provides for organizations and society, and the need to protect the availability of those resources for the future.

What environmental concerns are priorities for you and in your community? Is it toxic waste that may be getting dumped in a regional landfill? Could it be global warming prompted by unusual seasonal temperatures? Or is it fossil fuel consumption and the search for reliable and affordable alternative energy sources? All of these topics and more focus attention on "sustainable" practices—organizational and personal.[20] Just look around and you'll see people and organizations trying harder to reduce water consumption, cut back waste and increase recycling, improve energy efficiencies, buy and consume more local produce, and eliminate pollution. As consumers we are asking for and getting more access to "green products and services." And as job candidates, we seek and are finding more "green job" opportunities.[21]

We'll return to this discussion of environment and sustainability later in the chapter. For now, let's just recognize that we expect organizations and their managers to help preserve and respect the environment. When they don't, public criticism can be vocal and harsh. Just recall the outrage that quickly surfaced over the disastrous BP oil spill in the Gulf of Mexico and subsequent calls for stronger government oversight and control over corporate practices that put our natural world at risk.[22]

### LEARNING CHECK 1

**TAKEAWAY QUESTION 1 What is in the general or macro environment of organizations?**

**Be sure you can** • list the key elements in the general environments of organizations • give examples of how present conditions for each element pose immediate challenges to organizations • give examples of how possible future developments for each of these elements might require significant changes in how organizations operate

# The Specific or Task Environment

The **specific environment**, or **task environment**, includes the people and groups with whom an organization interacts.

In contrast to the general environment conditions, organizations and their managers deal every day with the **specific environment** or **task environment**. It comprises the actual organizations, groups, and persons with whom an organization interacts and conducts business. Picture it as standing between the level of the general environment and the boundary of the organization itself.

## Stakeholders and Value Creation

**Stakeholders** are the persons, groups, and institutions directly affected by an organization.

Members of the specific or task environment are often described as **stakeholders**, the persons, groups, and institutions affected by the organization's performance.[23] Stakeholders are key constituencies that have a stake in how an organization operates; they are influenced by it, and they can influence it in return. The important stakeholders for most organizations include customers, suppliers, competitors, regulators, advocacy groups, investors or owners, and employees. "Society at large" and "future generations" are also part of the stakeholder map; they introduce, in particular, concerns for sustainability and the natural environment.

Organizations should create value for and satisfy the needs of their multiple stakeholders. For example, businesses create value for customers through product pricing and quality; for owners the value is represented in realized profits and losses. Businesses create value for suppliers through the benefits of long-term business relationships. They create value for employees by wages earned and job

satisfaction. They can even create value for competitors by stimulating markets and innovations that didn't exist before. Businesses create value for local communities by the citizenship they display.

## Competitive Advantage

Speaking of competitors in an organization's specific or task environment, one of the goals is to gain **competitive advantage**—something that an organization does extremely well and that gives it an advantage over competitors in the marketplace.[24] The notion of competitive advantage may be best summed up as an answer to this question: "What does my organization do best?"

Legendary investor Warren Buffett of Berkshire Hathaway is often quoted as saying "sustainable competitive advantage" is what he first looks for in a potential investment. Examples might be Wal-Mart's inventory management technology which enables a low-cost structure, and Coca-Cola's brand management which helps maintain a loyal customer base. More generally, organizations pursue competitive advantage in the following ways:[25]

- *Competitive advantage can be achieved through costs*—finding ways and using technology to operate with lower costs than one's competitors and thus earn profits with prices that one's competitors have difficulty matching.
- *Competitive advantage can be achieved through quality*—finding ways and using technology to create products and services that are of consistently higher quality for customers than what is offered by one's competitors.
- *Competitive advantage can be achieved through delivery*—finding ways and using technology to outperform competitors by delivering products and services to customers faster and on time, and by developing timely new products.
- *Competitive advantage can be achieved through flexibility*—finding ways and using technology to adjust and tailor products and services to fit customer needs in ways that are difficult for one's competitor to match.

> **Competitive advantage** is something that an organization does extremely well, is difficult to copy, and gives it an advantage over competitors in the marketplace.

> **Environmental uncertainty** is a lack of information regarding what exists in the environment and what developments may occur.

## Uncertainty, Complexity, and Change

As managers deal with stakeholders and seek competitive advantage, things are often complicated by **environmental uncertainty**—a lack of complete information regarding what exists in the environment and what developments may occur. The more uncertain the environment, the harder it is to analyze environmental conditions and predict future states of affairs.

Two dimensions of environmental uncertainty are shown in Figure 4.2.[26] The first is the *degree of complexity*, or the number of different factors in the environment. An environment is typically classified as relatively simple or complex. The second is the *rate of change* in and among these factors. An environment

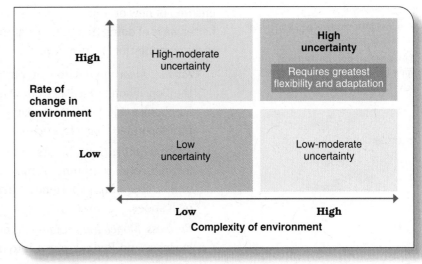

FIGURE 4.2 **Dimensions of uncertainty in the external environments of organizations.**

is typically classified as stable or dynamic. The most challenging and uncertain situation is an environment that is both complex and dynamic. High-uncertainty environments require flexibility and adaptability in organizational designs and work practices, as well as an ability of decision makers to respond quickly as new circumstances arise and new information becomes available.

---

**LEARNING CHECK 2**

**TAKEAWAY QUESTION 2   What are key elements and issues in the specific or task environment of organizations?**

**Be sure you can** • describe how a business can create value for four key stakeholders • explain *competitive advantage* and give examples of how a business might achieve it • analyze the uncertainty of an organization's external environment using degree of complexity and rate of change

---

# Environment and Innovation

**Innovation** is the process of taking a new idea and putting it into practice.

One of the things we can say for sure about organizational environments today is that change, uncertainty, and complexity call for constant **innovation**. It is the process of coming up with new ideas and putting them into practice. Innovation is often a high priority when executives and leaders try to steer organizations through complex and uncertain environments.[27] As IBM's former CEO, Samuel J. Palmisano, says: "The way you will thrive in this environment is by innovating—innovating in technologies, innovating in strategies, innovating in business models."[28]

## Types of Innovations

**Product innovations** result in new or improved goods or services.

**Process innovations** result in better ways of doing things.

**Business model innovations** result in ways for firms to make money.

When you think *innovation*, what comes to mind? Is it a product like the iPad or Kindle e-reader? Something fun like an online game or a Super-Soaker water gun? Or a customer experience, such as a self-scanning checkout at the grocery store or an online check-in for air travel? These are all part and parcel of a whole host of innovations that sort into three broad forms: (1) **Product innovations** result in the creation of new or improved goods and services. (2) **Process innovations** result in better ways of doing things. (3) **Business model innovations** result in new ways of making money for the firm. Consider these examples.

- *Product Innovation*—Groupon put coupons on the Web; Apple introduced us to the iPod, iPhone, and iPad world; Amazon's Kindle launched a new era of e-readers; Facebook made social media part of everyday life and Twitter introduced communication in 140 characters or less.

- *Process Innovation*—IKEA's "ready to assemble" furniture and fixtures transformed retail shopping; Amazon.com's "1-Click" ordering streamlined the online shopping experience; Nike allows online customers to design their own shoes.

- *Business Model Innovation*—Netflix turned movie rental into a subscription business and Redbox put it into a vending machine; Zynga made "paying for extras" profitable in free online games; eBay created the world's largest online marketplace.

Although the tendency is to view innovation in the business and economic context just described, it's important to remember that it applies equally well when we talk about the world's social problems—poverty, famine, literacy, diseases—and the general conditions for economic and social development. **Social business innovation** uses business models to address important social problems. Think of it as business innovation with a social conscience. And, the whole concept is very relevant. As management consultant Peter Drucker once said: "Every single social and global issue of our day is a business opportunity in disguise."[29]

Micro-credit lending is an example of social business innovation. It was pioneered in Bangladesh, where economist Mohammad Yunus started the Grameen Bank. Recognizing that many of the country's poor couldn't get regular bank loans because they didn't have sufficient collateral, Yunus came up with the "microcredit" idea. He set up the Grameen Bank to lend small amounts of money to the poor at very low interest rates and with the goal of promoting self-sufficiency through owning small enterprises. At one level this is a business model innovation—microcredit lending. But at another level it is a social business innovation—using microcredit lending to help tackle poverty.[30]

> **Social business innovation** finds ways to use business models to address important social problems.

## The Innovation Process

Whatever the goal—new product, improved process, unique business model, or social problem solving, the innovation process begins with *invention*—the act of discovery—and ends with *application*—the act of use. Consultant Gary Hamel describes it in the five steps of the *wheel of innovation* shown in Figure 4.3.[31] Step 1 is *imagining*—thinking about new possibilities. Step 2 is *designing*—building initial models, prototypes, or samples. Step 3 is *experimenting*—examining practicality and financial value through experiments and feasibility studies. Step 4 is *assessing*—identifying strengths and weaknesses, potential costs and benefits, and potential markets or applications. Step 5 is *scaling*—implementing what has been learned and commercializing new products or services. In business this final step involves commercializing innovation by turning it into actual products, services, or processes that increase profits by improving sales or lowering costs.

Something called **reverse innovation** is now getting lots of attention. It taps the potential for innovation existing at lower organizational levels and in diverse settings or locations.[32] The concept got its start as global firms moved away from viewing innovation as a "home market" activity that creates new products and services for distribution to "foreign markets." Instead, reverse innovation pulls new products and services from settings where they are often created under pricing constraints, and then pushes them into use elsewhere. GE, for example, developed low-priced and portable electrocardiogram and ultrasound machines in India and China. They were moved through reverse innovation into U.S. markets where their mobility and low prices made them popular with emergency units.

> **Reverse innovation** recognizes the potential for valuable innovations to be launched from lower organizational levels and diverse locations, including emerging markets.

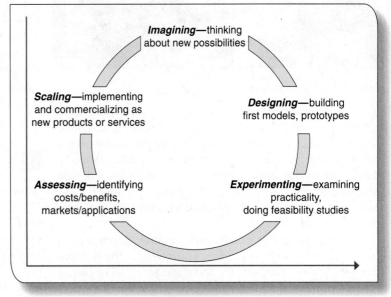

FIGURE 4.3 **The five steps in Hamel's "Wheel of Innovation."**

## Disruptive Innovation and Technology

**Disruptive innovation** creates products or services that become so widely used that they largely replace prior practices and competitors.

At times the innovation process is so successful that **disruptive innovation** occurs. It is defined by Harvard Scholar Clay Christensen as the creation of an innovative product or service that starts out small scale and then moves "up market" to where it becomes so widely used that it displaces prior practices and competitors.[33] Historical examples include cellular phones that disrupted traditional landlines and discount retailers that disrupted traditional full-line department stores. Online e-retailers are now disrupting fixed-place stores, while online gaming and movie streaming businesses that are disrupting the "buy and own" models.

As you think about disruptive innovation and technology, the world of Apple Computer and Steve Jobs can't be far away. His leadership at Apple is a model for harnessing technology and innovating—continuously and disruptively.[34] His influence at Apple turned raw technology into consumer friendly and captivating innovative products—from the Apple II to the Mac to the iPod to the iPhone to the iPad. Wouldn't you agree that we could also use the term *disruptive* to describe each of them?

**FOLLOW THE STORY**

> STEVE JOBS WAS A GENIUS FOR CUSTOMER-SAVVY INNOVATION. WHAT'S NEXT FOR APPLE?

## Disruptive Innovation the Steve Jobs Way (1955–2011)

Xinhua eyevine/Redux Pictures

Steve Jobs and Steve Wozniak built the first Apple computer in Jobs' parents' California garage. It was 1976 and within four years its successor, the Apple II, had turned Apple Computer Inc. into a fast-growing public company. Jobs' genius for customer-savvy innovation and design soon led to the MacIntosh in 1984. But a year later he was out, fired at the age of 30 by Apple's board from the company he helped create.

Jobs moved on. He bought an innovative graphics company, turned it into Pixar Studios, which created the first feature-length animated film, *Toy Story*, and sold it all to Disney for $7.4 billion. He founded NeXT Computer and created a core technology that eventually helped transform future Apple products. Jobs was brought back in charge of a struggling Apple in 1997. He and the firm never looked back—our world of iPad, iPhone, and iPod tells the rest of the story. When he died at home on October 5, 2011. The *Wall Street Journal* declared, "With Jobs Gone, a New Test for Apple 'Army.'" Many wondered: With Steve gone, what happens next for Apple?

*Creativity is about connecting things.*

*Simple can be harder than complex. You have to work hard to get your thinking clean to make it simple.*

*The only way to be satisfied is to do what you believe is great work.*

*Great companies must have a noble cause. Then it's the leader's job to transform that noble cause into such an inspiring vision that it will attract the most talented people in the world to want to join it.*

—Steve Jobs

 **YOUR TAKE?**

Steve Jobs had a keen eye for picking people—new CEO Tim Cook, for example. He built a corporate culture that encouraged creativity and innovation, and he left the firm with a strong talent pool. But is this legacy enough to secure Apple's future? Is innovation person or leader dependent, or can it be made part of an organization's DNA? Will Apple be able to keep delivering next great products?

**LEARNING CHECK 3**

**TAKEWAY QUESTION 3  How do organizations accomplish innovation?**

**Be sure you can** • define *innovation* • discuss differences between process, product, business model, and social business innovations • list the five steps in Hamel's wheel of innovation • explain how innovations get commercialized • define *reverse innovation* and *disruptive innovation* • give an example of a disruptive innovation that you use almost every day

# Environment and Sustainability

Think about issues of our day—climate change, carbon footprints, alternative energy; the link between people, organizations, and nature. They highlight **sustainability** as a core issue of the times. It's a commitment to live and work in ways that protect the rights of both present and future generations as co-stakeholders of the world's resources. This commitment applies to everything from the air we breathe and water we consume, to the spaces we inhabit, to the human

**Sustainability** is a commitment to protect the rights of present and future generations as co-stakeholders of the world's resources.

**ETHICS ON THE LINE**

> IT'S A LOT EASIER TO SEND HAZARDOUS WASTE TO ANOTHER COUNTRY THAN DISPOSE OF IT AT HOME

## Offshore E-Waste Graveyards Bury a Problem

Ermin Gutenberger/iStockphoto

 **G**ive me a plan," says the boss. "We need to get rid of this electronic waste."

This isn't an uncommon problem. Just think about all those old stereo components, out-of-date cell phones, used computers and displays, and so on. Did you know that they often end up in e-waste graveyards in countries like Ghana, China, and Vietnam? The waste arrives by sea container or barge and ends in huge dumps. Local laborers, perhaps including children, go to work disassembling the waste products to salvage

valuable scrap metals, often burning the plastic and motherboards to release the sought-after scraps.

Those who work in and live around e-waste graveyards face real hazards to health and welfare. But, it can be expensive for the source to dispose of electronic waste. That's the hidden problem behind the boss's directive here; an offshore e-waste graveyard is an attractive low-cost option. But the price is paid in adverse environmental and health effects. At what human and environmental price are the scrap materials being disassembled, recovered, and buried? It isn't a stretch to say that the workers often inhale toxic fumes; nearby streams can get polluted with runoff waste; and even streets and living areas of the workers get cluttered with electronic debris.

**ETHICS QUESTIONS**

Even as some countries become hosts for e-waste products, their governments may look the other way when it comes to the environmental and human costs. Whose responsibility is it to deal with bad consequences of e-waste disposal? Does the originating country and consumer have an obligation to reduce waste creation and assist with safe waste disposal? If the "plan" that is given to the boss in this case simply involves "ship it to Ghana," is that acceptable business practice?

labor that gives life to our best-loved devices and smart phones. Gavin Neath, vice president for Unilever, says "With a global population at 6.5 billion we are already consuming resources at a rate far in excess of nature's capacity to replenish them. Water is becoming scarce and global warming and climate change are accelerating."[35] Little wonder that 93% of CEOs in a recent survey admit that the future success of their firms depends in part on how well they meet sustainability challenges.[36]

## Sustainable Development

**Sustainable development** uses environmental resources to support societal needs today while also preserving and protecting them for future generations.

If sustainability is a priority, just what is **sustainable development**? Most often, the term describes the use of environmental resources to support societal needs today while also preserving and protecting them for use by future generations. The World Business Council for Sustainable Development, whose membership includes the CEOs of global corporations, defines sustainable development as "forms of progress that meet the needs of the present without compromising the ability of future generations to meet their needs."[37]

**Environmental capital** or **natural capital** is the storehouse of natural resources—atmosphere, land, water, and, minerals—that we use to sustain life and produce goods and services for society.

Sustainable development preserves our **environmental capital** or **natural capital**.[38] This is the world's storehouse of natural resources in the form of atmosphere, land, water, and minerals, which sustains life as we know it. The catch words are renew, recycle, conserve, and preserve. Rising oil prices, concerns for greenhouse-gas emissions and use of toxins, public values on climate change and clean energy, poverty and income disparities—all of these and more are driving the conversations.[39] We want prosperity, convenience, comfort, and luxury in our everyday lives. But, we are more and more aware of the costs of these aspirations and the threats these costs pose to the future.

The **triple bottom line** assesses the economic, social, and environmental performance of organizations.

The **3 P's of organizational performance** are profit, people, and planet.

PepsiCo CEO Indra Nooyi says: "All corporations operate with a license from society. It's critically important that we take that responsibility very, very seriously; we have to make sure that what corporations do doesn't add costs to society."[40] Her point directs attention toward the **triple bottom line**, evaluating not just an organization's economic performance but also its social and environmental performance.[41] It embraces the **3 Ps of organizational performance**—profit, people, and planet.

## Sustainable Business

A **sustainable business** operates in ways that meet the needs of customers while protecting or advancing the well-being of our natural environment.

The triple bottom line and the 3 P's are anchor points of **sustainable businesses**, ones that both meet the needs of customers and protect or advance the well-being of our natural environment.[42] Sustainable businesses try to operate in harmony with nature rather than by exploiting it. They set goals for things like "recycling percentage," "carbon reduction," "energy efficiency," "ethical sourcing," "food security," and more.[43] They employ people with job titles like corporate sustainability officer, green building manager, staff ecologist, sustainability program director, and sustainability planner. And, they pursue **sustainable innovation** or **green innovation** to create new products, practices, and methods that reduce any negative impact on the environment or, even better, enhance its positive impact.[44]

**Sustainable innovations** or **green innovations** help reduce an organization's negative impact and enhance its positive impact on the natural environment.

## Management in Popular Culture

### Sustainability Warms the Heart in Chipotle Commercial

TJP/Alamy

Some say the commercial makes them cry. Watch "Back to the Start" on YouTube and decide for yourself. As Willie Nelson sings Coldplay's "The Scientist," the viewer journeys through the animated world of a factory farm. It's pure assembly line. But after the farmer sends his animals to market, he realizes there's a better way. As Willie sings "I'm going back to the start . . . " he goes home and changes things for the better. The goal is still the same—producing food for people, but the means is a lot different in the end as the farm is recreated as a sustainable food venture. As for Chipotle, the tag line is: "Cultivate a Better World."

A sustainable business model strives for win–win outcomes where both the organization and the environment gain. There are lots of examples around. Stonyfield Farm saved over $1.7 million in energy costs over six years after putting in a large solar photovoltaic array. Clif Bar cut shrink-wrapping and saved $400,000 a year in plastic costs. Seventh Generation built revenues of $40+ million creating green personal care and household products.[45] Subaru of Indiana Automotive saved $5.3 million in one year as 98% of plant waste was recycled or reduced, paint solvents were filtered and reused, and compost from food waste was sold to local farmers.[46] Similar stories are found in organizations investing in more energy-efficient building designs, materials, and even work practices like using virtual teams and conferences instead of paying travel expenses to hold meetings.[47]

## Sustainability Goals, Measurement, and Reporting

As the public at large becomes more sustainability conscious, top management teams are giving increased attention to sustainability goals for their organizations. You'll find them in published materials and on websites. But a bit of caution is in order here. Sustainability goals achieve their greatest impact only when top management fully supports them by both committing resources to their accomplishment and regularly measuring performance results.

Procter & Gamble's annual Sustainability Report links a corporate vision with sustainability goals described as "long term operational end points" like these:[48]

- Powering our plants with 100% renewable energy
- Emitting no fossil-based $CO_2$ or toxic emissions
- Delivering effluent water quality that is as good as or better than influent water quality with no contribution to water scarcity
- Having zero manufacturing waste go to landfills

This list states lofty sustainability goals, ones it will take years to reach. But they keep P&G pointed in the right short-term directions. In terms of accomplishments

## ManagementSmarts

### Assessing Organizational Impact on Human Sustainability

*Get a start on assessing human sustainability by asking:*

To what extent do management decisions and organizational practices help support and advance human health and well-being?

- Provision of health insurance to employees?
- Provision of health and wellness programs for employees?
- Avoiding job layoffs?
- Structuring work hours to reduce stress?
- Structuring work hours to avoid and minimize work–family conflict?
- Designing jobs to reduce stress?
- Designing jobs to give people control over their work?
- Being transparent and fair in handling wage and status inequalities?

and accountability, for example, the firm's latest sustainability report identifies the following progress as measured against a 2007 baseline: 16% decrease in energy consumption, 12% decrease in $CO_2$ emissions, 22% decrease in water usage, and 57% decreased in waste disposal.[49] Such sustainability reporting not only documents and publicizes achieved successes, it also keeps management and the public alerted to what still remains to be accomplished.

## Human Sustainability

It's important to recognize that the notion of sustainability in management applies to more than the natural environment alone. Scholar Jeffrey Pfeffer offers a strong case for giving greater management attention to social and human sustainability—the People part of the 3 P's.[50] He says: "Just as there is concern for protecting natural resources, there could be a similar level of concern for protecting human resources.... Being a socially responsible business ought to encompass the effect of management practices on employee physical and psychological well-being."[51]

Pfeffer's concerns for human sustainability confirm the importance of employees as organizational stakeholders. They call attention to issues like those highlighted in Management Smarts. And they remind us that management practices can have major consequences for the health and well-being of people whose everyday work fuels the organizations of our society.

One example of human sustainability at risk came to public attention after problems with factory conditions in Apple's Asian supply chain made the news. An audit of Hon Hai Precision Industry (Foxconn) by the Fair Labor Association, for example, documented problems with excessive overtime and accidents among workers assembling Apple products. After Apple CEO Tim Cook made a personal visit to the China factories, his company spokesperson said "We think empowering workers and helping them understand their rights is essential." A Foxconn counterpart replied that they would ensure all workers had "safe, satisfactory, and healthy" working conditions.[52]

---

### LEARNING CHECK 4

**TAKEAWAY QUESTION 4** **What are the emerging issues of sustainability and the environment?**

**Be sure you can** • explain the triple bottom line and 3 P's of organizational performance • define the terms *sustainable development* and *environmental capital* • give examples of sustainability issues today • explain and give examples of *sustainable business practices* • discuss human sustainability as a management concern

# MANAGEMENT LEARNING REVIEW

## LEARNING CHECK SUMMARY

### TAKEAWAY QUESTION 1 What is in the general or macro environment of organizations?

- The general environment includes background economic, sociocultural, legal-political, technological, and natural environment conditions.
- The economic environment influences organizations through the health of the local, domestic, and global economies in terms of such things as financial markets, inflation, income levels, unemployment, and job outlook.
- The legal-political environment influences organizations through existing and proposed laws and regulations, government policies, and the philosophy and objectives of political parties.
- The sociocultural environment influences organizations through the norms, customs, and demographics of a society or region, as well as social values on such matters as ethics, human rights, gender roles, and lifestyles.
- The technological environment influences organizations through continuing advancement of information and computer technologies that affect the way we work, how we live, and how we raise our children.
- The natural environment conditions influence organizations through the abundance of natural resources provided, and the need for organizational practices that both meet the needs of customers and protect future well-being.

**For Discussion** If interests of a firm's owners/investors conflict with those of the community, which stakeholder gets preference?

### TAKEAWAY QUESTION 2 What are the key elements and issues in the specific or task environment of organizations?

- The specific environment or task environment consists of suppliers, customers, competitors, regulators, and other stakeholders with which an organization interacts.
- A competitive advantage is achieved when an organization does something very well that allows it to outperform its competitors.
- Environmental uncertainty is created by the rate of change of factors in the external environment and the complexity of this environment in terms of the number of factors that are relevant and important.

**For Discussion** Which among the two or three retail stores that you shop at weekly seems to have the strongest competitive advantage, and why?

### TAKEAWAY QUESTION 3 How do organizations accomplish innovation?

- Product innovations deliver new products and services to customers; process innovations improve operations; and business model innovations find new ways of creating value and making profits.
- Social business innovations use business models to help address social problems, things like poverty, famine, disease, and literacy.
- The innovation process involves moving from the stage of invention that involves discovery and idea creation all the way to final application that involves actual use of what has been created.
- The process of commercializing innovation turns new ideas into outcomes that add value or increase profits for organizations.
- Reverse innovation finds innovation opportunities in diverse locations, such as taking products and services developed in emerging markets and finding ways to utilize them elsewhere.
- Disruptive innovation, often involving technological advancements, is the creation of a new product or service that starts out small scale and then becomes so widely used that it displaces prior practices and competitors.

**For Discussion** Can a creative person prosper in an organization that doesn't have an innovation-driven culture?

### TAKEAWAY QUESTION 4 What are the emerging issues of sustainability and the environment?

- The concept of sustainability describes a commitment to recognize and protect the rights of both present and future generations as co-stakeholders of the world's natural resources.
- The triple bottom line evaluates how well organizations perform on economic, social, and environmental performance criteria; it is also called the 3 P's of organizational performance—profits, people, planet.
- Sustainable development uses environmental resources to support society today while also preserving and protecting those resources for use by future generations.
- Sustainable innovations pursue new ways for minimizing the negative impact and maximizing positive impact of organizations on the natural environment by reducing energy and natural resource consumption.

**For Discussion** When the costs of pursuing sustainability goals reduce business profits, which stakeholder interests should take priority, business owners or society at large?

## Multiple-Choice Questions

1. The general environment of an organization would include _____.
   - (a) population demographics
   - (b) activist groups
   - (c) competitors
   - (d) customers

2. Internet censorship faced in foreign countries by firms such as Google is an example of how differences in _____ factors in the general environment can cause complications for global business executives.
   - (a) economic
   - (b) legal-political
   - (c) natural environment
   - (d) demographic

3. If the term *offshoring* describes outsourcing of work and jobs to foreign locations, what is it called when firms like Caterpillar move jobs back into the United States from foreign locations?
   - (a) protectionism
   - (b) reshoring
   - (c) disrupting
   - (d) upscaling

4. Work preferences of different generations and public values over things like high pay for corporate executives are examples of developments in the _____ environment of organizations.
   - (a) task
   - (b) specific
   - (c) socio-cultural
   - (d) economic

5. A business that has found ways to use technology to outperform its rivals in the marketplace can be said to have gained _____.
   - (a) environmental capital
   - (b) competitive advantage
   - (c) sustainable development
   - (d) environmental certainty

6. Apps for an Apple iPhone or Google Android phone are examples of _____ innovations, whereas the use of robotics in performing manufacturing tasks previously done by humans is an example of _____ innovation.
   - (a) cost-benefit, process
   - (b) product, cost-benefit
   - (c) value-driven, service-driven
   - (d) product, process

7. Micro-credit lending that makes it possible for poor people to get small loans so they can start small businesses is an example of a business model innovation that is also a _____ innovation.
   - (a) social business
   - (b) technological
   - (c) disruptive
   - (d) green

8. Two dimensions that determine the level of environmental uncertainty are the number of factors in the external environment and the _____ of these factors.
   - (a) location
   - (b) rate of change
   - (c) importance
   - (d) interdependence

9. One of the ways that corporations might better take into account their responsibility for being good environmental citizens is to redefine the notion of profit to: Profit = Revenue − Cost of Goods Sold − _____.
   - (a) operating expenses
   - (b) dividends
   - (c) costs to society
   - (d) loan interest

10. The three P's of organizational performance are Profit, People, and _____.
    - (a) Philanthropy
    - (b) Principle
    - (c) Potential
    - (d) Planet

11. What organizational stakeholder must be considered in any serious discussion about how a firm can better fulfill its obligations for sustainable development?
    - (a) owners or investors
    - (b) customers
    - (c) suppliers
    - (d) future generations

12. The first step in Hamel's wheel of innovation is _____.
    - (a) imagining
    - (b) assessing
    - (c) experimenting
    - (d) scaling

13. When a medical device is developed in India so that it can sell at a low price and still deliver high-quality results, and then that device is transferred for sale in the United States also at a low price, this is an example of _____.
    - (a) trickle-down innovation
    - (b) disruptive innovation
    - (c) reverse innovation
    - (d) sustainable innovation

14. What term is used to describe the world's storehouse of natural resources, things like land, water, and minerals?
    - (a) sustainable development
    - (b) global warming
    - (c) climate justice
    - (d) environmental capital

15. Health insurance for employees, flexible work hours to balance work and family responsibilities, and programs to help employees deal with stress in their lives, are ways organizations might try to improve their accomplishments in respect to _____.
    - (a) profits
    - (b) human sustainability
    - (c) innovation
    - (d) natural capital

## Short-Response Questions

**16.** Who and/or what should be considered as key stakeholders by a business executive when mapping the task environment for her organization?

**17.** Exactly how should *sustainability* be best defined when making it part of a goal statement or performance objective for a business or an organization?

**18.** How do product, process, and business model innovations differ from one another?

**19.** How does the process of reverse innovation work?

## Essay Question

**20.** At a reunion of graduates from a college of business at the local university, two former roommates engaged in a discussion about environment and sustainability. One is a senior executive with a global manufacturer, and the other owns a sandwich shop in the college town.

*Global executive*: "We include sustainability in our corporate mission and have a chief sustainability officer on the senior management team. The CSO is really good and makes sure that we don't do anything that could cause a lack of public confidence in our commitment to sustainability."

*Sandwich shop owner*: "That's all well and good, but what are you doing on the positive side in terms of environmental care. It sounds like you do just enough to avoid public scrutiny. Shouldn't the CSO be a real advocate for the environment rather than just a protector of the corporate reputation? We, for example, use only natural foods and ingredients, recycle everything that is recyclable, and compost all possible waste."

*Question:* If you were establishing a new position called *corporate sustainability officer*, what would you include in the job description as a way of both clarifying the responsibilities of the person hired and establishing clear accountability for what sustainability means to your organization?

## MANAGEMENT SKILLS AND COMPETENCIES

# Further Reflection: Risk Taking

The chapter opener highlighted the importance of understanding our tendencies toward **risk taking** and its potential to work for us or against us. It discussed a "risk line" above which risk is a positive influence on our behavior and below which it is a negative influence. The former is driven by opportunity and confidence, the latter by fear and desperation. As you ponder the many complexities of the external environment of organizations, including opportunities of innovation and sustainability, would you agree that it's important to stop and ask: How do we individually, organizationally, and as a society deal with risk in our environments, and how can we do better?

 **DO IT NOW . . .**
**LOOK IN THE MIRROR**

- Use the figure in the chapter opener to do a quick self-check of your risk taking tendencies.

- Which side of the risk line are you most often on— positive or negative?

- Write short descriptions of risks you've taken at school and work and that were driven (a) by confidence and (b) by desperation.

- What do these observations suggest about how risk taking might affect your behavior in career and personal affairs?

# Self-Assessment: Tolerance for Ambiguity

## Instructions

To determine your level of tolerance for ambiguity, rate each of the following items on this 7-point scale.[53]

| 1 | strongly disagree |
| 2 | |
| 3 | slightly agree |
| 4 | |
| 5 | slightly agree |
| 6 | |
| 7 | strongly disagree |

___ 1. An expert who doesn't come up with a definite answer probably doesn't know too much.

___ 2. There is really no such thing as a problem that can't be solved.

___ 3. I would like to live in a foreign country for a while.

___ 4. People who fit their lives to a schedule probably miss the joy of living.

___ 5. A good job is one where what is to be done and how it is to be done are always clear.

___ 6. In the long run it is possible to get more done by tackling small, simple problems rather than large, complicated ones.

___ 7. It is more fun to tackle a complicated problem than it is to solve a simple one.

___ 8. Often the most interesting and stimulating people are those who don't mind being different and original.

___ 9. What we are used to is always preferable to what is unfamiliar.

___ 10. A person who leads an even, regular life in which few surprises or unexpected happenings arise really has a lot to be grateful for.

___ 11. People who insist upon a yes or no answer just don't know how complicated things really are.

___ 12. Many of our most important decisions are based on insufficient information.

___ 13. I like parties where I know most of the people more than ones where most of the people are complete strangers.

___ 14. The sooner we all acquire ideals, the better.

___ 15. Teachers or supervisors who hand out vague assignments give a chance for one to show initiative and originality.

___ 16. A good teacher is one who makes you wonder about your way of looking at things.

___ Total Score

## Scoring

To obtain a score, first *reverse* the scale score for the eight "reverse" items, 3, 4, 7, 8, 11, 12, 15, and 16 (i.e., a rating of 1 5 7, 2 5 6, 3 5 5, etc.), then add up the rating scores for all 16 items.

## Interpretation

Individuals with a *greater* tolerance for ambiguity are more likely to be able to function effectively in organizations and contexts with high turbulence, a high rate of change, and less certainty about expectations, performance standards, what needs to be done, and so on. They are likely to "roll with the punches" as organizations, environmental conditions, and demands change rapidly.

Individuals with a *lower* tolerance for ambiguity are more likely to be unable to adapt or adjust quickly in turbulence, uncertainty, and change. These individuals are likely to become rigid, angry, stressed, and frustrated when there is a high level of uncertainty and ambiguity in the environment.

# Team Exercise:
# Organizational Commitment to Sustainability Scorecard

## Instructions

In your assigned work teams do the following.

1. Agree on a definition of "sustainability" that should fit the operations of any organization.

2. Brainstorm and agree on criteria for an Organizational Commitment to Sustainability Scorecard (OCSS) that can be used to audit the sustainability practices of an organization. Be sure that an organization being audited would not only receive scores on individual dimensions or categories of sustainability performance, but also receive a total overall "Sustainability Score" that can be compared with results for other organizations.

3. Present and defend your OCSS to the class at large.

4. Use feedback received from the class presentation to revise your OCSS so that it can be used to conduct an actual organizational sustainability audit.

5. Use your OCSS to complete a sustainability audit for a local organization.

6. Present the results of your audit to the instructor and class at large. Include in the presentation not only the audit scores, but also: (a) recommendations for how this organization could improve its sustainability practices in the future, and (b) any benchmarks from this organization that might be considered as sustainability "best practices" for others to follow.

# Career Situations for a Complex Environment: What Would You Do?

1. **Diversity Is Here to Stay**   It was uncomfortable just to hear it. One of your friends brought his friend to lunch. When discussing a new female boss, he says: "It really irritates me not only that she gets the job just because she's a woman, but she's also Hispanic. No way that someone like me had a chance against her "credentials." Now has the gall to act as if we're all one big happy team and the rest of us should accept her leadership. As for me, I'll do my best to make it difficult for her to succeed." Your friend looks dismayed but isn't saying anything. What will you say or do?

2. **Innovation Isn't Everything**   A member of your team is in the office with a complaint. "You're a great boss," she says, "but . . . ." Well, it turns out the "but" has to do with an apparent bias on your part for praising in public only those members of the team who come up with new ideas. You seem to overlook or neglect the fact that other team members are working hard and producing good—albeit standard—work every day. Are you ready to accept the point that not all high performers are going to be great innovators? And, if so, what changes in your behavior might be made to reflect this belief?

3. **Humans Count, Too**   Your boss is high on making sustainability a top organizational priority. In a recent meeting he kept talking about "nature," "green practices," and "resource protection." You listened and finally said: "What about people—shouldn't they count when it comes to issues of sustainability?" After listening, perhaps after an initial thought to be sharp with you, he said in return: "Give me a proposal that we can discuss at the next staff meeting." What are you going to give him?

# Case Study

# Timberland

Go to *Management Cases for Critical Thinking* to find the recommended case for Chapter 4—"Timberland: Walking with Sustainability."

Jeff Greenberg/Alamy

# Wisdom
## Learning From Others

MORE TO LOOK
FOR INSIDE>

Navigation

GPS

## > GLOBALIZATION MAKES BUSINESSES WORLD TRAVELERS

*Question 1.* What do Victoria's Secret, C. O. Bigelow, Bath & Body Works, White Barn Candle Co., La Senza, and Henri Bendel have in common? Their roots go back to 1963 and a small women's clothing store in Columbus, Ohio that grew to be one of the world's most admired fashion retailers—Limited Brands.

The Limited's founder, chairman, and CEO, Leslie Wexner, has been called a "pioneer of specialty brands" with "vision and focus." He says success in a highly competitive industry comes from "better brands, best brands—I don't believe bigger is better; I believe better is better. Period."

*Question 2.* Where does the Limited get its products? The answer is global sourcing; it gets them anywhere in the world where it finds quality at low cost.

The Limited's global supply chains are to be envied. But they can also be risky for brand reputation. When things go wrong, child labor exposed in a foreign supplier, for example, the brand can be badly hurt.

Wexner makes sure The Limited's global reach is tightly managed to maintain ethical standards. Supplier and subcontractor relationships are guided by clear and unequivocal standards. If you don't meet the standards, you don't work with the Limited. Suppliers are expected to operate with no prison or forced labor or child labor, with protection of worker health and safety, and with nondiscrimination, among other matters.[1]

**FOLLOW THE STORY**
Wal-Mart Finds It Holds a Chinese Tiger by the Tail

**ETHICS ON THE LINE**
Who Wins When Nationalism Meets Protectionism

**FACTS FOR ANALYSIS**
Corruption and Bribes Haunt Global Business

**RESEARCH BRIEF**
Personality Traits, Behavioral Competencies, and Expatriate Effectiveness

# Global Management and Cultural Diversity

## > CULTURAL AWARENESS

The complications and dramas of global events are ever-present reminders that **cultural awareness** is one of the great challenges of our century. Consultant Richard Lewis warns of "cultural spectacles" that limit our vision, causing us to see and interpret things with the biases of our own culture.[2]

It's one thing to say we now live in a global community. It's quite another to participate effectively in this community. To do so we must remove blinders that limit our vision to the culture in which we were raised. We need to embrace the rich cultural diversity of the world's peoples.

It's hard to pass a day without bumping into Asia's influence on global politics and economics. When our business and government leaders venture into Asia, we want them to be successful. To do so they must be high in cultural awareness and sensitive to how cultural dynamics can affect their work.

How informed are you regarding Asian cultures? Are you aware that Confucian values such as those shown in the box are very influential?

Isn't cultural awareness a must-have competency? Look around your college campus. The cultural diversity of students offers a trip around the world. . . . if we're willing to reach out and embrace it.

Cross-cultural communication can be a bit awkward, but that shouldn't hold us back. Good old-fashioned sensitivity and a willingness to listen and learn can go a long way toward closing any cultural gaps.

## Insight
### Learning About Yourself

### CONFUCIAN VALUES IN ASIAN CULTURES

- **Harmony**—works well in a group, doesn't disrupt group order, puts group before self-interests
- **Hierarchy**—accepts authority and hierarchical nature of society; doesn't challenge superiors
- **Benevolence**—acts kindly and understandingly toward others; paternalistic, willing to teach and help subordinates
- **Loyalty**—loyal to organization and supervisor, dedicated to job, grateful for job and supportive of superior
- **Learning**—eager for new knowledge, works hard to learn new job skills, strives for high performance

## BUILD SKILLS AND COMPETENCIES AT END OF CHAPTER

- Engage in *Further Reflection on Cultural Awareness*
- Take the *Self-Assessment on Global Intelligence*
- Complete the *Team Exercise—American Football*
- Solve the *Career Situations in Global Management*
- Analyze the *Case Study—Harley-Davidson: Style and Strategy Have Global Reach*

## <GET TO KNOW YOURSELF BETTER

# Global Management and Cultural Diversity

5

**Management and Globalization**
- Global management
- Why companies go global
- How companies go global
- Global business environments

**Global Businesses**
- Types of global businesses
- Pros and cons of global businesses
- Ethics challenges for global businesses

**Culture and Global Diversity**
- Cultural intelligence
- Silent languages of culture
- Tight and loose cultures
- Values and national cultures

**Global Management Learning**
- Are management theories universal?
- Intercultural competencies
- Global learning goals

Our global community is rich with information, opportunities, controversies, and complications. We get on-the-spot news from around the world delivered to our smart devices. When crises like the Japanese tsunami or civil unrest happen, social media like Twitter and Facebook join major news networks to get the information out instantaneously. We play online games with competitors and partners from other countries, and our colleges and universities offer a growing variety of study-abroad programs.

Speaking of traveling the globe, companies like Limited Brands featured in the chapter opener are travelers, too. IBM employs more than 40,000 software developers in India. Anheuser-Busch, maker of "America's King of Beers," is owned by the Belgian firm InBev. Ben & Jerry's Ice Cream is owned by the British-Dutch firm Unilever. India's Tata Group owns Jaguar, Land Rover, Tetley Tea, and Eight-O'Clock Coffee. Japan's Honda, Nissan, and Toyota get 80 to 90% of their profits from sales in America.[3] Components for Boeing planes come from 5,400 suppliers in 40 countries.[4]

## Management and Globalization

In the **global economy**, resources, markets, and competition are worldwide in scope.

**Globalization** is the growing interdependence among elements of the global economy.

**World 3.0** is a world where nations cooperate in the global economy while still respecting different national characters and interests.

This is the age of the **global economy** in which resource supplies, product markets, and business competition are worldwide rather than local or national in scope. It is also a time heavily influenced by the forces of **globalization**, defined as the growing interdependence among the components in the global economy. Some see the effects as a "borderless world" where economic integration becomes so extreme that nation states hardly matter anymore.[5] But international management scholar Pakaj Ghemawat describes us as moving toward what he calls **World 3.0**.[6] It's where nations cooperate in the global economy while still respecting one another's national characters and special interests. They balance economic gains of global integration with local needs and priorities. In other words, World 3.0 is globalization in which national identities remain strong even as the opportunities of the global economy are sought.

There's no better way to illustrate the global economy than with the clothes we wear. Where did you buy your favorite t-shirt? Where was it made? Where will it end up? In a fascinating book called *The Travels of a T-Shirt in the Global Economy*, economist Pietra Rivoli tracks the origins and disposition of a t-shirt that she bought while on vacation in Florida.[7]

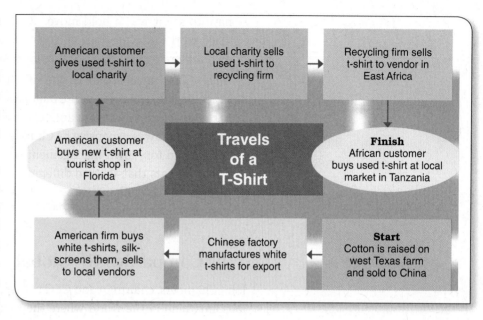

As shown here, Rivoli's t-shirt lived a complicated and very global life. That life began with cotton grown in Texas. It moved to China where the cotton was processed and white t-shirts were manufactured. The t-shirts were then sold to a firm in the United States that silk-screened and sold them to retail shops for resale to American customers. These customers eventually donated the used t-shirts to a charity that sold them to a recycler. The recycler sold them to a vendor in Africa who distributed them to local markets to be sold yet again to local customers.

It's quite a story, this t-shirt that travels the commercial highways and byways of the world. Along with the Limited Brands story and many other examples to follow, it all leaves little doubt why Harvard scholar and consultant Rosabeth Moss Kanter once described globalization as "one of the most powerful and pervasive influences on nations, businesses, workplaces, communities, and lives."[8]

## Global Management

The term used to describe management in businesses and organizations with interests in more than one country is **global management**. Procter & Gamble, for example, pursues a global strategy with customers in over 180 countries. The majority of McDonald's sales are now coming from outside the United States, with the "Golden Arches" prominent on city streets from Moscow to Tokyo to Budapest to Rio de Janeiro. Toyota has 14 plants in North America and employs over 35,000 locals. The success of firms like these depends on being able to attract and hire truly **global managers** who have strong global perspectives, are culturally aware, and always stay informed about international developments.

Global managers face unique challenges. Consider two short cases—one a success story and the other more of a "work in progress."

*Honda*—Allen Kinzer, now retired, was the first American manager Honda hired for its Marysville, Ohio, plant. Although people were worried whether or not U.S. workers could adapt to the Japanese firm's production methods, technology, and style, it all worked out. Says Kinzer: "It wasn't easy blending the cultures; anyone who knew anything about the industry at the time would

**Global management** involves managing business and organizations with interests in more than one country.

A truly **global manager** is culturally aware and informed on international affairs.

have to say it was a bold move." Bold move, indeed! Honda now employs 4,200 workers to produce 440,000 vehicles per year. It is one among hundreds of foreign firms offering employment opportunities to U.S. workers.[9]

*Haier*—The Haier Group is one of China's best-known appliance makers. When its CEO, Zhang Ruimin, built a factory in South Carolina, the idea was to manufacture in America and take a larger share of its refrigerator market. But the plant was expensive by Chinese standards and Haier's organizational culture and top-down management style were resented by American workers. Work hats that showed different ranks and seniority, for example, didn't go over well. But Zhang stayed with the project, saying "First the hard, then smooth. That's the way to win."[10]

## Why Companies Go Global

John Chambers, chairman and CEO of Cisco Systems Inc., once said: "I will put my jobs anywhere in the world where the right infrastructure is, with the right educated workforce, with the right supportive government."[11] Cisco, Honda, Haier, and other firms like them are classic **international businesses** that conduct for-profit transactions of goods and services across national boundaries. Nike is another; its swoosh is one of the world's most recognized brands.

Did you know that Nike does no domestic manufacturing? All of its products come from sources abroad, including 100+ factories in China alone. Its competitor, New Balance, takes a different approach. Even though making extensive use of global suppliers and licensing its products internationally, New Balance still produces at factories in the United States.[12] The two firms follow somewhat different strategies, but each is actively pursuing these common reasons for doing international business.

> *Profits*—Gain profits through expanded operations.
> *Customers*—Enter new markets to gain new customers.
> *Suppliers*—Get access to materials, products, and services.
> *Labor*—Get access to lower-cost talented workers.
> *Capital*—Tap a larger pool of financial resources.
> *Risk*—Spread assets among multiple countries.

Today you can add another reason to this list, *economic development*—where a global firm does business in foreign countries with direct intent to help the local economy. Coffee giants Green Mountain Coffee Roasters, Peet's Coffee & Tea, and Starbucks, for example, are helping Rwandan farmers improve production and marketing methods. They send advisers to teach coffee growers how to meet high standards so that their products can be sold worldwide. It's a win–win: The global coffee firm gets a quality product at a good price, the local coffee growers gain skills and market opportunities, and the domestic economy improves.[13]

## How Companies Go Global

The common forms of international business are shown in Figure 5.1. When a business is just getting started internationally, global sourcing, exporting/importing, and licensing and franchising are the usual ways to begin. These are *market-entry strategies* that involve the sale of goods or services to foreign markets without expensive investments. Strategic alliances, joint ventures, and wholly owned subsidiaries are

An **international business** conducts for-profit transactions of goods and services across national boundaries.

*direct investment strategies.* They require major capital commitments, but also create rights of ownership and control over operations in the foreign country.

## Global Sourcing

A common first step into international business is **global sourcing**—the process of purchasing materials, manufacturing components, or locating business services around the world. It is an international division of labor in which activities are performed in countries where they can be done well at the lowest cost. Global sourcing at Boeing, for example, means that components flow in from a complex global supply chain for final assembly into 787 Dreamliners at American plants. In the service sector, it may mean setting up toll-free customer support call centers in the Philippines, locating research and development centers in Brazil or Russia, or hiring physicians in India to read medical X-rays.[14]

> In **global sourcing**, materials or services are purchased around the world for local use.

Most manufacturers today—toys, shoes, electronics, furniture, clothing, aircraft—make extensive use of global sourcing. China is still a major outsourcing destination and in many areas has become the factory for the world. If you use an Apple iPod, iPhone, or iPad, for example, chances are it was assembled by a Taiwanese-owned company called Hon Hai Precision Instruments at plants located in China. The plants are huge—employing as many as 350,000+ workers, and they produce products not just for Apple, but for other firms like Sony and Hewlett-Packard. You may know of Hon Hai through its trade name, Foxconn, and for controversies that have reached the news regarding poor treatment of workers.[15] By its own admission, Apple audits found

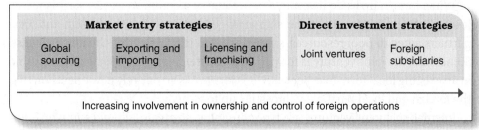

| Market entry strategies | | | Direct investment strategies | |
|---|---|---|---|---|
| Global sourcing | Exporting and importing | Licensing and franchising | Joint ventures | Foreign subsidiaries |

Increasing involvement in ownership and control of foreign operations

**FIGURE 5.1** **Common forms of international business—from market entry to direct investment increasing involvement in ownership and control of foreign operations strategies.**

that its global suppliers had problems with work hours (62%), worker safety (35%), and hazardous substance practices (32%).[16]

## Exporting and Importing

In **exporting**, local products are sold abroad to foreign customers.

**Importing** involves the selling in domestic markets of products acquired abroad.

A second form of international business involves **exporting**—selling locally made products in foreign markets. The flip side of exporting is **importing**—buying foreign-made products and selling them in domestic markets.

Because the growth of export industries creates local jobs, governments often offer special advice and assistance to businesses that are trying to develop or expand their export markets. After visiting a U.S. government-sponsored trade fair in China, Bruce Boxerman, president of a small Cincinnati firm, Richards Industries, decided to take advantage of the growing market for precision valves. In 10 years he doubled export sales to the point where they account for one-half the firm's revenues. One of his employees says: "It wasn't long ago that guys looked at globalization like it is going to cause all of us to lose our jobs. Now it's probably going to save our jobs."[17]

## Licensing and Franchising

In a **licensing agreement** a local firm pays a fee to a foreign firm for rights to make or sell its products.

Another form of international business is the **licensing agreement** whereby foreign firms pay a fee for rights to make or sell another company's products in a specified region. The license typically grants access to a unique manufacturing technology, special patent, or trademark. But, such licensing involves potential risk.[18] New Balance, for example, licensed a Chinese supplier to produce one of its brands. Even after New Balance revoked the license, the supplier continued to produce and distribute the shoes around Asia. It took costly and lengthy litigation in China's courts for New Balance to deal with the problem.[19]

In **franchising**, a fee is paid to a foreign business for rights to locally operate using its name, branding, and methods.

**Franchising** is a form of licensing in which the foreign firm buys the rights to use another's name and operating methods in its home country. The international version operates similar to domestic franchising agreements. Firms such as McDonald's, Wendy's, and Subway, for example, sell facility designs, equipment, product ingredients and recipes, and management systems to foreign investors, while retaining certain brand, product and operating controls.

## Joint Ventures and Strategic Alliances

**Insourcing** is job creation through foreign direct investment.

Sooner or later, some firms decide to make substantial investments in global operations. Foreign direct investment, or FDI, involves setting up and buying all or part of a business in another country. And, for many countries, the ability to attract foreign business investors has been a key to succeeding in the global economy. The term **insourcing** is often used to describe local job creation that results from foreign direct investment. Over 5 million U.S. jobs, for example, are linked to insourcing and China's foreign direct investment in the U.S. now runs close to $6 billion per year.[20]

A **joint venture** operates in a foreign country through co-ownership by foreign and local partners.

When foreign firms do invest in a new country, a common way to start is with a **joint venture**. This is a co-ownership arrangement in which the foreign and local partners agree to pool resources, share risks, and jointly operate the new business. Sometimes the joint venture is formed when a foreign partner buys part ownership in an existing local firm. In other cases it is formed as an entirely new operation that the foreign and local partners jointly start up together.

A **global strategic alliance** is a partnership in which foreign and domestic firms share resources and knowledge for mutual gains.

International joint ventures are types of **global strategic alliances** in which foreign and domestic firms work together for mutual benefit. Each partner hopes to gain through cooperation things they couldn't do or would have a hard time doing alone. For the local partner, an alliance may bring access to technology and opportunities to learn new skills. For the outside partner, an alliance may bring access to new markets and the expert assistance of locals that understand them and the local business context.

Joint ventures and strategic alliances pose potential risks, and partners must be carefully chosen.[21] Sometimes the goals of partners may not match, for example, when the foreign firm seeks profits and cost efficiencies while the local firm seeks maximum employment and acquisition of new technology.[22] Dishonesty and loss of business secrets are also risks. Not long ago GM executives noticed that a new car from a fast-growing local competitor, partially owned by GM's Chinese joint venture partner, looked very similar to one of its models. GM claims its design was copied. The competitor denied it and went on to become China's largest independent automaker, selling the "Chery" at home and abroad.[23]

> ### HOW TO CHOOSE A JOINT VENTURE PARTNER
>
> - Familiar with firm's major business
> - Employs a strong local workforce
> - Values its customers
> - Has potential for future expansion
> - Has strong local market
> - Has good profit potential
> - Has sound financial standing

## Foreign Subsidiaries

One way around some of the risks and problems associated with joint ventures and strategic alliances is full ownership of the foreign operation. A **foreign subsidiary** is a local operation completely owned and controlled by a foreign firm. These subsidiaries may be built ground up as so-called **greenfield ventures**. They can also be established by acquisition, where the outside firm purchases a local operation in its entirety.

A **foreign subsidiary** is a local operation completely owned by a foreign firm.

A **greenfield venture** is a foreign subsidiary built from the ground up by the foreign owner.

Although a foreign subsidiary represents the highest level of involvement in international operations, it can make very good business sense. When Nissan opened a plant in Canton, Mississippi, an auto analyst said: "It's a smart strategy . . . building more in their regional markets, as well as being able to meet consumers' needs more quickly."[24] The analyst could have also pointed out that this plant allowed Nissan to claim reputational benefits by dealing with American customers as a "local" employer rather than a "foreign" company.

# Global Business Environments

When Nissan comes to America or GM goes to China, a lot of what takes place in the foreign business environment is very different from what is common at home. Not only must global managers master the demands of operating with worldwide suppliers, distributors, customers, and competitors, they must deal successfully with many unique local challenges.

## Legal and Political Systems

Some of the biggest risk in international business comes from differences in legal and political systems. Global firms are expected to abide by local laws, some of which may be unfamiliar. And the more home-country and host-country laws differ, the harder it is for international businesses to adapt to local ways.

Common legal problems faced by international businesses involve incorporation practices and business ownership; negotiation and implementation of contracts with foreign parties; handling of foreign exchange; and intellectual property rights—patents, trademarks, and copyrights. You might know the intellectual property issue best in terms of movie and music downloads, sale of fake designer fashions, and software pirating. Companies like Microsoft, Sony, and Louis Vuitton know it as lost profits due to their products or designs being copied and sold as imitations by foreign firms. Microsoft CEO Steve Balmer says that it gets only about 5% of software revenues in China on the same number of computer sales as in the United States, and that pirated versions of its programs sell there for as little as $2.[25]

**Political risk** is the potential loss in value of a foreign investment due to instability and political changes in the host country.

Political turmoil, violence, and government changes constitute a further area of concern known as **political risk**—the potential loss in value of an investment in or managerial control over a foreign asset because of instability and political changes in the host country. The major threats of political risk today come from terrorism, civil wars, armed conflicts, and new government systems and policies. Although such things can't be prevented, they can be anticipated. Most global firms use a planning technique called **political-risk analysis** to forecast the probability of disruptive events that can threaten the security of a foreign investment. Consider, for example, the criminal drugs violence in Mexico. Gun battles, killings, and kidnappings are often in the news. What are the implications for business investors? Well, it's an exercise in political risk. So far, foreign investment in Mexico hasn't faltered. The country's proximity to the U.S. markets and low-cost skilled labor are still attractive. Gonzalo Cano, quality manager at a big Lego's plant in Monterrey, says: "Security is an issue but it does not get in the way. Companies are taking the long view."[26]

**Political-risk analysis** tries to forecast political disruptions that can threaten the value of a foreign investment.

## Trade Agreements and Trade Barriers

When international businesses believe they are being mistreated in foreign countries, or when local companies believe foreign competitors are disadvantaging them, their respective governments might take the cases to the **World Trade Organization**. The WTO is a global organization established to promote free trade and open markets around the world. Its member nations, presently 151 of them, agree to negotiate and resolve disputes about tariffs and trade restrictions.[27]

**World Trade Organization** member nations agree to negotiate and resolve disputes about tariffs and trade restrictions.

WTO members are supposed to give one another **most favored nation status**—the most favorable treatment for imports and exports. Yet trade barriers are still common. They include outright **tariffs**, which are basically taxes that governments impose on imports. They also include **nontariff barriers** that discourage imports in nontax ways. They include quotas, import restrictions, and other forms of **protectionism** that give favorable treatment to domestic businesses. Foreign firms complain, for example, that the Chinese government creates barriers that make it hard for them to succeed. A spokesperson for the U.S. Chamber of Commerce says that American multinationals like Caterpillar, Boeing, Motorola, and others, have been hurt by "systematic efforts by China to develop policies that build their domestic enterprises at the expense of U.S. firms."[28]

**Most favored nation status** gives a trading partner most favorable treatment for imports and exports.

**Tariffs** are taxes governments levy on imports from abroad.

**Nontariff barriers** to trade discourage imports in nontax ways such as quotas and government import restrictions.

**Protectionism** is a call for tariffs and favorable treatments to protect domestic firms from foreign competition.

One goal of most tariffs and protectionism is to protect local firms from foreign competition and save jobs for local workers. You can see such issues reflected in political campaigns and debates. And the issues aren't easy. Government leaders face the often conflicting goals of seeking freer international trade while still protecting domestic industries. Such political dilemmas create controversies for the WTO in its role as a global arbiter of trade issues. In one claim filed with the WTO, the United States complained that China's "legal structure for protecting and enforcing copyright and trademark protections" was "deficient" and not in compliance with WTO rules. China's response was that the suit was out of line with WTO rules and that "we strongly oppose the U.S. attempt to impose on developing members through this case."[29]

**ETHICS ON THE LINE**

> BOLIVIA'S PRESIDENT ANNOUNCED THAT HIS GOVERNMENT WAS NATIONALIZING "ALL NATURAL RESOURCES, WHAT OUR ANCESTORS FOUGHT FOR"

## When Nationalism Meets Protectionism, Who Wins?

AIZAR RALDES/AFP/Getty Images/Newscom

The headline read "Bolivia Seizes Control of Oil and Gas Fields." Although executives from the world's oil industry couldn't say that it wasn't anticipated, it still must have been a shocker when Bolivia's government announced that it was taking control of the country's oil and gas fields. The announcement said: "We are beginning by nationalizing oil and gas; tomorrow we will add mining, forestry, and all natural resources, what our ancestors fought for."

As soon as the announcement was made, Bolivia's armed forces secured all oil and gas fields in the country. The country's President Evo Morales set forth new terms that gave a state-owned firm 82% of all revenues, leaving 18% for the foreign firms. He said: "Only those firms that respect these new terms will be allowed to operate in the country." The implicit threat was that any firms not willing to sign new contracts would be sent home.

While foreign governments described this nationalization as an "unfriendly move," Morales considered it patriotic. His position was that any existing contracts with the state were in violation of the constitution, and that Bolivia's natural resources belonged to its people.

 **ETHICS QUESTIONS**

If you were the CEO at one of these global firms, how would you react to this nationalization? Do you resist and raise the ethics issue of honoring existing contracts with the Bolivian government? Or, do you comply and accept the new terms being offered? And as an everyday citizen of the world, do you agree or disagree with the argument that Bolivia's natural resources are national treasures that belong to the people, not foreign investors? Just what are the ethics of this decision to nationalize the oil and gas industry?

## Regional Economic Alliances

One of the characteristics of globalization is the growth of regional economic alliances, where nations agree to work together for economic gains. **NAFTA**, the North American Free Trade Agreement, is an example. Formed in 1994 by the United States, Canada, and Mexico, it created a trade zone that frees the flows of goods and services, workers, and investments among the three countries.

**NAFTA** is the North American Free Trade Agreement linking Canada, the United States, and Mexico in an economic alliance.

Many American firms have taken advantage of NAFTA by moving production facilities from the United States to Mexico, largely to benefit from lower wages paid to skilled Mexican workers. These job shifts have pros and cons, and NAFTA is still a hot topic in some political debates. Arguments on the positive side credit NAFTA with greater cross-border trade, greater productivity of U.S. manufacturers, and reform of the Mexican business environment. Arguments on the negative side blame NAFTA for substantial job losses to Mexico, lower wages being paid to American workers wanting to keep their jobs, and a wider trade deficit with Mexico.[30]

The **European Union** (EU) is a regional economic and political alliance of global importance. Indeed, the financial health of the EU is regularly in the news, as upswings and downswings in its economy affect the world at large. The EU now comprises 27

The **European Union** is a political and economic alliance of European countries.

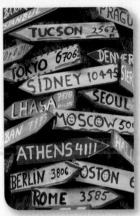

## "Focus on What You Do Best" and Gain from the World of Comparative Advantage

"Focus on what you do best," indeed. Does the message sound familiar? It's a common strategic management theme for organizations today. But, do you realize the words come from a book, *Principles of Political Economy and Taxation*, written in 1817 by British economist David Ricardo? He set forth the concept of comparative advantage where nations focus on their strengths, say agriculture or manufacturing, and trade with others to get the rest. Ricardo's theory is still a foundation for advocates of "free trade"—lowering trade barriers so that nations can fully benefit from comparative advantage. But not everyone thinks free trade is the route to travel. Perhaps this is a debate about which you have strong views.

Jerry Horbert/iStockphoto

The **euro** is now the common European currency.

countries that have agreed to support mutual interests by integrating themselves politically—there is now a European Parliament—and economically—member countries have removed barriers that previously limited cross-border trade and business development. Seventeen EU members are part of a common currency, the **euro**, that has grown to the point where it is a major alternative and competitor to the U.S. dollar in the global economy.

When one looks toward Asia and the Pacific Rim, 21 member nations established the *Asia Pacific Economic Cooperation* (APEC) to promote free trade and investment in the Pacific region. Businesses from APEC countries have access to a region of superstar economic status and containing some of the world's fastest growing economies such as China, Republic of Korea, Indonesia, Russia, and Australia. The market potential of member countries, close to 3 billion consumers, far exceeds NAFTA and the EU. Also in Asia, the 10 nations of the *Association of Southeast Asian Nations* (ASEAN) cooperate with a stated goal of promoting economic growth and progress.

Africa is also more and more center stage in world business headlines.[31] The region's economies are growing, the middle class is expanding, and there is a promising rise in entrepreneurship.[32] Companies like Harley-Davidson, Wal-Mart, Caterpillar, and Google are making their presence—and continental ambitions—known as they set up offices, invest in dealerships, and buy local companies.[33] The *Southern Africa Development Community* (SADC) links 14 countries of southern Africa in trade and economic development efforts. Its website posts this vision: "a future in a regional community that will ensure economic well-being, improvement of the standards of living and quality of life, freedom and social justice, and peace and security for the peoples of Southern Africa."[34]

---

**LEARNING CHECK 1**

**TAKEAWAY QUESTION 1 What are the management challenges of globalization?**

**Be sure you can** • define *globalization* and discuss its implications for international management • list five reasons companies pursue international business opportunities • describe and give examples of global sourcing, exporting/importing, franchising/licensing, joint ventures, and foreign subsidiaries • discuss how differences in legal environments can affect businesses operating internationally • explain the goals of the WTO • discuss the significance of regional economic alliances such as NAFTA, the EU, APEC, and SADC

# Global Businesses

If you travel abroad these days, many of your favorite brands and products will travel with you. You can have a McDonald's sandwich, follow it with a Haagen-Dazs ice cream, and then brush up with Procter & Gamble's Crest toothpaste. Economists even use the "Big Mac" index, which compares the U.S. dollar price of the McDonald's sandwich around the world, to track purchasing power parity among the world's currencies.[35]

**Global corporations**, also called **multinational enterprises** (MNEs) and **multinational corporations** (MNCs), are business firms with extensive international operations in many foreign countries. The largest global corporations are identified in annual listings such as *Fortune* magazine's Global 500 and the *Financial Times'* FT Global 500. They include familiar names such as Wal-Mart, BP, Toyota, Nestlé, BMW, Hitachi, Caterpillar, Sony, and Samsung, as well as others you might not recognize, such as the big oil and gas producers PetroChina (China), Gazprom (Russia), and Total (France).

| Big Mac Index 2011 | |
|---|---|
| United States | $4.07 |
| Australia | $4.94 |
| China | $2.27 |
| Euro area | $4.93 |
| Mexico | $2.74 |
| Sweden | $7.64 |
| Russia | $2.70 |

## Types of Global Businesses

Is there any doubt in your mind that Hewlett-Packard and General Motors are American firms, and that Sony and Honda are Japanese? Most likely not. But that may not be how their executives want the firms to be viewed. They and many other global firms act more like **transnational corporations** that do business around the world without being identified with one national home.[36]

Executives of transnationals view the entire world as their domain for acquiring resources, locating production facilities, marketing goods and services, and communicating brand image. The goal, says one, is to "source everywhere, manufacture everywhere, sell everywhere."[37] When shopping at an Aldi store or browsing Hugo Boss clothes, would you know they're German companies? And, which company is really more American—the Indian giant Tata, which gets some 50% of its revenues from North America, or IBM, which gets over 65% of its revenues from outside of the United States?[38]

A **global corporation** is a multinational enterprise (MNE) or multinational corporation (MNC) that conducts commercial transactions across national boundaries.

A **transnational corporation** is a global corporation or MNE that operates world-wide on a borderless basis.

## Pros and Cons of Global Businesses

What difference does a company's nationality make? Does it really matter to an American whether local jobs come from a domestic giant like IBM or a foreign one like Honda? How about size? Does it matter that Exxon/Mobil's revenues are larger than Sweden's GDP?[39] And what about wealth? Is what some call the "globalization gap"—large multinationals gaining disproportionately from globalization—a matter for social and personal concern?[40]

### Host-Country Issues

Global corporations and the countries that host them should ideally both reap benefits. But things can go right and wrong in these relationships.[41] The potential host-country benefits include larger tax bases, increased employment opportunities, technology transfers, introduction of new industries, and development of

FIGURE 5.2  **What should go right and what can go wrong in global corporation and host-country relationships.**

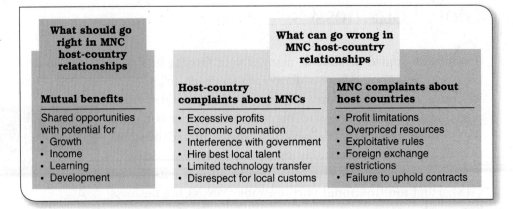

local resources. Potential host-country costs are also shown Figure 5.2. They include complaints that global corporations extract excessive profits, dominate the local economy, interfere with the local government, do not respect local customs and laws, fail to help domestic firms develop, hire the most talented of local personnel, and fail to transfer their most advanced technologies.

### Home-Country Issues

Global corporations can also get into trouble at home in the countries where they were founded and where their headquarters are located. Even as many global firms try to operate as transnationals, home-country governments and citizens still tend to identify them with local and national interests. They also expect the global firms to act as good domestic citizens.[42] Whenever a global business cuts back home-country jobs, or closes a domestic operation in order to shift work to lower-cost international destinations, the loss is controversial. Corporate decision makers are likely to be called upon by government and community leaders to reconsider and give priority to domestic social responsibilities. Other home-country criticisms of global firms include sending scarce investment capital abroad and engaging in corrupt practices in foreign settings.

## Ethics Challenges for Global Businesses

"Avon Products Says It Fired Four Executives Over Bribes" . . . "Mexico starts Investigation in Wal-Mart Bribery Case" . . . "International Effort Unveils Counterfeit Goods."[43] These are just a sampling of recent headlines. Where do you stand on the ethical issues challenging global businesses?

### Corruption

**Corruption** involves illegal practices to further one's business interests.

**Corruption** occurs when people engage in illlegal practices to further their personal business interests. It's a source of continuing controversy in any setting and often makes headline news in the international business context.[44] And, there is no doubt that corruption poses significant challenges for global managers. The civic society organization Transparency International is devoted to eliminating corrupt practices around the world. Its annual reports and publications track corruption and are a source of insight for executives and policy-makers alike.[45] But the issues aren't always neat and clear cut. An American executive, for example, says that payoffs are needed to get shipments through customs in Russia even though all legal taxes and tariffs are already paid. "We use customs brokers," he says, "and they build bribes into the invoice."[46]

> TRANSPARENCY INTERNATIONAL WANTS TO END THE "DEVASTATING IMPACT OF CORRUPTION ON MEN, WOMEN AND CHILDREN AROUND THE WORLD"

## Corruption and Bribes Haunt Global Business

If you want a world free of corruption and bribes, you have a lot in common with the global civil society organization Transparency International. TI's mission is to "create change for a world free of corruption." The organization publishes regular surveys and reports on corruption and bribery around the world. Here are some recent data.

**Corruption:** Best and worst out of 178 countries in perceived public sector corruption:

> *Best*—Denmark/New Zealand/Singapore (tie); Finland/Sweden (tie)
>
> *Worst*—Somalia; Myanmar/Afghanistan (tie); Iraq
>
> *In-Betweens*—Spain, Saudi Arabia, Brazil, China

**Bribery:** Best and worst of 20 countries in likelihood of home-country firms' willingness to pay bribes abroad:

> *Best*—Belgium/Canada (tie); Netherlands/Switzerland (tie); Germany
>
> *Worst*—Russia; China; Mexico; India; Italy/Brazil
>
> *In-Betweens*—Australia, France, United States, Spain, South Korea & Taiwan

 **YOUR THOUGHTS?**

Are there any patterns in these data? Does it surprise you that the United States didn't make the "best" lists? How could TI's website be used by a global business executive? Is there a meaningful difference between "corruption" and "bribery" in international business?

---

In the United States, the **Foreign Corrupt Practices Act (FCPA)** makes it illegal for U.S. firms and their representatives to engage in corrupt practices overseas.[47] They are not supposed to pay or offer bribes or excessive commissions—including nonmonetary gifts, to foreign officials in return for business favors.

Critics claim that the FCPA fails to recognize the realities of business as practiced in many foreign nations. They believe it puts U.S. companies at a competitive disadvantage because they can't offer the same "deals" or "perks" as businesses from other nations, deals locals may regard as standard business practices. But other nations, such as Great Britain with its Bribery Act, are starting to pass similar laws and the U.S. Department of Justice isn't backing down. Penalties levied by the U.S. government are now running over $1 billion per year.[48]

The **Foreign Corrupt Practices Act (FCPA)** makes it illegal for U.S. firms and their representatives to engage in corrupt practices overseas.

### Child Labor and Sweatshops

The facts are startling: 215 million child laborers worldwide, 115 million of them working in hazardous conditions.[49] **Child labor**—the employment of children to perform work otherwise done by adults, a major ethics issue that haunts global businesses as they follow the world's low-cost manufacturing from country to country. You've surely heard about its use to manufacture handmade carpets, but what about your favorite electronic device whose components are largely made by foreign suppliers?[50] When an internal audit by Apple Inc. discovered that five of its foreign contractors used underage workers, the firm's response was this: "We required the suppliers to support the younger workers' return to school and to improve their management systems—such as labor recruitment practices and age verification procedures—to prevent recurrences."[51]

**Child labor** is the employment of children for work otherwise done by adults.

**Sweatshops** employ workers at very low wages for long hours in poor working conditions.

Child labor isn't the only labor issue facing global managers. **Sweatshops**—business operations that employ workers at low wages for long hours in poor working conditions—are another concern. Microsoft, for example, is investigating complaints about workers being abused in a factory in China that supplies some of its electronic devices. The National Labor Committee, a U.S.-based human rights advocacy organization, claims that the Chinese factory owners were overworking employees and housing them in bad conditions. The NLC's director went so far as to say "the factory was really run like a minimum security prison." Microsoft's response was to send independent auditors "to conduct a complete and thorough investigation."[52]

---

**LEARNING CHECK 2**

**TAKEAWAY QUESTION 2** **What are global businesses, and what do they do?**

**Be sure you can** • differentiate a multinational corporation from a transnational corporation • list at least three host-country complaints and three home-country complaints about global business operations • give examples of corruption, sweatshops, and child labor in international businesses

---

# Culture and Global Diversity

*Situation:* A U.S. executive goes to meet a business contact in Saudi Arabia. He sits in the office with crossed legs and the sole of his shoe exposed. Both are unintentional signs of disrespect in the local culture. He passes documents to the host using his left hand, which Muslims consider unclean. He declines when coffee is offered, which suggests criticism of the Saudi's hospitality. *Results:* A $10 million contract is lost to a Korean executive better versed in Arab ways.[53]

**Culture** is a shared set of beliefs, values, and patterns of behavior common to a group of people.

**Culture shock** is the confusion and discomfort a person experiences when in an unfamiliar culture.

**Ethnocentrism** is the tendency to consider one's culture superior to others.

"Culture" matters, as we often say, and cultural miscues can be costly in international business and politics. **Culture** is the shared set of beliefs, values, and patterns of behavior common to a group of people.[54] **Culture shock** is the confusion and discomfort a person experiences when in an unfamiliar culture. Management Smarts is a reminder that these feelings must be mastered to travel comfortably and do business around the world.

## Management**Smarts**

### Culture Shock: Stages in Adjusting to a New Culture

- *Confusion:* First contacts with the new culture leave you anxious, uncomfortable, and in need of information and advice.
- *Small victories:* Continued interactions bring some "successes," and your confidence grows in handling daily affairs.
- *The honeymoon:* A time of wonderment, cultural immersion, and even infatuation, with local ways viewed positively.
- *Irritation and anger:* A time when the "negatives" overwhelm the "positives," and the new culture becomes a target of your criticism.
- *Reality:* A time of rebalancing; you are able to enjoy the new culture while accommodating its less desirable elements.

## Cultural Intelligence

The American's behavior in Saudi Arabia was self-centered; he ignored and showed no concern for the culture of his Arab host. This showed **ethnocentrism**, a tendency to view one's culture as superior to that of others. Some might excuse him as suffering from culture shock. Perhaps he was exhausted after a long international flight. Maybe he was so uncomfortable upon arrival that all he could think about was making a deal and leaving Saudi Arabia as quickly as possible. Still others might give him the benefit of the doubt as being well-intentioned but not having time to learn enough about Saudi culture before making the trip. But regardless of possible reasons for the cultural mistakes, they still worked to this executive's disadvantage. They also showed a lack of something critical to success in global management—**cultural intelligence**, the ability to adapt and adjust to new cultures.[55]

People with cultural intelligence are flexible in dealing with cultural differences and willing to learn from what is unfamiliar. They use that learning to self-regulate and modify their behaviors to act with sensitivity toward another culture's ways. In other words, someone high in cultural intelligence views cultural differences not as threats but as learning opportunities.[56]

Executives at China's Haier Group showed cultural intelligence in the way they responded to problems that popped up when the firm opened a factory in South Carolina.[57] Workers that make mistakes in Haier's Chinese factories are made to stand on special footprints and publicly criticize themselves by pointing out what they did wrong and what lessons they have learned. When this practice was implemented in the United States, American workers protested—they thought it was humiliating. But Haier executives didn't force the Americans to accept the practice; they changed it. The footprints and quality commitment still exist, but American workers stand in them as public recognition for exceptional work. Because the Chinese managers listened and learned from their American experiences, they ended up with a practice that fits both corporate values and the local culture.

> **Cultural intelligence** is the ability to accept and adapt to new cultures.

## Silent Languages of Culture

The capacities to listen, observe, and learn are building blocks of cultural intelligence. These skills and competencies can be developed by better understanding what anthropologist Edward T. Hall calls the "silent" languages of culture.[58] He believes that these silent languages are found in a culture's approach to context, time, and space.

### Context

If we look and listen carefully, Hall says we'll recognize how cultures differ in their use of language in communication.[59] Most communication in **low-context cultures** takes place via the written or spoken word. This is common in the United States, Canada, and Germany, for example. Americans in particular tend to say or write what they mean and mean what they say. Things aren't this way in many parts of the world.

In **high-context cultures** what is actually said or written may convey only part, and sometimes a very small part, of the real message. The rest must be interpreted from the situation, body language, physical setting, and even past relationships among the people involved. Dinner parties, social gatherings, and golf outings in high-context cultures such as Thailand and Malaysia, for example, are ways for potential business partners to get to know one another. Only after the social relationships are established and a context for communication exists is it possible to begin making business deals.

> **Low-context cultures** emphasize communication via spoken or written words.

> **High-context cultures** rely on nonverbal and situational cues as well as on spoken or written words in communication.

### Time

Hall describes differences in how cultures deal with time. People in **monochronic cultures** often do one thing at a time. It is common in the United States, for example, to schedule meetings with specific people and focus on a specific agenda

> In **monochronic cultures** people tend to do one thing at a time.

Igor Demchenkov/iStockphoto

## Silent Language Skills Do the Talking in China

Lots of people are doing business in China; many are working for employers with links to Chinese firms. What are the silent language lessons to remember? When meeting a Chinese counterpart, be sure to initiate the handshake when you are the lower ranking person. Act impressed when receiving a business card and don't quickly tuck it away. Don't point with your finger; use a folded hand with thumb on top. Mind your alcohol, but be ready to mix drinks with business during dinner. Speaking of dinner, get ready. There will be lots of new and interesting things on the menu. And don't eat too much too fast, the dishes may keep coming well past your "I'm full" point.

for an allotted time.[60] And if someone is late or brings an uninvited guest, we tend not to like it.

Members of **polychronic cultures** are more flexible toward time. They often try to work on many different things at once, perhaps not in any particular order, and give in to distractions and interruptions. A monochronic American visitor to the office of a polychronic Egyptian client may be frustrated. He may not get dedicated attention as the client greets and deals with a continuous stream of people flowing in and out of his office.

In **polychronic cultures** time is used to accomplish many different things at once.

### Space

The use of space is also one of the silent languages of culture. Hall describes these cultural tendencies in terms of **proxemics**, the study of how people use space to communicate.[61] Americans tend to like and value their own space, perhaps as much space as they can get. We like big offices, big cars, big homes, and big yards. We get uncomfortable in tight spaces and when others stand too close to us in lines. When someone "talks right in our face," we don't like it; the behavior may even be interpreted as an expression of anger.

**Proxemics** is how people use space to communicate.

Members of some cultures are quite comfortable surrounded by smaller spaces and closer physical distances. If you visit Japan you should notice very quickly that space is precious. Small homes, offices, and shops are the norm; gardens are tiny, but immaculate; public spaces are carefully organized for most efficient use; privacy is highly valued and protected. And in many Latin cultures the *abrazzo*, or strong embrace, is a common greeting. In Vietnam, men often hold hands or link arms as a sign of friendship when talking with one another.

## Tight and Loose Cultures

> *The nail that sticks up will be hammered down.*    Asian Proverb
>
> *The squeaking wheel gets the grease.*    American Idiom

Two sayings; two different cultural settings. What are their implications? Picture young children listening to parents and elders as they offer these words of wisdom. One child grows up being careful to not speak out, stand out, or attract attention. The other grows up trying to speak up and stand out in order to get attention.

# Personality Traits, Behavioral Competencies, and Expatriate Effectiveness

When organizations send employees to work as expatriates in foreign countries, the assignments can be challenging, and the expatriate's performance can turn out lower than anticipated. Nevertheless, many employers fail to make fully informed decisions on expatriate assignments. The results of three empirical studies reported in the *Journal of Applied Psychology* by Margaret Shaffer and her colleagues show that individual differences have an impact on expatriate effectiveness.

The researchers propose a model in which expatriate effectiveness is a function of individual differences in personalities and competencies. Specifically, they examine stable dispositions in terms of the "Big Five" personality traits (conscientiousness, emotional stability, agreeableness, intellectance, and extroversion) and the dynamic competencies of cultural flexibility, task orientation, people orientation, and ethnocentrism.

Data samples were gathered from expatriates working in Hong Kong and Korean expatriates working in other nations. Each of the Big Five traits, except conscientiousness, predicted some aspect of expatriate effectiveness. Emotional stability was the strongest predictor of withdrawal cognitions, while intellectance was the only predictor of task and contextual performance. The link between dynamic competencies and performance was less clear, and

**Expatriate Effectiveness Model**

**Individual Differences**
- Stable dispositions
- Dynamic competencies

**Expatriate Effectiveness**
- Adjustment
- Withdrawal cognitions
- Performance

the researchers believe that study design and/or the presence of unmeasured moderator variables might account for the mixed findings.

 **YOU BE THE RESEARCHER**

There may be international students in your class or on campus who have worked with or as expatriates. You may also have family and friends with expatriate experience. Why not interview them to gather their views about how expatriates adapt and perform in foreign cultures? Compare the results of your investigation with the model and findings of this research study.

*Reference:* Margaret A. Shaffer, David A. Harrison, Hal Gregersen, J. Steward Black, and Lori A. Ferzandi, "You Can Take It with You: Individual Differences and Expatriate Effectiveness," *Journal of Applied Psychology*, vol. 91 (2006), pp. 109–125.

---

The contrast in childhoods just described introduces the concept of **cultural tightness-looseness**. Scholars Michele J. Gelfand, Lisa H. Nishii, and Jana L. Raver describe it as "the strength of social norms and degree of sanctioning within societies."[62] Two things are at issue in this definition: (1) the strength of norms that govern social behavior, and (2) the tolerance that exists for any deviations from the norms. Empirical studies have classified 33 societal cultures around the world on their tightness and looseness.[63]

In a *tight culture*, such as ones found in Korea, Japan, or Malaysia, social norms are strong and clear. People know the prevailing norms and let them guide their behavior. They self-govern and try to conform. They also understand that any deviations are likely to be noticed, discouraged, and even sanctioned. The goal in tight cultures, as suggested in the Asian proverb, is to fit in with society's expectations and not stand out.

In a *loose culture*, such as ones found in Australia, Brazil, or Hungary, social norms are mixed and less clear cut. People may be more or less concerned with them, and conformity will vary a good deal. Deviations from norms tend to be tolerated unless they take the form of criminal behavior or reach toward the extremes

*Tight cultures*—Malaysia (tightest), South Korea, India, China, Japan

*Loose cultures*—Ukraine (loosest), Hungary, Netherlands, Brazil, Australia

## Management in Popular Culture

Brian Dowling/©AP/Wide World Photos

### Cultural Awareness Helps Find the Finish Line in *The Amazing Race*

The next time you watch an episode of "The Amazing Race," consider it a window into cultural awareness. The race pits teams of players in an around-the-world competition with challenges that are both physical and cultural. As contestants travel from one country to the next, they end up dealing with language barriers and customs unfamiliar to them—not to mention the jet lag. When Nat Strand and Kat Chang won the $1 million prize in Season 17, they were the first female team to do so. Their journey covered 30 cities, four continents, and 32,000 miles. They crossed a lot of national and cultural boundaries along the way, much as today's global executives do.

of morality. It is quite acceptable for individuals in loose cultures, as suggested in the American idiom, to show unique identities and express themselves independent from the masses.

It can be challenging to go from a tight to a loose culture, or vice-versa, for travel or work. This calls for lots of cultural awareness to understand differences and a similar amount of self-management to handle the differences well. One of the most common settings where the dynamics of tight and loose cultures play out is a course group or work team whose members come from different cultures. You've probably been there; what did you see and what might you expect?

A mix of cultural tightness and looseness on a cross-cultural team may result in soft or unstated conflict and missed performance opportunity. Members from tight cultures may be slow to volunteer, criticize, show emotion, or seek praise. They may look toward formal authority for direction while trying to always be on time and prepared. Members from loose cultures may be quick to voice opinion, criticize others, display emotions, and look for recognition. They may not show much respect for authority, and punctuality may be a hit-or-miss proposition. It takes a lot of cultural awareness for a team leader and team members to spot these culturally derived behaviors. And, it takes a lot of skill to create a team environment where everyone gets their chance to both contribute to team performance and take satisfaction from the experience.

## Values and National Cultures

The ideas of Geert Hofstede on value differences in national cultures are another useful way for considering how cultural differences can influence management and organizational practices. After studying employees of a global corporation operating in 40 countries, Hofstede identified four cultural dimensions: power distance, uncertainty avoidance, individualism–collectivism, and masculinity–femininity.[64] Later studies added a fifth called time orientation.[65]

Figure 5.3 shows how national cultures can vary on these dimensions. Imagine what these cultural differences might mean when global business executives try to

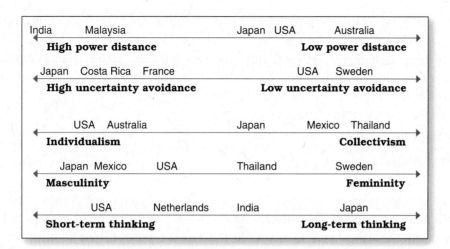

FIGURE 5.3  **How countries' short-term thinking and long-term thinking compare on Hofstede's dimensions of national culture.**

work and make deals around the world, or when representatives of national governments meet to seek agreements or resolve problems. But remember that Hofstede warns against falling prey to the **ecological fallacy**. This is acting with the mistaken assumption that a generalized cultural value, such as individualism in American culture or masculinity in Japanese culture, applies equally to all members of the culture.[66]

The **ecological fallacy** assumes that a generalized cultural value applies equally well to all members of the culture.

## Power Distance

**Power distance** is the degree to which a society accepts or rejects the unequal distribution of power among people in organizations and the institutions of society. In high-power-distance cultures we expect to find great respect for age, status, and titles. People in these cultures tend to be tolerant of power and are prone to follow orders and accept differences in rank. Picture a businesswoman from low-moderate rate power distance America visiting her firm's joint venture partner in high-power-distance Malaysia. Could her tendencies toward informality by using first names to address superiors and dressing casually in the office create discomfort for local executives less accustomed to such practices?

**Power distance** is the degree to which a society accepts unequal distribution of power.

## Individualism–Collectivism

**Individualism–collectivism** is the degree to which a society emphasizes individual accomplishments and self-interests versus collective accomplishments and the interests of groups.[67] The United States had the highest individualism score of any country in Hofstede's data. Do you find the "I" and "me" words used a lot in conversations and meetings, or even when students are making team presentations in class? Such expressions reflect a cultural tendency toward individualism. This contrasts with the importance placed on group harmony in the Confucian and more collectivist cultures of Asia, as pointed out in the chapter opener. What might go wrong when team members from individualistic cultures try to work with those from more collectivist ones?

**Individualism–collectivism** is the degree to which a society emphasizes individuals and their self-interests.

## Uncertainty Avoidance

**Uncertainty avoidance** is the degree to which a society is uncomfortable with risk, change, and situational uncertainty, versus having tolerance for them. Members of low-uncertainty-avoidance cultures display openness to change and innovation. In

**Uncertainty avoidance** is the degree to which a society tolerates risk and uncertainty.

high-uncertainty-avoidance cultures, by contrast, one would expect to find a preference for structure, order, and predictability. Persons in these cultures may have difficulties dealing with ambiguity, tend to follow rules, and prefer structure in their lives. Could high uncertainty avoidance be one of the reasons why Europeans seem to favor employment practices that provide job security?

## Masculinity–Femininity

**Masculinity–femininity** is the degree to which a society values assertiveness and materialism.

**Masculinity–femininity** is the degree to which a society values assertiveness and materialism versus feelings, relationships, and quality of life.[68] You might think of it as a tendency for members of a culture to show stereotypical masculine or feminine traits and reflect different attitudes toward gender roles. Visitors to Japan, with the highest masculinity score in Hofstede's research, may be surprised at how restricted career opportunities can still be for women. The *Wall Street Journal* has pointed out that "In Japan, professional women face a set of socially complex issues—from overt sexism to deep-seated attitudes about the division of labor." One female Japanese manager says: "Men tend to have very fixed ideas about what women are like."[69]

## Time Orientation

**Time orientation** is the degree to which a society emphasizes short-term or long-term goals.

**Time orientation** is the degree to which a society emphasizes short-term or long-term goals and gratifications.[70] American tendencies toward impatience and desire for quick, even instantaneous, gratifications show short-term thinking. Even our companies are expected to achieve short-term results; those failing to meet quarterly financial targets often suffer immediate stock price declines. Many Asian cultures are quite the opposite, displaying Confucian values of persistence, thrift, patience, and willingness to work for long-term success. This might help explain why Japan's auto executives were more willing than their American counterparts to invest years ago in hybrid engine technologies even though market demand was very low and any return on the investments would take a long time to materialize.

---

**LEARNING CHECK 3**

**TAKEAWAY QUESTION 3 What is culture, and how does it impact global management?**

**Be sure you can** • define *culture* • explain how ethnocentrism can create difficulties for people working across cultures • differentiate between low-context and high-context cultures, and monochronic and polychronic cultures • explain the differences between tight and loose cultures • list and illustrate Hofstede's five dimensions of value differences among national cultures

---

## Global Management Learning

**Comparative management** studies how management practices differ among countries and cultures.

Scholars in the area of **comparative management** study how management perspectives and practices systematically differ among countries and cultures.[71] They use the cultural models just described for Hall, Gelfand et al., and Hofstede, as well as those of others, in the search for meaningful insights on management around the globe.[72]

# Are Management Theories Universal?

You might think that all the management theories in this book and your course apply universally from one country and culture to the next. They don't. Differences in economic, legal-political, soiciocultural, technological, and natural environmental conditions all affect management. If anything, management scholars agree that the world is a very complicated place with lots left to understand.[73]

Geert Hofstede, whose framework for understanding national cultures was just discussed, worries that many management theories are ethnocentric because they come from a single cultural context, often North American.[74] He points out, for example, that the American emphasis on participation in leadership reflects the culture's moderate stance on power distance. The cultures of France and some Asian countries with higher power-distance scores, by contrast, show more tolerance for hierarchy and directive leadership. Hofstede also notes that the American cultural value of individualism shows up in management theories on individual performance, rewards, and job design. These theories may be less applicable in countries where cultural values are more collectivist. Sweden, for example, has a history of redesigning jobs for groups of workers rather than for individuals.

**FOLLOW THE STORY**    > "ANYONE WHO BREAKS THE LAW, NO MATTER FOREIGN OR DOMESTIC, BIG OR SMALL, WILL BE PUNISHED. IT IS A WARNING TO THEM."

## Wal-Mart Finds It Holds a Chinese Tiger by the Tail

SHI TOU/Newscom

"What we want is to be more effective than a local retailer because we are global. But to be so locally relevant that we are not disadvantaged against other retailers." These comments by Wal-Mart International's CEO Doug McMillon describe his vision for the firm's global reach—now cutting across 27 countries and 4,800+ stores. But vision is one thing; accomplishment is another. Wal-Mart is expanding internationally at a faster rate than within the United States. But, it's running into some rough spots.

*Dateline Chongqing, China:* After ordinary pork was found labeled as organic pork in a local Wal-Mart, the authorities closed all 13 of the company's Chongqing stores for two weeks, arrested two employees and detained 35 others, and fined Wal-Mart 3.65 million Yuan or $573,000. "Wal-Mart has been quick in admitting their wrongdoings, but slow in correcting them," said Tang Chuan of the local Bureau of Inspection and Enforcement. "Anyone who breaks the law, no matter foreign or domestic, big or small, will be punished. It is a warning to them." Wal-Mart accepted the penalties and pledged cooperation to operate its stores in ways that "exceed customer expectations." Shortly thereafter, the CEO and the human resources vice president for Wal-Mart China resigned.

Observers generally agree that Wal-Mart faces greater pressures as China's local and national governments assert themselves more and support local companies. But while a Chongqing customer said that local competitors are catching up and "are not known for cheating on quality or price," others saw the legal crackdown as a form of protectionism. An analyst with the Brookings Institution in Washington warned: "There has been concern across China that foreign companies like Wal-Mart will drive out Chinese competitors in a powerful way."

### WHAT'S YOUR TAKE?

Doug McMillon's responsibilities extend around the world. How can he keep up with everything? Is this situation in China one that he or others should have been more on top of? Or, is this situation indicative of a country that will do what it can to support local business development in the face of foreign competition? And if, as a Western lawyer says, "foreign companies in China have no effective remedies, judicial, administrative, or political, to counter what might be capricious governmental activities," is China's huge market worth the risk of huge investments?

## Intercultural Competencies

**Intercultural competencies** are skills and personal characteristics that help us be successful in cross-cultural situations.

Even though management theories are not always universal, it may well be that **intercultural competencies** are. These are skills and personal characteristics that help us function successfully in cross-cultural situations.

Intercultural competencies are "must haves" for anyone seeking career success as a global manager. They begin with but add specifics to the notion of cultural awareness that introduced this chapter. Rather than just a generalized openness to learning about other cultures and sensitivity to different cultural ways, the focus is on acting competent when working in another culture or in culturally-mixed settings. What scholars know in this regard is summarized in three pillars of intercultural competency-perception management, relationship management, and self management.[75]

In terms of *perception management* a person must be inquisitive and curious about cultural differences, and be flexible and nonjudgmental when interpreting and dealing with situations in which differences are at play. In terms of *relationship management* a person must be genuinely interested in others, sensitive to their emotions and feelings, and able to make personal adjustments while engaging in cross cultural interactions. In terms of *self management* a person must have a strong sense of personal identity, understand their own emotions and values, and be able to stay self confident even in situations that call for personal adaptations because of cultural differences.

**Foundations for Global Management Success**

*Goal:* Global Knowledge

*Goal:* Intercultral Competency

*Goal:* Management Skills

## Global Learning Goals

The small figure shows that intercultural competencies are essential global learning goals. They are irreplaceable foundations for success in cross-cultural work situations. It helps to think of them as the glue that binds together the benefits of global knowledge on the one hand with good solid management skills and systems understanding on the other.

We should always be strengthening our personal intercultural competencies, especially if we aspire to careers as global managers. And, we should always be looking everywhere and anywhere in the world for new management ideas. Our home country and home culture have no lock on good management and the best organizational practices. The intent of comparative management studies is to engage in critical thinking about the way managers around the world do things and about how they might do them better. As we try to engage in global management learning, however, we should hesitate before accepting any idea or practice as a universal prescription for action. Culture and cultural differences always have to be considered. As Hofstede once said: "Disregard of other cultures is a luxury only the strong can afford . . . increase in cultural awareness represents an intellectual and spiritual gain."[76]

---

**LEARNING CHECK 4**

**TAKEAWAY QUESTION 4 How can we benefit from global management learning?**

**Be sure you can** • describe the concept of global organizational learning • Define *intercultural competency* and identify three of its major components • answer this question: "Do management theories apply universally around the world?"

# MANAGEMENT LEARNING REVIEW

## LEARNING CHECK SUMMARY

### TAKEAWAY QUESTION 1 What are the management challenges of globalization?

- Global managers are informed about international developments and are competent in working with people from different cultures.
- The forces of globalization create international business opportunities to pursue profits, customers, capital, and low-cost suppliers and labor in different countries.
- Market entry strategies for international business include global sourcing, exporting and importing, and licensing and franchising.
- Direct investment strategies of international business establish joint ventures or wholly owned subsidiaries in foreign countries.
- General environment differences, including legal and political systems, often complicate international business activities.
- Regional economic alliances such as NAFTA, the EU, and SADC link nations of the world with the goals of promoting economic development.
- The World Trade Organization is a global institution that promotes free trade and open markets around the world.

**For Discussion What aspects of the U.S. legal-political environment could prove difficult for a Chinese firm setting up a factory in America?**

### TAKEAWAY QUESTION 2 What are global businesses, and what do they do?

- A global corporation is a multinational enterprise or multinational corporation with extensive operations in multiple foreign countries.
- A transnational corporation tries to operate globally without a strong national identity and with a worldwide mission and strategies.
- Global corporations can benefit host countries by offering broader tax bases, new technologies, and employment opportunities.
- Global corporations can cause problems for host countries if they interfere in local government, extract excessive profits, and dominate the local economy.

- The U.S. Foreign Corrupt Practices Act prohibits American multinational corporations from engaging in bribery and corrupt practices abroad.

**For Discussion Is the Foreign Corrupt Practices Act unfair to American firms trying to compete for business around the world?**

### TAKEAWAY QUESTION 3 What is culture, and how does it impact global management?

- Culture is a shared set of beliefs, values, and behavior patterns common to a group of people.
- Culture shock is the discomfort people sometimes experience when interacting with persons from cultures different from their own.
- Cultural intelligence is an individual capacity to understand, respect, and adapt to cultural differences.
- Hall's "silent" languages of culture include the use of context, time, and interpersonal space.
- Hofstede's five dimensions of value differences in national cultures are power distance, uncertainty avoidance, individualism–collectivism, masculinity–femininity, and time orientation.

**For Discussion Should religion be included on Hall's list of the silent languages of culture?**

### TAKEAWAY QUESTION 4 How can we benefit from global management learning?

- The field of comparative management studies how management is practiced around the world and how management ideas are transferred from one country or culture to the next.
- The foundations for intercultural competency are found in perception management, relationship management, and self management.
- Because management practices are influenced by cultural values, global management learning must recognize that successful practices in one culture may work less well in others.

**For Discussion Even though cultural differences are readily apparent, is the tendency today for the world's cultures to converge and become more alike?**

## Multiple-Choice Questions

1. The reasons why businesses go international include gaining new markets, finding investment capital, and reducing _____.
   (a) political risk     (b) protectionism
   (c) labor costs     (d) most favored nation status

2. When shoe maker Rocky Brands decided to buy full ownership of a manufacturing company in the Dominican Republic, Rocky was engaging in which form of international business?
   (a) import/export     (b) licensing
   (c) foreign subsidiary     (d) joint venture

3. A form of international business that falls into the category of a direct investment strategy is _____.
   (a) exporting     (b) joint venture
   (c) licensing     (d) global sourcing

4. The World Trade Organization would most likely become involved in disputes between countries over _____.
   (a) exchange rates     (b) ethnocentrism
   (c) nationalization     (d) tariffs

5. Business complaints about copyright protection and intellectual property rights in some countries illustrate how differences in _____ can impact international operations.
   (a) legal environments
   (b) political stability
   (c) sustainable development
   (d) economic systems

6. In _____ cultures, members tend to do one thing at a time; in _____ cultures, members tend to do many things at once.
   (a) monochronic, polychronic
   (b) polycentric, geocentric
   (c) collectivist, individualist
   (d) neutral, affective

7. A culture that places great value on expressing meaning in the written or spoken word is described as _____ by Hall.
   (a) monochronic     (b) proxemic
   (c) collectivist     (d) low-context

8. It is common in Malaysian culture for people to value teamwork and to display great respect for authority. Hofstede would describe this culture as high in both _____.
   (a) uncertainty avoidance and feminism
   (b) universalism and particularism
   (c) collectivism and power distance
   (d) long-term orientation and masculinity

9. In Hofstede's study of national cultures, America was found to be the most _____ compared with other countries in his sample.
   (a) individualistic     (b) collectivist
   (c) feminine     (d) long-term oriented

10. It is _____ when a foreign visitor takes offense at a local custom such as dining with one's fingers, considering it inferior to practices of his or her own culture.
    (a) universalist     (b) prescriptive
    (c) monochronic     (d) enthnocentric

11. When Limited Brands buys cotton in Egypt, has tops sewn from it in Sri Lanka according to designs made in Italy, and then offers the garments for sale in the United States, this form of international business is known as _____.
    (a) licensing     (b) importing
    (c) joint venturing     (d) global sourcing

12. The difference between an international business and a transnational corporation is that the transnational _____.
    (a) tries to operate around the world without a strong national identity
    (b) does business in only one or two foreign countries
    (c) is led by ethnocentric managers
    (d) is based outside North America

13. The Foreign Corrupt Practices Act makes it illegal for _____.
    (a) Americans to engage in joint ventures abroad
    (b) foreign businesses to pay bribes to U.S. government officials
    (c) U.S. businesses to make payoffs abroad to gain international business contracts
    (d) foreign businesses to steal intellectual property from U.S. firms operating in their countries

14. When a member of a cross-cultural team is hesitant to speak up and offer ideas, defers to the team leader, and avoids accepting praise for individual work, the person is displaying characteristics consistent with a _____ culture.
    (a) monochronic     (b) low-context
    (c) tight     (d) loose

15. Hofstede would describe a culture whose members respect age and authority and whose workers defer to the preferences of their supervisors as _____.
    (a) low masculinity     (b) high particularism
    (c) high power distance     (d) monochronic

## Short-Response Questions

**16.** Why do host countries sometimes complain about how global corporations operate within their borders?

**17.** Why is the "power-distance" dimension of national culture important in management?

**18.** What is the difference between a culture that is tight and one that is loose?

**19.** How do regional economic alliances impact the global economy?

## Essay Question

**20.** Kim has just returned from her first business trip to Japan. While there, she was impressed with the intense use of work teams. Now back in Iowa, she would like to totally reorganize the workflows and processes of her canoe manufacturing company and its 75 employees around teams. There has been very little emphasis on teamwork, and she now believes this is "the way to go." Based on the discussion of culture and management in this chapter, what advice would you offer Kim?

# MANAGEMENT SKILLS AND COMPETENCIES

# Further Reflection: Cultural Awareness

The forces of globalization are often discussed in respect to job migration, outsourcing, currency fluctuations, and the fortunes of global corporations. These and other similar issues best understood and dealt with in a context of **cultural awareness**. It's only natural that we become habitual and used to the ways of our culture. But many of these same values and patterns of behavior can be called into question when we work and interact with persons from different cultures. Although comfortable to us, our ways of doing things may seem strange. At the extreme they may even come across as offensive to others who come from different cultural backgrounds. It's only natural for cultural differences to be frustrating and even threatening when we come face to face with them. You should find the ideas and models discussed in this chapter are a good basis for cultural understanding.

 DO IT NOW . . .
**LOOK IN THE MIRROR**

- Take advantage of global diversity on your college campus to test your behavior in real cross-cultural situations.
- Observe and criticize yourself as you meet, interact with, and otherwise come into contact with persons from other cultures.
- Jot notes on what you perceive as cultural differences and on your "first tendencies" in reacting to these differences.
- Make a list of what could be your strengths and weaknesses as a global manager.
- Write down personal reflections on your capacity to work well across cultural boundaries.

# Self-Assessment: Global Intelligence

## Instructions

Use the following scale to rate yourself on each of these 10 items:[77]

1 Very Poor
2 Poor
3 Acceptable
4 Good
5 Very Good

1. I understand my own culture in terms of its expectations, values, and influence on communication and relationships.

2. When someone presents me with a different point of view, I try to understand it rather than attack it.

3. I am comfortable dealing with situations where the available information is incomplete and the outcomes are unpredictable.

4. I am open to new situations and am always looking for new information and learning opportunities.

5. I have a good understanding of the attitudes and perceptions toward my culture as they are held by people from other cultures.

6. I am always gathering information about other countries and cultures and trying to learn from them.

7. I am well informed regarding the major differences in the government, political, and economic systems around the world.

8. I work hard to increase my understanding of people from other cultures.

9. I am able to adjust my communication style to work effectively with people from different cultures.

10. I can recognize when cultural differences are influencing working relationships, and I adjust my attitudes and behavior accordingly.

## Interpretation

To be successful in the global economy, you must be comfortable with the cultural diversity that it holds. This requires a global mind-set that is receptive to and respectful of cultural differences, global knowledge that includes the continuing quest to know and learn more about other nations and cultures, and global work skills that allow you to work effectively across cultures.

## Scoring

The goal is to score as close to a perfect "5" as possible on each of the three dimensions of global intelligence. Develop your scores as follows:

1. Items (1 + 2 + 3 + 4)/4 = *Global Mindset Score*
2. Items (5 + 6 + 7)/3 = *Global Knowledge Score*
3. Items (8 + 9 + 10)/3 = *Global Work Skills Score*

# Team Exercise: American Football

## Instructions

Form into groups as assigned by the instructor. In the group do the following:[78]

1. Discuss "American Football"—the rules, the way the game is played, the way players and coaches behave, and the roles of owners and fans.

2. Use "American Football" as a metaphor to explain the way U.S. corporations run and how they tend to behave in terms of strategies and goals.

3. Prepare a class presentation for a group of visiting Japanese business executives. In this presentation, use the metaphor of "American Football" to (1) explain American business strategies and practices to the Japanese, and (2) critique the potential strengths and weaknesses of the American business approach in terms of success in the global marketplace.

## Career Situations in Global Management: What Would You Do?

1. **To Buy or Not to Buy**   You've just read in the newspaper that the maker one of your favorite brands of sports shoes is being investigated for using sweat-shop at factories in Asia. It really disturbs you, but the shoes are great! One of your friends says it's time to boycott the brand. You're not sure. Do you engage in a personal boycott or not, and why?

2. **China Beckons**   Your new design for a revolutionary golf putter has turned out to be a big hit with friends and members of the local golf course. You decide to have clubs with your design manufactured in China so that you can sell them to pro shops around the country. The question is: how can you make sure that your design won't be copied by the manufacturer and

then used to create a competing business? Is there any way you can protect your design and still get the manufacturing done in China? What should you do in this situation?

3. **Cross-Cultural Teamwork**   Incredible! You've just been asked to join a team being sent to Poland for 10 days to discuss with your firm's Polish engineers a new software development project. It's your first business trip out of the country. In fact, you've only been to Europe once, as part of a study tour when in college. How will you prepare for the trip and for work with Polish colleagues? What worries you the most under the circumstances? After all, if you do well here more international assignments are likely to come your way.

## Case Study

# Harley-Davidson

Go to *Management Cases for Critical Thinking* to find the recommended case for Chapter 5—"Harley-Davidson: Style and Strategy Have Global Reach."

Although the company has been exporting motor-cycles ever since it was founded, it was not until the late 1980s that Harley-Davidson management began to think seriously about going international. New ads were developed specifically for different foreign markets and the firm's famous rallies were adapted to fit local customs. The company also began to actively recruit and develop dealers in Europe and Japan. It purchased a Japanese distribution company and built a large parts warehouse in Germany.

Harley reached the point where it became the number one motorcycle brand in five European countries, and number two in four countries. Harley has learned a lot from its international activities and continues to make inroads in over-seas markets including China and India. But its competitors are watching every move and they're not going to sit still and let Harley's dominate the highways of the world.

Jeff Chiu/©AP/Wide World Photos

# Wisdom
## Learning
## From Others

### > ENTREPRENEURS ARE CHANGING OUR WORLD

Are you a FarmVille or CityVille or Empires & Allies player? If so, you're well into the world of Zynga—the online gaming brainchild of Marc Pincus.[1]

Self-described as having one part the DNA of an entrepreneur and second part the DNA of a competitive gamer, Pincus built Zynga to tap what he observed as the many opportunities of a new "app economy." And it's been a success so far—players log in for over 2 billion minutes each day.

Pincus didn't just create Zynga; he created it with a fun culture heavy on creativity and light on corporate control. Chefs cook meals—why waste time going out for food? A masseuse is on staff—who needs stress? And, yes, you can bring your pet to work.

Visiting Zynga's offices and looking for Pincus? He's just another guy in jeans and a loose shirt. But don't let appearances fool you; he's all business. There's a lot at stake as the online gaming industry grows more competitive every day. Zynga has launched HTML5 games compatible across mobile devices and the Web, it's embedded in Facebook and also running its own Zynga Direct game portal.

Like FarmVille's crops, Zynga's business keeps growing. Pincus is doing his best to make sure it has all the care and nourishment it needs.

## MORE TO LOOK FOR INSIDE>

# Entrepreneur-ship and New Ventures

6

## > SELF-MANAGEMENT

The many challenges of work and everyday living in uncertain times call upon our capacities for **self-management**. It's an ability to use objective understanding of personal strengths and weaknesses to keep improving and growing—individually and career-wise. Self-management is an essential skill that asks you to dig deep and continually learn from experience.

To be strong in self-management, you'll need lots of self-awareness plus the ability to self-regulate. In other words, you must have the ability to understand yourself as a person and in relationships with others, exercise initiative, accept responsibility for good and bad behavior and accomplishments, and keep adapting for self-improvement.

Look at the self-management tips.[2] These and other foundations for career success are within everyone's grasp. But the motivation and the effort required to succeed must come from within.

Only you can make the commitment to take charge of your destiny and become a self-manager.

## Insight
## Learning About Yourself

### SELF-MANAGEMENT TIPS FOR CAREER SUCCESS

**Perform to your best.** No matter what the assignment, you must work hard to quickly establish your credibility and work value.

**Be and stay flexible.** Don't hide from ambiguity. Don't wait for structure. You must always adapt to new work demands, new situations, and new people.

**Keep the focus.** You can't go forward without talent. Be a talent builder—always adding to and refining your talents to make them valuable to an employer.

**Figure out what you love to do and then do it well.** Practice makes perfect. Like a professional golfer, you have to hit lots and lots of practice balls in order to make perfect shots during the match.

**Don't give up; certainly never give up too soon.** You have to stick with it, even during tough times. Remember—resilience counts. If you have talent and know what you love, go for it. Self-management is a way to realize your dreams.

## BUILD MANAGEMENT SKILLS AND COMPETENCIES AT END OF CHAPTER

- Engage in *Further Reflection on Self-Management*
- Take the *Self-Assessment—Entrepreneurial Orientation*
- Complete the *Team Exercise—Entrepreneurs Among Us*
- Solve the *Career Situations for Entrepreneurs*
- Analyze the *Case Study—"In-N-Out Burger: Building a New Burger"*

## <GET TO KNOW YOURSELF BETTER

# Entrepreneurship and New Ventures

6

## The Nature of Entrepreneurship

- Who are the entrepreneurs?
- Characteristics of entrepreneurs
- Women and minority entrepreneurs
- Social entrepreneurship

## Entrepreneurship and Small Business

- Why and how to get started
- Web-based business models
- Family businesses
- Why small businesses fail
- Small business development

## New Venture Creation

- Life cycles of entrepreneurial firms
- Writing the business plan
- Choosing the form of ownership
- Financing the new venture

**LEARNING CHECK 1**          **LEARNING CHECK 2**          **LEARNING CHECK 3**

*Need a job? Why not create one?* That's what Jennifer Wright did after the financial crisis shut down her work as a credit analyst. While back at school in an MBA program she tweaked a friend's idea for a better pizza box and entered it in an entrepreneurship competition. She says the feedback was "so incredibly positive I felt I'd be crazy not to pursue this." Her "green box" breaks into plates and a storage container before it goes for recycling.

*Retired, feeling a bit old, and want to do more?* Not to worry; people aged 55 to 64 are the most entrepreneurially active in the United States. Realizing that he needed "someplace to go and something to do" after retirement, Art Koff, now 74, started RetireBrains.com. It's a job board for retirees that gets thousands of hits a day. It also employs seven people and keeps Koff as busy as he wants to be.

*Struggling with work–life balance as a mother?* Why not find flexibility and opportunity in entrepreneurship? Denise Devine did. Once a financial executive with Campbell Soup Co., she now has her own line of fiber-rich juice drinks for kids. Called **mompreneurs**, women like Devine find opportunity in market niches for safe, useful, and healthy products they spot as moms. Says Devine: "As entrepreneurs we're working harder than we did, but we're doing it on our own schedules."[3]

*Female, thinking about starting a small business, but don't have the money?* Get creative and reach out. You might find help with organizations like Count-Me-In. Started by co-founders Nell Merlino and Iris Burnett, it offers "microcredit" loans of $500 to $10,000 to help women start and expand small

**Mompreneurs** pursue business opportunities they spot as mothers.

businesses. Borrowers qualify by a unique credit scoring system that doesn't hold against them things such as a divorce, time off to raise a family, or age—all things that might discourage conventional lenders. Merlino says: "Women own 38% of all businesses in this country, but still have far less access to capital than men because of today's process."[4]

Are these examples inspiring? Hopefully so. In fact, this is really a chapter of examples. The goal is not only to inform, but also to get you thinking about starting your own business, becoming your own boss, and making your own special contributions to society. What about it? Can we count you in to join the world of entrepreneurship and small business management?

## The Nature of Entrepreneurship

The term **entrepreneurship** describes strategic thinking and risk-taking behavior that results in the creation of new opportunities. H. Wayne Huizenga started Waste Management with just $5,000 and once owned the Miami Dolphins. He says: "An important part of being an entrepreneur is a gut instinct that allows you to believe in your heart that something will work even though everyone else says it will not."[5]

**Entrepreneurship** is risk-taking behavior that results in new opportunities.

### Who Are the Entrepreneurs?

A **classic entrepreneur** is a risk-taking individual who takes action to pursue opportunities others fail to recognize, or even view as problems or threats. Some people become **serial entrepreneurs** that start and run new ventures over and over again, moving from one interest and opportunity to the next. We find such entrepreneurs both in business and nonprofit settings.

A **classic entrepreneur** is someone willing to pursue opportunities in situations others view as problems or threats.

A **serial entrepreneur** starts and runs businesses and nonprofits over and over again, moving from one interest and opportunity to the next.

On the business side, H. Wayne Huizenga, mentioned earlier, is a serial entrepreneur who made his fortune founding and selling businesses like Blockbuster Entertainment, Waste Management, and AutoNation. A member of the Entrepreneurs' Hall of Fame, he describes being an entrepreneur this way: "We're looking for something where we can make something happen: an industry where the competition is asleep, hasn't taken advantage. The point is, we're going to be busy."[6]

On the nonprofit side, Scott Beale is also a classic entrepreneur. He quit his job with the U.S. State Department to start Atlas Corps, something he calls a "Peace Corps in reverse." The organization brings nonprofit managers from India and Colombia to the United States to volunteer for local nonprofits while improving their management skills. After a year they return to a nonprofit in their home countries. "I am just like a business entrepreneur," Beale says, "but instead of making a big paycheck I try to make a big impact."[7]

A common pattern among successful entrepreneurs is **first-mover advantage**. They move quickly to spot, exploit, and deliver a product or service to a new market or an unrecognized niche in an existing one. Consider some other brief examples of entrepreneurs who were willing to take risks and sharp enough to pursue first-mover advantage.[8]

A **first-mover advantage** comes from being first to exploit a niche or enter a market.

### Caterina Fake

From idea to buyout it only took 16 months. That's quite a benchmark for would-be Internet entrepreneurs. Welcome to the world of Flickr, co-founded by Caterina Fake. Flickr took the notion of online photo sharing and turned it into an almost viral Internet phenomenon. Startup capital came from families, friends, and angel investors. The payoff came when Yahoo! bought them out for $30 million. Fake then started Hunch.com, a website designed to help people make decisions (e.g., should I buy that Porsche?). She sold it to eBay for $80 million. She says: "You pick a big, ambitious problem, and look for great people to solve it."

Peter Foley/Bloomberg/Getty Images, Inc.

### Earl Graves

Bebeto Matthews/©AP/Wide World Photos

Earl G. Graves, Sr. started *Black Enterprise* magazine with a vision and a $175,000 loan. Its success grew into the diversified business information company Earl G. Graves Ltd.—a multimedia venture spanning television, radio, and digital media including BlackEnterprise.com. Graves' accomplishments led *Fortune* magazine to call him one of the 50 most powerful and influential African Americans in corporate America. The author of the best-selling book, *How to Succeed in Business Without Being White*, Graves received a Lifetime Achievement Award from the National Association of Black Journalists. He is a member of many business and nonprofit boards, and the business school at his college alma mater—Baltimore's Morgan State University, is named after him. Graves says: "I feel that a large part of my role as publisher of *Black Enterprise* is to be a catalyst for Black economic development in this country."

### Anita Roddick

In 1973, Anita Roddick was a 33-year-old housewife looking for a way to support herself and her two children. She spotted a niche for natural-based skin and health-care products, and started mixing and selling them from a small shop in Brighton, England. It became Body Shop, a global retailer selling a product every half-second around the world. Known for her commitment to human rights, the environment, and economic development, Roddick was an early advocate of "profits with principles" and business social responsibility. She once said: "If you think you're too small to have an impact, try going to bed with a mosquito."

David Montgomery/Getty Images, Inc.

### Shawn Corey Carter

You probably know him as Jay Z, and there's an entrepreneurial story behind the name. Carter began rapping on the streets of Brooklyn where he lived with his single mom and three brothers. Hip Hop turned into his ticket to travel. "When I left the block," he told an interviewer, "everyone was saying I was crazy, I was doing well for myself on the streets, and cats around me were like, these rappers . . . just record, tour, and get separated from their families, while some white person takes all their money. I was determined to do it differently." He sure did. Carter used his music millions to found the media firm Roc Nation, co-found the apparel firm Rocawear, and become part owner of the New Jersey Nets.

## Characteristics of Entrepreneurs

Andrew Milligan/PA Photos/Landov LLC

Entrepreneurs and entrepreneurship are everywhere and there is no age prerequisite to join them. For starters, consider these stories of two "young" entrepreneurs. At the age of 22, Richard Ludlow turned down a full-time job offer and an MBA admission to start New York's Academic Earth. It's an online location for posting and sharing faculty lectures and other educational materials. His goal is to both make a profit and help society by lowering the cost of education. While in high school Jasmine Lawrence created her own natural cosmetics after having problems with a purchased hair relaxer. Products from her firm, Eden Body Works, can now be found at Wal-Mart and Whole Foods.[9]

There are lots of entrepreneurs to be found in any community. Just look around at those who take the risk of buying a local McDonald's or Subway Sandwich or Papa John's franchise, open a small retail shop selling used video games or bicycles, start a self-employed service business such as financial planning or management consulting, or establish a nonprofit organization to provide housing for the homeless or deliver hot meals to house-bound senior citizens. All are entrepreneurs in their own ways.[10]

Is there something in your experience that could be a pathway to business or nonprofit entrepreneurship? As you think about this question, don't let the myths shown in Management Smarts discourage you.[11]

### Attitudes and Personal Interests

Research suggests that entrepreneurs tend to share certain attitudes and personal characteristics. The general profile is an individual who is very self-confident, determined, re-

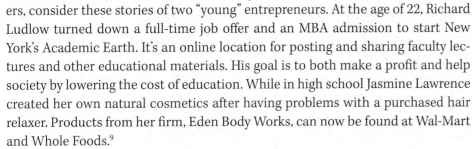

## Management**Smarts**

### Challenging the myths about entrepreneurs

- *Entrepreneurs are born, not made.*

Not true! Talent gained and enhanced by experience is a foundation for entrepreneurial success.

- *Entrepreneurs are gamblers.*

Not true! Entrepreneurs are risk-takers, but the risks are informed and calculated.

- *Money is the key to entrepreneurial success.*

Not true! Money is no guarantee of success. There's a lot more to it than that; many entrepreneurs start with very little.

- *You have to be young to be an entrepreneur.*

Not true! Age is no barrier to entrepreneurship; with age often comes experience, contacts, and other useful resources.

- *You have to have a degree in business to be an entrepreneur.*

Not true! You may not need a degree at all. Although a business degree is not necessary, it helps to study and understand business fundamentals.

silient, adaptable, and driven by excellence.[12] You should be able to identify these attributes in the prior examples. Look also at the typical personality traits and characteristics of entrepreneurs shown in Figure 6.1 and described here:[13]

- *Internal locus of control:* Entrepreneurs believe that they are in control of their own destiny; they are self-directing and like autonomy.
- *High energy level:* Entrepreneurs are persistent, hardworking, and willing to exert extraordinary efforts to succeed.
- *High need for achievement:* Entrepreneurs are motivated to accomplish challenging goals; they thrive on performance feedback.
- *Tolerance for ambiguity:* Entrepreneurs are risk takers; they tolerate situations with high degrees of uncertainty.
- *Self-confidence:* Entrepreneurs feel competent, believe in themselves, and are willing to make decisions.
- *Passion and action orientation:* Entrepreneurs try to act ahead of problems; they want to get things done and not waste valuable time.
- *Self-reliance and desire for independence:* Entrepreneurs want independence; they are self-reliant; they want to be their own bosses, not work for others.
- *Flexibility:* Entrepreneurs are willing to admit problems and errors, and are willing to change a course of action when plans aren't working.

## Background, Experiences, and Interests

Entrepreneurs tend to have unique backgrounds and personal experiences.[14] *Childhood experiences and family environment* seem to make a difference. Evidence links entrepreneurs with parents who were entrepreneurial and self-employed. And entrepreneurs are often raised in families that encourage responsibility, initiative, and independence. Another issue is *career or work history*. Entrepreneurs who try one venture often go on to others. Prior work experience in the business area or industry being entered is helpful.

Figure 6.1 **Personality traits and characteristics of entrepreneurs.**

A report in the *Harvard Business Review* further suggests that entrepreneurs may have unique and *deeply embedded life interests*.[15] The article describes entrepreneurs as having strong interests in starting things. They enjoy creative production—things like project initiation, working with the unknown, and finding unconventional solutions. Entrepreneurs also have strong interests in running things. They enjoy enterprise control—being in charge, being held accountable, and making decisions while moving others toward a goal.

Entrepreneurs also tend to emerge during certain *windows of career opportunity*. Most start their businesses between the ages of 22 and 45, an age spread that seems to allow for risk taking. However, age shouldn't be viewed as a barrier. When Tony DeSio was 50, he founded the Mail Boxes Etc.

chain. He sold it for $300 million when he was 67 and suffering heart problems. Within a year he launched PixArts, another franchise chain based on photography and art. When asked by a reporter what he liked most about entrepreneurship, DeSio replied: "Being able to make decisions without having to go through layers of corporate hierarchy—just being a master of your own destiny."[16]

## Women and Minority Entrepreneurs

When economists speak about entrepreneurs, they differentiate between ones driven by a quest for new opportunities and ones driven by absolute need. Those in the latter group pursue **necessity-based entrepreneurship,** meaning that they start new ventures because they have few or no other employment and career options. This was the case for Anita Roddick, the Body Shop founder introduced earlier. She said her entrepreneurship began because she needed "to create a livelihood for myself and my two daughters, while my husband, Gordon, was trekking across the Americas."[16]

Necessity-driven entrepreneurship is one way for people, including women and minorities who have hit the "glass ceiling" in their careers or are otherwise cut off from other employment choices, to strike out on their own and gain economic independence. One survey of women who left private-sector employment to work on their own found 33% saying they were not being taken seriously by their prior employer and 29% saying they had experienced glass ceiling issues.[17] As to entrepreneurship by women of color, the report *Women Business Owners of Color: Challenges and Accomplishments* points out that the glass ceiling problems include not being recognized or valued by their employers, not being taken seriously, and seeing others promoted ahead of them.[18]

The National Foundation for Women Business Owners (NFWBO) reports that women own close to 8 million of U.S. non-farm businesses. Their firms account for just over 6% of U.S. employment and are forecast to create one-third of the 15+ million new jobs predicted by 2018.[19] Although the top four industries for women entrepreneurs are the same as for men—construction, manufacturing, wholesale trade, and retail trade, a Kauffman report notes that only 19.8% of the female business owners earned $100,000+ per year compared to 32.8% for men. The report states that women "seem to be encountering 'glass walls' that keep their businesses from expanding."[20]

The last U.S. small business census identified almost 2 million small firms owned by African Americans, a growth of 60% over prior numbers and representing 7% of total businesses. Among new start-ups in 2010, 9% were led by African American entrepreneurs and 23% by Latinos.[21] Even with this record of accomplishment the obstacles to minority entrepreneurship, as with female entrepreneurs, are real and shouldn't be underestimated. Less than 1% of the available venture capital in the United States goes to minority entrepreneurs. High unemployment and declining wealth among black households also make it hard to find start-up financing. In an effort to address such issues the U.S. Minority Business Development Agency of the Department of Commerce has set up a nationwide network of 40 business development centers with the goal of helping them grow in "size, scale, and capacity."[22]

**Necessity-based entrepreneurship** takes place because other employment options don't exist.

## Minority Entrepreneurs Lead the Way

Economic necessity and career difficulties may help explain the growth of minority entrepreneurship. Consider these facts and trends.

- Minority-owned firms in America contribute $1 trillion annually to the economy.
- Minority-owned firms employ close to 6 million workers, with the largest employers Asian owned (2.9 million jobs), Hispanic owned (1.9 million jobs), and African American owned (921,000 jobs).
- If minorities owned businesses in proportion to their share of the U.S. population they would own more than 8 million firms and provide more than 17 million jobs.

- Minority businesses export to 41 countries on six continents, and generate twice the export activity of nonminority firms.

 **YOUR THOUGHTS?**

What factors can help or hinder the growth of minority-owned businesses? Should we invest more in minority entrepreneurship as a good way to fight economic disparities in society? What can be done to reduce or eliminate obstacles minorities and women face on their pathways toward entrepreneurship?

## Social Entrepreneurship

Speaking of entrepreneurship, don't forget it can play an important role in tackling social issues: housing and job training for the homeless; bringing technology to poor families; improving literacy among disadvantaged youth; reducing poverty and improving nutrition in communities. These examples and others like them are all targets for **social entrepreneurship**, a form of ethical entrepreneurship that seeks novel ways to solve pressing social problems. Social entrepreneurs take risks and create **social enterprises** whose missions are to help make lives better for underserved populations.[23]

**Social entrepreneurship** is a unique form of ethical entrepreneurship that seeks novel ways to solve pressing social problems.

**Social enterprises** have a social mission to help make lives better for underserved populations.

Social entrepreneurs and their enterprises, both nonprofit and for-profit, come up with new ways to meet needs that are not being sufficiently served through governments or the private sector.[24] *Fast Company* magazine tries to spot and honor social entrepreneurs that run their organizations with "innovative thinking that can transform lives and change the world." Here are two winners on its Honor Roll of Social Enterprises of the Year.[25]

- Chip Ransler and Manoj Sinha—tackled the lack of power in many of India's poor villages. As University of Virginia business students, they realized that 350 million people lived in India's rice-growing regions without reliable electricity. After discovering that tons of rice husks were being discarded with every harvest, Ransler and Sinha started Husk Power Systems. It creates biogas from the husks and uses the gas to fuel small power plants.
- Rose Donna and Joel Selanikio—tackled public health problems in sub-Saharan Africa. After realizing that public health services in developing nations are often bogged down in paperwork, they created software to make the process quicker and more efficient while increasing the reliability of databases. The UN, the World Health Organization, and the Vodafone Foundation are now helping their firm, DataDyne, move the program into 22 other African nations.

FOLLOW THE STORY > FRUGAL LIVING IN A RURAL HOME PLUS ENTREPRENEURIAL SKILLS LAUNCHED AN ALTERNATIVE ENERGY BUSINESS.

# Entrepreneurs Find Rural Setting Fuels Solar Power

Christian Baird Photography

When she was named as a recipient of the Ohio Department of Development's Keys to Success Award, Michelle Greenfield said: "It's exciting. It's kind of nice to be recognized as a good business owner. The goal is not to have the award: the goal is to have a good business and do well." She and her husband Geoff are co-founders of Third Sun Solar Wind and Power, Ltd.

The Greenfields began by building a rural home that used solar power in rural Athens county, Ohio. As friends became interested they helped others get into solar and the business kept growing from there. Soon after its birth, Third Sun moved into the Ohio University Innovation Center, a business incubator dedicated to helping local firms grow and prosper. Michelle says that they lived very frugally in their rural home and this helped them start the business on a low budget.

They have also benefited from tapping the local workforce in a university town and from having MBA students work with their firm in consulting capacities.

Third Sun has been ranked by *Inc.* magazine as the 32nd fastest-growing energy business in the United States. It is the largest provider of solar energy systems in the Midwest and experienced a 390% growth in three years—quite a story for an idea that began with a sustainable home! As the company grew, Geoff focused on technical issues while Michelle focused on business and managerial ones. She's now the CEO and primarily concerned with strategic issues.

Michelle is proud of her accomplishments and says: "I think it's nice to be able to point out that there are women in the field who also have enough brains to be successful." She also points out that the name "Third Sun . . . " was chosen to represent a "third son" for the couple, one requiring lots of nurturing in order to help it grow big and strong.

 **YOUR TAKE?**

What entrepreneurial characteristics are evident in Michelle's story? Is this an example of necessity-driven entrepreneurship, or is it one of making a great connection between personal interests and market opportunities? How easy would it be for others to take this path of building a business on principles of sustainability? What "growth" problems do you think Third Sun will have to master along the road to future success?

---

Lots of social entrepreneurship takes place without much notice. It flies under the radar, so to speak, as most attention often goes to business entrepreneurs making lots of money. But you should find social entrepreneurs right in your own community. Lewisville, Texas, for example, is the home of the housekeeping service Buckets & Bows, owned by Deborah Sardone. She became alarmed after noticing that many of her clients with cancer struggled hard with everyday household chores. Her response to this problem was to start Cleaning for a Reason. It's a nonprofit that builds networks of linkages with cleaning firms around the country whose owners are willing to offer free home cleaning to cancer patients.[26]

**LEARNING CHECK 1**

**TAKEAWAY QUESTION 1 What is entrepreneurship and who are the entrepreneurs?**

**Be sure you can** • define *entrepreneurship* and differentiate between classic and serial entrepreneurs • list key personal characteristics of entrepreneurs • explain the influence of background and experience on entrepreneurs • discuss motivations for entrepreneurship by women and minorities • define *social entrepreneurship* and *social enterprise*

## Entrepreneurship and Small Business

A **small business** has fewer than 500 employees, is independently owned and operated, and does not dominate its industry.

The U.S. Small Business Administration (SBA) defines a **small business** as one that has 500 or fewer employees, is independently owned and operated, and does not dominate its industry. Just over 99% of American businesses meet this definition. They provide employment for just over 55% of private-sector workers and create as many as 6 out of every 10 new jobs in the economy.[27] Small businesses employ 40% of high-tech workers such as scientists, engineers, and computer programmers. They produce more patents per employee than do large firms, receive 35% of federal government contract dollars, and export more than $500 billion worth of goods and services annually.[28] The most common small business areas are restaurants, skilled professions such as craftspeople and doctors, general services such as hairdressers and repair shops, and independent retailers.[29] The vast majority of small businesses employ fewer than 20 persons and over half are home based.

## Why and How to Get Started

There are many reasons why people start their own small businesses. They range from necessity, as discussed earlier as a stimulus to entrepreneurship, to wanting to be your own boss, control your future, and fulfill a dream.[30] Interestingly, the Gallup-Healthways Well-Being Index points to high satisfaction among small business owners. Self-employed business and store owners outrank working adults in 10 other occupations—including professional, manager/executive, and sales—on such factors as job satisfaction and emotional and physical health.[31]

A **franchise** is when one business owner sells to another the right to operate the same business in another location.

Once a decision is made to go the small business route, the most common ways to get involved are to start one, buy an existing one, or buy and run a **franchise**—where a business owner sells to another the right to operate the same business in another location. A franchise such as Subway, Quiznos, or Domino's Pizza runs under the original owner's business name and guidance. In return, the franchise parent receives a share of income or a flat fee from the franchisee.

A **business model** is a plan for making a profit by generating revenues that are greater than costs.

Any business—large or small, franchise or startup, needs a solid underlying **business model.** Think of this as a plan for making a profit by generating revenues

Brian Ramsay/Modesto Bee/ZUMA Press/Alamy

### Etsy Turns "Handmade" Into Entrepreneurship

Etsy's mission is described as empowering people and creating "a world in which very-very small businesses have much-much more sway in shaping the economy . . ." The original idea came from painter and photographer Rob Kalin who wanted an online market for his works. Along with Chris Maguire and Haim Schoppik he founded Etsy as an online marketplace where artisans could showcase their work and link with customers. The business model was as neat as a hand-stitched quilt: take a 3.5% transaction fee and 20¢ listing charge, and sell ads to artists. And it worked. Etsy now has 14 million members.

that are greater than the costs of doing business. Serial entrepreneur Steven Blank calls business **startups** temporary organizations that are trying "to discover a profitable, scalable business model."[32] In other words, a startup is just that—a "start"; it's a new venture that the entrepreneur is hoping will take shape and prove successful as things move forward.

Blank's advice for those starting up a new venture is to move fast and create a "minimum viable product" that will attract customers, and that can be further developed and made more sophisticated over time. An example is Facebook, which started with simple message sharing and quickly grew into the complex social media operation we know today. Blank also favors something called a **lean startup**. It takes maximum advantage of things like open-source software and free Web services to save on costs, while staying small and keeping operations as simple as possible.[33]

## Web-Based Business Models

Web access, open-source software, and social media have created major opportunities in **Internet entrepreneurship**—direct use of the Internet to pursue startup activities. Although giant firms like Amazon.com, Google, and Netflix may jump to mind, the Internet is also a major opportunity to create any variety of small web-based businesses. Just take a look at the action on eBay and imagine how many people are now running small trading businesses from their homes. A sample of proven web-based business models includes:

- **Advertising model**—providing free information or services and then generating revenues from paid advertising made available to viewers (e.g., Yahoo!, Google).
- **Brokerage model**—bringing buyers and sellers together for online business transactions and taking a percentage from the sales (e.g., eBay, Priceline).
- **Community model**—providing a meeting point sold by subscription or supported by advertising (e.g., eHarmony, Facebook).
- **Freemium model**—offering a free service and encouraging users to buy extras (e.g., Skype, Zynga).
- **Infomediary model**—providing free service in exchange for collecting information on users and selling it to other businesses (e.g., Epinions, Yelp).
- **Merchant model**—e-tailing or selling products direct to customers through the Web (e.g., Amazon, Netflix).
- **Referral model**—providing free listings and getting referral fees from online merchants for directing potential customers to them (e.g., Shopzilla, PriceGrabber).
- **Subscription model**—selling access to high-value content through a subscription website (e.g., Wall Street Journal Interactive, Consumer Reports Online).

## Family Businesses

In the little town of Utica, Ohio, there is a small child's desk in the corner of the president's office at Velvet Ice Cream Company. Its purpose is to help grow the next generation of leadership for the firm. "That's the way Dad did it," says Luconda Dager, the current head of the firm. "He exposed us all to the business at an early age." She and her two sisters, now both vice presidents, started working at the firm when they were 13 years old. And when it came time for Joseph Dager to retire and pass the business on to the next generation, he said: "It is very special for me to pass the baton to my oldest daughter. Luconda has been with us for 15 years. She understands and breathes the ice cream business, and there is no one better suited for this position."[34]

A **family business** is owned and controlled by members of a family.

Velvet Ice Cream is the classic **family business,** one owned and financially controlled by family members. The Family Firm Institute reports that family businesses account for 78% of new jobs created in the United States and provide 60% of the nation's employment.[35] These family businesses must solve the same problems of other small or large businesses—meeting the challenges of strategy, competitive advantage, and operational excellence. When everything goes right, as in the Velvet Ice Cream case, the family firm is almost an ideal situation—everyone working together, sharing values and a common goal, and knowing that what they do benefits the family. But it doesn't always work out this way or stay this way. Indeed, family businesses often face unique problems.

**RESEARCH BRIEF**

# Do Founders of New Ventures Take Less Compensation than Other Senior Managers in Their Firms?

In an article published in the *Academy of Management Journal*, Noam Wasserman examines two theories that might explain the founders' approaches to compensation. *Stewardship theory* argues that founders are likely to act as "stewards" of the firms they create, derive more psychic rewards from their roles in the enterprise, and, thus, take less monetary compensation. *Agency theory* argues that nonfounders are "agents" hired by founders to work in their behalf; agency costs are incurred because the interests of the founders and agents may diverge. Incentive compensation is one way of reducing those agency costs.

Wasserman hypothesized that founders will act more like stewards and nonfounders more like agents. He used data from 1,238 executives in 528 private companies to test his ideas. Results confirmed his hypotheses, with an interesting twist. Founders holding higher amounts of equity in a private firm earn less monetary compensation. Wasserman describes this as a "founder's discount," saying they essentially "pay to be founders" and take more "soft" compensation in the form of psychic rewards.

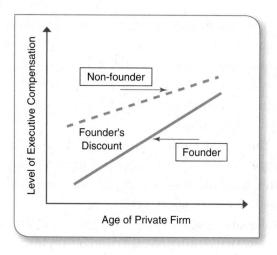

**YOU BE THE RESEARCHER**

Would you have predicted that founders may often get more psychic satisfactions than monetary compensation from their

firms? Could this be explained by the fact that they own most of the assets and will thus profit more in the long run, especially if the company is sold? Suppose founders gave more equity to other executives and lower-level employees? Is it possible that we would find that these firms would grow faster and prosper more than others?

*Reference:* Noam Wasserman, "Stewards, Agents and the Founder Discount: Executive Compensation in New Ventures," *Academy of Management Journal,* vol. 49 (2006), pp. 960–76.

"Okay, Dad, so he's your brother. But does that mean we have to put up with inferior work and an erratic schedule that we would never tolerate from anyone else in the business?"[36] This complaint introduces a problem that can all too often set the stage for failure in a family business—the **family business feud**. Simply put, members of the controlling family get into disagreements about work responsibilities, business strategy, operating approaches, finances, or other matters. The example is of an intergenerational problem, but the feud can be between spouses, among siblings, or between parents and children. It really doesn't matter. Unless family disagreements are resolved to the benefit of the business itself, the firm will have difficulty surviving in a highly competitive environment.

A **family business feud** occurs when family members have major disagreements over how the business should be run.

Family businesses can also suffer from the **succession problem**—transferring leadership from one generation to the next. A survey of small and midsized family businesses indicated that 66% planned on keeping the business within the family.[37] But the management question is: How will the assets be distributed, and who will run the business when the current head leaves? A family business that has been in operation for some time is often a source of both business momentum and financial wealth. Ideally, both are maintained in the succession process. But data on succession are eye-opening. About 30% of family firms survive to the second generation; only 12% survive to the third; and only 3% are expected to survive beyond that.[38]

The **succession problem** is the issue of who will run the business when the current head leaves.

Business advisers recommend having a **succession plan**—a formal statement that describes how the leadership transition and related financial matters will be handled when the time for changeover arrives. A succession plan should include procedures for choosing or designating the firm's new leadership, legal aspects of any ownership transfer, and financial and estate plans relating to the transfer. This plan should be shared and understood among all affected by it. And, the chosen successor should be prepared through experience and training to perform in the new role when the time comes.

A **succession plan** describes how the leadership transition and related financial matters will be handled.

## Why Small Businesses Fail

Small businesses have a high failure rate—one high enough to be intimidating. The SBA reports that as many as 60 to 80% of new businesses fail in their first five years of operation.[39] Part of this is a "counting" issue—the government counts as a "failure" any business that closes, whether it is because of the death or retirement of an owner, sale to someone else, or inability to earn a profit.[40] Nevertheless, the fact is that a lot of small business startups don't make it.

FIGURE 6.2 **Eight reasons why many small businesses fail.**

As shown in Figure 6.2, most small business failures are the result of insufficient financing, bad judgment, and management mistakes. These include:[41]

- *Insufficient financing*—not having enough money available to maintain operations while still building the business and gaining access to customers and markets.

- *Lack of experience*—not having sufficient know-how to run a business in the chosen market or geographical area.

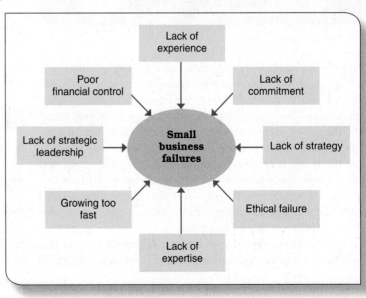

- *Lack of expertise*—not having expertise in the essentials of business operations, including finance, purchasing, selling, and production.
- *Lack of strategy and strategic leadership*—not taking the time to craft a vision and mission, nor to formulate and properly implement a strategy.
- *Poor financial control*—not keeping track of the numbers, and failure to control business finances and use existing monies to best advantage.
- *Growing too fast*—not taking the time to consolidate a position, fine-tune the organization, and systematically meet the challenges of growth.
- *Lack of commitment*—not devoting enough time to the requirements of running a competitive business.
- *Ethical failure*—falling prey to the temptations of fraud, deception, and embezzlement.

**ETHICS ON THE LINE**

> FOR EACH PAIR OF SHOES IT SELLS, THIS CARING CAPITALISM FIRM DONATES ANOTHER PAIR TO NEEDY CHILDREN

## Entrepreneurship Meets Caring Capitalism Meets Big Business

Todd Williamson/Getty Images, Inc.

Would you buy shoes just because they're also pledged to philanthropy? Blake Mycoskie, founder of TOMS Shoes, wants you to. Former President Bill Clinton once called him "the most interesting entrepreneur I've ever met."

Mycoskie's journey to entrepreneurship began on the reality TV show, *The Amazing Race*, which whetted his appetite for travel. He had a revelation while visiting Argentina and after coming face-to-face with lots of young children without shoes. He would return home and start a sustainable business to help address the problem. He named the business TOMS, short for "better tomorrow."

TOMS sells shoes made in a classic Argentinean style, but with a twist. For each pair of shoes sold TOMS donates a pair to needy children. Mycoskie calls this One for One, a "movement" that involves "people making everyday choices that improve the lives of children." The business model is caring capitalism or profits with principles.

TOMS has expanded to include eyewear. Buy a pair and the firm will pay for saving someone's eyesight with prescription glasses and medical care. Further expansion seems likely.

Who knows what the future holds for TOMS if it grows to the point where corporate buyers loom. It's happened to profits-with-principles businesses in the past. Ben & Jerry's is now owned by Unilever and Tom's of Maine is owned by Colgate-Palmolive. At least one state, Maryland, is concerned about such things. It passed a law creating the "benefit corporation" as a new legal entity. It is designed to protect firms whose charters spell out special values; it also requires them to report their social benefit activities and impact.

### ETHICS QUESTIONS

Is TOMS' business model one that other entrepreneurs should adopt? Is it ethical to link personal philanthropic goals with the products that your business sells? When an entrepreneurial firm is founded on a caring capitalism model, is it ethical for a future buyer of the business to reduce or limit the emphasis on social benefits? Is Maryland's concept of the benefit corporation the way we should be heading?

# Small Business Development

Individuals who start small businesses face a variety of challenges. Even though the prospect of being part of a new venture is exciting, the realities of working through complex problems during setup and the early life of the business can be especially daunting. Fortunately, there is often some assistance available to help entrepreneurs and owners of small businesses get started.

One way that startup difficulties can be managed is through participation in a **business incubator**. These are special facilities that offer space, shared administrative services, and management advice at reduced costs. The goal is helping new businesses become healthy enough to survive on their own. Some incubators are focused on specific business areas such as technology, light manufacturing, or professional services; some are located in rural areas, while others are urban based; some focus only on socially responsible businesses.

Regardless of their focus or location, business incubators hope to increase the survival rates for new startups. They want to help build new businesses that will create new jobs and expand economic opportunities in their local communities. An example is Y Combinator, an incubator located in Mountain View, California. It was founded by Paul Graham with a focus on Web businesses, and supports about 10 startups at any given time. Member entrepreneurs get offices, regular meetings with Graham and other business experts, and access to potential investors. They also receive $15,000 grants in exchange for the incubator taking a 6% ownership stake. Y Combinator hopes to capture a significant return on such investments as the new businesses succeed.[42]

Another source of assistance for small business development is the U.S. Small Business Administration. Because small business plays such a significant role in the economy, the SBA works with state and local agencies as well as the private sector to support a network of over 1,100 **Small Business Development Centers** (SBDCs) nationwide.[43] These SBDCs offer guidance to entrepreneurs and small business owners, actual and prospective, on how to set up and manage business operations. They are often associated with colleges and universities, and some give students a chance to work as consultants with small businesses at the same time that they pursue their academic programs.

> **Business incubators** offer space, shared services, and advice to help get small businesses started.

> **Small Business Development Centers** founded with support from the U.S. Small Business Administration provide advice to new and existing small businesses.

---

**LEARNING CHECK 2**

**TAKEAWAY QUESTION 2 What is special about small business entrepreneurship?**

**Be sure you can** • give the SBA definition of *small business* • illustrate opportunities for starting a Web-based business • discuss the succession problem in family-owned businesses and possible ways to deal with it • list several reasons why many small businesses fail • explain how business incubators work and how both they and SBDCs can help new small businesses

---

# New Venture Creation

Whether your interest is low-tech or high-tech, online or bricks and mortar, opportunities for new ventures are always there for the true entrepreneur. You start with good ideas and the courage to give them a chance. But then you must master the test of strategy and competitive advantage. Can you identify a market niche on

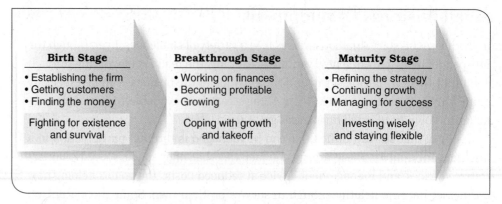

| **Birth Stage** | **Breakthrough Stage** | **Maturity Stage** |
|---|---|---|
| • Establishing the firm<br>• Getting customers<br>• Finding the money | • Working on finances<br>• Becoming profitable<br>• Growing | • Refining the strategy<br>• Continuing growth<br>• Managing for success |
| Fighting for existence<br>and survival | Coping with growth<br>and takeoff | Investing wisely<br>and staying flexible |

FIGURE 6.3 **Stages in the life cycle of an entrepreneurial firm.**

a new market that is being missed by other established firms? Can you generate first-mover advantage by exploiting a niche or entering a market before competitors? Do you have a viable business model? These are among the questions that entrepreneurs must ask and answer in the process of beginning a new venture.

## Life Cycles of Entrepreneurial Firms

Figure 6.3 describes the stages common to the life cycles of entrepreneurial companies. It shows relatively typical progression from birth to breakthrough to maturity.

The firm begins with the *birth stage*—where the entrepreneur struggles to get the new venture established and survive long enough to test the viability of the underlying business model in the marketplace. The firm then passes into the *breakthrough stage*—where the business model begins to work well, growth is experienced, and the complexity of managing the business operation expands significantly. Next comes the *maturity stage*—where the entrepreneur experiences the advantages of market success and financial stability, while also facing the continuing management challenge of remaining competitive in a changing environment.

Entrepreneurs often face control problems and other management dilemmas when their firms start to grow rapidly. The problems often involve the different

Kathy Willens/AP/Wide World Photos

## Grad School Startup Takes On Big Competitors

Why are fashionable glasses so expensive? When four classmates at Wharton's MBA program tackled this question they concluded it was because the industry was an oligopoly controlled by a few firms. They wrote a Web-driven business plan to sell cheap but fashionable eyewear. That plan became the firm Warby Parker with its mission "to create boutique-quality, classically crafted eyewear at a revolutionary price point." By offering glasses for as low as $95—frames with Rx lenses and free shipping—on the Web, with policies like "free home try-ons," and using the same suppliers as the major brands, Warby Parker quickly sold over 50,000 pairs. The company has a social mission, too: For every pair they sell they donate one pair to someone in need.

skills needed for entrepreneurial leadership in the early life cycle stages versus strategic leadership in the later ones. Entrepreneurial leadership brings the venture into being and sees it through the early stages of life. Strategic leadership manages and leads the venture into maturity as an ever-evolving and still-growing enterprise. If the founding entrepreneur doesn't have the skills or interests required to meet the firm's strategic leadership needs, its continued success may depend on selling to other owners or passing on day-to-day management to professionals.

## Writing the Business Plan

When people start new businesses or launch new units within existing ones, they can benefit from a good **business plan**. This plan describes the details needed to obtain startup financing and operate a new business.[44] Banks and other financiers want to see a business plan before they loan money or invest in a new venture; senior managers want to see a business plan before they allocate scarce organizational resources to support a new entrepreneurial project. And, there's good reason for this.

The detailed thinking required to prepare a business plan can contribute to the success of the new initiative. It forces the entrepreneur to think through important issues and challenges before starting out. Ed Federkeil, who founded a small business called California Custom Sport Trucks, says: "It gives you direction instead of haphazardly sticking your key in the door every day and saying, 'What are we going to do?'"[45] More thoughts on why you need a business plan are presented in Management Smarts.[46]

Although there is no single template, it is generally agreed that a good business plan includes an executive summary, covers certain business fundamentals, is well organized with headings and easy to read, and runs no more than about 20 pages in length. Here is a sample business plan outline.[47]

- *Executive summary*—overview of the business purpose and the business model for making money.
- *Industry analysis*—nature of the industry, including economic trends, important legal or regulatory issues, and potential risks.
- *Company description*—mission, owners, and legal form.
- *Products and services description*—major goods or services, with competitive uniqueness.
- *Market description*—size of market, competitor strengths and weaknesses, five-year sales goals.
- *Marketing strategy*—product characteristics, distribution, promotion, pricing, and market research.
- *Operations description*—manufacturing or service methods, supplies and suppliers, and control procedures.
- *Staffing description*—management and staffing skills needed and available, compensation, and human resource systems.
- *Financial projection*—cash flow projections for one to five years, breakeven points, and phased investment capital.

A **business plan** describes the direction for a new business and the financing needed to operate it.

## ManagementSmarts

### Why you need a business plan

- It forces you to be clear about your business model—how your business will make money.
- It makes you identify and confront the potential strengths and weaknesses of your proposed business.
- It makes you examine the market potential for your business's products or services.
- It makes you examine the strengths and weaknesses of the competitors for your proposed business.
- It helps you clarify the mission and key directions for the business, helping you to stay focused.
- It helps you determine how much money will be needed to launch and operate the business.
- It helps you communicate more confidently and credibly with potential lenders and investors.

- *Capital needs*—amount of funds needed to run the business, amount available, and amount requested from new sources.
- *Milestones*—a timetable of dates showing when key stages of the new venture will be completed.

## Choosing the Form of Ownership

One of the important choices that must be made in starting a new venture is the legal form of ownership. There are a number of alternatives, and the choice among them requires careful consideration of their respective advantages and disadvantages.

A **sole proprietorship** is simply an individual or a married couple pursuing business for a profit. This does not involve incorporation. One does business, for example, under a personal name—such as "Tiaña Lopez Designs." A sole proprietorship is simple to start, run, and terminate, and it is the most common form of small business ownership in the United States. However, the business owner is personally liable for business debts and claims.

A **partnership** is formed when two or more people agree to start and operate a business together. It is usually backed by a legal and written partnership agreement. Business partners agree on the contribution of resources and skills to the new venture, and on the sharing of profits and losses. The simplest and most common form is a *general partnership* where the partners share management responsibilities. A *limited partnership* consists of a general partner and one or more "limited" partners who do not participate in day-to-day business management. They share in the profits, but their losses are limited to the amount of their investment. A *limited liability partnership*, common among professionals such as accountants and attorneys, limits the liability of one partner for the negligence of another.

A **corporation**, commonly identified by the "Inc." designation in a name, is a legal entity that is chartered by the state and exists separately from its owners. The corporation can be for-profit, such as Microsoft, Inc., or nonprofit, such as Count-Me-In, Inc.—a firm featured early in the chapter for helping women entrepreneurs get started with small loans. The corporate form offers two major advantages: (1) It grants the organization certain legal rights (e.g., to engage in contracts), and (2) the corporation becomes responsible for its own liabilities. This separates the owners from personal liability and gives the firm a life of its own that can extend beyond that of its owners. The disadvantage of incorporation rests largely with the cost of incorporating and the complexity of the documentation required to operate as an incorporated business.

The **limited liability corporation**, or LLC, has gained popularity because it combines the advantages of the other forms—sole proprietorship, partnership, and

A **sole proprietorship** is an individual pursuing business for a profit.

A **partnership** is when two or more people agree to contribute resources to start and operate a business together.

A **corporation** is a legal entity that exists separately from its owners.

A **limited liability corporation** is a hybrid business form combining the advantages of the sole proprietorship, partnership, and corporation.

## Management in Popular Culture

MCT/NewsCom

### Self-Management Beats Mistreatment and Deception in the *Slumdog Millionaire*

Have you seen the rags-to-riches story of an orphan growing up in Mumbai, India, and finding his way to a TV game show offering him the chance to be "the slumdog millionaire"? When the police chief in *Slumdog Millionaire* has the main character, Jamal, roughed up the night before the big show, he asks: "What the hell can a slum boy possibly know?" Facing the chief and the prospect of more mistreatment, Jamal says in return: "The answers." He held up under the police chief's pressure. And, he didn't fall prey to the quizmaster's attempts to deceive and intimidate him into not believing his own right answers.

corporation. For liability purposes, it functions like a corporation and protects the assets of owners against claims made against the company. For tax purposes, it functions as a partnership in the case of multiple owners and as a sole proprietorship in the case of a single owner.

## Financing the New Venture

Have you seen the reality TV show, *Shark Tank*? It pits entrepreneurs against potential investors called "sharks." The entrepreneurs present their ideas, and the sharks, people with money to invest, debate the worthwhileness of investing in their businesses. Brian Duggan went on the show to pitch his Element Bars, a custom energy bar he developed as an MBA student. He previously tried to get a bank loan, but failed. But the sharks were impressed and gave him $150,000 in return for 30% ownership in his business.[48]

While being part of a reality TV show isn't common, Brian Duggan's situation is characteristic of that faced by entrepreneurs. Starting a new venture takes money, and that money must often be raised. The cost of setting up a new business or expanding an existing one can easily exceed the amount a would-be entrepreneur has available from personal sources. Initial startup financing might come from personal bank accounts and credit cards. Very soon, however, the chances are much more money will be needed to sustain and grow the business. There are two major ways an entrepreneur can obtain such outside financing for a new venture.

**Debt financing** involves going into debt by borrowing money from another person, bank, or financial institution. This loan must be paid back over time, with interest. It also requires collateral that pledges business assets or personal assets, such as a home, to secure the loan in case of default. The lack of availability of debt financing became a big issue during the recent financial crisis, and the problem hit entrepreneurs and small business owners especially hard.

**Debt financing** involves borrowing money that must be repaid over time, with interest.

**Equity financing** is an alternative to debt financing. It involves giving ownership shares in the business to outsiders in return for their cash investments. This money does not need to be paid back. It is an investment, and the investor assumes the risk for potential gains and losses. The equity investor gains some proportionate ownership control in return for taking that risk.

**Equity financing** involves exchanging ownership shares for outside investment monies.

**Venture capitalists** make large investments in new ventures in return for an equity stake in the business.

**An initial public offering,** or IPO, is an initial selling of shares of stock to the public at large.

**An angel investor** is a wealthy individual willing to invest in a new venture in return for an equity stake.

In **equity-based crowd funding** new ventures go online to sell equity stakes in their businesses to crowds of investors.

Equity financing is usually obtained from **venture capitalists,** companies and individuals that make investments in new ventures in return for an equity stake in the business. Most venture capitalists tend to focus on relatively large investments of $1 million or more, and they usually take a management role, such as a board of director's seat, in order to oversee business growth. The hope is that a fast-growing firm will gain a solid market base and be either sold at a profit to another firm or become a candidate for an **initial public offering,** or IPO. This is where shares of stock in the business are first sold to the public and begin trading on a stock exchange. When an IPO is successful and the share prices are bid up by the market, the original investments of the venture capitalist and entrepreneur rise in value. The quest for such return on investment is the business model of the venture capitalist.

When large amounts of venture capital aren't available to the entrepreneur, another financing option is the **angel investor**. This is a wealthy individual who is willing to make a personal investment in return for equity in a new venture. Angel investors are especially common and helpful in the very early startup stage. Their presence can raise investor confidence and help attract additional venture funding that would otherwise not be available. When Liz Cobb wanted to start her sales compensation firm, Incentive Systems, for example, she contacted 15 to 20 venture capital firms. She was interviewed by 10 and turned down by all of them. After she located $250,000 from two angel investors, the venture capital firms got interested again. She was able to obtain her first $2 million in financing and has since built the firm into a 70-plus-employee business.[49]

A new form of equity investing is closely regulated by law, and courts are debating whether or not it should be made more widely available. Called **equity-based crowd funding**, it involves new ventures going online to sell equity stakes in their businesses to crowds of small angel investors. The U.S. Securities and Exchange Commission oversees equity-based crowd funding. The law allows small start-ups to raise up to $1 million per year through online equity sales. The possible "crowd" for any one firm is limited to 2,000 investors. Those with net worths less than $100,000 can invest up to 5% of annual income with a $2,000 maximum. The limits for higher net worth investors are 10% of income and a maximum of $100,000. Advocates of equity-based crowd funding claim it spurs entrepreneurship by giving small start-ups a better shot at raising investment capital. Those against it worry that small investors in a crowd won't do enough analysis or have the financial expertise to ensure they are making good investments.[50]

---

**LEARNING CHECK 3**

**TAKEAWAY QUESTION 3 How do entrepreneurs start and finance new ventures?**

**Be sure you can** • explain the concept of first-mover advantage • illustrate the life cycle of an entrepreneurial firm • identify the major elements in a business plan • differentiate sole proprietorship, partnership, and corporation • differentiate debt financing and equity financing • explain the roles of venture capitalists and angel investors in new venture financing

# MANAGEMENT LEARNING REVIEW

## TAKEAWAY QUESTION 1  What is entrepreneurship and who are the entrepreneurs?

- Entrepreneurship is risk-taking behavior that results in the creation of new opportunities.
- A classic entrepreneur is someone who takes risks to pursue opportunities in situations that others may view as problems or threats.
- A serial entrepreneur is someone who starts and runs businesses and other organizations one after another.
- Entrepreneurs tend to be creative people who are self-confident, determined, resilient, adaptable, and driven to excel; they like to be masters of their own destinies.
- Women and minorities are well represented among entrepreneurs, with some being driven by necessity or the lack of alternative career options.
- Social entrepreneurs set up social enterprises to pursue novel ways to help solve social problems.

**For Discussion Given that "necessity is the mother of invention," can we expect that the poor economy we have been dealing with will result in lots of new and successful small business entrepreneurship?**

## TAKEAWAY QUESTION 2  What is special about small business entrepreneurship?

- Entrepreneurship results in the founding of many small businesses that offer new jobs and other benefits to local economies.
- The Internet has opened a whole new array of entrepreneurial possibilities for small businesses.
- Family businesses, ones owned and financially controlled by family members, represent the largest percentage of businesses operating worldwide; they sometimes suffer from a succession problem.

- Small businesses have a high failure rate, with as many as 60 to 80% failing within five years; many failures are the result of poor management.
- Entrepreneurs and small business owners can often get help in the startup stages by working with business incubators and Small Business Development Centers in their local communities.

**For Discussion Given that so many small businesses fail due to poor management practices, what type of advice and assistance should a Small Business Development Center offer?**

## TAKEAWAY QUESTION 3  How do entrepreneurs start and finance new ventures?

- Entrepreneurial firms tend to follow the life-cycle stages of birth, breakthrough, and maturity, with each stage offering different management challenges.
- A new startup should be guided by a good business plan that describes the intended nature of the business, how it will operate, and how financing will be obtained.
- An important choice is the form of business ownership for a new venture, with the proprietorship, corporate, and limited liability forms offering different advantages and disadvantages.
- Two basic ways of financing a new venture are through debt financing—by taking loans, and equity financing—exchanging ownership shares in return for outside investment.
- Venture capitalists pool capital and make investments in new ventures in return for an equity stake in the business; an angel investor is a wealthy individual who is willing to invest money in return for equity in a new venture.

**For Discussion If an entrepreneur has a good idea and his or her startup is starting to take off, is it better to take an offer for equity financing from an angel investor or try to get a business loan from a bank?**

## Multiple-Choice Questions

1. _____ is among the personality characteristics commonly found among entrepreneurs.
   (a) External locus of control    (b) Inflexibility
   (c) Self-confidence              (d) Low self-reliance

   (a) high tolerance for ambiguity
   (b) internal locus of control
   (c) need for achievement
   (d) action orientation

2. When an entrepreneur is comfortable with uncertainty and willing to take risks, these are indicators of someone with a(n) _____.

3. Somewhere around _____ % of American businesses meet the definition of "small business" used by the Small Business Administration.
   (a) 40    (b) 99    (c) 75    (d) 81

4. When a business owner sells to another person the right to operate that business in another location, this is a business form known as a _____.
   (a) conglomerate          (b) franchise
   (c) joint venture          (d) limited partnership

5. A small business owner who is concerned about passing the business on to heirs after retirement or death should prepare a formal _____ plan.
   (a) retirement            (b) succession
   (c) franchising           (d) liquidation

6. What is one of the most common reasons why new small business startups often fail?
   (a) The founders lack business expertise.
   (b) The founders are too strict with financial controls.
   (c) The founders don't want fast growth.
   (d) The founders have high ethical standards.

7. When a new business is quick to act and captures a market niche before competitors, this is called
   _____.
   (a) intrapreneurship      (b) an initial public offering
   (c) succession planning   (d) first-mover advantage

8. When a small business is just starting up, the business owner is typically most focused on _____.
   (a) gaining acceptance in the marketplace
   (b) finding partners for expansion
   (c) preparing an initial public offering
   (d) bringing professional skills into the management team

9. At which stage in the life cycle of an entrepreneurial firm does the underlying business model begin to work well and growth starts to occur?
   (a) birth                 (b) early childhood
   (c) maturity              (d) breakthrough

10. A venture capitalist who receives an ownership share in return for investing in a new business is providing _____ financing.
    (a) debt                  (b) equity
    (c) corporate             (d) partnership

11. In _____ financing, a business owner borrows money as a loan that must eventually be repaid to the lender along with agreed-upon interest.
    (a) debt                  (b) equity
    (c) partnership           (d) limited

12. The people who take ownership shares in new ventures in return for providing the entrepreneurs with critical start-up funds are called _____.
    (a) business incubators   (b) angel investors
    (c) SBDCs                 (d) intrapreneurs

13. The _____ form of small business ownership protects owners from any personal losses greater than their original investments; while the _____ form separates them completely from any personal liabilities.
    (a) sole proprietorship, partnership
    (b) general partnership, sole proprietorship
    (c) limited partnership, corporation
    (d) corporation, general partnership

14. The first component of a good business plan is usually a/an _____.
    (a) industry analysis
    (b) marketing strategy
    (c) executive summary of mission and business model
    (d) set of financial milestones

15. If a new venture has reached the point where it is pursuing an IPO, the firm is most likely _____.
    (a) going into bankruptcy
    (b) trying to find an angel investor
    (c) filing legal documents to become a LLC
    (d) successful enough that the public at large will want to buy its shares

## Short-Response Questions

16. What is the relationship between diversity and entrepreneurship?

17. What are the major stages in the life cycle of an entrepreneurial firm, and what are the management challenges at each stage?

18. What are the advantages of a limited partnership form of small business ownership?

19. What is the difference, if any, between a venture capitalist and an angel investor?

## Essay Question

20. Assume for the moment that you have a great idea for a potential Internet-based start-up business. In discussing the idea with a friend, she advises you to be very careful to tie your business idea to potential customers and then describe it well in a business plan. "After all," she says, "you won't succeed without customers, and you'll never get a chance to succeed if you can't attract financial backers through a good business plan." With these words to the wise, you proceed. What questions will you ask and answer to ensure that you are customer-focused in this business? What are the major areas that you would address in writing your initial business plan?

# MANAGEMENT SKILLS AND COMPETENCIES

## Further Reflection: Self-Management

The pathway to entrepreneurship involves risk, confidence, insight, and more. But for those who have both the desire to attempt new things and **self-management** skills, it's a path worth taking. Even in the absence of entrepreneurial aspirations, we need and depend upon self-management skills to do well in school, at work, and in everyday living. These are challenging times; what we are good at today may not serve us well tomorrow. There are lots of uncertainties. Now is a good time to test what you really know about yourself individually and in a social context, assess personal strengths and weaknesses, and make adjustments that better position you to achieve your goals.

 **DO IT NOW . . .
LOOK IN THE MIRROR**

- One of the best ways to check your capacity for self-management is to examine how you approach college, your academic courses, and the rich variety of development opportunities available on and off campus. Test yourself: What activities are you involved in? How well do you balance them with academic and personal responsibilities? Do you miss deadlines or turn in assignments pulled together at the last minute? Do you accept poor or mediocre performance? Do you learn from mistakes?

## Self-Assessment: Entrepreneurial Orientation Inventory

### Instructions

Distribute *five* points between each pair of statements to indicate the extent to which you agree with "a" and "b."[51]

1. _____ (a) Success as an entrepreneur depends on many factors. Personal capabilities may have very little to do with one's success. _____ (b) A capable entrepreneur can always shape his or her own destiny.

2. _____ (a) Entrepreneurs are born, not made. _____ (b) People can learn to be more enterprising even if they do not start out that way.

3. _____ (a) Whether or not a salesperson will be able to sell his or her product depends on how effective the competitors are. _____ (b) No matter how good the competitors are, an effective salesperson always will be able to sell his or her product.

4. _____ (a) Capable entrepreneurs believe in planning their activities in advance. _____ (b) There is no need for advance planning, because no matter how enterprising one is there always will be chance factors that influence success.

5. _____ (a) A person's success as an entrepreneur depends on social and economic conditions. _____ (b) Real entrepreneurs can always be successful irrespective of social and economic conditions.

6. _____ (a) Entrepreneurs fail because of their own lack of ability and perceptiveness. _____ (b) Entrepreneurs often fail because of factors beyond their control.

7. _____ (a) Entrepreneurs are often victims of forces that they can neither understand nor control. _____ (b) By taking an active part in economic, social, and political affairs, entrepreneurs can control events that affect their businesses.

8. _____ (a) Whether or not you get a business loan depends on how fair the bank officer you deal with is. _____ (b) Whether or not you get a business loan depends on how good your project plan is.

9. _____ (a) When purchasing something, it is wise to collect as much information as possible and then make a final choice. _____ (b) There is no point in collecting a lot of information; in the long run, the more you pay the better the product is.

10. _____ (a) Whether or not you make a profit in business depends on how lucky you are. _____ (b) Whether or not you make a profit in business depends on how capable you are as an entrepreneur.

11. _____ (a) Some types of people can never be successful entrepreneurs. _____ (b) Entrepreneurial ability can be developed in different types of people.

**12.** _____ (a) Whether or not you will be a successful entrepreneur depends on the social environment into which you were born. _____ (b) People can become successful entrepreneurs with effort and capability irrespective of the social strata from which they originated.

**13.** _____ (a) These days business and personal success depends on the actions of government, banks, and other outside institutions. _____ (b) It is possible to succeed without depending too much outside institutions. What is required is insight and a knack for dealing with people.

**14.** _____ (a) Even perceptive entrepreneurs falter quite often because the market situation is very unpredictable. _____ (b) When an entrepreneur's prediction of the market situation is wrong, he or she is to blame for failing to read things correctly.

**15.** _____ (a) With effort, people can determine their own destinies. _____ (b) There is no point in spending time planning. What is going to happen will happen.

**16.** _____ (a) There are many events beyond the control of entrepreneurs. _____ (b) Entrepreneurs are the creators of their own experiences.

**17.** _____ (a) No matter how hard a person works, he or she will achieve only what is destined. _____ (b) The rewards one achieves depend solely on the effort one makes.

**18.** _____ (a) Organizational success can be achieved by employing competent and effective people. _____ (b) No matter how competent the employees are, the organization will have problems if socioeconomic conditions are not good.

**19.** _____ (a) Leaving things to chance and letting time take care of them helps a person to relax and enjoy life. _____ (b) Working for things always turns out better than leaving things to chance.

**20.** _____ (a) The work of competent people will always be rewarded. _____ (b) No matter how competent one is, it is hard to succeed without contacts.

## Scoring

_____ *External Orientation Score*. Total your points for the following items: 1a, 2a, 3a, 4b, 5a, 6b, 7a, 8a, 9b, 10a, 11a, 12a, 13a, 14a, 15b, 16a, 17a, 18b, 19a, 20b.

_____ *Internal Orientation Score*. Total your points for the following items: 1b, 2b, 3b, 4a, 5b, 6a, 7b, 8b, 9a, 10b, 11b, 12b, 13b, 14b, 15a, 16b, 17b, 18a, 19b, 20a.

## Interpretation

This Inventory measures the extent to which a person is internally or externally oriented in entrepreneurial activities. Scores greater than fifty indicate more of that orientation. Those who score high on entrepreneurial internality tend to believe that entrepreneurs can shape their own destinies through their own capabilities and efforts. Those who score high on entrepreneurial externality believe that the success of entrepreneurs depends on factors such as chance, political climate, community conditions, and economic environment—factors beyond their own capabilities and control.

# Team Exercise: Entrepreneurs Among Us

## Question

Who are the entrepreneurs in your community and what are they accomplishing?

## Instructions

**1.** Make a list of persons in the local community that you believe are good examples of entrepreneurs.

**2.** Meet as a team to share and discuss your lists. Choose one entrepreneur as your team's "exemplar". Focus on the entrepreneur as a person, success and/or failure of the entrepreneur's business or nonprofit venture, and what the entrepreneur contributes to the local community.

**3.** Further Research:

- Contact as many local entrepreneurs as possible and interview them. Try to learn how and why they got started, what they encountered as obstacles or problems, and what they learned about entrepreneurship that could be passed along to others.

- Analyze your results for class presentation. Look for patterns and differences in the entrepreneurs as persons, their "founding stories," and their successes and failures.

## Career Situations for Entrepreneurs: What Would You Do?

1. **Becoming Your Own Boss** It could be very nice to be your own boss, do your own thing, and make a decent living in the process. What are your three top choices for potential business entrepreneurship? How would you rank them on potential for personal satisfaction and long-term financial success?

2. **Becoming a Social Entrepreneur** Make a list of social problems that exist in your local community. Choose one and identify how you might deal with it through social entrepreneurship. How will you be able to earn a living wage from this venture while still doing good?

2. **Making Your Startup Legal** Your small startup textbook-rating website is attracting followers. One angel investor is willing to put up $150,000 to help move things to the next level. But, you and your two co-founders haven't done anything to legally structure the business. You've managed so far on personal resources and a "handshake" agreement among friends. What is the best choice of ownership to prepare the company for future growth and outside investors?

## Case Study

# In-N-Out Burger

Go to *Management Cases for Critical Thinking* to find the recommended case for Chapter 6—"In-N-Out Burger: Building a Better Burger."

Taken at face value, In-N-Out Burger seems like a modest enterprise—only four food items on the menu, little to no advertising. For more than sixty years, In-N-Out has focused on providing customers the basics—fresh, well-cooked food served quickly in a sparkling clean environment—and has made consistency and quality their hallmarks.

In addition to making the best burgers around, In-N-Out's other primary successful trait is its insis-tence on playing by its own rules. A fierce entrepreneurial streak ran through the Snyders, In-N-Out's founding family, and from the sock-hop décor to the secret menu to its treatment of employees as long-term partners instead of disposable resources, the chain prefers to focus on its formula for success instead of conventional definitions like shareholder return or IPOs.

# Wisdom
## Learning From Others

Mel Evans/AP/Wide World Photos

## > DECISIONS TURN POTENTIAL INTO ACHIEVEMENT

Tom Szaky is an "eco-capitalist"—someone who turns sustainability into profits. While a freshman at Princeton University, Szaky ordered a million red worms, thinking he could use them to recycle campus waste. In conversations with classmate Jon Beyer, the idea shifted to selling liquid fertilizer made from worm excrement. But, they couldn't afford the expensive plastic bottles for packaging.

Many conversations led to creating TerraCycle with a mission to "find a meaningful use for waste materials." Szaky's book, *Revolution in a Bottle*, is all about "upcycling"—the art, if you will, of turning waste that isn't recyclable into reusable packaging.[1]

TerraCycle upcycles waste products like cookie wrappers, drink containers, and discarded juice packs into usable products like tote bags and other containers. Szaky says: "First we identify a waste stream, then we figure out what we can make from that material. This is our strength—creatively solving the 'what the hell do we make from it' issue."

Szaky's foray into the entrepreneurial world of eco-capitalism could have ended with the red worms experiment. But he and his friends didn't stop there. Learning from experience, they persevered and made decisions that turned ideas into accomplishments.

## MORE TO LOOK FOR INSIDE>

**FOLLOW THE STORY**
No. 2 at Facebook Is a Good Fit for Sheryl Sandberg

**ETHICS ON LINE**
Climber Left to Die on Mt. Everest

**FACTS FOR ANALYSIS**
Intelligent Enterprises Show How to Win with Data

**RESEARCH BRIEF**
Escalation Increases Risk of Unethical Decisions.

# Information and Decision Making

## > SELF-CONFIDENCE

Does confidence put a spring into your step and a smile on your face? It's a powerful force, something to be nurtured and protected. Managers need the **self-confidence** not only to make decisions but to take the actions required to implement them. Too many of us find all sorts of excuses for doing everything but that. Lacking confidence, we have difficulty deciding, and we have difficulty acting.

How would you proceed with the situation in the box—option A, or B, or C?

Jeff McCracken was the team leader who actually had to deal with this situation. He acted deliberately, with confidence, and in a collaborative fashion. After extensive consultations with the team, he decided to salvage the old track. They worked 24 hours a day and finished in less than a week. McCracken called it a "colossal job" and said the satisfaction came from "working with people from all parts of the company and getting the job done without anyone getting hurt."[2]

Self-confidence doesn't have to mean acting alone, but it does mean being willing to act. Management consultant Ram Charan calls self-confidence a willingness to "listen to your own voice" and "speak your mind and act decisively." It is, he says, an "emotional fortitude" that counteracts "emotional insecurities."[3]

## Insight
### Learning About Yourself

### DECISION TIME

*Situation:* A massive hurricane has damaged a railroad bridge over a large lake. The bridge is critical for relief efforts to aid a devastated city. You are leading a repair team of 100. Two alternatives are on the table: Rebuild using new tracks, or rebuild with old track salvaged from the lake.

*Question:* How do you proceed?

A. Decide to rebuild with new tracks; move quickly to implement.

B. Decide to rebuild with old tracks; move quickly to implement.

C. Consult with team; make decision; move quickly to implement.

## BUILD MANAGEMENT SKILLS AND COMPETENCIES AT END OF CHAPTER

- Engage in *Further Reflection on Self-Confidence*
- Take the *Self-Assessment—Cognitive Style*
- Complete the *Team Exercise—Lost at Sea*
- Solve the *Career Situations for Decision Makers*
- Analyze the *Case Study—"Amazon.com: One E-Store to Rule Them All"*

## <GET TO KNOW YOURSELF BETTER

| TAKEAWAY 1 | TAKEAWAY 2 | TAKEAWAY 3 | TAKEAWAY 4 |
|---|---|---|---|
| **Information, Technology, and Management** | **Information and Managerial Decisions** | **The Decision-Making Process** | **Issues in Managerial Decision Making** |
| • What is useful information? | • Managers as information processors | • Identify and define the problem | • Decision errors and traps |
| • Information systems and business intelligence | • Managers as problem solvers | • Generate and evaluate alternative courses of action | • Creativity in decision making |
| • Information needs in organizations | • Types of managerial decisions | • Choose a preferred course of action | |
| • How information technology is changing organizations | • Decision conditions | • Implement the decision | |
| | | • Evaluate results | |
| | | • At all steps—Check ethical reasoning | |

| LEARNING CHECK 1 | LEARNING CHECK 2 | LEARNING CHECK 3 | LEARNING CHECK 4 |
|---|---|---|---|

On August 5, 2010, the San José copper and gold mine collapsed in Chile; 32 miners and their shift leader, Carlos Urzua, were trapped inside.[4] "The most difficult moment was when the air cleared and we saw the rock," said Urzua. "I had thought maybe it was going to be a day or two days, but not when I saw the rock. . . ." In fact, the miners were trapped 2,300 feet below the surface for 69 days. Getting them out alive was a problem that caught the attention of the entire world. After the rescue shaft was completed, Urzua was the last man out. "The job was hard," he said. "They were days of great pain and sorrow." But the decisions Urzua made as shift leader—organizing the miners into work shifts, keeping them busy, studying mine diagrams, making escape plans, raising morale—all contributed to the successful rescue. After embracing Urzua when he arrived at the surface, Chile's President Sebastian Pinera said, "He was a shift boss who made us proud."

Most managers will never have to face such an extreme crisis, but decision making and problem solving are parts of every manager's job. Not all decisions are going to be easy ones; some will have to be made under tough conditions; and, not all decisions will turn out right. But as with the case of Urzua trapped in the Chilean mine, the goal is to do the best you can under the circumstances.

## Information, Technology, and Management

Tests of our abilities to make good decisions occur every day in situations that may not be crisis driven, but which nevertheless have real consequences for ourselves and others. The challenges begin with the fact that our society is now highly information-driven, digital, networked, and continuously evolving. Career and personal success increasingly requires three "must-have" competencies: **technological competency**—the ability to understand new technologies and to use them to their best advantage; **information competency**—the ability to locate, gather, organize, and display information; and **analytical competency**—the ability to evaluate and analyze information to make actual decisions and solve real problems.[5] How about it—are you ready?

## What Is Useful Information?

This sign should be on every manager's desk—*Warning: Data ≠ Information!* **Data** are raw facts and observations. **Information** is data made useful and meaningful for decision making. We all have lots of access to data, but we don't always turn it into useful information that meets the test of these five criteria:

1. *Timely*—The information is available when needed; it meets deadlines for decision making and action.

2. *High quality*—The information is accurate, and it is reliable; it can be used with confidence.

3. *Complete*—The information is complete and sufficient for the task at hand; it is as current and up to date as possible.

4. *Relevant*—The information is appropriate for the task at hand; it is free from extraneous or irrelevant materials.

5. *Understandable*—The information is clear and easily understood by the user; it is free from unnecessary detail.

Even when the information is good, we don't always make the right decisions based upon it. The term **analytics,** sometimes called *business analytics* or *management analytics*, describes the systematic evaluation and analysis of information to make decisions. Think of it as putting data to work for informed decision making.[6] Analytics is critically important to all aspects of the management process—planning, organizing, leading, and controlling. But even at the highest executive levels analytics often breaks down. Consider these miscues in situations of organizational complexity, environmental uncertainty, and business competition:

*Netflix Gets Lost in the Mail*—800,000 customers deserted Netflix after CEO Reed Hastings announced that the company was splitting into separate video streaming (the new Netflix) and mail-order DVD businesses (something called Quickster), and that the charge for each would be $7.99 instead of $9.99 previously charged for both. Less than two months later Hastings canceled the Quickster initiative and apologized to Netflix customers and shareholders.[7]

*Hewlett-Packard Hits the Delete Key*—HP's then-CEO Leo Apotheker announced that the firm was most likely going to get out of the PC business. Loyal PC customers yelled "foul," shareholders yelled "What's going on with our company?," and HP's board was left to wonder, "Why did we approve this possibility?" Five weeks later Apotheker was fired, Meg Whitman moved from the board to the CEO's job, and HP announced that it was sticking with its PC business after all. Whitman said the decision was made after "HP objectively evaluated the strategic, financial and operational impact . . . ."[8]

**Technological competency** is the ability to understand new technologies and to use them to their best advantage.

**Information competency** is the ability to locate, gather, and organize information for use in decision making.

**Analytical competency** is the ability to evaluate and analyze information to make actual decisions and solve real problems.

**Data** are raw facts and observations.

**Information** is data made useful for decision making.

Management with **analytics** involves systematic gathering and processing of data to make informed decisions.

## What's the Fastest Way to Board Passengers on a Plane?

Surely you've pondered this question while being stranded in a narrow aisle while someone ahead jostles their luggage into the carry-on rack. Airline executives do, too, since minutes saved in boarding can mean money saved. The tried–and-true method is boarding back to front; close behind is boarding in blocks—As and Bs by number. But airline execs may be as stuck in their thinking as their passengers are in the aisles. Research by astrophysicist Jason Steffen sheds new light on the problem. His data show that boarding alternating rows back to front and boarding window–middle–aisle for each row beats the other methods by a lot. Most airlines, though, say they don't plan to change.

What information fueled prior decisions? Where were the analytics? The lesson here is that managers at all levels need information, they need it all the time, and they have to use it well to make consistently good decisions.

## Information Systems and Business Intelligence

People perform best when they have available to them the right information at the right time and in the right place. This is the function served by **management information systems** that use the latest technologies to collect, organize, and distribute data. Silicon Valley pioneer and Cisco Systems CEO John Chambers once pointed out that he always has the information he needs to be in control—be it information on earnings, expenses, profitability, gross margins, and more. "Because I have my data in that format," he said, "every one of my employees can make decisions that might have had to come all the way to the president. . . . Quicker decision making at lower levels will translate into higher profit margins. . . . Companies that don't do that will be noncompetitive."[9]

Given the great power of technology today, information systems are indispensable executive tools. They also help bring financial transparency to all levels of an organization. In terms of *big picture information,* for example, companies can now easily share the latest financial results so that employees know current profits and how they compare to past results and desired targets. In terms *of business or function specific information,* they can make sure, that plant workers always know costs, marketing people know sales expenses relative to sales revenues, and customer service workers know cost per service contact.[10]

**Business intelligence** is the process of tapping or mining information systems to extract data that is most useful for decision makers. It sorts and reports data in organized ways that help decision makers detect, digest, and deal with patterns posing important implications. One of the trends in business intelligence is use of **executive dashboards** that visually display and update key performance metrics as graphs, charts, and scorecards on a real-time basis. The Chief Financial Officer of the manufacturing firm Ceradyne says: "If numbers are the language of business, then dashboards are the way we drive the business forward." He adds that they "take the daily temperature of a business."[11]

**Management information systems** use IT to collect, organize, and distribute data for use in decision making.

**Business intelligence** taps information systems to extract and report data in organized ways that are helpful to decision makers.

**Executive dashboards** visually display graphs, charts, and scorecards of key performance indicators and information on a real-time basis.

Use of executive dashboards helps managers focus on the most important things, spot trends that represent problems or opportunities to be addressed, and avoid getting bogged down either in a data vacuum or in a data overload. Picture a sales manager whose office wall has a large flat-panel computer display much like the one you use for TV and games at home. But this display calls up one or more dashboards rich with all sorts of up-to-the-moment information—things like sales by product, salesperson, sales area, as well as tracking comparisons with past performance and current sales targets. How can this manager fail to make well informed decisions?

## Information Needs in Organizations

Information serves the variety of needs described in Figure 7.1. At the organization's boundaries, information in the external environment is accessed. Managers use this *intelligence information* to deal with customers, competitors, and other stakeholders such as government agencies, creditors, suppliers, and stockholders. Organizations also send vast amounts of *public information* to stakeholders and the external environment. This often takes the form of advertising, public relations messages, and financial reports that serve a variety of purposes, ranging from image-building to product promotion to financial documentation. It also increasingly involves the use of social media such as Facebook and Twitter. The power of the Internet as a source for public information is very real, but it can work both to the negative and to the positive. When a YouTube video showing two Domino's Pizza employees doing all sorts of nasty things to sandwiches went viral, Domino's faced a crisis of customer confidence. Although the video was pulled by one of its creators—who apologized for "faking" how they worked—Domino's brand was already damaged in the public eye. In response, the firm's management created a Twitter account to present its own view of the situation and posted a YouTube video message from the CEO.[12]

Within organizations, people need vast amounts of *internal information* to make decisions and solve problems in their daily work. They need information from their immediate work setting and from other parts of the organization. Internal information

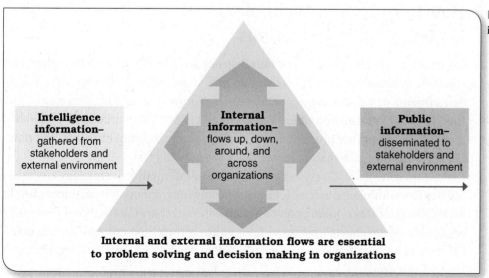

FIGURE 7.1 **Internal and external information needs in organizations.**

**Intelligence information**—gathered from stakeholders and external environment

**Internal information**—flows up, down, around, and across organizations

**Public information**—disseminated to stakeholders and external environment

**Internal and external information flows are essential to problem solving and decision making in organizations**

## Intelligent Enterprises Show How to Win with Data

A survey on "The New Intelligent Enterprise" conducted by the *Sloan Management Review* asked 3,000 executives from around the world to report on how their organizations use and deal with data for business intelligence. Results included the following:

- 60% of executives said their organizations were "overwhelmed" by data and have difficulty making it useful for performance results.
- Organizations outperforming competitors were three times better at managing and acting on the data than low performers.
- Top performers were two times more likely than low performers to say they needed to get even better with analytics.
- Most mentioned obstacles to adopting better analytics are lack of understanding, competing management priorities, and lack of skills.
- Analytic techniques projected to grow most in importance over the next 2 years are data visualization, use of simulations and scenarios development, and use of analytics within business processes.
- Top performers say their organizations use analytics most often in finance, strategy, operations, and sales and marketing; they make better use of analytics than do low performers in all business areas.

### YOUR THOUGHTS?

What are the implications of these data for your career planning and development? The consulting firm McKinsey & Co. projects that by 2018 the United States will be short 1.5 million managers who have the skills to "use data to shape business decisions." Are you prepared to compete for jobs and promotions in career situations where analytics count? How could your local schools, small businesses, and even government agencies gain by better harnessing the power of information and analytics?

---

flows downward in such forms as goals, instructions, and feedback; it flows horizontally in ways that assist in cross-functional coordination and problem solving; and it flows upward in such forms as performance reports, suggestions for improvement, and even disputes. The ability of technology to gather and move information quickly within an organization—up, down, and horizontally—can be a great asset to decision making. It helps top levels stay informed, while freeing lower levels to make speedy decisions and take the actions they need to best perform their jobs.

## How Information Technology Is Changing Organizations

Information technology, or IT, not only helps us acquire, store, process, analyze, and transmit information, it is also changing how organizations operate. Information departments or centers are now mainstream features on organization charts, and the CIO (chief information officer) or CKO (chief knowledge officer) or CTO (chief technology officer) are prominent members of top management teams. The number and variety of information career fields are growing fast.

As shown in Figure 7.2, ever-expanding uses of information technology are breaking barriers within organizations. IT helps people from different departments, levels, and physical locations more easily communicate and share information. IT-intensive organizations are able to operate with fewer levels than their more traditional counterparts as information systems replace people whose jobs were devoted primarily to moving it around.

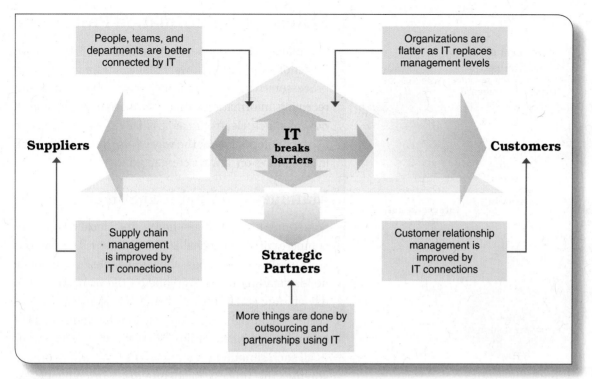

FIGURE 7.2   **Information technology is breaking barriers and changing organizations.**

IT is also breaking barriers between organizations and key elements in the external environment. It plays an important role in customer relationship management by quickly and accurately providing information regarding customer needs, preferences, and satisfactions. It helps in supply chain management to better control costs and streamline activities everywhere from initiation of purchase, to logistics and transportation, to point of delivery and ultimate use. And it helps maintain linkages with outsourcing clients and other strategic partners.

**LEARNING CHECK 1**

**TAKEAWAY QUESTION 1** **What is the role of information in the management process?**

**Be sure you can** • define and give examples of *technological competency, information competency,* and *analytical competency* • differentiate data and information • list the criteria of useful information • describe the role of information systems in organizations • explain the importance of analytics and business intelligence • discuss how IT is breaking barriers within organizations and between organizations and their environments

## Information and Managerial Decisions

In a book entitled *Judgment: How Winning Leaders Make Great Calls,* scholars and consultants Noel M. Tichy and Warren G. Bennis discuss the importance of what leaders do before a decision is made, while making it, and when implementing it.[13] Information is the anchor point for all three—information helps a leader sense the need for a decision, frame an approach to the decision, and communicate about the decision with others.[14]

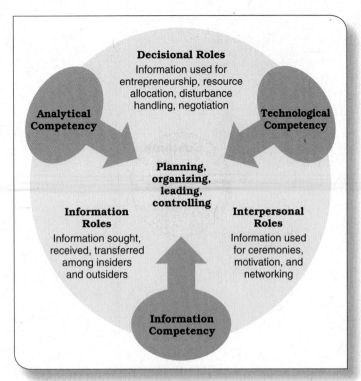

FIGURE 7.3 **The manager as an information processor and nerve center for planning, organizing, leading, and controlling.**

**Problem solving** involves identifying and taking action to resolve problems.

A **decision** is a choice among possible alternative courses of action.

A **performance threat** is a situation in which something is obviously wrong or has the potential to go wrong.

A **performance opportunity** is a situation that offers the chance for a better future if the right steps are taken.

## Managers as Information Processors

The manager's job is depicted in Figure 7.3 as a nerve center of information flows.[15] Managers are information processors who are continually gathering, giving, and receiving information. This information processing is now as much electronic as it is face to face. Managers use technology at work the way we use it in our personal lives—always on, always connected.

## Managers as Problem Solvers

Sometimes it's big things—how a small local retailer can compete with the big chains. Other times it's smaller but still consequential things—how to handle Fourth of July holiday staffing when everyone on the team wants the day off. And sometimes it's being able to recognize and correct an outright mistake—such as the Netflix and HP examples described earlier. What we are talking about in all such situations is a manager's skill with **problem solving,** the process of identifying a discrepancy between an actual and a desired state of affairs, and then taking action to resolve it.

Success in problem solving comes from using information to make good **decisions**—choices among alternative possible courses of action. Managers, in this sense, make decisions while facing a continuous stream of daily problems. The most obvious situation is a **performance threat** in which something is already wrong or has the potential to go wrong. This happens when actual performance is less than desired or is moving in an unfavorable direction. Examples are when turnover or absenteeism suddenly increases in the work unit, when a team member falls behind in work, or when a customer complains about service delays. Another important situation emerges as a **performance opportunity** that offers the chance for a better future if the right steps are taken. This happens when an actual situation either turns out better than anticipated or offers the potential to do so.

### Openness to Problem Solving

Even when presented with good information, managers often differ in their openness to problem solving. Some are more willing than others to accept the responsibilities it entails.

*Problem avoiders* ignore information that would otherwise signal the presence of a performance opportunity or threat. They are passive in information gathering, not wanting to make decisions and deal with problems. *Problem solvers* are willing to make decisions and try to solve problems, but only when forced by the situation. They are reactive in gathering information to solve problems after, but not before, they occur. They may deal reasonably well with performance threats, but miss many performance opportunities.

There is quite a contrast between the last two styles and *problem seekers* who constantly process information and look for problems to solve. True problem seekers are proactive and forward thinking. They anticipate performance threats and opportunities, and they take action to gain the advantage.

## Recommended Reading

THOMAS H. DAVENPORT, JEANNE G. HARRIS
Co authors of *Competing on Analytics*
and ROBERT MORISON

**Analytics at Work**
Smarter Decisions
Better Results

### Analytics at Work: Smarter Decisions, Better Results

(Harvard Business Press, 2010)

## by Thomas Davenport, Jeanne Harris, and Robert Morison

Decision maker beware: Those gut feelings might be misleading you. In *Analytics at Work*, authors Davenport, Harris, and Morison point out that we can often do a lot better when making decisions. All it takes is a willingness to use analytics and turn information into valuable decision insights. There are lots of data in and around organizations that could be well used, but they have to be gathered, sorted, and well analyzed if we are to avoid errors that come from "shooting from the hip" or "deciding from the gut" at the wrong times. For example, just where should those scarce advertising dollars be spent? In these and many other common decision situations, Davenport et al. say we should give more attention to facts. When we do, our organizations will act more intelligently.

Success at problem seeking is one of the ways to distinguish exceptional managers from the merely good or even bad ones. When Toyota faced a crisis over major quality defects and massive auto recalls, it turns out that data on these problems had been available within the system a long time. But, nothing was done about it until the crisis hit and executives were forced into a problem-solving mode. The top U.S. executive for the company said: "We did not hide it. But it was not properly shared."[16] Surely, customers and shareholders would have been better served by problem-seeking managers who were continuously alert to information suggesting the presence of quality problems and willing to quickly take corrective actions.

## Systematic and Intuitive Thinking

Managers also differ in their use of "systematic" and "intuitive" thinking when trying to solve problems and make decisions. In **systematic thinking** a person approaches problems in a rational, step-by-step, analytical fashion. The process is slow and analytical. Systematic thinking breaks a complex problem into smaller components and then addresses them in a logical and integrated fashion. Managers who are systematic can be expected to make a plan before taking action, and carefully search for information to facilitate problem solving in a step-by-step fashion.

**Systematic thinking** approaches problems in a rational and analytical fashion.

Someone using **intuitive thinking** is more flexible and spontaneous in problem solving.[17] This process uses a quick and broad evaluation of the situation and the possible alternative courses of action. Managers who are intuitive can be expected to deal with many aspects of a problem at once, jump from one issue to another, and consider "hunches" based on experience or spontaneous ideas. This approach is often imaginative and tends to work best in situations where facts are limited and few decision precedents exist.[18]

**Intuitive thinking** approaches problems in a flexible and spontaneous fashion.

Amazon.com's Jeff Bezos recognizes it's not always possible for the firm's top managers to make systematic fact-based decisions. There are times, he says, when "you have to rely on experienced executives who've honed their instincts" and are able to make good judgments.[19] In other words, there's a place for both systematic and

Jerzyworks/Masterfile

# Video Games May Be Good for Decision Making

Believe it or not, and contrary to lots of public opinion, researchers are starting to talk about gaming being good for our brains. Consider these data. Starcraft players show faster thought and movements; players of action video games were 25% faster than non-players in decision making; game players can track six things at once, while non-players track four; surgeons who play games at least three hours a week make fewer surgical errors. Of course there's a lot of downside risk too. Players of violent video games seem to have more aggressive thoughts and are less caring toward others. Perhaps your gaming, well considered, can be a decision-making asset—boosting creativity and multitasking skills.

intuitive decision making in management. Intuition balanced by support from good solid analysis, experience, and effort can be a great combination.[20]

## Multidimensional Thinking

**Multidimensional thinking** is an ability to address many problems at once.

**Strategic opportunism** focuses on long-term objectives while being flexible in dealing with short-term problems.

Managers often deal with portfolios of problems that consist of multiple and interrelated issues. This requires **multidimensional thinking**—an ability to view many problems at once, in relationship to one another and across both long and short time horizons.[21] The best managers are able to "map" multiple problems into a network that can be actively managed over time as priorities, events, and demands continuously change. They are able to make decisions and take actions in the short run that benefit longer-run objectives. And they avoid being sidetracked while sorting through a shifting mix of daily problems. Harvard scholar Daniel Isenberg calls this skill **strategic opportunism**—the ability to remain focused on long-term objectives while being flexible enough to resolve short-term problems and opportunities in a timely manner.[22]

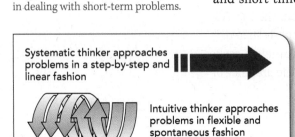

Systematic thinker approaches problems in a step-by-step and linear fashion

Intuitive thinker approaches problems in flexible and spontaneous fashion

## Cognitive Styles

**Cognitive styles** are shown by the ways individuals deal with information while making decisions.

When US Airways Flight 1549 was in trouble and pilot Chesley Sullenberger decided to land in the Hudson River, he had both a clear head and a clear sense of what he had been trained to do. The landing was successful and no lives were lost. Called a "hero" for his efforts, Sullenberger described his thinking this way:[23]

> I needed to touch down with the wings exactly level. I needed to touch down with the nose slightly up. I needed to touch down at . . . a descent rate that was survivable. And I needed to touch down just above our minimum flying speed but not below it. And I needed to make all these things happen simultaneously.

This example highlights **cognitive styles**, or the way individuals deal with information while making decisions. If you take the end-of-chapter self-assessment, it will examine your cognitive style in problem solving as a contrast of tendencies toward information gathering—*sensation versus intuition*—and information evaluation—*feeling versus thinking*. Most likely, pilot Sullenberger would score high in both sensation and thinking, and that is probably an ideal type for his job.

People with different cognitive styles may approach problems and make decisions in quite different ways. It is helpful to understand the four styles shown here along with their characteristics, both for yourself and as they are displayed by others.[24]

| | | **Information Processing** | |
|---|---|---|---|
| | | Sensing | Intuition |
| **Information Evaluation** — Thinking | | Sensation Thinkers "STs"—like facts, goals | Intuitive Thinkers "ITs"—idealistic, theoretical |
| **Information Evaluation** — Feeling | | Sensation Feelers "SFs"—like facts, feelings | Intuitive Feelers "IFs"—thoughtful, flexible |

- *Sensation Thinkers*—STs tend to emphasize the impersonal rather than the personal and take a realistic approach to problem solving. They like hard "facts," clear goals, certainty, and situations of high control.

- *Intuitive Thinkers*—ITs are comfortable with abstraction and unstructured situations. They tend to be idealistic, prone toward intellectual and theoretical positions; they are logical and impersonal but also avoid details.

- *Intuitive Feelers*—IFs prefer broad and global issues. They are insightful and tend to avoid details, being comfortable with intangibles; they value flexibility and human relationships.

- *Sensation Feelers*—SFs tend to emphasize both analysis and human relations. They tend to be realistic and prefer facts; they are open communicators and sensitive to feelings and values.

## Types of Managerial Decisions

Not all the problems we face and decisions we need to make are going to be easy ones. Some will present themselves under tough but manageable conditions; others may leave us wondering how anything could possibly turn out right. Yet through it all, we need to keep moving forward and stick with the goal—doing the best jobs we can under the circumstances.

### Programmed and Nonprogrammed Decisions

Managers sometimes face **structured problems** that are familiar, straightforward, and clear with respect to information needs. Because these problems are routine and occur over and over again, they can be dealt with by **programmed decisions** that use solutions or decision rules already available from past experience. Although not always predictable, routine problems can be anticipated. This allows for decisions to be programmed in advance and then put into use as needed. In human resource management, for example, problems are common whenever decisions are made on pay raises and promotions, vacation requests, committee assignments, and the like. Forward-looking managers use this understanding to decide in advance how to handle complaints and conflicts when and if they arise.

Managers also deal with **unstructured problems** that are new or unusual situations full of ambiguities and information deficiencies. These problems require **nonprogrammed decisions** that craft novel solutions to meet the demands of the unique situation at hand. Many, if not most, problems faced by higher-level managers are of this type, often involving the choice of strategies and objectives in situations of some uncertainty. In the recent financial crisis, for example, all eyes were on U.S. Treasury Secretary Timothy Geithner. His task was to solve the problems with billions of dollars in bad loans made by the nation's banks and restore

**Structured problems** are straightforward and clear with respect to information needs.

A **programmed decision** applies a solution from past experience to a routine problem.

**Unstructured problems** have ambiguities and information deficiencies.

A **nonprogrammed decision** applies a specific solution crafted for a unique problem.

stability to the financial markets. It was uncharted territory; no programmed solutions were readily available. Geithner and his team crafted what they believed were the best possible solutions at the time. But only time would tell if these non-programmed decisions were the right ones.

## Crisis Decisions

A **crisis decision** occurs when an unexpected problem arises that can lead to disaster if not resolved quickly and appropriately.

Think back to the opening example of shift leader Carlos Urzua and the Chilean mine disaster. It represents one of the most challenging of all decision situations—**crisis.** This appears as an unexpected problem that can lead to disaster if not resolved quickly and appropriately. The ability to handle crises could well be the ultimate test of any manager's decision-making capabilities.[25] Urzua certainly passed this test with flying colors. Not everyone does as well. In fact, a look back on Toyota's handling of a quality disaster shows that we sometimes react to crises by doing exactly the wrong things.

It caught most people by surprise when Toyota, the king of automobile quality, recalled over 5 million vehicles for quality defects—a real disaster for the brand. It wasn't just the size of the recall that caught our attention; the way Toyota's management handled the crisis was scrutinized as well. One observer called the situation a "public relations nightmare for Toyota" and said that "crisis management does not get any more woeful than this." This poor management was described as a fault of Toyota's insular corporate culture, one that discouraged early disclosure of quality problems and contributed to poor public relations when the crisis finally hit the news. By the time Toyota's CEO Akio Toyoda apologized in public and pledged a return to high standards of quality, customers and government regulators considered it too little and too late. Both he and the firm were criticized for "initially denying, minimizing and mitigating the problems."[26]

Managers err in crisis situations when they isolate themselves and try to solve the problem alone or in a small "closed" group.[27] This denies them access to crucial information at the very time that they need it the most. It not only sets them up for poor decisions, it may create even more problems. This is why it is getting more common for organizations to hold formal crisis management training, covering things like the rules in Management Smarts. The intent is to help managers and others prepare for unexpected high-impact events that threaten an organization's health and well-being.

While anticipation is one aspect of crisis management, preparation is another. People can be assigned ahead of time to crisis management teams, and crisis management plans can be developed to deal with various contingencies. Just as police departments and community groups plan ahead and train to best handle civil and natural disasters, so, too, can managers and work teams plan ahead and train to best deal with organizational crises.

## Management**Smarts**

### Six Rules for Crisis Management

1. *Figure out what is going on*—Take the time to understand what's happening and the conditions under which the crisis must be resolved.

2. *Remember that speed matters*—Attack the crisis as quickly as possible, trying to catch it when it is as small as possible.

3. *Remember that slow counts, too*—Know when to back off and wait for a better opportunity to make progress with the crisis.

4. *Respect the danger of the unfamiliar*—Understand the danger of all-new territory where you and others have never been before.

5. *Value the skeptic*—Don't look for and get too comfortable with agreement; appreciate skeptics and let them help you see things differently.

6. *Be ready to "fight fire with fire"*—When things are going wrong and no one seems to care, you may have to start a crisis to get their attention.

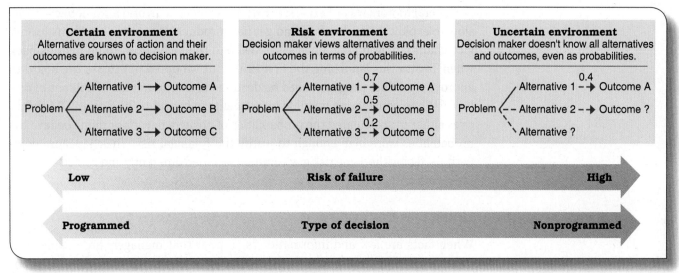

FIGURE 7.4   **Three environments for managerial decision making.**

## Decision Conditions

Figure 7.4 shows three different decision conditions or environments—certainty, risk, and uncertainty. Although managers make decisions in each, the conditions of risk and uncertainty are common at higher management levels where problems are more complex and unstructured.

### Certain Environment

The decisions just described were made in conditions quite different from the relative predictability of a **certain environment**. This is an ideal decision situation in which factual information is available about the possible alternative courses of action and their outcomes. The decision maker's task is simple: Study the alternatives and choose the best solution. Certain environments are nice, neat, and comfortable for decision makers. However, very few managerial problems are like this.

A **certain environment** offers complete information on possible action alternatives and their consequences.

### Risk Environment

Looking back on decisions he made during the financial crisis, GE's CEO Jeffrey Immelt says that he did "things I never thought I would have to do. I am sure my board and investors frequently wondered what in the heck I was doing. I had to act without perfect knowledge."[28] In this statement Immelt is stating a basic fact of managerial decision making: Many management problems emerge in **risk environments**—ones where facts and information on action alternatives and their consequences are incomplete.

A **risk environment** lacks complete information but offers "probabilities" of the likely outcomes for possible action alternatives.

Decision making in risk environments requires the use of *probabilities* to estimate the likelihood that a particular outcome will occur (e.g., 4 chances out of 10). Because probabilities are only possibilities, people vary in how they act under risk conditions.

Domino's Pizza CEO J. Patrick Boyle is a risk taker. He not only decided to change the firm's pizza recipe, he ran a television ad admitting that customers really disliked the old one because it was "totally devoid of flavor" and had a crust "like cardboard." Whereas some executives might want to hide or downplay such customer reviews, Boyle used them to help launch the new recipe. He says it was a "calculated risk" and that "we're proving to our customers that we are listening to them by brutally accepting the criticism that's out there."[29]

General Motors wasn't a risk taker when it comes to hybrid automobiles. It was slow to exploit the technology and get new products to market. The firm's former vice chairman, Bob Lutz, once said: "GM had the technology to do hybrids back when Toyota was launching the first Prius, but we opted not to ask the board to approve a product program that'd be destined to lose hundreds of millions of dollars."[30] When considering possible investments in hybrid technologies, GM executives either miscalculated the probabilities of positive payoffs or didn't believe the probabilities were high enough to justify the financial risk. Their Japanese competitors, facing the same risk environment, decided differently and gained the early mover advantage.

## Uncertain Environment

An **uncertain environment** lacks so much information that it is difficult to assign probabilities to the likely outcomes of alternatives.

When facts are few and information is so poor that managers are unable even to assign probabilities to the likely outcomes of alternatives, an **uncertain environment** exists. This is the most difficult decision condition. The high level of uncertainty forces managers to rely heavily on intuition, judgment, informed guessing, and hunches—all of which leave considerable room for error. Perhaps no better example exists of the challenges of uncertainty than the situation faced by government and business leaders as they struggle to deal with global economic turmoil. Even as they try hard to find the right pathways, great political, social, and economic uncertainties make their tasks difficult and the outcomes of their decisions efforts hard to predict.

---

**LEARNING CHECK 2**

**TAKEAWAY QUESTION 2 How do managers use information to make decisions?**

**Be sure you can** • describe how IT influences the four functions of management • define *problem solving* and *decision making* • explain systematic and intuitive thinking • list four cognitive styles in decision making • differentiate programmed and nonprogrammed decisions • describe the challenges of crisis decision making • explain decision making in certain, risk, and uncertain environments

---

# The Decision-Making Process

All of those case studies, experiential exercises, class discussions, and even essay exam questions in your courses are intended to engage students in experiencing the complexities of managerial decision making, the potential problems and pitfalls, and even the pressures of crisis situations. From the classroom forward, however, it's all up to you. Only you can determine whether you step up and make the best out of very difficult problems, or collapse under pressure.

The **decision-making process** begins with identification of a problem and ends with evaluation of implemented solutions.

Figure 7.5 describes five steps in the **decision-making process**: (1) Identify and define the problem, (2) generate and evaluate alternative solutions, (3) choose a preferred course of action, (4) implement the decision, and (5) evaluate results.[31] Importantly, ethical reasoning should be double checked in all five steps. The decision-making process can be understood in the context of the following short case.

*The Ajax Case.* On December 31, the Ajax Company decided to close down its Murphysboro plant. Market conditions were forcing layoffs, and the company

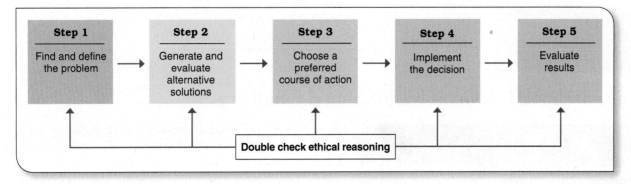

FIGURE 7.5  **Steps in the decision-making process.**

could not find a buyer for the plant. Some of the 172 employees had been with the company as long as 18 years; others as little as 6 months. All were to be terminated. Under company policy, they would be given severance pay equal to one week's pay per year of service.

This case reflects how competition, changing times, and the forces of globalization can take their toll on organizations, the people who work for them, and the communities in which they operate. Think about how you would feel as one of the affected employees. Think about how you would feel as the mayor of this small town. Think about how you would feel as a corporate executive having to make the difficult business decisions.

## Step 1—Identify and Define the Problem

The first step in decision making is to find and define the problem. Information gathering and deliberation are critical in this stage. The way a problem is defined can have a major impact on how it is resolved, and it is important to clarify exactly what a decision should accomplish. The more specific the goals, the easier it is to evaluate results after the decision is actually implemented. But, three common mistakes can occur in this critical first step in decision making.[32]

*Mistake number 1* is defining the problem too broadly or too narrowly. To take a classic example, the problem stated as "build a better mousetrap" might be better defined as "get rid of the mice." Managers should define problems in ways that give them the best possible range of problem-solving options.

*Mistake number 2* is focusing on symptoms instead of causes. Symptoms are indicators that problems may exist, but they shouldn't be mistaken for the problems themselves. Although managers should be alert to spot problem symptoms (e.g., a drop in performance), they must also dig deeper to address root causes (such as discovering that a worker needs training in the use of a new computer system).

*Mistake number 3* is choosing the wrong problem to deal with at a certain point in time. For example, which of these three problems would you address first on a busy workday? 1—An e-mail message from your boss is requesting a proposal "as soon as possible" on how to handle employees' complaints about lack of flexibility in their work schedules. 2—One of your best team members has just angered another by loudly criticizing her work performance. 3—Your working spouse has left a voice mail message that your daughter is sick at school and the nurse would like her to go home for the day. Choices like this are not easy. But we have to set priorities

# No. 2 at Facebook Is a Good Fit for Sheryl Sandberg

Dennis Van Tine/ABACAUSA.COM/Newscom

Take a great innovative company, mix in fast—even insane—growth, lawsuits over founding ownership rights, intense competition, and societal concerns for privacy, and what do you get? A fabulous opportunity to step in as the No. 2 and help run Facebook! That's just what Sheryl Sandberg was looking at when she decided to leave Google and become Facebook's chief operating officer. It was a good fit for Sandberg, whose new boss, CEO, Mark Zuckerberg, was long on tech skills and short on people skills. Sandberg's rocket ride at Facebook shows the worth of adding non-tech skills to top management decision making at high-tech firms.

Peek in at a meeting. Sandberg is sitting with 30 top managers from Facebook's business units. The managers present; Sandberg listens. After one speaks she exclaims, "Great accomplishment, whoever worked on this you guys should feel great." Another shows a slide depicting advertising revenues and volume both steadily rising while the number of person-hours spent stays pretty constant. It's business intelligence at work and Sandberg says: "This is a beautiful chart, I might frame it on the wall." The chart was communicating growing profits and Sandberg was a buyer. "Guys, this is the difference," she says.

Facebook has grown from just over 60 million users to 800+ million users while Sandberg has been COO. She's worked with Zuckerberg and others to clarify strategy, set and clean up procedures, and nurture talent. One of her most crucial accomplishments was gaining agreement on the underlying business model—where were profits to come from? Should users pay, or should advertisers pay? The decision was to go with advertising. That's the model that carried Facebook to one of the most anticipated IPOs in U.S. stock market history.

Of course not everything unfolds as smoothly. Take prospects for Facebook in China, for example. Zuckerberg seems to think Facebook can make a difference in China, notwithstanding the problems with government censorship of the Internet. Sandberg is more cautious and wonders if the firm would gain or lose from the compromises it would have to make to be in the China market. Ultimately, it will be the CEO's decision, she points out. But as No. 2 it's her job to argue the pros and cons.

## YOUR TAKE?

Does it take a special managerial skill set for someone like Sheryl Sandberg to succeed in a company driven by engineers? How about Sandberg's decision to become No. 2 to a personality as strong as Mark Zuckerberg's? How big of a gamble was it? And how about now, when she could surely be No. 1 someplace else? What might cause her to leave Facebook or stay?

and deal with the most important problems first. Perhaps the boss can wait while you telephone school to learn more about your daughter's illness and then spend some time with the employee who seems to be having "a bad day."

*Back to the Ajax Case.* Closing the Ajax plant will put a substantial number of people from the small community of Murphysboro out of work. The unemployment will have a negative impact on individuals, their families, and the town as a whole. The loss of the Ajax tax base will further hurt the community. The local financial implications of the plant closure will be great. The problem for Ajax management is how to minimize the adverse impact of the plant closing on the employees, their families, and the community.

# Step 2—Generate and Evaluate Alternative Courses of Action

Once a problem is defined, it is time to assemble the facts and information that will solve it. This is where we clarify exactly what is known and what needs to be known. Extensive information gathering should identify alternative courses of action, as well as their anticipated consequences. Key stakeholders in the problem should be identified, and the effects of possible courses of action on each of them should be considered. During a time when General Motors was closing plants and laying off thousands of workers, for example, a union negotiator said: "While GM's continuing decline in market share isn't the fault of workers or our communities, it is these groups that will suffer."[33]

A **cost-benefit analysis** is a useful approach for evaluating alternatives. It compares what an alternative will cost in relation to the expected benefits. The benefits of an alternative should be greater than its costs, and it should also be ethically sound. The following list includes costs, benefits, and other useful criteria for evaluating alternatives:

> **Cost-benefit analysis** involves comparing the costs and benefits of each potential course of action.

- *Costs:* What are the "costs" of implementing the alternative, including resource investments as well as potential negative side effects?
- *Benefits:* What are the "benefits" of using the alternative to solve a performance deficiency or take advantage of an opportunity?
- *Timeliness:* How fast can the alternative be implemented and a positive impact be achieved?
- *Acceptability:* To what extent will the alternative be accepted and supported by those who must work with it?
- *Ethical soundness:* How well does the alternative meet acceptable ethical criteria in the eyes of the various stakeholders?

Any course of action can ultimately be only as good as the quality of the alternatives considered. The better the pool of alternatives, the more likely that any actions taken will help solve the problem at hand. It's important to avoid a common decision-making error that occurs at this stage—*abandoning the search for alternatives too quickly.* This often happens under pressures of time and other circumstances. Just because an alternative is convenient doesn't make it the best. It could have damaging side effects, or it could be less good than others that might be discovered with extra effort. One way to minimize the risk of this error is through consultation and involvement. Adding more people to the decision-making process often brings new perspectives to bear on a problem, generates more alternatives, and results in a course of action more appealing to everyone involved.

> *Back to the Ajax Case.* The Ajax plant is going to be closed. Given that, the possible alternative approaches that can be considered are (1) close the plant on schedule and be done with it; (2) delay the plant closing until all efforts have been made to sell it to another firm; (3) offer to sell the plant to the employees and/or local interests; (4) close the plant and offer transfers to other Ajax plant locations; or (5) close the plant, offer transfers, and help the employees find new jobs in and around Murphysboro.

# Step 3—Choose a Preferred Course of Action

This is the point where an actual decision is made to select a preferred course of action. Just how this choice occurs and by whom must be successfully resolved in each

FIGURE 7.6  **Differences in the classical and behavioral decision-making models.**

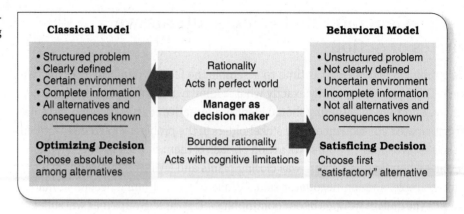

problem situation. Management theory recognizes rather substantial differences between the classical and behavioral models of decision making as shown in Figure 7.6.

## Classical Decision Model

The **classical decision model** de-scribes decision making with complete information.

The **classical decision model** views the manager as acting rationally in a certain world. The assumption is that a rational choice of the preferred course of action will be made by a decision maker who is fully informed about all possible alternatives. Here, the manager faces a clearly defined problem and knows all possible action alternatives, as well as their consequences. As a result, he or she makes an **optimizing decision** that gives the absolute best solution to the problem.

An **optimizing decision** chooses the alternative giving the absolute best solution to a problem.

## Behavioral Decision Model

Behavioral scientists question the assumptions of perfect information underlying the classical model. Perhaps best represented by the work of scholar Herbert Simon, they instead recognize *cognitive limitations* to our human information-processing capabilities.[34] These limits make it hard for managers to become fully informed and make optimizing decisions. They create a **bounded rationality**, such that manage-rial decisions are rational only within the boundaries set by the available informa-tion and known alternatives, both of which are incomplete.

**Bounded rationality** describes making decisions within the constraints of lim-ited information and alternatives.

The **behavioral decision model** describes decision making with limited information and bounded rationality.

Because of cognitive limitations and bounded rationalities, the **behavioral decision model** assumes that people act with only partial knowledge about the available action alternatives and their consequences. Consequently, the first alter-native that appears to give a satisfactory resolution of the problem is likely to be chosen. Simon, who won a Nobel Prize for his work, calls this the tendency to make **satisficing decisions**—choosing the first satisfactory alternative that comes to your attention. The behavioral model is useful in describing how many decisions get made in the ambiguous and fast-paced problem situations faced by managers.

A **satisficing decision** chooses the first satisfactory alternative that comes to one's attention.

*Back to the Ajax Case.* Ajax executives decided to close the plant, offer transfers to company plants in another state, and offer to help displaced employees find new jobs in and around Murphysboro.

## Step 4—Implement the Decision

Once a decision is made, actions must be taken to fully implement it. Nothing new can or will happen unless action is taken to actually solve the problem. Managers not only need the determination and creativity to arrive at a decision, they also need the ability and willingness to implement it.

> "HUMAN LIFE IS FAR MORE IMPORTANT THAN
> JUST GETTING TO THE TOP OF A MOUNTAIN"

## Climber Left to Die on Mt. Everest

Bobby Model/Getty Images, Inc.

Some 40 climbers are winding their ways to the top of Mount Everest. About 1,000 feet below the summit sits a British mountain climber in trouble, collapsed in a shallow snow cave. Most of those on the way up just look while continuing their climbs. Sherpas from one passing team pause to give him oxygen before moving on. Within hours David Sharp, 34, is dead of oxygen deficiency on the mountain.

A climber who passed by says: "At 28,000 feet it's hard to stay alive yourself . . . he was in very poor condition . . . , it was a very hard decision . . . he wasn't a member of our team."

Someone who made the summit in the past says: "If you're going to go to Everest . . . I think you have to accept responsibility that you may end up doing something that's not ethically nice . . . you have to realize that you're in a different world."

After hearing about this case, the late Sir Edmund Hillary, who reached the top in 1953, said: "Human life is far more important than just getting to the top of a mountain."

 **ETHICS QUESTIONS**

Who's right and who's wrong here? Should the climbers have ignored Sharp and continued on their way to the top of Mount Everest? Does this situation happen in real life—not on mountains but in our workplaces? How often do we meet people who are struggling or in trouble, but just pass them by as we pursue our own career interests and personal goals? When we encounter others who are having difficulties, what are our ethical or moral obligations to them? How do we make choices between what is best for us versus what is best for others?

---

Difficulties encountered when decisions get implemented may trace to **lack-of-participation error**. This is a failure to adequately involve in the process those persons whose support is necessary to put the decision into action. Managers who use participation wisely get the right people involved in problem solving from the beginning. When they do, implementation typically follows quickly, smoothly, and to everyone's satisfaction.

**Lack-of-participation error** is failure to involve in a decision the persons whose support is needed to implement it.

*Back to the Ajax Case.* Ajax ran ads in the local and regional newspapers. The ad called attention to an "Ajax skill bank" composed of "qualified, dedicated, and well-motivated employees with a variety of skills and experiences." Interested employers were urged to contact Ajax for further information.

## Step 5—Evaluate Results

The decision-making process is not complete until results are evaluated. If the desired outcomes are not achieved or if undesired side effects occur, corrective action should be taken. Evaluation is a form of managerial control. It involves gathering data to measure performance results and compare them against goals. If results are less than what was desired, it is time to reassess and return to earlier steps. In this way, problem solving becomes a dynamic and ongoing activity within the management process. Evaluation is always easier when clear goals, measurable targets, and timetables were established to begin with.

*Back to the Ajax Case.* How effective were Ajax's decisions? We don't know for sure. But after the advertisement ran for some 15 days, the plant's industrial relations manager said: "I've been very pleased with the results." That's all we know and more information would certainly be needed for a good evaluation of how well management handled this situation. Wouldn't you like to know how many of the displaced employees got new jobs locally and how the local economy held up? You can look back on the case as it was described and judge for yourself. Perhaps you would have approached the situation and the five steps in decision making somewhat differently.

## At All Steps—Check Ethical Reasoning

Each step in the decision-making process can and should be linked with ethical reasoning.[35] The choices made often have moral dimensions that might easily be overlooked. For example, job eliminations in the prior Ajax case might not be sufficiently considered for their implications on the affected persons, families, and community. We sometimes have to take special care to stay tuned into *virtues*—things like fairness, kindness, compassion, and generosity—and guard against *vices*—things like greed, anger, ignorance, and lust.[36]

One way to check ethical reasoning in decision making is to ask and answer pointed questions that bring critical thinking to the process. Gerald Cavanagh and his associates, for example, suggest that a decision should test positive on these four ethics criteria.[37]

1. *Utility*—Does the decision satisfy all constituents or stakeholders?

2. *Rights*—Does the decision respect the rights and duties of everyone?

3. *Justice*—Is the decision consistent with the canons of justice?

4. *Caring*—Is the decision consistent with my responsibilities to care?

The **spotlight questions** test the ethics of a decision by exposing it to scrutiny through the eyes of family, community members, and ethical role models.

Another way to test ethical reasoning is to consider consider a decision in the context of full transparency and the prospect of shame.[38] Three **spotlight questions** can be powerful in this regard. *Ask:* "How would I feel if my family found out about this decision?" *Ask:* "How would I feel if this decision were published in the local newspaper or posted on the Internet?" *Ask:* "What would the person you know or know of who has the strongest character and best ethical judgment do in this situation?"

It is also helpful to check decisions against the hazards of undue rationalizations. Caution is called for when you hear yourself or others saying, "It's just part of the job" . . . "We're fighting fire with fire" . . . "Everyone is doing it" . . . "I've got it coming" . . . "It's legal and permissible" . . . "I'm doing it just for you." Such comments or thoughts are warning signs that, if heeded, can prompt a review of the decision and perhaps lead to a more ethical outcome.

---

**LEARNING CHECK 3**

**TAKEAWAY QUESTION 3 What are the steps in the decision-making process?**

**Be sure you can** • list the steps in the decision-making process • apply these steps to a sample decision-making situation • explain cost-benefit analysis in decision making • discuss differences between the classical and behavioral decision models • define *optimizing* and *satisficing* • explain how lack-of-participation error can hurt decision making • list useful questions for double checking the ethical reasoning of a decision

# Issues in Managerial Decision Making

Once we accept the fact that we are likely to make imperfect decisions at least some of the time, it makes sense to try to understand why. Two common mistakes are falling prey to decision errors and traps, and not taking full advantage of creativity. Both can be easily avoided.

## Decision Errors and Traps

*Test:* Would you undergo heart surgery if the physician tells you the survival rate is 90%? Chances are you would. But if the physician tells you the mortality rate is 10%, the chances of you opting for surgery are lower.

What is happening here? Well-intentioned people often rely on simplifying strategies when making decisions with limited information, time pressures, and even insufficient energy. Psychologist Daniel Kahneman describes this as a triumph of *System 1 thinking*—automatic, effortless, quick, and associative—over *System 2 thinking*—conscious, slow, deliberate, and evaluative.[40] In the above test, the simplification of System 1 thinking is called "framing" because the decision to have surgery or not varies according to whether the information is presented as a survival rate—encouraging, or a mortality rate—threatening.[41] This and other simplifying strategies or rules of thumb are known as **heuristics**.[42] Although they can be helpful in dealing with complex and ambiguous situations, they also cause common decision-making errors.[43]

**Heuristics** are strategies for simplifying decision making.

### Framing Error

As just suggested, managers sometimes suffer from **framing error** that occurs when a problem is evaluated and resolved in the context in which it is perceived—either positively or negatively. Suppose, for example, data show a product that has a 40% market share. A negative frame views the product as deficient because it is missing 60% of the market. The likely discussion would focus on: "What are we doing wrong?" Alternatively, the frame could be a positive one, looking at the 40% share as a good accomplishment. In this case the discussion is more likely to proceed with "How do we do things better?" Sometimes people use framing as a tactic for presenting information in a way that gets other people to think inside the desired frame. In politics, this is often referred to as "spinning" the data.

**Framing error** is trying to solve a problem in the context in which it is perceived.

### Availability Bias

The **availability bias** occurs when people assess a current event or situation by using information that is "readily available" from memory. An example is deciding not to invest in a new product based on your recollection of a recent product failure. The potential bias is that the readily available information is fallible and irrelevant. For example, the product that recently failed may have been a good idea that was released to market at the wrong time of year.

The **availability bias** bases a decision on recent information or events.

### Representativeness Bias

The **representativeness bias** occurs when people assess the likelihood of something happening based on its similarity to a stereotyped set of occurrences. An

The **representativeness bias** bases a decision on similarity to other situations.

# Escalation Increases Risk of Unethical Decisions

When Marc and Vera L. Street reviewed research on escalating commitments to previously chosen courses of action, they realized that little has been done to investigate if escalation tendencies lead to unethical behaviors. To address this void, the researchers conducted an experiment with 155 undergraduate students working on a computerized investment task. They found that exposure to escalation situations increases tendencies toward unethical acts and that the tendencies further increase with the magnitude of the escalation.

Street and Street believe this link between escalation and poor ethics is driven by desires to get out of and avoid the increasing stress of painful situations. Additional findings from the study showed that students with an external locus of control were more likely to choose an unethical decision alternative than their counterparts with an internal locus of control.

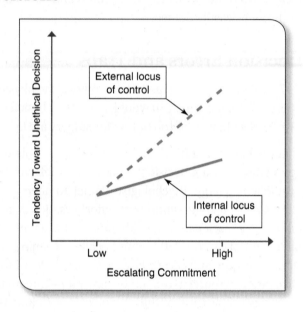

## YOU BE THE RESEARCHER

This study was done in the college classroom and under simulated decision conditions. How would you design a study that tests the same hypotheses in the real world? Also, is it possible to design a training program that would use the "Spotlight Questions" to help people better deal with unethical decision options in escalation situations?

*Reference:* Marc Street and Vera L. Street, "The Effects of Escalating Commitment on Ethical Decision Making," *Journal of Business Ethics*, vol. 64 (2006), pp. 343–56.

example is deciding to hire someone for a job vacancy simply because he or she graduated from the same school attended by your last and most successful new hire. The potential bias is that the representative stereotype masks factors important and relevant to the decision. For instance, the abilities and career expectations of the job candidate may not fit the job requirements; the school attended may be beside the point.

## Anchoring and Adjustment Bias

The **anchoring and adjustment bias** bases a decision on incremental adjustments from a prior decision point.

The **anchoring and adjustment bias** occurs when decisions are influenced by inappropriate allegiance to a previously existing value or starting point. An example is a manager who sets a new salary level for an employee by simply raising her prior year's salary by a small percentage amount. Although the increase may appear reasonable to the manager, the decision actually undervalues the employee relative to the job market. The small incremental salary adjustment, reflecting anchoring and adjustment bias, may end up prompting her to look for another, higher-paying job.

## Confirmation Error

One of our tendencies after making a decision is to try and find ways to justify it. In the case of unethical acts, for example, we try to "rationalize" them after the fact. This is called **confirmation error**. It means that we notice, accept, and even seek out only information that confirms or is consistent with a decision we have just made. Contrary information that shows what we are doing is incorrect is downplayed or denied.

> ## Management**Smarts**
>
> ### How to Avoid the Escalation Trap in Decision Making
>
> - Set advance limits on your involvement and commitment to a particular course of action; stick with these limits.
> - Make your own decisions; don't follow the leads of others, since they are also prone to escalation.
> - Carefully assess why you are continuing a course of action; if there are no good reasons to continue, don't.
> - Remind yourself of what a course of action is costing; consider saving these costs as a reason to discontinue.
> - Watch for escalation tendencies in your behaviors and those of others.

## Escalating Commitment

Another decision-making trap is **escalating commitment**. This occurs as a decision to increase effort and perhaps apply more resources to pursue a course of action that is not working.[44] Managers prone to escalation let the momentum of the situation and personal ego overwhelm them. They are unwilling to admit they were wrong and unable to "call it quits," even when facts indicate that this is the best thing to do. This is a common decision error, perhaps one that you are personally familiar with. It is sometimes called the *sunk-cost fallacy*. Management Smarts offers advice on how to avoid tendencies toward escalating commitments to previously chosen courses of action.

A **confirmation error** occurs when focusing only on information that confirms a decision already made.

**Escalating commitment** is the continuation of a course of action even though it is not working.

# Creativity in Decision Making

*Situation*—Elevator riders in a new high-rise building are complaining about long waiting times. *Building engineers' advice*—upgrade the entire system at substantial cost. Why? He assumed that any solutions to a slow elevator problem had to be mechanical ones. *Creativity consultant's advice*—place floor-to-ceiling mirrors by the elevators. Why? People, he suspected, would not notice waiting times because they were distracted by their and others' reflections. *Outcome*—the creativity consultant was right.[45]

**Creativity** in decision making occurs as a novel idea or unique approach to solving problems or exploiting opportunities.[46] The potential for creativity is one of our greatest personal assets, even though this fact may be unrecognized by ourselves and by others. One of the reasons is that we all too often we limit our thinking about creativity to what researchers call **Big-C creativity**—when extraordinary things are done by exceptional people.[47] Think Big-C creativity when you use or see someone using an iPhone or iPad—Steve Jobs' creativity, or browse Facebook—Mark Zuckerburg's creativity.

But don't get sidetracked by Big-C creativity alone. There is lots of **Little-C creativity** around also. It occurs when average people come up with unique ways to deal with daily events and situations. Think Little-C creativity, for example, the next time you solve relationship problems at home, build something for the kids, or even find ways to pack too many things into too small a suitcase.

**Creativity** is the generation of a novel idea or unique approach that solves a problem or crafts an opportunity.

**Big-C creativity** occurs when extraordinary things are done by exceptional people.

**Little-C creativity** occurs when average people come up with unique ways to deal with daily events and situations.

Yuri Arcurs/Alamy Limited

# Want Creativity? Don't Punish Mistakes, Reward Them

Would you like to work with a box of used kitty litter under your conference table? A group of executives had mixed reactions after finding out that was the case—many laughed; two left the room. The culprit was Amanda Zolten. She did the stunt as part of a pitch for her agency, Grey New York, to do ads for the firm's kitty litter products. Zolten says she was trying to achieve a "memorable experience." Her boss, Tor Myhren, said "there was enough chaos in the room we didn't know if it was a good or bad thing." But, it earned Zolten a Heroic Failure Award that Myhren gives out to stimulate risk taking and avoid risk aversion at the fast-growing ad agency.

**Design thinking** unlocks creativity in decision making through a process of experiencing, ideation, and prototyping.

Just imagine what can be accomplished with all the creative potential—Big-C and Little-C—that exists in an organization. How do you turn that potential into creative decisions? David Kelley, founder of the design firm IDEO, believes that a lot, perhaps most, of us start to lose our creativity skills in primary school.[48] It's something about being taught to look for answers to assigned problems and fearing failure when taking standardized tests. But, he also believes our creativity can be reenergized when we commit to learning by doing, reach out to collaborate with others, and stop fearing failure. This sets the stage for making creative decisions through what Kelly calls **design thinking**. First comes *experiencing*—defining problems by research and observation; not simply accepting them as delivered. Second comes *ideation*—visualizing and brainstorming potential solutions in collaboration with others. Third comes *prototyping*—testing and modifying the potential solution over and over to achieve the best outcome.

## Personal Creativity Drivers

The small figure identifies task expertise, task motivation, and creativity skills as personal creativity drivers.[49] This three-component model points us in useful directions for personal creativity development as well as toward management actions that can boost creativity in a team or work unit.

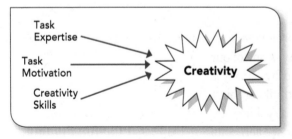

Creative decisions are more likely to occur when the person or team has a lot of *task expertise*. Creativity grows from something one is good at or knows about, while extending it in new directions. Creative decisions are more likely as well when someone is highly *task-motivated*. Creativity tends to occur in part because people work exceptionally hard to resolve a problem or exploit an opportunity.

Creative decisions are also more likely when the people involved have strong personal *creativity skills*. There is general agreement, for example, that creative people tend to work with high energy, hold their ground in the face of criticism, and act resourceful even in difficult situations. They have strong associative skills, meaning they are good at making connections among seemingly unrelated facts or events. They have strong behavioral skills of questioning, observing, networking, and experimenting.[50] They are also good at synthesizing information to find correct answers (convergent thinking), looking at diverse ways to solve problems (lateral thinking), and thinking "outside of the box" (divergent thinking).[51]

## Situational Creativity Drivers

If you mix creative people and traditional organization and management practices, what will you get? Perhaps not much; it takes more than individual creativity alone to make innovation a way of life in organizations. The situational creativity drivers shown here are important too.

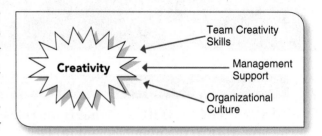

Managers should, of course, make sure that their organizations and teams are well staffed with creative members. But they should also realize these *team creativity skills* will blossom best when backed by good *management support* and the right *organizational culture*. This means things like having a team leader with the patience to allow for creative processes to work themselves through a decision situation. It means having top management that is willing to accept and even celebrate failure, and to provide the resources—time, technology, and space—that are helpful to the creative processes. It also means making creativity a top organizational priority and a core value in the organizational culture.

*Think creativity gained* the next time you see a young child playing with a really neat toy. It may be from Fisher-Price Toys—part of Mattel, Inc. In the firm's headquarters you'll find a special place called the "Cave," and it's not your typical office space. Picture bean-bag chairs, soft lighting, casual chairs, and couches. It's a place for brainstorming, where designers, marketers, engineers, and others can meet and join in freewheeling to come up with the next great toy for preschoolers. Consultants recommend that such innovation spaces be separated from the normal workplace and be large enough for no more than 15 to 20 people.[52]

*Think creativity wasted* the next time you watch TV on a beautiful, large, flat-panel screen. In 1964, George H. Heilmeier showed his employers at RCA Labs his new discovery—a liquid-crystal display, or LCD. They played with it until 1968 when RCA executives decided the firm was so heavily invested in color TV tubes that they weren't really interested. Today the market is dominated by Japanese, Korean, and Taiwanese producers, with not a single U.S. maker in the play. Ironically, Heilmeier received the Kyoto Prize, considered the Nobel Prize of Japan, for his pioneering innovation.[53]

---

**LEARNING CHECK 4**

**TAKEAWAY QUESTION 4 What are current issues in managerial decision making?**

**Be sure you can** • explain the availability, representativeness, anchoring, and adjustment heuristics • illustrate framing error, confirmation error, and escalating commitment in decision making • identify key personal and situational creativity drivers

# MANAGEMENT LEARNING REVIEW

## LEARNING CHECK SUMMARY

### TAKEAWAY QUESTION 1  What is the role of information in the management process?

- Technological, information, and analytical competencies are all needed to take advantage of information technology in decision making.
- Data are raw facts and figures; information is data made useful for decision making; useful information is timely, high quality, complete, relevant, and understandable.
- Analytics is the systematic evaluation and analysis of information for decision making.
- Management information systems collect, organize, store, and distribute data to meet the information needs of managers.
- Business intelligence systems organize and display data, often in the form of dashboards, so that patterns and trends are evident to decision makers.
- Information technology is breaking barriers within and between organizations as rapidly expanding developments help speed workflows and cut costs.

**For Discussion What are the potential downsides to the ways IT is changing organizations?**

### TAKEAWAY QUESTION 2  How do managers use information to make decisions?

- Managers serve as information nerve centers in the process of planning, organizing, leading, and controlling activities in organizations.
- Managers can display problem avoidance, problem solving, and problem seeking in facing problems.
- Managers vary in the use of systematic and intuitive thinking, and in tendencies toward multidimensional thinking.
- Managers must understand the different cognitive styles people use in decision making.
- Programmed decisions are routine solutions to recurring and structured problems; nonprogrammed decisions are unique solutions to novel and unstructured problems.
- Crisis problems occur unexpectedly and can lead to disaster if not handled quickly and properly.
- Managers face problems and make decisions under conditions of certainty, risk, and uncertainty.

**For Discussion When would a manager be justified in acting as a problem avoider?**

### TAKEAWAY QUESTION 3  What are the steps in the decision-making process?

- The steps in the decision-making process are (1) find and define the problem, (2) generate and evaluate alternatives, (3) decide on the preferred course of action, (4) implement the decision, and (5) evaluate the results.
- An optimizing decision, following the classical model, chooses the absolute best solution from a known set of alternatives.
- A satisficing decision, following the behavioral model, chooses the first satisfactory alternative to come to attention.
- To check the ethical reasoning of a decision at any step in the decision-making process, it is helpful to ask the ethics criteria questions of utility, rights, justice, and caring.
- To check the ethical reasoning of a decision at any step in the decision-making process, it is helpful to ask the spotlight questions that expose the decision to transparency in the eyes of family, community members, and ethical role models.

**For Discussion Do the steps in the decision-making process have to be followed in order?**

### TAKEAWAY QUESTION 4  What are current issues in managerial decision making?

- Common decision errors and traps include the availability, representation, and anchoring and adjustment biases, as well as framing error, confirmation error, and escalating commitment.
- Creativity in decision making can be enhanced by the personal creativity drivers of individual creativity skills, task expertise, and motivation.
- Creativity in decision making can be enhanced by the situational creativity drivers of group creativity skills, management support, and organizational culture.

**For Discussion Which decision trap seems most evident as an influence on bad choices made by business CEOs today?**

## SELF-TEST 7

## Multiple-Choice Questions

1. Among the ways information technology is changing organizations today, _____ is one of its most noteworthy characteristics.
   (a) eliminating need for top managers
   (b) reducing information available for decision making
   (c) breaking down barriers internally and externally
   (d) decreasing need for environmental awareness

2. Whereas management information systems use the latest technologies to collect, organize, and distribute data, _____ involves tapping the available data to extract and report it in organized ways that are most useful to decision makers.
   (a) analytics
   (b) business intelligence
   (c) anchoring and adjustment
   (d) optimizing

3. A manager who is reactive and works hard to address problems after they occur is known as a _____.
   (a) problem seeker
   (b) problem avoider
   (c) problem solver
   (d) problem manager

4. A(n) _____ thinker approaches problems in a rational and an analytic fashion.
   (a) systematic
   (b) intuitive
   (c) internal
   (d) external

5. A person likes to deal with hard facts and clear goals in a decision situation; she also likes to be in control and keep things impersonal. This person's cognitive style tends toward _____.
   (a) sensation thinking
   (b) intuitive thinking
   (c) sensation feeling
   (d) intuitive feeling

6. The assigning of probabilities for action alternatives and their consequences indicates the presence of _____ in the decision environment.
   (a) certainty
   (b) optimizing
   (c) risk
   (d) satisficing

7. The first step in the decision-making process is to _____.
   (a) identify alternatives
   (b) evaluate results
   (c) find and define the problem
   (d) choose a solution

8. Being asked to develop a plan to increase international sales of a product is an example of the types of _____ problems that managers must be prepared to deal with.
   (a) routine
   (b) unstructured
   (c) crisis
   (d) structured

9. Costs, timeliness, and _____ are among the recommended criteria for evaluating alternative courses of action.
   (a) ethical soundness
   (b) competitiveness
   (c) availability
   (d) simplicity

10. A common mistake made by managers in crisis situations is that they _____.
    (a) try to get too much information before responding
    (b) rely too much on group decision making
    (c) isolate themselves to make the decision alone
    (d) forget to use their crisis management plan

11. The _____ decision model views managers as making optimizing decisions, whereas the _____ decision model views them as making satisficing decisions.
    (a) behavioral, human relations
    (b) classical, behavioral
    (c) heuristic, humanistic
    (d) quantitative, behavioral

12. When a manager makes a decision about someone's annual pay raise only after looking at his or her current salary, the risk is that the decision will be biased because of _____.
    (a) a framing error
    (b) escalating commitment
    (c) anchoring and adjustment
    (d) strategic opportunism

13. When a problem is addressed according to the positive or negative context in which it is presented, this is an example of _____.
    (a) framing error
    (b) escalating commitment
    (c) availability and adjustment
    (d) strategic opportunism

14. When a manager decides to continue pursuing a course of action that facts otherwise indicate is failing to deliver desired results, this is called _____.
    (a) strategic opportunism
    (b) escalating commitment
    (c) confirmation error
    (d) the risky shift

15. Personal creativity drivers include creativity skills, task expertise, and _____.
    (a) emotional intelligence
    (b) management support
    (c) organizational culture
    (d) task motivation

## Short-Response Questions

16. What is the difference between an optimizing decision and a satisficing decision?

17. How can a manager double-check the ethics of a decision?

18. How would a manager use systematic thinking and intuitive thinking in problem solving?

19. How can the members of an organization be trained in crisis management?

## Essay Question

20. As a participant in a new mentoring program between your university and a local high school, you have volunteered to give a presentation to a class of sophomores on the challenges in the new "electronic office." The goal is to sensitize them to developments in information technology and motivate them to take the best advantage of their high school academics so as to prepare themselves for the workplace of the future. What will you say to them?

# MANAGEMENT SKILLS AND COMPETENCIES

## Further Reflection: Self-Confidence

If managers are to make consistently good decisions they must be skilled at gathering and processing information. But managers also have to be implementers. Once decisions are made, they are expected to rally people and resources to put them into action. This is how problems actually get solved and opportunities get explored. In order for all this to happen, managers need the **self-confidence** to turn decisions into real action accomplishments; they must believe in their decisions and the information foundations for them. A better understanding of your personal style in gathering and processing information can go a long way toward building your self-confidence as a decision maker.

 **DO IT NOW . . .**
**LOOK IN THE MIRROR**

- Opportunities to improve your self-confidence abound, but you have to act in order to take advantage of them. What about your involvement in student organizations, recreational groups, and community activities?
- Do a self-check: Make a list of things you are already doing that offer ways of building your self confidence. Just what are you gaining from these experiences?
- Make another list that describes what you could do to gain more experience and add more self-confidence to your skills portfolio between now and graduation.

## Self-Assessment: Cognitive Style

### Instructions

This assessment is designed to get an impression of your cognitive style based on the work of psychologist Carl Jung.[54] For each of the following 12 pairs, place a "1" next to the statement that best describes you. Do this for each pair, even though the description you choose may not be perfect.

1. (a) I prefer to learn from experience.
   (b) I prefer to find meanings in facts and how they fit together.

2. (a) I prefer to use my eyes, ears, and other senses to find out what is going on.
   (b) I prefer to use imagination to come up with new ways to do things.

3. (a) I prefer to use standard ways to deal with routine problems.
   (b) I prefer to use novel ways to deal with new problems.

4. (a) I prefer ideas and imagination.
   (b) I prefer methods and techniques.

5. (a) I am patient with details, but get impatient when they get complicated.
   (b) I am impatient and jump to conclusions, but I am also creative, imaginative, and inventive.

6. (a) I enjoy using skills already mastered more than learning new ones.
   (b) I like learning new skills more than practicing old ones.

7. (a) I prefer to decide things logically.
   (b) I prefer to decide things based on feelings and values.

8. (a) I like to be treated with justice and fairness.
   (b) I like to be praised and to please other people.

9. (a) I sometimes neglect or hurt other people's feelings without realizing it.
   (b) I am aware of other people's feelings.

10. (a) I give more attention to ideas and things than to human relationships.
    (b) I can predict how others will feel.

11. (a) I do not need harmony; arguments and conflicts don't bother me.
    (b) I value harmony and get upset by arguments and conflicts.

12. (a) I am often described as analytical, impersonal, unemotional, objective, critical, hard nosed, rational.
    (b) I am often described as sympathetic, people-oriented, unorganized, uncritical, understanding, ethical.

## Self-Assessment Scoring

Sum your scores as follows, and record them in the parentheses. (Note that the *Sensing* and *Feeling* scores will be recorded as negatives.)

- (−    ) *Sensing* (*S Type*) 5 1a 1 2a 1 3a 1 4a 1 5a 1 6a
- (    ) *Intuitive* (*N Type*) 5 1b 1 2b 1 3b 1 4b 1 5b 1 6b
- (    ) *Thinking* (*T Type*) 5 7a 1 8a 1 9a 1 10a 1 11a 1 12a
- (−    ) *Feeling* (*F Type*) 5 7b 1 8b 1 9b 1 10b 1 11b 1 12b

## Interpretation

This assessment contrasts personal tendencies toward information gathering (sensation vs. intuition) and information evaluation (feeling vs. thinking) in one's approach to problem solving. The result is a classification of four master cognitive styles and their characteristics. Read the descriptions provided in the chapter text and consider the implications of your suggested style, including how well you might work with persons whose styles are very different.

# Team Exercise:
# Lost at Sea

## Consider This Situation[55]

You are sailing on a private yacht in the South Pacific when a fire of unknown origin destroys the yacht and most of its contents. You and a small group of survivors are now in a large raft with oars. Your location is un-clear, but you estimate that you are about 1,000 miles south-southwest of the nearest land. One person has just found in her pockets five $1 bills and a packet of matches. Everyone else's pockets are empty. The items below are available to you on the raft.

| | Individual ranking | Team ranking | Expert ranking |
|---|---|---|---|
| Sextant | | | |
| Shaving mirror | | | |
| 5 gallons water | | | |
| Mosquito netting | | | |
| 1 survival meal | | | |
| Maps of Pacific Ocean | | | |
| Floatable seat cushion | | | |
| 2 gallons oil-gas mix | | | |
| Small transistor radio | | | |
| Shark repellent | | | |
| 20 square feet black plastic | | | |
| 1 quart 20-proof rum | | | |
| 15 feet nylon rope | | | |
| 24 chocolate bars | | | |
| Fishing kit | | | |

## Instructions

1. *Working alone*, rank the 15 items in order of their importance to your survival ("1" is most important and "15" is least important).

2. *Working in an assigned group*, arrive at a "team" ranking of the 15 items. Appoint one person as team spokesperson to report your team ranking to the class.

3. *Do not write in Column C* until your instructor provides the "expert" ranking.

## Career Situations for Decision Makers: What Would You Do?

1. **Tired of Excuses** Little problems are popping up at the most inconvenient times to make your work as team leader sometimes difficult and even aggravating. Today it's happened again. Trevor just called in "sick," saying his doctor advised him yesterday that it was better to stay home than to come to work and infect others with his flu. It makes sense, but it's also a hardship for you and the team. What can you do to best manage this type of situation since it's sure to happen again?

2. **Social Loafing Problem** You are under a lot of pressure because your team is having performance problems traced, in part at least, to persistent social loafing by one team member. You have come up with a reason to remove her from the team. But, you've done the ethics analysis and the decision you are about to make fails all three of the spotlight questions. As team leader, what will you do now?

3. **Task Force Selection** You have finally caught the attention of senior management. Top executives asked you to chair a task force to develop a creative new product that can breathe new life into an existing product line. To begin, you need to select the members of the task force. What criteria will you use to choose members who are most likely to bring high levels of creativity to this team?

## Case Study

# Amazon

Go to *Management Cases for Critical Thinking* to find the recommended case for Chapter 7—"Amazon.com: One E-Store to Rule Them All."

Amazon.com has soared ahead of other online merchants. What the firm can't carry in its many worldwide warehouses, affiliated retailers distribute for it. Not content to rest on past laurels, CEO Jeff Bezos keeps introducing new Amazon products and services. New versions of the Kindle keep rolling out to attract customers and keep them loyal to the Amazon store.

In just over a decade, Amazon.com has grown from a one-man operation into a global giant of commerce. By forging alliances to ensure that he has what customers want and making astute purchases, Jeff Bezos has made Amazon the go-to brand for online shopping. But with its significant investments in new media and services, does the company risk spreading itself too thin? Will customers continue to flock to Amazon as the go-to company for their every need?

HO/REUTERS/Newscom

# Wisdom
## Learning From Others

### > THINK NOW AND EMBRACE THE FUTURE

Having grown up poor, Oprah Winfrey says she is grateful for getting a good education, calling it "the most vital aspect of my life." She's now sharing that lesson through the Oprah Winfrey Leadership Academy for young women in South Africa.

When the academy's opened Winfrey said: "I wanted to give this opportunity to girls who had a light so bright that not even poverty could dim that light." Her goal was for the new academy to "be the best school in the world."

Nelson Mandela, first president of non-apartheid South Africa, spoke at the opening ceremony and praised her vision. "The key to any country's future is in educating its youth," said Mandela. "Oprah is therefore not only investing in a few young individuals, but in the future of our country." One of the first students said: "I would have had a completely different life if this hadn't happened to me."

Even the best intentions couldn't guarantee that everything would go according to Winfrey's plan. Not long after the academy launched, it was hit by scandal over alleged abuse of students by a dorm matron. Oprah quickly apologized to the students and their families, and rededicated herself to the school.

"I think that crisis is there to teach you about life," she said. "The school is going to be even better because that happened."[1]

### MORE TO LOOK FOR INSIDE>

# Planning Processes and Techniques

## > TIME MANAGEMENT

When it comes to planning, one of the first things that may come to mind is time. It is one of our most precious resources and **time management** is an essential career skill.

Some 77% of managers in one survey said that the new digital age has increased the number of decisions they have to make. Not too surprising perhaps. But what about this? Forty-three percent said there was less time available to make these decisions.[2] And, who hasn't complained or heard others complain "there's just not enough hours in the day to get everything done"?

Don't you wonder about the time you waste every day?—instant messages, voice and text messages, drop-in visitors, and more? Of course, you have to be careful in defining *waste*.

It isn't a waste of time to occasionally relax, take a breather from work or daily affairs, and find humor and pleasure in social interactions. Breaks help us gather and replenish energies.

It is a waste to let friends dominate your time so that you don't work on a term paper until it is too late to write a really good one, or delay a decision to apply for an internship until the deadline is passed.

Can the "Checkup" shown here help you keep time management on your side?

## Insight
### Learning About Yourself

---

**TIME MANAGEMENT CHECKUP**

*List 1—What I have to do tomorrow*
  (A) Most important, top priority—these are things you *must* do.
  (B) Important, not top priority—these are things you *should* do.
  (C) Least important, low priority—these are things you *might* do.
  (D) Not important, no priority—these are things you *should not* do.
  *Ask:* Do my actions match the priorities?

*List 2—Time wasters*
  (A) Things I can control—they won't happen if I don't let them.
  (B) Things I can't control—they happen and I can't do anything about it.
  *Ask:* Are you taking control where you can?

---

## BUILD MANAGEMENT SKILLS AND COMPETENCIES AT END OF CHAPTER

- Engage in *Further Reflection on Time Management*
- Take the *Self-Assessment—Time Management Profile*
- Complete the *Team Exercise—The Future Workplace/Personal Career Planning*
- Solve the *Career Situations for Planners*
- Analyze the *Case Study—"Walgreens: Staying One Step Ahead"*

<GET TO KNOW YOURSELF BETTER

| TAKEAWAY 1 | TAKEAWAY 2 | TAKEAWAY 3 | TAKEAWAY 4 |
|---|---|---|---|
| **Why and How Managers Plan**<br>• Importance of planning<br>• The planning process<br>• Benefits of planning<br>• Planning and time management | **Types of Plans Used by Managers**<br>• Long-range and short-range plans<br>• Strategic and tactical plans<br>• Operational plans | **Planning Tools and Techniques**<br>• Forecasting<br>• Contingency planning<br>• Scenario planning<br>• Benchmarking<br>• Use of staff planners | **Implementing Plans to Achieve Results**<br>• Goal setting<br>• Goal alignment<br>• Participation and involvement |
| LEARNING CHECK 1 | LEARNING CHECK 2 | LEARNING CHECK 3 | LEARNING CHECK 4 |

Managers need the ability to look ahead, make good plans, and help themselves and others meet the challenges of the future. But it can be easy to get so engrossed in the present that we forget about what lies ahead. Other times a mad rush to the future can go off track due to all sorts of uncertainties and lack of familiar reference points. The trick is to blend the lessons of past experiences with future aspirations, and with a willingness to adapt as new circumstances arise.

No one knows for sure what the future holds. The likelihood is that even the best of plans will have to be adjusted and changed at some point. We need the insight and courage to be flexible, and the discipline to stay focused on goals even as complications and problems arise.

## Why and How Managers Plan

The management process involves planning, organizing, leading, and controlling the use of resources to achieve performance objectives. The first of these functions, **planning**, sets the stage for the others by providing a sense of direction. It is a process of setting objectives and determining how best to accomplish them. Said a bit differently, planning involves deciding exactly what you want to accomplish and how best to go about it.

**Planning** is the process of setting objectives and determining how to accomplish them.

### Importance of Planning

When planning is done well it creates a solid platform for the other management functions. It helps with *organizing*—allocating and arranging resources to accomplish tasks, *leading*—guiding the efforts of human resources to ensure high levels of task accomplishment, and *controlling*—monitoring task accomplishments and taking necessary corrective action.

The centrality of planning in management is shown in Figure 8.1. Good planning helps us become better at what we are doing and to stay action-oriented. An Eaton Corporation annual report, for example, once stated: "Planning at Eaton means making the hard decisions before events force them upon you, and anticipating the future needs of the market before the demand asserts itself."[3]

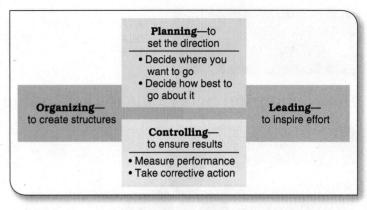

FIGURE 8.1 **The roles of planning and controlling in the management process.**

## The Planning Process

The five basic steps in the planning process are:

1. *Define your objectives*—Identify desired outcomes or results in very specific ways. Know where you want to go; be specific enough that you will know you have arrived when you get there, or know how far off the mark you are at various points along the way.

2. *Determine where you stand vis-à-vis objectives*—Evaluate current accomplishments relative to the desired results. Know where you stand in reaching the objectives; know what strengths work in your favor and what weaknesses may hold you back.

3. *Develop premises regarding future conditions*—Anticipate future events. Generate alternative "scenarios" for what may happen; identify for each scenario things that may help or hinder progress toward your objectives.

4. *Analyze alternatives and make a plan*—List and evaluate possible actions. Choose the alternative most likely to accomplish your objectives; describe what must be done to follow the best course of action.

5. *Implement the plan and evaluate results*—Take action and carefully measure your progress toward objectives. Follow through by doing what the plan requires; evaluate results, take corrective action, and revise plans as needed.

Planning should focus attention on **objectives** and **goals** that identify the specific results or desired outcomes that one intends to achieve. But the objectives and goals have to be good ones; they should push you to achieve substantial, not trivial, things. Jack Welch, former CEO of GE, believed in what he called **stretch goals**—performance targets that we have to work extra hard and really stretch to reach.[4] Would you agree that Welch's concept of stretch goals adds real strength to the planning process for both organizations and individuals?

> **Objectives** and **goals** are specific results that one wishes to achieve.

> **Stretch goals** are performance targets that we have to work extra hard and stretch to reach.

It's important not to forget the action side of planning. The process should always create a real and concrete **plan**, a statement of action steps to be taken in order to accomplish objectives and goals. These steps must be clear and compelling, so that the all-important follow through takes place. Plans alone don't deliver results; implemented plans do. Like other decision making in organizations, the best planning includes the active participation of those people whose work efforts will eventually determine whether or not the plans get put into action successfully.

> A **plan** is a statement of intended means for accomplishing objectives.

It's also important to remember that planning is not something managers do only on occasion and while working alone in quiet rooms, free from distractions, and at

## Don Thompson Sets Goals for a Winning Role at McDonald's

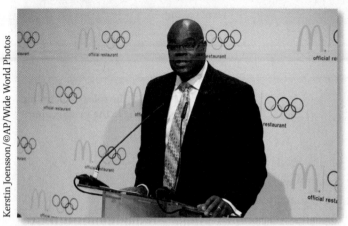

Kerstin Joensson/©AP/Wide World Photos

Some call Don Thompson, CEO of McDonald's, the accidental executive. He surely followed an unusual career path.

After graduating from Purdue with a degree in electrical engineering, Johnson went to work for Northrop Grumman, a leading global security company. One day he received a call from a head-hunter. Thompson listened, thinking the job being offered was at McDonnell Douglas Company, a firm in which engineering is central. Finding out it was at McDonald's, he almost turned the opportunity down. But he took the interview and his career changed course.

Thompson did well from the start but became frustrated after failing to win the annual McDonald's President's Award.

He confided to Raymond Mines, at the time the firm's highest-ranking African-American executive, that he "wanted to have an impact on decisions," Mines told him to move out of engineering and into the operations side of the business. Thompson did. His work excelled and got the attention he needed to move to higher responsibilities in restaurant operations, franchisee relations, and strategic management.

McDonald's was on a real run of success when Thompson took over as CEO. Some wonder if that record of past success is going to be hard to live up to in the future. But Thompson has created his own success story and seems well up to the task ahead.

Former mentor Raymond Mines describes Thompson this way: "He has the ability to listen, blend in, analyze, and communicate. People feel at ease with him. A lot of corporate executives have little time for those below them. Don makes everyone a part of the process." As for Thompson, he says "I want to make sure others achieve their goals, just as I have."

 **WHAT'S YOUR TAKE?**

Don Thompson has done very well in his career. How much of his success traces to strong motivation and clear goals? Is his resiliency when things didn't always go according to plan a strength that many others might lack? What skills does Thompson display that could be benchmarks for ones you might also develop for career success?

---

scheduled times. It is an ongoing process, done continuously while dealing with an otherwise busy and demanding work setting.

## Benefits of Planning

The pressures organizations face come from many sources. Externally, these include changing social norms and ethical expectations, government regulations, uncertainties of a global economy, changing technologies, and the sheer cost of investments in labor, capital, and other supporting resources. Internally, they include the quest for operating efficiencies, new structures and technologies, alternative work arrangements, greater workplace diversity, and concerns for work–life balance. As you would expect, planning in such conditions has a number of benefits for both organizations and individuals.

### Planning Improves Focus and Flexibility

Good planning improves focus and flexibility, both of which are important for performance success. An organization with focus knows what it does best, knows the needs of its customers, and knows how to serve them well. An individual with focus knows where he or she wants to go in a career or situation, and in life overall. An organization with flexibility is willing and able to change and adapt to shifting circumstances without losing focus, and it operates with an orientation toward the future rather than the past. An individual with flexibility adjusts career plans to fit new and developing opportunities.

## Planning Improves Action Orientation

Planning focuses our attention on priorities and helps avoid the **complacency trap**—simply being carried along by the flow of events. It is a way for people and organizations to stay ahead of the competition and become better at what they are doing. Planning keeps the future visible as a performance target and reminds us that the best decisions are often those made before events force problems upon us.

The **complacency trap** is being carried along by the flow of events.

Management consultant Stephen R. Covey points out that the most successful executives "zero in on what they do that 'adds value' to an organization."[5] Instead of working on too many things, they work on the things that really count. Covey says that good planning makes managers more (1) results oriented—creating a performance-oriented sense of direction; (2) priority oriented—making sure the most important things get first attention; (3) advantage oriented—ensuring that all resources are used to best advantage; and (4) change oriented—anticipating problems and opportunities so they can be best dealt with.

> ### GOOD PLANNING HELPS MAKE US
>
> - *Action oriented*—keeping a results-driven sense of direction;
> - *Priority oriented*—making sure the most important things get first attention;
> - *Advantage oriented*—ensuring that all resources are used to best advantage;
> - *Change oriented*—anticipating problems and opportunities so they can be best dealt with.

## Planning Improves Coordination and Control

Planning improves coordination.[6] The individuals, groups, and subsystems in organizations are each doing many different things at the same time. But their efforts must also be combined into meaningful contributions to the organization as a whole. Good plans help coordinate the activities of people and subsystems so that their accomplishments advance performance for the organization.

When planning is done well it facilitates control. The link between planning and controlling begins when objectives and standards are set. They make it easier to measure results and take action to improve things as necessary. After launching a costly information technology upgrade, for example, executives at McDonald's realized that the system couldn't deliver on its promises. They stopped the project, took a loss of $170 million, and refocused the firm's plans and resources on projects with more direct impact on customers.[7]

This is how planning and controlling work closely together in the management process. Without planning, control lacks objectives and standards for measuring how things are going and identifying what could be done to make them go better. Without control, planning lacks the follow-through needed to ensure that things work out as planned. With both, it's a lot easier to spot when things aren't going well and make the necessary adjustments.

# Planning and Time Management

Daniel Vasella is CEO of Novartis AG and responsible for operations spread across 140 countries. He's also calendar-bound. He says: "I'm locked in by meetings,

## ManagementSmarts

### Personal Time Management Tips

1. *Do* say "No" to requests that divert you from what you really should be doing.
2. *Don't* get bogged down in details that you can address later or leave for others.
3. *Do* have a system for screening telephone calls, e-mails, and requests for meetings.
4. *Don't* let drop-in visitors or instant messages use too much of your time.
5. *Do* prioritize what you will work on in terms of importance and urgency.
6. *Don't* become calendar-bound by letting others control your schedule.
7. *Do* follow priorities and work on the most important and urgent tasks first.

travel and other constraints. . . . I have to put down in priority things I like to do." Kathleen Murphy is president of Fidelity Personal Investing. She's also calendar-bound, with conferences and travel booked well ahead. Meetings can be scheduled at half-hour intervals and work days can last 12 hours. She spends lots of time traveling, but tries to make good use of her time on planes. "No one can reach me by phone," she says, "and I can get reading and thinking done."[8]

These are common executive stories—tight schedules, little time alone, lots of meetings and phone calls, and not much room for spontaneity. The keys to success in such classic management scenarios rest, in part at least, with another benefit of good planning—time management.

Management Smarts offers useful tips on developing time management skills. And, a lot comes down to discipline and priorities. Lewis Platt, former chairman of Hewlett-Packard, once said: "Basically, the whole day is a series of choices."[9] These choices have to be made in ways that allocate your time to the most important priorities. Platt says that he was "ruthless about priorities" and that you "have to continually work to optimize your time."

Most of us have experienced the difficulties of balancing available time with our many commitments and opportunities. As suggested in the chapter opener, it is easy to lose track of time and fall prey to what consultants identify as "time wasters." All too often we allow our time to be dominated by other people or to be misspent on nonessential activities.[10] "To-Do" lists can help, but they have to contain the right things. In daily living and in management, it is important to distinguish between things that you must do (top priority), should do (high priority), would be nice to do (low priority), and really don't need to do (no priority).

### LEARNING CHECK 1

**TAKEAWAY QUESTION 1 Why and how do managers plan?**

**Be sure you can** • explain the importance of planning as the first of four management functions • list the steps in the formal planning process • illustrate the benefits of planning for an organization familiar to you • illustrate the benefits of planning for your personal career development • list at least three things you can do now to improve your time management

## Types of Plans Used by Managers

"I am the master of my fate: I am the captain of my soul." How often have you heard this phrase? The lines are from *Invictus*, written by British poet William Earnest Henley in 1875. He was sending a message, one of confidence and control, as he moved forward into the future. That notion, however, worries a scholar by the name of Richard Levin. His response to Henley is: "Not without a plan you're not."[11]

Managers use a variety of plans as they face different challenges in organizations. In some cases the planning environment is stable and quite predictable; in others, it is more dynamic and uncertain. Different needs call for different types of plans.

## Long-Range and Short-Range Plans

It used to be that **long-term plans** looked three or more years into the future, while **short-term plans** covered one year or less. But, the environmental turmoil of recent years has put the concept of "long-term" planning to a stiff test. Would you agree that the complexities and uncertainties challenge how we go about planning and how far ahead we can really plan? At the very least we can say that there is a lot less permanency to long-term plans today and that they are subject to frequent revisions.

**Long-term plans** typically look three or more years into the future.

**Short-term plans** typically cover one year or less.

Even though the time frames of planning may be shrinking, top management is still responsible for setting longer-term plans and directions for the organization as a whole. They set the context for lower management to work on useful short-terms plans. And unless everyone understands an organization's long-term plans and objectives, there is always risk that the pressures of daily events will divert attention from important tasks. In other words, without a sense of long-term direction people can end up working hard and still not achieve significant results.

Management researcher Elliot Jaques suggests that people vary in their capability to think with different time horizons.[12] In fact, he believes that most people work comfortably with only 3-month time spans; a smaller group works well with a 1-year span; and only the very rare person can handle a 20-year time frame. These are provocative and personally challenging ideas. Although a team leader's planning may fall mainly in the weekly or monthly range, a chief executive is expected to have a vision extending years into the future. Career progress to higher management levels requires the conceptual skills to work well with longer-range time frames.

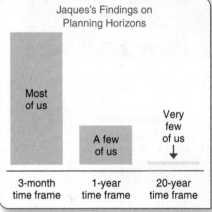

Jaques's Findings on Planning Horizons

Most of us — 3-month time frame

A few of us — 1-year time frame

Very few of us — 20-year time frame

## Plans Drive Rolls Royce into High-Wage Countries

imago stock & people/NewsCom

It's been common strategy for European and North American manufacturers to head toward Asia and Latin America to find low-wage destinations for their factories. But not Rolls Royce. You'll find the firm operating plants in places like England, Germany, and Norway. How does it compete? It keeps high-value work in high-wage locations and shifts low-value work to low-cost countries. One design manager for the firm says: "We aren't very good at cost per man-hour, so we have to be better on technology." Another executive states: "If you want to do complicated high-value engineering, you've got to have a good supply of skilled people and support from governments."

## Strategic and Tactical Plans

When a sports team enters a game, it typically does so with a "strategy" in hand. Most often this strategy is set by the head coach in conjunction with assistants. The goal is clear: Win the game. As the game unfolds, however, situations arise that require actions to solve problems or exploit opportunities. They call for "tactics" that deal with a current situation in ways that advance the overall strategy for winning. The same logic holds true for organizations. Plans at the top of the traditional organizational pyramid tend to be strategic in nature. Those at the middle and lower level are more tactical.

A **strategic plan** identifies long-term directions for the organization.

A **vision** clarifies the purpose of the organization and expresses what it hopes to be in the future.

**Strategic plans** are focused on the organization as a whole or a major component. They are longer-term plans that set broad action directions and create a frame of reference for allocating resources for maximum performance impact. Strategic plans ideally set forth the goals and objectives needed to accomplish the organization's **vision** in terms of mission or purpose and what it hopes to be in the future.

RESEARCH
BRIEF

# You've Got to Move Beyond Planning by the Calendar

Courtesy Harvard Business
School Publishing

**O**rganizations today need executives who can make faster and better decisions, and that means strategic planning must be done continuously. Michael C. Mankins and Richard Steele, writing in the *Harvard Business Review*, express their concerns that planning is too often viewed as an annual activity focused more on documenting plans for the record than on action. Little wonder, they suggest, that only 11% of executives in a survey of 156 firms with sales of $11 billion were highly satisfied that strategic planning is worthwhile.

The research, conducted in collaboration with Marakon Associates and the Economist Intelligence Unit, inquired as to how long-range strategic planning was conducted and how effective these planning activities were. Results showed that executives perceived a substantial disconnect between the way many firms approached strategic planning and the way they approached strategic decisions. Some 66% of the time, executives said that strategic planning at their firms was conducted only at set times, and very often was accomplished by a formal and structured process. Survey respondents also indicated that planning was often considered as only a "periodic event" and not something to be engaged in continuously. Mankins and Steele call such planning "calendar driven," and they question its effectiveness.

In calendar-driven planning, the researchers found that firms averaged only 2.5 major strategic decisions per year, with "major" meaning a decision that could move profits by more than 10%. They also point out that when planning is disconnected from the calendar, companies make higher-quality and more strategic decisions. The researchers call this alternative planning approach "continuous review" and argue it is more consistent with the way executives actually make decisions and business realities.

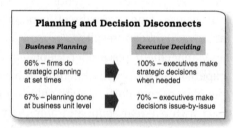

**Planning and Decision Disconnects**

| Business Planning | Executive Deciding |
|---|---|
| 66% – firms do strategic planning at set times | 100% – executives make strategic decisions when needed |
| 67% – planning done at business unit level | 70% – executives make decisions issue-by-issue |

### ■ YOU BE THE RESEARCHER

Why can tying planning to certain calendar dates end up being dysfunctional for a business? On the other hand, how can we plan almost continuously? Choose two or three organizations in your community for field research. Arrange interviews with their senior executives. Find out if they plan on a set schedule and if so, what that schedule might be. Probe further to find out how effective they consider planning in their organization to be, and what changes they might like to see made.

*Reference:* Michael C. Mankins and Richard Steele, "Stop Making Plans; Start Making Decisions," *Harvard Business Review* (January 2006), reprint R0601F.

**Tactical plans** are developed and used to implement strategic plans. They specify how the organization's resources can be used to put strategies into action. In the sports context you might think of tactical plans as having "special teams" or as "special plays" ready to meet a particular threat or opportunity. Tactical plans in business often take the form of **functional plans** that indicate how different components of the enterprise will contribute to the overall strategy. Such functional plans might include:

A **tactical plan** helps to implement all or parts of a strategic plan.

**Functional plans** indicate how different operations within the organization will help advance the overall strategy.

- *Production plans*—dealing with work methods and technologies.
- *Financial plans*—dealing with money and capital investments.
- *Facilities plans*—dealing with facilities and work layouts.
- *Logistics plans*—dealing with suppliers and acquiring resource inputs.
- *Marketing plans*—dealing with selling and distributing goods or services.
- *Human resource plans*—dealing with building a talented workforce.

## Operational Plans

**Operational plans** guide behavior and describe what needs to be done in the short term to support strategic and tactical plans. They include both *standing plans* like policies and procedures that are used over and over again, and *single-use plans* like budgets that apply to one specific task or time period.

An **operational plan** identifies short-term activities to implement strategic plans.

### Policies and Procedures

A **policy** communicates broad guidelines for making decisions and taking action in specific circumstances. Organizations operate with lots of policies, and they set expectations for many aspects of employee behavior. Typical human resource policies cover things like employee hiring, termination, performance appraisals, pay increases, promotions, and discipline. For example, Judith Nitsch made sexual harassment a top priority when starting her engineering-consulting business.[13] Nitsch

A **policy** is a standing plan that communicates broad guidelines for decisions and action.

---

**FACTS FOR ANALYSIS**

> SOME EMPLOYEES SIGN "LOVE CONTRACTS" SAYING OFFICE RELATIONSHIPS WON'T INTERFERE WITH THEIR WORK

## Policies on Office Romances Vary Widely

The press is quick to report when a top executive or public figure runs into trouble over an office affair. But the fact is that employer policies on office relationships vary. One survey finds the following.

- 24%—prohibit relationships among persons in the same department.
- 13%—prohibit relationships among persons who have the same supervisor.
- 80%—prohibit relationships between supervisors and subordinates.
- 5%—have no restrictions on office romances.

- New trend—"love contracts," where employees pledge that their romantic relationships in the office won't interfere with their work.

**YOUR THOUGHTS?**

Do you know anyone who has been involved in an office relationship? What is your thinking on this issue? Is this an area that employers should be regulating? Or should office romances be left to the best judgments of those involved? After all, it's their private business—isn't it?

defined a sexual harassment policy, took a hard line on its enforcement, and appointed both a male and a female employee for others to talk with about sexual harassment concerns.

**Procedures** describe specific rules for what actions are to be taken in various situations. They are stated in employee handbooks and often called SOPs—standard operating procedures. Whereas a policy sets a broad guideline, procedures define precise actions to be taken. In the prior example, Judith Nitsch was right to establish a sexual harassment policy for her firm. But, she should also put into place procedures that ensure everyone receives fair, equal, and nondiscriminatory treatment under the policy. Everyone in her firm should know both how to file a sexual harassment complaint and just how that complaint will be handled.

> A **procedure** is a rule describing actions that are to be taken in specific situations.

## Budgets

**Budgets** are single-use plans that commit resources for specific time periods to activities, projects, or programs. Managers typically spend a fair amount of time bargaining with higher levels to get adequate budgets to support the needs of their work units or teams. They are also expected to achieve work objectives while keeping within the allocated budget. To be "over budget" is generally bad; to come in "under budget" is generally good.

> A **budget** is a plan that commits resources to projects or activities.

Managers deal with and use a variety of budgets. *Financial budgets* project cash flows and expenditures; *operating budgets* plot anticipated sales or revenues against expenses; *nonmonetary budgets* allocate resources like labor, equipment, and space. A *fixed budget* allocates a stated amount of resources for a specific purpose, such as $50,000 for equipment purchases in a given year. A *flexible budget* allows resources to vary in proportion with various levels of activity, such as having extra money available to hire temporary workers when workloads exceed certain levels.

Because budgets link planned activities with the resources needed to accomplish them, they are useful for activating and tracking performance. But budgets can get out of control, creeping higher and higher without getting sufficient critical reviews. In fact, one of the most common budgeting problems is that resource allocations get "rolled over" from one time period to the next without rigorous scrutiny; the new budget is simply an incremental adjustment to the previous one. In a major division of Campbell Soups, for example, managers once discovered that 10% of the marketing budget was going to sales promotions no longer relevant to current product lines.

> A **zero-based budget** allocates resources as if each budget were brand new.

A **zero-based budget** deals with this roll-over budget problem by approaching each new budget period as it if were brand new. In zero-based budgeting there is no guarantee that any past funding will be renewed; all proposals—old and new, must compete for available funds at the start of each new budget cycle.

---

**LEARNING CHECK 2**

**TAKEAWAY QUESTION 2 What types of plans do managers use?**

**Be sure you can** • differentiate between short-range and long-range plans • differentiate between strategic and operational plans and explain how they relate to one another • define *policy* and *procedure* and give examples of each in a university setting • define *budget* and explain how zero-based budgeting works

# Planning Tools and Techniques

Planning delivers the most benefits when its foundations are strong. The useful planning tools and techniques include forecasting, contingency planning, scenario planning, benchmarking, and staff planning.

## Forecasting

Who would have predicted on New Year's Eve 2008 that General Motors and Chrysler would soon declare bankruptcy; that Italy's Fiat would buy a big stake in Chrysler; that GM's Pontiac and Saturn brands would be discontinued? Who would have predicted even a few years ago that Chinese firms would now own Volvo and Hummer or that China would now be the largest car market in the world? Would you believe that by the year 2025 (at the latest) China is expected to have more cars on the roads than the United States has today?

What are top executives around the world thinking about as they make plans for the future? Are they on top of the right trends? At least one corporate CEO, GE's Jeffery Immelt, is frank about his failure in this regard. "I should have done more to anticipate the radical changes that occurred," he says.[14]

Planning in business and our personal lives often involves **forecasting**, the process of predicting what will happen in the future.[15] Periodicals such as *Business Week*, *Fortune*, and *The Economist* regularly report forecasts of industry conditions, interest rates, unemployment trends, and national economies, among other issues. Some are based on *qualitative forecasting*, which uses expert opinions to predict the future. Others involve *quantitative forecasting*, which uses mathematical models and statistical analyses of historical data and surveys to predict future events.

**Forecasting** attempts to predict the future.

Although useful, all forecasts should be treated cautiously. They are planning aids, not substitutes. It is said that a music agent once told Elvis Presley: "You ought to go back to driving a truck, because you ain't going nowhere." He was obviously mistaken, and that's the problem with forecasts. They rely on human judgment—and they can be wrong.

## Contingency Planning

Picture the scene: A professional golfer is striding down the golf course with an iron in each hand. The one in her right hand is "the plan"; the one in her left is the "backup plan." Which club she uses will depend on how the ball lies on the fairway. One of her greatest strengths is being able to adjust to the situation by putting the right club to work in the circumstances she encounters.

Planning is often like that. By definition it involves thinking ahead. But the more uncertain the planning environment, the more likely that one's original forecasts and intentions may prove inadequate or wrong. The golfer deals with this by having backup clubs available. This amounts to **contingency planning**—identifying alternative courses of action that can be implemented if circumstances change. A really good contingency plan will even contain "trigger points" to indicate when to activate preselected alternatives. Given the uncertainties of our day, this is really an indispensable tool for managerial and personal planning.

**Contingency planning** identifies alternative courses of action to take when things go wrong.

## Recommended Reading

### The Shift: The Future of Work Is Already Here

(HarperBusiness UK, 2011)

## by Lynda Gratton

Eamonn McCabeCamera Press/Redux Pictures

As professor of management at the London Business School, Lynda Gratton is concerned that students fail to understand the nature, pace, and complexity of forces that will shape the future of work. Her book, *The Shift*, describes five key forces. They are technology (helpful but time consuming), globalization (workers from everywhere compete for the same jobs), demography (more people, less space), society (traditional communities under threat), and energy resources (too few and shrinking). In the face of it all, "What's the worker to do?" she asks. The answer is we can enter a bleak and default future or a bright and crafted one. To work on the bright side in the future she says we must shift from "shallow generalist to serial master" of things; shift from "isolated competitor to innovative connector" in vast networks; and shift from "voracious consumer to impassioned producer" who worries more about creating things than buying them. Are you ready for the shift?

Poor contingency planning was very much in the news when debates raged over how BP managed the disastrous Deepwater Horizon oil spill in the Gulf of Mexico. Everyone from the public at large to U.S. lawmakers to oil industry experts criticized BP not only for failing to contain the spill quickly, but also for failing to anticipate and have contingency plans in place to handle such a crisis.[16]

> *A BP spokesperson initially said*—"You have here an unprecedented event . . . the unthinkable has become thinkable and the whole industry will be asking questions of itself."

> *An oil industry expert responded*—"There should be a technology that is preexisting and ready to deploy at the drop of a hat. . . . It shouldn't have to be designed and fabricated now, from scratch."

> *Former BP CEO Tony Hayward finally admitted*—"There are some capabilities that we could have available to deploy instantly, rather than creating as we go."

The lesson here is hard-earned but very clear. Contingency planning can't prevent crises from occurring. But when things do go wrong, there's nothing better to have in place than good contingency plans.

## Scenario Planning

**Scenario planning** identifies alternative future scenarios and makes plans to deal with each.

**Scenario planning** is a long-term version of contingency planning. It involves identifying several possible future scenarios or states of affairs and then making plans to deal with each scenario should it actually occur.[17] In this sense, scenario planning forces us to think really far ahead and be open to lots of possibilities.

The scenario planning approach was developed years ago at Royal Dutch/Shell when top managers asked themselves a perplexing question: "What would Shell do after its oil supplies ran out?" Although recognizing that scenario planning can

# What Really Works When Fighting World Poverty?

DIPTENDU DUTTA/AFP/Getty Images/NewsCom

**D**eveloping countries send $100+ billion in aid to poor countries; private foundations and charities spend $70+ billion more fighting poverty and its effects around the world. Their plans and goals are praiseworthy, but are the monies well spent?

Not all of them, that's for sure. And that's a problem being tackled by the Poverty Action Lab at the Massachusetts Institute of Technology. The director, Abhijit Banerjee, a development economist, says: "We aren't really interested in the more-aid-less-aid debate. We're interested in seeing what works and what doesn't." The lab criticizes "feel-good" evaluations and pushes for rigorous evaluations of poverty-fighting programs using scientific methods. Here's an example.

The Indian antipoverty group Seva Mandir was concerned about teacher absenteeism and low performance by rural school children. Its original plan was to pay extra tutors to assist teachers in 120 rural schools. The Poverty Lab Plan suggested paying extra tutors in 60 schools, making no changes in the other 60, and then comparing outcomes to see if the plan worked. An evaluation of results showed no difference in children's performance, even with the higher costs of extra tutors.

A new plan was made to buy cameras for 60 teachers, have them take time/date-stamped photos with children at the start and end of each school day, and have the photos analyzed each month. Teachers would receive bonuses or fines based on their absenteeism and student performance. Again, no changes were made in the other 60 schools. Evaluation revealed that teacher absenteeism was 20% lower and student performance was significantly higher in the camera schools. With the Poverty Lab's help, Seva Mandir concluded that investing in closely monitored pay incentives could improve teacher attendance in rural schools.

 **ETHICS QUESTIONS**

Look around your organization and at cases reported in the news. How often do we draw conclusions that "plans are working" based on feel-good evaluations or anecdotal reports rather than solid scientific evaluations? What are the consequences at work and in society when plans are implemented at great cost, but without defensible systems of evaluation? Even if the objectives of a project are honorable, what ethical issues arise in situations where it isn't clear that the project is having the intended benefit?

---

never be inclusive of all future possibilities, a Shell executive once said that it helps "condition the organization to think" and better prepare for "future shocks."

Shell uses scenario planning to tackle such issues as climate change, sustainable development, fossil-fuel alternatives, human rights, and biodiversity. Most typically it involves descriptions of "worst cases" and "best cases." In respect to oil supplies, for example, a worst-case scenario might be—global conflict and devastating effects on the natural environment occur as nations jockey with one another to secure increasingly scarce supplies of oil and other natural resources. A best-case scenario might be—governments work together to find pathways that take care of our resource needs while supporting the sustainability of global resources. It's anyone's guess which scenario will materialize or if something else altogether will happen. But these words of former Shell CEO Jeroen van der Veer highlight the value of the scenario planning process: "This will require hard work and time is short."[18]

## Benchmarking

**Benchmarking** uses external and internal comparisons to plan for future improvements.

Planners sometimes become too comfortable with the ways things are going and overconfident that the past is a good indicator of the future. It is often better to keep challenging the status quo and not simply accept things as they are. One way to do this is through **benchmarking**—the use of external and internal comparisons to better evaluate one's current performance and identify possible ways to improve for the future.[19]

The purpose of benchmarking is to find out what other people and organizations are doing very well, and then plan how to incorporate these ideas into one's own operations. It is basically a way of learning from the successes of others. One benchmarking technique is to search for **best practices**—things people and organizations do that help them achieve superior performance.

**Best practices** are things people and organizations do that lead to superior performance.

Well-run organizations emphasize *internal benchmarking* that encourages members and work units to learn and improve by sharing one another's best practices. They also use *external benchmarking* to learn from competitors and non-competitors alike. Xerox, for example, has benchmarked L.L. Bean's warehousing and distribution methods, Ford's plant layouts, and American Express's billing and collections. Ford benchmarked BMW's 3 series. James D. Farley, Ford's global marketing head, says: "The ubiquity of the 3 series engenders trust in every part of the world, and its design always has a strong point of view."[20] And in the apparel industry, the Spanish retailer Zara has become a benchmark for excellence in "fast-fashion."[21] The firm's design and manufacturing systems allow it to get new fashions from design to stores in two weeks. Zara produces only in small batches that sell out and create impressions of scarcity. Shoppers know they have to buy now because an item will not be replaced. And if something doesn't sell at Zara, it's not a big problem; there wasn't a large stock of the item to begin with.

## Staff Planning

As organizations grow, so do the planning challenges. Cisco Systems, for example, has been planning for quite some time that a lot of its growth will come from investments overseas. And it wasn't too long ago that China was the big target in Asia. It still is a big one, but when Cisco's planners analyzed their planning premises and projected future scenarios, India emerged as a strong competitor. It turns out that they found a lot to like about India: excellence in software design, need for Cisco's products, and weak local competition. They also found some major things to worry about in China, including a government favoring local companies and poor intellectual property protection.[22]

Many organizations use staff planners to help coordinate and energize planning. These specialists are experts in all steps of the planning process, as well as in the use of planning tools and techniques. They can help bring focus and expertise to a wide variety of planning tasks. But one risk is a tendency for a communication gap to develop between the staff planners and line managers. Unless everyone works closely together, the resulting plans may be based on poor information. Also, people may lack commitment to implement the plans, no matter how good they are.

**TAKEAWAY QUESTION 3** **What are some useful planning tools and techniques?**

**Be sure you can** • define *forecasting, contingency planning, scenario planning,* and *benchmarking* • explain the benefits of contingency planning and scenario planning • describe pros and cons of using staff planners

# Implementing Plans to Achieve Results

In a book entitled *Doing What Matters*, Jim Kilts, the former CEO of Gillette, quotes an old management adage: "In business, words are words, promises are promises, but only performance is reality."[23] The same applies to plans—plans, we might say, are words with promises attached. These promises are only fulfilled when plans are implemented so that their purposes are achieved. The implementation of plans is largely driven by solid management practices discussed throughout the rest of this book, from organizing to leading to controlling. But, the foundations for successful implementation begin with the planning processes of goal setting, goal alignment, and participation and involvement.

## Goal Setting

Commitment to goals is standard practice among successful managers. When Jim Kilts took over as CEO of Gillette he realized that the firm needed work.[24] After analyzing the situation he was very disciplined in setting planning goals to deal with high priority problems. In respect to sales, Gillette's big brands were losing sales to competitors. Kilts made plans to *increase market shares* for these brands. In respect to earnings, the company had missed its estimates for 15 quarters in a row. Kilts made plans to *meet earnings estimates* and raise the company's stock price.

Although most of us are aware of the importance of goal setting in management, the tendency may be to mistakenly think it's an easy thing to accomplish. The reality is that the ways goals are set can make a big difference in how well they do in pointing people in the right directions and inspiring them to work hard. There's a big difference between having "no goals" or even just everyday run-of-the-mill "average goals," and having really "great goals" that result in plans being successfully implemented. Great goals tend to have these five characteristics:

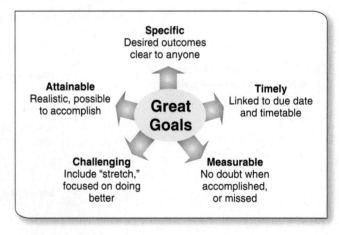

1. *Specific*—clearly targeted key results and outcomes to be accomplished.
2. *Timely*—linked to specific timetables and "due dates."
3. *Measurable*—described so results can be measured without ambiguity.
4. *Challenging*—include a stretch factor that moves toward real gains.
5. *Attainable*—although challenging, realistic and possible to achieve.

SUKREE SUKPLANG/Reuters/Lan dov LLC

### Goal Setting in Project Quark Helps Ford Preserve Supply Chains

When Ford and the other automakers were facing the impact of a global financial crisis, it became clear to CEO Alan Mulally that many of the firm's suppliers were at risk of business failure. And if Ford didn't have parts, it couldn't build vehicles. Mulally's response was to set up a cross-functional team with three goals: monitor parts suppliers, prevent supply chain breakdowns, and reduce the number of suppliers Ford was dealing with. He called it Project Quark and gave it his highest action priority. Team members had the goals, and Mulally wanted action follow-through. "Let's do it," he said. "I want regular reports every Thursday."

## Goal Alignment

It is one thing to set great goals and make them part of a plan. It is quite another to make sure that goals and plans are well integrated across the many people, work units, and levels of an organization as a whole. Goals set everywhere in the organization should ideally help advance its overall mission or purpose. Yet, we sometimes work very hard to accomplish things that simply don't make much of a difference in organizational performance. This is why goal alignment is an important part of managerial planning.

In a **hierarchy of goals** or **hierarchy of objectives**, lower-level goals and objectives are means to accomplishing higher-level ones.

Figure 8.2 shows how a **hierarchy of goals** or **hierarchy of objectives** helps with goal alignment. When such a hierarchy is well defined, the accomplishment of lower-level goals and objectives is the means to the accomplishment of higher-level ones. The example in the figure is built around quality goals in a manufacturing setting. Strategic goals set by top management cascade down the

FIGURE 8.2 **A sample hierarchy of objectives for quality management.**

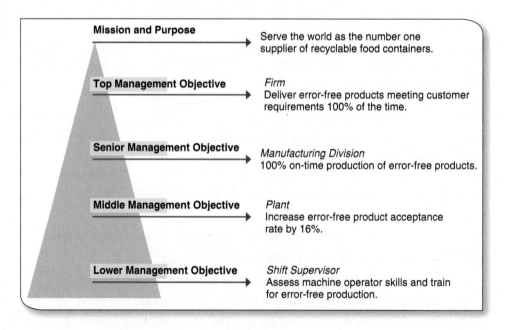

| | |
|---|---|
| **Mission and Purpose** | Serve the world as the number one supplier of recyclable food containers. |
| **Top Management Objective** | *Firm* Deliver error-free products meeting customer requirements 100% of the time. |
| **Senior Management Objective** | *Manufacturing Division* 100% on-time production of error-free products. |
| **Middle Management Objective** | *Plant* Increase error-free product acceptance rate by 16%. |
| **Lower Management Objective** | *Shift Supervisor* Assess machine operator skills and train for error-free production. |

organization step by step to become quality management objectives for lower levels. Everything ideally works together in a consistent "means–end" fashion so that the organization, as shown in the last figure, consistently performs as "the world's number one supplier of recyclable food containers."

Conversations between team leaders and team members or between supervisors and subordinates at each step in the hierarchy are essential to achieving the goal alignment just described. The conversations should result in agreements on: (1) performance objectives for a given time period, (2) plans through which they will be accomplished, (3) standards for measuring whether they have been accomplished, and (4) procedures for reviewing performance results. This process is sometimes called *management by objectives* (MBO), but it is really just old-fashioned good management.[25]

Goal alignment conversations should focus on objectives that are specific, timely, measurable, challenging, and attainable. An example is the improvement objective for a team member "to reduce quality rejects by 10% within three months." Another is the personal development objective "to learn by April 15 the latest version of our supply chain management software package."

| Goal Alignment Between Team Leader and Team Member | | |
| --- | --- | --- |
| **Jointly plan** | **Individually set** | **Jointly control** |
| • Set objectives<br>• Set standards<br>• Choose actions | • Perform tasks (member)<br>• Provide support (leader) | • Review results<br>• Discuss implications<br>• Renew cycle |

One of the more difficult aspects of goal alignment is making performance objectives as measurable as possible. It's best to achieve agreement on a *measurable end product*, for example, "to reduce travel expenses by 5% by the end of the fiscal year." But performance in some jobs, particularly managerial ones, can be hard to quantify. Rather than abandon the quest for a good objective in such cases, it is often possible to agree on *verifiable work activities*. Their accomplishment serves as an indicator of performance progress. An example is "to improve communications with my team in the next three months by holding weekly team meetings." Whereas it can be difficult to measure "improved communications," it is easy to document whether the "weekly team meetings" have been held.

## Participation and Involvement

Planning is a process and not an event. And "participation" and "involvement" are two of its core components. When 7-Eleven executives decided to offer new upscale products and services, such as selling fancy meals-to-go, they learned a planning lesson the hard way. Although their ideas sounded good at the top, franchise owners balked at the store level. The executives belatedly realized the value of taking time to involve the owners when making new plans for the stores.[26]

**Participatory planning** includes in all planning steps the people who will be affected by the plans and asked to help implement them. One of the things that research is most clear about is that when people participate in setting goals they gain motivation to work hard to accomplish them.[27] Whether the planning is for a team, a large division, or the entire organization, involving people goes a long way toward gaining their commitments to work hard and support the implementation of plans.

**Participatory planning** includes the persons who will be affected by plans and/or those who will implement them.

FIGURE 8.3 **How participation and involvement help build commitment to plans.**

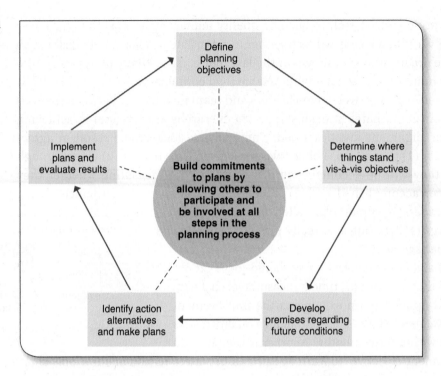

Figure 8.3 shows the role of participation and involvement in the planning process. Notice that participation can and should be engaged in all planning steps. Think of it using the metaphor of a big kitchen table. Everyone from family members to guests sits around the table and enjoys the meal while joining in the conversation. The same can happen with planning, if the manager invites others to the table. And when he or she does, the conversation focuses on defining objectives, assessing present and future states of affairs, identifying action alternatives, and discussing implementation successes and failures.

There are many benefits when and if this participatory planning approach is followed in practice. Participation can increase the creativity and information available for planning. It can also increase the understanding and acceptance of plans, as well as commitment to their success. And even though participatory planning takes more time, it can improve performance results by improving both the quality of any plans made and the effectiveness of their implementation.

---

**LEARNING CHECK 4**

**TAKEAWAY QUESTION 4 How can plans be well implemented?**

**Be sure you can** • list the criteria of great goals • describe the value of a hierarchy of objectives • give examples of improvement and personal development objectives • explain how goal alignment can take place between a team leader and team members

# MANAGEMENT LEARNING REVIEW

## TAKEAWAY QUESTION 1  Why and how do managers plan?

- Planning is the process of setting performance objectives and determining what should be done to accomplish them.
- A plan is a set of intended actions for accomplishing important goals and objectives.
- Five steps in the planning process are: (1) Define your objectives, (2) determine where you stand vis-à-vis your objectives, (3) develop your premises regarding future conditions, (4) identify and choose among alternative ways of accomplishing objectives, and (5) implement action plans and evaluate results.
- The benefits of planning include better focus and flexibility, action orientation, coordination, control, and time management.

  **For Discussion Which step in the planning process is likely to cause the most difficulties for managers?**

## TAKEAWAY QUESTION 2  What types of plans do managers use?

- Short-range plans tend to cover a year or less; long-range plans extend up to three years or more.
- Strategic plans set critical long-range directions; operational plans are designed to implement strategic plans.
- Policies, such as a sexual harassment policy, are plans that set guidelines for the behavior of organizational members.
- Procedures and rules are plans that describe actions to be taken in specific situations, such as the steps to be taken when persons believe they have been subjected to sexual harassment.
- Budgets are plans that allocate resources to activities or projects.

  **For Discussion Is there any real value to long-term planning in today's rapidly changing environment?**

## TAKEAWAY QUESTION 3  What are some useful planning tools and techniques?

- Forecasting, which attempts to predict what might happen in the future, is a planning aid but not a planning substitute.
- Contingency planning identifies alternative courses of action that can be implemented if and when circumstances change.
- Scenario planning analyzes the implications of alternative versions of the future.
- Planning through benchmarking utilizes external and internal comparisons to identify best practices for possible adoption.
- Staff planners with special expertise are often used to assist in the planning process, but the risk is a lack of involvement by managers and others who must implement the plans.

  **For Discussion Shouldn't all plans be supported by contingency plans?**

## TAKEAWAY QUESTION 4  How can plans be well implemented?

- Great goals are specific, timely, measurable, challenging, and attainable.
- A hierarchy of objectives helps to align goals from top to bottom in organizations.
- Goal alignment is facilitated by a participative process that clarifies performance objectives for individuals and teams, and identifies support that can and should be provided by managers.
- Participation and involvement open the planning process to valuable inputs from people whose efforts are essential to the effective implementation of plans.

  **For Discussion Given its potential advantages, why isn't goal alignment a characteristic of all organizations?**

## Multiple-Choice Questions

1. Planning is the process of _____ and _____.
   - (a) developing premises about the future, evaluating them
   - (b) measuring results, taking corrective action
   - (c) measuring past performance, targeting future performance
   - (d) setting objectives, deciding how to accomplish them

2. The benefits of planning include _____.
   (a) improved focus       (b) lower labor costs
   (c) more accurate forecasts   (d) higher profits

3. In order to help implement its corporate strategy, a business firm would likely develop a (an) _____ plan for the marketing department.
   (a) functional       (b) single-use
   (c) production       (d) zero-based

4. _____ planning identifies alternative courses of action that can be taken if and when certain situations arise.
   (a) Zero-based       (b) Participative
   (c) Strategic       (d) Contingency

5. The first step in the control process is to _____.
   (a) measure actual performance
   (b) establish objectives and standards
   (c) compare results with objectives
   (d) take corrective action

6. A sexual harassment policy is an example of _____ plans used by organizations.
   (a) long-range       (b) single-use
   (c) standing-use       (d) operational

7. When a manager is asked to justify a new budget proposal on the basis of projected activities rather than past practices, this is an example of _____ budgeting.
   (a) zero-based       (b) variable
   (c) fixed       (d) contingency

8. One of the benefits of participatory planning is _____.
   (a) reduced time for planning
   (b) less need for forecasting
   (c) greater attention to contingencies
   (d) more commitment to implementation

9. The ideal situation in a hierarchy of objectives is that lower level plans become the _____ for accomplishing higher-level plans.
   (a) means       (b) ends
   (c) scenarios       (d) benchmarks

10. When managers use the benchmarking approach to planning, they _____.
    (a) use flexible budgets
    (b) identify best practices used by others
    (c) are seeking the most accurate forecasts that are available
    (d) focus more on the short term than the long term

11. One of the problems in relying too much on staff planners is _____.
    (a) a communication gap between planners and implementers
    (b) lack of expertise in the planning process
    (c) short-term rather than long-term focus
    (d) neglect of budgets as links between resources and activities

12. The planning process isn't complete until _____.
    (a) future conditions have been identified
    (b) stretch goals have been set
    (c) plans are implemented and results evaluated
    (d) budgets commit resources to plans

13. When a team leader is trying to follow an approach known as management by objectives, who should set a team member's performance objectives?
    (a) the team member
    (b) the team leader
    (c) the team leader and team member
    (d) the team member, the team leader, and a lawyer

14. A good performance objective is written in such a way that it _____.
    (a) has no precise timetable
    (b) is general and not too specific
    (c) is almost impossible to accomplish
    (d) can be easily measured

15. Which type of plan is used to guide resource allocations for long-term advancement of the organization's mission or purpose?
    (a) tactical       (b) operational
    (c) strategic       (d) functional

## Short-Response Questions

16. List five steps in the planning process and give examples of each.

17. How might planning through benchmarking be used by the owner of a local bookstore?

18. How does planning help to improve focus?

19. Why does participatory planning facilitate implementation?

## Essay Question

20. Put yourself in the position of a management trainer. You have been asked to make a short presentation to the local Small Business Enterprise Association at its biweekly luncheon. The topic you are to speak on is "How Each of You Can Use Objectives to Achieve Better Planning and Control." What will you tell them and why?

# MANAGEMENT SKILLS AND COMPETENCIES

## Further Reflection: Time Management

Time management is a form of planning that is consistently rated one of the top "must-have" skills for new graduates entering fast-paced and complicated careers in business and management. Many, perhaps most, of us keep To-Do lists. But, it's the rare person who is consistently successful in living up to one.

Planning can easily suffer the same fate as the To-Do lists—it starts with the best of intentions, but may end up with little or nothing to show as real results. There were a lot of good ideas in this chapter on how to plan, both in management and in our personal lives. Now is a good time to improve your planning capabilities. It's a key management function and a critical life skill. Start by getting in touch with how you presently manage and use time.

 **DO IT NOW . . .
LOOK IN THE MIRROR**

• *Task 1*—Keep a daily time log for a day or two, listing what you do and how long it takes. Make such a log, and then write up an analysis of where you seem to be wasting time and where you are using it well.

• *Task 2*—Complete the lists requested in the Time Management Checkup from the chapter opener. Double-check List 1 "B" items and reclassify any that are really "As" or "Cs." Look at your "As" and reclassify any that are really "Bs" or "Cs." Write a priority To-Do list for your day tomorrow. Also check your time wasters in List 2. Write down a plan to take charge of the controllables.

## Self-Assessment: Time Management Profile

### Instructions

Complete the following questionnaire by indicating "Y" (yes) or "N" (no) for each item. Be frank and allow your responses to create an accurate picture of how you tend to respond to these kinds of situations.

1. When confronted with several items of urgency and importance, I tend to do the easiest first.

2. I do the most important things during that part of the day when I know I perform best.

3. Most of the time I don't do things someone else can do; I delegate this type of work to others.

4. Even though meetings without a clear and useful purpose upset me, I put up with them.

5. I skim documents before reading and don't finish any that offer little value for my time.

6. I don't worry much if I don't accomplish at least one significant task each day.

7. I save the most trivial tasks for that time of day when my creative energy is lowest.

8. My workspace is neat and organized.

9. My office door is always "open"; I never work in complete privacy.

10. I schedule my time completely from start to finish every workday.

11. I don't like To-Do lists, preferring to respond to daily events as they occur.

12. I block out a certain amount of time each day or week that is dedicated to high-priority activities.

### Scoring

Count the number of "Y" responses to items 2, 3, 5, 7, 8, 12. Enter that score here [   ]. Count the number of "N" responses to items 1, 4, 6, 9, 10, 11. Enter that score here [   ]. Add the two scores together here [   ].

## Self-Assessment Interpretation

The higher the total score, the closer your behavior matches recommended time management guidelines. Reread those items where your response did not match the desired one. Why don't they match? Do you have reasons why your behavior in this instance should be different from the recommended time management guideline? Think about what you can do to adjust your behavior to be more consistent with these guidelines.

# Team Exercise:
# The Future Workplace/Personal Career Planning

## Instructions

Form groups as assigned by the instructor. Brainstorm to develop a master list of the major characteristics you expect to find in the workplace in the year 2020. Use this list as background for completing the following tasks:

1. Write a one-paragraph description of what the typical "Workplace 2020" manager's workday will be like.

2. Draw a "picture" representing what the "Workplace 2020" organization will look like.

3. Summarize in list form what you consider to be the major planning implications of your future workplace scenario for management students today. That is, explain what this means in terms of using academic and extracurricular activities to best prepare for success in this future scenario.

4. Choose a spokesperson to share your results with the class as a whole and explain their implications for the class members.

## Personal Career Planning Add-On

After participating in the The Future Workplace exercise and using its implications for your career planning, complete the following activities as an individual assignment. Summarize everything in a report to be submitted to your instructor.

*Activity 1    Strengths and Weaknesses Inventory*
Different occupations require special talents, abilities, and skills. Each of us, you included, has a repertoire of existing strengths and weaknesses that are "raw materials" we presently offer a potential employer. Actions can (and should!) be taken over time to further develop current strengths and to turn weaknesses into strengths. Make a list identifying your most important strengths and weaknesses in relation to the career direction you are likely to pursue upon graduation. Place a * next to each item you consider most important to focus on for continued personal development.

*Activity 2    Five-Year Career Objectives*    Make a list of three career objectives that you hope to accomplish within five years of graduation. Be sure they are appropriate given your list of personal strengths and weaknesses.

*Activity 3    Five-Year Career Action Plans*    Write a specific action plan for accomplishing each of the five objectives. State exactly what you will do, and by when, in order to meet each objective. If you will need special support or assistance, identify it and state how you will obtain it. An outside observer should be able to read your action plan for each objective and end up feeling confident that he or she knows exactly what you are going to do and why.

## Career Situations for Planners: What Would You Do?

1. **The Planning Retreat** It's been a bit over two years since your promotion to division manager. You're now accountable for delivering about 10% of your firm's total revenues, and oversee more than 100 people working in five different departments. This year you'd like to make the annual planning retreat really valuable to everyone. All managers from team leaders to department heads will be present. You will have them off site for a full day. What goals will you state for the retreat in the e-mail you send out with the retreat agenda? Knowing the steps in the planning process, what will the retreat agenda look like, and why?

2. **Sexual Harassment** One of the persons under your supervision has a "possible" sexual harassment complaint about the behavior of a coworker. She says that she understands the sexual harassment policy of the organization, but the procedures are not clear. You're not clear, either, and take the matter to your boss. She tells you to draft a set of procedures that can be taken to top management for approval. What procedures will you recommend so that sexual harassment complaints like this one can be dealt with in a fair manner?

3. **Getting "Buy In"** A consulting firm has been hired to help write a strategic plan for your organization. The plan would be helpful, but you are worried about getting buy-in from all members, not just those at the top. What conditions can you set for the consultants so that they not only provide a solid strategic plan, but also create strong commitments to implementing it from members of your organization?

## Case Study

# Walgreens

Go to *Management Cases for Critical Thinking* to find the recommended case for Chapter 8—"Walgreen's—Staying One Step Ahead."

With a strong presence throughout the U.S., Walgreens has built a reputation as America's corner drugstore. But it's not alone on the corner. Squeezed on all sides by tough competitors like CVS, Wal-Mart, and the big grocery chains, it has had to keep fighting for its territory. Walgreens has found continued success through agility and an uncanny sense of how to extend its brand within this crowded marketplace. Even so, the firm's executives can't afford to rest on past laurels. It will take the right plans and the best implementation to stay ahead of the competition in an everchanging market.

# Wisdom
## Learning From Others

Michael Holahan/Augusta Chronicle/Zuma Press

### > CONTROL LEAVES NO ROOM FOR COMPLACENCY

You can get a tasty sandwich at one of its restaurants, but don't plan on stopping in on a Sunday. All of chick-fil-A's 1,270 stores are closed. It is a tradition started by founder Truett Cathy, who believed that employees deserve a day of rest.

Current President Dan T. Cathy says the rest day is part of the firm's success. "If we take care of our team members and operators behind the counter, then they are going to do a better job on Monday. In fact, I say our food tastes better on Monday because we are closed on Sunday."[1]

Chick-fil-A's mission is to "Be America's best quick-service restaurant." And president Truett believes in "continuous improvement" to upgrade menus and stores even after years of increasing sales. Woody Faulk, vice president of brand development, says: "It would be very easy for us to pause after a successful year, but in doing that, we would be in jeopardy of falling into a trap of complacency."

The results seem to speak for themselves. Chick-fil-A is the 2nd largest chicken restaurant chain in the United States. Its turnover among restaurant operators is only 3%, compared to an industry average as high as 50%. And, it has an enviable record of sales growth for 44 years.

## MORE TO LOOK FOR INSIDE>

# Control Processes and Systems

## > RESILIENCY

Managerial control is all about how to make sure things go right for organizations even as they deal with lots of complexities. It's the same for us. We need to be managed, we need to exercise control, and we need staying power to perform for the long term.

A person's success in life and work depends a lot on **resiliency.** This is the ability to call upon inner strength and keep moving forward even when things are tough.

Think of resiliency in personal terms—caring for an aging parent with a terrible disease or single parenthood with small children. Think of it in career terms—juggling personal and work responsibilities, continuously attending to e-mails, voice mails, instant messages, and rushing to many scheduled and unscheduled meetings.

Resilient people face and identify their challenges; they don't hide or back away from them. They develop strategies, make plans, and find opportunity even in bad situations.

"Resilient people are like trees bending in the wind," says Dr. Steven M. Southwick, professor of psychiatry at Yale University. "They bounce back." Does this description fit you . . . or not?[2]

## Insight
### Learning About Yourself

**BUILD MANAGEMENT SKILLS AND COMPETENCIES AT END OF CHAPTER**

- Engage in *Further Reflection on Resiliency*
- Take the *Self-Assessment—Internal/External Control*
- Complete the *Team Exercise—After-Meeting/Project Remorse*
- Solve the *Career Situations for Management Control*
- Analyze the *Case Study—"Electronic Arts: Inside Fantasy Sports"*

**<GET TO KNOW YOURSELF BETTER**

| TAKEAWAY 1 | TAKEAWAY 2 | TAKEAWAY 3 |
|---|---|---|
| **Managerial Control**<br>• Importance of controlling<br>• Types of controls<br>• Internal and external control | **The Control Process**<br>• Establish objectives and standards<br>• Measure actual performance<br>• Compare results with objectives<br>• Take corrective action | **Control Tools and Techniques**<br>• Project management and control<br>• Inventory control<br>• Breakeven analysis<br>• Financial controls<br>• Balanced scorecards |
| **LEARNING CHECK 1** | **LEARNING CHECK 2** | **LEARNING CHECK 3** |

Keeping in touch . . . staying informed . . . being in control: These are important responsibilities for every manager. But *control* is a word like *power*. If you aren't careful when and how it's used, the word carries a negative connotation. Yet, control plays a positive and necessary role in the management process. To have things "under control" is good; for things to be "out of control" is generally bad.

Nike and Groupon are well-known companies with different control stories. At Nike it's a positive. The firm's 5.6 ounce Flyknit is a marvel of a new manufacturing technique called micro-level precision engineering. Its style, fabric, and construction show Nike's continuous push for innovation. But the Flyknit was also driven by another of Nike's commitments—controlling costs of materials, time, and labor. It is, simply put, a lot cheaper to make.[3] At Groupon the control example is a negative. This innovative technology company made its reputation as a successful first-mover in the "daily deal" space. But its executives failed to spot what auditor Ernst & Young called "a material weakness in its internal control." Not enough money was being set aside to cover customer refunds. When the firm's financial results had to be restated its stock price fell 6%.[4] What's behind these different control stories? Are management practices just better and more sophisticated at Nike? Did Groupon's rapid growth make it slow to put the right control systems into place?

## Why and How Managers Control

Control is important for any organization, and we practice a lot of control quite naturally. Think of fun things you do—playing golf or tennis or Frisbee, reading, dancing, driving a car, or riding a bike. Through activities such as these you've already become quite expert in the control process. How? Most probably by having an objective in mind, always checking to see how well you are doing, and making continuous adjustments to get it right.

## Importance of Controlling

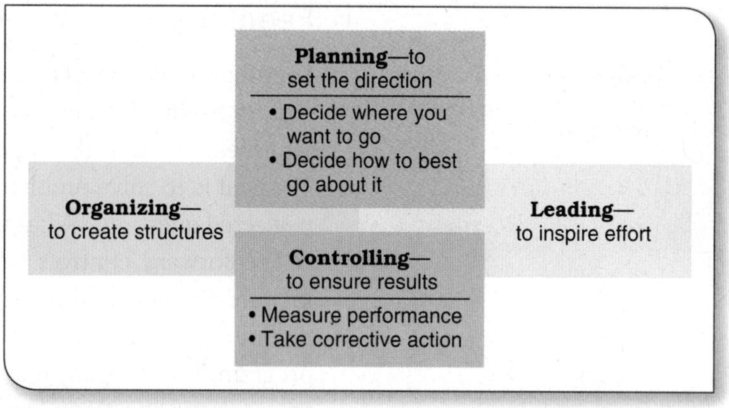

The management function of planning is all about setting goals and making plans. **Controlling** is the process of measuring performance and making sure things turn out as intended. And, information is its foundation. Henry Schacht, former CEO of Cummins Engine Company, discussed control in terms of what he called "friendly facts." He stated: "facts that reinforce what you are doing are nice, because they help in terms of psychic reward. Facts that raise alarms are equally friendly, because they give you clues about how to respond, how to change, where to spend the resources."[5]

Figure 9.1 shows how controlling fits in with the other management functions. *Planning* sets the directions and allocates resources. *Organizing* brings people and material resources together in working combinations. *Leading* inspires people to best utilize these resources. *Controlling* sees to it that the right things happen, in the right way, and at the right time. It helps ensure that performance is consistent with plans, and that accomplishments throughout an organization are coordinated in a means–ends fashion. It also helps ensure that people comply with organizational policies and procedures.

One of the great benefits of effective control is organizational learning. Consider, for example, the program of **after-action review** pioneered by the U.S. Army and now utilized in many corporate settings. It is a structured review of lessons learned and results accomplished in a completed project, task force assignment, or special operation. Participants answer questions such as: "What was the intent?" "What actually happened?" "What did we learn?"[6] The after-action review helps make continuous improvement a shared norm. It encourages those involved to take responsibility for how they acted and what they achieved, and for how they can do better in the future. The end-of-chapter team exercise is modeled on this approach.

**FIGURE 9.1** **The role of controlling in the management process.**

**Controlling** is the process of measuring performance and taking action to ensure desired results.

An **after-action review** is a systematic assessment of lessons learned and results accomplished in a completed project.

## Types of Controls

One of the best ways to understand control is in respect to the open-systems perspective in Figure 9.2. It shows how feedforward, concurrent, and feedback controls link with different phases of the input–throughput–output cycle.[7] Each type of control increases the likelihood of high performance.

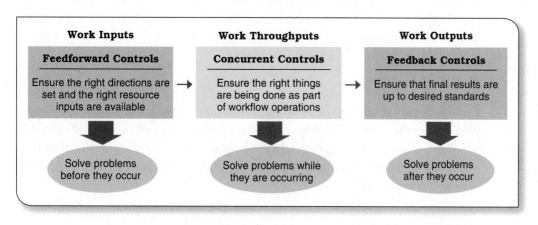

**FIGURE 9.2** **Feedforward, concurrent, and feedback controls.**

## Feedforward Controls

Feedforward control ensures that directions and resources are right before the work begins.

**Feedforward controls**, also called *preliminary controls*, take place before a work activity begins. They ensure that objectives are clear, that proper directions are established, and that the right resources are available to accomplish the objectives. The goal is to solve problems before they occur by asking an important but often neglected question: "What needs to be done before we begin?"

Feedforward controls are preventive in nature. Managers using them take a forward-thinking and proactive approach to control. At McDonald's, for example, preliminary control of food ingredients plays an important role in the firm's quality program. The company requires that suppliers of its hamburger buns produce them to exact specifications, covering everything from texture to uniformity of color. Even in overseas markets, the firm works hard to develop local suppliers that can offer dependable quality.[8]

## Concurrent Controls

Concurrent control focuses on what happens during the work process.

**Concurrent controls** focus on what happens during the work process. Sometimes called *steering controls*, they make sure things are being done according to plan. You can also think of this as control through direct supervision. In today's world, that supervision is as likely to be computer driven as face-to-face. Picture this scene at the Hyundai Motors headquarters in Seoul, South Korea, in what the firm calls its Global Command and Control Center.[9]

> . . . with dozens of computer screens relaying video and data, it [the Global Command and Control Center] keeps watch on Hyundai operations around the world. Parts shipments are traced from the time they leave the supplier until they reach a plant. Cameras peer into assembly lines from Beijing to Montgomery and keep a close watch on Hyundai's giant Ulsan, Korea, plant, the world's largest integrated auto factory.

The goal of concurrent controls is to solve problems as they occur. The key question is, "What can we do to improve things right now?" In the Hyundai example, operations are monitored and business intelligence is gathered in real time using sophisticated information systems. This helps managers to quickly spot and correct any problems in the manufacturing cycle. The same thing happens at McDonald's, but this time it all takes place face to face as ever-present shift leaders provide concurrent control through direct supervision. They constantly observe what is taking place, even while helping out with the work. They are trained to intervene immediately when something is not done right and to correct things on the spot. Detailed manuals also steer workers in the right directions as they perform their jobs.

## Feedback Controls

Feedback control takes place after an action is completed.

**Feedback controls**, also called *post-action controls*, take place after work is completed. They focus on the quality of end results rather than on inputs and activities. Feedback controls are largely reactive; the goals are to solve problems after they occur and prevent future ones. They ask the question: "Now that we are finished, how well did we do?"

## Members of the Elsewhere Class Blend Worlds of Work and Leisure

Are you *really* in control of your life, or are you always thinking about "elsewhere"? You may be at home or out shopping or at a sports event. Yet, you're thinking "it's time to check my messages on my smartphone." Today's young professionals, the "Elsewhere Class," are more and more living in what sociologist Dan Conley describes as "a blended world of work and leisure, home and office." He says: "We feel like we are in the right place at the right time only when in transit, moving from points A to B. Constant motion is a balm to an anxious culture where we are haunted by the feeling that we are frauds, expendable in the workplace because so much of our service work is intangible."

Kathrin Ziegler/Getty Images, Inc.

We are all familiar with feedback controls and probably recognize their weak points from a customer service perspective. Restaurants often ask how you liked a meal after it is eaten; course evaluations tell instructors how well they performed after the course is over; a budget summary identifies cost overruns after a project is completed. Such feedback about mistakes already made may not be able to correct them, but it can help improve things in the future.

## Internal and External Control

Managers have two broad options with respect to control systems. First, they can manage in ways that allow and expect people to control their own behavior. This puts priority on internal or self-control. Second, they can structure situations to make sure things happen as planned.[10] This is external control. The alternatives include bureaucratic or administrative control, clan or normative control, and market or regulatory control. Effective control typically involves a mix of these internal and external options.

### Self-Control

We all exercise internal control in our daily lives. We do so with regard to managing our money, our relationships, our eating and drinking, and more. Managers can take advantage of this human capacity for **self-control** by unlocking, allowing, and supporting it. This means helping people to be good at self-management, giving them freedom, and encouraging them to exercise self-discipline in performing their jobs. Any workplace that emphasizes participation, empowerment, and involvement will rely heavily on self-control.

> **Self-control** is internal control that occurs through self-discipline in fulfilling work and personal responsibilities.

Managers can gain a lot by assuming that people are ready and willing to exercise self-control in their work.[11] But an internal control strategy requires a high degree of trust. When people are willing to work on their own and exercise self-control, managers must have the confidence to give them the freedom to do so. Self control is most likely when the process setting objectives and standards is participative. The potential for self-control also increases when capable people have a clear sense of organizational mission and have the resources necessary to do their jobs well. It is further enhanced by inclusive organizational cultures in which everyone treats each other with respect and consideration.

It's also important to think about self-control as a personal capacity, even a life skill. How good are you at taking control of your time and maintaining a healthy work–life balance? Do you ever wonder who's in control, you or your smartphone? It used to be that we sometimes took work home in a briefcase, did a bit, closed the case up, and took it back to work the next day. Now work is always there, on the computer, in our e-mails, and streamed as text messages. It's habit forming and some of us handle this better than others.[12]

In San Jose, California, Elizabeth Safran works virtually. That's the way the 13-member public relations firm operates—by e-mails and instant messaging. But she is concerned about work–life balance, saying: "It [technology] makes us more productive, but everybody is working all the time—weekends, evenings. It's almost overkill." In London, England, Paul Renucci is managing director of a systems integration firm. He works at home on Fridays, saving two hours of traffic time and staying connected by computer. At 5 P.M. he turns the machine off, his workday over. He says: "I can work pretty hard, but at 5 P.M. exactly I stop working and the weekend starts."[13]

## Bureaucratic Control

Another form of external control uses authority, policies, procedures, job descriptions, budgets, and day-to-day supervision to make sure that people act in harmony with organizational interests. It's called **bureaucratic control** and you can think of it as control that flows through the organization's hierarchy of authority. Organizations typically have policies and procedures regarding sexual harassment, for example. Their goal is to make sure members behave toward one another respectfully

**Bureaucratic control** influences behavior through authority, policies, procedures, job descriptions, budgets, and day-to-day supervision.

---

**FACTS FOR ANALYSIS**  > MANY FIRMS PLANNING TO SPEND MORE TO DEFEND AGAINST THEFT, FRAUD, AND CYBERSPYS

## Corporate Thieves Thrive on Sticky Hands and Cyberheists

There's a lot of crime in the corporate world. A bad economy tends to bring out the worst in some of us; the race for technology and business competition raises the stakes of "cyberspying." Consider these survey results.

- 20% of employers say worker theft is a "moderate to very big problem"; 18% report an increase in money crimes such as stolen cash or fraudulent transactions; 17% have tightened security to prevent employee theft.
- In global business, 48% of firms report fear of fraud, keeping them from investing in places like China and Africa; 50% plan to spend more defending intellectual property.
- The U.S. government claims China and Russia are major cyberspys who attempt to steal U.S. technology and re-

search insights for domestic purposes; industrial espionage of military technology is also considered a threat to national security.

 **YOUR THOUGHTS?**

Do these data tell the real story? Is employee theft mainly a "bad economy" problem? Is it a smaller or larger problem than indicated here? Have you witnessed such theft and, if so, what did you do about it? And have you been a participant in such bad employee behavior? What about international cyberspying or cyberheists? How can a company or a nation protect itself in today's hyperlinked digital world?

and with no suggestion of sexual pressures or improprieties. Organizations also use budgets for personnel, equipment, travel expenses, and the like to keep behavior targeted within set limits.

Another level of bureaucratic control comes from laws and regulations in the organization's external environment. An example is the Sarbanes-Oxley Act (SOX), which establishes procedures to regulate financial reporting and governance in publicly traded corporations.[14] SOX was passed in response to major corporate scandals that raised serious questions about top management behavior and the accuracy of financial reports provided by the firms. Under SOX, chief executives and chief financial officers of firms must personally sign off on financial reports and certify their accuracy. Those who misstate their firm's financial records can go to jail and pay substantial personal fines.

## Clan Control

Whereas bureaucratic control emphasizes hierarchy and authority, **clan control** influences behavior through norms and expectations set by the organizational culture. Sometimes called *normative control,* it harnesses the power of group cohesiveness and collective identity.

> **Clan control** influences behavior through norms and expectations set by the organizational culture.

Clan control happens as persons who share values and identify strongly with one another behave in consistent ways. Just look around the typical college classroom and campus. You'll see clan control reflected in how students dress, use language, and act in class and at leisure. They often behave according to the expectations of peers and groups with whom they identify. The same holds true in organizations, where clan control influences members of teams and work groups to display common behavior patterns.

## Market Control

**Market control** is essentially the influence of customers and competition on the behavior of organizations and their members. Business firms show the influence of market control in the way that they adjust products, pricing, promotions, and other practices in response to customer feedback and what competitors are doing. A good example is the growing emphasis on green products and sustainability practices. When a firm like Wal-Mart starts to get positive publicity from its expressed commitment to eventually power all of its stores with renewable energy, for example,

> **Market control** is essentially the influence of market competition on the behavior of organizations and their members.

AFP PHOTO/VOISHMEL/NewsCom

## Many Wonder What Took Apple So Long to Act

What did Apple know and when? Could it have acted sooner? Its products are widely popular, but its global manufacturing chain may be out of control. After getting lots of bad press over working conditions at supplier factories in China—allegations about underage workers, low paid workers, poorly treated workers, unsafe conditions—Apple CEO Tim Cook responded. He said the firm had hired the Fair Labor Association to audit the makers of its popular products and that audit results will be posted monthly on its website. "We're determined to drive widespread change," said Cook.

the effect is felt by its competitors.[15] They have to adjust their practices in order to avoid losing the public relations advantage to Wal-Mart. In this sense the time-worn phrase "keeping up with the competition" is really another way of expressing the dynamics of market controls in action.

**LEARNING CHECK 1**

**TAKEAWAY QUESTION 1 Why and how do managers exercise control?**

**Be sure you can** • define *controlling* as a management function • explain benefits of after-action reviews • illustrate how a fast-food restaurant utilizes feedforward, concurrent, and feedback controls • discuss internal control and external control systems • give examples of bureaucratic, clan, and market controls

# The Control Process

The control process involves the four steps shown in Figure 9.3. They are (1) establish performance objectives and standards; (2) measure actual performance; (3) compare actual performance with objectives and standards; and (4) take corrective action as needed. Although essential to management, these steps apply equally well to personal affairs and careers. Think about it. Without career objectives, how do you know where you really want to go? How can you allocate your time and other resources to take best advantage of available opportunities? Without measurement, how can you assess any progress being made? How can you adjust current behavior to improve prospects for future results?

An **output standard** measures performance results in terms of quantity, quality, cost, or time.

## Step 1—Establish Objectives and Standards

The control process begins with planning, when performance objectives and standards for measuring them are set. It can't start without them. Performance objectives identify key results that one wants to accomplish, and the word *key* deserves emphasis. The focus in planning should be on describing "critical" or "essential" results that will make a substantial performance difference. Once these key results are identified, standards can be set to measure their accomplishment.

FIGURE 9.3 **Four steps in the control process.**

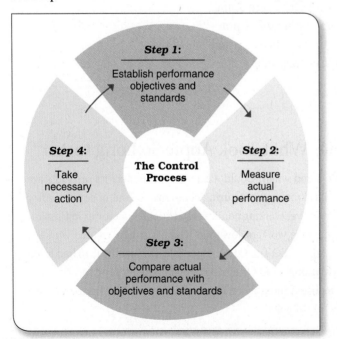

### Output Standards

**Output standards** measure actual outcomes or work results. Businesses use many output standards, such as earnings per share, sales growth, and market share. Others include quantity and quality of production, costs incurred, service or delivery time, and error rates. Based on your experience at work and as a customer, you can probably come up with even more examples.

When Allstate Corporation launched a new diversity initiative, it created a "diversity index" to quantify performance on diversity issues. The standards included how well employees met the goals of bias-free customer service and how well managers met the firm's diversity expectations.[16] When General Electric became concerned about managing ethics in its 320,000-member global workforce, it created measurement standards to track compliance. Each business unit was required to report quarterly on how many of its members attend ethics training sessions and signed the firm's "Spirit and Letter" ethics guide.[17]

How about output standards for other types of organizations, such as a symphony orchestra? When the Cleveland Orchestra wrestled with performance standards, the members weren't willing to rely on vague generalities like "we played well" or "the audience seemed happy" or "not too many mistakes were made." Rather, they decided to track standing ovations, invitations to perform in other countries, and how often other orchestras copied their performance style.[18]

**ETHICS ON THE LINE** > WHO WINS (AND LOSES) WHEN GLOBAL INTERNET FIRMS AND LOCAL GOVERNMENTS BATTLE FOR CONTROL?

# Firms Find Global Traveling Rough on Privacy and Censorship

Lv Jianshe/Imaginechina/Zuma Press

*London*—Reporters Without Borders raised concerns about Twitter's new censorship policy after the company said it will remove tweets in response to government requests in specific countries. These tweets will remain available elsewhere in the world and deleted tweets will be replaced with the message—deleted at government request.

Twitter points out that global expansion will take it to "countries that have different ideas about the contours of freedom of expression." CEO Dick Costolo says: "You can't reside in countries and not operate within the law." Lucie Morillon of Reporters Without Borders is still concerned. She says that "if Twitter is ready to abide by repressive countries then there are real consequences for journalists, bloggers . . . the chain of information is broken."

*Beijing*—Skype is told by the Chinese government that its software must filter words that the Chinese leadership considers offensive from text messages. If the company

doesn't, it can't do business in the country. After refusing at first, company executives finally agree: phrases such as "Falun Gong" and "Dalai Lama" are deleted from text messages delivered through Skype's Chinese joint venture partner, Tom Online.

Skype co-founder Niklas Zennstrom, says: "I may like or not like the laws and regulations to operate businesses in the UK or Germany or the U.S., but if I do business there I choose to comply."

*New Delhi*—An Indian citizen sues Google in local court claiming that some of its content is offensive to certain religious communities. The New Delhi district court issued an order for Google to remove the content. Google complies on its India site but keeps the content available outside of the country.

A Google spokesperson says: "This step is in accordance with Google's longstanding policy of responding to court orders." But, free speech advocates in India claim it is censorship.

 **ETHICS QUESTIONS**

Is it ethical for companies who want to do business in China or elsewhere to go along with policies that would clearly be considered to be a violation of human rights in other places? What determines whether companies should comply with local censorship requests? Should they follow local rules, challenge the status quo, or simply decline to operate in those markets? When should business executives stand up and challenge laws and regulations that are used to deny customers the rights or privacy that they expect?

## Input Standards

The control process also uses **input standards** that measure work efforts. These are common in situations where outputs are difficult or expensive to measure. Examples of input standards for a college professor might be the existence of an orderly course syllabus, meeting all class sessions, and returning exams and assignments in a timely fashion. Of course, as this example might suggest, measuring inputs doesn't mean that outputs such as high-quality teaching and learning are necessarily achieved. Other examples of input standards at work include conformance with rules, efficiency in the use of resources, and work attendance.

## Step 2—Measure Actual Performance

The second step in the control process is to measure actual performance. It is the point where output standards and input standards are used to carefully document results. When Linda Sanford, currently a senior vice president and one of the highest-ranking women at IBM, was appointed head of IBM's sales force, she came with a high performance record earned during a 22-year career with the company. Interestingly, Sanford grew up on a family farm where she developed an appreciation for measuring results. "At the end of the day, you saw what you did, knew how many rows of strawberries you picked." At IBM she was known for walking around the factory, just to see "at the end of the day how many machines were going out of the back dock."[19]

Performance measurements in the control process must be accurate enough to spot significant differences between what is really taking place and what was originally planned. Without measurement, effective control is not possible. With measurement tied to key results, however, an old adage often holds true: "What gets measured happens."

## Step 3—Compare Results with Objectives and Standards

Step 3 in the control process is to compare objectives with results. You can remember its implications by this **control equation**:

$$\text{Need for Action} = \text{Desired Performance} - \text{Actual Performance}$$

The question of what constitutes "desired" performance plays an important role in the control equation. Some organizations use *engineering comparisons*. United Parcel Service (UPS), for example, carefully measures the routes and routines of its drivers to establish the times expected for each delivery. When a delivery manifest is scanned as completed, the driver's time is registered in a performance log that is closely monitored by supervisors. Organizations also use *historical comparisons*, where past experience becomes the baseline for evaluating current performance. They also use *relative comparisons* that benchmark performance against that being achieved by other people, work units, or organizations.

## Step 4—Take Corrective Action

The final step in the control process is to take the action needed to correct problems or make improvements. **Management by exception** is the practice of giving

# Roger Ferguson Provides Strategic Leadership for Retirement Security

RAMINTALAIE/EPA/Newscom

It's a big challenge to lead a huge financial institution in today's economy. But Roger W. Ferguson, Jr. is well prepared and confident in his job as president and chief executive officer of TIAA-CREF. His firm manages over $402 billion in retirement savings for 3.6 million Americans in the academic, research, medical, and cultural fields. And when U.S. President Barack Obama set up a new Economic Advisory Board "to meet regularly so that I can hear different ideas and sharpen my own, and seek counsel that is candid and informed by the wider world," Roger W. Ferguson, Jr. was one of the members.

*Black Enterprise* magazine listed Ferguson as one of the "100 most powerful African Americans in corporate America." At TIAA-CREF he leads an organization that believes "Diversify isn't just smart financial advice. It's a sound hiring policy as well." The firm includes "promoting diversity" in its mission, and states the belief that "all benefit from a work environment that fosters respect, integrity and opportunity for people from a wide variety of backgrounds."

One of Ferguson's main themes is retirement security. He says the average American is short at least $250,000+ at retirement time. He wants a stronger retirement system that "is designed to help people through 30 years of retirement, not just 30 years of work," He advocates for a "holistic retirement system" that will "combine the best practices of defined benefit and defined contribution plans."

## WHAT'S YOUR TAKE?

Having sufficient financial resources to retire comfortably is a real goal. But who's in control? Are we talking individual responsibility and self-control in lifelong financial decision making, or reliance on an employer's choices or even those of government? What criteria should we use to assess whether companies like TIAA-CREF are good places to put our retirement savings? Do you have a retirement plan, and are you staying in control of your progress?

attention to situations that show the greatest need for action. It saves time, energy, and other resources by focusing attention on high-priority areas.

Managers should be alert to two types of exceptions. The first is a problem situation where actual performance is less than desired. It must be understood so that corrective action can restore performance to the desired level. The second is an opportunity situation where actual performance turns out higher than what was desired. It must be understood with the goal of continuing or increasing the high level of accomplishment in the future.

## LEARNING CHECK 2

**TAKEAWAY QUESTION 2 What are the steps in the control process?**

**Be sure you can** • list the steps in the control process • explain why planning is important to controlling • differentiate between output and input standards • state the control equation • define *management by exception*

# Control Tools and Techniques

Managers in most organizations use a variety of control systems and techniques. Some of the most common ones include special techniques of project management, inventory control, breakeven analysis, and financial controls, as well as the use of balanced scorecards.

## Project Management and Control

It might be something personal, like an anniversary party for one's parents, a renovation to your home, or the launch of a new product or service at your place of work. It might be the completion of a new student activities building on a campus, or the implementation of a new advertising campaign for a sports team. What these examples and others like them share in common is that they are relatively complicated tasks with multiple components that have to happen in a certain sequence, and that must be completed by a specified date. We call them **projects**, complex one-time events with unique components and an objective that must be met within a set time.

**Projects** are one-time activities with many component tasks that must be completed in proper order and according to budget.

**Project management** makes sure that activities required to complete a project are planned well and accomplished on time.

**Project management** is the responsibility for overall planning, supervision, and control of projects. A project manager's job is to ensure that a project is well planned and then completed according to plan—on time, within budget, and consistent with objectives. Two useful techniques for project management and control are Gantt charts and CPM/PERT.

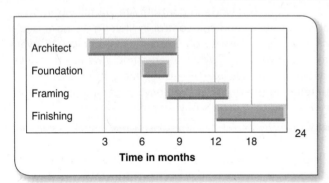

A **Gantt chart** graphically displays the scheduling of tasks required to complete a project.

**CPM/PERT** is a combination of the critical path method and the program evaluation and review technique.

A **Gantt chart** graphically displays the scheduling of tasks that go into completing a project. As developed in the early 20th century by Henry Gantt, an industrial engineer, this tool has become a mainstay of project management. The visual overview of what needs to be done on a project allows for easy progress checks to be made at different time intervals. It also helps with event or activity sequencing to make sure that things get accomplished in time for later work to build upon them. One of the biggest problems with projects, for example, is when delays in early activities create problems for later ones.

A more advanced use of the Gantt chart is a technique known as **CPM/PERT**—a combination of the critical path method and the program evaluation and review technique. Project planning based on CPM/PERT uses a network chart like the one shown here. Such charts break a project into a series of small sub-activities that each have clear beginning and end points. These points become "nodes" in the charts, and the arrows between nodes show in what order things must be done. The full diagram shows all the interrelationships that must be coordinated for the entire project to be successfully completed.

Use of CPM/PERT techniques helps project managers track activities to make sure they happen in the right sequence and on time. If you look at the network in the nearby figure, you should notice that the time required for each activity can be easily computed and tracked. The pathway from

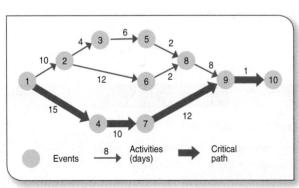

start to conclusion that involves the longest completion times is called the **critical path**. It represents the quickest time in which the entire project can be finished, assuming everything goes according to schedule and plans. In the example, the critical path is 38 days.

## Inventory Control

Cost control is always an important performance concern. And a very good place to start is with inventory. The goal of **inventory control** is to make sure that any inventory is only big enough to meet immediate needs.

The **economic order quantity** form of inventory control, shown in the figure, automatically orders a fixed number of items every time an inventory level falls to a predetermined point. The order sizes are mathematically calculated to minimize inventory costs. A good example is your local supermarket. It routinely makes hundreds of daily orders on an economic order quantity basis.

Another popular approach to inventory control is **just-in-time scheduling** (JIT). These systems reduce costs and improve workflow by scheduling materials to arrive at a workstation or facility just in time for use. Because JIT nearly eliminates the carrying costs of inventories, it is an important business productivity tool.

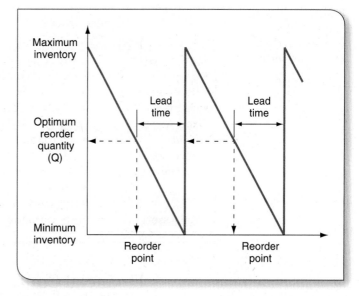

**Inventory control** ensures that inventory is only big enough to meet immediate needs.

The **economic order quantity** method places new orders when inventory levels fall to predetermined points.

**Just-in-time scheduling** (JIT) routes materials to workstations just in time for use.

## Breakeven Analysis

A frequent control question asked by business executives is: "What is the **breakeven point**?" Figure 9.4 shows that breakeven occurs at the point where revenues just equal costs. You can also think of it as where losses end and profit begins. A breakeven point is computed using this formula:

Breakeven Point = Fixed Costs ÷ (Price − Variable Costs)

Managers using **breakeven analysis** perform what-if calculations under different projected cost and revenue conditions. Suppose the proposed target price for a new product is $8 per unit, fixed costs are $10,000, and variable costs are $4 per unit. What sales volume is required to break even? (Answer: breakeven at 2,500 units.) What happens if you can keep variable costs to $3 per unit? (Answer: breakeven at 2,000 units.) If you can produce only 1,000 units in the beginning and at the original costs, at what price must you sell them to break even? (Answer: $14.) Business executives perform these types of cost control analyses every day.

The **breakeven point** occurs where revenues just equal costs.

**Breakeven analysis** performs what-if calculations under different revenue and cost conditions.

FIGURE 9.4 **Use of breakeven analysis to make informed "what-if" decisions.**

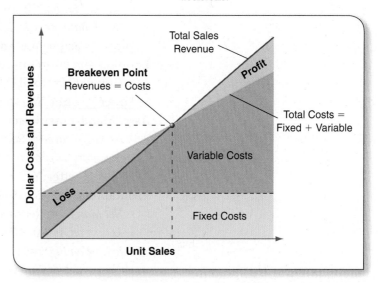

FIGURE 9.5  **Basic foundations of a balance sheet and income statement.**

**Balance Sheet**

| Assets | Liabilities |
|---|---|
| **Current Assets** | **Current Liabilities** |
| • Cash | • Accounts payable |
| • Receivables | • Accrued expenses |
| • Inventories | • Taxes payable |
| **Fixed Assets** | **Long-term Liabilities** |
| • Land | • Mortgages |
| • Buildings | • Bonds |
| **Less Depreciation** | **Owner's Equity** |
| | • Outstanding stock |
| | • Retained earnings |
| **Total Assets** | = **Total Liabilities** |

**Income Statement**

**Gross Sales**
  less Returns
**Net Sales**
  less Expenses and Cost of Goods Sold
**Operating Profits**
  plus Other Income
**Gross Income**
  less Interest Expense
**Income Before Taxes**
  less Taxes
**Net Income**

## Financial Controls

The pressure is ever present for all organizations to use their financial resources well. And the global economic recession has left no doubt that an important part of managerial control involves the analysis of financial performance. Control is all about measurement, and there are a number of ways that financial performance can be measured and tracked for control purposes.

The foundation for analysis using financial controls rests with the firm's balance sheet and income statement. The **balance sheet** shows assets and liabilities at a point in time. It will be displayed in an Assets = Liabilities format. The **income statement** shows profits or losses at a point in time. It will be displayed in a Sales − Expenses = Net Income format. You can remember both from an accounting course or as simply summarized in Figure 9.5.

Managers should be able to use information from balance sheets and income statements to understand a firm's financial performance. Financial controls of this nature often involve measures of *liquidity*—ability to generate cash to pay bills; *leverage*—ability to earn more in returns than the cost of debt; *asset management*—ability to use resources efficiently and operate at minimum cost; and *profitability*—ability to earn revenues greater than costs. Some of the common financial ratios are listed here.

A **balance sheet** shows assets and liabilities at one point in time.

An **income statement** shows profits or losses at one point in time.

**Liquidity**—measures ability to meet short-term obligations
  • *Current Ratio* = Current Assets/Current Liabilities
  • *Quick Ratio or Acid Test* = Current Assets − Inventories/Current Liabilities
  Higher is better: You want more assets and fewer liabilities.
**Leverage**—measures use of debt
  • *Debt Ratio* = Total Debts/Total Assets
  Lower is better: You want fewer debts and more assets.
**Asset Management**—measures asset and inventory efficiency
  • *Asset Turnover* = Sales/Total Assets
  • *Inventory Turnover* = Sales/Average Inventory
  Higher is better: You want more sales relative to assets and inventory.
**Profitability**—measures ability to earn revenues greater than costs
  • *Net Margin* = Net Income/Sales
  • *Return on Assets* (ROA) = Net Income/Total Assets
  • *Return on Equity* (ROE) = Net Income/Owner's Equity
  Higher is better: You want high net income relative to sales, assets, and equity.

Financial ratios are very common in executive dashboards that organize business intelligence information for decision making. The ratios lend themselves nicely to visual displays that provide neat historical comparisons within the firm and for industry benchmarking. They can also be used to set financial targets or goals to be shared with employees and tracked to indicate performance success or failure. Civco Medical Instruments, for example, distributes a monthly financial report to all employees. They always know factually how well the firm is doing. This helps them focus on what they can do better to improve on the firm's bottom line.[20]

## Balanced Scorecards

If an instructor takes class attendance and assigns grades based on it, students tend to come to class. If an employer tracks the number of customers each employee serves per day, employees tend to serve more customers. So if "what gets measured happens," shouldn't managers take advantage of "scorecards" to record and track performance results?

Strategic management consultants Robert S. Kaplan and David P. Norton advocate using the **balanced scorecard** for management control.[21] They say it gives top managers "a fast, but comprehensive view of the business." The basic principle is that to do well and to win, you have to keep score. And like sports teams, organizations tend to perform better when their members always know the score.

Developing a balanced scorecard for any organization begins with a clarification of the organization's mission and vision—what it wants to be and how it wants to be perceived by its key stakeholders. Next, the following questions are used to develop specific scorecard goals and measures:

A **balanced scorecard** tallies organizational performance in financial, customer service, internal process, and innovation and learning areas.

- *Financial Performance*—"How well do our actions directly contribute to improved financial performance? To improve financially, how should we appear to our shareholders?" Sample goals: survive, succeed, prosper. *Sample measures:* cash flow, sales growth and operating income, increased market share, and return on equity.

- *Customer Satisfaction*—"How well do we serve our customers and clients? To achieve our vision, how should we appear to our customers?" Sample goals: new products, responsive supply. *Sample measures:* percentage sales from new products, percentage on-time deliveries.

- *Internal Process Improvement*—"How well do our activities and processes directly increase the value we provide our customers and clients? To satisfy our customers and shareholders, at what internal business processes should we excel?" Sample goals: manufacturing excellence, design productivity, new product introduction. *Sample measures:* cycle times, engineering efficiency, new product time.

- *Innovation and Learning*—"How well are we learning, changing, and improving things over time? To achieve our vision, how will we sustain our ability to change and improve?" Sample goals: technology leadership, time to market. *Sample measures:* time to develop new technologies, new product introduction time versus competition.

When balanced scorecard measures are taken and routinely recorded for critical managerial review, Kaplan and Norton expect managers to make better decisions and organizations to perform better in these four performance areas. Like the financial ratios, the balanced scorecard is a good fit for executive dashboards and visual displays of business intelligence. Again, what gets measured happens.

# Restating Corporate Financial Performance Foreshadows Significant Executive Turnover

Control and accountability are core issues in research by Marne L. Arthaud-Day, S. Trevis Certo, Catherine M. Dalton, and Dan R. Dalton. Using a technique known as event history analysis, the researchers say that what happens subsequent to financial misstatements is an "opportunity to study the accountability of leaders for organizational outcomes, independent of firm performance."

Arthaud-Day et al. examined what happened in a two-year period for 116 firms that restated financials, in comparison with 116 others that did not. The firms were chosen from the Financial Statement Restatement Database and matched in pairs by industry and size for control purposes.

**CEO, CFO, Outside Director, Audit Committee Turnover**

↓

Higher

Lower

Firms Not Restating Financials | Firms Restating Financials

Results showed that higher turnover of CEOs, CFOs, outside directors, and audit committee members were higher in firms that restated their earnings.

The researchers point out that financial misstatements harm a firm's legitimacy in the eyes of key stakeholders, and this threatens the firm's ability to obtain resources and external support. Because financial misstatements are considered to be direct management failures, executives are more likely to be held accountable for them than for poor performance of an organization overall—even for bankruptcy, which might be explained by adverse external factors.

The researchers note that "companies often couch involuntary departures in nice-sounding clichés (i.e., an executive 'retires'), making it nearly impossible to determine the true reason for turnover." In terms of future research, they recommend looking at what happens after "tainted" leadership is removed. Does the firm regain stakeholder legitimacy and do better in the future, or not?

## ■ YOU BE THE RESEARCHER

If one looked not just at financial misstatements, but also at share price declines, profit and loss trends, and product successes and failures, would similar patterns of control and accountability for top managers be found? Given the increased concern for tightening financial controls and holding business executives accountable for performance, are executives in governments, schools, and nonprofits in your community being held accountable as well?

*Reference:* Marne L. Arthaud-Day, S. Trevis Certo, Catherine M. Dalton, and Dan R. Dalton, "A Changing of the Guard: Executive and Director Turnover Following Corporate Financial Restatements," *Academy of Management Journal*, vol. 49 (December 2006), pp. 119–136.

Think about the possibilities of using balanced scorecards in all types of organizations. How can this approach be used, for example, by an elementary school, a hospital, a community library, a mayor's office, a fast-food restaurant? How might the performance dimensions and indicators vary among these different organizations? And if balanced scorecards make sense, why is it that more organizations don't use them?

## LEARNING CHECK 3

**TAKEAWAY QUESTION 3 What are common control tools and techniques?**

**Be sure you can** • define *project management* • explain how Gantt charts and CPM/PERT analysis can assist in project management • explain how inventory controls and breakeven analysis can assist in cost control • list and explain common ratios used in financial control • identify the four main balanced scorecard components and give examples of how they may be used in organizations of various types

# MANAGEMENT LEARNING REVIEW

## TAKEAWAY QUESTION 1 Why and how do managers exercise control?

- Controlling is the process of measuring performance and taking corrective action as needed.
- Feedforward controls are accomplished before a work activity begins; they ensure that directions are clear and that the right resources are available to accomplish them.
- Concurrent controls make sure that things are being done correctly; they allow corrective actions to be taken while the work is being done.
- Feedback controls take place after an action is completed; they address the question "Now that we are finished, how well did we do, and what did we learn for the future?"
- Internal control is self-control and occurs as people take personal responsibility for their work.
- External control is based on the use of bureaucratic, clan, and market control systems.

  **For Discussion** Can strong input and output controls make up for poor concurrent controls?

## TAKEAWAY QUESTION 2 What are the steps in the control process?

- The first step in the control process is to establish performance objectives and standards that create targets against which later performance can be evaluated.
- The second step in the control process is to measure actual performance and specifically identify what results are being achieved.
- The third step in the control process is to compare performance results with objectives to determine if things are going according to plans.

- The fourth step in the control process is to take action to resolve problems or explore opportunities that are identified when results are compared with objectives.

  **For Discussion** What are the potential downsides to management by exception?

## TAKEAWAY QUESTION 3 What are common control tools and techniques?

- A project is a unique event that must be completed by a specified date; project management is the process of ensuring that projects are completed on time, on budget, and according to objectives.
- Gantt charts assist in project management and control by displaying how various tasks must be scheduled in order to complete a project on time.
- CPM/PERT analysis assists in project management and control by describing the complex networks of activities that must be completed in sequences for a project to be completed successfully.
- Economic order quantities and just-in-time deliveries are common approaches to inventory cost control.
- The breakeven equation is: Breakeven Point = Fixed Costs ÷ (Price − Variable Costs).
- Breakeven analysis identifies the points where revenues will equal costs under different pricing and cost conditions.
- Financial control of business performance is facilitated by a variety of financial ratios, such as those dealing with liquidity, leverage, assets, and profitability.
- The balanced scorecard measures overall organizational performance in four areas: financial, customers, internal processes, and innovation.

  **For Discussion** Should all employees of a business be regularly informed of the firm's overall financial performance?

## Multiple-Choice Questions

1. After objectives and standards are set, what step comes next in the control process?
   (a) Measure results.
   (b) Take corrective action.
   (c) Compare results with objectives.
   (d) Modify standards to fit circumstances.

2. When a soccer coach tells her players at the end of a game: I'm pleased you stayed with the game plan," she is using a/an _____ to a measure performance, even though in terms of outcomes her team lost.
   (a) input standard          (b) output standard
   (c) historical comparison   (d) relative comparison

3. When an automobile manufacturer is careful to purchase only the highest-quality components for use in production, this is an example of an attempt to ensure high performance through _____ control.
   (a) concurrent　　(b) statistical
   (c) inventory　　(d) feedforward

4. Management by exception means _____.
   (a) managing only when necessary
   (b) focusing attention where the need for action is greatest
   (c) the same thing as concurrent control
   (d) the same thing as just-in-time delivery

5. When a supervisor working alongside an employee corrects him or her when a mistake is made, this is an example of _____ control.
   (a) feedforward　　(b) concurrent
   (c) internal　　(d) clan

6. If an organization's top management visits a firm in another industry to learn more about its excellent record in hiring and promoting minority and female candidates, this is an example of using _____ for control purposes.
   (a) a balanced scorecard
   (b) relative comparison
   (c) management by exception
   (d) progressive discipline

7. The control equation states: _____ = Desired Performance − Actual Performance.
   (a) Problem Magnitude
   (b) Management Opportunity
   (c) Planning Objective
   (d) Need for Action

8. When a UPS manager compares the amount of time a driver takes to make certain deliveries against standards set through a quantitative analysis of her delivery route, this is known as _____.
   (a) a historical comparison
   (b) an engineering comparison
   (c) relative benchmarking
   (d) concurrent control

9. Projects are unique one-time events that _____.
   (a) have unclear objectives
   (b) must be completed by a specific time
   (c) have unlimited budgets
   (d) are largely self-managing

10. The _____ chart graphically displays the scheduling of tasks required to complete a project.
    (a) exception　　(b) Taylor
    (c) Gantt　　(d) after-action

11. When one team member advises another team member that "your behavior is crossing the line in terms of our expectations for workplace civility," she is exercising a form of _____ control over the other's inappropriate behaviors
    (a) clan　　(b) market
    (c) internal　　(d) preliminary

12. In a CPM/PERT analysis the focus is on _____ and the event _____ that link them together with the finished project.
    (a) costs, budgets　　(b) activities, sequences
    (c) timetables, budgets　　(d) goals, costs

13. If fixed costs are $10,000, variable costs are $4 per unit, and the target selling price per unit is $8, what is the breakeven point?
    (a) 2　　(b) 500
    (c) 2,500　　(d) 4,800

14. Among the financial ratios used for control, Current Assets/Current Liabilities is known as the _____.
    (a) debt ratio　　(b) net margin
    (c) current ratio　　(d) inventory turnover ratio

15. In respect to return on assets (ROA) and the debt ratio, the preferred directions when analyzing them from a control standpoint are _____.
    (a) decrease ROA, increase debt
    (b) increase ROA, increase debt
    (c) increase ROA, decrease debt
    (d) decrease ROA, decrease debt

## Short-Response Questions

16. List the four steps in the controlling process and give examples of each.

17. How might feedforward control be used by the owner/manager of a local bookstore?

18. How does Douglas McGregor's Theory Y relate to the concept of internal control?

19. What four questions could be used to organize the presentation of an up-to-the-moment balanced scorecard in the executive dashboard for a small business?

## Essay Question

**20.** Assume that you are given the job of project manager for building a new student center on your campus. List just five of the major activities that need to be accomplished to complete the new building in two years. Draw an AON network diagram that links the activities together in required event scheduling and sequencing. Make an estimate for the time required for each sequence to be completed and identify the critical path.

# MANAGEMENT SKILLS AND COMPETENCIES

# Further Reflection: Resiliency

The control process is one of the ways managers help organizations best use resources and systems to achieve productivity. In many ways our daily lives are similar quests for high performance, and the control process counts there too. We need to spot and understand whether things are going according to plan or going off course. We need to have the courage and confidence to change ways that aren't working well. And, we need to have the **resiliency** to hold on and keep things moving forward even in the face of adversity.

The way we use, or don't use, positive self-management makes a substantial difference in the results we achieve in work and personal affairs. It all begins with a strong commitment to both planning—getting the goals clear and right—and controlling—making sure that we are always moving forward to accomplish them.

 **DO IT NOW . . .
LOOK IN THE MIRROR**

- Go back to the chapter-opening Resiliency Quick Test. If you haven't already taken it, do it now. A score of 35 or better suggests you are highly resilient; with any lower score you should question how well you hold up under pressure.
- Double-check the test results by looking at your behavior. Write notes on how you handle situations like a poor grade at school, a put-down from a friend, a denial letter from a job application, or criticism from a boss or coworker on your job.
- Summarize what you've learned in a memo to yourself about how you might benefit from showing more resiliency in difficult situations.

# Self-Assessment: Internal/External Control[22]

## Instructions

Circle either a or b to indicate the item you most agree with in each pair of the following statements.

**1.** (a) Promotions are earned through hard work and persistence.
 (b) Making a lot of money is largely a matter of breaks.

**2.** (a) Many times the reactions of teachers seem haphazard to me.
 (b) In my experience I have noticed that there is usually a direct connection between how hard I study and the grades I get.

**3.** (a) The number of divorces indicates that more and more people are not trying to make their marriages work.
 (b) Marriage is largely a gamble.

**4.** (a) It is silly to think that one can really change another person's basic attitudes.
 (b) When I am right, I can convince others.

**5.** (a) Getting promoted is really a matter of being a little luckier than the next guy.
 (b) In our society, an individual's future earning power is dependent on his or her ability.

**6.** (a) If one knows how to deal with people, they are really quite easily led.

(b) I have little influence over the way other people behave.

**7.** (a) In my case, the grades I make are the results of my own efforts; luck has little or nothing to do with it.

(b) Sometimes I feel that I have little to do with the grades I get.

**8.** (a) People such as I can change the course of world affairs if we make ourselves heard.

(b) It is only wishful thinking to believe that one can really influence what happens in society at large.

**9.** (a) Much of what happens to me is probably a matter of chance.

(b) I am the master of my fate.

**10.** (a) Getting along with people is a skill that must be practiced.

(b) It is almost impossible to figure out how to please some people.

## Scoring

Give yourself 1 point for 1b, 2a, 3a, 4b, 5b, 6a, 7a, 8a, 9b, 10a. Total scores of: 8–10 = high *internal* locus of control, 6–7 = moderate *internal* locus of control, 5 = *mixed* locus of control, 3–4 = moderate *external* locus of control, 0–2 = high *external* locus of control.

## Interpretation

This instrument offers an impression of your tendency toward an *internal locus of control or external locus of control*. Persons with a high internal locus of control tend to believe they have control over their own destinies. They may be most responsive to opportunities for greater self-control in the workplace. Persons with a high external locus of control tend to believe that what happens to them is largely in the hands of external people or forces. They may be less comfortable with self-control and more responsive to external controls in the workplace.

# Team Exercise:
# After-Meeting/Project Remorse

## Instructions

A. Everyone on the team should complete the following assessment after participating in a meeting or a group project.[23]

**1.** How satisfied are you with the outcome of the meeting project?

Not at all satisfied  1 2 3 4 5 6 7  Totally satisfied

**2.** How would the other members of the meeting/project group rate your influence on what took place?

No influence  1 2 3 4 5 6 7  Very high influence

**3.** In your opinion, how ethical was any decision that was reached?

Highly unethical  1 2 3 4 5 6 7  Highly ethical

**4.** To what extent did you feel *pushed into* going along with the decision?

Not pushed into it at all  1 2 3 4 5 6 7  Very pushed into it

**5.** How committed are you to the agreements reached?

Not at all committed  1 2 3 4 5 6 7  Highly committed

**6.** Did you understand what was expected of you as a member of the meeting or project group?

Not at all clear  1 2 3 4 5 6 7  Perfectly clear

**7.** Were participants in the meeting/project group discussions listening to each other?

Never  1 2 3 4 5 6 7  Always

**8.** Were participants in the meeting/project group discussions honest and open in communicating with one another?

Never  1 2 3 4 5 6 7  Always

**9.** Was the meeting/project completed efficiently?

Not at all  1 2 3 4 5 6 7  Very much

**10.** Was the outcome of the meeting/project something that you felt proud to be a part of?

Not at all  1 2 3 4 5 6 7  Very much

B. Share results with all team members and discuss their meaning.

C. Summarize and share with the instructor and class the implications of this exercise for: (a) the future success of this team if it was to work on another project, and (b) each individual team member as he or she goes forward to work in other teams and on other group projects in the future.

## Career Situations for Management Control: What Would You Do?

1. **Adrift in Career** A work colleague comes to you and confides that she feels "adrift in her career" and "just can't get enthused about what she's doing anymore." You think this might be a problem of self-management and personal control. How can you respond most helpfully? How might she use the steps in the management control process to better understand and correct her situation?

2. **Too Much Socializing** You have a highly talented work team whose past performance has been outstanding. You've recently noticed team members starting to act like the workday is mainly a social occasion. Getting the work done too often seems less important than having a good time. Data show performance is on the decline. How can you use controls in positive ways to restore performance to high levels in this team?

3. **Yes or No to Graduate School** You've had three years of solid work experience after earning your undergraduate degree. A lot of your friends are talking about going to graduate school, and the likely target for you would be an MBA degree. Given all the potential costs and benefits of getting an MBA, how can breakeven analysis help you make the decision: (a) to go or not go, (b) to go full time or part time, and (c) even where to go?

## Case Study

# Electronic Arts

Go to *Management Cases for Critical Thinking* to find the recommended case for Chapter 9—"Electronic Arts: Inside Fantasy Sports."

Electronic Arts is one of the largest and most profitable third-party video game makers. Exclusive contracts with professional sports teams enabled it to dominate the sports gaming market. Until recently, EA's devotion to sports games was a winning asset.

But as gaming has shifted from consoles to laptops, smartphones, and tablets, it is struggling to stay ahead. The gaming market has radically and quickly changed. Can EA keep the pole position in a crowded, competitive, and contentious market?

# Wisdom
## Learning
## From Others

Kai Nedden/laif/Redux

### > PASSION AND VALUES MAKE FOR STRATEGIC SUCCESS

Patagonia is known for top-quality and high-priced outdoor clothing and gear. The firm is also driven by a commitment to sustainability and the natural environment. Its mission is to "build the best product, cause no unnecessary harm, use business to inspire and implement solutions to the environmental crisis."

You are as likely to find Patagonia's founder Yvon Chouinard climbing a mountain in Yosemite or the Himalayas as working in the office. But his values are ever present. "Most people want to do good things but don't," he says. "At Patagonia it's an essential part of your life." Chouinard has been called "nonconformist," "eco-conscious," and "employee friendly." And it all shows up

in his company. Patagonia's "Reason for Being" states in part: "For us at Patagonia, a love of wild and beautiful places demands participation in the fight to save them. . . . We know that our business activity—from lighting stores to dyeing shirts—creates pollution as a by-product. So we work steadily to reduce those."

What's the business payoff? Patagonia's earnings are consistently above the industry average. Its workforce is loyal and inspired. And Chouinard says, "I have an M.B.A. theory of management. Management by Absence. I take off for weeks at a time and never call in. We hire the best people we can and then leave them to do their jobs."[1]

## MORE TO LOOK FOR INSIDE>

# Strategy and Strategic Management

## > CRITICAL THINKING

Managers face significant challenges as they try to move their organizations forward with success in ever-changing environments. When things are complex and uncertain, **critical thinking** skills are especially important. They represent an ability to gather, organize, analyze, and interpret information to make good decisions in situations that range from difficult to utterly perplexing.

We rarely have the luxury of making decisions with full information that is boxed up to digest and analyze in a nice, neat format. How good are you at making critical connections in unusual situations? For starters, take a stab at the two puzzles shown here.[2]

The case studies and problem-solving projects in your courses help develop your critical thinking skills. But beware—a lot of information in circulation on and off the Internet is anecdotal, superficial, irrelevant, and even just plain inaccurate.

You must be disciplined, cautious, and discerning in interpreting the credibility and usefulness of available information. In other words, you must be good at critical thinking.

## Insight
### Learning About Yourself

**Puzzle 1**
Divide this shape into four shapes that are exactly the same size as one another.

**Puzzle 2**
Draw no more than four lines that cross all nine dots; don't lift your pencil while drawing.

## BUILD MANAGEMENT SKILLS AND COMPETENCIES AT END OF CHAPTER

- Engage in *Further Reflection on Critical Thinking*
- Take the *Self-Assessment—Intuitive Ability*
- Complete the *Team Exercise—Strategic Scenarios*
- Solve the *Career Situations for Strategic Management*
- Analyze the *Case Study—"Dunkin' Donuts: Betting Dollars on Donuts"*

## <GET TO KNOW YOURSELF BETTER

| TAKEAWAY 1 | TAKEAWAY 2 | TAKEAWAY 3 | TAKEAWAY 4 | TAKEAWAY 5 |
|---|---|---|---|---|
| **Strategic Management** | **Essentials of Strategic Analysis** | **Corporate-Level Strategy Formulation** | **Business-Level Strategy Formulation** | **Strategy Implementation** |
| • Competitive advantage <br> • Strategy and strategic intent <br> • Levels of strategy <br> • Strategic management process | • Analysis of mission, values, and objectives <br> • SWOT analysis of organization and environment <br> • Five forces analysis of industry attractiveness | • Portfolio planning model <br> • Growth and diversification strategies <br> • Retrenchment and restructuring strategies <br> • Global strategies <br> • Cooperative strategies | • Competitive strategies model <br> • Differentiation strategy <br> • Cost leadership strategy <br> • Focus strategy | • Management practices and systems <br> • Strategic control and corporate governance <br> • Strategic leadership |
| LEARNING CHECK 1 | LEARNING CHECK 2 | LEARNING CHECK 3 | LEARNING CHECK 4 | LEARNING CHECK 5 |

Set the opening story of Patagonia aside for a moment and switch to another well-recognized name—Wal-Mart. Whether or not you like the firm, its master plan is elegant in its simplicity: attract customers by delivering consistently everyday low prices.[3] It's all supported by the latest technology and sophisticated logistics with world-class distribution and inventories monitored around the clock. Stores are rarely out of the items customers want. All systems and people are rallied to deliver low prices and quality service. At least, that's the plan.

Times keep changing and Wal-Mart can't rest on past laurels. It's been challenged on everything from its wage levels to employee benefits, to its impact on local competition in communities, to its low-cost global supply chains, to the clutter and lack of attractiveness of its stores. Not too long ago Wal-Mart's competitors were consistently asking: "How can we keep up?" Now retailers like Dollar General and Target offer real alternatives, and the online giant Amazon.com is also taking its toll.[4]

Among conversations in Wal-Mart's Barksdale, Arkansas, headquarters, you're likely to hear the strategists asking: "Are we still ahead? If so, how can we stay ahead? If not, what can we do to get back on top?" Even though sticking with its master plan, Wal-Mart is constantly making adjustments—such as layaways, free online shipping, and matching rivals' prices—to stay in tune with economic trends, customer tastes, and the competition.[5]

# Strategic Management

The forces and challenges evident in the Wal-Mart example confront managers in all organizations and industries. Today's environment places a great premium on "competitive advantage" and how it is achieved, or not, through "strategy" and "strategic management."[6]

## Competitive Advantage

The term **competitive advantage** describes an organization's ability to use resources so well that it performs better than the competition. Typical sources of competitive advantage are:[7]

- *Technology*—using technology to gain operating efficiencies, market exposure, and customer loyalty.
- *Cost and quality*—operating with greater efficiency and product or service quality.
- *Knowledge and speed*—doing better at innovation and speed of delivery to market for new ideas.
- *Barriers to entry*—creating a market stronghold that is protected from entry by others.
- *Financial resources*—having better investments or loss absorption potential than competitors.

Finding and holding onto competitive advantage is a stiff challenge. Whenever organizations do things very well, rivals try to duplicate and copy the success stories. The ultimate goal is creating **sustainable competitive advantage**—competitive advantage that is durable and difficult or costly for others to copy or imitate. When you think sustainable competitive advantage, think about Apple's iPad. It was first to market as an innovative product linking design, technology, and customer appeal. It was also backed by Apple's super-efficient supply chain which made it a high-margin product. And so far, the iPad ball has kept on rolling. One analyst observes: "Apple moved the goal posts before most of their competitors even took the field."[8]

## Strategy and Strategic Intent

If sustainable competitive advantage is the goal, "strategy" is the means to its achievement.[9] A **strategy** is a comprehensive action plan that identifies the long-term direction for an organization and guides resource utilization to achieve sustainable competitive advantage. It is a "best guess" about what must be done for future success in the face of rivalry and changing conditions. *Fast Company* magazine once said: "If you want to make a difference as a leader, you've got to make time for strategy."[10]

Just as with our personal resources, organizational resources—such as time, money, and people—can get wasted when spent on things that don't really add up to much value. A strategy helps ensure that resources are used with consistent **strategic intent**, that is, with all energies directed toward accomplishing a long-term target or goal.[11] Pepsico's mission, for example, is "to be the world's premier consumer products company focused on convenient food and beverages." This mission is presently being pursued by investments in healthier products—a strategic intent described by the firm as "achieving business and financial success while leaving a positive imprint on society—delivering what we call 'Performance with Purpose.'"[12]

**Competitive advantage** is the ability to do something so well that one outperforms competitors.

**Sustainable competitive advantage** is the ability to outperform rivals in ways that are difficult or costly to imitate.

A **strategy** is a comprehensive plan guiding resource allocation to achieve long-term organization goals.

**Strategic intent** focuses and applies organizational energies on a unifying and compelling goal.

© Web Pix/Alamy

## LivingSocial Chases First-Mover Groupon in an Industry of Copycats

Groupon made the "daily deal" an enviable Web-driven business model. It also spawned a lot of copycats, many of which have since disappeared. LivingSocial started out as a copycat and has gained traction. Its CEO, Tim O'Shaughnessy, says that his firm is differentiating by making better connections among its merchant clients. But he has to be careful; the strategic table turns both ways. After LivingSocial debuted Escapes as a place to find discounts at luxury hotels, Groupon followed by starting its own and more successful one called Getaways.

## Levels of Strategy

*Motorola finally breaks up. What now?*
*Xerox chief looks beyond photocopiers toward services.*
*Chip maker thrives on virtual manufacturing.*

These headlines display the three levels of strategy in organizations. Shown in Figure 10.1, they are corporate-level strategy—Motorola splitting into Motorola Sales and Motorola Mobility; business-level strategy—Xerox shifting emphasis from selling photocopiers to selling services; and functional strategy—a semiconductor chip maker operating with a virtual factory.[13] To really understand the stories behind such headlines, you need to understand the strategy and its fit with both the business purpose and the current competitive conditions.

### Corporate-Level Strategy

A **corporate strategy** sets long-term direction for the total enterprise.

The level of **corporate strategy** directs the organization as a whole toward sustainable competitive advantage. It describes the scope of operations by answering this *corporate-level strategic question*: "In what industries and markets should we compete?" The headline example is of Motorola's CEO deciding that the firm will be better off in the future after being split into two separate entities.

FIGURE 10.1 **Corporate-level strategy, business-level strategy, and functional strategy.**

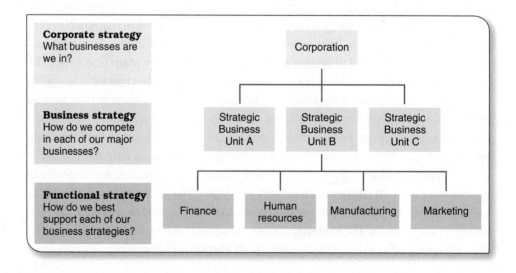

**Corporate strategy**
What businesses are we in?

**Business strategy**
How do we compete in each of our major businesses?

**Functional strategy**
How do we best support each of our business strategies?

Corporation

Strategic Business Unit A

Strategic Business Unit B

Strategic Business Unit C

Finance

Human resources

Manufacturing

Marketing

The purpose of corporate strategy is to set direction and guide resource allocations for the entire enterprise. It identifies how large and complex organizations can compete across multiple industries and markets. General Electric, for example, owns over 100 businesses in a wide variety of areas, including aircraft engines, appliances, capital services, medical systems, and power systems. Typical corporate-level strategic decisions for GE relate to things like new business acquisitions and existing business expansions and cutbacks.

## Business-Level Strategy

**Business strategy** is the strategy for a single business unit or product line. It involves asking and answering this *business-level strategic question*: "How are we going to compete for customers in this industry and market?" The headline example is Xerox shifting resources and attention toward providing more business services.

> A **business strategy** identifies how a division or strategic business unit will compete in its product or service domain.

Typical business strategy decisions include choices about product and service mix, facilities locations, new technologies, and the like. Business strategy is the corporate strategy in single-product enterprises. But multi-product firms like Xerox will follow a variety of business strategies. The term *strategic business unit* (SBU) is often used to describe a business firm that is part of a larger enterprise. Whereas the enterprise on a whole will have a corporate strategy, each SBU will have its own business strategy.

## Functional Strategy

**Functional strategy** guides the use of organizational resources to implement business strategy. This level of strategy focuses on activities within a specific functional area such as marketing, manufacturing, finance, or human resources. The *functional-level strategic question* is: "How can we best utilize resources within a function to implement our business strategy?"

> A **functional strategy** guides activities within one specific area of operations.

Functional-level strategies typically focus on management practices to improve things like operating efficiency, product quality, customer service, or innovativeness. Picochip, for example, is the firm behind the last of the earlier headlines. It produces specialized microchips to its own designs but without a factory. Its manufacturing strategy is based on a "virtual" model where all chip production is outsourced. CEO Nigel Toon says what the firm saves from not having expensive factories it invests in research and development on state-of-the-art chip designs.[14]

# Strategic Management Process

Developing strategy for an organization may seem a deceptively simple task: Find out what customers want, provide it for them at the best prices and service, and make sure competitors can't copy what you are doing well. In practice, things can get very complicated.[15] The reality is that strategies don't just happen; they must be developed and then be well implemented. And at the same time that managers in one organization are doing all this, their competitors are trying to do the same—only better.

**Strategic management** is the process of formulating and implementing strategies to accomplish long-term goals and sustain competitive advantage. You can think of it as making decisions that allocate an organization's resources so it will consistently outperform rivals. As shown in Figure 10.2, the process begins with

> **Strategic management** is the process of formulating and implementing strategies.

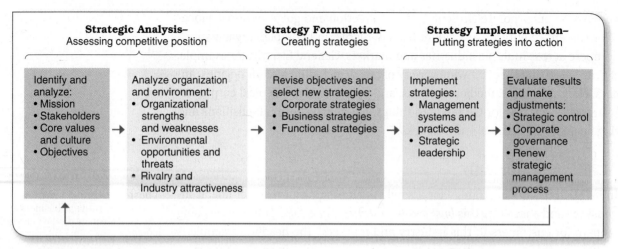

**FIGURE 10.2    Major elements in the strategic management process.**

**Strategic analysis** is the process of analyzing the organization, the environment, and the organization's competitive position and current strategies.

**Strategy formulation** is the process of crafting strategies to guide the allocation of resources.

**Strategy implementation** is the process of putting strategies into action.

**strategic analysis** to assess the organization, its environment, its competitive positioning, and its current strategies. Next comes **strategy formulation**, the process of developing a new or revised strategy. The final phase is **strategy implementation**, using resources to put strategies into action, and then evaluating results so that the implementation can be improved or the strategy itself changed. As the late management consultant and guru Peter Drucker once said: "The future will not just happen if one wishes hard enough. It requires decision—now. It imposes risk—now. It requires action—now. It demands allocation of resources, and above all, it requires work—now."[16]

---

**LEARNING CHECK 1**

**TAKEAWAY QUESTION 1 What is strategic management?**

**Be sure you can** • define *competitive advantage, strategy,* and *strategic intent* • explain the concept of sustainable competitive advantage • differentiate corporate, business, and functional strategies • differentiate strategy formulation from strategy implementation • list the major phases in the strategic management process

---

# Essentials of Strategic Analysis

Let's go back to Patagonia, the firm featured in the chapter opener. We'll talk more about it while examining the essentials of strategic analysis. Think, too, about this set of strategic questions that any top manager should be ready to answer: (1) What is our business mission? (2) Who are our customers? (3) What do our customers value? (4) What have been our results? (5) What is our plan?[17]

## Analysis of Mission, Values, and Objectives

The strategic management process begins with analysis of mission, values, and objectives. This sets the stage for assessing the organization's resources and capabilities, as well as opportunities and threats in its external environment.

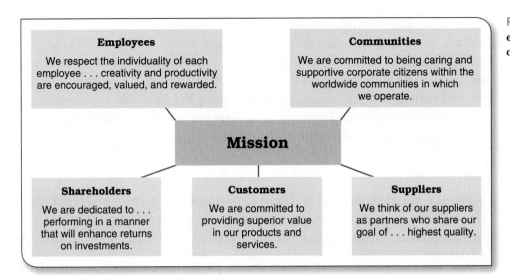

## Mission and Stakeholders

The **mission** or purpose of an organization describes its reason for existence in society.[18] Strategy consultant Michael Hammer believes that a mission should represent what the strategy or underlying business model is trying to accomplish. To clarify mission he suggests asking: "What are we moving to?" "What is our dream?" "What kind of a difference do we want to make in the world?" "What do we want to be known for?"[19]

The mission at Patagonia is to "Build the best product, cause no unnecessary harm, use business to inspire and implement solutions to the environmental crisis."[20] In this mission one finds not only a business direction but also a distinctive value commitment, one that gives Patagonia a unique identity as it competes with much larger rivals in its industry. Such a clear sense of mission helps managers inspire the support and respect of an organization's **stakeholders**. These are individuals and groups—including customers, shareholders, employees, suppliers, creditors, community groups, and others—who are directly affected by the organization and its accomplishments. Figure 10.3 gives an example of how stakeholder interests can be linked with the mission of a business firm.

A **mission** statement expresses the organization's reason for existence in society.

**Stakeholders** are individuals and groups directly affected by the organization and its strategic accomplishments.

## Core Values and Culture

Organizational values and culture should be analyzed in the strategic management process to determine how well they align with the mission.[21] **Core values** are broad beliefs about what is or is not appropriate behavior. Patagonia founder and chairman Yvon Chouinard says: "Most people want to do good things, but don't. At Patagonia it's an essential part of your life."[22] He leads Patagonia with a personal commitment to sustainability and expects the firm to live up to it as a core value. For example, the firm's Common Threads Initiative strives to "reduce excess consumption and give the planet's vital systems a rest from pollution, resource depletion and greenhouse gases." It pledges Patagonia to "build useful things that last, to repair what breaks and recycle what comes to the end of its useful life." It also asks customers to reduce consumption and then repair, reuse, and recycle their purchases.[23]

The presence of core values helps build a clear organizational identity. It gives the organization a sense of character as seen through the eyes of employees and

**Core values** are broad beliefs about what is or is not appropriate behavior.

**Organizational culture** is the predominant value system for the organization as a whole.

external stakeholders. This character is part of what we call the **organizational culture** or predominant value system of the organization as a whole.[24] A clear and strong organizational culture helps guide the behavior of organization members in ways consistent with mission and core values. When browsing Patagonia's website for job openings, for example, the message about the corporate culture is clear: "We're especially interested in people who share our love of the outdoors, our passion for quality, and our desire to make a difference."[25]

## Objectives

**Operating objectives** are specific results that organizations try to accomplish.

Whereas a mission statement sets forth an organization's purpose and core values set standards for accomplishing it, **operating objectives** direct activities toward key performance areas. Typical operating objectives of a business include the following:[26]

- *Profitability*—operating with a net profit.
- *Sustainability*—helping to preserve, not exploit, the environment.
- *Social responsibility*—acting as a good community citizen.
- *Financial health*—acquiring capital; earning positive returns.
- *Cost efficiency*—using resources well to operate at low cost.
- *Customer service*—meeting customer needs and maintaining loyalty.
- *Product quality*—producing high-quality goods or services.
- *Market share*—gaining a specific share of possible customers.
- *Human talent*—recruiting and maintaining a high-quality workforce.
- *Innovation*—developing new products and processes.

Well-chosen operating objectives turn a broad sense of mission into specific performance targets. In the case of Patagonia, mission, values, and operating objectives seem to fit well together as a coherent whole. Chouinard says that he wants to run Patagonia "so that it's here 100 years from now and always makes the best-quality stuff." Although one of the firm's objectives is revenue growth, this doesn't mean growth at any cost. Chouinard's objective is modest growth, not extreme or uncontrolled growth. Patagonia now is growing about 5% per year.[27]

## SWOT Analysis of Organization and Environment

A **SWOT analysis** examines organizational strengths and weaknesses and environmental opportunities and threats.

A technique known as **SWOT analysis** is a useful first step in analyzing the organization and its environment. As Figure 10.4 describes, it is an internal analysis of *organizational strengths and weaknesses* as well as an external analysis of *environmental opportunities and threats*. Although the examples and discussion to follow apply SWOT to organizational situations, you should also be thinking about how to use a personal SWOT analysis for career planning purposes.

### Organizational Strengths and Weaknesses

A **core competency** is a special strength that gives an organization a competitive advantage.

A SWOT analysis begins with a systematic evaluation of the organization's resources and capabilities—its basic strengths and weaknesses. You can think of this as an analysis of organizational capacity to achieve its objectives. A major goal is to identify **core competencies**—things that the organization has or does exceptionally well in comparison with competitors. They are capabilities that by virtue

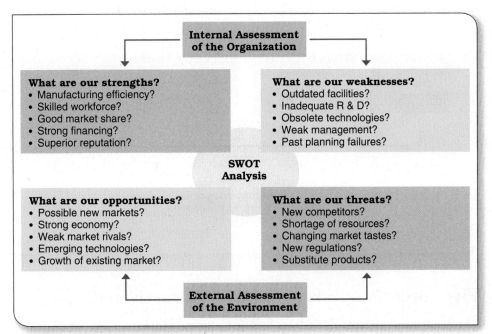

of being rare, costly to imitate, and nonsubstitutable, become potential sources of competitive advantage.[28] Core competencies may be found in special knowledge or expertise, superior technologies, efficient supply chains, or unique distribution systems, among many other possibilities.

Organizational weaknesses are the other side of the picture. The goal here is to identify things that inhibit performance and hold the organization back from fully accomplishing its objectives. Examples might be outdated products, lack of financial capital, shortage of talented workers, and poor or poorly used technology. Once weaknesses are identified plans can be set to eliminate or reduce them, or possibly to turn them into strengths. Even if some weaknesses cannot be corrected, they need to be understood. Strategies should ideally build on organizational strengths and minimize the negative impact of weaknesses.

## Environmental Opportunities and Threats

No SWOT analysis is complete until opportunities and threats in the external environment are also assessed. As shown in Figure 10.4, opportunities may exist as possible new markets, a strong economy, weaknesses in competitors, and emerging technologies. Environmental threats may be such things as the emergence of new competitors, resource scarcities, changing customer tastes, new government regulations, and a weak economy.

Imagine the threats faced by airline executives when global economies went into recession and oil prices rose sharply. These forces upset existing strategies and caused major rethinking about what to do next. Some airlines adjusted tactically. They reduced flight schedules, cutback fleets, and laid off employees. Others made strategy shifts. The large legacy carriers Northwest and Delta merged, for example, because their executives believed industry conditions favored larger carriers.

### TAKE ADVANTAGE OF INSIGHTS FROM SWOT ANALYSIS

- Build on and use strengths to create core competencies.

- Avoid relying on weaknesses that can't be turned into strengths.

- Move toward opportunities to capture advantage.

- Avoid threats or act in ways that minimize their impact.

FIGURE 10.5 **Porter's model of five strategic forces affecting industry competition.**

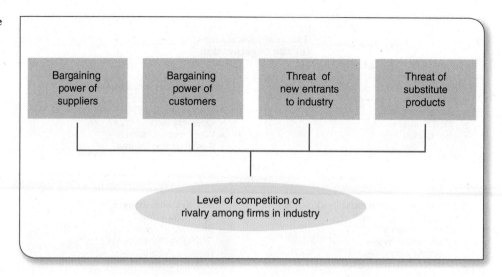

## Five Forces Analysis of Industry Attractiveness

The ideal strategic setting for any firm is to operate in *monopoly conditions* as the only player in an industry—that is, to have no rivals to compete with for resources or customers. But this is rare except in highly regulated settings. The reality for most businesses is rivalry and competition that unfolds either under conditions of *oligopoly*—facing just a few competitors, such as in a consolidated airline industry or *hypercompetition*—facing several direct competitors, such as in the fast-food industry.[29] Both oligopoly and hypercompetition are strategically challenging. Hypercompetition is especially so because any competitive advantage tends to be short-lived.

Harvard scholar and consultant Michael Porter describes the five forces shown in Figure 10.5 as a tool for strategic analysis in competitive industries.[30] He calls these five forces the "industry structure."

1. *Industry competition*—the intensity of rivalry among firms in the industry and the ways they behave competitively toward one another.
2. *New entrants*—the threat of new competitors entering the market, based on the presence or absence of barriers to entry.
3. *Substitute products or services*—the threat of substitute products or services, or ability of customers to get what they want from other sellers.
4. *Bargaining power of suppliers*—the ability of resource suppliers to influence the price that one has to pay for their products or services.
5. *Bargaining power of customers*—the ability of customers to influence the price that they will pay for the firm's products or services.

The status of these five forces determine an industry's attractiveness or potential to generate long-term business returns. The less attractive the industry structure, the harder it will be to make good strategic choices and realize a sustained competitive advantage. According to a five forces analysis, an

### FIVE FORCES ANALYSIS

| Attractive Industry | Unattractive Industry |
|---|---|
| • Few competitors | • Many competitors |
| • High barriers to entry | • Low barriers to entry |
| • Few substitute products | • Many substitute products |
| • Low power of suppliers | • High power of suppliers |
| • Low power of customers | • High power of customers |

*unattractive industry* is one in which rivalry among competitors is intense, substantial threats exist in the form of possible new entrants and substitute products, and suppliers and buyers are very powerful in bargaining over such things as prices and quality. An *attractive industry*, by contrast, has less existing competition, few threats from new entrants or substitutes, and low bargaining power among suppliers and buyers.

---

**LEARNING CHECK 2**

**TAKEAWAY QUESTION 2 What are the essentials of strategic analysis?**

**Be sure you can** • explain how a good mission statement helps organizations relate to stakeholders • define *core values* and *organizational culture* • list several operating objectives of organizations • define *core competency* • explain SWOT analysis • use Porter's five forces model to assess the attractiveness of an industry

---

# Corporate-Level Strategy Formulation

The CEO and the top management team are supposed to plot the overall direction of an organization in the competitive setting of its industry. But this is often easier said than done. If we had asked with GM executives a few years ago about their strategy, "growth" would have been the ready answer. Then recession hit. Growth is now back on the table in a much more modest way. GM is making a fresh start after a period of strategic restructuring and bankruptcy.[31]

Check the news. You can always find ready examples of organizations choosing and changing courses of action in search of the best strategy—one that keeps them moving forward in a complex and ever-changing competitive environment. We've got Netflix constantly trying to figure out how to deal with increasing competition in movie streaming from Apple, Amazon, and the cable companies. Then there's Yahoo! It's a great brand, but even after changing CEOs twice in one year no one is sure if it can hold up to competition.

## Portfolio Planning Model

General Electric's CEO Jeffrey Immelt faces a difficult strategic question all the time: How should GE's resources be allocated across a diverse mix of media, infrastructure, and finance businesses to advance the success of the conglomerate as a whole?[32] If you think about it, Immelt's strategic management problem is similar to what we face while managing our personal assets. How, for example, do you create a good mix of cash, stocks, bonds, and real estate investments? What do you buy more of, what do you sell, and what do you hold? These are the same questions that Immelt and other executives ask. They are *portfolio-planning* questions, and they have major strategic implications. Shouldn't they be made systematically rather than haphazardly?[33]

The Boston Consulting Group offers a portfolio planning approach known as the **BCG Matrix**. Although more complicated models of strategic portfolio planning are available, this is a good place to start.

**BCG matrix** analyzes business opportunities according to market growth rate and market share.

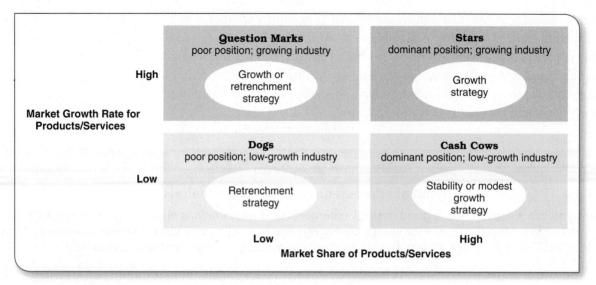

FIGURE 10.6 **The BCG matrix approach for portfolio planning in corporate-level strategy formulation.**

The BCG Matrix shown in Figure 10.6 asks managers to analyze business and product strategies based on two major factors: (1) market growth rate for the industry, and (2) market share held by the firm.[34] The analysis shown in the figure sorts businesses or products into four strategic types: Dogs, Stars, Question Marks, and Cash Cows. Each type comes with a recommended core or master strategy—*growth*, *stability*, or *retrenchment*.[35] These strategies become the guidelines for making resource allocation decisions.

- *Grow the Stars.* Businesses or products with high-market-shares in high-growth markets are "Stars" in the BCG Matrix. They produce large profits through substantial penetration of expanding markets. The preferred strategy for Stars is growth and the BCG Matrix recommends making further resource investments in them. Stars are not only high performers in the present, but they offer similar potential for the future. If we look at Apple today, the iPad would be a Star.

- *Milk the Cash Cows.* Businesses or products with high-market shares in low-growth markets are "Cash Cows" in the BCG Matrix. They produce good profits and a strong cash flow, but with little upside potential. Because the markets offer limited growth opportunity, the preferred strategy for Cash Cows is stability or modest growth. Like real dairy cows, the BCG Matrix advises firms to "milk" these businesses. They should invest just enough to keep them stable or growing just a bit. This keeps them generating cash that can be reinvested in other more promising areas. For Apple, we might wonder. Is yesterday's Star—the iPhone—now becoming a Cash Cow?

- *Grow or Retrench the Question Marks.* Businesses or products with low-market shares in high-growth markets are "Question Marks" in the BCG Matrix. Although they may not generate much profit at the moment, the upside potential is there because of the growing markets. But nothing is guaranteed. Question Marks make for difficult strategic decision making. The BCG Matrix recommends targeting only the most promising Question Marks for growth, while retrenching those that are less promising. What's the most promising

FOLLOW
THE STORY

> "SHE SHIFTED THE STRATEGY AWAY FROM SUPPLYING PHOTOCOPIERS TO PROVIDING BUSINESS PROCESS AND DOCUMENT HANDLING SERVICES"

## Ursula Burns Sets Strategic Directions for Xerox

Ramin Talaie/Bloomberg/Getty Images, Inc.

*F*rankness, sharp humor, willingness to take risks, deep industry knowledge, technical prowess: These are all adjectives used to describe Ursula Burns, CEO of Xerox Corporation. She began her career with the company as an intern and rose through the ranks to become the first African American woman to head a *Fortune* 500 firm. Her predecessor, Anne Mulcahy, was also a company veteran who had worked her way to the top over a 27-year career.

Burns took over Xerox at the height of financial crisis. The firm faced declining sales and profits and the stock price had lost half its value in a year's time. But her experience and leadership were up to the competitive challenges.

The traditional photocopier business was on the decline—less paper was being used in offices, less equipment was being bought or leased, and prices were falling. Burns responded by pushing for more sales in emerging markets, better efficiencies, and greater focus on high-margin services. She made tough decisions on downsizing, closed

Xerox manufacturing operations, and changed the product mix. And, she shifted the strategy away from supplying photocopiers to providing business process and document handling services.

One of Burns's key strategic moves was buying Affiliated Computer Services at a $6.4 billion price tag. The firm had more employees than Xerox and many questioned her wisdom. But this was part of Burns's strategy—move aggressively into services. She's now praised for the move.

Getting a new strategy in place requires lots of support, including from the Board of Directors. Burns has again been up to the task. Board member Robert A. McDonald says, "She understands the technology and can communicate it in a way that a director can understand it."

A working mother and spouse who was raised by a single mom in New York City public housing, Burns is proud of her accomplishments. In a speech to the YWCA in Cleveland, she once said: "I'm in this job because I believe I earned it through hard work and high performance. Did I get some opportunities early in my career because of my race and gender? Probably. . . . I imagine race and gender got the hiring guys' attention. And then the rest was really up to me."

### WHAT'S YOUR TAKE?

Does Burns' strategic intention to shift Xerox away from photocopiers and toward services make sense? What special internal management problems might she be facing to implement the shift? Can you picture the day when the photocopier part of Xerox is gone? Burns followed an internal career strategy to success at Xerox. What are the risk–reward trade-offs of sticking with one employer? In what ways can Burns be a role model for others?

Question Mark at Apple today? That's a good question and perhaps the answer is AppleTV. Will it be the Star of the future, or a Dog?

• *Retrench the Dogs.* Businesses or products with low-market shares in low-growth markets are "Dogs" in the BCG Matrix. They produce little if any profit, and they have low potential for future improvement. The preferred strategy for dogs in the BCG Matrix is retrenchment. Not too long ago Apple's iPod was a Star; then it become a Cash Cow. Is it now well on the road to being tomorrow's Dog?

# Growth and Diversification Strategies

A **growth strategy** involves expansion of the organization's current operations.

Among the core or master strategies just illustrated in the BCG matrix, **growth strategies** seek to expand the size and scope of operations. The goal is to increase things such as total revenue, product or service lines, and operating locations. When you hear terms like *acquisition*, *merger*, and *global expansion*, for example, the underlying master strategy is one of growth.

Growth is a common and popular business strategy. But it can be sometimes driven as much by executive egos as business realities. Although there is a tendency to equate growth with effectiveness, it is possible to get caught in an "expansion trap" where growth outruns an organization's capacity to manage it. Mark Zuckerberg faced this problem at Facebook. The firm grew incredibly fast and spending outran revenues. The *Wall Street Journal* claimed it had "growing pains" and Zuckerberg even asked: "Is being a CEO always this hard?" His response was to hire an experienced Google vice president, Sheryl Sandberg, to become chief operating officer and lead Facebook's continued expansion.[36] It's a decision that took some humility on his part; it's also one that history has shown to be a great move.

Growth through **concentration** is within the same business area.

Organizations pursue growth strategies in a variety of ways. One approach is to grow through **concentration**—expanding in the same business area. McDonald's, Dollar General, Auto Zone, and others pursue growth strategies by adding locations while concentrating on their primary businesses. And some, as their domestic markets become saturated, aggressively expand around the world to find new customers and push further sales growth. When McDonald's announced growth plans to open 1,325 new restaurants, only 225 were targeted for the U.S. and Canada; the rest were in Asia, the Middle East, Africa, Europe, and Latin America.[37]

Growth through **diversification** is by acquisition of or investment in new and different business areas.

Another way to grow is through strategic **diversification**—expanding into different business areas. A strategy of *related diversification* pursues growth by acquiring new businesses or entering business areas similar to what one already does. An example is Starbucks' purchase of the California fruit company Evolution Fresh. Starbucks is not only adding the juices to its existing stores, it is opening separate Evolution Fresh stores. The goal of this related diversification is to gain more nutrition-conscious customers and grow Starbucks' business as a whole.

A strategy of *unrelated diversification* pursues growth by acquiring businesses or entering business areas that are different from what one already does. India's Tata Group, for example, owns 98 companies in diverse industries such as steel, information and communications, hotels, energy, and consumer products. Its brands include Eight O'Clock Coffee and Tetley Tea as well as Jaguar and Land Rover. As Tata continues to grows by unrelated diversification, Chairman Ratan N. Tata says: "We have been thinking bigger . . . we have been bolder . . . we have been more aggressive in the marketplace."[38]

Growth through **vertical integration** occurs by acquiring suppliers or distributors.

Growth by diversification can also be done by **vertical integration** where a business acquires suppliers—*backward vertical integration,* or distributors—*forward vertical integration.* Backward vertical integration is evident at Apple Computer where the firm has bought chip manufacturers to give it more privacy and sophistication in developing microprocessors for its products. It's also evident at Rolex where the firm owns a foundry for the precious metals used in its luxury watches. Forward vertical integration is common in the beverage industry, where both Coca-Cola and PepsiCo own some of their major bottlers.[39]

Ma jian—Imaginechina/AP Wide World Photos

## Growth Is a Glamor Strategy for Louis Vuitton

"The paradox is how to grow without diluting our image," says CEO Yves Carcelle. Louis Vuitton is part of the large luxury goods conglomerate LVMH, which also owns Dom Perignon, Sephora, and Fendi. But while growth may be Vuitton's strategy, it has to do so while protecting its place as a luxury—not mass-market—brand. The firm's manufacturing strategy focuses on lean production methods, more teamwork, and better technology—such as using computer-guided lasers to more efficiently cut hides for purses. These moves have boosted production and cut costs while allowing the firm to maintain high-quality standards.

## Retrenchment and Restructuring Strategies

When organizations are in trouble, perhaps experiencing problems brought about by a bad economy or too much growth and diversification, the focus shifts toward **retrenchment and restructuring strategies** that pursue radical changes to solve problems. At the extreme a firm may be insolvent and unable to pay its bills. In some cases retrenchment may take the form of **bankruptcy**, which under U.S. law gives firms Chapter 11 protection while they reorganize to restore solvency. Both Chrysler and General Motors used this strategy during the recent economic crisis. In other cases an insolvent firm goes into outright **liquidation**, where business ceases and assets are sold to pay creditors.

Short of bankruptcy and liquidation, organizations in trouble can try other retrenchment strategies to get back on a path to high performance. Restructuring by **downsizing** decreases the size of operations, often by reducing the workforce.[40] During the peak of the recent recession, for example, Citigroup released 53,000 workers. When you learn of organizations downsizing by "across-the-board" cuts, however, you might be a bit skeptical. Research shows that downsizing is most successful when cutbacks are done selectively and with specific performance objectives. The term *rightsizing* is sometimes used to describe downsizing with a clear strategic focus.[41]

Restructuring by **divestiture** sells off parts of the organization to refocus the remainder on core competencies, cut costs, and improve operating efficiency. You'll see this strategy being followed by organizations that are overdiversified and have problems managing so much complexity. For example, eBay bought Skype with high expectations and later sold it to private investors at a loss. At the time of sale eBay's CEO said "Skype is a strong standalone business, but it does not have synergies with our e-commerce and online payments business."[42] In other words, the original purchase was a costly and bad idea. Skype is now owned by Microsoft. The strategic question is: Will the expected synergies pay off there, or will yet another divestiture be in Skype's future?

Restructuring by **turnaround** is an attempt to fix specific performance problems. It often occurs along with a change in top management. Check the latest on Yahoo!, a company that has struggled for traction even though its brand is well

**Retrenchment and restructuring strategies** pursue radical changes to solve problems.

Chapter 11 **bankruptcy** under U.S. law protects a firm from creditors while management reorganizes to restore solvency.

**Liquidation** is where a business closes and sells its assets to pay creditors.

A **downsizing strategy** decreases the size of operations.

**Divestiture** sells off parts of the organization to refocus attention on core business areas.

A **turnaround strategy** tries to fix specific performance problems.

established. Some time ago, founder Jerry Yang came back in as CEO in a turn-around attempt. But he stepped down 18 months later after investors complained he missed an opportunity by refusing a buyout offer from Microsoft. Carol Bartz was then hired as CEO in another turnaround attempt. She was fired after 30 months on the job. The first major move by her successor Scott Thompson was to sue Facebook—a strategic partner, over patent infringements. He lasted less than a year, and investors were left wondering what a new CEO would do next.[43]

## Global Strategies

A key issue in corporate strategy today is how to embrace the global economy and its mix of business risks and opportunities.[44] An easy way to spot differences in global strategies is to notice how products are developed and advertised around the world. A firm pursuing a **globalization strategy** tends to view the world as one large market. It makes most decisions from the corporate headquarters and tries as much as possible to standardize products and advertising for use everywhere. The latest Gillette razors from Procter & Gamble, for example, are likely to be sold and advertised similarly around the world.

> A **globalization strategy** adopts standardized products and advertising for use worldwide.

Firms using a **multidomestic strategy** try to customize products and advertising as much as possible to fit local preferences in different countries or regions. McDonald's is a good example. Although you can get your standard fries and Big Mac in most locations, you can have a McVeggie in India, a McArabia Kofta in Saudi Arabia, and a Croque McDo in France.

> A **multidomestic strategy** customizes products and advertising to best fit local needs.

A third approach is the **transnational strategy** where a firm tries to operate without a strong national identity and blend seamlessly with the global economy. Resources and management talents are acquired worldwide. Manufacturing and other business functions are performed wherever in the world they can be done best at lowest cost. Ford is an example. It's global strategy uses design, manufacturing, and distribution expertise all over the world to build five core car platforms with common parts and components. These platforms are then modified to meet regional tastes. When the Ford Fiesta ST was unveiled at the Frankfurt Auto Show, group vice president for Global Product Development, Derrick Kuzak, said: "By taking advantage of platform efficiencies and focusing our performance engineering resources globally, we can bring performance vehicles to more customers in more markets."[45]

> A **transnational strategy** seeks efficiencies of global operations with attention to local markets.

## Cooperative Strategies

It's quite common today to hear about **strategic alliances** where two or more organizations join in a targeted partnership to pursue an area of mutual interest. This is basically a strategy of cooperating for common gains. In an *outsourcing alliance*, one organization contracts to purchase important services, perhaps IT or human resources, from another. In a *supplier alliance*, preferred supplier relationships guarantee a smooth and timely flow of quality supplies among partners. And in a *distribution alliance*, firms join together as partners to sell and distribute products or services.

> In a **strategic alliance**, organizations join in partnership to pursue an area of mutual interest.

One interesting strategic direction is called **co-opetition**, or strategic alliances among competitors.[46] The idea is that you can still cooperate even as you compete. An example is the airline industry. United Airlines and Lufthansa are major

> **Co-opetition** is the strategy of working with rivals on projects of mutual benefit.

## Life and Death at an Outsourcing Factory

JASON LEE/REUTERS/Newscom

Foxconn is a major outsourcing firm owned by Hon Hai Precision Industry of Taiwan and having extensive operations in China. It makes products for Apple, Dell, and Hewlett-Packard, among others. Foxconn has over a million workers in China, with some 250,000 working in one huge complex stretching over 1 square mile in Shenzen. The site includes dormitories, restaurants, recreational facilities, and a hospital in addition to the factory spaces. Due to a number of employee suicides, netting has been draped from the dormitories to prevent employees from jumping to their death from the roofs.

One worker complains that the work is meaningless, no conversation is allowed on the production lines, and bathroom breaks are limited. Another says: "I do the same thing every day. I have no future." A supervisor points out that the firm provides counseling services since most workers are young and this is the first time they have been away from their homes. "Without their families," says the supervisor, "they're left without direction. We try to provide them with direction and help."

Recent moves by Hon Hai involve shifting more production to sites in rural China that are closer to many workers' homes and expanding automation through the use of more assembly-line robots. Wages have been increased and employees get counseling. This goes along with a broader commitment to the "highest possible safety practices," says a company spokesperson.

### ETHICS QUESTIONS

What ethical responsibilities do firms have when they contract for outsourcing in foreign plants? Whose responsibility is it to make sure workers are well treated—the global firm or the local supplier? What are our responsibilities as consumers? Should we support bad practices by buying products from firms whose outsourcing partners are known to treat workers poorly?

---

international competitors, but they also cooperate as "Star Alliance" partners. The alliance provides their customers code-sharing on flights and shared frequent-flyer programs. In the auto industry the cost of developing new technologies is a stimulus to co-opetition. Daimler cooperates with BMW to co-develop new motors and components for hybrid cars; it cooperates with Nissan to co-develop electric car batteries.[47]

FIGURE 10.7  **Porter's competitive strategies framework with soft-drink industry examples.**

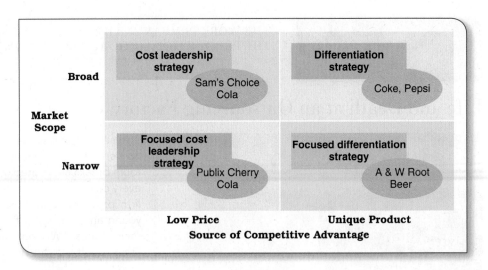

# Business-Level Strategy Formulation

Harvard's Michael Porter says that "the company without a strategy is willing to try anything."[48] But with a good strategy in place, he believes a business can achieve superior profitability or above-average returns within its industry. The key question in formulating business-level strategy is: "How can we best compete for customers in our market and with our products or services?"

## Competitive Strategies Model

Figure 10.7 shows Porter's model for choosing competitive strategies. He frames the strategy analysis in terms of: (1) market scope of the product or service, and (2) source of competitive advantage for the product or service.

In respect to *market scope* the strategic planner asks: "How broad or narrow is the market or target market?" In respect to *source of competitive advantage*, the question is: "Do we seek competitive advantage primarily through low price or product uniqueness?" Answers to these questions create a matrix like the one shown in the figure. Three business-level strategies are possible—cost leadership, differentiation, and focus. There are two combinations of the focus strategy— focused cost leadership and focused differentiation.

## Differentiation Strategy

A **differentiation strategy** offers products that are unique and different from the competition.

A **differentiation strategy** seeks competitive advantage through uniqueness. This means developing goods and services that are clearly different from the competition. The strategic objective is to attract customers who stay loyal to the firm's products and lose interest in those of its competitors.

Success with a differentiation strategy requires organizational strengths in marketing, research and development, and creativity. An example in the apparel industry is Polo Ralph Lauren, retailer of upscale classic fashions and accessories. In Ralph Lauren's words, "Polo redefined how American style and quality is perceived. Polo has always been about selling quality products by creating worlds and inviting our customers to be part of our dream."[49]

The differentiation strategy examples in Figure 10.7 are Coke and Pepsi from the soft drinks industry. These firms continually battle for customer attention and loyalty. Although part of their differentiation may be actual taste, another part is pure perception. Coke and Pepsi spend enormous amounts on advertising to create beliefs their products are somehow distinctly different from one another.

## Cost Leadership Strategy

A **cost leadership strategy** seeks competitive advantage by operating with lower costs than competitors. This allows organizations to make profits while selling products or services at low prices their competitors can't profitably match. The objective is to continuously improve operating efficiencies in purchasing, production, distribution, and other organizational systems.

Success with the cost leadership strategy requires tight cost and managerial controls, as well as products or services that are easy to create and distribute. This is what might be called the "Wal-Mart" strategy—do everything you can to keep costs so low that you can offer customers the lowest prices and still make a reasonable profit. The example in Figure 10.7 is Sam's Choice Colas. An example from the financial services industry is the Vanguard Group. It keeps operating costs low so that it can attract customers to buy mutual funds with low expense ratios and minimum fees.

You might be wondering if it's possible to combine cost leadership with differentiation. Porter says "No." He refers to this combination as a *stuck-in-the-middle strategy* and believes it is rarely successful because differentiation most often drives up costs. "You can compete on price or you can compete on product, but you can't compete on both," the marketers tend to say. And Porter agrees.

> ### PORTER'S COMPETITIVE STRATEGIES
>
> - *Differentiation*—Make products that are unique and different.
> - *Cost leadership*—Produce at lower cost and sell at lower price.
> - *Focused differentiation*—Use differentiation and target needs of a special market.
> - *Focused cost leadership*—Use cost leadership and target needs of a special market.

A **cost leadership strategy** seeks to operate with low cost so that products can be sold at low prices.

---

**FACTS FOR ANALYSIS** > AUTO FIRMS IN SOUTHERN STATES HAVE LOWER LABOR COSTS THAN FIRMS LOCATED IN THE NORTH

## Wage and Benefits as a Competitive Issue in the Auto Industry

When Volkswagen built a new plant in Tennessee, one of the advantages was gaining access to lower-cost labor. The labor costs (wages + benefits) of automakers using northern plants are much higher, as the following data from 2010 show:

- Volkswagen—Tennessee: cost of labor = $27/hour
- Hyundai—Alabama: cost of labor = $27/hour
- Honda—Ohio: cost of labor = $50/hour
- Ford—Michigan: cost of labor = $58/hour

One way that automakers are trying to deal with labor costs is through two-tier wage systems that give new workers lower wages and benefits than those received by existing hires. Even though the United Autoworkers Union has allowed two-tier plans, it is an issue in labor contract negotiations. Ford's 2011 labor contract with the United Autoworkers Union set new-hire wages at $15.78 per hour versus the $28 per hour average earned by senior workers. The overall cost of labor per hour with wages and benefits included was projected at $59. Because so few new workers are being hired, labor costs remain relatively higher for some firms.

 **YOUR THOUGHTS?**

Should other automakers like GM, Ford, and Chrysler "head South" in search of lower-labor-cost locations to gain more competitive advantage? Is it right for firms in any industry to deliberately "head South" when building new factories so that they avoid the union complications and higher labor costs often associated with northern locations? Is there any way to bridge the gap between company needs for cost controls and worker needs for good wages and benefits?

## Focus Strategy

A **focus strategy** concentrates on serving a unique market segment better than anyone else.

A **focus strategy** concentrates attention on a special market segment in the form of a niche customer group, geographical region, or product or service line. The objective is to serve the needs of the segment better than anyone else. Competitive advantage is achieved by combining focus with either differentiation or cost leadership.[50]

A **focused differentiation strategy** offers a unique product to a special market segment.

A **focused cost leadership** strategy seeks the lowest costs of operations within a special market segment.

NetJets offers private, secure, and luxury air travel for those who can pay a high fee, such as wealthy media stars and executives. This is a **focused differentiation strategy** because the firm sells a unique product to a special niche market. Also in airlines, carriers such as Ryan Air and Easy Jet in Europe offer heavily discounted fares and "no-frills" flying. This is a **focused cost leadership** strategy because it offers low prices to attract budget travelers. The airlines still make profits by keeping costs low. They fly to regional airports and cut out free services such as bag checks and in-flight snacks.[51]

Figure 10.7 shows both types of focus strategies in the soft drink industry. Specialty drinks such as A&W Root Beer, Dr. Pepper, and Mountain Dew represent the focused differentiation strategy. Each focuses on a special market segment and tries to compete on the basis of product uniqueness. Drinks like Sam's Diet Cola, Publix Cherry Cola, and Big K Cola with Lime represent the focused cost leadership strategy. They also focus on special market segments, but try to compete by selling colas at low prices made possible by low operating costs.

---

# Strategy Implementation

A discussion of the corporate history on Patagonia, Inc.'s website includes this statement: "During the past thirty years, we've made many mistakes but we've never lost our way for very long."[52] Not only is the firm being honest in its public information, it is also communicating an important point about strategic management—mistakes will be made. Sometimes those mistakes will be in poor strategy selection. Other times they will be failures of implementation.

## Management Practices and Systems

The rest of *Management 12/e* is really all about strategy implementation. In order to successfully put strategies into action, the entire organization and all of its resources must be mobilized in support of them. This involves the complete management process—from planning and controlling through organizing and leading. No matter how

## Recommended Reading

### Behind the Cloud: The Untold Story of How a Salesforce.com went from Idea to Billion-Dollar Company and Revolutionized an Industry (Jossey-Bass, 2009)
#### by Marc Benioff and Carlye Adler

Can a trip to India launch a new corporate strategy? It did for Marc Benioff. He started Salesforce.com after a transforming trip to India that included a meeting with a "hugging saint." In *Behind the Cloud* he tells the story of his pioneering work to build a business around cloud computing and a software-as-service business model. His playbook for strategic success includes mantras like these—"Have a Big Dream," "Define Your Values and Culture Up Front," and "Differentiate."

well or elegantly planned, a strategy requires supporting structures and workflows staffed by talented people. The strategy needs leaders who can motivate everyone so that individuals and teams do their very best work. And the strategy needs to be properly monitored and controlled to ensure that the desired results are achieved.

*Failures of substance* in strategic management show up in poor analysis and bad strategy selection. *Failures of process* reflect poor handling of the ways in which strategic management is accomplished. A common process failure is the **lack of participation error**. It shows up as a lack of commitment to action and follow-through by persons who were excluded from the strategic planning process.[53] Another process failure is *goal displacement*. This is the tendency to get so bogged down in details that the planning process becomes an end in itself, rather than a means to an end.

> **Lack of participation error** is a failure to include key persons in strategic planning.

## Strategic Control and Corporate Governance

Top managers exercise **strategic control** by making sure strategies are well implemented and that poor strategies are scrapped or modified quickly to meet performance demands of changing conditions. We expect them to always be "in control" by measuring results, evaluating the success of existing strategies, and taking action to improve things in the future. Yet the financial crisis and recent recession showed that strategic control was inadequate at many firms, like the automakers and big banks.

> **Strategic control** makes sure strategies are well implemented and that poor strategies are scrapped or modified.

When strategic control fails at the level of top management it is supposed to kick in at the level of **corporate governance**. This is the system of control and monitoring of top management performance exercised by boards of directors and boards of trustees. Good governance is supposed to make sure that the strategic management of the organization is successful.[54] But boards are sometimes too compliant and uncritical in endorsing or confirming what top management is doing. Instead of criticizing and requiring change, they condone and let things alone. Weak corporate governance doesn't subject top management to rigorous oversight and accountability. The result is that organizations may end up doing the wrong things or even bad things, or just performing poorly.

> **Corporate governance** is the system of control and performance monitoring of top management.

**RESEARCH BRIEF**

# Female Directors on Corporate Boards Linked with Positive Management Practices

Richard Vernardi, Susan Bosco, and Katie Vassill examined gender diversity of board membership and corporate performance. The research question guiding their article in *Business and Society* was: "Do firms listed in *Fortune's* '100 Best Companies to Work For' have a higher percentage of female directors than do *Fortune* 500 companies?" The researchers chose the "100 Best" listing because it includes firms whose employees consider them to have positive organizational cultures and supportive work practices. The evaluations were measured on a 225-item Great Place to Work Trust Index, sent to a random sample of employees in each company. Documentation of female board representatives was obtained by examining company annual reports.

Results confirmed expectations: the percentage of female directors was higher for firms on the "100 Best" list than for those in the *Fortune* 500 overall. The researchers suggest that gender diversity on boards of directors may bring about positive organizational changes that make firms better places to work. They also cite the growing presence of women on corporate boards as evidence that firms are changing board memberships to be "more representative of its employee and customer pools."

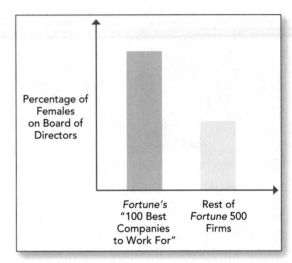

**YOU BE THE RESEARCHER**

Why would the presence of more female directors on a board result in a better workplace? Does board diversity, including minorities and women, lead to different agendas, deliberations, concerns, and strategies? Does it lead to better strategy implementation through greater employee involvement and loyalty? Look at organizations with which you are familiar. Can you see where greater membership diversity in general, not just at the top, makes a difference in the way an organization performs?

*Reference:* Richard A. Vernardi, Susan M. Bosco, and Katie M. Vassill, "Does Female Representation on Boards of Directors Associate with *Fortune's*, '100 Best Companies to Work For' List?" *Business and Society*, vol. 45 (June 2006), pp. 235–48.

---

When governance fails, blame sometimes traces back to the composition of the board overall. Most boards consist of *inside directors* chosen from the ranks of senior management and *outside directors* chosen from other organizations and positions external to the organization. In some boards insiders are too powerful. In others the board lacks outside members whose skills match well with the organization's strategic challenges. In still others the board members may be insufficiently observant or critical because they are friends of top management or at least sympathetic to them.

## Strategic Leadership

CEO Alan Mulally led Ford out of the recession and back onto a growth path. Paul Ingrassia, an auto analyst, called his success "one of the great turnarounds in corporate history" and praised Mulally's efforts "to simplify, relentlessly and systematically, a business that had grown way too complicated and costly to be managed effectively."[55] What Mulally showed at Ford is **strategic leadership**—the capability to inspire people to successfully engage in a process of continuous change, performance enhancement, and implementation of organizational strategies.[56]

One of the big lessons learned in studying how business firms fare during economic crisis is that a *strategic leader has to maintain strategic control*. This means that the CEO and other top managers should always be in touch with the strategy. They must know how well it is being implemented, whether the strategy is generating performance success or failure, and if the strategy needs to be tweaked or changed.

Other key responsibilities of strategic leadership have been described in these ways.[57]

- *A strategic leader has to be the guardian of trade-offs.* It is the leader's job to make sure that the organization's resources are allocated in ways consistent with the strategy. This requires the discipline to sort through many competing ideas and alternatives, to stay on course, and not to get sidetracked.

- *A strategic leader needs to create a sense of urgency.* The leader can't allow the organization and its members to grow slow and complacent. Even when doing well, the leader keeps the focus on getting better and being alert to conditions that require adjustments to the strategy.

- *A strategic leader needs to make sure that everyone understands the strategy.* Unless strategies are understood, the daily tasks and contributions of people lose context and purpose. Everyone might work very hard, but without alignment to strategy the impact is dispersed and fails to advance common goals.

- *A strategic leader needs to be a teacher.* It is the leader's job to teach the strategy and make it a "cause." In order for strategy to work it must become an ever-present commitment throughout the organization. This means that a strategic leader must be a great communicator. Everyone must understand the strategy and how it makes their organization different from others.

**Strategic leadership** inspires people to continuously change, refine, and improve strategies and their implementation.

---

### LEARNING CHECK 5

**TAKEAWAY QUESTION 5 What are the foundations for strategy implementation?**

**Be sure you can** • explain how the management process supports strategy implementation • define *corporate governance* • explain why boards of directors sometimes fail in their governance responsibilities • define *strategic control* and *strategic leadership* • list the responsibilities of a strategic leader in today's organizations

# MANAGEMENT LEARNING REVIEW

## LEARNING CHECK SUMMARY

### TAKEAWAY QUESTION 1  What is strategic management?

- Competitive advantage is achieved by operating in ways that allow an organization to outperform its rivals; a competitive advantage is sustainable when it is difficult for competitors to imitate.
- A strategy is a comprehensive plan that sets long-term direction and guides resource allocation for sustainable competitive advantage.
- Corporate strategy sets direction for an entire organization; business strategy sets direction for a business division or product/service line; functional strategy sets direction for the operational support of business and corporate strategies.
- Strategic management is the process of formulating and implementing strategies that achieve goals in a competitive environment.

**For Discussion Can an organization have a good strategy and still fail to achieve competitive advantage?**

### TAKEAWAY QUESTION 2  What are the essentials of strategic analysis?

- The strategic management process begins with analysis of mission, clarification of core values, and identification of objectives.
- A SWOT analysis systematically assesses organizational strengths and weaknesses, and environmental opportunities and threats.
- Porter's five forces model analyzes industry attractiveness in terms of competitive rivalry, new entrants, substitute products, and the bargaining powers of suppliers and buyers.

**For Discussion Would a monopoly get a perfect score for industry attractiveness in Porter's five forces model?**

### TAKEAWAY QUESTION 3  What are corporate-level strategies and how are they formulated?

- Growth strategies pursue greater sales and broader markets by concentration that expands in related product or business areas, and diversification that expands in new and different product and business areas.
- Restructuring strategies pursue ways to correct performance problems by such means as liquidation, bankruptcy, downsizing, divestiture, and turnaround.

- Global firms take advantage of international business opportunities through globalization, multi-domestic, and transnational strategies.
- Cooperative strategies create strategic alliances with other organizations to achieve mutual gains, including such things as outsourcing alliances, supplier alliances, and even co-opetition among competitors.
- The BCG matrix is a portfolio planning approach that classifies businesses or product lines as "stars," "cash cows," "question marks," or "dogs" for purposes of strategy formulation.

**For Discussion Is it good news or bad news for investors when a firm announces that it is restructuring?**

### TAKEAWAY QUESTION 4  What are business-level strategies and how are they formulated?

- Potential sources of competitive advantage in business-level strategy formulation are found in things like lower costs, better quality, more knowledge, greater speed, and strong financial resources.
- Porter's model of competitive strategy bases the choice of business-level strategies on two major considerations—market scope of product or service, and source of competitive advantage for the product or service.
- A differentiation strategy seeks competitive advantage by offering unique products and services that are clearly different from those of competitors.
- A cost leadership strategy seeks competitive advantage by operating at low costs that allow products and services to be sold to customers at low prices.
- A focus strategy seeks competitive advantage by serving the needs of a special market segment or niche better than anyone else; it can be done as focused differentiation or focused cost leadership.

**For Discussion Can a business ever be successful with a combined cost leadership and differentiation strategy?**

### TAKEAWAY QUESTION 5  What are the foundations for strategy implementation?

- Management practices and systems—including the functions of planning, organizing, leading, and controlling—must be mobilized to support strategy implementation.
- Pitfalls that inhibit strategy implementation include failures of substance—such as poor analysis of the

environment; and failures of process—such as lack of participation by key players in the planning process.

- Boards of directors play important roles in control through corporate governance, including monitoring how well top management fulfills strategic management responsibilities.

- Top managers exercise strategic control by making sure strategies are well implemented, and are changed if not working.

- Strategic leadership inspires the process of continuous evaluation and improvement of strategies and their implementation.

**For Discussion   Is strategic leadership by top managers capable of making up for poor corporate governance by board members?**

## SELF-TEST 10

## Multiple-Choice Questions

1. The most appropriate first question to ask in strategic planning is _____.
   (a) "Where do we want to be in the future?"
   (b) "How well are we currently doing?"
   (c) "How can we get where we want to be?"
   (d) "Why aren't we doing better?"

2. The ability of a firm to consistently outperform its rivals is called _____.
   (a) vertical integration
   (b) competitive advantage
   (c) incrementalism
   (d) strategic intent

3. In a complex conglomerate business such as General Electric, a(n) _____ level strategy sets strategic direction for a strategic business unit.
   (a) institutional
   (b) corporate
   (c) business
   (d) functional

4. The _____ is a predominant value system for an organization as a whole.
   (a) strategy
   (b) core competency
   (c) mission
   (d) corporate culture

5. Cost efficiency and product quality are two examples of _____ objectives of organizations.
   (a) official
   (b) operating
   (c) informal
   (d) institutional

6. An organization that is downsizing to reduce costs is implementing a grand strategy of _____.
   (a) growth
   (b) cost differentiation
   (c) retrenchment
   (d) vertical integration

7. When PepsiCo acquired Tropicana, a maker of orange juice, the firm's strategy was growth by _____.
   (a) related diversification
   (b) concentration
   (c) vertical integration
   (d) cooperation

8. In Porter's five forces framework, having _____ increases industry attractiveness.
   (a) many rivals
   (b) many substitute products
   (c) low bargaining power of suppliers
   (d) few barriers to entry

9. A _____ in the BCG matrix would have a high market share in a low-growth market, and the correct grand or master strategy is _____.
   (a) dog, growth
   (b) cash cow, stability
   (c) question mark, stability
   (d) star, retrenchment

10. The alliances that link together firms in supply chain management relationships are examples of how businesses try to use _____ strategies.
    (a) B2C
    (b) growth
    (c) cooperation
    (d) concentration

11. The two questions asked by Porter to identify competitive strategies for a business or product line are: 1—What is the market scope? 2—What is the _____?
    (a) market share
    (b) source of competitive advantage
    (c) core competency
    (d) industry attractiveness

**12.** According to Porter's model of competitive strategies, a firm that wants to compete with its rivals in a broad market by selling a very low-priced product would need to successfully implement a _____ strategy.
(a) retrenchment
(b) differentiation
(c) cost leadership
(d) diversification

**13.** When Coke and Pepsi spend millions on ads trying to convince customers that their products are unique, they are pursuing a/an _____ strategy.
(a) transnational
(b) concentration
(c) diversification
(d) differentiation

**14.** The role of the board of directors as an oversight body that holds top executives accountable for the success of business strategies is called _____.
(a) strategic leadership
(b) corporate governance
(c) logical incrementalism
(d) strategic opportunism

**15.** An example of a process failure in strategic planning is _____.
(a) lack of participation
(b) weak mission statement
(c) bad core values
(d) insufficient financial resources

## Short-Response Questions

**16.** What is the difference between corporate strategy and functional strategy?

**17.** What would a manager look at in a SWOT analysis?

**18.** What is the difference between focus and differentiation as competitive strategies?

**19.** What is strategic leadership?

## Essay Question

**20.** Kim Harris owns and operates a small retail store selling the outdoor clothing of an American manufacturer to a predominately college-student market. Lately, a large department store outside of town has started selling similar, but lower-priced clothing manufactured in China, Thailand, and Bangladesh.

Kim believes she is starting to lose business to this store. Assume you are part of a student team assigned to do a management class project for Kim. Her question for the team is: "How can I best deal with my strategic management challenges in this situation?" How will you reply?

# Further Reflection: Critical Thinking

Strategic management is one of the most significant planning challenges faced by managers. A complex array of forces and uncertainties must be consolidated and integrated to craft a strategy that moves an organization forward with success. **Critical thinking** is an essential foundation for success in strategic management. The same critical thinking that is part of a rigorous class discussion or case studies in your course is what helps managers create strategies that result in competitive advantage. But managers rarely have the luxury of full information that is boxed up for analysis in a nice, neat case format. Many life and career events are a lot like puzzles; everything looks pretty easy until you get down to the task. Is your critical thinking up to the challenges?

**DO IT NOW...**
**LOOK IN THE MIRROR**

**Is your personal career strategy well attuned to the future job market, not just the present one?**

- **Are you showing strong critical thinking skills as you make academic choices and prepare for your career?**
- **Make a list of information you need to best make solid career choices.**
- **Identify where you can obtain this information and how credible the sources might be.**
- **Write a short plan that uses this information and commits you to activities in this academic year that can improve your career readiness.**

# Self-Assessment: Intuitive Ability

## Instructions

Complete this survey as quickly as you can. Be honest with yourself. For each question, select the response that most appeals to you.[58]

1. When working on a project, do you prefer to
   (a) be told what the problem is but be left free to decide how to solve it?
   (b) get very clear instructions for how to go about solving the problem before you start?

2. When working on a project, do you prefer to work with colleagues who are
   (a) realistic?   (b) imaginative?

3. Do you most admire people who are
   (a) creative?   (b) careful?

4. Do the friends you choose tend to be
   (a) serious and hard working?
   (b) exciting and often emotional?

5. When you ask a colleague for advice on a problem you have, do you
   (a) seldom or never get upset if he or she questions your basic assumptions?
   (b) often get upset if he or she questions your basic assumptions?

6. When you start your day, do you
   (a) seldom make or follow a specific plan?
   (b) usually first make a plan to follow?

7. When working with numbers, do you find that you
   (a) seldom or never make factual errors?
   (b) often make factual errors?

8. Do you find that you
   (a) seldom daydream during the day and really don't enjoy doing so when you do it?
   (b) frequently daydream during the day and enjoy doing so?

9. When working on a problem, do you
   (a) prefer to follow the instructions or rules that are given to you?
   (b) often enjoy circumventing the instructions or rules that are given to you?

10. When you are trying to put something together, do you prefer to have
    (a) step-by-step written instructions on how to assemble the item?
    (b) a picture of how the item is supposed to look once assembled?

**11.** Do you find that the person who irritates you *the most* is the one who appears to be
(a) disorganized?    (b) organized?

**12.** When an unexpected crisis comes up that you have to deal with, do you
(a) feel anxious about the situation?
(b) feel excited by the challenge of the situation?

## Scoring

Total the number of "a" responses selected for questions 1, 3, 5, 6, 11; enter the score here [a = _____]. Total the number of "b" responses for questions 2, 4, 7, 8, 9, 10, 12; enter the score here [b = _____]. Add your "a" and "b" scores and enter the sum here [a + b = _____]. This is your intuitive score. The highest possible intuitive score is 12; the lowest is 0.

## Interpretation

In his book *Intuition in Organizations* (Newbury Park, CA: Sage, 1989), pp. 10–11, Weston H. Agor states, "Traditional analytical techniques . . . are not as useful as they once were for guiding major decisions. . . . If you hope to be better prepared for tomorrow, then it only seems logical to pay some attention to the use and development of intuitive skills for decision making." Agor developed the preceding survey to help people assess their tendencies to use intuition in decision making. Your score offers a general impression of your strength in this area. It may also suggest a need to further develop your skill and comfort with more intuitive decision-making approaches.

# Team Exercise:
# Strategic Scenarios

## Preparation

In today's turbulent economics it is no longer safe to assume that an organization that was highly successful yesterday will continue to be so tomorrow—or that it will even be in existence. Changing times exact the best from strategic planners. Think about the situations currently facing the following well-known organizations. Think, too, about the futures they may face in competitive markets.[59]

| | | |
|---|---|---|
| McDonald's | Domino's Pizza | Sony |
| Apple Computer | Nordstrom | Zynga |
| Netflix | National Public Radio | AT&T |
| Ann Taylor | *New York Times* | Federal Express |

## Instructions

Form into groups as assigned by your instructor. Choose one or more organizations from the prior list (or as assigned) and answer for the organization the following questions:

**1.** What in the future might seriously threaten the success, perhaps the very existence, of this organization? As a group, develop at least three such *future scenarios*.

**2.** Estimate the probability (0 to 100%) of each future scenario occurring.

**3.** Develop a strategy for each scenario that will enable the organization to deal with it successfully.

Thoroughly discuss these questions within the group and arrive at your best possible consensus answers. Be prepared to share and defend your answers in general class discussion.

## Career Situations for Strategic Management: What Would You Do?

1. **The Mission Statement** You've just been given a great assignment to serve as personal assistant to the company president. It will last for six months and then, if you've done a good job, the expectation is you'll be moved into a fast-track management position. The president comes to you and says: "It's time to revisit the mission statement and our corporate values. Set things up for us." There's about a dozen people on the top management team and the company as a whole employs 700+, all in one location. How will you proceed to get the mission and values of this company updated?

2. **Cooperate or Compete, or Both?** A neighborhood business association has this set of members: coffeeshop, bookstore, drugstore, dress shop, hardware store, and bicycle shop. The owners of these businesses are interested in how they might cooper-

ate for better success. As a business consultant to the association, what strategic alliances would you propose as ways to join sets of these businesses together for mutual gain?

3. **Saving a Bookstore** For some years you've owned a small specialty bookshop in a college town. You sell some textbooks but mainly cater to a broader customer base. The store always has the latest fiction, nonfiction, and children's books in stock. You've recently experienced a steep decline in overall sales, even for those books that would normally be considered bestsellers. You suspect this is because of the growing popularity of e-books and e-readers such as the Amazon Kindle and Barnes&Noble Nook. Some of your friends say it's time to close the store and call it quits because your market is dying. Is it hopeless? Or, is there a business strategy that might save you?

## Case Study

# Dunkin' Donuts

Go to *Management Cases for Critical Thinking* to find the recommended case for Chapter 10—"Dunkin' Donuts: Betting Dollars on Donuts."

Once a niche company operating in the northeast, Dunkin' Donuts is opening hundreds of stores and entering new markets domestically and around the world. At the same time, the java giant is expanding both its food and coffee menus to ride the wave of fresh trends, appealing to a new generation of customers. But is the rest of the world ready for Dunkin' Donuts? And can the company keep up with its own rapid growth?

Dunkin' Donuts is banking on mutually beneficial partnerships to help it achieve widespread marketplace prominence. If the company can find the sweet spot by being within most consumers' reach while falling just short of a Big Brother-like presence, the company's strategy of expansion may well reward it very handsomely. Can Dunkin' Donuts keep the coffee hot and the donuts sweet?

© Caro/Alamy Limited

# Wisdom
## Learning From Others

MORE TO LOOK
FOR INSIDE>

## > IT'S ALL ABOUT HOW YOU PUT THE PIECES TOGETHER

The next time you're in the mall check out what's happening in the Build-A-Bear store. You'll see lots of activity, excitement, and fun as kids and parents work together building memories.

The Build-A-Bear concept is simple but elegant: Pick out a bear or bunny or turtle shell that you like, add stuffing, and then outfit your pet with clothing, shoes, and accessories. Each pet is unique—soccer player, girl scout . . . you name it; it leaves the store personalized to the new owner's tastes and interests.

Every Build-A-Bear store is carefully organized. Guest Bear Builders move along the Bear Pathway from the Choose Me computer workstation on to Stuff Me and finally to Name Me as their personal creation takes shape. Sounds a lot like organizations, doesn't it? Until you get to the "making it personal" part. That's where organizations often struggle—how to bring together hundreds, thousands, even hundreds of thousands of people in arrangements that make sense and still allow for personal talents to shine through.

Build-A-Bear was started by Maxine Clark based on her retailing experience. She obviously had the talent, creativity, and drive to build a successful business. Her founding story is classic entrepreneurship. But Build-A-Bear's success is driven by classic management.[1]

Navigation    GPS

# Organization Structures and Design

## 11

## > EMPOWERMENT

It takes a lot of trust to be comfortable with **empowerment**—letting others make decisions and exercise discretion in their work. But if you aren't willing and able to empower others, you may try to do too much on your own and end up accomplishing too little.

How often are you stressed out by group projects at school, feeling like you're doing all the work? Do you have a problem "letting go," or letting others do their share? The reason may be the fear of losing control. People with control anxiety often end up trying to do too much. This unfortunately raises the risks of missed deadlines and poor performance.

If the prior description fits you, your assumptions probably align with those in the upper left box in the Empowerment Quick Test. Alternatively, you could be in the lower right box and perhaps find that you work smarter and better while making others happier, too.

The beauty of organizations is synergy—bringing together the contributions of many people to achieve something that is much greater than what any individual can accomplish alone. Empowerment gives synergy a chance. It means joining with others to get things done; allowing and even helping them to do things that you might be very good at doing yourself.

## Insight
### Learning About Yourself

**EMPOWERMENT QUICK TEST**

*In a team situation, which square best describes your beliefs and behaviors?*

It's faster to do things myself than explain how to do them to others

Some things are just too important not to do yourself

**?**

People make mistakes, but they also learn from them

Many people are ready to take on more work, but are too shy to volunteer

## BUILD MANAGEMENT SKILLS AND COMPETENCIES AT END OF CHAPTER

- Engage in *Further Reflection on Empowerment*
- Take the *Self-Assessment—Empowering Others*
- Complete the *Team Exercise—Designing a Network University*
- Solve the *Career Situations for Organizing*
- Analyze the *Case Study—"Nike: Spreading Out to Win the Race"*

## <GET TO KNOW YOURSELF BETTER

| TAKEAWAY 1 | TAKEAWAY 2 | TAKEAWAY 3 | TAKEAWAY 4 |
|---|---|---|---|
| **Organizing as a Management Function** <br>• What is organization structure? <br>• Formal structures <br>• Informal structures | **Traditional Organization Structures** <br>• Functional structures <br>• Divisional structures <br>• Matrix structures | **Horizontal Organization Structures** <br>• Team structures <br>• Network structures <br>• Boundaryless structures | **Organizational Designs** <br>• Contingency in organizational design <br>• Mechanistic and organic designs <br>• Trends in organizational designs |
| **LEARNING CHECK 1** | **LEARNING CHECK 2** | **LEARNING CHECK 3** | **LEARNING CHECK 4** |

It is much easier to talk about high-performing organizations than to actually create them. Going back to the opening example, we might just say that it's a lot harder to build an organization than to build a bear! And in true contingency fashion there is no one best way to do things; no one organizational form meets the needs of all circumstances. What works well at one moment in time can quickly become outdated or even dysfunctional in another. This is why you often read and hear about organizations making changes and reorganizing in an attempt to improve their performance.

Management scholar and consultant Henry Mintzberg says that people need to understand how their organizations work if they are to work well within them.[2] Whenever job assignments and reporting relationships change, whenever the organization grows or shrinks, whenever old ways of doing things are reconfigured, people naturally struggle to understand the new ways of working. They ask questions such as: "Who's in charge?" "How do the parts connect to one another?" "How should processes and people come together?" "Whose ideas have to flow where?" They also worry about the implications of the new arrangements for their jobs and careers. These are all critical issues about organization structures and how well they meet an organization's performance needs.

## Organizing as a Management Function

**Organizing** arranges people and resources to work toward a goal.

**Organizing** is the process of arranging people and other resources to work together to accomplish a goal. Its purpose as one of the basic functions of management is to create a division of labor and then coordinate results to achieve a common purpose.

Figure 11.1 shows the central role that organizing plays in the management process. Once plans are created, the manager's task is to see to it that they are carried out. Given a clear mission and strategy, organizing begins the process of implementation by clarifying jobs and working relationships. It identifies who is to do what, who is in charge of whom, and how different people and parts of the organization relate to and work with one another. All of this, of course, can be done in different ways. The manager's challenge is to choose the best organizational form to fit the strategy and other situational demands.

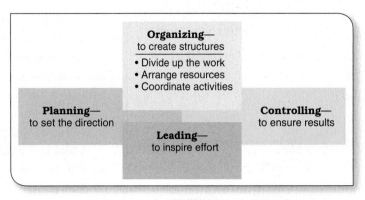

**FIGURE 11.1** **Organizing viewed in relationship with the other management functions.**

## What Is Organization Structure?

The way in which the various parts of an organization are arranged is usually referred to as the **organization structure**. It is the system of tasks, workflows, reporting relationships, and communication channels that link together the work of diverse individuals and groups. Any structure should do a good job of both allocating tasks through a division of labor and providing for the coordination of performance results. A structure that does both of these things well helps to implement an organization's strategy.[3] Unfortunately, it is easier to talk about good structures than it is to actually create them.

> **Organization structure** is a system of tasks, reporting relationships, and communication linkages.

## Formal Structures

You may know the concept of structure best in the form of an **organization chart**. It diagrams reporting relationships and the arrangement of work positions within an organization.[4] A typical organization chart identifies positions and job titles as well as the lines of authority and communication between them. It shows the **formal structure**, or how the organization is intended to function.

> An **organization chart** describes the arrangement of work positions within an organization.

Reading an organization chart should help you learn the basics of an organization's formal structure. This includes:

- *Division of work*—Positions and titles show work responsibilities.
- *Supervisory relationships*—Lines show who reports to whom.
- *Communication channels*—Lines show formal communication flows.
- *Major subunits*—Positions reporting to a common manager are shown.
- *Levels of management*—Vertical layers of management are shown.

> **Formal structure** is the official structure of the organization.

Even though organization charts are supposed to be helpful, the reality is that they sometimes don't make sense. They may be out of date or they may be just plain confusing. This happened to Carol Bartz when she took over as Yahoo!'s CEO. After looking at the organization chart, she said: "It was like a Dilbert cartoon. It was very odd." Her response was: "You need management here."[5]

## Informal Structures

Behind every formal structure typically lies an **informal structure**. This is a "shadow" organization made up of the unofficial, but often critical, working relationships

> **Informal structure** is the set of unofficial relationships among an organization's members.

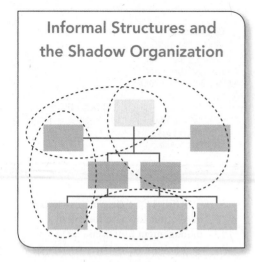

Informal Structures and the Shadow Organization

**Social network analysis** identifies the informal structures and their embedded social relationships that are active in an organization.

between organizational members. If the informal structure could be drawn, it would show who talks and interacts with whom, regardless of their formal titles and relationships. The lines of the informal structure would cut across levels and move from side to side. They would show people meeting for coffee, in exercise groups, and in friendship cliques. No organization can be fully understood without gaining insight into the informal structure as well as the formal one.[6]

A tool known as **social network analysis** is one way of identifying informal structures and their embedded social relationships. Such an analysis asks people to identify others to whom they turn for help most often, with whom they communicate regularly, and who give them energy and motivation.[7] Lines are then drawn from person to person according to frequency and type of relationship maintained. The result is a social network map that shows how a lot of work really gets done, in contrast to the formal arrangements shown in the organization chart. This information can be used to update the organization chart to better reflect the way things actually work. It also legitimates the informal networks people use in their daily work.

Informal structures and social networks are in many ways essential to organizational success. They allow people to make contacts with others who can help them get things done. They stimulate informal learning as people work and interact together throughout the workday. And, they are sources of emotional support and friendship that satisfy members' social needs.

Of course, informal structures also have potential disadvantages. They can be susceptible to rumor, carry inaccurate information, breed resistance to change, and even divert work efforts from important objectives. The Society for Human Resource Management, for example, reported that when the bad economy caused massive job losses, firms experienced an increase in workplace eavesdropping and in "gossip and rumors about downsizings and layoffs."[8] Another problem sometimes found in informal structures is the existence of "in" and "out" groups. Those who perceive themselves as "outsiders" may become less engaged in their work and more dissatisfied. Some American managers of Japanese firms, for example, have complained about being excluded from what they call the "shadow cabinet" consisting of Japanese executives who hold the real power and sometimes interact with one another while excluding others.[9]

**LEARNING CHECK 1**

**TAKEAWAY QUESTION 1 What is organizing as a management function?**

**Be sure you can** • define *organizing* as a management function • explain the difference between formal and informal structures • discuss the potential advantages and disadvantages of informal structures in organizations

## Traditional Organization Structures

A basic principle of organizing is that performance should improve when tasks are divided up and people are allowed to become experts in specific jobs. But there are different ways to accomplish this division of labor, and each has potential advantages and disadvantages. The traditional alternatives are the functional, divisional, and matrix structures.[10]

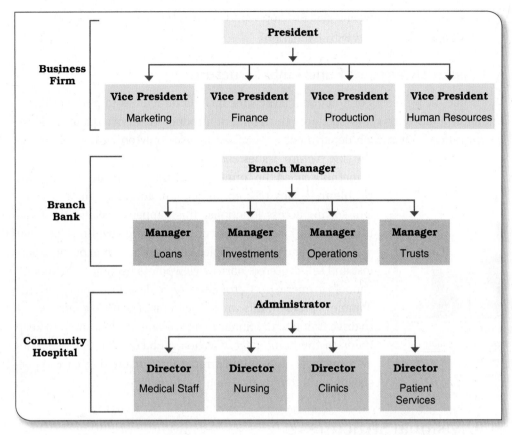

FIGURE 11.2   **Functional structures in a business, branch bank, and community hospital.**

# Functional Structures

In **functional structures**, people with similar skills and performing similar tasks are grouped together into formal work units. Members of functional departments share technical expertise, interests, and responsibilities. The first example in Figure 11.2 shows a functional structure common in business firms, with top management arranged by the functions of marketing, finance, production, and human resources. In this functional structure, manufacturing problems are the responsibility of the production vice president, marketing problems are the responsibility of the marketing vice president, and so on. Figure 11.2 also shows how functional structures are used in other types of organizations such as banks and hospitals.

A **functional structure** groups together people with similar skills who perform similar tasks.

## Advantages of Functional Structures

The key point of the functional structure is to put together people within the same expertise and help them work well together. If each function does its work properly, the expectation is that the organization as a whole will operate successfully. These structures work well for organizations dealing with only one or a few products or services. They also tend to work best in relatively stable environments where problems are predictable and the demands for change and innovation are limited. The major advantages of functional structures include the following:

- Economies of scale with efficient use of resources.
- Task assignments consistent with expertise and training.
- High-quality technical problem solving.

- In-depth training and skill development within functions.
- Clear career paths within functions.

## Disadvantages of Functional Structures

Common problems of functional structures include difficulties in pinpointing responsibilities for things like cost containment, product or service quality, and innovation. When each department or function focuses only on its own concerns, the "big picture" issues can easily get neglected. This relates to something called the **functional chimneys or functional silos problem**—a lack of communication, coordination, and problem solving across functions. This happens because the functions become formalized not only on the organization chart, but also in the mind-sets of people. A sense of common purpose gets lost and self-centered, narrow viewpoints become prominent.[11] Yahoo!'s former CEO Carol Bartz once described the functional chimneys problem this way: "The homepage people didn't want to drive traffic to the finance page because they wanted to keep them on the home page."[12] When problems like this occur, an alert manager steps in to correct things before they can do persistent harm to organizational performance.

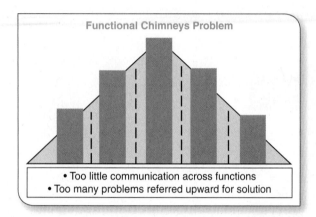

**Functional Chimneys Problem**

- Too little communication across functions
- Too many problems referred upward for solution

# Divisional Structures

A **divisional structure** groups together people working on the same product, in the same area, with similar customers, or on the same processes.

A second organizing alternative is the **divisional structure**. As illustrated in Figure 11.3, it groups together people who work on the same product or process, serve similar customers, or are located in the same area or geographical region.

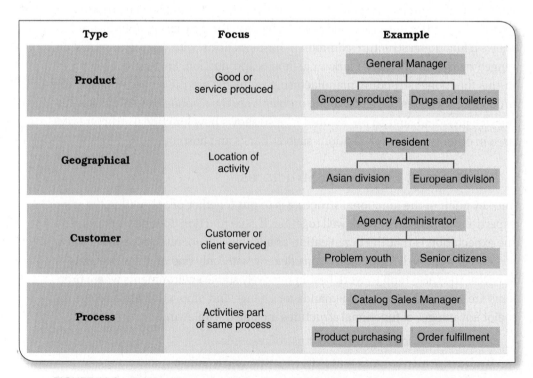

| Type | Focus | Example |
|---|---|---|
| **Product** | Good or service produced | General Manager → Grocery products, Drugs and toiletries |
| **Geographical** | Location of activity | President → Asian division, European division |
| **Customer** | Customer or client serviced | Agency Administrator → Problem youth, Senior citizens |
| **Process** | Activities part of same process | Catalog Sales Manager → Product purchasing, Order fulfillment |

FIGURE 11.3 **Divisional structures based on product, geography, customer, and process.**

Divisional structures are common in complex organizations with diverse operations that extend across many products, territories, customers, and work processes.[13] The idea is to use the divisional focus to overcome the disadvantages of a functional structure, such as the functional chimneys problem. For example, Toyota changed to a divisional structure in its North American operations. The new design brought together the engineering, manufacturing, and sales functions under a common boss instead of having each report to a top executive of its own. One analyst said: "The problem is every silo reported back to someone different, but now they need someone in charge of the whole choir."[14]

## Product Structures

**Product structures** group together jobs and activities focused on a single product or service. They clearly link costs, profits, problems, and successes in a market area with a central point of accountability. This prompts managers to be responsive to changing market demands and customer tastes.

A **product structure** groups together people and jobs focused on a single product or service.

Common in large organizations, product structures may even extend into global operations. When Fiat took over Chrysler, for example, CEO Sergio Marchionne said he wanted a "leaner, flatter structure" to decision making and to improve communication flow." His choice was to use product divisions. Each of the firm's three brands—Chrysler, Jeep, and Dodge—was given its own chief executive and assigned responsibility for its own profits and losses.[15] You'll find this same approach at General Motors, which is now organized around four product divisions—Buick, Cadillac, Chevrolet, and GMC. The goal of these product structures is to focus the technology and other firm resources on the core auto brands.[16]

## Geographical Structures

**Geographical structures**, sometimes called *area structures*, group together jobs and activities being performed in the same location. They are typically used when there is a need to differentiate products or services in various locations, such as in different parts of a country. They also help global companies focus attention on the unique cultures and requirements of particular regions. As United Parcel Service operations expanded worldwide, for example, the company announced a change from a product structure to a geographical structure. Two geographical divisions were created—the Americas and Europe/Asia. Each area was given responsibility for its own logistics, sales, and other business functions.

A **geographical structure** groups together people and jobs performed in the same location.

## Customer Structures

**Customer structures** group together jobs and activities that are serving the same customers or clients. The goal is to best serve the special needs of the different customer groups. This is a common structure in the consumer products industry. 3M Corporation structures itself to focus attention on such diverse markets as consumer and office, specialty materials, industrial, health care, electronics and communications, and safety. Customer structures are also useful in services. Banks, for example, use them to give separate attention to consumer and commercial customers for loans. If you look again at Figure 11.3 you'll see that it also shows a government agency using the customer structure to serve different client populations.

A **customer structure** groups together people and jobs that serve the same customers or clients.

## Dancing Deer Baking Sweetens Growth with Values

Courtesy Dancing Deer Baking Company, Inc

**D**ancing Deer Baking sells about $10 million of confectionary concoctions annually. Every product is made with all natural ingredients and packaged in recycled materials. And, they're all produced in inner-city Boston.

The bakery's story is entrepreneurship with social values. It began with partners Patricia Karter, Suzanne Lombardi, and Ayis Antoniou, a $20,000 investment, great recipes, and two ovens located in a former pizza shop. After Dancing Deer was recognized on national TV as having the "best cake in the nation," more expansion into mail-order sales quickly followed.

Growth like this can cause problems for any organization. Managers have to adjust practices, structures, and staffing to deal with increasing size. Dancing Deer is no exception. But its pathways to prosperity have been clear—let core values be the guide.

When offered a chance to make a large cookie sale to Williams-Sonoma, then-CEO Karter declined because the contract would have required use of preservatives. But Williams-Sonoma was so impressed with her products and principles that it contracted for the sale of her bakery mixes. Instead of lost opportunity, Karter's principles guided the firm to more sales and further growth.

Throughout Dancing Deer's growth, Karter never swayed from the firm's core principles—"passionate about food, nature, aesthetics, and community." This legacy thrives even though Karter has moved on to focus on community service and Frank Carpetino is in as the new CEO. All of Dancing Deer's employees get stock options and free lunches; 35% of profits from the firm's Sweet Home cakes are donated to help the homeless find accommodations and jobs. "There's more to life than selling cookies," says the firm's website, "but it's not a bad way to make a living."

 **YOUR TAKE?**

Tish Karter's experiences at Dancing Deer Baking show how business entrepreneurship and social values can combine for real accomplishments. But, what about tipping points like the first Williams-Sonoma offer? Isn't it easy for the quest for customers, contracts, and plain old cash to throw things off balance? Is it easier to stay on course with values in a small firm than in a large organization? And as an organization grows, can it be structured to protect core values, or is it really up to the leader and his or her day-to-day influence?

## Process Structures

A **work process** is a group of related tasks that collectively creates a valuable work product.

A **process structure** groups jobs and activities that are part of the same processes.

A **work process** is a group of related tasks that collectively creates something of value to a customer.[17] An example is order fulfillment by a catalog retailer, a process that takes an order from point of initiation by the customer to point of fulfillment by a delivered product. A **process structure** groups together jobs and activities that are part of the same processes. Figure 11.3 shows how this might take the form of product-purchasing teams and order-fulfillment teams for a mail-order catalog business.

## Advantages and Disadvantages of Divisional Structures

Organizations use divisional structures for a variety of reasons, including the desire to avoid the functional chimneys problem and other downsides of functional structures. The potential advantages of divisional structures include:

- More flexibility in responding to environmental changes.
- Improved coordination across functional departments.

- Clear points of responsibility for product or service delivery.
- Expertise focused on specific customers, products, and regions.
- Greater ease in changing size by adding or deleting divisions.

As with other structural alternatives, divisional structures have potential disadvantages. They can reduce economies of scale and increase costs through the duplication of resources and efforts across divisions. They can also create unhealthy rivalries as divisions compete for resources and top management attention, and as they emphasize division needs over the goals of the organization as a whole.

## Matrix Structures

The **matrix structure**, often called the *matrix organization*, combines the functional and divisional structures. It is an attempt to gain the advantages and minimize the disadvantages of each. This is accomplished by creating permanent teams that cut across functions to support specific products, projects, or programs.[18] As shown in Figure 11.4, workers in a matrix structure belong to at least two formal groups at the same time—a functional group and a product, program, or project team. They also report to two bosses—one within the function and the other within the team.

The matrix organization has gained a strong foothold in the workplace, with applications in such diverse settings as manufacturing (e.g., aerospace, electronics, pharmaceuticals), service industries (e.g., banking, brokerage, retailing), professional fields (e.g., accounting, advertising, law), and the nonprofit sector (e.g., city, state, and federal agencies, hospitals, universities). Matrix structures are also found in multinational corporations, where they offer the flexibility to deal with regional differences while still handling multiple product, program, or project needs.

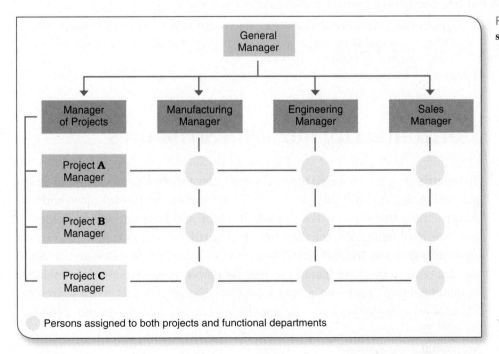

FIGURE 11.4   **Matrix structure in a small, multiproject business firm.**

## Advantages and Disadvantages of Matrix Structures

The main benefits of matrix structures rest with the teams whose members work closely together to share expertise and information in a timely manner. This goes a long way toward eliminating functional chimneys problems and poor cross-functional communication. The potential advantages of matrix structures include:

- Better communication and cooperation across functions.
- Improved decision making; problem solving takes place at the team level where the best information is available.
- Increased flexibility in adding, removing, or changing operations to meet changing demands.
- Better customer service; there is always a program, product, or project manager informed and available to answer questions.
- Better performance accountability through the program, product, or project managers.
- Improved strategic management; top managers are freed from lower-level problem solving to focus time on more strategic issues.

Predictably, matrix structures also have potential disadvantages. The two-boss system is susceptible to power struggles if functional supervisors and team leaders compete with one another to exercise authority. The two-boss system can be frustrating if it creates task confusion and conflicting work priorities. Team meetings in the matrix can take lots of time, and the teams may develop "groupitis"— strong team loyalties that cause a loss of focus on larger organizational goals. The requirement of adding the team leaders to a matrix structure can also result in higher costs.

---

**LEARNING CHECK 2**

**TAKEAWAY QUESTION 2 What are the traditional organization structures?**

**Be sure you can** • explain the differences between functional, divisional, and matrix structures • list advantages and disadvantages of a functional structure, divisional structure, and matrix structure • draw charts to show how each type of traditional structure could be used in organizations familiar to you

---

# Horizontal Organization Structures

The matrix structure is a step toward better cross-functional integration in an organization. But it is just one part of a broader movement toward more horizontal structures that harness the powers of teams and information technology to improve communication, collaboration, and flexibility. And as traditional vertical structures give way to more horizontal ones, the two "$Ts$" of teams and technology are used to decrease hierarchy, increase empowerment, and better mobilize human talents.[19] Consultant and scholar Gary Hamel says that today's "younger workers—the 'digital natives'—are impatient with old hierarchies and value systems."[20] They are among the driving forces behind the movement toward more horizontal organizations.

## Recommended Reading

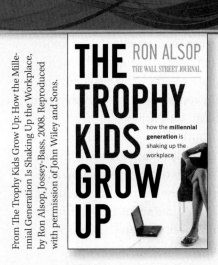

### *The Trophy Kids Grow Up: How the Millennial Generation Is Shaking Up the Workplace* (Jossey-Bass, 2008)
### by Ron Alsop

Chances are you are one of them; if not, you are or will be managing them. They're the Millennials, born 1980–2001, and they're bringing a lot of changes to organizations. Author Ron Alsop says that in their formative years members of this generation received trophies and rewards for efforts, not accomplishments. They're heavily into text messages and social media; they're informal, casual, and confident when it comes to work; they value family and are socially aware. What are the implications of this generation for traditional organizations and those who manage them?

## Team Structures

Organizations with **team structures** make extensive use of both permanent and temporary teams to solve problems, complete special projects, and accomplish day-to-day tasks.[21] As illustrated in Figure 11.5, these are often **cross-functional teams** composed of members drawn from different areas of work responsibility.[22] Like the matrix structure, the intention is to break down functional chimneys and create more effective working relations around and across the organization.

Team structures use many **project teams** that are convened to complete a specific task or "project." An example is a team convened to guide the changeover to a new information system. Such project teams are temporary and disband once the task is completed. The intention is to convene a team of people who have the needed talents, focus their efforts intensely to solve a problem or take advantage of a special opportunity, and then release them once the project is finished.

A **team structure** uses permanent and temporary cross-functional teams to improve lateral relations.

A **cross-functional team** brings together members from different functional departments.

**Project teams** are convened for a particular task or project and disband once it is completed.

### Advantages and Disadvantages of Team Structures

The advantages of team structures trace to the fact that putting people into teams and giving them common goals to work on together breaks down barriers and

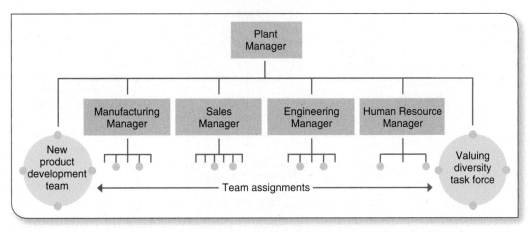

FIGURE 11.5   **How a team structure uses cross-functional teams for improved lateral relations.**

mobilizes talents. After a research team at Polaroid Corporation developed a new medical imaging system in one-half the predicted time, a senior executive said: "Our researchers are not any smarter, but by working together they get the value of each other's intelligence almost instantaneously."[23] Because teams focus shared knowledge and expertise on specific problems, they can improve performance by increasing the speed and quality of decisions in many situations. They can also boost morale. People working in teams often experience a greater sense of task involvement and identification, and this increases their enthusiasm for the job.

The complexities of teams and teamwork contribute to the potential disadvantages of team structures. These include conflicting loyalties for persons with both team and functional assignments. They also include issues of time management and group process. By their very nature, teams spend a lot of time in meetings. Whether these meetings are face-to-face or virtual, not all of the time spent together is productive. The quality of outcomes depends a lot on how well tasks, relationships, and overall team dynamics are managed. But, all of these challenges can be mastered with the right team talents and leadership.

## Network Structures

A **network structure** uses information technologies to link with networks of outside suppliers and service contractors.

Organizations using a **network structure**, like the one in Figure 11.6, have a central core of full-time employees surrounded by "networks" of outside contractors and partners that supply essential services.[24] Because the central core is relatively small and the surrounding networks can be expanded or shrunk as needed, the network structure helps lower costs and improve flexibility in dealing with changing environments.[25]

A **strategic alliance** is a cooperation agreement with another organization to jointly pursue activities of mutual interest.

Instead of doing everything for itself with full-time employees, the network organization employs a minimum staff and contracts out as much work as possible. This is done through **strategic alliances**, which are cooperation agreements with other firms to pursue business activities of mutual interest. Some are *outsourcing strategic alliances* in which they contract to purchase important services such as accounting or document processing from another organization. Others may be *supplier strategic*

**FIGURE 11.6  A network structure for a Web-based retail business.**

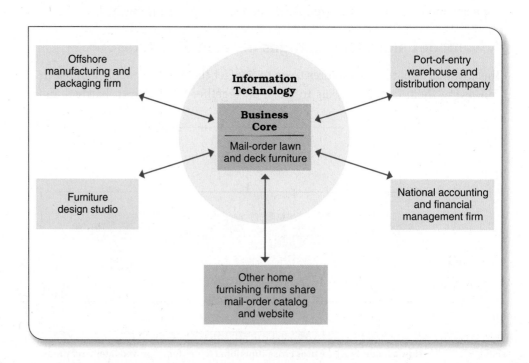

*alliances* that link businesses in preferred relationships that guarantee a smooth and timely flow of quality supplies among the partners. An example of a step toward the network organization is found in residential colleges and universities that traditionally owned their own dormitories. Many are now getting out of the campus housing business by entering public–private partnerships that turn dormitories over to private businesses to operate.[26]

The example in Figure 11.6 shows how a network structure might work for a mail-order company selling lawn and deck furniture through a catalog. The firm is very small, consisting of relatively few full-time core employees. Beyond that, it is structured as a network of outsourcing and partner relationships linked together by the latest in information technology. Merchandise is designed on contract with a furniture designer—which responds quickly as designs are shared and customized via computer networking. The furniture is manufactured and packaged by subcontractors located around the world—wherever materials are found at the lowest cost and best quality. Stock is maintained and shipped from a contract warehouse—ensuring quality storage and on-time expert shipping. Accounting and financial details are contracted with an outside firm—providing better technical expertise than the merchandiser could afford to employ on a full-time basis. The quarterly catalog is produced in cooperation with two other firms that sell different home furnishings with a related price appeal.

## Advantages and Disadvantages of Network Structures

In respect to advantages, network structures are lean and streamlined. They help organizations stay cost-competitive by reducing overhead and increasing operating efficiency. Network concepts allow organizations to employ outsourcing strategies and contract out specialized business functions. Within the operating core of a network structure, furthermore, interesting jobs are created for those who coordinate the entire system of relationships.

Network structures have potential disadvantages as well. The more complex the business or mission of the organization, the more complicated it is to control and coordinate the network of contracts and alliances. If one part of the network breaks down or fails to deliver, the entire system suffers. The organization may lose control over activities contracted out. It may also experience a lack of loyalty among contractors who are used infrequently rather than on a long-term basis. Some worry that outsourcing can become so aggressive as to be dangerous to the firm, especially when critical activities such as finance, logistics, and human resources management are outsourced.[27] Not too long ago, for example, Delta Air announced that it was shutting down its call-center operations in India because too many customers were complaining about communication difficulties with the Indian service providers.[28]

## Boundaryless Structures

It is popular today to speak about creating a **boundaryless organization** that eliminates many of the internal boundaries among subsystems and external boundaries with the external environment.[29] The boundaryless structure, as shown in Figure 11.7, can be viewed as a combination of the team and network structures just described, with the added feature of "temporariness." A photograph that documents

A **boundaryless organization** eliminates internal boundaries among subsystems and external boundaries with the external environment.

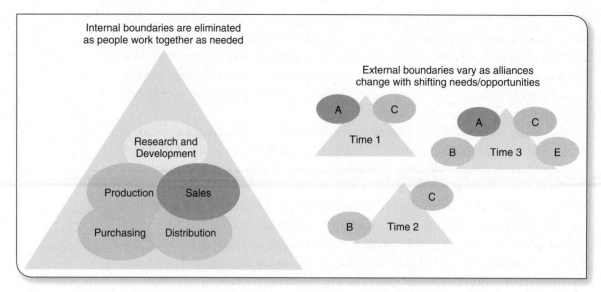

**FIGURE 11.7** **The boundaryless organization eliminates internal and external barriers.**

this organization's configuration today will look different from one taken tomorrow, as the form naturally adjusts to new pressures and circumstances.

Spontaneous teamwork and communication replace formal lines of authority within the boundaryless organization. Meetings and information sharing happen continuously. People work together in teams that form and disband as needed. There is little hierarchy but lots of empowerment and technology utilization. Impermanence is accepted. Knowledge sharing is both a goal and an essential component. At consulting giant PricewaterhouseCoopers, for example, knowledge sharing brings together 160,000 partners spread across 150 countries in a virtual-learning and problem-solving network. Partners collaborate electronically through online databases where information is stored, problems are posted, and questions are asked and answered in real time by those with experience and expertise relevant to the problem at hand.[30]

A **virtual organization** uses IT and the Internet to engage a shifting network of strategic alliances.

The **virtual organization** takes the boundaryless concept to the extreme.[31] It operates as a shifting network of alliances that are engaged as needed using IT and the Internet. The virtual organization calls an alliance into action to meet specific operating needs and objectives; when the work is complete, the alliance rests until next called into action. This mix of mobilized alliances is continuously shifting, and an expansive pool of potential alliances is always ready to be called upon. Do you see similarities with the Facebook or LinkedIn communities? Isn't the virtual organization concept similar to how we manage our relationships online—signing in, signing off, getting things done as needed with different people and groups, and all taking place instantaneously, temporarily, and without the need for face-to-face contacts?

**LEARNING CHECK 3**

**TAKEAWAY QUESTION 3 What are the types of horizontal organization structures?**

**Be sure you can** • describe how organizations can be structured to use cross-functional teams and project teams • define *network structure* • illustrate how a new retail venture might use a network structure to organize its various operations • discuss the potential advantages and disadvantages of a network structure • explain the concept of the boundaryless organization

> "IT DOESN'T MATTER WHAT INDUSTRY YOU'RE IN. PEOPLE HAVE BLIND SPOTS ABOUT WHERE THEY ARE WEAK"

## Bosses May Be Overestimating Their Managing Skills

A survey by Development Dimensions International, Inc., finds that managers may be overestimating their managing skills. "It doesn't matter what industry you're in. People have blind spots about where they are weak," says DDI vice president Scott Erker. These results are from a sample of 1,100 first-year managers:

- 72% never question their ability to lead others.
- 58% claim planning and organizing skills as strengths.
- 53% say they are strong in decision making.
- 50% say they are strong in communication.

- 32% claim proficiency in delegating.
- Skills rated as needing most development were delegating, gaining commitment, and coaching.

 **YOUR THOUGHTS?**

Would you, like managers in this survey, probably overestimate your strengths in management skills? What might explain such tendencies toward overconfidence? And among the skills needing work, why would delegating be the one about which even very confident managers still feel some inadequacy?

## Organizational Designs

**Organizational design** is the process of choosing and implementing structures to accomplish the organization's mission and objectives.[32] Because every organization faces its own set of unique problems and opportunities, no one design applies in all circumstances. The best design at any moment is the one that achieves a good match between structure and situational contingencies—including task, technology, environment, and people.[33] The choices among design alternatives are broadly framed in the distinction between mechanistic or bureaucratic designs at one extreme, and organic or adaptive designs at the other.

> **Organizational design** is the process of creating structures that accomplish mission and objectives.

### Contingency in Organizational Design

A classic **bureaucracy** is a form of organization based on logic, order, and the legitimate use of formal authority.[34] It is a vertical structure, and its distinguishing features include a clear-cut division of labor, strict hierarchy of authority, formal rules and procedures, and promotion based on competency.

> A **bureaucracy** emphasizes formal authority, order, fairness, and efficiency.

According to sociologist Max Weber, bureaucracies were supposed to be orderly, fair, and highly efficient.[35] But the bureaucracies we know are often associated with "red tape." And instead of being orderly and fair, they are often seen as cumbersome and impersonal to customer or client needs.[36] Rather than view all bureaucratic structures as inevitably flawed, however, management theory asks two contingency questions. When is a bureaucratic form a good choice for an organization? When it isn't, what alternatives are available?

Pioneering research conducted in England during the early 1960s by Tom Burns and George Stalker helps answer these questions.[37] After investigating 20 manufacturing firms they concluded that two quite different organizational forms could be successful, depending on the nature of a firm's external environment. A more

FIGURE 11.8 **Organizational design alternatives: From bureaucratic to adaptive organizations.**

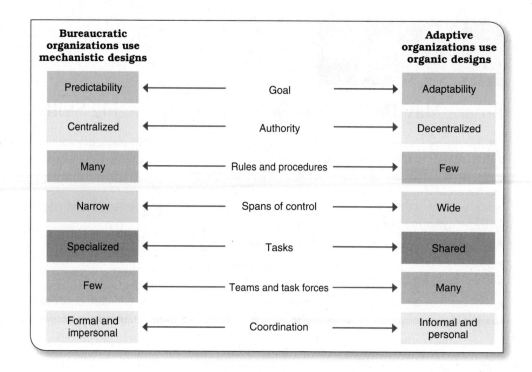

| Bureaucratic organizations use mechanistic designs | | Adaptive organizations use organic designs |
|---|---|---|
| Predictability | Goal | Adaptability |
| Centralized | Authority | Decentralized |
| Many | Rules and procedures | Few |
| Narrow | Spans of control | Wide |
| Specialized | Tasks | Shared |
| Few | Teams and task forces | Many |
| Formal and impersonal | Coordination | Informal and personal |

bureaucratic form, which Burns and Stalker called "mechanistic," thrived when the environment was stable. But it experienced difficulty when the environment was rapidly changing and uncertain. In dynamic situations a much less-bureaucratic form, called "organic," performed best. Figure 11.8 portrays these two approaches as opposite extremes on a continuum of organizational design alternatives.

## Mechanistic and Organic Designs

A **mechanistic design** is centralized, with many rules and procedures, a clear-cut division of labor, narrow spans of control, and formal coordination.

Organizations with more **mechanistic designs** are highly bureaucratic. As shown in the figure, they are vertical structures that typically operate with centralized authority, many rules and procedures, a precise division of labor, narrow spans of control, and formal means of coordination. They can be described as "tight" structures of the traditional pyramid form.[38]

Mechanistic designs work best for organizations doing routine tasks in stable environments. For a good example, visit your local fast-food restaurant. Each store is a relatively small operation that operates quite like others in the franchise chain and according to rules established by the corporate management. Service personnel work in orderly and disciplined ways, guided by training, rules and procedures, and by close supervision of crew leaders who work alongside them. Even personal appearance is carefully regulated, with everyone working in uniform. These mechanistic restaurants perform well as they repetitively deliver items that are part of their standard menus. You quickly discover their limits, however, if you try to order something not on the menu. The chains also are slow to adjust when consumer tastes change.

When organizations operate in dynamic and often uncertain environments, their effectiveness depends on being able to change with the times. This requires the more **organic designs** described in Figure 11.8.[39] These are horizontal structures with decentralized authority, fewer rules and procedures, less precise division of labor, wider spans of control, and more personal means of coordination.

An **organic design** is decentralized, with fewer rules and procedures, open divisions of labor, wide spans of control, and more personal coordination.

Organic designs create **adaptive organizations** that can perform well in environments that demand flexibility in dealing with changing conditions. They are relatively "loose" systems where a lot of work gets done through informal structures and networking.[40] And, they are built on a foundation of trust that people will do the right things on their own initiative. This means giving workers the freedom to use their ideas and expertise to do what they can do best—get the job done.

An **adaptive organization** operates with a minimum of bureaucratic features and encourages worker empowerment and teamwork.

## Trends in Organizational Designs

The complexity, uncertainty, and change inherent in today's environment are prompting more and more organizations to shift toward horizontal and organic structures. A number of trends in organizational design are evident as structures and practices are adjusted to gain performance efficiency and effectiveness in challenging conditions. The growth of new technologies, particularly in information systems and social media, is helping drive these trends by improving information availability and ease of communication within organizations.

### Fewer Levels of Management

A typical organization chart shows the **chain of command**, or the line of authority that vertically links each position with successively higher levels of management. When organizations grow in size they tend to get taller and add more levels of management to the chain of command. But high-performing firms like Nucor, a North Carolina-based steel producer, show preferences for fewer management levels. Nucor's management hierarchy is flat and compact. Its structure is described as "simple" and "streamlined" in order to "allow employees to innovate and make quick decisions."[41]

The **chain of command** links all persons with successively higher levels of authority.

One of the influences on management levels is **span of control**—the number of persons directly reporting to a manager. Narrow spans of control are characteristic of **tall structures** with many levels of management. Because tall organizations have more managers, they are more costly. They also tend to be less efficient, less flexible, and less customer-sensitive. Wider spans of control run with **flat structures** that have fewer levels of management. This not only reduces overhead costs, it also tends to give workers more empowerment and independence because less-direct supervision is available.[42]

**Span of control** is the number of subordinates directly reporting to a manager.

**Tall structures** have narrow spans of control and many hierarchical levels.

**Flat structures** have wide spans of control and few hierarchical levels.

When Procter & Gamble's CEO, Robert McDonald, was appointed, one of his first announcements was that he would be taking steps to "create a simpler, flatter and more agile organization." This involved cutting the number of levels of management in the firm from nine to seven. McDonald stated that streamlining the organization structure was important "because simplification reduces cost, improves productivity and enhances employee satisfaction."[43]

*Trend:* Organizations are cutting unnecessary levels of management and shifting to wider spans of control. Managers are taking responsibility for larger teams whose members operate with less direct supervision.

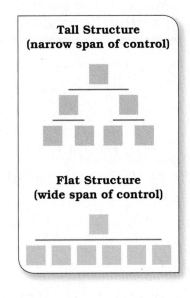

**Tall Structure (narrow span of control)**

**Flat Structure (wide span of control)**

### More Delegation and Empowerment

All managers must decide what work they should do themselves and what should be left for others. At issue here is **delegation**—the process of entrusting work to others by giving them the right to make decisions and take action. A classical princi-

**Delegation** is the process of distributing and entrusting work to other persons.

> "I EVEN FEEL GUILTY NOW TAKING TIME TO WATCH MY DAUGHTER
PLAY SOCCER ON SATURDAY MORNINGS"

## Help! I've Been Flattened into Exhaustion

Sean Locke/iStockphoto

As my organization "restructures" and cuts back staff, it puts a greater burden on those of us that remain. We get exhausted, and our families get short-changed and even angry. I even feel guilty now taking time to watch my daughter play soccer on Saturday mornings. Sure, there's some decent pay involved, but that doesn't make up for the heavy price in terms of lost family time.

But you know what? My boss doesn't get it. I never hear her ask: "Camille, are you working too much? Don't you think it's time to get back on a reasonable schedule?" No! What I often hear instead is "Look at Andy; he handles our new management model really well, and he's a real go-getter. I don't think he's been out of here one night this week before 8 PM."

What am I to do, just keep it up until everything falls apart one day? Is a flatter structure with fewer managers always best? Am I missing something in regard to this "new management"?

Sincerely,

Overworked in Cincinnati

D ear Stress Doctor:
   My boss has come up with this great idea of laying off some managers, assigning more workers to those of us who remain, and calling us "coaches" instead of supervisors. She says this is all part of a new management approach to operate with a flatter structure and more empowerment.

For me this means a lot more work coordinating the activities of 17 operators instead of the six that I previously supervised. I can't get everything cleaned up on my desk most days, and I end up taking a lot of work home.

### ■ ETHICS QUESTIONS

Is it ethical to restructure, cut management levels, and expect the remaining managers to do more work? Or is it simply the case that managers used to the "old" ways of doing things need extra training and care while learning "new" management approaches? And what about this person's boss—is she on track with her management skills? Aren't managers supposed to help people understand their jobs, set priorities, and fulfill them, while still maintaining a reasonable work–life balance?

---

The **authority-and-responsibility principle** is that authority should equal responsibility when work is delegated.

ple of organization warns managers not to delegate without giving the other person sufficient authority to perform. The **authority-and-responsibility principle** states that authority should equal responsibility when work is delegated from a supervisor to a subordinate. When done well the process of delegation involves these three action steps.

- *Step 1*—The manager assigns responsibility by carefully explaining the work or duties someone else is expected to do. This responsibility is an expectation for the other person to perform assigned tasks.

- *Step 2*—The manager grants authority to act. Along with the assigned task, the right to take necessary actions ( for example, to spend money, direct the work of others, or use resources) is given to the other person.

## Management in Popular Culture

### Empowerment and *Patch Adams*

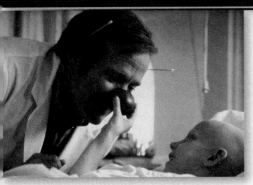

The movie *Patch Adams* is based on the true-life story of Hunter "Patch" Adams. It's also a lesson in organizational design. Adams (played by Robin Williams) is a doctor who becomes increasingly disillusioned with medical bureaucracy. He's inspired to create a new kind of hospital, free from the usual constraints, and using unconventional methods of treatment. At Patch's hospital doctors and patients work side-by-side, with patients taking responsibility for their own care. By empowering patients, Adams believed medical treatment would be more effective.

© AF archive/Alamy

• *Step 3*—The manager creates accountability. By accepting an assignment, the person takes on a direct obligation to the manager to complete the job as agreed.

On those days when you complain that "I just can't get everything done," the real problem may be that you are trying to do everything yourself. This unwillingness to delegate is a common management failure. Whether this comes from a lack of trust in others or from personal inflexibility, it can still be damaging. Too little delegation overloads the manager with work that could be done by others; it also denies others many opportunities to fully utilize their talents on the job.

Delegation that is done well leads to **empowerment**. This concept was defined in the chapter opener as letting others make decisions and exercise discretion in their work. Empowerment occurs when delegation gives decision-making authority to people who are most capable of doing the work. It builds performance potential by allowing people freedom to use their talents, contribute ideas, and do their jobs in the best possible ways. And because empowerment creates a sense of ownership, it also increases commitment to decisions and work goals.

> **Empowerment** allows others to make decisions and exercise discretion in their work.

*Trend:* Managers are delegating more. They are finding ways to empower people at all levels to make more decisions that affect themselves and their work.

### Decentralization with Centralization

Should most decisions be made at the top levels of an organization, or should they be dispersed by extensive delegation throughout all levels? The former approach is referred to as **centralization**; the latter is called **decentralization**. But the management issue they represent isn't necessarily an either/or choice. Today's organizations can operate with greater decentralization without giving up centralized control.[44]

High speed computer networks and advanced information systems allow managers at higher levels to easily stay informed about a wide range of day-to-day performance matters throughout an organization. Because they have information so readily available, they can allow more decentralization in decision making. If

> **Centralization** is the concentration of authority for most decisions at the top level of an organization.
>
> **Decentralization** is the dispersion of authority to make decisions throughout all organization levels.

## Making Schools Work Better with Organizational Design

Scholar and consultant William Ouchi believes that our public schools can be improved through organizational design. In his book, *Making Schools Work: A Revolutionary Plan to Get Your Children the Education They Need*, Ouchi points out that as organizations grow in size, they tend to "bulk up" with staff personnel and higher-level managers that are distant from customers and operating workers. He finds many less-successful schools following this pattern.

Ouchi's study of 223 school districts suggests that adding administrative weight and cost at the top does little to improve organizational performance and can actually harm it. Even though most school districts are highly centralized, he finds that decentralization is a characteristic of the more successful ones. The better districts in his study had fewer central office staff personnel per student and allowed maximum autonomy to school principals. Ouchi advocates redesigning schools so that decision making is more decentralized. He believes in allowing principals more autonomy to control school budgets and work with their staffs, and in allowing teachers more freedom to solve their own problems.

### ▪ YOU BE THE RESEARCHER

Does Ouchi offer us a general organizational design principle—systems perform best with streamlined designs and greater decentralization? Or can you come up with examples of

**Administrative Staffing Comparisons**

| School District A *Successful* | School District B *Less Successful* |
| --- | --- |
| 22 central office staff for 120,000 students; 1 per 5,455 students | 22,500 central office staff for 1.2 million students; 1 per 47 students |
| *Decentralized; schools have lots of autonomy* | *Centralized; schools have little autonomy* |

organizations that perform well with large staffs and lots of centralization?

Don't you wonder how School District B justifies its large administrative staff while School District A has a reputation for success? What is the ratio of administrative to instructional staff at your university? Could "performance" be improved along lines suggested by Ouchi?

*Reference:* William Ouchi, *Making Schools Work: A Revolutionary Plan to Get Your Children the Education They Need* (New York: Simon & Schuster, 2003); and Richard Riordan, Linda Lingle, and Lyman Porter, "Making Public Schools Work: Management Reform as the Key," *Academy of Management Journal*, vol. 48, no. 6 (2005), pp. 929–40.

---

something goes wrong, the information systems should sound an alarm and allow corrective action to be taken quickly.

*Trend:* Delegation, empowerment, and horizontal structures are contributing to more decentralization in organizations; at the same time, advances in information technology help top managers maintain centralized control.

### Reduced Use of Staff

**Staff positions** provide technical expertise for other parts of the organization.

When it comes to coordination and control in organizations, the issue of line–staff relationships is important. People in **staff positions** provide expert advice and guidance to line personnel. In a large retail chain, for example, line managers in each store typically make daily operating decisions regarding direct sales of merchandise. But, staff specialists at the corporate or regional levels often provide direction and support so that all the stores operate with the same credit, purchasing, employment, marketing, and advertising procedures.

Problems in line–staff distinctions can and do arise, and organizations sometimes find that staff size grows to the point where it costs more than it is worth. This is why cutbacks in staff positions are common during downsizing and other turnaround efforts. There is no one best solution to the problem of how to divide work between line and staff responsibilities. What is best for any organization will be a cost-effective staff component that satisfies, but doesn't overreact to, needs for specialized technical assistance to line operations. But overall, the trend toward reduced use of staff is quite clear.

*Trend:* Organizations are lowering costs and increasing efficiency by employing fewer staff personnel and using smaller staff units.

---

**LEARNING CHECK 4**

**TAKEAWAY QUESTION 4 How are organizational designs changing the workplace?**

**Be sure you can** • define *organizational design* • describe the characteristics of mechanistic and organic designs • explain when the mechanistic design and the organic design work best • describe trends in levels of management, delegation and empowerment, decentralization and centralization, and use of staff

# MANAGEMENT LEARNING REVIEW

## LEARNING CHECK SUMMARY

### TAKEAWAY QUESTION 1 What is organizing as a management function?

- Organizing is the process of arranging people and resources to work toward a common goal.
- Organizing decisions divide up the work that needs to be done, allocate people and resources to do it, and coordinate results to achieve productivity.
- Structure is the system of tasks, reporting relationships, and communication that links people and positions within an organization.
- The formal structure, such as that shown on an organization chart, describes how an organization is supposed to work.
- The informal structure of an organization consists of the unofficial relationships that develop among members.

**For Discussion If organization charts are imperfect, why bother with them?**

### TAKEAWAY QUESTION 2 What are the traditional organization structures?

- In functional structures, people with similar skills who perform similar activities are grouped together under a common manager.
- In divisional structures, people who work on a similar product, work in the same geographical region, serve the same customers, or participate in the same work process are grouped together under common managers.
- A matrix structure combines the functional and divisional approaches to create permanent cross-functional project teams.

**For Discussion Why use functional structures if they are prone to functional chimneys problems?**

### TAKEAWAY QUESTION 3 What are the types of horizontal organization structures?

- Team structures use cross-functional teams and task forces to improve lateral relations and problem solving at all levels.
- Network structures use contracted services and strategic alliances to support a core organizational center.
- Boundaryless structures or boundaryless organizations combine team and network structures with the advantages of technology to accomplish tasks and projects.
- Virtual organizations utilize information technology to mobilize a shifting mix of strategic alliances to accomplish tasks and projects.

**For Discussion How can problems with group decision making hurt team structures?**

### TAKEAWAY QUESTION 4 How are organizational designs changing the workplace?

- Contingency in organizational design basically means finding a design that best fits situational features.
- Mechanistic designs are bureaucratic and vertical, performing best for routine and predictable tasks.
- Organic designs are adaptive and horizontal, performing best in conditions requiring change and flexibility.
- Key organizing trends include fewer levels of management, more delegation and empowerment, decentralization with centralization, and fewer staff positions.

**For Discussion Which of the organizing trends is most subject to change under current conditions?**

## SELF-TEST 11

### Multiple-Choice Questions

1. The main purpose of organizing as a management function is to _____.
   (a) make sure that results match plans
   (b) arrange people and resources to accomplish work
   (c) create enthusiasm for the work to be done
   (d) match strategies with operational plans

2. _____ is the system of tasks, reporting relationships, and communication that links together the various parts of an organization.
   (a) Structure          (b) Staff
   (c) Decentralization   (d) Differentiation

**3.** Rumors and resistance to change are potential disadvantages often associated with _____.
(a) virtual organizations (b) informal structures
(c) delegation (d) specialized staff

**4.** An organization chart showing vice presidents of marketing, finance, manufacturing, and purchasing all reporting to the president is depicting a _____ structure.
(a) functional (b) matrix
(c) network (d) product

**5.** The functional chimneys problem occurs when people in different functions _____.
(a) fail to communicate with one another
(b) try to help each other work with customers
(c) spend too much time coordinating decisions
(d) focus on products rather than functions

**6.** A manufacturing business with a functional structure has recently developed three new product lines. The president of the company might consider shifting to a/an _____ structure to gain a stronger focus on each product.
(a) virtual (b) informal
(c) divisional (d) network

**7.** _____ structure tries to combine the best elements of the functional and divisional forms.
(a) Virtual (b) Boundaryless
(c) Team (d) Matrix

**8.** The "two-boss" system of reporting relationships is found in the _____ structure.
(a) functional (b) matrix
(c) network (d) product

**9.** Better lower-level teamwork and more top-level strategic management are among the expected advantages of a _____ structure.
(a) divisional (b) matrix
(c) geographical (d) product

**10.** "Tall" organizations tend to have long chains of command and _____ spans of control.
(a) wide (b) narrow
(c) informal (d) centralized

**11.** A student volunteers to gather information on a company for a group case analysis project. The other members of the group agree, and tell her to go ahead and choose the information sources. In terms of delegation, this group is giving the student _____ to fulfill the agreed-upon task.
(a) responsibility (b) accountability
(c) authority (d) decentralization

**12.** The current trend in the use of staff in organizations is to _____.
(a) give staff personnel more authority over operations
(b) reduce the number of staff personnel
(c) remove all staff from the organization
(d) combine all staff functions in one department

**13.** The bureaucratic organization described by Max Weber is similar to the _____ organization described by Burns and Stalker.
(a) adaptive (b) mechanistic
(c) organic (d) adhocracy

**14.** Which type of organization design best fits an uncertain and changing environment?
(a) mechanistic (b) bureaucratic
(c) organic (d) traditional

**15.** An organization that employs just a few "core" or essential full-time employees and outsources a lot of the remaining work show signs of using a _____ structure.
(a) functional (b) network
(c) matrix (d) mechanistic

## Short-Response Questions

**16.** What symptoms might indicate that a functional structure is causing problems for the organization?

**17.** Explain by example the concept of a network organization structure.

**18.** Explain the practical significance of this statement: "Organizational design should be done in contingency fashion."

**19.** Describe two trends in organizational design and explain their importance to managers.

## Essay Question

**20.** Faisal Sham supervises a group of seven project engineers. His unit is experiencing a heavy workload, as the demand for different versions of one of his firm's computer components is growing. Faisal finds that he doesn't have time to follow up on all design details for each version. Up until now he has tried to do this all by himself. Two of the engineers have shown interest in helping him coordinate work on the various designs. As a consultant, how would you advise Faisal in terms of delegating work to them?

# Further Reflection: Empowerment

Organization structures help bring order to organizational complexity. They put people together in ways that, on paper at least, make good sense in terms of getting tasks accomplished.

One thing we know is that all structural alternatives struggle for success at times. Things can change fast and you might think of today's structures as solutions to yesterday's problems. This puts a great burden on people to fill in the gaps and deal spontaneously with things that structures don't or can't cover at any point in time.

**Empowerment** is a way of unlocking talent. It gives people freedom to make decisions about how they work. Many managers fail when it comes to empowerment. And when they do, their organizations often underperform.

### DO IT NOW... LOOK IN THE MIRROR

- Are you someone who easily and comfortably empowers others? Or, do you suffer from control anxiety and lack the willingness to delegate?
- The next time you are in a study or work group, be a self-observer. The question is: How well do you handle empowerment?
- Write a short narrative that would accurately describe your behavior to someone who wasn't present. Focus on both your tendencies to empower others and how you respond when others empower you.
- Compare that narrative with the results from the Self-Assessment—Empowering Others.

# Self-Assessment: Empowering Others

## Instructions

Think of times when you have been in charge of a group in a work or student situation. Complete the following questionnaire by recording how you feel about each statement according to this scale:[45]

| 1 | 2 | 3 | 4 | 5 |
|---|---|---|---|---|
| Strongly disagree | Disagree | Neutral | Agree | Strongly agree |

When in charge of a team, I find that:

1. Most of the time other people are too inexperienced to do things, so I prefer to do them myself.
2. It often takes more time to explain things to others than to just do them myself.
3. Mistakes made by others are costly, so I don't assign much work to them.
4. Some things simply should not be delegated to others.
5. I often get quicker action by doing a job myself.
6. Many people are good only at very specific tasks, so they can't be assigned additional responsibilities.
7. Many people are too busy to take on additional work.
8. Most people just aren't ready to handle additional responsibilities.
9. In my position, I should be entitled to make my own decisions.

## Scoring

Total your responses to get an overall score. Possible scores range from 9 to 45.

## Interpretation

The lower your score, the more willing you appear to be to delegate to others. Willingness to delegate is an important managerial characteristic. It is how you, as a manager, can "empower" others and give them opportunities to assume responsibility and exercise self-control in their work. With the growing importance of horizontal organizations and empowerment in the new workplace, your willingness to delegate is worth thinking about seriously.

# Team Exercise:
## Designing a Network University

### Instructions

Form into groups as assigned by the instructor. In the group do the following:

1. Discuss the concept of the network organization structure as described in the textbook.

2. Create a network organization structure for your college or university. Identify the "core staffing" and what will be outsourced. Identify how outsourcing will be managed.

3. Draw a diagram depicting the various elements in your "Network U."

4. Identify why "Network U" will be able to meet two major goals: (a) Create high levels of student learning and (b) operate with cost efficiency.

5. Present and justify your design for "Network U" to the class.

## Career Situations for Organizing:
## What Would You Do?

1. **The New Branch Manager** As the newly promoted manager of a branch bank location, you will be leading a team of 22 people. Most members have worked together for a number of years. How can you discover the informal structure of the branch? Once you understand it, how will you try to use informal structure to advantage while establishing yourself as an effective manager in this situation?

2. **Advisor to the Business School** The typical university business school is organized on a functional basis, with departments heads in accounting, finance, information systems, management, and marketing all reporting to a dean. You are on your alma mater's advisory board and the dean is asking for advice. What suggestions might you give for redesigning this structure to increase communication and collaboration across departments, as well as improve curriculum integration for students in all areas of study?

3. **Entrepreneur's Dilemma** As the owner of a small computer repair and services business, you would like to allow employees more flexibility in their work schedules. But you also need consistent coverage to handle drop-in customers as well as at-home service calls. There are also times when customers need what they consider to be "emergency" help outside of normal 8 A.M. to 5 P.M. office times. You've got a meeting with employees scheduled for next week. Your goal is to come out of the meeting with a good plan to deal with this staffing dilemma. How can you achieve this goal?

# Case Study

# Nike

Go to *Management Cases for Critical Thinking* to find the recommended case for Chapter 11—"Nike: Spreading Out to Win the Race."

Bill Hogan/Chicago Tribune/MCT/NewsCom

# Wisdom
## Learning From Others

### > HEALTHY LIVING SETS THE TONE AT CLIF BAR

Have you had your Clif Bar today? Lots of people have, thanks to a long bike ride during which Gary Erickson decided he just couldn't eat another of the available energy bars. He went back to experiment in his mother's kitchen and produced the first Clif Bar two years later.

Despite its growth from a one-man operation to one employing 270+ people, Clif's still runs with a commitment to what it calls the "5 aspirations"—"sustaining our planet … community … people … business … brands."

Clif's core values are evident not only in the firm's healthy organic foods and philanthropy, but also in the quality of working life offered to employees.

Picture the "Clifies," working this way:[1]

- Every employee an owner.
- Paid sabbatical leaves of 6 to 8 weeks after seven years.
- If you want, work a flexible schedule to get every other Friday free.
- Get paid for 2.5 hours of workout time each week.
- Bring your pet to work and wear casual clothes.
- Use the in-house concierge service for car washes, laundry, dry cleaning, haircuts, and more.
- Get $6,500 toward a hybrid or bio-diesel automobile.

Why can't more of us find jobs in places like this?

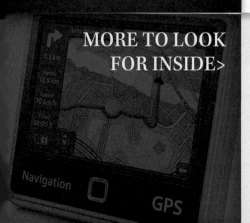

# Organization Culture and Change

## > TOLERANCE FOR AMBIGUITY

Change creates anxiety and breaks us from past habits and conditions. Uncertainty puts many things out of our control. Depending on your **tolerance for ambiguity**, you may be more or less comfortable dealing with these realities.

Which alternatives in the Tolerance for Ambiguity Double Check box best describe you? What are the insights for your tolerance for ambiguity?

It takes personal flexibility and lots of confidence to cope well with unpredictability, whether in a college course or in a work situation. Some people struggle with the unfamiliar. They prefer structure, security, and clear directions. They get comfortable with fixed patterns in life and can be afraid of anything "new."

Have we been talking about you? Or are you willing and able to work with less structure? Do you enjoy flexibility, setting your own goals, and making decisions? Are you excited by prospects of change and new opportunities?

It's important to find a good fit between your personal preferences and the pace and nature of change in the career field and organizations in which you choose to work. To achieve this fit, you have to understand your tolerance for ambiguity and how you react in change situations.

## Insight
### Learning About Yourself

An instructor who gives precise assignments and accepts no deviations *or* one who gives open-ended assignments and lets students suggest alternatives?

⬇ **In a typical course, do you prefer...** ⬆

An instructor who keeps modifying the course syllabus using student feedback *or* one who gives out a detailed syllabus and sticks to it?

## BUILD SKILLS AND COMPETENCIES AT END OF CHAPTER

- Engage in *Further Reflection on Your Tolerance for Ambiguity*
- Take the *Self-Assessment—Change Leadership IQ*
- Prepare for the *Team Exercise—Force-Field Analysis*
- Solve the *Career Situations for Organizational Culture and Change*
- Analyze the *Case Study—"Apple, Inc.: People and Design Create the Future"*

## <GET TO KNOW YOURSELF BETTER

There's little doubt that discomfort with change can bog organizations and their leaders down, making it hard for them to keep pace with new environmental challenges. When General Motors was struggling to restructure during the financial crisis, board chairman Ed Whitacre fired then CEO Fritz Henderson. Whitacre and GM's board were frustrated with the slow pace of change and wanted more measurable progress. They believed the firm and its executives should take more risks; and, they held Henderson accountable for being slow to make needed changes happen. Notably, they were critical of what was being called "GM's cautious culture."[2]

## Organizational Cultures

Think of the stores where you shop; the restaurants that you patronize; the place where you work. What is the "climate" like? Do you notice, for example, that the stores of major retailers like Anthropologie, Gap, Hollister, and Banana Republic have atmospheres that seem to fit their brands and customer identities?[3] Such aspects of the internal environments of organizations are important in management, and the term used to describe them is **organizational culture**. This is the system of shared beliefs and values that shapes and guides the behavior of its members.[4] It is also often called the *corporate culture*, and through its influence on employees and customers it can have a big impact on performance.[5]

The organizational culture is what you see and hear when walking around an organization as a visitor, a customer, or an employee. Look carefully, check the atmosphere, and listen to the conversations. Whenever someone speaks of "the way we do things here," for example, that person is shedding insight into the organization's culture. Just as nations, ethnic groups, and families have cultures, organizations also have cultures that create unique identities and help to distinguish them from one another.

**Organizational culture** is the system of shared beliefs and values that guides behavior in organizations.

# Understanding Organizational Culture

At Zappos.com, a popular e-tailer of shoes, CEO Tony Hsieh has built a fun, creative, and customer-centered culture. He says: "The original idea was to add a little fun," and then everyone joined in the idea that "We can do it better." Now the notion of an unhappy Zappos customer is almost unthinkable. "They may only call once in their life," says Hsieh, "but that is our chance to wow them."[6] Hsieh's advice is that if you "get the culture right, most of the other stuff, like brand and the customer service, will just happen."[7] Amazon.com CEO Jeff Bezos liked Zappos so much he bought the company, and the Girl Scouts send executives to study Zappos' culture and bring back ideas for improving their own.

## ManagementSmarts

### Questions for reading an organization's culture

- How tight or loose is the structure?
- Do most decisions reflect change or the status quo?
- What outcomes or results are most highly valued?
- What is the climate for risk taking and innovation?
- How widespread are empowerment and worker involvement?
- What is the competitive style, internal and external?
- What value is placed on people, as customers and employees?
- Is teamwork a way of life in this organization?

## Types of Organization Cultures

Management Smarts offers ideas for reading organizational cultures based on things such as innovation and risk taking, teamwork, people orientation, and emphasis on outcomes. When such questions are asked and answered, different culture types can be identified. The consulting firm LeadershipIQ, for example, describes four common organizational cultures this way. *Hierarchical cultures* emphasize tradition and clear roles; *dependable cultures* emphasize process and slow change; *enterprising cultures* emphasize creativity and competition; and, *social cultures* emphasize collaboration and trust. How do these options sound to you? According to LeadershipIQ, employees give enterprising cultures the highest marks for engagement and motivation, and as good places to work.[8]

## Strong Organizational Cultures

The best organizations are likely to have strong cultures that are clear, well defined, and widely shared among members. These cultures encourage positive work behaviors and discourage dysfunctional ones. Have you visited Disneyland or Disney World? Think about how the employees acted, how the park ran, and how consistently and positively all visitors were treated. Strong organizational cultures like Disney's respect members while being customer driven and performance oriented.[9]

One of the ways organizations build strong and positive cultures is through **socialization**. This is the process of helping new members learn the culture and values of the organization.[10] Socialization often begins in an anticipatory sense with one's education, such as teaching business students the importance of professional appearance and interpersonal skills. It continues with an employer's orientation and training programs, which, when well done, can have a strong influence on the new member. Disney's strong culture is supported by major investments in socializing and training new hires. Founder Walt Disney is quoted as saying: "You can dream, create, design and build the most wonderful place in the world, but it requires people to make the dream a reality."[11]

**Socialization** is the process through which new members learn the culture of an organization.

## Respect for Traditions Helps Strong Disney Culture Travel the World

Organizational culture is a core competency at Disney, Inc. Each new hire attends a program called Traditions. It informs them on the company history, its language and lore, and its founding story. The goal is to make sure people learn the culture and commit to making the Disney dream a reality. Attention to detail, organizational pride, and keeping the magic alive are described and taught as essential parts of shared Disney identities. And it works—the Disney culture is strong and clear to employees and visitors alike. Walt Disney's legacy has endured as families around the world continue to enter his lands of enchantment.

Ke Xin/Color China Photos/Zuma Press

# The Observable Culture of Organizations

Organizational culture is usually described from the perspective of the two levels shown in Figure 12.1. The outer level is the "observable" culture, and the inner level is the "core" culture.[12] As suggested by the figure, you might think of organizational culture as an iceberg. That which stands out above the surface and is more visible to the discerning eye is the observable culture. What lies below the surface and is harder to see is the core culture.

The observable culture is visible and readily apparent at the surface of every organization. It is expressed in the way people dress at work, how they arrange their offices, how they speak to and behave toward one another, the nature of their conversations, and how they talk about and treat their customers. Test this out the next time you go in a store, restaurant, or service establishment. How do people look, act, and behave? How do they treat one another? How do they treat customers? What's in their conversations? Are they enjoying themselves? When you answer these questions, you are starting to identify the observable culture of the organization.

The observable culture is also found in the stories, heroes, rituals, and symbols that are part of daily organizational life. In the university it includes the pageantry of graduation and honors ceremonies; in sports teams it's the pregame rally, sidelines peptalk, and all the "thumping and bumping" that takes place after a good play. In workplaces like Apple, Zappos, and Amazon, it's in the stories told about the founders and the firm's history. It's also present in spontaneous celebrations of a work accomplishment or personal milestone such as a coworker's birthday.

FIGURE 12.1 **Levels of organizational culture—observable culture and core culture in the organizational "iceberg."**

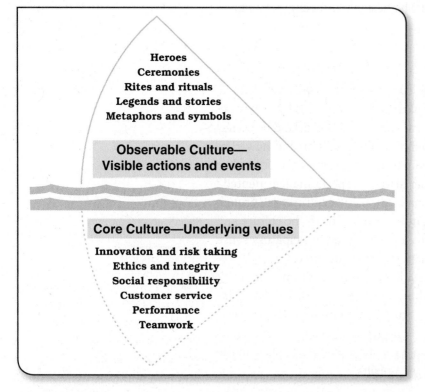

Heroes
Ceremonies
Rites and rituals
Legends and stories
Metaphors and symbols

**Observable Culture—
Visible actions and events**

**Core Culture—Underlying values**

Innovation and risk taking
Ethics and integrity
Social responsibility
Customer service
Performance
Teamwork

When you are trying to understand the observable culture of an organization, look for the following:[13]

- *Heroes*—the people singled out for special attention and whose accomplishments are recognized with praise and admiration; they include founders and role models.
- *Ceremonies, rites, and rituals*—the ceremonies and meetings, planned and spontaneous, that celebrate important events and accomplishments.
- *Legends and stories*—oral histories and tales, told and retold among members, about dramatic sagas and incidents in the life of the organization.
- *Metaphors and symbols*—the special use of language and other nonverbal expressions that communicate important themes and values of the organization.

## Values and the Core Culture of Organizations

A second and deeper level of organizational culture is the **core culture**. It consists of the **core values** or underlying assumptions and beliefs that shape and guide people's behaviors. You know core values, so to speak, when you experience them. This may be when you are trying to claim lost luggage at an airline counter and are treated really well, or are returning a product to a retail store and are greeted with a smile and "no questions asked." Values set in the core culture are a strong influence on how such transactions play out. And when customer experiences aren't as positive as these, the culprit may well be weak or just plain bad core values.

Values in some of the best companies have been found to emphasize performance excellence, innovation, social responsibility, integrity, worker involvement, customer service, and teamwork.[14] Examples of values driving strong-culture firms include "service above all else" at Nordstrom; "science-based innovation" at Merck; "encouraging individual initiative and creativity" at Sony; and "fanatical attention to consistency and detail" at Disney.[15]

The **core culture** consists of the core values, or underlying assumptions and beliefs that shape and guide people's behaviors in an organization.

**Core values** are beliefs and values shared by organization members.

### Value-Based Management

Don't be fooled by values statements alone when trying to read or understand an organization's core culture. It's easy to write a set of values, post them on the Web, and talk about them. It's a lot harder to live up to them. If core values as stated are to have any positive effects, everyone in the organization from top to bottom must reflect the values in day-to-day actions. In this sense managers have a special responsibility to "walk the values talk" and make the expressed values real.

Glen Argov/Landov LLC.

## Management Decisions at Tom's of Maine Are Guided by Core Values

After a big investment in a new deodorant, Tom's of Maine founder Tom Chappell was dismayed when he learned that customers were not happy with it. But having founded the company on values that include fairness and honesty in all matters, he decided to pull the product from the market and reimburse customers who had purchased it. Even though the costs of the recall were high, Tom did what he believed was the right thing. In this case, his decision not only lived up to the full spirit of the company's values, it set a positive example for others in the firm to follow.

How would you react if you found out senior executives in your organization talked up values such as honesty and ethical behavior, but then acted quite differently—perhaps by spending company funds on lavish private parties and personal travel? Most likely you'd be upset and justifiably so.

The term **value-based management** describes managers who actively help develop, communicate, and enact core values within an organization. Although you might tend to associate value-based management with top executives only, the responsibility extends to all managers and team leaders. Like the organization as a whole, any work team or group will have a culture. The nature of this culture and its influence on team outcomes will have a lot to do with how the team leader behaves as a values champion and role model.

**Value-based management** actively develops, communicates, and enacts shared values.

---

**FOLLOW THE STORY**

> ONE OF FORD'S SENIOR MANAGERS SAYS: "I'VE NEVER HAD SUCH CONSISTENCY OF PURPOSE BEFORE."

## Alan Mulally Makes His Mark on Ford's Culture

Laura Rauch/©AP/Wide World Photos

Why is it that a CEO brought in from outside the industry fared the best as the Big Three automakers went into crisis mode during the economic downturn? That's a question that Ford Motor Company's chairman, William Clay Ford Jr., is happy to answer. And the person he's talking about is Alan Mulally, a former Boeing executive hired by Ford to retool the firm and put it back on a competitive track.

Many wondered at the time if an "airplane guy" could run an auto company. It isn't easy to come in from outside an industry and successfully lead a huge firm. But Mulally's management experience and insights proved well up to the task. One consultant says: "The speed with which Mulally has

transformed Ford into a more nimble and healthy operation has been one of the more impressive jobs I've seen."

In addition to making changes to modernize plants and streamline operations, Mulally tackled Ford's bureaucracy—particularly functional chimneys and a lack of open communication. Ford previously had a culture that "loved to meet" and in which managers got together to discuss the message they wanted to communicate to the top executives. Mulally changed all that. He pushed transparency and data-based decision making, cooperation between divisions, and global operations that build vehicles to sell in many markets. When some of the executives balked, he says, "I didn't permit it." And after four years, one of Ford's senior managers says: "I've never had such consistency of purpose before."

Ford is a dividend-paying stock once again. Of course, the future for the global economy is still uncertain and lots of challenges lie ahead. But for now Mulally has certainly done his job well and gained lots of respect for his executive prowess. That's pretty good for an airplane executive who stepped in to drive a firm in the auto industry. Now the next big question for Ford may well be: who's going to replace Mulally? He's due for retirement soon.

 **WHAT'S YOUR TAKE?**

What are the advantages of taking a top leadership job and coming from outside of the industry? What are the potential disadvantages? Can part of Mulally's success be attributed to confidence and a willingness to make major changes at Ford right from the beginning? What are the lessons here for any manager taking a new position in any organization? And how about the person who follows Mulally as Ford's next CEO. Will Mulally's success make the task easier or harder?

## Workplace Spirituality

It is becoming popular to discuss **workplace spirituality** along with value-based management. Although the first tendency might be to associate "spirituality" with religion, the term is used more broadly in management to describe an organizational culture in which people find meaning and a sense of shared community in their work. The foundation for workplace spirituality is respect for the full value of human beings. The guiding principle is that people are inwardly enriched by meaningful work and a sense of personal connection with others inside and outside of the organization.[16]

A culture of workplace spirituality will have strong ethics foundations, recognize human dignity, respect diversity, and focus on linking jobs with an organization's contributions to society. Anyone who works in or leads a culture of workplace spirituality should derive pleasure from knowing that what is being accomplished is personally meaningful, created through community, and valued by others. The decision making at Tom's of Maine by CEO Tom Chappell in the last photo essay meets this test. Even though his decision to recall an unpopular product and give customer refunds had a high monetary cost for the company, it lived up to his sense of ethics and his firm's core values.[17]

**Workplace spirituality** creates meaning and shared community among organizational members.

> ### SAMPLE VALUES IN SPIRITUAL ORGANIZATIONAL CULTURES
>
> - Meaningful purpose
> - Trust and respect
> - Honesty and openness
> - Personal growth and development
> - Worker friendly practices
> - Ethics and social responsibility

---

### LEARNING CHECK 1

**TAKEAWAY QUESTION 1 What is organizational culture?**

**Be sure you can** • define *organizational culture* and explain the importance of strong cultures to organizations • define and explain the process of *socialization* • distinguish between the observable and core cultures • explain how value-based management helps build strong culture organizations • describe how workplace spirituality gets reflected, or not, in an organization's culture

---

# Multicultural Organizations

In his book, *Beyond Race and Gender*, consultant R. Roosevelt Thomas Jr. makes the link between organizational culture and diversity.[18] He believes that the way people are treated at work—with respect and inclusion, or with disrespect and exclusion—is a direct reflection of the organization's culture and its leadership. He also believes that organizations whose cultures respect diversity gain performance advantages from the wide mixture of talents and perspectives they can draw upon.

The term **multiculturalism** refers to inclusiveness, pluralism, and respect for diversity in the workplace. In a truly **multicultural organization** the organizational culture communicates and supports core values that respect and empower the full diversity of its members. Such a multicultural organization has these characteristics.[19]

- *Pluralism*—Members of both minority cultures and majority cultures are influential in setting key values and policies.
- *Structural integration*—Minority-culture members are well represented in jobs at all levels and in all functional responsibilities.
- *Informal network integration*—Various forms of mentoring and support groups assist in the career development of minority-culture members.

**Multiculturalism** in organizations involves inclusiveness, pluralism, and respect for diversity.

A **multicultural organization** has a culture with core values that respect diversity and support multiculturalism.

- *Absence of prejudice and discrimination*—A variety of training and task-force activities address the need to eliminate culture-group biases.
- *Minimum intergroup conflict*—Diversity does not lead to destructive conflicts between members of majority and minority cultures.

## Multicultural Organizations and Performance

What many call the "business case for diversity" is increasingly clear. The *Gallup Management Journal* reports that a racially and ethnically inclusive workplace is good for morale. In a study of 2,014 American workers, those who felt included were more likely to stay with their employers and recommend them to others.[20] And in respect to gender diversity, a Catalyst study also found that firms with at least three female board members achieved a higher return on equity than did firms with no women on their boards.[21] But Thomas Kochan and his colleagues at MIT warn that the presence of diversity alone does not guarantee a positive performance impact. It's only when diversity is backed by training and supportive human resource practices that the advantages are gained. In other words, respect for diversity must be firmly embedded in the organizational culture. Kochan et al. summarize their findings with this guidance.[22]

> To be successful in working with and gaining value from diversity requires a sustained, systemic approach and long-term commitment. Success is facilitated by a perspective that considers diversity to be an opportunity for everyone in an organization to learn from each other how better to accomplish their work and an occasion that requires a supportive and cooperative organizational culture as well as group leadership and process skills that can facilitate effective group functioning.

## Organizational Subcultures

Like society as a whole, organizations contain a mixture of **organizational subcultures**. These are cultures common to groups of people that share similar values and beliefs based on their work responsibilities and social identities. Subcultures often complicate the task of tapping the full potential of diverse workforces and creating truly multicultural organizations. Just as with life in general, **ethnocentrism**—the belief that one's membership group or subculture is superior to all others—can creep into organizations and adversely affect the way people relate to one another.

Age differences create **generational subcultures** in organizations.[23] Several generations can mix in an organization today, ranging from post–World War II Baby Boomers to the latest Internet generation.[24] Just imagine the possible conflicts when today's college graduates end up working for older managers who grew up with quite different life experiences and values. Harris and Conference Board polls report that younger workers tend to be more dissatisfied than older workers.[25] They are also described as more short-term oriented, giving higher priority to work–life balance, and expecting to hold several jobs during their careers.[26]

**Gender subcultures** form in organizations as persons of the same gender share identities. Research shows that when men

**Organizational subcultures** are groups of people who share similar beliefs and values based on their work or personal characteristics.

**Ethnocentrism** is the belief that one's membership group or subculture is superior to all others.

**Generational subcultures** form among persons who work together and share similar ages, such as Millennials and Baby Boomers.

**Gender subcultures** form among persons who work together and share the same gender identities.

### TIPS FOR WORKING WITH THE MILLENNIAL GENERATION

- Challenge them—give meaningful work.
- Reward them with responsibility and recognition for accomplishments.
- Ask their opinion, avoid command-and-control approaches.
- Link them with an experienced mentor.
- Give frequent feedback; they're used to instantaneous gratification.

## Organization Cultures Must Face Up to Emerging Work–Life Trends

If you have any doubts regarding the importance of work–life issues and their implications for organizational cultures and management practices, consider these facts:

- 78% of American couples are dual-wage earners.
- 63% believe they don't have enough time for their spouses or partners.
- 74% believe they don't have enough time for their children.
- 35% are spending time caring for elderly relatives.
- Both Baby Boomers (87%) and Millennials (89%) rate flexible work as important.

- Both Baby Boomers (63%) and Millennials (69%) want opportunities to work remotely at least part of the time.

 **YOUR THOUGHTS?**

What organizational culture issues are raised by these facts? What should employers do to best respond to the situation described here? And when it comes to you, are you prepared to succeed in a work culture that doesn't respect these facts? Or, are you preparing right now to always find and be attractive to employers that do?

---

work together, a subgroup culture may form around a competitive climate where sports metaphors are common and games and stories often deal with winning and losing.[27] When women work together, the subculture may give more emphasis to personal relationships and collaboration.[28]

**Ethnic subcultures** or **national subcultures** form in the workplace among people sharing the same background in terms of ethnicities, home countries, or world regions. The world of work today is one of diverse cultural communities. And it's often a more complicated world than it looks at first glance. Current events, for example, sometimes show how difficult it can be for members of "African American" or "Latino" or "Anglo" cultures to fully understand and respect one another.[29] We often talk about improving cross-cultural understandings across national boundaries. Shouldn't the same understandings help us relate better to one another in the same workplace?

> **Ethnic subcultures** or **national subcultures** form among people who work together and have roots in the same ethnic community, country, or region of the world.

The many possible subcultures in organizations also include **occupational and functional subcultures** that form among persons that share the same professions and skills.[30] And, people from different occupations and functions can have difficulty understanding and working well with one another. Employees in a business firm, for example, may consider themselves "systems people" or "marketing people" or "manufacturing people" or "finance people." When such identities are overemphasized, members of the functional groups spend most of their time with each other, develop a shared "jargon" or technical language, and view their roles in the organization as more important than those of the other functions. It's easy under such conditions for teamwork across the occupational or functional boundaries to suffer.

> **Occupational and functional subcultures** form among persons who share the same skills and work responsibilities.

## Diversity Issues and Organizational Cultures

The very term *diversity* basically means the presence of differences. But what happens when those differences are distributed unequally among organizational subcultures and power structures? That is, what happens when one subculture is in "majority" status while others become "minorities"?

FIGURE 12.2 **Glass ceilings as barriers to women and minority cultures in traditional organizations.**

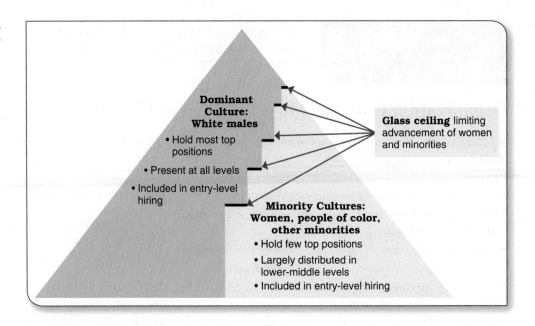

## Glass Ceilings

The **glass ceiling** is an invisible barrier to advancement by women and minorities in organizations.

Even though organizations are changing, there is still likely to be more workforce diversity at lower and middle levels than at the top. Look at Figure 12.2. It depicts the **glass ceiling** as an invisible barrier that limits the advancement of women and minorities in some organizations. What are the implications for minority members seeking to advance and prosper in an organization where the majority culture consists of white males? How easy is it for women and persons of color to move up when promotions are controlled by decision makers who are part of an alternative and dominant culture?

Take the case of women. They constitute more than 50% of the U.S. workforce and hold 53% of entry-level jobs. So, why were there only 18 female CEOs of *Fortune* 500 firms in 2012? Why did women hold just 3% of CEO positions and 19% of top executive jobs in publicly traded companies?[31]

One reason why more women aren't getting to the top is that so many plateau or drop out at earlier career stages. Sometimes called "falling off the cliff," this glass ceiling effect isn't always based on outright gender prejudice. But it can trace to male-dominant organizational cultures that make it hard for women to advance.[32] Ambitious women may lack female role models and have difficulty finding top managers to advocate and sponsor their career progress. Executive mindsets may have a hard time tolerating women who want both families and careers. Even as employers put into place family-friendly human resource policies, some women still feel forced at times to choose between career and family—a choice that career often loses. The term **leaking pipeline problem** is used to describe situations where qualified and high-performing women drop out of upward career paths for these and other glass ceiling reasons.

The **leaking pipeline problem** is where glass ceilings and other obstacles cause qualified and high-performing women to drop out of upward career paths.

## Harassment and Discrimination

The subculture challenges faced by minorities and women can range from misunderstandings and lack of sensitivity on the one hand to outright sexual harassment and discrimination on the other. Data from the U.S. Equal Employment Opportunity Commission (EEOC), for example, show that a growing number of bias suits are being filed by workers and that sex discrimination is a factor in some 30% of them.[33] The EEOC also reports an increase in pregnancy discrimination complaints.[34] Pay discrimination is another issue. A senior executive in the computer industry reported her surprise at finding out that the top performer in her work group, an African American male, was paid 25% less than anyone else. This wasn't because his pay had been cut to that level, she said. It was because his pay increases had always trailed those given to his white coworkers. The differences added up significantly over time, but no one noticed or stepped forward to make the appropriate adjustment.[35]

Sometimes members of minority cultures try to adapt through tendencies toward **biculturalism**. This is the display of majority culture characteristics that seem necessary to succeed in the work environment. For example, one might find gays and lesbians hiding their sexual orientation from coworkers out of fear of prejudice or discrimination. Similarly, one might find an African American carefully training herself to not use certain words or phrases at work that might be considered as subculture slang by white coworkers.

> **Biculturalism** is when minority members adopt characteristics of majority cultures in order to succeed.

## Diversity Leadership

There should be no doubt that all workers want the same things everyone wants—respect for their talents and a work setting that allows them to achieve their full potential. It takes an inclusive organizational culture and the best in diversity leadership at all levels of organizational management to meet these expectations.

R. Roosevelt Thomas describes the continuum of leadership approaches to diversity shown here. The first is *affirmative action*, in which leadership commits the organization to hiring and advancing minorities and women. The second is *valuing diversity*, in which leadership commits the organization to education and training programs designed to help people better understand and respect individual differences. The third and most comprehensive is **managing diversity**, in which leadership creates an orga-

> **Managing diversity** is a leadership approach that creates an organizational culture that respects diversity and supports multiculturalism.

nizational culture that allows all members, minorities and women included, to reach their full potential.[36] Leaders committed to managing diversity build organization cultures that are what Thomas calls diversity mature.[37] They have a diversity mission as well as an organizational mission, and they view diversity as a strategic imperative.

| *Affirmative Action* Create upward mobility for minorities and women | *Valuing Differences* Build quality relationships with respect for diversity | *Managing Diversity* Achieve full utilization of diverse human resources |
|---|---|---|

---

**LEARNING CHECK 2**

**TAKEAWAY QUESTION 2 What is a multicultural organization?**

**Be sure you can** • define *multiculturalism* and explain the concept of a multicultural organization • identify common organizational subcultures • discuss glass ceilings and employment problems faced by minorities and women • explain Thomas's concept of managing diversity

# Organizational Change

What if the existing culture of an organization is flawed, doesn't drive high performance, and needs to be changed? What if organizational subcultures are clashing and adjustments must be made? What can a leader do if diversity isn't valued on a team or in an organization?

We use the word *change* so much that the tendency may be to make culture changes like these seem easy, almost a matter of routine. But that's not always the case.[38] Former British Airways CEO Sir Rod Eddington once said that "Altering an airline's culture is like trying to perform an engine change in flight."[39]

## Models of Change Leadership

A **change leader** takes initiative in trying to change the behavior of another person or social system.

A **change leader** is someone who takes initiative to change the existing pattern of behavior of another person or social system. These are managers who act as *change agents* and make things happen, even when inertia has made systems and people reluctant to embrace new ways of doing things. Managers who are strong change leaders are alert to cultures, situations, and people needing change, open to good ideas and opportunities, and ready and able to support the implementation of new ideas in actual practice.

In theory, every manager should act as a change leader. But the reality is that people show major tendencies toward staying with the status quo—accepting things as they are and not wanting to change. Figure 12.3 contrasts a true "change leader" with a "status quo manager." Whereas the status quo manager is backward-looking, reactive, and comfortable with habit, the change leader is forward-looking, proactive, supportive of new ideas, and comfortable with criticism. At Xerox, for example, CEO Ursula Burns talks about the "Xerox family" when referring to her firm's corporate

---

ETHICS
ON THE LINE

> SOME MANAGERS USE DECEPTION TO AVOID LOSING POWER
WHILE GIVING THE APPEARANCE OF SHARING POWER

## Hidden Agendas in Organizational Change

Image Source/Alamy

Some managers are afraid of losing power while sharing power during organizational change. So, they resort to hidden agendas. They handpick key members to be on change teams. They ask them to also take prominent roles in discussions and support only the "right" ideas. The goal is to make sure that change heads in the preferred direction while still giving everyone a sense of being included and empowered. It's a way of sharing power but still getting your way.

### ETHICS QUESTIONS

Although this situation happens frequently in organizations, does that make it right? What are the ethical issues involved? When is such an approach more or less likely to be ethical? As a manager, would you handpick the leaders of a change effort in order to get your way—even if that meant that alternative points of view were excluded from the process? What if your boss selected you to represent your department on a task force just because you agreed with his or her favored approach? If you knew that most people in your department disagreed, would you do what your boss wanted or would you try to represent the wishes of the majority of your department?

Sharing power is a popular choice for change strategy. It means allowing others to have a role in decision making and be involved throughout the change process. It gets a lot of good ideas on the table and helps generate all-important "buy-in" to support the proposed change. But, suppose the ideas offered and the ensuing conversations move in a direction that top management thinks is the wrong pathway? What happens then?

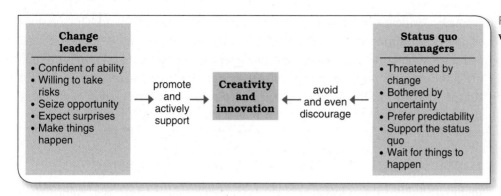

FIGURE 12.3 **Change leaders versus status quo managers.**

culture. But when speaking to employees as a change leader, she also says: "When we're in the family, you don't have to be as nice as when you're outside the family. I want us to stay civil and kind, but we have to be frank—and the reason we can be frank is because we're all in the same family."[40]

## Top-Down Change

**Top-down change** is where senior managers initiate changes with the goal of improving organizational performance. Although it sounds straightforward, research indicates that some 70% or more of large-scale change efforts in American firms actually fail; only 20% of European firms report "substantial success" with large-scale change, while 63% report "occasional" success.[41]

> In **top-down change**, the change initiatives come from senior management.

The most common reason for the failure of top-down change is poor implementation. And without doubt, people are more committed to implement plans that they have played a part in creating. Change programs have little chance of success without the support of those who must implement them. Any change that is driven from the top and perceived as insensitive to the needs of lower-level personnel can easily fail. As the lessons in Management Smarts show, successful top-down change is led in ways that earn the support of others throughout the organization.[42]

## Bottom-Up Change

**Bottom-up change** tries to tap into ideas and initiative at lower organizational levels and let them percolate upward. Such change is made possible by management commitments to empowerment, involvement, and participation.

> In **bottom-up change**, change initiatives come from all levels in the organization.

Many organizations are so large it is easy for good ideas to get lost. One way to unlock the potential for bottom-up change is through "diagonal slice meetings" where top managers meet with samples of workers from across functions and levels. They solicit ideas about what might be wrong and what changes might be made to improve things. Another way is to build an organizational culture around the belief that workers should be encouraged to use their job knowledge and common sense to improve things.

At General Electric, former CEO Jack Welch harnessed bottom-up change

## Management**Smarts**

### How to lead organizational change

- Establish a sense of urgency for change.
- Form a powerful coalition to lead the change.
- Create and communicate a change vision.
- Empower others to move change forward.
- Celebrate short-term "wins" and recognize those who help.
- Build on success; align people and systems with the new ways.
- Stay with it; keep the message consistent; champion the vision.

through a widely benchmarked program called Work-Out. In Work-Out sessions employees confront their managers in a "town meeting" format with the manager in front listening to suggestions. The managers are expected to respond immediately and support positive change initiatives raised during the session. Welch felt that approaches like this facilitate change because they "bring an innovation debate to the people closest to the products, services, and processes."[43]

## Incremental and Transformational Change

Planned changes at top levels are likely to be large-scale and strategic repositioning changes focused on big issues that affect the organization as a whole. Lower-level changes often deal with adjustments in structures, systems, technologies, products, and people to support strategic positioning. Both types of changes—incremental and transformational— are important in the organizational change pyramid shown here.[44]

**Incremental change** is modest, frame-bending change. It basically bends or nudges existing systems and practices to better align them with emerging problems and opportunities. The intent isn't to break and remake the system, but to move it forward through continuous improvements. Common incremental changes in organizations involve evolutions in products, processes, technologies, and work systems. **Transformational change**, by contrast, is radical or frame-breaking change that results in a major and comprehensive redirection of the organization.[45] It is usually led from the top and creates fundamental shifts in strategies, culture, structures, and even the underlying sense of purpose or mission. Incremental changes keep things tuned up—like the engine in a car, in between transformations—as when the old car is replaced with a new one.

**Incremental change** bends and adjusts existing ways to improve performance.

**Transformational change** results in a major and comprehensive redirection of the organization.

## Phases of Planned Change

Managers seeking to lead change in organizations can benefit from a simple but helpful model developed many years ago by the psychologist Kurt Lewin. He recommends that any planned change be viewed as a process with the three phases. Phase 1 is *unfreezing*—preparing a system for change; phase 2 is *changing*—making actual changes in the system; and phase 3 is *refreezing*—stabilizing the system after change.[46] In today's fast-paced organizational environments we can also talk about another phase called *improvising*—making adjustments as needed while change is taking place.[47]

### Unfreezing

**Unfreezing** is the phase during which a situation is prepared for change.

Planned change has a better chance for success when people are ready for it and open to doing things differently. **Unfreezing** is the phase in which a situation is prepared for change and felt needs for change are developed. The goal is to get people to view change as a way of solving a problem or pursuing an opportunity.

Some call unfreezing the "burning bridge" phase of change, arguing that in order to get people to jump off a bridge you might just have to set it on fire. Managers can

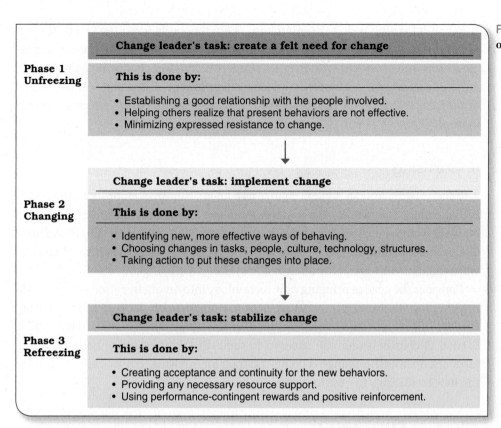

FIGURE 12.4   **Lewin's three phases of planned organizational change.**

simulate the burning bridge by engaging people with facts and information that communicate the need for change—environmental pressures, declining performance, and examples of benchmarks or alternative approaches. And as you have probably experienced, conflict can help people to break old habits and recognize new ways of thinking about or doing things. Errors at the unfreezing stage include not creating a sense of urgency for change and neglecting to build a coalition of influential persons who support it.

## Changing

Figure 12.4 shows that unfreezing is followed by the **changing** phase, where actual changes are made in such organizational targets as tasks, people, culture, technology, and structure. Lewin believes that many change agents commit the error of entering the changing phase prematurely. They are too quick to change things and end up creating harmful resistance. In this sense the change process is like building a house; you need to put a good foundation in place before you begin the framing. If you try to implement change before people are prepared and feel a need for it, there is an increased likelihood of failure.

**Changing** is the phase where a planned change actually takes place.

## Refreezing

The final phase in Lewin's planned change process is **refreezing**. Here, the manager is concerned about stabilizing the change. Refreezing is accomplished by linking change with appropriate rewards, positive reinforcement, and resource support. It is important in this phase to evaluate results, provide feedback to the people involved, and make any required modifications in the original change.

**Refreezing** is the phase at which change is stabilized.

When refreezing is done poorly, changes are too easily forgotten or abandoned with the passage of time. The most common error at the refreezing stage is declaring victory too soon and withdrawing support before the change is really fixed in normal routines. Also, in today's dynamic environments there may not be a lot of time for refreezing before things are ready to change again. We end up preparing for more change even before the present one is fully implemented.

## Improvising

Although Lewin's model depicts change as a linear, step-by-step process, the reality is that change is dynamic and complex. Managers must not only understand each phase of planned change, they must be prepared to deal with them simultaneously. They should also be willing to engage in the process of **improvisational change** where adjustments are continually made as things are being implemented.[48]

Consider the case of bringing new technology into an organization or work unit. A technology that is attractive in concept may appear complicated to the new users. The full extent of its benefits or inadequacies may not become known until it is tried. A change leader can succeed in such situations by continually gathering feedback on how the change is going and then improvising to revise and customize the new technology to best meet users' needs.

**Improvisational change** makes continual adjustments as changes are being implemented.

# Change Strategies

Strategy is a major issue when a manager actually tries to move people and systems toward change. Figure 12.5 summarizes three common strategies used to make things happen during the planned change process—force-coercion, rational persuasion, and shared power.[49] Managers, as change agents and leaders, should understand each strategy and its likely results.

## Force-Coercion Strategies

A **force-coercion strategy** uses formal authority as well as rewards and punishments as the primary inducements to change. A change agent that seeks to create change through force-coercion believes that people are motivated by self-interest and by what the situation offers in terms of potential personal gains or losses.[50]

A **force-coercion strategy** pursues change through formal authority and/or the use of rewards or punishments.

FIGURE 12.5  **Alternative change strategies and their leadership implications.**

| Change Strategy | Power Bases | Managerial Behavior | Likely Results |
|---|---|---|---|
| **Force–Coercion**<br><br>Using formal authority to create change by decree and position power | Legitimacy<br><br>Rewards<br><br>Punishments | *Direct forcing* and unilateral action<br><br>*Political maneuvering* and indirect action | Faster, but low commitment and only temporary compliance |
| **Rational Persuasion**<br><br>Creating change through rational persuasion and empirical argument | Expertise | *Informational efforts* using credible knowledge, demonstrated facts, and logical argument | |
| **Shared power**<br><br>Developing support for change through personal values and commitments | Reference | *Participative efforts* to share power and involve others in planning and implementing change | Slower, but high commitment and longer-term internalization |

In *direct forcing*, the change agent takes direct and unilateral action to "command" that change take place. In *political maneuvering*, the change agent works indirectly to gain special advantage over other persons and thereby make them change. This involves bargaining, obtaining control of important resources, forming alliances, or granting small favors.

The force-coercion strategy of change usually produces limited results. Although it can be quickly tried, most people respond to this strategy out of fear of punishment or hope for a reward. The likely outcome is temporary compliance; the new behavior continues only as long as the rewards and punishments are present. For this reason, force-coercion may be most useful as an unfreezing strategy that helps people break old patterns and gain willingness to try new ones. The earlier example of General Electric's Work-Out program applies here.[51] Jack Welch started Work-Out to create a forum for active employee empowerment of continuous change. But he didn't make the program optional; participation in Work-Out was mandatory. Part of Welch's commitment to change leadership was a willingness to use authority to unfreeze the situation and get Work-Out started. Once the program was under way, he was confident it would survive and prosper on its own—and it did.

## Rational Persuasion Strategies

Change agents using a **rational persuasion strategy** attempt to bring about change through persuasion backed by special knowledge, empirical data, and rational argument. A change agent following this strategy believes that people are inherently rational and guided by reason. Once the value of a specific course of action is demonstrated by information and facts, the change agent assumes that reason and rationality will cause the person to adopt it. A good rational persuasion strategy helps both unfreeze and refreeze a change situation. Although slower than force-coercion, it can result in longer-lasting and more internalized change.

A **rational persuasion strategy** pursues change through empirical data and rational argument.

To succeed with the rational persuasion strategy, a manager must convince others that a change will leave them better off than before. This persuasive power can come directly from the change agent if she or he has personal credibility as an

©Euler/AP/Wide World Photos

### *Change by Design: How Design Thinking Transforms Organizations and Inspires Innovation* (HarperCollins, 2009)
### by Tim Brown

Tim Brown is CEO of the respected design firm IDEO, serving clients like Fisher-Price, Procter & Gamble, and Target. He says that organizations that unlock "design thinking" can achieve radical and highly beneficial changes that improve performance dramatically. Brown describes design thinking as combining "the designer's creative problem-solving skills" with the "larger strategic initiatives" of the organization. An example is IDEO's work with Kaiser Permanente health centers. After a team brought together design experts, nurses, and technologists, they ended up making major changes in how nurses staff hospital shifts.

"expert." It can also be borrowed in the form of advice from consultants and other outside experts, or gained from credible demonstration projects and identified benchmarks. Many firms, for example, benchmark Disney to demonstrate to their own employees the benefits of a customer-oriented culture. A Ford vice president says: "Disney's track record is one of the best in the country as far as dealing with customers."[52] In this sense, the power of rational persuasion is straightforward: if the culture works for Disney, why can't it work for us?

### Shared Power Strategies

> A **shared power strategy** pursues change by participation in assessing change needs, values, and goals.

A **shared power** strategy uses collaboration to identify values, assumptions, and goals from which support for change will naturally emerge. Sometimes called a *normative–reeducative strategy*, this approach is empowerment based and highly participative. It involves others in examining personal needs and values, group norms, and operating goals as they relate to the issues at hand. Power is shared as the change agent and others work together to develop consensus to support needed change. Because it entails a high level of involvement, this strategy is often slow and time consuming. But power sharing is likely to result in longer-lasting, internalized change.

A change agent shares power by recognizing that people have varied needs and complex motivations. He or she understands that organizational changes involve changes in attitudes, values, skills, and significant relationships, not just changes in knowledge, information, or practices. Thus, this change agent is sensitive to the way group pressures can support or inhibit change. Every attempt is made to gather opinions, identify feelings and expectations, and incorporate them fully into the change process.

The great "power" of sharing power in the change process lies with unlocking the creativity, experience, and energies of people within the system. Some managers hesitate to engage this strategy for fear of losing control or of having to compromise on important organizational goals. But Harvard scholar Teresa M. Amabile points out that they should have the confidence to share power regarding means and processes, if not overall goals. "People will be more creative," she says, "if you give them freedom to decide how to climb particular mountains. You needn't let them choose which mountains to climb."[53]

## Resistance to Change

When people resist change, they are most often defending something important to them that now appears threatened. A change leader can learn a lot by listening to resistance and then using it as a resource for improving the change and change process.[54] Check the common

---

## Management**Smarts**

### Why People May Resist Change

- *Fear of the unknown*—not understanding what is happening or what comes next.
- *Disrupted habits*—feeling upset to see the end of the old ways of doing things.
- *Loss of confidence*—feeling incapable of performing well under the new ways of doing things.
- *Loss of control*—feeling that things are being done "to" you rather than "by" or "with" you.
- *Poor timing*—feeling overwhelmed by the situation or that things are moving too fast.
- *Work overload*—not having the physical or emotional energy to commit to the change.
- *Loss of face*—feeling inadequate or humiliated because the "old" ways weren't "good" ways.
- *Lack of purpose*—not seeing a reason for the change and/or not understanding its benefits.

# Top Management Must Get—and Stay—Committed for Shared Power to Work in Tandem with Top-Down Change

Harry Sminia and Antonie Van Nistelrooij's case study of a public-sector organization in the Netherlands sheds light on what happens when top-down change and organization development based on shared power are used simultaneously.

Writing in the *Journal of Change Management,* they describe how top management initiated a strategic change involving organization design, procedures, work standards, and systems. Called the "project strand," this change was well structured with deadlines and a management hierarchy. Simultaneously, a "change strand" was initiated with organization development interventions to develop information and create foundations helpful to the success of the project strand. The change strand involved conferences, workshops, and meetings. The goal was for both strands to operate in parallel and eventually converge in joint implementation.

What the researchers found was that top management favored the project strand and resisted challenges to its decision-making prerogatives that came from the change strand. Eventually, the shared power aspects of the change pretty much disappeared and activities centered around completing the project on schedule. Sminia and Van Nistelrooij conclude that the change was hampered by "management refusal to share power with the employees."

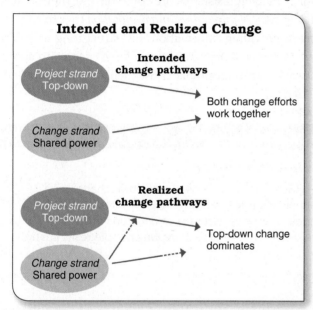

**Intended and Realized Change**

Project strand
Top-down

**Intended
change pathways**

Change strand
Shared power

Both change efforts
work together

Project strand
Top-down

**Realized
change pathways**

Change strand
Shared power

Top-down change
dominates

### ◼ YOU BE THE RESEARCHER

Is it realistic to expect that top-down and bottom-up changes can operate simultaneously? Can any shared power change strategy be successful without full and continuing support from top management? How would you design research projects to test these questions?

*Reference:* Harry Sminia and Antonie Van Nistelrooij, "Strategic Management and Organizational Development: Planned Change in a Public Sector Organization," *Journal of Change Management,* vol. 6 (March 2006), pp. 99–113.

sources of resistance as shown in Management Smarts. Surely you've seen some or all of them. And honestly, haven't you been a resistor at times?

Instead of viewing resistance as something that must be "overcome," it's often better viewed as feedback. The presence of resistance usually means that something can be done to achieve a better "fit" among the planned change, the situation, and the people involved. Things to check when listening to feedback for clues on how to improve the change process include the following.[55]

1. *Check the benefits*—Make sure the people involved see a clear advantage in making the change. People should know "what is in it for me" or "what is in it for our group or the organization as a whole."

2. *Check the compatibility*—Keep the change as close as possible to the existing values and ways of doing things. Minimizing the scope of change helps keep it more acceptable and less threatening.

3. *Check the simplicity*—Make the change as easy as possible to understand and use. People should have access to training and assistance to make the transition to new ways as easy as possible.

4. *Check the triability*—Allow people to try the change little by little, making adjustments as they go. Don't rush the change, and be sure to adjust the timing to best fit work schedules and cycles of high/low workloads.

In addition to these checkpoints, there are other positive ways to deal with resistance to change.[56] *Education and communication* uses discussions, presentations, and demonstrations to educate people beforehand about a change. *Participation and involvement* allows others to contribute ideas and help design and implement the change. *Facilitation and support* provides encouragement and training, actively listens to problems and complaints, and finds ways to reduce performance pressures. *Negotiation and agreement* provides incentives to gain support from those who are actively resisting or ready to resist.

Two other approaches for managing resistance are common, but they are also risky in terms of negative side effects. *Manipulation and co-optation* tries to covertly influence others by selectively providing information and structuring events in favor of the desired change. *Explicit and implicit coercion* forces people to accept change by threatening resistors with undesirable consequences if they don't do what is being asked.

---

**LEARNING CHECK 3**

**TAKEAWAY QUESTION 3 What is the nature of organizational change?**

**Be sure you can** • define *change leader* and *change agent* • discuss pros and cons of top-down change and bottom-up change • differentiate incremental and transformational change • describe Lewin's three phases of planned change • discuss improvising as an approach to planned change • discuss pros and cons of the force-coercion, rational persuasion, and shared power change strategies • list several reasons why people resist change • describe strategies for dealing with resistance to change

# MANAGEMENT LEARNING REVIEW

## LEARNING CHECK SUMMARY

### TAKEAWAY QUESTION 1 What is organizational culture?

- Organizational culture is an internal environment that establishes a personality for the organization and influences the behavior of members.
- The observable culture is found in the rites, rituals, stories, heroes, and symbols of the organization; the core culture consists of the core values and fundamental beliefs on which the organization is based.
- In organizations with strong cultures, members behave with shared understandings and act with commitment to core values.
- Key dimensions of organizational culture include such things as innovation and risk taking, team emphasis, concern for people, and performance orientation.
- Among trends in managing organizational cultures, value-based management and workplace spirituality are popular directions and considerations.

**For Discussion Of the various dimensions of organizational culture, which are most important to you as an employee?**

### TAKEAWAY QUESTION 2 What is a multicultural organization?

- Multicultural organizations operate with internal cultures that value pluralism, respect diversity, and build strength from an environment of inclusion.
- Organizations have many subcultures, including those based on occupational, functional, ethnic, age, and gender differences.
- Challenges faced by members of minority subcultures in organizations include sexual harassment, pay discrimination, job discrimination, and the glass ceiling effect.
- Managing diversity is the process of developing an inclusive work environment that allows everyone to reach their full potential.

**For Discussion What can a manager do, at the work team level, to reduce diversity bias in the workplace?**

### TAKEAWAY QUESTION 3 What is the nature of organizational change?

- Change leaders are change agents who take initiative to change the behavior of people and organizational systems.
- Organizational change can proceed with a top-down emphasis, with a bottom-up emphasis, or a combination of both.
- Incremental change makes continuing adjustments to existing ways and practices; transformational change makes radical changes in organizational directions.
- Lewin's three phases of planned change are unfreezing—preparing a system for change; changing—making a change; and refreezing—stabilizing the system.
- Change agents should understand the force-coercion, rational persuasion, and shared power change strategies.
- People resist change for a variety of reasons, including fear of the unknown and force of habit.
- Good change agents deal with resistance in a variety of ways, including education, participation, support, and facilitation.

**For Discussion Can the refreezing stage of planned change ever be satisfied in today's dynamic environments?**

## SELF-TEST 12

### Multiple-Choice Questions

1. Pluralism and the absence of discrimination and prejudice in policies and practices are two important hallmarks of _____.
   (a) the glass ceiling effect
   (b) a multicultural organization
   (c) quality circles
   (d) affirmative action

2. When members of minority cultures feel that they have to behave in ways similar to the majority culture, this is called _____.
   (a) biculturalism
   (b) symbolic leadership
   (c) the glass ceiling effect
   (d) inclusivity

**3.** Engineers, scientists, and information systems specialists are likely to become part of separate _____ subcultures in an organization.
(a) ethnic  (b) generational
(c) functional  (d) occupational

**4.** Stories told about an organization's past accomplishments and heroes such as company founders are all part of what is called the _____ culture.
(a) observable  (b) underground
(c) functional  (d) core

**5.** Honesty, social responsibility, and customer service are examples of _____ that can become foundations for an organization's core culture.
(a) rites and rituals  (b) values
(c) subsystems  (d) ideas

**6.** Which leadership approach is most consistent with an organizational culture that values the full utilization of all diverse talents of all the organization's human resources?
(a) Managing diversity  (b) Affirmative action
(c) Status quo  (d) Rational persuasion

**7.** When members of a dominant subculture, such as white males, make it hard for members of minority subcultures, such as women, to advance to higher level positions in the organization, this is called the _____ effect.
(a) dominator  (b) glass ceiling
(c) brick wall  (d) end-of-line

**8.** An executive pursuing transformational change would give highest priority to which one of these change targets?
(a) an out-of-date policy
(b) the organizational culture
(c) a new information system
(d) job designs in a customer service department

**9.** _____ change results in a major change of direction for an organization, while _____ makes small adjustments to current ways of doing things.
(a) Frame breaking; radical
(b) Frame bending; incremental

(c) Transformational; frame breaking
(d) Transformational; incremental

**10.** The presence or absence of a felt need for change is a key issue in the _____ phase of the planned change process.
(a) improvising  (b) evaluating
(c) unfreezing  (d) refreezing

**11.** When a manager listens to users, makes adaptations, and continuously tweaks and changes a new MIS as it is being implemented, the approach to technological change can be described as _____.
(a) top-down  (b) improvisational
(c) organization development  (d) frame breaking

**12.** A manager using a force-coercion strategy will rely on _____ to bring about change.
(a) expertise  (b) benchmarking
(c) formal authority  (d) information

**13.** The most participative of the planned change strategies is _____.
(a) force-coercion  (b) rational persuasion
(c) shared power  (d) command and control

**14.** True internalization and commitment to a planned change is most likely to occur when a manager uses a(n) _____ change strategy.
(a) education and communication
(b) rational persuasion
(c) manipulation and co-optation
(d) shared power

**15.** Trying to covertly influence others, offering only selective information, and structuring events in favor of the desired change, is a way of dealing with resistance by _____.
(a) participation
(b) manipulation and co-optation
(c) force-coercion
(d) facilitation

## Short-Response Questions

**16.** What core values might be found in high-performance organizational cultures?

**17.** Why is it important for managers to understand subcultures in organizations?

**18.** What are the three phases of change described by Lewin, and what are their implications for change leadership?

**19.** What are the major differences in potential outcomes of using the force-coercion, rational persuasion, and shared power strategies of planned change?

## Essay Question

**20.** Two businesswomen, former college roommates, are discussing their jobs and careers over lunch. You overhear one saying to the other: "I work for a large corporation, while you own a small retail business. In my company there is a strong corporate culture and everyone feels its influence. In fact, we are always expected to act in ways that support the culture and serve as role models for others to do so as well. This includes a commitment to diversity and multiculturalism. Because of the small size of your firm, things like corporate culture, diversity, and multiculturalism are not so important to worry about." Do you agree or disagree with this statement? Why?

# MANAGEMENT SKILLS AND COMPETENCIES

# Further Reflection: Tolerance for Ambiguity

The next time you are driving somewhere and following a familiar route only to encounter a "detour" sign, test your **tolerance for ambiguity**. Is the detour just a minor inconvenience and you go forward without any further thought? Or is it a big deal, perhaps causing anxiety and anger, and showing tendencies to resist change in your normal routines? The chapter opener links tolerance for ambiguity with organizational cultures and the processes of organizational change. People are being asked today to be ever more flexible in their work; organizations are, too. Managers are expected to support change initiatives launched from the top; they are also expected to be change leaders in their own teams and work units. This is a good time to check your readiness to meet career challenges cultures and change processes in today's organizations.

 **DO IT NOW . . . LOOK IN THE MIRROR**

- Write a short narrative describing your "ideal" employer in terms of organization culture, management styles, and frequency of major changes.
- Add a comment that explains how this ideal organization fits your personality, including insights from self-assessments completed in other chapters.
- What does this say about how you may have to change and adapt to make your career aspirations come true?

# Self-Assessment: Change Leadership IQ

## Instructions

Indicate whether each of the following statements is true (T) or false (F).[57]

T F 1. People invariably resist change.

T F 2. One of the most important responsibilities of any change effort is that the leader clearly describes the expected future state.

T F 3. Communicating what will remain the same after change is as important as communicating what will be different.

T F 4. Planning for change should be done by a small, knowledgeable group, and then that group should communicate its plan to others.

T F 5. Managing resistance to change is more difficult than managing apathy about change.

T F 6. Complaints about a change effort are often a sign of change progress.

T F 7. Leaders find it more difficult to change organizational goals than to change the ways of reaching those goals.

T F 8. Successful change efforts typically involve changing reward systems to support change.

T F 9. Involving more members of an organization in planning a change increases commitment to making the change successful.

T F 10. Successful organizational change requires certain significant and dramatic steps or "leaps," rather than moderate or "incremental" ones.

## Scoring

Questions 2, 3, 6, 8, 9, 10 are true; the rest are false. Tally the number of correct items to indicate the extent to which your change management assumptions are consistent with findings from the discipline.

# Team Exercise: Force-Field Analysis

## Instructions

1. Form into your class discussion groups and review this model of **force-field analysis**—the consideration of forces driving in support of a planned change and forces resisting the change.

2. Use force-field analysis and make lists of driving and resisting forces for one of the following situations:

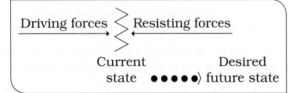

Driving forces ⋛ Resisting forces

Current state ●●●●) Desired future state

(a) *"Home Schooling" at College Level.* Things are changing in colleges and universities as budget declines create pressures for a rethinking of educational programming. Home schooling has grown popular at primary and secondary levels. Why can't it work for college as well, at least for the first two years? At least one vice president at the local university is in favor of making a proposal to move her campus to a 3rd/4th-year-only status and have years 1 and 2 go online. She wonders what she should prepare for when sharing her ideas with the rest of the executive team.

(b) *Scheduling Dilemma.* A new owner has just taken over a small walk-in-and-buy-by-the-slice pizza shop in a college town. There are presently eight employees, three of whom are full-time and five of whom are part-time. The shop is open seven days a week from 10:30 A.M. to midnight. The new owner believes there is a market niche available for late-night pizza and would like to stay open each night until 4 A.M. She wants to make the change as soon as possible.

(c) *Instructor's Choice.* A situation assigned by the instructor.

3. Choose the three driving forces that are most significant for the proposed change. For each force, develop ideas on how it could be further increased or mobilized in support of the change.

4. Choose the three resisting forces that are most significant for the proposed change. For each force, develop ideas on how it could be reduced or turned into a driving force.

5. Be prepared to participate in a class discussion led by your instructor.

## Career Situations for Organizational Culture and Change: What Would You Do?

1. **Two Job Offers**   You will soon have to choose between two really nice job offers. They are in the same industry, but you wonder which employer would be the "best fit." You have a sense that their "cultures" are quite different. Fortunately, you've been invited back to spend a full day at each before making your decision. One of your friends suggests that doing a balance-sheet assessment of cultural pluses and minuses for each employer could be helpful. What aspects of organizational culture would you identify as important to your job choice? Given the items on the list, what can you look for or do in the coming visits to discover the real organizational cultures pluses and minuses for each item?

2. **Team Culture Nightmare**   The promotion to team manager puts you right where you want to be in terms of career advancement. Even though you've had to move to a new location it's a great opportunity . . . if you can do well as team leader. That's the problem. Now that you're in the job you realize that the culture of the team is really bad. Some of the ways you've heard members describe it to one another are "toxic," "dog-eat-dog," "watch your back," and "keep your head down." Realizing that culture change takes time but that's it's also necessary in this situation, what can you do right away as the new team leader to set the team on course for a positive change to its culture?

3. **Tough Situation**   Times are tough at your organization, and, as the director of human resources, you have a problem. The company's senior executives have decided that 10% of the payroll has to be cut immediately. Instead of laying off about 30 people, you would like to have everyone cut back their work hours by 10%. This way the payroll would be cut but everyone would get to keep their jobs. But you've heard that this idea isn't popular with all the workers. Some are already grumbling that it's a "bad idea" and the company is just looking for excuses "to cut wages." How can you best handle this situation as a change leader?

## Case Study

# Apple Inc.

Go to *Management Cases for Critical Thinking* to find the recommended case for Chapter 12—"Apple Inc.: People and Design Create the Future."

Over a span of more than 30 years, Apple Computer has generated some of America's greatest business successes and has also experienced major failures. Apple Inc. ignited the personal computer industry in the 1970s with a major challenge to behemoth IBM. The company then stagnated as co-founder Steve Jobs was ousted from leadership and a series of CEOs lost opportunities. It rebounded tremendously when Jobs returned as CEO. Now Jobs has died and the firm faces new challenges in trying to live up to his legacy in a hugely competitive business world. Apple represents a fascinating microcosm of American business as it continues to leverage its strengths while reinventing itself. With the world reveling in iPads, iPods, iPhones, and iMacs, what's next for a firm that continues to face a tough economy and stiff competition without its founder and guiding genius?

# Wisdom
## Learning From Others

© Purestock/Age Fotostock America, Inc.

## > GREAT EMPLOYERS RESPECT DIVERSITY AND VALUE PEOPLE

*Working Mother* magazine's annual listing of the "100 Best Companies for Working Mothers" is a management benchmark—both for employers that want to be able to say that they are among the best and for potential employees who only want to work for the best. Employers like IBM, Johnson & Johnson, American Express, Marriott International, Merck, and Procter & Gamble are regulars on the list.

Top practices of the "100 Best Companies" include flextime, telecommuting, and maternity leave, compressed work weeks, and job-sharing opportunities. These firms are also strong on mentoring programs.

Companies on the *Working Mother* list stand out for providing employees with services that help working moms achieve work–life balance. Teddi

Hernandez, an employee of Hallmark Cards, was able to adopt her five children by using the company's generous allowances for time off and adoption aid. When one child was diagnosed with Asperger's Syndrome, the company allowed Teddi to reduce her work schedule 20 hours per week, enough to keep the company-sponsored family health insurance. Hernandez also attends Hallmark's support group for parents of children with autism.[1]

*Working Mother* is a major supporter of mothers with careers. Self-described as helping women "integrate their professional lives, their family lives and their inner lives," the magazine covers timely issues and highlights the challenges and needs experienced by working women.

## MORE TO LOOK FOR INSIDE>

# Human Resource Management

## 13

## > CONSCIENTIOUSNESS

**Conscientiousness** is the degree to which an individual is achievement-oriented, careful, hard-working, organized, persevering, responsible, and thorough. People low on conscientiousness tend to be laid back, less goal-oriented, less driven by success, and less self-disciplined. They are often procrastinators.

Conscientiousness is linked with successful academic and work performance. It's a personality characteristic that is positively related to work performance across a wide range of jobs. Conscientiousness improves job performance directly because conscientious individuals simply pay more attention to the details of their jobs. It also

improves success in training programs, which in turn improves job knowledge and future performance.

Many employers tend to hire for attitude and train for skill.[2] They try to identify future top performers by focusing on key personality characteristics that are likely to predict job success.

Conscientiousness is often at the top of recruiters' "must-have" lists. Their search for clues about an individual job candidate covers things like those shown in the box. How about you? Can your credentials meet a recruiter's conscientiousness test?

## Insight
### Learning
### About Yourself

### HOW TO SHOW RECRUITERS YOU ARE CONSCIENTIOUS

- Professional Résumé—Carefully proofed, well-designed, and organized, it shows you value a high-quality product and attend to details.
- Interview Preparation—Doing research beforehand and being well informed shows conscientiousness.
- Self-Presentation—First impressions count; conscientiousness shows up in dressing appropriately and acting professionally in manners and engagement.
- Career Plans—Being able to thoughtfully discuss career and personal plans shows you are goal-oriented and conscientious.

---

**BUILD SKILLS AND COMPETENCIES AT END OF CHAPTER**

- Engage in *Further Reflection on Conscientiousness*
- Take the *Self-Assessment on Performance Appraisal Assumptions*
- Complete the *Team Exercise—Upward Appraisal*
- Solve the *Career Situations for Human Resource Management*
- Analyze the *Case Study—Two-Tier Wages: Same Job, Different Pay*

## <GET TO KNOW YOURSELF BETTER

| TAKEAWAY 1 | TAKEAWAY 2 | TAKEAWAY 3 | TAKEAWAY 4 |
|---|---|---|---|
| **Human Resource Management** | **Attracting a Quality Workforce** | **Developing a Quality Workforce** | **Maintaining a Quality Workforce** |
| • Human resource management process | • Human resource planning | • Orientation and socialization | • Flexibility and work–life balance |
| • Strategic human resource management | • Recruiting process | • Training and development | • Compensation and benefits |
| • Legal environment of human resource management | • Selection techniques | • Performance management | • Retention and turnover |
| | | | • Labor–management relations |

| LEARNING CHECK 1 | LEARNING CHECK 2 | LEARNING CHECK 3 | LEARNING CHECK 4 |
|---|---|---|---|

The key to managing people in ways that lead to profit, productivity, innovation, and real organizational learning ultimately lies in how you think about your organization and its people. . . . When you look at your people, do you see costs to be reduced? . . . Or, when you look at your people do you see intelligent, motivated, trustworthy individuals—the most critical and valuable strategic assets your organization can have?

With these words from his book, *The Human Equation: Building Profits by Putting People First*, scholar Jeffrey Pfeffer challenges managers to invest in people and their talents.[3] He believes, and has research evidence to back up his claims, that organizations that invest more in people outperform those that don't. High-performing organizations thrive on strong foundations of **human capital**—the economic value of people with job-relevant knowledge, skills, abilities, experience, ideas, energies, and commitments. They put people first and benefit from it. This chapter explores how organizations build human capital by managing their human resources in ways that unlock and respect talents and value diversity.

**Human capital** is the economic value of people with job-relevant knowledge, skills, abilities, ideas, energies, and commitments.

## Human Resource Management

A marketing manager at IDEO, a Palo Alto-based consulting design firm, once said: "If you hire the right people . . . if you've got the right fit . . . then everything will take care of itself."[4] This is what **human resource management**, or HRM, is all about—attracting, developing, and maintaining a talented and energetic workforce. If an organization can't do this well and therefore doesn't have talented and committed people available to do the required work, it has very little chance of long-term success.

**Human resource management** is a process of attracting, developing, and maintaining a talented workforce.

There are many career opportunities in a wide variety of areas in human resource management. HRM specialists within organizations deal with hiring, compensation and benefits, training, employee relations, and more. Specific job titles include human resource planner, corporate recruiter, training and development specialist, compensation analyst, salary and benefits manager, and director of diversity. HRM expertise is highly important in an environment complicated by legal issues, economic turmoil, new corporate strategies, and changing social values. Scholar and consultant Edward E. Lawler III argues that the HRM staff should be experts "on the state of an organization's workforce and its ability to perform."[5]

## Human Resource Management Process

The goal of human resource management is to enhance organizational performance through the effective utilization of people. All managers, not just human resource specialists, share the responsibility to ensure that highly capable and enthusiastic people are in the right positions and working with the support they need to be successful. The three major tasks in human resource management are typically described as

1. *Attracting a quality workforce*—human resource planning, employee recruitment, and employee selection.

2. *Developing a quality workforce*—employee orientation, training and development, and performance management.

3. *Maintaining a quality workforce*—career development, work–life balance, compensation and benefits, retention and turnover, and labor–management relations.

A key concept in HRM is "fit." In fact, an organization's HRM approach should always seek to ensure a good fit between the employee and the specific job to be accomplished, and between the employee and the overall culture of the organization. Hiring the wrong person can be a very expensive mistake. **Person–job fit** is the extent to which an individual's knowledge, skills, experiences, and personal characteristics are consistent with the requirements of their work.[6] **Person–organization fit** is the extent to which an individual's values, interests, and behavior are consistent with the culture of the organization.[7]

**Person–job fit** is the extent to which an individual's knowledge, skills, experiences and personal characteristics are consistent with the requirements of their work.

**Person–organization fit** is the extent to which an individual's values, interests, and behavior are consistent with the culture of the organization.

## Strategic Human Resource Management

When Sheryl Sandberg left her senior management post with Google to become Facebook's chief operating officer, one of her first steps was to strengthen the firm's human resource management systems. She updated the approach for employee performance reviews, established new recruiting methods, and launched new management training programs.[8] Sandberg's initiatives are consistent with the concept of **strategic human resource management**—mobilizing human capital through the HRM process to best implement organizational strategies.[9]

Strategic human resource management translates the strategic goals of the organization into human resource plans that make sure the organization always has the right people in the right places at the right times. This is essential for an organization to successfully implement its strategies and accomplish its objectives.

**Strategic human resource management** mobilizes human capital to implement organizational strategies.

## Management in Popular Culture

© AF archive/Alamy Limited

### *The Office* Sensationalizes Dysfunction

Watch *The Office* and learn what you shouldn't do at work. Although many of the politically incorrect situations may make you cringe, the show's diverse and outrageous characters also challenge us to think about how we could improve our workplaces. Episodes call attention to questions like: What behavior violates employment law? Should employees attend diversity training sessions? How can we do a better job of handling rivalries between colleagues? When does trying to be funny cross the line into being unprofessional?

One indicator that HRM is truly strategic to an organization is when it is headed by a senior executive reporting directly to the chief executive officer. When Laszlo Bock became Google's first-ever vice president of people operations he not only helped Google sustain its standing as an innovator and market leader, he also created an HR function that could strategically deal with the explosive growth the company was experiencing.[10] HRM also plays a strategic role in supporting core values and the corporate culture. Reacting to a spate of corporate ethics scandals, Susan Meisinger, former president of the Society for Human Resource Development, said: "It was a failure of people and that isn't lost on those in the executive suite."[11]

## Legal Environment of Human Resource Management

Hire a relative? Promote a friend? Fire an enemy? Hold on! Managers and employers can't simply do whatever they please when it comes to human resource management practices. Everything must be done within the framework of laws and regulations that govern employment practices.

### Equal Employment Opportunity

**Equal employment opportunity** is the requirement that employment decisions be made without regard to race, color, national origin, religion, gender, age, or disability status.

The foundations of our legal protection against discrimination in employment rest with Title VII of the Civil Rights Act of 1964, as amended by the Equal Employment Opportunity Act of 1972 and the Civil Rights Act of 1991. These acts provide for **equal employment opportunity**—the requirement that employment decisions be made without regard to race, color, national origin, religion, gender, age, or disability status.

The intent of equal employment opportunity is to ensure all citizens the right to gain and keep employment based only on ability to do the job and performance once on the job. This right is federally enforced by the Equal Employment Opportunity Commission, or EEOC. This agency has the power to file civil lawsuits against organizations that do not provide timely resolution of discrimination charges lodged against them. The laws generally apply to all public and private organizations employing 15 or more people.

Under Title VII, organizations are expected to show **affirmative action** in setting goals and having plans to ensure equal employment opportunity for members of protected groups, those historically underrepresented in the workforce. The purpose of affirmative action plans is to ensure that women and minorities are represented in the workforce in proportion to their labor market availability.[12] The pros and cons of affirmative action are debated at both the federal and state levels. Criticisms tend to focus on the use of group membership, such as female or minority status, as a criterion in employment decisions.[13] The issues include claims of reverse discrimination by members of majority populations. White males, for example, may claim that preferential treatment given to minorities interferes with their individual rights.

As a general rule, legal protections for equal employment opportunity do not restrict an employer's right to establish **bona fide occupational qualifications**. These are criteria for employment that can be clearly justified as being a reasonable necessity for the normal operation of a business and are clearly related to a person's capacity to perform a job. The use of bona fide occupational qualifications based on race and color is not allowed under any circumstances. Those based on sex, religion, age, and national origin are possible, but organizations must take great care to support these requirements.[14]

**Affirmative action** is an effort to give preference in employment to women and minority group members who have traditionally been underrepresented.

**Bona fide occupational qualifications** are employment criteria justified by capacity to perform a job.

## Laws Against Employment Discrimination

"Why didn't I get invited for a job interview—is it because my first name is Abdul?" "Why didn't I get the promotion—is it because I'm so visibly pregnant?" These are questions that relate to possible **discrimination** in employment. It occurs when someone is denied a job or a job assignment for reasons that are not job-relevant. The possibilities raised in these questions shouldn't happen, and Figure 13.1 provides a sample of major U.S. laws prohibiting employment discrimination. The legal protections in the following areas are quite extensive.

**Discrimination** occurs when someone is denied a job or job assignment for reasons that are not job-relevant.

*Race, Sex, or Religion—Title VII of the Civil Rights Act of 1964* banned discrimination in all aspects of employment (including hiring, promotion, compensation, and termination) based on race, color, religion, sex, or national origin.[15]

*Disabilities—The Americans with Disabilities Act of 1990* (ADA) outlaws discrimination against qualified individuals with disabilities—physical or mental impairments that substantially limit one or more major life activities, and requires employers to provide reasonable accommodations for disabled employees.[16]

*Age—The Age Discrimination in Employment Act* (ADEA) *of 1967 as amended in 1978 and 1986* prohibits employment discrimination against persons 40 years of age or older.[17] Age discrimination occurs when a qualified individual is adversely affected by a job action that replaces him or her with a younger worker. The ADEA includes a broad ban against age discrimination, and specifically outlaws discrimination in hiring, promotion, compensation, or firing. It forbids statements in job notices or advertisements of age preference and limitations. It also prohibits mandatory retirement ages in most employment sectors.

*Pregnancy—The Pregnancy Discrimination Act of 1978* protects women from discrimination because of pregnancy. This law forbids discrimination when it comes to any aspect of employment, including hiring, firing, pay, job assignments, promotions, layoffs, training, fringe benefits, such as leave and health insurance, and any other term or condition of employment.[18]

FIGURE 13.1 **Sample of U.S. laws against employment discrimination.**

| | |
|---|---|
| Equal Pay Act of 1963 | Requires equal pay for men and women performing equal work in an organization. |
| Title VII of the Civil Rights Act of 1964 (as amended) | Prohibits discrimination in employment based on race, color, religion, sex, or national origin. |
| Age Discrimination in Employment Act of 1967 | Prohibits discrimination against persons over 40; restricts mandatory retirement. |
| Occupational Health and Safety Act of 1970 | Establishes mandatory health and safety standards in workplaces. |
| Pregnancy Discrimination Act of 1978 | Prohibits employment discrimination against pregnant workers. |
| Americans with Disabilities Act of 1990 | Prohibits discrimination against a qualified individual on the basis of disability. |
| Civil Rights Act of 1991 | Reaffirms Title VII of the 1964 Civil Rights Act; reinstates burden of proof by employer, and allows for punitive and compensatory damages. |
| Family and Medical Leave Act of 1993 | Allows employees up to 12 weeks of unpaid leave with job guarantees for childbirth, adoption, or family illness. |

*Family matters*—The *Family and Medical Leave Act of 1993* (FMLA) entitles eligible employees to take up to 12 weeks of unpaid, job-protected leave in a 12-month period for specified family and medical reasons such as childbirth, adoption, or serious health conditions involving the employee or his/her family member. To be eligible, an employee must have worked for a covered employer for 12 months and at least 1,250 hours over the previous 12 months. Employers must have at least 50 employees to be covered by this act.[19]

## Current Legal Issues

Because the legal environment is complex and dynamic, managers and human resource professionals have to stay informed about new laws and changes to existing ones. Failure to follow the laws is not only unjustified in civil society, it can also be an expensive mistake that results in fines and penalties. But things aren't always clear-cut and managers must be alert to current issues of potential legal consequence. A brief sampler follows.

**Sexual harassment** is behavior of a sexual nature that affects a person's employment situation.

**Sexual harassment** occurs when a person experiences conduct or language of a sexual nature that affects his or her employment situation. The EEOC defines sexual harassment as behavior of a sexual nature that creates a hostile work environment, interferes with a person's ability to do a job, or impedes a person's promotion potential. *Quid pro quo sexual harassment* is where job decisions are made based on whether the employee submits to or rejects sexual advances. *Hostile work environment sexual harassment* occurs when any unwelcome form of sexual conduct (inappropriate touching, teasing, dirty jokes, vulgar conversations, or the display of sexually explicit pictures) creates an intimidating, hostile, or offensive work setting. Organizations should have clear sexual harassment policies in place, along with fair and equitable procedures for implementing them.

> SINCE WHEN IS SOMEONE'S FACEBOOK PROFILE MEANT
TO BE AN ONLINE RÉSUMÉ?

# Personality Test? Drug Test? Facebook Test?

Arda Guildogan/iStockphoto

It used to be that preparing for a job interview meant being ready to answer questions about your education, work experience, interests, and activities. Now there's another question to prepare for: What's your Facebook user name and password?

It's true. Many interviewers are now asking for access to an applicant's Facebook page. They don't want just a quick glance at the public stuff; they want access to the private profile too. And by the way, the recruiter's request for access may be an indirect "Please friend me."

"It's akin to requiring someone's house keys," says a law professor. "I needed the job to feed my family. I had to," said one job candidate. Another turned down the request and withdrew her application. She didn't want to work for an employer that would even ask to view her private web pages.

While a Facebook profile can be a treasure chest of information for recruiters and employers, it is less clear whether it is ethical for a firm to tap into this resource to measure a candidate's character and make employment decisions. Since when is one's Facebook profile meant to be an online résumé?

According to a survey by Microsoft Research, 70% of recruiters said that they had rejected applicants based on information they found online. Warren Ashton, group marketing manager at Microsoft, says: "For the first time ever, you suddenly have very public information about almost any candidate."

Sometimes negative decisions are made based on information involving relatively mild forms of questionable behavior such as using poor grammar, posting negative comments about prior employees, or uploading drinking pictures. Other decisions may be based on information or pictures that the individual has little control over. What happens if a "friend" posts a picture of someone from a party that occurred years ago, or if untrue information is posted as a joke among friends?

### ETHICS QUESTIONS

What are the ethical issues involved with regard to recruiters asking for access to personal Facebook pages? Should it be held against an applicant to refuse? Is it okay for a manager to search online sites to check up on what employees are doing outside of work? And, should what one does outside of work cost someone their job? On the other hand, shouldn't individuals who knowingly post online information understand that it may end up in the hands of their employers?

---

The Equal Pay Act of 1963 requires that men and women in the same organization be paid equally for doing work that is equivalent in terms of skills, responsibilities, and working conditions. But a lingering issue over gender disparities in pay involves **comparable worth**, the notion that persons performing jobs of similar importance should be paid at comparable levels. Why should a long-distance truck driver, for example, be paid more than an elementary teacher in a public school? Does it make any difference that truck driving is a traditionally male occupation and teaching is a traditionally female occupation? Advocates of comparable worth argue that historical disparities in pay across occupations can result from gender bias. They would like to have the issue legally resolved.

The legal status and employee entitlements of part-time workers and **independent contractors** are also being debated. As organizations seek to reduce costs

**Comparable worth** holds that persons performing jobs of similar importance should be paid at comparable levels.

**Independent contractors** are hired as needed and are not part of the organization's permanent workforce.

and increase staffing flexibility, more and more persons are being hired as temporary workers who do not become part of an organization's permanent workforce. Even though they work only "as needed," however, many are engaged regularly by the same organization and become what some call "permatemps." Because these employees often work without benefits such as health insurance and pensions, legal cases are now being brought before the courts seeking to make independent contractors eligible for benefits.

**Workplace privacy** is the right to privacy while at work.

**Workplace privacy** is the right of individuals to privacy on the job.[20] It is legal for employers to monitor the work performance and behavior of their employees. But employer practices can become invasive and cross legal and ethical lines, especially with the capabilities that information technology now provides. Computers can easily monitor e-mails and track Internet searches for unauthorized usage; they can identify who is called by telephone and how long conversations last; they can document work performance moment to moment; and they can check online profiles for key words. All of this information, furthermore, can be stored in vast databases, even without the individual's permission. Until the legal status of electronic surveillance is cleared up, one consultant says the best approach is to "assume you have no privacy at work."[21]

---

**LEARNING CHECK 1**

**TAKEAWAY QUESTION 1  What is human resource management?**

**Be sure you can** • explain the human resource management process • define *discrimination, equal employment opportunity, affirmative action,* and *bona fide occupational qualification* • identify major laws that protect against discrimination in employment • discuss legal issues of sexual harassment, comparable worth, independent contractors, and workplace privacy.

---

# Attracting a Quality Workforce

The first responsibility of human resource management is to attract to the organization a high-quality workforce whose talents fit the jobs to be done. An advertisement once run by the Motorola Corporation clearly states the goal: "Productivity is learning how to hire the person who is right for the job." To attract the right people, an organization must first know exactly what it is looking for; it must have a clear understanding of the jobs to be done and the talents required to do them well. Then it must have the systems in place to excel at employee recruitment and selection.

## Human Resource Planning

**Human resource planning** analyzes staffing needs and identifies actions to fill those needs.

**Human resource planning** is the process of analyzing an organization's staffing needs and determining how to best fill them. As shown in Figure 13.2, human resource planning identifies staffing needs, assesses the existing workforce, and decides what additions or replacements are required for the future. The process becomes strategic when all this is done in specific reference to organizational mission, objectives, and strategies.

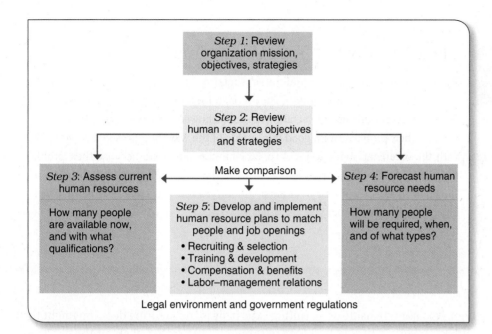

FIGURE 13.2  **Steps in strategic human resource planning.**

The foundations for human resource planning begin with **job analysis**—the orderly study of job facets to determine what is done when, where, how, why, and by whom.[22] This information is then used to write or update **job descriptions** that describe specific job duties and responsibilities. The information in a job analysis is used to create **job specifications**. These are lists of the qualifications—such as education, prior experience, and skills—needed by someone hired for a given job. These specifications become important inputs to the recruiting process.

A **job analysis** studies exactly what is done in a job, and why.

A **job description** details the duties and responsibilities of a job holder.

**Job specifications** list the qualifications required of a job holder.

## Recruiting Process

**Recruitment** is a set of activities designed to attract a talented pool of job applicants to an organization. Three steps in a typical recruitment process are: (1) advertisement of a job vacancy, (2) preliminary contact with potential job candidates, and (3) initial screening to create a pool of applicants potentially meeting the organization's staffing needs.

**Recruitment** is a set of activities designed to attract a talented pool of job applicants.

### External and Internal Recruitment

The recruiting that takes place on college campuses is one example of **external recruitment**, in which job candidates are sought from outside the hiring organization. External recruits are found through company websites and social media sites, virtual job fairs, specialized recruiting websites such as Monster and CareerBuilder, employment agencies and headhunters, university placement centers, personal contacts, and employee referrals. **Internal recruitment**, by contrast, seeks applicants from inside the organization. Most organizations have a procedure for announcing vacancies through newsletters, electronic postings, and the like. They also rely on managers and team leaders to recommend internal candidates for advancement.

**External recruitment** seeks job applicants from outside the organization.

**Internal recruitment** seeks job applicants from inside the organization.

Both recruitment methods have potential advantages and disadvantages. External recruitment brings outside applicants with fresh perspectives, expertise, and work experience. But extra effort is needed to get reliable information on

# Make the Most of Your Online Image

Recruiters who check job candidates' social media sites are not just looking for bad or inappropriate things. They're also looking for positive indicators. A survey on recruiters' use of social media sites showed that 39% hired a candidate because their profiles gave a good impression of the way their personality would fit with the organizational culture. Also, 36% hired a candidate because their profile supported their professional qualifications, and 34% hired a candidate because of the good references posted by others. The impression you create online may well determine whether or not you get hired.

Vicky Kasala/Alamy

them. A major downside of recruiting externally is that a hiring decision might turn out bad because either not enough information was gathered about the applicant, or what was discovered turned out to be inaccurate.

Internal recruitment is usually quicker and focuses on persons whose performance records are well known. A history of internal recruitment builds loyalty and motivation in a workforce by showing that opportunities exist to advance within the organization. It also helps to reduce turnover rates and aids in the retention of high-quality employees. But internal recruiting has downsides as well. Limiting job searches to only internal talent pools raises the risks that the best candidate may not be chosen for a position. A valuable opportunity to bring in outside expertise and viewpoints might be lost at the very time when new insights, skills, and creativity are most needed by the organization.

## Realistic Job Previews

**Traditional recruitment** focuses on selling the job and organization to applicants.

In what may be called **traditional recruitment**, the emphasis is on selling the job and organization to applicants. The focus is on communicating the most positive features of the position, perhaps to the point where negatives are downplayed or concealed. This may create unrealistic expectations that cause costly turnover when new hires become disillusioned and quit. The individual suffers a career disruption; the employer suffers lost productivity and the added costs of having to recruit again.

**Realistic job previews** provide job candidates with all pertinent information about a job and an organization, both positive and negative.

The alternative to traditional recruitment is a **realistic job preview** that gives the candidate all pertinent information about the job and organization without distortion, and before the job is accepted.[23] Instead of "selling" the applicant on the positive features of the job or organization, realistic job previews try to be open and balanced. Both favorable and unfavorable aspects are covered.

The interviewer in a realistic job preview might use phrases such as "Of course, there are some downsides . . ."; "Something that you will want to be prepared for is . . ."; and "We have found that some new hires have difficulty with. . ." And, such conversations may lead some applicants to decide that the job is not for them. But this avoids a mismatch that could prove troublesome later. For those who do take the job, knowing both the positive and negative features ahead of time builds realistic expectations and better prepares them for the inevitable ups and downs of a new position. The expected benefits of realistic recruiting practices include higher levels of early job satisfaction, greater trust in the organization, and less inclination to quit prematurely.

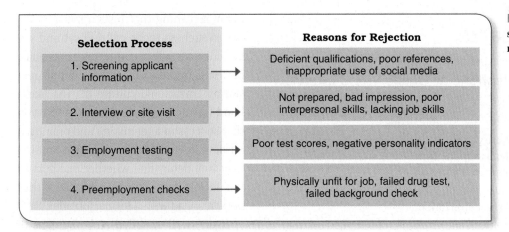

## Selection Techniques

Once a manager has a pool of candidates, the next step is to select whom to hire. The process of **selection** as outlined in Figure 13.3 involves gathering and assessing information about job candidates and making a hiring decision.

**Selection** is choosing individuals to hire from a pool of qualified job applicants.

### Hiring the Best Qualifications or the Best Person?

There are two sometimes-competing viewpoints when it comes to making selection decisions: Hire the best qualifications or hire the best person? Most employers select based on qualifications like knowledge, skills, and past work experiences. Their focus is getting someone ready for immediate job performance. Others, however, focus on the person. They pay less attention to qualifications and prior experiences, and give more attention to finding an individual whose personal traits—say intelligence and conscientiousness—offer long-term success potential. Which approach is best? To a large extent, that depends on the situation. If an organization needs to fill an immediate need or is not able to invest in training, then hiring for best existing qualifications is generally preferred. But in situations that are dynamic and fast-changing, then hiring the best person may result in better long-term performance.[24]

### Reliability and Validity

Whether the focus is on qualifications or the best person, the selection process is always a prediction exercise. This makes the reliability and validity of the selection techniques very important. **Reliability** means that the selection technique is consistent in how it measures something. That is, it returns the same results time after time. For example, a personality test is reliable if the same individual receives a similar score when taking the test on two separate occasions. **Validity** means that there is a clear relationship between what the selection device is measuring and eventual job performance. That is, there is clear evidence that once on the job, individuals with high scores on an employment test, for example, outperform individuals with low scores.

**Reliability** means that a selection device gives consistent results over repeated measures.

**Validity** means that scores on a selection device have demonstrated links with future job performance.

### Interviews

Very few individuals are hired for professional positions without first sitting through one or more interviews. And, the traditional *face-to-face interview* with HR staff and/or hiring manager remains the most common method of assessment in the selection process. But the *telephone interview* and the *virtual or online video interview* are rapidly increasing in frequency and importance. Both are often part of an

## ManagementSmarts

### How to Succeed in a Telephone or Online Video Interview

- *Prepare ahead of time*—Study the organization; carefully list your strengths and capabilities; have a materials ready for note taking.
- *Take the call in private*—Make sure you are in a quiet room, with privacy and without the possibility of interruptions; turn cell phones and computer alerts off so that you are not interrupted.
- *Dress as a professional*—Don't be casual; dressing right increases confidence and sets a tone for your side of the conversation.
- *Practice your interview "voice" and "screen presence"*—Your impression will be made quickly; how you sound and look counts; speak slowly, look at the camera, and enunciate clearly; it helps to smile when you talk because it will change the tone of your voice.
- *Have reference materials handy*—Your résumé and other supporting documents should be within easy reach.
- *Have a list of questions ready*—Don't be caught unprepared; intersperse your best questions during the interview.
- *Ask what happens next*—Find out how to follow up by telephone or e-mail; ask what other information you can provide; ask about the time frame for a decision.
- *Follow up*—Don't forget to send a thank-you note to reiterate your interest in the job.

In **unstructured interviews** the interviewer does not work from a formal and preestablished list of questions that is asked of all interviewees.

**Behavioral interviews** ask job applicants about past behaviors.

**Situational interviews** ask job applicants how they would react in specific situations.

initial screening that tests applicants for basics such as technical skill set and experience, as well as communication skills, personal impression, and potential person-organizational culture fit. The likelihood for most college graduates today is that success in a telephone and online interview, featured in Management Smarts, may well determine whether one gets to the face-to-face on-site interviews that hopefully end with a formal job offer.

Even well-qualified job applicants may perform poorly in a job interview. They may be unprepared for questions related to the specific organization with which they are interviewing. They may be nervous or may be poor communicators. Or, they may simply fail at answering unusual and demanding questions. Google is famous for asking questions like: "A man pushed his car to a hotel and lost his fortune. What happened?" Other employers are now pushing the interview envelop as well. Whole Foods might ask: "What's your perfect last meal?" Expedia might ask: "If you could go camping anywhere, where would you put your tent?"[25] These types of interview questions are designed less for testing "right" answers and more for finding, through a candidate's responses, how well they might fit with the organization overall and its culture.

It may surprise you to find out that interviews often have relatively low validity as selection devices. This is especially true of **unstructured interviews** where the interviewer doesn't work from a formal and preestablished list of questions that is asked of all interviewees. Some interviewers rush to judgement on a candidate's first impression and fail to dig deeper for relevant information. Or, they dominate the conversation and spend more time talking about themselves or the organization than focusing on the applicant and his or her readiness for the position.

The predictive validity of interviews increases as the amount of structure increases. In this respect, behavioral interviews and situational interviews are much more effective at predicting successful job performance than the traditional interview.[26] **Behavioral interviews** ask job candidates about their past behavior, focusing specifically on actions that are likely to be important in the work environment. For example: "Describe a situation in which you have been in conflict with a co-worker and how you resolved that situation." **Situational interviews** ask applicants how they would react when confronted with specific work situations they would be likely to experience on the job. For example: "How would you as team leader handle two team members who do not get along with one another?"[27]

### Employment Tests

Employment tests are often used to identify a candidate's intelligence, aptitudes, personality, interests, and even ethics. But organizations need to be careful about

## Employers Use Sophisticated Software to Match Applicants with Jobs

Don't count on someone reading a résumé you post on an online job site. Most likely a computer reads it first. Online résumés are often churned through filtering software that checks for key words or phrases that match well with hiring indicators. It's as much necessity-driven as anything else. Starbucks had 65,000 job openings in 12 months and received 7.6 million applications. Procter & Gamble had 2,000 openings and screened 1 million applicants. If you're going to compete for résumé attention online, make sure you match the words to the targeted employer.

Frances M. Roberts/Newscom

the way that they use tests and make sure that they are documented as valid predictors of job performance. **Biodata methods** usually take the form of multiple-choice, self-report questionnaires. They collect "hard" biographical information and also include "soft" items that inquire about more abstract things such as value judgments, aspirations, motivations, attitudes, and expectations. When used in conjunction with ability tests, biodata methods can increase the reliability and validity of the selection process.[28] If you apply for a job at Google, for example, you may be asked to answer a biodata survey. The company will analyze your responses using an algorithm that compares your answers to those of existing top performers at the company.[29]

Other types of employment tests involve actual demonstrations of job-relevant skills and personal characteristics. An **assessment center** evaluates a person's potential by observing his or her performance in experiential activities designed to simulate daily work. When using **work sampling**, companies ask applicants to do actual job tasks while being graded by observers on their performance. Generally speaking, organizations should use a combination of methods in order to increase the predictive validity of the selection process.

> **Biodata methods** collect certain biographical information that has been proven to correlate with good job performance.

> An **assessment center** examines how job candidates handle simulated work situations.
>
> In **work sampling**, applicants are evaluated while performing actual work tasks.

### LEARNING CHECK 2

**TAKEAWAY QUESTION 2   How do organizations attract a quality workforce?**

**Be sure you can** • explain the difference between external recruitment and internal recruitment • discuss the value of realistic job previews to employers and to job candidates • differentiate reliability and validity as two criteria of selection devices • discuss the pros and cons of job interviews and employment tests

## Developing a Quality Workforce

When people join an organization they have to "learn the ropes" and become familiar with "the way things are done." Newcomers need to learn about the organizational culture so they can best fit into the work setting. The best employers don't leave all this to chance. They step in and try to guide this learning process in the right directions.

## Orientation and Socialization

The first formal experience of newcomers often begins with some form of **orientation**—a set of activities designed to familiarize new employees with their jobs, coworkers, and key aspects of the organization as a whole. A good orientation program clarifies the organization's mission and goals, explains the culture, and communicates key policies and procedures. It's well known, for example, that at the Disney World Resort in Buena Vista, Florida, new employees learn that everyone, regardless of her or his specific job title—be it entertainer, ticket seller, or groundskeeper—is a "cast member" who is there "to make the customer happy."

    **Socialization** is a process through which new members learn and adapt to the ways of the organization.[30] The socialization that occurs during the first six months or so of employment often determines how well someone is going to fit in and perform. A good orientation program helps ensure that socialization sets the right foundations for high performance, job satisfaction, and work enthusiasm. When orientation is weak or neglected, socialization largely takes place informally as newcomers learn about the organization and their jobs through casual interactions with coworkers.[31] It is easy in such situations for even well-intentioned and capable people to learn the wrong things and pick up bad attitudes.

## Training and Development

**Training** is a set of activities that helps people acquire and improve job-related skills. This applies both to initial training of an employee and to upgrading or improving skills to meet changing job requirements. Organizations that value their human resources invest in extensive training and development programs to ensure that everyone always has the capabilities needed to perform well.[32]

    On-the-job training takes place in the work setting while someone is doing a job. A common approach is **job rotation**, which allows people to spend time working in different jobs or departments or even geographical locations, and thus expand the range of their job capabilities. LG Electronics, IBM, and McDonald's are some of the companies that are using job rotation.[33] Another approach is **coaching,** in which an experienced person provides performance advice to someone else. **Mentoring** is a form of coaching in which early-career employees are formally assigned as protégés to senior persons. The mentoring relationship gives them regular access to advice on developing skills and getting better informed about the organization.

    Off-the-job training is accomplished outside the work setting. It provides an opportunity to enhance important skills or even to develop skills that might be needed before a promotion or transfer. An example is **management development**—formal training designed to improve a person's knowledge and skill in the fundamentals of management. Beginning managers often benefit from training that emphasizes team leadership and communication. Middle managers may benefit from training to better understand multifunctional viewpoints or techniques for motivating employees. Top managers may benefit from advanced management training to sharpen their decision-making and negotiating skills, as well as to expand their awareness of corporate strategy and direction.

# Performance Management

An important part of human resource management is the design and implementation of a successful **performance management system**. This system ensures that performance standards and objectives are set, that performance is regularly assessed, and that actions are taken to improve future performance.

**Performance appraisal** is the process of formally assessing someone's work accomplishments and providing feedback. Such a performance review serves both evaluation and development purposes.[34] The *evaluation purpose* focuses on past performance and measures results against standards. Performance is documented for the record and for allocating rewards. The manager provides an evaluation of the job holder's accomplishments and areas of weakness. The *development purpose* focuses on future performance. Performance goals and obstacles are identified, along with areas where training or supervisory support may be needed. The manager acts in a counseling role and gives attention to the job holder's developmental needs.

Many managers say that conducting annual reviews is their second-most-disliked task, trailing only by firing someone in the extent to which they find it unpleasant. The focus on employee assessment is the main thing that makes the annual review so often unpleasant for all involved. However, ongoing **performance coaching** helps minimize this problem. It focuses on providing employees with more frequent and more developmental feedback in an effort to improve their job performance. The ongoing dialog in performance coaching helps to clarify expectations and prevent small performance issues from becoming bigger ones. At the same time it increases trust and improves the supervisor–subordinate relationship. By providing more frequent feedback and discussing both individual and organizational goals more regularly, performance coaching also helps integrate individual and team performance efforts into the overall organizational mission.

When it comes to the variety of performance appraisal methods used in organizations, they should be as reliable and valid as possible.[35] To be reliable, the method should consistently yield the same result over time or for different raters. To be valid, it should be unbiased and measure only factors directly relevant to job performance. At a minimum, written documentation of rigorous performance appraisals and a record of consistent past actions will be required to back up any contested evaluations. Performance appraisal methods can be classified as focusing on traits, behaviors, results, or 360-degree feedback.

## Trait-Based Performance Appraisals

Trait-based approaches are designed to measure the extent to which the employee possesses characteristics or traits that are considered important in the job. For example, trait-based measures often assess characteristics such as dependability, initiative, and leadership. One of the oldest and most widely used performance appraisal methods is a **graphic rating scale**. It is basically a checklist for rating an individual on traits or performance characteristics such as quality of work, job attitude, and punctuality. Although this approach is quick and easy, it tends to be very subjective and, as a result, has poor reliability and validity.

A **performance management system** sets standards, assesses results, and plans for performance improvements.

**Performance appraisal** is the process of formally evaluating performance and providing feedback to a job holder.

**Performance coaching** provides frequent and developmental feedback for how a worker can improve job performance.

A **graphic rating scale** uses a checklist of traits or characteristics to evaluate performance.

**RESEARCH BRIEF**

# Racial Bias May Exist in Supervisor Ratings of Workers

That is a conclusion of a research study by Joseph M. Stauffer and M. Ronald Buckley reported in the *Journal of Applied Psychology*. The authors point out that it is important to have performance criteria and supervisory ratings that are free of bias. They cite a meta-analysis by Kraiger and Ford (1985) that showed white raters tending to rate white employees more favorably than black employees, whereas black raters rated blacks more favorably than did whites. They also cite a later study by Dackett and DuBois (1991) that disputed the finding that raters tended to favor members of their own racial groups.

In their study, Stauffer and Buckley re-analyzed the Dackett and DuBois data for possible interactions between rater and ratee. The data included samples of military and civilian workers, each of whom was rated by black and white supervisors. In both samples, white supervisors gave significantly higher ratings to white workers than they did to black workers; black supervisors also tended to favor white workers in their ratings.

Stauffer and Buckley advise caution in concluding that the rating differences are the result of racial prejudice, saying the data aren't sufficient to address this issue. They call for future studies to examine both the existence of bias in supervisory ratings and the causes of such bias. In terms of present implications, the authors say: "If you are a White ratee, then it doesn't matter if your supervisor is Black or White. If you are a Black ratee, then it is important whether your supervisor is Black or White."

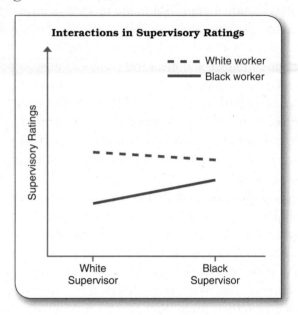

**Interactions in Supervisory Ratings**

- - - White worker
——— Black worker

Supervisory Ratings

White Supervisor      Black Supervisor

### ■ YOU BE THE RESEARCHER

Why would white supervisors rate black workers lower than white workers in this study if the ratings weren't based on racial prejudice? Why might black supervisors favor white workers over black workers in their ratings? What research questions come to mind that you would like to see definitively answered through rigorous scientific studies in the future? Is it possible that the present findings could be replicated with respect to teacher ratings of student performance? Suggest a study design that would examine this possibility.

*References:* Joseph M. Stauffer and M. Ronald Buckley, "The Existence and Nature of Racial Bias in Supervisory Ratings," *Journal of Applied Psychology*, vol. 90 (2005), pp. 586–91. Also cited: K. Kraiger and J. K. Ford, "A Meta-analysis of Ratee Race Effects in Performance Ratings," *Journal of Applied Psychology*, vol. 70 (1985), pp. 56–65; and P. R. Dackett and C. L. Z. DuBois, "Rater-Ratee Race Effects on Performance Evaluations: Challenging Meta-Analytic Conclusion," *Journal of Applied Psychology*, vol. 76 (1991), pp. 873–77.

## Behavior-Based Performance Appraisals

A **behaviorally anchored rating scale** uses specific descriptions of actual behaviors to rate various levels of performance.

Behavior-based approaches evaluate employees on specific actions that are important parts of the job. The **behaviorally anchored rating scale**, or BARS, describes actual behaviors for various levels of performance achievement in a job. In the case of the customer-service representative illustrated in Figure 13.4, "extremely poor" performance is clearly defined as rude or disrespectful treatment of a customer.

The BARS is more reliable and valid than the graphic rating scale because it anchors performance assessments to specific descriptions of work behavior. Behavioral-based appraisals are also more consistent with the developmental purpose of the performance appraisal since they provide specific feedback to employees on

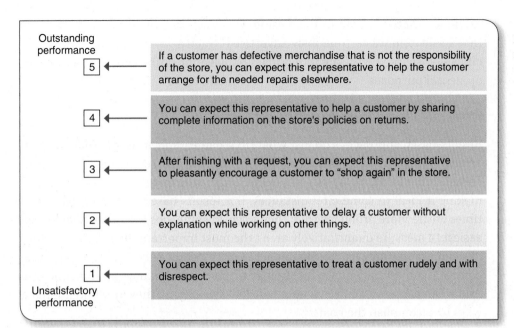

FIGURE 13.4 **Sample of a behaviorally anchored rating scale for performance appraisal.**

Outstanding performance

5 — If a customer has defective merchandise that is not the responsibility of the store, you can expect this representative to help the customer arrange for the needed repairs elsewhere.

4 — You can expect this representative to help a customer by sharing complete information on the store's policies on returns.

3 — After finishing with a request, you can expect this representative to pleasantly encourage a customer to "shop again" in the store.

2 — You can expect this representative to delay a customer without explanation while working on other things.

1 — You can expect this representative to treat a customer rudely and with disrespect.

Unsatisfactory performance

what they need to do better. But one problem is that a BARS evaluation may be influenced by **recency bias**. This is the tendency for evaluations to focus on recent behaviors rather than on behavior that occurred throughout the evaluation period.

The **critical-incident technique** is a behavior-based approach that can make recency bias less likely. This technique keeps a running log or inventory of a person's effective and ineffective job behaviors. Using the case of the customer-service representative, a critical-incidents log might contain the following entries: Positive example—"Took extraordinary care of a customer who had purchased a defective item from a company store in another city"; negative

**Recency bias** overemphasizes the most recent behaviors when evaluating individual performance.

The **critical-incident technique** keeps a log of someone's effective and ineffective job behaviors.

## Recommended Reading

### Profit at the Bottom of the Ladder: Creating Value by Investing in Your Workforce

(Harvard Business Press Books, 2010)

### by Jody Heymann

It is said that employees are responsible for 90% of a company's profitability. Yet many firms invest only in their most highly skilled, best-educated workers, while cutting wages and benefits for workers at the bottom of the ladder as a quick way to improve profits. Researcher Jody Heymann challenges this approach by providing evidence that investing in frontline employees has a powerful impact on the corporate profitability. Drawing on thousands of interviews with organizations around the world, Heymann shows how organizations have profited by improving the working conditions of their least-skilled employees. Examples of practices that improve productivity are higher pay, flexible working opportunities, increased training, and career development.

example—"Acted rudely in dismissing the complaint of a customer who felt that a sale item was erroneously advertised." Such a written record can be specifically discussed with the individual and used for both evaluative and developmental purposes.

## Results-Based Performance Appraisals

Results-based approaches do just what their name implies. Rather than focusing on employee traits or specific behaviors, results-based assessments center on accomplishments. This type of assessment is typically quantitative and objective, making it ideal in some circumstances. But results-based measures can sometimes create more problems than they solve. In some jobs the things that are the easiest to measure quantitatively aren't the most important. In addition, results-based measures may ignore the impact of circumstances beyond the employee's control, such as inadequate technology or poor performance by someone else. And when people are only evaluated on goal attainment, they may find unethical ways to accomplish the goals.[36]

> **Leniency** is the tendency to give employees a higher performance rating than they deserve.

One of the common performance appraisal errors is **leniency**—the tendency for supervisors to rate employees more favorably than they deserve in order to avoid the unpleasant task of giving negative feedback.[37] While leniency tends to be less pronounced in results-based performance appraisals, it may be further reduced by the use of **multiperson comparisons** that formally compare one person's results with that of one or more others. In *rank ordering*, all persons being rated are arranged in order of performance achievement. The best performer goes at the top of the list, the worst performer at the bottom; no ties are allowed. In *forced distribution*, each person is placed into a frequency distribution, which requires that a certain percentage of employees fall into specific performance classifications, such as top 10%, next 40%, next 40%, and bottom 10%. These systems are usually put in place to guard against supervisors giving their employees too lenient or overly positive evaluations.[38]

> A **multiperson comparison** compares one person's performance with that of others.

## 360-Degree Feedback

> **360-degree appraisals** include superiors, subordinates, peers, and even customers in the appraisal process.

It is increasingly popular to include more than the immediate boss in the performance appraisal process.[39] **360-degree appraisals** gather feedback from multiple sources in order to provide a more comprehensive evaluation of the employee's performance. They typically include input not only from the employee's supervisor but from peers, subordinates, and even customers—individuals inside and outside the organization who depend on the job-holder's performance. Most 360-degree appraisals also include self-evaluations by the job holder. Assessments from all these sources are used to identify strengths, weaknesses, and development needs.[40]

---

**LEARNING CHECK 3**

**TAKEAWAY QUESTION 3   How do organizations develop a quality workforce?**

**Be sure you can** • define *orientation* and *socialization* and describe their importance to organizations • give examples of on-the-job and off-the-job training • discuss strengths and weaknesses of trait-based, behavior-based, and results-based performance appraisals • explain how 360-degree appraisals work

# Maintaining a Quality Workforce

"Hiring good people is tough . . . keeping them can be even tougher" states an article in the *Harvard Business Review*.[41] The point is that it isn't enough to hire and train workers to meet an organization's immediate needs; they must also be successfully nurtured, supported, and retained. A Society for Human Resource Management survey of employers shows that popular tools for maintaining a quality workforce include flexible work schedules and personal time off, competitive salaries, and good benefits—especially health insurance.[42]

## Flexibility and Work–Life Balance

Today's fast-paced and complicated lifestyles have contributed to increased concerns about **work–life balance**—how people balance the demands of careers with their personal and family needs.[43] Not surprisingly, the "family-friendliness" of an employer is now frequently used as a screening criterion by job candidates. It is also used in "best employer" rankings found in magazines like *Working Mother* and *Fortune*.

> **Work–life balance** involves balancing career demands with personal and family needs.

Work–life balance is enhanced when workers have flexibility in scheduling work hours, work locations, and even such things as vacations and personal time off. Flexibility allows people to more easily balance personal affairs and work responsibilities. And, research shows that workers who have flexibility, at least with start and stop times, are less likely to leave their jobs.[44] The health-care company Pfizer encourages employees to customize their work schedules around their families' needs. In one year 86% of all employees adjusted their hours at some point, while 50% occasionally worked from their homes or other off-site locations.[45]

Flexibility programs are becoming essential for many employers to attract and retain the talented workers they need. Some are helping workers handle family matters through such things as on-site day-care and elder-care, and concierge services for miscellaneous needs such as dry cleaning and gift purchasing. Others have moved into innovative programs like work sabbaticals—FedEx, Genentech, and General Mills are now offering sabbaticals as a means of motivating (and retaining) their best performers.[46] A few even offer limitless vacation time. At investment research firm Morningstar, employees can take as much vacation time as they want whenever they want. The same goes for online investment information website Motley Fool and software company HubSpot.[47]

## Compensation and Benefits

It may be that no other work issue receives as much attention as pay. **Base compensation** in the form of a market-competitive salary or hourly wage helps in hiring the right people. The way pay increases are subsequently handled can have a big impact on employees' job attitudes, motivation, and performance, and also influences their tendencies to look around for better jobs elsewhere.

> **Base compensation** is a salary or hourly wage paid to an individual.

Benefits rank right up there in importance with pay as a way of helping to attract and retain workers. How many times does a graduating college student hear "Be sure to get a job with benefits!"?[48] But with rising costs, these benefits—retirement plans and health insurance in particular, are becoming harder to get. Most employers that still offer them require employees to pay at least part of the costs.[49]

## Merit Pay Systems

**Merit pay** awards pay increases in proportion to performance contributions.

The trend in compensation today is largely toward "pay-for-performance."[50] If you are part of a **merit pay** system, your pay increases will be based on some assessment of how well you perform. The notion is that a good merit raise is a positive signal to high performers; no merit raise or a low merit raise sends a negative signal to low performers. Because their pay is contingent on performance, both groups are expected to work hard in the future.

---

**FOLLOW THE STORY**  > ZAPPOS' "WORK-HARD PLAY-HARD" SETTING INCLUDES FREE FOOD AND FULLY PAID MEDICAL AND DENTAL INSURANCE

## Tony Hsieh Taps HRM to Keep Zappos One Step Ahead

Brad Swonetz/Redux Pictures

As the CEO of Zappos.com, a popular online retailer that sells shoes, clothing, handbags, and more, Tony Hsieh (pronounced *shay*) has led the company through an amazing growth spurt. He's also forged a creative and unique approach to human resources management. Zappos' distinctive corporate culture gives it an edge over the competition, and Hsieh is determined to hire and retain only those employees who are truly committed to the values of the company.

Before becoming "Zapponians," prospective hires go through two different interviews. In the first one, Zappos interviewers assess their technical proficiency. In the second one, they evaluate the applicant's ability to fit into the Zappos culture, which is characterized by 10 core values. Hsieh actually created the "cultural fit interview" himself. He included questions such as: "On a scale of 1 to 10, how weird are you?" "If they say 'one,' we won't hire them. . . . We like 7s or 8s," says Hsieh. He also notes that "qualified egotists need not apply" because one of our core values is to "be humble."

Once hired, all employees, even executives, are required to go through a four-week customer loyalty training, where they not only spend time on the phone with customers but also work at the company's giant warehouse in Kentucky. At the end of this "KY Boot Camp," boot camp trainees are offered a $2,000 bonus to quit and walk away. When asked why he offers to pay new employees to leave the company, Hsieh says that he wants only people who are committed to his long-term vision. Interestingly, 97% of the trainees turn down the buyout.

Hsieh also believes in creating a "work hard, play hard" atmosphere. To keep Zapponians inspired, he throws a weekly costume party at the main office. Hsieh has also implemented several employee-friendly practices such as providing free food in the company's cafeterias and vending machines as well as paying 100% of medical and dental expenses for employees.

The latest object of Hsieh's entrepreneurial and creative interests is downtown Las Vegas. He's relocating Zappos' corporate offices there to help reinvigorate the center city. He's also spending $350 million of his own money to buy land, renovate buildings, subsidize schools, and back new entrepreneurial start-ups there. Hsieh, who lives modestly, says he isn't worried about making money. "No matter what happens, I don't see my lifestyle changing."

 **WHAT'S YOUR TAKE?**

Is Hsieh's approach to human resource management just an interesting oddity? Or, is it representative of the directions more organizations should be following to attract today's new generation of talented workers? What Zappos approach could be used by just about any employer? What might not fit at all? And if Hsieh moves more and more toward community development projects like the one in downtown Las Vegas, can his practices survive at Zappos without him?

Although they make sense in theory, merit systems are not problem free. A survey reported by the *Wall Street Journal* found that only 23% of employees understood their companies' reward systems.[51] Typical questions include: Who assesses performance? What happens if the employee doesn't agree with the assessment? Is the system fair and equitable to everyone involved? Is there enough money available to make the merit increases meaningful?

## Bonuses and Profit-Sharing Plans

How would you like to someday receive a letter like this one, once sent to two top executives by Amazon.com's chairman Jeff Bezos? "In recognition and appreciation of your contributions," his letter read, "Amazon.com will pay you a special bonus in the amount of $1,000,000."[52] **Bonus pay** plans provide one-time or lump-sum payments to employees who meet specific performance targets or make some other extraordinary contribution, such as an idea for a work improvement. These pay plans have been most common at the executive level, but many companies now use them more extensively across all levels. At Applebee's, for example, "Applebucks" are small cash bonuses given to reward employee performance and raise loyalty to the firm.[53]

**Bonus pay** plans provide one-time payments based on performance accomplishments.

In contrast to straight bonuses, **profit-sharing** plans give employees a proportion of the net profits earned by the organization in a performance period. **Gain-sharing** plans extend the profit-sharing concept by allowing groups of employees to share in any savings or "gains" realized when their efforts or ideas result in measurable cost reductions or productivity increases. As incentive systems, profit-sharing plans, gain-sharing plans, and bonus plans have the advantage of helping to ensure that individual employees work hard by linking their pay to the performance of the organization as a whole.

**Profit-sharing** plans distribute to employees a proportion of net profits earned by the organization.

**Gain-sharing** plans allow employees to share in cost savings or productivity gains realized by their efforts.

## Stock Ownership and Stock Options

Some employers provide employees with ways to accumulate stock in their companies and thus develop a sense of ownership. The idea is that stock ownership will motivate employees to work hard so that the company becomes and stays successful. In an **employee stock ownership plan**, employees purchase stock directly through their employing companies and sometimes at special discounted rates. At Anson Industries, a Chicago construction firm, almost 95% of employees are stock owners.[54] An administrative assistant says it has made a difference in her job performance: "You have a different attitude . . . everyone here has the same attitude because it's our money." Of course, recent economic events show the risks of such ownership. When the company's market value falls, so too does the value of any employee-owned stock.

**Employee stock ownership plans** help employees purchase stock in their employing companies.

Another approach is to grant employees **stock options** linked to their performance or as part of their hiring packages. Stock options give the owner the right to buy shares of stock at a future date at a fixed price. Employees gain financially if the stock price rises above the option price, but the stock options lose value if the stock price ends up lower. The logic is that option holders will work hard so that the company performs well and they can reap some of the financial benefits. The Hay Group, a global human resource management consulting firm, reports that the most admired U.S. companies are also those that offer stock options to a greater proportion of their workforces.[55]

**Stock options** give the right to purchase shares at a fixed price in the future.

## Benefits

**Employee benefits** are nonmonetary forms of compensation such as health insurance and retirement plans.

**Employee benefits** packages include nonmonetary forms of compensation that are intended to improve the work and personal lives of employees. Some benefits are required by law, such as contributions to Social Security, unemployment insurance, and workers' compensation insurance. Also, some types of unpaid leave are mandated by the Family and Medical Leave Act. Many organizations traditionally offered additional benefits in order to attract and retain highly qualified employees. These discretionary benefits include health care, retirement plans, pay for time not worked (personal days, vacations, and holidays), sick leave, and numerous other perks.

The ever-rising costs of benefits, especially medical insurance and retirement, are a major worry for employers. Many are attempting to gain control over health care expenses by shifting more of the insurance costs to the employee and by restricting choices among health care providers. Some are also encouraging healthy lifestyles as a way of decreasing health insurance claims.

**Flexible benefits** programs allow employees to choose from a range of benefit options.

**Family-friendly benefits** help employees achieve better work–life balance.

**Flexible benefits** programs are increasingly common. They let the employee choose a set of benefits within a certain dollar amount. The trend is also toward more **family-friendly benefits** that help employees balance work and nonwork responsibilities. These include child care, elder care, flexible schedules, parental leave, and part-time employment options, among others. Increasingly common as well are **employee assistance programs** that help employees deal with troublesome personal problems. Such programs may offer assistance in dealing with stress, counseling on alcohol and substance abuse, referrals for domestic violence and sexual abuse, and sources for family and marital counseling.

**Employee assistance programs** help employees cope with personal stresses and problems.

**FACTS FOR ANALYSIS**

> UNDEREMPLOYMENT IS MUCH LOWER AMONG COLLEGE GRADUATES THAN FOR THOSE WITH JUST HIGH SCHOOL DIPLOMAS

# Underemployment Affects One-Fifth of U.S. Workers

One-fifth (20%) of the U.S. workforce was underemployed in 2010 according to Gallup, Inc.'s assessment of U.S. employment patterns. Gallup defines "underemployment" as either being unemployed or working part-time when you would prefer to work full-time. This means that close to 30 million Americans were either unemployed or working less than they desired.

- Underemployment declines with increasing education levels. Whereas 38% of respondents with less than a high school diploma were underemployed, only 12% of college graduates and 10% of those with postgraduate work were underemployed. Women are only slightly more likely than men to be underemployed (21% of women versus 19% of men).

- Adults aged 18 to 29 are almost twice as likely (31%) to be underemployed as 30-to-49-year-olds (17%) and 50-to-65-year-olds (17%).

- Underemployed Americans report spending 36% less than their employed counterparts on average, costing the U.S. economy hundreds of millions of dollars.

- Underemployed individuals in the South (42%) and East (40%) are more optimistic about finding full-time employment than those in the West (38%) and Midwest (36%).

**YOUR THOUGHTS?**

Check these facts against the latest data available. Are things getting better or worse for job seekers? What are the implications of underemployment for organizations and the people involved? What are the implications for the economy as a whole? Is there anything an organization can do to keep the underemployed high performing, motivated, and loyal? Is a high level of underemployment likely to affect the wages of those workers who are fully employed?

## Retention and Turnover

All organizations experience turnover, and handling it is part of the human resource management process. Some of the most difficult decisions involve terminations, layoffs, and retirements.

Retirement is one of those things that can raise fears and apprehensions when it is close at hand. Many organizations offer special counseling and other forms of support for retiring employees, including advice on company benefits, financial management, estate planning, and use of leisure time. Increasingly, you hear about **early retirement incentive programs**. These programs give workers financial incentives to retire early. The potential benefits for employers are opportunities to lower payroll costs by reducing positions, replacing higher-wage workers with less expensive newer hires, or creating openings that can be used to hire workers with different skills and talents.

The most extreme replacement decisions involve **termination**, or the involuntary and permanent dismissal of an employee. In some cases the termination is based on performance problems or violations of organizational policy. In other cases the persons involved may be performing well, but may be terminated as part of strategic restructuring by workforce reduction. In all cases, terminations should be handled fairly according to organizational policies and in full legal compliance.

Many employment relationships are governed by the **employment-at-will** doctrine. This principle assumes that employers can terminate employees at any time for any reason. Likewise, employees may quit their job at any time for any reason. In other cases, the principle of **wrongful discharge** gives workers legal protections against discriminatory firings, and employers must have bona-fide job-related reasons for a termination. In situations where workers belong to unions, terminations also become subject to labor contract rules and specifications.

**Early retirement incentive programs** offer workers financial incentives to retire early.

**Termination** is the involuntary dismissal of an employee.

**Employment-at-will** means that employees can be terminated at any time for any reason.

**Wrongful discharge** is a doctrine giving workers legal protections against discriminatory firings.

## Labor–Management Relations

**Labor unions** are organizations to which workers belong and that deal with employers on the workers' behalf.[56] They are found in many industrial and business occupations, as well as among public-sector employees like teachers, police officers, and government workers. Unions have historically played an important role

A **labor union** is an organization that deals with employers on the workers' collective behalf.

### Employers Focus on Wellness Benefits

NBC NewsWire/Getty Images, Inc.

Want to take a work break?—try employer-sponsored Zumba. True enough. More and more employers are focusing their benefits contributions on things that can help the bottom line, and employee wellness is one of them. That's why employees at Dallas/Forth Worth International Airport get their Zumba class as a perk. Other benefits include "lunch and learn" seminars on healthy eating and handling chronic diseases. As just one measure of success, the airport notes that the number of sick days fell by 47% in a year. Employer surveys also show increasing use of work-at-home policies, lactation rooms, legal counseling, and paid or subsidized off-site fitness.

in American society. Although they are often associated with wage and benefit issues, workers also join unions because of things like poor relationships with supervisors, favoritism or lack of respect by supervisors, little or no influence with employers, and failure of employers to provide a mechanism for grievance and dispute resolution.[57]

The National Labor Relations Act of 1935 (known as the Wagner Act) protects employees by recognizing their right to join unions and engage in union activities. It is enforced by the National Labor Relations Board (NLRB). The Taft-Hartley Act of 1947 protects employers from unfair labor practices by unions and allows workers to decertify unions. And, the Civil Service Reform Act of 1978 clarifies the right of government employees to join and be represented by labor unions.

Although union membership has been on the decline in the United States and now covers only about 12% of American workers, unions remain important forces in the workplace. They serve as a collective "voice" for their members and act as bargaining agents to negotiate **labor contracts** with employers. These contracts specify the rights and obligations of employees and management with respect to wages, work hours, work rules, seniority, hiring, grievances, and other conditions of employment.

The foundation of any labor and management relationship is **collective bargaining**, the process through which labor and management representatives negotiate, administer, and interpret labor contracts. It typically involves face-to-face meetings between labor and management representatives. During this time, a variety of demands, proposals, and counterproposals are exchanged. Several rounds of bargaining may be required before a contract is reached or a dispute over a contract issue is resolved.

As you might expect, the collective bargaining process is time-consuming and can lead to problems. When negotiations break down and labor-management relations take on an adversarial character, the conflict can be prolonged and costly for both sides. This happens mostly when labor and management view each other as "win-lose" adversaries. In these situations the collective bargaining becomes more of a battle than a constructive conversation. The ideal process, by contrast, is "win-win" and the ideal outcome is one that offers benefits to labor in terms of fair treatment and to management in terms of workforce quality.

A **labor contract** is a formal agreement between a union and an employer about the terms of work for union members.

**Collective bargaining** is the process of negotiating, administering, and interpreting a labor contract.

---

**LEARNING CHECK 4**

**TAKEAWAY QUESTION 4 How do organizations maintain a quality workforce?**

**Be sure you can** • define *work–life balance* • explain why compensation and benefits are important elements in human resource management • explain potential benefits and problems for merit pay plans • differentiate between bonuses, profit sharing, and stock options • define *flexible benefits plans* and discuss their advantages • define *labor union* and *collective bargaining*

# MANAGEMENT LEARNING REVIEW

## LEARNING CHECK SUMMARY

### TAKEAWAY QUESTION 1  What is human resource management?

- The human resource management process involves attracting, developing, and maintaining a quality workforce.
- Human resource management becomes strategic when it is integrated into the organization's strategic management process.
- Employees have legal protections against employment discrimination; equal employment opportunity requires that employment and advancement decisions be made without discrimination.
- Current legal issues in human resource management include sexual harassment, comparable worth, rights of independent contractors, and employee privacy.

**For Discussion What gaps in legal protection against employment discrimination still exist?**

### TAKEAWAY QUESTION 2  How do organizations attract a quality workforce?

- Human resource planning analyzes staffing needs and identifies actions to fill these needs over time.
- Recruitment is the process of attracting qualified job candidates to fill positions.
- Realistic job previews provide candidates with both positive and negative information about the job and organization.
- Selection involves gathering and assessing information about job candidates and making decisions about whom to hire.
- The selection process often involves screening applicants for qualifications, interviewing applicants, administering employment tests, and doing preemployment checks.

**For Discussion Is it realistic to expect that a potential employer will give you a "realistic" job preview?**

### TAKEAWAY QUESTION 3  How do organizations develop a quality workforce?

- Orientation is the process of formally introducing new employees to their jobs, performance expectations, and the organization.
- On-the-job training includes job rotation, coaching, modeling, and mentoring; off-the-job training includes things like management development programs.
- Performance appraisal serves both evaluation and development purposes.
- Common performance appraisal methods focus on evaluating employees' traits, behaviors, or performance achievements.

**For Discussion What are some of the potential downsides to using 360-degree feedback?**

### TAKEAWAY QUESTION 4  How do organizations maintain a quality workforce?

- Complex demands of job and family responsibilities have made work–life balance programs increasingly important in human resource management.
- Compensation and benefits packages must be attractive so that an organization stays competitive in labor markets.
- Merit pay plans link compensation and performance; bonuses, profit sharing, and stock options are also forms of incentive compensation.
- Retention decisions in human resource management involve promotions, retirements, and/or terminations.
- The collective bargaining process and labor–management relations are carefully governed by law.

**For Discussion What creative options could employers offer lower-wage employees to help attract and retain them?**

## SELF-TEST 13

### Multiple-Choice Questions

1. Human resource management is the process of _____, developing, and maintaining a high-quality workforce.
   - (a) attracting
   - (b) compensating
   - (c) appraising
   - (d) training

2. _____ programs are designed to ensure equal employment opportunities for persons historically underrepresented in the workforce.
   - (a) Realistic recruiting
   - (b) External recruiting
   - (c) Affirmative action
   - (d) Employee assistance

3. The Age Discrimination in Employment Act prohibits discrimination against persons _____.
   (a) 40 years and older    (b) 50 years and older
   (c) 65 years and older    (d) of any age

4. _____ is the idea that jobs that are similar in terms of their importance to the organization should be compensated at the same level.
   (a) Affirmative action    (b) Realistic pay
   (c) Merit pay    (d) Comparable worth

5. A _____ is a criterion that can be legally justified for use in screening candidates for employment.
   (a) job description
   (b) bona fide occupational qualification
   (c) job specification
   (d) BARS

6. The first step in strategic human resource management is to _____.
   (a) forecast human resource needs
   (b) forecast labor supplies
   (c) assess the existing workforce
   (d) review organizational mission, objectives, and strategies

7. In human resource planning, a/an _____ is used to determine exactly what is done in an existing job.
   (a) critical-incident technique
   (b) assessment center
   (c) job analysis
   (d) multiperson comparison

8. If an employment test yields different results over time when taken by the same person, it lacks _____; if it bears no relation to actual job performance, it lacks _____.
   (a) equity, reliability    (b) specificity, equity
   (c) realism, idealism    (d) reliability, validity

9. Which phrase is most consistent with a recruiter offering a job candidate a realistic job preview?
   (a) "There are just no downsides to this job."
   (b) "No organization is as good as this one."
   (c) "There just aren't any negatives."
   (d) "Let me tell you what you might not like once you start work."

10. Socialization of newcomers occurs during the _____ step of the staffing process.
    (a) recruiting    (b) orientation
    (c) selecting    (d) training

11. The _____ purpose of performance appraisal is being addressed when a manager describes training options that might help an employee improve future performance.
    (a) development    (b) evaluation
    (c) judgment    (d) legal

12. When a team leader is required to rate 10% of team members as "superior," 80% as "good," and 10% as "unacceptable" for their performance on a project, this is an example of the _____ approach to performance appraisal.
    (a) graphic
    (b) forced distribution
    (c) behaviorally anchored rating scale
    (d) realistic

13. An employee with domestic problems due to substance abuse would be pleased to learn that his employer had a(n) _____ plan to help on such matters.
    (a) employee assistance    (b) cafeteria benefits
    (c) comparable worth    (d) collective bargaining

14. Whereas bonus plans pay employees for special accomplishments, gain-sharing plans reward them for _____.
    (a) helping to increase social responsibility
    (b) regular attendance
    (c) positive work attitudes
    (d) contributing to cost reductions

15. In labor–management relations, the process of negotiating, administering, and interpreting a labor contract is known as _____.
    (a) arbitration    (b) mediation
    (c) reconciliation    (d) collective bargaining

## Short-Response Questions

16. What are the different advantages of internal and external recruitment?

17. Why is orientation an important part of the human resource management process?

18. Why is a BARS potentially superior to a graphic rating scale for use in performance appraisals?

19. How does mentoring work as a form of on-the-job training?

### Essay Question

**20.** Sy Smith is not doing well in his job. The problems began to appear shortly after Sy's job was changed from a manual to a computer-based operation. He has tried hard but is just not doing well in learning to use the computer; as a result, he is having difficulty meeting performance expectations. As a 55-year-old employee with over 30 years with the company, Sy is both popular and influential among his work peers. Along with his performance problems, you have also noticed that Sy seems to be developing a more negative attitude toward his job. As Sy's manager, what options would you consider in terms of dealing with the issue of his retention in the job and in the company? What would you do, and why?

# MANAGEMENT SKILLS AND COMPETENCIES

## Further Reflection: Conscientiousness

**Conscientiousness** is the degree to which an individual is achievement-oriented, careful, hard-working, organized, persevering, responsible, and thorough. Just how conscientious are you, not only in work and school situations but also in everyday life?

Are you someone whom others would describe as efficient, prompt, systematic, thorough, careful, practical, neat, and steady? If you can check off each of these as a positive personal characteristic, you're on the right path when it comes to conscientiousness. And it's a good path to be on. Conscientiousness often links with job success. Remember too that conscientiousness is easy to monitor. Its presence or absence will always be evident in the way you approach work and how you follow through with the tasks and challenges you face.

 **DO IT NOW...
LOOK IN THE MIRROR**

- Take the conscientiousness test by scoring yourself on the adjectives listed in the paragraph to the left. Ask: "How would others rate me on these same characteristics?"
- Ask also: "Should I just accept where I am in terms of conscientiousness, or are there things I can do to change my behavior in ways that can make me more conscientious in the future?"
- Put your thoughts about conscientiousness as one of your personal traits down on paper. Share it with someone who knows you well and ask whether they agree, or not.

## Self-Assessment: Performance Appraisal Assumptions

### Instructions

In each of the following pairs, check the statement that best reflects your assumptions about performance assessment and appraisal.[58]

**Performance appraisal is:**

1. (a) a formal process that is done annually.
   (b) an informal process done continuously.

2. (a) a process that is planned for subordinates.
   (b) a process that is planned with subordinates.

3. (a) a required organizational procedure.
   (b) a process done regardless of requirements.

4. (a) a time to evaluate subordinates' performance.
   (b) a time for subordinates to evaluate their manager.

5. (a) a time to clarify standards.
   (b) a time to clarify the subordinate's career needs.

6. (a) a time to confront poor performance.
   (b) a time to express appreciation.

7. (a) an opportunity to clarify issues and provide direction and control.
   (b) an opportunity to increase enthusiasm and commitment.

8. (a) only as good as the organization's forms.
   (b) only as good as the manager's coaching skills.

## Scoring

There is no formal scoring for this assessment, but there may be a pattern to your responses.

## Interpretation

The "a" responses represent a more traditional approach to performance appraisal that emphasizes its evaluation function. This role largely puts the supervisor in the role of documenting a subordinate's performance for control and administrative purposes. The "b" responses represent more emphasis on the counseling or development role. Here, the supervisor is concerned with helping the subordinate perform better and learn how he or she might be of help.

# Team Exercise:
# Upward Appraisal

## Instructions

Form into work groups as assigned by the instructor. After the instructor leaves the room, complete the following tasks.[59]

1. Create a master list of comments, problems, issues, and concerns about the course experience to date that members would like to communicate to the instructor.

2. Select one person from the group to act as the spokesperson who will give your feedback to the instructor when he or she returns to the classroom.

3. The spokespersons should meet to rearrange the room (placement of tables, chairs, etc.) for the feedback session. This arrangement should allow the spokespersons and instructor to communicate in view of the other class members.

4. While spokespersons are meeting, group members should discuss what they expect to observe during the feedback session.

5. The instructor should be invited in; spokespersons should deliver feedback while observers make notes.

6. After the feedback session is complete, the instructor will call on observers for comments, ask the spokespersons for their reactions, and engage the class in general discussion about the exercise and its implications.

# Career Situations for Human Resource Management:
# What Would You Do?

1. **Gender Equity Being Questioned**   You have been chosen to serve on a high-level committee appointed by the CEO of your company. The task is to investigate gender equity in the organization. The first meeting is coming up and the chair has asked every member to bring a list of gender equity issues and concerns they would like to raise for discussion by the committee. What will you put on your list, and what short point would you make about each item when first presenting it to the committee?

2. **Bad Appraisal System**   As the new head of retail merchandising at a local department store, you are disappointed to find that the sales associates are evaluated on a graphic rating scale that uses a simple list of traits to gauge their performance. You believe that better alternatives are available, ones that will not only meet the employer's needs but also be helpful to the sales associates themselves. After raising this issue with your boss, she says "Fine, I hear you. Give me a good proposal and I'll take it to the store manager for approval." What will you propose, and how will you justify it as being good for both the sales associates and the boss?

3. **The Union Wants In**   There's a drive to organize the faculty of your institution and have them represented by a union. The student leaders on campus are holding a forum to gather opinions on the pros and cons of a unionized faculty. Because you represent a popular student organization in your college, you are asked to participate in the forum. You are expected to speak for about 3 minutes in front of the other student leaders. What will you say, and why?

## Case Study

# Two-Tier Wages: Same Job, Different Pay

Go to *Management Cases for Critical Thinking* to find the recommended case for Chapter 13 —"Two-Tier Wages: Same Job, Different Pay."

The recession hit automakers hard. It was tough to sell cars and trucks when consumers were struggling. It was tough to earn a profit when costs, especially labor and legacy pension costs, were high. And it was tough to compete with foreign carmakers who were building new cost efficient plants in states where unions weren't strong and wages were lower. America's big firms—Chrysler, Ford, General Motors—had to reduce labor costs if they were to survive. The solution was to introduce a "two-tier" wage system that pays new workers substantially less than existing workers doing the same job. In some cases the new wages are half as large as the old ones. The benefits received by the new workers, including insurance and paid time off, are also lower. So far the labor unions have gone along with the two-tier system. Now that the auto industry is on the rebound, however, questions are being raised. Were two-tier wages just a stop-gap measure that will fade away in an improving economy? Or, are two-tier wages here to stay?

JACKY NAEGELEN/Reuters/Landov

# Wisdom
## Learning From Others

## > LEADERS PROVIDE THE ROADMAPS

When Kraft Foods was bidding to buy the British candy maker Cadbury against its wishes, CEO Irene Rosenfeld was often in the news. The purchase was a key to Rosenfeld's strategy for transforming Kraft. She wanted it to be a global powerhouse in snacks and confectionery, and she didn't give in until she succeeded.

When first made CEO, Rosenfeld said she found a firm that "was not living up to our potential." She focused on engaging the firm's employees and stakeholders in frank discussions, and then embarking on strategies—such as the Cadbury acquisition—to meet her lofty goals. Her latest move is to break up Kraft into two separate companies—snacks and grocery—something she believes will unlock value for shareholders and make each new company a stronger competitor.

Rosenfeld leads with confidence—pushing decision making down the hierarchy, building teams with companywide perspectives, and targeting resources on key markets. She's been called "a risk taker" who makes "bold" moves.

Throughout her life, from school to work, Rosenfeld says "I just never gave much thought to the fact I couldn't do it." Her advice to leaders is "Get the right people on the bus . . . Second, give them a roadmap . . . engage their hearts and minds . . . move quickly . . . communicate frequently, consistently and honestly.[1]

## MORE TO LOOK FOR INSIDE>

# Leading and Leadership Development

## > INTEGRITY

Whether you call it ethical leadership or moral leadership, the lesson is the same: Respect flows toward leaders who behave with **integrity**. If you have integrity, you'll be honest, credible, and consistent in all that you do. This description seems like a no-brainer. "This is what we have been taught since we were kids," you might say.

So, why do we find so many examples of people who act without integrity? Where, so to speak, does integrity go when some people find themselves in positions of leadership?

CEO coach Kenny Moore says that our personal character gets "revealed by how we treat those with no power." Look closely at how people in leadership positions treat everyday workers—servers, technicians, custodians, and clerks, for example. Moore says that the ways we deal with people who are powerless "brings out our real dispositions."

The "integrity line" in the figure marks the difference between where we should and should not be. Below the line are leaders who lie, blame others for personal mistakes, want others to fail, and take credit for others' ideas. They're conceited, and they're also selfish.

Above the integrity line are honest, consistent, humble, and selfless leaders. Some call such leaders "servants" of the organization and its members.[2]

## Insight
### Learning About Yourself

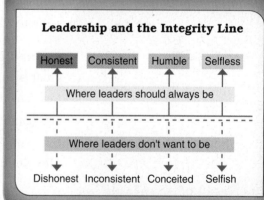

**Leadership and the Integrity Line**

| Honest | Consistent | Humble | Selfless |
|---|---|---|---|

Where leaders should always be

Where leaders don't want to be

| Dishonest | Inconsistent | Conceited | Selfish |
|---|---|---|---|

## BUILD SKILLS AND COMPETENCIES AT END OF CHAPTER

- Engage in *Further Reflection on Your Integrity*
- Take the *Self-Assessment—Least-Preferred Coworker Scale*
- Prepare for the *Team Exercise—Leading by Participation*
- Solve the *Career Situations for Leadership*
- Analyze the *Case Study—Zappos: They Did It with Humor*

**<GET TO KNOW YOURSELF BETTER**

| TAKEAWAY 1 | TAKEAWAY 2 | TAKEAWAY 3 | TAKEAWAY 4 |
|---|---|---|---|
| **The Nature of Leadership** <br> • Leadership and power <br> • Leadership and vision <br> • Leadership as service | **Leadership Traits and Behaviors** <br> • Leadership traits <br> • Leadership behaviors <br> • Classic leadership styles | **Contingency Approaches to Leadership** <br> • Fiedler's contingency model <br> • Hersey-Blanchard situational model <br> • Path–goal theory <br> • Leader–member exchange theory <br> • Leader–participation model | **Personal Leadership Development** <br> • Charismatic and transformational leadership <br> • Emotional intelligence and leadership <br> • Gender and leadership <br> • Moral leadership <br> • Drucker's "old-fashioned" leadership |
| LEARNING CHECK 1 | LEARNING CHECK 2 | LEARNING CHECK 3 | LEARNING CHECK 4 |

The late Grace Hopper, management expert and the first female admiral in the U.S. Navy, once said: "You manage things; you lead people."[3] Leadership scholar and consultant Barry Posner says: "The present moment is the domain of managers. The future is the domain of leaders."[4] Consultant and author Tom Peters claims the leader is "rarely—possibly never?—the best performer."[5] All seem to agree that leaders thrive through and by the successes of others.

If we go right to the heart of the matter, the consensus is that leaders become great by bringing out the best in people. Although this message is clear, the task isn't easy. Managers today often face daunting responsibilities. Resources are scarce and performance expectations are high. Time frames for getting things accomplished are becoming shorter. Problems to be resolved are complex, ambiguous, and multidimensional.[6]

It takes hard work to be a great leader. There are lots of challenges to be mastered. But at the bottom of it all, say scholars Beth Benjamin and Charles O'Reilly, "Leadership is . . . about what you do, how you think, and who you are."[7] So, why not use this chapter as an opportunity to find out more about the leader who resides in you?

## The Nature of Leadership

**Leadership** is the process of inspiring others to work hard to accomplish important tasks.

A glance at the shelves in your local bookstore will quickly confirm that **leadership**—the process of inspiring others to work hard to accomplish important tasks—is one of the most popular management topics.[8] As shown in Figure 14.1, it is also one of the four functions that constitute the management process. *Planning* sets the direction and objectives; *organizing* brings together resources to turn plans into action; *leading* builds the commitments and enthusiasm for people to apply their talents to help accomplish plans; and *controlling* makes sure things turn out right.

## Leadership and Power

Leadership success begins with the ways a manager uses power to influence the behavior of other people. Harvard professor Rosabeth Moss Kanter once called *power* "America's last great dirty word."[9] She was concerned that too many people, managers included, are uncomfortable with the concept of power. They don't realize how indispensable it is to leadership.

**Power** is the ability to get someone else to do something you want done, or to make things happen the way you want. And, the "positive" face of power is the foundation of effective leadership. This means using power not with the desire to influence others for the sake of personal satisfaction. It means using power to influence others for the good of the group or organization as a whole.[10]

Anyone in a managerial position theoretically has power, but how well it is used will vary from one person to the next. Leaders gain power from both the positions they hold and their personal qualities.[11] The three bases of position power are reward power, coercive power, and legitimate power. The two bases of personal power are expertise and reference.

### Position Power

When it comes to the position of being a manager, **reward power** is the ability to influence through rewards. It is the capacity to offer something of value—a positive outcome—as a means of influencing another person's behavior. This involves use of incentives such as pay raises, bonuses, promotions, special assignments, and verbal or written compliments. To mobilize reward power, a manager says, in effect: "If you do what I ask, I'll give you a reward." And as you might expect, this approach can work well as long as people want the reward and the manager or leader makes it continuously available. But take the value of the reward or the reward itself away, and the power is quickly lost.

**Coercive power** is the ability to influence through punishment. It is the capacity to punish or withhold positive outcomes as a way to influence the behavior of other people. A manager may attempt to coerce someone by threatening him or her with verbal reprimands, pay penalties, and even termination. To mobilize coercive power, a manager says, in effect: "If you don't do what I want, I'll punish you." How do you or would you feel when threatened in these ways? If you're like many, you'll most likely resent both the threat and the person making it. You might act as requested or at least go through the motions. But, you're unlikely to continue doing so once the threat no longer exists.

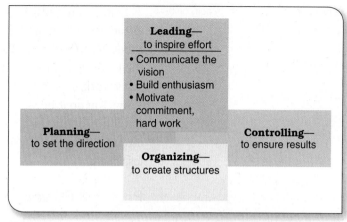

FIGURE 14.1 **Leading viewed in relationship to the other management functions.**

**Power** is the ability to get someone else to do something you want done or to make things happen the way you want.

**Reward power** is the capacity to offer something of value as a means of influencing other people.

**Coercive power** is the capacity to punish or withhold positive outcomes as a means of influencing other people.

---

**Power of the POSITION:**
*Based on things managers can offer to others.*

**Rewards:** "If you do what I ask, I'll give you a reward."

**Coercion:** "If you don't do what I ask, I'll punish you."

**Legitimacy:** "Because I am the boss; you *must* do as I ask."

**Legitimate power** is the capacity to influence other people by virtue of formal authority, or the rights of office.

**Legitimate power** is the ability to influence through authority. It is the right by virtue of one's organizational position or status to exercise control over persons in subordinate positions. To mobilize legitimate power, a manager says, in effect: "I am the boss; therefore, you are supposed to do as I ask." When the instructor assigns homework, exams, and team projects, don't you most often do what is requested? Why? You do it because the requests seem legitimate in the context of the course. But if the instructor moves outside of the course boundaries, such as telling you to attend a campus sports event, the legitimacy is lost and your compliance is much less likely.

## Personal Power

After all is said and done, position power isn't sufficient for any manager. It's very often the amount of personal power you can mobilize through expertise and reference that makes the difference between success and failure in a leadership situation, and even in your career.

**Expert power** is the capacity to influence other people because of specialized knowledge.

**Expert power** is the ability to influence through special skills, knowledge, and information. It is the capacity to influence the behavior of other people because of expertise. When a manager uses expert power, the implied message is: "You should do what I want because of what I know." This expertise can be gained from experience and accomplishments as well as access to useful information. It is maintained by protecting one's credibility by not overstepping boundaries and pretending to expertise that really isn't there. Although some people are granted at least temporary expertise due to credentials, such as medical doctors and attorneys, they can quickly lose it through mistakes and bad behavior. Most of us acquire expertise at work one step at a time. Gaining it, in fact, may be one of your biggest early career challenges.

> **Power of the PERSON:**
> *Based on how managers are viewed by others.*
>
> **Expertise**—as a source of special knowledge and information.
>
> **Reference**—as a person with whom others like to identify.

**Referent power** is the capacity to influence other people because of their desire to identify personally with you.

**Referent power** is the ability to influence through identification. It is the capacity to influence the behavior of other people because they admire you and want to identify positively with you. Reference is a power derived from charisma or interpersonal attractiveness. When a manager uses referent power, the implied message is: "You should do what I want in order to maintain a positive, self-defined relationship with me." It's helpful to view reference power as something that can be developed and maintained through good interpersonal relationships, ones that encourage the admiration and respect of others. Simply put, it's a lot easier to get people to do what you want when they like you than when they dislike you.

## Leadership and Vision

"Great leaders," it is said, "get extraordinary things done in organizations by inspiring and motivating others toward a common purpose."[12] In other words, they use their power exceptionally well. And that use of power is associated with **vision**—a future that one hopes to create or achieve in order to improve upon the present state of affairs. But simply having the vision of a desirable future is not enough. Truly exceptional leaders are really good at turning their visions into accomplishments.

**Vision** is a clear sense of the future.

The term **visionary leadership** describes a leader who brings to the situation a clear and compelling sense of the future, as well as an understanding of the actions

**Visionary leadership** brings to the situation a clear sense of the future and an understanding of how to get there.

### Power: Why Some People Have It and Others Don't (HarperBusiness, 2010)
### by Jeffrey Pfeffer

Eric Risberg/©AP/Wide World Photos

According to Jeffrey Pfeffer, there's no doubt about it. Power plays a major role in a person's career success, salary level, and job performance. He even claims it positively affects one's life span. With power being the engine that helps people get things done in social situations, both work and personal, it's something to be cultivated and not avoided. Pfeffer believes people in organizations need to be politically savvy, they should know the power centers, and be diligent and adept at getting the resources and making decisions. Focus, energy, and ambition are desirable personal qualities for power seekers. But raw intelligence, says Pfeffer, is no guarantee of power.

needed to get there successfully.[13] This means having a clear vision, communicating the vision, and getting people motivated and inspired to pursue the vision in their daily work. Think of it this way. Visionary leadership gives meaning to people's work; it makes what they do seem worthy and valuable. Noted educational leader Lorraine Monroe says: "The job of a good leader is to articulate a vision that others are inspired to follow."[14] Her views match those of the late John Wooden, former stand-out men's basketball coach at UCLA. He once said: "Effective leadership means having a lot of people working toward a common goal." If you can achieve that with no one caring who gets the credit, you're going to accomplish a lot.[15]

## Leadership as Service

*Institutions function better when the idea, the dream, is to the fore, and the person, the leader, is seen as servant to the dream.*

> —Robert Greenleaf of the Greenleaf Center for Servant Leadership[16]

*The real leader is a servant of the people she leads. A really great boss is not afraid to hire smart people. You want people who are smart about things you are not smart about.*

> —Lorraine Monroe of the Monroe Leadership Institute[17]

When thinking about leadership, power, and vision, it is important to remember personal integrity as described in the chapter opener. According to Peter Drucker, the concept of "service" is central to integrity, and leaders who have integrity act as "servants of the organization."[18] More and more today you'll hear conversations about **servant leadership** that is based on serving others and helping them fully use their talents so that organizations benefit society.[19] Ask this question: Who is most important in leadership, the leader or the followers? For those who believe in servant leadership there is no doubt about the correct answer. It's the followers. A servant leader is "other-centered" and not "self-centered."

**Servant leadership** is follower-centered and committed to helping others in their work.

FOLLOW
THE STORY

> "THE JOB OF THE LEADER IS TO UPLIFT HER PEOPLE ... AS INDIVIDUALS
OF INFINITE WORTH ..."

## Educator's Leadership Turns Vision into Inspiration

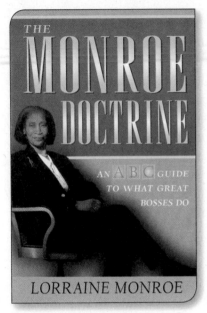

THE
MONROE
DOCTRINE

AN A B C GUIDE
TO WHAT GREAT
BOSSES DO

LORRAINE MONROE

Copyright © 2003 by Lorraine Monroe. Reprinted by permission of PUBLICAFFAIRS,
a member of Perseus Books Group. All
rights reserved.

Dr. Lorraine Mon-
roe's career in the
New York City schools
began as a teacher. She
went on to serve as as-
sistant principal, principal, and vice-chancel-
lor for curriculum and
instruction. Then she
founded the Frederick
Douglass Academy, a
public school in Har-
lem, where she grew
up. Like its namesake,
an escaped slave who
later became a promi-
nent abolitionist and
civil rights leader, the
school became highly
respected for educa-
tional excellence.

Through her experi-
ences, Monroe formed
a set of beliefs cen-
tered on a leader being vision-driven and follower-centered.
They are summarized in what is called the "Monroe Doctrine."
It begins with this advice: "The job of the leader is to uplift her

people—not just as members of and contributors to the organization, but as individuals of infinite worth in their own right.

Monroe believes leaders must always start at the "heart
of the matter" and that "the job of a good leader is to articulate a vision that others are inspired to follow." She also
believes in making sure all workers know they are valued and
that their advice is welcome, and that workers and managers
should always try to help and support one another. "I have
never undertaken any project," she says, "without first imagining on paper what it would ultimately look like. . . . all the
doers who would be responsible for carrying out my imagin-
ings have to be informed and let in on the dream."

Now retired and serving as a leadership consultant, Monroe
retains her commitment to public leadership. "We can reform
society," she says, "only if every place we live—every school,
workplace, church, and family—becomes a site of reform."

### ■ WHAT'S YOUR TAKE?

Is visionary leadership something that works only at the
very top of organizations? Should the leader of a work team
also have a vision? And what about this notion that a leader
should be follower centered? Does that mean that followers
get to determine what gets done and when? What are the
lessons of the Monroe Doctrine for everyday leaders at all
levels in organizations of all types and sizes? Could this doctrine serve you well someday?

---

**Empowerment** enables others to gain
and use decision-making power.

When a leader shifts the focus away from himself or herself and toward others,
what happens? The answer is **empowerment**. This is the process of allowing others
to exercise power and achieve influence within the organization. Servant leaders
realize that power in organizations is not a "zero-sum" quantity. They reject the idea
that in order for one person to gain power someone else needs to give it up.[20] They
empower others by providing them with the information, responsibility, authority,
and trust to make decisions and act independently. And, they expect that people
who are empowered will work hard so that the organization as a whole is more
powerful in pursuing its cause or mission.

---

**LEARNING CHECK 1**

### TAKEAWAY QUESTION 1  What is the nature of leadership?

**Be sure you can** • define *power* • illustrate three types of position power and discuss how managers use each
• illustrate two types of personal power and discuss how managers use each • define *vision* • explain the
concept of visionary leadership • define *empowerment* • explain the notion and benefits of servant leadership

# Leadership Traits and Behaviors

People have recognized for centuries that some persons perform very well as leaders while others do not. The question still debated is *why*. Historically, the issue has been studied from the perspective of the trait, behavioral, and contingency approaches. Although they differ in how leadership effectiveness is explained, each still offers useful insights on leadership development.

## Leadership Traits

**Question**—*What personal traits and characteristics are associated with leadership success?*

An early direction in leadership research involved the search for universal traits or distinguishing personal characteristics that separate effective from ineffective leaders.[21] Sometimes called the "great person theory," the results of many years of research in this direction can be summarized as follows.

Physical characteristics such as a person's height, weight, and physique make no difference in determining leadership success. On the other hand, certain personal traits are common among the best leaders. A study of more than 3,400 managers, for example, found that followers rather consistently admired leaders who were honest, competent, forward looking, inspiring, and credible.[22] And, a comprehensive review by Shelley Kirkpatrick and Edwin Locke identifies these personal traits of many successful leaders:[23]

- *Drive*—Successful leaders have high energy, display initiative, and are tenacious.
- *Self-confidence*—Successful leaders trust themselves and have confidence in their abilities.
- *Creativity*—Successful leaders are creative and original in their thinking.
- *Cognitive ability*—Successful leaders have the intelligence to integrate and interpret information.

**FACTS FOR ANALYSIS** > ONLY 37% OF WORKERS IN A HARRIS SURVEY BELIEVE THEIR MANAGERS DISPLAY "INTEGRITY AND MORALITY"

## Workers Report Shortcomings of Leaders and Top Managers

Harris Interactive periodically conducts surveys of workers' attitudes toward their jobs and employers. The results for "leaders" and "top managers" reveal lots of shortcomings:

- 37% believe their top managers display integrity and morality.
- 39% believe leaders most often act in the best interest of organization.
- 22% see leaders as ready to admit mistakes.
- 46% believe their organizations give them freedom to do their jobs.

- 25% of women and 16% of men believe their organizations pick the best people for leadership.
- 33% of managers are perceived by followers as "strong leaders."

### YOUR THOUGHTS?

How do the leaders you have experienced stack up? Which ones rate as "strong or weak," or as "moral or immoral"? How would you describe your best leader and his or her impact on you? What makes the greatest difference in the ways leaders are viewed in the eyes of followers?

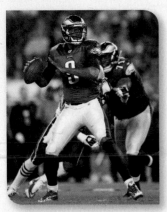

Sportschrome/NewsCom

## Researchers Find Bias against Black Leaders on the Football Field

Are black leaders at a disadvantage when leadership success is evaluated? The answer is "yes" according to research reported in the *Academy of Management Journal*. Scholars Andrew M. Carton and Ashleigh Shelby Rosette studied how the performance of football quarterbacks was reported in the news. They found that successful performances by black quarterbacks were attributed less often to leadership competence—such as "making decisions under pressure," and more often to factors that made up for incompetence—such as having "the speed to get away." Black quarterbacks were more likely than whites to be perceived as incompetent, especially when their teams lost. The researchers expressed concern that black leaders may suffer poor career advancement because of biased evaluations.

- *Job-relevant knowledge*—Successful leaders know their industry and its technical foundations.
- *Motivation*—Successful leaders enjoy influencing others to achieve shared goals.
- *Flexibility*—Successful leaders adapt to fit the needs of followers and the demands of situations.
- *Honesty and integrity*—Successful leaders are trustworthy; they are honest, predictable, and dependable.

## Leadership Behaviors

**Question**—*How is leadership success affected by the ways leaders behave when engaging with followers?*

Moving on from the early trait studies, researchers next turned their attention to the issue of how leaders behave when dealing with followers.[24] If the most effective behaviors could be identified, they reasoned, then it would be possible to train leaders to become skilled at using them.

A stream of research that began in the 1940s, spearheaded by studies at Ohio State University and the University of Michigan, focused attention on two dimensions of leadership behavior: (1) concern for the task to be accomplished, and (2) concern for the people doing the work. The Ohio State studies used the terms *initiating structure* and *consideration* for the respective dimensions; the University of Michigan studies called them *production-centered* and *employee-centered*.[25] Regardless of the terminology used, the characteristics of each dimension of leadership behavior were quite clear.

- *A leader high in concern for task*—plans and defines the work to be done, assigns task responsibilities, sets clear work standards, urges task completion, and monitors performance results.
- *A leader high in concern for people*—acts with warmth and supportiveness toward followers, maintains good social relations with them, respects their feelings, is sensitive to their needs, and shows trust in them.

The results of leader behavior research at first suggested that followers of people-oriented leaders would be the most productive and satisfied.[26] However, researchers eventually moved toward the position that effective leaders were high in concerns for both people and task. Figure 14.2 shows one of the popular versions of this conclusion—

the Leadership Grid™ of Robert Blake and Jane Mouton.[27] The preferred combination of "high-high" leadership on the grid is called the team manager. This leader shares decisions with team members, empowers them, encourages participation, and supports teamwork.

## Classic Leadership Styles

Work in the leader behavior tradition made it easy to talk about different **leadership styles**—the recurring patterns of behaviors exhibited by leaders. When people talk about the leaders with whom they work, even today, their vocabulary often describes classic styles of leadership from the behavioral theories.[28]

A leader identified with an **autocratic style**, Blake and Mouton's authority-obedience manager, emphasizes task over people, retains authority and information, and acts in a unilateral, command-and-control fashion. A leader with a **human relations style**, the country club manager in the grid, does just the opposite and emphasizes people over task. A leader with a **laissez-faire style**, the impoverished manager in the grid, shows little concern for the task, lets the group make decisions, and acts with a "do the best you can and don't bother me" attitude. A leader with a **democratic style**, Blake and Mouton's "high-high" team manager, is committed to both task and people. This leader tries to get things done while sharing information, encourages participation in decision making, and otherwise helps others develop their skills and capabilities.

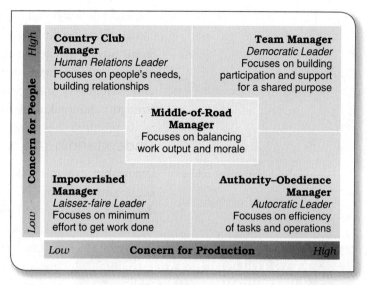

FIGURE 14.2 **Blake and Mouton's Leadership Grid.**

**Leadership style** is a recurring pattern of behaviors exhibited by a leader.

An **autocratic** leader acts in a command-and-control fashion.

A **human relations** leader emphasizes people over task.

A **laissez-faire** leader has a "do the best you can and don't bother me" attitude.

A **democratic** leader emphasizes both tasks and people.

---

**LEARNING CHECK 2**

**TAKEAWAY QUESTION 2 What are the important leadership traits and behaviors?**

**Be sure you can** • contrast the trait and leader-behavior approaches to leadership research • identify five personal traits of successful leaders • illustrate leader behaviors consistent with a high concern for task • illustrate leader behaviors consistent with a high concern for people • describe behaviors associated with four classic leadership styles

---

## Contingency Approaches to Leadership

Over time, scholars became increasingly uncomfortable with the notion of a "high-high" leader. They concluded that no one set of behaviors or style works best all of the time. And, they developed a number of contingency approaches to explain the conditions for leadership success in different situations.

### Fiedler's Contingency Model

**Question**—*Which leadership styles work best in the different types of situations that leaders face?*

One of the first contingency leadership models was developed by Fred Fiedler. He proposed that good leadership depends on a match or fit between a person's leadership style and situational demands.[29]

Fiedler believed that leadership style is part of one's personality and is difficult to change. Thus, he didn't place much hope in trying to train leaders to behave in different ways. He instead suggested that leadership success comes from putting our existing styles to work in situations for which they are the best fit. This requires both self-awareness of one's leadership style and a good understanding of the situational strengths and weaknesses of that style.[30]

## Understanding Leadership Styles and Situations

The **least-preferred coworker scale**, LPC, is used in Fiedler's contingency model to measure a person's leadership style.

Leadership style in Fiedler's model is measured on the **least-preferred coworker scale**, known as the LPC scale and found as the end-of-chapter self-assessment. It describes tendencies to behave either as a *task-motivated leader* (low LPC score) or *relationship-motivated leader* (high LPC score).

Leadership situations in Fiedler's model are assessed according to the amount of control they offer the leader. Three contingency variables measure situational control. The *quality of leader–member relations* (good or poor) measures the degree to which the group supports the leader. The degree of *task structure* (high or low) measures the extent to which task goals, procedures, and guidelines are clearly spelled out. The amount of *position power* (strong or weak) measures the degree to which the position gives the leader power to reward and punish subordinates.

> **KEYS TO UNDERSTANDING LEADERSHIP SITUATIONS**
>
> 1. Leader–member relations—good or poor?
> 2. Task structure—high or low?
> 3. Position power—strong or weak?

Figure 14.3 shows eight leadership situations that result from different combinations of these contingency variables. They range from the most favorable situation of high control (good leader–member relations, high task structure, strong in position power) to the least favorable situation of low control (poor leader–member relations, low task structure, weak in position power).

## Matching Leadership Style and Situation

Fiedler's research showed that neither the task-oriented nor the relationship-oriented leadership style was effective all the time. Instead, as summarized here and shown in Figure 14.4, each style seemed to work best when used in the right situation.

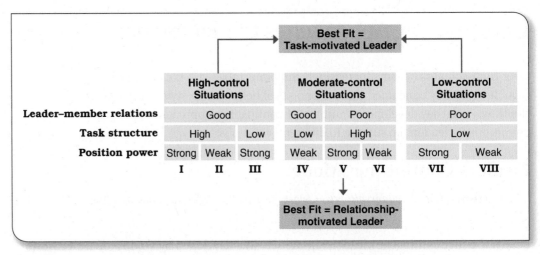

FIGURE 14.3   **Predictions on style–situation fit from Fiedler's contingency leadership model.**

*Task-motivated style*—This leader will be most successful in either very favorable (high-control) or very unfavorable (low-control) situations.

*Relationship-motivated style*—This leader will be most successful in situations of moderate control.

Consider some examples. Assume you are the leader of a team of market researchers. The researchers seem highly supportive of you, and their job is clearly defined regarding what needs to be done. You have the authority to evaluate their performance and to make pay and promotion recommendations. This is a high-control situation consisting of good leader–member relations, high task structure, and high position power. Figure 14.4 shows that a task-motivated leader would be most effective in this situation.

Suppose now that you are the faculty chairperson of a committee asked to improve student–faculty relationships in a university. Although the goal is clear, no one can say for sure how to accomplish it and task structure is low. Because the committee is voluntary and members are free to quit any time, the chairperson has little position power. Because student members thought that the chair should be a student rather than a faculty member, leader–member relations are mixed. According to the figure, this low-control situation also calls for a task-motivated leader.

Finally, assume that you are the new head of a fashion section in a large department store. Because you were selected over one of the popular sales associates you now supervise, leader–member relations are poor. Task structure is high because the associate's job is well-defined. Your position power is low because associates work under a seniority system and fixed wage schedule. Figure 14.4 shows that a relationship-motivated leader is the best fit for this moderate-control situation.

## Hersey-Blanchard Situational Leadership Model

> **Question**—*How should leaders adjust their leadership styles according to the task readiness of followers?*

In contrast to Fiedler's notion that leadership style is hard to change, the Hersey-Blanchard situational leadership model suggests that successful leaders do adjust their styles. But they do so wisely and based on the task readiness, or task maturity, of followers.[31] "Readiness," in this sense, refers to how able and willing or confident followers are to perform required tasks. The four leadership styles to choose from are shown in Figure 14.4 as:

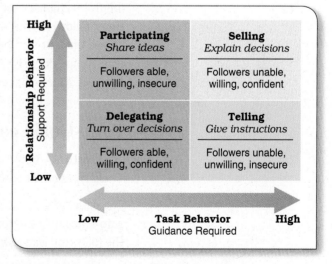

- *Delegating*—allowing the group to take responsibility for task decisions; a low-task, low-relationship style.

- *Participating*—emphasizing shared ideas and participative decisions on task directions; a low-task, high-relationship style.

- *Selling*—explaining task directions in a supportive and persuasive way; a high-task, high-relationship style.

- *Telling*—giving specific task directions and closely supervising work; a high-task, low-relationship style.

The delegating style works best in high-readiness situations with able, willing, and confident followers. The telling style works best at the other extreme of low readiness, where

FIGURE 14.4 **Leadership implications of the Hersey-Blanchard situational leadership model.**

## Would You Put Your Boss Above Your Organization?

Masterfile

**M**anagement scholars like to talk about the "zone of indifference" in leadership. It basically identifies the range of requests that a follower is willing to comply with just because someone is his or her boss.

Most of the time this zone is clear to all. Bosses stick to legitimate requests that others have no qualms about following. But, some bosses take things into ambiguous territory. They ask us to do things that are outside the job description and/or that don't really benefit the employing organization.

Sure, we're getting paid to do these things, but is it only the boss that benefits?

What if your boss wants to pay you overtime to make PowerPoint slides for a presentation he is giving at a conference? It doesn't sound wrong until you learn that he hopes the presentation will lead to a job offer from another employer. What if your boss is active in a local community group? It sounds great, until she asks you to spend part of your workday helping organize one of its fundraising events. The group has no connection to work. What do you say?

By helping your boss with requests like these, you may benefit from extra pay or by building up goodwill in the boss–subordinate relationship. Yet it's also clear that the work you would do on company time has no direct benefit for the organization. In fact, the organization may end up being worse off.

### ETHICS QUESTION

Is it ethical to help your supervisor in the situations described above? Are you doing a disservice to the organization's other stakeholders if you go along with these requests? How far does a supervisor's authority extend? Is it acceptable for a supervisor to ask for help with things that are not directly tied to work? Just where do you draw the line for your zone of indifference?

---

followers are unable and unwilling, or insecure. The participating style is recommended for low-to-moderate-readiness followers—able but unwilling, or insecure. And, the selling style is for moderate-to-high-readiness followers—unable, but willing or confident.

Hersey and Blanchard also believe that leadership styles should be adjusted as followers change over time. If the correct styles are used in lower-readiness situations, followers will "mature" and grow in ability, willingness, and confidence. This allows the leader to become less directive and more participative as followers mature. Although the Hersey-Blanchard model is intuitively appealing, limited research has been accomplished on it to date.[32]

## Path–Goal Leadership Theory

**Question**—*How can leaders use alternative leadership styles to add value in different types of situations?*

The path–goal theory advanced by Robert House seeks the right fit between leadership style and situation.[33] Unlike Fiedler, House believes that a leader can use all of the following leadership styles and actually shift back and forth among them:

• *Directive leadership*—letting followers know what is expected; giving directions on what to do and how; scheduling work to be done; maintaining definite standards of performance; clarifying the leader's role in the group.

- *Supportive leadership*—doing things to make work more pleasant; treating team members as equals; being friendly and approachable; showing concern for the well-being of subordinates.
- *Achievement-oriented leadership*—setting challenging goals; expecting the highest levels of performance; emphasizing continuous improvement in performance; displaying confidence in meeting high standards.
- *Participative leadership*—involving team members in decision making; consulting with them and asking for suggestions; using these suggestions when making decisions.

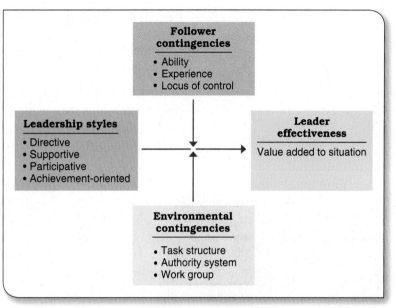

FIGURE 14.5  **Contingency relationships in House's path–goal leadership theory.**

## Path–Goal Contingencies

The path–goal theory advises leaders to shift among the four styles in ways that best fit situational needs. The critical thing is to use the style that adds real value to a situation by contributing something that is missing or needs strengthening. Leaders should avoid redundancy and doing things that are already taken care of. When team members are already expert and competent at their tasks, for example, it is unnecessary and even dysfunctional for the leader to tell them how to do things.

The details of path–goal theory, as summarized in Figure 14.5, provide a variety of research-based guidance on how to contingently match leadership styles with situational characteristics. When job assignments are unclear, *directive leadership* helps to clarify task objectives and expected rewards. When worker self-confidence is low, *supportive leadership* can increase confidence by emphasizing individual abilities and offering needed assistance. When task challenge is insufficient in a job, *achievement-oriented leadership* helps to set goals and raise performance aspirations. When performance incentives are poor, *participative leadership* might clarify individual needs and identify appropriate rewards.[34]

## Substitutes for Leadership

Path–goal theory contributed to the recognition of what we call **substitutes for leadership**.[35] These are aspects of the work setting and the people involved that can reduce the need for active leader involvement. In effect, they make leadership from the "outside" unnecessary because leadership is already provided from within the situation.

**Substitutes for leadership** are factors in the work setting that direct work efforts without the involvement of a leader.

Possible substitutes for leadership include follower characteristics such as ability, experience, and independence; task characteristics such as the presence or absence of routine and the availability of feedback; and organizational characteristics such as clarity of plans and formalization of rules and procedures. When these substitutes for leadership are present, managers are advised in true path–goal fashion to avoid duplicating them. Instead, they should concentrate on making other and more important leadership contributions.

## Leader–Member Exchange Theory

**Question**—*How do in-group and out-group dynamics influence leader–follower relationships?*

One of the things you may have noticed is the tendency of leaders to develop "special" relationships with some team members, even to the point where not everyone is always treated in the same way. This notion is central to leader–member exchange theory, or LMX theory as it is often called.[36]

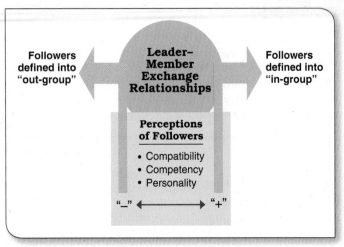

**FIGURE 14.6** **Elements of leader–member exchange (LMX) theory.**

Described in Figure 14.6, LMX theory recognizes that not everyone is treated the same by the leader. People fall into "in-groups" and "out-groups," and the group you are in can make a big difference in your experience with the leader.[37] In-group members enjoy special and trusted high-exchange relationships with the leaders and often get special rewards, assignments, privileges, and access to information. For a follower in the leader's in-group, it's motivating and satisfying to receive such favorable treatments. Out-group members have a low-exchange relationship and may be marginalized, ignored, and even get fewer benefits. For someone in the out-group, it can be frustrating to receive fewer rewards, less information, and little or no special attention.

Just look around. You're likely to see examples of this in classroom situations between instructors and certain students, and in work teams between leaders and certain members. The notion of leader in-groups and out-groups seems to make sense and corresponds to working realities experienced by many people. Interestingly, research shows that members of leaders' in-groups get more positive performance evaluations and report higher levels of job satisfaction. They are also more loyal as followers and less prone to turnover than are members of out-groups.[38]

An **authority decision** is made by the leader and then communicated to the group.

A **consultative decision** is made by a leader after receiving information, advice, or opinions from group members.

A **group decision** is made by group members themselves.

## Leader-Participation Model

**Question**—*How should leaders make decisions in different types of problem situations?*

The Vroom-Jago leader-participation model links leadership success with use of alternative decision-making methods. It suggests that leaders are most effective when they make decisions in ways that best fit the problem situation.[39]

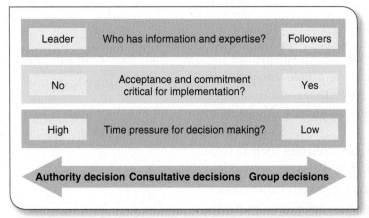

**FIGURE 14.7** **Leadership implications of Vroom-Jago leader-participation model.**

Figure 14.7, shows that a leader's decision-making alternatives fall into three broad categories—authority, consultative, or group decisions.[40] An **authority decision** is made by the leader and then communicated to the group. A **consultative decision** is made by the leader after gathering information and advice from others. A **group decision** is made by the group with the leader's support as a contributing member.

A leader's choice among alternative decision-making methods is governed by three factors: (1) *Decision quality*—based on who has the information needed for problem solving; (2) *Decision acceptance*—based on the importance of follower acceptance to the decision's eventual implementation; (3) *Decision time*—based on the time available to make and implement the decision. Because each decision method has its advantages and disadvantages in respect to these factors, effective leaders continually shift methods as they deal with daily problems and opportunities.[41]

Authority decisions work best when leaders have the expertise needed to solve the problem and are confident and acting alone. They also work best when followers are likely to accept and implement the leader's decision, and when there is little or no time available for group discussion.

Consultative and group decisions work best when the leader lacks the expertise and information needed to solve the problem. They also work best when the problem is unclear, follower acceptance is uncertain but necessary for implementation, and adequate time is available.

Although all decision methods are potentially useful (see Management Smarts), Vroom and Jago believe the consultative and group decisions offer special benefits.[42] Participation helps improve decision quality by bringing more information to bear on the problem. It helps improve decision acceptance as participants gain understanding and commitment. It also contributes to leadership development by allowing others to gain experience in the problem-solving process. Of course, the lost efficiency of consultative and group decisions is a potential negative. Participative decision making is time consuming and leaders don't always have extra time available. When problems must be resolved immediately, the authority decision may be the only option.[43]

---

## ManagementSmarts

### Five Ways for Leaders to Make Decisions

1. *Decide alone*—This is an authority decision; the manager decides how to solve the problem and communicates the decision to the group.
2. *Consult individually*—The manager makes the decision after sharing the problem and consulting individually with group members to get their suggestions.
3. *Consult with group*—The manager makes the decision after convening the group, sharing the problem, and consulting with everyone to get their suggestions.
4. *Facilitate group*—The manager convenes the group, shares the problem, and facilitates discussion to make a decision.
5. *Delegate to group*—The manager convenes the group and delegates authority to define the problem and make a decision.

---

**LEARNING CHECK 3**

**TAKEAWAY QUESTION 3 What are the contingency approaches to leadership?**

**Be sure you can** • contrast the leader-behavior and contingency leadership approaches • explain Fiedler's contingency model • identify the four leadership styles in the Hersey–Blanchard situational model • explain House's path–goal theory • define *substitutes for leadership* • explain LMX theory • contrast the authority, consultative, and group decisions in the Vroom-Jago model

---

# Personal Leadership Development

The opening questions posed for the trait, behavioral, and contingency theories should have prompted you to think seriously about your leadership qualities, tendencies, styles, and effectiveness in various situations. There's no one answer to the question of what makes a particular person—say you—an effective leader. Personal leadership development is best viewed as an ongoing goal that benefits from knowing the concepts and models, but also requires continuous learning as you move from one experience to the next. And, there is always room to grow. If you consider the various theories just visited, listen to what people say about leaders in their workplaces, are open to feedback about your leadership successes and failures, and understand the contextual issues presented next, the pathways of leadership development should be clear and full of opportunities.

## Charismatic and Transformational Leadership

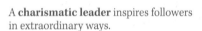

A **charismatic leader** inspires followers in extraordinary ways.

It is popular to talk about "superleaders," persons whose visions and strong personalities have an extraordinary impact on others.[44] Martin Luther King, Jr.'s famous "I Have a Dream" speech delivered in August 1963 on the Washington Mall is a good example. Some call people like King **charismatic leaders** because of their ability to inspire others in exceptional ways. We used to think charisma was limited to only a few lucky persons. It's now considered one of several personal qualities—including honesty, credibility, and competence—that we should be able to develop with foresight and practice.

**Transformational leadership** is inspirational and arouses extraordinary effort and performance.

Leadership scholars James MacGregor Burns and Bernard Bass link charismatic qualities like enthusiasm and inspiration with something called **transformational leadership**.[45] They also lament its absence in the ways of many leaders.

Transformational leaders use their personalities to inspire followers. They get them so highly excited about their jobs and organizational goals that they strive for extraordinary performance accomplishments. Indeed, the easiest way to spot a truly transformational leader is through his or her followers. They are likely to be enthusiastic about the leader, loyal and devoted to his or her ideas, and willing to work exceptionally hard to achieve the leader's vision.

The pathway to transformational leadership starts with a willingness to bring real emotion to the leader–follower relationship. It involves acting with integrity and living up to the trust of others. It requires both having a compelling vision of the future and the ability to communicate that vision in ways that cause others to work hard together to achieve it. Transformational leaders excel in part because of the strong sense of high aspiration, confidence, and contagious enthusiasm they bring to a situation.

RollsPress/Popperfoto/
Getty Images

## Martin Luther King, Jr. Shared An Inspiring Dream

When Martin Luther King, Jr. delivered his famous "I Have a Dream" speech, on August 28, 1963, at the Washington Mall, he connected with a massive audience of civil rights supporters. His choice of words and emotional delivery are exemplars of transformational leadership skill. "I have a dream today," said Martin Luther King, "that my four little children will one day live in a nation where they will not be judged by the color of their skin but by the content of their character." Indeed! The U.S. Congress passed the Civil Rights Act in 1964, and King received the Nobel Peace Prize in 1965.

# Emotional Intelligence and Leadership

The role of personality in transformational leadership relates to another area of inquiry in leadership development—**emotional intelligence**. Popularized by the work of Daniel Goleman, emotional intelligence, or EI for short, is an ability to understand emotions in yourself and others and use this understanding to handle social relationships effectively.[46] "Great leaders move us," say Goleman and his colleagues. "Great leadership works through emotions."[47]

**Emotional intelligence** is the ability to manage our emotions in social relationships.

Emotional intelligence shows up in research as an important influence on leadership success, especially in more senior management positions. In Goleman's words: "the higher the rank of the person considered to be a star performer, the more emotional intelligence capabilities showed up as the reason for his or her effectiveness."[48] This is a pretty strong endorsement for paying attention to Goleman's belief that not only is EI a key leadership asset, it is one that we can each develop.

Consider the four emotional intelligence competencies shown nearby.[49] A leader strong in emotional intelligence possesses *self-awareness*. This is the ability to understand our own moods and emotions, and to understand their impact on our work and on others. The emotionally intelligent leader is good at *self-management*, or self-regulation. This is the ability to think before we act and to control otherwise disruptive impulses. Emotional intelligence in leadership involves *motivation and persistence* in being willing to work hard for reasons other than money and status. Leaders who are high in emotional intelligence display *social awareness*, or empathy. They have the ability to understand the emotions of others and to use this understanding to better relate to them. And, a leader high in emotional intelligence is good at *relationship management*. This is the ability to establish rapport with others and to build social capital through relationships and networks.

# Gender and Leadership

When Sara Levinson was president of NFL Properties, Inc., she asked the all-male members of her NFL management team this question: "Is my leadership style different from a man's?" "Yes," they replied, and even suggested that the very fact that she was asking the question was evidence of the difference. They said her leadership style emphasized communication as well as gathering ideas and opinions from others. When Levinson probed further by asking, "Is this a distinctly 'female' trait?" the men said they thought it was.[50]

Are there gender differences in leadership? In pondering this question, three background points deserve highlighting. First, social science research largely supports the **gender similarities hypothesis**. That is, males and females are very similar to one another in terms of psychological properties.[51] Second, research leaves no doubt that both women and men can be equally effective as leaders.[52] Third, research does show that men and women are sometimes perceived as using somewhat different styles, and perhaps arriving at leadership success from different angles.[53]

The **gender similarities hypothesis** holds that males and females have similar psychological properties.

When men and women are perceived differently as leaders, the perceptions fit traditional stereotypes.[54] Men may be expected to act as "take-charge" leaders who are task-oriented, directive, and assertive while trying to get things done in traditional command-and-control ways. Women may be expected to act as "take-care"

RESEARCH
BRIEF

# Charismatic Leaders Display Positive Emotions That Followers Find Contagious

Reprinted from LEAD-
ERSHIP QUARTERLY,
Vol. 17, Issue 2, 2006.
Reproduced with permis-
sion from Elsevier.

When leaders show positive emotions, the effect on followers is positive, creating positive moods and also creating tendencies toward positive leader ratings and feelings of attraction to the leader. These are the major conclusions from four research studies conducted by Joyce E. Bono and Remus Ilies, and reported in *Leadership Quarterly.*

Bono and Ilies set out to examine how charismatic leaders "use emotion to influence followers." They advanced hypotheses as indicated in the figure. They expected to find that charismatic leaders display positive emotions, that positive leader emotions create positive follower moods, and that positive follower moods generate both positive ratings of the leader and attraction toward the leader. These hypotheses were examined in a series of four empirical studies.

The researchers concluded that positive emotions are an important aspect of charismatic leadership. They found that leaders who rated high in charisma chose words with more positive emotional content for vision statements and speeches. They also found that the positive emotions of leaders were transferred into positive moods among followers; that is, the positive leader moods were contagious. They also found that followers with positive moods had more positive perceptions of leader effectiveness.

These studies, by Bono and Ilies, focused only on positive leader emotions. This leaves open the questions of how

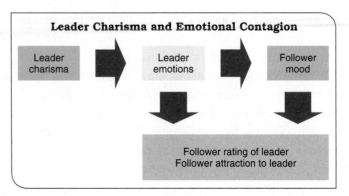

leaders use negative emotions and how these emotions affect followers. Also, the researchers suggest we need to know more about the impact of leader moods on follower performance and creativity.

 **YOU BE THE RESEARCHER**

Is this logic of emotional contagion insightful? What are the implications? Should we conclude that a leader can never allow herself or himself to have a "bad" day, and can never communicate, verbally or nonverbally, anything other than positive emotional messages? Is it realistic for managers to live up to these expectations to always be positive? Could you design a research study to examine these questions?

*Reference:* Joyce E. Bono and Remus Ilies, "Charisma, Positive Emotions and Mood Contagion," *Leadership Quarterly*, vol. 17 (2006), pp. 317–34.

---

leaders who behave in supportive and nurturing ways. Studies report, for example, that female leaders are viewed as more participative than male leaders. They are also rated by peers, subordinates, and supervisors as strong on motivating others, emotional intelligence, persuading, fostering communication, listening to others, mentoring, and supporting high-quality work.[55] In research using 360-degree assessments, women were rated more highly than men in all but one area of leadership—visioning. The possible explanation was that because women are less directive as leaders, they aren't perceived as visionaries.[56]

Harvard scholar Rosabeth Moss Kanter says that in many ways "Women get high ratings on exactly those skills required to succeed in the global information age, where teamwork and partnering are so important."[57] The pattern of behaviors sometimes attributed to women is called **interactive leadership**.[58] Leaders with this style are democratic, participative, and inclusive. They approach problems and decisions through teamwork, show respect for others, and share power and information. They use communication and

**Interactive leaders** are strong communicators and act democratic and participative with followers.

involvement to build good interpersonal relations and seek consensus.[59] They also tend to get things done more through personal power and good interpersonal relationships than through command-and-control use of position power.

One of the risks in any discussion of gender and leadership is falling prey to stereotypes that place individual men and women into leadership boxes in which they don't necessarily belong.[60] Perhaps we should set gender issues aside, accept the gender similarities hypothesis, and focus instead on the notion of interactive leadership. The likelihood is that an interactive leader is a very good fit with the needs of today's organizations and their members. Furthermore, there is no reason why men and women can't do it equally well.[61]

## Moral Leadership

As highlighted in the chapter opener on integrity, society expects organizations to be run with **moral leadership**. This is leadership with ethical standards that clearly meet the test of being "good" and "correct."[62] Anyone in a leadership position will ideally practice high ethical standards of behavior, try to build and maintain an ethical organizational culture, and both help and require others to behave ethically in their work. Unfortunately, the facts don't always support this aspiration.

> **Moral leadership** is always "good" and "right" by ethical standards.

Would you be surprised to learn that a *Business Week* survey found that just 14% of top executives at large U.S. firms rated "having strong ethical values" as a top leadership characteristic?[63] Likely not. But how about this? A Harris Poll found that only 37% of U.S. adults in a survey described their top managers as acting with "integrity and morality."[64]

Moral leadership begins with personal integrity, a concept fundamental to the notion of transformational leadership. Leading with **integrity** means acting in an honest, credible, and consistent manner in putting one's values into action. When a leader has integrity, he or she earns the trust of followers. And when followers believe leaders are trustworthy, they try to behave in ways that live up to the leader's expectations.

> Leaders show **integrity** by acting with honesty, credibility, and consistency in putting values into action.

In his book, *Transforming Leadership: A New Pursuit of Happiness*, James Mac-Gregor Burns explains that transformational leadership creates significant, even revolutionary, change in social systems, while still based on integrity. He notably eliminates certain historical figures from this definition: Napoleon is out—too much order-and-obey in his style; Hitler is out—no moral foundations; Mao is out, too—no true empowerment of followers. Among Burns's positive role models from history are Mahatma Gandhi, George Washington, and both Eleanor and Franklin Delano Roosevelt. Burns firmly believes that great leaders follow agendas true to the wishes of their followers. He also says that wherever in the world great leadership is found, it will always have a moral anchor point.[65]

One of the risks we face in living up to the expectations of moral leadership is **moral overconfidence**. Dean Nitin Nohria of the Harvard Business School describes this as an overly positive view of one's strength of character. He believes this is quite common and we must be vigilant to guard against it.[66] Leaders with moral overconfidence may act unethically without recognizing it or while justifying it by inappropriate rationalizations. "I'm a good person, so I can't be wrong," one might say with overconfidence. "The world isn't neatly divided into good people and bad people," Nohria says. "Most will behave well or poorly, depending on the context."[67]

> **Moral overconfidence** is an overly positive view of one's strength of character.

The concept of servant leadership fits with the concept of a moral leader. So, too, does the notion of **authentic leadership**. Fred Luthans and Bruce Avolio describe an authentic leader as one with a high level of self-awareness and a clear understanding

> **Authentic leadership** activates positive psychological states to achieve self-awareness and positive self-regulation.

Bettmann/©Corbis

## Nonviolence Was Moral Path for Mahatma Gandhi

Mohandas Karamchand Gandhi is praised as a moral leader who rallied nonviolent civil disobedience to support India's independence from Great Britain. He is most often addressed with the honorific "Mahatma," meaning great-souled. Although not known for giving inspirational and emotional speeches, his symbolic and determined behavior was a contagious role model for others. Gandhi's example might prompt us to ask: Where are the exemplars of moral leadership today?

of his or her personal values.[68] An authentic leader acts consistent with those values, being honest and avoiding self-deceptions. Because of this the leader is perceived by followers as genuine, gains their respect, and develops a capacity to positively influence their behaviors.[69] The values and actions of authentic leaders create a positive ethical climate in their organizations.[70]

## Drucker's "Old-Fashioned" Leadership

The late and respected consultant Peter Drucker took a time-tested and very pragmatic view of leadership. His many books and articles remind us that leadership effectiveness must have strong foundations, something he refers to as the "good old-fashioned" hard work of a successful leader.[71]

Drucker believes that the basic building block for success as a leader is defining and establishing a sense of mission. A good leader sets the goals, priorities, and standards. And a good leader keeps them all clear and visible. As Drucker puts it: "The leader's first task is to be the trumpet that sounds a clear sound."[72] Next, Drucker believes that leadership should be accepted as a responsibility rather than a rank. He adds that good leaders surround themselves with talented people, aren't afraid to develop strong and capable followers, and don't blame others when things go wrong. The adage—"The buck stops here," is still good to remember.

Finally, Drucker stresses the importance of earning and keeping the trust of others. The key here is the leader's personal integrity, the point on which the chapter began. The followers of good leaders trust them. They believe the leader means what he or she says, and know his or her actions will be consistent with what is said. In Drucker's words again: "Effective leadership is not based on being clever; it is based primarily on being consistent."[73]

### DRUCKER'S STRAIGHT TALK ON LEADERSHIP

- Define and communicate a clear vision.
- Accept leadership as a responsibility, not a rank.
- Surround yourself with talented people.
- Don't blame others when things go wrong.
- Keep your integrity; earn the trust of others.
- Don't be clever, be consistent.

### LEARNING CHECK 4

**TAKEAWAY QUESTION 4 What are current issues in personal leadership development?**

**Be sure you can** • define *transformational leadership* • explain how emotional intelligence contributes to leadership success • discuss research insights on the relationship between gender and leadership • define *interactive leadership* • discuss integrity as a foundation for moral leadership • list Drucker's essentials of good old-fashioned leadership

# MANAGEMENT LEARNING REVIEW

## TAKEAWAY QUESTION 1  What is the nature of leadership?

- Leadership is the process of inspiring others to work hard to accomplish important tasks.
- The ability to communicate a vision—a clear sense of the future—is essential for effective leadership.
- Power is the ability to get others to do what you want them to do through leadership.
- Sources of position power include rewards, coercion, and legitimacy or formal authority; sources of personal power include expertise and reference.
- Effective leaders empower others, allowing them to make job-related decisions on their own.
- Servant leadership is follower-centered, focusing on helping others fully utilize their talents.

**For Discussion When is a leader justified in using coercive power?**

## TAKEAWAY QUESTION 2  What are the important leadership traits and behaviors?

- Traits that seem to have a positive impact on leadership include drive, integrity, and self-confidence.
- Research on leader behaviors has focused on alternative leadership styles based on concerns for the task and concerns for people.
- One suggestion of leader-behavior researchers is that effective leaders are team-based and participative, showing both high task and people concerns.

**For Discussion Are any personal traits indispensable "must haves" for success in leadership?**

## TAKEAWAY QUESTION 3  What are the contingency approaches to leadership?

- Contingency leadership approaches point out that no one leadership style always works best; the best style

is one that properly matches the demands of each unique situation.
- Fiedler's contingency model matches leadership styles with situational differences in task structure, position power, and leader–member relations.
- The Hersey-Blanchard situational model recommends using task-oriented and people-oriented behaviors, depending on the "maturity" levels of followers.
- House's path–goal theory points out that leaders add value to situations by using supportive, directive, achievement-oriented, or participative styles.
- The Vroom-Jago leader-participation theory advises leaders to choose decision-making methods—individual, consultative, group—that best fit the problems to be solved.

**For Discussion What are the career development implications of Fiedler's contingency model of leadership?**

## TAKEAWAY QUESTION 4  What are current issues in personal leadership development?

- Transformational leaders use charisma and emotion to inspire others toward extraordinary efforts and performance excellence.
- Emotional intelligence—the ability to manage our relationships and ourselves effectively—is an important leadership capability.
- The interactive leadership style emphasizes communication, involvement, and interpersonal respect.
- Managers are expected to be moral leaders who communicate high ethical standards and show personal integrity in all dealings with other people.

**For Discussion Is transformational leadership always moral leadership?**

## Multiple-Choice Questions

1. Someone with a clear sense of the future and the actions needed to get there is considered a _____ leader.
   (a) task-oriented   (b) people-oriented
   (c) transactional   (d) visionary

2. Leader power = _____ power + _____ power.
   (a) reward, punishment   (b) reward, expert
   (c) legitimate, position   (d) position, personal

3. A manager who says "because I am the boss, you must do what I ask" is relying on _____ power.
   (a) reward          (b) legitimate
   (c) expert          (d) referent

4. When a leader assumes that others will do as she asks because they want to positively identify with her, she is relying on _____ power to influence their behavior.
   (a) expert          (b) reference
   (c) legitimate      (d) reward

5. The personal traits now considered important for managerial success include _____.
   (a) self-confidence    (b) gender
   (c) age                (d) height

6. In the leader-behavior approaches to leadership, someone who does a very good job of planning work, setting standards, and monitoring results would be considered a(n) _____ leader.
   (a) task-oriented        (b) control-oriented
   (c) achievement-oriented (d) employee-centered

7. According to the Blake and Mouton leadership grid, the most successful leader is one who acts with _____.
   (a) high initiating structure and low consideration
   (b) high concern for task and high concern for people
   (c) high emotional intelligence and high integrity
   (d) low job stress and high task goals

8. A leader whose actions indicate an attitude of "do as you want, and don't bother me" would be described as having a(n) _____ leadership style.
   (a) autocratic      (b) country club
   (c) democratic      (d) laissez-faire

9. In Fiedler's contingency model, both highly favorable and highly unfavorable leadership situations are best dealt with by a _____ leader.

   (a) task-motivated       (b) laissez-faire
   (c) participative        (d) relationship-motivated

10. _____ leadership model suggests that leadership style is strongly anchored in personality and therefore hard to change.
    (a) Trait             (b) Fiedler's
    (c) Transformational  (d) Blake and Mouton's

11. House's _____ theory of leadership says that successful leaders find ways to add value to leadership situations.
    (a) trait             (b) path–goal
    (c) transformational  (d) life-cycle

12. A leader who _____ would be described as achievement-oriented in the path–goal theory.
    (a) sets challenging goals for others
    (b) works hard to achieve high performance
    (c) gives directions and monitors results
    (d) builds commitment through participation

13. The critical contingency variable in the Hersey-Blanchard situational model of leadership is _____.
    (a) followers' maturity    (b) LPC
    (c) task structure         (d) LMX

14. Vision, charisma, integrity, and symbolism are all on the list of attributes typically associated with _____ leaders.
    (a) contingency        (b) informal
    (c) transformational   (d) transactional

15. The interactive leadership style, sometimes associated with women, is characterized by _____.
    (a) inclusion and information sharing
    (b) use of rewards and punishments
    (c) command and control
    (d) emphasis on position power

## Short-Response Questions

16. Why does a person need both position power and personal power to achieve long-term managerial effectiveness?

17. What is the major insight of the Vroom-Jago leader-participation model?

18. What are the three variables that Fiedler's contingency model uses to diagnose the favorability of leadership situations, and what does each mean?

19. How does Peter Drucker's view of "good old-fashioned leadership" differ from the popular concept of transformational leadership?

## Essay Question

20. When Marcel Henry took over as leader of a new product development team, he was both excited and apprehensive. "I wonder," he said to himself on the first day in his new assignment, "if I can meet the challenges of leadership." Later that day, Marcel shared this concern with you during a coffee break. Based on the insights of this chapter, how would you describe to him the implications for his personal leadership development of current thinking on transformational leadership and moral leadership?

## MANAGEMENT SKILLS AND COMPETENCIES

# Further Reflection: Integrity

Even though we can get overly enamored with the notion of the "great" or "transformational" leader, it is just one among many leadership fundamentals that are enduring and important. This chapter covered a range of concepts, models, and theories useful for leadership development. Each is best supported by a base of personal **integrity** that keeps the leader above the "integrity line" depicted in the chapter opener—high in honesty, consistency, humility, and selflessness. Servant leadership represents integrity; Drucker's notion of good old-fashioned leadership requires integrity; Gardner's concept of moral leadership is centered on integrity. Why is it, then, that in the news and in everyday experiences we so often end up wondering where leadership integrity has gone?

 **DO IT NOW . . .**
**LOOK IN THE MIRROR**

- Ask: How often have I worked for someone who behaved below the "integrity line"? How did I feel about it, and what did I do?
- Write a set of notes on your behavior in situations where your own leadership integrity could be questioned. What are the lessons for the future?
- Who are your leadership exemplars, the ones you most admire and would like to emulate?
- At this point in your life, who is the real leader in you?

# Self-Assessment: Least-Preferred Coworker Scale

## Instructions

Think of all the different people with whom you have ever worked—in jobs, in social clubs, in student projects, or whatever. Next think of the one person with whom you could work least well—that is, the person with whom you had the most difficulty getting a job done. This is the one person—a peer, boss, or subordinate—with whom you would least want to work. Describe this person by circling numbers at the appropriate points on each of the following pairs of bipolar adjectives. Work rapidly. There are no right or wrong answers.[74]

| | | | | | | | | | |
|---|---|---|---|---|---|---|---|---|---|
| Pleasant | 8 | 7 | 6 | 5 | 4 | 3 | 2 | 1 | Unpleasant |
| Friendly | 8 | 7 | 6 | 5 | 4 | 3 | 2 | 1 | Unfriendly |
| Rejecting | 1 | 2 | 3 | 4 | 5 | 6 | 7 | 8 | Accepting |
| Tense | 1 | 2 | 3 | 4 | 5 | 6 | 7 | 8 | Relaxed |
| Distant | 1 | 2 | 3 | 4 | 5 | 6 | 7 | 8 | Close |
| Cold | 1 | 2 | 3 | 4 | 5 | 6 | 7 | 8 | Warm |
| Supportive | 8 | 7 | 6 | 5 | 4 | 3 | 2 | 1 | Hostile |
| Boring | 1 | 2 | 3 | 4 | 5 | 6 | 7 | 8 | Interesting |
| Quarrelsome | 1 | 2 | 3 | 4 | 5 | 6 | 7 | 8 | Harmonious |
| Gloomy | 1 | 2 | 3 | 4 | 5 | 6 | 7 | 8 | Cheerful |
| Open | 8 | 7 | 6 | 5 | 4 | 3 | 2 | 1 | Guarded |
| Backbiting | 1 | 2 | 3 | 4 | 5 | 6 | 7 | 8 | Loyal |
| Untrustworthy | 1 | 2 | 3 | 4 | 5 | 6 | 7 | 8 | Trustworthy |
| Considerate | 8 | 7 | 6 | 5 | 4 | 3 | 2 | 1 | Inconsiderate |
| Nasty | 1 | 2 | 3 | 4 | 5 | 6 | 7 | 8 | Nice |
| Agreeable | 8 | 7 | 6 | 5 | 4 | 3 | 2 | 1 | Disagreeable |
| Insincere | 1 | 2 | 3 | 4 | 5 | 6 | 7 | 8 | Sincere |
| Kind | 8 | 7 | 6 | 5 | 4 | 3 | 2 | 1 | Unkind |

## Self-Assessment Scoring

Compute your "least-preferred coworker" (LPC) score by totaling all the numbers you circled; enter that score here [LPC _____ ].

## Interpretation

The LPC scale is used by Fred Fiedler to identify a person's dominant leadership style. He believes that this style is a relatively fixed part of our personality and is therefore difficult to change. Thus, he suggests the key to leadership success is finding (or creating) good "matches" between style and situation. If your score is 73 or above, Fiedler considers you a "relationship-motivated" leader. If your score is 64 or below, he considers you a "task-motivated" leader. If your score is between 65 and 72, Fiedler leaves it up to you to determine which leadership style is most like yours.

# Team Exercise:
# Leadership and Participation in Decision Making

## Procedure

1. For the 10 situations described here, decide which of the three styles you would use for that unique situation. Place the letter A, P, or L on the line before each situation's number.

   A—authority; make the decision alone without additional inputs.
   P—consultative; make the decision based on group inputs.
   L—group; allow the group to which you belong to make the decision.

### Decision Situations

_____ 1. You have developed a new work procedure that will increase productivity. Your boss likes the idea and wants you to try it within a few weeks. You view your employees as fairly capable and believe that they will be receptive to the change.

_____ 2. The industry of your product has new competition. Your organization's revenues have been dropping. You have been told to lay off three of your ten employees in two weeks. You have been the supervisor for over one year. Normally, your employees are very capable.

_____ 3. Your department has been facing a problem for several months. Many solutions have been tried and have failed. You finally thought of a solution, but you are not sure of the possible consequences of the change required or its acceptance by the highly capable employees.

_____ 4. Flextime has become popular in your organization. Some departments let each employee start and end work whenever they choose. However, because of the cooperative effort of your employees, they must all work the same eight hours. You are not sure of the level of interest in changing the hours. Your employees are a very capable group and like to make decisions.

_____ 5. The technology in your industry is changing faster than the members of your organization can keep up. Top management hired a consultant who has given the recommended decision. You have two weeks to make your decision. Your employees are capable, and they enjoy participating in the decision-making process.

_____ 6. Your boss called you on the telephone to tell you that someone has requested an order for your department's product with a very short delivery date. She asked that you call her back with the decision about taking the order in 15 minutes. Looking over the work schedule, you realize that it will be very difficult to deliver the order on time. Your employees will have to push hard to make it. They are cooperative, capable, and enjoy being involved in decision making.

_____ 7. A change has been handed down from top management. How you implement it is your decision. The change takes effect in one month. It will personally affect everyone in your department. The acceptance of the department members is critical to the success of the change. Your employees are usually not too interested in being involved in making decisions.

_____ 8. You believe that productivity in your department could be increased. You have thought of some ways that may work, but you're not sure of them. Your employees are very experienced; almost all of them have been in the department longer than you have.

_____ **9.** Top management has decided to make a change that will affect all of your employees. You know that they will be upset because it will cause them hardship. One or two may even quit. The change goes into effect in 30 days. Your employees are very capable.

_____ **10.** A customer has offered you a contract for your product with a quick delivery date. The offer is open for two days. Meeting the contract

deadline would require employees to work nights and weekends for six weeks. You cannot require them to work overtime. Filling this profitable contract could help get you the raise you want and feel you deserve. However, if you take the contract and don't deliver on time, it will hurt your chances of getting a big raise. Your employees are very capable.

**2.** Form groups as assigned by your instructor. Share and compare your choices for each decision situation. Reconcile any differences and be prepared to defend your decision preferences in general class discussion.

## Career Situations for Leadership: What Would You Do?

**1. Autocratic Boss** Some might say it was bad luck. Others will tell you it's life and you'd better get used to it. You've just gotten a new boss, and within the first week it was clear to everyone that she is as "autocratic" as can be. The previous boss was very "democratic," and so is the next-higher-level manager, with whom you've always had a good working relationship. Is there anything you and your coworkers can do to remedy this situation without causing anyone, including the new boss, to lose their jobs?

**2. New to the Team** You've just been hired as a visual effects artist by a top movie studio. The team you are joining has already been together for about two months. There's obviously an in-group when it comes to team leader and team member relationships. This job is important to you; the movie is going to be

great résumé material. But you're worried about the leadership dynamics and your role as a newcomer to the team. What can you do to get on board as soon as possible, work well with the team leader, and be valued by other team members?

**3. Out of Comfort Zone** Okay, it's important to be "interactive" in leadership. By personality, though, you tend to be a bit withdrawn. If you could do things by yourself, that's the way you would behave. That's your comfort zone. Yet you are talented and ambitious. Career growth in your field requires taking on management responsibilities. So, here you are agreeing to take over as a team leader in your first upward career move. Can you succeed by leading within your comfort zone? If not, what can you do to "stretch" your capabilities into new leadership territories?

## Case Study

# Zappos

Go to *Management Cases for Critical Thinking* to find the recommended case for Chapter 14—"Zappos: They Did It with Humor."

# Wisdom
## Learning
## From Others

Andrew H. Walker/Stringer/Getty Images

## > THERE ARE PERSONALITIES BEHIND THOSE FACES

*The story:* Woman, unhappy with the way she looks in white slacks, cuts feet off a pair of panty hose, puts them on under slacks, attends party, and feels great. *The result:* Sara Blakely founds Spanx, Inc.

"I knew this could open up so many women's wardrobes," Blakely says. "All women have that clothing in the back of the closet that they don't wear because they don't like the way it looks." With $5,500 and the idea for "body-shaping" underwear, she set out to start a business. But the pathway to profits wasn't a straight line. Others with the same idea might not have succeeded.

Blakely brought a unique experience and personality to the task. She had a passion for direct selling and diligently researched patents and trademarks. When manufacturers balked—with one calling it "a crazy idea"—she persisted. When department stores turned her down, she persisted. Finally, she persuaded a buyer at Neiman Marcus to give Spanx its first big chance.

As sales grew, Blakely realized her limits; additional skills were needed to handle the firm's fast-paced growth. Saying she "was eager to delegate my weaknesses," she turned day-to-day operations over to CEO Laurie Ann Goldman and freed herself for brand development and philanthropy.[1]

## MORE TO LOOK
## FOR INSIDE>

# Individual Behavior

## > AMBITION

When it comes to understanding people at work, one of the big differences is often **ambition**, the desire to achieve or to accomplish something. It shows up in personality as a sense of competitiveness and the urge to be the best at something.[2]

Scholar and consultant Ram Charan calls ambition a "personal differentiator" that separates "people who perform from those who don't."[3] It was a driving force in Sara Blakely's success story at Spanx. Less ambitious persons could have gotten the same idea, but failed to pursue it as a business venture. Or they might have tried to make a business out of it, but ended up quitting when the first obstacles appeared. Ambition in this sense is something to be admired and developed both in others and in ourselves.

But there's also a potential downside to ambition. Charan says people blinded by ambition can end up sacrificing substance for superficiality and even sacrificing right for wrong. Overly ambitious people may overstate their accomplishments to themselves and others. They may try to do too much and end up accomplishing too little. And, ambitious people who lack integrity can also get trapped by corruption and misbehavior.[4]

## Insight
### Learning About Yourself

### PERSONAL TRAITS ASSOCIATED WITH PEOPLE WHO PERFORM

- Ambition—to achieve
- Drive—to solve
- Tenacity—to persevere
- Confidence—to act
- Openness—to experience
- Realism—to accept
- Learning—to grow
- Integrity—to fulfill

## BUILD SKILLS AND COMPETENCIES AT END OF CHAPTER

- Engage in *Further Reflection on Your Ambition*
- Take the *Self-Assessment—Internal/External Control*
- Prepare for the *Team Exercise—Job Satisfaction Preferences*
- Solve the *Career Situations in Individual Behavior*
- Analyze the *Case Study—"Panera: Growing a Company with Personality"*

## <GET TO KNOW YOURSELF BETTER

| TAKEAWAY 1 | TAKEAWAY 2 | TAKEAWAY 3 | TAKEAWAY 4 |
|---|---|---|---|
| **Perception**<br>• Perception and psychological contracts<br>• Perception and attribution<br>• Perception tendencies and distortions<br>• Perception and impression management | **Personality**<br>• Big five personality dimensions<br>• Myers-Briggs personality type indicator<br>• Personal conception and emotional adjustment traits | **Attitudes**<br>• What is an attitude?<br>• What is job satisfaction?<br>• Job satisfaction and its outcomes | **Emotions, Moods, and Stress**<br>• Emotions<br>• Moods<br>• Stress<br>• Sources of stress |
| **LEARNING CHECK 1** | **LEARNING CHECK 2** | **LEARNING CHECK 3** | **LEARNING CHECK 4** |

In his books, *Leadership Is an Art* and *Leadership Jazz*, Max DePree, former chairperson of furniture maker Herman Miller, Inc., talks about a millwright who worked for his father. When the man died, DePree's father, wishing to express his sympathy to the family, went to their home. There he listened as the widow read some beautiful poems which, to his father's surprise, the millwright had written. DePree says that he and his father often wondered, "Was the man a poet who did millwright's work, or a millwright who wrote poetry?" He summarizes the lesson this way: "It is fundamental that leaders endorse a concept of persons."[5]

Contrast that story with this one. Some years ago, Karen Nussbaum founded an organization called 9 to 5 devoted to improving women's salaries and promotion opportunities in the workplace. She started it after leaving her job as a secretary at Harvard University. Describing what she calls "the incident that put her over the edge," Nussbaum says: "One day I was sitting at my desk at lunchtime, when most of the professors were out. A student walked into the office and looked me dead in the eye and said, 'Isn't anyone here?'"[6] Nussbaum founded 9 to 5 to support her commitment to "remake the system so that it does not produce these individuals."

Such things as perceptions, personalities, attitudes, emotions, and moods influence individual behavior—the good and the bad. When people work without respect, as in

### INDIVIDUAL BEHAVIOR SETS

*Performance behaviors*—task performance, customer service, productivity

*Withdrawal behaviors*—absenteeism, turnover, job disengagement

*Citizenship behaviors*—helping, volunteering, job engagement

*Dysfunctional behaviors*—antisocial behavior, intentional wrongdoing

Nussbaum's story, they can tend toward low performance, poor customer service, absenteeism, and even antisocial behavior. But when they work in supportive settings, positive behavior sets—higher performance, less withdrawal and dysfunction, and helpful citizenship—are more likely. As Max DePree says: "We need to give each other space so that we may both give and receive such beautiful things as ideas, openness, dignity, joy, healing, and inclusion."[7]

# Perception

**Perception** is a major influence on individual behavior. It is the process through which people receive and interpret information from the environment. It affects the impressions we form about ourselves, other people, and daily life experiences. And importantly, we behave according to these perceptions.[8] Perception acts as a screen or filter through which information passes before we respond to it. Because perceptions are influenced by such things as cultural background, values, and other personal and situational circumstances, people can and do perceive the same people, things, or situations differently.

> **Perception** is the process through which people receive, organize, and interpret information from the environment.

## Perception and Psychological Contracts

One way in which perception influences individual behavior is through the **psychological contract**, or what the individual expects in the employment relationship.[9] Figure 15.1 shows that a healthy psychological contract offers a balance between individual contributions made to the organization and inducements received. Contributions are work activities, such as effort, time, creativity, and loyalty. Inducements are what the organization gives to the individual in exchange for these contributions. They include pay, fringe benefits, training and opportunities for personal growth and advancement, and job security.

> A **psychological contract** is the set of individual expectations about the employment relationship.

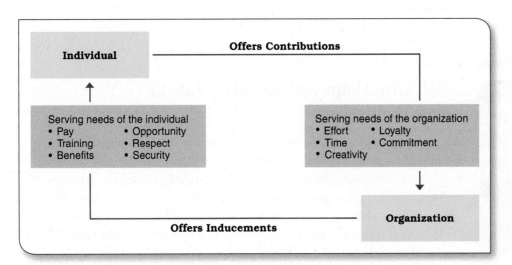

**FIGURE 15.1** **Components in the psychological contract.**

The ideal psychological contract is one in which the exchange of values is perceived as fair. Problems are likely to occur when the psychological contract is perceived as unbalanced or broken. Individuals who sense they are getting less from the organization than they are giving, for example, might try to compensate through lower performance, withdrawal, and poor citizenship.

## Perception and Attribution

**Attribution** is the process of explaining events.

Perception also influences individual behavior through **attribution**, the process of developing explanations for events. What happens when you perceive that someone else in a job or student group isn't performing up to expectations? How do you explain it? And given your explanation, how do you react?

Attribution theory describes how people try to explain the behavior of themselves and other people, while often making errors in the process.[10] **Fundamental attribution error** occurs when someone's performance problems are blamed more on internal failures of the individual than external factors relating to the environment. In the case of poor-quality work, for example, a team leader might blame a person's lack of job skills or laziness—an unwillingness to work hard enough. In response, the leader may try to resolve the problem through training, reward or punishment, or even replacement. Because fundamental attribution error neglects possible external explanations for the poor-quality work, such as unrealistic time pressures or bad technology, opportunities to improve these factors easily get missed.

**Fundamental attribution error** overestimates internal factors and underestimates external factors as influences on someone's behavior.

Fundamental Attribution Error — "It's their fault." ← They are performing poorly | I am performing poorly → Self-Serving Bias — "It's not my fault."

**Self-serving bias** explains personal success by internal causes and personal failures by external causes.

Attribution theory also recognizes tendencies toward **self-serving bias**. This happens when individuals blame personal failures or problems on external causes while attributing successes to internal causes. You can recognize it as the "It's not my fault!" error when something is wrong and as the "It was me, I did it!" error when things go right. Think of this the next time you blame your instructor for a poor course grade or are quick to claim credit for a team project that received a high grade. Self-serving bias creates a false sense of confidence. It causes us to overlook opportunities for personal change and development.

Courtesy Root Learning

## Small Firm Helps People Take Pride in Being Themselves

The individual counts at Root Learning, a small management consulting firm in Sylvania, Ohio, ranked by the *Wall Street Journal* as one of America's Top Small Workplaces. Individual differences are a source of pride. Caricature drawings of each employee are prominently hung in the lobby. The goal is to celebrate diversity and uniqueness while highlighting each person's special interests and talents. CEO Jim Haudan sees this as a way of making sure that everyone is viewed as a whole person. "If we pigeon-hole or just identify any of our people as a 'proofer' or an 'analyst,' it grossly limits what they're capable of," he says.

## Recommended Reading

### Women Count: A Guide to Changing the World
(Purdue University Press, 2010)
### by Susan Bulkeley Butler

Author Susan Bulkeley Butler says women need to think big, take action, assert their leadership value, and help one another. She speaks from experience as the first female partner at Accenture. If some rebalancing of work and home lives is necessary, employers should work with women to redefine the roles to achieve a better fit. Supportive human resource policies can only pay off. Women have real leadership advantages when it comes to things like communication, compassion, listening, and even keeping egos in check. The world needs the qualities they have to offer. "Women count," says Butler. They "have the numbers, the education, the track record, and the characteristics to change the world." Her final appeal is to men and women alike: "It's time to join the new movement. Let's get going."

## Perception Tendencies and Distortions

A variety of perceptual tendencies and distortions also influence the way we communicate with and behave toward one another. They include the use of stereotypes, halo effects, selective perception, and projection. And importantly, they can each cause us to lose sight of important individual differences.

### Stereotypes

A **stereotype** occurs when someone is identified with a group or category, and then oversimplified attributes associated with the group or category are used to describe the individual. We all make use of stereotypes, and they are not always negative or ill-intended. But those based on such things as gender, age, and race can, and unfortunately do, bias perceptions.

Although employment barriers caused by gender stereotypes are falling, for example, they can still cause even everyday behavior to be misconstrued. Scene: A man is talking with coworkers—stereotyped interpretation: he's discussing a new project. Scene: A woman is talking with coworkers—stereotyped interpretation: she's gossiping.[11] And, only a small portion of U.S. managers sent on international assignments are women. Why? A Catalyst study of women in global business blames gender stereotypes that place women at a disadvantage to men for these jobs. The perception seems to be that women lack the abilities or willingness for working abroad.[12]

A **stereotype** occurs when attributes commonly associated with a group are assigned to an individual.

### Halo Effects

A **halo effect** occurs when one attribute is used to develop an overall impression of a person or situation. When meeting someone new, for example, the halo effect may cause one trait, such as a pleasant smile, to trigger overall positive perceptions. A unique hairstyle or manner of dressing, by contrast, may trigger negative perceptions. Halo effect errors often show up in performance evaluations. One factor, such as a person's punctuality or pleasant personality, may become the "halo" for a positive overall performance assessment even though a full set of facts would show it is not deserved.

A **halo effect** occurs when one attribute is used to develop an overall impression of a person or situation.

## Selective Perception

**Selective perception** is the tendency to define problems from one's own point of view.

**Selective perception** is the tendency to single out for attention those aspects of a situation or person that reinforce one's existing beliefs, values, or needs.[13] Information that makes us uncomfortable is screened out; comfortable information is allowed in. What this often means in organizations is that people from different departments or functions—such as marketing and manufacturing—see things from their own points of view and fail to recognize other points of view. One way to reduce this tendency and avoid the negative impact of selective perception is to be sure to gather and be open to inputs and opinions from many people.

## Projection

**Projection** is the assignment of personal attributes to other individuals.

**Projection** involves the assignment of personal attributes to other individuals. A classic projection error is to assume that other people share our needs, desires, and values. Suppose that you enjoy a lot of responsibility and challenge in your work. Suppose,

---

**FOLLOW THE STORY**

> "YOU CAN DECIDE YOU'RE GOING TO BE HAPPY TODAY . . . THE LITTLE THINGS IN LIFE ARE THE BIG THINGS"

## Little Things Are Big Things at Life Is Good

Erick Jacobs/The New York Times/Redux Pictures

*Imagine! Yes, you can! Go for it! Life is good.* We'll make that: *Life is really good!* These thoughts can turn dreams into realities. They're also part and parcel of a multimillion-dollar company that really *is* named Life is Good.

It all began with two brothers—Bert and John Jacobs—making t-shirts for street sales. Picture a card-table set up at a Boston street fair and two young brothers setting out 48 t-shirts printed with a smiling face—Jake—and the words "Life is good." Then picture the cart empty, with all shirts sold for $10 apiece, and two brothers happily realizing they might—just *might*—have a viable business idea.

From that modest beginning, Bert—Chief Executive Optimist—and John—Chief Creative Optimist—built a company devoted to humor and humility. John says: "It's important that we're saying 'Life is good,' not 'Life is great' or 'Life is perfect'; there's a big difference. . . . Don't determine that you're going to be happy when you get the new car or the big promotion or meet that special person. You can decide that you're going to be happy today." According to Bert: "The little things in life are the big things." And that's the message of the Life Is Good brand.

So how did the two brothers turn a belief in happiness into a successful firm? Well, they didn't start with business degrees or experience. They paved the road for prosperity with good instincts, creativity, and positive views on life. And they stuck to their values while learning about business as their firm grew. They still live the brand while enjoying leisure pursuits like kayaking and ultimate Frisbee. They also support philanthropies like Camp Sunshine for children with serious illnesses and Playmakers for traumatized children.

### YOUR TAKE?

Bert and John Jacobs built a successful company with a smile and feel-good approach to life. Just how far can positive thinking carry them? Does there come a point where business need for good old-fashioned management kicks in? How about us? Is there more to be gained by looking for positives than negatives in our everyday experiences and relationships? And when it comes to our lives—*your* life—who's in charge of the "good" factor?

too, that you are the newly appointed manager for a team whose jobs you consider dull and routine. You might move quickly to give team members more responsibilities and challenge. But this may not be a good decision. Instead of designing jobs to best fit members' needs, you have designed the jobs to fit your needs. The fact is that some people might be quite satisfied doing jobs that seem overly routine to you. Projection errors can be controlled through self-awareness and a willingness to communicate and empathize with other persons. To do this you must try to see things through their eyes.

## Perception and Impression Management

Richard Branson, CEO of the Virgin Group, is one of the richest and most famous executives in the world. He's also known for informality and being a casual dresser. One of his early successes was launching Virgin Airlines as a competitor of British Airways (BA). The former head of BA, Lord King, said: "If Richard Branson had worn a shirt and tie instead of a goatee and jumper, I would not have underestimated him."[14] This shows how much impressions can count—both positive and negative.

Scholars discuss **impression management** as the systematic attempt to influence how others perceive us.[15] It's really a matter of routine in everyday life. We dress, talk, act, and surround ourselves with things that convey a desirable image to other persons. When well done, impression management can help us to advance in jobs and careers, form relationships with people we admire, and even create pathways to group memberships. And some of its basic tactics are worth remembering. Dress in ways that convey positive appeal—for example, know when to "dress up" and when to "dress down." Use words to flatter other people in ways that generate positive feelings toward you. Make eye contact and smile when engaged in conversations so as to create a personal bond. Display a high level of energy that is suggestive of lots of work commitment and initiative.[16]

**Impression management** is the systematic attempt to influence how others perceive us.

---

**LEARNING CHECK 1**

**TAKEAWAY QUESTION 1 How do perceptions influence individual behavior?**

**Be sure you can** • define *perception* • explain the benefits of a healthy psychological contract • explain fundamental attribution error and self-serving bias • define *stereotype, halo effect, selective perception,* and *projection* and illustrate how each can adversely affect work behavior • explain impression management

---

## Personality

How often do you complain about someone's "bad personality" or tell a friend how much you like someone because of their "nice personality"? Well, the same holds true at work. Perhaps you have been part of conversations like these: "I can't give him that job; with a personality like that there's no way he can work with customers." "Put Erika on the project—her personality is perfect for the intensity that we expect from the team."

We use the term **personality** in management to describe the profile of enduring characteristics that makes each of us unique. No one can doubt that a person's personality can have consequences for how she or he behaves and how that behavior is regarded by others. The implications extend to our relationships with everyone from family to friends to coworkers.

**Personality** is the profile of characteristics making a person unique from others.

## Big Five Personality Dimensions

Although there are many personality traits, some of the best known are on a short list of five that are especially significant in the workplace. Known as the *Big Five*,[17] these personality traits are:

**Extraversion** is being outgoing, sociable, and assertive.

1. *Extraversion*—the degree to which someone is outgoing, sociable, and assertive. An extravert is comfortable and confident in interpersonal relationships; an introvert is more withdrawn and reserved.

**Agreeableness** is being good-natured, cooperative, and trusting.

2. *Agreeableness*—the degree to which someone is good-natured, cooperative, and trusting. An agreeable person gets along well with others; a disagreeable person is a source of conflict and discomfort for others.

**Conscientiousness** is being responsible, dependable, and careful.

3. *Conscientiousness*—the degree to which someone is responsible, dependable, and careful. A conscientious person focuses on what can be accomplished and meets commitments; a person who lacks conscientiousness is careless, often trying to do too much and failing, or doing little.

**Emotional stability** is being relaxed, secure, and unworried.

4. *Emotional stability*—the degree to which someone is relaxed, secure, and unworried. A person who is emotionally stable is calm and confident; a person lacking in emotional stability is anxious, nervous, and tense.

**Openness to experience** is being curious, receptive to new ideas, and imaginative.

5. *Openness to experience*—the degree to which someone is curious, open to new ideas, and imaginative. An open person is broad-minded, receptive to new things, and comfortable with change; a person who lacks openness is narrow-minded, has few interests, and is resistant to change.

**ETHICS ON THE LINE** > IF YOU WANT THE JOB, TAKE THE PERSONALITY TEST

## Is Personality Testing in Your Future?

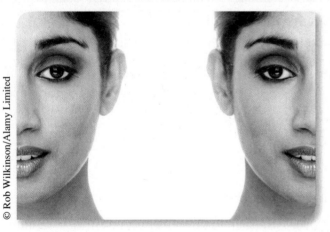

© Rob Wilkinson/Alamy Limited

Thank you again for your interest in XYZ Corp. I look forward to meeting you during the next step in our recruiting process.

Sincerely,

[signed]

Human Resource Director

Getting a letter like this is great news. It's a nice confirmation of your hard work and performance in college. You obviously made a good first impression. But have you thought about this "personality test" thing? What do you know about them and how they are used for employment screening? Some people might even consider their use an invasion of privacy.

### ETHICS QUESTIONS

What are the ethical issues associated with the use of personality testing? What responsibilities does an employer have if they are being used? Should they be required to have data showing that personality tests actually predict key areas of employee performance on the job? Just when is personality testing inappropriate and an invasion of privacy? How should all this be handled by a job candidate as in the case just presented?

Dear [your name goes here]:

I am very pleased to invite you to a second round of screening interviews with XYZ Corporation. Your on-campus session with our representative went very well, and we would like to consider you further for a full-time position. Please contact me to arrange a visit date. We will need a full day. The schedule will include several meetings with executives and your potential team members, as well as a round of personality tests.

A considerable body of literature links the personality dimensions of the Big Five model with individual behavior at work and in life overall. For example, conscientiousness is a good predictor of job performance for most occupations. Extraversion is often associated with success in management and sales.[18] Indications are that extraverts tend to be happier than introverts in their lives overall, that conscientious people tend to be less risky, and that those more open to experience are more creative.[19]

You can easily spot the Big Five personality traits in people with whom you work, study, and socialize. But don't forget that they also apply to you. Others form impressions of your personality, and respond to it, just as you do with theirs. Managers often use personality judgments when making job assignments, building teams, and otherwise engaging in the daily social give-and-take of work.

## Myers-Briggs Type Indicator

The Myers-Briggs Type Indicator is another popular approach to personality assessment. It "types" personalities based on a questionnaire that probes into how people act or feel in various situations. Called the *MBTI* for short, it was developed by Katherine Briggs and her daughter Isabel Briggs-Myers from foundations set forth in the work of psychologist Carl Jung.[20]

Jung's model of personality differences included three main distinctions. First is how people differ in the ways they relate with others—by extraversion or introversion, as just discussed. Second is how they differ in the ways they gather information—by sensation (emphasizing details, facts, and routine) or by intuition (looking for the "big picture" and being willing to deal with various possibilities). Third is how they differ in ways of evaluating information—by thinking (using reason and analysis) or by feeling (responding to the feelings and desires of others). Briggs and Briggs-Myers used all three of Jung's personality dimensions in developing the MBTI. But they also added a fourth dimension that describes how people differ in the ways they relate to the outside world— judging or perceiving. The four MBTI dimensions are:

- *Extraverted vs. introverted (E or I)*—social interaction: whether a person tends toward being outgoing and sociable or shy and quiet.
- *Sensing vs. intuitive (S or I)*—gathering data: whether a person tends to focus on details or on the big picture in dealing with problems.
- *Thinking vs. feeling (T or F)*—decision making: whether a person tends to rely on logic or emotions in dealing with problems.
- *Judging vs. perceiving (J or P)*—work style: whether a person prefers order and control or acts with flexibility and spontaneity.

Sixteen possible MBTI personality types result from combinations of four dimensions just described.[21] A sample of Myers-Briggs types often found in work settings is shown in the box. Such neat and understandable personality classifications have made the Myers-Briggs Type Indicator popular in management.[22] Employers and trainers like it because people can be taught both to understand their own personality types, for example as an ESTJ or ISJF, and to learn how to work better with people having different ones.

### SAMPLE MYERS-BRIGGS TYPES

- ESTJ (extraverted, sensing, thinking, judging)—decisive, logical, and quick to dig in; common among managers.

- ENTJ (extraverted, intuitive, thinking, judging)—analytical, strategic, quick to take charge; common for leaders.

- ISJF (introverted, sensing, judging, feeling)—conscientious, considerate, and helpful; common among team players.

- INTJ (introverted, intuitive, thinking, judging)—insightful, free thinking, determined; common for visionaries.

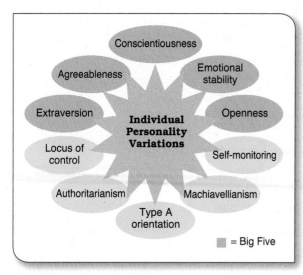

FIGURE 15.2 **Common personality dimensions that influence human behavior at work.**

**Locus of control** is the extent to which one believes that what happens is within one's control.

**Authoritarianism** is the degree to which a person tends to defer to authority.

# Personal Conception and Emotional Adjustment Traits

In addition to the Big Five dimensions and the Myers-Briggs Type Indicator, psychologists have long studied many other personality traits. As shown in Figure 15.2, some with special relevance to people at work include the personal conception traits of locus of control, authoritarianism, Machiavellianism, and self-monitoring, as well as the emotional adjustment trait of Type A orientation.[23] In general, you can think of a *personal conception trait* as describing how people by personality tend to relate with the environment, while an *emotional adjustment trait* describes how they are inclined toward handling stress and uncomfortable situations.

## Locus of Control

Scholars have a strong interest in **locus of control**, recognizing that some people believe they are in control of their destinies, while others believe that what happens to them is beyond their control.[24] "Internals" are more self-confident and accept responsibility for their own actions. "Externals" are more prone to blame others and outside forces for what happens to them. Research suggests that internals tend to be more satisfied and less alienated from their work.

## Authoritarianism

**Authoritarianism** is the degree to which a person defers to authority and accepts status differences.[25] Someone with an authoritarian personality tends to act rigidly and be control-oriented when in a leadership capacity. This same person is likely to act subservient and comply with rules when in a follower capacity. The tendency of people with authoritarian personalities to obey can cause problems if they follow orders to the point of acting unethically or even illegally.

## Machiavellianism

In his 16th-century book, *The Prince*, Niccolo Machiavelli gained lasting fame for giving his prince advice on how to use power to achieve personal goals.[26] The

# Does Success Come from Hard Work, Good Luck, or a Bit of Both?

A survey of LinkedIn members in 15 countries reports that 84% believe that luck influences their careers—for good and bad. But they also say that luck is something we create for ourselves, with good luck coming mostly to those who have a strong work ethic. In addition to work ethic, other things believed to drive good luck include communication skills, networking, being flexible, and acting on opportunities when they arise. Japanese survey respondents considered themselves most lucky in their careers while Americans—with 49% feeling career luck—ranked in the middle.

personality trait of **Machiavellianism** describes the extent to which someone is emotionally detached and manipulative in using power.[27] A person with a "high-Mach" personality is viewed as exploitative and unconcerned about others, often acting with the assumption that the end justifies the means. A person with a "low-Mach" personality, by contrast, would be deferential in allowing others to exert power over him or her.

> **Machiavellianism** describes the extent to which someone is emotionally detached and manipulative.

## Self-Monitoring

**Self-monitoring** reflects the degree to which someone is able to adjust and modify behavior in response to the immediate situation and to external factors.[28] A person high in self-monitoring tends to be a learner, comfortable with feedback, and both willing and able to change. Because high self-monitors are flexible in changing behavior from one situation to the next, it may be hard to get a clear reading on where they stand. A person low in self-monitoring, by contrast, is predictable and tends to act consistently regardless of circumstances.

> **Self-monitoring** is the degree to which someone is able to adjust behavior in response to external factors.

## Type A Personality

A **Type A personality** is high in achievement orientation, impatience, and perfectionism. One of the important tendencies of Type A persons is to bring stress on themselves, even in situations others may find relatively stress free. You can spot Type A personality tendencies in yourself and others through the following patterns of behavior.[29]

> A **Type A personality** is a person oriented toward extreme achievement, impatience, and perfectionism.

- Always moving, walking, and eating rapidly.
- Acting impatient, hurrying others, put off by waiting.
- Doing, or trying to do, several things at once.
- Feeling guilty when relaxing.
- Hurrying or interrupting the speech of others.

---

**LEARNING CHECK 2**

**TAKEAWAY QUESTION 2 What should we know about personalities in the workplace?**

**Be sure you can** • list the Big Five personality traits and give work-related examples of each • list and explain the four dimensions used to assess personality in the MBTI • list five personal conception and emotional adjustment personality traits and give work-related examples for each

---

# Attitudes

When Challis M. Lowe was executive vice president at Ryder System, she was one of only two African American women among the five highest-paid executives in over 400 U.S. companies.[30] She rose to the top after a 25-year career that included several changes of employers and lots of stressors—working-mother guilt, a failed marriage, gender bias on the job, and an MBA degree earned part-time. Through it all, she once said: "I've never let being scared stop me from doing something. Just because you haven't done it before doesn't mean you shouldn't try." That, simply put, is what we would call a "can-do" attitude!

## What Is an Attitude?

An **attitude** is a predisposition to act in a certain way.

**Attitudes** are predispositions to act in a certain way toward people and things in our environment.[31] To fully understand them, it helps to recognize the three components shown in the small box. First, the *cognitive component* reflects a belief or an opinion. You might believe, for example, that your management course is very interesting.

Second, the *affective or emotional component* of an attitude reflects a specific feeling. For example, you might feel very good about being a management major. Third, the *behavioral component* of an attitude reflects an intention to behave in a manner consistent with the belief and feeling. Using the same example again, you might say to yourself: "I am going to work hard and try to get an A in all my management courses."

The intentions reflected in an attitude may or may not be confirmed in actual behavior. Despite having a positive attitude and all good intentions in your management courses, for example, the demands of family, friends, or leisure activities might use up time you would otherwise devote to studying. You end up not working hard enough to get an A, and fail to live up to your original intentions.

**Components of Individual Attitudes**

Cognition → Affect → Behavior

| "This job isn't challenging; work is important to me." | "I really don't like my job." | "I'm going to ask for a better job, or quit." |

Cognitive dissonance is discomfort felt when attitude and behavior are inconsistent.

The psychological concept of **cognitive dissonance** describes the discomfort felt when one's attitude and behavior are inconsistent.[32] For most people, dissonance is very uncomfortable and results in changing the attitude to fit the behavior ("Oh, I really don't like management that much anyway"), changing future behavior to fit the attitude (dropping out of intramural sports to get extra study time), or rationalizing to force the two to be compatible ("Management is an okay major, but being a manager also requires the experience I'm gaining in my extracurricular activities").

## What Is Job Satisfaction?

**Job satisfaction** is the degree to which an individual feels positive or negative about a job.

People hold attitudes about many things at work—bosses, each other, tasks, policies, goals, and more. One of the most discussed work attitudes is **job satisfaction,** the degree to which an individual feels positive or negative about various aspects of work.[33] The following are among the job satisfaction facets most commonly discussed and measured:

- *Work itself*—Does the job offer responsibility, interest, challenge?
- *Quality of supervision*—Are task help and social support available?
- *Coworkers*—How much harmony, respect, friendliness exists?
- *Opportunities*—Are there avenues for promotion, learning, growth?
- *Pay*—Is compensation, actual and perceived, fair and substantial?
- *Work conditions*—Do conditions offer comfort, safety, support?
- *Security*—Is the job and employment secure?

### Job Satisfaction Trends

If you watch or read the news, you'll regularly find reports on job satisfaction. You'll also find lots of job satisfaction studies in the academic literature. The results don't always agree, but they do show that job satisfaction tends to be higher in small firms and lower in large ones, that it tends to run together with overall life satisfaction, and that the general trend has been down for several years.[34]

RESEARCH
BRIEF

# Business Students More Satisfied with Their Lives Perform Better

Wondering if "a happy student is a high-performing student," Joseph C. Rode, Marne L. Arthaud-Day, Christine H. Mooney, Janet P. Near, Timothy T. Baldwin, William H. Bommer, and Robert S. Rubin hypothesized that students' satisfaction with their life and student domains would, along with cognitive abilities, have a positive influence on academic performance.

A sample of 673 business students completed satisfaction and IQ questionnaires, and their academic performance was measured by self-reported GPAs and performance on a 3-hour simulation exercise. The findings confirmed the expected relationships between students' leisure and family satisfaction and overall life satisfaction. Also confirmed were links between both life satisfaction and IQ scores, and self-reported GPA and simulation performance. Expected relationships between students' university and housing satisfaction and overall life satisfaction proved not to be significant.

Rode et al. point out that "it is time to more fully acknowledge that college students also live 'integrated lives' and are heavily influenced by the milieu that surrounds them."

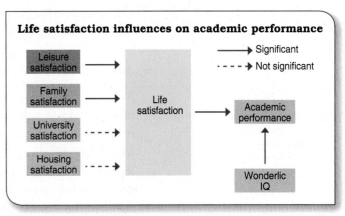

**Life satisfaction influences on academic performance**

→ Significant
┅┅→ Not significant

Leisure satisfaction → Life satisfaction → Academic performance
Family satisfaction →
University satisfaction ┅┅→
Housing satisfaction ┅┅→
Wonderlic IQ →

 **YOU BE THE RESEARCHER**

Does your everyday experience as a student support these results or contradict them? Build a model that describes how you would predict student academic performance, not limiting yourself to directions used in this study. If it is true that students' academic performance is influenced by overall life satisfaction, what does this mean to an instructor or to a college administrator?

*Reference:* Joseph C. Rode, Marne L. Arthaud-Day, Christine H. Mooney, Janet P. Near, Timothy T. Baldwin, William H. Bommer, and Robert S. Rubin, "Life Satisfaction and Student Performance," *Academy of Management Learning & Education*, vol. 4 (2005), pp. 421–33.

---

Conference Board surveys identify a slide in reported job satisfaction. In 1987 about 61% of workers said they were satisfied. By 2008 that dropped to 49% and by 2010, after the effects of the recession were in full force, it dropped further to 45%. Younger workers under 25 were the least happy, with 64% reporting dissatisfaction. Among other findings, only 51% of all workers surveyed said their jobs were interesting, 56% liked their co-workers, and 51% were satisfied with their bosses. These data say "something troubling about work in America," according to a Conference Board analyst.[35]

## Job Satisfaction and Its Outcomes

An effective manager helps others achieve both high performance and job satisfaction. Surely you can accept that job satisfaction is an important goal on quality-of-work-life grounds alone; people deserve to have satisfying work experiences. But, is job satisfaction important in other than a "feel-good" sense? Here is what we know.

### Job Satisfaction and Withdrawal Behaviors

A strong relationship exists between job satisfaction and the **withdrawal behaviors** of temporary absenteeism and actual job turnover. With regard to *absenteeism*, workers who are more satisfied with their jobs are absent less often than those

**Withdrawal behaviors** occur as temporary absenteeism and actual job turnover.

who are dissatisfied. With regard to *turnover*, satisfied workers are more likely to stay and dissatisfied workers are more likely to quit their jobs.[36]

Both findings are important. Absenteeism and turnover are costly in terms of the recruitment and training needed to replace workers, as well as in the productivity lost while new workers are learning how to perform up to expectations.[37] In fact, one study found that changing retention rates up or down results in magnified changes to corporate earnings. It also warns about the negative impact on corporate performance of declining employee loyalty and high turnover.[38]

## Job Satisfaction and Employee Engagement

**Employee engagement** is a strong positive feeling about one's job and the organization.

A survey of 55,000 American workers by the Gallup organization suggests that business profits rise with higher levels of **employee engagement**—a strong sense of belonging or connection with one's job and employer.[39] It shows up as being willing to help others, always trying to do something extra to improve performance, and feeling and speaking positively about the organization. Things that counted most toward employee engagement among workers in the Gallup research were believing they had the opportunity to do their best every day, believing their opinions count, believing fellow workers are committed to quality, and believing there is a direct connection between their work and the company's mission.[40]

**Job involvement** is the extent to which an individual feels dedicated to a job.

**Organizational commitment** is the loyalty an individual feels toward the organization.

Employee engagement also links with two other attitudes that influence individual behavior at work. **Job involvement** is the extent to which an individual feels dedicated to a job. Someone with high job involvement psychologically identifies with her or his job, and, for example, would be expected to work beyond expectations to complete a special project. **Organizational commitment** reflects the degree of loyalty an individual feels toward the organization. Individuals with a high organizational commitment identify strongly with the organization and take pride in considering themselves a member. Researchers find that strong *emotional commitments* to the organization—based on values and interests of others, are as much

**FACTS FOR ANALYSIS**

> ONLY 30% OF YOUNG ADULTS CONSIDER THEIR
  PRESENT JOBS AS PART OF A REAL CAREER

# Tough Times Shown in Employment Trends for Younger Workers

Ongoing research on job satisfaction and employment among young adults (ages 18 – 34) shows the difficulties they face in dealing with hard economic times.

- 30% consider their present jobs a real career.
- 49% took jobs they didn't like in order to pay their bills.
- 24% have taken unpaid jobs to get experience on their resumes.
- 46% believe they have the education and skills needed to do well.
- 35% went back to school because of the recession.
- 20% put off marriage and 22% put off having a baby.
- 24% moved back in with parents to save money.

 **YOUR THOUGHTS?**

Do these data seem consistent with your work experiences and those of your friends and family? Are people with jobs going to be "satisfied" just because they're employed and earning a paycheck? Or, does uncertainty in the economy change the relationship between what we want from work and what we expect in return? What can a concerned employer do to create conditions for high job satisfaction given these data?

as four times more powerful in positively influencing performance than are *rational commitments*—based primarily on pay and self-interests.[41]

## Job Satisfaction and Organizational Citizenship

Have you ever wondered about those people who are always willing to "go beyond the call of duty" or "go the extra mile" in their work?[42] Such behaviors represent **organizational citizenship** and are also linked with job satisfaction.[43] A person who is a good organizational citizen does things that, although not required, help advance the performance of the organization. Examples are a service worker who goes to extraordinary lengths to take care of a customer, a team member who is always willing to take on extra tasks, or an employee who always volunteers to stay late at no pay just to make sure a key job gets done right.

**Organizational citizenship** is a willingness to "go beyond the call of duty" or "go the extra mile" in one's work.

## Job Satisfaction and Job Performance

The job satisfaction and job performance relationship is somewhat complicated.[44] Three plausible arguments are depicted in the small figure.

There is probably a modest link between job satisfaction and performance.[45] But, keep the stress on the word *modest* in the last sentence. We shouldn't rush to conclude that making people happy is a surefire way to improve their job performance. The reality is that some people will like their jobs, be very satisfied, and still will not perform very well. That's just part of the complexity regarding individual differences. When you think of this, remember a sign that once hung in a tavern near a Ford plant in Michigan: "I spend 40 hours a week here, am I supposed to work too?"

> **Arguments in the Job Satisfaction and Performance Relationship**
>
> "The happy worker is a productive worker."
>
> **Satisfaction ⟶ Performance**
>
> "The productive worker is a happy worker."
>
> **Performance ⟶ Satisfaction**
>
> "Performance followed by rewards creates satisfaction; satisfaction influences future performance."
>
> **Performance ⟶ Rewards ⟶ Satisfaction**

There is also a link between performance and job satisfaction. High-performing workers are likely to feel satisfied. Here again, caution is called for; not everyone is likely to fit the model. Some people may get their jobs done and meet high performance expectations while still not feeling satisfied. Given that job satisfaction is a good predictor of absenteeism and turnover, managers might be well advised to worry about losing highly productive but unhappy workers unless changes are made to increase their job satisfaction.

Finally, job satisfaction and job performance most likely influence one another. But the relationship is also most likely to hold under certain "conditions," particularly those related to rewards. We know that job performance followed by rewards that are valued and perceived as fair tends to create job satisfaction. This experienced satisfaction is likely to increase motivation to work hard and achieve high performance in the future.

---

**LEARNING CHECK 3**

**TAKEAWAY QUESTION 3 How do attitudes influence individual behavior?**

**Be sure you can** • define *attitude* and list the three components of an attitude • define *job satisfaction* and list its components • explain the potential consequences of high and low job satisfaction • define *employee engagement, job involvement, organizational commitment,* and *organizational citizenship* • explain three arguments in the job satisfaction and performance relationship

# Emotions, Moods, and Stress

*Situation:* Hewlett-Packard's former CEO, Mark V. Hurd, faced an unusual corporate scandal. Information leaks by members of HP's board of directors had been uncovered and the board chairman had resigned. When trying to explain this to the press, Hurd called the actions "very disturbing" and said that "I could have and I should have" read an internal report that he had been given on the matter. The *Wall Street Journal* described him as speaking with "his voice shaking."[46]

Looking in from the outside, we might say that Hurd was emotional and angry that this incident was causing public humiliation for him and the company. He ended up in a bad mood because of it. And, the whole episode was very stressful.

## Emotions

**Emotional intelligence** is an ability to understand emotions and manage relationships effectively.

**Emotions** are strong feelings directed toward someone or something.

**Emotional intelligence** is an important human skill for managers and an essential leadership capability. Daniel Goleman defines "EI" as an ability to understand emotions in ourselves and in others, and to use this understanding to manage relationships effectively.[47] His point is that we perform best when we are good at recognizing and dealing with emotions. Simply put, we should avoid letting our emotions "get the better of us." We should also show restraint when the emotions of others are getting the better of them."[48]

An **emotion** is a strong feeling directed toward someone or something. For example, you might feel positive emotion or elation when an instructor congratulates you on a fine class presentation; you might feel negative emotion or anger when an instructor criticizes you in front of the class. In both cases the object of your emotion is the instructor, but the impact of the instructor's behavior on your feelings is quite different. How you respond to the aroused emotions is likely to differ as well—perhaps breaking into a wide smile with the compliment, or making a nasty side comment after the criticism.

### UNDERSTANDING EMOTIONS

"I was really mad when Prof. Nitpicker criticized my presentation."

- Linked with a specific cause
- Tends to be brief or episodic
- Specific effect on attitude, behavior
- Might turn into a mood

## Moods

**Moods** are generalized positive and negative feelings or states of mind.

**Mood contagion** is the spillover of one's positive or negative moods onto others.

Whereas emotions tend to be short term and clearly targeted, **moods** are more generalized positive and negative feelings or states of mind that may persist for some time.[49] Everyone seems to have occasional moods, and we each know the full range of possibilities they represent. How often do you wake up in the morning and feel excited, refreshed, and just happy, or wake up feeling low, depressed, and generally unhappy? What are the consequences of these different moods for your behavior with friends and family, and at work or school?

Positive and negative emotions can be "contagious," causing others to display similarly positive and negative moods. Researchers call this **mood contagion**, and it can easily extend to one's followers, coworkers, and teammates, as well as family and friends.[50] When a leader's mood contagion is positive, followers display more positive moods, report being more attracted to their leaders, and rate their leaders more highly.[51]

With regard to CEO moods, a *BusinessWeek* article claims it pays to be likable.[52] If a CEO goes to a meeting in a good mood and gets described as "cheerful," "charming," "humorous," "friendly," and "candid," she or he may be viewed as on the upswing. But if the CEO is in a bad mood and comes away perceived as "prickly," "impatient," "remote," "tough," "acrimonious," or even "ruthless," she or he may be seen as on the downhill slope. Some CEOs are even hiring executive coaches to help them manage emotions and moods so that they will come across as more personable and friendly in their relationships with others.

## UNDERSTANDING MOODS

"I just feel lousy today and don't have any energy. I've been down all week."

- Hard to identify cause
- Tends to linger, be long-lasting
- General effect on attitude, behavior
- Can be "negative" or "positive"

## Stress

Closely aligned with a person's emotions and moods is **stress**, a state of tension caused by extraordinary demands, constraints, or opportunities.[53] It's a life force to be reckoned with. In one survey of college graduates, for example, 31% reported working over 50 hours per week, 60% rushed meals and 34% ate lunches "on the run," and 47% of those under 35 and 28% of those over 35 had feelings of job burnout.[54] A study by the Society for Human Resources Management found that 70% of those surveyed worked over and above scheduled hours, including putting in extra time on the weekends; over 50% said that the pressure to do the extra work was "self-imposed."[55]

**Stress** is a state of tension caused by extraordinary demands, constraints, or opportunities.

## Sources of Stress

**Stressors** are the things that cause stress. Whether they come from work or nonwork situations, or from personality, stressors can influence our attitudes, emotions and moods, behavior, job performance, and even health.[56] Having the Type A personality discussed earlier is an example of a personal stressor. Stressful life situations include such things as family events (e.g., the birth of a new child), economics (e.g., a sudden loss of extra income), and personal affairs (e.g., a preoccupation with a bad relationship). Importantly, stressors from one space—work or nonwork—can spill over to affect the other.

A **stressor** is anything that causes stress.

Work factors have an obvious potential to create job stress. Some 34% of workers in one survey said that their jobs were so stressful they were thinking of quitting.[57] We experience stress from long hours of work, excessive e-mails, unrealistic work deadlines, difficult bosses or coworkers, unwelcome or unfamiliar work, and unrelenting change. It is also associated with excessively high or low task demands, role conflicts or ambiguities, poor interpersonal relations, and career progress that is too slow or too fast.

One common work-related stress syndrome is *set up to fail*—where the performance expectations are impossible or the support is totally inadequate to the task. Another is *mistaken identity*—where the individual ends up in a job that doesn't at all match talents, or that he or she simply doesn't like.[58]

## Constructive and Destructive Stress

**Constructive stress**, sometimes called *eustress*, is personally energizing and performance-enhancing.[59] It encourages increased effort, stimulates creativity, and

**Constructive stress** acts in a positive way to increase effort, stimulate creativity, and encourage diligence in one's work.

## Tension Must Be Fine Tuned

Stockbyte/Getty Images

When the tension on a violin string is just right, a talented artist can create a beautiful sound. But if the string is too loose the sound is weak, and if it's too tight the sound is shrill and the string can snap. Stress is a lot like that. It sometimes adds a creative high-performance edge to what we are doing. But other times there's too little or too much tension on the system. With too little tension we can get lazy and underperform. With too much tension we may also underperform even though working too many hours, eating too many lunches "on the run," missing too many family and leisure activities . . . and ending up with feelings of burnout.

enhances diligence, while still not overwhelming the individual and causing negative outcomes. Individuals with a Type A personality, for example, are likely to work long hours and to be less satisfied with poor performance. Challenging task demands move them toward ever-higher levels of task accomplishment. Even non-work stressors such as new family responsibilities may cause them to work harder in anticipation of greater financial rewards.

Achieving the right balance of stress for each person and situation is difficult. **Destructive stress**, or *distress*, is dysfunctional. It occurs when intense or long-term stress overloads and breaks down a person's physical and mental systems. This can lead to **job burnout**—a form of physical and mental exhaustion that can be personally incapacitating.

Figure 15.3 shows how productivity suffers when people with exhaustion and burnout react through turnover, absenteeism, errors, accidents, dissatisfaction, and reduced performance. An extreme by-product of destructive stress is **workplace rage**—aggressive behavior toward coworkers and the work setting in general. Lost tempers are common examples; the unfortunate extremes are tragedies that result in physical harm to others.[60]

Medical research is concerned that too much stress causes poor health. Stress becomes destructive to health when it reduces resistance to disease and increases the likelihood of physical and/or mental illness. Other possible stress-related health problems include hypertension, ulcers, substance abuse, overeating, depression, and muscle aches, among others.[61]

**Destructive stress** impairs the performance of an individual.

**Job burnout** is physical and mental exhaustion from work stress.

**Workplace rage** is aggressive behavior toward coworkers or the work setting.

FIGURE 15.3 **Potential negative consequences of a destructive job stress–burnout cycle.**

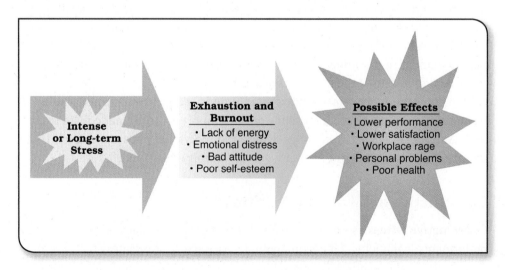

## Stress Management

The best stress management strategy is to prevent it from reaching excessive levels in the first place. A top priority for individuals and employers alike is **personal wellness**. Individually this means taking personal responsibility for your physical and mental health through a disciplined approach to such things as smoking, alcohol use, diet, exercise, and physical fitness. As an employer this means setting up wellness programs and assistance plans to help employees follow through with wellness commitments to healthy living.

> **Personal wellness** is the pursuit of one's full potential through a personal health-promotion program.

Stress can also be managed by taking actions to cope with and, hopefully, minimize the impact of personal and nonwork stressors. Family difficulties may be relieved by a change in work schedule, or the anxiety they cause may be reduced by an understanding supervisor. Work stress can sometimes be dealt with by role clarification through frank and open communication between bosses and coworkers. Jobs can sometimes be redesigned to eliminate poor fits between individual abilities and job demands.

Some employers are trying to curb tendencies to "work too much" as a way of helping people "do better work." The consulting firm KPMG, for example, uses a wellness scorecard to track and counsel workers who skip vacations and work excessive overtime. Harvard scholar Leslie Perlow says the goal is to avoid "a feeling of having no time truly free from work, no control over work and no opportunity to ask questions to clarify foggy priorities."[62]

---

**LEARNING CHECK 4**

**TAKEAWAY QUESTION 4 What are the dynamics of emotions, moods, and stress?**

**Be sure you can** • define *emotion, mood,* and *stress* • explain how emotions and moods influence behavior • identify the common stressors found in work and in personal life • differentiate constructive and destructive stress • define *job burnout* and *workplace rage* • discuss personal wellness as a stress management strategy

# MANAGEMENT LEARNING REVIEW

## TAKEAWAY QUESTION 1 How do perceptions influence individual behavior?

- Perception acts as a filter through which people receive and process information from the environment.
- Because people perceive things differently, a situation may be interpreted and responded to differently by different people.
- A healthy psychological contract occurs with perceived balance between work contributions, such as time and effort, and inducements received, such as pay and respect.
- Fundamental attribution error occurs when we blame others for performance problems while excluding possible external causes; self-serving bias occurs when we take personal credit for successes and blame failures on external factors.
- Stereotypes, projection, halo effects, and selective perception can distort perceptions and result in errors as people relate with one another.

**For Discussion Are there times when self-serving bias is actually helpful?**

## TAKEAWAY QUESTION 2 What should we know about personalities in the workplace?

- Personality is a set of traits and characteristics that cause people to behave in unique ways.
- The personality factors in the Big Five model are extraversion, agreeableness, conscientiousness, emotional stability, and openness to experience.
- The Myers-Briggs Type Indicator profiles personalities in respect to tendencies toward extraversion-introversion, sensing-intuitive, thinking-feeling, and judging-perceiving.
- Additional personality dimensions of work significance include the personal conception traits of locus of control, authoritarianism, Machiavellianism, and behavioral self-monitoring, as well as the emotional adjustment trait of Type A orientation.

**For Discussion What dimension would you add to make the "Big Five" the "Big Six" personality model?**

## TAKEAWAY QUESTION 3 How do attitudes influence individual behavior?

- An attitude is a predisposition to respond in a certain way to people and things.
- Cognitive dissonance occurs when a person's attitude and behavior are inconsistent.
- Job satisfaction is an important work attitude that reflects a person's evaluation of the job, coworkers, and other aspects of the work setting.
- Job satisfaction influences work attendance and turnover, and is related to other attitudes, such as job involvement and organizational commitment.
- Three possible explanations for the job satisfaction and performance relationship are: satisfaction causes performance, performance causes satisfaction, and rewards cause both performance and satisfaction.

**For Discussion What should a manager do with someone who has high job satisfaction but is a low performer?**

## TAKEAWAY QUESTION 4 What are the dynamics of emotions, moods, and stress?

- Emotions are strong feelings that are directed at someone or something; they influence behavior, often with intensity and for short periods of time.
- Moods are generalized positive or negative states of mind that can be persistent influences on one's behavior.
- Stress is a state of tension experienced by individuals facing extraordinary demands, constraints, or opportunities.
- Stress can be destructive or constructive; a moderate level of stress typically has a positive impact on performance.
- Stressors are found in a variety of personal, work, and nonwork situations.
- Stress can be managed through both prevention and coping strategies, including a commitment to personal wellness.

**For Discussion Is a Type A personality required for managerial success?**

## SELF-TEST 15

## Multiple-Choice Questions

1. In the psychological contract, job security is a/an _____, whereas loyalty is a/an _____.
   (a) satisfier factor, hygiene factor
   (b) intrinsic reward, extrinsic reward
   (c) inducement, contribution
   (d) attitude, personality trait

2. Self-serving bias is a form of attribution error that involves _____.
   (a) blaming yourself for problems caused by others
   (b) blaming the environment for problems you caused
   (c) poor emotional intelligence
   (d) authoritarianism

3. If a new team leader changes job designs for persons on her work team mainly "because I would prefer to work the new way rather than the old," the chances are that she is committing a perceptual error known as _____.
   (a) halo effect
   (b) stereotype
   (c) selective perception
   (d) projection

4. If a manager allows one characteristic of a person, say a pleasant personality, to bias performance ratings of that individual overall, the manager is committing a perceptual distortion known as _____.
   (a) halo effect
   (b) stereotype
   (c) selective perception
   (d) projection

5. Use of special dress, manners, gestures, and vocabulary words when meeting a prospective employer in a job interview are all examples of how people use _____ in daily life.
   (a) projection
   (b) selective perception
   (c) impression management
   (d) self-serving bias

6. A person with a/an _____ personality would most likely act unemotionally and manipulatively when trying to influence others to achieve personal goals.
   (a) extraverted
   (b) sensation-thinking
   (c) self-monitoring
   (d) Machiavellian

7. When a person believes that he or she has little influence over things that happen in life, this indicates a/an _____ personality.
   (a) low emotional stability
   (b) external locus of control
   (c) high self-monitoring
   (d) intuitive-thinker

8. Among the Big Five personality traits, _____ indicates someone who is responsible, dependable, and careful with respect to tasks.
   (a) authoritarianism
   (b) agreeableness
   (c) conscientiousness
   (d) emotional stability

9. The _____ component of an attitude is what indicates a person's belief about something, whereas the _____ component indicates a specific positive or negative feeling about it.
   (a) cognitive, affective
   (b) emotional, affective
   (c) cognitive, attributional
   (d) behavioral, attributional

10. The term used to describe the discomfort someone feels when his or her behavior is inconsistent with an expressed attitude is _____.
    (a) alienation
    (b) cognitive dissonance
    (c) job dissatisfaction
    (d) person–job imbalance

11. Job satisfaction is known from research to be a good predictor of _____.
    (a) job performance
    (b) job burnout
    (c) conscientiousness
    (d) absenteeism

12. A person who is always willing to volunteer for extra work or to help someone else with his or her work is acting consistent with strong _____.
    (a) job performance
    (b) self-serving bias
    (c) emotional intelligence
    (d) organizational citizenship

13. Which statement about the job satisfaction-job performance relationship is most likely based on research?
    (a) A happy worker will be a productive worker.
    (b) A productive worker will be a happy worker.
    (c) A productive worker well rewarded for performance will be a happy worker.
    (d) There is no link between being happy and being productive in a job.

14. A/an _____ represents a rather intense but short-lived feeling about a person or a situation, whereas a/an _____ describes a more generalized positive or negative state of mind.
    (a) stressor, role ambiguity
    (b) external locus of control, internal locus of control
    (c) self-serving bias, halo effect
    (d) emotion, mood

15. Through _____, the stress people experience in their personal lives can create problems for them at work while the stress experienced at work can create problems for their personal lives.
    (a) eustress
    (b) self-monitoring
    (c) spillover effects
    (d) selective perception

## Short-Response Questions

16. What is a healthy psychological contract?

17. What is the difference between self-serving bias and fundamental attribution error?

18. Which three of the Big Five personality traits do you believe most affect how well people work together in organizations, and why?

19. Why is it important for a manager to understand the Type A personality?

## Essay Question

20. When Scott Tweedy picked up a magazine article on how to manage health care workers, he was pleased to find some advice. Scott was concerned about poor or mediocre performance on the part of several respiratory therapists in his clinic. The author of the article said that the "best way to improve performance is to make your workers happy." Scott was glad to have read this and made a pledge to himself to start doing a much better job of making workers happy. But should Scott follow this advice? What do we know about the relationship between job satisfaction and performance, and how can this apply to the performance problems at Scott's clinic?

# MANAGEMENT SKILLS AND COMPETENCIES

## Further Reflection: Ambition

People differ in the ways they work, relate to others, and even in how they view themselves. One difference you might observe when interacting with other people is in **ambition**, or the desire to succeed and reach for high goals. Ambition is one of those traits that can certainly have a big impact on individual behavior. As discussed in the chapter opener, it is evident in how we act and what we try to achieve at work, at home, and in leisure pursuits. The more we understand ambition in our lives, and the more we understand how personality traits like those in the Big Five model, the Myers-Briggs Type Indicator, and others influence our behavior, the more successful we're likely to be in accomplishing our goals and helping others do the same.

**DO IT NOW ...
TAKE THE MIRROR TEST**

- Review the "personal differentiators" in the small box in the chapter opener. How do you score?
- Can you say that your career ambition is backed with a sufficient set of personal traits and skills to make success a real possibility?
- Ask others to comment on the ambition you display as you go about your daily activities.
- Write a short synopsis of two situations—one in which you showed ambition and one in which you did not. Consider the implications for your career development.

## Self-Assessment: Internal/External Control

### Instructions

Circle either (a) or (b) to indicate the item you most agree with in each pair of the following statements.[63]

1. (a) Promotions are earned through hard work and persistence.
   (b) Making a lot of money is largely a matter of breaks.
2. (a) Many times the reactions of teachers seem haphazard to me.
   (b) In my experience there is usually a direct connection between how hard I study and grades I get.
3. (a) The number of divorces indicates more and more people are not trying to make their marriages work.
   (b) Marriage is largely a gamble.
4. (a) It is silly to think that one can really change another person's basic attitudes.
   (b) When I am right, I can convince others.
5. (a) Getting promoted is really a matter of being a little luckier than the next guy.
   (b) In our society an individual's future earning power is dependent on his or her ability.

6. (a) If one knows how to deal with people, they are really quite easily led.
   (b) I have little influence over the way other people behave.
7. (a) In my case, the grades I make are the result of my own efforts; luck has little or nothing to do with it.
   (b) Sometimes I feel that I have little to do with the grades I get.
8. (a) People like me can change the course of world affairs if we make ourselves heard.
   (b) It is only wishful thinking to believe that one can really influence what happens in society at large.
9. (a) Much of what happens to me is probably a matter of chance.
   (b) I am the master of my fate.
10. (a) Getting along with people is a skill that must be practiced.
    (b) It is almost impossible to figure out how to please some people.

## Self-Assessment Scoring

Give yourself 1 point for 1a, 2b, 3a, 4b, 5b, 6a, 7a, 8a, 9b, 10a.

- 8–10 = high *internal* locus of control
- 6–7 = moderate *internal* locus of control
- 5 = mixed locus of control
- 3–4 = moderate *external* locus of control

## Interpretation

This instrument offers an impression of your tendency toward an internal locus of control or an external locus of control. Persons with a high internal locus of control tend to believe they have control over their own destinies. They may appreciate opportunities for greater self-control at the workplace. Persons with a high external locus of control tend to believe that what happens to them is largely in the hands of external people or forces. They may be less comfortable with self-control and more responsive to external controls at work.

# Team Exercise:
# Job Satisfaction Preferences

## Preparation

Rank the following items for how important (1 = least important to 9 = most important) they are to your future job satisfaction.[64]

*My job will be satisfying when it—*

- (a) is respected by other people.
- (b) encourages continued development of knowledge and skills.
- (c) provides job security.
- (d) provides a feeling of accomplishment.
- (e) provides the opportunity to earn a high income.
- (f) is intellectually stimulating.
- (g) rewards good performance with recognition.
- (h) provides comfortable working conditions.
- (i) permits advancement to high administrative responsibility.

## Instructions

Form into groups as designated by your instructor. Within each group, the men should develop a consensus ranking of the items as they think women ranked them. The reasons for the rankings should be shared and discussed so they are clear to everyone. The women in the group should not participate in this ranking task. They should listen to the discussion and be prepared to comment later in class discussions. A spokesperson for the men in the group should share the group's rankings with the class.

## Optional Instructions

Form into groups consisting entirely of men or women. Each group should meet and decide which of the work values members of the opposite sex will rank first. Do this again for the work value ranked last. The reasons should be discussed, along with the reasons why each of the other values probably was not ranked first or last. A spokesperson for each group should share group results with the rest of the class.

## Career Situations in Individual Behavior: What Would You Do?

1. **Putting Down Seniors**   While standing on line at the office coffee machine, you overhear the person in front of you saying this to his friend: "I'm really tired of having to deal with the old-timers here. It's time for them to call it quits. There's no way they can keep up the pace and handle all the new technology we're getting these days." You can listen and forget, or you can listen and act. What would you do or say here, and why?

2. **Compulsive Coworker**   You've noticed that one of your coworkers is always rushing, always uptight, and constantly criticizing herself while on the job. She never takes breaks when the rest of you do, and even at lunch it's hard to get her to stay and just talk for awhile. Your guess is that she's fighting stress from some sources other than work and the job itself. How can you help her out?

3. **Bad Mood in the Office**   Your department head has just told you that some of your teammates have complained to him that you have been in a really bad mood lately. They like you and point out that this isn't characteristic of you at all. But, they also think your persistent bad mood is rubbing off on others in this situation. What can you do? Is there anything your boss or co-workers might do to help?

## Case Study

# Panera Bread Company

Go to *Management Cases for Critical Thinking* to find the recommended case for Chapter 15—"Panera: Growing a Company with Personality."

Panera's success runs with founder Ron Shaich's personality—open, conscientious, extraverted. It's also part and parcel of his ability to predict long-term trends and orient the company toward innovation to fulfill consumers' desires. Panera's self-perception as a purveyor of artisan bread predated the current national trend for fresh bread and an explosion of both large-chain and small artisan bakeries.

So far, Panera's fresh breads, deli sandwiches and soups, all followed with fresh pastries, have been a combination proven to please the hungry masses. The company has been able to stick with the founder's values even while growing rapidly. But competition and changing times are ever-present challenges. The low-carb craze didn't faze Panera, but can this company continue to navigate the changing dietary trends tastes in today's unstable market?

# Wisdom
## Learning
## From Others

### > GREAT EMPLOYERS BRING OUT THE BEST IN US

A regular on *Fortune* magazine's "Best Companies to Work For," it recently ranked number one for two years in a row. Who are we talking about? The company is SAS, headquartered in North Carolina and the world's largest privately owned software firm. Here's what it is like to be one of SAS's 4,800 employees.

The typical workweek is 35 hours and no one monitors what time you show up or leave. There are two day-care centers. You can get dry cleaning, car detailing, and haircuts on site. Work–life and wellness centers provide everything from workout rooms to special programs in weight management to counseling on family issues. For a fee you can even schedule an in-house masseur at the company's fitness center.

SAS offers no stock options and does not offer the highest salaries. CEO Jim Goodnight believes pampering makes up for the lack of outright financial incentives. "My chief assets walk out the door every day," he says. "My job is to make sure they come back."

SAS employee Bev Brown says: "Some may think that because SAS is family-friendly and has great benefits that we don't work hard, but people do work hard here because they're motivated to care for a company that takes care of them."[1]

### MORE TO LOOK FOR INSIDE>

**FOLLOW THE STORY**
The King of Coffee Brews for Engagement

**ETHICS ON THE LINE**
Information Goldmine Creates Equity Dilemma

**FACTS FOR ANALYSIS**
Gender Differences in Motivation

**RESEARCH BRIEF**
Generational Differences in Extrinsic and Intrinsic Work Values

# Motivation Theory and Practice

**16**

## > ENGAGEMENT

One of the hot topics in management these days is **engagement**. You might think of it as personal initiative and the willingness to "go the extra mile" at work. Tim Galbraith, vice president of people development at Yum Brands, Inc., says: "A person who's truly engaged says 'I'm willing to give a little bit more; I'm willing to help my team members when I see they're in need.'"

The Conference Board defines engagement as "a heightened emotional connection" with the organization that influences an employee to "exert greater discretionary effort in his or her work." Its surveys show that high engagement generates positive outcomes like lower turnover, higher productivity, and better customer service.[2]

Engagement varies greatly among people at work, as it does among students. Consider your experiences as a customer. When you're disappointed, perhaps with how a banking transaction or how a flight delay is handled, ask: Would a high level of employee engagement generate better customer service in such situations?

Scholars tend to believe that giving workers the authority to act goes a long way to unlocking the powers of employee engagement.[3] Doesn't it make sense that letting workers make decisions could result in them doing their jobs better?

## Insight
### Learning About Yourself

## BUILD SKILLS AND COMPETENCIES AT END OF CHAPTER

- Engage in *Further Reflection on Engagement*
- Take the *Self-Assessment—Student Engagement Survey*
- Solve the *Career Situations for Motivation*
- Complete the *Team Exercise—Why We Work*
- Analyze the *Case Study—SAS: Business Success Starts on the Inside*

**<GET TO KNOW YOURSELF BETTER**

| TAKEAWAY 1 | TAKEAWAY 2 | TAKEAWAY 3 | TAKEAWAY 4 |
|---|---|---|---|
| **Individual Needs and Motivation** | **Process Theories of Motivation** | **Reinforcement Theory** | **Motivation and Job Design** |
| • Hierarchy of needs theory | • Equity theory | • Reinforcement strategies | • Job simplification |
| • ERG theory | • Expectancy theory | • Positive reinforcement | • Job enrichment |
| • Two-factor theory | • Goal-setting theory | • Punishment | • Alternative work schedules |
| • Acquired needs theory | • Self-efficacy theory | | |
| **LEARNING CHECK 1** | **LEARNING CHECK 2** | **LEARNING CHECK 3** | **LEARNING CHECK 4** |

Did you know that J. K. Rowling's first *Harry Potter* book was rejected by 12 publishers; that their "sound" cost the Beatles a deal with Decca Records; and that Walt Disney once lost a newspaper job because he supposedly "lacked imagination"?[4] Thank goodness they didn't give up. In fact, we might say that their "motivation" to stay engaged and confident with their work paid off handsomely—to them and to those who have enjoyed the fruits of their labors.

Did you also know that studies show almost 20% of U.S. workers report themselves as "disengaged" on any given workday? Or, that 25% of American employers believe their workers have low morale? And that up to 40% of workers say that they have trouble staying motivated?[5]

Why do some people work enthusiastically, persevere in the face of difficulty, and often exceed the requirements of their job? Why do others hold back, quit at the first negative feedback, and do the minimum needed to avoid reprimand or termination? What can be done to ensure that the best possible performance is achieved by every person, in every job, on every workday?[6]

## Individual Needs and Motivation

**Motivation** accounts for the level, direction, and persistence of effort expended at work.

The term **motivation** describes forces within the individual that account for the level, direction, and persistence of effort expended at work. Simply put, a highly motivated person works hard at a job while an unmotivated person does not. One of the most important managerial responsibilities is to create conditions under which other persons feel consistently inspired to work hard.

A **need** is an unfulfilled physiological or psychological desire.

Most discussions of motivation begin with the concept of individual **needs**— the unfulfilled physiological or psychological desires of an individual. Although each of the following theories discusses a slightly different set of needs, all agree that needs create tensions that lead individuals to act in ways to help meet their needs. They suggest that managers should attempt to help people satisfy important needs through their work, and try to eliminate obstacles that block need satisfactions.

## Hierarchy of Needs Theory

Abraham Maslow's theory of human needs is an important foundation in the history of management thought. The **lower-order needs** in his hierarchy include physiological, safety, and social concerns, while **higher-order needs** include esteem and self-actualization concerns.[7] Whereas lower-order needs focus on desires for physical and social well-being, the higher-order needs focus on desires for psychological development and growth.

> **Lower-order needs** are physiological, safety, and social needs in Maslow's hierarchy.
>
> **Higher-order** needs are esteem and self-actualization needs in Maslow's hierarchy.

Maslow uses two principles to describe how these needs affect human behavior. The **deficit principle** states that a satisfied need is not a motivator of behavior. People are expected to act in ways that satisfy deprived needs—that is, needs for which a "deficit" exists. The **progression principle** states that the need at one level does not become activated until the next-lower-level need in the hierarchy is already satisfied. People are expected to advance step by step up the hierarchy in their quest for need satisfaction. This progression principle ends at the level of self-actualization. According to the theory, the need to self-actualize can never be fully met. The more the needs for self-actualization are satisfied, the stronger they are supposed to grow.

> The **deficit principle** states that a satisfied need does not motivate behavior.
>
> The **progression principle** states that a need isn't activated until the next lower-level need is satisfied.

Figure 16.1 illustrates how managers can use Maslow's ideas to better meet the needs of the people with whom they work. Notice that higher-order self-actualization needs are served by things like creative and challenging work, and job autonomy; esteem needs are served by respect, responsibility, praise, and recognition. The satisfaction of lower-order social, safety, and physiological

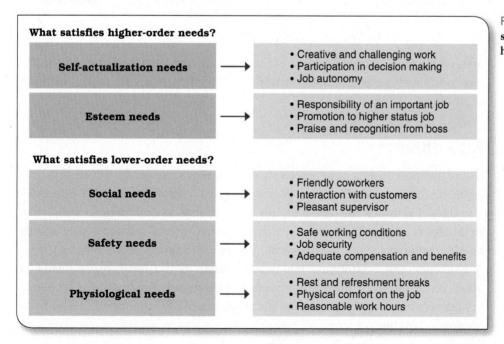

## The King of Coffee Brews with a Recipe for Engagement

BOBBY YIP/Reuters/Landov

When Howard Schultz returned to Starbucks as CEO after an eight year absence, he was concerned that the famous chain of coffee shops had lost its way. Schultz was determined to restore not only the company's financial health but also its "soul." And, he has done well indeed. *Fortune* magazine named Schultz "The 2011 Business Person of the Year." He was praised for helping the company achieve record profits without compromising its core values.

Schultz believes that "employees should be valued as much as profit" and deserve a great work environment. His moves as CEO were designed to realign practice with his principles. All the firm's employees—even part-timers—are called "partners." They are offered stock options and are covered by the company's medical insurance. Even during the worst part of the recent financial crisis, Schultz didn't abandon or scale back his health-care plan despite its $300 million annual cost.

By way of philosophy, Schultz believes leaders must have empathy and be able to see things from their employees' perspectives. The notion that frontline employees are keys to customer satisfaction and bottom-line success underlies Starbucks' motivation strategy.

But Starbucks has thousands of locations around the world and the number keeps growing. It's quite a challenge to make sure each store offers its employees a motivating work environment every single day.

 **YOUR TAKE?**

To what extent is the success of an organization dependent on the quality of its products versus the quality and motivation of its workforce? Why don't more companies provide entry-level employees, even part-timers, with benefits like health care? Can good benefits alone motivate lower-pay employees to high performance levels? Can Schultz maintain a highly motivated workforce as Starbucks continues to grow rapidly worldwide?

---

needs rests more with conditions of the work environment, such as positive interactions with others, compensation and benefits, and reasonable working conditions.

## ERG Theory

**Existence needs** are desires for physical well-being.

**Relatedness needs** are desires for good interpersonal relationships.

**Growth needs** are desires for personal growth and development.

One of the most promising efforts to build on Maslow's work is the ERG theory proposed by Clayton Alderfer.[8] This theory collapses Maslow's five needs categories into three. **Existence needs** are desires for physiological and material well-being. **Relatedness needs** are desires for satisfying interpersonal relationships. **Growth needs** are desires for continued psychological growth and development.

Existence and relatedness needs are similar to the lower-order needs in Maslow's hierarchy, while growth needs are essentially the higher-order needs in Maslow's hierarchy. Beyond that, the dynamics of ERG theory differ a bit from Maslow's thinking.

ERG theory doesn't accept the progression principle that certain needs must be satisfied before other needs become activated. Instead, it suggests the various needs can influence individual behavior at any given time. Alderfer also rejects the deficit principle that only unsatisfied needs have motivational impact. According to his **frustration-regression principle**, an already satisfied need can become reactivated and influence behavior when a higher-level need cannot be satisfied. Workers who are stuck in simple and repetitive jobs that offer little room for growth and limited opportunities for promotion, for example, will be frustrated in attempts to satisfy their growth needs. Their response could be to refocus attention on getting better work schedules, work conditions, and even pay and benefits to further fulfill their existence needs.

The **frustration-regression principle** states that an already satisfied need can become reactivated when a higher-level need is blocked.

## Two-Factor Theory

Frederick Herzberg developed the two-factor theory of motivation from a pattern discovered in almost 4,000 interviews.[9] When asked what "turned them on" about their job, respondents talked mostly about things relating to the nature of the work itself. Herzberg calls these **satisfier factors** (or motivator factors). When asked what "turned them off," they talked more about things relating to the work environment. Herzberg calls these **hygiene factors**. As shown in Figure 16.2, Herzberg suggests that these two factors affect people in different ways.

Two-factor theory links hygiene factors with job dissatisfaction. That is, job dissatisfaction goes up as hygiene quality goes down. Hygiene factors are found in the job context—the environment in which the work takes place—and include such things as working conditions, interpersonal relations, organizational policies and administration, and compensation. Herzberg argues that making improvements in these factors, such as remodeling the work environment or adding piped-in music, can make people less dissatisfied at work. But, it will not increase job satisfaction and motivation.

Satisfier factors are linked with job satisfaction. They are found in the job content—nature of the work itself—and include things like job challenge, recognition for work well done, a sense of responsibility, the opportunity for advancement, and feelings of personal growth. Herzberg believes that the more satisfier factors are present in a job, the higher the individual's work motivation. The way to build such

A **satisfier factor** is found in job content, such as challenging and exciting work, recognition, responsibility, advancement opportunities, or personal growth.

A **hygiene factor** is found in the job context, such as working conditions, interpersonal relations, organizational policies, and compensation.

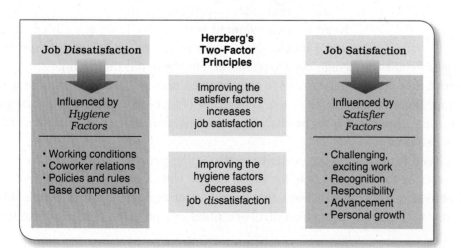

FIGURE 16.2  **Elements in Herzberg's two-factor theory.**

## What Do Workers Say They Dread the Most About Their Jobs?

Lots of times the answer to this question is: "It's my boss." A survey by Development Dimensions International reports that difficult conversations with bosses are what employees often dread the most. Those conversations rank ahead of going back to work after vacation. They even rank higher than getting a speeding ticket or paying taxes. The influence of boss behavior—words and actions—on motivation was clear. Some 98% of those working for their "best boss ever" said they were highly motivated in their jobs; only 13% of those working for their "worst boss ever" said so.

Ice Tea Images/AgeFotostock America, Inc.

high-content jobs, he suggests, is to make the job holder responsible for not just doing the work, but also planning and controlling its accomplishment.

Scholars have criticized Herzberg's research on this theory as being method-bound and difficult to replicate.[10] But he reports confirming studies from around the world.[11] At the very least, the two-factor theory is a reminder that all jobs have two important aspects: *job content*—what people do in terms of job tasks—and *job context*—the work setting in which they do it. And Herzberg's advice to managers makes good sense: (1) Correct poor job context to eliminate potential job dissatisfaction; (2) build satisfier factors into job content to maximize job satisfaction.

## Acquired Needs Theory

Yet another approach to the study of human needs was developed by David McClelland and his colleagues. They began by asking people to view pictures and write stories about what they saw.[12] The stories were then content-analyzed for themes that display the strengths of three needs—achievement, power, and affiliation. According to McClelland, people acquire or develop these needs over time as a result of individual life experiences. Because each need can be linked with a distinct set of work preferences, he encourages managers to understand these needs in themselves and in others, and try to create work environments responsive to them.

**Need for achievement** is the desire to do something better or more efficiently, to solve problems, or to master complex tasks. People with a high need for achievement like to put their competencies to work; they take moderate risks in competitive situations, and they are willing to work alone. As a result, the work preferences of high-need achievers include individual responsibility for results, achievable but challenging goals, and feedback on performance.

**Need for power** is the desire to control other people, to influence their behavior, or to be responsible for them. People with a high need for power are motivated to behave in ways that have a clear impact on other people and events. They enjoy being in control of a situation and being recognized for this

### WORK PREFERENCES OF HIGH-NEED ACHIEVERS

- Challenging but achievable goals
- Feedback on performance
- Individual responsibility

**Need for achievement** is the desire to do something better, to solve problems, or to master complex tasks.

**Need for power** is the desire to control, influence, or be responsible for other people.

responsibility. Importantly, though, McClelland distinguishes between two forms of the power need. The *need for personal power* is exploitative and involves manipulation for the pure sake of personal gratification. This type of power need is not successful in management. The *need for social power* involves the use of power in a socially responsible way, one that is directed toward group or organizational objectives rather than personal gains. This need for social power is essential to managerial leadership.

**Need for affiliation** is the desire to establish and maintain friendly and warm relations with other people. People with a high need for affiliation seek companionship, social approval, and satisfying interpersonal relationships. They tend to like jobs that involve working with people and offer opportunities for social approval. This is consistent with managerial work. But, McClelland believes that managers must be careful that high needs for affiliation don't interfere with decision making. There are times when managers and leaders must act in ways that other persons may disagree with. If the need for affiliation limits someone's ability to make these decisions, managerial effectiveness gets lost. In McClelland's view, the successful executive is likely to possess a high need for social power that is greater than an otherwise strong need for affiliation.

**Need for affiliation** is the desire to establish and maintain good relations with people.

---

**LEARNING CHECK 1**

**TAKEAWAY QUESTION 1 How do individual needs influence motivation?**

**Be sure you can** • define *motivation* and *needs* • describe work practices that satisfy higher-order and lower-order needs in Maslow's hierarchy • contrast Maslow's hierarchy with ERG theory • describe work practices that influence hygiene factors and satisfier factors in Herzberg's two-factor theory • explain McClelland's needs for achievement, power, and affiliation • describe work conditions that satisfy a person with a high need for achievement

---

# Process Theories of Motivation

Although the details vary, each of the needs theories offers insights on individual differences and on how managers can deal effectively with them. Another set of motivation theories, the process theories, add further to this understanding. They include the equity, expectancy, goal-setting, and self-efficacy theories.

## Equity Theory

*Fact:* In 1965, the average CEO pay was 24 times that of the typical worker; in 1980 it was 42 times; by 2010 it was 343 times.

*Fact:* The $3.4 billion paid in 2010 to the CEOs of 299 companies in the AFL-CIO Executive PayWatch database would be enough to support the wages of over 102,325 employees making the median salary of all workers.

How do these data strike you?[13] Do they motivate you as an aspiring CEO? Or, do they concern you as someone who empathizes with hourly and lower-wage workers? For many people, facts like these bring the words *equity* and *fairness* immediately to mind.

FIGURE 16.3 **Equity theory and the role of social comparison.**

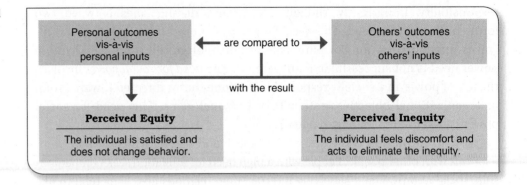

The equity theory of motivation is best known through the work of J. Stacy Adams.[14] It is based on the idea that we all want to be treated fairly in comparison to others. The theory suggests that being unfairly treated (whether we receive too little or too much when compared to someone else) makes people uncomfortable. When this happens, they are motivated to eliminate the discomfort and restore a sense of perceived equity to the situation.

## Equity and Social Comparison

Figure 16.3 shows how the equity dynamic works. According to equity theory, people compare their outcomes-to-inputs ratio to the outcomes-to-inputs ratio of another person (called a *referent*). Outcomes are what an individual receives from work—things like pay, benefits, job security, advancement opportunities, autonomy, interesting work experiences, and anything else that the employee values. Inputs are the qualifications an individual possesses and the contributions made to the organization—things like education, experience, special skills and training, the quality and quantity of work completed, and a positive attitude and loyalty.

Perceived inequities occur whenever people feel that the outcomes they receive for their work contributions are unfair in comparison to the outcomes received by others. Equity comparisons are especially common whenever managers allocate rewards such as pay raises, preferred job assignments, work privileges, and even office space or new technology. Equity comparisons can be made with coworkers (individual equity comparisons), others at different levels within the same organization (internal equity comparisons), or even persons employed by other organizations (external equity comparisons).

## Equity Dynamics

A key point in the equity theory is that people behave according to their perceptions. In the case of a pay raise, for example, it isn't the reward's absolute value or the manager's intentions that influences individual behavior; the recipient's perceptions determine the motivational impact.

An individual who perceives that she or he is being treated unfairly in comparison to others will be motivated to act in ways that reduce the perceived inequity. There are two basic types of inequity: over-reward (or positive) inequity and under-reward (or negative) inequity. **Over-reward inequity** occurs when an individual perceives that he or she is receiving more than what is fair. That is, the outcomes-to-inputs ratio is greater than that of his or her referent. While such perceptions do occur, it is much more common for individuals to experience

In **over-reward inequity** (positive inequity) an individual perceives that rewards received are more than what is fair for work inputs.

**under-reward inequity**. The perception here is receiving less than deserved in comparison to someone else. Adams predicts that people will try to deal with such perceived negative inequity in the following ways:

- Changing their work inputs by putting less effort into their jobs—"If that's all I'm going to get, I'm going to do a lot less."
- Changing the rewards received by asking for better treatment—"Next stop, the boss's office; I should get what I deserve."
- Changing the inputs or outcomes of their referent—"Bob either needs to work as hard as the rest of us or else he shouldn't get the same bonus that we get."
- Changing the person to whom you compare yourself to make things seem better—"Well, if I look at Marissa's situation, I'm still pretty well off."
- Changing the situation by leaving the job—"No way I'm going to stick around here if this is the way you get treated."

In **under-reward inequity** (negative inequity) an individual perceives that rewards received are less than what is fair for work inputs.

## Equity Research and Insights

The research on equity theory is most conclusive with respect to perceived negative inequity. Those who feel they are under-rewarded appear to be more likely to make active attempts to restore equity than those who feel they are over-rewarded.[15] But, there is evidence that the equity dynamic can occur among people who feel perceived positive inequity from being over-rewarded. In such cases, the attempt to restore perceived equity may involve increasing the quantity or quality of work, taking on more difficult assignments, or advocating for others to be compensated more fairly.

Managers should anticipate that perceptions of negative inequity can arise when especially visible rewards such as pay or promotions are given. And, they should make sure that processes for allocating rewards are both objectively fair and perceived to be fair. One way to do this is to be as transparent as possible. At a minimum managers should communicate the intended value of rewards being given, clarify the performance appraisals on which they are based, and suggest appropriate comparison points. This advice is especially relevant in organizations using merit-based pay-for-performance systems. A common problem in these systems is that what constitutes "meritorious" performance can be a source of debate. Any disagreement over performance ratings makes negative equity dynamics problems more likely.

## Equity Sensitivity

While equity theory is based on the premise that all employees desire fairness, research suggests that equity considerations are not equally important to all individuals. The idea of **equity sensitivity** proposes that people have different preferences for equity and thus react differently to perceptions of inequity. Differences in equity sensitivity are usually described as follows.[16] *Benevolents* are less concerned about being under-rewarded. They more readily accept situations of negative inequity while situations of positive inequity make them very uncomfortable. *Sensitives* have a strong preference for rewards to be distributed equitably. They react as the basic theory proposes. *Entitleds* have a desire to be over-rewarded. They try to create situations of positive inequity for themselves and react very negatively in situations of perceived negative inequity.

**Equity sensitivity** reflects that people have different preferences for equity and react differently to perceptions of inequity.

ETHICS
ON THE LINE

> "WHY DON'T I PASS THIS INFORMATION ALONG ANONYMOUSLY
SO THAT EVERYONE KNOWS WHAT'S GOING ON?"

## Information Goldmine Creates Equity Dilemma

Siri Stafford/Getty Images, Inc.

A worker opens the top of the office photocopier and finds a document someone has left behind. It's a list of performance evaluations, pay, and bonuses for 80 coworkers.

Lo and behold, someone considered a "slacker"" by peers is getting paid more than others regarded as better employees. New hires are being brought in at substantially higher pay and bonuses than are paid to existing staff.

And to make matters worse, she's in the middle of the list, not near the top where she would expect to be. She makes a lot less money than some others are getting.

Looking at the data, the worker wonders why she is spending extra hours on her laptop evenings and weekends at home, trying to do a really great job for the firm. The thought occurs to her: "Why don't I pass this information around anonymously so that everyone knows what's going on?" But then she thinks, "Maybe I should just quit and find another employer who fully values me for my talents and hard work."

 **ETHICS QUESTIONS**

What would you do? Would you hit "print," make about 80 copies, and then put them in everyone's mailboxes? That would get the gossip chain started and might force some changes. Would you meet privately with your supervisor and demand a raise, leaving others to fend for themselves? What is the right thing to do? What are the ethical issues that need to be considered?

## Expectancy Theory

Victor Vroom's expectancy theory of motivation asks the question: What determines the willingness of an individual to work hard at tasks important to the organization?[17] The answer is that motivation depends on the relationships between three expectancy factors depicted in Figure 16.4 and described here:

**Expectancy** is a person's belief that working hard will result in high task performance.

**Instrumentality** is a person's belief that various outcomes will occur as a result of task performance.

**Valence** is the value a person assigns to work-related outcomes.

- **Expectancy**—a person's belief that working hard will result in a desired level of task performance being achieved (this is sometimes called effort-performance expectancy).

- **Instrumentality**—a person's belief that successful performance will be followed by rewards and other work-related outcomes (this is sometimes called performance-outcome expectancy).

- **Valence**—the value a person assigns to the possible rewards and other work-related outcomes.

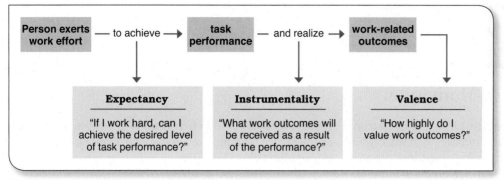

FIGURE 16.4    **Elements in the expectancy theory of motivation.**

## Motivation = Expectancy × Instrumentality × Valence

In expectancy theory, motivation (M), expectancy (E), instrumentality (I), and valence (V) are related to one another in a multiplicative fashion: $M = E \times I \times V$. In other words, motivation is determined by expectancy times instrumentality times valence. Mathematically speaking, a zero at any location on the right side of the equation (that is, for E, I, or V) will result in zero motivation. What this means in practice is that all three factors must be high and positive for someone's motivation to also be high.[18]

Suppose, for example, that a manager is wondering whether or not the prospect of earning a promotion will be motivational to a job holder. Expectancy theory predicts that a person's motivation to work hard for a promotion will be low if any one or more of the following three conditions apply. First, if expectancy is low, motivation will suffer. This is the "If I try hard will I succeed?" question. The person may not believe that he or she can achieve the performance level necessary to get promoted. So why try? Second, if instrumentality is low, motivation will suffer. This is the "If I succeed will I be rewarded?" question. The person may lack confidence that a high level of task performance will result in being promoted. Perhaps the manager is notorious for promoting only those who are his close friends, so why try? Third, if valence is low, motivation will suffer. This is the "What does the possible reward for this hard work and performance achievement mean to me?" question. The person may place little value on receiving a promotion because it would require longer hours away from home or because it would require relocation to another city. It simply isn't a desired reward. So, why try for it?

## Expectancy Theory Applications

Expectancy theory reminds managers that people answer the question "Why should I work hard today?" in different ways. Every person has unique needs, preferences, and concerns at work. Knowing this, a manager should try to build work environments that respect individual differences so that expectancies, instrumentalities, and valences all support motivation.

---

### MANAGING BY EXPECTANCY THEORY

*Create high expectancies*—Select capable workers, train them well, support them with adequate resources.

*Create high instrumentalities*—Clarify rewards earned by performance, give rewards on performance-contingent basis.

*Create positive valences*—Identify individual needs, offer rewards that satisfy these needs.

# Gender Differences in Motivation

Men and women tend to differ somewhat in their perceptions of what is important and motivating at work. Men seem to place a higher motivational value on extrinsic rewards such as salary and bonuses; whereas women place more importance on interpersonal factors such as respectful treatment by the boss and work–life balance. The following data report male and female differences on the importance of various work aspects with regard to motivation and commitment.

Pay—Men 85%, Women 80%

Bonuses—Men 58%, Women 53%

Work–Life Balance—Men 59%, Women 66%

Being Treated with Respect—Men 69%, Women 76%

These differences tend to fade away when women are in management jobs, and tend to be magnified among those not in managerial roles.

 **YOUR THOUGHTS?**

Do these data seem consistent or inconsistent with your experiences? Why do you think gender differences regarding motivation disappeared when the researchers looked at managers? Could it be that women in management, either consciously or subconsciously, change their values to fit in with the prevailing organizational culture?

*To maximize expectancy people must believe in their abilities.* They must believe that if they try, they can perform. Managers can build positive expectancies by selecting workers with the right abilities for the jobs to be done, providing them with the best training and development, and supporting them with resources so that the jobs can be accomplished. *To maximize instrumentality people must see the link between high performance and work outcomes.* Managers can create positive instrumentalities by clarifying the possible rewards for high performance and then allocating these rewards fairly and on a performance-contingent basis. *To maximize positive valence people must value the outcomes associated with high performance.* Managers can use the content theories or increase communication with their subordinates to help identify important employee needs. Steps can then be taken to link these needs with rewards that offer positive valences and that can be earned through high performance.

## Goal-Setting Theory

Steven A. Davis rose through a variety of management jobs to become CEO of Bob Evans Farms in Columbus, Ohio.[19] His parents gave him lots of encouragement when he was a child. "They never said that because you are an African-American, you can only go this far or do only this or that," he says, "they just said 'go for it'." Davis set goals when he graduated from college—to be a corporate vice president in 10 years and a president in 20. Expectancy theory would say that his parents increased his motivation by creating high positive expectancy during his school years. Goal-setting theory would add that Davis found lots of motivation through the goals he set as a college graduate.

### Goal-Setting Essentials

The basic premise of Edwin Locke's goal-setting theory is that task goals can be highly motivating if they are properly set and if they are well managed.[20] Goals give direction to people in their work. They clarify the performance expectations in supervisory relationships, between coworkers, and across subunits in an organization. They establish a frame of reference for task feedback. And, goals also set a foundation for behavioral self-management.

The motivational benefits of goal setting occur when managers and team leaders work with others to set the right goals in the right ways. Management Smarts points out that things such as goal specificity, goal difficulty, goal acceptance, and goal commitment are all important. Managers can use goal setting in these and related ways to enhance individual work performance and job satisfaction.

## ManagementSmarts

### How to Make Goal Setting Work for You

- *Set specific goals:* They lead to higher performance than do more generally stated ones, such as "do your best."
- *Set challenging goals:* When viewed as realistic and attainable, more difficult goals lead to higher performance than do easy goals.
- *Build goal acceptance and commitment:* People work harder for goals they accept and believe in; they resist goals forced on them.
- *Clarify goal priorities:* Make sure that expectations are clear as to which goals should be accomplished first, and why.
- *Provide feedback on goal accomplishment:* Make sure that people know how well they are doing with respect to goal accomplishment.
- *Reward goal accomplishment:* Don't let positive accomplishments pass unnoticed; reward people for doing what they set out to do.

## Goal Setting and Participation

Participation goes a long way toward unlocking the motivational power of task goals. When managers and team members join in a participative process of goal setting and performance review, members are likely to experience greater motivation. The participation increases understanding of task goals, increases acceptance and commitment to them, and creates more readiness to receive feedback on goal accomplishment.

It isn't always possible to allow participation when selecting which goals need to be pursued. But it can be possible to allow participation in deciding how to best pursue them. It's also true that the constraints of time and other factors in some situations may not allow for participation. But Locke's research suggests that workers will respond positively to externally imposed goals if supervisors assigning them are trusted and if workers believe they will be adequately supported in their attempts to achieve them.

## Self-Efficacy Theory

Closely related to both the expectancy and goal-setting approaches to motivation is self-efficacy theory, also referred to as social learning theory. Based on the work of psychologist Albert Bandura, the notion of **self-efficacy** refers to a person's belief that she or he is capable of performing a specific task.[21] You can think of self-efficacy using such terms as confidence, competence, and ability. From a manager's perspective, the major point is that anything done to boost feelings of self-efficacy among people at work is likely to pay off with increased levels of motivation.

**Self-efficacy** is a person's belief that she or he is capable of performing a task.

Mahatma Gandhi once said: "If I have the belief that I can do it, I shall surely acquire the capacity to do it, even if I may not have it at the beginning."[22] This is the essence of self-efficacy theory. When people believe themselves to be capable, they will set higher goals for themselves, be more motivated to work hard at these goals, and persist longer

## Recommended Reading

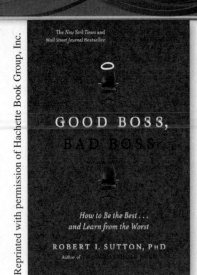

### Good Boss, Bad Boss: How to Be the Best—and Learn from the Worst (Hachette Book Group, 2010)
### by Robert I. Sutton

In *Good Boss, Bad Boss*, Stanford Professor Robert Sutton combines psychological and management research with personal case stories to identify the mindsets and behaviors of the best and worst bosses. After listening to stories people told him about their work experiences, he realized they wanted a lot more than just a jerk-free workplace; they wanted to become or work for an all-around great boss. This "great" boss is someone who inspires the best in others and treats them with dignity and respect. Sutton says the best bosses realize their success depends on controlling their own moods, accurately predicting the impact of their actions on others, and treating others in ways that affirm their worth.

in the face of any obstacles that impede their progress. The *Wall Street Journal* has called this "the unshakable belief some people have that they have what it takes to succeed."[23]

There is a clear link between Bandura's self-efficacy theory elements of Vroom's expectancy theory, and Locke's goal-setting theory. With respect to Vroom, a person with higher self-efficacy will have greater expectancy that he or she can achieve a high level of task performance. With respect to Locke, a person with higher self-efficacy should be more willing to set challenging performance goals. In terms of expectancy and goal setting, managers who help create feelings of self-efficacy in others should boost their motivation to work.

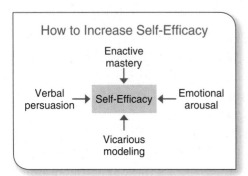

How to Increase Self-Efficacy

Enactive mastery → Self-Efficacy ← Emotional arousal; Verbal persuasion → Self-Efficacy; Vicarious modeling ↑

Bandura states that there are four major ways to enhance self-efficacy.[24] First is *enactive mastery*—when a person gains confidence through positive experience. The greater the initial success and the more experience you have with a task, the more confident you become at doing it. Second is *vicarious modeling*—learning by observing others. When someone else is good at a task and we are able to observe how they do it, we gain confidence in being able to do it ourselves. Third is *verbal persuasion*—when someone tells us that we can or encourages us to perform the task. Hearing others praise our efforts and link those efforts with performance successes is often very motivational. Fourth is *emotional arousal*—when we are highly stimulated or energized to perform well in a situation. A good analogy for arousal is how athletes get "psyched up" and highly motivated to perform in key competitions.

### LEARNING CHECK 2

**TAKEAWAY QUESTION 2** **What are the process theories of motivation?**

**Be sure you can** • explain the role of social comparison in Adams's equity theory • describe how people with felt negative inequity behave • define *equity sensitivity* • define *expectancy, instrumentality,* and *valence* • explain Vroom's expectancy theory equation: $M = E \times I \times V$ • explain Locke's goal-setting theory • define *self-efficacy* and explain four ways to increase it

# Reinforcement Theory

The motivation theories discussed so far are concerned with explaining "why" people do things in terms of satisfying needs, resolving felt inequities, evaluating expectancies, and pursuing task goals. Reinforcement theory, by contrast, views human behavior as determined by its environmental consequences. Instead of looking within the individual to explain motivation, this theory focuses on the external environment and its consequences.

The basic premises of reinforcement theory are based on what E. L. Thorndike called the **law of effect**. It states: Behavior that results in a pleasant outcome is likely to be repeated; behavior that results in an unpleasant outcome is not likely to be repeated.[25]

The **law of effect** states that behavior followed by pleasant consequences is likely to be repeated; behavior followed by unpleasant consequences is not.

## Reinforcement Strategies

Psychologist B. F. Skinner popularized the concept of **operant conditioning** as the process of applying the law of effect to control behavior by manipulating its consequences.[26] You may think of operant conditioning as learning by reinforcement. In management, the goal is to use reinforcement principles to systematically reinforce desirable work behavior and discourage undesirable work behavior.[27] The four strategies of reinforcement that can be used in operant conditioning are positive reinforcement, negative reinforcement, punishment, and extinction.

**Operant conditioning** is the control of behavior by manipulating its consequences.

Figure 16.5 shows how the four reinforcement strategies can be used in management. The example applies the strategies to influence quality practices by employees. Note that both positive and negative reinforcement strategies strengthen desirable behavior when it occurs; punishment and extinction strategies weaken or eliminate undesirable behaviors.

**Positive reinforcement** strengthens or increases the frequency of desirable behavior. It does so by making a pleasant consequence contingent on its occurrence. *Example:* A manager compliments an employee on his or her creativity in making a helpful comment during a staff meeting. **Negative reinforcement** also strengthens or increases the frequency of desirable behavior, but it does so by making the avoidance of an unpleasant consequence contingent on its occurrence. *Example:* A

**Positive reinforcement** strengthens behavior by making a desirable consequence contingent on its occurrence.

**Negative reinforcement** strengthens behavior by making the avoidance of an undesirable consequence contingent on its occurrence.

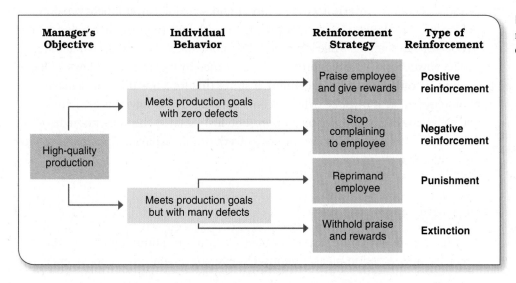

FIGURE 16.5 **Four reinforcement strategies: Case of total quality management.**

manager who has been nagging a worker every day about tardiness does not nag when the worker comes to work on time.

**Punishment** discourages behavior by making an unpleasant consequence contingent on its occurrence.

**Extinction** discourages behavior by making the removal of a desirable consequence contingent on its occurrence.

**Punishment** decreases the frequency of or eliminates an undesirable behavior. It does so by making an unpleasant consequence contingent on its occurrence. *Example:* A manager issues a written reprimand to an employee whose careless work is creating quality problems. **Extinction** also decreases the frequency of or eliminates an undesirable behavior, but does so by making the removal of a pleasant consequence contingent on its occurrence. *Example:* A manager observes that a disruptive employee is receiving social approval from coworkers who laugh at his jokes during staff meetings; the manager counsels coworkers to ignore the jokes and stop providing approval of this behavior.

## Positive Reinforcement

Positive reinforcement deserves special attention among the reinforcement strategies. It should be part of any manager's motivational tool kit. Sir Richard Branson, founder of Virgin Group, is a believer. "For the people who work for you or with you, you must lavish praise on them at all times," he says. "If a flower is watered, it flourishes. If not it shrivels up and dies." And besides, he adds, "It is much more fun looking for the best in people."[28] David Novak, CEO of Yum! Brands, Inc., is also a believer. He claims that one of his most important tasks as CEO is "to get people fired up" and that "you can never underestimate the power of telling someone he's doing a good job." Novak advocates celebrating "first downs and not just touchdowns," which means publicly recognizing and rewarding small wins that keep everyone motivated for the long haul.[29]

Management Smarts presents useful guidelines for positive reinforcement. One way to put them into action is through a process known as **shaping**.[30] This is the creation of a new behavior by the positive reinforcement of successive approximations to it. A **continuous reinforcement** schedule administers a reward each time a desired behavior occurs. An **intermittent reinforcement** schedule rewards behavior only periodically. Continuous reinforcement tends to work best to draw forth a desired behavior through shaping, while intermittent reinforcement works best to maintain it.

The power of positive reinforcement is governed by two important laws.[31] First is the **law of contingent reinforcement**. It states that for a reward to have maximum reinforcing value, it must be delivered only if the desired behavior is exhibited. Second is the **law of immediate reinforcement**. It states that the more immediate the delivery of a reward after the occurrence of a desirable behavior, the greater the reinforcing value of the reward.

### ManagementSmarts

#### Guidelines for Positive Reinforcement

- Clearly identify desired work behaviors.
- Maintain a diverse inventory of rewards.
- Inform everyone what must be done to get rewards.
- Recognize individual differences when allocating rewards.
- Follow the laws of immediate and contingent reinforcement.

**Shaping** is positive reinforcement of successive approximations to the desired behavior.

**Continuous reinforcement** rewards each time a desired behavior occurs.

**Intermittent reinforcement** rewards behavior only periodically.

The **law of contingent reinforcement** is that a reward should only be given when a desired behavior occurs.

The **law of immediate reinforcement** is that a reward should be given as soon as possible after a desired behavior occurs.

## Punishment

As a reinforcement strategy, punishment attempts to eliminate undesirable behavior by making an unpleasant consequence contingent on its occurrence. For example, a manager may punish an employee by issuing a verbal reprimand, suspending the employee, or reducing the employee's pay. Just as with positive reinforcement, punishment can be done poorly or it can be done well. But because punishment often has a harmful effect on relationships, it should be used sparingly. Management Smarts offers advice on how best to handle punishment as a reinforcement strategy.

## Management**Smarts**

### Guidelines for Punishment

- Tell the person what is being done wrong.
- Tell the person what is being done right.
- Focus on the undesirable behavior, not on characteristics of the person.
- Make sure the punishment matches the behavior so that it is neither too harsh nor too lenient.
- Administer the punishment in private.
- Follow the laws of immediate and contingent reinforcement.

---

**LEARNING CHECK 3**

**TAKEAWAY QUESTION 3 What role does reinforcement play in motivation?**

**Be sure you can** • explain the law of effect and operant conditioning • illustrate how positive reinforcement, negative reinforcement, punishment, and extinction influence work behavior • explain the reinforcement technique of shaping • describe how managers can use the laws of immediate and contingent reinforcement • list guidelines for positive reinforcement and punishment

---

# Motivation and Job Design

One place where motivation theories come into play is **job design**, the process of arranging work tasks for individuals and groups. Building jobs so that satisfaction and performance go hand in hand is in many ways an exercise in "fit" between task requirements and people's needs, capabilities, and interests.[32] The alternatives range from job simplification at one extreme to job enrichment at the other.

**Job design** is arranging work tasks for individuals and groups.

## Job Simplification

**Job simplification** standardizes work procedures and employs people in well-defined and highly specialized tasks.[33] Simplified jobs, such as those in classic automobile assembly lines, are narrow in *job scope*—the number and variety of different tasks a person performs.

**Job simplification** employs people in clearly defined and specialized tasks with narrow job scope.

The logic of job simplification is straightforward. Because the jobs don't require complex skills, workers should be easier and quicker to train, less difficult to supervise, and easy to replace if they leave. And because tasks are well defined, workers should become more efficient by performing them over and over again. But, things don't always work out as planned.[34] The routine, structured, and repetitive tasks can cause problems if workers become bored and alienated. Productivity can go down when unhappy workers do poor work. Costs can go up when lack of satisfaction causes higher levels of absenteeism and turnover.

One way to eliminate the problems with job simplification is **automation,** the total mechanization of a job. One example is in manufacturing where robots are being used to perform tasks previously done by humans. A second is evident each

**Automation** is the total mechanization of a job.

## Management in Popular Culture

### Motivation Was the Game in the *Blind Side*

The movie *The Blind Side* tells the true story of Michael Oher, a homeless African American teenager who meets and ends up being adopted by a caring white family. After overcoming many challenges, he becomes a star football player at the University of Mississippi and is drafted by the Baltimore Ravens of the NFL. If you watch the movie, ask: Just how was Michael able to overcome so much adversity? What motivated him and kept him going? You should see Maslow's hierarchy of needs at play—with both his lower-level and higher-level needs being addressed. Michael experiences self-efficacy as his confidence grows with his success. And, there is the power of positive reinforcement for his football talents and self-esteem, so that he grows as a person both on and off the field.

*Warner Bros./Photofest*

**Job rotation** increases task variety by periodically shifting workers between different jobs.

**Job enlargement** increases task variety by combining into one job two or more tasks previously done by separate workers.

time you use an ATM machine; this technology is basically an automated replacement for a human teller.

Another way to deal with job simplification problems is **job rotation**. It gives workers more variety by periodically shifting them between jobs. Also, **job enlargement** increases task variety by combining into one job two or more tasks that were previously assigned to separate workers. It is sometimes called *horizontal loading*, which simply means making a job bigger by allowing the worker to do tasks from earlier and later stages in the workflow.

## Job Enrichment

Frederick Herzberg, whose two-factor theory of motivation was discussed earlier, not only questions the motivational value of job simplification, he is also critical of job enlargement and rotation. "Why," he asks, "should a worker become motivated when one or more meaningless tasks are added to previously existing ones, or when work assignments are rotated among equally meaningless tasks?" By contrast, he says: "If you want people to do a good job, give them a good job to do."[35] Herzberg believes this is best done through **job enrichment** that expands job content and increases *job depth*—the extent to which planning and controlling duties are performed by the individual worker rather than the supervisor. Job enrichment is a form of *vertical loading*, which means increasing job depth and giving employees more responsibility for the way they carry out their tasks.

**Job enrichment** increases job depth by adding work planning and evaluating duties normally performed by the supervisor.

### Job Characteristics Model

Management theory now takes job enrichment a step beyond Herzberg's suggestions. It adopts a contingency perspective that recognizes job enrichment may not be good for everyone. This thinking is evident in the job characteristics model developed by Hackman and Oldham and shown in Figure 16.6.[36] It focuses attention on the extent to which these five characteristics are present or absent in a job:

1. *Skill variety*—the degree to which a job requires a variety of different activities to carry out the work, and involves the use of a number of different skills and talents of the individual.

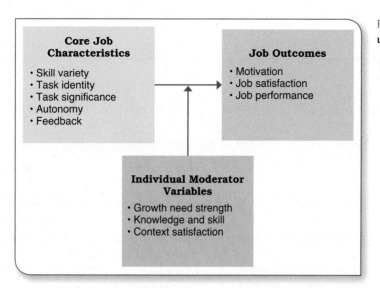

FIGURE 16.6  **Job design essentials using the job characteristics model.**

2. *Task identity*—the degree to which the job requires completion of a "whole" and identifiable piece of work, one that involves doing a job from beginning to end with a visible outcome.

3. *Task significance*—the degree to which the job has a substantial impact on the lives or work of other people elsewhere in the organization, or in the external environment.

4. *Autonomy*—the degree to which the job gives the individual freedom, independence, and discretion in scheduling work and in choosing procedures for carrying it out.

5. *Feedback from the job itself*—the degree to which work activities required by the job result in the individual obtaining direct and clear information on his or her performance.

A job that is high in the five core characteristics is considered enriched. But in true contingency fashion, an enriched job will not affect everyone in the same way. Generally speaking, people who respond most favorably to enriched jobs will have strong growth needs as described in Alderfer's ERG theory, appropriate job knowledge, skills, and abilities, and be otherwise satisfied with job context as discussed in Herzberg's two-factor theory. This creates a good person–job fit. When people without these characteristics are given enriched jobs, however, there is a poor person–job fit. Their satisfaction and performance may fall instead of rise.

## Improving Job Characteristics

For people and situations in which job enrichment is a good choice, Hackman and his colleagues recommend five ways to improve the core job characteristics. First, *combine tasks*. Expand job responsibilities by pulling a number of smaller tasks previously done by others into one larger job. Second, *form natural units of work*. Make sure that the tasks people perform are logically related to one another and provide a clear and meaningful task identity. Third, *establish client relationships*. Put people in contact with others who, as clients inside or outside

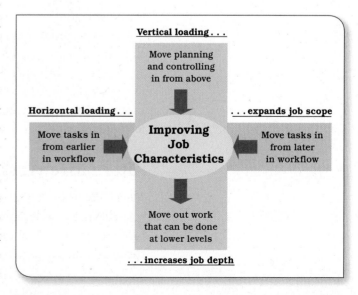

# Generational Differences in Extrinsic and Intrinsic Work Values

Jean M. Twenge and her colleagues used a time-lag method to examine generational differences in work values among Baby Boomers (born between 1946 and 1964), Gen Xers (1965-1981), and Millennials (1982-1999). They did so by looking at 16,507 graduating high school seniors in 1976, 1991, and 2006.

The research studied how much each generation valued the outcomes of leisure (schedule flexibility and time off), extrinsic rewards (money and status), intrinsic rewards (interesting and challenging work and opportunities for growth), social rewards (making friends and contact with others), and altruistic rewards (helping others and contributing to society).

The findings shown in the small box support the popular notion that Millennials have a sense of entitlement. While they place a relatively high emphasis on money and status, they do not want to work harder to achieve these outcomes. Instead, they place a higher value on leisure and work–life balance than prior generations. Because leisure is so highly valued, companies might want to consider offering it through such things as flexible schedules, a compressed workweek, and increased vacation time as an incentive to attract members of the Millennial generation. Also, contrary to popular belief, Millennials do not place a higher value on either social or altruistic rewards than members of previous generations.

**YOU BE THE RESEARCHER**

Take a survey of your classmates and ask them to describe which aspects of work they value the most. How closely do

> **Summary of Study Findings**
>
> - Leisure is more important to Millennials than to Baby Boomers or Gen Xers.
> - Millennials value extrinsic rewards more than Baby Boomers but less than Gen Xers.
> - Millennials value intrinsic rewards less than Baby Boomers and Gen Xers.
> - Social interactions at work (social rewards) are less important to Millennials than to Baby Boomers and Gen Xers.
> - Altruistic rewards were equally valued across all generations.

your results match the findings of Twenge's study? Do you think these results would be different if you asked your parents and their colleagues?

Companies are currently experiencing a big change in the makeup of their workforce. Baby Boomers are starting to retire and companies are seeking to hire, develop, and retain a new generation of talent. What are some practical implications of this study's findings? What will companies and managers need to do in order to attract and get the best performance from members of the Millennial generation?

*Reference:* Jean M. Twenge, Stacy M. Campbell, Brian J. Hoffman, and Charles E. Lance, "Generational Differences in Work Values: Leisure and Extrinsic Values Increasing, Social and Intrinsic Values Decreasing," *Journal of Management*, vol. 36, no. 5 (September 2010), pp. 1117–42.

the organization, use the results of their work. Fourth, *practice vertical loading* that gives people authority to perform the planning and controlling previously done by supervisors. Fifth, *open feedback channels.* Provide opportunities for people both to receive performance feedback as they work and to learn how performance changes over time. In contrast to job enlargement and job rotation, which merely make jobs bigger horizontally by expanding job scope, the small figure shows that job enrichment expands job depth to make jobs vertically bigger as well.

## Alternative Work Schedules

"Flexibility" is the key word driving the emergence of alternative ways for people to schedule their work time.[37] Employers are finding that alternative work schedules help attract and retain motivated workers by offering them flexibility to deal with the many complications of work–life balance.

## Flexible Working Hours

The term **flexible working hours**, also called *flextime*, describes any work schedule that gives employees some choice in how to allocate their daily work hours. Flexible schedules of starting and ending times give employees greater autonomy while meeting their work responsibilities. Some may choose to come in earlier and leave earlier while still completing a full work day; others may choose to start later and leave later. Flexible scheduling allows employees to handle personal and family needs—such as medical appointments, home emergencies, child care issues, as long as they get their work done. Reports indicate that flexible schedules reduce stress and lower job turnover.[38] All top 100 companies in *Working Mother* magazine's list of best employers for working moms offer it.

> **Flexible working hours** give employees some choice in daily work hours.

## Compressed Workweek

A **compressed workweek** is any work schedule that allows a full-time job to be completed in less than the standard five days of 8-hour shifts. The most common form is the "4–40," that is, accomplishing 40 hours of work in four 10-hour days. A key feature of the 4–40 schedule is that the employee receives three consecutive days off from work each week. Many employees are on a four-day schedule at USAA, a diversified financial services company listed among the 100 best companies to work for in America. Its advantages include improved employee morale, lower overtime costs, less absenteeism, fewer days lost to sick leave, as well as lower costs of commuting.[39] Potential disadvantages of the compressed workweek include increased fatigue and family adjustment problems for the individual, as well as scheduling problems for the employer.

> A **compressed workweek** allows a full-time job to be completed in less than five days.

## Job Sharing

**Job sharing** splits one full-time job between two or more persons. This can be done in a variety of ways, from half day to weekly or monthly sharing arrangements. Organizations benefit by employing talented people who are unable or unwilling to commit to a full-time job. A parent with young children, for example, might be unable to stay away from home for a full workday, but able to work half a day.

> **Job sharing** splits one job between two people.

## Telecommuting

It is increasingly popular for people to work by **telecommuting**, an arrangement that allows at least a portion of scheduled work hours to be completed outside the office. It is facilitated by computers and smart devices that allow easy electronic links with customers and coworkers. New terms are even associated with telecommuting practices. We speak of *hoteling* when telecommuters come to the central office and use temporary office facilities; we also refer to *virtual offices* that include everything from an office at home to a mobile workspace in an automobile.

When asked what they like about this work arrangement, telecommuters report increased productivity, fewer distractions, less time spent commuting to and from work, and the freedom to schedule their own time. On the negative side, they may complain about working too much, difficulty separating work and personal life, and having less time for family.[40] One telecommuter offers this advice: "You have to have self-discipline and pride in what you do, but you also have to have a boss that trusts you enough to get out of the way."[41]

> **Telecommuting** involves using IT to work at home or outside the office.

Zak Kendal/Zuma Press

## Co-Working Spaces Gain Popularity for Flexible Schedulers

Want to telecommute, but not work at home all the time? Try office sharing. As more people work on their own and away from the corporate office, and as more budding entrepreneurs try their hand at start-ups, the notion of work flexibility has entered a new dimension—co-working spaces. They typically allow people to pay by the month and get not only their workspace and back office support; they get a fixed address as well. Plug and Play Tech Center is one example. It provides co-working spaces to 1,000 people in Sunnyvale, California. Founder Saeed Amidi says: "You don't need to buy furniture, you don't need to set up Internet, you don't need to sign a long term lease."

## Contingency and Part-Time Work

**Contingency workers** are employed on a part-time and temporary basis to supplement a permanent workforce.

If there is one trend that has been reinforced by our tight economy, it's the use of more **contingency workers** hired on a temporary and part-time basis to supplement the regular workforce.[42] You'll hear them called temps, freelancers, and contract hires. They provide just-in-time and as-needed work for employers who want to avoid the cost and responsibilities of hiring full-timers. One business analyst says the appeal to the employer is "easy to lay off, no severance; no company funded retirement plan; pay own health insurance; get zero sick days and no vacation."[43]

It is now possible to hire on a part-time basis everything from executive support, such as a chief financial officer, to special expertise in areas like engineering, computer programming, and market research. While some worry that they lack the commitment of permanent workers and thus may lower productivity and product or service quality, others argue that contingent employees frequently do just as good a job and offer cost savings of up to 30% over full-time workers.[44] But these cost advantages are also controversial. Contingency workers are generally paid less than their full-time counterparts, can experience stress and anxiety from their part-time and non-secure job status, and generally do not receive important benefits such as health care, life insurance, pension plans, and paid vacations.

### LEARNING CHECK 4

**TAKEAWAY QUESTION 4 What is the link between job design and motivation?**

**Be sure you can** • illustrate a job designed by simplification, rotation, and enlargement • list five core job characteristics • describe how an enriched job scores on these characteristics • describe advantages of the compressed workweek, flexible work hours, job sharing, and telecommuting • discuss the role of part-time contingency workers in the economy

# MANAGEMENT LEARNING REVIEW

## TAKEAWAY QUESTION 1  How do individual needs influence motivation?

- Motivation predicts the level, direction, and persistence of effort expended at work; simply put, a highly motivated person works hard.
- Maslow's hierarchy of human needs suggests a progression from lower-order physiological, safety, and social needs to higher-order esteem and self-actualization needs.
- Alderfer's ERG theory identifies existence, relatedness, and growth needs.
- Herzberg's two-factor theory describes the importance of both job content and job context to motivation and performance.
- McClelland's acquired needs theory identifies the needs for achievement, affiliation, and power, all of which may influence what a person desires from work.

**For Discussion** How can managers balance the competing desires of attempting to meet the unique needs of individual employees while treating all employees fairly and equitably?

## TAKEAWAY QUESTION 2  What are the process theories of motivation?

- Adams's equity theory recognizes that social comparisons take place when rewards are distributed in the workplace.
- People who feel inequitably treated are motivated to act in ways that reduce the sense of inequity; perceived negative inequity may result in someone working less hard in the future.
- The concept of equity sensitivity suggests that not all employees are equally concerned about being treated equitably and that not all employees respond to different types of inequity in the same way.
- Vroom's expectancy theory states that Motivation = Expectancy × Instrumentality × Valence.
- Locke's goal-setting theory emphasizes the motivational power of goals; task goals should be specific rather than ambiguous, difficult but achievable, and set through participatory means.
- Bandura's self-efficacy theory indicates that when people believe they are capable of performing a task, they experience a sense of confidence and will be more highly motivated to work hard at it.

**For Discussion** In which job aspects are people most likely to be upset by inequity? In which job aspects are people more likely to be accepting of, or less concerned about, inequity?

## TAKEAWAY QUESTION 3  What role does reinforcement play in motivation?

- Reinforcement theory recognizes that human behavior is influenced by its environmental consequences.
- The law of effect states that behavior followed by a pleasant consequence is likely to be repeated; behavior followed by an unpleasant consequence is unlikely to be repeated.
- Reinforcement strategies used by managers include positive reinforcement, negative reinforcement, punishment, and extinction.
- Positive reinforcement works best when applied according to the laws of contingent and immediate reinforcement.

**For Discussion** Is it possible for a manager or a parent to rely solely on positive reinforcement strategies?

## TAKEAWAY QUESTION 4  What is the link between job design and motivation?

- Job design is the process of creating or defining jobs by assigning specific work tasks to individuals and groups.
- Job simplification creates narrow and repetitive jobs consisting of well-defined tasks with many routine operations, such as the typical assembly-line job.
- Job enlargement allows individuals to perform a broader range of simplified tasks; job rotation allows individuals to shift among different jobs with similar skill levels.
- The job characteristics model of job design analyzes jobs according to skill variety, task identity, task significance, autonomy, and feedback; a job high in them is considered enriched.
- Alternative work schedules make work hours more convenient and flexible to better fit workers' needs and personal responsibilities; options include the compressed workweek, flexible working hours, job sharing, telecommuting, and part-time work.

**For Discussion** Is it reasonable to enrich someone's job without increasing his or her pay as well?

## Multiple-Choice Questions

1. Lower-order needs in Maslow's hierarchy match well with _____ needs in ERG theory.
   (a) growth
   (b) affiliation
   (c) existence
   (d) achievement

2. When a team member shows strong ego needs in Maslow's hierarchy, the team leader should find that _____ will be motivating to him or her.
   (a) alternative work schedules
   (b) praise and recognition for job performance
   (c) social interactions with other team members
   (d) easy performance goals

3. A worker with a high need for _____ power in McClelland's theory tries to use power for the good of the organization.
   (a) position
   (b) expert
   (c) personal
   (d) social

4. In Herzberg's two-factor theory, base pay is considered a(n) _____ factor.
   (a) valence
   (b) satisfier
   (c) equity
   (d) hygiene

5. Which of the following is a correct match?
   (a) McClelland—ERG theory
   (b) Skinner—reinforcement theory
   (c) Vroom—equity theory
   (d) Locke—expectancy theory

6. The expectancy theory of motivation says that motivation = expectancy × _____ ×

   _____.
   (a) rewards, valence
   (b) instrumentality, valence
   (c) equity, instrumentality
   (d) rewards, valence

7. When someone has a high and positive "expectancy" in the expectancy theory of motivation, this means that the person _____.
   (a) believes he or she can meet performance expectations
   (b) highly values the rewards being offered
   (c) sees a link between high performance and available rewards
   (d) believes that rewards are equitable

8. In the _____ theory of motivation, someone who perceives herself under-rewarded relative to a coworker might be expected to reduce his or her performance in the future.
   (a) ERG
   (b) acquired needs
   (c) two-factor
   (d) equity

9. In goal-setting theory, the goal of "doing a better job" would not be considered a good source of motivation because it fails the test of goal _____.
   (a) acceptance
   (b) specificity
   (c) challenge
   (d) commitment

10. The law of _____ states that behavior followed by a positive consequence is likely to be repeated, whereas behavior followed by an undesirable consequence is not likely to be repeated.
    (a) reinforcement
    (b) contingency
    (c) goal setting
    (d) effect

11. _____ is a positive reinforcement strategy that rewards successive approximations to a desirable behavior.
    (a) Extinction
    (b) Negative reinforcement
    (c) Shaping
    (d) Merit pay

12. B. F. Skinner would argue that "getting a paycheck on Friday" reinforces a person for coming to work on Friday, but it does not reinforce the person for having done an extraordinary job on Tuesday. This is because the Friday paycheck fails the law of _____ reinforcement.
    (a) negative
    (b) continuous
    (c) immediate
    (d) intermittent

13. When a job is redesigned to allow a person to do a whole unit of work from beginning to end, it becomes high on which core characteristic?
    (a) task identity
    (b) task significance
    (c) task autonomy
    (d) feedback

14. A typical compressed workweek schedule involves 40 hours work done in _____ days.
    (a) 3
    (b) 4
    (c) 5
    (d) a flexible number of

15. A term often used to describe someone who is a long-term but part-time hire is _____ worker.
    (a) contingency
    (b) virtual
    (c) flexible
    (d) permatemp

### Short-Response Questions

**16.** What preferences does a person with a high need for achievement bring to the workplace?

**17.** Why is participation important to goal-setting theory?

### Essay Question

**20.** How can a manager combine the powers of goal setting and positive reinforcement to create a highly motivational work environment for workers with high needs for achievement?

**18.** What is the common ground in Maslow's, Alderfer's, and McClelland's views of human needs?

**19.** Why might an employer not want to offer employees the option of a compressed workweek schedule?

## MANAGEMENT SKILLS AND COMPETENCIES

## Further Reflection: Engagement

There's a lot of attention being given these days to the levels of **engagement** displayed by people at work. Differences in job engagement show up many ways. Is someone enthusiastic or lethargic, diligent or lazy, willing to do more than expected or willing to do only what is expected? Managers obviously want high levels of engagement by members of their work units and teams. The ideas of this chapter offer many insights on how to create engagement by using the content, process, and reinforcement theories of motivation. We expect engagement from others when our outcomes are dependent on how well they perform, say on a team project. Take a look around the classroom. What do you see and what would you predict for the future of your classmates based on the engagement they now show as students?

 DO IT NOW ...
LOOK IN THE MIRROR

• Ask: "How engaged am I in projects at school and at work?

• Ask also: "What could my instructor do to help increase my engagement? By the same token, what could I do?

• Write a summary of your answers. Discuss their implications for both (a) your remaining time as a student, and (b) your future career and how you will behave in the workplace.

## Self-Assessment: Student Engagement Survey

### Instructions

Use this scale to show the degree to which you agree with the following statements. Write your choices in the margin next to each question.[45]

1—No agreement; 2—Weak agreement; 3—Some agreement; 4—Considerable agreement; 5—Very strong agreement

1. I know what is expected of me in this course.

2. I have the resources and support I need to do my coursework correctly.

3. In this course, I have the opportunity to do what I do best all the time.

4. In the last week, I have received recognition or praise for doing good work in this course.

5. My instructor seems to care about me as a person.

6. There is someone in the course who encourages my development.

7. In this course, my opinions seem to count.

8. The mission/purpose of the course makes me feel my area of study is important.

9. Other students in the course are committed to doing quality work.

10. I have a good friend in the course.

11. In the last six class sessions, someone has talked to me about my progress in the course.

12. In this course, I have had opportunities to learn and grow.

## Scoring

Score the instrument by adding up all your responses. A score of 0–24 suggests you are "actively disengaged" from the learning experience; a score of 25–47 suggests you are "moderately engaged"; a score of 48–60 indicates you are "actively engaged."

## Interpretation

This instrument is a counterpart to a survey used by the Gallup Organization to measure the "engagement" of American workers. The Gallup results are surprising—indicating that up to 19% of U.S. workers are actively disengaged, with the annual lost productivity estimated at some $300 billion per year. One has to wonder: What are the costs of academic disengagement by students?

## Team Exercise: Why We Work

## Preparation

Read this "ancient story."[46]

In days of old, a wandering youth happened upon a group of men working in a quarry. Stopping by the first man, he said: "What are you doing?" The worker grimaced and groaned as he replied: "I am trying to shape this stone, and it is backbreaking work." Moving to the next man, the youth repeated the question. This man showed little emotion as he answered: "I am shaping a stone for a building." Moving to the third man, our traveler heard him singing as he worked. "What are you doing?" asked the youth. "I am helping to build a cathedral," the man proudly replied.

## Instructions

In groups assigned by your instructor:

1. Discuss this short story.

2. Ask and answer the question: "What are the motivation and job design lessons of this ancient story?"

3. Discuss the question: How can managers help employees feel more inspired about what they are doing?

4. Have someone prepared to report and share the group's responses with the class as a whole.

## Career Situations for Motivation: What Would You Do?

1. **Paying the Going Rate** As the manager of a small engineering company, you need to hire a replacement for a senior employee who just retired. The salaries you pay have always been a little below average, but it has never been an issue because you offer excellent benefits and a great work environment. The individual you want to hire has made it clear that she will not accept the job unless you increase the offer by $5,000 to match the market rate for the position. If you pay the going rate, you'll risk alienating your current workforce. If you don't, you'll miss out on a great new hire. What can you do to best handle this dilemma?

2. **Across-the-Board Raises** Because of the poor economy your company has not been able to offer pay raises to its employees for the past 3 years. Now the salary budget has been increased by 5%. Your initial thought was to give every employee a 5% raise. Is this a good idea as seen through the lens of equity theory and expectancy theory? How should you allocate salary increases in this situation?

3. **Is Job Redesign a Good Idea?** As the manager of a small manufacturing operation, you have come up with a plan to redesign operations to give workers more autonomy and control over the way they do their jobs. Your assistant manager believes this is a bad idea. She says that the workers show no capacity to act on their own, and that both productivity and quality will suffer. You think they're bored and disengaged, but otherwise capable. How should you approach this decision?

## Case Study

**SAS**

Go to *Management Cases for Critical Thinking* to find the recommended case for Chapter 16—SAS: Business Success Starts on the Inside.

Short for *Statistical Analysis System*, SAS is a set of integrated software tools that help decision makers cope with unwieldy amounts of unrelated data. It's the primary product of North Carolina-based SAS Institute, self-described as the "leader in business analytics software." One user describes SAS products as "empowering people with data to make efficient, effective decisions earlier." With Jim Goodnight at the helm, the firm has gained an impressive roster of clients from Fortune Global 500 companies to universities and government agencies. Its reach extends to customers in over 100 different countries.

But there's more to SAS than great products. If you look below the surface, you'll find that Goodnight's special approach to building a talented and motivated workforce is as great as the firm's software. SAS employees aren't always paid the best, but they work in a great setting that goes a long way toward meeting their needs for both satisfying work and work-life balance.

# Wisdom
## Learning From Others

### > THE BEAUTY IS IN THE TEAMWORK

What distinguishes a group of people from a high-performance team? For an answer, look no further than your favorite NASCAR pit crew.

The difference between winning and losing in NASCAR often comes down to just seconds. When a driver pulls in for a pit stop, the team must jump in to perform multiple tasks flawlessly and in perfect order and unison. A second gained or lost can be crucial to a driver. Pit team members must be well trained and rehearsed to perform efficiently on race day.

The members of a pit crew are often former college and professional athletes. All are conditioned and trained to execute intricate maneuvers while taking care of tire changes, car adjustments, fueling, and related matters—all on a crowded pit lane.

Each crew member is an expert at one task. But each is fully aware of how that job fits with every other in a few-second pit-stop interval. The individual duties are carefully scripted and choreographed to fit together seamlessly at the team level. There's no room for error. If the jacker is late, the wheel changer can't pull the wheel.

Practice makes for perfection. And it's the job of the crew chief to make sure that everyone is in shape, well trained, and ready to go on race day. One crew chief says: "I don't want seven all-stars, I want seven guys who work as a team."[1]

## MORE TO LOOK FOR INSIDE>

**FOLLOW THE STORY**
Teams and Teamwork Add Lift to Boeing's New Planes

**ETHICS ON THE LINE**
Social Loafing Is Getting in the Way of Team Performance

**FACTS FOR ANALYSIS**
Unproductive Meetings Are Major Time Wasters

**RESEARCH BRIEF**
Demographic Faultlines Pose Implications for Managing Teams

# Teams and Teamwork

## > TEAM CONTRIBUTIONS

The benefits of team performance aren't realized unless members make positive **team contributions**. These are things people do to help teams succeed at their tasks and help members enjoy the team experience.

*Scene—Hospital operating room:* Scholars notice that heart surgeons have lower death rates for similar procedures performed in hospitals where they do more operations than those performed where they do fewer operations.

Why? Researchers say the operations go better because the doctors in the better hospitals spend more time working together with members of their surgery teams. It's not only the surgeon's skills that count, they say, ". . . the skills of the team, and of the organization, matter."[2]

*Scene—NBA basketball court:* Scholars find that basketball teams win more games the longer the players have been together.

Why? Researchers claim it's a "teamwork effect." Teams whose members play together longest win more because the players get to know each other's moves and playing tendencies.[3]

A large part of your career success will depend on how well you work in and lead teams. Take a look at the list of "must-have" team skills. Do you have the skills portfolio and personal commitment to make truly valuable team contributions?

## Insight
### Learning About Yourself

### "MUST HAVE" TEAM SKILLS

- Encouraging and motivating others
- Accepting suggestions
- Listening to different points of view
- Communicating information and ideas
- Persuading others to cooperate
- Resolving and negotiating conflict
- Building consensus
- Fulfilling commitments
- Avoiding disruptive acts and words

## BUILD SKILLS AND COMPETENCIES AT END OF CHAPTER

- Engage in *Further Reflection on Your Team Contributions*
- Take the *Self-Assessment—Team Leader Skills*
- Prepare for the *Team Exercise—Work Team Dynamics*
- Solve the *Career Situations in Teamwork*
- Analyze the *Case Study—Auto Racing!—"When the Driver Takes a Back Seat"*

## <GET TO KNOW YOURSELF BETTER

| TAKEAWAY 1 | TAKEAWAY 2 | TAKEAWAY 3 | TAKEAWAY 4 |
|---|---|---|---|
| **Teams in Organizations**<br><br>• Teamwork pros<br>• Teamwork cons<br>• Meetings, meetings, meetings<br>• Organizations as networks of teams | **Trends in the Use of Teams**<br><br>• Committees, project teams, and task forces<br>• Cross-functional teams<br>• Self-managing teams<br>• Virtual teams<br>• Team building | **How Teams Work**<br><br>• Team inputs<br>• Stages of team development<br>• Norms and cohesiveness<br>• Task and maintenance roles<br>• Communication networks | **Decision Making in Teams**<br><br>• Ways teams make decisions<br>• Advantages and disadvantages of team decisions<br>• Groupthink<br>• Creativity in team decision making |
| **LEARNING CHECK 1** | **LEARNING CHECK 2** | **LEARNING CHECK 3** | **LEARNING CHECK 4** |

"Sticks in a bundle are hard to break"—*Kenyan proverb*

"Never doubt that a small group of thoughtful, determined people can change the world"—*Margaret Mead,* anthropologist

"Pick good people, use small teams and give them great tools so that they are very productive. . ."—*Bill Gates*, businessman and philanthropist

"Gettin' good players is easy. Gettin' 'em to play together is the hard part"—*Casey Stengel*, baseball manager

From proverbs to societies to sports to business, teams and teamwork are rich topics of conversation and major pathways to great accomplishments.[4] But even so, just the words *group* and *team* elicit both positive and negative reactions in the minds of many people. Although it is said that "two heads are better than one," we are also warned that "too many cooks spoil the broth." The true skeptic can be heard to say: "A camel is a horse put together by a committee."

Teams are both rich in performance potential and very complex in the way they work; they can be great successes and they can also be colossal failures.[5] More than a third of workers report dissatisfaction with teamwork, and less than half say they receive training in group dynamics.[6] Still, many people prefer to work in teams rather than independently.

## Teams in Organizations

A **team** is a collection of people who regularly interact to pursue common goals.

**Teamwork** is the process of people actively working together to accomplish common goals.

A **team** is a small group of people with complementary skills who interact and work with one another to achieve shared goals.[7] **Teamwork** is the process of people working together to accomplish these goals.

Managers must be prepared to perform at least four important teamwork roles. A *team leader* serves as the appointed head of a team or work unit. A *team member* serves as a helpful contributing part of a project team. A *network facilitator* serves as the peer leader and networking hub for a special task force. And, a *coach or developer* serves as a team's advisor on ways to improve processes and performance.

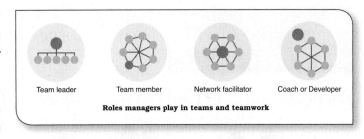

Team leader    Team member    Network facilitator    Coach or Developer

**Roles managers play in teams and teamwork**

## Teamwork Pros

Although teams can be hard work, they are worth it when things turn out right.[8] Their beauty is accomplishing something far greater than what's possible for an individual alone. This is called **synergy**, the creation of a whole that is greater than the sum of its parts.

**Synergy** is the creation of a whole greater than the sum of its individual parts.

Synergy pools individual talents and efforts to create extraordinary results through collective action. When Jens Voigt, one of the top racers on the Tour de France, was asked to describe a "perfect cyclist," for example, he created a composite of his nine-member team: "We take the time trial legs of Fabian Cancellara, the speed of Stuart O'Grady, the climbing capacity of our leaders and my attitude." His point was that the tour is way too hard for a single rider to win on his own talents. Like so many other things in any workplace, the synergies made possible by teamwork are the keys to success.[9]

Just being part of a team is often good for its members. The personal connections can help people do their jobs better—getting help, making contacts, sharing ideas, responding to favors, and avoiding roadblocks. The personal relationships can help satisfy important needs that may be difficult to meet in the regular work setting or life overall, providing things like positive interactions, a sense of security and belonging, or emotional support.[10]

### THE MANY BENEFITS OF TEAMS

• Performance gains through synergy
• More resources for problem solving
• Improved creativity and innovation
• Improved quality of decision making
• Greater member commitment to tasks
• Increased motivation of members
• Increased need satisfaction of members

## Teamwork Cons

We all know that things don't always work out as intended with teams and teamwork. Problems can easily turn their great potential into frustration and failure.[11]

Personality conflicts and work style differences can disrupt a team. Unclear tasks, ambiguous agendas, and ill-defined problems can cause teams to work too long on the wrong things. Sometimes people start out motivated and then lose it because teamwork takes too much time from other tasks, deadlines, and priorities. A lack of success also hurts morale. And, it's easy for members to lose motivation when the team is poorly organized and led, or other members slack off.[12]

Who hasn't encountered **social loafing**? This is the presence of "free-riders" who slack off because responsibility is diffused in teams and others are present to do the work.[13] But don't despair, there are things a leader or concerned team members can do in such cases. The possibilities include making individual contributions more visible, rewarding individuals for their contributions, making task assignments more interesting, and keeping group size small so that free-riders are more subject to peer pressure and leader evaluation.[14]

**Social loafing** is the tendency of some people to avoid responsibility by "free-riding" in groups.

ETHICS
ON THE LINE

> THE STUDENT COMPLAINED THAT FREE RIDERS WERE
MAKING IT HARD FOR HER TEAM TO PERFORM WELL

## Social Loafing Is Getting in the Way of Team Performance

Masterfile

1. *Psychology study:* A German researcher asked people to pull on a rope as hard as they could. First, individuals pulled alone. Second, they pulled as part of a group. The results showed that people pull harder when working alone than when working as part of a team. Such "social loafing" is the tendency to reduce effort when working in groups.

2. *Faculty office:* A student wants to speak with the instructor about his team's performance on the last group project. There were four members, but two did almost all of the work. The other two largely disappeared, showing up only at the last minute to be part of the formal presentation.

His point is that the team was disadvantaged because two free-riders caused reduced performance capacity.

3. *Telephone call from the boss:* "John, I really need you to serve on this committee. Will you do it? Let me know tomorrow." In thinking about this, I ponder: I'm overloaded, but I don't want to turn down the boss. I'll accept but let the committee members know about my situation. I'll be active in discussions and try to offer viewpoints and perspectives that are helpful. However, I'll let them know up front that I can't be a leader or volunteer for any extra work.

### ETHICS QUESTIONS

What are the ethical issues involved in team situations when some people sit back and let others do more of the work? When you join a group, do all members have an ethical obligation to do a similar amount of work—why or why not? When it comes to John, does the fact that he intends to be honest with the other committee members make any difference? Isn't he still going to be a social loafer while earning credit from his boss for serving on the committee? Is his approach ethical—or should he simply decline to participate on the committee?

## Meetings, Meetings, Meetings

"We have the most ineffective meetings of any company," says a technology executive. "We just seem to meet and meet and meet, and we never seem to do anything," says another in the package delivery industry. "We realize our meetings are unproductive. A consulting firm is trying to help us, but we've got a long way to go," says a corporate manager.[15]

What do you think when someone says: "Let's have a meeting"? Are you ready and willing, or apprehensive and even perturbed? We aren't always happy to get a request to add another meeting to our busy schedules. And the problems described in Management Smarts don't help.[16] You might even be able to add to the list from personal experience.

Good meetings don't happen by chance. People have to work hard and work together to make them productive and rewarding. Face-to-face and virtual meetings are where lots of information is shared, decisions get made, and people gain understanding

### Management**Smarts**

#### Spotting the Seven Sins of Deadly Meetings

1. People arrive late, leave early, and don't take things seriously.
2. The meeting is too long, sometimes twice as long as necessary.
3. People don't stay on topic; they digress and are easily distracted.
4. The discussion lacks candor; people are unwilling to tell the truth.
5. The right information isn't available, so decisions are postponed.
6. Nothing happens when the meeting is over; no one puts decisions into action.
7. Things never get better; the same mistakes are made meeting after meeting.

of issues and one another. They're important and necessary. This is why knowing more about teams and teamwork is so useful.

## Organizations as Networks of Teams

**Formal groups** are officially recognized and supported by the organization. They may be called departments (e.g., market research department), units (e.g., audit unit), teams (e.g., customer service team), or divisions (e.g., office products division), among other possibilities. These formal groups form interlocking networks that set the foundations of organization structure, and managers are key "linking pins" among them. Managers lead formal groups at one level while also serving as members of others at the next higher level and in groups formed across functions.[17]

**Informal groups** are also present and important in all organizations. They emerge from natural or spontaneous relationships among people. Some are *interest groups* in which workers band together to pursue a common cause such as better working conditions. Some emerge as *friendship groups* that develop for a wide variety of personal reasons, including shared non-work interests. Others exist as *support groups*, in which the members basically help one another do their jobs or cope with common problems.

Although people may sometimes air gripes and spread rumors in informal groups, the social connections they offer play many positive roles in organizations. Tapping into relationships within informal groups can help speed the workflow or allow people to "get things done" in ways not possible within the formal structure. Members of informal groups can also satisfy needs that are otherwise unmet in their formal work assignments. These include gaining such things as friendship, security, support, and a sense of belonging.

> A **formal group** is a team officially recognized and supported by the organization.

> An **informal group** is unofficial and emerges from relationships and shared interests among members.

---

**LEARNING CHECK 1**

**TAKEAWAY QUESTION 1 How do teams contribute to organizations?**
**Be sure you can** • define *team* and *teamwork* • identify four roles managers perform in teams • define *synergy* • explain teamwork pros and cons • discuss the implications of social loafing • explain the potential benefits of informal groups

---

## Trends in the Use of Teams

A trend toward greater empowerment in organizations today shows up as an emphasis on committees, project teams, task forces, cross-functional teams, and self-managing teams. And importantly, any and all of these teams function in both face-to-face and virtual forms.

## Committees, Project Teams, and Task Forces

A **committee** brings people together outside of their daily job assignments to work in a small team for a specific purpose. The task agenda is typically narrow, focused,

> A **committee** is designated to work on a special task on a continuing basis.

## Management in Popular Culture

### Mysterious Island Was a Window into Teamwork

A plane crash deposits a group of strangers on a mysterious island with little hope of rescue. Sound familiar? It's all part of the background for a television series you might recall, *Lost.* An early episode shows a doctor, Jack Shephard (Matthew Fox), walking off on his own. He ends up finding a source of clean water, something that can keep them all alive. He returns to the crash site only to witness a fight for the last of the bottled water. He breaks up the fight and declares we "live together, die alone." His lesson in teamwork was that each person should find a way to contribute to the good of all, and then make the commitment to really do it.

ABC/Photofest

and ongoing. Organizations usually have a variety of permanent or standing committees dedicated to a wide variety of concerns, such as diversity, quality, and product development. Committees are led by a designated head or chairperson, who is held accountable for performance results.

**Project teams** or **task forces** bring people together to work on common problems, but on a temporary rather than permanent basis. The goals and task assignments are specific and completion deadlines are clear. Creativity and innovation may be part of the agenda. Project teams, for example, might be formed to develop a new advertising message, redesign an office layout, or streamline a work process.[18]

> A **project team** or **task force** is convened for a specific purpose and disbands when its task is completed.

## Cross-Functional Teams

> A **cross-functional team** operates with members who come from different functional units of an organization.
> The **functional chimneys problem** is a lack of communication across functions.

Many organizations make use of **cross-functional teams** that pull together members from across functional units to work on common goals. These teams help reduce the **functional chimneys problem** by eliminating "walls" that may otherwise limit communication and cooperation among people from different departments and functions. Target CEO Gregg Steinhafel, for example, says that his firm uses cross-functional teams from "merchandising, marketing, design, communications, presentation, supply chain and stores" to create and bring to customers new limited edition fashions.[19]

## Self-Managing Teams

> Members of a **self-managing work team** have the authority to make decisions about how they share and complete their work.

Traditional work groups consisting of first-level supervisors and their immediate subordinates are being replaced in a growing number of organizations with **self-managing work teams**. As shown in Figure 17.1, these teams operate with a high degree of task interdependence, authority to make many decisions about how they work, and collective responsibility for results.[20] The expected advantages are better performance, reduced costs, and good morale.

Multitasking is a key feature of any self-managing team, whose members each have the skills to perform several different jobs. And within a team the emphasis

# Unproductive Meetings Are Major Time Wasters

A survey of some 38,000 workers around the world links low productivity with bad meetings, poor communication, and unclear goals.

- 69% of meetings attended are considered ineffective.
- 32% of workers complain about team communication.
- 31% complain about unclear objectives and priorities.

**■ YOUR THOUGHTS?**

Do these data match your experiences with team meetings? Given the common complaints about meetings, what can a team leader do to improve them? Think about the recent meetings you have attended. In what ways were the best meetings different from the worst ones? Did your behavior play a significant role in both these cases?

is always on participation. Self-managing teams operate with members sharing tasks and taking collective responsibility for management functions performed by supervisors in more traditional settings. The "self-management" responsibilities include planning and scheduling work, training members in various tasks, distributing tasks, meeting performance goals, ensuring high quality, and solving day-to-day operating problems. In some settings, the team's authority may even extend to "hiring" and "firing" members. Typical characteristics of self-managing teams include:

- Members are held collectively accountable for performance results.
- Members have discretion in distributing tasks within the team.
- Members have discretion in scheduling work within the team.
- Members are able to perform more than one job on the team.
- Members train one another to develop multiple job skills.
- Members evaluate one another's performance contributions.
- Members are responsible for the total quality of team products.

**FIGURE 17.1** Organizational and management implications of self-managing work teams.

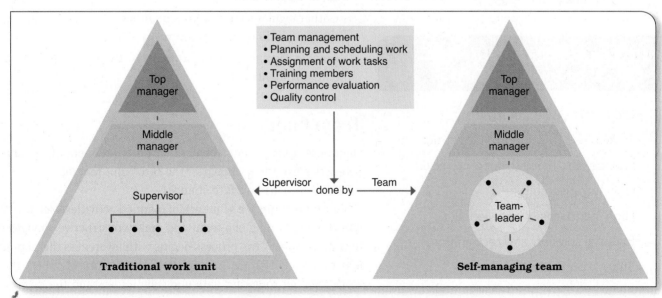

## Virtual Teams

*Scene:* U.S.-based IT manager needs to meet with team members located in Brazil, the Philippines, and Poland. Rather than pay for everyone to fly to a common location, he checks world time zones, sends e-mail to schedule, and then simply turns on his Webcam to join the others online at the appointed time.

The constant emergence of new technologies is making virtual collaboration both easier and more common. At home it may be Facebook; at the office it's likely to be a wide variety of online meeting resources. Members of **virtual teams**, also called **distributed teams**, work together through computer-mediation rather than face-to-face.[21] They operate like other teams in respect to what gets done. It's the way they get things done that is different. And this difference has both potential advantages and disadvantages.[22]

In terms of potential advantages, virtual teams can save time and travel expenses when members work in different locations. They can also be easily expanded to include more members as needed, and the discussions and shared information can be archived for later access. Virtual teams are usually quite efficient because members are less prone to stray off task and get sidetracked by interpersonal difficulties. A vice president for human resources at Marriott, for example, once called electronic meetings "the quietest, least stressful, most productive meetings you've ever had."[23]

The lack of face-to-face interaction in virtual teams creates potential disadvantages. It limits the role of emotions and nonverbal cues in communication and allows relationships to stay depersonalized.[24] "Human beings are social animals for whom building relationships matters a great deal," says one scholar. "Strip away the social side of teamwork and, very quickly, people feel isolated and unsupported."[25] The following guidelines can help keep the possible downsides of virtual teamwork to a minimum.[26]

- Select team members high in initiative and capable of self-starting.
- Select members who will join and engage the team with positive attitudes.
- Select members known for working hard to meet team goals.
- Begin with social messaging that allows members to exchange information about each other to personalize the process.
- Assign clear goals and roles so that members can focus while working alone and also know what others are doing.
  - Gather regular feedback from members about how they think the team is doing and how it might do better.
  - Provide regular feedback to team members about team accomplishments.

## Team Building

High-performance teams of all the prior types operate with characteristics like those shown in the box.[27] But real teamwork and great results can't be left to chance.

**Team building** is a sequence of planned activities used to analyze the functioning of a team and make constructive changes in how it operates.[28] The process begins with awareness that a problem may exist or may develop within the team. Members then work together to gather data and fully understand the problem,

---

*Members of a **virtual team** or **distributed team** work together and solve problems through computer-based interactions.*

*Team building is a sequence of activities to analyze a team and make changes to improve its performance.*

---

**CHARACTERISTICS OF HIGH-PERFORMANCE TEAMS**

- Clear and elevating goals
- Task-driven, results-oriented structure
- Competent, hard-working members
- Collaborative culture
- High standards of excellence
- External support and recognition
- Strong, principled leadership

© Mikael Dubois/AgeFotostock America, Inc.

## Outdoor Team Building Can Be Quite an Experience

When a team of employees from American Electric Power (AEP) went to an outdoor camp for a day of team-building activities, they had to get six members through a spider-web maze of bungee cords strung two feet above the ground. When her teammates lifted Judy Gallo into their hands to pass her over the obstacle, she was nervous. But a trainer told the team the spider web was just another performance constraint, much like the difficult policy issues or financial limits they might face at work. After "high-fives" for making it through the web, Judy's team went on to jump tree stumps together, pass hula hoops while holding hands, and more.

make plans to correct it, implement the plans, and evaluate results. This whole process is repeated as difficulties or new problems are discovered.

There are many ways to gather data for team building, including structured and unstructured interviews, questionnaires, and team meetings. Regardless of the method used, the basic principle of team building remains the same. It is a careful and collaborative assessment of all aspects of the team ranging from how members work together to the results they achieve.

Team building can be done with consulting assistance or under managerial direction. It can also be done in the workplace or in outside locations. A popular approach is to bring team members together in special outdoor settings where their capacities for teamwork are put to the test in unusual and even physically demanding experiences. Says one team-building trainer: "We throw clients into situations to try and bring out the traits of a good team."[29]

---

**LEARNING CHECK 2**

**TAKEAWAY QUESTION 2 What are current trends in the use of teams?**

**Be sure you can** • differentiate a committee from a task force • explain the benefits of cross-functional teams • discuss potential advantages and disadvantages of virtual teams • list the characteristics of self-managing work teams • explain how self-managing teams are changing organizations • describe the typical steps in team building

---

# How Teams Work

An **effective team** does three things well—perform its tasks, satisfy its members, and remain viable for the future.[30] On the *task performance* side, a work group or team is expected to transform resource inputs (such as ideas, materials, and information) into product outputs (such as a report, decision, service, or commodity). In respect to *member satisfaction*, members should take pleasure from both the team's performance accomplishments and their contributions toward making it happen. And as to *future viability*, the team should have a social fabric and work climate that makes its members willing and able to work well together in the future, again and again as needed.

An **effective team** achieves high levels of task performance, membership satisfaction, and future viability.

FIGURE 17.2 **An open-systems model of team effectiveness.**

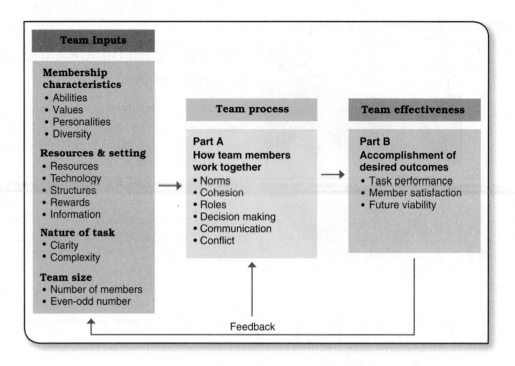

You sometimes hear top executives saying that team effectiveness comes together when you have "the right players in the right seats on the same bus, headed in the same direction."[31] The open-systems model in Figure 17.2 supports this view. It shows that a team's effectiveness is influenced by inputs—"right players in the right seats"—and by process—"on the same bus, headed in the same direction."[32] You can remember the implications of this figure by the following **Team Effectiveness Equation.**[33]

Team effectiveness = Quality of inputs + (Process gains − Process losses)

**Team Effectiveness Equation**
Team effectiveness = Quality of inputs + (Process gains − Process losses)

## Team Inputs

Among the important inputs that influence team effectiveness are membership characteristics, resources and setting, nature of the task, and team size.[34] You can think of these as the things that load or prepare the team for action. Simply said, a team with the right inputs has a greater chance of having a positive process and being effective.

### Membership Characteristics

The blend of member characteristics on a team is critically important. Teams need members with the right abilities, or skill sets, to master and perform tasks well. Teams must also have members whose attitudes, values, and personalities are sufficiently compatible for everyone to work well together. How often, for example, have you read or heard about college sports teams where a lack of the right "chemistry" among talented players meant sub-par team performance? As one of the chapter opening quotes said: "Gettin' good players is easy. Gettin' 'em to play together is the hard part."[35]

**Team diversity** is the differences in values, personalities, experiences, demographics, and cultures among the membership.

**Team diversity,** in the form of different values, personalities, experiences, demographics, and cultures among the membership, affects how teams work.[36] It is easier

# Demographic Faultlines Pose Implications for Managing Teams

Membership of organizations is becoming more diverse, and teams are becoming more important. According to Dora Lau and Keith Murnighan, these trends raise some important research issues. They believe that strong "faultlines" occur when demographic diversity results in the formation of two or more subgroups whose members are similar to and strongly identify with one another. Examples include teams with subgroups forming around age, gender, race, ethnic, occupational, or tenure differences. When strong faultlines are present, members tend to identify more strongly with their subgroups than with the team as a whole. Lau and Murnighan predict that this affects what happens within the team in terms of conflict, politics, and performance.

Using subjects from 10 organizational behavior classes at a university, the researchers created different conditions of faultline strengths by randomly assigning students to case work groups based on sex and ethnicity. After working on cases, the students completed questionnaires about group processes and outcomes. Results showed members of strong faultline groups evaluated those in their subgroups more favorably than did members of weak faultline groups. Members of strong faultline groups also experienced less conflict, more psychological safety, and more satisfaction than did those in weak faultline groups.

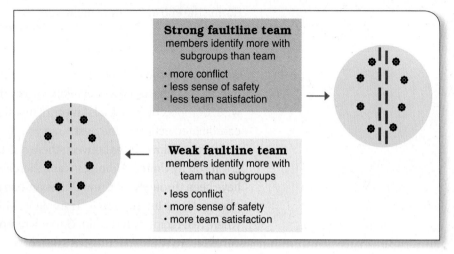

**YOU BE THE RESEARCHER**

How might faultlines operate in groups of different sizes and in the contexts of different organizational cultures? Are faultlines influencing the processes and outcomes of groups in which you participate—at the university and at work? And if you are a member or leader of a team with strong faultlines, what can you do to help minimize any negative effects?

*References:* Dora C. Lau and J. Keith Murnighan, "Interactions within Groups and Subgroups: The Effects of Demographic Faultlines," *Academy of Management Journal,* vol. 48 (2005), pp. 645–59; "Demographic Diversity and Faultlines: The Compositional Dynamics of Organizational Groups," *Academy of Management Review,* vol. 23 (1998), pp. 325–40.

to manage relationships among members of more *homogeneous teams*—ones whose members share similar characteristics. It is harder to manage relationships among members of more *heterogeneous teams*—ones whose members are quite dissimilar to one another. As team diversity increases, so does the complexity of interpersonal relationships among members. But the potential complications of membership diversity also come with special performance opportunities. When heterogeneous teams are well managed, the variety of ideas, perspectives, and experiences within them can become valuable problem solving and performance assets.

## Resources and Setting

The available resources and organizational setting can affect how well team members use and pool their talents to accomplish team tasks. Teams function best when members have good information, material resources, technology, organization structures, and rewards. The physical work space counts too, and many organizations are being architecturally designed to directly facilitate teamwork. At SEI Investments, employees work in a large, open space without cubicles or dividers; each has a private set of office furniture and fixtures—but all on wheels; all technology easily plugs and unplugs from suspended power beams that run overhead. This makes it easy for project teams to convene and disband as needed, and for people to meet and communicate during the ebb and flow of daily work.[37]

### Nature of the Task

The nature of the task not only sets standards for the talents needed by team members, it also affects how they work together. Clearly defined tasks are easier to deal with. Complex tasks ask a lot more of members in things like information sharing and coordinated action.[38] The next time you fly, check out the ground crews. You should notice some similarities between them and teams handling pit stops for NASCAR racers. If you fly United Airlines, in fact, there's a chance the members of the ramp crews have been through "Pit Crew U." It is among many organizations that are sending employees to Pit Instruction & Training in Mooresville, North Carolina. At this facility, where real racing crews train, United's ramp workers learn to work intensely and under pressure while meeting the goals of teamwork, safety, and job preparedness. The goal is better teamwork to reduce aircraft delays and service inadequacies.[39]

### Team Size

Team size affects how members work together, handle disagreements, and make decisions. The number of potential interactions increases geometrically as teams grow larger. This creates communication problems and congestion. Teams with odd numbers of members help prevent "ties" when votes need to be taken. Also, teams larger than about six or seven members can be difficult to manage for creative problem solving. Amazon.com's founder and CEO Jeff Bezos is a great fan of teams. But he also has a simple rule when it comes to sizing the firm's product development teams: No team should be larger than two pizzas can feed.[40]

## Stages of Team Development

Although having the right inputs is important, it doesn't guarantee team effectiveness. **Team process** counts too. This is the way the members of any team actually work together as they transform inputs into output. Also called *group dynamics*, the process aspects of any group or team include how members develop norms and cohesiveness, share roles, make decisions, communicate with one another, and handle conflicts.[41] And importantly, we know that teams experience different process challenges as they pass through the stages of team development—forming, storming, norming, performing, and adjourning.[42]

### Forming Stage

The forming stage of team development involves the first entry of individual members into a team. This is a time of initial task orientation and interpersonal testing. When people first come together, they ask questions: "What can or does the team offer me?" "What will I be asked to contribute?" "Can my needs be met while my efforts serve the task needs of the team?"

**Team process** is the way team members work together to accomplish tasks.

It is in the forming stage that people begin to identify with other members and with the team itself. They are concerned about getting acquainted, establishing relationships, discovering what is acceptable behavior, and learning how others perceive the team's task. This may also be a time when some members rely on others who appear "powerful" or especially "knowledgeable." Such things as prior experience with team members in other contexts and personal impressions of organization culture, goals, and practices may affect emerging relationships. Difficulties in the forming stage tend to be greater in more culturally and demographically diverse teams.

## Storming Stage

The storming stage is a period of high emotionality and can be the most difficult stage to pass through successfully. Tensions often emerge over tasks and interpersonal concerns. There may be periods of outright hostility and infighting. Coalitions or cliques may form around personalities or interests. Subteams may form around areas of agreement and disagreement. Conflict may develop as individuals compete to impose their preferences on others and to become influential.

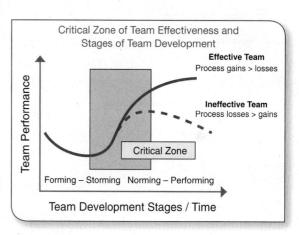

Important changes occur in the storming stage as task agendas become clarified and members begin to understand one another's styles. Attention begins to shift toward obstacles that may stand in the way of task accomplishment. Efforts are made to find ways to meet team goals while also satisfying individual needs. The storming stage is part of a "critical zone" in team development, where successes create long-term gains while failures create long-lasting problems.

## Norming Stage

It is in the norming stage that team members begin to cooperate well with one another. Shared rules of conduct emerge and the team feels a sense of leadership as each member starts to fulfill useful roles. Interpersonal hostilities start to diminish and harmony is emphasized, but minority viewpoints may still be discouraged.

The norming stage is also part of the critical zone of team development. As members develop initial feelings of closeness, a division of labor, and shared expectations, this helps protect the team from disintegration. In fact, holding the team together may seem more important than accomplishing important tasks.

## Performing Stage

Teams in the performing stage are more mature, organized, and well-functioning. They score high on the criteria of team maturity shown in Figure 17.3.[43] Performing is a stage of total integration in which team members are able to deal in creative ways with complex tasks and any interpersonal conflicts. The team operates with a clear and stable structure and members are motivated by team goals. The primary challenges are to continue refining how the team operates and building member relationships to keep everyone working well together as an integrated unit.

## Adjourning Stage

The final stage of team development is adjourning, when team members prepare to achieve closure and disband. Temporary committees, task forces, and project

| | Very poor | | | Very good | |
|---|---|---|---|---|---|
| 1. Trust among members | 1 | 2 | 3 | 4 | 5 |
| 2. Feedback mechanisms | 1 | 2 | 3 | 4 | 5 |
| 3. Open communications | 1 | 2 | 3 | 4 | 5 |
| 4. Approach to decisions | 1 | 2 | 3 | 4 | 5 |
| 5. Leadership sharing | 1 | 2 | 3 | 4 | 5 |
| 6. Acceptance of goals | 1 | 2 | 3 | 4 | 5 |
| 7. Valuing diversity | 1 | 2 | 3 | 4 | 5 |
| 8. Member cohesiveness | 1 | 2 | 3 | 4 | 5 |
| 9. Support for each other | 1 | 2 | 3 | 4 | 5 |
| 10. Performance norms | 1 | 2 | 3 | 4 | 5 |

FIGURE 17.3 **Criteria for assessing the maturity of a team.**

A **norm** is a behavior, rule, or standard expected to be followed by team members.

**Cohesiveness** is the degree to which members are attracted to and motivated to remain part of a team.

teams should disband with a sense that important goals have been accomplished. But this can be an emotional period after team members have worked together intensely for some time. Adjourning is a time when it is important to acknowledge everyone for their contributions, praise them, and celebrate the team's success. A team ideally disbands with everyone feeling they would like to work with one another again sometime in the future.

## Norms and Cohesiveness

A **norm** is a behavior expected of team members.[44] It is a "rule" or "standard" that guides behavior. Typical team norms relate to such things as helpfulness, participation, timeliness, work quality, and creativity and innovation. A team's performance norm is one of the most important, since it defines the level of work effort and performance that members are expected to contribute. Work groups and teams with positive performance norms are more successful in accomplishing task objectives than are teams with negative performance norms.

### Managing Team Norms

Team leaders should help and encourage members to develop positive norms. During the forming and storming steps of development, for example, norms relating to expected attendance and levels of commitment are important. By the time the stage of performing is reached, norms relating to adaptability and change become relevant. Here are some things leaders can do to help their teams build positive norms.[46]

- Act as a positive role model.
- Reinforce the desired behaviors with rewards.
- Control results by performance reviews and regular feedback.
- Train and orient new members to adopt desired behaviors.
- Recruit and select new members who exhibit the desired behaviors.
- Hold regular meetings to discuss progress and ways of improving.
- Use team decision-making methods to reach agreement.

### Managing Team Cohesiveness

Team members vary in adherence to group norms. Conformity to norms is largely determined by the strength of team **cohesiveness**, the degree to which members are attracted to and motivated to remain part of a team.[45] Persons in a highly cohesive team value their membership and strive to maintain positive relationships with other team members. Because of this, they tend to conform to the norms. In the extreme, violation of a norm on a highly cohesive team can result in a member being expelled or socially ostracized.

Figure 17.4 shows the power of group cohesiveness. The "best-case" scenario is a team with high cohesiveness and a high performance norm. Strong conformity to norms by members of this team has a beneficial effect on team performance.

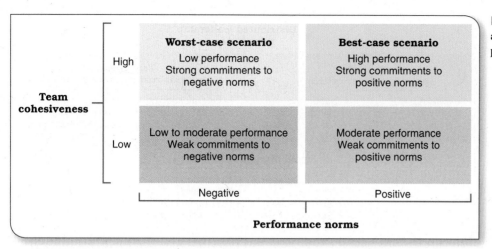

FIGURE 17.4 **How cohesiveness and norms influence team performance.**

Contrast this with the "worst-case" scenario of high cohesiveness and a low performance norm. Members of this team conform to the low performance norm and restrict their work efforts.

We have already talked about ways to build positive norms. But, the implications of Figure 17.4 suggest that managers must also be good at building high cohesiveness. This can be done in the following ways.

- Create agreement on team goals.
- Reward team rather than individual results.
- Increase membership homogeneity.
- Increase interactions among members.
- Decrease team size.
- Introduce competition with other teams.
- Provide physical isolation from other teams.

## Task and Maintenance Roles

Research on the social psychology of groups identifies two types of roles or activities that are essential if team members are to work well together.[47] **Task activities** contribute directly to the team's performance purpose, while **maintenance activities** support the emotional life of the team as an ongoing social system.

Although the team leader or supervisor should give them special attention, the responsibility for task and maintenance activities should be shared and distributed among all team members. Anyone can help lead a team by acting in ways that satisfy these needs. This concept of **distributed leadership** in teams makes every member continually responsible for both recognizing when task or maintenance activities are needed and taking actions to provide them.

*Leading through task activities* involves making an effort to define and solve problems and to advance work toward performance results. Without the relevant task activities such as initiating agendas, sharing information, and others shown in Figure 17.5, teams will have difficulty accomplishing their objectives. *Leading through maintenance activities*, by contrast, helps strengthen the team as a social system. When maintenance activities such as gatekeeping, encouraging others, and reducing tensions are performed well, good interpersonal relationships are achieved and the ability of the team to stay together over the longer term is ensured.

A **task activity** is an action taken by a team member that directly contributes to the group's performance purpose.

A **maintenance activity** is an action taken by a team member that supports the emotional life of the group.

**Distributed leadership** is when all members of a team contribute helpful task and maintenance behaviors.

FIGURE 17.5 **Distributed leadership helps teams meet task and maintenance needs.**

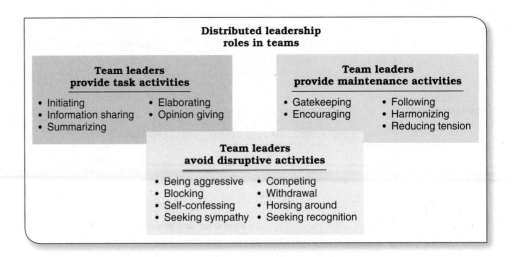

Both team task and maintenance activities stand in distinct contrast to the **disruptive activities** described in Figure 17.5. Activities such as showing incivility toward other members, withdrawing from the discussion, and fooling around are self-serving and detract from, rather than enhance, team effectiveness. Unfortunately, very few teams are immune to dysfunctional behavior. And, every team member shares in the responsibility for minimizing its occurrence.

**Disruptive activities** are self-serving behaviors that interfere with team effectiveness.

## Communication Networks

There is considerable research on the team interaction patterns and communication networks shown in Figure 17.6.[48] When team members must interact intensively and work closely together on complex tasks, this need is best met by a **decentralized communication network**. Sometimes called the *all-channel or star communication network*, this is where all members communicate directly with one another. At other

A **decentralized communication network** allows all members to communicate directly with one another.

FIGURE 17.6 **Interaction patterns and communication networks in teams.**

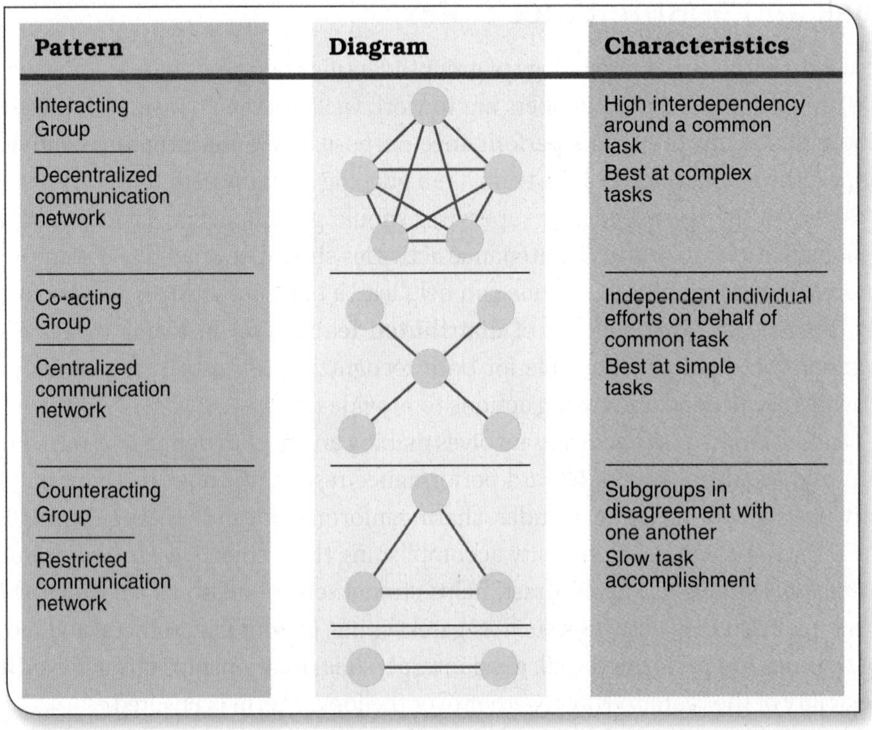

| Pattern | Diagram | Characteristics |
|---|---|---|
| Interacting Group ——— Decentralized communication network | | High interdependency around a common task ——— Best at complex tasks |
| Co-acting Group ——— Centralized communication network | | Independent individual efforts on behalf of common task ——— Best at simple tasks |
| Counteracting Group ——— Restricted communication network | | Subgroups in disagreement with one another ——— Slow task accomplishment |

times team members can work on tasks independently, with the required work being divided up among them. This creates a **centralized communication network**, sometimes called a *wheel or chain communication structure*. Its activities are coordinated and results pooled by a central point of control.

When teams are composed of subgroups experiencing issue-specific disagreements, such as a temporary debate over the best means to achieve a goal, the resulting interaction pattern often involves a **restricted communication network**. Here, polarized subgroups contest one another and may even engage in conflict. Communication between the subgroups is limited and biased, with negative consequences for group process and effectiveness.

The best teams use each of these communication networks, but they use them in the right ways and at the right times. Centralized communication networks seem to work better on simple tasks.[49] These tasks lend themselves to more centralized control because they require little creativity, information processing, and problem solving. The reverse is true for more complex tasks, where interacting groups do better. Their decentralized communication networks support the more intense interactions and information sharing required to perform complicated tasks. Even coacting groups can be useful. When teams get complacent, the conflict that emerges from them can be a source of creativity and critical evaluation. But when these subgroups stop communicating and helping with one another, task accomplishment typically suffers—for the short run at least.

> In a **centralized communication network**, communication flows only between individual members and a hub, or center point.

> In a **restricted communication network**, subgroups have limited communication with one another.

---

**LEARNING CHECK 3**

**TAKEAWAY QUESTION 3 How do teams work?**

**Be sure you can** • define *team effectiveness* • identify inputs that influence group effectiveness • discuss how membership diversity influences team effectiveness • list five stages of group development • define *group norm* and list ways to build positive group norms • define *cohesiveness* and list ways to increase group cohesion • explain how norms and cohesiveness influence team performance • differentiate between task, maintenance, and disruptive activities • describe use of decentralized and centralized communication networks

---

# Decision Making in Teams

**Decision making**, the process of making choices among alternative possible courses of action, is one of the most important group processes. The best teams will use a variety of decision-making methods over time as they face different kinds of problems.[50] But as with other aspects of teamwork, decision making can be challenging.[51] Edgar Schein, a respected scholar and consultant, says all this can be better understood when we recognize that teams use at least six methods to make decisions: lack of response, authority rule, minority rule, majority rule, consensus, and unanimity.[52]

> **Decision making** is the process of making choices among alternative possible courses of action.

## Ways Teams Make Decisions

In *decision by lack of response*, one idea after another is suggested without any discussion taking place. When the team finally accepts an idea, all others have been bypassed by simple lack of response rather than by critical evaluation.

## Teams and Teamwork Add Lift to Boeing's New Planes

Larry W. Smith/©AP/WideWorld Photos

Lots of productivity and innovation opportunities get lost every day when good ideas are buried in organizational bureaucracy. Sometimes managers don't listen or ask for suggestions. Sometimes employees don't volunteer or let their voices get lost in the crowd. So what's a company that faces enormous complexity—say a company that builds some of the world's most sophisticated airplanes—do? At Boeing the answer is teams, lots of them.

*Situation:* Production is bogging down because of slow engine assemblies. *Teamwork:* A team comes up with a way to rearrange workspace so that four engines can be assembled at one time, instead of just three.

*Situation:* A paint shop has long been doing things the same way. *Teamwork:* A team decides they could do things better and comes up with ways to speed up each job by five minutes per worker.

*Situation:* Installers got crowded and delayed while trying to assemble 640 tubes in a plane's wheel well. *Teamwork:* A team saved 30 hours per plane by breaking the process into smaller subassemblies done outside the wells.

Boeing has over 1,300 teams working on its commercial jets. The ideas generated by members of these teams are crucially important as the company tries to deal with large order backlogs and delivery delays. But assembling passenger airplanes is a complicated, time consuming, and physically large task. All this places a premium on employee voice and creativity. Vice President Eric Lindblad says: "How do you produce more aircraft without expanding the space? Space is the forcing function that means you've got to be creative."

Unlocking creativity through teamwork is one management response to Boeing's need for innovation and efficiency. The expertise and ideas exist with the workers, but it often takes the best of teamwork to bring them to the surface.

### WHAT'S YOUR TAKE?

Boeing is turning to its skilled workforce and asking for suggestions on how to boost productivity. But can you get creative ideas from just putting people into teams and saying "give us your best ideas?" Or, is there more to it? What roles do supportive leadership, a culture of openness and trust, and perhaps more, play in making teams and teamwork the asset that companies like Boeing and others would like them to be?

In *decision by authority rule*, the leader, manager, committee head, or some other authority figure makes a decision for the team. This can be done with or without discussion and is very time-efficient. Whether the decision is a good one or a bad one, however, depends on whether the authority figure has the necessary information and expertise, and on how well this approach is accepted by other team members.

In *decision by minority rule*, two or three people are able to dominate or "railroad" the team into making a decision that they prefer. This is often done by providing a suggestion and then forcing quick agreement by challenging the team with such statements as "Does anyone object? No? Well let's go ahead, then."

One of the most common things teams do, especially when signs of disagreement arise, is to take a vote and arrive at a *decision by majority rule*. Although this is consistent with the democratic political process, it has some potential problems. The very process of voting can create coalitions as some people become "winners" and others "losers." Those in the minority—the "losers"—may feel left out or discarded without having had a fair say. They may be unenthusiastic about implementing the decision of the "majority," and lingering resentments may impair team effectiveness in the future. Such possibilities are well illustrated in the political arena, where candidates receiving only small and controversial victory margins end up struggling against entrenched opposition from the losing party.

Teams are often encouraged to achieve *decision by consensus*. This is where full discussion leads to one alternative being favored by most members, and the other members agree to support it. When a consensus is reached, even those who may have opposed the decision know that their views have been heard by everyone involved. Consensus does not require unanimity, but it does require that team members are able to argue, engage in reasonable conflict, and still get along with and respect one another.[53] As pointed out in Management Smarts, true consensus occurs only when any dissenting members have been able to speak their minds and know they have been listened to.[54]

A *decision by unanimity* may be the ideal state of affairs. "Unanimity" means that all team members agree on the course of action to be taken. This is a logically perfect method, but it is also extremely difficult to achieve in actual practice. One of the reasons that teams sometimes turn to authority decisions, majority voting, or even minority decisions, is the difficulty of managing the team process to achieve consensus or unanimity.

## Advantages and Disadvantages of Team Decisions

When teams take time to make decisions by consensus or unanimity, they gain special advantages over those relying more on individual or minority decision methods.[55] The process of making a true team decision makes more information, knowledge, and expertise available. It expands the number of action alternatives that are examined, and helps to avoid getting trapped by tunnel vision and considering only one or a few options. Team decisions also increase understanding and acceptance by members. This helps build commitments of members to work hard to implement the decisions they have made together.

The potential disadvantages of team decision making trace largely to the difficulties with group process. It can be hard to reach agreement when many people are trying to make a team decision. There may be social pressure to conform and even minority domination, where some members feel forced or "railroaded" to accept a decision advocated by one vocal individual or small coalition. And for sure, the time required to make team decisions can sometimes be a disadvantage. As more people are involved in the dialogue and discussion, decision making takes longer. This added time may be costly, even prohibitively so, in certain circumstances.

## Management**Smarts**

### How to Achieve Consensus

1. Don't argue blindly; consider others' reactions to your points.
2. Don't change your mind just to reach quick agreement.
3. Avoid conflict reduction by voting, coin tossing, bargaining.
4. Keep everyone involved in the decision process.
5. Allow disagreements to surface so that things can be deliberated.
6. Don't focus on winning versus losing; seek acceptable alternatives.
7. Discuss assumptions, listen carefully, and encourage inputs by all.

## When Teams Stand Up, Decisions Speed Up

Did you ever wonder what it would take to move decisions along a lot faster in a team meeting? One solution is simple: Take away the seats. At the software firm Atomic Object, seats are out and speed is in. At the regular team meeting that starts each workday, everyone stands up. They also have to be on time and are expected to stay on task; no playing Angry Birds or chit-chatting. Even tables are out at many Atomic Object meetings. A vice president declares "They make it too easy to lean or rest laptops." Stand up meetings are popular in the tech industry, where some call them "agile meetings." At Atomic Object, agile they are; the typical meeting lasts less than five minutes.

Cultura Creative/Alamy

## Groupthink

**Groupthink** is a tendency for highly cohesive teams to lose their evaluative capabilities.

One of the potential downsides of team decision making is what psychologist Irving Janis calls **groupthink**, the tendency for highly cohesive teams to lose their critical evaluative capabilities.[56] Although it may seem counterintuitive, a high level of cohesiveness can be a disadvantage if strong feelings of team loyalty make it hard for members to criticize and evaluate one another's ideas and suggestions. Members of very cohesive teams may feel so strongly about the group that they won't say or do anything that might harm the goodwill. They end up publicly agreeing with actual or suggested courses of action that they have serious doubts about. Groupthink occurs as desires to hold the team together and avoid disagreements result in poor decisions.

Janis suggests that groupthink played a role in well-known historical cases such as the lack of preparedness of U.S. naval forces for the Japanese attack on Pearl Harbor, the Bay of Pigs invasion under President Kennedy, and the many roads that led to the United States' difficulties in the Vietnam War. But he also says that when the groupthink symptoms listed here are spotted, managers and team leaders can prevent them from causing too much harm.

- *Illusions of invulnerability:* Members assume that the team is too good for criticism, or beyond attack.

- *Rationalizing unpleasant and disconfirming data:* Members refuse to accept contradictory data or to thoroughly consider alternatives.

- *Belief in inherent group morality:* Members act as though the group is inherently right and above reproach.

- *Stereotyping competitors as weak, evil, and stupid:* Members refuse to look realistically at other groups.

## ManagementSmarts

### How to Avoid Groupthink

- Assign the role of critical evaluator to each team member; encourage a sharing of viewpoints.
- As a leader, don't seem partial to one course of action; do absent yourself from meetings at times to allow free discussion.
- Create subteams to work on the same problems and then share their proposed solutions.
- Have team members discuss issues with outsiders and report back on their reactions.
- Invite outside experts to observe team activities and react to team processes and decisions.
- Assign one member to play a "devil's advocate" role at each team meeting.
- Hold a "second-chance" meeting to review the decision after consensus is apparently achieved.

- *Applying direct pressure to deviants to conform to group wishes:* Members refuse to tolerate anyone who suggests the team may be wrong.
- *Self-censorship by members:* Members refuse to communicate personal concerns to the whole team.
- *Illusions of unanimity:* Members accept consensus prematurely, without testing its completeness.
- *Mind guarding:* Members protect the team from hearing disturbing ideas or outside viewpoints.

## Creativity in Team Decision Making

When team creativity is needed in special situations, managers shouldn't hesitate to use the time tested brainstorming and nominal group techniques. Both can be done in face-to-face or virtual team settings.

Classic **brainstorming** usually asks members to follow these strict guidelines. *Don't criticize each other*—withhold judging or evaluating ideas as they are being presented. *Welcome "freewheeling"*—the wilder or more radical the idea, the better. *Go for quantity*—the more ideas generated, the greater the likelihood that one or more will be outstanding. *Keep building on one another's ideas*—don't hesitate to piggyback and tweak one or more existing ideas into new forms.

> **Brainstorming** engages group members in an open, spontaneous discussion of problems and ideas.

At the Aloft Group, Inc., a small advertising firm in Newburyport, Massachusetts, President Matt Bowen says brainstorming works best if he specifies the goal—ideally in a sentence that he distributes a day or two ahead of the session. He limits the brainstorming session to an hour, and keeps the group small—ideally five to seven members. He allows no criticisms—there is no such thing as a "bad" idea. He also encourages everyone to build on one another's ideas and is sure to follow up by implementing something from the brainstorming session.[57]

In situations where brainstorming won't work, such as in a situation prone to intense disagreement and interpersonal conflicts, an approach known as the **nominal group technique** can sometimes help.[58] It uses a highly structured meeting agenda that allows everyone to contribute ideas without the interference of evaluative comments by others. Participants are first asked to work alone and respond in writing with possible solutions to a stated problem. Ideas are then shared in round-robin fashion without any criticism or discussion, and all ideas are recorded as they are presented. Ideas are next discussed and clarified in another round-robin sequence, with no evaluative comments allowed. Finally, members individually and silently follow a written voting procedure that ranks all alternatives in priority order.

> The **nominal group technique** structures interaction among team members discussing problems and ideas.

---

**LEARNING CHECK 4**

**TAKEAWAY QUESTION 4 How do teams make decisions?**

**Be sure you can** • illustrate how groups make decisions by authority rule, minority rule, majority rule, consensus, and unanimity • list advantages and disadvantages of group decision making • define *groupthink* and identify its symptoms • illustrate how brainstorming and the nominal group technique can improve creativity in team decision making

# MANAGEMENT LEARNING REVIEW

## LEARNING CHECK SUMMARY

### TAKEAWAY QUESTION 1 How do teams contribute to organizations?

- A team is a collection of people working together to accomplish a common goal.
- Teams help organizations perform through synergy—the creation of a whole that is greater than the sum of its parts.
- Teams help satisfy important needs for their members by providing sources of job support and social satisfactions.
- Social loafing and other problems can limit the performance of teams.
- Organizations operate as networks of formal and informal groups.

**For Discussion** Why do people often tolerate social loafers at work?

### TAKEAWAY QUESTION 2 What are current trends in the use of teams?

- Committees and task forces are used to accomplish special tasks and projects.
- Cross-functional teams bring members together from different departments, and help improve lateral relations and integration in organizations.
- New developments in information technology are making virtual teams commonplace at work, but virtual teams also pose special management challenges.
- Self-managing teams are changing organizations, as team members perform many tasks previously done by their supervisors.
- Team building engages team members in a process of assessment and action planning to improve teamwork and future performance.

**For Discussion** What are some of the things that virtual teams probably can't do as well as face-to-face teams?

### TAKEAWAY QUESTION 3 How do teams work?

- An effective team achieves high levels of task performance, member satisfaction, and team viability.

- Important team inputs include the organizational setting, nature of the task, size, and membership characteristics.
- A team matures through various stages of development, including forming, storming, norming, performing, and adjourning.
- Norms are the standards or rules of conduct that influence the behavior of team members; cohesion is the attractiveness of the team to its members.
- In highly cohesive teams, members tend to conform to norms; the best situation is a team with positive performance norms and high cohesiveness.
- Distributed leadership occurs as members share in meeting a team's task and maintenance needs.
- Effective teams make use of alternative communication structures, such as the centralized and decentralized networks, to best complete tasks.

**For Discussion** What can be done if a team gets trapped in the storming stage of group development?

### TAKEAWAY QUESTION 4 How do teams make decisions?

- Teams can make decisions by lack of response, authority rule, minority rule, majority rule, consensus, and unanimity.
- Although group decisions often make more information available for problem solving and generate more understanding and commitment, they are slower than individual decisions and may involve social pressures to conform.
- Groupthink is a tendency of members of highly cohesive teams to lose their critical evaluative capabilities and make poor decisions.
- Techniques for improving creativity in teams include brainstorming and the nominal group technique.

**For Discussion** Is it possible that groupthink doesn't only occur when groups are highly cohesive, but also when they are pre-cohesive?

## SELF-TEST 17

### Multiple-Choice Questions

1. When a group of people is able to achieve more than what its members could by working individually, this is called _____.
   (a) social loafing
   (b) consensus
   (c) viability
   (d) synergy

2. One of the recommended strategies for dealing with a group member who engages in social loafing is to _____.
   (a) redefine tasks to make individual contributions more visible
   (b) ask another member to encourage this person to work harder
   (c) give the person extra rewards and hope he or she will feel guilty
   (d) just forget about it

3. In an organization operating with self-managing teams, the traditional role of _____ is replaced by the role of team leader.
   (a) chief executive officer
   (b) first-line supervisor
   (c) middle manager
   (d) general manager

4. An effective team is defined as one that achieves high levels of task performance, member satisfaction, and _____.
   (a) resource efficiency
   (b) future viability
   (c) consensus
   (d) creativity

5. In the open-systems model of teams, the _____ is an important input factor.
   (a) communication network
   (b) decision-making method
   (c) performance norm
   (d) set of membership characteristics

6. The team effectiveness equation states the following: Team effectiveness = Quality of inputs + (_____ − Process losses).
   (a) Process gains
   (b) Leadership impact
   (c) Membership ability
   (d) Problem complexity

7. A basic rule of team dynamics states that the greater the _____ in a team, the greater the conformity to norms.
   (a) membership diversity
   (b) cohesiveness
   (c) task structure
   (d) competition among members

8. Members of a team tend to start to get coordinated and comfortable with one another in the _____ stage of team development.
   (a) forming
   (b) norming
   (c) performing
   (d) adjourning

9. One way for a manager to build positive norms within a team is to _____.
   (a) act as a positive role model
   (b) increase group size
   (c) introduce groupthink
   (d) isolate the team

10. To increase the cohesiveness of a group, a manager would be best off _____.
    (a) starting competition with other groups
    (b) increasing the group size
    (c) acting as a positive role model
    (d) introducing a new member

11. Groupthink is most likely to occur in teams that are _____.
    (a) large in size
    (b) diverse in membership
    (c) high-performing
    (d) highly cohesive

12. A team member who does a good job at summarizing discussion, offering new ideas, and clarifying points made by others is providing leadership by contributing _____ activities to the group process.
    (a) required
    (b) task
    (c) disruptive
    (d) maintenance

**13.** A _____ decision is one in which all members agree on the course of action to be taken.
(a) consensus
(b) unanimous
(c) majority
(d) nominal

**14.** A team performing very creative and unstructured tasks is most likely to succeed using _____.
(a) a decentralized communication network
(b) decisions by majority rule
(c) decisions by minority rule
(d) more task than maintenance activities

**15.** Which of the following approaches can help groups achieve creativity in situations where lots of interpersonal conflicts are likely to occur?
(a) nominal group technique
(b) minority rule
(c) consensus
(d) brainstorming

## Short-Response Questions

**16.** How can a manager improve team effectiveness by modifying inputs?

**17.** What is the relationship among a team's cohesiveness, performance norms, and performance results?

**18.** How would a manager know that a team is suffering from groupthink (give two symptoms), and what could the manager do about it (give two responses)?

**19.** What makes a self-managing team different from a traditional work team?

## Essay Question

**20.** Marcos Martinez has just been appointed manager of a production team operating the 11 PM to 7 AM shift in a large manufacturing firm. An experienced manager, Marcos is pleased that the team members really like and get along well with one another, but they also appear to be restricting their task outputs to the minimum acceptable levels. What could Marcos do to improve things in this situation, and why should he do them?

## MANAGEMENT SKILLS AND COMPETENCIES

# Further Reflection: Team Contributions

Given that teams and teamwork are a major part of how organizations operate today, **team contributions** are essential career skills. We need to be able to contribute as team members in many different ways so that our teams can reach their performance potential. But experience also proves time and time again that teams often underperform.

Time and effectiveness can easily get lost when members struggle with a variety of process difficulties. Things run more smoothly when everyone understands how teams work. On some teams you'll be the leader; on others you'll be one of the members. But in all cases your behavior will play an important role in determining whether your teams achieve satisfying, high-performance outcomes, or turn out to be time-wasting failures.

 DO IT NOW ...
LOOK IN THE MIRROR

- Speak seriously with others who know and work with you about your performance as a team member and team leader. What do they say?
- Ask for suggestions on how you could improve your team contributions.
- Prepare a short presentation to a potential employer describing your team skills. Write a set of notes on how you will describe yourself and what examples you will give to support your potential as a team leader and member.

# Self-Assessment: Team Leader Skills

## Instructions

Consider your experience in groups and work teams while completing the following inventory. Rate yourself on each item using the following scale (circle the number that applies):[59]

1 = Almost never   2 = Seldom   3 = Sometimes
4 = Usually   5 = Almost always

*Question: "How do I behave in team leadership situations?"*

1 2 3 4 5   **1.** Facilitate communications with and among team members between team meetings.

1 2 3 4 5   **2.** Provide feedback/coaching to individual team members on their performance.

1 2 3 4 5   **3.** Encourage creative and "out-of-the-box" thinking.

1 2 3 4 5   **4.** Continue to clarify stakeholder needs/expectations.

1 2 3 4 5   **5.** Keep team members' responsibilities and activities focused within the team's objectives and goals.

1 2 3 4 5   **6.** Organize and run effective and productive team meetings.

1 2 3 4 5   **7.** Demonstrate integrity and personal commitment.

1 2 3 4 5   **8.** Have excellent persuasive and influencing skills.

1 2 3 4 5   **9.** Respect and leverage the team's cross-functional diversity.

1 2 3 4 5   **10.** Recognize and reward individual contributions to team performance.

1 2 3 4 5   **11.** Use the appropriate decision-making style for specific issues.

1 2 3 4 5   **12.** Facilitate and encourage border management with the team's key stakeholders.

1 2 3 4 5   **13.** Ensure that the team meets its team commitments.

1 2 3 4 5   **14.** Bring team issues and problems to the team's attention and focus on constructive problem solving.

1 2 3 4 5   **15.** Provide a clear vision and direction for the team.

## Self-Assessment Scoring

The inventory measures seven dimensions of team leadership. Add your scores for the items listed next to each dimension below to get an indication of your potential strengths and weaknesses.

| | |
|---|---|
| 1, 9 | Building the Team |
| 2, 10 | Developing People |
| 3, 11 | Team Problem Solving and Decision Making |
| 4, 12 | Stakeholder Relations |
| 5, 13 | Team Performance |
| 6, 14 | Team Process |
| 7, 8, 15 | Providing Personal Leadership |

## Interpretation

The higher the score, the more confident you are on the particular skill and leadership capability. Consider giving this inventory to people who have worked with you in teams and have them rate you. Compare the results to your self-assessment. Also, remember it is doubtful that any one team leader is capable of exhibiting all the skills listed. More and more, organizations are emphasizing teams that blend a variety of skills, rather than depending on the vision of the single, heroic leader figure. As long as the necessary leadership skills are represented within the membership, it is more likely that the team will be healthy and achieve high performance. Of course, the more skills you bring with you to team leadership situations, the better.

# Team Exercise:
# Work Team Dynamics

## Preparation

Think about your course work group, a work group you are involved in for another course, or any other group suggested by your instructor. Use this scale to indicate how often each of the following statements accurately reflects your experience in the group.[60]

1 All the time   2 Very often   3 Sometimes
4 Never happens

1. My ideas get a fair hearing.

2. I am encouraged to give innovative ideas and take risks.

3. Diverse opinions within the group are encouraged.

4. I have all the responsibility I want.

5. There is a lot of favoritism shown in the group.

6. Members trust one another to do their assigned work.

7. The group sets high standards of performance excellence.

8. People share and change jobs a lot in the group.

9. You can make mistakes and learn from them in this group.

10. This group has good operating rules.

## Instructions

Form teams as assigned by your instructor. Ideally, this will be the group you have just rated. Have all members share their ratings, and then make one master rating for the team as a whole. Circle the items for which there are the biggest differences of opinion. Discuss those items and try to find out why they exist. In general, the better a team scores on this instrument, the higher its creative potential. Make a list of the five most important things members believe they can do to help groups perform better. Nominate a spokesperson to summarize your discussion for the class as a whole.

## Career Situations in Teamwork: What Would You Do?

1. **New Task Force**   It's time for the first meeting of the task force that you have been assigned to lead. This is a big opportunity, since it's the first time your boss has given you this level of responsibility. There are seven members of the team, all of whom are your peers and coworkers. The task is to develop a proposal for increased use of flexible work schedules and telecommuting in the organization. What will your agenda be for the first meeting, and what opening statement will you make?

2. **Declining Performance**   You've been concerned for quite some time now about a drop in the performance of your work team. Although everyone seems to like one another, the "numbers" in terms of measured daily accomplishments are on the decline. It's

   time to act. What will you look at, and why, to determine where and how steps might be taken to improve the effectiveness of this work team?

3. **Groupthink Possibilities**   The members of the executive compensation committee that you are chairing show a high level of cohesiveness. It's obvious that they enjoy being part of the committee and are proud to be on the board of directors. But the committee is about to approve extraordinarily high bonuses for the CEO and five other senior executives. This is occurring at a time when executive pay is getting lots of criticism from the press, unions, and the public at large. What can you do to make sure groupthink isn't causing this committee to potentially make a bad decision?

## Case Study

# Auto Racing

Go to *Management Cases for Critical Thinking* to find the recommended case for Chapter 17—Auto Racing—"When the Driver Takes a Back Seat."

Cars running in NASCAR races hit speeds over 200 mph. But winning or losing can be decided by tenths of a second. Although it's the driver who gets featured in the winner's circle and in all the advertisements, the difference between crossing the finish line first or later often comes down to the pit crews. It's in a crowded pit lane that tires get

changed, windshields cleaned, fenders bent back into shape, and spring and balance adjustments fine tuned. Any seconds saved by pit crews are a driver's best friends. Little wonder that racing teams give high priority to hiring the right crew chiefs and building high performance pit crew teams to maximize their winning chances on race days.

# Wisdom
## Learning
## From Others

Don Simpson/Alamy

### > IMPACT IS JUST A TWEET AWAY

"My Siamese cat Skimbleshanks is up a tree . . . At Wilco concert—Jeff Tweedy is so cool . . . Home alone . . . Flying to Ireland, wish me luck driving . . . Just saw Todd with Stephanie!"

So who cares? Lots of people do, just as Evan Williams and Biz Stone, co-founders of Twitter, had anticipated. They took micro-blogging into the upper limits. And it isn't just for friends and family. Twitter is now the "voice" of the people. It carries their messages around the world in situations of oppression and civil unrest.

More than 250 million tweets fly through cyberspace each day. Twitter's "digital handshake" connects people instantaneously, and companies have taken notice. Whole Foods has 2.1 million followers for tweets that deliver recipes and answer customer questions. Southwest Airlines has 1.2 million followers who get special promotions and help when they encounter flight problems.

Twitter's growth and popularity have been challenging for the firm and its founders. The business model is still a work in process. Lots of people wonder how Twitter will make money from all those tweets. But CEO Dick Costolo has no doubt about the firm, the technology, or the social impact it creates. "We're trying to build a lasting company," he says, "a company that will change the world in interesting and beneficial ways."[1]

### MORE TO LOOK FOR INSIDE>

**FOLLOW THE STORY**
Linda Heasley Gives Others Reasons to Work with Her

**ETHICS ON THE LINE**
Blogging Is Easy, but Bloggers Beware

**FACTS FOR ANALYSIS**
Value of Performance Reviews Gets Increasing Scrutiny

**RESEARCH BRIEF**
Words Affect Outcomes in Online Dispute Resolution

# Communication and Collaboration

## > COMMUNICATION AND NETWORKING

Recruiters give **communication and networking** skills high priority when screening candidates for college internships and first jobs. They're looking for people who can communicate well both orally and in writing, and network well with others for collaboration and teamwork. But if you're like many of us, there's work to be done to master the challenge.

The American Management Association found that workers rated their bosses only slightly above average on transforming ideas into words, being credible, listening and asking questions, and giving written and oral presentations. Over three-quarters of university professors rated incoming high school graduates as only "fair" or "poor" in writing clearly, and in spelling and use

of grammar.[2] And when it comes to decorum or just plain old "good manners," a *BusinessWeek* survey reported that 38% of women complain about "sexual innuendo, wisecracks and taunts" at work.[3]

Social networking is in on the college campus and among young professionals, as everyone wants to be linked in. The same skills transfer to the workplace. A good networker acts as a *hub*—connected with others; *gatekeeper*—moving information to and from others; and *pulse-taker*—staying abreast of what is happening.[4]

## Insight
### Learning About Yourself

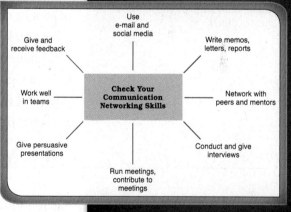

## BUILD SKILLS AND COMPETENCIES AT END OF CHAPTER

- Engage in *Further Reflection on Your Communication and Networking*
- Take the *Self-Assessment—Conflict Management Strategies*
- Prepare for the *Team Exercise—Feedback Sensitivities*
- Solve the *Career Situations in Communication and Collaboration*
- Analyze the *Case Study—Facebook: Making the World More Open*

## <GET TO KNOW YOURSELF BETTER

| TAKEAWAY 1 | TAKEAWAY 2 | TAKEAWAY 3 | TAKEAWAY 4 |
|---|---|---|---|
| **The Communication Process**<br>• Effective communication<br>• Persuasion and credibility in communication<br>• Communication barriers<br>• Cross-cultural communication | **Improving Collaboration Through Communication**<br>• Transparency and openness<br>• Use of electronic media<br>• Active listening<br>• Constructive feedback<br>• Space design | **Managing Conflict**<br>• Functional and dysfunctional conflict<br>• Causes of conflict<br>• Conflict resolution<br>• Conflict management styles<br>• Structural approaches to conflict management | **Managing Negotiation**<br>• Negotiation goals and approaches<br>• Gaining agreements<br>• Negotiation pitfalls<br>• Third-party dispute resolution |
| **LEARNING CHECK 1** | **LEARNING CHECK 2** | **LEARNING CHECK 3** | **LEARNING CHECK 4** |

Whether you work at the top of an organization—building support for strategies and goals, or at lower levels—interacting with others to support their work efforts and your own, your career toolkit must include abilities to achieve positive impact through communication and collaboration. They are foundations for **social capital**, the capacity to attract support and help from others in order to get things done. Whereas intellectual capital is basically what you know, social capital comes from the people you know and how well you relate to them. It's something all managers need. Pam Alexander, former CEO of Ogilvy Public Relations Worldwide, says: "Relationships are the most powerful form of media. Ideas will only get you so far these days. Count on personal relationships to carry you further."[5]

> **Social capital** is a capacity to get things done with the support and help of others.

## The Communication Process

> **Communication** is the process of sending and receiving symbols with meanings attached.

Figure 18.1 describes **communication** as an interpersonal process of sending and receiving symbols with messages attached to them. This process can be understood as a series of questions: "Who?" (sender) "says what?" (message) "in what ways?" (channel) "to whom?" (receiver) "with what result?" (interpreted meaning). It is through this process that people build and use social capital, exchange and share information, and influence one another's attitudes, behaviors, and understandings.

The communication process is the glue that binds together the four functions of planning, organizing, leading, and controlling.[6] *Planning* is accomplished and plans are shared through the communication of information. *Organizing* identifies and structures communication links among people and positions. *Leading* uses communication to achieve positive influence over organization members and stakeholders. And, *controlling* relies on communication to process information to measure performance results.

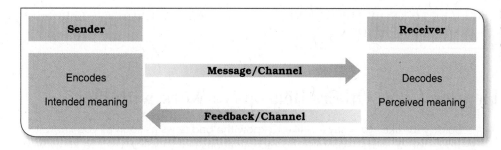

## Effective Communication

One problem often encountered in the communication process is that we take our abilities for granted and end up being disappointed when things break down. It always helps to be alert to issues of "effectiveness" and "efficiency" in the ways we communicate.

**Effective communication** occurs when the sender's message is fully understood by the receiver. **Efficient communication** occurs at minimum cost in terms of resources expended. It's nice for our communications to be both effective and efficient. But as we all know, this isn't always achieved.

In **effective communication** the intended meaning is fully understood by the receiver.

**Efficient communication** occurs at minimum cost.

Many times we are too busy or too lazy to invest enough time to make sure that communication is effective. Instead, we shoot for efficiency. Picture your instructor taking the time to communicate individually with each student about this chapter. It would be virtually impossible. Even if it were possible, it would be costly. This is why managers often leave voice-mail messages and interact by SMS and e-mail rather than visit people face-to-face. These are efficient but not always effective alternatives. Although an e-mail note to many people on a distribution list may save time, not everyone might get the same meaning from the message.

By the same token, an effective communication may not always be efficient. If a team leader visits each team member individually to explain a new change in procedures, this may guarantee that everyone truly understands the change. But it may also take a lot of the leader's time. In these and other ways, potential trade-offs between effectiveness and efficiency must be recognized in communication.

## Persuasion and Credibility in Communication

Communication is not only about sharing information or being "heard." It's about the intent of one party to influence or motivate the other in a desired way. **Persuasive communication** results in a recipient agreeing with or supporting the message being presented.[7] Managers, for example, get things done through relationships with peers, teammates, coworkers, and bosses. Their success is often due more to convincing than to giving orders.

**Persuasive communication** presents a message in a manner that causes the other person to support it.

Scholar and consultant Jay Conger says that without credibility there is little chance that persuasion can be successful.[8] He describes **credible communication** as that which is based on trust, respect, and integrity in the eyes of others. His advice to managers is to build credibility for persuasive communication through expertise and relationships.

**Credible communication** earns trust, respect, and integrity in the eyes of others.

To build credibility through expertise, you must be knowledgeable about the issue in question or have a successful track record in dealing with similar issues in the past. In a hiring situation where you are trying to persuade team members

## The Limited's Linda Heasley Gives Others Reasons to Work with Her

Will Ragozzino/BFA/SIPA/Newscom

Would you like to work for a boss who encourages you to keep your eyes open for other job opportunities? That's the message Linda Heasley's team at The Limited hears. She says it's her job as president and CEO to "re-recruit them every day and give them a reason to choose to work for us and for me as opposed to anyone else." This is part of a leadership philosophy based on the belief that "it's not about me . . . it's very much about the team."

Newcomers to Heasley's team are advised to follow a 90-day rule when it comes to communication. Based on her experience living in Thailand as a high school exchange student, she believes in taking the first 90 days to "watch and listen," trying "not to talk at meetings," and working to build relationships. And when it comes to performance, she also says: "I like to know the bad news as soon as you know it—I promise no recriminations—but I will expect to know what we could've avoided so it doesn't happen again."

Heasley took over The Limited when the company's stores were struggling for profitability. She acted decisively to refocus on core target customers while reducing costs and remodeling sales spaces. And she focused on recruiting staff who would find excitement in the challenges ahead.

When asked what she looks for in new hires, Heasley highlights things like passion, curiosity, energy, willingness to take risks, and a sense of humor. During interviews she uses proven questions to try to draw out job candidates and discover their capabilities. She might ask "What books have you read lately?" or "Can you describe a challenging situation you've been in and where you took a controversial position?"

 **YOUR TAKE?**

Linda Heasley seems very comfortable with herself and her role as president and CEO of this major company. Can you see where communication is one of her strengths? Would you respond well to a leader like this? In what respects might Heasley become a role model for making communication skills part of your personal leadership approach?

---

to select candidate A rather than B, for example, you must be able to defend your reasons. It will always be better if your past recommendations turned out to be good ones.

To build credibility for communication, you must have a good working relationship with the person to be persuaded. In a hiring situation where you want to persuade your boss to provide a special bonus package to attract top job candidates, for example, having a good relationship with your boss can add credibility to your request. Remember: It is always easier to get someone to do what you want if that person likes you.

## Communication Barriers

*Scene:* A Japanese executive used an interpreter when meeting with representatives of the firm's American joint venture partner. *Result:* He estimates that 20% of his intended meaning was lost in the exchange between himself and the interpreter, while another 20% was lost between the interpreter and the Americans.[9]

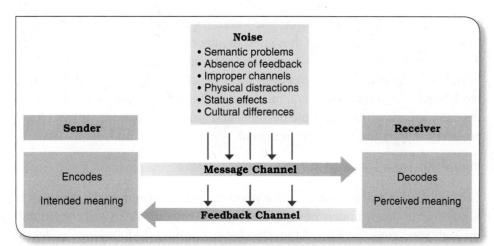

FIGURE 18.2 **Downsides of noise, shown as anything that interferes with the effectiveness of the communication process.**

**Noise**, as shown in Figure 18.2, is anything that interferes with the effectiveness of the communication process. And it isn't just a cross-cultural issue. Do you recognize its potential in everyday conversations, such as the nearby text messages exchanged between a high-tech Millennial and her low-tech Baby Boomer manager? Common sources of noise include information filtering, poor choice of channels, poor written or oral expression, failures to recognize nonverbal signals, and physical distractions.

## Information Filtering

"Criticize my boss? I don't have the right to." "I'd get fired." "It's her company, not mine." These comments display **information filtering**—the intentional distortion of information to make it appear favorable to the recipient. Management author and consultant Tom Peters calls it "Management Enemy Number 1." He even goes so far as to say that "once you become a boss you will never hear the unadulterated truth again."[10]

The problem with information filtering is that someone tells the boss only what they think he or she wants to hear. Whether the reason is a fear of retribution for bringing bad news, unwillingness to identify personal mistakes, or just a general desire to please, the end result is the same. The higher-level gets biased and inaccurate information from below and ends up making bad decisions. It's a continuing challenge for managers to fight this problem.

When Stephen Martin was head of a firm in England, he once "went underground" for two weeks and posed under an assumed name as an office worker. He says: "They (workers) said things to me that they never have told their managers. . . . Our key messages were just not getting through to people. . . . We were asking the impossible of some of them." And when Martin shared these findings with his firm's managers, they replied: "They never told us that!"[11]

## Poor Choice of Channels

A **communication channel** is the pathway or medium through which a message is conveyed from sender to receiver. Good communicators choose the right channel or combination of channels to accomplish their intended purpose.[12]

**MILLENNIAL TEXT TO BABY BOOMER**

• Sry abt mtg b rdy nxt time g2g

**BABY BOOMER TEXT TO MILLENNIAL**

• Missed you at important meeting. Don't forget next one. Stop by to discuss.

**Noise** is anything that interferes with the effectiveness of communication.

**Information filtering** is the intentional distortion of information to make it appear most favorable to the recipient.

A **communication channel** is the pathway through which a message moves from sender to receiver.

*Written channels*—paper or electronic—are most acceptable for simple messages that are easy to convey and for those that require extensive dissemination quickly. They are also useful when it is important to document that policies or directives have been conveyed. *Spoken channels,* such as face-to-face or virtual meetings, work best for complex and difficult messages and where immediate feedback to the sender is valuable. They are more personal and more likely to be perceived by the receiver as supportive or even inspirational.

## Poor Written or Oral Expression

Communication will only be effective when the sender expresses the message in a way that is clearly understood by the receiver. Words must be well chosen and properly used, something we all too often fail at. Consider the following "bafflegab" found among some executive communications.

> *A business report said:* "Consumer elements are continuing to stress the fundamental necessity of a stabilization of the price structure at a lower level than exists at the present time." *Translation:* Consumers keep saying that prices must go down and stay down.

> *A manager said:* "Substantial economies were affected in this division by increasing the time interval between distributions of data-eliciting forms to business entities." *Translation:* The division saved money by sending out fewer questionnaires.

## Failure to Recognize Nonverbal Signals

**Nonverbal communication** takes place through gestures, facial expressions, body posture, eye contact, and the use of interpersonal space. Research shows that up to 55% of a message's impact may come through nonverbal communication.[13] The absence of gestures and other nonverbal signals is one of the weaknesses of voice mail, text messaging, and other electronic communications. It's hard for things like clickable emoticons to make up for their loss.

Think of how nonverbal signals play out in your own communications.[14] Sometimes our body language "talks" even as we maintain silence. And when we do speak, our body may "say" different things than our words convey. This is called a

*Nonverbal communication takes place through gestures and body language.*

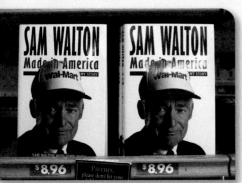

Gilles Mingasson/Getty Images, Inc.

## Wal-Mart Founder's Success Backed by Skills as the "Great Communicator"

The late Sam Walton, Wal-Mart's founder, was considered a master of persuasive communication. Picture him in a store and wearing a Wal-Mart baseball cap. "Northeast Memphis," he says, "you must have the best floor-cleaning crew in America. This floor is so clean, let's sit down on it." He continues after a pause: "I thank you. The company is so proud of you we can hardly stand it. But you know that confounded Kmart is getting better, and so is Target. So what's our challenge?" Walton smiles and answers his own question: "Customer service!"

**mixed message**—where words communicate one message while actions and body language communicate something else. Watch how people behave in a meeting. A person who feels under attack may move back in a chair or lean away from the presumed antagonist, even while expressing verbal agreement. All of this may be done quite unconsciously, but the mixed message will be picked up by those who are on the alert for nonverbal signals.

> A **mixed message** results when words communicate one message while actions, body language, or appearance communicate something else.

## Physical Distractions

Any number of physical distractions can interfere with communication effectiveness. Some of these distractions, such as telephone interruptions, drop-in visitors, and lack of privacy, are evident in the following meeting between an employee, George, and his manager.[15]

> Okay, George, let's hear your problem [phone rings, boss answers it and promises caller to deliver a report "just as soon as I can get it done"]. Uh, now, where were we—oh, you're having a problem with your technician. She's . . . [manager's assistant brings in some papers that need his immediate signature] . . . you say she's overstressed lately, wants to leave. I tell you what, George, why don't you [phone beeps a reminder, boss looks and realizes he has a luncheon meeting] . . . uh, take a stab at handling it yourself. I've got to go now.

It's obvious that this manager did not do a good job of communicating with George. The errors could be easily avoided. At a minimum, the manager should set aside adequate time and privacy for the meeting. Additional interruptions such as the telephone and drop-in visitors could be easily eliminated by good planning.

# Cross-Cultural Communication

After taking over as the CEO of the Dutch publisher Wolters Kluwer, Nancy McKinstry initiated major changes in strategy and operations—cutting staff, restructuring divisions, and investing in new business areas. She was the first American to head the firm, and described herself as "aggressive" when first meeting with her management team. After learning her use of that word wasn't well received by Europeans, she switched to "decisive." McKinstry says: "I was coming across as too harsh, too much of a results-driven American to the people I needed to get on board."[16]

Robert Churchill/iStockphoto

## Don't Let Gestures Cause Mistakes in Cross-Cultural Communication

Mistakes can happen when crossing cultural boundaries if gestures from home send the wrong messages. The firm handshake preferred by Americans can be viewed as aggressive in Asia where a limp meeting of the hands is more acceptable. And in Japan, a bow is the preferred form of greeting. Americans often point toward someone with an index finger extended. But this can be insulting to Asians who point with the thumb and a closed fist. Most such things can be quickly spotted and corrected by the alert and sensitive traveler. But cultural miscues await those who are ethnocentric.

Communicating across cultures requires lots of sensitivity, awareness, and an ability to quickly learn the rights and wrongs. The most difficult situation is when you don't speak the local language, or when one or both of you are weak in a shared second language. Advertising messages are notorious for getting lost in translation. A Pepsi ad in Taiwan that was intended to say "The Pepsi Generation" came out as "Pepsi will bring your ancestors back from the dead." A KFC ad in China that was intended to say "finger lickin' good" came out as "eat your fingers off."[17]

**Ethnocentrism** is the tendency to consider one's culture superior to any and all others.

**Ethnocentrism** is a major enemy of effective cross-cultural communication. This is the tendency to consider one's culture superior to any and all others. And, it hurts communication in at least three major ways. First, it may cause someone to not listen well to what others have to say. Second, it may cause someone to address or speak with others in ways that alienate them. Third, it may lead to the use of inappropriate stereotypes when dealing with persons from other cultures.[18]

One of the ways ethnocentrism may show up is a failure to respect cultural differences in nonverbal communication.[19] The American "thumbs-up" sign is an insult in Ghana and Australia; signaling "OK" with thumb and forefinger circled together is not okay in parts of Europe. Waving "hello" with an open palm is an insult in West Africa, suggesting the other person has five fathers.[20]

---

**LEARNING CHECK 1**

**TAKEAWAY QUESTION 1 What is the communication process?**

**Be sure you can** • describe the communication process and identify its key components • differentiate between effective and efficient communication • explain the role of credibility in persuasive communication • list the common sources of noise that limit effective communication • explain how mixed messages interfere with communication • explain how ethnocentrism affects cross-cultural communication

---

# Improving Collaboration Through Communication

Effective communication is essential as people work together in organizations. The better the communication, the more likely it is that collaboration will be successful. Pathways through which better communication can improve collaboration in organizations are found in such things as attention to transparency and openness, good use of electronic media, active listening practices, focusing on constructive feedback, and appropriate space design.

## Transparency and Openness

At HCL Industries, a large technology outsourcing firm, CEO Vineet Nayar believes that one of his most important tasks is to create transparency so that a "culture of trust" exists within the firm. Transparency at HCL means that the firm's financial information is fully posted on the internal Web. "We put all the dirty linen on the table," Nayar says. Transparency also means that the results of 360-degree feedback reviews for HCL's 3,800 managers get posted as well, including Nayar's own reviews. And when managers present plans to the top management team, Nayar insists that they also get posted so that everyone can read them and offer comments. His intent is to stimulate what he calls a company-wide process of "massive

## Manager Finds Workers' Ideas Really Sweet

Hammond's Candies was in business for 90 years when the Denver, Colorado, business was bought by entrepreneur Andrew Schuman. But the firm was losing money, and Schuman didn't know the candy business. He had what he calls an "aha" moment when learning that Hammond's famous ribbon snowflake candy was the brainchild of an assembly-line worker. "I thought," he says, "wow, we have a lot of smart people back here, and we're not tapping their knowledge." By encouraging a flow of more such ideas, Schuman was able to move his new company out of the red and into the black.

Courtesy of Hammond's Candies,
Since 1920, LLC

collaborative learning." This ensures that by the time a plan gets approved, it's most likely to be a good one.[21]

**Communication transparency** involves being honest in sharing accurate and complete information about the organization and workplace affairs. A lack of communication transparency is evident when managers try to hide information and restrict the access of organizational members to it. High communication transparency, such as that just illustrated in the HCL case, is evident when managers openly share information throughout an organization.

> **Communication transparency** involves openly sharing honest and complete information about the organization and workplace affairs.

The term **open book management** describes a form of communication transparency where employees are provided with essential financial information about their companies. At Bailard, Inc., a private investment firm, this openness extends to salaries. If you want to know what others are making at the firm, all you need to do is ask the chief financial officer. The firm's co-founder and CEO Thomas Bailard believes this is a good way to defeat office politics. "As a manager," he says, "if you know that your compensation decisions are essentially going to be public, you have to have pretty strong conviction about any decision you make."[22]

> **Open book management** is where managers provide employees with essential financial information about their companies.

As the prior examples suggest, the benefits of communication transparency start with better decision making. When people are well informed they can be expeted to make good decisions that serve the best interests of the organization. But, the benefits of transparency also extend into the realm of motivation and engagement. When people are trusted with information they can also be expected to feel more loyal and show more engagement as members of the organization.

## Use of Electronic Media

Are you part of the Twitter community on Facebook, married to your choice of smart mobile devices? Technology hasn't just changed how we communicate. It has created a social media revolution—one that can be a performance asset or detriment in the world of work.[23]

To begin, we may be getting so familiar with writing online short-hand that we use it in the wrong places. Sending a message like "Thnx for the IView! I Wud Luv to Work 4 U!! ;)" isn't the follow-up most employers like to receive from job candidates. When Tory Johnson, president of Women for Hire, Inc., received a thank-you note by e-mail from an intern candidate, it included "hiya," "thanx," three exclamation points, and two emoticons. She says: "That e-mail just ruined it for me."[24] Textspeak and emoticons may be the norm in social networks, but their use can be inappropriate in work settings.

Privacy is a concern in electronic communication.[25] And when Facebook's CEO, Mark Zuckerberg, says privacy is "no longer a social norm," it's time to take the issue seriously. An American Management Association survey of 304 U.S. companies found that 66% monitor Internet connections; 43% store and review computer files and monitor e-mail; 45% monitor telephone time and numbers dialed; and 30% have fired employees for misuse of the Internet.[26] When it comes to Web browsing and using social media at work, the best advice comes down to this: Find out the employer's policy and follow it. Don't ever assume that you have electronic privacy, chances are the employer is checking or can easily check on you.[27]

The **electronic grapevine** is now a fact of life as electronic messages—both accurate and inaccurate—fly with great speed around our world. When a law professor told his class that Chief Justice John Roberts was resigning from the U.S. Supreme Court, it was supposed to be a lesson on checking facts of stories. By the time they realized what he was doing, class members had already spread the false story by instant messaging and e-mails to the point of it almost making the national news.[28] And then there's YouTube. Domino's Pizza executives felt its sting when a posted video showed two employees doing nasty things to sandwiches. It was soon viewed over a million times. By the time the video was pulled (by one of its authors who apologized for "faking"), Domino's faced a crisis in customer confidence. The CEO finally created a Twitter account and posted a YouTube video message to present the company's own view of the story.[29]

> **Electronic grapevines** use electronic media to pass messages and information among members of social networks.

> **Active listening** helps the source of a message say what he or she really means.

## Active Listening

Whether trying to communicate electronically or face to face, managers must be very good at listening. When people "talk," they are trying to communicate something. That "something" may or may not be what they are saying.

**Active listening** is the process of taking action to help someone say exactly what he or she really means.[30] It involves being sincere and trying to find out the full meaning of what is being said. It also involves being disciplined in controlling emotions and withholding premature evaluations or interpretations. Different responses to the following two questions contrast how a "passive" listener and an "active" listener might act in real workplace conversations.[31]

*Question 1:* "Don't you think employees should be promoted on the basis of seniority?" *Passive listener's response:* "No, I don't!" *Active listener's response:* "It seems to you that they should, I take it?"

*Question 2:* "What does the supervisor expect us to do about these out-of-date computers?" *Passive listener's response:* "Do the best you can, I guess." *Active listener's response:* "You're pretty frustrated with those machines, aren't you?"

### GUIDELINES FOR ACTIVE LISTENING

1. *Listen for message content:* Try to hear exactly what content is being conveyed in the message.

2. *Listen for feelings:* Try to identify how the source feels about the content in the message.

3. *Respond to feelings:* Let the source know that her or his feelings are being recognized.

4. *Note all cues:* Be sensitive to nonverbal and verbal messages; be alert for mixed messages.

5. *Paraphrase and restate:* State back to the source what you think you are hearing.

## Constructive Feedback

> **Feedback** is the process of telling someone else how you feel about something that person did or said.

The process of telling other people how you feel about something they did or said, or about the situation in general, is called **feedback**. It occurs in the normal give-and-

> ONLY 3% OF HR EXECUTIVES GIVE "A" GRADES TO THEIR FIRMS' PERFORMANCE MEASUREMENT SYSTEMS

## Value of Performance Reviews Gets Increasing Scrutiny

Surveys show people aren't always pleased with the way managers in their organizations do performance reviews. Some are so concerned that they suggest dropping them altogether. Check these survey findings:

- Only 30% of HR executives believed that employees trust their employer's performance measurement system.
- 60% of HR executives give their performance management systems "C" grades or worse.
- Top concerns of HR executives are that managers aren't willing to face employees and give constructive feedback, and employees don't have a clear understanding of what rates as good and bad performance.
- 1% of firms are completely doing away with performance reviews and shifting to regular one-on-one meetings where performance is discussed.

 **YOUR THOUGHTS?**

Performance review is often a hot topic these days. The buzzwords are *merit pay* and *performance accountability*. But is it really possible to have a performance measurement system that is respected by managers and workers alike? Do the data reported here fit with your own experiences? What are their implications for management practice? Will we soon see a dramatic increase in the number of employers who shift away from the formal annual review to something less formal and more regular?

---

take of working relationships, and it occurs more formally during scheduled performance reviews.

The art of giving feedback is an indispensable skill, particularly for managers who must regularly give feedback to other people. When poorly done, feedback can be threatening to the recipient and cause resentment. When properly done, feedback—even performance criticism—can be listened to, accepted, and used to good advantage by the receiver.[32] Consider someone who comes late to meetings. Feedback from the meeting chair might be *evaluative*—"You are unreliable and always late for everything." It might be *interpretive*—"You're coming late to meetings; you might be spreading yourself too thin and have trouble meeting your obligations." And it might be *descriptive*—"You were 30 minutes late for today's meeting and missed a lot of the context for our discussion."[33]

Feedback is most useful and constructive, rather than harmful, when it offers real benefit to the receiver and doesn't just satisfy some personal need of the sender. A supervisor who berates a computer programmer for errors, for example, may actually be angry about failing to give clear instructions in the first place. Common advice on making feedback constructive includes the following guidelines:[34]

- Give feedback directly and with real feeling, based on trust between you and the receiver.
- Make sure that feedback is specific rather than general; use good, clear, and preferably recent examples to make your points.
- Give feedback at a time when the receiver seems most willing or able to accept it.
- Make sure the feedback is valid; limit it to things the receiver can be expected to do something about.
- Give feedback in small doses; never give more than the receiver can handle at any particular time.

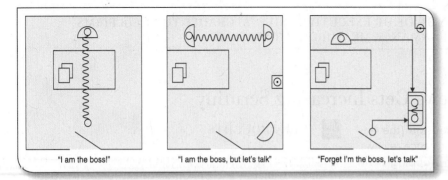

"I am the boss!"  "I am the boss, but let's talk"  "Forget I'm the boss, let's talk"

**Proxemics** involves the use of space in communication.

## Space Design

**Proxemics** is the study of how we use space.[35] And, space counts in communication. The distance between people conveys varying intentions in terms of intimacy, openness, and status in interpersonal communications. Even the physical layout of an office or room is a form of nonverbal communication. Think about it. Offices with chairs available for side-by-side seating convey different messages than offices where the manager's chair sits behind the desk and those for visitors sit facing it in front.

An extreme example of space design and communication confronted Tim Armstrong when he became CEO of AOL. One of his first decisions was to remove the doors separating executive offices from other workers. Previously, the only way to open them had been with a company key card.[36]

**LEARNING CHECK 2**

**TAKEAWAY QUESTION 2 How can we improve our communications?**

**Be sure you can** • explain how transparency and openness improves communication • explain how interactive management and practices like MBWA can improve upward communication • discuss possible uses of electronic media by managers • define *active listening* and list active listening rules • illustrate the guidelines for constructive feedback • explain how space design influences communication

# Managing Conflict

**Conflict** is a disagreement over issues of substance and/or an emotional antagonism.

**Substantive conflict** involves disagreements over goals, resources, rewards, policies, procedures, and job assignments.

**Emotional conflict** results from feelings of anger, distrust, dislike, fear, and resentment, as well as from personality clashes.

The ability to deal with conflicts is a critical communication and collaboration skill. **Conflict** occurs as a disagreement between people on substantive or emotional issues.[37] **Substantive conflicts** involve disagreements over such things as goals and tasks, allocation of resources, distribution of rewards, policies and procedures, and job assignments. **Emotional conflicts** result from feelings of anger, distrust, dislike, fear, and resentment, as well as from personality clashes and relationship problems. Both forms of conflict can cause difficulties. But when managed well, they can also stimulate creativity and high performance.

## Functional and Dysfunctional Conflict

**Functional conflict** is constructive and helps task performance.

**Dysfunctional conflict** is destructive and hurts task performance.

The inverted "U" curve depicted in Figure 18.3 shows that conflict of moderate intensity can be good for performance. This **functional conflict**, or constructive conflict, moves people toward greater work efforts, cooperation, and creativity. It helps teams achieve their goals and avoid making poor decisions because of groupthink. **Dysfunctional conflict**, or destructive conflict, harms performance, relationships, and even individual well-being. It occurs when there is too much or too little conflict in the situation. Too much conflict is distracting and overwhelming. Too little conflict promotes groupthink, complacency, and the loss of a high-performance edge.

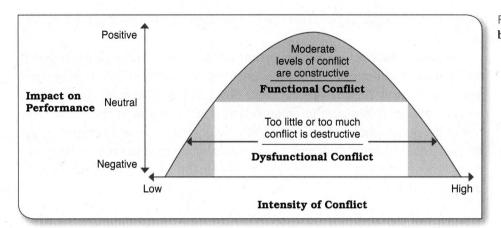

FIGURE 18.3 **The relationship between conflict and performance.**

## Causes of Conflict

A number of things can cause or set the stage for conflict. *Role ambiguities* in the form of unclear job expectations and other task uncertainties increase the likelihood for people to work at cross-purposes. *Resource scarcities* cause conflict when people have to share or compete for them. *Task interdependencies* breed

ETHICS ON THE LINE > A CHRISTMAS PARTY WAS DESCRIBED IN DETAIL, INCLUDING AN EXECUTIVE'S "UNFORGIVABLE FAUX PAS"

## Blogging Is Easy, but Bloggers Should Beware

Magali Delporte/eyevine/Redux Pictures

It is easy and tempting to set up your own blog, write about your experiences and impressions, and then share your thoughts with others online. So, why not do it?

Catherine Sanderson, a British citizen living and working in Paris, might have asked this question before launching her blog, "Le Petite Anglaise." At one point it was so "successful" that she had 3,000 readers. But the Internet diary included reports on her experiences at work—and her employer, an accounting firm, wasn't at all happy when it became public knowledge.

Even though Sanderson was blogging anonymously, her photo was on the site, and the connection was eventually discovered. Noticed, too, was her running commentary about bosses, colleagues, and life at the office. One boss, she wrote, "calls secretaries 'typists.'" A Christmas party was described in detail, including an executive's "unforgivable faux pas."

News reports said that one of the firm's partners was "incandescent with rage" after learning what Sanderson had written about him. Sanderson was upset too, claiming she was "dooced"—a term used to describe being fired for what one writes in a blog. She sued for financial damages and confirmation of her rights, on principle, to have a private blog. The court awarded her a year's salary for unfair dismissal.

### ETHICS QUESTIONS

Just what are the ethical issues here, from both the blogger's and the employer's perspective? What rights do employees have with regard to communicating about their work experiences? Is it ethical for a supervisor to fire an employee any time the employee says something negative about the organization? For example, which is the bigger "crime," to get drunk at the office holiday party or to write a blog that reports that your supervisor got drunk at the office party? What obligations do employees have to their employers even when they are off the clock, and, in contrast, where does the employer's ability to control employee behaviors outside of work end?

conflict when people depend on others to perform well in order to perform well themselves.

*Competing objectives* are also opportunities for conflict. When goals are poorly set or reward systems are poorly designed, individuals and groups may come into conflict by working to one another's disadvantage. *Structural differentiation* breeds conflict. Differences in organization structures and in the characteristics of the people staffing them may foster conflict because of incompatible approaches toward work. And, *unresolved prior conflicts* tend to erupt in later conflicts. Unless a conflict is fully resolved, it may remain latent only to emerge again in the future.

## Conflict Resolution

When conflicts do occur, they can either be "resolved," in the sense that the causes are corrected, or "suppressed," in that the causes remain but the conflict behaviors are controlled. True **conflict resolution** eliminates the underlying causes of conflict and reduces the potential for similar conflicts in the future. Suppressed conflicts tend to fester and recur at a later time.

> **Conflict resolution** is the removal of the substantial and emotional reasons for a conflict.

## Conflict Management Styles

People tend to respond to interpersonal conflict through different combinations of cooperative and assertive behaviors.[38] *Cooperativeness* is the desire to satisfy another party's needs and concerns. *Assertiveness* is the desire to satisfy one's own needs and concerns. Figure 18.4 shows five interpersonal styles of conflict management that result from various combinations of these two tendencies.[39]

- **Avoidance** or *withdrawal*—being uncooperative and unassertive, downplaying disagreement, withdrawing from the situation, and/or staying neutral at all costs.
- **Accommodation** or *smoothing*—being cooperative but unassertive, letting the wishes of others rule, smoothing over or overlooking differences to maintain harmony.

> **Avoidance,** or withdrawal, pretends that a conflict doesn't really exist.

> **Accommodation,** or smoothing, plays down differences and highlights similarities to reduce conflict.

FIGURE 18.4 **Alternative conflict management styles.**

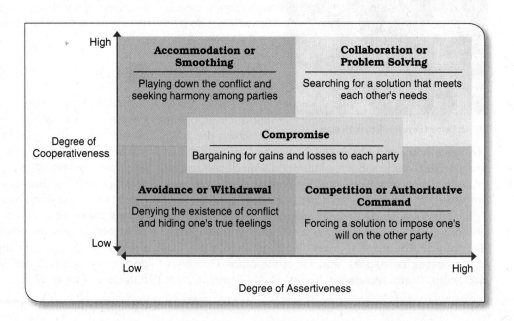

- **Competition** or *authoritative command*—being uncooperative but assertive, working against the wishes of the other party, engaging in win-lose competition, and/or forcing through the exercise of authority.
- **Compromise**—being moderately cooperative and assertive, bargaining for "acceptable" solutions in which each party wins a bit and loses a bit.
- **Collaboration** or *problem solving*—being cooperative and assertive, trying to fully satisfy everyone's concerns by working through differences, finding and solving problems so that everyone gains.

Avoiding and accommodating styles often create **lose–lose conflict**.[40] No one achieves her or his true desires, and the underlying reasons for conflict remain unaffected. Although the conflict appears settled or may even disappear for a while, it tends to recur in the future. Avoidance pretends that conflict doesn't really exist. Everyone withdraws and hopes it will simply go away. Accommodation plays down differences and highlights areas of agreement. Peaceful coexistence is the goal, but the real essence of a conflict may be ignored.

Competing and compromising styles tend to create **win–lose conflict** where each party strives to gain at the other's expense. Because win–lose methods don't address the root causes of conflict, future conflicts of the same or a similar nature are likely to occur. In competition, one party wins because superior skill or outright domination allows his or her desires to be forced on the other. An example is authoritative command where a supervisor simply dictates a solution to subordinates. Compromise occurs when trade-offs are made such that each party to the conflict gives up and gains something. But because each party loses something, antecedents for future conflicts are established.

A collaborating or problem-solving style is a form of **win–win conflict** where issues get resolved to everyone's benefit. Parties to the conflict recognize that something is wrong and needs attention, and they confront the issues head on. Win–win outcomes eliminate the underlying causes of the conflict because all matters and concerns are raised and discussed openly.

**Competition**, or authoritative command, uses force, superior skill, or domination to "win" a conflict.

**Compromise** occurs when each party to the conflict gives up something of value to the other.

**Collaboration**, or problem solving, involves working through conflict differences and solving problems so everyone wins.

In **lose–lose conflict** no one achieves his or her true desires, and the underlying reasons for conflict remain unaffected.

In **win–lose conflict** one party achieves its desires, and the other party does not.

In **win–win conflict** the conflict is resolved to everyone's benefit.

## Structural Approaches to Conflict Management

Not all conflict management in groups and organizations can be resolved at the interpersonal level. Think about it. Aren't there likely to be times when personalities and emotions prove irreconcilable? In such cases a structural approach to conflict management can often help.[41]

When conflict traces back to a resource issue, the structural solution is to *make more resources available* to everyone. Although costly and not always possible, this is a straightforward way to resolve resource-driven conflicts. When people are stuck in conflict and just can't seem to appreciate one another's points of view, *appealing to higher-level goals* can sometimes focus their attention on one mutually desirable outcome. In a student team where members are arguing over content choices for a Power-Point presentation, for example, it might help to remind everyone that the goal is to get an "A" from the instructor. An appeal

**STRUCTURAL WAYS TO MANAGE CONFLICT**

- Make resources available.
- Appeal to higher goals.
- Change the people.
- Change the environment.
- Use integrating devices.
- Provide training.
- Change reward systems.

to higher goals offers a common frame of reference for analyzing differences and reconciling disagreements.

It may be that *changing the people* is necessary. There are times when a manager may need to replace or transfer one or more of the conflicting parties to eliminate the conflict. When the people can't be changed, they may have to be separated by *altering the physical environment*. Sometimes it is possible to rearrange facilities, work space, or workflows to physically separate conflicting parties and decrease opportunities for contact with one another. Organizations can also use *integrating devices* to help manage conflicts between groups. These approaches include assigning people to formal liaison roles, convening special task forces, setting up cross-functional teams, and even switching to the matrix form of organization.

By *changing reward systems* it is sometimes possible to reduce conflicts that arise when people feel they have to compete with one another for attention, pay, and other rewards. An example is shifting pay bonuses or even student project grades to the group level so that individuals benefit in direct proportion to how well the team performs as a whole. This is a way of reinforcing teamwork and reducing the tendencies of team members to compete with one another. And finally, people who get good *training in interpersonal skills* are better prepared to communicate and work effectively in conflict-prone situations. When employers list criteria for recruiting new college graduates, such "soft" or "people" skills are often right at the top. You can't succeed in today's horizontal and team-oriented organizations if you can't work well with other people, even when disagreements are inevitable.

---

**LEARNING CHECK 3**

**TAKEAWAY QUESTION 3 How can we deal positively with conflict?**

**Be sure you can** • differentiate substantive and emotional conflict • differentiate functional and dysfunctional conflict • explain the common causes of conflict • define *conflict resolution* • explain the conflict management styles of avoidance, accommodation, competition, compromise, and collaboration • discuss lose–lose, win–lose, and win–win conflicts • list the structural approaches to conflict management

---

# Managing Negotiation

*Situation:* Your employer offers you a promotion, but the pay raise being offered is disappointing.

*Situation:* You have enough money to send one person for training from your department, but two really want to go.

*Situation:* Your team members are having a "cook-out" on Saturday afternoon and want you to attend; your husband wants you to go with him to visit his mother in a neighboring town.

*Situation:* Someone on your sales team has to fly to Texas to meet an important client; you've made the last two trips out of town and don't want to go; another member of the team hasn't been out of town in a long time and "owes" you a favor.

**Negotiation** is the process of making joint decisions when the parties involved have different preferences.

These are examples of the many work situations that lead to **negotiation**—the process of making joint decisions when the parties involved have different preferences.

Stated a bit differently, negotiation is a way of reaching agreement. People negotiate over job assignments, work schedules, work locations, and salaries, as pointed out in Management Smarts.[42] Any and all negotiations are ripe for conflict. They are stiff tests of anyone's communication and collaboration skills.[43]

## Negotiation Goals and Approaches

Two important goals should be considered in any negotiation. **Substance goals** are concerned with negotiation outcomes. They are tied to content issues. **Relationship goals** are concerned with negotiation processes. They are tied to the way people work together while negotiating and how they (and any constituencies they represent) will be able to work together again in the future.

**Effective negotiation** occurs when issues of substance are resolved and working relationships among the negotiating parties are maintained or even improved. The three criteria of effective negotiation are:

> ### ManagementSmarts
>
> #### "Ins" and "Outs" of Negotiating Salaries
>
> - *Prepare, prepare, prepare*—Do the research and find out what others make for a similar position inside and outside the organization, including everything from salary to benefits, bonuses, incentives, and job perks.
> - *Document and communicate*—Identify and communicate your performance value; put forth a set of accomplishments that show how you have saved or made money and created value in your present job or for a past employer.
> - *Identify critical skills and attributes*—Make a list of your strengths and link each of them with potential contributions to the new employer; show how "you" offer talents and personal attributes of immediate value to the work team.
> - *Advocate and ask*—Be your own best advocate; the rule in salary negotiation is "Don't ask, don't get." But don't ask too soon; your boss or interviewer should be the first to bring up salary.
> - *Stay focused on the goal*—Your goal is to achieve as much as you can in the negotiation; this means not only doing well at the moment but also getting better positioned for future gains.
> - *View things from the other side*—Test your requests against the employer's point of view; ask if you are being reasonable, convincing, and fair; ask how the boss could explain to higher levels and to your peers a decision to grant your request.
> - *Don't overreact to bad news*—Never "quit on the spot" if you don't get what you want; be willing to search for and consider alternative job offers.

1. *Quality*—negotiating a "wise" agreement that is truly satisfactory to all sides.
2. *Cost*—negotiating efficiently, using a minimum of resources and time.
3. *Harmony*—negotiating in a way that fosters, rather than inhibits, good relationships.[44]

## Gaining Agreements

In **distributive negotiation** each party makes claims for certain preferred outcomes.[45] This emphasis on substance can become self-centered and competitive, with each party thinking the only way for him or her to gain is for the other to lose. Relationships often get sacrificed as process breaks down in these win–lose conditions.

In **principled negotiation**, sometimes called **integrative negotiation**, the orientation is win–win. The goal is to achieve a final agreement based on the merits of each party's claims. No one should lose in a principled negotiation, and positive relationships should be maintained in the process. Four pathways or rules for gaining such integrated agreements are set forth by Roger Fisher and William Ury in their book, *Getting to Yes*:[46]

1. Separate the people from the problem.
2. Focus on interests, not on positions.
3. Generate many alternatives before deciding what to do.
4. Insist that results be based on some objective standard.

**Substance goals** in negotiation are concerned with outcomes.

**Relationship goals** in negotiation are concerned with the ways people work together.

**Effective negotiation** resolves issues of substance while maintaining a positive process.

**Distributive negotiation** focuses on win–lose claims made by each party for certain preferred outcomes.

**Principled negotiation** or **integrative negotiation** uses a "win–win" orientation to reach solutions acceptable to each party.

FIGURE 18.5  **The bargaining zone in classic two-party negotiation.**

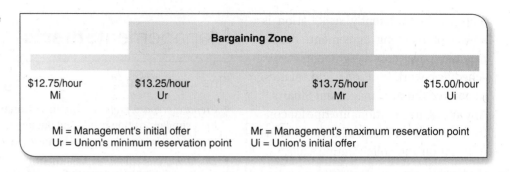

The attitudinal foundations of principled negotiation involve the willingness of each party to trust, share information, and ask reasonable questions. The information foundations involve both parties knowing what is important to them and finding out what is important to the other party.

Attitudes and information both come into play during a classic two-party labor–management negotiation over a new contract and salary increase.[47] Look at Figure 18.5 and consider the situation from the labor union's perspective. The union negotiator has told her management counterpart that the union wants a new wage of $15.00 per hour. This expressed preference is the union's initial offer. However, she also has in mind a minimum reservation point of $13.25 per hour. This is the lowest wage she is willing to accept for the union. Now look at it from the perspective of the management negotiator. His initial offer is $12.75 per hour. But his maximum reservation point, the highest wage he is prepared to eventually offer the union, is $13.75 per hour.

A **bargaining zone** is the space between one party's minimum reservation point and the other party's maximum reservation point.

The **bargaining zone** in a negotiation is defined as the space between one party's minimum reservation point and the other party's maximum reservation point. In this case it lies between $13.25 per hour and $13.75 per hour. It is a "positive" zone since the reservation points of the two parties overlap. If the union's minimum reservation point was greater than management's maximum reservation point, no room would exist for bargaining. A key task for any negotiator is to discover the other party's reservation point. It is difficult to negotiate effectively until this is known and each party realizes that a positive bargaining zone exists.

## Negotiation Pitfalls

The negotiation process is admittedly complex and negotiators must guard against common pitfalls. The first is the *myth of the "fixed pie."* This involves acting on the distributive win–lose assumption that in order for you to gain the other person must give something up. This fails to recognize the integrative assumption that the "pie" can sometimes be expanded or utilized to everyone's advantage. A second negotiation error is *nonrational escalation of conflict.* The negotiator gets locked into previously stated "demands" and allows personal needs for "ego" and "saving face" to inflate the perceived importance of satisfying them.

A third negotiating error is *overconfidence and ignoring the other's needs.* The negotiator becomes overconfident, believes his or her position is the only correct one, and fails to consider the needs of the other party. The fourth error is *too*

**BEWARE OF NEGOTIATION PITFALLS**

- Myth of fixed pie
- Escalation of conflict
- Overconfidence
- Too much telling
- Too little listening
- Cultural miscues
- Unethical behavior

much *"telling"* and too little *"hearing."* The "telling" error occurs when parties to a negotiation don't really make themselves understood to each other. The "hearing" error occurs when they fail to listen well enough to understand what each other is saying.[48]

Another potential negotiation pitfall in our age of globalization is *premature cultural comfort*. This occurs when a negotiator is too quick to assume that he or she understands the intentions, positions, and meanings of a negotiator from a different culture. A negotiator from a low-context culture, for example, is used to getting information through direct questions and answers. But this style might have difficulties if used with a negotiator from a high-context culture

# Words Affect Outcomes in Online Dispute Resolution

The National Consumer League reports that 41% of participants in online trading had problems, often associated with late deliveries. A study of online dispute resolution among eBay buyers and sellers found that using words that "give face" were more likely than words that "attack face" to result in settlement. Jeanne Brett, Mara Olekalns, Ray Friedman, Nathan Goates, Cameron Anderson, and Cara Cherry Lisco studied real disputes being addressed through Square Trade, an online dispute resolution service to which eBay refers unhappy customers. A "dispute" was defined as a form of conflict in which one party to a transaction makes a claim that the other party rejects.

The researchers adopted what they call a "language-based" approach using "face theory," essentially arguing that how participants use language to give and attack the face of the other party will have a major impact on results. For example, in filing a claim an unhappy buyer might use polite words that preserve the positive self-image, or face, of the seller, or the buyer might use negative words that attack this sense of face. Examples of negative words are "agitated, angry, apprehensive, despise, disgusted, frustrated, furious, and hate."

This study examined 386 eBay-generated disputes processed through Square Trade. Results showed that expressing negative emotions and giving commands to the other party inhibited dispute resolution, whereas providing a causal explanation, offering suggestions, and communicating firmness all made dispute resolution more likely. The hypothesis that expressing positive emotions would increase the likelihood of dispute resolution was not supported. The study also showed that the longer a dispute played out, the less likely it was to be resolved.

### Online Dispute Resolution

| Dispute resolution less likely when | Dispute resolution more likely when |
|---|---|
| • Negative emotions are expressed<br>• Commands are issued | • Causal explanations given<br>• Suggestions are offered<br>• Communications are firm |

In terms of practical implications, the researchers say: "Watch your language: Avoid attacking the other's face either by showing your anger toward them, or by expressing contempt. Avoid signaling weakness, and be firm in your claim. Provide causal accounts that take responsibility and give face."

 **YOU BE THE RESEARCHER**

Why is it that using words that express negative emotions seems to have adverse effects on dispute resolution, but the use of words expressing positive emotions does not have positive effects? How might this result be explained? Also, why is it that using words that communicate "firmness" seems important in resolving disputes? Can you apply these ideas and findings to other contexts? Suppose a student is unhappy about a grade. How does dispute resolution with the course instructor play out? Suppose an employee is unhappy about a performance evaluation or pay raise. How does dispute resolution with the boss proceed?

*References:* Jeanne Brett, Mara Olekalns, Ray Friedman, Nathan Goates, Cameron Anderson, and Cara Cherry Lisco, "Sticks and Stones: Language and On-Line Dispute Resolution," *Academy of Management Journal*, vol. 50 (February 2007), pp. 85–99.

whose tendency is to communicate indirectly, use nondeclarative language and nonverbal signals, and avoid hard-and-fast position statements.[49]

It is also important to avoid the *trap of ethical misconduct*. The motivation to negotiate unethically sometimes arises from pure greed and undue emphasis on the profit motive. This may be experienced as a desire to "get just a bit more" or to "get as much as you can" from a negotiation. The motivation to behave unethically may also result from a sense of competition. This is a desire to "win" a negotiation just for the sake of winning it, or because of the misguided belief that someone else must "lose" in order for you to gain.

When unethical behavior occurs in negotiation, the persons involved may try to explain it away with inappropriate rationalizing: "It was really unavoidable." "Oh, it's harmless." "The results justify the means." "It's really quite fair and appropriate."[50] These and other excuses for questionable behavior are morally unacceptable. They also run the risk that any short-run gains will be offset by long-run losses. Unethical negotiators risk being viewed with distrust, disrespect, and dislike, and even being targeted for revenge in later negotiations.

## Third-Party Dispute Resolution

In **mediation** a neutral party tries to help conflicting parties improve communication to resolve their dispute.

Even with the best of intentions, it may not always be possible to achieve integrative agreements. When disputes reach the point of impasse, third-party assistance with dispute resolution can be useful. **Mediation** involves a neutral third party who tries to improve communication between negotiating parties and keep them focused on relevant issues. The mediator does not issue a ruling or make a decision, but can take an active role in discussions. This may include making suggestions in an attempt to move the parties toward agreement.

In **arbitration** a neutral third party issues a binding decision to resolve a dispute.

**Arbitration**, such as salary arbitration in professional sports, is a stronger form of dispute resolution. It involves a neutral third party, the arbitrator, who acts as a "judge" and issues a binding decision. This usually includes a formal hearing in which the arbitrator listens to both sides and reviews all facets of the case before making a ruling.

An **ombudsperson** is a designated neutral third party who listens to complaints and disputes in an attempt to resolve them.

Some organizations provide for a process called *alternative dispute resolution*. This approach utilizes mediation or arbitration, but does so only after direct attempts to negotiate agreements between the conflicting parties have failed. An **ombudsperson**, a designated neutral third party who listens to complaints and disputes, often plays a key role in this process.

**LEARNING CHECK 4**

**TAKEAWAY QUESTION 4 How can we negotiate successful agreements?**

**Be sure you can** • differentiate between distributive and principled negotiation • list four rules of principled negotiation • define *bargaining zone* and use this term to illustrate a labor–management wage negotiation • describe the potential pitfalls in negotiation • differentiate between mediation and arbitration

# MANAGEMENT LEARNING REVIEW

## LEARNING CHECK SUMMARY

### TAKEAWAY QUESTION 1  What is the communication process?

- Communication is the interpersonal process of sending and receiving symbols with messages attached to them.
- Effective communication occurs when the sender and the receiver of a message both interpret it in the same way.
- Efficient communication occurs when the message is sent at low cost for the sender.
- Persuasive communication results in the recipient acting as intended by the sender; credibility earned by expertise and good relationships is essential to persuasive communication.
- Noise is anything that interferes with the effectiveness of communication; common examples are poor utilization of channels, poor written or oral expression, physical distractions, and status effects.

**For Discussion When is it okay to accept less effectiveness to gain efficiency in communication?**

### TAKEAWAY QUESTION 2  How can we improve our communications?

- Transparency in the sense that information conveyed to others is honest, credible, and fully disclosed is an important way to improve communication in the workplace.
- Interactive management through MBWA, such as structured meetings, use of electronic media, and advisory councils can improve upward communication.
- Active listening, through reflecting back and paraphrasing, can help overcome barriers and improve communication.
- Constructive feedback is specific, direct, well-timed, and limited to things the receiver can change.
- Office architecture and space designs can be used to improve communication in organizations.
- Proper choice of channels and use of information technology can improve communication in organizations.
- Greater cross-cultural awareness and sensitivity are important if we are to overcome the negative influences of ethnocentrism on communication.

**For Discussion What rules of active listening do most people break?**

### TAKEAWAY QUESTION 3  How can we deal positively with conflict?

- Conflict occurs as disagreements over substantive or emotional issues.
- Moderate levels of conflict are functional for performance and creativity; too little or too much conflict becomes dysfunctional.
- Conflict may be managed through structural approaches that involve changing people, goals, resources, or work arrangements.
- Personal conflict management styles include avoidance, accommodation, compromise, competition, and collaboration.
- True conflict resolution involves problem solving through a win–win collaborative approach.

**For Discussion When is it better to avoid conflict rather than engage it?**

### TAKEAWAY QUESTION 4  How can we negotiate successful agreements?

- Negotiation is the process of making decisions in situations in which the participants have different preferences.
- Substance goals concerned with outcomes and relationship goals concerned with processes are both important in successful negotiation.
- Effective negotiation occurs when issues of substance are resolved while the process maintains good working relationships.
- Distributive negotiation emphasizes win–lose outcomes; integrative negotiation emphasizes win–win outcomes.
- Common negotiation pitfalls include the myth of the fixed pie, overconfidence, too much telling and too little hearing, and ethical misconduct.
- Mediation and arbitration are structured approaches to third-party dispute resolution.

**For Discussion How do you negotiate with someone who is trapped in the "myth of the fixed pie"?**

## Multiple-Choice Questions

1. When the intended meaning of the sender and the interpreted meaning of the receiver are the same, a communication is _____.
   (a) effective      (b) persuasive
   (c) selective      (d) efficient

2. The use of paraphrasing and reflecting back what someone else says in communication is characteristic of _____.
   (a) mixed messages      (b) active listening
   (c) projection      (d) lose–lose conflict

3. Which is the best example of a supervisor making feedback descriptive rather than evaluative?
   (a) You are a slacker.
   (b) You are not responsible.
   (c) You cause me lots of problems.
   (d) You have been late to work three days this month.

4. When interacting with an angry co-worker who is complaining about a work problem, a manager skilled at active listening would most likely try to _____.
   (a) suggest that the conversation be held at a better time
   (b) point out that the conversation would be better held at another location
   (c) express displeasure in agreement with the co-worker's complaint
   (d) rephrase the co-worker's complaint to encourage him to say more

5. When a manager uses e-mail to send a message that is better delivered face-to-face, the communication process suffers from _____.
   (a) semantic problems
   (b) a poor choice of communication channels
   (c) physical distractions
   (d) information overload

6. If a visitor to a foreign culture makes gestures commonly used at home even after learning that they are offensive to locals, the visitor can be described as _____.
   (a) a passive listened
   (b) ethnocentric
   (c) more efficient than effective
   (d) an active listener

7. In order to be consistently persuasive when communicating with others in the workplace, a manager should build credibility by _____.
   (a) making sure rewards for compliance are clear
   (b) making sure penalties for noncompliance are clear
   (c) making sure they know who is the boss
   (d) making sure good relationships have been established

8. A manager who understands the importance of proxemics in communication would be likely to _____.
   (a) avoid sending mixed messages
   (b) arrange work spaces so as to encourage interaction
   (c) be very careful in the choice of written and spoken words
   (d) make frequent use of e-mail messages to keep people well informed

9. A conflict is most likely to be functional and have a positive impact on performance when it is _____.
   (a) based on emotions
   (b) resolved by arbitration
   (c) caused by resource scarcities
   (d) of moderate intensity

10. An appeal to superordinate goals is an example of a(n) _____ approach to conflict management.
    (a) avoidance      (b) structural
    (c) dysfunctional      (d) self-serving

11. The conflict management style with the greatest potential for true conflict resolution involves _____.
    (a) compromise      (b) competition
    (c) smoothing      (d) collaboration

12. When a person is highly cooperative but not very assertive in approaching conflict, the conflict management style is referred to as _____.
    (a) avoidance      (b) authoritative
    (c) smoothing      (d) collaboration

13. The three criteria of an effective negotiation are quality, cost, and _____.
    (a) harmony      (b) timeliness
    (c) efficiency      (d) effectiveness

14. In classic two-party negotiation, the difference between one party's minimum reservation point and the other party's maximum reservation point is known as the _____.
    (a) BATNA      (b) arena of indifference
    (c) myth of the fixed pie      (d) bargaining zone

15. The first rule of thumb for gaining integrative agreements in negotiations is to _____.
    (a) separate the people from the problems
    (b) focus on positions
    (c) deal with a minimum number of alternatives
    (d) avoid setting standards for measuring outcomes

## Short-Response Questions

**16.** Briefly describe how a manager would behave as an active listener when communicating with subordinates.

**17.** Explain the relationship between conflict intensity and performance.

## Essay Question

**20.** After being promoted to store manager for a new branch of a large department store chain, Kathryn was concerned about communication in the store. Six department heads reported directly to her, and 50 full-time and part-time sales associates reported to

**18.** How do tendencies toward assertiveness and cooperativeness in conflict management result in win–lose, lose–lose, and win–win outcomes?

**19.** What is the difference between substance and relationship goals in negotiation?

them. Given this structure, Kathryn worried about staying informed about all store operations, not just those coming to her attention as senior manager. What steps might Kathryn take to establish and maintain an effective system of upward communication in this store?

---

## MANAGEMENT SKILLS AND COMPETENCIES

# Further Reflection: Communication and Networking

You might think that **communication and networking** are overdone or over-pitched as critical management and career skills. The reality is they aren't. Recruiters give them high priority when screening job candidates. Employers expect all employees, to communicate well both orally and in writing. They expect them to be capable of networking with others to find pathways for individual and team performance.

Communication and networking must be done well to build all-important social capital, the capacity to enlist the help and support of others when needed. Someone with communication and networking skills earns social capital that facilitates positive collaboration, even in conflict and negotiation situations.

 **DO IT NOW . . .
LOOK IN THE MIRROR**

- Can you convince a recruiter that you are ready to run effective meetings? . . . write informative reports? . . . deliver persuasive presentations? . . . conduct job interviews? . . . use e-mail and social media well? . . . keep conflicts constructive and negotiations positive? . . . network well with peers and mentors?

- Where does social capital rank on your list of personal strengths? Ask friends, co-workers, family to rate your communication and networking skills.

- Turn these ratings into a personal development "To Do" list you can share with your instructor.

# Self-Assessment: Conflict Management Strategies

## Instructions

Think of how you behave in conflict situations in which your wishes differ from those of others.[51] In the space to the left, rate each of the following statements on a scale of "1" = "not at all" to "5" = "very much." *When I have*

*a conflict at work, school, or in my personal life, I do the following:*

**1.** I give in to the wishes of the other party.

**2.** I try to realize a middle-of-the-road solution.

**3.** I push my own point of view.

**4.** I examine issues until I find a solution that really satisfies me and the other party.

**5.** I avoid a confrontation about our differences.

**6.** I concur with the other party.

**7.** I emphasize that we have to find a compromise solution.

**8.** I search for gains.

**9.** I stand for my own and the other's goals.

**10.** I avoid differences of opinion as much as possible.

**11.** I try to accommodate the other party.

**12.** I insist we both give in a little.

**13.** I fight for a good outcome for myself.

**14.** I examine ideas from both sides to find a mutually optimal solution.

**15.** I try to make differences seem less severe.

**16.** I adapt to the other party's goals and interests.

**17.** I strive whenever possible toward a 50–50 compromise.

**18.** I do everything to win.

**19.** I work out a solution that serves my own as well as other's interests as much as possible.

**20.** I try to avoid a confrontation with the other person.

## Scoring

Total your scores for items as follows.

Yielding tendency: 1 + 6 + 11 + 16 = _____.

Compromising tendency: 2 + 7 + 12 + 17 = _____.

Forcing tendency: 3 + 8 + 13 + 18 = _____.

Problem-solving tendency: 4 + 9 + 14 + 19 = _____.

Avoiding tendency: 5 + 10 + 15 + 20 = _____.

## Interpretation

Each of the scores above approximates one of the conflict management styles discussed in the chapter. Look back to Figure 18.4 and make the matchups. Although each style is part of management, only collaboration or problem solving leads to true conflict resolution. You should consider any patterns that may be evident in your scores and think about how to best handle the conflict situations in which you become involved.

---

# Team Exercise:
# Feedback Sensitivities

## Preparation

Indicate the degree of discomfort you would feel in each situation below by circling the appropriate number:[52]

**1.** high discomfort   **2.** some discomfort   **3.** undecided
**4.** very little discomfort   **5.** no discomfort

1 2 3 4 5    **1.** Telling an employee who is also a friend that she or he must stop coming to work late.

1 2 3 4 5    **2.** Talking to an employee about his or her performance on the job.

1 2 3 4 5    **3.** Asking an employee for comments about your rating of her or his performance.

1 2 3 4 5    **4.** Telling an employee who has problems in dealing with other employees that he or she should do something about it.

1 2 3 4 5    **5.** Responding to an employee who is upset over your rating of his or her performance.

1 2 3 4 5    **6.** Responding to an employee's becoming emotional and defensive when you tell her or him about mistakes on the job.

1 2 3 4 5    **7.** Giving a rating that indicates improvement is needed to an employee who has failed to meet minimum requirements of the job.

1 2 3 4 5    **8.** Letting a subordinate talk during an appraisal interview.

1 2 3 4 5    **9.** Having an employee challenge you to justify your evaluation during an appraisal interview.

1 2 3 4 5    **10.** Recommending that an employee be discharged.

1 2 3 4 5    **11.** Telling an employee that you are uncomfortable having to judge his or her performance.

1 2 3 4 5    **12.** Telling an employee that her or his performance can be improved.

1 2 3 4 5    **13.** Telling an employee that you will not tolerate his or her taking extended coffee breaks.

1 2 3 4 5    **14.** Telling an employee that you will not tolerate her or his making personal telephone calls on company time.

## Instructions

Form three-person teams as assigned by your instructor. Identify the three behaviors with which each person indicates the most discomfort. Then each team member should practice performing these behaviors with another member, while the third member acts as an observer. Be direct, but try to perform the behavior in an appropriate way. Listen to feedback from the observer and try the behaviors again, perhaps with different members of the group practicing each behavior. When finished, discuss the overall exercise.

# Career Situations in Communication and Collaboration: What Would You Do?

1. **Work vs. Family**   Your boss just sent a text message that he wants you at a meeting starting at 3 P.M. Your daughter is performing in a program at her elementary school at 2:45 P.M., and she wants you to attend. You're out of the office making sales calls and previously scheduled appointments to put you close to the school in the early afternoon. The office is a long way across town. Do you call him, text him, or send him an e-mail? What exactly will you say?

2. **Bearer of Bad News**   The restaurant you own is hit hard by a bad economy. Customer count is down. So is the average dinner bill. You have a staff of 12, but it's obvious that you have to cut back so that the payroll covers no more than 8. One of the servers has just told you that a regular customer is tweeting that the restaurant is going to close its doors after the weekend. The staff is "buzzing" about the news and customers are asking questions. How do you deal with this situation?

3. **Can't Get Along**   Two of your coworkers are constantly bickering. They just can't seem to get along, and it's starting to affect the rest of the team members—including you. As far as you can tell their bickering has something to do with a difference in wages. One has been there a long time while the other is relatively new. But, the newcomer earns more than the other. The other team members think it's time to approach the supervisor and try to resolve the problem, and they want you to do it. You're willing, but want to give the supervisor a suggested plan of action. What will it be?

# Case Study

# Facebook

Go to *Management Cases for Critical Thinking* to find the recommended case for Chapter 18—"Facebook: Making the World More Open."

# Management Cases for Critical Thinking

# Trader Joe's

## Keeping a Cool Edge

*The average Trader Joe's stocks only a small percentage of the products of local supermarkets in a space little larger than a corner store. How did this neighborhood market grow to earnings of $9 billion, garner superior ratings, and become a model of management? Take a walk down the aisles of Trader Joe's and learn how sharp attention to the fundamentals of retail management made this chain more than the average Joe.*

Ruaridh Stewart/Zuma Press

## From Corner Store to Foodie Mecca

In more than 365 stores across the United States, hundreds of thousands of customers are treasure hunting.[1] Driven by gourmet tastes but hungering for deals, they are led by cheerful guides in Hawaiian shirts who point them to culinary discoveries such as ahi jerky, ginger granola, and baked jalapeño cheese crunchies.

It's just an average day at Trader Joe's, the gourmet, specialty, and natural-foods store that offers staples such as milk and eggs along with curious, one-of-a-kind foods at below average prices in thirty-odd states.[2] With their plethora of kosher, vegan, and gluten-free fare, Trader Joe's has products to suit every dietary need.[3] Foodies, hipsters, and recessionistas alike are attracted to the chain's charming blend of low prices, tasty treats, and laid-back but enthusiastic customer service. Shopping at Trader Joe's is less a chore than it is immersion into another culture. In keeping with its whimsical faux-nautical theme, crew members and managers wear loud tropical-print shirts. Chalkboards around every corner unabashedly announce slogans such as, "You don't have to join a club, carry a card, or clip coupons to get a good deal."

"When you look at food retailers," says Richard George, professor of food marketing at St. Joseph's University, "there is the low end, the big middle, and then there is the cool edge—that's Trader Joe's."[4] But how does Trader Joe's compare with other stores with an edge, such as Whole Foods? Both obtain products locally and from all over the world. Each values employees and strives to offer the highest quality. However, there's no mistaking that Trader Joe's is cozy and intimate, whereas Whole Foods' spacious stores offer an abundance of choices. By limiting its stock and selling quality products at low prices, Trader Joe's sells twice as much per square foot than other supermarkets.[5] Most retail megamarkets, such as Whole Foods, carry between 25,000 and 45,000 products; Trader Joe's stores carry only 4,000.[6] But this scarcity benefits both Trader Joe's and its customers. According to Swarthmore professor Barry Schwartz, author of *The Paradox of Choice: Why Less Is More*, "Giving people too much choice can result in paralysis. . . .[R]esearch shows that the more options you offer, the less likely people are to choose any."[7]

David Rogers of DSR Marketing Systems expects other supermarkets to follow the Trader Joe's model toward a smaller store size. He cites several reasons, including excessive competitive floor space, development costs, and the aging population.[8]

Named by *Fast Company* as one of this year's 50 Most Influential Companies, Trader Joe's didn't always stand for brie and baguettes at peanut butter and jelly prices.[9] In 1958, the company began life in Los Angeles as a chain of 7-Eleven–style corner stores called Pronto Markets. Striving to differentiate his stores from those of his competitors in order to survive in a crowded marketplace, founder "Trader" Joe Coulombe, vacationing in the Caribbean, reasoned that consumers are more likely to try new things while on vacation. In 1967 the first Trader Joe's store opened in Pasadena. Mr. Coulombe had transformed his stores into oases of value by replacing humdrum sundries with exotic, one-of-a-kind foods priced persuasively below those of any reasonable competitor.[10] In 1979, he sold his chain to the Albrecht family, German billionaires and owners of an estimated 8,700 Aldi markets in the United States, Europe, and Australia.[11]

The Albrechts shared Coulombe's relentless pursuit of value, a trait inseparable from Trader Joe's success. Recent annual sales are estimated at $9 billion, landing Trader Joe's in the top third of *Supermarket News's* Top 75 Retailers.[12] Because it's not easy competing with such giants as Whole Foods and Dean & DeLuca, the company applies its pursuit of value to every facet of management. By keeping stores comparatively small—they average about 10–15,000 square feet—and shying away from prime locations, Trader Joe's keeps real estate costs down.[13] The chain prides itself on its thriftiness and cost-saving measures, proclaiming, "Every penny we save is a penny you save" and "Our CEO doesn't even have a secretary."[14,15]

## Trader Giotto, Trader José, Trader Ming, and Trader Darwin

Trader Joe's strongest weapon in the fight to keep costs low may also be its greatest appeal to customers: its stock. The company follows a deliciously simple approach to stocking stores: (1) search out tasty, unusual foods from all around the world; (2) contract directly with manufacturers; (3) label each product under one of several catchy house brands; and (4) maintain a small stock, making each product fight for its place on the shelf. This commonsense, low-overhead approach to retail serves Trader Joe's well, embodying its commitment to aggressive cost-cutting.

Most Trader Joe's products are sold under a variant of their house brand—dried pasta under the "Trader Giotto's" moniker, frozen enchiladas under the "Trader Jose's" label, vitamins under "Trader Darwin's," and so on. But these store brands don't sacrifice quality—readers of *Consumer Reports* awarded Trader Joe's house brands top marks.[16] The house brand success is no accident. According to Trader Joe's President Doug Rauch, "the company pursued the strategy to put our destiny in our own hands."[17]

But playing a role in this destiny is no easy feat. Ten to fifteen new products debut each week at Trader Joe's—and the company maintains a strict "one in, one out" policy. Items that sell poorly or whose costs rise get the heave-ho in favor of new blood, something the company calls the "gangway factor."[18] If the company hears that customers don't like something about a product, out it goes. In just such a move, Trader Joe's phased out single-ingredient products (such as spinach and garlic) from China. "Our customers have voiced their concerns about products from this region and we have listened," the company said in a statement, noting that items would be replaced with "products from other regions until our customers feel as confident as we do about the quality and safety of Chinese products."[19]

Conversely, discontinued items may be brought back if customers are vocal enough, making Trader Joe's the model of an open system. "We feel really close to our customers," says Audrey O'Connell, vice president of marketing for Trader Joe's East. "When we want to know what's on their minds, we don't need to put them in a sterile room with a swinging bulb. We like to think of Trader Joe's as an economic food democracy."[20] In return, customers keep talking, and they recruit new converts. Word-of-mouth advertising has lowered the corporation's advertising budget to approximately 0.2% of sales, a fraction of the 4% spent by supermarkets.[21]

## Customer Connection

Trader Joe's connects with its customers because of the culture of product knowledge and customer involvement that its management cultivates among store employees. Each employee is encouraged to taste and learn about the products and to engage customers to share what they've experienced. Most shoppers recall instances when helpful crew members took the time to locate or recommend particular items. Despite the lighthearted tone suggested by marketing materials and in-store ads, Trader Joe's aggressively courts friendly, customer-oriented employees by writing job descriptions highlighting desired soft skills ("ambitious and adventurous, enjoy smiling and have a strong sense of values") as much as actual retail experience.[22]

A responsible, knowledgeable, and friendly "crew" is critical to Trader Joe's success. Therefore, it nurtures its employees with a promote-from-within philosophy, and its employees earn more than their counterparts at other chain grocers. In California, Trader Joe's employees can earn almost 20% more than counterparts at supermarket giants Albertsons or Safeway.[23] Starting benefits include medical, dental, and vision insurance; company paid retirement; paid vacation; and a 10% employee discount.[24] Assistant store managers earn a compensation package averaging $94,000 a year, and store managers' packages average $132,000. One analyst estimates that a Wal-Mart store manager earning that much would need to run an outlet grossing six or seven times that of an average Trader Joe's.[25]

Outlet managers are highly compensated, partly because they know the Trader Joe's system inside and out (managers are hired only from within the company). Future leaders enroll in training programs such as Trader Joe's University that foster in them the loyalty necessary to run stores according to both company

and customer expectations, teaching managers to imbue their part-timers with the customer-focused attitude shoppers have come to expect.[26]

For all of its positive buzz, Trader Joe's narrowly avoided a boycott recently when it became embroiled in a controversy over its opposition to the Campaign for Fair Food, an initiative organized by the Coalition of Immokalee Workers (CIW) to push for better wages and working conditions in Florida's produce fields.[27] Trader Joe's insisted that it already followed the guidelines stipulated by the Fair Food campaign, but the CIW demanded increased transparency. Trader Joe's finally signed an agreement with the CIW in February 2012, mere days before the nationally organized boycott of its stores was scheduled to begin.[28]

If Trader Joe's has any puzzling trait, it's that the company is more than a bit media-shy. Executives have granted no interviews since the Aldi Group took over. Company statements and spokespersons have been known to be terse—the company's leases even stipulate that no store opening may be formally announced until a month before the outlet opens![29]

The future looks bright for Trader Joe's. In 2012, between 25–30 locations are slated to open, and the company continues to break into markets hungry for reasonably priced gourmet goodies. But will Trader Joe's struggle to sustain its international flavor in the face of rising fuel costs and shrinking discretionary income, or will the allure of cosmopolitan food at provincial prices continue to tempt consumers?

### Discussion Questions

**1.** In what ways does Trader Joe's demonstrate the importance of each responsibility in the management process—planning, organizing, leading, and controlling?

**2.** Trader Joe's is owned by a German company operating in America. What are the biggest risks that international ownership and global events pose for Trader Joe's performance effectiveness and performance efficiency?

### Problem Solving

At the age of 22 and newly graduated from college, Hazel has just accepted a job with Trader Joe's as a shift leader. She'll be supervising 4 team members who fill part-time jobs in the produce section. Given Trader Joe's casual and nontraditional work environment, what should she do and what should she avoid doing in the first few days of work to establish herself as a skillful manager of this team?

### Further Research

Study news reports to find more information on Trader Joe's management and organization practices. Look for comparisons with its competitors and try to identify whether or not Trader Joe's has the right management approach and business model for continued success. Are there any internal weaknesses or external competitors or industry forces that might cause future problems?

# Zara International

## Fashion at the Speed of Light

Gregory Wrona/Alamy

*At the announcement of her engagement to Spain's Crown Prince Felipe, Letizia Ortiz Rocasolano wore a chic white pantsuit. Within a few weeks, hundreds of European women sported the same look. Welcome to fast fashion, a trend that sees clothing retailers frequently purchasing small quantities of merchandise to stay on top of emerging trends. In this world of "hot today, gauche tomorrow," no company does fast fashion better than Zara International. Shoppers in 78 countries are fans of Zara's knack for bringing the latest styles from sketchbook to clothing rack at lightning speed and reasonable prices.[1]*

## In Fast Fashion, Moments Matter

Because style-savvy customers expect shorter and shorter delays from runway to store, Zara International employs a creative team of more than 200 professionals to help it keep up with the latest fashions.[2] It takes just two weeks for the company to update existing garments and get them into its stores; new pieces hit the market twice a week.

Defying the recession with its cheap-and-chic Zara clothing chain, Zara's parent company Inditex posted strong sales gains. Low prices and a rapid response to fashion trends are enabling it to challenge Gap, Inc., for top ranking among global clothing vendors. The improved results highlight how Zara's formula continues to work even in the downturn. The chain specializes in lightning-quick turnarounds of the latest designer trends at prices tailored to the young—about $27 an item.[3] Louis Vuitton fashion director Daniel Piette described Zara as "possibly the most innovative and devastating retailer in the world."[4]

Inditex Group shortens the time from order to arrival by utilizing a complex system of just-in-time production and inventory reporting that keeps Zara ahead. Their distribution centers can have items in European stores within 24 hours of receiving an order, and in American and Asian stores in under 48 hours.[5] "They're a fantastic case study in terms of how they manage to get product to their stores so quick," said Stacey Cartwright, executive vice-president and CFO of Burberry Group PLC. "We are mindful of their techniques."[6]

Inditex's history in fabrics manufacturing made it good business sense to internalize as many points in the supply chain as possible. Inditex controls design, production, distribution, and retail sales to optimize the flow of goods, without having to share profits with wholesalers or intermediary partners. Customers win by having access to new fashions while they're still fresh off the runway. During a Madonna concert tour in Spain, Zara's quick turnaround let young fans at the last show wear Madonna's outfit from the first one.[7]

Twice a week Zara's finished garments are shipped to logistical centers that all simultaneously distribute products to stores worldwide. These small production batches help the company avoid the risk of oversupply. Because batches always contain new products, Zara's stores perpetually energize their inventories.[8] Most clothing lines are not replenished. Instead they are replaced with new designs to create scarcity value—shoppers cannot be sure that designs in stores one day will be available the next.

Store managers track sales data with handheld computers. They can reorder hot items in less than an hour. This lets Zara know what's selling and what's not; when a look doesn't pan out, designers promptly put together new products. According to Dilip Patel, managing director for Inditex, new arrivals are rushed to store sales floors still on the black plastic hangers used in shipping. Shoppers who are in the know recognize these designs as the newest of the new; soon after, any items left over are rotated to Zara's standard wood hangers.[9]

Inside and out, Zara's stores are specially dressed to strengthen the brand. Inditex considers this to be of the greatest importance because that is where shoppers ultimately decide which fashions make the cut. In a faux shopping street in the basement of the company's headquarters, stylists craft and photograph eye-catching layouts that are e-mailed every two weeks to store managers for replication.[10]

Zara stores sit on some of the world's glitziest shopping streets—including New York's Fifth Avenue, near the flagship stores of leading international fashion brands—which make its reasonable prices stand out. "Inditex gives people the most up-to-date fashion at accessible prices, so it is a real alternative to high-end fashion lines," said Luca Solca, senior research analyst with Sanford C. Bernstein in London. That is good news for Zara as many shoppers trade down from higher priced chains.[11]

## Catfights on the Catwalk

Zara is not the only player in fast fashion. Competition is fierce, but Zara's overwhelming success (recent sales were over $16 billion) has the competition scrambling to keep up.[12] San Francisco-based Gap, Inc., which had been the largest independent clothing retailer by revenue until Zara bumped them to second place in 2009, posted a 21% decline in the first half of 2011 and has plans to close 700 stores by the end of 2013.[13] Only time will tell if super-chic Topshop's entry into the American market will make a wrinkle in Zara's success.

Some fashion analysts are referring to all of this as the democratization of fashion: bringing high(er) fashion to low(er) income shoppers. According to James Hurley, managing director and senior research analyst with New York-based Telsey Advisory Group LLC, big-box discount stores such as Target and Wal-Mart are emulating Zara's ability to study emerging fashions and knock out look-alikes in a matter of weeks. "In general," Hurley said, "the fashion cycle is becoming sharper and more immediately accessible."[14]

But making fashion more accessible can have its costs: Zara faced some controversy last year when Brazilian authorities discovered and shut down a São Paulo sweatshop run by AHA, one of Zara's contractors. Inditex denied knowledge of the working conditions, but it acknowledged that the conditions in the sweatshop ran counter to its code of conduct and compensated the affected workers.[15]

## A Single Fashion Culture

With a network of over 1,600 stores around the world, Zara International is Inditex's largest and most profitable brand, bringing home 77% of international sales and nearly 67% of revenues.[16] The first Zara outlet opened shop in 1975 in La Coruña.[17] It remained solely a Spanish chain until opening a store in Oporto, Portugal, in 1988. The brand reached the United States and France in 1989 and 1990 with outlets in New York and Paris, respectively.[18] Zara went into mainland China in 2001, India in 2009, and Japan, Jordan, Lebanon, Oman, Qatar, and Russia last year.[19]

Essential to Zara's growth and success are Inditex's 100-plus textile design, manufacturing, and distribution companies that employ more than 92,000 workers.[20,21] The Inditex group began in 1963 when Amancio Ortega Gaona, chairman and founder of Inditex, got his start in textile manufacturing.[22] After a period of growth, he assimilated Zara into a new holding company, Industria de Diseño Textil.[23] Inditex has a tried-and-true strategy for entering new markets: start with a handful of stores and gain a critical mass of customers. Generally, Zara is the first Inditex chain to break ground in new countries, paving the way for the group's other brands, including Pull and Bear, Massimo Dutti, and Bershka.[24]

Inditex farms out much of its garment production to specialist companies, located on the Iberian Peninsula, which it often supplies with its own fabrics. Although some pieces and fabrics are purchased in Asia—many of them not dyed or only partly finished—the company manufactures about half of its clothing in its hometown of La Coruña, Spain.[25]

H&M, one of Zara's top competitors, uses a slightly different strategy. Around one quarter of its stock is made up of fast-fashion items that are designed in-house and farmed out to independent factories. As at Zara, these items move quickly through the stores and are replaced often by fresh designs. But H&M also keeps a large inventory of basic, everyday items sourced from cheap Asian factories.[26]

Inditex CEO Pablo Isla believes in cutting expenses wherever and whenever possible. Zara spends just 0.3% of sales on ads, making the 3–4% typically spent by rivals seem excessive in comparison. Isla disdains markdowns and sales as well.[27]

Few can criticize the results of Isla's frugality: Inditex opened 358 new stores by the end of Q3 last year and was simultaneously named Retailer of the Year during the World Retailer Congress meeting.[28,29] Perhaps most important in an industry based on image, Inditex secured bragging rights as Europe's largest fashion retailer by overtaking H&M.[30] According to José Castellano, former deputy chairman of Inditex, the group plans to double in size in the coming years while making sales of more than $15 billion. He envisioned most of this growth taking place in Europe—especially in trend-savvy Italy.[31]

## Fashion of the Moment

Although Inditex's dominance of fast fashion seems virtually complete, it isn't without its challenges. For instance, keeping production so close to home becomes difficult when an increasing number of Zara stores are far-flung across the globe. "The efficiency of the supply chain is coming under more pressure the farther abroad they go," notes Nirmalya Kumar, a professor at London Business School.[32]

Inditex launched its Zara online store in the United States in the fall of 2011, offering free 2–3 day shipping and free returns in the model of uber-successful e-retailer Zappos.[33] A Zara application for the iPhone has been downloaded by more prospective clients in the United States than in any other market, according to chief executive Pablo Isla—more than a million iPhone users in just three months. Beginning in 2010, Zara rolled out its online store in sixteen European countries and plans to progressively add the remaining countries where Zara operates.[34]

Analysts worry that Inditex's rapid expansion may bring undue pressure to its business. The rising number of overseas stores, they warn, adds cost and complexity and is straining its operations. Inditex may no longer be able to manage everything from Spain. But Inditex isn't worried. By closely managing costs, Inditex says its current logistics system can handle its growth until 2012.[35]

José Luis Nueno of IESE, a business school in Barcelona, agrees that Zara is here to stay. Consumers have become more demanding and more arbitrary, he says—and fast fashion is better suited to these changes.[36] But is Zara International trying to expand too quickly? Do you think it will be able to introduce a new logistics system able to carry it into another decade of intense growth?

### Discussion Questions

1. In what ways are elements of the classical and behavioral management approaches evident in how things are done at Zara International?

2. How can systems concepts and the notion of contingency thinking explain the success of some of Zara's distinctive practices?

### Problem Solving

Zara states that its existing logistics system can handle the company's current pace of growth but will need updating soon. How could Zara employ the concept of evidence-based management to inform its next logistics system?

### Further Research

Gather the latest information on competitive trends in the apparel industry, and on Zara's latest actions and innovations. Is the firm continuing to do well? Is it adapting in ways needed to stay abreast of both its major competition and the pressures of a changing global economy? Is Inditex still providing worthy management benchmarks for other firms to follow?

# Patagonia

## Leading a Green Revolution

*How has Patagonia managed to stay both green and profitable at a time when the economy is down, consumers are tight for cash, and "doing the profitable thing" is not necessarily doing the right thing? Are Patagonia's business practices good for outdoor enthusiasts, good for the environment, or just good for Patagonia?*

KaiNedden/laif/Redux Pictures

Twelve hundred Wal-Mart buyers, a group legendary for their tough-as-nails negotiating tactics, sit in rapt attention in the company's Bentonville, AR, headquarters. They're listening to a small man in a mustard-yellow corduroy sportcoat lecture them on the environmental impact of Wal-Mart's purchasing choices.[1]

He's not criticizing the company, per se—*he's criticizing them.* Yet when he finishes speaking, the buyers leap to their feet and applaud enthusiastically.

Such is the authenticity of Yvon Chouinard. Since founding Patagonia in 1972, he's built it into one of the most successful outdoor clothing companies, and one that is steadfastly committed to environmental sustainability.

It's hard to discuss Patagonia without constantly referencing Chouinard, because for all practical purposes, the two are one. Where Chouinard ends, Patagonia begins. Chouinard breathes life into the company, espousing the outdoorsy athleticism of Patagonia's customers. In turn, Patagonia's business practices reflect Chouinard's insistence on minimizing environmental impact, even at the expense of the bottom line.

## Taking Risks to Succeed

For decades, Patagonia has been at the forefront of a cozy niche: high-quality, performance-oriented outdoor clothes and gear sold at top price points. Derided as *Pradagonia* or *Patagucci* by critics, the brand is aligned with top-shelf labels like North Face and Royal Robbins. Patagonia clothes are designed for fly fishermen, rock climbers, and surfers. They are durable, comfortable, and sustainably produced. And they are not cheap.

It seems counterintuitive, almost dangerous to market a $400 raincoat in a down economy. But the first thing you learn about Yvon Chouinard is that he's a risk taker. The second thing you learn is that he's usually right.

"Corporations are real weenies," he says. "They are scared to death of everything. My company exists, basically, to take those risks and prove that it's a good business."[2]

And it is a good business. With estimated 2011 revenues of $400 million, up from $333 million last year, Patagonia succeeds by staying true to Chouinard's vision.[3] "They've become the Rolls-Royce of their product category," says Marshal Cohen, chief industry analyst with market research firm NPD Group. "When people were stepping back, and the industry became copycat, Chouinard didn't sell out, lower prices, and dilute the brand. Sometimes, the less you do, the more provocative and true of a leader you are."[4]

Chouinard concurs. "I think the key to surviving a conservative economy is quality," he says. "The number one reason is

that in a recession, consumers stop being silly. Instead of buying fashion, they'll pay more for a multifunctional product that will last a long time."[5]

## Ideal Corporate Behavior

Chouinard is not shy about espousing the environmentalist ideals intertwined with Patagonia's business model. "It's good business to make a great product, and do it with the least amount of damage to the planet," he says. "If Patagonia wasn't profitable or successful, we'd be an environmental organization."[6]

In many ways, Patagonia is an environmental organization. The company publishes online a library of working documents, *The Footprint Chronicles,* that guides employees in making sustainable decisions in even the most mundane office scenarios. Its mission statement: "Build the best product, cause no unnecessary harm, use business to inspire and implement solutions to the environmental crisis." Patagonia is revamping *Footprints* for a May 2012 rerelease and will include a world map that shows where all of Patagonia's products are made, profiles of the social and environmental practices of key suppliers and mills, and profiles of key independent partners.[7]

Patagonia's solutions extend well beyond the lip service typically given by profitable corporations. The company itself holds an annual environmental campaign, this year's being *Our Common Waters.*[8]

Chouinard has cofounded a number of external environmental organizations, including 1% For the Planet, which secures pledges from companies to donate 1% of annual sales to a worldwide network of nearly 2,400 environmental causes. To date, almost 1,480 companies participate, raising more than $50 million since 2002.[9]

The name comes from Patagonia's thirty-year practice of contributing 10% of pre-tax profits or 1% of sales—whichever is *greater*—to environmental groups each year. Whatever you do, don't call it a handout. "It's not a charity," Chouinard flatly states. "It's a cost of doing business. We use it to support civil democracy."[10]

Another core value at Patagonia is providing opportunities for motivated volunteers to devote themselves to sustainable causes. Employees can leave their jobs for up to two months to volunteer full-time for the environmental cause of their choice, while continuing to receive full pay and benefits from Patagonia.[11] And every eighteen months, the company hosts the Tools for Grassroots Activists Conference, where it invites a handful of participants to engage in leadership training, much of it derived from the advocacy experiences of Patagonia management.[12] Patagonia of Japan team members also contributed to cleanup efforts following the devastating March 2011 earthquake and subsequent tsunami.[13]

## Growing Green

Patagonia has demonstrated a remarkable ability to thrive even despite the unplanned obsolescence of several of its key products. What makes this even more notable is that Chouinard is often the force driving his own best sellers out of the marketplace.

Chouinard Equipment, Ltd., Patagonia's precursor, was a successful vendor in America's nascent rock climbing community. Chouinard himself was well known on the circuit, having made the first successful climbs of several previously unconquered Californian peaks. For more than a decade, Chouinard had been hand forging his own steel pitons (pegs driven into rock or ice to support climbers) that were far more durable than the soft iron pitons coming from Europe. Because his pitons could be used again and again, climbing was suddenly more affordable and less of a fringe activity.

But during a 1970 ascent of El Capitan, Chouinard saw that the very invention that brought his company success was also irreparably damaging the wilderness he so loved. Though Chouinard Equipment's pitons brought more climbers into the sport, the climbers tended to follow the same routes. And the constant hammering and removal of steel pitons was scarring the delicate rock face of these peaks.

Ignoring the fact that pitons were a mainstay of their success, Chouinard and partner Tom Frost decided to phase themselves out of the piton business. Two years later, the company coupled a new product—aluminum chocks that could be inserted or removed by hand—with a fourteen-page essay in their catalog on the virtues of *clean climbing*. A few months later, demand for pitons had withered and orders for chocks outstripped supplies.[14]

Fast forward nearly twenty years. Chouinard Equipment spinoff Patagonia is a booming manufacturer of outdoor clothing. And though they'd seen success with products woven with synthetic threads, the majority of their items were still spun with natural fibers like cotton and wool. Patagonia commissioned an external audit of the environmental impact of their four major fibers, anticipating bad news about petroleum-derived nylon and polyester.

Instead, they were shocked to learn that the production of cotton, a mainstay of the American textile market for hundreds of years, had a more negative impact on the environment than any of their other fibers. The evidence was clear: destructive soil and water pollution, unproven but apparent health consequences for fieldworkers, and the astounding statistic that 25% of all toxic pesticides used in agriculture are spent in the cultivation of cotton.

To Chouinard and Patagonia, the appropriate response was equally clear: Source organic fibers for all sixty-six of their cotton clothing products. They gave themselves until 1996 to complete the transition, which was a manageable lead time of eighteen months.

But due to the advance nature of fashion production, they had only four months to lock in fabric suppliers. Worse, at the time, there wasn't enough organic cotton being commercially produced to fill their anticipated fabric needs.

Taking a page from their own teaching on grassroots advocacy, Patagonia representatives went directly to organic cotton farmers, ginners, and spinners, seeking pledges from them to increase production, dust off dormant processing equipment, and do whatever it would take to line up enough raw materials to fulfill the company's promise to its customers and the environment.

Not surprisingly, Patagonia met its goal, and every cotton garment made since 1996 has been spun from organic cotton.

## Sustaining Momentum

At 73, Chouinard can't helm Patagonia forever. But that's not to say he isn't continuing to find better ways for Patagonia to do business.

"I think entrepreneurs are like juvenile delinquents who say, 'This sucks. I'll do it my own way,'" he says. "I'm an innovator because I see things and think I can make it better. So I try it. That's what entrepreneurs do."[15]

Patagonia's current major project is their Common Threads initiative. To demonstrate that it's possible to minimize the number of Patagonia clothes that wind up in landfills, the company is committing to making clothes built to last, fixing wear-and-tear items for consumers that can be repaired, and collecting and recycling worn-out fashions as efficiently and responsibly as possible.[16]

"It'll be in the front of the catalog—our promise that none of our stuff ever ends up in a landfill," Chouinard says. "We'll make sure of it with a liberal repair policy and by accepting old clothing for recycling. People will talk about it, and we'll gain business like crazy."[17]

It's doubtful that Chouinard will ever stop thinking about how Patagonia can responsibly innovate and improve. "Right now, we're trying to convince zipper companies to make teeth out of polyester or nylon synths, which can be recycled infinitely," he says. "Then we can take a jacket and melt the whole thing down back to its original polymer to make more jackets."[18]

Despite his boundless enthusiasm for all things green, Chouinard admits that no process is truly sustainable. "I avoid using that word as much as I can," he says. He pauses for a moment and adds: "I keep at it, because it's the right thing to do."[19]

---

### Discussion Questions

1. Patagonia has a history of putting sustainability ahead of profits. Based on what you learned about Patagonia's ideals, how do you think the company determines what possible ventures will be both business practical and environmentally friendly?

2. What could Patagonia do today to make sure that Yvon Chouinard's ideals become a permanent part of the company's culture after he leaves the company?

### Problem Solving

It seems Yvon Chouinard is never satisfied. He comes to you and asks for a proposal on a new—"forward looking"—sustainability agenda for the firm. What would you include in this agenda to stretch the firm beyond what it is already doing, and why?

### Further Research

Business decisions can be a compromise between ethics and profitability. Could ethics lose out to greed even in a company with the idealism of Patagonia? See if you can find a decision that appeared to or could put profits ahead of the company's publicly stated environmental goals. Explain why you think that company made this decision and the competing factors you believe were involved.

 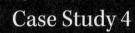 

# Timberland

## From Bootmaker to Earthkeeper

*An iconic American brand for sixty years, Timberland has built a reputation for creating simple, durable footwear and outdoor accessories. And guided by the moral compass of its most recent CEO, the company has developed a reputation as a leader in environmental stewardship. But will the company's recent sale to a clothing conglomerate change that?*

RICHARD B. LEVINE/NewsCom

A New Englander to the bone, Jeffrey Swartz is a straight-talking man.

So when you ask him how he feels about the recent sale of Timberland, the outdoor shoe and apparel company founded by his grandfather and formerly run by his father, to clothing giant VF Corporation, you expect a characteristically honest answer.

"It's a magnificent day and a bittersweet day," he said, "but the shareholders had to be our only concern."[1]

Natural, unpracticed humility is an uncommon trait of CEOs. But during his fourteen-year stint running Timberland, Swartz made a successful career of putting the interests of consumers, partners, and virtually everyone on planet Earth ahead of his own, even in his last days at the family business.

As business writer Marc Gunther notes, "It's interesting—and very much in character—that as part of the acquisition, Jeff didn't negotiate a contract for himself to stay on at Timberland, either as CEO or as an adviser. Executives of companies that are being sold often do that, but they are, in effect, using the leverage they have during a negotiation to take care of themselves, potentially at the expense of other shareholders."[2]

Unsurprisingly, Swartz is demure about this too. "[Staying on after a merger] is standard procedure," Swartz said. But, he continued, "I need to live by a higher standard than standard procedure. I didn't want there to be any appearance of self-dealing."[3]

And while Swartz can be confident that he left his family's sixty-year-old company on high moral standing, he has to wonder about Timberland's future. When VF Corporation acquired Timberland in the summer of 2011 for $2.3 billion, an outdoors brand that had made its name by charting a confidently independent path became just another holding of one of the world's largest clothing companies, whose stable of nearly two-dozen brands includes The North Face, Nautica, and Vans.[4]

### Boot, Brand, Belief

Timberland describes its eras of evolution in terms of "Boot, Brand, Belief." *Boot* depicts Timberland's roots as the Abington Shoe Company, purchased by Jeffrey Swartz's grandfather, Nathan, partially in 1952 and then fully in 1955. For decades, the company specialized in tough-as-nails boots, only branching out to shoemaking in 1979. When he took over in 1986, Sidney Swartz

(Nathan's son and Jeffrey's father) extended the Timberland *Brand* internationally and added clothing, accessories, and women's and children's shoes to the product lineup. And when Jeffrey assumed the post of CEO in 1998, he inoculated the family business with his *Belief* in social justice, environmental sustainability, and corporate social responsibility.[5]

And while Nathan's "do one thing and do it right" focus and Sidney's years of continuous corporate growth built a robust company to inherit, Jeffrey's deep moral convictions have come to define Timberland among outdoor brands perhaps more than any of its products.

"If I think there's a big gap between belief and execution in corporate governance," Jeffrey once said, "I also think there's a big gap in what I espouse and how I live. And I investigate both gaps daily." To do that in terms of a business, he noted, involved asking the right questions. "As always, the decisions aren't hard—the questions are hard. If you have the right questions, and you have the right people that care—and we do have bright, caring people—you will almost always get a right answer."[6]

Timberland's emphasis on social responsibility began as early as 1989, when it partnered with Boston's City Year, an "urban Peace Corps," to promote community service. But it took declining profits and a stagnant economy to inspire Timberland to forge its current identity as a protector of the earth.

"About four years ago, the winds shifted against us," said Mike Harrison, Timberland's chief brand officer. "We really had to dig deep and figure out how to create demand. In doing that, we reached back to what the brand had always stood for. We went back to what we're known for, which was an authentic outdoor brand with a very strong heritage of social responsibility and environmental sustainability. So, out of necessity, we made a decision to refocus on our strengths."[7]

That refocusing ultimately spawned Timberland's Earthkeeping campaign. Defined as "taking actions that enable us to be good stewards of the earth," Earthkeeping is a tidy encapsulation of the environmental virtues that Timberland has both espoused and lived in recent years. While it is hip for companies to adopt a green posture, perhaps no other American company in recent memory has so deeply committed itself to sustainable and environmentally and socially conscious business practices.

Guided by the moral compass of Jeffrey Swartz, Timberland shows its commitment to Earthkeeping in several key areas:

**Production.** Like an increasing number of apparel companies, Timberland found that using partially or wholly recycled materials can be just as cost-effective as using virgin components. Many of Timberland's boots now bear Green Rubber soles, which are made from nearly 50% recycled materials. Other footwear components are produced from recycled PET bottles, by which Timberland hopes to offset some of the 2,500,000 plastic bottles used by Americans every hour.[8] The company also participates in environmentally focused working groups such as the Outdoor Industry Association and the Sustainable Apparel Coalition.

**Retail.** From Boston, Massachusetts, to Milan, Italy, Timberland retail stores use reclaimed materials, such as industrial machine base tables, nineteenth-century window shutters, and a 1930s wooden wardrobe from Oxford University, to display shoes and garments.[9] Even the stone and wooden flooring in many Timberland stores is reclaimed from original sources.[10] And a recent store retrofit replaced the incandescent spotlights in nearly all North American stores with LED spotlights, saving approximately $170,000 in one year and reducing the carbon emissions produced by Timberland's retail stores by more than 15%.[11]

**Community Service.** Timberland gives every employee forty paid hours each year to volunteer in their community and sponsors two annual company-wide service events—one coinciding with Earth Day (April 22) and Serv-a-palooza, a worldwide service effort marked by participation from Timberland's employees and partners.

**Manufacturing Partners.** Timberland products are made in thirty-eight different countries by roughly 247,000 craftspeople working in more than 300 factories.[12] And because environmental standards are still evolving in many of these countries, these areas may be at greater risk from pollution and erosion. So Timberland assists its manufacturing partners in improving the land, water, and air near their plants and tanneries, resulting in the planting of more than one million trees in the last ten years, including 300,000 fruit trees in Haiti.[13]

"The news in the world today shows us if you can make a good green product then people will want it," said John Healy, general manager of Timberland's Invention Factory.[14]

And that's been a sound strategy for Timberland. Sales are strong, with the company providing $549 million to VF's $2.9 billion of revenue in the most recent quarter.[15] But it's fair to say that everyone—from Timberland's employees to its manufacturing partners to even Jeffrey Swartz—has to wonder what, if anything, will change in the years to come following Timberland's acquisition by VF. As Swartz said in the days preceding his departure, "When you change the signature in the bottom-right corner of the paycheck, that means they will get to make decisions that I now get to make."[16]

For now, Timberland remains ever focused on doing business the only way it knows how. "Business success, for us, is defined not only by the return we earn for our shareholders but also by the positive impact we have on our communities and the environment," said Betsy Blaisdell, Timberland's senior manager of environmental stewardship. "Bottom-line results are obviously critical—if we cease to be profitable, we cease to exist—but if we earn them at the expense of our values and commitment to be a responsible corporate citizen, we've failed."[17]

And what will become of Jeffrey Swartz, the former CEO whose deep moral convictions inspired Timberland's current stance in the marketplace? He's not saying for now, but it should be noted that the noncompete clause he signed does not limit him from "noncommercial activity, either by himself or with, for, or on behalf of any other person or entity, including, without limitation, any corporate social responsibility activity or charitable or philanthropic activity."[18]

"I hope this deal will help show the critics and the skeptics and even the cynics that they're wrong when they say our strategy can't work," Swartz said shortly before his departure. "You can run a for-profit business and be mindful of basic human rights and your environmental impact. You can run a for-profit business in a way you'd be proud to tell your children about and face your God about."[19]

---

### Discussion Questions

1. Who would Timberland identify as its stakeholders? Does its stakeholder map contain stakeholders that aren't on the maps of other apparel companies?

2. What competitive advantages does Timberland's focus on environmental sustainability offer the company? List three examples.

### Problem Solving

Like many other American manufacturers, Timberland is heavily reliant on offshore production facilities. Be a global supply chain consultant. How would you describe the environmental uncertainty Timberland exposes itself to by sending work overseas? What might you suggest as ways to manage supply chain risks to the firm's profits with principles strategy?

### Further Research

Timberland's acquisition by VF Corporation puts the company at a pivotal point in its history. Research other apparel companies held by VF as well as the corporation itself. Describe how you believe Timberland's emphasis on Earthkeeping will help or hinder its integration into the VF family of brands.

# Harley-Davidson

## Style and Strategy Have Global Reach

*Harley-Davidson recently celebrated a century in business with a year-long International Road Tour. The party culminated in the company's hometown, Milwaukee.[1] Harley is a true American success story. Once near death in the face of global competition, Harley reestablished itself as the dominant maker of big bikes in the United States. However, as a weak economy tightened credit lending, consumers shied away from the purchase of luxury items, including Harley's high-end heavyweight motorcycles. Can a relatively new CEO with a revised vision help Harley-Davidson weather the economic storm?*

NIR ELIAS/Reuters/Landov LLC

### Harley-Davidson's Roots

When Harley-Davidson was founded in 1903, it was one of more than 100 firms producing motorcycles in the United States. The U.S. government became an important customer for the company's high-powered, reliable bikes, using them in both world wars. By the 1950s, Harley-Davidson was the only remaining American manufacturer.[2] But by then British competitors were entering the market with faster, lighter-weight bikes. And Honda Motor Company of Japan began marketing lightweight bikes in the United States, moving into middleweight vehicles in the 1960s. Harley initially tried to compete by manufacturing smaller bikes but had difficulty making them profitably. The company even purchased an Italian motorcycle firm, Aermacchi, but many of its dealers were reluctant to sell the small Aermacchi Harleys.[3]

### Consolidation and Renewal

American Machine and Foundry Co. (AMF) took over Harley in 1969, expanding its portfolio of recreational products. AMF increased production from 14,000 to 50,000 bikes per year. This rapid expansion led to significant problems with quality, and better-built Japanese motorcycles began to take over the market. Harley's share of its major U.S. market—heavyweight motorcycles—was only 23%.[4] A group of 13 managers bought Harley-Davidson back from AMF in 1981 and began to turn the company around with the rallying cry "The Eagle Soars Alone." As Richard Teerlink, former CEO of Harley, explained, "The solution was to get back to detail. The key was to know the business, know the customer, and pay attention to detail."[5] The key elements in this process were increasing quality and improving service to customers and dealers. Management kept the classic Harley style and focused on the company's traditional strength—heavyweight and super heavyweight bikes.

In 1983, the Harley Owners Group (H.O.G.) was formed; H.O.G. membership now exceeds 1 million members, and there are 1,400 chapters worldwide.[6,7] Also in 1983, Harley-Davidson asked the International Trade Commission (ITC) for tariff relief on the basis that Japanese manufacturers were stockpiling inventory in the United States and providing unfair competition. The request was granted, and a tariff relief for five years was placed

on all imported Japanese motorcycles that were 700 cc or larger. By 1987, Harley was confident enough to petition the ITC to have the tariff lifted because the company had improved its ability to compete with foreign imports. Once Harley's image had been restored, the company began to increase production.[8] The firm opened new facilities in Franklin, Milwaukee, and Menomonee Falls, Wisconsin; Kansas City, Missouri; and York, Pennsylvania; and opened a new assembly plant in Manaus, Brazil.[9]

In the 1980s, the average Harley purchaser was in his late thirties, with an average household income of over $40,000. Teerlink didn't like the description of his customers as "aging" Baby Boomers: "Our customers want the sense of adventure that they get on our bikes. . . . Harley-Davidson doesn't sell transportation, we sell transformation. We sell excitement, a way of life."[10] However, the average age and income of Harley riders has continued to increase. Recently, the median age of a Harley rider was 49, and the median income exceeded $87,000.[11] The company also created a line of Harley accessories available online, by catalog, or through dealers, all adorned with the Harley-Davidson logo. These jackets, caps, t-shirts, and other items became popular with non-bikers as well. In fact, the clothing and parts had a higher profit margin than the motorcycles; non-bike products made up as much as half of sales at some dealerships.

### International Efforts

Although the company had been exporting motorcycles ever since it was founded, it was not until the late 1980s that Harley-Davidson management began to think seriously about international markets. Traditionally, the company's ads had been translated word for word into foreign languages. New ads were developed specifically for different markets, and rallies were adapted to fit local customs.[12] The company also began to actively recruit and develop dealers in Europe and Japan. It purchased a Japanese distribution company and built a large parts warehouse in Germany. Harley learned a great deal from its international activities. Recognizing, for example, that German motorcyclists rode at high speeds–often more than 100 mph—the company began studying ways to give Harleys a smoother ride and emphasizing accessories that would give riders more protection.[13]

Harley continues to make inroads in overseas markets. At one time, it had 30% of the worldwide market for heavyweight motorcycles—chrome-laden cruisers, aerodynamic rocket bikes mostly produced by the Japanese, and oversize touring motorcycles. In Europe, Harley ranked third, with only 10.7% of the market share behind Honda and Suzuki.[14] However, in the Asia/Pacific market, where one would expect Japanese bikes to dominate, Harley had the largest market shares in the early part of the decade. Harley had 21.3% of the market share, compared to 19.2% for Honda.[15]

Harley motorcycles are among America's fastest-growing exports to Japan. Harley's Japanese subsidiary adapted the company's marketing approach to Japanese tastes, even producing shinier and more complete tool kits than those available in the United States. Harley bikes have long been considered symbols of prestige in Japan; many Japanese enthusiasts see themselves as rebels on wheels.[16]

The company has also made inroads into the previously elusive Chinese market, with the first official Chinese Harley-Davidson dealership opening its doors just outside downtown Beijing. To break into this emerging market, Harley partnered with China's Zongshen Motorcycle Group, which makes more than 4 million small-engine motorcycles each year.[17] Like other Harley stores, the Chinese outlet stocks bikes, parts and accessories, and branded merchandise, and offers post-sales service. Despite China's growing disposable income, the new store has several hurdles ahead of it, including riding restrictions imposed by the government in urban areas.

## The Future

Although its international sales have grown, the domestic market still represents almost 75% of Harley's sales.[18] Given the climbing price of gas, Harley is uniquely positioned to take advantage of this economic factor. Many riders report in-town fuel consumption rates in excess of 50 miles per gallon.[19] Analyst Todd Sullivan notes, "I know plenty of F150, Suburban, and Silverado drivers who ride Harleys. They are doubling or even tripling their gas mileage and savings by making the switch."[20] Executives attribute Harley's success to loyal customers and the Harley-Davidson name. "It is a unique brand that is built on personal relationship and deep connections with customers, unmatched riding experiences, and proud history," said Jim Ziemer, Harley's former president and chief executive.[21]

However, Harley-Davidson has been in a fight not just with its competitors, but also with the recession and a sharp consumer spending slowdown, with the aging of its customer base, and with a credit crisis that has made it difficult for both the motorcycle maker and its loyal riders to get financing.[22] For the first time in 16 years, the company posted a loss—$218.7 million in the fourth quarter of 2009. As part of the strategy put into place by CEO Keith E. Wandell, the company has laid off workers, closed factories, and begun selling brands. In early 2010 Harley discontinued its Buell product line and divested its MV Agusta unit. Considering all that turmoil and transition, some loyalists felt they had been taken for a ride when Wandell received a $6.4 million pay package during his first eight months on the job.[23]

Wandell's compensation may be justified, however, if he's successful in his plan to drive growth through a single-minded focus of efforts and resources on the unique strengths of the Harley-Davidson brand, and to enhance productivity and profitability through continuous improvement. Part of his approach focuses company resources on Harley-Davidson products and experiences, global expansion, demographic outreach, and commitment to core customers.[24] Through Harley's demographic outreach, Garage Party Events have been developed specifically for women—creating an intimidation-free zone where female riders can connect with one another. Harley-Davidson's global expansion into the fast-growing luxury market in India may help offset tough times at home.[25]

Since the beginning of the Great Recession, Harley has managed to work its way back to profitability. After earning just $70.6 million in 2009, the company took in $259.7 million in 2010 and a breathtaking $548.1 million in 2011.[26] This is due in part to improved motorcycle sales: In 2011, the company saw its first domestic sales increase since 2006 and sold 10.9 percent more units in the U.S. compared to 2010.[27] Sales were also up in foreign markets, where Harley sold 11.8 percent more bikes than in 2010.[28] The company also claims to have saved $217 million due to the company restructuring that began in 2009 under Wandell.

Having survived the Great Depression, only time and customers' wallets will determine whether Harley-Davidson will make it through the Great Recession.

## Discussion Questions

1. If you were CEO of Harley-Davidson, how would you compare the advantages and disadvantages of using exports, joint ventures, and foreign subsidiaries as ways of expanding international sales?

2. In America and Japan, Harley has shifted the positioning of its products away from simply motorcycles and more toward being status symbols of a particular way of life. Can this positioning succeed in Asia, Africa, and South America? Why or why not?

## Problem Solving

Assume the CEO of Harley has decided to set up new manufacturing facilities in both China and India. Which of the general environment conditions should be analyzed before Harley makes strategic investments in each country? Should Harley set up wholly owned subsidiaries to do the manufacturing, or would it be better off entering into joint ventures with local partners?

## Further Research

Is it accurate to say that Harley is still "on top of its game"? How well is the company performing today in both domestic and global markets? Who are its top competitors in other parts of the world, and how is Harley faring against them?

# In-N-Out Burger

## Building a Better Burger

E.J. Baumeister Jr./Alamy

*At face value, In-N-Out Burger seems like a modest enterprise—only four food items on the menu, little to no advertising. So how has this West Coast chain achieved near-cult status among regular joes and foodies alike? For more than sixty years, In-N-Out has focused on providing customers the basics—fresh, well-cooked food served quickly in a sparkling clean environment—and has made consistency and quality their hallmarks.*

Gordon Ramsay is not an easy man to satisfy. The celebrity chef and star of Hell's Kitchen is well known for his culinary prowess, perfectionism, and earth-shaking, profanity-strewn tantrums. He is one of only four chefs in England to maintain a rating of three Michelin Stars for his restaurant. And he is infamous for finding fault with simple and extravagant dishes alike.

So it came as a shock to more than a few foodies when Ramsay revealed his affinity for the best kept open secret in West Coast fast food.

"In-N-Out burgers [are] extraordinary," Ramsay admits, recounting a recent visit. "I was so bad: I sat in the restaurant, had my double cheeseburger, then minutes later I drove back round and got the same thing again."[1]

Walk into any of the more than Two hundred seventy-five In-N-Out Burger locations, and you'll only find four food items on the menu: Hamburger, Cheeseburger, Double-Double, and French Fries. You can wash those down with a Coke or a milkshake. In addition, there's . . . nothing else. That's the entire menu.

Or so In-N-Out would have you think.

Stand next to the ordering counter long enough, and you'll hear customers recite a litany of curious requests. None are on the menu, but sure enough, the cashier rings each one up with a smile: Animal Style (a mustard-cooked patty with extra pickles, extra spread, and grilled onions), Flying Dutchman (two patties, two slices of cheese, no bun or garnish), Protein Style (heavy on the fixings, wrapped in lettuce instead of a bun), or any permutation of patties and cheese slices up to a 4 × 4 (four patties and four slices of cheese barely contained in one bun).

It's as if you've gone through the looking glass, and the menu is not what it seems. But the open secret of the secret menu is only part of what keeps customers coming back for more.

## A Simple Formula for Success

In-N-Out's motto is straightforward: "Give customers the freshest, highest quality foods you can buy and provide them with friendly service in a sparkling clean environment." And so is the chain's formula for success—it only makes a few food items, it consis-

tently makes them well, and it earns the trust of its customers by not deviating from this premise.

Customers aren't the only ones to notice In-N-Out's fastidious focus on quality. In a recent survey of fifty-three fast food restaurants, several thousand *Consumer Reports* readers ranked In-N-Out #1 with regards to the best food, service, and value to customers.[2]

In addition to making the best burgers around, In-N-Out's other primary successful trait is its insistence on playing by its own rules. A fierce entrepreneurial streak ran through the Snyders, In-N-Out's founding family, and from the sock-hop décor to the secret menu to its treatment of employees as long-term partners instead of disposable resources, the chain prefers to focus on its formula for success instead of conventional definitions like shareholder return or IPOs.

The funny thing is, it works. Unwilling to grow at a speed that would sacrifice quality or consistency of the customer experience, In-N-Out has resisted going public or franchising. Yet—or maybe, because of this—they handily beat rivals Burger King and McDonald's in per-store sales.[3]

## All in the Family

Harry Snyder and his wife Esther opened the first In-N-Out Burger in Baldwin Park, CA, in 1948. Unlike other carhop-oriented fast food restaurants of the era, Harry installed a two-way speaker through which drivers could order without leaving their car, thus creating California's first drive-thru hamburger stand. Harry brought sons Rich and Guy to work at an early age, where the boys learned their father's insistence on complementing fresh, promptly cooked food with great customer service.

The Snyder's second restaurant opened three years later, and franchising continued slowly until 1976, when Rich took over after his father's death. At that time, In-N-Out managed eighteen locations throughout California.

Though he was only twenty-four when he became CEO, Rich Snyder had big plans for In-N-Out. The next seventeen years would see Rich expand In-N-Out into new cities but still maintain exacting control over the quality of both ingredients and employees.

Harry and Rich understood that you can't truthfully attest to the quality of your ingredients unless you've inspected them yourself. So with the help of younger brother Guy, one of Rich's first projects was to build a commissary in Baldwin Park, CA, where all In-N-Out's ingredients are inspected for quality and prepared for distribution to their stores. The commissary location in part explains why In-N-Out restaurants are clustered in the American Southwest: establishing locations longer than one day's drive from the commissary is "not even negotiable," executive Carl Van Fleet told the Orange County Register in 2006, as doing so would require longer delivery runs or additional processing hubs, both of which could reduce quality control. (Yet a few years later, In-N-Out caved to consumer demand and built a second patty plant in Dallas, TX, to support their inevitable expansion into the Lone Star state, which now totals fifteen locations.)[4]

Unlike Harry, who hoped employees would transfer skills learned at In-N-Out to a "better" job, Rich thought differently: "Why let good people move on when you can use them to help your company grow?"[5] Knowing that his expansion plans would require a pool of talented and loyal store managers, Rich opened In-N-Out University in 1984. Store associates had to please hungry diners, show initiative, and exhibit strong decision-making skills for at least one year before being invited to attend the management training program. Reasoning that the same high-tech tools for performance analysis employed by pro sports teams could also improve his team, Rich videotaped trainees to analyze their performance and produced training films.[6]

## The Best Advertising Is Free

Whether by preference or accident, In-N-Out's infrequent forays into paid advertising are oblique at best—with radio ads that simply tout, "In-N-Out, In-N-Out. That's what a hamburger's all about", and holiday ads that explain the meaning of the holidays instead of the weekly specials.

You're more likely to see a simple visual ad for In-N-Out. Like other stores in the early days of roadside diners, the company placed locations along interstate off ramps, relying on their yellow boomerang logo and plain billboards reading, "In-N-Out Burger 2.5 Miles Ahead" to draw customers.[7]

For years they gave customers free bumper stickers with the company's name, thousands of which were modified by rabid fans to say, "In-N-Out urge." Stores have also sold clothing bearing the company logo.[8] In-N-Out customers tend to be deeply polarized—you either think their food is OK or you can't get enough. And because fans have been more than willing to do most of the

company's promotion for it, its marketing formula could be paraphrased as, "Our fans are our billboards."

Because the company has long been press and advertising shy, and because their burgers aren't available in most of the U.S., In-N-Out has cultivated a considerable mystique around ultimately simple products.

William Martin, who composed In-N-Out University's training regimen, says that during his time with the company, the Snyders and other top brass were definitely conscious of the magic surrounding their brand. "They were all aware of it, and they loved it," he says. "But they had no explanation for it."[9]

In an era of celebrity chefs and high-tech cuisine, In-N-Out Burger draws rave reviews for making only a handful of items with great attention to quality. How did this family-owned burger chain with roadside diner roots inspire such a passionate following?

---

### Discussion Questions

1. Rich Snyder was twenty-four years old when his father passed away and he assumed leadership of In-N-Out. Was his young age an asset or a liability for leadership of the company? Explain your answer. Take a position: Does age really matter in the first place?

2. In an era of jalapeño poppers and extreme fajitas, how risky is In-N-Out's long-term strategy of offering only four simple food items? Is the strategy still on track?

### Problem Solving

A would-be entrepreneur walks into your bank and asks to receive financing for a business plan modeled after In-N-Out's approach and extremely simple menu. But all the ingredients would come from local suppliers and growers within a thirty-mile radius of town. Is this a winning recipe deserving of financing from your bank?

### Further Research

Imagine you were asked by In-N-Out Burger to modernize its advertising mix while maintaining the modesty and simplicity that's characterized its brand for over sixty years. Do research on the current industry and social trends, and consumer values and tastes. Craft an advertising concept that fits the scene and speaks to In-N-Out's core values: quality, consistency, friendliness, and cleanliness. How would you illustrate this concept to consumers? Explain why you would choose to include or exclude TV, print, radio, or online advertising based on your premise. How would you pitch this concept to In-N-Out's marketing department in a way that would emphasize In-N-Out's core values?

# Amazon

## One E-Store to Rule Them All

*Amazon.com has soared ahead of other online merchants. What the firm can't carry in its 65 worldwide fulfillment centers, affiliated retailers distribute for it. Not content to rest on past laurels, CEO Jeff Bezos has introduced a number of new services to keep customers glued to the Amazon site. His latest innovation is the Kindle Fire, a seven-inch tablet that's easy on the wallet and is the iPad's first real competitor. But can Amazon afford to go head to head with Apple for the long haul?*

### The Rocket Takes Off

From its modest beginning in Jeff Bezos's garage in 1995 as an online bookstore, Amazon.com has quickly sprouted into the pre-eminent online retailer. Once Bezos saw that Amazon could outgrow its role as an immense book retailer, he began to sell CDs and DVDs. Even its logo was updated to symbolize that Amazon.com sells almost anything you can think of, from A to Z.

And that only takes into account Amazon's U.S. presence. At latest count, customers in eight other countries, including China, Japan, and France, can access Amazon sister sites built especially for them.[1] Amazon's 65 "fulfillment centers" around the world enclose more than 26 million square feet of operating space.[2,3]

And that's only the warehouse space required to store the products Amazon itself stocks. Hundreds of other companies also list their products through Amazon in a program known as the Amazon Marketplace. The companies profit from the additional exposure and sales (without undercutting their existing business), and Amazon's brand thrives from the opportunity to keep customers who might otherwise shop elsewhere.

### From Bookseller to Book Publisher

Not forgetting its roots as a bookseller, Amazon enhanced its media offerings by making several key acquisitions. Its purchase of on-demand book self-publisher BookSurge reinforces Amazon's literary heritage: Customers publishing memoirs or first books of poetry may, for a small fee, have their work made available for sale via Amazon's website.[4] Considering how many sets of eyes visit the site in the average week, this is a very compelling offer to a writer who may be considering other on-demand services.

And it won't hurt that Bezos lured Larry Kirshbaum, a former head of Time Warner Book Group and veteran publishing mogul, away from the print world to run Amazon Publishing, an in-house imprint formed with no less of a goal than to "publish bestselling books by big-name authors." Kirshbaum's offerings will lean heavily on the Kindle platform for distribution, of course. "We're building [...] an in-house laboratory where authors and editors and marketers can test new ideas," said Jeff Belle, vice-president of Amazon Publishing. "Success to us means working with authors who want to find new ways to connect with more readers."[5]

David Strick/Redux Pictures

### Taking a Bite Out of Apple

Time and time again, Amazon has squared off against tech industry giant Apple. First, Amazon launched its Amazon MP3 music downloading service and then, in a move of digital one-upmanship, offered all of its tracks from the Big 4 record labels without proprietary digital rights management (DRM) software, allowing Amazon customers to play the files on any MP3 player.[6] Amazon also bought top-shelf audiobook vendor Audible.com for $300 million, adding more than 100,000 audio titles to its arsenal.

And just as the iPod turned the music industry on its head, the Amazon Kindle is revamping the publishing industry. Sales of the books for the Kindle recently outnumbered Amazon's sales of hardcover books.[7] Part e-book reader, part wireless computer, the Kindle can download and store e-books, RSS feeds, Microsoft Word documents, and digital pictures in most major formats. Bezos sees this as a natural evolution of technology. "Books are the last bastion of analog," he said to *Newsweek*. "Music and video have been digital for a long time, and short-form reading has been digitized, beginning with the early Web. But long-form reading really hasn't."[8]

Last year, Amazon made headlines by announcing the Kindle Fire, the first color touchscreen device to bear the Kindle name. As a tablet computer, it invited comparisons to the iPad, but in reality the Fire is a bit simpler than Apple's tablet: It allows users to purchase, download, and view books, movies, music, TV shows, and games from Amazon's online storefronts. Contrary to other iPad competitors, the Kindle Fire has sold well; Amazon does not provide exact Kindle sales figures, but analysts predicted that Amazon would sell six million in the last quarter of 2011 alone.[9]

### Sensing Competition

Apple unleashed its own e-reader application, iBooks. And while Apple is still courting publishers, it's fair to say that iBooks hasn't quite received the same widespread adoption as the Kindle apps, which now exist for most major smartphone and desktop platforms, as well as a Kindle Cloud Reader that supports several web browsers.

Apple isn't the only company in Amazon's sights—already among the largest sellers of DVDs, it also moved to compete with streaming video companies like Hulu and Netflix by announcing Amazon Prime Instant Videos, a library of streaming movies and TV shows available at no extra cost to customers with a $79-per-year Amazon Prime membership.[10] Originally a service that offered unlimited free two-day shipping on many products for a flat annual fee, Amazon Prime is quickly becoming even more attractive to frequent Amazon shoppers. Prime subscribers may also "borrow" select Kindle books for a set period of time at no additional cost.[11]

Beyond simply finding more and more products to sell, Bezos realized that to prevent his brand from becoming stagnant, he would have to innovate, creating new levels of service to complement existing products. "We have to say, 'What kind of innovation can we layer on top of that that will be meaningful for our customers?'" he explains.[12]

So far, much of this innovation has come from the depth of the free content available to Amazon customers. Far from being a loss leader, Amazon's free content spurs sales and reinforces customers' perception of Amazon's commitment to customer service.

As David Meerman Scott put it in *eContent*, "Here is the flip side of free in action—a smart content company figuring out how to get people to contribute compelling content for free and then building a for-profit business model around it. Amazon.com has built a huge content site by having content provided to it for no cost. Of course, Amazon.com makes money by selling products based on the contributed content on the site—another example of the flip side of free."[13]

## Pressing Too Hard?

While it often feels as if Amazon can't lose, this isn't always the case. Recently, a number of high-profile retailers have pulled their products from The Amazon Marketplace, including Target, The Gap, and Macy's. According to Neel Grover, CEO of Buy.com—another retailer who recently abandoned ship—"We didn't want to give them information on products and sales that Amazon could potentially use against us." Participation in the Marketplace requires retailers to share information about their customer base with Amazon. And while Amazon clearly isn't hurting for customers, don't forget that the Marketplace accounted for more than 30% of Amazon's recent quarterly profits.[14]

Amazon continues to face opposition from state governments that can collect no sales tax from the company, and many states are discussing so-called "Amazon taxes" to force the company to collect state taxes from its customers. Most states require online retailers to collect sales tax only if they also have a physical presence in the state. By not having to collect state sales taxes, which can exceed 8%, Amazon retains yet another means of undercutting brick-and-mortar stores. An investigation by *The Wall Street Journal* indicates the company believes that steering clear of sales tax is critical to its performance.[15]

Despite Amazon's success in so many new markets, some critics question whether Amazon.com, let alone the Internet, is the best place to make high-involvement purchases. Bezos is characteristically confident. "We sell a lot of high-ticket items," he counters. "We sell diamonds that cost thousands of dollars and $8,000 plasma TVs. There doesn't seem to be any resistance, and, in fact, those high-priced items are growing very rapidly as a percentage of our sales."[16]

## Looking Ahead

Even as Amazon's stock values fluctuate, Bezos still believes that customer service and anticipating customers' needs, not the stock ticker, define the Amazon experience. "I think one of the things people don't understand is we can build more shareholder value by lowering product prices than we can by trying to raise margins," he says. "It's a more patient approach, but we think it leads to a stronger, healthier company. It also serves customers much, much better."[17]

In less than two decades, Amazon.com has grown from a one-man operation into a global giant of commerce. By forging alliances to ensure that he has what customers want and making astute purchases, Jeff Bezos has made Amazon the go-to brand for online shopping. But with its significant investments in new media and services, does the company risk spreading itself too thin? Will customers continue to flock to Amazon, the go-to company for their every need?

### Discussion Questions

1. In what ways does Bezos's decision to develop and deliver the Kindle and Kindle Fire show systematic and intuitive thinking?

2. How do you describe the competitive risk in Amazon's environment as Wal-Mart, Barnes and Noble, and other retailers strengthen their online offerings?

### Problem Solving

Amazon is continuously looking for new markets to exploit. As CEO Bezos addresses the strategic opportunity of delivering streaming video, he calls on you for advice. Amazon's presence and technology are already established in this market. But what decision error and traps might cause him to make the wrong decisions regarding Amazon's future moves, and why? What can he do to best avoid these mistakes?

### Further Research

What are the latest initiatives coming out of Amazon? How do they stack up in relation to actual or potential competition? How has the decision to produce the Fire turned out? Is Bezos making the right decisions as he guides the firm through today's many business challenges?

# Walgreens
## Staying One Step Ahead

*Squeezed on one side by tough competitors like CVS and on the other side by dynamic and ever-changing relationships with partner companies, Walgreens has found success through agility and an uncanny sense of how to extend their brand within a very crowded marketplace. How has Walgreens managed to stay competitive and thrive among close competition in an ever-changing market?*

You don't hope for surprises at the corner drugstore, an American staple since the nineteenth century. Today's customers expect a certain range of products, from vitamins to bandages to prescription medicines.

But Walgreens, one of the oldest players in the drugstore game, wants to redefine your image of the contemporary drugstore. By broadening their portfolio to include the counseling of genetic and long-term diseases, selling health insurance, and even installing EV (electric vehicle) charging stations outside hundreds of their stores, Walgreens is betting that consumers will like their range of expanded services.

## Evading the Competition

It's been a whirlwind year for the 111-year-old drugstore chain. It lost critical negotiations with Express Scripts, one of the oldest pharmacy benefit managers in the U.S.; acquired Drugstore.com; filled 25% of prescriptions via their mobile app, and added disease counseling and health insurance sales to its growing roster of services.

Like a prizefighter, Walgreens is learning how to duck a punch while going in for the uppercut. It's an aggressive game of cat-and-mouse that Walgreens and competitors like CVS play, each trying to crowd the other out of profitable marketplaces, woo new and vital collaborators, or be the first to host a new product or service.

"They've had a lot of other retailers get into their space, and their competitors have expanded into other spaces, too," said David Magee, an analyst at Atlanta-based SunTrust Robinson Humphrey. "They were lagging; now they're shaking things up."[1]

Walgreens CEO Gregory Wasson agrees, telling shareholders that Walgreens is moving beyond the traditional drugstore format to create "something unique, new, and special."[2]

## Steady Growth, Unsteady Future

Charles R. Walgreen, Sr. opened his first store on the south of Chicago in 1901. He purchased the dusty, dimly lit store of a former employer and set about making it one of Chicago's most successful drugstores by thinking carefully about what customers wanted—and couldn't find at the time—in competing stores. He slowly expanded the store's product line, adding hot food to augment the standard ice cream and soda fountain offerings in 1910, and introducing the malted milkshake in 1920.[3]

RICHARD B. LEVINE/Newscom

Walgreen's habit of listening to customers, adding the products and services they desired, and growing in a controlled, predictable manner paid handsomely and set a long-term strategy for Walgreens's growth for decades to come. In many states, the name *Walgreens* became synonymous with the very image of the corner drugstore.

According to Jim Collins, an author who profiled blue-chip companies in his 2001 best-seller *Good to Great*, if you invested in Walgreens at the end of 1975, in 2000 your returns would have beat the stock market by more than fifteen times, Coca-Cola Co. by almost eight times, and General Electric Co. by almost five times. He praised the company for adhering with "fanatical consistency" to a strategy of convenience.[4]

John Palizza, a twenty-three-year Walgreens vet and former head of its investor relations department, concurred. The company's "terrific formula" matched constant, 5% annual expansion with a strict eye for cost containment. "But in the mid-2000s, they got so enamored of growth that they lost sight of the expense line."[5]

Walgreens thrived by steadily dotting the U.S. map with new stores. But once they reached saturation in a number of key markets, even after buying NYC drugstore chain Duane Reade, the company was forced to redefine how it could continue to expand.

## The "New" Corner Drugstore

Unfortunately for Walgreens, in an increasingly complex medical regulatory environment, the business of filling prescriptions isn't as simple as it used to be. And though the company never lost sight of its consumer-focused strategy of convenience and one-stop shopping, price now matters more than anything to many shoppers, who find that sometimes the corner drugstore isn't the only option worth considering.

Two additional factors made business challenging for Walgreens in recent years. First, increased competition: While the company was once the clear retail pharmaceutical leader, Wal-Mart fundamentally changed the game in 2006 when it introduced $4 refills on generic prescriptions. Only two years later, CVS dramatically multiplied its number of stores when it beat out Walgreens with a last-minute $2.9 billion bid for Longs Drugs.[6]

The second squeeze came from increasingly tight negotiations with pharmacy benefit managers (PBMs)—third-party organizations that contract with pharmacies and negotiate discounts and rebates with drug manufacturers. As of today, roughly half of all Americans receive drug benefits administered by PBMs, which handle about 70% of all prescriptions.[7] Walgreens created its own PBM, Walgreens Health Initiatives, in 1995, but the business never achieved enough success to justify its existence.

Increasingly reliant on PBMs to drive prescription sales, Walgreens found itself in unproductive negotiations last year with Express Scripts, one of the largest PBMs. When talks fell apart, Walgreens stood to lose up to $5.3 billion in prescription sales.[8]

## A New Chapter

Luckily, CEO Gregory Wasson had been focused for years on re-defining Walgreens, and he brought a sweeping set of changes to the company in 2011.

First, Wasson got Walgreens out of failing lines of business, which included spinning off its PBM to Catalyst Health Solutions Inc. for $525 million.

"They made a very public sale of it, really just to kind of rub it in CVS's face," said Jeff Jonas, analyst at Gabelli & Co. "[The launch of CVS's PBM] was pitched as this big transformational thing, but Walgreens wanted to point out that the PBM business is pretty rocky and not what they do."[9]

Next, Wasson is keen to deliver customers whatever they want from Walgreens, a strategy dubbed *customer-centric retailing*. One phase involves store makeovers that add food, beer, wine, and liquor; eliminate unpopular products; and expand the beauty aisles. More than 4,000 stores have been remodeled at a cost of approximately $45,000 each.[10]

And after introducing Walgreens apps for the iOS and Android platforms, the company soon found consumers using the apps to submit 25% of all prescription refills. Using the apps, customers can select store pickup locations as well as the date and time of pickup; they can also receive SMS alerts when their prescriptions are ready.[11]

The company is also creating a clever niche for itself by appealing to customers' environmental sensibilities. "A green drugstore?" consumers might ask, "Why not?" Starting in 2007, Walgreens began installing rooftop solar panels on many of its stores, looking to complete one hundred thirty installations by the end of last year. With fifty-three installations in Ohio, Walgreens is one of the largest solar power users in the state. The rooftop panels typically offset 15–20% of a store's energy consumption.[12] In addition, the company debuted its first EV (electric vehicle) charging station in an Orlando, Florida, location in October 2011. Earlier that year, Walgreens announced that it hoped to have up to 800 EV charging stations installed outside stores by the end of the year.[13]

And then there's Walgreens' acquisition of Drugstore.com, which it purchased last March for $429 million. With new access to three million customers and over 60,000 health and beauty products, this acquisition pushes the company another notch ahead of CVS and into more direct competition with Wal-Mart and Target.

But analysts are torn over the value of this purchase. In thirteen years, Drugstore.com never posted a full-year profit, despite being purchased at a 113% premium on its stock price. And it doesn't even have prescription drug business to bring Walgreens, having sold off that line in 2010.

"I think they were sold a bill of goods," John Palizza said. "They paid a lot of money for an unsuccessful company."[14]

## Looking Forward

Despite this, Walgreens performed respectably in fiscal year 2011: It posted $72.2 billion in sales, $20.5 billion in gross profit, and $3.6 billion in cash flow from operations.[15]

And despite ever-tighter competition, Walgreens is poised to profit from 76 million aging baby boomers who are increasingly reliant on prescription drugs, along with the 36 million Americans who may get access to health care when reforms are enacted in 2014. This makes sense considering that Walgreens has long depended on prescription sales for the better portion of its profit. It filled 778 million prescriptions last year, up from 651 million in the year before.[16]

In addition, Wasson continues to freshen up the executive team, offering early retirement to old-timers and inviting outsiders into key top-management spots, a move previously unheard of in a company that prided itself on promoting from within.

According to John Palizza, "Walgreens's success lies in whether the store managers, the district managers, the regional VPs buy into this transformation."

Meredith Adler, an analyst at Barclays Capital, agrees. "No one had opened the windows there for way too long," she said. "Now they're getting some fresh air."[17]

## Discussion Questions

1. What planning objectives and goals can you identify in CEO Gregory Wasson's plans to revitalize Walgreens?

2. What benchmarks can Walgreens use to measure its success and control progress in its pursuit of these plans?

## Problem Solving

You've got a great assignment to serve as special assistant to Walgreen's CEO during a summer internship. But the first task you are assigned is a bit daunting. The CEO says "You're my conscience. You're going to be present for every decision I make. I want you to be critical and make sure my decisions and plans stay on track. Be ready to speak out and defend yourself." What planning errors will you be watching for? What planning techniques will you be ready to recommend if the CEO seems to be straying off course?

## Further Research

Imagine that you have been retained by Walgreens CEO Gregory Wasson as a scenario planning consultant. Research what is happening to describe three possible long-term scenarios in which Walgreens could face environmental, competitive, and strategic challenges. Explain from where Walgreens's threats emerge, possible weaknesses these threats exploit, and strengths Walgreens can draw upon to counter these challenges.

# Electronic Arts

## Inside Fantasy Sports

MIKE SEGAR/Reuters/Landov LLC

*Electronic Arts is one of the largest and most profitable third-party video game makers. Exclusive contracts with professional sports teams have enabled it to dominate the sports gaming market. But as gaming has shifted from consoles to laptops, phones, and tablets, it is struggling to stay relevant. Can EA regain the pole position in a crowded and contentious market?*

Founded in 1982 by William "Trip" Hawkins, an early director of strategy and marketing for Apple Computer, EA gained quick distinction for its detail-oriented sports titles compatible with the Nintendo and Sega platforms. Although EA has also received good reviews for its strategy and fighting games, it left its heart on the gridiron, diamond, court, or any other playing field long ago. According to former EA Sports marketing chief Jeffrey Karp, EA wants to be "a sports company that makes games."

### Ad Revenue In, Ad Revenue Out

Word of mouth may still be the most trusted form of advertising, and EA has always depended on fans to spread its gaming gospel. But in a highly competitive—and lucrative—gaming market, EA knows better than to skimp on brand building: it spends two to three times as much marketing and advertising a title as it does developing it.[1] EA knows its audience, and it promotes as heavily to *Game Informer* readers as it does to subscribers of ESPN's *The Magazine*.

The realism of EA's graphics set it apart from competitors long ago, but the energy and talent used to depict that realism might be wasted if EA games didn't include the one element fans most want to see: their favorite players. However, top athletes aren't cheap, and neither are their virtual depictions. Players such as Tim Tebow, Donovan McNabb, and Carmelo Anthony expect a tidy sum to promote any product, including video games that use their likenesses. EA spends $100 million annually—three times its ad budget—to license athletes, players' associations, and teams. It's a complex dance: the *FIFA Soccer 2012 for iPad*, for example, requires hundreds of different licenses from a total of 22 club leagues, 500 teams, and 15,000 players.[2] Cheap? Anything but, though it's doubtful you'll hear EA complain about the 15 million digital and physical copies of *FIFA 2011* it sold last year, netting $150 million in revenue in the first week alone.[3]

### Paying to Be Seen

Even the most dedicated *Madden* fans may wonder whether the sports video gaming market has enough muscle to shoulder EA's gargantuan costs. Enter the promotional alliance. Just as EA pays to license the use of NFL logos in its games, big-name sports companies such as Nike and Reebok pay to the tune of $3.5 mil-

lion a year to get their logos on digital players. One game, *NBA Live*, offers players the opportunity to switch up the color and style of players' logo-friendly footwear. The shoe styles may be virtual, but the value of brand recognition is very real for companies that pony up for sponsorship.

Such brand reinforcement isn't limited to sports games either. EA's *Need for Speed Underground 2*, a fast-paced racing game, takes endorsement beyond the omnipresent billboard ads and vehicle logos found in typical driving simulators. Here players receive "text messages" on the screen suggesting game hints, each bearing the AT&T logo. The significance may be lost on adults, but for a younger generation raised on instant messaging, the placement makes perfect sense.

It makes financial sense, too. A recent poll by Nielsen Entertainment and Activision indicates that this kind of placement may result in notable improvements in both brand recall and favorable brand perception. "I think truly that no other media type can deliver the persuasion that in-game ads can if executed properly," said Michael Dowling, general manager at Nielsen Interactive, Los Angeles.

### Losing Ground in a Crowded Market

Until recently, EA's devotion to sports games was a winning asset—it dominated the market as the world's largest video-game publisher. But a funny thing happened on the way to the bank—over the course of a few short years, the gaming market radically changed. Now EA finds itself in third place behind two strong competitors whose successes represent areas in which EA needs to double down to stay in the game.

Blame the Wii. Or blame *Guitar Hero*. Both led popular interest in gaming away from complex sports games played with standard controllers to new types of games, and new ways of interacting with consoles. Nintendo's Wii has been tremendously popular, and although EA has several successful titles for the platform, many of the top games—like *Wii Sports Resort and Super Mario Galaxy 2*—are published by Nintendo itself. The nontraditional controller lends itself to movement-based games, not EA's button-mashing bread and butter.

Emerging nearly parallel with the Wii was the popularity of *Guitar Hero* and *Rock Band*. It didn't take long for casual gamers to take up cheap plastic guitars and drum sets, leaving their traditional controllers to gather dust in the corner. Small gaming shop Harmonix pulled double duty in this market, first publishing *Guitar Hero*, then selling it to EA adversary Activision only to follow up with the arguably better *Rock Band* series. EA came to the party late; sensing the market for rock-along music games was sufficiently saturated, it resorted to striking a deal with Harmonix to help distribute *Rock Band*.

While the Wii's popularity seems to have peaked for the time being and plastic instruments are on their way out (parent company Viacom recently sold Harmonix for the bargain-basement price of $50), these emerging trends ultimately diluted EA's chokehold on the popular gaming market.[4] Meanwhile, Activision found a comfortable home with the Wii, scoring big hits with several *Guitar Hero* titles and hitting the bullseye by porting their massively successful *Call of Duty* franchise.

And then there's Apple. When Steve Jobs launched the iOS App Store in the summer of 2008, he decreed that one-third of the first 500 apps would be games.[5] Before long, specs improved in iOS devices to make them serious portable gaming machines. Successive generations of iPad improved iOS gaming with a large, high-resolution screen, and the App Store suddenly became a self-sufficient gaming platform faster than you can say *Angry Birds*.

At the same time, Facebook was coming into its own as a singular destination for simple but time-swallowing games. Together, these platforms heralded a new way of acquiring and playing games in which EA had little to no experience: digital distribution. Quick on the draw, however, was Zynga, an upstart publisher who quickly dominated Facebook games with *Farmville* and *Frontierville*, among others. Games on iOS and Facebook are portable, easy, and you can step away from them as long as you like and pick up just where you left off. That kind of gaming is worlds away from EA's traditions, and it's forced the company to do some serious reckoning on its future as well as its executive time—Zynga lured former EA marketing chief Jeffrey Karp to take on a parallel position there.[6]

As of today, EA is the third-place publisher behind Activision and Zynga, and while things are starting to look up, it's a long, hard road back to the top. CEO John Riccitiello even admitted recently, "What we've described as a two-year comeback is clearly taking longer."[7]

EA knows that the road to riches is paved with recurring sales. And though its annualized releases of many popular sports titles for some time, they haven't done so for the growing market of massive multiplayer online games (MMOG), which Activision has been lucratively exploiting for years with *Call of Duty* and *World of Warcraft*. EA's entry into the MMOG fray was last year's *Star Wars: The Old Republic*.

Especially in the last few years, EA has been remarkably successful in creating new franchises, which has historically been difficult in the sequel-heavy video game market. EA's successes include *Mass Effect*, a sci-fi action series that has sold over seven million units, not counting the sales from the recently released third entry in the series.[8] *Dead Space*, a survival horror series, sold over four million units and received significant critical acclaim.[9]

The company has also seen continued success with older franchises: *Battlefield 3* drew favorable comparisons to the competing *Call of Duty* franchise and has shipped over 12 million units.[10] EA has also recently launched *The Sims Social*, a popular Facebook game that has performed well against titles from social game heavyweight Zynga.[11]

And the company is showing signs that it's shifting gears to compete successfully in the new gaming landscape. It spent $300 million last year to snatch up social gaming developer Playfish, and it also brought *Madden NFL Superstars* to Facebook, where it has been intensely popular, scoring almost 800,000 "Likes."[12] Origin, EA's digital distribution business, which it's been quietly building, offers profile management, the ability to connect with friends via chat, and integration of scores and game stats to social media and online gaming sites.[13] As of last count, 9.3 million users installed Origin, earning EA more than $100 million and helping it to do battle with rival online platform Steam.[14]

## Playing for Keeps

Despite its wild success in the video game market, Electronic Arts faces substantial challenges to its power by competing game companies, the cost of doing business, and even dissatisfied gamers. Can EA overcome these threats and continue producing the sports franchises that brought the company considerable success?

### Discussion Questions

1. How can feedforward, concurrent, and feedback controls help Electronic Arts meet its quality goals for video games?

2. Can you see the principle of management by exception at play in any of EA's recent business decisions? Why or why not?

### Problem Solving

Control is an essential and important management function. It's also something that even the best managers and organizations can always improve upon. Break the video game production process down into its various components, a start-to-finish workflow model so to speak. Now identify for each phase in the process the control standards that could be set so that managers make the process work best overall.

### Further Research

What is the latest in Electronic Arts' quest to regain its former glory as the top gaming publisher? How well is EA positioned for future competitive advantage? Overall, is EA's executive team still on "top of its game?"

## Case Study 10

# Dunkin' Donuts

## Betting Dollars on Donuts

*Once a niche company operating in the northeast, Dunkin' Donuts is opening hundreds of stores and entering new markets. At the same time, the java giant is broadly expanding both its food and its coffee menus to ride the wave of fresh trends, appealing to a new generation of customers. But is the rest of America ready for Dunkin' Donuts? Can the company keep up with its own rapid growth? With Starbucks rethinking its positioning strategy and McDonald's offering a great tasting coffee at a reasonable price, Dunkin' Donuts is hoping they "Kin Do It."*

JESSICA RINALDI/REUTERS/Newscom

### Serving the Caffeinated Masses

There's a lot more to a coffee shop than just change in the tip jar. Some 400 billion cups of coffee are consumed every year, making it the most popular beverage globally. Estimates indicate that more than 150 million Americans drink a total of 465 million cups of coffee a day.[1] And with Starbucks driving tastes for upscale coffee, some customers may wonder whether any coffee vendors remember the days when drip coffee came in only two varieties—regular and decaf. But Dunkin' Donuts does, and it's betting dollars to donuts that consumers nationwide will embrace its reputation for value, simplicity, and a superior Boston Kreme donut.

### Winning New Customers

Most of America has had an occasional relationship with the Dunkin' Donuts brand through its more than 6,700 domestic outlets, which have their densest cluster in the northeast and a growing presence in the rest of the country.[2] But the brand has also managed to carve out an international niche with nearly 3,000 international shops in 30 countries. The shops are not only found in expected markets such as Canada and Brazil, but also in some unexpected ones, including Qatar, South Korea, Pakistan, and the Philippines.[3] And Dunkin' Brands recently hired Giorgio Minardi—a veteran of McDonald's and Burger King—as president of its international operations at the same time it unveiled plans to expand aggressively into China, Southeast Asia, and Latin America.[4]

If the company has its way, in the future you won't have to go very far to pick up a box of donuts. "We're only represented large-scale in the northeastern market," said Jayne Fitzpatrick, strategy officer for Dunkin' Brands, mentioning plans to expand "as aggressively" as possible. "We're able to do that because we're a franchise system, so access to operators and capital is easier."[5] How aggressively? According to CNN, Dunkin' plans to double the number of its locations over the next twenty years.[6] According to social media manager Jessica Gioglio, the brand plans a strategy of westward expansion into new markets adjacent to those already served by Dunkin' Donuts, including Denver, Baton Rouge, New Orleans, and Albuquerque.[7]

### Changing Course to Follow Demand

For most of its existence, Dunkin' Donuts' main product focus has been implicit in its name: donuts, and coffee in which to dip them. First-time customers acquainted with this simple reputation were often overwhelmed by the wide varieties of donuts stacked end-to-end in neat, mouthwatering rows. Only in recent years has the company expanded its offerings to include breakfast sandwiches, previously the sole domain of fast food restaurants like McDonalds.

None of Dunkin' Donuts' moves makes much difference unless consumers buy into the notion that the company has the culinary imperative to sell more than its name suggests. If plans prove successful, more customers than ever may flock to indulge in the company's breakfast-to-go menu. If they don't, the only thing potentially worse for Dunkin' Donuts than diluted coffee could be a diluted brand image. After 60 years, the company has a reputation for doing two things simply and successfully—coffee and donuts. Even when consumers see the line of products expand into what was once solely the realm of the company's competitors, they may be unconvinced that Dunkin' Donuts is the shop to go to for breakfast.

Dunkin' Donuts sells more than one billion cups of coffee a year, for 62% of the company's annual store revenue.[8,9] Considering that coffee is the most profitable product on the menu, it's a good bet that those margins give the company room to experiment with its food offerings.

Faced with the challenge of maintaining a relevant brand image in the face of fierce and innovative competition, Dunkin' Donuts pursued a time-honored business tradition—following the leader. The company now offers a competitive variety of espresso-based drinks complemented with a broad number of sugar-free flavorings, including caramel, vanilla, and Mocha Swirl.[10] And considering the growing popularity of single-shot coffee makers like Keurig's K-Cup, it is a logical format for Dunkin' to apply to package their coffee. Ever-increasing competition in the morning meal market made an update to Dunkin' Donuts' food selection inevitable, too. The company currently focuses on bagel and croissant-based breakfast sandwiches, sausage pancake bites, and the Big N' Toasted.

### On Every Corner

Starbucks is known for its aggressive dominance of the coffee marketplace. When competitors opened a new store in town, Starbucks didn't worry. It just opened a new store across the street, in a vigorous one-upmanship that conquered new ground and deterred competitors. But many who have struggled to compete with Starbucks have had to do so with limited resources or only a few franchises. Not so with Dunkin' Donuts. Its parent brand, Dunkin' Brands, also owns Baskin-Robbins. And in the time since Dunkin' Donuts went public last summer, it's earned a nearly $500 million coffer from which it can draw to fund its westward expansion.[11] The number of Starbucks outlets has shrunk in recent years; at its current pace of growth, the number of Dunkin' stores may easily eclipse Starbucks' in the next decade.

## Simple Food for Simple People

Dunkin Donuts' history of offering simple and straightforward morning snacks has given it the competitive advantage of distinction as *the* anti-Starbucks—earnest and without pretense. Like Craftsman tools and Levi's jeans, the company appeals to unpretentious people who enjoy well-crafted products.

## The Sweet Spot Has a Jelly Center

Dunkin' Donuts is trying to grow in all directions, reaching more customers in more places with more products. Achieving proper retail placement can be a delicate balance.

Although Dunkin' Donuts often partners with a select group of grocery retailers—such as Stop & Shop and Wal-Mart—to create a store-within-a-store concept, the company won't set up shop in just any grocery store. "We want to be situated in supermarkets that provide a superior overall customer experience," he said. "Of course, we also want to ensure that the supermarket is large enough to allow us to provide the full expression of our brand . . . which includes hot and iced coffee, our line of high-quality espresso beverages, donuts, bagels, muffins, and even our breakfast sandwiches." Furthermore, the outlet's location within the supermarket is critical for a successful relationship. "We want to be accessible and visible to customers, because we feel that gives us the best chance to increase incremental traffic and help the supermarket to enhance their overall performance," said John Fassak, vice president of business development.

But why stop at grocery stores? Taking this philosophy a step further, Dunkin' Donuts has also entered the lodging market with their first hotel restaurant at the Great Wolf Lodge® in Concord, North Carolina—one of North America's largest indoor water parks. Dunkin' Donuts offers a variety of store models to suit any lodging property, including full retail shops, kiosks, and self-serve hot coffee stations perfect for gift shops and general stores, snack bars, and convention registration areas.[12] Who knows where they'll pop up next?

The launch into the lodging market coincides with Dunkin' Donuts' worldwide expansion program. Steadily and strategically expanding, Dunkin' Donuts unveiled the brand's first-ever theme park restaurant at Hershey Park, new coffee kiosks at sporting venues such as Fenway Park, Yankee Stadium, and the TD Banknorth (Boston) Garden, and new stores at airports including Boston, Dallas-Fort Worth, and New York City.[13]

The company is banking on these mutually beneficial partnerships to help it achieve widespread marketplace prominence. Dunkin' Donuts is a nationally known brand with a long reputation for quality, giving the company the benefit of not having to work hard to earn many customers' trust. And if Dunkin' Donuts can find the sweet spot by being within most consumers' reach while falling just short of a Big Brother-like omnipresence, the company's strategy of expansion may well reward it handsomely. But this strategy is not without its risks. In the quest to appeal to new customers, offering too many original products and placements could dilute the essential brand appeal and alienate long-time customers who respect simplicity and authenticity. On the other hand, new customers previously unexposed to Dunkin' Donuts might see it as "yesterday's brand."

If Dunkin' Donuts' executives focus too narrowly on franchising new stores, they might not be aware of issues developing in long-standing or even recently established stores. Some older franchises seem long overdue for a makeover, especially when compared to the Starbucks down the block. To combat the perception that many of Dunkin' Donuts' stores are outdated, the company unveiled a new prototype restaurant design in Pawtucket, Rhode Island providing a glimpse into the future look and feel of the brand. The contemporary design includes retro elements inspired by the very first shop built in 1950, and two-thirds of the planned stores will be built in this style.[14]

For the time being, Dunkin' Donuts seems determined in its quest for domination of the coffee and breakfast market. Will Dunkin' Donuts strike the *right* balance of products and placement needed to mount a formidable challenge against competitors?

## Discussion Questions

1. What does a Porter's Five Forces analysis reveal about the industry in which Dunkin' Donuts and Starbucks compete? What are its strategic implications for Dunkin' Donuts?

2. Is Dunkin' Donuts presently using strategic alliances to full advantage? How could cooperative strategies further assist with its master plan for growth?

## Problem Solving

Until recently, the Starbucks brand was much better known around the world than Dunkin' Donuts. As Dunkin's CEO, what global strategy—globalization, multidomestic, or transnational—would you follow to position Dunkin' as a real challenge to Starbucks in the international markets, and why?

## Further Research

Gather information on industry trends, as well as current developments—domestic and international, affecting Dunkin' Donuts and its competitors. Use this information to build an up-to-date SWOT analysis for Dunkin' Donuts. Based on implications of this analysis, is Dunkin's top leadership doing the right things when it comes to strategic management, or not?

# Nike

## Spreading Out to Win the Race

*Nike is indisputably a giant in the athletics industry. But the Portland, Oregon, company has grown large precisely because it knows how to stay small. By focusing on its core competencies—and outsourcing all others—Nike has managed to become a sharply focused industry leader. But can it stay in front?*

Robert Haidinger/Anzenberger/Redux Pictures

## What Do You Call a Company of Thinkers?

It's not a joke or a Buddhist riddle. Rather, it's a conundrum about one of the most successful companies in the United States—a company known worldwide for its products, none of which it actually makes. This begs two questions: If you don't make anything, what do you actually do? If you outsource everything, what's left? A whole lot of brand recognition, for starters. Nike, famous for its trademark Swoosh™, is still among the most recognized brands in the world and is an industry leader in the $74.2 billion U.S. sports footwear and apparel market.[1] And its 33% market share dominates the global athletic shoe market.[2]

Since captivating the shoe-buying public in the early 1980s with legendary spokesperson Michael Jordan, Nike continues to outpace the athletic shoe competition while spreading its brand through an ever-widening universe of sports equipment, apparel, and paraphernalia. The ever-present Swoosh graces everything from bumper stickers to sunglasses to high school sports uniforms.

Not long after Nike's introduction of Air Jordans, the first strains of the "Just Do It" ad campaign sealed the company's reputation as a megabrand. When Nike made the strategic image shift from simply selling products to embodying a love of sport, discipline, ambition, practice, and all other desirable traits of athleticism, it became among the first in a long line of brands to represent itself as aiding customers in their self-expression as part of its marketing strategy.

Advertising has played a large part in Nike's continued success. The largest seller of athletic footwear and apparel in the world, Nike recently spent nearly $2.5 billion annually on advertising.[3]

Portland ad agency Wieden & Kennedy has been instrumental in creating and perpetuating Nike's image—so much so that the agency has a large division in-house at Nike headquarters. This intimate relationship between the two companies allows the agency's creative designers to focus solely on Nike work and gives them unparalleled access to executives, researchers, and anyone else who might provide advertisers with their next inspiration for marketing greatness.

## What's Left, Then?

Although Nike has cleverly kept its ad agency nestled close to home, it has relied on outsourcing many nonexecutive responsibilities in order to reduce overhead. It can be argued that Nike, recognizing that its core competency lies in the design—not the manufacturing—of shoes, was wise to transfer production overseas.

But Nike has taken outsourcing to a new level, barely producing any of its products in its own factories. All of its shoes, for instance, are made by subcontractors. Although this allocation of production hasn't hurt the quality of the shoes at all, it has challenged Nike's reputation among fair-trade critics.

After initial allegations of sweatshop labor surfaced at Nike-sponsored factories, the company tried to reach out and reason with its more moderate critics. But this approach failed, and Nike found itself in the unenviable position of trying to defend its outsourcing practices while withholding the location of its favored production shops from the competition.

Boldly, in a move designed to turn critics into converts, Nike posted information on its Web site detailing every one of the more than 700 factories it uses to make shoes, apparel, and other sporting goods.[4] It released the data in conjunction with a comprehensive new corporate responsibility report summarizing the environmental and labor situations of its contract factories.[5]

According to a 2011 Associated Press report, two-thirds of Nike's Converse factories still fail to meet Nike's own standards for contract manufacturers. Hannah Jones, a Nike exec overseeing efforts to improve factory working conditions, acknowledged that workers in two Indonesian plants were subjected to "serious and egregious" physical and verbal abuse. "We have been working every time we can [. . .] to influence the licensee and their subcontractors much more directly," she said.[6]

Nike's critics find the company's claims that it can't control labor conditions in contract plants far-fetched. "I simply find it impossible that a company of the size and market power of Nike is impotent in persuading a local factory in Indonesia or anywhere else in meeting its code of conduct," counters Prakash Sethi, a corporate strategy professor at Baruch College CUNY.[7]

## Jordan Isn't Forever

Knowing that shoe sales alone wouldn't be enough to sustain continued growth, Nike decided, in a lateral move, to learn more about its customers' interests and involvement in sports, identifying what needs it might be able to fill. Nike's success in the running category, for example, was largely driven by the Apple iPod-linked Nike Plus, which now ranks as the world's largest running club. The technology not only motivates runners with music and tracking their pace, but it also uploads their times and distances into a global community of runners online, creating a social-networking innovation that lets runners race in different countries.[8]

Banking on the star power of its Swoosh, Nike has successfully branded apparel, sporting goods, and even sunglasses. Like many large companies who have found themselves at odds with the possible limitations of their brands, Nike realized that it would have to master the one-two punch: identifying new needs and supplying creative and desirable products to fill those needs.

In fitting with the times, Nike's VP of Global Design, John R. Hoke III, is encouraging his designers to develop environmentally sustainable designs like the Nike Free, a lightweight running shoe that boosted sales 18% to $6.08 billion last quarter, topping analysts' estimates.[9,10] And Nike's Sustainable Business & Innovation Lab will fund outside startups focused on alternative energies, more efficient approaches to manufacturing, and the promotion of healthy lifestyles.[11]

Nike first stepped into sustainability in 1993 when it began grinding up old shoes and donating the material and other scraps from the manufacturing process to builders of sports surfaces like tracks and basketball courts.[12] While the original program continues, the company has shifted from one-of-a-kind initiatives to a long-term plan that will "achieve zero waste throughout the supply chain and have products and materials that can be continuously reused—no pre or post consumer waste."[13] In fact, when the world's greatest soccer players stepped on the field at the FIFA World Cup hosted by South Africa in 2010, many were wearing Nike jerseys made almost entirely from plastic bottles salvaged from landfills in Japan and Taiwan.[14]

## Nipping at Nike's Heels

Despite Nike's success and retention of its market share, things haven't been a bed of roses in the past few years. Mark Parker, a 27-year Nike vet, was promoted to CEO after Phil Knight's first choice, former S.C. Johnson & Sons CEO Bill Perez, stepped down after less than a year in the job when Knight decided Perez couldn't "get his arms around the company."[15]

And pressures are mounting from outside its Beaverton, Oregon, headquarters. German rival adidas drew a few strides closer to Nike when it purchased Reebok for approximately $3.8 billion.[16] Joining forces will collectively help the brands negotiate shelf space and other sales issues in American stores and will aid the adidas group in its price discussions with Asian manufacturers. With recent combined global sales of almost $15 billion,[17] the new supergroup of shoes isn't far off from Nike's $20.3 billion.[18,19]

According to Jon Hickey, senior vice president of sports and entertainment marketing for the ad agency Mullen, Nike has its "first real, legitimate threat since the '80s. There's no way either one would even approach Nike, much less overtake them, on their own." But now, adds Hickey, "Nike has to respond. This new, combined entity has a chance to make a run. Now, it's game on."[20]

But when faced with a challenge, Nike simply knocks its bat against its cleats and steps up to the plate. "Our focus is on growing our own business," said Nike spokesman Alan Marks. "Of course we're in a competitive business, but we win by staying focused on our strategies and our consumers. And from that perspective nothing has changed."[21]

## Putting It All Together

Nike has balanced its immense size and tremendous pressures to remain successful by leveraging a decentralized corporate structure. Individual business centers—such as research, production, and marketing—are free to focus on their core competencies without worrying about the effects of corporate bloat.

A recent organizational change is part of a wider Nike restructuring that may result in an overall reduction of up to 5% of the company's workforce.[22] "This new model sharpens our consumer focus and will allow us to make faster decisions, with fewer management layers," said Charlie Denson, President of the Nike Brand.[23]

It looks like his plan may have worked: Shares of Nike jumped to an all-time high in 2010 and have continued to climb since then. The company has found continued marketplace success by positioning itself not simply as a sneaker company but as a brand that fulfills the evolving needs of today's athletes. Will Nike continue to profit from its increasingly decentralized business model, or will it spread itself so thin that its competition will overtake it?

### Discussion Questions

1. How does Nike's decision to retain an in-house arm of ad agency Wieden & Kennedy exemplify the concept of organizational design?

2. Given the problems Nike has had with sweatshop labor being used by some of its foreign contractors, are there parts of the firm that need to be run with a mechanistic rather than organic design? Give examples to support your answer.

### Problem Solving

Nike seems to be using some form of network structure. Draw a diagram that shows what you believe its present structure looks like. Be sure to include all possible components; make and explain your assumptions in doing so. Now be an organization design consultant. Look at your diagram and ask: How can this network structure be improved? How can Nike gain even more operating efficiencies without losing its performance edge in terms of high quality and top design shoes? Explain and defend your answers to this question.

### Further Research

Gather information on Nike's recent moves and accomplishments, and those of its rivals. Are the firms following the same strategies and using the same structures to support them? Or is one doing something quite different from the others? Based on what you learn, what do you predict for the future? Can Nike stay on top, or is some other firm destined to be the next industry leader?

# Apple Inc.

## People and Design Create the Future

*Over a span of more than 30 years, Apple Inc. paradoxically existed both as one of America's greatest business successes and as a company that sometimes failed to realize its potential. Beginning with the 1996 return of ousted CEO Steve Jobs, Apple embarked on a mission to dominate the PC market and invent more than a few new markets along the way. Skeptics wonder if current CEO Tim Cook can muster the productivity and imagination that Jobs inspired in Apple employees before he passed away. Can Apple chart a continued course for success without Jobs at the helm?*

ROBERT RIZZUTO/TheRepublican/Landov LLC

## Corporate History

The history of Apple Inc. is a history of passion, whether on the part of its founders, its employees, or its loyal users.[1] It was begun by a pair of Stevens who, from an early age, had an interest in electronics. Steven Wozniak and Steven Jobs initially put their skills to work at Hewlett Packard and Atari, respectively. But then Wozniak constructed his first personal computer—the Apple I—and, along with Jobs, created Apple Computer on April 1, 1976. Right from the start, Apple exhibited an extreme emphasis on new and innovative styling in its computer offerings. Jobs took a personal interest in the development of new products, including the Lisa and the first, now legendary, Macintosh, or "Mac."

The passion that Apple is so famous for was clearly evident in the design of the Mac. Project teams worked around the clock to develop the machine and its operating system, Mac OS. The use of graphical icons to create simplified user commands was an immensely popular alternative to the command-line structure of DOS found on IBM's first PCs. When Apple and IBM began to clash head-on in the personal computer market, Jobs recognized the threat and realized that it was time for Apple to "grow up" and be run in a more businesslike fashion. In early 1983, he persuaded John Sculley, at that time president of Pepsi-Cola, to join Apple as president. The two men clashed almost from the start, with Sculley eventually ousting Jobs from the company.

The launch of the Mac reinvigorated Apple's sales. However, by the 1990s, IBM PCs and clones were saturating the personal computer market. Furthermore, Microsoft launched Windows 3.0, a greatly improved version of the Wintel operating system, for use on IBM PCs and clones. Although in 1991 Apple had contemplated licensing its Mac operating system to other computer manufacturers, making it run on Intel-based machines, the idea was nixed by then chief operating officer Michael Spindler in a move that would ultimately give Windows the nod to dominate the market.

## Innovative Design to the Rescue

Apple continued to rely on innovative design to remain competitive in the 1990s. It introduced the very popular Power-

Book notebook computer line, as well as the unsuccessful Newton personal digital assistant. Sculley was forced out and replaced by Michael Spindler. He oversaw a number of innovations, including the PowerMac family—the first Macs based on the PowerPC chip, an extremely fast processor co-developed with IBM and Motorola. In addition, Apple finally licensed its operating system to a number of Mac-cloners, although never in significant numbers.

After a difficult time in the mid-1990s, Spindler was replaced with Gil Amelio, the former president of National Semiconductor. This set the stage for one of the most famous returns in corporate history.

## Returning Home

After leaving Apple, Steve Jobs started NeXT computer, which produced an advanced personal computer with a sleek, innovative design. However, the computer, which entered the market late in the game and required proprietary software, never gained a large following. Jobs then cofounded the Pixar computer-animation studio, which coproduced a number of movies with Walt Disney Studios, including the *Toy Story Series*, *Monsters, Inc.*, *Finding Nemo*, *Ratatouille*, and *Up*.[2] When Jobs was running Pixar and it was struggling, his cofounder Alvy Ray Smith says: "We should have failed, but Steve just wouldn't let it go."[3]

In late 1996, Apple purchased NeXT, and Jobs returned to Apple in an unofficial capacity as advisor to the president. When Amelio resigned, Jobs accepted the role of "interim CEO" of Apple Computer and wasted no time in making his return felt. He announced an alliance with Apple's former rival, Microsoft. In exchange for $150 million in Apple stock, Microsoft and Apple would share a five-year patent cross-license for their graphical interface operating systems. He revoked licenses allowing the production of Mac clones and started offering Macs over the Web through the Apple Store. The first retail Apple Store opened in 2001, and just over ten years and 322 stores later, they're phenomenally profitable, earning an estimated $5,000 per square foot, approximately five times that of Best Buy.[4]

Beginning with the iMac and the iBook, its laptop cousin, Jobs continually introduced a series of increasingly popular products that captured the buying public's imagination. Upon their release, the iPod, MacBook, Apple TV, iPhone, and iPad instantly spawned imitators that mimicked the look of these products, but they couldn't duplicate Apple's acute ability to integrate design with usability. Once again, Apple became an industry innovator by introducing certifiably attractive—and powerful—consumer electronics products. Its recent successes have included growing to command approximately 35% of operating profits in the computer market and 90% of the market share for computers priced over $1,000.[5] In the mobile handset market, Apple earned 52% of profits in a recent quarter despite carrying only 4.2% of the global handset market.[6]

## Life After Steve?

Since he helped found Apple, Steve Jobs has been inextricably linked to the company and its brand.[7] And when Jobs passed away in October 2011, there was great concern expressed over Apple's ability to stay on its creative course without Jobs at the helm.

Although current CEO Tim Cook has not been credited with the showmanship or visibility of Steve Jobs, he is best known as the operations wizard who transformed Apple from within by eliminating expensive internal production processes by outsourcing to contract manufacturers, cutting the time inventory sat on Apple's balance sheet from months to days, and utilizing Apple's multi-billion-dollar cash reserve to purchase manufacturers' entire supply of cutting-edge components for one to two years into the future.[8] Skeptics suggested that Apple could fall into disarray if Jobs permanently left the company, but since his August 2011 resignation, Apple released stunning new versions of the iPhone, iPad, and Apple TV; issued notable updates to several of its computer lines; and boosted its stock value 44%.[9]

## The iOS Era and Beyond

The iPad and iPhone continue to be huge growth engines for Apple, respectively selling 32.1 million and 72.3 million units in 2011, 334% and 88% over their 2010 numbers.[10] By continuing to sell older phone models, Apple has expanded its lineup to cover multiple price points, from a high-end $849 iPhone 4S sold without a contract to the free-with-contract iPhone 3GS. The iPhone 3GS, iPhone 4, and iPhone 4S were the top three bestselling phone handsets in the United States in 2011.[11] Free yearly updates to iOS, the iPhone and iPad operating system, help the devices keep pace with the competition.

To mirror this yearly release cycle, Apple recently announced that it would be moving to a similar yearly release cycle for OS X, the operating system used by its line of Mac computers.[12] Recent releases of OS X, including Lion and Mountain Lion, ported features from the successful iOS platform to Macs. The most prominent is iCloud, a new cloud computing service that seamlessly syncs email, notes, bookmarks, music, and other data across multiple Apple devices, making it even more advantageous for people to buy their phone, tablet, *and* computer from Apple.[13]

Apple also recently announced an initiative to revolutionize the textbook industry: The latest version of its iBooks app brings textbooks to the iPad, and Apple partnered with publishing companies like Pearson, McGraw-Hill, Houghton Mifflin Harcourt, and DK Publishing to offer textbooks that would normally cost students $100 or more for $15 apiece. Apple also announced an iBooks authoring tool to facilitate the creation of ebooks. Mac users can download the app for free.[14]

So let's look into the future. Though Tim Cook is a celebrated operational leader, will he need to muster the charisma and personality of Steve Jobs to effectively lead Apple? If Jobs was the driving force behind Apple's successful comeback, how well can the firm do without him? And how long can Apple continue to sell iPad after iPad, iPhone after iPhone, without saturating their respective markets?

### Discussion Questions

1. Apple sells stylish and functional computers as well as a variety of electronic devices, and it operates retail stores. How does Apple's organization culture help the firm keep its creative edge in all these areas?

2. Stepping into his new role as CEO following the passing of one-of-a-kind visionary Steve Jobs, should Tim Cook be pushing transformational change, incremental change, or both?

### Problem Solving

Apple has had to deal with Jobs's death and the advancement of Tim Cook to the CEO position. Leadership succession issues like this are inevitable and the best firms will be prepared and ready for them. If you were a member of Apple's board, what steps would you recommend the firm be taking now to get ready for Cook's eventual replacement? What practices should be put into place so that the firm won't suffer if he suddenly isn't available? What criteria should be on the table as the board discusses Apple's future leadership needs given current events and trends?

### Further Research

Review what the analysts are presently saying about Apple. Make a list of all of the praises and criticisms, organize them by themes, and then put them in the priority order for a change leadership agenda. What does Apple most have to fear in its quest to maintain a sustainable competitive advantage?

# Two-Tier Wages

## Same Job, Different Pay

*Like many other American manufacturing and service industries, the domestic auto manufacturers were hit particularly hard by the Great Recession. Struggling to overcome rising material and pension costs, the automakers felt they couldn't compete with foreign carmakers unless they drastically cut their labor costs. The solution: Introduce a two-tier system where new workers earn significantly less than existing workers doing the same job. Was this the right choice for the Big Three? And how does it impact their employees?*

In Ford, General Motors, and Chrysler manufacturing plants across the country, thousands of newly hired workers are joining the assembly lines. It's a sign of both a rebounding economy and the American auto industry's methodical return from their economic struggles of the last decade.

But unlike their counterparts with a few years of service under their belts, these new hires earn an hourly wage as low as $14, nearly half that of their more experienced coworkers performing precisely the same assembly tasks. In addition, the new hires' auxiliary benefits—health insurance, paid time off, and retirement funding—don't compare to those of experienced plant workers.

## A New Contract with Organized Labor

These differences are the result of *two-tier contracts*—arrangements in which labor unions permit corporations to hire new workers at wages below those earned by existing unionized employees who perform the same jobs. The compensation differences between the two tiers may be marked by lower wages, slower progression toward raises, alternate health benefits, or reduced or restructured pension plans. Employers may also invoke tier arrangements by creating new job classifications with comparable responsibilities to existing jobs but with lower pay and by expanding part-time positions with inherently lower benefit levels.[1]

More commonly, unions may agree to concessionary contracts which include "tunnel" or "graduation" provisions; in these cases, newer workers can eventually reach the higher wage scales if they stay on the job long enough, which, in most cases, is longer than existing workers would take to reach the same compensation levels.[2]

Though two-tier contracts have existed in one form or another since the 1930s, they're getting more attention than ever now because they play an integral part in the Big Three automakers' plans to return to profitability. And it's easy to see why: By the early 2000s, the Big Three were struggling to survive; unlike foreign automakers with manufacturing plants in the United States, American manufacturers had long paid unionized workers a comfortable salary and a healthy pension. And with labor costs rising and sales in a slump, the Big Three felt they had two choices—restructure labor costs to match wages offered by Toyota and Honda or drastically cut production. In separate talks with each of the Big Three, United Auto Workers (UAW) negotiators conceded to two-tier contracts in order

Andreas Gebert/DPA/Zuma Press

to prevent further layoffs and protect the union's presence in domestic auto plants.

## Putting a New Face on an Old Practice

Two-tier contracts drew national attention in the early 1980s after the Airline Deregulation Act of 1978 prompted airlines to reconsider existing salary arrangements. American Airlines led the way, successfully negotiating two-tier plans with the Transportation Workers Union and airline pilots in 1983.[3] A few years later, grocery unions in many states reluctantly agreed to two-tier wages after a massive wave of grocery store consolidations closed 7,000 stores and cut 100,000 union jobs.[4]

In industries with high turnover, it may not take long for employers who implement two-tier contracts to see the benefits, as new employees may quickly replace their higher-earning predecessors. In addition, companies may offer buyouts to higher-tier workers to speed the transition and increase the percentage of workers paid at lower-tier wages. For example, following 2007 UAW negotiations, 19,000 workers at General Motors (GM) and 4,200 at Ford took a buyout.[5]

In the past, two-tier contracts have been stop-gap measures at best, since the diminished wages often disappeared once the economy picked up again. Companies that put two-tier plans into place often experienced higher turnover, lower morale, and reduced productivity. And in some instances, unions have been able to block two-tier contracts altogether, such as the United Food and Commercial Workers (UFCW) union's negotiations in the 2007 Southern California grocery workers' contract.[6]

## Tough Times for the Big Three

In 1993 talks with Ford, the UAW agreed temporarily to two-tier wages. And four years later, it reluctantly accepted negotiations including a permanent two-tier system for some workers—the first permanent implementation among the Big Three's workers.[7] Though neither autoworkers nor automakers forgot this concession, further talk of two-tier plans subsided for the meantime.

Fast-forward to 2007. The U.S. economy is tumbling, and executives at each of the Big Three automakers claim that their companies must undergo substantial restructuring to get out of debt and stay in business. Despite each company's individual circumstances, a common contention is that the automakers must slash labor costs and pension obligations in order to remain competitive with foreign automakers. The UAW fights to retain comfortable salaries and benefits for existing employees but concedes to lowering wages for new workers to forestall further layoffs.

In accordance with the U.S. government's bailouts of Chrysler and GM, the UAW conceded that second-tier workers would not be eligible for promotion to top-tier wages until 2015. Ford, which did not undergo government-managed bankruptcy, forged a UAW contract permitting it to fill 20% of its union jobs with second-tier workers before any are eligible for top-tier wages.[8]

Thus far, roughly 12% of Chrysler's 23,000 union employees earn second-tier wages,[9] as will most of Ford's 12,000 anticipated new hires.[10]

"This is not going away," said Kristin Dziczek, a labor analyst at Ann Arbor's Center for Automotive Research. "It has allowed the Big Three to reduce labor costs without cutting the pay of incumbent workers. Is it good for the health and competitiveness of the companies? Yes. And is that good for job security? Yes."[11]

That the Big Three are hiring assembly workers at lower wages means that the automakers are on sufficiently stable ground to hire new laborers in the first place, a vast improvement over their financial straits in recent years. And so far, so good: Last year, the Big Three saw their first increases in market share in decades.[12] Chrysler's yearly sales skyrocketed 26%; GM and Ford showed positive gains of 13% and 11% respectively.[13]

## What About Workers?

The labor market's reaction to the Big Three's implementation of two-tier wages has been predictably mixed. While no one relishes the thought of earning 50% as much as the worker across the aisle, "Everybody is appreciative of a job and glad to be working," said Derrick Chatman, a recent hire at Chrysler's Jefferson North plant. Before coming on at Chrysler for $14.65 per hour, Chatman was laid off from Home Depot, worked the odd construction job, and collected unemployment.[14]

While new hires may have mixed feelings about joining a labor force with uneven pay for its workers, they may be encouraged that some of their top-tier cohorts gladly extend a helping hand, like Gary Wurtz. A line worker at GM's Orion Township, MI, plant, where 40% of his fellow workers receive lower-tier wages, Kurtz offered, "In order to get those guys up, we'll take a signing bonus or profit sharing instead."[15]

That said, two-tier plans still bear the potential to divide workers across salary lines. As Gary Chaison, a professor of industrial relations at Clark University, pointed out in a 2008 paper, "[Lower-tier workers] might even feel sufficiently aggrieved to someday negotiate away the benefits of retired higher-tier workers. For example, a higher-tier autoworker observed: 'After we retire, the next generation may ask, "Why should we defend your pensions? You didn't defend our pay when we were young."'"

Forty-one thousand UAW workers for Ford, the U.S. automaker least adversely affected by the economic slowdown, gained notable benefits for their lower-tier employees in late 2011 negotiations, including some paid vacation and personal time, paid bereavement and jury duty time, and co-pays for office visits.[16] Lower-tier workers making $15.50 received a raise to $19.28, bringing their salary in line with comparable GM laborers. And in exchange for future pay raises, new lower-tier workers will each receive a $6,000 signing bonus, $7,000 in inflation protection payments, and $3,700 in profit sharing.

In the agreement, Ford also committed to create 5,750 additional manufacturing jobs, for a total of 12,000 jobs it intends to add by 2015. It also promised more than $6.2 billion for U.S. factories.[17]

## Will It Last?

For now, expect two-tier plans to be a fixture of the domestic automakers for the visible future. Employment is up in Detroit and throughout the auto manufacturing sector. Analysts classify these new jobs as permanent, which is a positive sign for economists, investors, and politicians eager for recent examples of economic growth in a challenged market. And as Pat Walsh, manager at Chrysler's Jefferson North plant, pointed out, the advent of two-tier wages has not hurt production. "Our quality numbers have been very good," he said. "And our data doesn't show any differences per shift or per workstation."[18]

But will workers buy into two-tier systems in the long term? The Big Three will likely find that laborers will insist on opportunities for advancement. "If you know you're going to get to the top wage eventually, the system can work," said Peter Cappelli, a professor at the University of Pennsylvania's Wharton School. "The big problem is when you think you'll never get there."[19]

# Zappos

## They Did It with Humor

*Zappos.com customers are known for their fierce loyalty, and it's easy to see why. CEO Tony Hsieh has built a billion-dollar business providing happiness to his customers, employees, and even fellow businesspeople seeking to learn more about Zappos' unique blend of humor, compassion, and high-quality customer service. How does Zappos do it?*

### Unusual Leader Faces Unusual Circumstances

No stranger to high-pressure conversations, Zappos CEO Tony Hsieh recently found himself discussing a very familiar topic under unusual circumstances.

Hsieh was the featured guest on *The Colbert Report*, where host Stephen Colbert was grilling Hsieh to learn the secrets of Zappos' phenomenal success and rabid customer loyalty. Hsieh simply replied that it's Zappos' goal to deliver *WOW* in every shoe or clothing box. When Colbert pressed him to explain, Hsieh elaborated that among other tactics, loyal Zappos customers are sometimes treated to a complementary upgrade to overnight shipping. "A lot of people order as late as midnight Eastern, and the shoes show up on their doorstep eight hours later," he explained.

Seemingly speechless, Colbert peered over his glasses and only said, "Wow."[1]

Noah Berger/Bloomberg/Getty Images, Inc

### From Startup to One of *Fortune*'s Best Places to Work

The brainchild of Hsieh and founder Nick Swinmurn, Zappos.com launched in 1999, selling only shoes complemented with the unique premise to deliver happiness with every customer interaction. By 2001, gross sales had reached $8.6 million. That number nearly quadrupled to $32 million in 2002. A few years later, Zappos caught the eye of Amazon's Jeff Bezos. He liked what he saw and spent $928 million to buy the firm for Amazon's business stable in 2009.

Today, the company is one of *Fortune*'s 15 Best Companies to Work For and continues to earn more than $1 billion annually. Zappos Fulfillment Centers currently stock more than three million shoes, handbags, clothing items, and accessories from over 1,130 brands.[2]

### Zappos Grows, Amazon Buys In

Zappos sees a lot of potential in continuing to expand beyond shoes. While footwear still constituted 80–85% of Zappos' business last year, Hsieh wants Zappos' clothing lineup to be an-

other billion-dollar business, and he's working hard to attain that goal within the next three years. "Hopefully, ten years from now, people won't even realize that we started selling shoes," he said.[3]

Under Amazon, Zappos has maintained its focus on customer service. For Hsieh, the Zappos brand is less about a particular type of product and more about providing good customer service. He remarked that he could see the Zappos name on things as large as airlines or hotels, as long as the service was up to his exacting standards. "We could be in any industry that we can differentiate ourselves through better customer service and better customer experience," he said.[4] This customer-first strategy is working out in a big way for the company: At last count, over 75% of its customers are repeat customers.[5]

### Customers Get Special Handling

The blog search engine *Land* calls Zappos "the poster child for how to connect with customers online." It uses Facebook and Twitter to connect with their customers, distributors, employees, and other businesses.

The company's relentless pursuit of the ultimate customer experience is the stuff of legend. Zappos offers extremely fast shipping at no cost and will cover the return shipping if you are dissatisfied for any reason at any time.

Hsieh, who was unsurprisingly named "The Smartest Dude in Town" by business magazine *Vegas Inc.*, feels employees have to be free to be themselves. That means no-call times or scripts for customer service representatives, regular costume parties, and parades and decorations in each department. Customer service reps are given a lot of leeway to make sure every customer is an enthusiastic customer.

## A Culture to Thrive In

Zappos' past success comes down to the company's culture and the unusual amount of openness Hsieh encourages among employees, vendors, and other businesses. "If we get the culture right," he says, "most of the other stuff, like the brand and the customer service will just happen. With most companies, as they grow, the culture goes downhill. We want the culture to grow stronger and stronger as we grow."

Like other CEOs in it for the long haul, Hsieh is forecasting Zappos' success and the brand experience he intends to deliver years into the future. "Many companies think only one quarter ahead, or one year ahead," he said. "We like to think about what we want our brand and culture to be like ten or even twenty years down the line. In general, with a ten- to twenty-year timeline versus a three- to five-year timeline, relationships are much more important. What you do after taking someone's money, such as customer service, matters much more than what you do to get their money, such as marketing."[6]

## A Culture to Share

In fact, Hsieh believes so strongly in the organizational culture that encompasses Zappos's desire to satisfy that he's on a mission to share it with anyone who will listen via tours of their headquarters, leadership retreats, and even two new books.

It comes together in a program called Zappos Insights. The core experience is a tour of Zappos's Las Vegas headquarters. "Company Evangelists" lead groups of twenty around the cubicles, which often overflow with kitschy action figures and brightly colored balloons, giving participants a glimpse of a workplace that prizes individuality and fun as much as satisfied customers. Staffers blow horns and ring cowbells to greet participants in the sixteen weekly tours, and each department tries to offer a more outlandish welcome than the last. "The original idea was to add a little fun," Hsieh says, but it grew into a friendly competition "as the next aisle said, 'We can do it better.'"[7]

The tours are free, but many visitors actually come for paid one- and two-day seminars that immerse participants in the Zappos culture. Want to learn how to recruit employees who are committed to your company culture? You'll get face time with Zappos HR staff. Yearn to learn what keeps customers coming back? Ask their Customer Loyalty Team. Hungry for a home-cooked meal? The capstone of the two-day boot camp is dinner at Tony Hsieh's house, with ample time to talk customer service with the CEO himself. Seminars range from $497 to $3,997.

"There are management consulting firms that charge really high rates," says Hsieh. "We wanted to come up with something that's accessible to almost any business."[8]

Those who want to learn Zappos' secrets without venturing to Las Vegas have a few options. For $39 a month, you can subscribe to a members-only community that grants access to video interviews and chats with Zappos management. Ask nicely, and the company will send you a free copy of their *Zappos Family Culture Book*, an annual compilation of every employee's ideas about Zappos's mission and core values. Hsieh has his own tome, too—*Delivering Happiness.*

They may be giving away hard-earned knowledge, but Zappos definitely isn't losing money on the Insights project—profits from the seminars pay for the entire program, and Hsieh hopes it will someday represent 10% of Zappos' operating profit.

"There's a huge open market," says Robert Richman, co-leader of Zappos Insights. "We were afraid that we've been talking about this for free for so long. 'Are people going to be upset we are charging for it?' Instead, the reaction is opposite."[9] Now that Zappos is part of Amazon, will it still prosper and grow? Will the company continue to put customers first?

### Discussion Questions

1. What traits of effective leadership does Tony Hsieh demonstrate at Zappos? What aspects of his leadership can you criticize, if any? Is his approach transferable to other leaders and other organizations, or is it person and situation specific?

2. Can you find examples of where House's path-goal theory of leadership can be confirmed or disconfirmed in the Zappos setting? Explain your answer.

### Problem Solving

Tony Hsieh is a big thinker and Zappos is clearly his baby. But he's also into philanthropy and community development activities that are taking up more of his time. And, perhaps he'll come up with other new business ideas as well. As a leadership coach, what steps would you recommend that he take now to ensure that his leadership approach and vision lives on at Zappos long after his departure? What can a strong and secure leader like him do to ensure a positive leadership legacy in any situation?

### Further Research

Compare and contrast the leadership style and characteristics of Tony Hsieh with those of his new boss at Amazon, Jeff Bezos. How are the leadership styles of the two CEOs alike? In what ways do they differ? For whom would you rather work? Is one better than the other in its situation?

# Panera Bread

## Growing a Company with Personality

*Panera Bread is in the business of satisfying customers. With fresh-baked breads, gourmet soups, and efficient service, the franchise has surpassed all expectations for success. But how did a startup food company get so big, so fast? By watching and carefully timing market trends.*

### French Roots, American Tastes

What's so exciting about bread and soup? For some people, it conjures up images of bland food that soothes an upset stomach. Others think of the kind of simple gruel offered to jailed prisoners in movies. But for Panera Bread, a company able to successfully spot long-term trends in the food industry, artisan-style bread served with deli sandwiches and soups is a combination proven to please the hungry masses.

Despite its abundance of restaurants, Panera Bread is a relatively new company, known by that name only since 1997. Its roots go back to 1981, when Louis Kane and Ron Shaich founded Au Bon Pain Company Inc., which merged Kane's three existing Au Bon Pain stores with Shaich's Cookie Jar store.

The chain of French-style bakeries offered baguettes, coffee, and sandwiches served on either French bread or croissants. It soon became the dominant operator in the bakery/café category on the East Coast. To expand its domestic presence, Au Bon Pain purchased the Saint Louis Bread Company, a Missouri-based chain of about 20 bakery-cafés, in 1993. It renovated the Saint Louis Bread Company stores, renamed them Panera Bread, and their sales skyrocketed.

### Birth of a Brand

Executives at Au Bon Pain invested heavily toward building the new brand. In 1999, Panera Bread was spun off as a separate company. Since then, the firm has sought to distinguish itself in the soup-and-sandwich restaurant category. Its offerings have grown to include not only a variety of soups and sandwiches, but also soufflés, salads, panini, breakfast sandwiches, and a variety of pastries and sweets. Most of the menu offerings somehow pay homage to the company name and heritage—bread. Panera takes great pride in noting that its loaves are handmade and baked fresh daily. To conserve valuable real estate in the retail outlets, as well as to reduce the necessary training for new employees, many bread doughs are manufactured off-site at one of the company's 17 manufacturing plants. The dough is then delivered daily by trucks—driving as many as 9.7 million miles per year—to the stores for shaping and baking.[1] At this point, there are more than 1,500 Panera Bread bakery/cafés in 40 states and Canada: Panera's 801 franchise stores slightly outnumber its 740 company-owned outlets.[2,3]

### Modern Tastes, Modern Trends

Panera's success has come partly from its ability to predict long-term trends and orient the company toward innovation to fulfill consumers' desires. Its self-perception as a purveyor of artisan bread well predated the current national trend (now rebounded from the brief low-carb craze) for fresh bread and the explosion of artisan bakeries throughout metropolitan America.

Consumers' desire for organic and all-natural foods, once thought to be a marginal market force, has become the norm. Keenly positioning itself at the forefront of retail outlets supporting this trend, Panera recently introduced a children's menu called Panera Kids. Kids can choose from items such as peanut butter and jelly, grilled cheese, and yogurt, and the all-natural and organic foods will please choosy parents.[4]

In addition, Panera proactively responded to unease in the marketplace about the negative impact of trans fats on a healthy diet by voluntarily removing trans fats from its menu. "Panera recognized that trans fat was a growing concern to our customers and the medical community; therefore we made it a priority to eliminate it from our menu," said Tom Gumpel, vice-president of bakery development for Panera Bread. Though reformulating the menu incurred unexpected costs, all Panera menu items are now free from trans fats, except for some small amounts that occur naturally in dairy and meat products, as well as in some condiments.[5]

According to Ron Shaich, former CEO and now executive chairman of the board of Panera, "Real success never comes by simply responding to the day-to-day pressures; in fact, most of that is simply noise. The key to leading an organization is understanding the long-term trends at play and getting the organization ready to respond to it."[6]

© Tom Gannam/AP/Wide World Photos

And let's not forget, we are a coffee nation. For customers who just want to come in, grab a quick cup, and get out, Panera has just the thing. In many stores, coffee customers can avoid the normal line and head straight for the cash register, where they can pick up a cup, drop a small fee into a nearby can, and go directly to the java station. Caffeine-crazed customers can avoid the maddening line during a morning rush and cut the wait for that first steaming sip.

## What Makes a Customer Stay?

Panera learned from mega-competitor Starbucks that offering wireless Internet access can make customers linger after their initial purchase, thus increasing the likelihood of a secondary purchase. Now most of its stores offer customers free Wi-Fi access. According to spokesperson Julie Somers, the decision to offer Wi-Fi began as a way to separate Panera from the competition and to exemplify the company's welcoming atmosphere. "We are the kind of environment where all customers are welcome to hang out," Somers said. "They can get a quick bite or a cup of coffee, read the paper or use a computer, and stay as long as they like. And in the course of staying, people may have a cappuccino and a pastry or a soup." She went on to note that the chief corporate benefit to offering Wi-Fi is that wireless customers tend to help fill out the slow time between main meal segments.[7]

Executive Vice President Neal Yanofsky concurred. "We just think it's one more reason to come visit our cafés," he said. And wireless users' tendency to linger is just fine with him. "It leads to food purchases," he concluded. And he's right—the average Panera store has an annualized unit volume of $2.3 million.[8]

## Profits Rise Along with the Dough

All of Panera's attention to the monitoring of trends has paid off handsomely. Since Panera went public, the company's stock has grown thirteen-fold, creating more than $1 billion in shareholder value. *BusinessWeek* recognized Panera as one of its "100 Hot Growth Companies." And *Forbes* named it #4 on its list of "Top 20 Franchises for the Buck."

And even more recently, the *Wall Street Journal* recognized the company as the top performer in the Restaurants and Bars category for one-year returns (63% return), five-year returns (42% return), and ten-year returns (32% return) to shareholders. In addition, a Sandleman & Associates survey of customer satisfaction ranked Panera #2 among 120 other competitors last year; it had held the top spot for the prior eight years.

Panera continued its rapid growth in the face of the recession: In 2011, its company-owned stores saw a 4.9% increase in same-store sales, while franchise stores saw a 3.4% increase. These numbers helped contribute to a record $1.8 billion in revenues for the year—a 15% increase over 2010—and brought the company's market cap to just over $4 billion.[9] As a result of these increased sales and also new store openings, Panera hired about 25,000 new employees in 2010 and 2011.[10]

## Sticking It Out

Through wise financial management, Panera Bread found itself in the enviable position of having no debt, stable liabilities, and $250 million in the bank.[11] Taking advantage of a weak U.S. real estate market, the company opened nearly 80 new stores last year, having only closed six stores in the last three fiscal years.[12] With a debt-free balance sheet, the company plans to better position itself for the end of the financial crisis. Panera Bread has demonstrated that sticking to company ideals while successfully forecasting, and then leading the response to long-term industry trends will please customers time and time again. The low-carb craze didn't faze Panera, but can this company continue to navigate the changing dietary trends in today's unstable market?

### Discussion Questions

1. How might consumers' perception of Panera's menu and atmosphere affect their dining experience and tendencies to return as customers?

2. Describe how stereotypes about the fast-food industry might positively and negatively impact Panera. Do you think of Panera as a fast-food restaurant, or has the company managed to distinguish itself from this group?

### Problem Solving

Can an entrepreneurial and leadership personality like Ron Shaich's be replaced? But how much of its success comes directly from Shaich as a person? Is it possible for his personal qualities to be ingrained in the corporate culture to the extent they will continue after he departs? As a consultant, what would you identify as the three or four most important of Shaich's personal qualities? What would you suggest be done to firmly embed these qualities in the Panera culture?

### Further Research

Find data reporting on how Panera's sales were affected by the recent economic downturn. See if the effects were different in various regions of the country. Does Panera have special strengths that help it deal better than others with challenges such as those posed by a difficult economy?

# SAS

## Success Starts on the Inside

Charly Kurz/laif/Redux Pictures

Dr. Bruce Bedford is a learned man. He spent years pursuing collegiate and postgraduate education. After leaving school, he joined Oberweis Dairy and is currently its vice president of marketing analytics and consumer insight. He uses complex diagnostic tools to study the intricacies of Oberweis's business and suggest micro-adjustments that could have million-dollar outcomes.

Recently, he was tasked with a career-defining challenge: Stop milk bottle fraud. It echoes an episode of *Seinfeld* where Kramer and Newman hatched a scheme to take thousands of recyclable bottles to Michigan to redeem them for a nickel more than in New York. But bottle fraud cuts into dairy companies' profits, and Dr. Bedford is investigating it using high-tech software that combines predictive modeling, data mining, and state-of-the-art visualization tools. Sounds like *CSI* ? It's more like SAS.

## Powerful Tools, Rapid Responses

Short for *Statistical Analysis System*, SAS (pronounced *sass*) is a set of integrated software tools that help decision makers cope with unwieldy amounts of unrelated data. "It is a very powerful tool," says Mu Hu, director of customer relationship management for Golfsmith. "I can pretty much do anything with SAS."[1]

At its core is Base SAS—a set of analyzing, reporting, and data output tools that compile and present information stored in tables or databases. Base SAS can interpret data from almost any source—like spreadsheets, sales records, or annual reports—so that non-programmers can make business decisions based on that information.

Companies can couple base SAS with more than 200 specialized software tools intended for specific applications or industries. Examples include tools for supply chain analysis, K–12 teacher evaluation, and anti-money laundering.

SAS is the primary product of the SAS Institute, the self-described "leader in business analytics software." While SAS is its primary product, the company has developed a peripheral business around supporting and training SAS users. Anthony J. Barr wrote the first version of SAS in 1966, incorporating the SAS Institute in 1976 with co-contributors James Goodnight, John Sall, and Jane T. Helwig. Since then, with Goodnight at the helm, it's gained an impressive roster of clients: 92 of the top 100 Fortune Global 500 companies, more than 45,000 businesses, universities, and government agencies, with customers in 121 different countries.[2]

## A New Way of Making Old Decisions

To understand the success of SAS, you must first grasp the concept of business analytics. According to Michael J. Beller and Alan Barnett, business analytics is the "continuous iterative exploration and investigation of past business performance to gain insight and drive business planning." It chiefly focuses on "developing new insights and understanding of business performance based on data and statistical methods."[3]

Business analytics help an organization's leaders and researchers understand why something is happening, what might happen next, what will happen if trends continue, and what the optimum result or decision might be.[4]

This focused measurement of business data has been employed since the late 19th century. But since the widespread implementation of business computing systems that began in the late 1960s, organizations have been collecting exponentially more data and have sought to analyze it to more effectively model business possibilities. This lead to the advent of computer-based decision support systems like SAS, as well as other tools like enterprise resource planning (ERP) systems and data warehouses.

## For Every Problem, a Solution

SAS brings an organization's decision makers the data they need to solve a problem in the absence of sufficient expertise or information. For example, Mu Hu and Golfsmith used SAS to shrink data merging costs by 50% and reduce time spent preparing marketing campaign results by 70%. Using other data gleaned from SAS, they increased their direct mail response rates from 10% to 60%.[5]

Business leaders often need to interpret separate sets of information to effectively forecast market conditions or gain greater organizational insight. "We had a lot of islands of data without any sort of enterprise information view of the college," says Dr. Jim Riha, chief information technology officer for Oklahoma City Community College (OCCC), noting his desire for "a more consistent and improved view of the organization."

Using SAS, Riha can "bring additional insight to the right people at the right time, while changing the focus from arguing about data to having a better understanding of the issues and making more informed decisions."[6]

And too often, leaders don't get to choose when they must make a key business decision, and they need the right data in order to act quickly. "We need to maintain rapid access to our global data to make informed decisions, and it has to be done cost-effectively," says John Wise, senior director of Informatics at drug developer Daiichi Sankyo. "We want to spend money on drug development, not IT."[7]

Stu Harvey, executive director of planning and research at OCCC, concurs. "The real value comes when you are empowering people with data to make efficient, effective decisions earlier."[8]

SAS also makes it easier for business leaders and analysts to share critical information without the need to extensively reformat data—its Office Analytics tools make it easy to repurpose reports, graphs, and spreadsheets directly into Microsoft Office programs like Excel and PowerPoint without massive copy-and-paste sessions.

"We work with a lot of data and need to analyze it quickly and effectively," said Mike Swinson, vice president of analytics, research and development at TrueCar, an online car pricing and forecasting service. "With SAS Office Analytics, we're able to compile data from multiple sources and get it in front of the right people in less than an hour—a task that once took nine hours."[9]

## Making the Complex Simple(r)

While leadership may come naturally to some managers, predictive analytics and data mining often do not. And though the SAS Institute takes great pains to make its tools user-friendly for non-programmers, it recognizes that SAS administrators and end-users alike need help from time to time.

Beyond the knowledge base and documentation you expect to find behind any major program, SAS Institute goes to great lengths to provide a constant stream of support for its users. Employees write more than 600 SAS blogs, many focused on tips, tricks, and shortcuts.[10] The SAS web site is chock full of useful sample queries, webinars, and articles with titles like, "Jedi SAS Tricks" and "The Bayes Theorem, Explained to an Above-Average Squirrel," and the company also maintains active Facebook, Google[1], and Twitter presences

## Inspiring Loyalty

Though competitors like Cognos, Oracle, and SAP are trying to catch up to SAS by rapidly gobbling up smaller business intelligence companies, SAS still leads the pack. And most of its success derives from its extremely dedicated staff. Number three on *Fortune Magazine*'s 2012 list of Companies to Work For, SAS attracts and keeps brainpower through such perks as private offices for every employee and a 35-hour work week.[11] The company snatches up thousands of undeveloped acres near its North Carolina headquarters, which it sells to employees at a steep discount so they'll establish roots nearby. And the corporate campus is a small town unto itself—it boasts a state-of-the art nursery school, health center, and even private junior and senior high schools.

Mark Moorman, senior director in the Advanced Analytics Lab at SAS, summarizes the strategy as, "We're willing to take care of you if you're willing to take care of us." It must be working: Employee turnover is less than 4% per year, compared with 15% turnover at typical U.S. software houses.[12]

Customers are equally enamored with the company. In fact, 95% of companies renew their annual lease of SAS software.

That's likely because CEO Jim Goodnight lets customers tell him where the company should go next. Users rave about SAS's

technical support representatives, who are required to record every product improvement users suggest. These suggestions are sorted, ranked, and sent to customers via the annual SASware Ballot. The results are analyzed (doubtlessly using SAS), and the top ten results are nearly always put into action. "It's an amazingly effective business practice, listening to your customers," says Goodnight.[13]

And it's a successful practice, too: SAS recently posted record-breaking 2011 global revenue of $2.725 billion, marking the company's thirty-sixth profitable year. "Innovation is what has kept SAS growing for the past thirty-six years," Goodnight said. "We can't succeed without innovation, new products, ideas and services. Loyal, creative, healthy employees are innovative."[14]

### Discussion Questions

1. In what ways is the work environment at SAS consistent or inconsistent with the implications of Maslow's hierarchy of needs theory, Alderfer's ERG theory, and Herzberg's two-factor theory?

2. If Goodnight's approach to leadership is evaluated from the perspectives of Vroom's expectancy theory and Locke's goal-setting theory, where is he on track and where is he in danger of going off track when it comes to employee motivation?

### Problem Solving

As a compensation consultant you've been called in to review how SAS pays its employees and the benefits it offers them. You've heard in some employee interviews that they are attracted to other employers because of the high salaries available. They still like SAS benefits and the working climate, but the fact is that the higher pay available elsewhere is looking increasingly hard to say "no" to. What do motivation theories say about the implications of pay for turnover, engagement, and motivation? How do you suggest this problem with external pay opportunities be dealt with at SAS? Is this a case where time will take its course and those who leave will depart for good reason, while those who stay will continue to be motivated to work hard by the current system?

### Further Research

What's the latest on SAS? How is the company doing in its industry? How is Goodnight faring as CEO? Are the employees still as motivated and happy as they appear in this case? Have any changes been made in compensation, benefits, or work practices at SAS? Are any planned? In short, can SAS still be held up as a motivational role model for other employers to follow, or is it starting to show some rough edges?

# Auto Racing

## When the Driver Takes a Back Seat

© Crystal Alison Macleod/CSM/Landov LLC

*When you think of auto racing, do you think of teamwork? Watch any televised race, and the better majority of the camera time is dedicated to the drivers and their cars. But in each of the three major forms of auto racing, the driver is simply one member of a larger team that works together to achieve maximum performance. And when the driver wins, the team wins as well.*

In the world of competitive auto racing, the drivers are the sports' rock stars. They're courted by sponsors, adored by fans, and portrayed as the subject of interview upon interview by the racing press. And while it goes without saying that drivers are absolutely essential to earning a trophy, racing enthusiasts, teammates, and especially drivers will tell you that they can't win the race by themselves—it takes a successful team to win a race.

Furthermore, while the driver is the most visible member of the team and certainly the one responsible for guiding the car, he's not always calling the shots. The most successful teams rely on multiple sets of eyes to assess track conditions and identify opportunities to advance that drivers themselves can't see from the cockpit.

Ray Evernham, crew chief and team manager for Hendrick Motorsports' DuPont car, describes teamwork this way: "We're all spark plugs. If one doesn't fire just right, we can't win the race. So no matter whether you are the guy that's doing the fabricating or changing tires on Sundays and that's the only job responsibility you have, if you don't do your job then we're not going to win. And no one is more or less important than you."[1]

While three of the major forms of professional auto racing—NASCAR, Formula One, and rally car racing—each utilize different vehicles, rules, and team structures, teamwork is the common denominator among them.

What are the qualities of successful racing teams? Let's take a look.

## NASCAR

NASCAR is the most widely known and watched racing sport in the United States, and the popularity and success of Jeff Gordon has more than a little to do with that. Gordon has the most wins in NASCAR's modern era, has the third-most all-time wins, and has become a spokesperson for the importance of teamwork in NASCAR racing.[2,3]

"My job to communicate is probably the most important thing," Gordon has said. "Because I've got to send a message from the race car and the race track back to the team so that they can make the proper adjustments."

NASCAR has come a long way since its origins in the late 1940s in racing stock cars purchased directly from auto dealerships. Today's NASCAR vehicles are custom fabricated from the ground up, though their thin metal bodies are molded in the shape of popular American sedans to reflect the sport's heritage. And

while most fans would be quick to point out the driver, manager, and pit crew as racing team members, shop mechanics, parts fabricators, and even aerodynamics experts are just as essential to a team's performance.

In his analysis of successful NASCAR teams, Robert Williamson notes that an essential characteristic is a team's sense of ownership for all actions—"We won the race, we hit the wall, we had a tire problem, we missed the setup for the track, we nailed that pit stop," rather than noting the success or shortcoming of an individual.[4]

It's impossible for a car to complete a NASCAR race without multiple visits to the pit, and these pit stops are often the best example of teamwork in the sport. Pit crew members practice routine maintenance tasks like tire changes and refueling until they can execute them with lightning speed and the utmost precision. Aside from the skill and muscle memory of the pit crew members, other teammates contribute by modifying parts and equipment so they can be changed out in less time. In Sprint Cup racing, NASCAR's highest designation, pit stops that would take a single Jiffy Lube mechanic twenty minutes or more to complete happen in less than twenty seconds.[5]

Two-time Sprint Cup winner Jimmie Johnson cites the importance of cohesive teamwork even before a car is assembled and tested on the track. "If you really get inside each other's heads, as the car is developed, you're looking to split hairs," Johnson said. "If you really know each other then, you know what each other is looking for, you've built that foundation and belief on the teammates [and] the engineers, you can split those hairs and get it right."[6]

## Formula One

Formula One drivers, team members, and fans have one quality that sets them above all other racing participants: the need for speed. Formula One vehicles are the fastest circuit racing cars in the world, screaming down the track at top speeds as high as 225 miles per hour.

But there's another buzzword that equally defines Formula One racing: *performance*. Because of the high speeds racers achieve and the intense G-forces drivers and cars are subjected to, ensuring that Formula One cars perform efficiently and successfully throughout a race is literally a life-and-death matter.

The term *formula* refers to a strict set of regulations teams must abide by when building their cars in order to keep the races competitive. Unlike in other racing sports, Formula One teams have been required to build their own chassis since 1981, so although teams procure specialized engines from specific manufacturers, they are primarily responsible for building their cars from the ground up.

Each formula has its own set of rules that eligible cars must meet (*Formula One* being the highest and fastest of these designations), the idea being that these limitations will produce cars that are roughly equivalent in performance. Of course, that won't always be the case, as teams work furiously to seek out every last bit of efficiency and performance while adhering to sport guidelines.[7] Team members often lean heavily on aerodynamics, racing suspensions, and tires to achieve maximum performance.

The McLaren team is one of the most successful Formula One teams, and engineering director Paddy Lowe understands the behind-the-scenes dynamics that helps great racing teams succeed. Speaking on the challenge of incorporating a new component into an existing car, he noted, "There weren't actually that many issues, but we kept experiencing a variety of failures with our new exhaust system. We'd come into the circuit each morning thinking we'd fixed the problems of the previous day, only to be met with a fresh series of trials the next day. Those days were very difficult for the team.

"You have to factor in the skill of the team to work together in a very short period of time to push in a completely different direction; to understand all the different issues. The reliability, the performance, the skills of the team, all the tools they've created over the years—they all came through to our profit. In those instances, there's not a big discussion about who's going to do what; there are very few instructions. Everybody moves seamlessly. They know what they've got to do."[8]

BMW Motorsport Director Mario Theissen put it simply: "Teamwork is the key to success," he said. "Of course the basis is formed by a competitive technical package, but without a well-integrated, highly motivated team, even the best car will not achieve prolonged success."[9]

## Rally Car Racing

Whereas NASCAR and Formula One racers speed around a paved track, rally car racing frequently heads off the circuit and into territory that would make Dale Earnhardt step on the brakes: Finnish rallies feature long, treacherous stretches of ice and snow. The famed French *Méditerranée-le Cap* ran 10,000 miles from the Mediterranean to South Africa. And the reputed Baja 1000 Rally ran the length of the Baja California peninsula, largely over deserts without a road in sight.

In rally car racing, drivers race against the clock instead of each other. Races generally consist of several stages that the driver must compete as quickly as possible, and the winning driver completes all stages in the least amount of time.[10]

You could argue that of all racing sports, rally drivers are the most reliant on teamwork to win. Unlike other forms of circuit racing, not only is the driver not racing on a fixed track, but he does not get to see the course before the race begins. Instead, he is wholly reliant on a teammate, the navigator, for information on upcoming terrain. Part coach and part copilot, the navigator relies on page notes (detailed information on the sharpness of turns and the steepness of gradients) to keep the driver on course from his place in the car's passenger seat.[11]

Turkish driver Burcu Çetinkaya had already made a name for herself as a successful snowboarder before she decided to take up rally car racing at the age of twenty-four. "I grew up with cars," she said. "After visiting my first rally when I was twelve, I made up my mind to be a rally driver."[12]

"The thing that hooked me about rally driving was working together with a team for a common goal with nature working against you," she said. "I love cars, first of all—I grew up with them and I love every part of them. And I love competition. I have been competing all my life. In a rally, these things come together: nature, competition, teamwork and cars."[13]

## You Can't Have One Without the Other

Though they may receive the lion's share of the notoriety and adulation, racing drivers are only one member of a larger team, wherein every team member's performance contributes to the team's success. The best drivers don't let the fame go to their heads. As Jeff Gordon—who knows a thing or two about success—put it, "The only way I can do my job correctly is to be totally clear in my mind and have 100% confidence in every person's job that went into this team so that they can have 100% confidence in what I'm doing as a driver."[14]

### Discussion Questions

1. What types of formal and informal groups would you expect to find in a racing team? What roles could each play in helping the team toward a winning season?

2. Racing teams and their leaders have to make lots of decisions—from the pressures of race day to the routines of everyday team management. When and in what situations would you see them making decisions by authority rule, minority rule, majority rule, consensus, or unanimity? Are all of these decision approaches acceptable at some times and situations, or are some unacceptable at any time? Defend your answer.

### Problem Solving

Assume you have been retained as a teambuilding consultant by a famous and successful racing team whose performance fell bad! during the prior season. Design a series of teambuilding activities you will lead the team in performing to strengthen their trust in each other and improve their individual and collective efforts.

### Further Research

Choose a racing team of interest to you. Research the team, its personnel, and its performance in the most recent racing season. Try to answer this question: What accounts for this team's success or lack of success—driver talent, technology, teamwork, or all three? Can you find lessons in the racing team that might apply to teams and organizations in any setting? If so, list at least three that you believe are valuable and transferable insights.

# Facebook

## Making the World More Open

Julian Stratenschulte DPA/Landov LLC

*Facebook is the second-most accessed website in the U.S., according to Nielsen Media Research; it is also the most popular social networking site, besting new rival Google+ by leaps and bounds.[1] Facebook now accounts for 16% of all time spent online in the U.S.[2]*

### Something for Everyone

Regardless of age or profession, what keeps users coming back to Facebook? The simple answer is *each other*. Facebook has the world's largest community of users, and love it or hate it, if you're looking to connect with someone, you'll probably find them on Facebook. In fact, the company boasts of the interconnectedness it creates: According to a recent press release, 99.6% of all pairs of Facebook users are connected by paths with five degrees of separation, and 92% are connected by only four degrees.[3]

Since 2004, Facebook has cleverly added feature after feature to ensure that its users don't need to leave the site to connect with each other. Beyond status updates and Wall posts, Facebook added its own private messaging system, Facebook Chat, and even recently unveiled in-site video chat through a partnership with Skype.

Noting that visitors to the site tripled after Facebook unveiled its international presence, the company has translated its content into 70 different languages. Because more than 80% of Facebook's 845 million users live outside the United States, Facebook has opted to simply translate its entire site for non-English speakers.[4] "Through the translations we are seeing mass adoption in those markets," said Javier Olivan, an international manager at Facebook, adding that because the site is by its nature a tool for communication, Facebook doesn't need to spend much energy localizing it. "The translation approach allows us to support literally every language in the world," he said.[5]

But the best potential for bringing users together lies in Facebook's ability to integrate applications, including ultrapopular games like Words with Friends, Gardens of Time, and The Sims. The site's photo viewing app, for example—the number-one photo sharing application on the Web—receives more than 6 billion photos uploaded to the site each month.[6] Some 1,000,000 developers and entrepreneurs from over 180 countries are involved in developing the Facebook Platform. More than 550,000 apps have been developed so far.[7] More than 95% of its members have used at least one application built on the Facebook Platform, and advertisers are betting that they can improve that statistic.[8]

### Advertisers Want to Connect with You

Commercial marketers are taking note more closely than ever of Facebook's propensity for attracting page views, hoping to benefit from the halo effect surrounding such a successful brand. Facebook now accounts for about a third of all online ad impressions in the United States.[9] Companies are integrating their logos and brands into Facebook's built-in culture of sharing and sending. According to Derek Dabrowski, marketing director at Dr. Pepper Snapple Group, it's a success. In a promotion to give away 250,000 virtual Sunkist sodas, "We got 130 million brand impressions through that 22-hour time frame. A Super Bowl ad, if you compare it, would have generated somewhere between 6 to 7 million."

As much as advertisers need Facebook users' page views, Facebook needs those advertisers as loyal customers to make money. Rather than use banner advertisements, Facebook continues to experiment with ad concepts—first with "engagement ads" which appear on the basis of status changes, and now "featured ads" which appear directly in users' news feeds. Featured ads appear on the behalf of a page users previously liked, and only pay for those specific impressions. Facebook defends the placement of featured ads in users' news feeds, claiming that they are more relevant because "they're seeing content from a page or person they have chosen to connect to."[10]

Facebook brand and artist pages and complementary ad space to promote it are the hottest ticket in brand marketing right now, along with the much sought after "Like" designation from users. They won't always be, and Facebook will have to maintain that front-runner status in plenty of advertising innovations down the road as the industry evolves faster than ever.[11] Facebook's strategic partnership with PayPal makes it quicker and easier to run campaigns on Facebook, especially for small and international companies. However, the pressure is on Facebook to continue to differentiate itself from other social networking sites, according to Jeff Ratner, a managing partner at WPP's MindShare Interaction. If not, "Facebook doesn't look that different," he said. "It just becomes another buy, and there are cheaper, more efficient ways to reach eyes."[12]

That may be the case, but advertisers have not been shy about utilizing Facebook: Last year's ad revenue was $3.2 billion, up 69% from the year before. In that time, Facebook delivered 42% more ads than the year before while simultaneously increasing ad rates 18%. Any way you look at it, ad revenue accounts for the largest slice of Facebook's profits. (Other payments, such as game fees from Zynga and other developers, accounted for the other 15% of Facebook's revenue.)[13]

## Becoming a Better Communicator

On several occasions during his reign at Facebook, the youthful Zuckerberg has fought the common Silicon Valley stereotype of young CEOs who are brash and unripe to lead. His flat rejection of Yahoo!'s $1 billion bid to buy Facebook was criticized by some at the time as a lost opportunity, so he's working to create a professional impression for his company by hiring some experienced Web personalities. Zuckerberg persuaded Sheryl Sandberg to leave Google, where she had developed cash cows Adwords and Adsense, to join Facebook as chief operating officer. Fourteen years older than her boss, Sandberg is charged with bringing a mature personality to the laid-back, collegiate work environment. To do this, she's integrated performance reviews, refined the recruiting model, and developed a mature, sustainable advertising program that will support Facebook as it evolves.

But for a company whose product is centered around communication and openness, critics charge that Facebook has been poor about communicating policy and privacy changes to users, even to the point of reorganizing and obscuring privacy settings. In an interview with *Ad Age*, Zuckerberg acknowledged a "natural tension" between maintaining Facebook's openness and the desire to give users control, and in the past he described privacy as an "evolving social norm."[14]

It's hard to tell how much of this talk is a result of Zuckerberg's known social awkwardness and how much is calculated. He told *The New Yorker* that privacy is the "third-rail issue" online. "A lot of people who are worried about privacy and those kinds of issues will take any minor misstep that we make and turn it into as big a deal as possible," Zuckerberg said. "We realize that people will probably criticize us for this for a long time, but we just believe that [openness] is the right thing to do."[15]

To add insult to injury, *The Social Network*, a movie about Facebook's controversial founding, recently hit theaters. Based on the book, *The Accidental Billionaires*, by Ben Mezrich, it describes Zuckerberg in less than flattering terms.[16] What does Zuckerberg think about the movie? "Honestly, I wish that when people tried to do journalism or write stuff about Facebook, they at least try to get it right," said Zuckerberg. He called the book the movie was based on a work of "fiction."[17]

## Competition for Connection

Myspace has long since gone by the wayside, but that doesn't mean that there aren't plenty of other services vying for users' time. While social networking sites like Twitter, Tumblr, and Pinterest don't offer a complete replacement for everything Facebook does, they have the advantage of simplicity. By choosing one or two core functions and continuously improving upon them, they can capture a sizable audience. As of September 2011, Twitter said that it had over 100 million active users.[18]

Another competitor has emerged in Google+, a full-featured social media site from the search giant. Its major innovation is a feature called "circles," which allows a user to sort his or her friends into different groups based on what the user wants them to see, letting people rest easy knowing that those embarrassing pictures from Friday night won't be seen by co-workers or family. While the service has seen respectable growth since its introduction in June of 2011; CEO Larry Page recently claimed it had 90 million users.[19] A report from comScore said that users spent an average of just 3.3 minutes on the service in January 2012, compared to 7.5 hours for Facebook.[20]

## What Do You Think?

While there's no doubt that Facebook has brought users all over the world closer together, the management team of Facebook knows that they have serious work ahead in order to change the perception of users concerned about their online privacy. And while no direct competitor to Facebook has emerged in recent years, the company knows it can't rest on its laurels. Will adding experienced management help bring the company into an era of improved communication with its users?

### Discussion Questions

1. What are the positive and negative implications of Facebook for the development of effective interpersonal communication skills among young users?

2. CEO Mark Zuckerberg has stated that he fundamentally believes in openness, to the point that he shares his email address and phone number with his Facebook friends. But who should have the final say when it comes to determining the visibility of personal information on Facebook—the company or individual Facebook's users?

### Problem Solving

Sheryl Sandberg was and still is under pressure to bring a mature edge to Facebook. What are the most significant challenges that she faces when communicating with her "young" boss and the firm's "younger" workforce? If you were asked to provide her with reverse mentoring—that is, advising her through the eyes of the younger generation of workers and Facebook users, what priorities would you suggest for her leadership attention? Why?

### Further Research

Find as much information as you can about Mark Zuckerberg and his communication skills. Is he considered a persuasive communicator outside of Facebook? Can you find examples of his conflict management style? Is he considered to be an effective negotiator? What does Facebook's current situation tell us about his personal leadership qualities and potential for long-term business success?

# Case Endnotes

## Chapter 1

[1]"Trader Joe's." *Hoover's Company Records*. Posted 2/14/12. http://w3.lexisnexis.com.proxy.ohiolink.edu:9099/dossier/companyreporting/resolvefs.do?prod=CD&host=Rosetta_US_Academic&cdcomp=24426cbd7ff7f1975fa3ab40836e4163:24426cbd7ff7f1975fa3ab40836e4163:6_T444833821&reportKey=snapshot_report&docLinkId=-5CADFED7E16F7D4266BCDB71E45F1DCB04DC3B374726707EF41BD665EE2F75A315D90F7F3979FA5627906731F2F8280A17B31295F7C88380145D36F9FADF66D3&view=FULL&docName=Hoover%27s+Company+Records+-+In-depth+Records&reportKey=snapshot_report. Accessed 2/14/12.

[2]"Where in the Dickens Can You Find a Trader Joe's?" *Trader Joe's*. http://www.traderjoes.com/pdf/locations/all-llocations.pdf. Accessed 2/23/12.

[3]www.traderjoes.com/static/lists.html

[4]Deborah Orr, "The Cheap Gourmet," *Forbes* (April 10, 2006).

[5]*BusinessWeek Online*. February 21, 2008.

[6]"11: Trader Joe's." *Fast Company*. http://www.fastcompany.com/most-innovative-companies/2011/profile/trader-joes.php. Accessed 2/21/12.

[7]Marianne Wilson, "When Less Is More," *Chain Store Age* (November 2006).

[8]supermarketnews.com/retail_financial/food-retailing-0301/index3.html

[9]"11: Trader Joe's."

[10]Orr.

[11]"Aldi." *Wikipedia*. http://en.wikipedia.org/wiki/Aldi#Geographic_distribution. Accessed 2/23/12.

[12]"Trader Joe's Co. 2012." *Supermarket News*. http://supermarketnews.com/trader-joe-s-co-2012. Accessed 2/21/12. *Supermarket News's* Top 75 Retailers January 12, 2009.

[13]Shan Li. "Trader Joe's Tries To Keep Quirky Vibe as It Expands Quickly." *Los Angeles Times*. Posted 10/26/11. http://articles.latimes.com/2011/oct/26/business/la-fi-trader-joes-20111027. Accessed 2/23/12.

[14]www.traderjoes.com/value.html

[15]www.traderjoes.com/how_we_do_biz.html

[16]"Win at the Grocery Game," *Consumer Reports* (October 2006), p. 10.

[17]Orr.

[18]ww.traderjoes.com/tjs_faqs.asp#DiscontinueProducts

[19]www.latimes.com/business/la-fi-tj12feb12,1,1079460.story

[20]Jena McGregor, "2004 Customer 1st," *Fast Company* (October 2004).

[21]Orr.

[22]Irwin Speizer, "The Grocery Chain That Shouldn't Be," *Fast Company* (February 2004).

[23]Heidi Brown, "Buy German," *Forbes* ( January 12, 2004).

[24]www.traderjoes.com/benefits.html

[25]Irwin Speizer, "Shopper's Special," *Workforce Management* (September 2004).

[26]Ibid.

[27]Tom Broderick. "Why We Picketed Trader Joe's." *OakPark.com*. Posted 11/29/11, 10:00 PM. http://www.oakpark.com/News/Articles/11-29-2011/Why_we_picketed_Trader_Joe%27s. Accessed 2/23/12.

[28]"Welcome Aboard...Trader Joe's and CIW Sign Fair Food Agreement!" *CIW Online*. Posted 2/9/12. http://ciw-online.org/index.html#tjs_announcement. Accessed 2/23/12.

[29]"Retailer Spotlight," *Gourmet Retailer* ( June 2006).

## Chapter 2

[1]"Inditex: Who We Are: Concepts: Zara." *Inditex*. http://www.inditex.com/en/who_we_are/concepts/zara. Accessed 2/21/12.

[2]Inditex Press Dossier: www.inditex.com/en/press/information/press_kit (accessed March 2010).

[3]"Zara Grows as Retail Rivals Struggle." *Wall Street Journal* (March 26, 2009).

[4]Zara, a Spanish Success Story. CNN June 15, 2001

[5]Inditex Press Dossier.

[6]Cecile Rohwedder and Keith Johnson, "Pace-setting Zara Seeks More Speed to Fight Its Rising Cheap-Chic Rivals," *Wall Street Journal* (February, 20, 2008), page B1.

[7]"The Future of Fast Fashion."

[8]Zara: Taking the Lead in Fast-Fashion. *BusinessWeek*. (April 4, 2006).

[9]Rohwedder and Johnson.

[10]Ibid.

[11]"Zara Grows as Retail Rivals Struggle." *Wall Street Journal*. (March 26, 2009).

[12]"Inditex FY2010 Results." *Inditex*. http://www.inditex.com/en/downloads/resanual_10.pdf. Accessed 2/17/12

[13]Dana Mattioli and Kris Hudson. "Gap to Slash Its Store Count." *The Wall Street Journal*. Posted 10/14/11, 11:15 A.M. http://online.wsj.com/article/SB10001424052970204002304576628953628772370.html. Accessed 2/17/12.

[14]Diana Middleton, "Fashion for the Frugal," *The Florida Times Union* (October 1, 2006).

[15]Stephen Burgen and Tom Phillips. "Zara Accused in Brazil Sweatshop Inquiry." *The Guardian*. Posted 8/18/11, 1:09 PM. http://www.guardian.co.uk/world/2011/aug/18/zara-brazil-sweatshop-accusation. Accessed 2/23/12.

[16]Inditex Press Dossier.

[17]"Our Group," www.inditex.com/en/who_we_are/timeline (accessed May 18, 2008).

[18]"Who We Are," www.inditex.com/en/who_we_are/timeline (accessed May 18, 2008).

[19]Zara España, S.A." *Hoover's Company Records*. Posted 2/14/12. Lexis-Nexis Academic. Accessed on 2/14/12.

[20]"Our Group."

[21]"Inditex: Our Team." *Inditex*. http://www.inditex.es/en/who_we_are/our_team. Accessed 2/21/12.

[22]Inditex Press Dossier.

[23]Ibid.

[24]Ibid.

[25]"Shining Examples." *Economist* ( June 17, 2006).

[26]Inditex Press Dossier.

[27]"The Future of Fast Fashion."

[28]"Inditex Achieves Net Sales of 9,709 Million Euros, an Increase of 10%." *Inditex*. Posted 12/14/11. http://www.inditex.es/en/press/press_releases/extend/00000899. Accessed 2/21/12.

[29]"Inditex Recognized as International Retailer of the Year at the World Retail Congress." *Inditex*. Posted 3/10/11. http://www.inditex.com/en/press/other_news/extend/00000884. Accessed 2/21/12.

[30]"Ortega's Empire Showed Rivals New Style of Retailing," *The Times* (United Kingdom) ( June 14, 2007).

[31]"The Future of Fast Fashion."

[32]Rohwedder and Johnson.

[33]"Zara Launches Online Shopping in the USA." *College Fashion*. Posted 9/7/11. http://www.collegefashion.net/fashion-news/zara-launches-online-shopping-in-the-usa/. Accessed 2/23/12.

[34]Christopher Bjork. Zara Has Online Focus for US Expansion Inditex Says. *Dow Jones Newswires*. (Accessed March 8, 2010) online.wsj.com/article/BT-CO-20100317-709288. html?mod=WSJ_World_MIDDLEHeadlinesEurope

[35]Zara Grows as Retail Rivals Struggle. *Wall Street Journal*. (March 26, 2009).

[36]"The Future of Fast Fashion."

## Chapter 3

[1]Monte Burke. "Wal-Mart, Patagonia Team To Green Business." *Forbes*. Posted 5/6/10, 12:20 PM. http://www.forbes.com/forbes/2010/0524/rebuilding-sustainability-eco-friendly-mr-green-jeans.html. Accessed 2/2/11.

[2]Kent Garber. "Yvon Chouinard: Patagonia Founder Fights for the Environment." *U.S. News.* Posted 10/22/09. http://www.usnews.com/news/best-leaders/articles/2009/10/22/yvon-chouinard-patagonia-founder-fights-for-the-environment. Accessed 2/2/11.

[3]Diana Random. "Finding Success by Putting Company Culture First." *Entrepreneur.* Posted 4/19/11. http://www.entrepreneur.com/article/219509. Accessed 3/1/12.

[4]Jennifer Wang. "Patagonia, From the Ground Up." *Entrepreneur.* Posted 6/10. http://www.entrepreneur.com/magazine/entrepreneur/2010/june/206536.html. Accessed 2/2/11.

[5]Ibid.

[6]Ibid.

[7]"The Footprint Chronicles." Patagonia. http://www.patagonia.com/us/patagonia.go?assetid=23429. Accessed 3/1/12.

[8]"Environmentalism: Our Common Waters." *Patagonia.* http://www.patagonia.com/us/patagonia.go?assetid=1865. Accessed 2/3/11.

[9]"Home page." *1% For the Planet.* http://www.onepercentfortheplanet.org/en/. Accessed 3/1/12

[10]Kristall Lutz. "What Makes Patagonia 'The Coolest Company on the Planet': Insights from Founder Yvon Chouinard." *Opportunity Green.* Posted 1/27/11. http://opportunitygreen.com/green-business-blog/2011/01/27/what-makes-patagonia-the-coolest-company-on-the-planet-insights-from-founder-yvon-chouinard/. Accessed 2/2/11.

[11]"Environmental Internships." *Patagonia.* http://www.patagonia.com/eu/enSE/patagonia.go?assetid=9153. Accessed 2/3/11.

[12]"Tools for Grassroots Activists Conference." *Patagonia.* http://www.patagonia.com/us/patagonia.go?assetid=15372. Accessed 2/3/11.

[13]Takayuki Tsujii. "A Look Back: Following the Devastation of Tohoku Region Pacific Coast Earthquake." The Cleanest Line. Posted 3/11/12. http://www.thecleanestline.com/2012/03/a-look-back-following-the-devastation-of-tohoku-region-pacific-coast-earthquake.html. Accessed 3/11/12.

[14]"Our History." *Patagonia.* http://www.patagonia.com/us/patagonia.go?assetid=3351. Accessed 2/3/11.

[15]*Entrepreneur.*

[16]"Introducing the Common Threads Initiative." *Patagonia.* http://www.patagonia.com/us/patagonia.go?assetid=1956. Accessed 2/3/11.

[17]*Entrepreneur.*

[18]Ibid.

[19]*U.S. News.*

## Chapter 4

[1]Bob Sanders. "Swartz: Timberland Deal 'Magnificent and Bittersweet.'" *New Hampshire Business Review.* Posted 6/14/11. http://www.nhbr.com/businessnewsstatenews/922680-257/swartz-timberland-deal-magnificent-and-bittersweet.html. Accessed 2/15/11.

[2]Marc Gunther. "Timberland's Jeff Swartz: 'This Is Hard.'" *MarcGunther.com.* Posted 6/14/11. http://www.marcgunther.com/2011/06/14/timberlands-jeff-swartz-this-is-hard/. Accessed 2/15/12.

[3]"This Is Hard."

[4]"V.F. Corp. Completes Acquisition Of Timberland Company." *RTT News.* Posted 9/13/11. http://www.rttnews.com/1712588/v-f-corp-completes-acquisition-of-timberland-company.aspx. Accessed 2/15/12.

[5]"Service." *Timberland.* http://responsibility.timberland.com/service/. Accessed 2/15/12.

[6]Jonathan Birchall. "Outdoor Boss Who Treads an Ethical Path." *Financial Times.* Posted 10/3/10. http://www.ft.com/intl/cms/s/0/dd93e490-cda1-11df-9c82-00144feab49a.html#axzz1mljYGtn2. Accessed 2/15/12.

[7]Craig Hayman. "Argyle Conversation: Mike Harrison, Chief Brand Officer, Timberland." *Argyle Journal.* Posted 5/7/11. www.argylejournal.com/articles/argyle-conversation-mike-harrison-chief-brand-officer-timberland/. Accessed 2/15/12.

[8]"Product Philosophy." *Timberland.* http://community.timberland.com/Product-Philosophy. Accessed 2/15/12.

[9]"What's New." *Timberland.* http://community.timberland.com/Whats-New. Accessed 2/15/12.

[10]"What Makes It Sustainable?" *Timberland.* http://community.timberland.com/Earthkeeping/What-Makes-it-Sustainable. Accessed 2/15/12.

[11]"Climate." *Timberland.* http://responsibility.timberland.com/climate/. Accessed 2/15/12.

[12]"Climate."

[13]*Argyle Journal.*

[14]"How Timberland Made the Move to Recycled Rubber Soles." *Environmental Leader.* Posted 3/18/09. www.environmentalleader.com/2009/03/18/sole-purveyors-of-green-rubber-shoes-strike-partnership/. Accessed 2/15/12.

[15]Bob Sanders. "VF Corp. Profits from Timberland Acquisition." *New Hampshire Business Review.* Posted 2/17/12. http://www.nhbr.com/businessnewsstatenews/950377-257/vf-corp.-profits-from-timberland-acquisition.html. Accessed 2/18/12.

[16]"This Is Hard."

[17]Michael McCord. "Timberland Achieves Profits While Helping the Environment." *Seacoast Online.* Posted 5/4/10. http://www.seacoastonline.com/articles/20100504-NEWS-5040309. Accessed 2/15/12.

[18]"Swartz: Timberland Deal 'Magnificent and Bittersweet.'"

[19]Dan Primack. "Q&A with Timberland CEO Jeff Swartz." *Fortune.* Posted 6/13/11. http://finance.fortune.cnn.com/2011/06/13/timberlands-ceo-talks-deal-mission/. Accessed 2/15/12.

## Chapter 5

[1]www.harley-davidson.com/wcm/Content/Pages/Events/100th_anniversary.jsp?locale=en_US (accessed May 25, 2009).

[2]Malia Boyd, "Harley-Davidson Motor Company," *Incentive* (September 1993), pp. 26–27.

[3]Shrader et al., "Harley-Davidson, Inc.—1991," in Fred David (ed.), *Strategic Management*, 4th ed. (New York: Macmillan, 1993), p. 655.

[4]Ibid.

[5]Marktha H. Peak, "Harley-Davidson: Going Whole Hog to Provide Stakeholder Satisfaction," *Management Review*, vol. 82 (June 1993), p. 53.

[6]www.harley-davidson.com/wcm/Content/Pages/HOG/about_hog.jsp?locale=en_US (accessed May 18, 2008).

[7]www.motorcyclistonline.com/calendar/122_0709_hog_members_ad-irondacks/index.html (accessed May 18, 2009).

[8]Harley-Davidson, 1992 Form 10K, p. 33.

[9]Harley-Davidson home page.

[10]Peak, op. cit.

[11]Susanna Hanner. "Harley, You're Not Getting Any Younger." *New York Times.* Posted 3/21/09. http://www.nytimes.com/2009/03/22/business/economy/22harley.html?pagewanted=all. Accessed 2/17/12.

[12]Kevin Kelly and Karen Miller, "The Rumble Heard Round the World: Harley's," *BusinessWeek* (May 24, 1993), p. 60.

[13]Ibid.

[14]www.harley-davidson.com/en_US/Media/downloads/Annual_Reports/2007/10k_2007.pdf?locale=en_US&bmLocale=en_US.

[15]Harley Davidson home page.

[16]Sandra Dallas and Emily Thornton, "Japan's Bikers: The Tame Ones," *BusinessWeek* (October 20, 1997), p. 159.

[17]"Introduction of Chongqing Zongshen Automobile Industry Manufacturing Co., Ltd." *Zongshen International.* http://www.zongsheninternational.com/Company/Company_qygk.aspx?id=1. Accessed 2/18/12.

[18]"Global Customer Focus." *Harley-Davidson.* http://investor.harley-davidson.com/phoenix.zhtml?c=87981&p=irol-demographics&locale=en_US&bmLocale=en_US. Accessed 2/23/12.

[19]"Improving Harley Fuel Efficiency, Harley Davidson Maintenance." *Harley-Davidson Maintenance.* http://www.harleydavidsonmaintenance.com/harley-fuel-mileage.html. Accessed 2/18/12.

[20]seekingalpha.com/article/75695-high-gas-prices-mayhelp-harley-davidson-more-evidence (accessed May 21, 2008).

[21]www.businessweek.com/investor/content/apr2009/pi20090416_239475_page_2.htm.

[22]www.businessweek.com/investor/content/apr2009/pi20090416_239475.htm?chan=rss_topEmailedStories_ssi_5.

[23]www.google.com/hostednews/ap/article/ALeq M5hu2rSpkXHX8Vhb-H_9JM0Nh3fOEgD9EDCVPG0.

[24]www.harley-davidson.com/wcm/Content/Pages/HD_News/Company/newsarticle.jsp?locale=en_US&articleLink=News/0581_press_release.hdnews&newsYear=2009&history=news (accessed March 22, 2010).

[25]"India's Luxury Market Up 20% in 2010." *Forbes*. Posted 10/27/11, 2:05 PM. http://www.forbes.com/sites/anthonydemarco/2011/10/17/indias-luxury-market-up-20-in-2010/. Accessed 2/26/12.

[26]"Harley-Davidson Earnings, Retail Motorcycles Show Continued Strength." *Harley-Davidson*. Posted 1/24/12. http://investor.harley-davidson.com/phoenix.zhtml?c=87981&p=irol-newsArticle&ID=1651657&highlight=. Accessed 2/26/12.

[27]Mark Clothier. "Harley-Davidson Profit Rises 37% on U.S. Bike Sales Gain." *Bloomberg*. Posted 7/19/11, 4:09 PM. http://www.bloomberg.com/news/2011-07-19/harley-davidson-profit-rises-37-on-increased-u-s-bike-sales.html. Accessed 2/26/12.

[28]"Harley-Davidson Earnings, Retail Motorcycles Show Continued Strength." *Harley-Davidson*. Posted 1/24/12. http://investor.harley-davidson.com/phoenix.zhtml?c=87981&p=irol-newsArticle&ID=1651657&highlight=. Accessed 2/26/12.

## Chapter 6

[1]Jill Scott. "Gordon Ramsay admits secret passion for fast food burgers." *Daily Record*. Posted 4/20/08. http://www.dailyrecord.co.uk/life/2008/04/20/burger-king-78057-20388483/. Accessed 2/17/11.

[2]Chris Morran. "Science Confirms In-N-Out Burger Is The Best And McDonald's The Worst." *The Consumerist*. Posted 6/30/11. http://consumerist.com/2011/06/science-confirms-in-n-out-burger-is-the-best-and-mcdonalds-the-worst.html. Accessed 2/24/12.

[3]Stacy Perman. "In-N-Out Burger: Professionalizing Fast Food." *Bloomberg Businessweek*. Posted 4/9/09, 5:00 PM. http://www.businessweek.com/magazine/content/09_16/b4127068288029.htm. Accessed 2/17/11.

[4]"In-N-Out Burger to open restaurants in Texas." *OC Register*. Posted 5/26/10. http://articles.ocregister.com/2010-05-26/food/24553290_1_burger-chain-open-restaurants-beef-processing-plant. Accessed 2/17/11.

[5]"Professionalizing Fast Food"

[6]*Ibid.*

[7]Stacy Perman. "In-N-Out Burger's Marketing Magic." *Bloomberg Businessweek*. Posted 4/24/09, 12:15 PM. http://www.businessweek.com/smallbiz/content/apr2009/sb20090424_877655.htm. Accessed 2/17/11.

[8]Frank Pellegrini. "Restaurant Review: The In-N-Out Burger." *TIME*. Posted 8/21/2000. http://www.time.com/time/nation/article/0,8599,53002,00.html. Accessed 2/17/11.

[9]"Marketing Magic."

## Chapter 7

[1]*Amazon*. http://www.amazon.com/. Accessed 2/18/12.

[2]Leena Rao. "Amazon Has Opened 15 Fulfillment Centers In 2011, Will Build 'A Few More' By End Of The Year." *Tech Crunch*. Posted 7/26/11. http://techcrunch.com/2011/07/26/amazon-has-opened-15-fulfillment-centers-in-2011-will-build-a-few-more-by-end-of-the-year/. Accessed 2/18/12.

[3]"About Amazon." *Amazon*. http://www.amazon.com/Careers-Homepage/b/ref=amb_link_5763692_2?ie=UTF8&node=239364011&pf_rd_m=ATVPDKIKX0DER&pf_rd_s=left-4&pf_rd_r=17QYG39JC2VTS9V736JY&pf_rd_t=101&pf_rd_p=1337714982&pf_rd_i=239366011. Accessed 2/18/12.

[4]"Amazon CEO Takes Long View." *USA Today*, July 6, 2005.

[5]Brad Stone. "Amazon's Hit Man." Businessweek. Posted 1/25/12. http://www.businessweek.com/magazine/amazons-hit-man-01252012.html. Accessed 1/29/12.

[6]Thomas Ricker. "Amazon adds Audible to its digital empire." Accessed at www.engadget.com/2008/01/31/amazon-adds-audible-to-its-digital-empire/May 28, 2008.

[7]www.nytimes.com/2010/07/20/technology/20kindle.html, *New York Times* (July 19, 2010).

[8]Steven Levy. "The Future of Reading," *Newsweek*, November 26, 2007.

[9]Zach Epstein. "Amazon To Sell 6 million Kindle Fire Tablets, 8 Million eReaders in Q4." *Boy Genius Report*. Posted 12/13/11. http://www.bgr.com/2011/12/13/amazon-to-sell-6-million-kindle-fire-tablets-8-million-ereaders-in-q4/. Accessed 2/29/12.

[10]"Amazon Prime Members Now Get Unlimited, Commercial-free, Instant Streaming of More Than 5,000 Movies and TV Shows at No Additional Cost." *Amazon Media Room*. Posted 2/22/11. http://phx.corporate-ir.net/phoenix.zhtml?c=176060&p=irol-newsArticle&ID=1531234. Accessed 2/29/12.

[11]Jason Boog. "Kindle Owners' Lending Library Unveiled." *Galleycat*. Posted 11/3/11, 3:47 PM. http://www.mediabistro.com/galleycat/kindle-owners-lending-library-opens_b41463. Accessed 2/29/12.

[12]Scott, David Meerman. "The Flip Side of Free." *eContent*, vol. 28, no. 10 (October 2005).

[13]"Long View."

[14]Patricio Robles. "Major Retailers Ditch the Amazon Marketplace." *Econsultancy*. Posted 2/8/11, 3:33 PM. http://econsultancy.com/us/blog/7133-major-retailers-ditch-the-amazon-marketplace. Accessed 2/29/12.

[15]Stu Woo. "Amazon Battles States Over Sales Tax." *Wall Street Journal*. Posted 8/3/11. http://online.wsj.com/article/SB10001424053111904772304576468753564916130.html. Accessed 2/29/12.

[16]Ressner, Jeffrey. "10 Questions for Jeff Besoz." *Time*, August 1, 2005. Vol. 166, Issue 5.

[17]"Long View."

## Chapter 8

[1]Brigid Sweeney. "Drugstore Drama: The Old Ways No Longer Work for Walgreen." *Crain's Chicago Business*. Posted 7/18/11. http://www.chicagobusiness.com/article/20110716/ISSUE01/307169974/drugstore-drama. Accessed 2/14/12.

[2]Marianne Wilson. "Walgreens Executives Outline Growth Strategies at Annual Meeting." *Chain Store Age*. Posted 1/11/12. http://www.chainstoreage.com/article/walgreens-executives-outline-growth-strategies-annual-meeting. Accessed 2/14/12.

[3]"Our Past." *Walgreens*. http://www.walgreens.com/marketing/about/history/hist5.jsp. Accessed 2/14/12.

[4]"Drugstore Drama."

[5]*Ibid.*

[6]"CVS Caremark Acquires Longs Drug Stores for $2.9 Billion." *GCI*. Posted 8/13/08. http://www.gcimagazine.com/marketstrends/channels/drugstores/26928849.html. Accessed 2/14/12.

[7]"Drugstore Drama."

[8]Jondi Gumz. "CVS Gains New Prescription Customers as Walgreens' Agreement with Express Scripts Expires." *Mercury News*. Posted 01/04/12, 7:10 PM. http://www.mercurynews.com/breaking-news/ci_19675244. Accessed 2/14/12.

[9]"Drugstore Drama."

[10]*Ibid.*

[11]Rimma Kats. "Walgreens: Mobile is Key Component of Multichannel Loyalty Strategy." *Mobile Commerce Daily*. Posted 3/4/11. http://www.mobilecommercedaily.com/2011/03/04/walgreens-finds-more-than-half-of-prescription-refills-come-from-mobile-app. Accessed 2/14/12.

[12]Cameron Chai. "Walgreens Completes Solar Installation at Ohio Facility." *AZoCleantech.com*. Posted 9/26/11. http://www.azocleantech.com/news.aspx?newsID=15602. Accessed 2/14/12.

[13]"First Walgreens Electric Vehicle Charging Station in Orlando Unveiled." *Walgreens*. Posted 10/12/11. http://news.walgreens.com/article_display.cfm?article_id=5482. Accessed 2/14/11.

[14]"Drugstore Drama."

[15]"Walgreens Executives Outline Growth Strategies at Annual Meeting."

[16]"Drugstore Drama."

[17]*Ibid.*

# Chapter 9

[1]Dean Takahashi. "EA's chief creative officer describes game industry's re-engineering." *GamesBeat*. Posted 8/26/09. http://venturebeat.com/2009/08/26/eas-chief-creative-officer-describes-game-industrys-re-engineering/. Accessed 2/20/11.

[2]"FIFA 12 for iPad and iPhone." *Electronic Arts*. http://www.ea.com/fifa-12-ios. Accessed 3/10/12.

[3]Eric Fisher. "EA Sports to North America: 'Even If You Don't Necessarily Love Soccer, 'You'll Still Love New 'FIFA 12' Game." *Sports Business Journal Daily*. Posted 9/26/11. http://m.sportsbusinessdaily.com/Journal/Issues/2011/09/26/Marketing-and-Sponsorship/EA-Sports-FIFA.aspx. Accessed 2/22/12.

[4]Ben Fritz. "Viacom sold Harmonix for $50, saved $50 million on taxes." *Los Angeles Times*. Posted 1/4/11. http://latimesblogs.latimes.com/entertainmentnewsbuzz/2011/01/viacom-sold-harmonix-for-50-saved-50-million-on-taxes.html. Accessed 2/20/11.

[5]Christopher Grant. "Jobs: 1/3 of iPhone App Store launch apps are games." Website *Joystiq*. Posted 7/10/08. http://www.joystiq.com/2008/07/10/jobs-1-3-of-iphone-app-store-launch-apps-are-games/. Accessed 2/20/11.

[6]Dean Takahashi. "Zynga Confirms It Hired EA's Jeff Karp As Marketing And Sales Chief." *Venture Beat*. Posted 8/21/11. http://venturebeat.com/2011/08/21/zynga-confirms-it-hired-eas-jeff-karp-as-marketing-and-sales-chief/. Accessed 2/29/12.

[7]Chris Morris. "Video Game Faceoff: EA vs Activision." *CNBC*. Posted 2/11/2010. http://www.cnbc.com/id/35352043/Video_Game_Faceoff_EA_vs_Activision. Accessed 2/20/11.

[8]Matt W. "Mass Effect Sales Top 7 Million." *The Sixth Axis*. Published 4/22/11. http://www.thesixthaxis.com/2011/04/22/mass-effect-sales-top-7-million/. Accessed 2/20/12.

[9]"Electronic Arts F1Q11 Earnings Call Transcript." *Seeking Alpha*. Posted 8/4/10. http://seekingalpha.com/article/218456-electronic-arts-f1q11-earnings-call-transcript. Accessed 2/20/12.

[10]Jake Denton. "News: Battlefield 3 Ships 12 Million Copies." *Computer and Video Games*. Posted 11/30/11. http://www.computerandvideogames.com/327893/battlefield-3-ships-12-million-copies/. Accessed 2/20/12.

[11]Alex Pham. "The Sims Social Bests Farmville As Second-Largest Facebook Game." *Los Angeles Times*. Posted 9/9/11. http://latimesblogs.latimes.com/entertainmentnewsbuzz/2011/09/sims-social-surpasses-farmville-as-second-largest-facebook-game.html. Accessed 2/20/12.

[12]"Faceoff."

[13]"PDF E3 2011 Investor Presentation". *Electronic Arts*. http://investor.ea.com/common/download/download.cfm?companyid=ERTS&fileid=475188&filekey=6d4ea4b7-0389-4c68-964f-af21a86c5a7d&filename=E3_2011_IR_Breakfast_-_6-8_-_small_file_size.pdf. Accessed 2/22/12.

[14]Tom Senior. "Origin Is Doing Quite Well: 9.3 Million Registered Users, $100 Million Revenue Since Launch." *PC Gamer*. Posted 2/2/12. http://www.pcgamer.com/2012/02/02/origin-is-doing-quite-well-9-3-million-registered-users-100-million-revenue-since-launch/. Accessed 2/22/12.

# Chapter 10

[1]"Coffee Business Statistics Report." *E-Imports*. http://www.e-importz.com/Support/specialty_coffee.htm. Accessed 2/26/12.

[2]www.dunkindonuts.com/aboutus/company/

[3]"Company Snapshot." *Dunkin' Donuts*. http://www.dunkindonuts.com/content/dunkindonuts/en/company.html. Accessed 2/18/12.

[4]Agustino Fontevecchia. "Dunkin' Brands CEO Travis: We've Got the Best K-cup Out There." *Forbes*. Posted 2/9/12. http://www.forbes.com/sites/afontevecchia/2012/02/09/dunkins-brands-ceo-travis-weve-got-the-best-k-cup-out-there/. Accessed 2/26/12.

[5]Susan Spielberg. "For Snack Chains, Coffee Drinks the Best Way to Sweeten Profits," *Nation's Restaurant News* (June 27, 2005).

[6]Annalyn Censky. "Dunkin' Donuts to Double U.S. Locations." *CNNMoney*. Posted 1/4/12. http://money.cnn.com/2012/01/04/news/companies/dunkin_donuts_locations/?source=cnn_bin. Accessed 2/29/12.

[7]"Dunkin' Donuts Expansion: Chain Says It Will Double Number of U.S. Stores." *Huffington Post*. Posted 1/4/12, 4:33 PM. http://www.huffingtonpost.com/2012/01/04/dunkin-donuts-expansion_n_1184139.html. Accessed 2/29/12.

[8]www.dunkindonuts.com/downloads/pdf/DD_Press_Kit.pdf.

[9]Kara Kridler. "Dunkin Donuts to Add 150 Stores in Baltimore-Washington Area," *Daily Record* (Baltimore) (May 26, 2005).

[10]dunkindonuts.com/aboutus/products/HotCoffee.aspx

[11]"Dunkin' Donuts Expansion.

[12]www.dunkindonuts.com/aboutus/press/PressRelease.aspx?viewtype=current&id=100140 (Accessed April 4, 2010).

[13]www.dunkindonuts.com/aboutus/press/PressRelease.aspx?viewtype=current&id=100157 (Accessed April 4, 2010).

[14]"Dunkin' Donuts New Look." *Boston.com*. http://www.boston.com/business/gallery/dunkin/. Accessed 2/18/12.

# Chapter 11

[1]"Sports Industry Overview." *Plunkett Research, Ltd*. http://www.plunkettresearch.com/sports-recreation-leisure-market-research/industry-statistics. Accessed 2/14/12.

[2]"NIKE 2008 10-K, Item 6, pg. 20.

[3]CCA LiveE. "Old Is New Again: Nike's Push Towards Sustainable Advertising." *Triple Pundit*. Posted 5/11/11. http://www.triplepundit.com/2011/05/nike-sustainable-advertising/. Accessed 2/24/12.

[4]nikeresponsibility.com/#workers-factories/active_factories

[5]"Improving Conditions in Our Contract Factories." *Nikebiz*. https://secure.nikebiz.com/responsibility/workers_and_factories.html. Accessed 2/24/12.

[6]The Associated Press. "Nike Faces New Abuse Claims by Contract Workers in Indonesia." *Oregon Live*. Posted 7/13/11. http://www.oregonlive.com/business/index.ssf/2011/07/nike_faces_new_abuse_claims_by.html. Accessed 2/24/12.

[7]*Ibid*.

[8]Stanley Holmes, "Green Foot Forward," *BusinessWeek*, November 28, 2005. Issue 3961.

[9]"Nike Replaces CEO After 13 Months," *USA Today*, January 24, 2006.

[10]Olga Kharif and Matt Townsend. "Nike Betting on Venture Capital in Effort to Step Up Innovation." *Bloomberg Businessweek*. Posted 9/28/11. http://www.businessweek.com/technology/nike-betting-on-venture-capital-in-effort-to-step-up-innovation-09282011.html. Accessed 2/24/12.

[11]*Ibid*.

[12]www.nikebiz.com/responsibility/ (accessed August 29, 2010).

[13]www.nytimes.com/2010/06/12/business/energy-environment/12sustain.html?_r=1, *New York Times* ( June 11, 2010).

[14]Ibid.

[15]findarticles.com/p/articles/mi_m0EIN/is_2008_March_5/ai_n24363712

[16]premium.hoovers.com/subscribe/co/factsheet.xhtml?ID-14254

[17]Adidas Annual Report 2009.

[18]Nike 2009 Annual Report. Select Financials accessed at media.corporate-ir.net/media_files/irol/10/100529/AnnualReport/nike-sh09-rev2/index.html#select_financialsApril 6, 2010).

[19]"2011 Letter to the Shareholder." *Nike*. Posted 7/13/11. http://investors.nikeinc.com/Theme/Nike/files/doc_financials/AnnualReports/2011/index.html#mark_parker_letter. Accessed 2/24/12.

[20]Thomaselli, Rich. "Deal Sets Stage for Full-Scale War with Nike." *Advertising Age*, August 8, 2005. Vol. 76, Issue 32.

[21]"Adidas-Reebok Merger Lets Rivals Nip at Nike's Heels." *USA Today*, August 4, 2005.

[22]www.nikebiz.com/media/pr/2009/05/14_NikeRestructuringStatement.html (April 6, 2010).

[23]"Adidas-Reebok Merger."

## Chapter 12

[1]Apple Inc. home page: HYPERLINK "http://www.apple.com" www.apple.com.

[2]Pixar home page: www.pixar.com.

[3]www.businessinsider.com/chart-of-the-day-revenues-operating-profit-share-of-top-pc-vendors-2010-3.

[4]John Paczkowski. "Apple Store Customers Satisfied Even if They Don't Buy Anything." *All Things D*. Posted 2/25/11. http://allthingsd.com/20110525/apples-retail-juggernaut/. Accessed 2/24/12.

[5]Joe Wilcox. "Apple Has 91% of Market for $1,000+ PCs, Says NPD." *Betanews*. Posted 7/22/09. http://betanews.com/2009/07/22/apple-has-91-of-market-for-1-000-pcs-says-npd/. Accessed 2/24/12.

[6]Damon Poeter. "Apple, with 4 Percent of Handset Market, Captures 52 Percent of Profits." *PC Magazine*. Posted 11/5/11. http://www.pcmag.com/article2/0,2817,2395951,00.asp. Accessed 2/24/12.

[7]Brad Stone, "Apple's Chief Takes a Medical Leave."

[8]Adam Lashinsky. "The Genius Behind Steve." *CNNMoney*. Posted 11/10/2008. http://money.cnn.com/2008/11/09/technology/cook_apple.fortune/index.htm. Accessed 2/24/12.

[9]"Apple Inc." *Google Finance*. Posted 3/10/12. https://www.google.com/finance?client=ob&q=NASDAQ:AAPL. Accessed 3/10/12.

[10]"2011 Apple Annual Report." *Apple*. Posted 10/26/11. Accessed 2/29/12.

[11]Mikey Campbell. "iPhones Sweep List of 2011's Best-Selling Smartphones in U.S." *AppleInsider*. Posted 2/23/12. http://www.appleinsider.com/articles/12/02/23/iphones_sweep_list_of_2011s_best_selling_smartphones_in_us.html. Accessed 2/29/12.

[12]Andrew Cunningham. "Apple Releases OS X 10.8 'Mountain Lion' Preview." *AnandTech*. Posted 2/16/12. http://www.anandtech.com/Show/Index/5544?cPage=3&all=False&sort=0&page=1&slug=apple-releases-os-x-108-mountain-lion-preview. Accessed 2/29/12.

[13]"iCloud." *Apple*. http://www.apple.com/icloud/. Accessed 2/29/12.

[14]"iBooks textbooks for iPad." *Apple*. http://www.apple.com/education/ibooks-textbooks/. Accessed 2/29/12.

## Chapter 13

[1]James Martin. "Two-Tier Compensation Structures: Their Impact on Union Employers and Employees." W.E. Upjohn Institute for Employment Research (1990).

[2]Sanford M. Jacoby and Daniel J.B. Mitchell. "Management Attitudes toward Two-Tier Pay Plans." *Journal of Labor Research*, Vol. VII, No. 3 (Summer 1986).

[3]"Two-Tier Compensation Structures."

[4]*Ibid.*

[5]Nick Bunkley. "Big Number for G.M.: 19,000 Take a Buyout." *New York Times*. Posted 5/30/08. http://www.nytimes.com/2008/05/30/business/30auto.html. Accessed 2/13/12.

[6]Ken Jacobs. "A Tale of Two Tiers." *UC Berkeley Labor Center*. http://laborcenter.berkeley.edu/jobquality/jacobs_two_tiers09.pdf. Accessed 2/13/12.

[7]Donald W. Neuss. "Ford-UAW Pact Would Create 2-Tier Pay Scale." *The Los Angeles Times*. Posted 9/18/96. http://articles.latimes.com/1996-09-18/business/fi-45010_1_ford-uaw-pact. Accessed 2/13/12.

[8]Bill Vlasic. "Detroit Sets Its Future on a Foundation of Two-Tier Wages." *The New York Times*. Posted 9/12/11. http://www.nytimes.com/2011/09/13/business/in-detroit-two-wage-levels-are-the-new-way-of-work.html?pagewanted=all. Accessed 2/13/12.

[9]*Ibid.*

[10]Akito Yoshikane. "Two-Tier System Remains in UAW Deal with Ford." *In These Times*. Posted 10/5/11. http://www.inthesetimes.com/working/entry/12047/two_tier_system_remains_in_uaw_deal_with_ford/. Accessed 2/13/12.

[11]"Detroit Sets Its Future on a Foundation of Two-Tier Wages."

[12]"Two-Tier Wage System Shortchanging Workers?" *NPR*. Posted 1/31/12. http://www.npr.org/templates/story/story.php?storyId=146143334. Accessed 2/13/12.

[13]Jeff Bennett. "U.S. Auto Sales Finish Year Strong." *Wall Street Journal*. Posted 1/5/12. http://online.wsj.com/article/SB10001424052970203513604577140440852581080.html. Accessed 2/13/12.

[14]"Detroit Sets Its Future on a Foundation of Two-Tier Wages."

[15]*Ibid.*

[16]"Two-Tier Wage System Shortchanging Workers?"

[17]Akito Yoshikane. "Two-Tier System Remains in UAW Deal with Ford." *In These Times*. Posted 10/5/11, 8:04 AM. http://www.inthesetimes.com/working/entry/12047/two_tier_system_remains_in_uaw_deal_with_ford/. Accessed 2/13/12.

[18]"Detroit Sets Its Future on a Foundation of Two-Tier Wages."

[19]*Ibid.*

## Chapter 14

[1]Kimberly Schaefer. "Zappos.com CEO Tony Hsieh Named the 'Smartest' in Town." *Vegas Inc*. Posted 9/5/11. http://www.vegasinc.com/news/2011/sep/05/tony-hsieh/. Accessed 2/27/12.

[2]"Looking Ahead - Let There Be Anything and Everything." *Zappos*. http://about.zappos.com/zappos-story/looking-ahead-let-there-be-anything-and-everything. Accessed 2/18/12.

[3]Jeremy Twitchell. "From Upstart to $1 Billion Behemoth, Zappos Marks 10 Years." *Las Vegas Sun*. Posted 6/16/09. http://www.lasvegassun.com/news/2009/jun/16/upstart-1-billion-behemoth-zappos-marks-10-year-an/. Accessed 2/27/12.

[4]Andria Cheng. "Zappos, Under Amazon, Keeps its Independent Streak." *MarketWatch*. Posted 6/11/10. http://www.marketwatch.com/story/zappos-under-amazon-keeps-its-independent-streak-2010-06-11. Accessed 2/27/12.

[5]Jeff Cerny. "10 Questions on Customer Service and 'Delivering Happiness': An Interview with Zappos CEO Tony Hsieh." *TechRepublic*. Posted 10/1/09. http://www.techrepublic.com/blog/10things/10-questions-on-customer-service-and-delivering-happiness-an-interview-with-zappos-ceo-tony-hsieh/1067. Accessed 2/27/12.

[6]*Ibid.*

[7]"Zappos Retails Its Culture." *Business Week*. Posted 12/30/09, 5:00 PM. http://www.businessweek.com/magazine/content/10_02/b4162057120453.htm. Accessed 2/27/12.

[8]"Zappos Launches Insights Service." *AdWeek*. Posted 12/15/08. http://www.adweek.com/aw/content_display/news/digital/e3i1ccc5c91366de3d9c9a65c32df3b5cdc. Accessed 2/27/12.

[9]"Zappos's grand mission doesn't involve selling shoes." *MarketWatch*. Posted 9/13/10. http://www.marketwatch.com/story/zapposs-grand-mission-goes-beyond-selling-shoes-2010-09-13. Accessed 2/27/12.

## Chapter 15

[1]http://www.bakingbusiness.com/bs/channel.asp?ArticleID_73003. Accessed August 2, 2006.

[2]"Panera Company Overview: Company FAQs." *Panera*. http://www.panerabread.com/about/company/. Accessed 2/18/12.

[3]"Panera Bread Financial Fact Sheet." *Panera*. http://www.panerabread.com/about/press/kit/#financial. Accessed 2/18/12.

[4]"Panera Bread(r) Introduces Panera Kids." Panera Bread press release, June 2, 2006.

[5]"Panera Bread Removes Trans Fat from Menu." Panera Bread press release. February 23, 2006.

[6]Shaich, Ron. Speech at Annual Meeting 2006, Temple Israel, June 28, 2006.

[7]Miller, Ron. "Wi-Fi Continues Its Extended Coffee Break." *Information Week*, January 4, 2006. Accessed August 2, 2006, at http://www.informationweek.com/story/showArticle.jhtml?articleID_175801232.

[8]"Panera Bread Financial Fact Sheet."

[9]"Panera Bread Financial Fact Sheet."

[10]"Panera expects to hire 25K employees: Exec Shaich." *CNBC*. Posted 7/28/10. http://www.cnbc.com/id/38451966/Panera_Expects_to_Hire_25K_Employees_Exec_Shaich. Accessed 2/27/12.

[11]Jefferson Starship. "Chipotle vs. Panera: Battle of the Fast Casual Restaurants." *Seeking Alpha*. Posted 6/23/11. http://seekingalpha.com/article/276304-chipotle-vs-panera-battle-of-the-fast-casual-restaurants. Accessed 2/18/12.

[12]J. J. Colao. "Top 20 Franchises For The Buck." *Forbes*. Posted 2/8/12, 2:33PM. http://www.forbes.com/sites/jjcolao/2012/02/08/top-20-franchises-for-the-buck/. Accessed 2/28/12.

## Chapter 16

[1]"Golfsmith Shoots Well Below Par with Help From SAS." *SAS*. http://www.sas.com/success/golfsmithint.html. Accessed 2/10/11.

[2]"Customer Success." *SAS*. http://www.sas.com/success/. Accessed 2/10/11.

[3]Michael J. Beller and Alan Barnett. "Next Generation Business Analytics". Lightship Partners LLC. http://www.slideshare.net/LightshipPartners/next-generation-business-analytics-presentation. Accessed 2/10/11

[4]Thomas H. Davenport and Jeanne G Harris. *Competing on Analytics : The New Science of Winning*. Harvard Business School Press, 2007.

[5]"Golfsmith"

[6]"Oklahoma City Community College uses SAS Business Analytics to make proactive decisions for student success." *SAS*. http://www.sas.com/success/occc.html. Accessed 2/10/11.

[7]"Daiichi Sankyo demonstrates a significant ROI with SAS Drug Development." *SAS*. http://www.sas.com/success/daiichisankyo.html. Accessed 2/10/11.

[8]"Oklahoma City Community College."

[9]"All Business Users Can Now Easily Access Analytic Results Through Well-Known Windows Applications." *SAS*. Posted 2/6/12. http://www.sas.com/news/preleases/officeanalytics.html. Accessed 2/18/12.

[10]Kelly Kass. "SAS Delivers a Personalized Internal Communication Strategy for Employees." *Simply Communicate*. http://www.simply-communicate.com/case-studies/internal-communications/sas-delivers-personalized-internal-communication-strategy-emplo. Accessed 2/18/12.

[11]"100 Best Companies to Work for." *CNNMoney*. http://money.cnn.com/magazines/fortune/best-companies/2012/snapshots/3.html. Accessed 2/18/12.

[12]Randall Lane. "Pampering The Customers, Pampering The Employees." *Forbes*. Posted 10/14/96, 11:37 AM. <http://www.forbes.com/2007/11/08/sas-corestates-goognight-biz-cz_rl_1108sas.html. Accessed 2/10/11>.

[13]*Forbes*

[14]"SAS Achieves Double-Digit Growth, Rockets 12 Percent to Record $2.725 Billion." *SAS*. Posted 1/19/2012. http://www.sas.com/news/preleases/2011financials.html. Accessed 2/18/12.

[15]"Oklahoma City Community College."

## Chapter 17

[1]Robert M. Williamson. "NASCAR Racing: A Model for Equipment Reliability & Teamwork." *Strategic Work Systems*. http://www.swspitcrew.com/articles/NASCAR%200999.pdf. Accessed 2/13/12.

[2]"Modern Era Race Winners." *NASCAR.com*. http://www.nascar.com/kyn/nbtn/cup/data/race_winners.html. Accessed 2/13/12.

[3]Mike Hembree. "CUP: Gordon's Ride Has Been One Of Sport's Grandest." *SpeedTV*. Posted 11/6/11. http://nascar.speedtv.com/article/cup-jeff-gordons-ride-has-been-one-of-nascars-grandest/. Accessed 2/13/12.

[4]"NASCAR Racing."

[5]*Ibid*.

[6]Dave Rodman. "Teamwork More Important with COT Going Full Time." *NASCAR.com*. Posted 1/14/08. http://www.nascar.com/2008/news/headlines/cup/01/14/cot.teamwork.kbusch.rnewman.jjohnson.index.html. Accessed 2/13/12.

[7]"Formula Racing." *Bethelame Indy*. http://www.bethelame-indy.org/formula-racing.php. Accessed 2/13/12.

[8]Adam Cooper. "F1: Lowe Credits McLaren Teamwork for Success." *Speed TV*. Posted 4/27/11. http://formula-one.speedtv.com/article/f1-lowe-credits-mclaren-teamwork-for-success/. Accessed 2/13/12.

[9]"Teamwork Is the Key to Success—Theissen." *F1 Technical*. http://www.f1technical.net/news/8632. Accessed 2/13/12.

[10]"Rallying." *Bethelame Indy*. http://www.bethelame-indy.org/rallying.php. Accessed 2/13/12.

[11]*Ibid*.

[12]Biser3a. "Turkish Ladies Take on the Men in Dubai Rally." *Biser3a*. http://biser3a.com/rally/turkish-ladies-take-on-the-men-in-dubai-rally/. Accessed 2/14/12.

[13]Nick Hardy. "The Fastest Woman on Four Wheels?" *Gulf News*. Posted 11/18/11. http://gulfnews.com/life-style/motoring/the-fastest-woman-on-four-wheels-1.930540. Accessed 2/14/12.

[14]"NASCAR Racing."

## Chapter 18

[1]Rossi Fernandes. "Facebook Second Most Accessed Site, Behind Google in the US." Posted 12/31/11, Tech2. Accessed 2/18.12.

[2]Mark Gongloff. "Facebook Sucks Up a Ridiculously Huge and Growing Share of Our Time Wasted Online." *Wall Street Journal*. Posted 9/26/11. http://blogs.wsj.com/marketbeat/2011/09/26/facebook-sucks-up-a-ridiculously-huge-and-growing-share-of-our-time-wasted-online/.Accessed 2/12/12.

[3]Sam Biddle. "Facebook Says Literally Everyone Is Only 4.74 Degrees Away." *Gizmodo*. Posted 11/22/11. http://gizmodo.com/5861806/facebook-says-literally-everyone-is-only-4.74-degrees-away. Accessed 2/18/12.

[4]Facebook Fact Sheet. *Facebook*. http://newsroom.fb.com/content/default.aspx?NewsAreaId=22. Accessed 2/18/12.

[5]Catherine Holahan, "Facebook's New Friends Abroad," *BusinessWeek Online* (May 14, 2008).

[6]Sarah Kessler. "Facebook Photos by Numbers." *Mashable*. Posted 2/14/11. http://mashable.com/2011/02/14/facebook-photo-infographic/. Accessed 2/18/12.

[7]Facebook Press Room, Statistics at www.facebook.com/press/info.php?statistics (accessed April 18, 2010).

[8]Ibid.

[9]Erick Schonfeld. "comScore: Facebook Now Serves One Third of Online Ads in US." *TechCrunch*. Posted 4/4/11. http://techcrunch.com/2011/05/04/facebook-one-third-online-ads/. Accessed 2/28/12.

[10]Jaime Condliffe. "Facebook's News Feed Ads Are Here and They're 'Featured,' Not Sponsored." *Gizmodo*. Posted 1/12/12. http://gizmodo.com/5875426/facebooks-news-feed-ads-are-here-and-theyre-featured-not-sponsored. Accessed 2/18/12.

[11]Caroline McCarthy. Facebook's $1B Revenues: Now Keep It Up. *CNet News* (Accessed April 10, 2010 at news.cnet.com/8301-13577_3-10462824-36.html).

[12]Jessi Hempel, "Finding Cracks in Facebook," *Fortune* (May 26, 2008).

[13]Jim Edwards. "Facebook's Advertising Revenue by Year." *Business Insider*. Posted 2/1/12. http://articles.businessinsider.com/2012-02-01/news/31011945_1_ad-revenue-zynga-sec. Accessed 2/18/12.

[14]Brian Morrissey. "Mark Zuckerberg's Dream of an Open World." *Adweek*. Posted 6/23/10. http://www.adweek.com/news/big-kahunas/mark-zuckerbergs-dream-open-world-94283. Accessed 2/18/12.

[15]Jose Antonio Vargas. "The Face of Facebook." *The New Yorker*. Posted 9/20/10. http://www.newyorker.com/reporting/2010/09/20/100920fa_fact_vargas?currentPage=all. Accessed 2/20/12.

[16]www.newsweek.com/blogs/techtonic-shifts/2010/05/13/as-facebook-takes-a-beating-a-brutal-movie-is-set-to-makethings-much-worse.html, *Newsweek* (May 13, 2010).

[17]blogs.forbs.com/velocity/2010/07/22/mark-zuckerbergstake-on-the-facebook-movie/, *Forbes* ( July 22, 2010).

[18]"One Hundred Million Voices." *Twitter*. Posted 9/8/11. http://blog.twitter.com/2011/09/one-hundred-million-voices.html. Accessed 3/1/12.

[19]"Larry Page: Google+ Now Has 90 Million Users." *Mashable*. Posted 1/19/12. http://mashable.com/2012/01/19/google-plus-90-million/.Accessed 3/1/12.

[20]Todd Wasserman. "Google Plus Users Spent Just 3.3 Minutes There Last Month." *CNN*. Posted 2/28/12. http://edition.cnn.com/2012/02/28/tech/social-media/google-plus-comscore/ Accessed 3/1/12.

# Self-Test Answers

**1.** d **2.** c **3.** a **4.** b **5.** a **6.** a **7.** c **8.** a **9.** b **10.** b **11.** c **12.** a **13.** b **14.** c **15.** c

**16.** Managers must value people and respect subordinates as mature, responsible, adult human beings. This is part of their ethical and social responsibility as persons to whom others report at work. The work setting should be organized and managed to respect the rights of people and their human dignity. Included among the expectations for ethical behavior would be actions to protect individual privacy, provide freedom from sexual harassment, and offer safe and healthy job conditions. Failure to do so is socially irresponsible. It may also cause productivity losses due to dissatisfaction and poor work commitments.

**17.** The manager is held accountable by her boss for performance results of her work unit. The manager must answer to her boss for unit performance. By the same token, the manager's subordinates must answer to her for their individual performance. They are accountable to her.

**18.** If the glass ceiling effect were to operate in a given situation, it would act as a hidden barrier to advancement beyond a certain level. Managers controlling promotions and advancement opportunities in the firm would not give them to African American candidates, regardless of their capabilities. Although the newly hired graduates might progress for a while, sooner or later their upward progress in the firm would be halted by this invisible barrier.

**19.** Globalization means that the countries and peoples of the world are increasingly interconnected and that business firms increasingly cross national boundaries in acquiring resources, getting work accomplished, and selling their products. This internationalization of work will affect most everyone in the new economy. People will be working with others from different countries, working in other countries, and certainly buying and using products and services produced in whole or in part in other countries. As countries become more interdependent economically, products are sold and resources purchased around the world, and business strategies increasingly target markets in more than one country.

**20.** One approach to this question is through the framework of essential management skills offered by Katz. At the first level of management, technical skills are important, and I would feel capable in this respect. However, I would expect to learn and refine these skills through my work experiences.

Human skills, the ability to work well with other people, will also be very important. Given the diversity anticipated for this team, I will need good human skills. Included here would be my emotional intelligence, or the ability to understand my emotions and those of others when I am interacting with them. I will also have a leadership responsibility to help others on the team develop and utilize these skills so that the team itself can function effectively.

Finally, I would expect opportunities to develop my conceptual or analytical skills in anticipation of higher-level appointments. In terms of personal development, I should recognize that the conceptual skills will increase in importance relative to the technical skills as I move upward in management responsibility. The fact that the members of the team will be diverse, with some of different demographic and cultural backgrounds from my own, will only increase the importance of my abilities in the human skills area.

It will be a challenge to embrace and value differences to create the best work experience for everyone and to fully value everyone's potential contributions to the audits we will be doing. Conceptually I will need to understand the differences and try to utilize them to solve problems faced by the team, but in human relationships I will need to excel at keeping the team spirit alive and keeping everyone committed to working well together over the life of our projects.

**1.** c **2.** b **3.** d **4.** a **5.** a **6.** b **7.** a **8.** c **9.** a **10.** a **11.** c **12.** a **13.** d **14.** c **15.** b

**16.** Theory Y assumes that people are capable of taking responsibility and exercising self-direction and control in their work. The notion of self-fulfilling prophecies is that managers who hold these assumptions will act in ways that encourage workers to display these characteristics, thus confirming and reinforcing the original assumptions. The emphasis on greater participation and involvement in the modern workplace is an example of Theory Y assumptions in practice. Presumably, by valuing participation and involvement, managers will create self-fulfilling prophecies in which workers behave this way in response to being treated with respect. The result is a positive setting where everyone gains.

**17.** According to the deficit principle, a satisfied need is not a motivator of behavior. The social need will only motivate if it is not present, or in deficit. According to the progression principle, people move step-by-step up Maslow's hierarchy as they strive to satisfy needs. For example, once the social need is satisfied, the esteem need will be activated.

**18.** Contingency thinking takes an "if–then" approach to situations. It seeks to modify or adapt management approaches to fit the needs of each situation. An example would be to give more customer contact responsibility to workers who want to satisfy social needs at work, while giving more supervisory responsibilities to those who want to satisfy their esteem or ego needs.

**19.** The external environment is the source of the resources an organization needs to operate. In order to continue to obtain these resources, the organization must be successful in selling its goods and services to customers. If customer feedback is negative, the organization must make adjustments or risk losing the support needed to obtain important resources.

**20.** A bureaucracy operates with a strict hierarchy of authority, promotion based on competency and performance, formal rules and procedures, and written documentation. Enrique can do all of these things in his store, since the situation is probably quite stable and most work requirements are routine and predictable. However, bureaucracies are quite rigid and may deny employees the opportunity to make decisions on their own. Enrique must be careful to meet the needs of the workers and not to make the mistake—identified by Argyris—of failing to treat them as mature adults. While remaining well organized, the store manager should still be able to help workers meet higher-order esteem and self-fulfillment needs, as well as assume responsibility consistent with McGregor's Theory Y assumptions.

## CHAPTER 3

**1.** b **2.** a **3.** d **4.** c **5.** c **6.** d **7.** b **8.** a **9.** b **10.** d **11.** c **12.** d **13.** b **14.** d **15.** c

**16.** The individualism view is that ethical behavior is that which best serves long-term interests. The justice view is that ethical behavior is fair and equitable in its treatment of people.

**17.** The rationalizations are believing that: (1) The behavior is not really illegal, (2) the behavior is really in everyone's best interests, (3) no one will find out, and (4) the organization will protect you.

**18.** The socioeconomic view of corporate social responsibility argues that socially responsible behavior is in a firm's long-run best interest. It should be good for profits, it creates a positive public image, it helps avoid government regulation, it meets public expectations, and it is an ethical obligation.

**19.** Management scholar Archie Carroll describes the immoral, amoral, and moral manager this way: An immoral manager does bad things on purpose, choosing to behave unethically. The amoral manager does bad things sometimes, but this is not intentional or calculated; it happens because the amoral manager just doesn't incorporate ethics into his or her analysis of the situation. The moral manager, by contrast, always includes ethics as a criterion for evaluating his or her approach to decisions and situations. This manager strives to act ethically and considers ethical behavior a personal goal.

**20.** The manager could make a decision based on any one of the strategies. As an obstructionist, the manager may assume that Bangladesh needs the business and that it is a local matter as to who will be employed to make the gloves. As a defensive strategy, the manager may decide to require the supplier to meet the minimum employment requirements under Bangladeshi law. Both of these approaches represent cultural relativism. As an accommodation strategy, the manager may require that the supplier go beyond local laws and meet standards set by equivalent laws in the United States. A proactive strategy would involve the manager in trying to set an example by operating in Bangladesh only with suppliers who not only meet local standards, but also actively support the education of children in the communities in which they operate. These latter two approaches would be examples of universalism.

## CHAPTER 4

**1.** a **2.** b **3.** b **4.** c **5.** b **6.** d **7.** a **8.** b **9.** c **10.** d **11.** d **12.** a **13.** c **14.** d **15.** b

**16.** When it comes to organizational stakeholders, the list should always begin with customers and suppliers to establish the output/input players in the value chain. Employees should be included as well as shareholders/investors to identify the interests of the "producers" and the "owners." Given the importance of sustainability it is important to include society at large and future generations in the stakeholder map; it is also important to include the local communities in which the organization operates. Beyond these basic map components the stakeholders for any given organization will include a broad mix of people, groups, and organizations from regulators to activist organizations to government agencies, and more.

**17.** To make "sustainability" part of any goal statement or objective for an organization the basic definition should reflect the concept of sustainable development. That is: the organization should act in ways that while making use of the environment to produce things of value today the potential for that environment to meet the needs of future generations is also being protected and ideally being enhanced.

**18.** Product innovations affect what goods and services an organization offers to its customers. Process innovations affect how the organization goes about its daily work in producing goods and services. Business model innovations affect the way the organization makes money and adds value to society.

**19.** Reverse innovation means finding innovations in alternative settings such as emerging markets and moving them into uses in established markets. An example would be portable and low cost medical diagnostic equipment developed in markets like India and China and then brought to the United States and sold there.

**20.** First of all it sounds like a good idea to have a Chief Sustainability Officer, or CSO, in order to focus attention on sustainability goals and also bring some point of accountability at the senior executive level for their accomplishment. In terms of the job description I would argue that things like this would need to be reflected. First, there should be some acknowledgment of the "triple bottom line" of economic, social, and environmental performance. Second, there should be a clear focus on sustainable development in respect to moving the organization forward in ways that while making use of the environment and its resources, the capacity of the environment to nurture and serve future generations is also being protected. This sets the foundation for further priorities or objectives to be set in the areas of pushing for green management practices that support sustainability in all aspects of an organization's operations. And finally, there should be a responsibility to serve as the "champion" for sustainable innovations that advance the capability of the organization to be sustainable by green products, green processes and even green business models.

## CHAPTER 5

**1.** c **2.** c **3.** b **4.** d **5.** a **6.** a **7.** d **8.** c **9.** a **10.** d **11.** d **12.** a **13.** c **14.** c **15.** c

**16.** The relationship between a global corporation and a host country should be mutually beneficial. Sometimes, however, host countries complain that MNCs take unfair advantage of them and do not include them in the benefits of their international operations. The complaints against MNCs include taking excessive profits out of the host country, hiring the best local labor, not respecting local laws and customs, and dominating the local economy. Engaging in corrupt practices is another important concern.

**17.** The power-distance dimension of national culture reflects the degree to which members of a society accept status and authority inequalities. Since organizations are hierarchies with power varying from top to bottom, the way power differences are viewed from one setting to the next is an important management issue. Relations between managers and subordinates, or team leaders and team members, will be very different in high-power-distance cultures than in low-power-distance ones. The significance of these differences is most evident in international operations, when a manager from a high-power-distance culture has to perform in a low-power-distance one, or vice versa. In both cases, the cultural differences can cause problems as the manager deals with local workers.

**18.** A tight culture is one in which clear norms for social behavior exist and members know that deviance from these norms will not be tolerated. There are both norms and a high degree of conformity to those norms. In a loose culture the norms and social expectations are often general and ambiguous. Individuals tend to behave with independence and in recognition that deviation is generally tolerated.

**19.** For each region of the world you should identify a major economic theme, issue, or element. For example: Europe—the European Union should be discussed for its economic significance to member countries and to outsiders; the Americas—NAFTA should be discussed for its importance to Mexico, the United States, and Canada, and also for implications in political debates within these countries; Asia—the Asia-Pacific Economic Forum should be identified as a platform for growing regional economic cooperation among a very economically powerful group of countries, including China; Africa—the nonracial democracy in South Africa should be cited as an example of growing foreign investor interest in the countries of Africa.

**20.** Kim must recognize that the cultural differences between the United States and Japan may affect the success of group-oriented work practices such as quality circles and work teams. The United States was the most individualistic culture in Hofstede's study of national cultures; Japan is much more collectivist. Group practices such as the quality circle and teams are natural and consistent with the Japanese culture. When introduced into a more individualistic culture, these same practices might cause difficulties or require some time for workers to get used to them. At the very least, Kim should proceed with caution; discuss ideas for the new practices with the workers before making any changes; and then monitor the changes closely, so that adjustments can be made to improve them as the workers gain familiarity with them and have suggestions of their own.

**CHAPTER 6**

**1.** c **2.** a **3.** b **4.** b **5.** b **6.** a **7.** d **8.** a **9.** d **10.** b
**11.** a **12.** b **13.** c **14.** c **15.** d

**16.** Entrepreneurship is rich with diversity. It is an avenue for business entry and career success that is pursued by many women and members of minority groups. Data show that almost 40% of U.S. businesses are owned by women. Many report leaving other employment because they had limited opportunities. For them, entrepreneurship made available the opportunities for career success that they had lacked. Minority-owned businesses are one of the fastest-growing sectors, with the growth rates highest for Hispanic-owned, Asian-owned, and African American–owned businesses, in that order.

**17.** The three stages in the life cycle of an entrepreneurial firm are birth, breakthrough, and maturity. In the birth stage, the leader is challenged to get customers, establish a market, and find the money needed to keep the business going. In the breakthrough stage, the challenges shift to becoming and staying profitable, and managing growth. In the maturity stage, a leader is more focused on revising/maintaining a good business strategy and more generally managing the firm for continued success, and possibly for more future growth.

**18.** The limited partnership form of small business ownership consists of a general partner and one or more "limited partners." The general partner(s) play an active role in managing and operating the business; the limited partners do not. All contribute resources of some value to the partnership for the conduct of the business. The advantage of any partnership form is that the partners may share in profits, but their potential for losses is limited by the size of their original investments.

**19.** A venture capitalist, often a business, makes a living by investing in and taking large ownership interests in fledgling companies, with the goal of large financial gains eventually, when the company is sold. An angel investor is an individual who is willing to make a financial investment in return for some ownership in the new firm.

**20.** My friend is right—it takes a lot of forethought and planning to prepare the launch of a new business venture. In response to the question of how to ensure that I am really being customer-focused, I would ask and answer for myself the following questions. In all cases I would try to frame my business model so that the answers are realistic, but still push my business toward a strong customer orientation. The "customer" questions might include: "Who are my potential customers? What market niche am I shooting for? What do the customers in this market really want? How do these customers make purchase decisions? How much will it cost to produce and distribute my product/service to these customers? How much will it cost to attract and retain customers?" After preparing an overall executive summary, which includes a commitment to this customer orientation, I would address the following areas in writing up my initial business plan: a company description—mission, owners, and legal form—as well as an industry analysis, product and services description, marketing description and strategy, staffing model, financial projections with cash flows, and capital needs.

## CHAPTER 7

**1.** c **2.** b **3.** c **4.** a **5.** a **6.** c **7.** c **8.** b **9.** a **10.** c
**11.** b **12.** c **13.** a **14.** b **15.** d

**16.** An optimizing decision is one that represents the absolute "best" choice of alternatives. It is selected from a set of all known alternatives. A satisficing decision selects the first alternative that offers a "satisfactory" choice, not necessarily the absolute best choice. It is selected from a limited or incomplete set of alternatives.

**17.** The ethics of a decision can be checked with the "spotlight" question: "How would you feel if your family found out?" "How would you feel if this were published in the local newspaper?" Also, one can test the decision by evaluating it on four criteria: (1) Utility—does it satisfy all stakeholders? (2) Rights—does it respect everyone's rights? (3) Justice—is it consistent with fairness and justice? (4) Caring—does it meet responsibilities for caring?

**18.** A manager using systematic thinking is going to approach problem solving in a logical and rational fashion. The tendency will be to proceed in a linear, step-by-step fashion, handling one issue at a time. A manager using intuitive thinking will be more spontaneous and open in problem solving. He or she may jump from one stage in the process to another and deal with many different things at once.

**19.** It almost seems contradictory to say that one can prepare for crisis, but it is possible. The concept of crisis management is used to describe how managers and others prepare for unexpected high-impact events that threaten an organization's health and well-being. Crisis management involves both anticipating possible crises and preparing teams and plans ahead of time for how to handle them if they do occur. Many organizations today, for example, are developing crisis management plans to deal with terrorism and computer "hacking" attacks.

**20.** This is what I would say in the mentoring situation: continuing developments in information technology are changing the work setting for most employees. An important development for the traditional white-collar worker falls in the area of office automation—the use of computers and related technologies to facilitate everyday office work. In the "electronic office" of today and tomorrow, you should be prepared to work with and take full advantage of the following: smart workstations supported by desktop computers; voice messaging systems, whereby computers take dictation, answer the telephone, and relay messages; database and word processing software systems that allow storage, access, and manipulation of data, as well as the preparation of reports; electronic mail systems that send mail and data from computer to computer; electronic bulletin boards for posting messages; and computer conferencing and videoconferencing that allow people to work with one another every day over great distances. These are among the capabilities of the new workplace. To function effectively, you must be prepared not only to use these systems to full advantage, but also to stay abreast of new developments as they become available.

## CHAPTER 8

**1.** d **2.** a **3.** a **4.** d **5.** b **6.** c **7.** a **8.** d **9.** a **10.** b
**11.** a **12.** c **13.** c **14.** d **15.** c

**16.** The five steps in the formal planning process are: (1) Define your objectives, (2) determine where you stand relative to objectives, (3) develop premises about future conditions, (4) identify and choose among action alternatives to accomplish objectives, and (5) implement action plans and evaluate results.

**17.** Benchmarking is the use of external standards to help evaluate one's own situation and develop ideas and directions for improvement. The bookstore owner/manager might visit other bookstores in other towns that are known for their success. By observing and studying the operations of those stores and then comparing her store to them, the owner/manager can develop plans for future action.

**18.** Planning helps improve focus for organizations and for individuals. Essential to the planning process is identifying your objectives and specifying exactly where it is you hope to get in the future. Having a clear sense of direction helps keep us on track by avoiding getting sidetracked on things that might not contribute to accomplishing our objectives. It also helps us to find discipline in stopping periodically to assess how well we are doing. With a clear objective, present progress can be realistically evaluated and efforts refocused on accomplishing the objective.

**19.** Very often plans fail because the people who make the plans aren't the same ones who must implement them. When people who will be implementing are allowed to participate in the planning process, at least two positive results may happen that help improve implementation: (1) Through involvement they better understand the final plans, and (2) through involvement they become more committed to making those plans work.

**20.** I would begin the speech by describing the importance of goal alignment as an integrated planning and control approach. I would also clarify that the key elements are objectives and participation. Any objectives should be clear, measurable, and time-defined. In addition, these objectives should be set with the full involvement and participation of the employees; they should not be set by the manager and then told to the employees. That understood, I would describe how each business manager should jointly set objectives with each of his or her employees and jointly review progress toward their accomplishment. I would suggest that the employees should work on the required activities while staying in communication with their managers. The managers in turn should provide any needed support or assistance to their employees. This whole process could be formally recycled at least twice per year.

## CHAPTER 9

**1.** a **2.** b **3.** d **4.** b **5.** b **6.** b **7.** d **8.** b **9.** b **10.** c **11.** a **12.** b **13.** c **14.** c **15.** c

**16.** The four steps in the control process are: (1) Establish objectives and standards, (2) measure actual performance, (3) compare actual performance with objectives and standards, and (4) take necessary action.

**17.** Feedforward control involves the careful selection of system inputs to ensure that outcomes are of the desired quality and up to all performance standards. In the case of a local bookstore, one of the major points of influence over performance and customer satisfaction is the relationship between the customers and the store's employees who serve them. Thus, a good example of feedforward control is exercising great care when the manager hires new employees and then trains them to work according to the store's expectations.

**18.** Douglas McGregor's concept of Theory Y involves the assumption that people can be trusted to exercise self-control in their work. This is the essence of internal control—people controlling their own work by taking personal responsibility for results. If managers approach work with McGregor's Theory Y assumptions, they will, according to him, promote more self-control—or internal control—by people at work.

**19.** The four questions to ask when developing a balanced scorecard for inclusion on an executive dashboard are: (1) *Financial Performance*—To improve financially, how should we appear to our shareholders? (2) *Customer Sat-isfaction*—To achieve our vision, how should we appear to our customers? (3) *Internal Process Improvement*—To satisfy our customers and shareholders, at what internal business processes should we excel? (4) *Innovation and Learning*—To achieve our vision, how will we sustain our ability to change and improve?

**20.** There are a very large number of activities required to complete a new student center building on a college campus. Among them, one might expect the following to be core requirements: (1) land surveys and planning permissions from local government, (2) architect plans developed and approved, (3) major subcontractors hired, (4) site excavation completed, (5) building exterior completed, (6) building interior completed and furnishings installed. Use the figure from the chapter as a guide for developing your AON diagram.

## CHAPTER 10

**1.** a **2.** b **3.** c **4.** d **5.** b **6.** c **7.** a **8.** c **9.** b **10.** c **11.** a **12.** c **13.** d **14.** b **15.** a

**16.** A corporate strategy sets long-term direction for an enterprise as a whole. Functional strategies set directions so that business functions such as marketing and manufacturing support the overall corporate strategy.

**17.** A SWOT analysis is useful during strategic planning. It involves the analysis of organizational strengths and weaknesses, and of environmental opportunities and threats.

**18.** The focus strategy concentrates attention on a special market segment or niche. The differentiation strategy concentrates on building loyalty to a unique product or service.

**19.** Strategic leadership is the ability to enthuse people to participate in continuous change, performance enhancement, and the implementation of organizational strategies. The special qualities of the successful strategic leader include the ability to make trade-offs, create a sense of urgency, communicate the strategy, and engage others in continuous learning about the strategy and its performance responsibilities.

**20.** Porter's competitive strategy model involves the possible use of three alternative strategies: differentiation, cost leadership, and focus. In this situation, the larger department store seems better positioned to follow the cost leadership strategy. This means that Kim may want to consider the other two alternatives.

A differentiation strategy would involve trying to distinguish Kim's products from those of the larger store.

This might involve a "Made in America" theme, or an emphasis on leather, canvas, or some other type of clothing material. A focus strategy might specifically target college students and try to respond to their tastes and needs, rather than those of the larger community population. This might involve special orders and other types of individualized services for the college student market.

## CHAPTER 11

**1.** b **2.** a **3.** b **4.** a **5.** a **6.** c **7.** d **8.** b **9.** b **10.** b **11.** c **12.** b **13.** b **14.** c **15.** b

**16.** The functional structure is prone to problems of internal coordination. One symptom may be that the different functional areas, such as marketing and manufacturing, are not working well together. This structure is also slow in responding to changing environmental trends and challenges. If the firm finds that its competitors are getting to market faster with new and better products, this is another potential indicator that the functional structure is not supporting operations properly.

**17.** A network structure often involves one organization "contracting out" aspects of its operations to other organizations that specialize in them. The example used in the text was of a company that contracted out its mailroom services. Through the formation of networks of contracts, the organization is reduced to a core of essential employees whose expertise is concentrated in the primary business areas. The contracts are monitored and maintained in the network to allow the overall operations of the organization to continue, even though they are not directly accomplished by full-time employees.

**18.** The term *contingency* is used in management to indicate that management strategies and practices should be tailored to fit the unique needs of individual situations. There is no universal solution that fits all problems and circumstances. Thus, in organizational design, contingency thinking must be used to identify and implement particular organizational points in time. What works well at one point in time may not work well at another, as the environment and other conditions change. For example, the more complex, variable, and uncertain the elements in the environment, the more difficult it is for the organization to operate. This situation calls for a more organic design. In a stable and more certain environment, the mechanistic design is appropriate, because operations are more routine and predictable.

**19.** Several options for answering this question are described in the chapter.

**20.** Faisal must first have confidence in the two engineers—he must trust them and respect their capabilities. Second, he must have confidence in himself, trusting his own judgment to give up some work and allow the others to do it. Third, he should follow the rules of effective delegation. These include being very clear on what must be accomplished by each engineer. Their responsibilities should be clearly understood. He must also give them the authority to act in order to fulfill their responsibility, especially in relationship to the other engineers. And he must not forget his own final accountability for the results. He should remain in control and, through communication, make sure that work proceeds as planned.

## CHAPTER 12

**1.** b **2.** a **3.** d **4.** a **5.** b **6.** a **7.** b **8.** b **9.** d **10.** c **11.** b **12.** c **13.** c **14.** d **15.** b

**16.** Core values indicate important beliefs that underlie organizational expectations about the behavior and contributions of members. Sample values for high-performance organizations might include expressed commitments to honesty and integrity, innovation, customer service, quality, and respect for people.

**17.** Subcultures are important in organizations because of the many aspects of diversity found in the workforce. Although working in the same organization and sharing the same organizational culture, members differ in subculture affiliations based on such aspects as gender, age, and ethnic differences, as well as in respect to occupational and functional affiliations. It is important to understand how subculture differences may influence working relationships. For example, a 40-year-old manager of 20-year-old workers must understand that the values and behaviors of the younger workforce may not be totally consistent with what she or he believes in, and vice versa.

**18.** Lewin's three phases of planned change and the relevant change leadership responsibilities are: unfreezing—preparing a system for change; changing—moving or creating change in a system; and refreezing—stabilizing and reinforcing change once it has occurred. In addition, we might talk about an additional or parallel phase of "improvising." This calls for change leadership that is good at gathering feedback, listening to resistance, and making constructive modifications as the change is in progress to smooth its implementation and make sure what is implemented is a best fit for the circumstances and people involved.

**19.** Use of force-coercion as a strategy of planned change is limited by the likelihood of compliance being the major outcome. People comply with force only so long as it remains real, visible, and likely, but they have no personal commitment to the behavior. So, when the force goes away, so does the behavior. Also, a manager who relies on forcing people to get changes made is likely to be viewed negatively by them and suffer from additional negative halo effects in other work with them. Rational persuasion and shared power are likely to have more long-lasting impact on behavior since the person responds to the change strategy by internalization of the value of the behavior being encouraged. Because of this commitment the influence on their actions is more likely to be long-lasting rather than temporary as in the case of force-coercion.

**20.** I disagree with this statement, because a strong organizational or corporate culture can be a positive influence on any organization, large or small. Also, issues of diversity, inclusiveness, and multiculturalism apply as well. In fact, such things as a commitment to pluralism and respect for diversity should be part of the core values and distinguishing features of the organization's culture. The woman working for the large company is mistaken in thinking that the concepts do not apply to her friend's small business. In fact, the friend—as owner and perhaps founder of the business—should be working hard to establish the values and other elements that will create a strong and continuing culture and respect for diversity. Employees of any organization should have core organizational values to serve as reference points for their attitudes and behavior. The rites and rituals of everyday organizational life are also important ways to recognize positive accomplishments and add meaning to the employment relationships. It may even be that the friend's roles as diversity leader and creator and sponsor of the corporate culture are more magnified in the small business setting. As the owner and manager, she is visible every day to all employees. How she acts will have a great impact on any "culture."

## CHAPTER 13

**1.** a **2.** c **3.** a **4.** d **5.** b **6.** d **7.** c **8.** d **9.** d **10.** b **11.** a **12.** b **13.** a **14.** d **15.** d

**16.** Internal recruitment deals with job candidates who already know the organization well. It is also a strong motivator because it communicates to everyone the opportunity to advance in the organization through hard work. External recruitment may allow the organization to obtain expertise not available internally. It also brings in employees with new and fresh viewpoints who are not biased by previous experience in the organization.

**17.** Orientation activities introduce a new employee to the organization and the work environment. This is a time when the individual may develop key attitudes and when performance expectations will also be established. Good orientation communicates positive attitudes and expectations and reinforces the desired organizational culture. It formally introduces the individual to important policies and procedures that everyone is expected to follow.

**18.** The graphic rating scale simply asks a supervisor to rate an employee on an established set of criteria, such as quantity of work or attitude toward work. This leaves a lot of room for subjectivity and debate. The behaviorally anchored rating scale asks the supervisor to rate the employee on specific behaviors that had been identified as positively or negatively affecting performance in a given job. This is a more specific appraisal approach and leaves less room for debate and disagreement.

**19.** Mentoring is when a senior and experienced individual adopts a newcomer or more junior person with the goal of helping him or her develop into a successful worker. The mentor may or may not be the individual's immediate supervisor. The mentor meets with the individual and discusses problems, shares advice, and generally supports the individual's attempts to grow and perform. Mentors are considered very useful for persons newly appointed to management positions.

**20.** As Sy's supervisor, you face a difficult but perhaps expected human resource management problem. Not only is Sy influential as an informal leader, he also has considerable experience on the job and in the company. Even though he is experiencing performance problems using the new computer system, there is no indication that he doesn't want to work hard and continue to perform for the company. Although retirement is an option, Sy may also be transferred, promoted, or simply terminated. The latter response seems unjustified and may cause legal problems. Transferring Sy, with his agreement, to another position could be a positive move; promoting Sy to a supervisory position in which his experience and networks would be useful is another possibility. The key in this situation seems to be moving Sy out so that a computer-literate person can take over the job, while continuing to utilize Sy in a job that better fits his talents. Transfer and/or promotion should be actively considered, both in his and in the company's interest.

## CHAPTER 14

**1.** d **2.** d **3.** b **4.** b **5.** a **6.** a **7.** b **8.** d **9.** a **10.** b **11.** b **12.** a **13.** a **14.** c **15.** a

**16.** Position power is based on reward; coercion, or punishment; and legitimacy, or formal authority. Managers, however, need to have more power than that made available to them by the position alone. Thus, they have to develop personal power through expertise and reference. This personal power is essential in helping managers to get things done beyond the scope of their position power alone.

**17.** Leader-participation theory suggests that leadership effectiveness is determined in part by how well managers or leaders handle the many different problem or decision situations that they face every day. Decisions can be made through individual or authority, consultative, or group-consensus approaches. No one of these decision methods is always the best; each is a good fit for certain types of situations. A good manager or leader is able to use each of these approaches and knows when each is the best approach to use in particular situations.

**18.** The three variables used in Fiedler's model to diagnose situational favorableness are: (1) position power—how much power the leader has in terms of rewards, punishments, and legitimacy; (2) leader–member relations—the quality of relationships between the leader and followers; and (3) task structure—the degree to which the task is either clear and well defined, or open-ended and more ambiguous.

**19.** Drucker says that good leaders have more than the "charisma" or "personality" being popularized in the concept of transformational leadership. He reminds us that good leaders work hard to accomplish some basic things in their everyday activities. These include: (1) establishing a clear sense of mission; (2) accepting leadership as a responsibility, not a rank; and (3) earning and keeping the respect of others.

**20.** In his new position, Marcel must understand that the transactional aspects of leadership are not sufficient to guarantee him long-term leadership effectiveness. He must move beyond the effective use of task-oriented and people-oriented behaviors and demonstrate through his personal qualities the capacity to inspire others. A charismatic leader develops a unique relationship with followers, in which they become enthusiastic, highly loyal, and high achievers. Marcel needs to work very hard to develop positive relationships with the team members. In those relationships he must emphasize high aspirations for performance accomplishments, enthusiasm, ethical behavior, integrity and honesty in all dealings, and a clear vision of the future. By working hard with this agenda and by allowing his personality to positively express itself in the team setting, Marcel should make continuous progress as an effective and moral leader.

## CHAPTER 15

**1.** c **2.** b **3.** d **4.** a **5.** c **6.** d **7.** b **8.** c **9.** a **10.** b **11.** d **12.** d **13.** c **14.** d **15.** c

**16.** A psychological contract is the individual's view of the inducements he or she expects to receive from the organization in return for his or her work contributions. The contract is healthy when the individual perceives that the inducements and contributions are fair and in a state of balance.

**17.** Self-serving bias is the attribution tendency to blame the environment when things go wrong—"It's not my fault; 'they' caused all this mess." Fundamental attribution error is the tendency to blame others for problems that they have—"It's something wrong with 'you' that's causing the problem."

**18.** All the Big Five personality traits are relevant to the workplace. Consider the following basic examples. Extraversion suggests whether or not a person will reach out to relate and work well with others. Agreeableness suggests whether a person is open to the ideas of others and willing to go along with group decisions. Conscientiousness suggests whether or not someone can be depended on to meet commitments and perform agreed-upon tasks. Emotional stability suggests whether someone will be relaxed and secure, or uptight and tense, in work situations. Openness to experience suggests whether or not someone will be open to new ideas or resistant to change.

**19.** The Type A personality is characteristic of people who bring stress on themselves by virtue of personal characteristics. These tend to be compulsive individuals who are uncomfortable waiting for things to happen, who try to do many things at once, and who generally move fast and have difficulty slowing down. Type A personalities can be stressful for both themselves and the people around them. Managers must be aware of Type A personality tendencies in their own behavior and among others with whom they work. Ideally, this awareness will help the manager take precautionary steps to best manage the stress caused by this personality type.

**20.** Scott needs to be careful. Although there is modest research support for the relationship between job satisfaction and performance, there is no guarantee that simply doing things to make people happier at work will cause them to be higher performers. Scott needs to take a broader perspective on this issue and his responsibilities as a manager. He should be interested in job satisfaction for his therapists and do everything he can to help them to experience it. But he should also be performance-oriented, and should understand that performance is achieved through a combination of skills, support, and motivation. He should be helping the therapists to achieve and maintain high levels of job competency. He should also work with them to find out what obstacles they are facing and what support they need—things that perhaps he can deal with in their behalf. All of this relates as well to research indications that performance can be a source of job satisfaction. And finally, Scott should make sure that the therapists believe they are being properly rewarded for their work, because rewards are shown by research to have an influence on both job satisfaction and job performance.

### CHAPTER 16

**1.** c **2.** b **3.** d **4.** d **5.** b **6.** b **7.** a **8.** d **9.** b **10.** d **11.** c **12.** c **13.** a **14.** b **15.** d

**16.** People high in need for achievement will prefer work settings and jobs in which they have (1) challenging but achievable goals, (2) individual responsibility, and (3) performance feedback.

**17.** Participation is important to goal-setting theory because, in general, people tend to be more committed to the accomplishment of goals they have helped to set. When people participate in the setting of goals, they also understand them better. Participation in goal setting improves goal acceptance and understanding.

**18.** Maslow, McClelland, and Herzberg would likely find common agreement in respect to a set of "higher order" needs. For Maslow these are self-actualization and ego; they correspond with Alderfer's growth needs, and with McClelland's needs for achievement and power. Maslow's social needs link up with relatedness needs in Alderfer's theory and the need for affiliation in McClelland's theory. Maslow's safety needs correspond to Alderfer's existence

needs. Herzberg's "satisfier-factors" correspond to satisfactions of Maslow's higher needs, Alderfer's growth needs, and McClelland's need for achievement.

**19.** The compressed workweek, or 4-40 schedule, offers employees the advantage of a three-day weekend. However, it can cause problems for the employer in terms of ensuring that operations are covered adequately during the normal five workdays of the week. Labor unions may resist, and the compressed workweek will entail more complicated work scheduling. In addition, some employees find that the schedule is tiring and can cause family adjustment problems.

**20.** It has already been pointed out in the answer to question 16 that a person with a high need for achievement likes moderately challenging goals and performance feedback. Participation of both manager and subordinate in goal setting offers an opportunity to choose goals to which the subordinate will respond, and which also will serve the organization. Furthermore, through goal setting the manager and individual subordinates can identify performance standards or targets. Progress toward these targets can be positively reinforced by the manager. Such reinforcements can serve as indicators of progress to someone with a high need for achievement, thus responding to their desire for performance feedback.

### CHAPTER 17

**1.** d **2.** a **3.** b **4.** b **5.** c **6.** a **7.** b **8.** b **9.** a **10.** a **11.** d **12.** b **13.** b **14.** a **15.** a

**16.** Input factors can have a major impact on group effectiveness. In order to best prepare a group to perform effectively, a manager should make sure that the right people are put in the group (maximize available talents and abilities), that these people are capable of working well together (membership characteristics should promote good relationships), that the tasks are clear, and that the group has the resources and environment needed to perform up to expectations.

**17.** A group's performance can be analyzed according to the interaction between cohesiveness and performance norms. In a highly cohesive group, members tend to conform to group norms. Thus, when the performance norm is positive and cohesion is high, we can expect everyone to work hard to support the norm—high performance is likely. By the same token, high cohesion and a low performance norm will yield the opposite result—low performance is likely. With other combinations of norms and cohesion, the performance results will be more mixed.

**18.** The textbook lists several symptoms of groupthink, along with various strategies for avoiding groupthink. For example, a group whose members censor themselves from contributing "contrary" or "different" opinions and/or whose members keep talking about outsiders as "weak" or the "enemy" may be suffering from groupthink. This may be avoided or corrected, for example, by asking someone to be the "devil's advocate" for a meeting, and by inviting in an outside observer to help gather different viewpoints.

**19.** In a traditional work group, the manager or supervisor directs the group. In a self-managing team, the members of the team provide self-direction. They plan, organize, and evaluate their work, share tasks, and help one another develop skills; they may even make hiring decisions. A true self-managing team does not need the traditional "boss" or supervisor, because the team as a whole takes on the supervisory responsibilities.

**20.** Marcos is faced with a highly cohesive group whose members conform to a negative, or low-performance norm. This is a difficult situation that is ideally resolved by changing the performance norm. In order to gain the group's commitment to a high-performance norm, Marcos should act as a positive role model for the norm. He must communicate the norm clearly and positively to the group and should not assume that everyone knows what he expects of them. He may also talk to the informal leader and gain his or her commitment to the norm. He might carefully reward high-performance behaviors within the group and may introduce new members with high-performance records and commitments. And he might hold group meetings in which performance standards and expectations are discussed, with an emphasis on committing to new high-performance directions. If his attempts to introduce a high-performance norm fail, Marcos may have to take steps to reduce group cohesiveness so that individual members can pursue higher-performance results without feeling bound by group pressures to restrict their performance.

## CHAPTER 18

**1.** a **2.** b **3.** d **4.** d **5.** b **6.** b **7.** d **8.** b **9.** d **10.** b **11.** d **12.** c **13.** a **14.** d **15.** a

**16.** The manager's goal in active listening is to help the subordinate say what he or she really means. To do this, the manager should carefully listen for the content of what someone is saying, paraphrase or reflect back what the person appears to be saying, remain sensitive to nonverbal cues and feelings, and not be evaluative.

**17.** The relationship between conflict intensity and performance can be pictured as an inverted "U" curve. It shows that performance increases as conflict intensity increases from low to moderate levels,. Conflict of moderate intensity creates the zone of *constructive conflict*, where its impact on performance is most positive. As conflict intensity moves into extreme levels, performance tends to decrease. This is the zone of *destructive conflict*. When conflict is too low, performance may also suffer.

**18.** Win-lose outcomes are likely when conflict is managed through high-assertiveness and low-cooperativeness styles. In this situation of competition, the conflict is resolved by one person or group dominating another. Lose-lose outcomes occur when conflict is managed through avoidance (where nothing is resolved), and possibly when it is managed through compromise (where each party gives up something to the other). Win-win outcomes are associated mainly with problem solving and collaboration in conflict management, which result from high assertiveness and high cooperativeness.

**19.** In a negotiation, both substance and relationship goals are important. Substance goals relate to the content of the negotiation. A substance goal, for example, may relate to the final salary agreement between a job candidate and a prospective employer. Relationship goals relate to the quality of the interpersonal relationships among the negotiating parties. Relationship goals are important, because the negotiating parties most likely have to work together in the future. For example, if relationships are poor after a labor–management negotiation, the likelihood is that future problems will occur.

**20.** Kathryn can do a number of things to establish and maintain a system of upward communication for her department store branch. To begin, she should, as much as possible, try to establish a highly interactive style of management based upon credibility and trust. Credibility is earned by building personal power through expertise and reference. In regard to credibility, she might set the tone for the department managers by using MBWA—"managing by wandering around." Once this pattern is established, trust will build between her and other store employees, and she should find that she learns a lot from interacting directly with them. Kathryn should also set up a formal communication structure, such as bimonthly store meetings, where she communicates store goals, results, and other issues to the staff and listens to them in return. An e-mail system whereby Kathryn and her staff could send messages to one another from their workstation computers would also be beneficial.

# Glossary

A **balance sheet** shows assets and liabilities at one point in time.

A **balanced scorecard** tallies organizational performance in financial, customer service, internal process, and innovation and learning areas.

A **bargaining zone** is the space between one party's minimum reservation point and the other party's maximum reservation point.

A **behaviorally anchored rating scale** uses specific descriptions of actual behaviors to rate various levels of performance.

A **boundaryless organization** eliminates internal boundaries among subsystems and external boundaries with the external environment.

A **budget** is a plan that commits resources to projects or activities.

A **bureaucracy** emphasizes formal authority, order, fairness, and efficiency.

A **business model** is a plan for making a profit by generating revenues that are greater than costs.

A **business plan** describes the direction for a new business and the financing needed to operate it.

A **business strategy** identifies how a division or strategic business unit will compete in its product or service domain.

A **certain environment** offers complete information on possible action alternatives and their consequences.

A **change leader** takes initiative in trying to change the behavior of another person or social system.

A **charismatic leader** inspires followers in extraordinary ways.

A **classic entrepreneur** is someone willing to pursue opportunities in situations others view as problems or threats.

A **code of ethics** is a formal statement of values and ethical standards.

A **committee** is designated to work on a special task on a continuing basis.

A **communication channel** is the pathway through which a message moves from sender to receiver.

A **compressed workweek** allows a full-time job to be completed in less than five days.

A **conceptual skill** is the ability to think analytically to diagnose and solve complex problems.

A **confirmation error** occurs when focusing only on information that confirms a decision already made.

A **consultative decision** is made by a leader after receiving information, advice, or opinions from group members.

A **core competency** is a special strength that gives an organization a competitive advantage.

A **corporate strategy** sets long-term direction for the total enterprise.

A **corporation** is a legal entity that exists separately from its owners.

A **cost leadership strategy** seeks to operate with low cost so that products can be sold at low prices.

A **crisis decision** occurs when an unexpected problem arises that can lead to disaster if not resolved quickly and appropriately.

A **cross-functional team** brings together members from different functional departments.

A **customer structure** groups together people and jobs that serve the same customers or clients.

A **decentralized communication network** allows all members to communicate directly with one another.

A **decision** is a choice among possible alternative courses of action.

A **defensive strategy** does the minimum legally required to display social responsibility.

A **democratic** leader emphasizes both tasks and people.

A **differentiation strategy** offers products that are unique and different from the competition.

A **divisional structure** groups together people working on the same product, in the same area, with similar customers, or on the same processes.

A **downsizing strategy** decreases the size of operations.

A **family business** is owned and controlled by members of a family.

A **family business feud** occurs when family members have major disagreements over how the business should be run.

A **first-mover advantage** comes from being first to exploit a niche or enter a market.

A **focus strategy** concentrates on serving a unique market segment better than anyone else.

A **focused cost leadership** strategy seeks the lowest costs of operations within a special market segment.

A **focused differentiation strategy** offers a unique product to a special market segment.

A **force-coercion strategy** pursues change through formal authority and/or the use of rewards or punishments.

A **foreign subsidiary** is a local operation completely owned by a foreign firm.

A **formal group** is a team officially recognized and supported by the organization.

A **franchise** is when one business owner sells to another the right to operate the same business in another location.

A **functional strategy** guides activities within one specific area of operations.

A **functional structure** groups together people with similar skills who perform similar tasks.

A **Gantt chart** graphically displays the scheduling of tasks required to complete a project.

A **geographical structure** groups together people and jobs performed in the same location.

A **global corporation** is a multinational enterprise (MNE) or multinational corporation (MNC) that conducts commercial transactions across national boundaries.

A **global strategic alliance** is a partnership in which foreign and domestic firms share resources and knowledge for mutual gains.

A **globalization strategy** adopts standardized products and advertising for use worldwide.

A **graphic rating scale** uses a checklist of traits or characteristics to evaluate performance.

A **greenfield venture** is a foreign subsidiary built from the ground up by the foreign owner.

A **group decision** is made by group members themselves.

A **growth strategy** involves expansion of the organization's current operations.

A **halo effect** occurs when one attribute is used to develop an overall impression of a person or situation.

A **human relations** leader emphasizes people over task.

A **human skill** or interpersonal skill is the ability to work well in cooperation with other people.

A **hygiene factor** is found in the job context, such as working conditions, interpersonal relations, organizational policies, and compensation.

A **job analysis** studies exactly what is done in a job, and why.

A **job description** details the duties and responsibilities of a job holder.

A **joint venture** operates in a foreign country through co-ownership by foreign and local partners.

A **knowledge worker** is someone whose mind is a critical asset to employers.

A **labor contract** is a formal agreement between a union and an employer about the terms of work for union members.

A **labor union** is an organization that deals with employers on the workers' collective behalf.

A **laissez-faire** leader has a "do the best you can and don't bother me" attitude.

A **learning organization** continuously changes and improves, using the lessons of experience.

A **limited liability corporation** is a hybrid business form combining the advantages of the sole proprietorship, partnership, and corporation.

A **maintenance activity** is an action taken by a team member that supports the emotional life of the group.

A **manager** is a person who supports, activates, and is responsible for the work of others.

A **mechanistic design** is centralized, with many rules and procedures, a clear-cut division of labor, narrow spans of control, and formal coordination.

A **mission** statement expresses the organization's reason for existence in society.

A **mixed message** results when words communicate one message while actions, body language, or appearance communicate something else.

A **moral manager** makes ethical behavior a personal goal.

A **multicultural organization** has a culture with core values that respect diversity and support multiculturalism.

A **multidomestic strategy** customizes products and advertising to best fit local needs.

A **multiperson comparison** compares one person's performance with that of others.

A **need** is a physiological or psychological deficiency that a person wants to satisfy.

A **network structure** uses information technologies to link with networks of outside suppliers and service contractors.

A **nonprogrammed decision** applies a specific solution crafted for a unique problem.

A **norm** is a behavior, rule, or standard expected to be followed by team members.

A **partnership** is when two or more people agree to contribute resources to start and operate a business together.

A **performance management system** sets standards, assesses results, and plans for performance improvements.

A **performance opportunity** is a situation that offers the chance for a better future if the right steps are taken.

A **performance threat** is a situation in which something is obviously wrong or has the potential to go wrong.

A **plan** is a statement of intended means for accomplishing objectives.

A **policy** is a standing plan that communicates broad guidelines for decisions and action.

A **proactive strategy** actively pursues social responsibility by taking discretionary actions to make things better in the future.

A **procedure** is a rule describing actions that are to be taken in specific situations.

A **process structure** groups jobs and activities that are part of the same processes.

A **product structure** groups together people and jobs focused on a single product or service.

A **programmed decision** applies a solution from past experience to a routine problem.

A **project team** or **task force** is convened for a specific purpose and disbands when its task is completed.

A **psychological contract** is the set of individual expectations about the employment relationship.

A **rational persuasion strategy** pursues change through empirical data and rational argument.

A **risk environment** lacks complete information but offers "probabilities" of the likely outcomes for possible action alternatives.

A **satisficing decision** chooses the first satisfactory alternative that comes to one's attention.

A **satisfier factor** is found in job content, such as challenging and exciting work, recognition, responsibility, advancement opportunities, or personal growth.

A **self-fulfilling prophecy** occurs when a person acts in ways that confirm another's expectations.

A **serial entrepreneur** starts and runs businesses and nonprofits over and over again, moving from one interest and opportunity to the next.

A **shamrock organization** operates with a core group of full-time long-term workers supported by others who work on contracts and part-time.

A **shared power strategy** pursues change by participation in assessing change needs, values, and goals.

A **Six Sigma program** sets a quality standard of 3.4 defects or less per million products or service deliveries.

A **skill** is the ability to translate knowledge into action that results in desired performance.

A **small business** has fewer than 500 employees, is independently owned and operated, and does not dominate its industry.

A **social responsibility audit** measures an organization's performance in various areas of social responsibility.

A **sole proprietorship** is an individual pursuing business for a profit.

A **startup** is a new and temporary venture that is trying to discover a profitable business model for future success.

A **stereotype** occurs when attributes commonly associated with a group are assigned to an individual.

A **strategic alliance** is a cooperation agreement with another organization to jointly pursue activities of mutual interest.

A **strategic plan** identifies long-term directions for the organization.

A **strategy** is a comprehensive plan guiding resource allocation to achieve long-term organization goals.

A **stressor** is anything that causes stress.

A **subsystem** is a smaller component of a larger system.

A **succession plan** describes how the leadership transition and related financial matters will be handled.

A **sustainable business** operates in ways that meet the needs of customers while protecting or advancing the well-being of our natural environment.

A **SWOT analysis** examines organizational strengths and weaknesses and environmental opportunities and threats.

A **system** is a collection of interrelated parts working together for a purpose.

A **tactical plan** helps to implement all or parts of a strategic plan.

A **task activity** is an action taken by a team member that directly contributes to the group's performance purpose.

A **team** is a collection of people who regularly interact to pursue common goals.

A **team structure** uses permanent and temporary cross-functional teams to improve lateral relations.

A **technical skill** is the ability to use expertise to perform a task with proficiency.

A **transnational corporation** is a global corporation or MNE that operates worldwide on a borderless basis.

A **transnational strategy** seeks efficiencies of global operations with attention to local markets.

A **truly global manager** is culturally aware and informed on international affairs.

A **turnaround strategy** tries to fix specific performance problems.

A **Type A personality** is a person oriented toward extreme achievement, impatience, and perfectionism.

A **virtual organization** uses IT and the Internet to engage a shifting network of strategic alliances.

A **vision** clarifies the purpose of the organization and expresses what it hopes to be in the future.

A **whistleblower** exposes the misdeeds of others in organizations.

A **work process** is a group of related tasks that collectively creates a valuable work product.

A **zero-based budget** allocates resources as if each budget were brand new.

**Accommodation**, or smoothing, plays down differences and highlights similarities to reduce conflict.

According to the **deficit principle** a satisfied need does not motivate behavior.

According to the **progression principle** a need is activated only when the next-lower-level need is satisfied.

**Accountability** is the requirement to show performance results to a supervisor.

**Active listening** helps the source of a message say what he or she really means.

**Affirmative action** is an effort to give preference in employment to women and minority group members, who have traditionally been underrepresented.

**Agenda setting** develops action priorities for accomplishing goals and plans.

**Agreeableness** is being good-natured, cooperative, and trusting.

An **accommodative strategy** accepts social responsibility and tries to satisfy society's basic ethical expectations.

An **adaptive organization** operates with a minimum of bureaucratic features and encourages worker empowerment and teamwork.

An **administrator** is a manager in a public or nonprofit organization.

An **amoral manager** fails to consider the ethics of her or his behavior.

An **angel investor** is a wealthy individual willing to invest in a new venture in return for an equity stake.

An **assessment center** examines how job candidates handle simulated work situations.

An **attitude** is a predisposition to act in a certain way.

An **authority decision** is made by the leader and then communicated to the group.

An **autocratic** leader acts in a command-and-control fashion.

An **effective manager** helps others achieve high performance and satisfaction at work.

An **effective team** achieves high levels of task performance, membership satisfaction, and future viability.

An **ethical dilemma** is a situation that offers potential benefit or gain and that may also be considered unethical.

An **ethical framework** is a personal rule or strategy for making ethical decisions.

An **immoral manager** chooses to behave unethically.

An **income statement** shows profits or losses at one point in time.

An **informal group** is unofficial and emerges from relationships and shared interests among members.

An **initial public offering**, or IPO, is an initial selling of shares of stock to the public at large.

An **input standard** measures work efforts that go into a performance task.

An **international business** conducts for-profit transactions of goods and services across national boundaries.

An **obstructionist strategy** tries to avoid and resist pressures for social responsibility.

An **ombudsperson** is a designated neutral third party who listens to complaints and disputes in an attempt to resolve them.

An **open system** interacts with its environment and transforms resource inputs into outputs.

An **operational plan** identifies short-term activities to implement strategic plans.

An **optimizing decision** chooses the alternative giving the absolute best solution to a problem.

An **organic design** is decentralized, with fewer rules and procedures, open divisions of labor, wide spans of control, and more personal coordination.

An **organization chart** describes the arrangement of work positions within an organization.

An **organization** is a collection of people working together to achieve a common purpose.

An **output standard** measures performance results in terms of quantity, quality, cost, or time.

An **uncertain environment** lacks so much information that it is difficult to assign probabilities to the likely outcomes of alternatives.

**Analytical competency** is the ability to evaluate and analyze information to make actual decisions and solve real problems.

**Analytics** is the systematic analysis of large databases to solve problems and make informed decisions.

**Attribution** is the process of explaining events.

**Authentic leadership** activates positive psychological states to achieve self-awareness and positive self-regulation.

**Authoritarianism** is the degree to which a person tends to defer to authority.

**Automation** is the total mechanization of a job.

**Avoidance**, or withdrawal, pretends that a conflict doesn't really exist.

## B

**Base compensation** is a salary or hourly wage paid to an individual.

**BCG matrix** analyzes business opportunities according to market growth rate and market share.

**Behavioral interviews** ask job applicants about past behaviors.

**Benchmarking** uses external and internal comparisons to plan for future improvements.

**Best practices** are things people and organizations do that lead to superior performance.

**Biculturalism** is when minority members adopt characteristics of majority cultures in order to succeed.

**Big-C creativity** occurs when extraordinary things are done by exceptional people.

**Biodata methods** collect certain biographical information that has been proven to correlate with good job performance.

**Bona fide occupational qualifications** are employment criteria justified by capacity to perform a job.

**Bonus pay** plans provide one-time payments based on performance accomplishments.

**Bounded rationality** describes making decisions within the constraints of limited information and alternatives.

**Brainstorming** engages group members in an open, spontaneous discussion of problems and ideas.

**Breakeven analysis** performs what-if calculations under different revenue and cost conditions.

**Bureaucratic control** influences behavior through authority, policies, procedures, job descriptions, budgets, and day-to-day supervision.

**Business incubators** offer space, shared services, and advice to help get small businesses started.

**Business intelligence** taps information systems to extract and report data in organized ways that are helpful to decision makers.

**Business model innovations** result in ways for firms to make money.

## C

**Centralization** is the concentration of authority for most decisions at the top level of an organization.

**Changing** is the phase where a planned change actually takes place.

Chapter 11 **bankruptcy** under U.S. law protects a firm from creditors while management reorganizes to restore solvency.

**Child labor** is the employment of children for work otherwise done by adults.

**Clan control** influences behavior through norms and expectations set by the organizational culture.

**Coaching** occurs as an experienced person offers performance advice to a less experienced person.

**Coercive power** is the capacity to punish or withhold positive outcomes as a means of influencing other people.

**Cognitive dissonance** is discomfort felt when attitude and behavior are inconsistent.

**Cognitive styles** are shown by the ways individuals deal with information while making decisions.

**Cohesiveness** is the degree to which members are attracted to and motivated to remain part of a team.

**Collaboration**, or problem solving, involves working through conflict differences and solving problems so everyone wins.

**Collective bargaining** is the process of negotiating, administering, and interpreting a labor contract.

**Communication** is the process of sending and receiving symbols with meanings attached.

**Communication transparency** involves openly sharing honest and complete information about the organization and workplace affairs.

**Commutative justice** is the degree to which an exchange or a transaction is fair to all parties.

**Comparable worth** holds that persons performing jobs of similar importance should be paid at comparable levels.

**Comparative management** studies how management practices differ among countries and cultures.

**Competition**, or authoritative command, uses force, superior skill, or domination to "win" a conflict.

**Competitive advantage** is something that an organization does extremely well, is difficult to copy, and gives it an advantage over competitors in the marketplace.

**Compromise** occurs when each party to the conflict gives up something of value to the other.

**Concurrent control** focuses on what happens during the work process.

**Conflict** is a disagreement over issues of substance and/or an emotional antagonism.

**Conflict resolution** is the removal of the substantial and emotional reasons for a conflict.

**Conscientiousness** is being responsible, dependable, and careful.

**Constructive stress** acts in a positive way to increase effort, stimulate creativity, and encourage diligence in one's work.

**Contingency planning** identifies alternative courses of action to take when things go wrong.

**Contingency thinking** tries to match management practices with situational demands.

**Contingency workers** are employed on a part-time and temporary basis to supplement a permanent workforce.

**Continuous improvement** involves always searching for new ways to improve work quality and performance.

**Continuous reinforcement** rewards each time a desired behavior occurs.

**Control charts** graphically plot quality trends against control limits.

**Controlling** is the process of measuring performance and taking action to ensure desired results.

**Co-opetition** is the strategy of working with rivals on projects of mutual benefit.

**Core values** are beliefs and values shared by organization members.

**Corporate governance** occurs when a board of directors holds top management accountable for organizational performance.

**Corporate social responsibility** is the obligation of an organization to serve the interests of society in addition to its own interests.

**Corruption** involves illegal practices to further one's business interests.

**Cost-benefit analysis** involves comparing the costs and benefits of each potential course of action.

**CPM/PERT** is a combination of the critical path method and the program evaluation and review technique.

**Creativity** is the generation of a novel idea or unique approach that solves a problem or crafts an opportunity.

**Credible communication** earns trust, respect, and integrity in the eyes of others.

**Cultural intelligence** is the ability to accept and adapt to new cultures.

**Cultural relativism** suggests there is no one right way to behave; ethical behavior is determined by its cultural context.

**Culture** is a shared set of beliefs, values, and patterns of behavior common to a group of people.

**Culture shock** is the confusion and discomfort a person experiences when in an unfamiliar culture.

## D

**Data** are raw facts and observations.

**Debt financing** involves borrowing money that must be repaid over time, with interest.

**Decentralization** is the dispersion of authority to make decisions throughout all organization levels.

**Decision making** is the process of making choices among alternative possible courses of action.

**360-degree appraisals** include superiors, subordinates, peers, and even customers in the appraisal process.

**Delegation** is the process of distributing and entrusting work to other persons.

**Demand legitimacy** indicates the validity and legitimacy of a stakeholder's interest in the organization.

**Design thinking** unlocks creativity in decision making through a process of experiencing, ideation, and prototyping.

**Destructive stress** impairs the performance of an individual.

**Discrimination** actively denies minority members the full benefits of organizational membership.

**Disruptive activities** are self-serving behaviors that interfere with team effectiveness.

**Disruptive innovation** creates products or services that become so widely used that they largely replace prior practices and competitors.

**Distributed leadership** is when all members of a team contribute helpful task and maintenance behaviors.

**Distributive justice** focuses on the degree to which outcomes are distributed fairly.

**Distributive negotiation** focuses on win–lose claims made by each party for certain preferred outcomes.

**Divestiture** sells off parts of the organization to refocus attention on core business areas.

**Dysfunctional conflict** is destructive and hurts task performance.

**E**

**Early retirement incentive programs** offer workers financial incentives to retire early.

**Effective negotiation** resolves issues of substance while maintaining a positive process.

**Efficient communication** occurs at minimum cost.

**Electronic grapevines** use electronic media to pass messages and information among members of social networks.

**Emotional conflict** results from feelings of anger, distrust, dislike, fear, and resentment, as well as from personality clashes.

**Emotional intelligence** is an ability to understand emotions and manage relationships effectively.

**Emotional stability** is being relaxed, secure, and unworried.

**Emotions** are strong feelings directed toward someone or something.

**Employee assistance programs** help employees cope with personal stresses and problems.

**Employee benefits** are nonmonetary forms of compensation such as health insurance and retirement plans.

**Employee engagement** is a strong positive feeling about one's job and the organization.

**Employee stock ownership plans** help employees purchase stock in their employing companies.

**Employment-at-will** means that employees can be terminated at any time for any reason.

**Empowerment** allows others to make decisions and exercise discretion in their work.

**Entrepreneurship** is risk-taking behavior that results in new opportunities.

**Environmental capital** or **natural capital** is the storehouse of natural resources—atmosphere, land, water, and, minerals—that we use to sustain life and produce goods and services for society.

**Environmental uncertainty** is a lack of information regarding what exists in the environment and what developments may occur.

**Equal employment opportunity** is the requirement that employment decisions be made without regard to race, color, national origin, religion, gender, age, or disability status.

**Equity financing** involves exchanging ownership shares for outside investment monies.

**Equity sensitivity** reflects that people have different preferences for equity and thus react differently to perceptions of inequity.

**Escalating commitment** is the continuation of a course of action even though it is not working.

**Ethical behavior** is "right" or "good" in the context of a governing moral code.

**Ethical imperialism** is an attempt to impose one's ethical standards on other cultures.

**Ethics** establish standards of good or bad, or right or wrong, in one's conduct.

**Ethics intensity** or **issue intensity** indicates the degree to which an issue or a situation is recognized to pose important ethical challenges.

**Ethics self-governance** is making sure day-to-day performance is achieved ethically and in socially responsible ways.

**Ethics training** seeks to help people understand the ethical aspects of decision making and to incorporate high ethical standards into their daily behavior.

**Ethnic subcultures** or **national subcultures** form among people who work together and have roots in the same ethnic community, country, or region of the world.

**Ethnocentrism** is the belief that one's membership group or subculture is superior to all others.

**Evidence-based management** involves making decisions based on hard facts about what really works.

**Executive dashboards** visually update and display key performance indicators and information on a real-time basis.

**Existence needs** are desires for physical well-being.

**Expectancy** is a person's belief that working hard will result in high task performance.

**Expert power** is the capacity to influence other people because of specialized knowledge.

**External recruitment** seeks job applicants from outside the organization.

**Extinction** discourages behavior by making the removal of a desirable consequence contingent on its occurrence.

**Extraversion** is being outgoing, sociable, and assertive.

## F

**Family-friendly benefits** help employees achieve better work–life balance.

**Feedback** is the process of telling someone else how you feel about something that person did or said.

**Feedback control** takes place after an action is completed.

**Feedforward control** ensures that directions and resources are right before the work begins.

**Flat structures** have wide spans of control and few hierarchical levels.

**Flexible benefits** programs allow employees to choose from a range of benefit options.

**Flexible working hours** give employees some choice in daily work hours.

**Forecasting** attempts to predict the future.

**Formal structure** is the official structure of the organization.

**Framing error** is trying to solve a problem in the context in which it is perceived.

**Functional conflict** is constructive and helps task performance.

**Functional managers** are responsible for one area, such as finance, marketing, production, personnel, accounting, or sales.

**Functional plans** indicate how different operations within the organization will help advance the overall strategy.

**Fundamental attribution error** overestimates internal factors and underestimates external factors as influences on someone's behavior.

## G

**Gain-sharing** plans allow employees to share in cost savings or productivity gains realized by their efforts.

**Gender subcultures** form among persons who work together and share the same gender identities.

**General managers** are responsible for complex, multifunctional units.

**Generational cohorts** consist of people born within a few years of one another and who experience somewhat similar life events during their formative years.

**Generational subcultures** form among persons who work together and share similar ages, such as Millennials and Baby Boomers.

**Globalization** is the growing interdependence among elements of the global economy.

**Global management** involves managing business and organizations with interests in more than one country.

**Groupthink** is a tendency for highly cohesive teams to lose their evaluative capabilities.

**Growth needs** are desires for personal growth and development.

Growth through **concentration** is within the same business area.

Growth through **diversification** is by acquisition of or investment in new and different business areas.

Growth through **vertical integration** occurs by acquiring suppliers or distributors.

## H

**Heuristics** are strategies for simplifying decision making.

**High-context cultures** rely on nonverbal and situational cues as well as on spoken or written words in communication.

**Higher-order** needs are esteem and self-actualization needs in Maslow's hierarchy.

**Human capital** is the economic value of people with job-relevant knowledge, skills, abilities, ideas, energies, and commitments.

**Human resource management** is a process of attracting, developing, and maintaining a talented workforce.

**Human resource planning** analyzes staffing needs and identifies actions to fill those needs.

## I

**Importing** involves the selling in domestic markets of products acquired abroad.

**Impression management** is the systematic attempt to influence how others perceive us.

**Improvisational change** makes continual adjustments as changes are being implemented.

In a **centralized communication network**, communication flows only between individual members and a hub, or center point.

In a **free-agent economy** people change jobs more often, and many work on independent contracts with a shifting mix of employers.

In a **hierarchy of goals** or **hierarchy of objectives**, lower-level goals and objectives are means to accomplishing higher-level ones.

In a **licensing agreement** a local firm pays a fee to a foreign firm for rights to make or sell its products.

In a **restricted communication network** subgroups have limited communication with one another.

In a **strategic alliance**, organizations join in partnership to pursue an area of mutual interest.

In **arbitration** a neutral third party issues a binding decision to resolve a dispute.

In **bottom-up change**, change initiatives come from all levels in the organization.

In **continuous-process production**, raw materials are continuously transformed by an automated system.

In **effective communication** the intended meaning is fully understood by the receiver.

In **exporting**, local products are sold abroad to foreign customers.

In **franchising**, a fee is paid to a foreign business for rights to locally operate using its name, branding, and methods.

In **global sourcing**, materials or services are purchased around the world for local use.

In **job rotation** people switch tasks to learn multiple jobs.

In **lose–lose conflict** no one achieves his or her true desires, and the underlying reasons for conflict remain unaffected.

In **mediation** a neutral party tries to help conflicting parties improve communication to resolve their dispute.

In **monochronic cultures** people tend to do one thing at a time.

In **over-reward inequity** (positive inequity) an individual perceives that rewards received are more than what is fair for work inputs.

In **polychronic cultures** time is used to accomplish many different things at once.

In the **global economy**, resources, markets, and competition are worldwide in scope.

In the **individualism view** ethical behavior advances long-term self-interests.

In the **justice view** ethical behavior treats people impartially and fairly.

In the **moral rights view** ethical behavior respects and protects fundamental rights.

In the **utilitarian view** ethical behavior delivers the greatest good to the most people.

In **top-down change**, the change initiatives come from senior management.

In **under-reward inequity** (negative inequity) an individual perceives that rewards received are less than what is fair for work inputs.

In **unstructured interviews** the interviewer does not work from a formal and preestablished list of questions that is asked of all interviewees.

In **win–lose** conflict one party achieves its desires, and the other party does not.

In **win–win** conflict the conflict is resolved to everyone's benefit.

In **work sampling**, applicants are evaluated while performing actual work tasks.

**Incremental change** bends and adjusts existing ways to improve performance.

**Independent contractors** are hired as needed and are not part of the organization's permanent workforce.

**Individualism–collectivism** is the degree to which a society emphasizes individuals and their self-interests.

**Informal structure** is the set of unofficial relationships among an organization's members.

**Information competency** is the ability to locate, gather, and organize information for use in decision making.

**Information** is data made useful for decision making.

**Information filtering** is the intentional distortion of information to make it appear most favorable to the recipient.

**Innovation** is the process of taking a new idea and putting it into practice.

**Insourcing** is job creation through foreign direct investment.

**Instrumentality** is a person's belief that various outcomes will occur as a result of task performance.

**Instrumental values** are preferences regarding the means to desired ends.

**Intellectual capital** is the collective brainpower or shared knowledge of a workforce.

**Interactional justice** is the degree to which others are treated with dignity and respect.

**Interactive leaders** are strong communicators and act democratic and participative with followers.

**Intercultural competencies** are skills and personal characteristics that help us be successful in cross-cultural situations.

**Intermittent reinforcement** rewards behavior only periodically.

**Internal recruitment** seeks job applicants from inside the organization.

**Internet censorship** is the deliberate blockage and denial of public access to information posted on the Internet.

**Internet entrepreneurship** is the use of the Internet to pursue an entrepreneurial venture.

**Intrapreneurs** display entrepreneurial behavior as employees of larger firms.

**Intuitive thinking** approaches problems in a flexible and spontaneous fashion.

**Inventory control** ensures that inventory is only big enough to meet immediate needs.

**ISO certification** indicates conformance with a rigorous set of international quality standards.

**Issue urgency** indicates the extent to which a stakeholder's concerns need immediate attention.

## J

**Job burnout** is physical and mental exhaustion from work stress.

**Job design** is arranging work tasks for individuals and groups.

**Job enlargement** increases task variety by combining into one job two or more tasks previously done by separate workers.

**Job enrichment** increases job depth by adding work planning and evaluating duties normally performed by the supervisor.

**Job involvement** is the extent to which an individual is dedicated to a job.

**Job migration** occurs when firms shift jobs from one country to another.

**Job rotation** increases task variety by periodically shifting workers between different jobs.

**Job satisfaction** is the degree to which an individual feels positive or negative about a job.

**Job sharing** splits one job between two people.

**Job simplification** employs people in clearly defined and specialized tasks with narrow job scope.

**Job specifications** list the qualifications required of a job holder.

**Just-in-time scheduling (JIT)** routes materials to workstations just in time for use.

## K

**Knowledge management** is the process of using intellectual capital for competitive advantage.

## L

**Lack of participation error** is a failure to include key persons in strategic planning.

**Leaders show integrity** by acting with honesty, credibility, and consistency in putting values into action.

**Leadership** is the process of inspiring others to work hard to accomplish important tasks.

**Leadership style** is a recurring pattern of behaviors exhibited by a leader.

**Leading** is the process of arousing enthusiasm and inspiring efforts to achieve goals.

**Lean startups** use things like open-source software, while containing costs, staying small, and keeping operations as simple as possible.

**Learning** is a change in behavior that results from experience.

**Legitimate power** is the capacity to influence other people by virtue of formal authority, or the rights of office.

**Leniency** is the tendency to give employees a higher performance rating than they deserve.

**Lifelong learning** is continuous learning from daily experiences.

**Line managers** directly contribute to producing the organization's goods or services.

**Liquidation** is where a business closes and sells its assets to pay creditors.

**Little-C creativity** occurs when average people come up with unique ways to deal with daily events and situations.

**Locus of control** is the extent to which one believes that what happens is within one's control.

**Long-term plans** typically look three or more years into the future.

**Low-context cultures** emphasize communication via spoken or written words.

**Lower-order needs** are physiological, safety, and social needs in Maslow's hierarchy.

## M

**Machiavellianism** describes the extent to which someone is emotionally detached and manipulative.

**Management by exception** focuses attention on substantial differences between actual and desired performance.

**Management development** is training to improve knowledge and skills in the management process.

**Management information systems** use IT to collect, organize, and distribute data for use in decision making.

**Management with analytics** involves systematic gathering and processing of data to make it useful as information.

**Managing diversity** is a leadership approach that creates an organizational culture that respects diversity and supports multiculturalism.

**Market control** is essentially the influence of market competition on the behavior of organizations and their members.

**Masculinity–femininity** is the degree to which a society values assertiveness and materialism.

Members of a **board of directors** or board of trustees are supposed to make sure an organization is run right.

Members of a **self-managing work team** have the authority to make decisions about how they share and complete their work.

Members of a **virtual team** or **distributed team** work together and solve problems through computer-based interactions.

**Mentoring** assigns early-career employees as protégés to more senior ones.

**Merit pay** awards pay increases in proportion to performance contributions.

**Middle managers** oversee the work of large departments or divisions.

**Moods** are generalized positive and negative feelings or states of mind.

**Mood contagion** is the spillover of one's positive or negative moods onto others.

**Moral absolutism** suggests ethical standards apply universally across all cultures.

**Moral leadership** is always "good" and "right" by ethical standards.

**Moral overconfidence** is an overly positive view of one's strength of character.

**Most favored nation status** gives a trading partner most favorable treatment for imports and exports.

**Motion study** is the science of reducing a task to its basic physical motions.

**Motivation** accounts for the level, direction, and persistence of effort expended at work.

**Multiculturalism** in organizations involves inclusiveness, pluralism, and respect for diversity.

**Multidimensional thinking** is an ability to address many problems at once.

# N

**NAFTA** is the North American Free Trade Agreement linking Canada, the United States, and Mexico in an economic alliance.

**Necessity-based entrepreneurship** takes place because other employment options don't exist.

**Need for achievement** is the desire to do something better, to solve problems, or to master complex tasks.

**Need for affiliation** is the desire to establish and maintain good relations with people.

**Need for power** is the desire to control, influence, or be responsible for other people.

**Negative reinforcement** strengthens behavior by making the avoidance of an undesirable consequence contingent on its occurrence.

**Negotiation** is the process of making joint decisions when the parties involved have different preferences.

**Networking** is the process of creating positive relationships with people who can help advance agendas.

**Noise** is anything that interferes with the effectiveness of communication.

**Nontariff barriers** to trade discourage imports in nontax ways such as quotas and government import restrictions.

**Nonverbal communication** takes place through gestures and body language.

# O

**Objectives** and **goals** are specific results that one wishes to achieve.

**Occupational and functional subcultures** form among persons who share the same skills and work responsibilities.

**Offshoring** is the outsourcing of jobs to foreign locations.

**Open book management** is where managers provide employees with essential financial information about their companies.

**Openness to experience** is being curious, receptive to new ideas, and imaginative.

**Operant conditioning** is the control of behavior by manipulating its consequences.

**Operating objectives** are specific results that organizations try to accomplish.

**Organization structure** is a system of tasks, reporting relationships, and communication linkages.

**Organizational behavior** is the study of individuals and groups in organizations.

**Organizational citizenship** is a willingness to "go beyond the call of duty" or "go the extra mile" in one's work.

**Organizational commitment** is the loyalty of an individual to the organization.

**Organizational culture** is the predominant value system for the organization as a whole.

**Organizational design** is the process of creating structures that accomplish mission and objectives.

**Organizational subcultures** are groups of people who share similar beliefs and values based on their work or personal characteristics.

**Organizing** is the process of assigning tasks, allocating resources, and coordinating work activities.

**Orientation** familiarizes new employees with jobs, coworkers, and organizational policies and services.

# P

**Participatory planning** includes the persons who will be affected by plans and/or those who will implement them.

**Perception** is the process through which people receive, organize, and interpret information from the environment.

**Performance appraisal** is the process of formally evaluating performance and providing feedback to a job holder.

**Performance coaching** provides frequent and developmental feedback for how a worker can improve job performance.

**Performance effectiveness** is an output measure of task or goal accomplishment.

**Performance efficiency** is an input measure of resource cost associated with goal accomplishment.

**Personality** is the profile of characteristics making a person unique from others.

**Personal wellness** is the pursuit of one's full potential through a personal health-promotion program.

**Person–job fit** is the extent to which an individual's knowledge, skills, experiences, and personal characteristics are consistent with the requirements of their work.

**Person–organization fit** is the extent to which an individual's values, interests, and behavior are consistent with the culture of the organization.

**Persuasive communication** presents a message in a manner that causes the other person to support it.

**Planning** is the process of setting objectives and determining how to accomplish them.

**Political risk** is the potential loss in value of a foreign investment due to instability and political changes in the host country.

**Political-risk analysis** tries to forecast political disruptions that can threaten the value of a foreign investment.

**Positive reinforcement** strengthens behavior by making a desirable consequence contingent on its occurrence.

**Power** is the ability to get someone else to do something you want done or to make things happen the way you want.

**Power distance** is the degree to which a society accepts unequal distribution of power.

**Prejudice** is the display of negative, irrational attitudes toward members of diverse populations.

**Principled negotiation** or **integrative negotiation** uses a "win–win" orientation to reach solutions acceptable to each party.

**Problem solving** involves identifying and taking action to resolve problems.

**Procedural justice** is concerned that policies and rules are fairly applied.

**Process innovations** result in better ways of doing things.

**Product innovations** result in new or improved goods or services.

**Productivity** is the quantity and quality of work performance, with resource utilization considered.

**Profit-sharing** plans distribute to employees a proportion of net profits earned by the organization.

**Project management** makes sure that activities required to complete a project are planned well and accomplished on time.

**Project teams** are convened for a particular task or project and disband once it is completed.

**Projection** is the assignment of personal attributes to other individuals.

**Projects** are one-time activities with many component tasks that must be completed in proper order and according to budget.

**Protectionism** is a call for tariffs and favorable treatments to protect domestic firms from foreign competition.

**Proxemics** involves the use of space in communication.

**Punishment** discourages behavior by making an unpleasant consequence contingent on its occurrence.

## Q

**Quality of work life** is the overall quality of human experiences in the workplace.

## R

**Realistic job previews** provide job candidates with all pertinent information about a job and an organization, both positive and negative.

**Recency bias** overemphasizes the most recent behaviors when evaluating individual performance.

**Recruitment** is a set of activities designed to attract a qualified pool of job applicants.

**Referent power** is the capacity to influence other people because of their desire to identify personally with you.

**Refreezing** is the phase at which change is stabilized.

**Relatedness needs** are desires for good interpersonal relationships.

**Relationship goals** in negotiation are concerned with the ways people work together.

**Reliability** means that a selection device gives consistent results over repeated measures.

**Reshoring** is the return of jobs from foreign locations as companies establish new domestic operations.

**Retrenchment and restructuring strategies** pursue radical changes to solve problems.

**Reverse innovation** recognizes the potential for valuable innovations to be launched from lower organizational levels and diverse locations, including emerging markets.

**Reward power** is the capacity to offer something of value as a means of influencing other people.

## S

**Scenario planning** identifies alternative future scenarios and makes plans to deal with each.

**Scientific management** emphasizes careful selection and training of workers and supervisory support.

**Selection** is choosing individuals to hire from a pool of qualified job applicants.

**Selective perception** is the tendency to define problems from one's own point of view.

**Self-control** is internal control that occurs through self-discipline in fulfilling work and personal responsibilities.

**Self-efficacy** is a person's belief that she or he is capable of performing a task.

**Self-management** is the ability to understand oneself, exercise initiative, accept responsibility, and learn from experience.

**Self-monitoring** is the degree to which someone is able to adjust behavior in response to external factors.

**Self-serving bias** explains personal success by internal causes and personal failures by external causes.

**Servant leadership** is follower-centered and committed to helping others in their work.

**Sexual harassment** is behavior of a sexual nature that affects a person's employment situation.

**Shaping** is positive reinforcement of successive approximations to the desired behavior.

**Shared value** approaches business decisions with the understanding that economic and social progress are interconnected.

**Short-term plans** typically cover one year or less.

**Situational interviews** ask job applicants how they would react in specific situations.

**Small Business Development Centers** founded with support from the U.S. Small Business Administration provide advice to new and existing small businesses.

**Social business innovation** finds ways to use business models to address important social problems.

**Social capital** is a capacity to get things done with the support and help of others.

**Social enterprises** have a social mission to help make lives better for underserved populations.

**Social entrepreneurship** is a unique form of ethical entrepreneurship that seeks novel ways to solve pressing social problems.

**Social loafing** is the tendency of some people to avoid responsibility by "free-riding" in groups. .

**Social network analysis** identifies the informal structures and their embedded social relationships that are active in an organization.

**Socialization** is the process through which new members learn the culture of an organization.

**Span of control** is the number of subordinates directly reporting to a manager.

**Staff managers** use special technical expertise to advise and support line workers.

**Staff positions** provide technical expertise for other parts of the organization.

**Stakeholders** are the persons, groups, and other organizations that are directly affected by the behavior of the organization and that hold a stake in its performance.

**Stakeholder power** refers to the capacity of the stakeholder to positively or negatively affect the operations of the organization.

**Stewardship** in management means taking personal responsibility to always respect and protect the interests of society at large.

**Stock options** give the right to purchase shares at a fixed price in the future.

**Strategic analysis** is the process of analyzing the organization, the environment, and the organization's competitive position and current strategies.

**Strategic control** makes sure strategies are well implemented and that poor strategies are scrapped or modified.

**Strategic human resource management** mobilizes human capital to implement organizational strategies.

**Strategic intent** focuses and applies organizational energies on a unifying and compelling goal.

**Strategic leadership** inspires people to continuously change, refine, and improve strategies and their implementation.

**Strategic management** is the process of formulating and implementing strategies.

**Strategic opportunism** focuses on long-term objectives while being flexible in dealing with short-term problems.

**Strategy formulation** is the process of crafting strategies to guide the allocation of resources.

**Strategy implementation** is the process of putting strategies into action.

**Stress** is a state of tension caused by extraordinary demands, constraints, or opportunities.

**Stretch goals** are performance targets that we have to work extra hard and stretch to reach.

**Structured problems** are straightforward and clear with respect to information needs.

**Substance goals** in negotiation are concerned with outcomes.

**Substantive conflict** involves disagreements over goals, resources, rewards, policies, procedures, and job assignments.

**Substitutes for leadership** are factors in the work setting that direct work efforts without the involvement of a leader.

**Sustainability** in management means acting in ways that support a high quality of life for present and future generations.

**Sustainable competitive advantage** is the ability to outperform rivals in ways that are difficult or costly to imitate.

**Sustainable development** uses environmental resources to support societal needs today while also preserving and protecting them for future generations.

**Sustainable innovations** or **green innovations** help reduce an organization's negative impact and enhance its positive impact on the natural environment.

**Sweatshops** employ workers at very low wages for long hours in poor working conditions.

**Synergy** is the creation of a whole greater than the sum of its individual parts.

**Systematic thinking** approaches problems in a rational and analytical fashion.

# T

**Tall structures** have narrow spans of control and many hierarchical levels.

**Tariffs** are taxes governments levy on imports from abroad.

**Team building** is a sequence of activities to analyze a team and make changes to improve its performance.

**Team diversity** is the differences in values, personalities, experiences, demographics, and cultures among the membership.

**Team Effectiveness Equation** is Team effectiveness = Quality of inputs + (Process gains − Process losses).

**Team leaders** report to middle managers and supervise nonmanagerial workers.

**Team process** is the way team members work together to accomplish tasks.

**Teamwork** is the process of people actively working together to accomplish common goals.

**Tech IQ** is ability to use technology and commitment to stay informed on the latest technological developments.

**Technological competency** is the ability to understand new technologies and to use them to their best advantage.

**Telecommuting** involves using IT to work at home or outside the office.

**Terminal values** are preferences about desired end states.

**Termination** is the involuntary dismissal of an employee.

**The 3 P's of organizational performance** are profit, people, and planet.

**The anchoring and adjustment bias** bases a decision on incremental adjustments from a prior decision point.

**The availability bias** bases a decision on recent information or events.

**The behavioral decision model** describes decision making with limited information and bounded rationality.

The **breakeven point** occurs where revenues just equal costs.

The **chain of command** links all persons with successively higher levels of authority.

The **classical decision model** describes decision making with complete information.

The **classical view of CSR** is that business should focus on profits.

The **complacency trap** is being carried along by the flow of events.

The **control equation** states: Need for Action = Desired Performance − Actual Performance.

The **core culture** consists of the core values, or underlying assumptions and beliefs that shape and guide people's behaviors in an organization.

The **critical-incident technique** keeps a log of someone's effective and ineffective job behaviors.

The **critical path** is the pathway from project start to conclusion that involves activities with the longest completion times.

The **decision-making process** begins with identification of a problem and ends with evaluation of implemented solutions.

The **deficit principle** states that a satisfied need does not motivate behavior.

The **ecological fallacy** assumes that a generalized cultural value applies equally well to all members of the culture.

The **economic order quantity** method places new orders when inventory levels fall to predetermined points.

The **euro** is now the common European currency.

The **European Union** is a political and economic alliance of European countries.

The **Foreign Corrupt Practices Act (FCPA)** makes it illegal for U.S. firms and their representatives to engage in corrupt practices overseas.

The **frustration-regression principle** states that an already satisfied need can become reactivated when a higher-level need is blocked.

The **functional chimneys or functional silos problem** is a lack of communication and coordination across functions.

The **gender similarities hypothesis** holds that males and females have similar psychological properties.

The **general environment** consists of economic, legal-political, sociocultural, technological, and natural environment conditions.

The **glass ceiling** is an invisible barrier to advancement by women and minorities in organizations.

The **Hawthorne effect** is the tendency of persons singled out for special attention to perform as expected.

The **intellectual capital equation** states: Intellectual Capital = Competency + Commitment.

The **law of effect** states that behavior followed by pleasant consequences is likely to be repeated; behavior followed by unpleasant consequences is not.

The **leaking pipeline problem** is where glass ceilings and other obstacles cause qualified and high-performing women to drop out of upward career paths.

The **least-preferred coworker scale**, LPC, is used in Fiedler's contingency model to measure a person's leadership style.

The **management process** is planning, organizing, leading, and controlling the use of resources to accomplish performance goals.

The **nominal group technique** structures interaction among team members discussing problems and ideas.

The **observable culture** is what one sees and hears when walking around an organization as a visitor, a customer, or an employee.

The **productivity equation** is: Productivity = Output/Input.

The **progression principle** states that a need isn't activated until the next lower-level need is satisfied.

The **representativeness bias** bases a decision on similarity to other situations.

The **socioeconomic view of CSR** is that business should focus on broader social welfare as well as profits.

The **specific environment,** or **task environment,** includes the people and groups with whom an organization interacts.

The **spotlight questions** test the ethics of a decision by exposing it to scrutiny through the eyes of family, community members, and ethical role models.

The **succession problem** is the issue of who will run the business when the current head leaves.

The **triple bottom line** assesses the economic, social, and environmental performance of organizations.

The **upside-down pyramid** view of organizations shows customers at the top being served by workers who are supported by managers.

The **virtuous circle** occurs when socially responsible behavior improves financial performance, which leads to more responsible behavior in the future.

**Theory X** assumes people dislike work, lack ambition, act irresponsibly, and prefer to be led.

**Theory Y** assumes people are willing to work, like responsibility, and are self-directed and creative.

**Time orientation** is the degree to which a society emphasizes short-term or long-term goals.

**Top managers** guide the performance of the organization as a whole or of one of its major parts.

**Total quality management** is an organization-wide commitment to continuous improvement, product quality, and customer needs.

**Traditional recruitment** focuses on selling the job and organization to applicants.

**Training** provides learning opportunities to acquire and improve job-related skills.

**Transformational change** results in a major and comprehensive redirection of the organization.

**Transformational leadership** is inspirational and arouses extraordinary effort and performance.

## U

**Uncertainty avoidance** is the degree to which a society tolerates risk and uncertainty.

**Unfreezing** is the phase during which a situation is prepared for change.

**Unstructured problems** have ambiguities and information deficiencies.

## V

**Valence** is the value a person assigns to work-related outcomes.

**Validity** means that scores on a selection device have demonstrated links with future job performance.

**Value-based management** actively develops, communicates, and enacts shared values.

**Values** are broad beliefs about what is appropriate behavior.

**Venture capitalists** make large investments in new ventures in return for an equity stake in the business.

**Vision** is a clear sense of the future.

**Visionary leadership** brings to the situation a clear sense of the future and an understanding of how to get there.

## W

**Withdrawal behaviors** occur as temporary absenteeism and actual job turnover.

**Workforce diversity** describes differences among workers in gender, race, age, ethnicity, religion, sexual orientation, and able-bodiedness.

**Work–life balance** involves balancing career demands with personal and family needs.

**Workplace privacy** is the right to privacy while at work.

**Workplace rage** is aggressive behavior toward coworkers or the work setting.

**Workplace spirituality** creates meaning and shared community among organizational members.

**World 3.0** is a world where nations cooperate in the global economy while still respecting different national characters and interests.

**World Trade Organization** member nations agree to negotiate and resolve disputes about tariffs and trade restrictions.

**Wrongful discharge** is a doctrine giving workers legal protections against discriminatory firings.

# Endnotes

## Chapter 1

### Endnotes

[1] Information and quotes from Jessi Hempel, "How LinkedIn Will Fire Up Your Career," *Fortune*, Kindle Edition (April 13, 2010); Shayndi Raice, "Friend—and Possible Employee," *Wall Street Journal* (October 24, 2011), p. R7; and, Spencer E. Ante, "Reid Hoffman: Search for Breakout Ideas," *The Wall Street Journal* (February 29, 2012), p. 89.

[2] See monster.com; linkedin.com; Bridget Carey, "Old Resume Just the Start These Days," *Columbus Dispatch* (March 16, 2008), p. D3; Joseph De Avila, "CEO Reorganizes Job-Search Pioneer, *Wall Street Journal* (May 12, 2008), p. B1.

[3] For a good discussion see Pino Audia, "A New B-School Specialty: Self-Awareness," *Forbes* (December 4, 2009): www.forbes.com.

[4] The Johari Window was originally described by Joseph Luft and Harry Ingham, "The Johari Window; A Graphic Model of Interpersonal Awareness," *Proceedings of the Western Training Laboratory in Group Development* (Los Angeles: UCLA, 1955).

[5] James O'Toole and Edward E. Lawler III, *The New American Workplace* (New York: Palgrave Macmillan, 2006).

[6] Quote from Philip Delves Broughton, "A Compelling Vision of a Dystopian Future for Workers and How to Avoid it," *Financial Times*, Kindle edition (May 19, 2011). See also Lynda Gratton, *The Shift: The Future of Work is Already Here* (London: HarperCollins UK, 2011).

[7] Thomas A. Stewart, *Intellectual Capital: The Wealth of Organizations* (New York: Bantam, 1998).

[8] Charles O'Reilly III and Jeffrey Pfeffer, *Hidden Value: How Great Companies Achieve Extraordinary Results with Ordinary People* (Boston: Harvard Business School Press, 2000), p. 2.

[9] Dave Ulrich, "Intellectual Capital = Competency + Commitment," *Harvard Business Review* (Winter 1998), pp. 15–26.

[10] See Peter F. Drucker, *The Changing World of the Executive* (New York: T.T. Times Books, 1982), and *The Profession of Management* (Cambridge, MA: Harvard Business School Press, 1997); and Francis Horibe, *Managing Knowledge Workers: New Skills and Attitudes to Unlock the Intellectual Capital in Your Organization* (New York: Wiley, 1999).

[11] Daniel Pink, *A Whole New Mind: Moving from the Information Age to the Conceptual Age* (New York: Riverhead Books, 2005).

[12] Gary Hamel, "Gary Hamel Sees More Options . . . Fewer Grand Visions," *Wall Street Journal*, Special Advertising Section (October 6, 2009), p. Akl16.

[12] Information from Sarah E. Needleman, "A New Job Is Just a Tweet Away," *Wall Street Journal* (September 6, 2009), pp. B7, B12.

[13] See Kenichi Ohmae's books *The Borderless World: Power and Strategy in the Interlinked Economy* (New York: Harper, 1989); *The End of the Nation State* (New York: Free Press, 1996); *The Invisible Continent: Four Strategic Imperatives of the New Economy* (New York: Harper, 1999); and *The Next Global Stage: Challenges and Opportunities in Our Borderless World* (Philadelphia: Wharton School Publishing, 2006).

[14] Information from Micheline Maynard, "A Lifeline Not Made in the USA," *New York Times* (October 18, 2009): nytimes.com (accessed April 15, 2010).

[15] See Joseph E. Stiglitz, *Globalization and Its Discontents* (New York: W.W. Norton, 2003); and Joseph E. Stiglitz, *Making Globalization Work* (New York: W.W. Norton, 2007).

[16] Michael E. Porter, *The Competitive Advantage of Nations: With a New Introduction* (New York: Free Press, 1998).

[17] See for example, John Bussey, "Buck Up America: China Is Getting Too Expensive," *Wall Street Journal* (October 7, 2011), pp. B1, B2.

[18] "Intel's Ambitions Bloom in Arizona Desert," *Financial Times*, Kindle Edition (January 23, 2012).

[19] Esmé E. Deprez, "Madoff Sentenced to Maximum 150 Years," *Business Week* (June 29, 2009): businessweek.com (accessed April 15, 2010).

[20] For discussions of ethics in business and management, see Linda K. Trevino and Katherine A. Nelson, *Managing Business Ethics*, 4th Edition (Hoboken, NJ: John Wiley & Sons, 2010); and Richard DeGeorge, *Business Ethics*, 7th ed. (Englewood Cliffs, NJ: Prentice-Hall, 2009).

[21] Daniel Akst, "Room at the Top for Improvement," *Wall Street Journal* (October 26, 2004), p. D8; and Herb Baum and Tammy King, *The Transparent Leader* (New York: Collins, 2005).

[22] *Workforce 2000: Work and Workers for the 21st Century* (Indianapolis, IN: Towers Perrin/Hudson Institute, 1987); Richard W. Judy and Carol D'Amico (eds.), *Work and Workers for the 21st Century* (Indianapolis, IN: Hudson Institute, 1997). See also Richard D. Bucher, *Diversity Consciousness: Opening Our Minds to People, Cultures, and Opportunities* (Upper Saddle River, NJ: Prentice-Hall, 2000); R. Roosevelt Thomas, "From Affirmative Action to Affirming Diversity," *Harvard Business Review* (March–April 1990), pp. 107–17; and *Beyond Race and Gender: Unleashing the Power of Your Total Workforce by Managing Diversity* (New York: AMACOM, 1992).

[23] June Dronholz, "Hispanics Gain in Census," *Wall Street Journal* (May 10, 2006), p. A6; Phillip Toledano, "Demographics: The Population Hourglass," *Fast Company* (March 2006), p. 56; June Kronholz, "Racial Identity's Gray Area," *Wall Street Journal* (June 12, 2008), p. A10; "We're Getting Old," *Wall Street Journal* (March 26, 2009), p. D2; Les Christie, "Hispanic Population Boom Fuels Rising U.S. Diversity," *CNNMoney*: www.cnn.com; Betsy Towner, "The New Face of 501 America," *AARP Bulletin* (June 2009), p. 31; Kelly Evans, "Recession Drives More Women in the Workforce," *Wall Street Journal* (November 12, 2009), p. A21; and "Minority Report: U.S. Sees Surge in Asian, Hispanic Populations," *Wall Street Journal* (May 28–29, 2011), p. A3.

[24] Information from "Women and Work: We Did It!" *Economist* (December 31, 2009); and Joann S. Lublin, "Female Directors: Why So Few?" *The Wall Street Journal* (December 27, 2011), p. B5.

[25] Information from "Racism in Hiring Remains, Study Says," *Columbus Dispatch* (January 17, 2003), p. B2.

[26] Ashleigh Shelby Rosette, Geoffrey J. Leonardelli, and Katherine W. Phillips, "The White Standard: Racial Bias in Leader Categorization," *Journal of Applied Psychology*, Vol. 93 (2008), pp. 758–777. See also, "Race Influences How Leaders Are Assessed," *The Wall Street Journal* (January 3, 2012), p. B7.

[27] Survey data reported in Sue Shellenbarger, "New Workplace Equalizer: Ambition," *The Wall Street Journal* (March 26, 2009), p. D5.

[28] Judith B. Rosener, "Women Make Good Managers. So What?" *BusinessWeek* (December 11, 2000), p. 24.

[29] See Leslie Kwoh, "Firms Hail New Chief (of Diversity)," *The Wall Street Journal* (January 5, 2012), p. B10.

[30] Charles Handy, *The Age of Unreason* (Cambridge, MA: Harvard Business School Press, 1990); Also see Charles Handy, *A Business Guru's Portfolio Life* (New York: Amacom, 2008), and *Myself and Other Important Matters* (New York: Amacom, 2008).

[31] See Peter Coy, Michelle Conlin, and Moira Herbst, "The Disposable Worker," *BusinessWeek* (January 18, 2010), pp. 33–39.

[32] See Gareille Monaghan, "Don't Get a Job, Get a Portfolio Career," *Sunday Times* (April 26, 2009), p. 15.

[33] Tom Peters, "The New Wired World of Work," *BusinessWeek* (August 28, 2000), pp. 172–73.

[34] Quotes from "IBM vs. the Carnegie Corporation: Making the World Work Better," *Economist*, Kindle edition (June 9, 2011); and "Corporate Responsibility at IBM: A Foreword by IBM's Chairman," ibm.com/ibm/responsibility/letter.shtml (accessed October 3, 2011).

[35] Quote from Stephen Moore, "The Conscience of a Capitalist," *Wall Street Journal* (October 3–4, 2009), p. A11; see also www.wholefoods.com/company.

[36] For an overview of organizations and organization theory, see W. Richard Scott, *Organizations: Rational, Natural and Open Systems*, 4th ed. (Englewood Cliffs, NJ: Prentice-Hall, 1998).

[37] Information from Paul F. Nunes, Geoffrey Godbey, and H. James Wilson, "Bet the Clock," *Wall Street Journal* (October 26, 2009), p. R6; and Steve Hamm, "The King of the Cloud," *BusinessWeek* (November 30, 2009), p. 77.

[38] Includes ideas from Jay A. Conger, *Winning 'em Over: A New Model for Managing in the Age of Persuasion* (New York: Simon & Schuster, 1998), pp. 180–81; Stewart D. Friedman, Perry Christensen, and Jessica DeGroot, "Work and Life: The End of the Zero-Sum Game," *Harvard Business Review* (November–December 1998), pp. 119–29; Chris Argyris, "Empowerment: The Emperor's New Clothes," *Harvard Business Review* (May–June 1998), pp. 98–105; and John A. Byrne, "Management by Web," *BusinessWeek* (August 28, 2000), pp. 84–98. See also emerging reports such as O'Toole and Lawler, op. cit.; Jon Nicholson and Amanda Nairn, *The Manager of the 21st Century: 2020 Vision* (Sydney: Boston Consulting Group, 2008); and, Jeffrey Pfeffer, "Building Sustainable Organizations: The Human Factor," *Academy of Management Perspectives*, vol. 24 (February 2010), pp. 34–45.

[39] Jeffrey Pfeffer and John F. Veiga, "Putting People First for Organizational Success," *Academy of Management Executive*, vol. 13 (May 1999), pp. 37–48; Jeffrey Pfeffer, *The Human Equation: Building Profits by Putting People First* (Boston: Harvard Business School Press, 1998).

[40] Henry Mintzberg, "The Manager's Job: Folklore and Fact," *Harvard Business Review*, Vol. 53 (July–August 1975), p. 61. See also his book *The Nature of Managerial Work* (New York: Harper-Row, 1973: HarperCollins, 1997).

[41] For an example of research on corporate boards see Marta Geletkanycz and Brian Boyd, "CEO Outside Directorships and Firm Performance: A Reconciliation of Agency and Embeddedness Views," *Academy of Management Journal*, vol. 54 (April, 2011), pp. 335–52.

[42] Ellen Byron, "P&G's Lafley Sees CEOs as Link to World," *Wall Street Journal* (March 23, 2009), p. B6; and Stefan Stern, "What Exactly Are Chief Executives For?" *Financial Times* (May 15, 2009).

[43] For a perspective on the first-level manager's job, see Leonard A. Schlesinger and Janice A. Klein, "The First-Line Supervisor: Past, Present and Future," pp. 370–82 in Jay W. Lorsch (ed.), *Handbook of Organizational Behavior* (Englewood Cliffs, NJ: Prentice-Hall, 1987).

[44] Jordan Robinson, "HP Fires Second CEO in 2 Years: Whitman in Charge," *Forbes.com* (September 23, 2011).

[45] Pfeffer, op. cit.

[46] George Anders, "Overseeing More Employees—With Fewer Managers," *Wall Street Journal* (March 24, 2008), p. B6.

[47] This running example is developed from information from "Accountants Have Lives, Too, You Know," *BusinessWeek* (February 23, 1998), pp. 88–90; Silvia Ann Hewlett and Carolyn Buck Luce, "Off-Ramps and On-Ramps: Keeping Talented Women on the Road to Success," *Harvard Business Review* (March 2005), reprint 9491; and the Ernst-Young website: www.ey.com.

[48] Mintzberg (1973/1997), op. cit., p. 30.

[49] See Mintzberg (1973/1997), op. cit., Henry Mintzberg, "Covert Leadership: The Art of Managing Professionals," *Harvard Business Review* (November–December 1998), pp. 140–47; and Jonathan Gosling and Henry Mintzberg, "The Five Minds of a Manager," *Harvard Business Review* (November 2003), pp. 1–9.

[50] For research on managerial work see Morgan W. McCall Jr., Ann M. Morrison, and Robert L. Hannan, *Studies of Managerial Work: Results and Methods. Technical Report #9* (Greensboro, NC: Center for Creative Leadership, 1978), pp. 7–9. See also John P. Kotter, "What Effective General Managers Really Do," *Harvard Business Review* (November–December 1982), pp. 156–57.

[51] Mintzberg (1973/1997), op. cit., p. 60.

[52] Kotter, op. cit., p. 164. See also his book *The General Managers* (New York: Free Press, 1986) and David Barry, Catherine Durnell Crampton, and Stephen J. Carroll, "Navigating the Garbage Can: How Agendas Help Managers Cope with Job Realities," *Academy of Management Executive*, vol. II (May 1997), pp. 43–56.

[53] Robert L. Katz, "Skills of an Effective Administrator," *Harvard Business Review* (September–October 1974), p. 94.

[54] Ibid.

[55] See, for example, Melissa Korn and Joe Light, "On the Lesson Plan: Feelings," *Wall Street Journal* (May 5, 2011) p. B6; and Alina Dizik, "Women Embrace the Skills and Strategies for a Corporate Life," *Financial Times* (September 12, 2011), p. 12.

[56] See Daniel Goleman's books *Emotional Intelligence* (New York: Bantam, 1995) and *Working with Emotional Intelligence* (New York: Bantam, 1998); and his articles "What Makes a Leader," *Harvard Business Review* (November–December 1998), pp. 93–102, and "Leadership That Makes a Difference," *Harvard Business Review* (March–April 2000), pp. 79–90; quote from p. 80.

[57] See Daniel Goleman, Richard Boyatzis, and Annie McKee, *Primal Leadership: Realizing the Power of Emotional Intelligence* (Boston: Harvard Business School Press, 2002).

[58] See Richard E. Boyatzis, *The Competent Manager: A Model for Effective Performance* (New York: Wiley, 1982); Richard E. Boyatzis, "Competencies in the 21st Century," *Journal of Management Development*, vol. 27 (1) (2008), pp. 5–12; and Richard Boyatzis (Guest Editor), "Competencies in the EU," *Journal of Management Development*, vol. 28 (2009), special issue.

[59] Audia, op cit.

[60] Suggested by and some items included from *Outcome Measurement Project, Phase I and Phase II Reports* (St. Louis: American Assembly of Collegiate Schools of Business, 1986).

### Feature Notes

Follow the Story—Information from Kate Klonick, "Pepsi's CEO a Refreshing Change" (August 15, 2006), www.abcnews.go.com; Diane Brady, "Indra Nooyi: Keeping Cool in Hot Water," *BusinessWeek* (June 11, 2007), special report; Indra Nooyi, "The Best Advice I Ever Got," *CNNMoney* (April 30, 2008), www.cnnnmoney.com; "Indra Nooyi," *Wall Street Journal* (November 10, 2008), p. R3; Andrew Hill, "The Women Who Mean Business, *Financial Times,* Kindle edition (September 26,

2009); "PepsiCo's Nooyi on 'New Capitalism'," money.cnn.com (accessed April 16, 2010); "Benefits Flow as Top People Join the Battle," *Financial Times*, Kindle edition (June 23, 2011); and, Mike Esterl, "PepsiCo Board Stands by Nooyi," *The Wall Street Journal* (January 13, 2012), pp. B1, B2; Duane Stanford, "At Pepsi, a Renewed Focus on Pepsi," *Bloomberg BusinessWeek* (February 6–12, 2012), pp. 25–26.

Ethics on the Line—Based on incident reported in "FBI Nabs 3 Over Coca-Cola Secrets," cnn.com (retrieved July 6, 2006); Betsy McKay, "Coke Employee Faces Charges in Plot to Sell Secrets," *Wall Street Journal* (July 6, 2006), p. B1; and "Man Gets Two Years in Coke Secrets Case," *Wall Street Journal* (June 7, 2007), p. A12.

Facts for Analysis—Information from Catalyst research reports at www.Catalyst.org; "Nicking the Glass Ceiling," *BusinessWeek* (June 9, 2009), p. 18; Francesco Guerrera and Alan Rappeport, "Women Still to Break Through 'Glass Ceiling' in U.S. Boardroom," *Financial Times*, Kindle edition (October 19, 2010); "Women on Wall Street Fall Further Behind," *Bloomberg BusinessWeek* (October 11–17, 2010), pp. 46–47; Dan Fitzpatrick and Liz Rappaport, "Women on Wall Street Still Hit a Glass Ceiling," *Wall Street Journal* (September 9–11, 2011), p. 24; Laura Petrecca, "More Women on Tap to Lead Top Companies," *USA Today* (October 27, 2011), p. 3b.; and Lublin, op cit.; Carol Hymowitz, "Behind Every Great Woman," *Bloomberg BusinessWeek* (January 9–15, 2012), pp. 54–57; April Dembosky, "A Social Networked Executive Finds the Perfect Job," *Financial Times*, Kindle Edition (February 3, 2012).

### Photo Essay Notes

Salesforce.com—Information from Jessica Hodgson, "Selling and Software," *Wall Street Journal* (December 17, 2009), p. A25; and Steve Hamm, "The King of the Cloud," *BusinessWeek* (November 30, 2009), p. 77. Teach for America—Information from teachforamerica.org; and "Wendy Kopp's Mission: Ensure Educational Opportunity for All Students," *VOANews.com* (November 2, 2009).

## Chapter 2

### Endnotes

[1] Information from Venture Capital Dispatch, "Facebook and Zappos's Different Views on Worker Retention," *Wall Street Journal* (October 29, 2009): wsj.com.

[2] See David A. Kolb, *Experiential Learning: Experience as the Source of Learning and Development* (Englewood Cliffs, NJ: Prentice-Hall, 1984); and David A. Kolb, "Experiential Learning Theory and the Learning Style Inventory," *The Academy of Management Review*, vol. 6 (1981), pp. 289–96.

[3] A thorough review and critique of the history of management thought, including management in ancient civilizations, is provided by Daniel A. Wren, *The Evolution of Management Thought*, 4th ed. (New York: Wiley, 1993).

[4] Pauline Graham, *Mary Parker Follett—Prophet of Management: A Celebration of Writings from the 1920s* (Boston: Harvard Business School Press, 1995).

[5] For a time line of 20th-century management ideas, see "75 Years of Management Ideas and Practices: 1922–1997," *Harvard Business Review*, supplement (September–October 1997).

[6] For a sample of this work, see Henry L. Gantt, *Industrial Leadership* (Easton, MD: Hive, 1921; Hive edition published in 1974); Henry C. Metcalfe and Lyndall Urwick (eds.), *Dynamic Administration: The Collected Papers of Mary Parker Follett* (New York: Harper-Brothers, 1940); James D. Mooney, *The Principles of Administration*, rev. ed. (New York: Harper-Brothers, 1947); Lyndall Urwick, *The Elements of Administration* (New York: Harper-Brothers, 1943); and *The Golden Book of Management* (London: N. Neame, 1956).

[7] *Frederick W. Taylor, The Principles of Scientific Management* (New York: W.W. Norton, 1967), originally published by Harper-Brothers in 1911. See also the biography, Robert Kanigel, *The One Best Way* (New York: Viking, 1997).

[8] For criticisms of Taylor and his work, see Charles W. Wrege and Amedeo G. Perroni, "Taylor's Pig-Tale: A Historical Analysis of Frederick W. Taylor's Pig Iron Experiments," *Academy of Management Journal*, vol. 17 (March 1974), pp. 6–27; Charles W. Wrege and Richard M. Hodgetts, "Frederick W. Taylor's 1899 Pig Iron Observations: Examining Fact, Fiction and Lessons for the New Millennium," *Academy of Management Journal*, vol. 43 (2000), pp. 1283–91; and Jill Lepore, "Not So Fast," *The New Yorker* (October 12, 2009); www.newyorker.com.

[9] For a discussion of the contemporary significance of Taylor's work, see Edwin A. Lock, "The Ideas of Frederick W. Taylor: An Evaluation," *Academy of Management Review*, vol. 7 (1982), p. 14.

[10] Information from Raymund Flandez and Kelly K. Sports, "Tackling the Energy Monster," *Wall Street Journal* (June 16, 2008), p. R1; and Jennifer Levitz, "Delivery Drivers to Pick up Pace by Surrendering Keys," *Wall Street Journal*, Kindle edition (September 16, 2011).

[11] Frank B. Gilbreth, *Motion Study* (New York: Van Nostrand, 1911).

[12] Ben Worthen, "Do You Need to Work Faster? Get a Bigger Computer Monitor," *Wall Street Journal* (March 25, 2008), p. B8; and "Plant Seeks Savings with Shot-Clock Approach," *The Messenger, Athens, Ohio* (November 15, 2009), p. A3.

[13] Available in English as *Henri Fayol, General and Industrial Administration* (London: Pitman, 1949); subsequent discussion is based on M. B. Brodie, *Fayol on Administration* (London: Pitman, 1949).

[14] A. M. Henderson and Talcott Parsons (eds. and trans.), *Max Weber: The Theory of Social Economic Organization* (New York: Free Press, 1947).

[15] Ibid., p. 337.

[16] For classic treatments of bureaucracy, see Alvin Gouldner, *Patterns of Industrial Bureaucracy* (New York: Free Press, 1954); and Robert K. Merton, *Social Theory and Social Structure* (New York: Free Press, 1957).

[17] M. P. Follett, *Freedom and Coordination* (London: Management Publications Trust, 1949).

[18] Judith Garwood, "A Review of Dynamic Administration: The Collected Papers of Mary Parker Follett," *New Management*, vol. 2 (1984), pp. 61–62; eulogy from Richard C. Cabot, *Encyclopedia of Social Work*, vol. 15, "Follett, Mary Parker," p. 351.

[19] The Hawthorne studies are described in detail in F. J. Roethlisberger and William J. Dickson, *Management and the Worker* (Cambridge, MA: Harvard University Press, 1966) and G. Homans, *Fatigue of Workers* (New York: Reinhold, 1941). For an interview with three of the participants in the relay–assembly test–room studies, see R. G. Greenwood, A. A. Bolton, and R. A. Greenwood, "Hawthorne a Half Century Later: Relay Assembly Participants Remember," *Journal of Management*, vol. 9 (1983), pp. 217–31.

[20] The criticisms of the Hawthorne studies are detailed in Alex Carey, "The Hawthorne Studies: A Radical Criticism," *American Sociological Review*, vol. 32 (1967), pp. 403–16; H. M. Parsons, "What Happened at Hawthorne?" *Science*, vol. 183 (1974), pp. 922–32; and B. Rice, "The Hawthorne Defect: Persistence of a Flawed Theory," *Psychology Today*, vol. 16 (1982), pp. 70–74. See also Wren, op. cit.

[21] This discussion of Maslow's theory is based on Abraham H. Maslow, *Eupsychian Management* (Homewood, IL: Richard D. Irwin, 1965) and Abraham H. Maslow, *Motivation and Personality*, 2nd ed. (New York: Harper-Row, 1970).

[22] Douglas McGregor, *The Human Side of Enterprise* (New York: McGraw-Hill, 1960).

[23] This notion is also discussed in terms of the "pygmalion effect." See Dov Eden, *Pygmalion in Management* (Lexington, MA: Lexington Books, 1990) and Dov Eden, Dvorah Geller, and Abigail Gerwirtz, "Implanting Pygmalion Leadership Style through Workshop Training: Seven Field Experiments," *Leadership Quarterly*, vol. 11 (2) (2000), pp. 171–210.

[24] Gary Heil, Deborah F. Stevens, and Warren G. Bennis, *Douglas McGregor on Management: Revisiting the Human Side of Enterprise* (New York: Wiley, 2000).

[25] Chris Argyris, *Personality and Organization* (New York: Harper-Row, 1957).

[26] Stefan Stern, "Smarter Leaders Are Betting Big on Data," *Financial Times*, Kindle edition (March 9, 2010). See also Thomas H. Davenport, Jeanne G. Harris, and Robert Morison, *Analytics at Work: Smarter Decisions, Better Results* (Cambridge, MA: Harvard Business Press, 2010).

[27] Scott Morrison, "Google Searches for Staffing Answers," *Wall Street Journal* (May 19, 2009), p. B1; and Dennis K. Berman, "So, What's Your Algorithm?" *The Wall Street Journal* (January 4, 2012), pp. B1, B2.

[28] The ideas of Chester I. Bamard, *Functions of the Executive* (Cambridge, MA: Harvard University Press, 1938), and Ludwig von Bertalanffy, "The History and Status of General Systems Theory," *Academy of Management Journal*, vol. 15 (1972), pp. 407–26, contributed to the emergence of this systems perspective on organizations. The systems view is further developed by Daniel Katz and Robert L. Kahn in their classic book, *The Social Psychology of Organizations* (New York: Wiley, 1978). For an integrated systems view see Lane Tracy, *The Living Organization* (New York: Quorum Books, 1994). For an overview, see W. Richard Scott, *Organizations: Rational, Natural, and Open Systems*, 4th ed. (Upper Saddle River, NJ: Prentice-Hall, 1998).

[29] For an overview, see Scott, op. cit., pp. 95–97.

[30] See, for example, the classic studies of Tom Burns and George M. Stalker, *The Management of Innovation* (London: Tavistock, 1961, and republished by Oxford University Press, London, 1994) and Paul R. Lawrence and Jay W. Lorsch, *Organizations and Environment* (Boston: Division of Research, Graduate School of Business Administration, Harvard University, 1967).

[31] W. Edwards Deming, *Quality, Productivity, and Competitive Position* (Cambridge, MA: MIT Press, 1982); and Rafael Aguay, *Dr. Deming: The American Who Taught the Japanese about Quality* (New York: Free Press, 1997).

[32] See Howard S. Gitlow and Shelly J. Gitlow, *The Deming Guide to Quality and Competitive Position* (Englewood Cliffs, NJ: Prentice-Hall, 1987).

[33] Peter F. Drucker, "The Future That Has Already Happened," *Harvard Business Review*, vol. 75 (September–October 1997), pp. 20–24; and Peter F. Drucker, Esther Dyson, Charles Handy, Paul Daffo, and Peter M. Senge, "Looking Ahead: Implications of the Present," *Harvard Business Review*, vol. 75 (September–October 1997).

[34] See, for example, Thomas H. Davenport and Laurence Prusak, *Working Knowledge: How Organizations Manage What They Know* (Cambridge, MA: Harvard Business School Press, 1997).

[35] Peter Senge, *The Fifth Discipline* (New York: Harper, 1990).

[36] See Bruce G. Resnick and Timothy L. Smunt, "From Good to Great to . . . " *Academy of Management Perspectives* (November 2008), pp. 6–12; and Bruce Niendorf and Kristine Beck, "Good to Great, or Just Good?" *Academy of Management Perspectives* (November 2008), pp. 13–20.

[37] See Denise M. Rousseau, "On Organizational Behavior," *BizEd* (May/June, 2008), pp. 30–31; and David G. Allen, Phillip C. Bryant, and James A. Vardaman, "Retaining Talent: Replacing Misconceptions with Evidence-Based Strategies," *Academy of Management Perspectives*, vol. 24 (May, 2010).

[38] Jeffrey Pfeffer and Robert I. Sutton, *Hard Facts, Dangerous Half-Truths, and Total Nonsense: Profiting from Evidence-Based Management* (Boston: Harvard Business School Press, 2006).

[39] Jeffrey Pfeffer and Robert I. Sutton, "Management Half-Truths and Nonsense," *California Management Review*, vol. 48(3) (2006), 77–100; and Jeffrey Pfeffer and Robert I. Sutton, "Evidence-Based Management," *Harvard Business Review* (January 2006), reprint R0601E.

[40] Rob B. Viner, David Denyer, and Denise M. Rousseau, "Evidence-Based Management: Concept Cleanup Time?" *Academy of Management Perspectives*, vol. 23 (November 2009), pp. 19–28. For debate on the concept, see the exchange between ibid. and Trish Reay, Whitney Berta, and Melanie Kazman Kohn, "What's the Evidence on Evidence-Based Management?" *Academy of Management Perspectives*, vol. 23 (November 2009), pp. 5–18.

[41] Jeffrey Pfeffer, *The Human Equation: Building Profits by Putting People First* (Boston: Harvard Business School Press, 1998); and Charles O'Reilly III and Jeffrey Pfeffer, *Hidden Value: How Great Companies Achieve Extraordinary Results with Ordinary People* (Boston: Harvard Business School Press, 2000).

[42] Developed from Sara L. Rynes, Tamara L. Giluk, and Kenneth G. Brown, "The Very Separate Worlds of Academic and Practitioner Periodicals in Human Resource Management: Implications for Evidence-Based Management," *Academy of Management Journal*, Vol. 50 (October 2008), p. 986; and, David G. Allen, Phillip C. Bryant, and James M. Vardaman, "Retaining Talent: Replacing Misconceptions with Evidence-Based Strategies," *Academy of Management Perspectives*, vol. 24 (May, 2010).

### Feature Notes

Follow the Story—Information from "Chapter 2," *Kellogg* (Winter 2004), p. 6; David Pilling, "Establishing Libraries to Help Children Gain a Love of Books," *Financial Times* (December 8, 2009); *Leaving Microsoft to Change the World* (New York: HarperCollins), 2006; and David Pilling, "Establishing Libraries to Help Gain a Love of Books," *Financial Times*, Kindle edition (December 8, 2009).

Ethics on the Line—Information from Aaron Task, "Another Corporate Outrage: 'Golden Parachutes' for Failed CEOs," *Yahoo! Finance* (September 30, 2011): http://finance.yahoo.com/blogs. See also John Helyar, "After Much Hoopla, Investor 'Say on Pay' Is a Bust," *Bloomberg BusinessWeek* (June 20–26, 2011), pp. 23–24.

Facts for Analysis—Generations and Bosses: Information and quotes from "Generation Gap: On Their Bosses, Millennials Happier Than Boomers," *Wall Street Journal* (November 15, 2010), p. B6.

### Photo Essay Notes

Great Choice—See the book review by Alan Murray, "Turbulent Tiimes, Steady Success," *Wall Street Journal* (October 11, 2011), p. A15.

## Chapter 3

### Endnotes

[1] Information and quotes from www.stonyfield.com/about_us; www.stonyfield.com/youtube/index.jsp; Gary Hirshberg biography retrieved from www.notablebiographies.com; "25 Rich Ass Greenies Who Made Their Fortune Saving the Environment," Earthfirst.com (August 25, 2008); and, "Stonyfield Founder Gary Hirshberg Steps Into New Role, Selects Mission-Driven Successor Walt Freese as Stonyfield CEO," Londonderry, NH (January 12, 2012): stonyfield.com/about-us/press-room.

[2] J. J. Graafland, "Do Markets Crowd Out Virtues? An Aristotelian Framework," *Journal of Business Ethics*, vol. 91 (2010), pp. 1–19.

[3] R. M. Ryckman, M. Hammer, L. M. Kaczor, and J. A. Gold, "Construction of a Hypercompetitive Attitude Scale," *Journal of Personality Assessment*, vol. 55 (1990), pp. 630–39.

[4] Desmond Tutu, "Do More Than Win," *Fortune* (December 30, 1991), p. 59.

[5] For an overview, see Linda K. Trevino and Katherine A. Nelson, *Managing Business Ethics*, 3rd ed. (New York: Wiley, 2003).

[6] M. J. O'Fallon and K. D. Butterfield, "A Review of the Empirical Ethical Decision-making Literature: 1996–2003," *Journal of Business Ethics*, vol. 59 (2005), pp. 375–413; and S. J. Vitell and E. R. Hidalgo, "The Impact of Corporate Ethical Values and Enforcement of Ethical Codes on the Perceived Importance of Ethics in Business: A Comparison of U.S. and Spanish Managers," *Journal of Business Ethics*, vol. 64 (2006), pp. 31–43.

[7] D. Lyons, *Ethics and the Rule of Law* (Cambridge: Cambridge University Press, 1984).

[8] See, for example, James Oliver Horter and Lois E. Horton, *Slavery and the Making of America* (New York: Oxford University Press, 2004).

[9] Trevino and Nelson, op. cit.

[10] Milton Rokeach, *The Nature of Human Values* (New York: Free Press, 1973). See also W. C. Frederick and J. Weber, "The Values of Corporate Executives and Their Critics: An Empirical Description and Normative Implications," in W. C. Frederick and L. E. Preston (eds.), *Business Ethics: Research Issues and Empirical Studies* (Greenwich, CT: JAI Press, 1990).

[11] Philip Delves Broughton, "MBA Students Sway Integrity for Plagiarism," *Financial Times* (May 19, 2008), p. 13.

[12] Case reported in Michelle Conlin, "Cheating—Or Postmodern Learning?" *BusinessWeek* (May 14, 2007), p. 42.

[13] See Gerald F. Cavanagh, Dennis J. Moberg, and Manuel Velasquez, "The Ethics of Organizational Politics," *Academy of Management Review*, vol. 6 (1981), pp. 363–74; Justin G. Locknecker, Joseph A. McKinney, and Carlos W. Moore, "Egoism and Independence: Entrepreneurial Ethics," *Organizational Dynamics* (Winter 1988), pp. 64–72; and Justin G. Locknecker, Joseph A. McKinney, and Carlos W. Moore, "The Generation Gap in Business Ethics," *Business Horizons* (September–October 1989), pp. 9–14.

[14] Raymond L. Hilgert, "What Ever Happened to Ethics in Business and in Business Schools?" *The Diary of Alpha Kappa Psi* (April 1989), pp. 4–8.

[15] The Universal Declaration of Human Rights was adopted by General Assembly resolution 217 A (III), December 10, 1948, in the United Nations. See un.org/ Overview/rights.html.

[16] Jerald Greenburg, "Organizational Justice: Yesterday, Today, and Tomorrow," *Journal of Management*, vol. 16 (1990), pp. 399–432; and Mary A. Konovsky, "Understanding Procedural Justice and Its Impact on Business Organizations," *Journal of Management*, vol. 26 (2000), pp. 489–511.

[17] For a review see Russell Cropanzano, David E. Bown, and Stephen W. Gilliland, "The Management of Organizational Justice," *Academy of Management Perspectives* (November 2007), pp. 34–48.

[18] Interactional justice is described by Robert J. Bies, "The Predicament of Injustice: The Management of Moral Outrage," in L. L. Cummings and B. M. Staw (eds.), *Research in Organizational Behavior*, vol. 9 (Greenwich, CT: JAI Press, 1987), pp. 289–319. The example is from Carol T. Kulik and Robert L. Holbrook, "Demographics in Service Encounters: Effects of Racial and Gender Congruence on Perceived Fairness," *Social Justice Research*, vol. 13 (2000), pp. 375–402.

[19] M. Fortin and M. R. Fellenz, "Hypocrisies of Fairness: Towards a More Reflexive Ethical Base in Organizational Justice Research and Practice," *Journal of Business Ethics*, vol. 78 (2008), pp. 415–33; and, W.

Sadurski, "Social Justice and Legal Justice," *Law and Philosophy*, vol. 3 (1984), pp. 329–54.

[20] Robert D. Haas, "Ethics—A Global Business Challenge," *Vital Speeches of the Day* (June 1, 1996), pp. 506–9.

[21] This discussion is based on Thomas Donaldson, "Values in Tension: Ethics Away from Home," *Harvard Business Review*, vol. 74 (September–October 1996), pp. 48–62.

[22] Thomas Donaldson and Thomas W. Dunfee, "Towards a Unified Conception of Business Ethics: Integrative Social Contracts Theory," *Academy of Management Review*, vol. 19 (1994), pp. 252–85.

[23] Donaldson, op. cit.

[24] Reported in Barbara Ley Toffler, "Tough Choices: Managers Talk Ethics," *New Management*, vol. 4 (1987), pp. 34–39. See also Barbara Ley Toffler, *Tough Choices: Managers Talk Ethics* (New York: Wiley, 1986).

[25] See, for example, Steven N. Brenner and Earl A. Mollander, "Is the Ethics of Business Changing?" *Harvard Business Review*, vol. 55 (January–February 1977).

[26] Survey results from Del Jones, "48% of Workers Admit to Unethical or Illegal Acts," *USA Today* (April 4, 1997), p. A1.

[27] For a discussion of similar approaches see Denis Collins, *Business Ethics: How to Design and Manage Ethical Organizations* (Hoboken, NJ: John Wiley & Sons, 2012), pp. 146–147.

[28] Reported in Adam Smith, "Wall Street's Outrageous Fortunes," *Esquire* (April 1987), p. 73. See also Long Wang and J. Keith Murnighan, "on great," *The Academy of Management Annals*, Vol. 5 (2011), pp. 279–316.

[29] Lawrence Kohlberg, *The Psychology of Moral Development: The Nature and Validity of Moral Stages* (*Essays in Moral Development*, Volume 2) (New York: HarperCollins, 1984). See also the discussion by Linda K. Trevino, "Moral Reasoning and Business Ethics: Implications for Research, Education, and Management," *Journal of Business Ethics*, vol. 11 (1992), pp. 445–59.

[30] See Thomas M. Jones, "Ethical Decision Making by Individuals in Organizations: An Issue Contingent Model," *Academy of Management Review*, vol. 16 (1991), pp. 366–95; Sara Morris and Robert A. McDonald, "The Role of Moral Intensity in Moral Judgments: An Empirical Investigation," *Journal of Business Ethics*, vol. 14 (9) (1995), pp. 715–726; and Tim Barnett, "Dimensions of Moral Intensity and Ethical Decision Making: An Empirical Study," *Journal of Applied Social Psychology*, vol. 31 (2001), pp. 1038–57.

[31] Information on this case from William M. Carley, "Antitrust Chief Says CEOs Should Tape All Phone Calls to Each Other," *Wall Street Journal* (February 15, 1983), p. 23; "American Air, Chief End Antitrust Suit, Agree Not to Discuss Fares with Rivals," *Wall Street Journal* (July 15, 1985), p. 4; "American Airlines Loses Its Pilot," *Economist* (April 18, 1998), p. 58.

[32] Situations from Alison Damast and Erin Zlomek, "Top B-School Stories of 2011," *Bloomberg BusinessWeek* (December 28, 2011): businessweek.com; and, Joe Palazzolo and Emily Glazer, "Grand Jury Gets Evidence," *The Wall Street Journal* (February 13, 2012), pp. A1, A2.

[33] Saul W. Gellerman, "Why 'Good' Managers Make Bad Ethical Choices," *Harvard Business Review*, vol. 64 (July–August 1986), pp. 85–90.

[34] Archie B. Carroll, "In Search of the Moral Manager," *Business Horizons* (March/April 2001), pp. 7–15.

[35] Kohlberg, op. cit.

[36] Alan L. Otten, "Ethics on the Job: Companies Alert Employees to Potential Dilemmas," *Wall Street Journal* (July 14, 1986), p. 17; and "The Business Ethics Debate," *Newsweek* (May 25, 1987), p. 36.

[37] Information from corporate website: www.gapinc.com/communitysourcing/vendor_conduct.htm.

[38] See "Whistle-Blowers on Trial," *BusinessWeek* (March 24, 1997), pp. 172–78, and "NLRB Judge Rules for Massachusetts Nurses in Whistle-Blowing Case," *American Nurse* (January–February 1998), p. 7.

[39] For a review of whistleblowing, see Marcia P. Micelli and Janet P. Near, *Blowing the Whistle* (Lexington, MA: Lexington Books, 1992); see also Micelli and Near, "Whistleblowing: Reaping the Benefits," *Academy of Management Executive*, vol. 8 (August 1994), pp. 65–72; and, M. J. Gundlach, S. C. Douglas, and M. J. Martinko, "The Decision to Blow the Whistle: A Social Information Processing Framework." *Academy of Management Review*, vol. 28, no. 1 (2003), pp. 107–23.

[40] "A Tip for Whistleblowers: Don't," *Wall Street Journal* (May 31, 2007), p. B6.

[41] Information from Ethics Resource Center, "Major Survey of America's Workers Finds Substantial Improvements in Ethics," www.ethics.org/releases/nr_20030521_nbes.html.

[42] James A. Waters, "Catch 20.5: Mortality as an Organizational Phenomenon," *Organizational Dynamics*, vol. 6 (Spring 1978), pp. 3–15.

[43] Definition from www.pgsupplier.com/environmental-sustainability-scorecard (accessed: May 12, 2010).

[44] Examples are from Dancing Deer Bakery website retrieved from http://www.dancingdeer.com/index.cfm?page_id=45; "Growing Green Business," *Northwestern* (Winter 2007), p. 19; Regina McEnery, "Cancer Patients Getting the White-Glove Treatment," *The Columbus Dispatch* (March 1, 2008); and, Nanett Byrnes, "Heavy Lifting at the Food Bank," *BusinessWeek* (December 17, 2007), pp. SC08–SC09.

[45] Alfred A. Marcus and Adam R. Fremeth, "Green Management Matters Regardless," *Academy of Management Perspectives*, Vol. 23 (August, 2009), pp. 17–26.

[46] Jeffrey Pfeffer, "Building Sustainable Organizations: The Human Factor," *Academy of Management Perspectives*, Vol. 24 (February, 2010), pp. 34–45.

[47] Joe Biesecker, "What Today's College Graduates Want: It's Not All about Paychecks," *Central Penn Business Journal* (August 10, 2007).

[48] Ibid. Sarah E. Needleman, "The Latest Office Perk: Getting Paid to Volunteer," *Wall Street Journal* (April 29, 2008), p. D1.

[49] See Thomas Donaldson and Lee Preston, "The Stakeholder Theory of the Corporation," *Academy of Management Review*, vol. 20 (January 1995), pp. 65–91.

[50] R. K. Bradley, R. Agle, and D. J. Wood, "Toward a Theory of Stakeholder Identification and Salience: Defining the Principle of Who and What Really Counts," *Academy of Management Review*, vol. 22 (1997), pp. 853–86.

[51] Michael E. Porter and Mark R. Kramer, "Strategy & Society: The Link between Competitive Advantage and Corporate Social Responsibility," *Harvard Business Review* (December 2006), Reprint R0612D.

[52] The historical framework of this discussion is developed from Keith Davis, "The Case for and against Business Assumption of Social Responsibility," *Academy of Management Journal* (June 1973), pp. 312–22; Keith Davis and William Frederick, *Business and Society: Management: Public Policy, Ethics*, 5th ed. (New York: McGraw-Hill, 1984). The debate is also discussed by Makower, op. cit., pp. 28–33. For further perspective on this debate see, for example, Marcus and Fremeth, op cit., and, Donald S. Siegel, "Green Management Matters Only if It Yields More Green: An Economic/Strategic Perspective," *Academy of Management Perspectives*, Vol. 23 (August 2009), pp. 5–16.

[53] The Friedman quotation is from Milton Friedman, *Capitalism and Freedom* (Chicago: University of Chicago Press, 1962). See also Henry G. Manne, "Milton Friedman Was Right," *Wall Street Journal* (November 24, 2006), p. A12.

[54] For more on this line of thinking see "Aneel Kamari, "The Case Against Corporate Social Responsibility," *Wall Street Journal* (August 23, 2010), wsj.com.

[55] The Samuelson quotation is from Paul A. Samuelson, "Love That Corporation," *Mountain Bell Magazine* (Spring 1971). Both are cited in Davis, op. cit.

[56] Michael E. Porter and Mark R. Kramer, "Shared Value: How to Reinvent Capitalism and Unleash a Wave of Innovation and Growth," *Harvard Business Review* (January–February, 2011), pp. 62–77.

[57] Ibid. p. 64.

[58] See Makower, op. cit. (1994), pp. 71–75; Sandra A. Waddock and Samuel B. Graves, "The Corporate Social Performance—Financial Performance Link," *Strategic Management Journal* (1997), pp. 303–19, Michael E. Porter and Mark R. Kramer, "Strategy-Society: The Link between Competitive Advantage and Corporate Social Responsibility," *Harvard Business Review* (December 2006), pp. 78–92.

[59] Information and quotes from Mara Lemos-Stein, "Talking About Waste with P&G," *Wall Street Journal* (September 13, 2011), p. R8; and "Benefits Flow as Top People Join the Battle," *Financial Times*, Kindle edition (June 23, 2011); and, http://www.nestle.com/csv/ruraldevelopment/responsiblesourcing (retrieved February 18, 2012); and, "How to Create a Green Supply Chain," *Financial Times*, Kindle Edition (November 11, 2010).

[60] Ioannis Ioannou and George Serafeim, "The Consequences of Mandatory Corporate Sustainability Reporting," *HBS Working Paper Number 11-100*, Harvard Business School (March, 2011).

[61] The "compliance–conviction" distinction is attributed to Mark Goyder in Martin Waller, "Much Corporate Responsibility Is Box-Ticking," *The Times Business* (July 8, 2003), p. 21. See also Archie B. Carroll, "A Three-Dimensional Model of Corporate Performance," *Academy of Management Review*, vol. 4 (1979), pp. 497–505.

[62] Elizabeth Gatewood and Archie B. Carroll, "The Anatomy of Corporate Social Response," *Business Horizons*, vol. 24 (September–October 1981), pp. 9–16; and Mark S. Schwartz and Archie B. Carroll, "Corporate Social Responsibility: A Three Domain Approach," *Business Ethics Quarterly*, vol. 13 (2003), pp. 503–30.

[63] Judith Burns, "Everything You Wanted to Know about Corporate Governance . . . But Didn't Know How to Ask," *Wall Street Journal* (October 27, 2003), pp. R1, R7.

### *Feature Notes*

Follow the Story—Information from Carolyn Y. Woo, "Lives, Not Just Livlihoods," *BizEd Magazine* (May/June, 2011), pp. 41–45; John Rivera, "CRS Names Carolyn Woo New President, CEO," crs.org (accessed February 21, 2012); and, "The Ten Principles," www.unglobalcompact.org.

Ethics on the Line—Information and quotes from Diane Staffor, "Can You Be Fired for Trashing the Boss on Facebook?" *The Columbus Dispatch* (June 12, 2011), p. D3; and Jennifer Preston, "Social Media History Becomes a New Job Hurdle," *New York Times* (July 7, 2011), nytimes.com.

Facts for Analysis—Manager Behavior: Information from Deloitte LLP, "Leadership Counts: 2007 Deloitte & Touche USA Ethics & Workplace Survey Results," *Kiplinger Business Resource Center* (June, 2007), www.kiplinger.com.

### *Photo Essay Notes*

Child Labor—Data from International Labour Organization, *Facts on Child Labor 2010* (Geneva, Switzerland: April 1, 2010). The Social Network—Eric Ditzian, "The Social Network: The Reviews are In!" mtv.com (October 1, 2010); and Ethan Smith, "'Social Network' Opens at No. 1," *Wall Street Journal* (October 4, 2010), p. B5. Shared Value—Information from Steve Lohr, "First, Make Money. Also, Do Good." The *New York Times* (August 13, 2011): nytimes.com.

## Chapter 4

### *Endnotes*

[1] Information and quotes from Jessica Hodgson, "Selling and Software," *Wall Street Journal* (December 17, 2009), p. A25; Steve Hamm, "The King of the Cloud," *BusinessWeek* (November 30, 2009), p. 77, and, "Charlie Rose talks to Marc Benioff," *Bloomberg Businessweek* (December 5–11, 2011),
p. 52. See also Marc Benioff, *Behind the Cloud: The Untold Story of How Salesforce.com Went from Idea to Billion-Dollar Company and Revolutionized an Industry* (San Francisco, CA: Jossey-Bass, 2009).

[2] See "Risk," *Psychology Today* (October 1, 2009), www.psychology-today.com (accessed February 3, 2010); Nathan Washburn, "Hard Times Can Inspire Wrong Type of Risk Taking," http://knowledgenet-work.thunderbird.edu (accessed January 12, 2010).

[3] Opening quotes from Joseph B. White and Peter Landers, "Toyoda Is Wary Star of Kabuki at Capitol," *Wall Street Journal* (February 25, 2010), pp. A1, A7; and *Associated Press*, "U.S. May Require Accelerator Override in New Cars," www.clickondetroit.com/automotive/22711707/detail.html (accessed March 8, 2010).

[4] See, For example, Ellen Byron, "P&G Tweaks Its Products as U.S. Shoppers Trade Down," *Wall Street Journal* (September 13, 2011), pp. 14–15; and, Conor Dougherty "Young Men Suffer Worst as Economy Staggers," The *Wall Street Journal* (November 7, 2011), pp. B1, B2.

[5] Information from Byron, op cit.

[6] See Kris Maher and Bob Tita, "Caterpillar Joins 'Onshoring' Trend," *Wall Street Journal* (March 10, 2010), pp. B1, B7.

[7] Information from John Letzing and Ian Sherr, "HTC Sues Apple via Google," *Wall Street Journal* (September 9–11, 2011), p. 22; Ian Sherr and Jessica & Vascellaro, "Apple Hits Samsung Phone," The *Wall Street Journal* (February 13, 2012), p. B1; and, John Letzing, "Yahoo Threatens Suit vs. Facebook," The *Wall Street Journal* (February 29, 2012) p. B5.

[8] Charles Forelle, "EU Fines Microsoft $1.35 Billion," *Wall Street Journal* (February 28, 2008), p. B2.

[9] Elaine Kurtenbauch, "Apple's 'iPad' Skirmish Moves to the U.S.," *USA Today*, usatoday.com (February 28, 2012).

[10] Ibid; and, Ben Worthen and Siobhan Gorman, "Google Prepares to Stop Censoring in China," *Wall Street Journal* (March 12, 2010), p. B1.

[11] See "It's Time for a Breakthrough," Special Advertising Section, *Bloomberg BusinessWeek* (July 4–10, 2011), pp. S1–S9; and Miriam Jordan, "White-Minority Wealth Gulf Widens," *Wall Street Journal*, Kindle Edition (July 26, 2011).

[12] See Jean M. Twenge, Stacy M. Campbell, Brian J. Hoffman, and Charles E. Lance, "Generational Difference in Work Values: Leisure and Extrinsic Values Increasing, Social and Intrinsic Values Decreasing," *Journal of Management Online First* (March 1, 2010): www.jom.sagepub.com.

[13] See, for example, Sharon Jayson, "'iGeneration' Has No Off Switch," *USA Today* (February 10, 2010), pp. D1, D2.

[14] Roger Lowenstein, "Is Any CEO Worth $189,000 per Hour?" *Bloomberg BusinessWeek* (February 20–26, 2012), pp. 8, 5.

[15] See Cara Pring, "100 More Social Media Statistics, 2012," www.thesocialskinny.com (accessed February 28, 2012).

[16] Bobby White, "The New Workplace Rules: No Video-Watching," *Wall Street Journal* (March 4, 2008), pp. B1, B3.

[17] Reported in "Surprising Attitudes Toward Texting," *BizEd* (May–June, 2011), p. 72.

[18] Information from Martin Giles, "Online Social Networks Are Changing the Way People Communicate," *Economist*, Kindle Edition (February 4, 2010).

[19] See, for example, Martin Fackler, "Large Zone Near Japanese Reactors to Be Off Limits," *New York Times* (August 22, 2011); nytimes.com.

[20] See Thomas L. Freedman, "Efficiency Must be the Wave of the Future," The Columbus Dispatch (March 6, 2012), p. A9.

[21] See Ibid; and, Bradfield Moody and Bianca Nogrady, *The Sixty Wave: How to Succeed in a Resource Limited World* (Sydney: Random House Australia, 2012).

[22] "Selling Green," *The Wall Street Journal* (March 26, 2012), p. R8.

[23] See Thomas Donaldson and Lee Preston, "The Stakeholder Theory of the Corporation," *Academy of Management Review*, vol. 20 (January 1995), pp. 65–91.

[24] See Michael E. Porter, *Competitive Strategy: Techniques for Analyzing Industries and Competitors* (New York: Free Press, 1980); and *Competitive Advantage: Creating and Sustaining Superior Performance* (New York: Free Press, 1986); see also Richard A. D'Aveni, *Hyper-Competition: Managing the Dynamics of Strategic Maneuvering* (New York: Free Press, 1994).

[25] Michael E. Porter, "Strategy and the Internet," *Harvard Business Review*, vol. 79, no. 3 (March 2001).

[26] James D. Thompson, *Organizations in Action* (New York: McGraw-Hill, 1967); and Robert B. Duncan, "Characteristics of Organizational Environments and Perceived Environmental Uncertainty," *Administrative Science Quarterly*, vol. 17 (1972), pp. 313–27. For discussion of the implications of uncertainty see Hugh Courtney, Jane Kirkland, and Patrick Viguerie, "Strategy under Uncertainty," *Harvard Business Review* (November–December 1997), pp. 67–79.

[27] Tom Peters, *The Circle of Innovation* (New York: Knopf, 1997).

[28] Quote from Jena McGregor, "The World's Most Innovative Companies," *BusinessWeek* (April 24, 2006), pp. 63–74.

[29] Peter F. Drucker, *Management: Tasks, Responsibilities, and Practices* (New York: Harper-Row, 1973), p. 797.

[30] See, for example, Muhammad Yunus, *Creating a World Without Poverty: Social Business and the Future of Capitalism* (New York: Public Affairs, 2008). Note that abuses of micro-credit lending have been publicized in the press and both the microfinance industry as a whole and the Grameen Bank in particular have been criticized by the Bangladesh government. Muhammad Yunus published his own criticism of the industry and defense of the Grameen Bank model in "Sacrificing Microcredit for Megaprofits," *New York Times* (January 14, 2011); nytimes.com. A Norwegian documentary that aired criticisms of how Yunus and Grameen Bank handled funds has largely been refuted, but Yunus continues to be criticized by the Bangladesh government.

[31] Gary Hamel, *Leading the Revolution: How to Thrive in Turbulent Times* (Boston: Harvard Business School Press, 2002).

[32] "The Joys and Perils of 'Reverse Innovation,'" *BusinessWeek* (October 5, 2009), p. 12; "How to Compete in a World Turned Upside Down," *Financial Times*, Kindle edition (October 6, 2009).

[33] See Clay Christensen, *The Innovator's Dilemma: When New Technologies Cause Great Firms to Fail*, Reprint edition (New York: Harper Paperbacks, 2011); and Clay Christensen, Jeff Dyer, and Hal Gregersen, *The Innovator's DNA: Mastering the Five Skills of Disruptive Innovators* (Cambridge, MA: Harvard Business Press, 2011).

[34] See the chronicle of Steve Jobs' life and work in "Steve Jobs (1955–2011)," Special edition, *Bloomberg BusinessWeek* (October 10–16, 2011), pp. 1–65.

[35] Information from Helen Jones, "CEOs Now Find that Principles and Profits Can Mix Well," *Wall Street Journal* (November 22, 2010), p. R5.

[36] Ibid.

[37] www.wbcsd.org.

[38] Economics—Creating Environmental Capital," *Wall Street Journal* (March 8, 2010), p. R1.

[39] See, for example, "The Long Road to an Alternative Energy Future," *Wall Street Journal* (February 22, 2010), p. R4.

[40] "Indra Nooyi of PepsiCo," View from the Top, *Financial Times* (February 1, 2010), www.ft.com (retrieved March 11, 2010).

[41] Marcus and Fremeth, op. cit.

[42] Definition from www.sustainablebusiness.com.

[43] See Sarah Murray, "Companies Ensure Efforts Are Not Beyond Description," *Financial Times*, Kindle Edition (June 23, 2011).

[44] David Cooperrider, "Sustainable Innovation," *BizEd* (July/August, 2008), pp. 32–38.

[45] Examples from "The Eco Advantage: The Pioneers," *Inc.* (November 1, 2006); inc.com.

[46] Information from *Bloomberg BusinessWeek* (June 6–12, 2011), pp. 70–74.

[47] "Clean-Tech Companies: Ranking the Top Venture-Backed Firms," *Wall Street Journal* (March 8, 2010), p. R4.

[48] http://www.pg.com/en_US/sustainability/environmental_sustainability/environmental_vision.shtml (accessed: April 3, 2012).

[49] http://www.pg.com/en_US/downloads/sustainability/reports/PG_2011_Sustainability_Overview.pdf (accessed: April 3, 2012).

[50] Jeffrey Pfeffer, "Building Sustainable Organizations: The Human Factor," *Academy of Management Perspectives*, Vol. 24 (February, 2010), pp. 34–45.

[51] Quotes from Ibid.

[52] Information and quote from Jessica E. Vascellaro, "Audit Faults Apple Supplier," *The Wall Street Journal* (March 30, 2012), pp. B1, B2.

[53] Based on Budner, S. "Intolerance of Ambiguity as a Personality Variable," *Journal of Personality*, Vol. 30, No. 1, (1962), pp. 29–50.

### Feature Notes

Follow the story—Information from Geoffrey A. Fowler and Jessica E. Vascellaro, "With Jobs Gone, a New Test for Apple 'Army,'" *Wall Street Journal* (October 7, 2011), pp. B1, B4; Joseph Menn and Richard Waters, "Cook Tasked with Replacing Apple Icon," *Financial Times* (August 26, 2011), P. 17; and quotes and information from "Steve Jobs (1955–2011)," Special edition, *Bloomberg BusinessWeek* (October 10–16, 2011), pp. 1–65.

Facts for Analysis—Information from Mike Dorning, "Grateful to Be Employed, Bored Half to Death," *Bloomberg BusinessWeek* (June 20–26, 2011), pp. 35–36; Joe Light, "Unhappy Workers Stay in Current Jobs, for Now," *The Wall Street Journal* (June 20, 2011), p. B7; Conor Dougherty, "Young Men Suffer Worst as Economy Staggers," *The Wall Street Journal* (November 7, 2011), pp. B1, B2.

### Photo Essay Notes

Nobel Prize—Information and quote from Jeanne Whalen, Paul Sonne, and Hakin Almasmari, "Three Women Share Nobel Peace Prize," *The Wall Street Journal* (October 8–9. 2011), p. A7. Chipotle Commercial, http://www.youtube.com/watch?v=aMfSGt6rHos. Nobel Peace Prize—see Jeanne Whalen, Paul Sonne, and Hakim Almasmari, "Three Women Share Nobel Peace Prize," *Wall Street Journal* (October 8–9, 2011), p. A7.

## Chapter 5

### Endnotes

[1] Quotes from www.limited.com/feature.jsp and www.limited.com/who/index.jsp. pp. 40–43: and limitedbrands.com.

[2] Richard D. Lewis, *The Cultural Imperative: Global Trends in the 21st Century* (Yarmouth, ME: Intercultural Press, 2002).

[3] See, for example, Dan Gearino, "Made in This Hemisphere," *Columbus Dispatch* (January 11, 2010), pp. A10, A11; and David Welch, "One Man, One Car, One World," *BusinessWeek* (January 25, 2010), pp. 48–49.

[4] "Boeing: Faster, Faster, Faster," *The Economist*, Kindle Edition (January 29, 2012).

[5] See, for example, Kenichi Ohmae's books, *The Borderless World: Power and Strategy in the Interlinked Economy* (New York: Harper, 1989); *The End of the Nation State* (New York: Free Press, 1996); and *The Next Global Stage: Challenges and Opportunities in Our Borderless World* (Philadelphia. Wharton School Publishing, 2006). See also Thomas L. Friedman, *Hot, Flat, and Crowded: Why We Need a Green Revolution—and How It Can Renew America* (New York: Farrar, Straus and Giroux, 2008).

[6] Pankaj Ghemawat, *World 3.0: Global Prosperity and How to Achieve It* (Cambridge, MA: Harvard Business Press, 2011).

[7] Pietra Rivoli, *The Travels of a T-Shirt in the Global Economy*, 2nd ed. (Hoboken, NJ: John Wiley & Sons, 2009).

[8] Rosabeth Moss Kanter, *World Class: Thinking Locally in the Global Economy* (New York: Simon and Schuster, 1995), preface.

[9] Information from Mark Niquette, "Honda's 'Bold Move' Paid Off," *Columbus Dispatch* (November 16, 2002), pp. C1, C2; and "Marysville Auto Plant," ohio.honda.com.

[10] Information from Mei Fong, "Chinese Refrigerator Maker Finds U.S. Chilly," *Wall Street Journal* (March 18, 2008), pp. B1, B2.

[11] Quote from John A. Byrne, "Visionary vs. Visionary," *BusinessWeek* (August 28, 2000), p. 210.

[12] Information from newbalance.com/corporate; and, "Nike Strategy Leaves It Room to Run," *Wall Street Journal* (March 16, 2010), p. C10.

[13] Steve Hamm, "Into Africa: Capitalism from the Ground Up," *BusinessWeek* (May 4, 2009), pp. 60–61.

[14] See "U. S. R&D Jobs Shift to Asia," *The Wall Street Journal* (January 18, 2012), p. B2; and, "Thomas L. Friedman, "Made in the World," *The New York Times* (January 28, 2012); nytimes.com.

[15] David Murphy, "A Foxconn Breakdown: It's Strengths, Strangeness, and Scrutiny," *PC Magazine* (January 22, 2012): pcmag.com.

[16] Jessica E. Vascellaro and Own Fletcher, "Apple Navigates China Maze," *The Wall Street Journal* (January 14–15, 2012), pp. B1, B2.

[17] Information from Michael A. Fletcher, "Ohio Profits from Exports," *Columbus Dispatch* (December 30, 2007), p. B3.

[18] "Survey: Intellectual Property Theft Now Accounts for 31 Percent of Global Counterfeiting," Gieschen Consultancy, February 25, 2005.

[19] Information from "Not Exactly Counterfeit," *Fortune* (April 26, 2006): money.cnn.com/magazines/fortune.

[20] Matthew J. Slaughter, "What Tata Tells Us," *Wall Street Journal* (March 27, 2008), p. A15; and Michelle Maynard, "A La Feline Not Made in the USA," *The New York Times* (October 18, 2009): www.nytimes.com; and, Jose W. Fernandez, "Foreign Direct Investment Supports U.S. Jobs," *DipNote: U.S. Department of State Official Blog* (October 07, 2011): accessed March 3, 2012; and, Joseph B. White and Norihiko Shirouzu, "In the Heart of the Rust Belt, Chinese Funds Provide the Grease," *The Wall Street Journal* (February 11–12, 2012), pp. A1, A8.

[21] Criteria for choosing joint venture partners developed from Anthony J. F. O'Reilly, "Establishing Successful Joint Ventures in Developing Nations: A CEO's Perspective," *Columbia Journal of World Business* (Spring 1988), pp. 65–71; and "Best Practices for Global Competitiveness," *Fortune* (March 30, 1998), pp. S1–S3, special advertising section.

[22] See James T. Areddy, "Danone Pulls Out of Disputed China Venture," *Wall Street Journal* (October 1, 2009), p. B1.

23 Karby Leggett, "U.S. Auto Makers Find Promise—and Peril—in China," *Wall Street Journal* (June 19, 2003), p. B1; "Did Spark Spark a Copycat?" *BusinessWeek* (February 7, 2005), p. 64; and "New Height, New Growth," News Release (July 28, 2011), cheryinternational.com.

24 "Best Practices for Global Competitiveness," *Fortune* (March 30, 1998), pp. S1–S3, special advertising.

25 Information from Own Fletcher and Jaon Dean, "Ballmer Bares China Travails," *Wall Street Journal* (May 2, 2011), pp. B1, B2.

26 Information and quote from "Multinational Groups Shrug off Mexican Drugs Violence," *Financial Times*, Kindle edition (July 30, 2011).

27 www.wto.org/English/thewto_e/whatis_e/tif_e/fact3_e.htm (March 25, 2008).

28 Information and quotes from Dexter Roberts, "Closing for Business?" *Bloomberg Businessweek* (April 5, 2010), pp. 32–37.

29 Information and quote from "WTO Takes Up U.S. Complaint against China Patent Regime," *AFP* (September 7, 2007): afp.google.com/article/ALeqM5hASBbePC8gtbmtfz ExtmfkdNDvKQ.

30 Pete Engardio, Geri Smith, and Jane Sasseen, "Refighting NAFTA," *BusinessWeek* (March 31, 2008), pp. 55–59.

31 The *Economist* is a good weekly source of information on Africa; and "Embracing Africa," *BusinessWeek* (December 18, 2006), p. 101.

32 See Robert Farzad, "Can Greed Save Africa?" *BusinessWeek* (December 10, 2007), pp. 46–54; "The Big Bounce," *Bloomberg Business-Week* (May 17–23, 2010), pp. 48–57; and, Will Connors and Sarah Childress, "Africa's Local Champions Begin to Spread Out," *Wall Street Journal* (May 26, 2010), p. B8.

33 See, for example, Patrick McGroarty, "Middle Class in Africa Set to Boom, but Risks Remain," *Wall Street Journal* (October 13, 2011), p. A17; and "U.S. Firms in Africa Hustle to Catch Up," *Wall Street Journal* (June 6, 2011), p. A16.

34 www.sadc.int/about_sadc/vision.php.

35 Data from "The Big Mac Index: Currency Comparisons to Go," *The Economist* (July 28, 2011): economist.com.

36 See Peter F. Drucker, "The Global Economy and the Nation-State," *Foreign Affairs*, vol. 76 (September–October 1997), pp. 159–71.

37 Friedman, op. cit. (2012).

38 Information from Steve Hamm, "IBM vs. TATA: Which Is More American?" *BusinessWeek* (May 5, 2008), p. 28; and, Greg Farrell, "McDonald's Continues to Rely on European Restaurants for Growth," *Financial Times*, Kindle edition (April 20, 2010).

39 "Sweden vs. Exxon," *Bloomberg Businessweek* (March 5–11, 2012), p. 91.

40 Michael Mandel, "Multinationals: Are They Good for America?," *BusinessWeek* (February 28, 2008): businessweek.com.

41 Developed from R. Hall Mason, "Conflicts Between Host Countries and Multinational Enterprise," *California Management Review*, vol. 17 (1974), pp. 6, 7.

42 Mandel, op. cit.; Engardio, op. cit.

43 Headlines from Matthew Boyle and Joel Rosenblatt, "Avon Products Says It Fired Four Executives Over Bribes to China Officials" *Bloomberg* (May 5, 2011): bloomberg.com; Miqual Guterary and Elisor Comlag, "Mexico Starts Investigation in Wal-Mart Bribery Case," news, yahoo.com (April 25, 2012). "International Effort Unveils Counterfeit Goods Op." *The Washington Post* (March 2, 2012): thewashingtonpost.com.

44 See transparency.org. See also Blake E. Ashforth, Dennis A. Gioia, Sandra L. Robinson, and Linda K. Trevino, "Special Topic Forum on Corruption," *Academy of Management Review*, vol. 33 (July 2008), p. 6701.

45 Transparency International, "Corruption Perceptions Index 2009," www.transparency.org: accessed April 23, 2010.

46 Quote from Carol Matlack, "The Peril and Promise of Investing in Russia," *BusinessWeek* (October 5, 2009), pp. 48–51.

47 See Dionne Searcey, "U.S. Cracks Down on Corporate Bribes," *Wall Street Journal* (May 26, 2009), pp. A1, A4.

48 John Bussey, "The Rule of Law Finds Its Way Abroad, However Painfully," *Wall Street Journal* (June 24, 2011), pp. B1, B2.

49 International Labour Organization, *Facts on Child Labor 2010* (Geneva, Switzerland: April 1, 2010).

50 See, for example, Jason Dean and Ting-I Tsai, "Suicides Spark Inquiries," *Wall Street Jounal* (May 27, 2010), pp. B1, B7.

51 "Apple Supplier Responsibility 2012 Progress Report," apple.com/supplierresponsibility (accessed March 4, 2012), p. 9.

52 Information and quote from Andrew Morse and Nick Wingfield, "Microsoft Will Investigate Conditions at Chinese Plant," *Wall Street Journal* (April 16, 2010), p. B7.

53 Examples reported in Neil Chesanow, *The World-Class Executive* (New York: Rawson Associates, 1985).

54 For alternative definitions of culture, see Martin J. Gannon, *Paradoxes of Culture and Globalization* (Thousand Oaks, CA: Sage, 2008), Chapter 2.

55 P. Christopher Earley and Elaine Mosakowski, "Toward Cultural Intelligence: Turning Cultural Differences Into Workplace Advantage," *Academy of Management Executive*, vol. 18 (2004), pp. 151–57.

56 For a good overview of the practical issues, see Lewis, op. cit.; and Martin J. Gannon, *Understanding Global Cultures* (Thousand Oaks, CA: Sage, 1994).

57 Example from Fong, op. cit.

58 Edward T. Hall, *The Silent Language* (New York: Anchor Books, 1959).

59 Edward T. Hall, *Beyond Culture* (New York: Doubleday, 1976).

60 Edward T. Hall, *The Hidden Dimension* (New York: Anchor Books, 1969) and *Hidden Differences* (New York: Doubleday, 1990).

61 Ibid.

62 Michele J. Gelfand, Lisa H. Nishii, and Jana L. Raver, "On the Nature and Importance of Cultural Tightness-Looseness," *Journal of Applied Psychology*, Vol. 91 (2006), pp. 1225–1244.

63 Michele J. Gelfand and 42 co-authors, "Differences Between Tight and Loose Cultures: A 33 Nation Study," *Science*, Vol. 332 (May 2011), pp. 100–1104.

64 Geert Hofstede, *Culture's Consequences* (Beverly Hills, CA: Sage, 1984), and *Culture's Consequences: Comparing Values, Behaviors, Institutions and Organizations across Nations*, 2nd ed. (Thousand Oaks, CA: Sage, 2001). See also Michael H. Hoppe, "An Interview with Geert Hofstede," *Academy of Management Executive*, vol. 18 (2004), pp. 75–79.

65 Geert Hofstede and Michael H. Bond, "The Confucius Connection: From Cultural Roots to Economic Growth," *Organizational Dynamics*, vol. 16 (1988), pp. 4–21.

66 See Geert Hofstede, *Culture and Organizations: Software of the Mind* (London: McGraw-Hill, 1991).

67 For another perspective see Harry Triandis and M. Gelfand, "Convergent Measurement of Horizontal and Vertical Collectivism," *Journal of Personality & Social Psychology*, vol. 74 (1998), pp. 118–28.

68 This dimension is explained more thoroughly by Geert Hofstede et al., *Masculinity and Femininity: The Taboo Dimension of National Cultures* (Thousand Oaks, CA: Sage, 1998).

69 Information for "Stay Informed" from "The Conundrum of the Glass Ceiling," *Economist* (July 23, 2005), p. 634, and "Japan's Diversity Problem," *Wall Street Journal* (October 24, 2005), pp. B1, B5.

70 See Hofstede and Bond, op. cit.

71 See, for example, Nancy Adler and Allison Gundersen, *International Dimensions of Organizational Behavior*, 5th ed. (New York: Thomson South-Western, 2008).

[72] For additional cultural models and research see Fons Trompenaars, *Riding the Waves of Culture: Understanding Cultural Diversity in Business* (London: Nicholas Brealey, 1993); Harry C. Triandis, *Culture and Social Behavior* (New York: McGraw-Hill, 1994); Steven H. Schwartz, "A Theory of Cultural Values and Some Implications for Work," *Applied Psychology: An International Review*, vol. 48 (1999), pp. 23–47; and Martin J. Gannon, *Understanding Global Cultures*, 3rd ed. (Thousand Oaks, CA: Sage, 2004). See also research known as Project GLOBE: Robert J. House, Paul J. Hanges, Mansour Javidan, Peter W. Dorfman, and Vipin Gupta (eds.), *Culture, Leadership and Organizations: The GLOBE Study of 62 Societies* (Thousand Oaks, CA: Sage., 2004). Further issues on Project GLOBE are developed in George B. Graen, "In the Eye of the Beholder: Cross-Cultural Lessons in Leadership from Project GLOBE: A Response Viewed from the Third Culture Bonding (TCB) Model of Cross-Cultural Leadership," *Academy of Management Perspectives*, vol. 20 (November 2006), pp. 95–101, and Robert J. House, Mansour Javidan, Peter W. Dorfman, and Mary Sully de Luque, "A Failure of Scholarship: Response to George Graen's Critique of GLOBE," *Academy of Management Perspectives*, vol. 20 (November 2006), pp. 102–14.

[73] See, for example, Rosalie L. Tung and Alain Verbeke, "Beyond Hofstede and GLOBE: Improving the Quality of Cross-Cultural Research," *Journal of International Business Studies*, Vol. 41 (2010), pp. 1259–1274.

[74] Geert Hofstede, "Motivation, Leadership, and Organization: Do American Theories Apply Abroad?" *Organizational Dynamics* (1980), p. 43; Geert Hofstede, "The Cultural Relativity of Organizational Practices," *Journal of International Business Studies* (Fall 1983), pp. 75–89. See also Hofstede's "Cultural Constraints in Management Theories," *Academy of Management Review*, vol. 7 (1993), pp. 81–94.

[75] Discussion based on Allan Bird, Mark Mendenhall, Michael J. Stevens, and Gary Oddou, "Defining the Content Domain of Intercultural Competence for Global Leaders," *Journal of Managerial Psychology*, vol. 25 (2010), pp. 810–28.

[76] Geert Hofstede, "A Reply to Goodstein and Hunt," *Organizational Dynamics*, vol. 10 (Summer 1981), p. 68.

[77] Developed from "Is Your Company Really Global?" *BusinessWeek* (December 1, 1997).

[78] Martin J. Gannon, *Understanding Global Cultures* (Thousand Oaks, Calif.: Sage, 1994), Chapter 16: American Football.

### Feature Notes

Follow the Story—Information and quotes from "Walmart's Asian Growth Set Trend for Global Empire," *Financial Times*, Kindle edition (December 31, 2010); Laurie Burkitt, "Foreign Firms Feel the Heat," *Wall Street Journal* (October 18, 2011): wsj.com; Laurie Burkitt, "Wal-Mart China Woes Add Up," *Wall Street Journal* (October 19, 2011), p. B3; "Years of Wal-Mart Violations Forced China Action, Official Says," *Bloomberg News* (October 19, 2011): businessweek.com; "China Rounds Up the Usual Suspects," *Bloomberg BusinessWeek* (October 31–November 6, 2011), pp. 27–28; C. Douglas McMillon, president and CEO, Walmart International: walmartstores.com.

Ethics Check—Information from Raul Burgoa, "Bolivia Seizes Control of Oil and Gas Fields," *Bangkok Post* (May 3, 2006), p. B5

Facts for Analysis—Information from Transparency International, "Corruption Perceptions Index 2010," and "Bribe Payers Index" (December 9, 2008), both available from: www.transparency.org.

### Photo Essay Notes

Recommended Reading—John Bowes, *The Fair Trade Revolution* (London: Pluto Press, 2011); see also Andrew Stark, "The Price of Moral Purity," *Wall Street Journal* (February 4, 2011), p. A13. Comparative Advantage—David Ricardo's book *Principles of Political Economy and Taxation* is available from Prometheus Books (New York: 1996). *Silent Language*—Information from Eric Spitznagel, "How to Impress Your Chinese Boss," *Bloomberg BusinessWeek* (January 5, 2012): businessweek.com.

## Chapter 6

### Endnotes

[1] Information from Douglas MacMillan, Peter Burrows, and Spencer E. Ante, "The App Economy," *BusinessWeek* (November 2, 2009), pp. 44–49; Douglas MacMillan, "Zynga and Facebook. It's Complicated," *Bloomberg BusinessWeek* (April 26–May 2, 2010), pp. 50, 51; Dean Takahashi, "On Strength of New Social Games, Zynga Files for $1B IPO," venturebeat.com (July 1, 2011); Dean Takahashi, "Zynga Launches Three HTML5 Games to Run on Mobile Browsers," venturebeat.com (October 11, 2011); "Seeking Freedom from Facebook," *Bloomberg BusinessWeek* (October 17–21, 2011), p. 35.

[2] See also Stephen Covey, "How to Succeed in Today's Workplace," *USA Weekend* (August 29–31, 1997), pp. 4–5.

[3] Information and quotes for these examples from Alison Damasi, "No Job? Create One," *Bloomberg Businessweek* (March 22 & 29, 2010), p. 89; Laura Lorber, "Older Entrepreneurs Target Peers," *Wall Street Journal* (February 16, 2010), p. B6; and Dale Buss, "The Mothers of Invention," *Wall Street Journal* (February 8, 2010), p. R7.

[4] Information from "Women Business Owners Receive First-Ever Micro Loans Via the Internet," *Business Wire* (August 9, 2000); Jim Hopkins, "Non-Profit Loan Group Takes Risks on Women in Business," *USA Today* (August 9, 2000), p. 2B; and "Women's Group Grants First Loans to Entrepreneurs," *Columbus Dispatch* (August 10, 2000), p. B2.

[5] Quote from "Working for Somebody Else Never Amounted to Anything—Wayne Huizenga," http://www.youngentrepreneur.com (accessed Janaury 22, 2010).

[6] Speech at the Lloyd Greif Center for Entrepreneurial Studies, Marshall School of Business, University of Southern California, 1996.

[7] Information from Thomas Heath, "Value Added: The Nonprofit Entrepreneur," voices.washingtonpost.com/washbizblog/2009/03.

[8] Information and quotes from the corporate websites; Entrepreneur's Hall of Fame at www.1tbn.com/halloffame.html; "Disruptor of the Day: Caterina Fake-Because She Had a Flickr of a Hunch about an Etsy." *Daily Disruption* (January 31, 2012): dailydisruption.com; and, Zack O'Malley Greenburg, "Jay-Z's Business Commandments" (March 16, 2011): forbes.com; and, "Shawn 'Jay Z' Carter," BlackEntrepreneurProfile.com (accessed March 8, 2012). www.hunch.com. See also Anita Roddick, *Business As Unusual: My Entrepreneurial Journey, Profits with Principles* (West Sussex, England: Anita Roddick Books, 2005).

[9] Examples from "America's Best Young Entrepreneurs 2008," *BusinessWeek* (September 8, 2009): www.businessweek.com.

[10] For the top-selling franchises, see "Top 10 Franchises for 2009," *Entrepreneur Magazine* (January 2009): www.entrepreneur.com.

[11] This list is developed from Timmons, op. cit, pp. 47–48; and Hisrich and Peters, op. cit., pp. 67–70.

[12] For a review and discussion of the entrepreneurial mind, see Jeffry A. Timmons, *New Venture Creation: Entrepreneurship for the 21st Century* (New York: Irwin/McGraw-Hill, 1999), pp. 219–25; and, "Can Entrepreneurship Be Taught?" *The Wall Street Journal* (March 19, 2012), p. R4.

[13] See the review by Robert D. Hisrich and Michael P. Peters, *Entrepreneurship*, 4th ed. (New York: Irwin/McGraw-Hill, 1998), pp. 67–70; and Paulette Thomas, "Entrepreneurs' Biggest Problems and

How They Solve Them," *Wall Street Journal Reports* (March 17, 2003), pp. R1, R2.

[14] Based on research summarized by Hisrich and Peters, op. cit., pp. 70–74.

[15] Information from Jim Hopkins, "Serial Entrepreneur Strikes Again at Age 70," *USA Today* (August 15, 2000).

[16] Quote from www.anitaroddick.com/aboutanita.php (accessed: April 24, 2010).

[17] Data from *Paths to Entrepreneurship: New Directions for Women in Business* (New York: Catalyst, 1998), as summarized on the National Foundation for Women Business Owners website: www.nfwbo.org/key.html.

[18] National Foundation for Women Business Owners, *Women Business Owners of Color: Challenges and Accomplishments* (1998).

[19] Data from "New Census Data Reinforces the Economic Power of Women-Owned Businesses in the U.S. Says NAWBO," press release, National Association of Women Business Owners (July 15, 2010); and Mark D. Wolfe, "Women-Owned Businesses: America's New Job Creation Engine," *Forbes* (January 12, 2010): forbes.com.

[20] Leah Yomtovian, "The Funding Landscape for Minority Entrepreneurs," *ideacrossing.org* (February 16, 2011); and, www.mbda.gov.

[21] "Wanted: More Black Entrepreneurs," *Bloomberg BusinessWeek* (January 23–29, 2012), pp. 4–16.

[22] Information and quote from Rieva Lesonsky, "Women Owned Businesses Have Come a Long Way But It's Not Far Enough," *Small Business Trends* (October 12, 2011); smallbiztrends.com.

[23] David Bornstein, *How to Change the World: Social Entrepreneurs and the Power of New Ideas* (Oxford, UK: Oxford University Press, 2004).

[24] Sharon Shinn, "Profit and Purpose," *BizEd* (May–June, 2011), pp. 24–31.

[25] "The 10 Best Social Enterprises of 2009," *Fast Company* (December 1, 2009): www.fastcompany.com/magazine (accessed April 24, 2010).

[26] Examples are from Byrnes and "Growing Green Business," *Northwestern* (Winter 2007), p. 19; and Byrnes, op. cit.; and Regina McEnery, "Cancer Patients Getting the White-Glove Treatment," *Columbus Dispatch* (March 1, 2008).

[27] See U.S. Small Business Administration website: http://www.sba.gov/advocacy/7495/8420 (accessed October 21, 2011); Carl Bialik, "Sizing Up the Small-Business Jobs Machine," *Wall Street Journal* (October 15–16, 2011), p. A2.

[28] Angus Loten, "Films Face Hurdles Overseas." *Wall Street Journal*, Kindle edition (August 25, 2011).

[29] Charles Kenny, "Small Isn't Beautiful," *Bloomberg BusinessWeek* (October 3–9, 2011), pp. 10–11.

[30] Information reported in "The Rewards," *Inc. State of Small Business* (May 20–21, 2001), pp. 50–51.

[31] Information from Sue Shellenbarger, "Plumbing for Joy? Be Your Own Boss," *Wall Street Journal* (September 16, 2009), pp. D1, D2.

[32] Information and quotes from Steve Lohr, "The Rise of the Fleet-Footed Start-Up," *New York Times* (April 23, 2010): www.nytimes.com.

[33] Ibid.

[34] Information and quotes from Tracy Turner, "Smooth Transition: Three Sisters Take over Family's Velvet Ice Cream Business," *Columbus Dispatch* (September 25, 2009), pp. A12, A13.

[35] Data reported by The Family Firm Institute: www.ffi.org/looking/factsfb.html.

[36] Conversation from the case "Am I My Uncle's Keeper?" by Paul I. Karofsky (Northeastern University Center for Family Business) and published at: www.fambiz.com/contprov.cfm? ContProvCode5NECFB[ANGELO]ID5140.

[37] Survey of Small and Mid-Sized Businesses: Trends for 2000 (Arthur Andersen, 2000).

[38] Ibid.

[39] See U.S. Small Business Administration website: www.sba.gov.

[40] George Gendron, "The Failure Myth," *Inc.* (January 2001), p. 13.

[41] Discussion based on "The Life Cycle of Entrepreneurial Firms," in Ricky Griffin (ed.), *Management*, 6th ed. (New York: Houghton Mifflin, 1999), pp. 309–10; and Neil C. Churchill and Virginia L. Lewis, "The Five Stages of Small Business Growth," *Harvard Business Review* (May–June 1993), pp. 30–50.

[42] Anne Field, "Business Incubators Are Growing Up," *BusinessWeek* (November 16, 2009), p. 76.

[43] See www.sba.gov/aboutsba. For arguments pro and con on the SBA see "Should the Small Business Administration Be Abolished?" *The Wall Street Journal* (March 19, 2012), p. R2.

[44] Developed from William S. Sahlman, "How to Write a Great Business Plan," *Harvard Business Review* (July–August 1997), pp. 98–108.

[45] Marcia H. Pounds, "Business Plan Sets Course for Growth," *Columbus Dispatch* (March 16, 1998), p. 9; see also the firm's website: www.calcustoms.com.

[46] Information from Colleen DeBaise, "Why You Need a Business Plan," *Wall Street Journal* (September 27, 2009): www.wsj.com.

[47] Standard components of business plans are described in many text sources such as Linda Pinson and Jerry Jinnett, *Anatomy of a Business Plan: A Step-by-Step Guide to Starting Smart, Building the Business, and Securing Your Company's Future*, 4th ed. (Dearborn Trade, 1999); and on websites such as American Express Small Business Services, Business Town.com, and Bizplanlt.com.

[48] Example from Matt Golsinski, "Entrepreneurs Score on 'Shark Tank,'" *Kellogg* (Winter 2009), p. 9.

[49] "You've Come a Long Way Baby," *BusinessWeek Frontier* (July 10, 2000).

[50] Information from "Should Equity-Based Crowd Funding Be Legal?" *The Wall Street Journal* (March 19, 2012), p. R3; and, Angus Loten, "Avoiding the Equity Crowd Funding," *The Wall Street Journal* (March 29, 2012): wsj/com.

[51] Adapted from Norman M. Scarborough and Thomas W. Zimmerer, *Effective Small Business Management*, 3rd ed. (Columbus, OH: Merrill, 1991), pp. 26–27. Used by permission.

[52] Quote from http://www.woopidoo.com/businessquotes/authors/michaelgerber/index.htm (retrieved September 16, 2006); see also Michael Gerber, The *E-Myth Revisited: Why Most Small Businesses Don't Work and What to Do About It* (New York: HarperCollins, 2001).

### Feature Notes

Follow the Story—Information and quotes from Joe Higgins, "Athens Business Owner Presented State Award," *Athens Messenger* (November 18, 2009), p. 3; and Samantha Pirc, "A Local Success Story: Q&A with Michelle Greenfield of Third Sun," *Ohio Today* (Fall/Winter, 2009), pp. 14, 15.

Ethics on the Line—TOMS: Information from Jessica Shambora, "The Story Behind the World's Hottest Shoemaker," *Financial Times*, Kindle Edition (March 21, 2010); www.toms.com/movement-one-for-one; John Tozzi, "The Ben & Jerrys' Law: Principles Before Profit," *Bloomberg Businessweek* (April 26—May 2, 2010), pp. 69, 70; and toms.com/eyewear/our-movement.

Facts for Analysis—Minority Entrepreneurs: Data reported by Karen E. Klein, "Minority Start Ups: A Measure of Progress," *Business Week* (August 25, 2005), retrieved from www.businessweekonline; and press release, Minority Business Development Agency (March 5, 2009): www.mbda.gov.

**Photo Essay Notes**

Etsy—Information from Etsy.com; and "Space Oddities," *Bloomberg BusinessWeek* (February 13-1, 2012), pp. 78–79. Warby Parker—Information from "A Startup's New Prescription for Eyewear," *Bloomberg BusinessWeek* (July 4–10, 2011), pp. 49–551; and warbyparker.com/Our-Story. Slumdog Millionaire—Information and quotes from Manohla Dargis, "Orphan's Lifeline Out of Hell Could Be a Game Show in Mumbai," *New York Times* (November 12, 2008), movies.nytimes.com; and James Christopher, "Slumdog Millionaire," *The Times* (January 8, 2009), entertainment.timesonline.co.uk. Social entrepreneur—Information from Patrick Clark, "Innovator Cleaning Up," *Bloomberg BusinessWeek* (October 17–23, 2011), p. 45; and, "Global Social Entrepreneurship Competition," *BizED* (May/June, 2011), p. 37.

## Chapter 7

**Endnotes**

[1] Information from David A. Price, "From Dorm Room to Wal-Mart," *Wall Street Journal* (March 11, 2009), p. A13; "Huddler.com Interview with CEO and Founder Tom Szaky," www.greenhome.huddler.com/wiki/terracycle; and Tom Szaky, *Revolution in a Bottle* (Knoxville, TN: Portfolio Trade, 2009).

[2] Situation from Carol Hymowitz, "Middle Managers Are Unsung Heroes on Corporate Stage," *Wall Street Journal* (September 19, 2005), p. B1.

[3] Ram Charan, "Six Personality Traits of a Leader," career-advice.monster.com/leadership-skills (retrieved August 6, 2008).

[4] Information and quotes from "Last Miner Out Hailed as a Shift Boss Who Kept Group Alive," news:blog.cnn.com (October 14, 2010): and Eva Bergara, "Chilean Miners Honored in Ceremony, Football Game," news.yahoo.com (October 25, 2010).

[5] For a good discussion see Micheal S. Hopkins, Steve LaValle, Fred Balboni, Nina Krusehwitz, and Rehecca Shokley. "10 Insights: First Look at the New Intelligent Enterprise Survey on Winning with Data." *Sloan Management Review*; Vol. 52 (Fall 2010). pp. 22–27.

[6] See Stefan Stern, "Smarter Leaders Are Betting Big on Data," *Financial Times,* Kindle edition (March 9, 2010); and, Thomas H. Davenport, Jeanne G. Harris, and Robert Morison, *Analytics at Work: Smarter Decisions, Better Results* (Cambridge, MA: Harvard Business Press, 2010).

[7] See, for example, "Netflix Gets Lost in the Mail." *Wall Street Journal* (October 29–30, 2011), p. C4: "Netflix, Netflix, Netflix, Netflix," *Bloomberg BusinessWeek* (October 24–30, 2011), pp. 21–22.

[8] See, for example, Ben Worthen. "In U-Turn. H-P Will Hold on to PCs," *Wall Street Journal* (October 28, 2011), pp. A1, A2.

[9] Information from John A. Byrne, "Visionary vs. Visionary," *BusinessWeek* (August 28, 2000), pp. 10–14.

[10] Information from Karen Berman and Joe Knight, "What Your Employees Don't Know Will Hurt You," *The Wall Street Journal* (February 27, 2012), p. R4.

[11] Information on executive dashboards and quote from Jessica Tennyman, "Dashboards Make the Corporate Drive Easier," *Financial Times*, Kindle Edition (March 21, 2012).

[12] Stephanie Clifford," Video Prank at Domino's Taints Brand." *New York Times* (April 16, 2009): www.nytimes.com: and Deborah Stead," An Unwelcome Delivery," *BusinessWeek* (May 4, 2009), p. 15.

[13] Noel M. Tichy and Warren G. Bennis, *Judgment: How Winning Leaders Make Great Calls* (Knoxville, TN: Portfolio Hardcover, 2007).

[14] Noel M. Tichy and Warren G. Bennis, "Judgment: How Winning Leaders Make Great Calls," *BusinessWeek* (November 19, 2007), pp. 68–72.

[15] Henry Mintzberg, *The Nature of Managerial Work* (New York: Harper Collins, 1997).

[16] Richard Tedlow, "Toyota Was in Denial. How About You?" *Bloomberg Businessweek* (April 19, 2010), p. 76.

[17] For a good discussion, see Watson H. Agor, *Intuition in Organizations: Leading and Managing Productively* (Newbury Park, CA: Sage, 1989); Herbert A. Simon, "Making Management Decisions: The Role of Intuition and Emotion," *Academy of Management Executive*, vol. 1 (1987), pp. 57–64; Orlando Behling and Norman L. Eckel, "Making Sense Out of Intuition," *Academy of Management Executive*, vol. 5 (1991), pp. 46–54.

[18] See, for example, William Duggan, *Strategic Intuition: The Creative Spark in Human Achievement* (New York: Columbia Business School, 2007).

[19] Alan Deutschman, "Inside the Mind of Jeff Bezos," *Fast Company*, Issue 85 (August 2004); www.fastcompany.com.

[20] See Susan Berfield, "The Limits of Going with Your Gut," *BusinessWeek* (December 21, 2009), p. 90. See also Michael J. Mauboussin, *Think Twice: Harnessing the Power of Counterintuition* (Boston: Harvard Business, 2009).

[21] Daniel J. Isenberg, "How Senior Managers Think," *Harvard Business Review*, vol. 62 (November–December 1984), pp. 81–90.

[22] Daniel J. Isenberg, "The Tactics of Strategic Opportunism," *Harvard Business Review*, vol. 65 (March–April 1987), pp. 92–97.

[23] Quote from Susan Carey, "Pilot 'in Shock' as He Landed Jet in River," *Wall Street Journal* (February 9, 2009), p. A6.

[24] Based on Carl Jung's typology as described in Donald Bowen, "Learning and Problem-Solving: You're Never Too Jung," in Donald D. Bowen, Roy J. Lewicki, Donald T. Hall, and Francine S. Hall, eds., *Experiences in Management and Organizational Behavior,* 4th ed. (New York: Wiley, 1997), pp. 7–13; and John W. Slocum Jr., "Cognitive Style in Learning and Problem Solving," ibid., pp. 349–53.

[25] Developed from Anna Muoio, "Where There's Smoke It Helps to Have a Smoke Jumper," *Fast Company*, vol. 33, p. 290.

[26] Information and quotes from Jeff Kingston. "A Crisis Made in Japan." *Wall Street Journal* (February 6–7, 2010), pp. W1, W2: Kate Linebaugh, Dionne Searcey, and Norihiko Shirouzu. "Secretive Culture Led Toyota Astray." *Wall Street Journal* (February 10, 2010), pp. A1, A16; and Richard Fedlow, "Toyota Was in Denial, How About You?" *Bloomberg Businessweek* (April 19, 2010). p. 76.

[27] For scholarly reviews, see Dean Tjosvold, "Effects of Crisis Orientation on Managers' Approach to Controversy in Decision Making," *Academy of Management-Journal*, vol. 27 (1984), pp. 130–38; and Jan I. Mitroff, Paul-Shrivastava, and Firdaus E. Udwadia, "Effective Crisis Management," *Academy of Management Executive*, vol. 1 (1987), pp. 283–92.

[28] Paul Glader, "GE's Immelt to Cite Lessons Learned," *Wall Street Journal* (December 15, 2009), p. B2.

[29] Information from Paul Farhi, "Behind Domino's Mea Culpa Ad Campaign," *Washington Post* (January 13, 2010): www.washingtonpost.com, accessed June 5, 2010; and J. Patrick Doyle, "Hard Choices," *Bloomberg BusinessWeek* (May 3–9, 2010), p. 84.

[30] Information and quotes from Terry Kosdrosky and John D. Stoll, "GM Puts Electric-Car Testing on Fast Track to 2010," *Wall Street Journal* (April 4, 2008), p. B2.

[31] See George P. Huber, *Managerial Decision Making* (Glenview, IL: Scott, Foresman, 1975). For a comparison, see the steps in Xerox's problem-solving process as described in David A. Garvin, "Building a Learning Organization," *Harvard Business Review* (July–August 1993), pp. 78–91; and the Josephson model for ethical decision making described at www.josephsoninstitute.org.

[32] Peter F. Drucker, *Innovation and Entrepreneurship: Practice and Principles* (New York: Harper Row, 1985).

[33] Joseph B. White and Lee Hawkins Jr., "GM Cuts Deeper in North America," *Wall Street Journal* (November 22, 2005), p. A3.

[34] For a sample of Simon's work, see Herbert A. Simon, *Administrative Behavior* (New York: Free Press, 1947); James G. March and Herbert A. Simon, *Organizations* (New York: Wiley, 1958); Herbert A. Simon, *The New Science of Management Decision* (New York: Harper, 1960).

[35] This figure and the related discussion are developed from conversations with Dr. Alma Acevedo of the University of Puerto Rico at Rio Piedras, and her articles "Of Fallacies and Curricula: A Case of Business Ethics," *Teaching Business Ethics*, vol. 5 (2001), pp. 157–70; and, "Business Ethics: An Introduction," Working Paper (2009).

[36] See the discussion by Denis Collins, *Business Ethics: How to Design and Manage Ethical Organizations* (Hoboken, NJ: John Wiley & Sons, 2012), p. 158.

[37] Based on Gerald F. Cavanagh, *American Business Values*, 4th ed. (Upper Saddle River, NJ: Prentice-Hall, 1998).

[38] Josephson, op. cit.

[39] For rationalizations, see ibid., p. 163. For time pressures see "Take a Deep Breath, Make Ethical Choices," *The Wall Street Journal* (March 7, 2012), p. B9.

[40] Damel Kahneman. *Thinking Fast and Slow* (New York: Farrar, Straus & Giroux. 2011).

[41] Example from Roger Lowenstein. "Better Think Twice," *Bloomberg BusinessWeek* (October 31, November 6, 2011), pp. 98–99. This article is a review of Daniel Kahneman. op cit. (2011).

[42] Daniel Kahneman and Amos Tversky, "Psychology of Preferences," *Scientific American*, vol. 246 (1982), pp. 161–73; and, Kahneman, op cit., 2011.

[43] This presentation is based on the discussion in Max H. Bazerman, *Judgment in Managerial Decision Making*, 6th ed. (Hoboken, NJ: Wiley, 2005).

[44] Barry M. Staw, "The Escalation of Commitment to a Course of Action," *Academy of Management Review*, vol. 6 (1981), pp. 577–87; and Barry M. Staw and Jerry Ross, "Knowing When to Pull the Plug," *Harvard Business Review*, vol. 65 (March–April 1987), pp. 68–74.

[45] Example from Dayton Fandray, "Assumed Innocent: Hidden and Unexamined Assumptions Can Ruin Your Day," *Continental.com/ Magazine* (December 2007), p. 100.

[46] See, for example, Roger von Oech's books *A Whack on the Side of the Head* (New York: Warner Books, 1983) and *A Kick in the Seat of the Pants* (New York: Harper & Row, 1986); and, John Lehrer, "How to Be Creative," *The Wall Street Journal* (March 10–11, 2012), pp. C1, C2; and, John Lehrer, *Imagine: How Creativity Works* (New York; Houghton Mifflin Harcourt, 2012).

[47] For discussions of Big-C creativity and Little-C creativity see James C. Kaufman and Ronald A. Beghetto, "Beyond Big and Little: The Four C Model of Creativity," *Review of General Psychology,* Vol. 13 (2009), pp. 1–12. My thanks go to Dr. Erin R. Flvegge of Southeastern Missouri State University for bringing this useful distinction to my attention.

[48] Carolyn T. Geer. "Innovation 101." *Wall Street Journal* (October 17, 2011). p. R5.

[49] Teresa M. Amabile, "Motivating Creativity in Organizations," *California Management Review*, vol. 40 (Fall 1997), pp. 39–58.

[50] See Jeff Dyer, Hal Gregersen, and Clayton M. Christensen. *The Innovator's DNA Mastering the Five Skills of Disruptive Innovators* (Cambridge, MA: Harvard Business Press 2011).

[51] Developed from discussions by Edward De Bono, *Lateral Thinking: Creativity Step-by-Step* (New York: HarperCollins, 1970); John S. Dacey and Kathleen H. Lennon, *Understanding Creativity* (San Francisco: Jossey-Bass, 1998); and Bettina von Stamm, *Managing Innovation, Design & Creativity* (Chichester, England: Wiley, 2003).

[52] Josephson, op. cit.

[53] Information from Stephen H. Wildstrom, "Video iPod, I Love You," *BusinessWeek* (November 7, 2005), p. 20; "Voices of Innovation," *BusinessWeek* (December 12, 2005), p. 22.

[54] Developed from Donald Bowen, "Learning and Problem-Solving: You're Never Too Jung," in Donald D. Bowen, Roy J. Lewicki, Donald T. Hall, and Francine S. Hall (eds), *Experiences in Management and Organizational Behavior,* 4th ed. (New York: Wiley, 1997), pp. 7–13; and John W. Slocum Jr., "Cognitive Style in Learning and Problem Solving," ibid., pp. 349–353.

[55] Adapted from "Lost at Sea: A Consensus-Seeking Task," in the *1975 Handbook for Group Facilitators*. Used with permission of University Associates, Inc.

### Feature Notes

Follow the Story—Information from Brad Stone, "Everybody Needs a Sheryl Sandberg," *Bloomberg BusinessWeek* (May 16–22, 2011), pp. 50–58; and, "Charlie Rose Talks to Mark Zuckerberg and Sheryl Sandberg," *Bloomberg BusinessWeek* (November 14–21, 2011), p. 50.

Ethics on the Line—Information from *Economist*, vol. 379, no. 8482, (June 17, 2006), pp. 65–66, 2p, 1c.

Facts for Analysis—Information and quotes from Michael S. Hopkins, Steve LaValle, Fred Balboni, Nina Kruschwitz, and Rebecca Shokley, "10 Insights: First Look at the New Intelligent Enterprise Survey on Winning with Data" and, "10 Data Points: Information and Analytics at Work," *Sloan Management Review*, Vol. 52 (Fall, 2010), pp. 22–27 and pp. 28–31; and Melissa Korn and Shara Tibken, "Business Schools Plan Leap into Data," *Wall Street Journal*, Kindle edition (August 4, 2010).

### Photo Essay Notes

Airline Passengers—Information from "What's the Quickest Way to Board a Plane?" *CNNGo*: cnn.com (September 2, 2011). Kitty Litter—Information from Sue Shellenbarger, "Better Ideas Through Failure," *Wall Street Journal* (September 27, 2011), pp. D1, D4. Video games—Information from Robert Lee Hotz, "When Gaming Is Good for You," *The Wall Street Journal* (March 6, 2012), pp. D1, D2.

## Chapter 8

### Endnotes

[1] Information and quotes from the Associated Press, "Oprah Opens School for Girls in S. Africa," "Lavish Leadership Academy Aims to Give Impoverished Chance to Succeed," MSNBC.com (January 2, 2007); "Oprah Winfrey Leadership Academy for Girls—South Africa Celebrates Its Official Opening," www.oprah.com/about; Jed Dreben, "Oprah Winfrey: 'I Don't Regret' Opening School," www.people.com (December 12, 2007); and, "Givson Foundation Builds Relationship with Oprah Winfrey Leadership Academy to Support Music Education," news release (April 14, 2009), www.gibson.com (accessed January 26, 2010).

[2] Data from "Hurry Up and Decide," *BusinessWeek* (May 14, 2001), p. 16; and *BusinessWeek* (June 23, 2008), p. 56.

[3] Eaton Corporation Annual Report, 1985.

[4] Paul Ingrassia, "The Right Stuff," *Wall Street Journal* (April 18, 2005), p. D5.

[5] Quote from Stephen Covey and Roger Merrill, "New Ways to Get Organized at Work," *USA Weekend* (February 6–8, 1998), p. 18. Books by Stephen R. Covey include *The 7 Habits of Highly Effective People: Powerful Lessons in Personal Change* (New York: Fireside, 1990); and Stephen R. Covey and Sandra Merrill Covey, *The 7 Habits of Highly Effective Families: Building a Beautiful Family Culture in a Turbulent World* (New York: Golden Books, 1996).

[6] See Stanley Thune and Robert House, "Where Long-Range Planning Pays Off," *Business Horizons*, vol. 13 (1970), pp. 81–87. For a critical review of the literature, see Milton Leontiades and Ahmet Teel, "Planning Perceptions and Planning Results," *Strategic Management Journal*, vol. 1 (1980), pp. 65–75; and J. Scott Armstrong. "The Value of Formal Planning for Strategic Decisions," *Strategic Management Journal*, vol. 3 (1982), pp. 197–211. For special attention to the small business setting, see Richard B. Robinson Jr., John A. Pearce II, George S. Vozikis, and Timothy S. Mescon, "The Relationship between Stage of Development and Small Firm Planning and Performance," *Journal of Small Business Management*, vol. 22 (1984), pp. 45–52; and Christopher Orphen, "The Effects of Long-Range Planning on Small Business Performance: A Further Examination," *Journal of Small Business Management*, vol. 23 (1985), pp. 16–23. For an empirical study of large corporations, see Vasudevan Ramanujam and N. Venkataraman, "Planning and Performance: A New Look at an Old Question," *Business Horizons*, vol. 30 (1987), pp. 19–25.

[7] "McDonald's Tech Turnaround," *Harvard Business Review* (November 2004), p. 128.

[8] Information from Carol Hymowitz, "Packed Calendars Rule Over Executives," *Wall Street Journal* (June 16, 2008), p. B1.

[9] Quote from *BusinessWeek* (August 8, 1994), pp. 78–86.

[10] See William Oncken Jr. and Donald L. Wass, "Management Time: Who's Got the Monkey?" *Harvard Business Review*, vol. 52 (September–October 1974), pp. 75–80, and featured as an HBR classic, *Harvard Business Review* (November–December 1999).

[11] Dick Levin, *The Executives Illustrated Primer of Long Range Planning* (Englewood Cliffs, NJ: Prentice-Hall, 1981).

[12] See Elliot Jaques, *The Form of Time* (New York: Russak-Co., 1982). For an executive commentary on his research, see Walter Kiechel III, "How Executives Think," *Fortune* (December 21, 1987), pp. 139–44.

[13] Information from "Avoiding a Time Bomb: Sexual Harassment," *BusinessWeek*, Enterprise issue (October 13, 1997), pp. ENT20–21.

[14] Paul Glader, "GE's Immelt to Cite Lessons Learned," *Wall Street Journal* (December 15, 2009), p. B2.

[15] For a thorough review of forecasting, see J. Scott Armstrong, *Long-Range Forecasting*, 2nd ed. (New York: Wiley, 1985).

[16] Information and following quotes from Guy Chazan and Neil King. "BP's Preparedness for Major Crisis Is Questioned." *Wall Street Journal* (May 10, 2010), p. A6, and Ben Casselman and Guy Chazan. "Disaster Plans Lacing at Deep Rigs," *Wall Street Journal.* (May 18, 2010), p. A1.

[17] The scenario-planning approach is described in Peter Schwartz, *The Art of the Long View* (New York: Doubleday/Currency, 1991).

[18] The scenario-planning approach is described in Peter Schwartz. *The Art of Long View* (New York: Doubleday/Currency, 1991); and Arie de Geus, *The Living Company. Habits for Survival in a Turbulent Business Environment* (Boston: Harvard Business School Press. 1997).

[19] See, for example, Robert C. Camp, *Business Process Benchmarking* (Milwaukee: ASQ Quality Press 1994); Michael J. Spendolini, *The Benchmarking Book* (New York: AMACOM, 1992); and Christopher E. Bogan and Michael J. English, *Benchmarking for Best Practices: Winning through Innovative Adaptation* (New York: McGraw-Hill, 1994).

[20] David Kiley, "One Ford for the Whole World," *BusinessWeek* (June 15, 2009), pp. 58–59.

[21] Rachel Tiplady, "Taking the Lead in Fast-Fashion," *BusinessWeek Online* (August 29, 2006); and Cecile Rohwedder and Keith Johnson, "Pace-Setting Zara Seeks More Speed to Fight Its Rising Cheap-Chic Rivals," *Wall Street Journal* (February 20, 2008), pp. B1, B6.

[22] Information from Peter Burrows and Manjeet Kripalani, "Cisco: Sold on India," *BusinessWeek* (November 28, 2005), pp. 50–51.

[23] Quote from Kenneth Roman, "The Man Who Sharpened Gillette," *Wall Street Journal* (September 5, 2007), p. D8.

[24] Example from Roman, op. cit.

[25] See Dale D. McConkey, *How to Manage by Results*, 3rd ed. (New York: AMACOM, 1976); Stephen J. Carroll Jr. and Henry J. Tosi Jr., *Management by Objectives: Applications and Research* (New York: Macmillan, 1973); and Anthony P. Raia, *Managing by Objectives* (Glenview, IL: Scott, Foresman, 1974). See also Steven Kerr, "Overcoming the Dysfunctions of MBO," *Management by Objectives*, vol. 5, no. 1 (1976).

[26] "How Classy Can 7-Eleven Get?" *BusinessWeek* (September 1, 1997), pp. 74–75; and Kellie B. Gormly, "7-Eleven Moving Up a Grade," *Columbus Dispatch* (August 3, 2000), pp. C1–C2.

[27] The work on goal-setting theory is well summarized in Edwin A. Locke and Gary P. Latham, *Goal Setting: A Motivational Technique That Works!* (Englewood Cliffs, NJ: Prentice Hall, 1984). See also Edwin A. Locke, Kenneth N. Shaw, Lisa A. Saari, and Gary P. Latham, "Goal Setting and Task Performance 1969–1980," *Psychological Bulletin*, vol. 90 (1981), pp. 125–52; Mark E. Tubbs, "Goal Setting: A Meta-Analytic Examination of the Empirical Evidence," *Journal of Applied Psychology*, vol. 71 (1986), pp. 474–83; and Terence R. Mitchell, Kenneth R. Thompson, and Jane George-Falvy, "Goal Setting: Theory and Practice," Chapter 9 in Cary L. Cooper and Edwin A. Locke, eds., *Industrial and Organizational Psychology: Linking Theory with Practice* (Malden, MA: Blackwell Business, 2000), pp. 211–49.

### Feature Notes

Follow the Story—Information from Julie Bennitt, "Don Thompson Engineers Winning Role as McDonald's President," *Franchise Times* (February 2008): www.franchisetimes.com; and Julie Jargon, "Can McDonald's Keep Up the Pace?" *Wall Street Journal* (March 23, 2012), pp. B1, B2.

Ethics on the Line—Information from "Trial and Error," *Forbes* (June 19, 2006), pp. 128–30; Drake Bennett, "Measures of Success," *Boston Globe Online* (July 2, 2006); William Easterly, "Measuring How and Why Aid Works—Or Doesn't," *Wall Street Journal* (April 30–May 1, 2011), p. C5.

Facts for Analysis—Information from Phred Dvorak, Baob Davis, and Louise Radnofsky, "Firms Confront Boss–Subordinate Love Affairs," *Wall Street Journal* (October 27, 2008), p. B5. Survey data from Society for Human Resource Management.

### Photo Essay Notes

*The Shift*—Information and quotes from Philip Delves Broughton, "The Shift: The Work," *Financial Times*, Kindle edition (May 19, 2011). See also Lynda Gratton, *The Shift: The Future of Work Is Already Here* (London: HarperCollins UK, 2011). *Rolls Royce*—Information and quotes from Daniel Michaels, "Rolls-Royce Powers Ahead in High-Wage Countries," *Wall Street Journal* (October 20, 2011), pp. A1, A13. *Ford*—Information and quotes from Bryce G. Hoffman, "Inside Ford's Fight to Avoid Disaster," *The Wall Street Journal* (March 9, 2012), pp. B1, B7.

## Chapter 9

### Endnotes

[1] Information and quotes from, "Chick-fil-A Reaches 20,000th Scholarship Milestone" (July 28, 2005), Chick-fil-A press release: www.csrwire.com; Daniel Yee, "Chick-fil-A Recipe Winning Customers,"

*Columbus Dispatch* (September 9, 2006), p. D1; Tom Murphy, "Chick-fil-A plans aggressive product rollout initiatives," *Rocky Mount Telegram* (May 28, 2008), retrieved from: www.rockymounttelegram.com; Robert D. Reid, "Ethical Business Leadership in Action," *BGS International Exchange*, Vol. 7 (Summer, 2008), pp. 14, 15; and, chick-fil-a.com.

[2] Information from Beth Howard, "The Secrets of Resilient People," *AARP* (November–December 2009), pp. 26, 37; Resiliency Quick Test developed from "How Resilient Are You?" *AARP* (November–December 2009), p. 37.

[3] Information from "Is Nike's Flyknit the Swoosh of the future?" *Bloomberg Business Week* (March 19-25, 2012), pp. 31, 32.

[4] Information and quote from Shayndi Raice and John Letzing, "Group Reveals Weak Controls," The Wall Street Journal (March 31-April 1, 2012), pp. A1, A4.

[5] "The Renewal Factor: Friendly Fact, Congenial Controls," *BusinessWeek* (September 14, 1987), p. 105.

[6] Rob Cross and Lloyd Baird, "Technology Is Not Enough: Improving Performance by Building Institutional Memory," *Sloan Management Review* (Spring 2000), p. 73.

[7] Based on discussion by Harold Koontz and Cryril O'Donnell, *Essentials of Management* (New York: McGraw-Hill, 1974), pp. 362–65; see also Cross and Baird, op. cit.

[8] See John F. Love, *McDonald's: Behind the Arches* (New York: Bantam Books, 1986); Ray Kroc and Robert Anderson, *Grinding It Out: The Making of McDonald's* (New York: St. Martin's Press, 1990).

[9] Information and quote from Gregg Segal, "Hyundai Smokes the Competition," *Financial Times* (January 5, 2010).

[10] This distinction is made in William G. Ouchi, "Markets, Bureaucracies and Clans," *Administrative Science Quarterly*, vol. 25 (1980), pp. 129–41.

[11] Douglas McGregor, *The Human Side of Enterprise* (New York: McGraw-Hill, 1960).

[12] See Sue Shellenbarger, "If You Need to Work Better, Maybe Try Working Less," *Wall Street Journal* (September 23, 2009), p. D1.

[13] Examples from Alan Cane, "Are Virtual Offices a Benefit or Burden? *Irish Times* (July 14, 2006), p. 12.

[14] For an overview, see www.soxlaw.com

[15] Martin LaMonica, "Wal-Mart Readies Long-Term Move into Solar Power," *CNET News.com* (January 3, 2007).

[16] Information from Leon E. Wynter, "Allstate Rates Managers on Handling Diversity," *Wall Street Journal* (October 1, 1997), p. B1.

[17] Information from Kathryn Kranhold, "U.S. Firms Raise Ethics Focus," *Wall Street Journal* (November 28, 2005), p. B4.

[18] Example from George Anders, "Management Guru Turns Focus to Orchestras, Hospitals," *Wall Street Journal* (November 21, 2005), pp. B1, B5.

[19] Information from Raju Narisetti, "For IBM, a Groundbreaking Sales Chief," *Wall Street Journal* (January 19, 1998), pp. B1, B5.

[20] Information from Karen Carney, "Successful Performance Measurement: A Checklist," *Harvard Management Update* (No. U9911B), 1999.

[21] Robert S. Kaplan and David P. Norton, "The Balanced Scorecard: Measures That Drive Performance," *Harvard Business Review* (July–August 2005); see also Robert S. Kaplan and David P. Norton, *The Balanced Scorecard* (Cambridge, MA: Harvard Business School Press, 1996).

[22] Julian P. Rotter, "External Control and Internal Control," *Psychology Today* (June, 1971). p. 42. Used by permission.

[23] Developed from Roy J. Lewicki, Donald D. Bowen, Douglas T. Hall, and Francine S. Hall, *Experiences in Management and Organizational Behavior*, 4th ed. (New York: Wiley, 1997), pp. 195–97.

### Feature Notes

Follow the Story—Information and quotes from "Who's Who on Obama's New Economic Advisory Board," LATimesBlog (February 6, 2009): www.latimesblogs.latimes.com; "'Diversify' Isn't Just Smart Financial Advice," *BlackMBA* (Winter, 2008/2009), p. 54; "*Black Enterprise* Announces 100 Most Powerful African Americans in Corporate America," Press Release (February 5, 2009): TIAA-CREF CEO Roger Ferguson Outlines Measures to Improve Retirement Security, www.tiaa-cref.org (February 3, 2010): accessed May 8, 2010.

Ethics on the Line—Amaol Sharma, "Google Pulls Some Content in India," *Wall Street Journal* (February 7, 2012), p. B3; Richard Waters, "Twitter, Darling of Political Activitists, Bows to Business Reality on Censorship,"*Financial Times*, Kindle Edition (January 29, 2012); Rachel McArthy, "Twitter Censorship' Raises Concerns from Press Freedom Group,"*Journalism.com.uk* (January 27, 2012): accessed March 12, 2012.Alison Maitland, "Skype Says Text Messages Censored by Partner in China," *Financial Times* (April 19, 2006), p. 15; and, "Web Firms Criticized Over China," CNN.com (July 20, 2006).

Facts for Analysis—Information from Sarah E. Needleman, "Businesses Say Theft by Their Workers Is Up," *Wall Street Journal* (December 11, 2008), p. B8; Michelle Conlin, "To Catch a Corporate Thief," *Business Week* (February 16, 2009), p. 52; Simona Covel, "Small Businesses Face More Fraud in Downturn," *Wall Street Journal* (February 19, 2009), p. B5; "Increase in Data Theft Outstrips Physical Loss," *Financial Times* (October 18, 2010) Kindle edition; and Siobhan Gorman, "China Singled Out for 'Cyberspying,'" *Wall Street Journal* (November 4, 2011), p. A8.

### Photo Essay Notes

Elsewhere Class—Information from Dalton Conley, "Welcome to Elsewhere," *Newsweek* (January 26, 2009), pp. 25–26. Apple—Information and quotes from Jessica E. Vascellaro and Owen Fletcher, "Apple Navigates China Maze," *The Wall Street Journal* (January 14-15, 2012), pp. B1,B2; and, Dan Simon "Apple 'Determined' to Improve Conditions at Plants in China," *CNN* (February 15, 2012): cnn.com. Employee Fraud—Information from Sarah E. Needleman, "Businesses Say Theft by Their Workers Is Up," *Wall Street Journal* (December 11, 2008), p. B8; Michelle Conlin, "To Catch a Corporate Thief," *Business Week* (February 16, 2009), p. 52; and Simona Covel, "Small Businesses Face More Fraud in Downturn," *Wall Street Journal* (February 19, 2009), p. B5.

## Chapter 10

### Endnotes

[1] Information and quotes from Yvon Chouinard. *Let My People Go Surfing: The Education of a Reluctant Businessman* (New York: Penguin Press HC, 2005; Steve Hamm, "A Passion for the Plan." *Business Week* (August 21, 28, 2006), pp. 92–94; Seth Stevenson, "America's Most Unlikely Corporate Guru," *Wall Street Journal Magazine* (May 2012), pp. 56–60. www. patagonia.com.

[2] Examples from Edward De Bono, *Lateral Thinking: Creativity Step by Step* (New York: Harper & Row, 1970).

[3] For an overview of Wal-Mart see Charles Fishman, *The Wal-Mart Effect* (New York: Penguin, 2006).

[4] See Michelle Conlin, "Look Who's Stalking Wal-Mart," *BusinessWeek* (December 7, 2009), pp. 30–33; and, John Jannarone, "Will Dollar General be Leading Retailers into Battle?" *Wall Street Journal* (June 6, 2011), p. C8.

[5] Karen Talley, "Wal-Mart Stocks to Low Prices," *The Wall Street Journal* (November 16, 2001), p. B3; Jackie Crosby, "Retail Makeover," *Columbus Dispatch* (December 30, 2009), pp. A10, A12; and "Why Wal-Mart Is Worried about Amazon," *Bloomberg BusinessWeek* (April 8, 2012), pp. 25–26.

[6] See, for example, Walter Kiechel III, *The Lords of Strategy* (Cambridge, MA: Harvard Business Press, 2010).

[7] Michael E. Porter, *Competitive Strategy: Techniques for Analyzing Industries and Competitors* (New York: Free Press, 1980).

[8] Geoffrey A. Fowler and Nick Wingfield, "Apple's Showman Takes the Stage," *Wall Street Journal* (March 3, 2011), p. B1.

[9] See Porter, op. cit., Michael E. Porter, *Competitive Advantage: Creating and Sustaining Superior Performance* (New York: Free Press, 1986); and Richard A. D'Aveni, *Hyper-Competition: Managing the Dynamics of Strategic Maneuvering* (New York: Free Press, 1994).

[10] Jim Collins, "Bigger, Better, Faster," *Fast Company*, vol. 71 (June 2003), p. 74; and www.fastcompany.com/magazine/71/walmart.html.

[11] Gary Hamel and C. K. Prahalad, "Strategic Intent." *Harvard Business Review* (May–June 1989), pp. 63–76.

[12] www.pepsico.com/Company/PepsiCo-Values-and-Philosophy. html.

[13] Headline examples from Paul R. La Monica, "Motorola Breaks Up What Now?" *CNNMoney* (January 4, 2011), cnn.com: Dana Mattioli," Xerox Chief Looks Beyond Photocopiers Towards Services." *Wall Street Journal* (June 13, 2011), p. B9; and Peter Marsh, "Virtual Maker of Chips Conjures Up Real Advances." *Financial Times* (August 24, 2011). p. 16.

[14] Marsh, op cit.

[15] For research support, see Daniel H. Gray, "Uses and Misuses of Strategic Planning," *Harvard Business Review*, vol. 64 (January–February 1986), pp. 89–97.

[16] Peter F. Drucker, *Management: Tasks, Responsibilities, Practices* (New York: Harper-Row, 1973), p. 122.

[17] Peter F. Drucker, "Five Questions," *Executive Excellence* (November 6, 1994), pp. 6–7.

[18] See Laura Nash. "Mission Statements—Mirrors and Windows," *Harvard Business Review* (March–April 1988), pp. 155–56; James C. Collins and Jerry I. Porras, "Building Your Company's Vision," *Harvard Business Review* (September–October 1996), pp. 65–77; and James C. Collins and Jerry I. Porras, *Built to Last: Successful Habits of Visionary Companies* (New York: Harper Business, 1997).

[19] Gary Hamel, *Leading the Revolution* (Boston: Harvard Business School Press, 2000), pp. 72–73.

[20] Values quote from www.patagonia.com/web/us/patagonia.go? assetid53351.

[21] www.patagonia.com/web/us/patagonia.go?assetid52047&ln524.

[22] Steve Hamm, "A Passion for the Plan," *BusinessWeek* (August 21/28, 2006), pp. 92–94; quote in box from "Yvon Chouinard: Patagonia's Founder Turned His Passion into Profit," *Spirit* (August, 2008), p. 40.

[23] www.patagonia.com/us/common-threads.

[24] Terrence E. Deal and Allen A. Kennedy, *Corporate Cultures: The Rites and Rituals of Corporate Life* (Reading, MA: Addison-Wesley, 1982), p. 22. For more on organizational culture see Edgar H. Schein, *Organizational Culture and Leadership*, 2nd ed. (San Francisco: Jossey-Bass, 1997).

[25] www.patagonia.com.

[26] Peter F. Drucker's views on organizational objectives are expressed in his classic books: *The Practice of Management* (New York: Harper-Row, 1954) and *Management: Tasks, Responsibilities, Practices* (New York: Harper-Row, 1973). For a more recent commentary, see his article, "Management: The Problems of Success," *Academy of Management Executive*, vol. 1 (1987), pp. 13–19.

[27] Hamm, op. cit., 2006.

[28] C. K. Prahalad and Gary Hamel, "The Core Competencies of the Corporation," *Harvard Business Review* (May–June 1990), pp. 79–91.

[29] See D'Aveni, op. cit.

[30] For a discussion of Michael Porter's approach to strategic planning, see his books *Competitive Strategy* and *Competitive Advantage*; and his article, "What Is Strategy?" *Harvard Business Review* (November–December 1996), pp. 61–78; and Richard M. Hodgetts's interview, "A Conversation with Michael E. Porter. A Significant Extension toward Operational Improvement and Positioning," *Organizational Dynamics* (Summer 1999), pp. 24–33.

[31] See Jonathan Welsh, "The Long Goodbye for Dying Brands," *Wall Street Journal* (December 23, 2009), pp. D1, D3.

[32] Richard G. Hammermesh, "Making Planning Strategic," *Harvard Business Review*, vol. 64 (July/August 1986), pp. 115–120; and Richard G. Hammermesh, *Making Strategy Work* (New York: Wiley, 1986).

[33] See Gerald B. Allan, "A Note on the Boston Consulting Group Concept of Competitive Analysis and Corporate Strategy," Harvard Business School, Intercollegiate Case Clearing House, ICCH9-175-175 (Boston: Harvard Business School, June 1976).

[34] Hammermesh, op. cit.

[35] The four grand strategies were described by William F. Glueck, in *Business Policy: Strategy Formulation and Management Action* (New York: McGraw-Hill, 1976).

[36] Information from Vauhini Vara, "Facebook CEO Seeks Help as Site Suffers Growing Pains," *Wall Street Journal* (March 5, 2008), pp. A1, A14.

[37] *See* "Fast-Food Giant Plans to Increase Capital Spending," *Wall Street Journal* (October 11, 2011), p. B4.

[38] Information and quote from Rajesh Mahapatra, "Tata Group Catapults into Global Marketplace," *Columbus Dispatch* (April 3, 2008), pp. C1, C9.

[39] Liam Denning, "Vertical Integration Isn't Just for Christmas," *Wall Street Journal* (December 30, 2009), p. C12.

[40] See William McKinley, Carol M. Sanchez, and A. G. Schick, "Organizational Downsizing: Constraining, Cloning, Learning," *Academy of Management Executive*, vol. 9 (August 1995), pp. 32–44.

[41] Kim S. Cameron, Sara J. Freeman, and A. K. Mishra, "Best Practices in White-Collar Downsizing: Managing Contradictions," *Academy of Management Executive*, vol. 4 (August 1991), pp. 57–73.

[42] Information and quote from Steven Musil and Jonathan E. Skillings, "Sold! eBay Jettisons Skype in $2 Billion Deal," *CNET News* (September 1, 2009): www.news.cnet.com (accessed April 25, 2010).

[43] Amir Efrat and John Letzing, "Yahoo, Facebook in Patent Row," *The Wall Street Journal* (March 13, 2012), p. B9.

[44] This strategy classification is found in Hitt et al., op. cit.; the attitudes are from a discussion by Howard V. Perlmutter, "The Tortuous Evolution of the Multinational Corporation," *Columbia Journal of World Business*, vol. 4 (January–February 1969). See also Pankaj Ghemawat, "Managing Differences," *Harvard Business Review* (March 2007), Reprint R0703C.

[45] News Release, "Ford Global Performance Strategy Accelerates at Frankfurt; New Fiesta ST Concept Joins Focus ST Production Model" (September 13, 2011) media ford.com.

[46] Adam M. Brandenburger and Barry J. Nalebuff, *Co-Opetition: A Revolutionary Mindset That Combines Competition and Cooperation* (New York: Bantam, 1996).

[47] See Jack Ewing: "2 Carmakers Prefer to Take Cooperation One Step at a Time," *International Herald Tribune* (September 15, 2011), p. 16.

[48] For a discussion of Michael Porter's approach to strategic planning, see his books *Competitive Strategy and Competitive Advantage*, and his article, "What Is Strategy?" *Harvard Business*

*Review* (November/December, 1996), pp. 61–78; and Richard M. Hodgetts' interview "A Conversation with Michael E. Porter: A Significant Extension Toward Operational Improvement and Positioning," *Organizational Dynamics* (Summer 1999), pp. 24–33.

49 Information from www.polo.com.

50 Porter, op. cit. (1996).

51 See Eric Bellman and Deniel Michaels, "In Asia, Budget Flights Multiply," *Wall Street Journal* (February 27, 2012), p. B5.

52 www.patagonia.com/web/us/patagonia.go?assetid53351.

53 For research support, see Daniel H. Gray, "Uses and Misuses of Strategic Planning," *Harvard Business Review*, vol. 64 (January–February 1986), pp. 89–97.

54 See Judith Burns, "Everything You Wanted to Know about Corporate Governance . . . But Didn't Know How to Ask," *Wall Street Journal* (October 27, 2003), pp. R1, R7.

55 Paul Ingrassia, "The Auto Makers Are Already Bankrupt," *Wall Street Journal* (November 21, 2008), p. A23.

56 See R. Duane Ireland and Michael A. Hitt, "Achieving and Maintaining Strategic Competitiveness in the 21st Century," *Academy of Management Executive*, vol. 13 (1999), pp. 43–57.

57 Hodgetts, op. cit.

58 *AIM Survey* (El Paso, TX: ENFP Enterprises, 1989), Copyright ©1989 by Weston H. Agor. Used by permission.

59 Suggested by an exercise in John F. Veiga and John N. Yanouzas, *The Dynamics of Organization Theory: Gaining a Macro Perspective* (St. Paul, MN: West, 1979), pp. 69–71.

### Feature Notes

Follow the Story—Information and quotes from William M. Bulkeley, "Xerox Names Burns Chief as Mulcahy Retires Early," *Wall Street Journal* (May 22, 2009), pp. B1, B2; Nanette Byrnes and Roger O. Crockett, "An Historic Succession at Xerox," *Business Week* (June 9, 2008), pp. 18–21; Ben Baker and Geoff Colvin, "Less Than a Year Into the Job, the Xerox CEO Is Already Transforming the Company," *Fortune*, Kindle edition (April 19, 2010); and, Dana Mattioli, "Xerox Chief Looks Beyond Photocopiers Towards Services," *Wall Street Journal* (June 13, 2011), p. B9.

Ethics on the Line—Information and quotes from "Life and Death at the iPad Factory," *Bloomberg BusinessWeek* (June 7–13, 2010), pp. 35–36; and, John Bussey, "Measuring the Human Cost of an iPad Made in China," *Wall Street Journal* (June 3, 2011), pp. B1, B2.

Facts for Analysis—Information from Mike Ramsey, "VW Alters Labor-Cost Equation," *Wall Street Journal* (May 23, 2011), pp. B1, B2; and Keith Naughton, "Ford Says New UAW Contract Boosts Labor Costs Less Than 1%," *Bloomberg* (October 20, 2011): bloomberg.com/news.

### Photo Essay Notes

Groupon—Information and quotes from Douglas MacMillan, "Who You Calling a Copycat?" *Bloomberg BusinessWeek* (September 26–October 2, 2011), pp. 45–46. Louis Vuitton—Information and quotes from Christina Passariello, "At Vuitton, Growth in Small Batches," *Wall Street Journal* (June 27, 2011), pp. B1, B10; and "Overheard," *Wall Street Journal* (October 10, 2011), p. C8.

## Chapter 11

### Endnotes

1 Information from "Build-A-Bear Workshop, Inc., Funding Universe": www.fundinguniverse.com/company-histories/BuildABear-Workshop-Inc (accessed March 9, 2009); and www.buildabear.com. See also Maxine Clark and Amy Joyner, *The Bear Necessities of Business: Building a Company with Heart* (Hoboken, NJ: Wiley, 2007).

2 Henry Mintzberg and Ludo Van der Heyden, "Organigraphs: Drawing How Companies Really Work," *Harvard Business Review* (September–October 1999), pp. 87–94.

3 The classic work is Alfred D. Chandler, *Strategy and Structure* (Cambridge, MA: MIT Press, 1962).

4 See Alfred D. Chandler, Jr., "Origins of the Organization Chart," *Harvard Business Review* (March–April 1988), pp. 156–57.

5 "A Question of Management," *Wall Street Journal* (June 2, 2009), p. R4.

6 Information from Jena McGregor, "The Office Chart that Really Counts," *BusinessWeek* (February 27, 2006), pp. 48–49.

7 See David Krackhardt and Jeffrey R. Hanson, "Informal Networks: The Company Behind the Chart," *Harvard Business Review* (July–August 1993), pp. 104–11.

8 Information from Dana Mattioli, "Job Fears Make Offices All Ears," *Wall Street Journal* (January 20, 2009): www.wsj.com.

9 See Kenneth Noble, "A Clash of Styles: Japanese Companies in the U.S.," *New York Times* (January 25, 1988), p. 7.

10 For a discussion of departmentalization, see H. I. Ansoff and R. G. Bradenburg, "A Language for Organization Design," *Management Science*, vol. 17 (August 1971), pp. B705–B731; Mariann Jelinek.

11 "A Question of Management," *Wall Street Journal* (June 2, 2009), p. R4.

12 Information and quotes from Luis Garicanco and Richard A. Posner, "What Our Spies Can Learn from Toyota," *Wall Street Journal* (January 13, 2010), p. A23.

13 "Organization Structure: The Basic Conformations," in Mariann Jelinek, Joseph A. Litterer, and Raymond E. Miles, eds., *Organizations by Design: Theory and Practice* (Plano, TX: Business Publications, 1981), pp. 293–302; Henry Mintzberg, "The Structuring of Organizations," in James Brian Quinn, Henry Mintzberg, and Robert M. James, eds., *The Strategy Process: Concepts, Contexts, and Cases* (Englewood Cliffs, NJ: Prentice-Hall, 1988), pp. 276–304.

14 Norihiko Shirouzu, "Toyota Plans a Major Overhaul in U.S.," *Wall Street Journal* (April 10, 2009), p. B3.

15 Information and quotes from "Management Shake-Up to Create 'Leaner Structure'," *Financial Times* (June 11, 2009).

16 Information and quote from "Revamped GM Updates Image of Core Brands," *Financial Times* (June 18, 2009).

17 The focus on process is described in Michael Hammer, *Beyond Reengineering* (New York: Harper Business, 1996).

18 Excellent reviews of matrix concepts are found in Stanley M. Davis and Paul R. Lawrence, *Matrix* (Reading, MA: Addison-Wesley, 1977); Paul R. Lawrence, Harvey F. Kolodny, and Stanley M. Davis, "The Human Side of the Matrix," *Organizational Dynamics*, vol. 6 (1977), pp. 43–61; and Harvey F. Kolodny, "Evolution to a Matrix Organization," *Academy of Management Review*, vol. 4 (1979), pp. 543–53.

19 Developed from Frank Ostroff, *The Horizontal Organization: What the Organization of the Future Looks Like and How It Delivers Value to Customers* (New York: Oxford University Press, 1999).

20 Quote from Andrew Hill, "Are Radical Innovations a Thing of the Past?" *Financial Times*, Kindle edition (September 27, 2011).

21 Susan Albers Mohrman, Susan G. Cohen, and Allan M. Mohrman Jr., *Designing Team-Based Organizations* (San Francisco: Jossey-Bass, 1996).

22 See Glenn M. Parker, *Cross-Functional Teams* (San Francisco: Jossey-Bass, 1995).

23 Information from William Bridges, "The End of the Job," *Fortune* (September 19, 1994), pp. 62–74; Alan Deutschman, "The Managing Wisdom of High-Tech Superstars," *Fortune* (October 17, 1994), pp. 197–206.

[24] See the discussion by Jay R. Galbraith, "Designing the Networked Organization: Leveraging Size and Competencies," in Susan Albers Mohrman, Jay R. Galbraith, Edward E. Lawler III, and associates, *Tomorrow's Organizations: Crafting Winning Strategies in a Dynamic World* (San Francisco: Jossey-Bass, 1998), pp. 76–102. See also Rupert F. Chisholm, *Developing Network Organizations: Learning from Practice and Theory* (Reading, MA: Addison-Wesley, 1998).

[25] See the discussion by Michael S. Malone, *The Future Arrived Yesterday: The Rise of the Protean Corporation and What It Means for You* (New York: Crown Books, 2009).

[26] See, for example, Dawn Wotapka, "School Wants to Get Out of Campus Housing," *Wall Street Journal* (December 13, 2011), p. B6.

[27] See Jerome Barthelemy, "The Seven Deadly Sins of Outsourcing," *Academy of Management Executive*, vol. 17 (2003), pp. 87–98.

[28] Paulo Prada and Jiraj Sheth, "Delta Air Ends Use of India Call Centers," *Wall Street Journal* (April 18–19, 2009), pp. B1, B5.

[29] See Ron Ashkenas, Dave Ulrich, Todd Jick, and Steve Kerr, *The Boundaryless Organization: Breaking the Chains of Organizational Structure* (San Francisco: Jossey-Bass, 1996).

[30] Information from "Scott Livengood and the Tasty Tale of Krispy Kreme," *BizEd* (May/June 2003), pp. 16–20.

[31] Information from John A. Byrne, "Management by Web," *BusinessWeek* (August 28, 2000), pp. 84–97; see the collection of articles by Cary L. Cooper and Denise M. Rousseau, eds., *The Virtual Organization: Vol. 6, Trends in Organizational Behavior* (New York: Wiley, 2000).

[32] For a classic work, see Jay R. Galbraith, *Organizational Design* (Reading, MA: Addison-Wesley, 1977).

[33] This framework is based on Harold J. Leavitt, "Applied Organizational Change in Industry," in James G. March, *Handbook of Organizations* (New York: Rand McNally, 1965), pp. 1144–70; and Edward E. Lawler III, *From the Ground Up: Six Principles for the New Logic Corporation* (San Francisco: Jossey-Bass Publishers, 1996), pp. 44–50.

[34] Max Weber, *The Theory of Social and Economic Organization*, A. M. Henderson, trans., and H. T. Parsons (New York: Free Press, 1947).

[35] Ibid.

[36] For classic treatments of bureaucracy, see Alvin Gouldner, *Patterns of Industrial Bureaucracy* (New York: Free Press, 1954); and Robert K. Merton, *Social Theory and Social Structure* (New York: Free Press, 1957).

[37] Tom Burns and George M. Stalker, *The Management of Innovation* (London: Tavistock, 1961; republished by Oxford University Press, London, 1994). See also Paul R. Lawrence and Jay W. Lorsch, *Organizations and Environment* (Boston: Division of Research, Graduate School of Business Administration, Harvard University, 1967).

[38] See Henry Mintzberg, *Structure in Fives: Designing Effective Organizations* (Englewood Cliffs, NJ: Prentice-Hall, 1983).

[39] See Rosabeth Moss Kanter, *The Changing Masters* (New York: Simon & Schuster, 1983). Quotation from Rosabeth Moss Kanter and John D. Buck, "Reorganizing Part of Honeywell: From Strategy to Structure," *Organizational Dynamics*, vol. 13 (Winter 1985), p. 6.

[40] See, for example, Jay R. Galbraith, Edward E. Lawler III, and associates, *Organizing for the Future* (San Francisco: Jossey-Bass, 1993); and Mohrman, Galbraith, Lawler, and associates, *Tomorrow's Organizations*.

[41] www.nucor.com/aboutus.htm

[42] David Van Fleet, "Span of Management Research and Issues," *Academy of Management Journal*, vol. 26 (1983), pp. 546–52.

[43] Information and quotes from Ellen Byron and Joann S. Lublin, "Appointment of New P&G Chief Sends Ripples through Ranks," *Wall Street Journal* (June 11, 2009), p. B3.

[44] Burns and Stalker, op. cit.

[45] Questionnaire adapted from L. Steinmetz and R. Todd, *First Line Management*, 4th ed. (Homewood, IL: BPI/Irwin, 1986), pp. 64–67. Used by permission.

### Feature Notes

Follow the Story—Information and quotes from Stacy Perman, "Scones and Social Responsibility," *BusinessWeek* (August 21/28, 2006), p. 38; www.simmons.edu/som/docs/Karter%281%29.pdf; Megan Woolhouse, "Dancing Deer Executive Leaves Post," *Boston Globe* (June 26, 2010): www.boston.com/business/articles/2010/06/26/dancing_deer_executive_leaves_post/; and, www.dancingdeer.com/about us.

Facts for Analysis—Information and quote from "Bosses Overestimate Their Managing Skills," *Wall Street Journal* (November 1, 2010), p. B10.

## Chapter 12

### Endnotes

[1] Information from Marnie Hanel, "Clif Bar's Offices Keep Employees Limber," *Bloomberg BusinessWeek* (November 21–27, 2011), pp. 104–105; and, www.clifbar.com.

[2] Information from David Welch, "GM: His Way or the Highway," *BusinessWeek* (October 5, 2009), pp. 62–63.

[3] See the discussion of Anthropologie in William C. Taylor and Polly LaBarre, *Mavericks at Work: Why the Most Original Minds in Business Win* (New York: William Morrow, 2006).

[4] Edgar H. Schein, "Organizational Culture," *American Psychologist*, vol. 45 (1990), pp. 109–19. See also *Schein's Organizational Culture and Leadership*, 2nd ed. (San Francisco: Jossey-Bass, 1997) and *The Corporate Culture Survival Guide* (San Francisco: Jossey-Bass, 1999).

[5] James Collins and Jerry Porras, *Built to Last* (New York: HarperBusiness, 1994).

[6] Information and quotes from Christopher Palmeri, "Now for Sale, the Zappos Culture," *BusinessWeek* (January 11, 2010), p. 57. See also Tony Hsieh, *Delivering Happiness! A Path to Profits, Passion, and Purpose* (New York: BusinessPlus, 2010).

[7] Jena McGregor, "Zappos' Secret: It's an Open Book," *BusinessWeek* (March 23/30, 2009), p. 62.

[8] Information from "Workplace Cultures Come in Four Kinds," *The Wall Street Journal* (February 7, 2012), p. B6.

[9] In their book *Corporate Culture and Performance* (New York: Macmillan, 1992), John P. Kotter and James L. Heskett make the point that strong cultures have the desired effects over the long term only if they encourage adaptation to a changing environment. See also Collins and Porras, op. cit.

[10] John P. Wanous, *Organizational Entry*, 2nd ed. (New York: Addison-Wesley, 1992).

[11] Scott Madison Patton, *Service Quality, Disney Style* (Lake Buena Vista, FL: Disney Institute, 1997).

[12] This is a simplified model developed from Schein, op. cit. (1997).

[13] Schein, op. cit. (1997); Terrence E. Deal and Alan A. Kennedy, *Corporate Cultures: The Rites and Rituals of Corporate Life* (Reading, MA: Addison-Wesley, 1982); Ralph Kilmann, *Beyond the Quick Fix* (San Francisco: Jossey-Bass, 1984).

[14] James C. Collins and Jerry I. Porras, "Building Your Company's Vision," *Harvard Business Review* (September–October 1996), pp. 65–77.

[15] David Rocks, "Reinventing Herman Miller," *BusinessWeek eBiz* (April 2, 2000), pp. E88–E96; www.hermanmiller.com.

[16] See Robert A. Giacalone and Carol L. Jurkiewicz (eds.), *Handbook of Workplace Spirituality and Organizational Performance* (Armonk, NY: M. E. Sharpe, 2005).

[17] McCune, op. cit.

[18] R. Roosevelt Thomas Jr., *Beyond Race and Gender* (New York: AMACOM, 1992), p. 10. See also R. Roosevelt Thomas Jr., "From 'Affirmative Action' to 'Affirming Diversity,'" *Harvard Business Review* (November–December 1990), pp. 107–17; R. Roosevelt Thomas Jr., with Marjorie I. Woodruff, *Building a House for Diversity* (New York: AMACOM, 1999).

[19] Taylor Cox Jr., *Cultural Diversity in Organizations* (San Francisco: Berrett Koehler, 1994).

[20] Survey reported in "The Most Inclusive Workplaces Generate the Most Loyal Employees," *Gallup Management Journal* (December 2001), retrieved from http://gmj.gallup.com/ press_room/release.asp?i=117.

[21] Data reported in Laura Petrecca. "Number of Female 'Fortune' 500 CEOs at Record High." *USA Today* (October 26, 2011); www.usa.com.

[22] Thomas Kochan, Katerina Bezrukova, Robin Ely, Susan Jackson, Aparna Joshi, Karen Jehn, Jonathan Leonard, David Levine, and David Thomas, "The Effects of Diversity on Business Performance: Report of the Diversity Research Network," reported in *SHRM Foundation Research Findings*, retrieved from www.shrm.org/foundation/findings. asp. Full article published in *Human Resource Management* (2003).

[23] Information from "Demographics: The Young and the Restful," *Harvard Business Review* (November 2004), p. 25.

[24] See, for example, Richard Donkin, "Caught Somewhere between the Ys and the Boomers," *Financial Times*, Kindle Edition (December 31, 2009).

[25] "Many U.S. Employees Have Negative Attitudes to Their Jobs, Employers and Top Managers." *The Harris Poll #38* (May 6, 2005), available from www.harrisinteractive.com; and "U.S. Job Satisfaction Keeps Falling," *The Conference Board Reports Today* (February 25, 2005; retrieved from www.conference-board.org).

[26] Mayo Clinic, "Workplace Generation Gap: Understand Differences Among Colleagues" (July 6, 2005), retrieved from http://www. cnn.com/HEALTH/library/WL/00045.html).

[27] Barbara Benedict Bunker, "Appreciating Diversity and Modifying Organizational Cultures: Men and Women at Work," Chapter 5 in Suresh Srivastava and David L. Cooperrider, *Appreciative Management and Leadership* (San Francisco: Jossey-Bass, 1990).

[28] See Gary N. Powell, *Women-Men in Management* (Thousand Oaks, CA: Sage, 1993), and Cliff Cheng (ed.), *Masculinities in Organizations* (Thousand Oaks, CA: Sage, 1996). For added background, see also Sally Helgesen, *Everyday Revolutionaries: Working Women and the Transformation of American Life* (New York: Doubleday, 1998).

[29] See Anthony Robbins and Joseph McClendon III, *Unlimited Power: A Black Choice* (New York: Free Press, 1997), and Augusto Failde and William Doyle, *Latino Success: Insights from America's Most Powerful Latino Executives* (New York: Free Press, 1996).

[30] See Joseph A. Raelin, *Clash of Cultures* (Cambridge, MA: Harvard Business School Press, 1986).

[31] Petrecca, op. cit; and, John Bussey, "Women, Welch Clash at Forum," *Wall Street Journal* (May 4, 2012), pp. B1, B2.

[32] Laurie Landro, "Of Women and Working," *Wall Street Journal*, online edition (December 5, 2009); and, Sue Shellenbarger, "The XX Factor: What's Holding Women Back?" *Wall Street Journal* (May 7, 2012), pp. B7-B12 .

[33] "Bias Cases by Workers Increase 9%," *Wall Street Journal* (March 6, 2008), p. D6.

[34] Sue Shellenbarger, "More Women Pursue Claims of Pregnancy Discrimination," *Wall Street Journal* (March 27, 2008), p. D1; and Rob Walker, "Sex vs. Ethics." *Fast Company* (June 2008), pp. 73–78.

[35] Ibid.

[36] Thomas, op. cit. (1992); and, Shellenbarger, op. cit. (2012).

[37] Ibid.

[38] For a review of scholarly work on organizational change, see Arthur G. Bedian, "Organizational Change: A Review of Theory and Research," *Journal of Management*, vol. 25 (1999), pp. 293–315; and W. Warner Burke, *Organizational Change: Theory and Practice*, 2nd ed. (Thousand Oaks, CA: Sage, 2008).

[39] Quote from Pilita Clark, "Delayed, Not Cancelled," *Financial Times* (December 19, 2009).

[40] Information and quote from Adam Bryant, "Xerox's New Chief Tries to Redefine Its Culture," *New York Times* (February 21, 2010): www.nytimes.com.

[41] For a review of data on change failures see Bernard Burnes, "Introduction: Why Does Change Fail, and What Can We Do About It?" *Journal of Change Management*, Vol. 11, No. 4 (2011), pp. 445–50; and, Mark Hughes, "Do 70 Per Cent of All Organizational Change Initiatives Fail?" *Journal of Change Management*, Vol. 11, No. 4 (2011), pp. 451–64.

[42] Based on John P. Kotter, "Leading Change: Why Transformation Efforts Fail," *Harvard Business Review* (March–April 1995), pp. 59–67.

[43] Jack and Suzy Welch, "Finding Innovation Where It Lives," *BusinessWeek* (April 21, 2008), p. 84.

[44] This is based on Rosabeth Moss Kanter's "Innovation Pyramid," *BusinessWeek* (March 2007), p. IN 3.

[45] For a discussion of alternative types of change, see David A. Nadler and Michael L. Tushman, *Strategic Organizational Design* (Glenview, IL: Scott, Foresman, 1988); Kotter, op. cit; and W. Warner Burke, *Organization Change* (Thousand Oaks, CA.: Sage, 2002).

[46] Kurt Lewin, "Group Decision and Social Change," in G. E. Swanson, T. M. Newcomb, and E. L. Hartley (eds.), *Readings in Social Psychology* (New York: Holt, Rinehart, 1952), pp. 459–73.

[47] See Wanda J. Orlikowski and J. Debra Hofman, "An Improvisational Model for Change Management: The Case of Groupware Technologies," *Sloan Management Review* (Winter 1997), pp. 11–21.

[48] Ibid.

[49] This discussion is based on Robert Chin and Kenneth D. Benne, "General Strategies for Effecting Changes in Human Systems," in Warren G. Bennis, Kenneth D. Benne, Robert Chin, and Kenneth E. Corey (eds.), *The Planning of Change*, 3rd ed. (New York: Holt, Rinehart, 1969), pp. 22–45.

[50] The change agent descriptions here and following are developed from an exercise reported in J. William Pfeiffer and John E. Jones, *A Handbook of Structured Experiences for Human Relations Training*, vol. 2 (La Jolla, CA: University Associates, 1973).

[51] Ram N. Aditya, Robert J. House, and Steven Kerr, "Theory and Practice of Leadership: Into the New Millennium," Chapter 6 in Cary L. Cooper and Edwin A. Locke, *Industrial and Organizational Psychology: Linking Theory with Practice* (Malden, MA: Blackwell, 2000).

[52] Information from Mike Schneider, "Disney Teaching Excess Magic of Customer Service." *Columbus Dispatch* (December 17, 2000), p. G9.

[53] Teresa M. Amabile, "How to Kill Creativity," *Harvard Business Review* (September–October 1998), pp. 77–87.

[54] For an overview see Jeffrey D. Ford, Laurie W. Ford, and Angelo D'Amoto, "Resistance to Change: The Rest of the Story," *Academy of Management Review*, vol. 33, no. 2 (2008), pp. 362–77; and, Jeffrey D. Ford and Laurie W. Ford, "Decoding Resistance to Change," *Harvard Business Review* (April 2009), pp. 99–103.

[55] These checkpoints are developed from Everett M. Rogers, *Communication of Innovations*, 3rd ed. (New York: Free Press, 1993).

[56] John P. Kotter and Leonard A. Schlesinger, "Choosing Strategies for Change," *Harvard Business Review*, vol. 57 (March–April 1979), pp. 109–12. Example from *Fortune* (December 1991), pp. 56–62; additional information from corporate website: www.toro.com.

[57] Based on an instrument developed by W. Warner Burke. Used by permission.

### Feature Notes

Follow the Story—Information and quotes from David Kiley, "Ford's Savior?" *BusinessWeek* (March 16, 2009), pp. 31–34; and Alex Taylor III, "Fixing Up Ford," *Fortune* (May 14, 2009).

Ethics on the Line—Information from "Can Business Be Cool?" *Economist* (June 10, 2006), pp. 59–60; and Aubrey Henretty, "A Brighter Day," *Kellogg* (Summer 2006), pp. 32–34; Competitive Enterprise Institute, http://www.cei.org/pages/co2.cfm (retrieved September 29, 2006); Joseph Stiglitz, *Making Globalization Work* (New York: Norton, 2006), p. 172; and, Jim Phillips, "Business Leaders Say 'Green' Approach Doable," *Athens News* (March 27, 2008), from www.athensnews.com.

Facts to Consider—Data reported in "A Saner Workplace," *Business Week* (June 1, 2009), pp. 66–69, and based on excerpt from Claire Shipman and Katty Kay, *Womenomics: Write Your Own Rules for Success* (New York: Harper Business, 2009); and "A to Z of Generation Y Attitudes," *Financial Times* (June 18, 2009).

### Photo Essay Notes

Tom's of Maine—This incident is reported in Jenny C. McCune, "Making Lemonade," *Management Review* (June 1997), pp. 49–53. Recommended Reading—Information and quotes from Tim Brown, "Change by Design," *BusinessWeek* (October 5, 2009), pp. 54–56. See also Tim Brown, *Change by Design* (New York: Harper Business, 2009).

## Chapter 13

### Endnotes

[1] Information from *Working Mother* (retrieved November 25, 2011, from http://www.workingmother.com/best-companies/2011-working-mother-100-best-companies).

[2] Orlando Behling, "Employee Selection: Will Intelligence and Conscientiousness Do the Job?," *Academy of Management Executive*, February 1998, vol. 12, no. 1, pp. 77–86.

[3] Jeffrey Pfeffer, *The Human Equation: Building Profits by Putting People First* (Boston: Harvard University Press, 1998), p. 292.

[4] Quote from William Bridges, "The End of the Job," *Fortune* (September 19, 1994), p. 68.

[5] Edward E. Lawler III, "The HR Department: Give It More Respect," *Wall Street Journal* (March 10, 2008), p. R8.

[6] *Dictionary of Business Management* (New York: Oxford University Press, 2006).

[7] T. Sekiguchi, "Person–Organization Fit and Person–Job Fit in Employee Selection: A Review of the Literature," *Osaka Keidai Ronshu*, vol. 54, no. 6 (2004), p. 179.

[8] Information from "New Face at Facebook Hopes to Map Out a Road to Growth," *Wall Street Journal* (April 15, 2008), pp. B1, B5.

[9] James N. Baron and David M. Kreps, *Strategic Human Resources: Framework for General Managers* (New York: Wiley, 1999).

[10] "Google's Laszlo Bock Named 2010 HR Executive of the Year," *Marketwire* (retrieved October 1, 2010 from http://www.marketwire.com/press-release/Googles-Laszlo-Bock-Named-2010-HR-Executive-of-the-Year-1328227.htm).

[11] Ibid.

[12] For a discussion of affirmative action see R. Roosevelt Thomas Jr., "From 'Affirmative Action' to 'Affirming Diversity,'" *Harvard Business Review* (November–December 1990), pp. 107–17.

[13] See the discussion by David A. DeCenzo and Stephen P. Robbins, *Human Resource Management*, 6th ed. (New York: Wiley, 1999), pp. 66–68 and 81–83.

[14] Ibid., pp. 77–79.

[15] Information from the U.S. Equal Employment Opportunity Commission (retrieved from www.eeoc.gov/laws/statutes/titlevii.cfm).

[16] Information from ADA National Network retrieved from www.adata.org/whatsada-definition.aspx.

[17] Information from the U.S. Equal Employment Opportunity Commission retrieved from www.eeoc.gov/laws/types/ages.cfm.

[18] Information from the U.S. Equal Employment Opportunity Commission retrieved from www.eeoc.gov/laws/types/pregnancy.cfm.

[19] Information from the U.S. Department of Labor, retrieved from http://www.dol.gov/whd/fmla/index.htm.

[20] See Frederick S. Lane, *The Naked Employee: How Technology Is Compromising Workplace Privacy* (New York: AMACOM, 2003).

[21] Quote from George Myers, "Bookshelf," *Columbus Dispatch* (June 9, 2003), p. E6.

[22] See Ernest McCormick, "Job and Task Analysis," in Marvin Dunnette (ed.), *Handbook of Industrial and Organizational Psychology* (Chicago: Rand McNally, 1976), pp. 651–96.

[23] See John P. Wanous, *Organizational Entry: Recruitment, Selection, and Socialization of Newcomers* (Reading, MA: Addison-Wesley, 1980), pp. 34–44.

[24] Behling, op. cit.

[25] Information and quotes from William Poundstone, "How to Ace a Google Interview," *The Wall Street Journal* (December 24–25, 2012), pp. C1,C2.

[26] Theresa Feathers, *Three Major Selection and Assessment Techniques, Their Popularity in Industry and Their Predictive Validity*, December 2000.

[27] See Michael A. D. McDaniel, Deborah L. Whetzel, Frank L. Schmidt, and Steven Maurer, "The Validity of Employment Interviews: A Comprehensive Review and Meta-analysis," *Journal of Applied Psychology*, vol. 79, no. 4 (August 1994), pp. 599–616.

[28] Information from "Biodata: The Measure of an Applicant?" *New York Law Journal* (May 21, 2007).

[29] Information from "Google Answer to Filling Jobs Is an Algorithm," *New York Times* (January 3, 2007).

[30] For a scholarly review, see John Van Maanen and Edgar H. Schein, "Toward a Theory of Socialization," in Barry M. Staw (ed.), *Research in Organizational Behavior*, vol. 1 (Greenwich, CT: JAI Press, 1979), pp. 209–64; for a practitioner's view, see Richard Pascale, "Fitting New Employees into the Company Culture," *Fortune* (May 28, 1984), pp. 28–42.

[31] This involves the social information processing concept as discussed in Gerald R. Salancik and Jeffrey Pfeffer, "A Social Information Processing Approach to Job Attitudes and Task Design," *Administrative Science Quarterly*, vol. 23 (June 1978), pp. 224–53.

[32] Boxed material developed from Alan Fowler, "How to Decide on Training Methods," *People Management*, vol. 25 (1995), pp. 36–38.

[33] Gouri Shukla, "Job Rotation and How It Works," April 27, 2005, retrieved from http://www.rediff.com/money/2005/apr/27spec1.htm.

[34] See Larry L. Cummings and Donald P. Schwab, *Performance in Organizations: Determinants and Appraisal* (Glenview, IL: Scott, Foresman, 1973).

[35] Dick Grote, "Performance Appraisal Reappraised," *Harvard Business Review Best Practice* (1999), Reprint F00105.

[36] See Gary P. Latham, Joan Almost, Sara Mann, and Celia Moore, "New Developments in Performance Management," *Organizational Dynamics*, vol. 34, no. 1 (2005), pp. 77–87.

[37] See Jeffrey S. Kane, John H. Bernardin, Peter Villanova, and Joseph Peyrefitte, "Stability of Rater Leniency: Three Studies," *Academy of Management Journal*, Vol. 38, no. 4 (1995), pp. 1036–1051.

[38] See Edward E. Lawler III, "Reward Practices and Performance Management System Effectiveness," *Organizational Dynamics*, vol. 32, no. 4 (November 2003), pp. 396–404.

[39] Information from Ilana DeBare, "360 Degrees of Evaluation—More Companies Turn to Full-Circle Job Reviews," *San Francisco Chronicle* (May 5, 1997).

[40] Latham, op. cit.

[41] Timothy Butler and James Waldroop, "Job Sculpting: The Art of Retaining Your Best People," *Harvard Business Review* (September–October 1999), pp. 144–52.

[42] Information from "What Are the Most Effective Retention Tools?" *Fortune* (October 9, 2000), p. S7.

[43] See Betty Friedan, *Beyond Gender: The New Politics of Work and the Family* (Washington, DC: Woodrow Wilson Center Press, 1997); and James A. Levine, *Working Fathers: New Strategies for Balancing Work and Family* (Reading, MA: Addison-Wesley, 1997).

[44] Study reported in Ann Belser, "Employers Using Less-Costly Ways to Retain Workers," *Columbus Dispatch* (June 1, 2008), p. D3.

[45] Information from *Working Mother* (http://www.workingmother.com/best-companies/2011-working-mother-100-best-companies).

[46] "Should Companies Offer Sabbaticals?," *CNNMoney* (retrieved January 3, 2011 from http://management.fortune.cnn.com/2011/01/03/should-companies-offer-sabbaticals).

[47] "Vacation Policies Are Here to Stay," *CNNMoney* (retrieved February 1, 2011 from http://money.cnn.com/2011/01/31/news/companies/no_vacation_policies.fortune/index.htm).

[48] A good overview of trends and issues is found in the special section on "Employee Benefits," *Wall Street Journal* (April 22, 2008), pp. A11–A17.

[49] "What Is the Typical Cost of Benefits per Employee?" *eHow.com* (retrieved June 29, 2011 from http://www.ehow.com/info_8663999_typical-cost-benefits-per-employee.html#ixzz1kRAYVptc).

[50] See Kaja Whitehouse, "More Companies Offer Packages Pay Plans to Performance," *Wall Street Journal* (December 13, 2005), p. B6.

[51] Ibid.

[52] Information from Susan Pulliam, "New .Dot-Com Mantra: 'Just Pay Me in Cash, Please,'" *Wall Street Journal* (November 28, 2000), p. C1.

[53] White, op. cit.

[54] Information from Andrew Blackman, "You're the Boss," *Wall Street Journal* (April 11, 2005), p. R5.

[55] Information from www.intel.com and "Stock Ownership for Everyone," Hewitt Associates (November 27, 2000).

[56] For reviews see Richard B. Freeman and James L. Medoff, *What Do Unions Do?* (New York: Basic Books, 1984); Charles C. Heckscher, *The New Unionism* (New York: Basic Books, 1988); and Barry T. Hirsch, *Labor Unions and the Economic Performance of Firms* (Kalamazoo, MI: W. E. Upjohn Institute for Employment Research, 1991).

[57] Ibid.

[58] Developed in part from Robert E. Quinn, Sue R. Faerman, Michael P. Thompson, and Michael R. McGrath, *Becoming a Master Manager: A Contemporary Framework* (New York: Wiley, 1990), p. 187. Used by permission.

[59] Developed from Eugene Owens, "Upward Appraisal: An Exercise in Subordinate's Critique of Superior's Performance," *Exchange: The Organizational Behavior Teaching Journal*, vol. 3 (1978), pp. 41–42.

### Feature Notes

Follow the Story—http://zappos.com; http://about.zappos.com/meet-our-monkeys/tony-hsieh-ceo; http://www.mahalo.com/tony-hsieh; Tony Hsieh, *Delivering Happiness: A Path to Profits, Passion, and Purpose* (New York: BusinessPlus, 2010); Interview of Tony Hsieh by Victoria Brown on May 27, 2010 (retrieved from http://bigthink.com/ideas/20673); and Brad Stone, "What Starts Up in Vegas Stays in Vegas," *Bloomberg BusinessWeek* (February 6–12, 2012), pp. 37–39.

Ethics on the Line—Information from "What Prospective Employers Hope to See in Your Facebook Account," Forbes.com (October 3, 2011): accessed November 26, 2011; and, Manuel Valdes and Shannon McFarland, "Drug Test? Now It's Facebook Password," *The Columbus Dispatch* (March 21, 2012), pp. A1, A4.

Facts for Analysis—Jenny Marlar, "Underemployed Report Spending 36% Less Than Employed," *Gallup.com*, February 23, 2010 (retrieved December 8, 2011).

### Photo Essay Notes

Managing Your Online Image in Social Networks—See "Managing Your Online Image Across Social Networks," Reppler.com, September 27, 2011.

Resume Software—Information from Lauren Weber, "Your Resume vs. Oblivion," *The Wall Street Journal* (January 24, 2012), p. B1. Zumba—Information from Brad Eagan, "Perks with a Payoff," *The Wall Street Journal* (October 24, 2011), p. R3. Google—See Bernard Girard, *The Google Way: How One Company Is Revolutionizing Management as We Know It* (San Francisco: No Starch Press, 2009).

## Chapter 14

### Endnotes

[1] Information and quotes from Irene Rosenfeld, "Irene Rosenfeld Drives Change with 'Rules of the Road'," *Wall Street Journal*, Special Advertising Section (October 6, 2009), p. A17; David Kesmodel and Ceceilie Rohwedder, "Sugar and Spice: A Clash of Two Change Agents," *Wall Street Journal* (September 8, 2009), p. A17; Ilan Brat, "A Jar of New Vegemite: A Window into Kraft," *Wall Street Journal* (September 30, 2009), pp. B1, B2; Susan Verfield and Michael Arndt, "Kraft's Sugar Rush," *BusinessWeek* (January 25, 2010), pp. 37–39; and, "Women at the Top," *Financial Times* (November 16, 2012), p. 3.

[2] List developed from S. Bartholomew Craig and Gigrid B. Qustafson, "Perceived Leader Integrity Scale: An Instrument for Assessing Employee Perceptions of Leader Integrity," *Leadership Quarterly*, vol. 9 (1998), pp. 127–45.

[3] Quote from Marshall Loeb, "Where Leaders Come From," *Fortune* (September 19, 1994), pp. 241–42. For additional thoughts, see Warren Bennis, *Why Leaders Can't Lead* (San Francisco: Jossey-Bass, 1996).

[4] Barry Z. Posner, "On Leadership," *BizEd* (May–June 2008), pp. 26–27.

[5] Tom Peters, "Rule #3: Leadership Is Confusing as Hell," *Fast Company* (March 2001), pp. 124–40.

[6] See Jean Lipman-Blumen, *Connective Leadership: Managing in a Changing World* (New York: Oxford University Press, 1996), pp. 3–11.

[7] Beth Benjamin and Charles O'Reilly, "Becoming a Leader: Early Career Challenges Faced by MBA Graduates," *Academy of Management Learning & Education*, vol. 10 (2011), p. 453.

[8] Abraham Zaleznick, "Leaders and Managers: Are They Different?" *Harvard Business Review* (May–June 1977), pp. 67–78.

[9] Rosabeth Moss Kanter, "Power Failure in Management Circuits," *Harvard Business Review* (July–August 1979), pp. 65–75.

[10] For a good managerial discussion of power, see David C. McClelland and David H. Burnham, "Power Is the Great Motivator," *Harvard Business Review* (March–April 1976), pp. 100–10.

[11] The classic treatment of these power bases is John R. P. French Jr. and Bertram Raven, "The Bases of Social Power," in Darwin Cartwright, ed., *Group Dynamics: Research and Theory* (Evanston, IL: Row, Peterson, 1962), pp. 607–13. For managerial applications of this basic framework, see Gary Yukl and Tom Taber, "The Effective Use of Managerial Power," *Personnel*, vol. 60 (1983), pp. 37–49; and Robert C. Benfari, Harry E. Wilkinson, and Charles D. Orth, "The Effective Use of Power," *Business Horizons*, vol. 29 (1986), pp. 12–16; Gary A. Yukl, *Leadership in Organizations*, 4th ed. (Englewood Cliffs, NJ: Prentice-Hall, 1998); includes "information" as a separate, but related, power source.

[12] James M. Kouzes and Barry Z. Posner, "The Leadership Challenge," *Success* (April 1988), p. 68. See also their books *Credibility: How Leaders Gain and Lose It; Why People Demand It* (San Francisco: Jossey-Bass, 1996); *Encouraging the Heart: A Leader's Guide to Rewarding and Recognizing Others* (San Francisco: Jossey-Bass, 1999); and *The Leadership Challenge: How to Get Extraordinary Things Done in Organizations*, 3rd ed. (San Francisco: Jossey-Bass, 2002).

[13] Burt Nanus, *Visionary Leadership: Creating a Compelling Sense of Vision for Your Organization* (San Francisco: Jossey-Bass, 1992).

[14] Lorraine Monroe, "Leadership Is about Making Vision Happen—What I Call 'Vision Acts,'" *Fast Company* (March 2001), p. 98; School Leadership Academy website: www.lorrainemonroe.com.

[15] Quote from Andy Serwer, "Game Changers: Legendary Basketball Coach John Wooden and Starbucks' Howard Schultz Talk about a Common Interest—Leadership," *Fortune* (August 11, 2008): www.cnnmoney.com.

[16] Robert K. Greenleaf and Larry C. Spears, *The Power of Servant Leadership: Essays* (San Francisco: Berrett-Koehler, 1996), p. 78.

[17] Monroe, op. cit., p. 98; School Leadership Academy website: www.lorrainemonroe.com.

[18] Loeb, op. cit.

[19] A classic work is Greenleaf and Spears, op. cit.

[20] Jay A. Conger, "Leadership: The Art of Empowering Others," *Academy of Management Executive*, vol. 3 (1989), pp. 17–24.

[21] The early work on leader traits is well represented in Ralph M. Stogdill, "Personal Factors Associated with Leadership: A Survey of the Literature," *Journal of Psychology*, vol. 25 (1948), pp. 35–71. See also Edwin E. Ghiselli, *Explorations in Management Talent* (Santa Monica, CA: Goodyear, 1971); and Shirley A. Kirkpatrick and Edwin A. Locke, "Leadership: Do Traits Really Matter?" *Academy of Management Executive* (1991), pp. 48–60.

[22] See also John W. Gardner's article, "The Context and Attributes of Leadership," *New Management*, vol. 5 (1988), pp. 18–22; John P. Kotter, *The Leadership Factor* (New York: Free Press, 1988); and Bernard M. Bass, *Stogdill's Handbook of Leadership* (New York: Free Press, 1990).

[23] Kirkpatrick and Locke, op. cit., 1991.

[24] This work traces back to classic studies by Kurt Lewin and his associates at the University of Iowa. See, for example, K. Lewin and R. Lippitt, "An Experimental Approach to the Study of Autocracy and Democracy: A Preliminary Note," *Sociometry*, vol. 1 (1938), pp. 292–300; K. Lewin, "Field Theory and Experiment in Social Psychology: Concepts and Methods," *American Journal of Sociology*, vol. 44 (1939), pp. 886–96; and K. Lewin, R. Lippitt, and R. K. White, "Patterns of Aggressive Behavior in Experimentally Created Social Climates," *Journal of Social Psychology*, vol. 10 (1939), pp. 271–301.

[25] The original research from the Ohio State studies is described in R. M. Stogdill and A. E. Coons, eds., *Leader Behavior: Its Description and Measurement*, Research Monograph No. 88 (Columbus: Ohio State University Bureau of Business Research, 1951); see also Chester A. Schreisham, Claudia C. Cogliser, and Linda L. Neider, "Is It 'Trustworthy'? A Multiple-Levels-of-Analysis Reexamination of an Ohio State Leadership Study with Implications for Future Research," *Leadership Quarterly*, vol. 2 (Summer 1995), pp. 111–45. For the University of Michigan studies, see Robert Kahn and Daniel Katz, "Leadership Practices in Relation to Productivity and Morale," in Dorwin Cartwright and Alvin Alexander, eds., *Group Dynamics: Research and Theory*, 3rd ed. (New York: Harper-Row, 1968).

[26] See Bass, op. cit., 1990.

[27] Robert R. Blake and Jane Srygley Mouton, *The New Managerial Grid III* (Houston: Gulf Publishing, 1985).

[28] See Lewin and Lippitt, op. cit., 1938.

[29] For a good discussion of this theory, see Fred E. Fiedler, Martin M. Chemers, and Linda Mahar, *The Leadership Match Concept* (New York: Wiley, 1978); Fiedler's current contingency research with the cognitive resource theory is summarized in Fred E. Fiedler and Joseph E. Garcia, *New Approaches to Effective Leadership* (New York: Wiley, 1987).

[30] See Pino Audia, "A New B-School Specialty: Self-Awareness," Forbes.com (December 4, 2009).

[31] Paul Hersey and Kenneth H. Blanchard, *Management and Organizational Behavior* (Englewood Cliffs, NJ: Prentice-Hall, 1988). For an interview with Paul Hersey on the origins of the model, see John R. Schermerhorn Jr., "Situational Leadership: Conversations with Paul Hersey," *Mid-American Journal of Business* (Fall 1997), pp. 5–12.

[32] See Claude L. Graeff, "The Situational Leadership Theory: A Critical View," *Academy of Management Review*, vol. 8 (1983), pp. 285–91; and Carmen F. Fernandez and Robert P. Vecchio, "Situational Leadership Theory Revisited: A Test of an Across-Jobs Perspective," *Leadership Quarterly*, vol. 8 (Summer 1997), pp. 67–84.

[33] See, for example, Robert J. House, "A Path–Goal Theory of Leader Effectiveness," *Administrative Sciences Quarterly*, vol. 16 (1971), pp. 321–38; Robert J. House and Terrence R. Mitchell, "Path–Goal Theory of Leadership," *Journal of Contemporary Business* (Autumn 1974), pp. 81–97. The path–goal theory is reviewed by Bass, op. cit. A supportive review of research is offered in Julie Indvik, "Path–Goal Theory of Leadership: A Meta-Analysis," in John A. Pearce II and Richard B. Robinson Jr., eds., *Academy of Management Best Paper Proceedings* (1986), pp. 189–92. The theory is reviewed and updated in Robert J. House, "Path–Goal Theory of Leadership: Lessons, Legacy and a Reformulated Theory," *Leadership Quarterly*, vol. 7 (Autumn 1996), pp. 323–52.

[34] See the discussions of path–goal theory in Bernard M. Bass, "Leadership: Good, Better, Best," *Organizational Dynamics* (Winter 1985), pp. 26–40.

[35] See Steven Kerr and John Jermier, "Substitutes for Leadership: Their Meaning and Measurement," *Organizational Behavior and Human Performance*, vol. 22 (1978), pp. 375–403; Jon P. Howell and Peter W. Dorfman, "Leadership and Substitutes for Leadership Among Professional and Nonprofessional Workers," *Journal of Applied Behavioral Science*, vol. 22 (1986), pp. 29–46.

[36] An early presentation of the theory is F. Dansereau Jr., G. Graen, and W. J. Haga, "A Vertical Dyad Linkage Approach to Leadership Within Formal Organizations: A Longitudinal Investigation of the Role-Making Process," *Organizational Behavior and Human Performance*, vol. 13, pp. 46–78.

[37] This discussion is based on Yukl, op. cit., pp. 117–22.

[38] Ibid.

[39] Victor H. Vroom and Arthur G. Jago, *The New Leadership: Managing Participation in Organizations* (Englewood Cliffs, NJ: Prentice-Hall, 1988). This is based on earlier work by Victor H. Vroom, "A New Look in Managerial Decision-Making," *Organizational Dynamics* (Spring 1973), pp. 66–80; and Victor H. Vroom and Phillip Yetton, *Leadership and Decision-Making* (Pittsburgh: University of Pittsburgh Press, 1973).

[40] Vroom and Jago, op. cit.

[41] For a related discussion, see Schein, op. cit.

[42] For a review, see Yukl, op. cit.

[43] See the discussion by Victor H. Vroom, "Leadership and the Decision-Making Process," *Organizational Dynamics*, vol. 28 (2000), pp. 82–94.

[44] Among the popular books addressing this point of view are Warren Bennis and Burt Nanus, *Leaders: The Strategies for Taking Charge* (New York: Harper Business 1997); Max DePree, *Leadership Is an Art* (New York: Doubleday, 1989); and Kouzes and Posner, op. cit. (2002).

[45] These terms are from James MacGregor Burns, *Leadership* (New York: Harper & Row, 1978), and further developed by Bernard Bass, *Leadership and Performance Beyond Expectations* (New York: Free Press, 1985), and Bernard M. Bass, "Leadership: Good, Better, Best," *Organizational Dynamics* (Winter 1985), pp. 26–40. See also Bernard M. Bass, "Does the Transactional-Transformational Leadership Paradigm Transcend Organizational and National Boundaries?" *American Psychologist*, vol. 52 (February 1997), pp. 130–39.

[46] Daniel Goleman, "Leadership That Gets Results," *Harvard Business Review* (March/April 2000), pp. 78–90. See also his books, *Emotional Intelligence* (New York: Bantam Books, 1995) and *Working with Emotional Intelligence* (New York: Bantam Books, 1998).

[47] Daniel Goleman, Annie McKee, and Richard E. Boyatzis, *Primal Leadership: Realizing the Power of Emotional Intelligence* (Boston, MA: Harvard Business School Press, 2002), p. 3.

[48] Daniel Goleman, "What Makes a Leader?" *Harvard Business Review* (November–December 1998), pp. 93–102.

[49] Goleman, op. cit., 1998.

[50] Information from "Women and Men, Work, and Power," *Fast Company*, issue 13 (1998), p. 71.

[51] Jane Shibley Hyde, "The Gender Similarities—Hypothesis," *American Psychologist*, vol. 60, no. 6 (2005), pp. 581–92.

[52] A. H. Eagley, S. J. Daran, and M. G. Makhijani, "Gender and the Effectiveness of Leaders: A Meta-Analysis," *Psychological Bulletin*, vol. 117 (1995), pp. 125–45.

[53] Research on gender issues in leadership is reported in Sally Helgesen, *The Female Advantage: Women's Ways of Leadership* (New York: Doubleday, 1990); Judith B. Rosener, "Ways Women Lead, "*Harvard Business Review* (November/December 1990), pp. 119–25; and Alice H. Eagley, Steven J. Karau, and Blair T. Johnson, "Gender and Leadership Style Among School Principals: A Meta Analysis," *Administrative Science Quarterly*, vol. 27 (1992), pp. 76–102; Jean Lipman-Blumen, *Connective Leadership: Managing in a Changing World* (New York: Oxford University Press, 1996); Alice H. Eagley, Mary C. Johannesen-Smith, and Marloes L. van Engen, "Transformational, Transactional and Laissez-Faire Leadership: A Meta-Analysis of Women and Men, *Psychological Bulletin*, vol. 124, no. 4 (2003), pp. 569–91; and Carol Hymowitz, "Too Many Women Fall for Stereotypes of Selves, Study Says," *Wall Street Journal* (October 24, 2005), p. B.1.

[54] Ibid.

[55] Eagley et al., op. cit.; Hymowitz, op. cit.; Rosener, op. cit.; Vroom, op. cit.; Herminia Ibarra and Otilia Obodaru, "Women and the Vision Thing," *Harvard Business Review* (January, 2009): Reprint R0901E.

[56] Ibarra and Obodaru, op. cit.

[57] Quote from "As Leaders, Women Rule," *BusinessWeek* (November 2, 2000), pp. 75–84. Rosabeth Moss Kanter is the author of *Men and Women of the Corporation*, 2nd ed. (New York: Basic Books, 1993).

[58] Rosener, op. cit.

[59] For debate on whether some transformational leadership qualities tend to be associated more with female than male leaders, see "Debate: Ways Women and Men Lead," *Harvard Business Review* (January–February 1991), pp. 150–60.

[60] Hyde, op. cit.; Hymowitz, op. cit.

[61] Julie Bennett, "Women Get a Boost Up that Tall Leadership Ladder," *Wall Street Journal* (June 10, 2008), p. D6.

[62] Based on the discussion by John W. Dienhart and Terry Thomas, "Ethical Leadership: A Primer on Ethical Responsibility," in John R. Schermerhorn, Jr., *Management*, 7th ed. (New York: Wiley, 2003).

[63] Vroom and Jago, op. cit.

[64] Schein, op. cit.

[65] James MacGregor Burns, *Transforming Leadership: A New Pursuit of Happiness* (New York: Atlantic Monthly Press, 2003); information from Christopher Caldwell, book review, *International Herald Tribune* (April 29, 2003), p. 18.

[66] See Nitin Nohria, "The Big Question: What Should We Teach Our Business Leaders?" *Bloomberg BusinessWeek* (November 14–20, 2011), p. 68.

[67] Ibid.

[68] Fred Luthans and Bruce Avolio, "Authentic Leadership: A Positive Development Approach," in K. S. Cameron, J. E. Dutton, and R. E. Quinn, eds., *Positive Organizational Scholarship* (San Francisco: Berrett-Koehler, 2003), pp. 241–58.

[69] Doug May, Adrian Chan, Timothy Hodges, and Bruce Avolio, "Developing the Moral Component of Authentic Leadership," *Organizational Dynamics*, vol. 32 (2003), pp. 247–60.

[70] See Arménio Rego, Filipa Sousa, Carla Marques, and Miguel Pina e Cunha, "Authentic Leadership Promoting Employee's Capital and Creativity," *Journal of Business Research*, vol. 65 (2012), pp. 429–37.

[71] Peter F. Drucker, "Leadership: More Doing than Dash," *Wall Street Journal* (January 6, 1988), p. 16. For a compendium of writings on leadership, sponsored by the Drucker Foundation, see Frances Hesselbein, Marshall Goldsmith, and Richard Beckhard, *Leader of the Future* (San Francisco: Jossey-Bass, 1997).

[72] Quote from ibid.

[73] Ibid.

[74] Fred E. Fiedler and Martin M. Chemers, *Improving Leadership Effectiveness: The Leader Match Concept*, 2nd ed. (New York: Wiley, 1984). Used by permission.

[75] Victor H. Vroom and Arthur G. Jago, *The New Leadership* (Englewood Cliffs, NJ: Prentice-Hall, 1988). Used by permission.

### Feature Notes

Follow the Story—Information and quotes from Lorraine Monroe, "Leadership Is about Making Vision Happen—What I Call 'Vision Acts,'" *Fast Company* (March 2001), p. 98; Lorraine Monroe Leadership Institute website: www.lorrainemonroe.com. See also, Lorraine Monroe, *Nothing's Impossible: Leadership Lessons from Inside and Outside the Classroom* (New York: PublicAffairs Books, 1999), and *The Monroe Doctrine: An ABC Guide to What Great Bosses Do* (New York: PublicAffairs Books, 2003).

Facts for Analysis—Information from "Many U.S. Employees Have Negative Attitudes to Their Jobs, Employers and Top Managers,"

Harris Poll #38 (May 6, 2005), retrieved from www.harrisinteractive.com.

### Photo Essay Notes

Recommended Reading—See also Gary Hamel, "The Purpose of Power," *Wall Street Journal* (May 11, 2011): wsj.com. Football Quarterbacks—Andrew M. Carton and Ashleigh Shelby Rosette, "Explaining Bias against Black Leaders: Integrating Theory on Information Processing and Goal-Based Stereotyping," *Academy of Management Journal*, vol. 56, no. 6 (2011), pp. 1141–58. Martin Luther King, Jr.—Full texts of the "I Have a Dream" speech are available online; see, for example, www.usconstitution.net/dream.html. Mahatma Gandhi—Information from "140 Years Ago: Civil but Disobedient," *Smithsonian* (October 2009), p. 20.

## Chapter 15

### Endnotes

[1] Information from Andrew Ward, "Spanx Queen Firms Up the Bottom Line," *Financial Times* (November 30, 2006), p. 7; and Simona Covel, "A Dated Industry Gets a Modern Makeover," *Wall Street Journal* (August 7, 2008), p. B9.

[2] See, for example, Ram Charan, *Know-How: The 8 Skills that Separate People Who Perform from Those that Don't* (New York: Crown Business, 2007); and Ram Charan, "Six Personality Traits of a Leader," www.career-advice.monster.com (accessed August 6, 2008).

[3] Ibid.

[4] Quotes from Charan, op. cit., 2008.

[5] Max DePree, "An Old Pro's Wisdom: It Begins with a Belief in People," *New York Times* (September 10, 1989), p. F2; Max DePree, *Leadership Is an Art* (New York: Doubleday, 1989); David Woodruff, "Herman Miller: How Green Is My Factory," *BusinessWeek* (September 16, 1991), pp. 54–56; and Max DePree, *Leadership Jazz* (New York: Doubleday, 1992); quote from www.depree.org/html/maxdepree.html.

[6] This example is reported in *Esquire* (December 1986), p. 243. Emphasis is added to the quotation. *Note:* Nussbaum became director of the Labor Department's Women's Bureau during the Clinton administration and subsequently moved to the AFL–CIO as head of the Women's Bureau.

[7] degree.org, op. cit.

[8] See H. R. Schiffman, *Sensation and Perception: An Integrated Approach*, 3d ed. (New York: Wiley, 1990).

[9] John P. Kotter, "The Psychological Contract: Managing the Joining Up Process," *California Management Review*, vol. 15 (Spring 1973), pp. 91–99; Denise Rousseau, ed., *Psychological Contracts in Organizations* (San Francisco: Jossey-Bass, 1995); Denise Rousseau, "Changing the Deal While Keeping the People," *Academy of Management Executive*, vol. 10 (1996), pp. 50–59; and Denise Rousseau and Rene Schalk, eds., *Psychological Contracts in Employment: Cross-Cultural Perspectives* (San Francisco: Jossey-Bass, 2000).

[10] A good review is E. L. Jones, ed., *Attribution: Perceiving the Causes of Behavior* (Morristown, NJ: General Learning Press, 1972). See also John H. Harvey and Gifford Weary, "Current Issues in Attribution Theory and Research," *Annual Review of Psychology*, vol. 35 (1984), pp. 427–59.

[11] These examples are from Natasha Josefowitz, *Paths to Power* (Reading, MA: Addison-Wesley, 1980), p. 60. For more on gender issues, see Gray N. Powell, ed., *Handbook of Gender and Work* (Thousand Oaks, CA: Sage, 1999).

[12] Information from "Misconceptions about Women in the Global Arena Keep Their Numbers Low," Catalyst Study: www.catalystwomen.org/home.html.

[13] The classic work is Dewitt C. Dearborn and Herbert A. Simon, "Selective Perception: A Note on the Departmental Identification of Executives," *Sociometry*, vol. 21 (1958), pp. 140–44. See also J. P. Walsh, "Selectivity and Selective Perception: Belief Structures and Information Processing, *Academy of Management Journal*, vol. 24 (1988), pp. 453–70.

[14] Quotation from Sheila O'Flanagan, "Underestimate Casual Dressers at Your Peril," *Irish Times* (July 22, 2005). See also Christina Binkley, "How to Pull Off 'CEO Casual,'" *Wall Street Journal* (August 7, 2008), pp. D1–D8.

[15] See William L. Gardner and Mark J. Martinko, "Impression Management in Organizations," *Journal of Management* (June 1988), p. 332.

[16] Sandy Wayne and Robert Liden, "Effects of Impression Management on Performance Ratings," *Academy of Management Journal* (February 2005), pp. 232–52.

[17] See M. R. Barrick and M. K. Mount, "The Big Five Personality Dimensions and Job Performance: A Meta-Analysis," *Personnel Psychology*, vol. 44 (1991), pp. 1–26.

[18] Ibid.

[19] For a good summary see Stephen P. Robbins and Timothy A. Judge, *Organizational Behavior*, 12th ed. (Upper Saddle River, NJ: Prentice-Hall), 2007, p. 112.

[20] Carl G. Jung, *Psychological Types*, H. G. Baynes trans. (Princeton, NJ: Princeton University Press, 1971).

[21] I. Briggs-Myers, *Introduction to Type* (Palo Alto, CA: Consulting Psychologists Press, 1980).

[22] See, for example, William L. Gardner and Mark J. Martinko, "Using the Myers-Briggs Type Indicator to Study Managers: A Literature Review and Research Agenda," *Journal of Management*, vol. 22 (1996), pp. 45–83; Naomi L. Quenk, *Essentials of Myers-Briggs Type Indicator Assessment* (New York: Wiley, 2000).

[23] See the discussion in John R. Schermerhorn, Jr., James G. Hunt, Richard N. Osborn, and Mary UhlBlen, *Organizational Behavior*, 11th Edition (Hoboken, N.J.: John Wiley & Sons, 2010), pp. 31–37.

[24] J. B. Rotter, "Generalized Expectancies for Internal versus External Control of Reinforcement," *Psychological Monographs*, vol. 80 (1966), pp. 1–28; see also Thomas W. Ng, Kelly L. Sorensen, and Lillian T. Eby, "Cocos of Control at Work: A Meta-Analysis," *Journal of Organizational Behavior* (2006).

[25] T. W. Adorno, E. Frenkel-Brunswick, D. J. Levinson, and R. N. Sanford, *The Authoritarian Personality* (New York: Harper-Row, 1950).

[26] Niccolo Machiavelli, *The Prince*, trans. George Bull (Middlesex, UK: Penguin, 1961).

[27] Richard Christie and Florence L. Geis, *Studies in Machiavellianism* (New York: Academic Press, 1970).

[28] See M. Snyder, *Public Appearances/Private Realities: The Psychology of Self-Monitoring* (New York: Freeman, 1987).

[29] The classic work is Meyer Friedman and Ray Roseman, *Type A Behavior and Your Heart* (New York: Knopf, 1974).

[30] Information and quote from Joann S. Lublin, "How One Black Woman Lands Her Top Jobs: Risks and Networking," *Wall Street Journal* (March 4, 2003), p. B1.

[31] Martin Fishbein and Icek Ajzen, *Belief, Attitude, Intention and Behavior: An Introduction to Theory and Research* (Reading, MA: Addison-Wesley, 1973).

[32] See Leon Festinger, *A Theory of Cognitive Dissonance* (Palo Alto, CA: Stanford University Press, 1957).

[33] Timothy A. Judge and Allan H. Church, "Job Satisfaction: Research and Practice," Chapter 7 in Cary L. Cooper and Edwin A. Locke, eds., *Industrial and Organizational Psychology: Linking Theory with Practice* (Malden, MA: Blackwell Business, 2000); and Timothy

A. Judge, "Promote Job Satisfaction through Mental Challenge," Chapter 6 in Edwin A. Locke, ed., *The Blackwell Handbook of Organizational Behavior* (Malden, MA: Blackwell, 2004).

[34] See ibid; Timothy A. Judge, "Promote Job Satisfaction through Mental Challenge," Chapter 6 in Edwin A. Locke, ed., *The Blackwell Handbook of Organizational Behavior* (Malden, MA: Blackwell, 2004); "U.S. Employees More Dissatisfied with Their Jobs," *Associated Press* (February 28, 2005), retrieved from www.msnbc.com; "U.S. Job Satisfaction Keeps Falling, The Conference Board Reports Today," The Conference Board (February 28, 2005), retrieved from www.conference-board.org; and, "Americans' Job Satisfaction Falls to Record Low," *USA Today* (January 5, 2010): usatoday.com (accessed March 27, 2012).

[35] Data reported in Jeannine Aversa, "Happy Workers Harder to Find," *Columbus Dispatch* (January 5, 2010), pp. A1, A4. Data from "U.S. Job Satisfaction the Lowest in Two Decades," press release, The Conference Board (January 5, 2010), retrieved January 6, 2010 from: http://www.conference-board.org; "Americans' Job Satisfaction Falls to Record Lows," op. cit.

[36] Judge and Church, op. cit., 2000; Judge, op. cit., 2004.

[37] Reported in "When Loyalty Erodes, So Do Profits," *BusinessWeek* (August 13, 2001), p. 8.

[38] Data reported in "When Loyalty Erodes, So Do Profits," *Business-Week* (August 13, 2001), p. 8.

[39] Tony DiRomualdo, "The High Cost of Employee Disengagement" (July 7, 2004): www.wistechnology.com.

[40] See "The Things They Do for Love," *Harvard Business Review* (December 2004), pp. 19–20.

[41] Information from Sue Shellenbarger, "Employers Are Finding It Doesn't Cost Much to Make a Staff Happy," *Wall Street Journal* (November 19, 1997), p. B1. See also "Job Satisfaction on the Decline," The Conference Board (July 2002).

[42] See Mark C. Bolino and William H. Turnley, "Going the Extra Mile: Cultivating and Managing Employee Citizenship Behavior," *Academy of Management Executive*, vol. 17 (August 2003), pp. 60–67.

[43] Dennis W. Organ, *Organizational Citizenship Behavior: The Good Soldier Syndrome* (Lexington, MA: Lexington Books, 1988).

[44] These relationships are discussed in Charles N. Greene, "The Satisfaction-Performance Controversy," *Business Horizons*, vol. 15 (1982), p. 31. Michelle T. Iaffaldano and Paul M. Muchinsky, "Job Satisfaction and Job Performance: A Meta-Analysis," *Psychological Bulletin*, vol. 97 (1985), pp. 251–73; Judge, op. cit., 2004; and, Michael Riketta, "The Causal Relation between Job Attitudes and Performance: A Meta-Analysis of Panel Studies," *Journal of Applied Psychology*, vol. 93, no. 2 (March, 2008), pp. 472–81.

[45] This discussion follows conclusions in Judge, op. cit., 2004.

[46] Damon Darlin and Matt Richtel, "Chairwoman Leaves Hewlett in Spying Furor," *Wall Street Journal* (September 23, 2006), pp. A1, A9.

[47] Daniel Goleman, "Leadership That Gets Results," *Harvard Business Review* (March–April 2000), pp. 78–90. See also his books *Emotional Intelligence* (New York: Bantam Books, 1995) and *Working with Emotional Intelligence* (New York: Bantam Books, 1998).

[48] Goleman, op. cit., 1998.

[49] See Robert G. Lord, Richard J. Klimoski, and Ruth Knafer (eds.), *Emotions in the Workplace; Understanding the Structure and Role of Emotions in Organizational Behavior* (San Francisco: Jossey-Bass, 2002); and Roy L. Payne and Cary L. Cooper (eds.), *Emotions at Work: Theory Research and Applications for Management* (Chichester, UK: Wiley, 2004); and, Daniel Goleman and Richard Boyatzis, "Social Intelligence and the Biology of Leadership," *Harvard Business Review* (September 2008), Reprint R0809E.

[50] Joyce E. Bono and Remus Ilies, "Charisma, Positive Emotions and Mood Contagion," *Leadership Quarterly*, vol. 17 (2006), pp. 317–34; and Goleman and Boyatzis, op. cit.

[51] Bono and Ilies, op. cit.

[52] See "Charm Offensive: Why America's CEOs Are So Eager to Be Loved," *BusinessWeek* (June 26, 2006): retrieved from businessweek.com (September 20, 2008).

[53] See Arthur P. Brief, Randall S. Schuler, and Mary Van Sell, *Managing Job Stress* (Boston: Little, Brown, 1981), pp. 7, 8.

[54] Data from Michael Mandel, "The Real Reasons You're Working So Hard," *BusinessWeek* (October 3, 2005), pp. 60–70; "Many U.S. Employees Have Negative Attitudes to Their Jobs, Employers and Top Managers," The Harris Poll #38 (May 6, 2005), retrieved from www.harrisinteractive.com.

[55] Data from Sue Shellenbarger, "If You Need to Work Better, Maybe Try Working Less," *Wall Street Journal* (September 23, 2009), p. D1.

[56] Sue Shellenbarger, "Do We Work More or Not? Either Way, We Feel Frazzled," *Wall Street Journal* (July 30, 1997), p. B1.

[57] Michael Mandel, "The Real Reasons You're Working So Hard," *BusinessWeek* (October 3, 2005), pp. 60–70; "Many U.S. Employees Have Negative Attitudes to Their Jobs, Employers and Top Managers," The Harris Poll #38 (May 6, 2005), retrieved from www.harrisinteractive.com.

[58] Carol Hymowitz, "Impossible Expectations and Unfulfilling Work Stress Managers, Too," *Wall Street Journal* (January 16, 2001), p. B1.

[59] See Steve M. Jex, *Stress and Job Performance* (San Francisco: Jossey-Bass, 1998).

[60] See "workplace violence" discussed by Richard V. Denenberg and Mark Braverman, *The Violence-Prone Workplace* (Ithaca, NY: Cornell University Press, 1999).

[61] See Daniel C. Ganster and Larry Murphy, "Workplace Interventions to Prevent Stress-Related Illness: Lessons from Research and Practice," Chapter 2 in Cooper and Locke (eds.), op. cit., 2000; Long working hours linked to high blood pressure," www.Gn.com/2006/Health (retrieved August 29, 2006).

[62] Information and quote from Shellenbarger, op. cit., 2009.

[63] Instrument from Julian P. Rotter, "External Control and Internal Control," *Psychology Today* (June 1971), p. 42. Used by permission.

[64] Adapted from Roy J. Lewicki, Donald D. Bowen, Douglas T. Hall, and Francine S. Hall, "What Do You Value in Work?" *Experiences in Management and Organizational Behavior*, 3rd ed. (New York: Wiley, 1988), pp. 23–26. Used by permission.

### Feature Notes

Follow the Story—Information from Leigh Buchanan, "Life Lessons," *Inc.* (retrieved June 6, 2006: from www.inc.com/magazine). "A Fortune Coined from Cheerfulness Entrepreneurship," *Financial Times* (May 20, 2009); and, www.lifeisgood.com/about.

Ethics on the Line—Information from Victoria Knight, "Personality Tests as Hiring Tools," *Wall Street Journal* (March 15, 2006), p. B3C.

Facts for Analysis—Information from "Young, Unemployed and Optimistic: Coming of Age Slowly in a Tough Economy," Pew Research Center (February 9, 2012): pewsocialtrends.org (accessed March 27, 2002); and, "A Star Customer Falls Back to Earth," *Bloomberg BusinessWeek* (March 26–April 1, 2012), p. 19.

### Photo Essay Notes

Root Learning—Information and quote from Kelly K. Spors, "Top Small Workplaces 2009," *Wall Street Journal* (September 28, 2009), p. R7. Recommended Reading—Quotes from Susan Bulkeley Butler, *Women Count: A Guide to Changing the World* (Lafayette, IN: Purdue

University Press), p. 2. Luck—Information from Lauren Weber, "Luck Is Hard Work," The *Wall Street Journal* (March 14, 2012), p. B8.

## Chapter 16

### Endnotes

[1] Information and quotes from David A. Kaplan, "#1 SAS: The Best Company to Work For," *Fortune* (January 26, 2010), Kindle edition.

[2] Conference Board research reported in Patricia Soldati, "Employee Engagement: What Exactly Is It?" *Management Issues* (March 8, 2007): www.managementissues.com (retrieved August 10, 2008). Yum Brands information from Erin White, "How Surveying Workers Can Pay Off," *Wall Street Journal* (June 18, 2007), p. B3.

[3] Information from "Executive Briefing: A New Approach for Airlines," *Wall Street Journal* (May 12, 2008), p. R3. See also Greg J. Bamber, Jody Hoffer Gittel, Thomas A. Kochan, and Andrew Von Nordenflycht, *Up in the Air: How the Airlines Can Improve Performance by Engaging Their Employees* (Ithaca, NY: Cornell University Press, 2009).

[4] Information from Melinda Beck, "If at First You Don't Succeed, You're in Excellent Company," *Wall Street Journal* (April 29, 2008), p. D1.

[5] Information from Jerry Krueger and Emily Killham, "At Work, Feeling Good Matters," *Gallup Management Journal* (December 8, 2005): gmj.gallup.com; and, Ellen Wulfhorst, "Morale Is Low, Say Quarter of Employers in Poll," *Reuters Bulletin* (November 17, 2009): reuters.com.

[6] See Paul Glader, "Firms Move Gingerly to Remove Salary Cuts," *Wall Street Journal* (March 1, 2010), pp. B, B7.

[7] See Abraham H. Maslow, *Eupsychian Management* (Homewood, IL: Richard D. Irwin, 1965); Abraham H. Maslow, *Motivation and Personality*, 2d ed. (New York: Harper-Row, 1970). For a research perspective, see Mahmoud A. Wahba and Lawrence G. Bridwell, "Maslow Reconsidered: A Review of Research on the Need Hierarchy," *Organizational Behavior and Human Performance*, vol. 16 (1976), pp. 212–40.

[8] See Clayton P. Alderfer, *Existence, Relatedness, and Growth* (New York: Free Press, 1972).

[9] The two-factor theory is in Frederick Herzberg, Bernard Mausner, and Barbara Block Synderman, *The Motivation to Work*, 2d ed. (New York: Wiley, 1967); Frederick Herzberg, "One More Time: How Do You Motivate Employees?" *Harvard Business Review* (January–February 1968), pp. 53–62, and reprinted as an HBR classic (September–October 1987), pp. 109–20.

[10] Critical reviews are provided by Robert J. House and Lawrence A. Wigdor, "Herzberg's Dual-Factor Theory of Job Satisfaction and Motivation: A Review of the Evidence and a Criticism," *Personnel Psychology*, vol. 20 (Winter 1967), pp. 369–89; Steven Kerr, Anne Harlan, and Ralph Stogdill, "Preference for Motivator and Hygiene Factors in a Hypothetical Interview Situation," *Personnel Psychology*, vol. 27 (Winter 1974), pp. 109–24.

[11] Frederick Herzberg, "Workers' Needs: The Same Around the World," *Industry Week* (September 21, 1987), pp. 29–32.

[12] For a collection of McClelland's work, see David C. McClelland, *The Achieving Society* (New York: Van Nostrand, 1961); "Business Drive and National Achievement," *Harvard Business Review*, vol. 40 (July–August 1962), pp. 99–112; David C. McClelland and David H. Burnham, "Power Is the Great Motivator," *Harvard Business Review* (March–April 1976), pp. 100–10; David C. McClelland, *Human Motivation* (Glenview, IL: Scott, Foresman, 1985); David C. McClelland and Richard E. Boyatsis, "The Leadership Motive Pattern and Long-Term Success in Management," *Journal of Applied Psychology*, vol. 67 (1982), pp. 737–43.

[13] Information from money.cnn.com/2011/04/19/news/economy/ceo_pay/index.htm; aflcio.org/corporatewatch/paywatch/.

[14] See, for example, J. Stacy Adams, "Toward an Understanding of Inequity," *Journal of Abnormal and Social Psychology*, vol. 67 (1963), pp. 422–36; J. Stacy Adams, "Inequity in Social Exchange," in L. Berkowitz, ed., *Advances in Experimental Social Psychology*, vol. 2 (New York: Academic Press, 1965), pp. 267–300.

[15] See, for example, J. W. Harder, "Play for Pay: Effects of Inequity in a Pay-for-Performance Context," *Administrative Science Quarterly*, vol. 37 (1992), pp. 321–35.

[16] L. A. Clark, D. A. Foote, W. R. Clark, and J. L. Lewis, "Equity Sensitivity: A Triadic Measure and Outcome/Input Perspectives. *Journal of Managerial Issues*, vol. 22, no. 3 (2010), pp. 286–305; R.C., Huseman, J. D. Hatfield, and E.W. Miles, "A New Perspective on Equity Theory: The Equity Sensitivity Construct," *Academy of Management Review*, vol. 12, no. 2, pp. 222–34.

[17] Victor H. Vroom, *Work and Motivation* (New York: Wiley, 1964; republished by Jossey-Bass, 1994).

[18] Ibid.

[19] Information and quotes from "The Boss: Goal by Goal," *The New York Times* (August 31, 2008), p. 10.

[20] The work on goal-setting theory is well summarized in Edwin A. Locke and Gary P. Latham, *Goal Setting: A Motivational Technique That Works!* (Englewood Cliffs, NJ: Prentice Hall, 1984). See also Edwin A. Locke, Kenneth N. Shaw, Lisa A. Saari, and Gary P. Latham, "Goal Setting and Task Performance 1969–1980," *Psychological Bulletin*, vol. 90 (1981), pp. 125–52; Mark E. Tubbs, "Goal Setting: A Meta-Analytic Examination of the Empirical Evidence," *Journal of Applied Psychology*, vol. 71 (1986), pp. 474–83; Gary P. Latham and Edwin A. Locke, "Self-Regulation Through Goal Setting," *Organizational Behavior and Human Decision Processes*, vol. 50 (1991), pp. 212–47; and Terence R. Mitchell, Kenneth R. Thompson, and Jane George-Falvy, "Goal Setting: Theory and Practice," Chapter 9 in Cary L. Cooper and Edwin A. Locke (eds), *Industrial and Organizational Psychology: Linking Theory with Practice* (Malden, MA: Blackwell Business, 2000), pp. 211–49.

[21] Albert Bandura, *Social Learning Theory* (Englewood Cliffs, NJ: Prentice-Hall, 1977); and Albert Bandura, *Self-Efficacy: The Exercise of Control* (New York: W. H. Freeman, 1997).

[22] Quote from www.des.emory.edu/mfp/self--efficacy.html.

[23] Beck, op. cit.

[24] Bandura, op. cit., 1977 and 1997.

[25] E. L. Thorndike, *Animal Intelligence* (New York: Macmillan, 1911), p. 244.

[26] See B. F. Skinner, *Walden Two* (New York: Macmillan, 1948); *Science and Human Behavior* (New York: Macmillan, 1953); *Contingencies of Reinforcement* (New York: Appleton-Century-Crofts, 1969).

[27] Fred Luthans and Robert Kreitner, *Organizational Behavior Modification* (Glenview, IL: Scott, Foresman, 1975); and Fred Luthans and Robert Kreitner, *Organizational Behavior Modification and Beyond* (Glenview, IL: Scott, Foresman, 1985); see also Fred Luthans and Alexander D. Stajkovic, "Reinforce for Performance: The Need to Go Beyond Pay and Even Rewards," *Academy of Management Executive*, vol. 13 (1999), pp. 49–57.

[28] Knowledge@Wharton, "The Importance of Being Richard Branson," Wharton School Publishing (June 3, 2005): www.whartonsp.com.

[29] Information and quote from Frederik Broden, "Motivate Without Spending Millions," *Fortune*, Kindle edition (April 13, 2010). See also David Novak, *The Education of an Accidental CEO: Lessons Learned from the Trailer Park to the Corner Office* (New York: Crown Business, 2007); and, D. Novak, *Taking People with You: The Only Way to Make BIG Things Happen* (New York: Portfolio Penguin, 2012).

30 See Luthans and Kreitner, op. cit.

31 Ibid.

32 For a review, see Arne L. Kalleberg, "The Mismatched Worker: When People Don't Fit their Jobs," *Academy of Management Perspectives* (February 2008), pp. 24–40.

33 See Frederick W. Taylor, *The Principles of Scientific Management* (New York: W.W. Norton, 1967), originally published by Harper-Brothers in 1911; and, Robert Kanigel, *The One Best Way* (New York: Viking, 1997).

34 Greg R. Oldham and J. Richard Hackman, "Not What It Was and Not What It Will Be: The Future of Job Design Research," *Journal of Organizational Behavior*, vol. 31 (2010), pp. 463–479.

35 See Frederick Herzberg, Bernard Mausner, and Barbara Block Synderman, *The Motivation to Work*, 2d ed. (New York: Wiley, 1967). The quotation is from Frederick Herzberg, "One More Time: How Do You Motivate Employees?" *Harvard Business Review* (January–February 1968), pp. 53–62, and reprinted as an HBR Classic in September–October 1987, pp. 109–20.

36 For a complete description of the core characteristics model, see J. Richard Hackman and Greg R. Oldham, *Work Redesign* (Reading, MA: Addison-Wesley, 1980). See also, Oldham and Hackman, op. cit. (2010).

37 See Allen R. Cohen and Herman Gadon, *Alternative Work Schedules: Integrating Individual and Organizational Needs* (Reading, MA: Addison-Wesley, 1978), p. 125; Simcha Ronen and Sophia B. Primps, "The Compressed Work Week as Organizational Change: Behavioral and Attitudinal Outcomes," *Academy of Management Review*, vol. 6 (1981), pp. 61–74.

38 Sue Shellenbarger, "What Makes a Company a Great Place to Work," *Wall Street Journal* (October 4, 2007), p. D1.

39 Information from Lesli Hicks, "Workers, Employers Praise Their Four-Day Workweek," *Columbus Dispatch* (August 22, 1994), p. 6; and Walsh, op. cit., 2001.

40 For a review, see Wayne F. Cascio, "Managing a Virtual Workplace," *Academy of Management Executive*, vol. 14 (2000), pp. 81–90.

41 Quote from Phil Porter, "Telecommuting Mom Is Part of a National Trend," *Columbus Dispatch* (November 29, 2000), pp. H1, H2.

42 Kris Maher, "Slack U.S. Demand Spurs Cut in Work Hours," *Wall Street Journal* (January 8, 2008), *Career Journal*, p. 29.

43 Quotes from Sudeep Reddy, "Wary Companies Rely on Temporary Workers," *The Wall Street Journal* (March 6–7, 2010), p. A. 4.

44 Michael Orey, "They're Employees, No, They're Not," *Business-Week* (November 16, 2009), pp. 73–74.

45 This survey was developed from a set of "Gallup Engagement Questions" presented in John Thackray, "Feedback for Real," *Gallup Management Journal* (March 15, 2001), gmj.gallup.com/management, accessed: (June 5, 2003); data reported from James K. Harter, "The Cost of Disengaged Workers," *Gallup Poll* (March 13, 2001).

46 Developed from Brian Dumaine, "Why Do We Work?" *Fortune* (December 26, 1994), pp. 196–204.

### Feature Notes

Follow the Story—Information from Howard Schultz, "Onward: How Starbucks Fought for Its Life without Losing Its Soul" (March 29, 2011, www.youtube.com; http://money.cnn.com/galleries/2011/fortune/1111/gallery.business_person_year.fortune/2.html); and, "Starbucks Refuses to Cut Benefits," CNNMoney (April 24, 2010).

Ethics on the Line—Information from Jared Sandberg, "Why You May Regret Looking at Papers Left on the Office Copier," *Wall Street Journal* (June 20, 2006), p. B1.

Facts for Analysis—Information based on an analysis conducted by the Research Institute of Labour and Social Affairs in a project titled "Measuring the Quality of Working Life" (Retrieved from http://www.eurofound.europa.eu/ewco/2006/01/CZ0601NU04.htm).

### Photo Essays Notes

Recommended Reading—Information from Leslie Kwoh, "Difficult Bosses Hurt Workers' Motivation," *The Wall Street Journal* (February 29, 2012), p. B8. Co-Working Spaces—Information and quotes from Emily Glazer, "Can't Afford an Office? Rent a Desk for $275," *The Wall Street Journal* (October 4, 2011), p. B4.

## Chapter 17

### Endnotes

1 Information and quotes from Allen St. John, "Racing's Fastest Pit Crew," *Wall Street Journal* (May 9, 2008), p. W4; and, Bonnie Berkowitz, "Pit Crews Keep NASCAR Racers on Track," *Columbus Dispatch* (May 28, 2008), p. D6.

2 Information from Scott Thurm, "Teamwork Raises Everyone's Game," *Wall Street Journal* (November 7, 2005), p. B7.

3 Ibid.

4 Chambers quote from Charles O'Reilly III and Jeffrey Pfeffer, *Hidden Value: How Great Companies Achieve Extraordinary Results through Ordinary People* (Boston: Harvard Business School Publishing, 2000), p. 4; other quotes from www.quotegarden.com.

5 For a discussion, see Jon R. Katzenbach and Douglas K. Smith, *The Wisdom of Teams: Creating the High Performance Organization* (Boston: Harvard Business School Press, 1993).

6 Lynda C. McDermott, Nolan Brawley, and William A. Waite, *World-Class Teams: Working across Borders* (New York: Wiley, 1998), p. 5; "White Collar Workers Shoulder Together—Like It or Not," *BusinessWeek* (April 28, 2008), p. 58.

7 Katzenbach and Smith, op. cit.

8 See, for example, Edward E. Lawler III, Susan Albers Mohrman, and Gerald E. Ledford Jr., *Employee Involvement and Total Quality Management: Practices and Results in Fortune 1000 Companies* (San Francisco: Jossey-Bass, 1992); Susan A. Mohrman, Susan A. Cohen, and Monty A. Mohrman, *Designing Team-based Organizations: New Forms for Knowledge Work* (San Francisco: Jossey-Bass, 1995).

9 Joe Lindsey, "Nine Riders, and Nearly as Many Jobs." *Wall Street Journal* (July 9, 2008): www.online.wsj.com.

10 Harold J. Leavitt, "Suppose We Took Groups More Seriously," in Eugene L. Cass and Frederick G. Zimmer (Eds.), *Man and Work in Society* (New York: Van Nostrand Reinhold, 1975), pp. 67–77.

11 See Marvin E. Shaw, *Group Dynamics: The Psychology of Small Group Behavior*, 2d ed. (New York: McGraw-Hill, 1976); Harold J. Leavitt, "Suppose We Took Groups More Seriously," in Eugene L. Cass and Frederick G. Zimmer, eds., *Man and Work in Society* (New York: Van Nostrand Reinhold, 1975), pp. 67–77.

12 For insights on how to conduct effective meetings, see Mary A. De Vries, *How to Run a Meeting* (New York: Penguin, 1994).

13 A classic work is Bib Latané, Kipling Williams, and Stephen Harkins, "Many Hands Make Light the Work: The Causes and Consequences of Social Loafing," *Journal of Personality and Social Psychology*, vol. 37 (1978), pp. 822–32.

14 John M. George, "Extrinsic and Intrinsic Origins of Perceived Social Loafing in Organizations," *Academy of Management Journal* (March 1992), pp. 191–202; and W. Jack Duncan, "Why Some People Loaf in Groups While Others Loaf Alone," *Academy of Management Executive*, vol. 8 (1994), pp. 79–80.

[15] Survey reported in "Meetings among Top Ten Time Wasters," *San Francisco Business Times* (April 7, 2003): www.bizjournals.com/sanfrancisco/stories/2003/04/07/daily21.html.

[16] Developed from Eric Matson, "The Seven Sins of Deadly Meetings," *Fast Company* (April/May 1996).

[17] The "linking pin" concept is introduced in Rensis Likert, *New Patterns of Management* (New York: McGraw-Hill, 1962).

[18] See Susan D. Van Raalte, "Preparing the Task Force to Get Good Results," *S.A.M. Advanced Management Journal*, vol. 47 (Winter 1982), pp. 11–16; Walter Kiechel III, "The Art of the Corporate Task Force," *Fortune* (January 28, 1991), pp. 104–6.

[19] Matt Golosinski, "With Teamwork, Gregg Steinhafel Hits the Bulls Eye at Target," *Kellogg* (Summer 2007), p. 32.

[20] See, for example, Paul S. Goodman, Rukmini Devadas, and Terri L. Griffith Hughson, "Groups and Productivity: Analyzing the Effectiveness of Self-Managing Teams," Chapter 11 in John R. Campbell and Richard J. Campbell, *Productivity in Organizations* (San Francisco: Jossey-Bass, 1988); Jack Orsbrun, Linda Moran, Ed Musslewhite, and John H. Zenger, with Craig Perrin, *Self-Directed Work Teams: The New American Challenge* (Homewood, IL: Business One Irwin, 1990); Dale E. Yeatts and Cloyd Hyten, *High Performing Self-Managed Work Teams* (Thousand Oaks, CA: Sage, 1997).

[21] Greg R. Oldham and J. Richard Hackman, "Not What It Was and Not What It Will Be: The Future of Job Design Research," *Journal of Organizational Behavior*, vol. 31 (2010), pp. 463–479.

[22] See Wayne F. Cascio, "Managing a Virtual Workplace," *Academy of Management Executive*, vol. 14 (2000), pp. 81–90; Sheila Simsarian Webber, "Virtual Teams: A Meta-Analysis," http://www.shrm.org/foundation/findings.asp; Stacie A. Furst, Martha Reeves, Benson Rosen, and Richard S. Blackburn, "Managing the Life Cycle of Virtual Teams," *Academy of Management Executive*, vol. 18 (2004), pp. 6–20; and, J. Richard Hackman and Nancy Katz, "Group Behavior and Performance," Chapter 32 (pp. 1208-1251) in Susan T. Fiske, Daniel T. Gilbert, and Gardner Lindzey (Eds.), *Handbook of Social Psychology*, Fifth Edition (Hoboken, NJ: John Wiley & Sons, 2010).

[23] R. Brent Gallupe and William H. Cooper, "Brainstorming Electronically," *Sloan Management Review* (Winter 1997), pp. 11–21.

[24] Cascio, op. cit.; Hackman and Katz, op. cit.

[25] Quote from Chris Tosic, "Tactics for Remote Teamwork," *Financial Times*, Kindle Edition (February 14, 2010).

[26] See Ibid.; Cascio, op. cit.; Furst et al., op. cit.

[27] Edgar Schein, *Process Consultation* (Reading, MA: Addison-Wesley, 1988), pp. 69–75.

[28] A good overview is William D. Dyer, *Team-Building* (Reading, MA: Addison-Wesley, 1977).

[29] Dennis Berman, "Zap! Pow! Splat!" *BusinessWeek*, Enterprise issue (February 9, 1998), p. ENT22.

[30] For a discussion of effectiveness in the context of top management teams, see Edward E. Lawler III, David Finegold, and Jay A. Conger, "Corporate Boards: Developing Effectiveness at the Top," in Mohrman, op. cit. (1998), pp. 23–50.

[31] Quote from Alex Markels, "Money & Business," *U.S. News online* (October 22, 2006).

[32] Mathew A. Cronin, Laurie R. Weingart, and Gergana Todoroya, "Dynamics in Groups: Are We There Yet?" *Academy of Management Annals*, vol. 5 (June 2011), pp. 571–612.

[33] For a review of research on group effectiveness, see J. Richard Hackman, "The Design of Work Teams," in Jay W. Lorsch (ed.), *Handbook of Organizational Behavior* (Englewood Cliffs, NJ: Prentice-Hall, 1987), pp. 315–42; and J. Richard Hackman, Ruth Wageman, Thomas M. Ruddy, and Charles L. Ray, "Team Effectiveness in Theory and Practice," Chapter 5 in Cary L. Cooper and Edwin A. Locke,

*Industrial and Organizational Psychology: Linking Theory with Practice* (Malden, MA: Blackwell, 2000).

[34] Ibid; Lawler et al., op. cit., 1998; Linda Hill and Michel J. Anteby, "Analyzing Work Groups," *Harvard Business School*, 9-407-032 (August 2007).

[35] Casey Stengel, www.quotegarden.com.

[36] See for example, Warren Watson. "Cultural Diversity's Impact on Interaction Process and Performance" *Academy of Management Journal*, vol. 16 (1993); Christopher Earley and Elaine Mosakowski, "Creating Hybrid Team Structures: An Empirical Test of Transnational Team Functioning," *Academy of Management Journal*, vol. 5 (February 2000), pp. 26–49; Eric Kearney, Diether Gebert, and Sven C. Voilpel, "When and How Diversity Benefits Teams: The Importance of Team Members' Need for Cognition," *Academy of Management Journal*, vol. 52 (2009), pp. 582–98; and Aparna Joshi and Hyuntak Roh, "The Role of Context in Work Team Diversity Research: A Meta-Analytic Approach," *Academy of Management Journal*, vol. 52 (2009), pp. 599–628.

[37] Example from "Designed for Interaction," *Fortune* (January 8, 2001), p. 150.

[38] See, for example, Lynda Gratton and Tamara J. Erickson, "Eight Ways to Build Collaborative Teams," *Harvard Business Review*, Reprint R0711F (November 2007).

[39] Information from Susan Carey, "Racing to Improve," *Wall Street Journal* (March 24, 2006). pp. B1, B6.

[40] Robert D. Hof, "Amazon's Risky Bet," *BusinessWeek* (November 13, 2006), p. 52.

[41] Shaw, op. cit.; and Cronin, Weingart, and Todorova, op. cit.

[42] J. Steven Heinen and Eugene Jacobson, "A Model of Task Group Development in Complex Organizations and a Strategy of Implementation," *Academy of Management Review*, vol. 1 (1976), pp. 98–111; Bruce W. Tuckman, "Developmental Sequence in Small Groups," *Psychological Bulletin*, vol. 63 (1965), pp. 384–99; Bruce W. Tuckman and Mary Ann C. Jensen, "Stages of Small-Group Development Revisited," *Group Organization Studies*, vol. 2 (1977), pp. 419–27.

[43] See, for example, Edgar Schein, *Process Consultation* (Reading, MA: Addison-Wesley, 1988); and Linda C. McDermott, Nolan Brawley, and William A. Waite, *World-Class Teams: Working across Borders* (New York: Wiley, 1998).

[44] For a good discussion, see Robert F. Allen and Saul Pilnick, "Confronting the Shadow Organization: How to Detect and Defeat Negative Norms," *Organizational Dynamics* (Spring 1973), pp. 13–16.

[45] See Schein, op. cit., pp. 76–79.

[46] Ibid.; Shaw, op. cit.

[47] A classic work in this area is K. Benne and P. Sheets, "Functional Roles of Group Members," *Journal of Social Issues*, vol. 2 (1948), pp. 42–47; see also Likert, op. cit., pp. 166–69; Schein, op. cit., pp. 49–56.

[48] Based on John R. Schermerhorn Jr., James G. Hunt, and Richard N. Osborn, *Organizational Behavior*, 9th ed. (New York: Wiley, 2005).

[49] Research on communication networks is found in Alex Bavelas, "Communication Patterns in Task-Oriented Groups," *Journal of the Acoustical Society of America*, vol. 22 (1950), pp. 725–30; Shaw, op. cit.

[50] See Victor H. Vroom and Arthur G. Jago, *The New Leadership: Managing Participation in Organizations* (Englewood Cliffs, NJ: Prentice-Hall, 1988); Victor H. Vroom, "A New Look in Managerial Decision-Making," *Organizational Dynamics* (Spring 1973), pp. 66–80; Victor H. Vroom and Phillip Yetton, *Leadership and Decision-Making* (Pittsburgh: University of Pittsburgh Press, 1973).

[51] Norman F. Maier, "Assets and Liabilities in Group Problem Solving," *Psychological Review*, vol. 74 (1967), pp. 239–49.

[52] Schein, op. cit.

53 See Kathleen M. Eisenhardt, Jean L. Kahwajy, and L. J. Bourgeois III, "How Management Teams Can Have a Good Fight," *Harvard Business Review* (July–August 1997), pp. 77–85.

54 Consensus box developed from a classic article by Jay Hall, "Decisions, Decisions, Decisions," *Psychology Today* (November 1971), pp. 55–56.

55 See Maier, op. cit.

56 See Irving L. Janis, "Groupthink," *Psychology Today* (November 1971), pp. 43–46; *Victims of Groupthink*, 2d ed. (Boston: Houghton Mifflin, 1982).

57 Information from Kelly K. Spors, "Productive Brainstorms Take the Right Mix of Elements," *Wall Street Journal* (July 28, 2008): www.wsj.online.com.

58 Delbecq et al., op. cit.

59 Developed from Lynda McDermott, Nolan Brawley, and William Waite, *World-Class Teams: Working across Borders* (New York: Wiley, 1998).

60 Adapted from William Dyer, *Team Building*, 2nd ed. (Reading, MA: Addison-Wesley, 1987), pp. 123–25.

### Feature Notes

Follow the Story—Information and quotes from David Kemodel, "Boeing Teams Speed Up 737 Output," *The Wall Street Journal* (February 7, 2012), p. B10.

Ethics on the Line—See Bib Latané, Kipling Williams, and Stephen Harkins, "Many Hands Make Light the Work: The Causes and Consequences of Social Loafing," *Journal of Personality and Social Psychology*, vol. 37 (1978), pp. 822–32; and W. Jack Duncan, "Why Some People Loaf in Groups and Others Loaf Alone," *Academy of Management Executive*, vol. 8 (1994), pp. 79–80.

Facts for Analysis—Survey data reported in "Two Wasted Days at Work," *CNNMoney.com* (March 16, 2005): www.cnnmoney.com.

### Photo Essay Notes

Management in Popular Culture—Developed from Robert (Lenie) Holbrook," Management Line: Team Contributions and *Lost,* John R. Schermerhorn, Jr., *Exploring Management*, Third Edition (Hoboken, NJ: John Wiley & Sons, 2011), p. 331. Team Building—Information from Dennis Berman, "Zap! Pow! Splat!" *BusinessWeek*, Enterprise issue (February 9, 1998), p. ENT22. Stand Up Meetings—Information and quote from Rachael Emma Silverman, "No More Angling for the Best Seat: More Meetings Are Stand-Up Jobs," *The Wall Street Journal* (February 2, 2012), pp. A9, A10.

## Chapter 18

### Endnotes

1 Information from Elizabeth Holmes. "Tweeting without Fear," *Wall Street Journal* (December 9, 2011), pp. B1, B7; and, "Idiot Proof," *Bloomberg BusinessWeek* (March 5–11, 2012), pp. 63–67.

2 Information from American Management Association. "The Passionate Organization Fast-Response Survey," September 25–29, 2000, and organization website: http://www.amanct.org/aboutama/index.htm.

3 Data from "Is the Workplace Getting Raunchier?" *BusinessWeek* (March 17, 2008), p. 19.

4 "Cultivating Personal Awareness," *BizEd* (May/June 2009), p. 26.

5 See Henry Mintzberg, *The Nature of Managerial Work* (New York: Harper & Row, 1973 and Harper-Collins, 1997); John P. Kotter, "What Effective General Managers Really Do," *Harvard Business Review,* vol.

60 (November/December 1982), pp. 156–57; and *The General Managers* (New York Macmillan, 1986).

6 "Relationships Are the Most Powerful Form of Media," *Fast Company* (March 2001), p. 100.

7 Jay A. Conger, *Winning 'Em Over: A New Model for Managing in the Age of Persuasion* (New York: Simon & Schuster, 1998), pp. 24–79.

8 Ibid.

9 *BusinessWeek* (February 10, 1992), pp. 102–8.

10 Tom Peters and Nancy Austin, *A Passion for Excellence* (New York: Random House, 1985); and, "Epigrams and Insights from the Original Modern Guru," *Financial Times*, Kindle Edition (March 4, 2010). See also Tom Peters, *The Little Big Things: 163 Ways to Pursue EXCELLENCE* (New York: HarperStudio, 2010).

11 Information and quotes from "Undercover Boss Gets the Communication Message," *Financial Times* (June 9, 2009).

12 See Robert H. Lengel and Richard L. Daft, "The Selection of Communication Media as an Executive Skill," *Academy of Management Executive*, vol. 2 (August 1988), pp. 225–32.

13 Martin J. Gannon, *Paradoxes of Culture and Globalization* (Los Angeles: Sage, 2008), p. 76.

14 David McNeill, *Hand and Mind: What Gestures Reveal about Thought* (Chicago: University of Chicago Press, 1992).

15 Adapted from Richard V. Farace, Peter R. Monge, and Hamish M. Russell, *Communicating and Organizing* (Reading, MA: Addison-Wesley, 1977), pp. 97–98.

16 Information from Carol Hymowitz, "More American Chiefs Are Taking Top Posts at Overseas Concerns," *Wall Street Journal* (October 17, 2005), p. B1.

17 Examples reported in Martin J. Gannon, *Paradoxes of Culture and Globalization* (Los Angeles: Sage Publications, 2008), p. 80.

18 See Edward T. Hall, *The Silent Language* (New York: Doubleday, 1973).

19 Gannon, op. cit.

20 Information from Ben Brown, "Atlanta Out to Mind Its Manners," *USA Today* (March 14, 1996), p. 7.

21 Information and quotes from Adam Bryant, "Creating Trust by Destroying Hierarchy," *The Global Edition of the New York Times* (February 15, 2010), p. 19.

22 Information and quote from Kelly K. Spors, "Top Small Workplaces 2009," *Wall Street Journal* (September 28, 2009), pp. R1–R4.

23 See, for example, John Freeman, *The Tyranny of E-mail* (New York: Scribner, 2009).

24 Information and quotes from Sarah E. Needleman, "Thnx for the IView! I Wud Luv to Work 4 U!!)," *Wall Street Journal Online* (July 31, 2008).

25 For a review of legal aspects of e-mail privacy, see William P. Smith and Filiz Tabak, "Monitoring Employee E-mails: Is There Any Room for Privacy?" *Academy of Management Perspectives*, vol. 23 (November 2009), pp. 33–48.

26 Information from American Management Association, "Electronic Monitoring & Surveillance Survey" (February 8, 2008); www.press.amaner. org/press-releases; and Liz Wolgemuth, "Why Web Surfing is a Nonproblem, *U.S. News & World Report* (August 22, 2008); www.usnews.com/blogs.

27 "Tread: Rethinking the Workplace," *BusinessWeek* (September 25, 2006), p. IN.

28 Information from "'Roberts Quits' Rumor Only a Class Exercise," *The Columbus Dispatch* (March 6, 2010), p. A5.

29 Stephanie Clifford, "Video Prank at Domino's Taints Brand," *New York Times* (April 16, 2009): www.nytimes.com; and, Deborah Stead, "An Unwelcome Delivery," *BusinessWeek* (May 4, 2009), p. 15.

30 This discussion is based on Carl R. Rogers and Richard E. Farson, "Active Listening" (Chicago: Industrial Relations Center of the University of Chicago, n.d.); see also Carl R. Rogers and Fritz J.

Roethlisberger, "Barriers and Gateways to Communication," *Harvard Business Review* (November–December 2001), Reprint 91610.

[31] Ibid.

[32] A useful source of guidelines is John J. Gabarro and Linda A. Hill, "Managing Performance," Note 996022 (Boston: Harvard Business School Publishing, n.d.).

[33] Sue DeWine, *The Consultant's Craft* (Boston: Bedford/St. Martin's Press, 2001), pp. 307–14.

[34] Developed from John Anderson, "Giving and Receiving Feedback," in Paul R. Lawrence, Louis B. Barnes, and Jay W. Lorsch, eds., *Organizational Behavior and Administration*, 3rd ed. (Homewood, IL: Richard D. Irwin, 1976), p. 109.

[35] A classic work on proxemics is Edward T. Hall's book, *The Hidden Dimension* (Garden City, NY: Doubleday, 1986).

[36] Information from Rachel Metz, "Office Décor First Change by New AOL Executive," *Columbus Dispatch* (May 25, 2009), p. A7.

[37] Richard E. Walton, *Interpersonal Peacemaking: Confrontations and Third-Party Consultation* (Reading, MA: Addison-Wesley, 1969), p. 2.

[38] See Robert R. Blake and Jane Strygley Mouton, "The Fifth Achievement," *Journal of Applied Behavioral Science*, vol. 6 (1970), pp. 413–27; Alan C. Filley, *Interpersonal Conflict Resolution* (Glenview, IL: Scott, Foresman, 1975).

[39] See Kenneth W. Thomas, "Conflict and Conflict Management," in M. D. Dunnett, ed., *Handbook of Industrial and Organizational Behavior* (Chicago: Rand McNally, 1976), pp. 889–935.

[40] This and following discussion developed from Alan C. Filley, *Interpersonal Conflict Resolution* (Glenview, IL: Scott, Foresman, 1975).

[41] See, also Walton, op. cit.

[42] See, for example, Robert Moskowitz, "How to Negotiate an Increase," www.worktree.com (retrieved March 8, 2007); Mark Gordon, "Negotiating What You're Worth," *Harvard Management Communication Letter*, vol. 2, no. 1 (Winter 2005); and Dona DeZube, "Salary Negotiation Know-How," www.monster.com (retrieved March 8, 2007).

[43] Portions of this treatment of negotiation originally adapted from John R. Schermerhorn, Jr., James G. Hunt, and Richard N. Osborn, *Managing Organizational Behavior*, 4th ed. (New York: Wiley, 1991), pp. 382–87. Used by permission.

[44] See Roger Fisher and William Ury, *Getting to Yes: Negotiating Agreement Without Giving In* (New York: Penguin, 1983); James A. Wall, Jr., *Negotiation: Theory and Practice* (Glenview, IL: Scott, Foresman, 1985); William L. Ury, Jeanne M. Brett, and Stephen B. Goldberg, *Getting Disputes Resolved* (San Francisco: Jossey-Bass, 1997).

[45] Fisher and Ury, op. cit.

[46] Fisher and Ury, op. cit.

[47] Developed from Max H. Bazerman, *Judgment in Managerial Decision Making*, 4th ed. (New York: Wiley, 1998), Chapter 7.

[48] Fisher and Ury, op. cit.

[49] "A Classes Grapher's Care," *Kellogg* (Summer 2006), p. 40.

[50] Roy J. Lewicki and Joseph A. Litterer, *Negotiation* (Homewood, IL: Irwin, 1985).

[51] This instrument is described in Carsten K. W. De Drew, Arne Evers, Bianca Beersma, Esther S. Kluwer, and Aukje Nauta, "A Theory-Based Measure of Conflict Management Strategies in the Workplace," *Journal of Organizational Behavior*, vol. 22 (2001), pp. 645–68. Used by permission.

[52] Feedback questionnaire is from Judith R. Gordon, *A Diagnostic Approach to Organizational Behavior*, 3rd ed. (Boston: Allyn & Bacon, 1991), p. 298. Used by permission.

### Feature Notes

Follow the Story—Information and quotes from Adam Bryant, "Give Your Staff a Reason to Work for You," *International Herald Tribune* (July 5, 2010), p. 17.

Ethics on the Line—Information from Bridget Jones, Blogger Fire Fury, CNN.com (July 19, 2006); and Bobbie Johnson, "Briton Sacked for Writing Paris Blog Wins Tribunal Case, *The Guardian* (March 29, 2007): guardian.co.uk/technology/2007/mar/30/news, France.

Facts for Analysis—Information from Joe Light, "Human-Resource Executives Say Reviews Are Off the Mark," *Wall Street Journal* (November 8, 2010), p. B8; and Rachel Emma Silverman, "Work Reviews Losing Steam," *Wall Street Journal* (December 19, 2011), p. B7.

### Photo Essay Notes

Hammond's Candies—Information and quotes from Teri Evans, "Entrepreneurs Seek to Elicit Workers' Ideas," *Wall Street Journal* (December 29, 2009), p. B7. Sam Walton—Quotations from John Huey, "America's Most Successful Merchant," *Fortune* (September 23, 1991), pp. 46–59; see also Sam Walton and John Huey, *Sam Walton: Made in America: My Story* (New York: Bantam Books, 1993).

# Organization Index

# Name Index

# Subject Index

## ETHICS ON THE LINE

Access to Coke's Secret Formula Is a Tantalizer

CEO Golden Parachutes Fly in Face of Public Outrage

Your Social Media History Might Be a Job Hurdle

Offshore E-Waste Graveyards Bury a Problem

When Nationalism Meets Protectionism, Who Wins?

Entrepreneurship Meets Caring Capitalism Meets Big Business

Climber Left to Die on Mt. Everest

What Really Works When Fighting World Poverty?

Firms Find Global Traveling Rough on Privacy and Censorship

Life and Death at an Outsourcing Factory

Flattened into Exhaustion

Hidden Agendas in Organizational Change

Are Employers Checking Your Facebook Page?

Would You Put Your Boss Above Your Organization?

Is Personality Testing in Your Future?

Information Goldmine Creates Equity Dilemma

Social Loafing Is Getting in the Way

Blogging Is Easy, But Bloggers Should Beware

## FACTS FOR ANALYSIS

Employment Contradictions in Workforce Diversity

Generations Differ When Rating Their Bosses

Behavior of Managers Key to Ethical Workplace

Workers May Be Unhappy, But They Aren't Changing Jobs

Corruption and Bribes Haunt Global Business

Minority Entrepreneurs Lead the Way

Intelligent Enterprises Show How to Win with Data

Policies on Office Romances Vary Widely

Corporate Thieves Thrive on Sticky Hands and Cyberheists

Wage and Benefits as a Competitive Issue in the Auto Industry

Bosses May Be Overestimating Their Managing Skills

Organization Cultures Must Face Up to Emerging Work–Life Trends

Underemployment Affects One-fifth of U.S. Workers

Workers Report Shortcomings of Managers

Job Satisfaction Trends

Gender Differences in Motivation

Unproductive Meetings Are Major Time Wasters

Performance Reviews Get Increasing Scrutiny

## RESEARCH BRIEF

Worldwide Study Identifies Success Factors in Global Leadership

Setting Personal Goals Improves Academic Performance

Prioritizing Stakeholders for Organizational Action

Generations Show Differences on Important Values

Personality Traits, Behavioral Competencies, and Expatriate Effectiveness

Do Founders of New Ventures Take Less Compensation than Other Senior Managers in Their Firms?

Escalation Increases Risk of Unethical Decisions

You've Got to Move Beyond Planning by the Calendar

Restating Corporate Financial Performance Foreshadows Significant Executive Turnover

Female Directors on Corporate Boards Linked with Positive Management Practices

Making Schools Work Better with Organizational Design

Top Management Must Get—and Stay—Committed for Shared Power to Work in Tandem with Top-Down Change

Racial Bias May Exist in Supervisor Ratings of Workers

Charismatic Leaders Display Positive Emotions That Followers Find Contagious

Business Students More Satisfied with Lives Perform Better

Generational Differences in Work Values

Demographic Faultlines Pose Implications for Managing Teams

Words Affect Outcomes in Online Dispute Resolution

## FOLLOW THE STORY

Indra Nooyi Pushes Pepsi Toward Responsibility and Sustainability

Former Microsoft Executive Finds Fulfillment Fighting Illiteracy

Business School Students Challenged to Serve the Greater Good

Disruptive Innovation the Steve Jobs Way (1955–2011)

Wal-Mart Holds a Chinese Tiger by the Tail

Entrepreneurs Find Rural Setting Fuels Solar Power

No. 2 at Facebook a Good Fit for Sheryl Sandberg

Don Thompson Sets Goals for Winning Role at McDonald's

Roger Ferguson Provides Strategic Leadership for Retirement Security

Ursula Burns Sets Strategic Directions for Xerox

Dancing Deer Baking Sweetens Growth with Values

Alan Mulally Makes His Mark on Ford's Culture

Tony Hsieh Taps HRM to Keep Zappos One Step Ahead

Educator's Leadership Turns Vision into Inspiration

Little Things Are Big Things at Life Is Good

The King of Coffee Brews for Engagement

Teams and Teamwork Help Put the Lift into Boeing's New Planes

The Limited's Linda Heasley Gives Others Reasons to Work with Her